-23

66-84

33-37

51-66

FEMINIST FRONTIERS

353-363   312-324

110-119   327-331

94-108   302-306

372-386

119-128

306-312

FEMINIST FRONTIERS

Sixth Edition

LAUREL RICHARDSON

VERTA TAYLOR

NANCY WHITTIER

McGraw
Hill

Boston   Burr Ridge, IL   Dubuque, IA   Madison, WI   New York
San Francisco   St. Louis   Bangkok   Bogotá   Caracas   Kuala Lumpur
Lisbon   London   Madrid   Mexico City   Milan   Montreal   New Delhi
Santiago   Seoul   Singapore   Sydney   Taipei   Toronto

The **McGraw·Hill** Companies

Higher Education

FEMINIST FRONTIERS, SIXTH EDITION
Published by McGraw-Hill, a business unit of The McGraw-Hill Companies, Inc., 1221 Avenue of the
Americas, New York, NY, 10020. Copyright © 2004, 2001, 1997, 1993, 1989, 1983 by The McGraw-Hill
Companies, Inc. All rights reserved. No part of this publication may be reproduced or distributed in
any form or by any means, or stored in a database or retrieval system, without the prior written
consent of The McGraw-Hill Companies, Inc., including, but not limited to, in any network or other
electronic storage or transmission, or broadcast for distance learning.
Some ancillaries, including electronic and print components, may not be available to customers outside
the United States.

This book is printed on acid-free paper.

1 2 3 4 5 6 7 8 9 0 FGR/FGR 0 9 8 7 6 5 4 3

ISBN 0–07–282423–9

Publisher: *Phillip A. Butcher*
Sponsoring editor: *Sherith H. Pankratz*
Developmental editor: *Katherine Blake*
Senior marketing manager: *Daniel M. Loch*
Producer, media technology: *Jessica Bodie*
Senior project manager: *Jean Hamilton*
Production supervisor: *Carol A. Bielski*
Senior designer: *Violeta Diaz*
Cover design: *Yvo Riezebos*
Interior design: *Michael Remener*
Compositor: *Shepherd Incorporated*
Typeface: *9/11 Palatino*
Printer: *Quebecor World Fairfield Inc.*

Library of Congress Control Number: 2003108637

www.mhhe.com

For our mothers,
Rose Foreman Richardson,
Alice Taylor Houston,
and Sally Kennedy;

to our sisters,
Jessica Richardson Phillips
and Sarah Whittier;

and to the special children in our lives,
Shana West,
Akiva Walum,
Natasha Woods,
Katerina Woods,
Maxwell Phillips,
Sara Beth Taylor Porter,
Jason Searcy Taylor,
Jonah Weigand-Whittier,
Eva Weigand-Whittier,
and Isaac Weigand-Whittier

A B O U T   T H E   A U T H O R S

LAUREL RICHARDSON is Professor Emerita of Sociology and Visiting Professor of Cultural Studies at The Ohio State University. She has published seven books and over 100 articles. *Fields of Play: Constructing an Academic Life* (Rutgers University Press, 1997) tells the story of her strategies to create a university that is more inviting to women and minorities. The book received the prestigious C. H. Cooley award. She is currently working on two books, *Confessions of a Retirement Resistor* and *Double Vision: Seeing Through the Ethnographic–Literary Divide* (with Ernest Lockridge).

VERTA TAYLOR is Professor of Sociology at the University of California at Santa Barbara. She teaches courses on gender, feminism, women's studies, and social movements and has won numerous teaching awards, including an Ohio State University Distinguished Teaching Award, a Multicultural Teaching Award, an Outstanding Faculty Award from the Office of Gay, Lesbian, and Bisexual Studies, and—most recently—a University Distinguished Diversity Enhancement Award for her role as Chair of Undergraduate Studies in the Department of Sociology at The Ohio State University. Professor Taylor also received the Sociologists for Women in Society's Mentoring Award and has served as Feminist Lecturer for Sociologists for Women in Society. She has served on more than a dozen editorial boards, as Chair of the Sex and Gender and the Collective Behavior and Social Movements Sections of the American Sociological Association, and as Chair of the Committee on the Status of Gay, Lesbian, Bisexual, and Transgender Sociologists of the American Sociological Association. She is the author of *Rock-a-by Baby: Feminism, Self-Help and Postpartum Depression;* and coauthor with Leila J. Rupp of *Survival in the Doldrums: The American Women's Rights Movement, 1945 to the 1960s,* and *Drag Queens at the 801 Cabaret.* Her writings have appeared in numerous scholarly collections and journals such as *Signs, Gender & Society, The American Sociological Review, Social Problems, Mobilization, Qualitative Sociology, Journal of Women's History, Journal of Homosexuality,* and *Journal of Marriage and the Family.*

NANCY WHITTIER is Associate Professor of Sociology and a member of the Women's Studies Program Committee at Smith College. She teaches courses on gender, social movements, queer politics, and research methods. She is the author of *Feminist Generations: The Persistence of the Radical Women's Movement,* and co-editor of *Social Movements: Identity, Culture, and the State.* Her work on the women's movement, social movement culture and collective identity, activist generations, and activism against child sexual abuse has appeared in numerous scholarly collections and journals.

P R E F A C E

The first edition of *Feminist Frontiers* was conceived in the late 1970s at a time when many women inside and outside academia were beginning to recognize and challenge male domination. At the time of its publication, only a handful of books and anthologies written for classroom use presented a feminist perspective on the status of women.

The evolution of this book through six editions reflects both the success of the women's movement and the development of feminist scholarship over the past three decades. Women's studies courses have blossomed and spread to campuses in even the most conservative regions of the country. Feminist scholars have, in the meantime, refined and enlarged our understanding of how gender inequality operates and how it intersects with other systems of domination based on race, ethnicity, nationality, class, and sexuality. There is no doubt that the situation of women has changed since the publication of the first edition of *Feminist Frontiers*. Gender inequality has not, however, disappeared.

We write this preface to *Feminist Frontiers* 6 with pride and excitement. We are proud to be part of the continuing women's movement; we are excited by the burgeoning knowledge about how gender is connected to race, class, sexuality, nationality, and other differences. We feel fortunate to be writing, teaching, and learning at a time when feminist thought and research are flourishing and deepening. It is, simultaneously, a time to enjoy the bounty of feminist scholarship and to sow new feminist seeds. We are proud as well that this book represents the collective effort of scholars from two generations of feminists. We have enjoyed our collaboration across intellectual and generational perspectives, and we think that it has enriched the book.

We developed *Feminist Frontiers* for use as the major—or supplementary—text in courses on the sociology of women, women's studies, gender studies, or sex roles. Because this book offers a general framework for analyzing the status of women, it can also be used as a supplementary text in introductory sociology courses and in courses on social problems, foundations of society, comparative studies, and American Studies.

Although we have retained some of the articles from previous editions of *Feminist Frontiers*—particularly writings that have become feminist classics—the book has been comprehensively updated to include the more recent scholarship on gender. Approximately half of the readings and boxes are new to this edition. We have selected readings that continue to emphasize the diversity of women's experiences and multicultural perspectives. We have strengthened several sections, bringing in discussion of the most current issues in feminist scholarship, including more thorough coverage of men and masculinity.

ORGANIZATION

Feminist Frontiers 6 is organized into four parts, each introduced by a sociological-feminist analysis. **Part One: Introduction** begins with a section representing the diversity of women's experiences and gender systems. Its section on "Theoretical Perspectives" presents social constructionist and intersectional theoretical approaches to gender. **Part Two: Gender, Culture, and Representation** has two sections, "Representation, Language, and Culture" and "Socialization." **Part Three: Social Organization of Gender** has five sections, providing readings on work, families, sexualities, bodies and medicine, and violence against women. **Part Four: Social Change** includes articles on global politics and the state and on social protest and the feminist movement.

CRITERIA FOR SELECTION

As we set about selecting articles for this edition, we found an abundance of excellent pieces. We used the following criteria for choosing what to include:

- We wanted each selection to be engagingly written and accessible in style and language to readers from different disciplinary backgrounds.
- As a testament to the tremendous growth in depth and understanding of feminist scholarship, we sought selections exploring a wide range of theoretical and substantive issues.
- We wanted this anthology to reflect a diversity of racial, ethnic, generational, sexual, and cultural experiences.
- We sought to capture the cross-disciplinary nature of gender research.

The result is a collection that links well-written and significant articles within a general feminist sociological perspective.

CHANGES IN THE SIXTH EDITION

The sixth edition contains 21 new articles and six new boxed inserts, representing the most current scholarship and public debates and expanding our coverage of numerous issues important to feminist scholarship. Dated pieces have been deleted or revised, while retained readings are classics in the field.

Central topics that continue to receive coverage in this edition include social constructionist theories of gender; feminist intersectionality theory; gender socialization; child-raising in egalitarian families; Chicana and Mexican women's motherhood and employment; lesbian history; intersexuality; affirmative action; gender segregation in the workplace; differences in women's and men's wages; women and welfare; eating disorders among African American, Latina, and White women; lesbian health; American Indian women; men's organizing to end violence against women; hate crimes against lesbians; sex education; adolescent girls' sexuality; disabled women's body images; male violence and school shootings; rape as a war crime; rape on college campuses; sweatshop labor; media images of Asian American and Black women; the medicalization of gender; women's movements; third-wave feminism; black feminism; and queer politics.

Additions to the text focus especially on improving coverage of **globalization**, with new articles on such topics as the marriage market in the Vietnamese diaspora, Hindu women's violence against Muslims in India, the globalization of beauty, the status of women in Iraq, and Middle Eastern women's participation in sports.

This edition offers coverage of many **new and central topics** including:

- Sex segregation in the labor force (Reading 19)
- The glass ceiling for women in male-dominated occupations (Reading 20)
- Latina immigrant domestic workers (Reading 21)
- Dual-career couples balancing work and family life (Reading 22)
- Trans-Pacific marriages between Vietnamese women and men (Reading 24)
- Lesbian and gay families (Reading 25)
- The exclusion of lesbians from traditional family rituals (Sect. 6 Box)
- The history of lesbian identity (Reading 26)
- Cosmetic surgery (Reading 10)
- Radicalized images of Black women's bodies (Reading 11)
- Internalized sexism among women in the southern U.S. (Sect. 3 Box)
- The globalization of beauty (Reading 11; Sect. 10 Box)
- Media images of lesbian women (Reading 25)
- Male bodies and sexuality (Readings 27 & 29)
- Sexism in gynecological examinations (Sect. 8 Box)
- Reproductive rights (Reading 32)
- Reproductive rights and abortion (Reading 36)
- Women and men in sports (Readings 29 & 33)
- Women's participation in electoral politics (Reading 39)

- Male privilege (Reading 5)
- The socialization of boys into violence (Reading 16)
- Violence against women of color (Reading 36)
- Masculinity and war (Sect. 4 Box)
- Women's and men's participation in anti-feminist movements (Readings 42 & 43)
- Hate movements and violent fundamentalist movements around the globe (Readings 41 & 42)
- Muslim and Hindu women (Readings 33 & 41)
- The status of women in Iraq (Sect. 10 Box)

Although the core focus remains on women and gender, this edition offers consistent coverage of masculinity. Every section includes articles dealing with men and masculinity, or articles dealing with both men and women, with an emphasis on the inter-relations between constructions of masculinity and femininity within gendered practices, cultures, and institutions. Thus, *Feminist Frontiers* is useful for courses in gender as well as courses in women's studies or the sociology of women.

New Readings in the Sixth Edition

Every section has been updated with new selections, and many have been comprehensively revised. Section One includes a popular article by **Steven Shacht** on male privilege. The section on *Theoretical Perspectives* includes a new piece by **Patricia Hill Collins** on intersectionality in feminist theory, allowing better coverage of this central topic. The section on *Representation, Language, and Culture* includes a previously unpublished article by **Ingrid Banks** on black women's hair, improving the coverage of the intersections of race and sexuality in television, music, and the mass media. In addition, there are new articles on representation in other sections, notably the article by **Suzanna Danuta Walters** on media representations of gay and lesbian families (Section Six). We have also reprinted a chapter from **Debra Gimlin's** recent book that describes women's experiences with cosmetic surgery.

We have expanded the section on socialization to focus on masculinity, by including an article by **Michael Kimmel** on the socialization of boys and

a well-known article on men and war by journalist **Grace Paley.** Our coverage of work includes two up-to-date overviews of gender in the workplace: an article on sex segregation in the U.S. labor force by **Christine E. Bose** and **Rachel Bridges Whaley** and a chapter by **Irene Padavic** and **Barbara Reskin** on factors that influence women's upward mobility in male dominated occupations and the professions. We also reprint a chapter from **Pierrette Hondagneu-Sotelo's** award-winning book on immigrant Latina domestic workers.

In the *Families* section, there are three new articles that improve coverage of the diversity of family forms. In addition to **Walters's** article on lesbian and gay families in the media, a new selection by **Rosanna Hertz** describes strategies used by families to balance work and family life, while **Hung Cam Thai** examines trans-national marriages between immigrant men in the U.S. and Vietnamese women. The section on *Sexualities* has been significantly revised, with three new selections out of four: **Leila Rupp** on lesbian identity, **Susan Bordo** on male bodies and sexuality, and **Michael Messner** on compulsory heterosexuality.

The section on *Bodies* includes two new readings aimed at improving our coverage of the crucial areas of reproductive rights and sports: **Laurie Nsiah-Jefferson's** piece on reproductive laws and women of color and **Jennifer Hargreaves's** piece on Islamic Middle-Eastern women's participation in organized sports. **Michael Messner's** new article in the *Sexualities* section adds to the coverage of sport by discussing sport as an institution that maintains and reinforces compulsory heterosexuality.

We have added coverage of domestic violence in the section on *Violence Against Women* with **Kimberle Crenshaw's** groundbreaking article on intersectionality and the race and gender dimensions of domestic violence. Crenshaw's article also allows coverage of feminist legal theory and its application to women's lives.

The final two sections, *Global Politics and the State* and *Social Protest and the Feminist Movement*, contain several changes. We include a selection by **Harriet Woods** focusing on how gender inequality influences women's participation in local, state, and national politics. We also provide newly expanded coverage of women's movements, focusing on racial, ethnic, class, national, sexual, and generational differences in women's activism. We have added several selections on anti-feminist movements as well. **Amrita Basu** provides new coverage of women's participation in violent fundamentalist movements in India directed against Muslims. A new selection by **Kathleen Blee** examines the way gender influences women's participation in contemporary hate movements in the United States. Another piece, by **Melanie Heath,** discusses the gender politics of the men's organization the Promise Keepers. This section also makes *Feminist Frontiers* unique among texts in its attention to third-wave feminism and queer activism.

SUPPLEMENTS

Companion Web site

The *Feminist Frontiers* Web site provides general information about the book and offers separate areas for students and instructors.

For the Student: The Student side of the site is organized to correspond to the 11 sections in the text. There are practice test questions, an annotated list of Web links, links to Census 2000 updates, a glossary, and a comprehensive annotated film/video guide.

For the Instructor: The Instructor's side of the Web site, which is password-protected, includes the Instructor's Manual, an annotated list of Web links and links to Census 2000 updates, a glossary, and a comprehensive annotated film/video guide.

Visit the companion Web site at:
www.mhhe.com/richardson6

Instructor's Resource CD (IRCD)

The following supplements are available to instructors on an Instructor's Resource CD:

Instructor's Manual
The Instructor's Manual is organized to correspond to the 11 sections in the text. It offers learning ob-jectives, discussion questions, summaries of the key points of the section introductions and readings, suggestions for assignments and exercises, and an annotated list of Web links. The Instructor's Manual is also available (password-protected) on the companion Web site.

Test Bank
The Test Bank offers multiple-choice, true-false, and essay questions on the section introductions and the individual readings. It can be printed from the CD. It is also included as a **Computerized Test Bank.**

ACKNOWLEDGMENTS

We gratefully acknowledge the support, skill, and help of many people. We extend thanks to contribution authors, not only for writing the selected pieces but also for allowing us to reprint them here. At McGraw-Hill, we especially thank Sally Constable for her friendship, encouragement, and help in shaping this book over the years; Sherith Pankratz, sponsoring editor; and Kathy Blake, developmental editor, for her patience, astute advice, and attention to detail in shepherding the book through its development. We also thank Jean Hamilton for her skill in seeing the production of the manuscript to completion, and Fred Courtright for his services as permissions editor. Amber Ault was instrumental in shaping some section introductions for the third edition of the book; we appreciate her contributions. We also thank her for developing some of the content for both the Instructor's Manual and the companion Web site. Nicole Raeburn provided invaluable research assistance on earlier editions of the book, and we continue to be grateful for her excellent work revising the Test Bank. Lindsey Dawson, Lisa Leitz, and Morgan Lynn provided clerical support and feedback from students' perspectives. Lindsey Dawson provided help in assembling the manuscript that went far beyond the call of duty. Lisa Leitz put her knowledge of feminism and her charisma as a teacher to use in creating much of the content for the Web site that accompanies this book. Without Lisa Leitz's intellectual contributions, hard work, support, and friendship, this revision would never have been completed. In addition, Mary Margaret Fonow, Elizabeth Kaminski, Claire Robertson, and Leila Rupp have given us valuable feedback on their teaching experiences with earlier editions of *Feminist Frontiers*. Finally, we express our appreciation to students in our classes on the sociology of women, sex and gender, and women's studies at Smith College, the University of California–Santa Barbara, and Ohio State University. They have contributed to the development of this anthology by their thoughtful responses to proposed articles.

The following scholars served as reviewers in the development of *Feminist Frontiers 6*:

Sandra Albrecht, University of Kansas
Maria Bevacqua, Minnesota State
   University–Mankato
Vicky Brockman, Southwest State University
Heather Dillaway, Wayne State University
Connie Frey, University of Nebraska–Lincoln
Margaret Gentry, Hamilton College
Naomi Gerstel, University of Massachusetts
Kathleen Gillum-Harris, Wichita State University
Linda Grant, University of Georgia
Marie Laberge, University of Delaware
Melissa Latimer, West Virginia University
Beth Mintz, University of Vermont

Special thanks go to those close to us who inspired both the work and the authors. Ernest Lockridge was steadfast in his belief in and support for the project in the early years. Leila Rupp critically reviewed the entire collection at every stage of the revision and offered the friendship, intellectual wisdom, support, and caring necessary to complete the project. Kate Weigand provided feedback and insight into the collection's organization and offered consistent encouragement and companionship. Jonah, Eva, and Isaac Weigand-Whittier are a constant source of inspiration as we seek to reconstruct gender. To them and to the many other students and colleagues who have touched our lives positively, we express our gratitude.

Laurel Richardson
Verta Taylor
Nancy Whittier

CONTENTS

P A R T   O N E

Introduction

What is gender? To answer the question requires thinking about what it means to individuals to be men or women and how these meanings affect the ways we interact with each other, the kinds of relationships we form, and our positions in our communities. It also entails thinking about the institutions that distribute power, resources, and status among various groups of women and men. Gender is an element of social relationships that operates at multiple levels to categorize and distinguish the sexes; as we shall see, it interacts with race, class, ethnicity, and sexuality to rank men above women of the same social group.

What does it mean to be a woman? Thinking about women's experiences is a complicated task because women have as many differences from each other as commonalities. On the one hand, women everywhere suffer restrictions, oppression, and discrimination because they are living in patriarchal societies. Yet gender is not the sole influence on any woman's life. Differences of race, ethnicity, class, sexuality, age, nation, region, and religion shape women's experiences. Moreover, these differences intersect with each other. For example, Asian-American women of various ages, sexual orientations, classes, and ethnic and national origins, have different experiences.

The experience of being a woman may be quite different for distinct groups of women. For a white, upper-class, heterosexual American woman, for example, femininity might entail being economically dependent on her husband, perfecting a delicate and refined physical appearance, and achieving social influence through child-raising and volunteer work. Womanhood for a middle-class African–American woman might mean providing financial support for her children, holding influential and respected positions within her church and community, yet being stereotyped by the dominant white culture as sexually promiscuous or unintelligent. For a Mexican immigrant to the United States, femininity might mean being a good mother—which, as Denise Segura suggests in Reading 26, may mean working long hours in order to support her children.

The experiences of men are similarly varied. Although men benefit from power and privilege over women, some groups of men also exercise power over other men, while other men are excluded from economic or political influence. To understand the position of a particular man, in other words, we must consider his gender, race, class, sexuality, age, and so forth, in order to understand the particular advantages and disadvantages he faces.

In short, gender is defined in various ways for different groups. Gender definitions bring with them a distinct set of restrictions and disadvantages for members in each group, as well as privileges and sources of power or resistance. The task for you, as students, as for scholars of gender, is to recognize the patterns and persistence of male dominance while simultaneously recognizing these variations.

As if matters were not complex enough, feminist scholars also recognize that individuals have unique constellations of experiences. Each of us has her own story to tell. Each of us has multiple alliances and identifications with groups that shift through time and social context. The religious identity of childhood may be shunted aside during young adulthood, for example, only to be reclaimed in later years. Self-definitions as heterosexual may give way later in life to new identities as lesbian or bisexual. As biracial or bicultural or mixed-religion daughters, we might identify with the heritage of either parent or both. Social forces such as sexism, racism, heterosexism, and class inequality shape our biographies, but it is as individuals that we experience and make sense of our lives. Individuals do not easily attribute our experiences to class, race, or gender as *separate* or *separable* entities. We rarely see our own biographies as sociohistorically situated.

The task of feminist scholarship, and of this volume, is to illuminate the social and structural roots of our gendered experiences, while simultaneously recognizing the complicated and unique factors that shape our lives. Feminist research builds upon and links two levels of analysis: structure and biography. The *structural* level looks at social institutions and cultural practices that create and sustain gender inequalities and links those inequalities to other systems of oppression, such as racism, ageism, and homophobia. The *biographical* level honors each individual's expression of her own experience. It pays attention to how individuals represent themselves and recognizes personal voice. As a result, we can learn how difference and commonality are structurally rooted and personally experienced. We can see how larger social forces affect our own and others' lives.

Feminist research is not just about analyzing the ways that social structures shape and restrict the lives of women. Of course, it is important to document the inequalities faced by various groups of women and to examine the ways that women have been oppressed and victimized based on gender. Experiences such as discrimination in hiring and pay, sexual violence, and legal subordination, for example, are undeniably central to gender. Yet feminist scholarship also emphasizes the sources of power that women find: how they define themselves, influence their social contexts, and resist the restrictions that they face. The articles in this volume view women not as passive victims of patriarchal social structures, but as actors who exercise control over their own lives, find pleasure and fulfillment, and resist social constraints.

Further, feminist research is not just about documenting women's experiences. It is about recognizing the ways that gender shapes the lives of both women and men and analyzing a broad system of gender. By documenting the influence of social structures and highlighting individuals' complex mixture of domination, resistance, and complicity, feminist scholarship leads us to rethink the structural changes necessary to meet the needs of actual women and men.

Feminist theory and scholarship on gender, then, face a broad set of questions. The approaches to answering these questions vary enormously; we hope that you will recognize disagreement and debate, as well as cooperation, in the readings that follow. There are, however, some shared assumptions that run through the chapters in this book.

First, feminist scholars view gender as *pervasive,* as part of every feature of social life and individual identity. It is impossible, therefore, to analyze any part of social life as if it were gender neutral. As a result, feminist scholars challenge the male bias hidden under claims of scientific objectivity in academic research. As you read these articles and those in other classes, ask yourself how the social conditions and practices of doing research reinforce or challenge gender inequities.

Second, feminist researchers understand systems of oppression as *interlocking*. Race, class, ethnicity, sexuality, and other systems of domination affect how one experiences gender. Therefore, although gender is a basic fact of social life, women and men in different positions in society experience their gender and the power or oppression that results from it differently. Just as feminist researchers challenge knowledge claims about "people" based on research on men, they question knowledge about "women" based on research on white, middle-class women.

Third, feminist scholars experiment with *new ways of doing research*, rethinking the relationship between the researcher and the researched. Scientific research assumes that there is a separation between the scholar and the subjects of research and that this separation is necessary to produce "objective" and "valid" research. Feminist researchers challenge this tenet. Treating women as "objects" of research contravenes feminist goals of equality by elevating the researcher's agenda and perspective above those of the researched. One of the major questions of feminist thought is how to do research that empowers both the researcher and the researched. How do we create social research practices in which researcher and researched collaborate in the process of interpreting the world? For some, the solution has been to write about their own lives; some acknowledge directly how their own biases affect their work; some study groups of which they are a part; others do "participatory" or "action" research in which the researcher and the researched determine together the topics, methods, goals, and political action to follow from the project, so that the scholar is a participant in the project, but not its leader.

These are not only theoretical concerns; they are important *ethical* questions. What right does a scholar have to write about another woman's life? How should scholars write about the lives of those women and men who are different from themselves? How can feminist scholars use the skills and privileges of academic practice to diminish social inequality?

We invite you to engage in reading, thinking about, and doing feminist research. We hope that you will consider some of the central questions that run through this book. What are the commonalities and differences among women (or among men)? What, if anything, do women of different classes, races, or sexualities share in common? We hope you will reflect on the complicated balance between oppression and resistance, between the pervasive influence of the society and the ways that individuals and groups find to define themselves and carve out meaningful lives. We encourage you to discuss your ideas, to debate the issues this volume raises with your friends and classmates, to agree or disagree with the authors here, and to come to your own conclusions. We hope that through this engagement, you will consider how gender has shaped your life and how gender intersects with the other systems of inequality that affect you. We hope that you will share your understandings with others, becoming a researcher yourself and a theorist of your own and others' lives so that you might help empower us all and transform society.

Diversity and Difference

Conducting research about women has been the focus of feminist scholars from the 1960s to the present. In recent years, researchers have looked especially closely at the differences and commonalities among women and have also begun to examine how men's lives are shaped by cultural expectations of masculinity. Scholars are interested in learning about the rich complexities of how gender shapes women's and men's lives and in discovering ways of knowing that stand true to these experiences and also offer the prospect of effecting positive change. Women everywhere live with a ubiquitous "monotone" of male advantage, in all its manifestations. Yet differences among women arise from factors like race, ethnicity, class, sexual orientation, age, geographic region, and religion. Further, not all men possess the same advantages or social power. Men of subordinate racial or ethnic groups, classes, or sexual orientations may have power relative to women in their own group but are subordinate in some ways to other men and to women in more powerful groups.

Recognizing that women are not a homogeneous group raises questions about the basis of comparison and the grounds for affiliation among women. Can we even speak of "women" as a meaningful category, or is the diversity among women too great for any generalization? The readings in this section discuss points of similarity and difference among women and among men. Although the readings in this section give only a sampling of the varied and rich experiences of women and men, they begin to illustrate the vast range of meanings that gender has for women and men in different groups.

One source of commonality that has attracted and shaped feminist understanding is the idea of *oppression*. As a concept, oppression has a long history in contemporary feminist scholarship. What does it mean? Why is it important to think about? The first selection, "Oppression," addresses these questions and raises some others. In that article, Marilyn Frye defines oppression as "living one's life confined and shaped by forces and barriers which are not accidental or occasional and hence avoidable, but are systematically related to each other in such a way as to catch one between and among them and restrict or penalize motion in any direction."

The multiple sources of interrelated oppressions make it difficult for people to recognize how the systems of oppression impinge on their lives or the lives of others. Knowing about the larger social forces helps one to understand the shape of one's life and the difference between "suffering" and "suffering from oppression." As you read the other articles in this section, can you use Frye's concept of oppression to think about the experiences they describe?

Whereas Frye emphasizes how structures of oppression constrict all women, the remaining readings in this section examine the distinctions among women's experiences. Rosalinda Méndez González discusses the history of the western United States from the point of view of women of various classes and ethnicities in "Distinctions in Western Women's Experience: Ethnicity, Class, and Social Change." She suggests that the traditional history of westward expansion across the frontier is the story of only one group of women, the "pioneer" settlers of European descent. Considering the lives of Indian, Mexican, and Chinese women means reconstructing our understanding of the development of the West. This article illustrates the task of contemporary feminist researchers: to examine the experiences of diverse groups of women, consider the impact of class and race inequalities, and rethink the biased assumptions and histories that scholars have long taken for granted.

Paula Gunn Allen, similarly, suggests that assumptions about what it means to be a woman in Anglo-European culture do not hold in American Indian cultures. In "Where I Come From Is Like This," she draws on her bicultural experiences to explore the incongruity of the images of women embedded in Anglo and American Indian cultures. The images of American Indian women she grew up with are images of "practicality, strength, reasonableness, intelligence, wit, and competence," in contrast to non-Indian ideas about women as "passive and weak." Again, we see the difficulty of generalizing about women's experiences. What are the assumptions about women embedded in your own culture?

The next selection emphasizes the difficulties of accurately analyzing how systems of oppression affect peoples' lives. In "The Master's Tools Will Never Dismantle the Master's House," Audre Lorde argues that feminists must critically examine their own use of dominant concepts in their analyses of women's lives. She suggests that academic knowledge is based in an institution that historically has excluded women and people of color, and asks whether academic knowledge can undermine the inequalities on which it is based. Do you think that the "regular" methods of scholarship and science are adequate to the task of understanding the diversity among women? Will new tools be necessary? Lorde argues that encouraging women to relate to each other at the points of their differences promotes growth, creativity, and social change. Do these conversations across differences happen on your campus?

In "Teaching about Being an Oppressor," Steven Schact discusses the invisible systems and taken-for-granted practices that privilege men over women. He argues that much of what men take for granted in daily life is in fact a result of their dominant social status. Documenting his own largely unrecognized male privilege helps him understand how he benefits from this system. How does his list of benefits from male privilege change your understanding of sexism? Can you think of other advantages to add to his list? If you are a member of another privileged group, can you construct a list of the benefits you receive by virtue of your race, class, sexual orientation, religion or nationality? If you are a member of a subordinated group, can you list some of the ways you are disadvantaged?

Oppression

✌ Marilyn Frye

It is a fundamental claim of feminism that women are oppressed. The word "oppression" is a strong word. It repels and attracts. It is dangerous and dangerously fashionable and endangered. It is much misused, and sometimes not innocently.

The statement that women are oppressed is frequently met with the claim that men are oppressed too. We hear that oppressing is oppressive to those who oppress as well as to those they oppress. Some men cite as evidence of their oppression their much-advertised inability to cry. It is tough, we are told, to be masculine. When the stresses and frustrations of being a man are cited as evidence that oppressors are oppressed by their oppressing, the word "oppression" is being stretched to meaninglessness; it is treated as though its scope includes any and all human experience of limitation or suffering, no matter the cause, degree, or consequence. Once such usage has been put over on us, then if ever we deny that any person or group is oppressed, we seem to imply that we think they never suffer and have no feelings. We are accused of insensitivity; even of bigotry. For women, such accusation is particularly intimidating, since sensitivity is one of the few virtues that have been assigned to us. If we are found insensitive, we may fear we have no redeeming traits at all and perhaps are not real women. Thus are we silenced before we begin: the name of our situation drained of meaning and our guilt mechanisms tripped.

But this is nonsense. Human beings can be miserable without being oppressed, and it is perfectly consistent to deny that a person or group is oppressed without denying that they have feelings or that they suffer. . . .

The root of the word "oppression" is the element "press." *The press of the crowd; pressed into military service; to press a pair of pants; printing press; press the button.* Presses are used to mold things or flatten them or reduce them in bulk, sometimes to reduce them by squeezing out the gases or liquids in them. Something pressed is something caught between or among forces and barriers which are so related to each other that jointly they restrain, restrict, or prevent the thing's motion or mobility. Mold. Immobilize. Reduce.

The mundane experience of the oppressed provides another clue. One of the most characteristic and ubiquitous features of the world as experienced by oppressed people is the double bind—situations in which options are reduced to a very few and all of them expose one to penalty, censure or deprivation. For example, it is often a requirement upon oppressed people that we smile and be cheerful. If we comply, we signal our docility and our acquiescence in our situation. We need not, then, be taken note of. We acquiesce in being made invisible, in our occupying no space. We participate in our own erasure. On the other hand, anything but the sunniest countenance exposes us to being perceived as mean, bitter, angry, or dangerous. This means, at the least, that we may be found "difficult" or unpleasant to work with, which is enough to cost one one's livelihood; at worst, being seen as mean, bitter, angry, or dangerous has been known to result in rape, arrest, beating, and murder. One can only choose to risk one's preferred form and rate of annihilation.

Another example: It is common in the United States that women, especially younger women, are in a bind where neither sexual activity nor sexual inactivity is all right. If she is heterosexually active, a woman is open to censure and punishment for being loose, unprincipled, or a whore. The "punishment" comes in the form of criticism, snide and embarrassing remarks, being treated as an easy lay by men, scorn from her more restrained female friends. She may have to lie and hide her behavior from her parents. She must juggle the risks of unwanted pregnancy and dangerous contraceptives. On the other hand, if she refrains from heterosexual activity, she is fairly constantly harassed by men who try to persuade her into it and pressure her to "relax" and "let her hair down"; she is threatened with labels like "frigid," "uptight," "man-hater," "bitch" and "cocktease." The same parents who would be disapproving of her sexual activity may be worried by her inactivity because it suggests she is not or will not be popular, or is not sexually normal. She may be charged with lesbianism. If a woman is raped, then if she has been heterosexually active she is subject to the presumption that she liked it (since her activity is presumed to show that she likes sex), and if she has not been heterosexually active, she is subject to the presumption that she liked it (since she is supposedly "repressed and frustrated"). Both heterosexual activity and heterosexual nonactivity are likely to be taken as proof that you wanted to be raped, and hence, of course, weren't *really* raped at all. You can't win. You are caught in a bind, caught between systematically related pressures.

Women are caught like this, too, by networks of forces and barriers that expose one to penalty, loss, or contempt whether one works outside the home or not, is on welfare or not, bears children or not, raises children or not, marries or not, stays married or not, is heterosexual, lesbian, both, or neither. Economic necessity; confinement to racial and/or sexual job ghettos; sexual harassment; sex discrimination; pressures of competing expectations and judgments about *women*, *wives*, and *mothers* (in the society at large, in racial and ethnic subcultures, and in one's own mind); dependence (full or partial) on husbands, parents, or the state; commitment to political ideas; loyalties to racial or ethnic or other "minority" groups; the demands of self-respect and responsibilities to others. Each of these factors exists in complex tension with every other, penalizing or prohibiting all of the apparently available options. And nipping at one's heels, always, is the endless pack of little things. If one dresses one way, one is subject to the assumption that one is advertising one's sexual availability; if one dresses another way, one appears to "not care about oneself" or to be "unfeminine." If one uses "strong language," one invites categorization as a whore or slut; if one does not, one invites categorization as a "lady"—one too delicately constituted to cope with robust speech or the realities to which it presumably refers.

The experience of oppressed people is that the living of one's life is confined and shaped by forces and barriers which are not accidental or occasional and hence avoidable, but are systematically related to each other in such a way as to catch one between and among them and restrict or penalize motion in any direction. It is the experience of being caged in: all avenues, in every direction, are blocked or booby-trapped.

Cages. Consider a birdcage. If you look very closely at just one wire in the cage, you cannot see the other wires. If your conception of what is before you is determined by this myopic focus, you could look at that one wire, up and down the length of it, and be unable to see why a bird would not just fly around the wire any time it wanted to go somewhere. Furthermore, even if, one day at a time, you myopically inspected each wire, you still could not see why a bird would have trouble going past the wires to get anywhere. There is no physical property of any one wire, *nothing* that the closest scrutiny could discover, that will reveal how a bird could be inhibited or harmed by it except in the most accidental way. It is only when you step back, stop looking at the wires one by one, microscopically, and take a macroscopic view of the whole cage, that you can see why the bird does not go anywhere; and then you will see it in a moment. It will require no great subtlety of mental powers. It is perfectly *obvious* that the bird is surrounded by a network of systematically related barriers, no one of which would be the least hindrance to its flight, but which, by their relations to each other, are as confining as the solid walls of a dungeon.

It is now possible to grasp one of the reasons why oppression can be hard to see and recognize: one can study the elements of an oppressive structure with great care and some good will without seeing the structure as a whole, and hence without seeing or being able to understand that one is looking at a cage and that there are people there who are caged, whose motion and mobility are restricted, whose lives are shaped and reduced.

The arresting of vision at a microscopic level yields such common confusion as that about the male door-opening ritual. This ritual, which is remarkably widespread across classes and races, puzzles many people, some of whom do and some of whom do not find it offensive. Look at the scene of the two people approaching a door. The male steps slightly ahead and opens the door. The male holds the door open while the female glides through. Then the male goes through. The door closes after them. "Now how," one innocently asks, "can those crazy women's libbers say that is oppressive? The guy *removed* a barrier to the lady's smooth and unruffled progress." But each repetition of this ritual has a place in a pattern, in fact in several patterns. One has to shift the level of one's perception in order to see the whole picture.

The door-opening pretends to be a helpful service, but the helpfulness is false. This can be seen by noting that it will be done whether or not it makes any practical sense. Infirm men and men burdened with packages will open doors for able-bodied women who are free of physical burdens. Men will impose themselves awkwardly and jostle everyone in order to get to the door first. The act is not determined by convenience or grace. Furthermore, these very numerous acts of unneeded or even noisome "help" occur in counterpoint to a pattern of men not being helpful in many practical ways in which women might welcome help. What *women* experience is a world in which gallant princes charming commonly make a fuss about being helpful and providing small services when help and services are of little or no use, but in which there are rarely ingenious and adroit princes at hand when substantial assistance is really wanted either in mundane affairs or in situations of threat, assault, or terror. There is no help with the (his) laundry; no help typing a report at 4:00 AM; no help in mediating disputes among relatives or children. There is nothing but advice that women should stay indoors after dark, be chaperoned by a man, or when it comes down to it, "lie back and enjoy it."

The gallant gestures have no practical meaning. Their meaning is symbolic. The door-opening and similar services provided are services which really are needed by people who are for one reason or another incapacitated—unwell, burdened with parcels, etc. So the message is that women are incapable. The detachment of the acts from the concrete realities of what women need and do not need is a vehicle for the message that women's actual needs and interests are unimportant or irrelevant. Finally, these gestures imitate the behavior of servants toward masters and thus mock women, who are in most respects the servants and caretakers of men. The message of the false helpfulness of male gallantry is female dependence, the invisibility or insignificance of women, and contempt for women.

One cannot see the meanings of these rituals if one's focus is riveted upon the individual event in all its particularity, including the particularity of the individual man's present conscious intentions and motives and the individual woman's conscious perception of the event in the moment. It seems sometimes that people take a deliberately myopic view and fill their eyes with things seen microscopically in order not to see macroscopically. At any rate, whether it is deliberate or not, people can and do fail to see the oppression of women because they fail to see macroscopically and hence fail to see the various elements of the situation as systematically related in larger schemes.

As the cageness of the birdcage is a macroscopic phenomenon, the oppressiveness of the situations in which women live our various and different lives is a macroscopic phenomenon. Neither can be *seen* from a microscopic perspective. But when you look macroscopically you can see it—a network of forces and barriers which are systematically related and which conspire to the immobilization, reduction, and molding of women and the lives we live.

Distinctions in Western Women's Experience: Ethnicity, Class, and Social Change

✺ Rosalinda Méndez González

The issues of ethnicity, class, and social change as they relate to women in western history and to historical reevaluation derive in part from the social-change movements of the 1950s and 1960s. Until then academic research had tended to neglect the experiences of minorities, women, and the laboring classes or to justify their subordinate social condition. Then the civil rights, feminist, and nationalist movements raised challenges to these approaches.

The new research born of the rebellions of those exciting years sought to uncover and document the historical facts of the neglected groups; to critique the existing myths, stereotypes, and paradigms that veiled or rationalized the inequalities and the historical contributions of the affected social groups; and to examine and expose the structures of domination and subordination in our society.

At first, these investigations took a rigidly protective stance toward their subjects. Black or Chicano nationalist analyses tended to question all traditional assumptions and to defend all that was black or brown; women's analyses attacked institutions and ideologies as patriarchal without distinction as to class or ethnic inequalities; radicals imbued with class analysis criticized imperialism abroad and class structures at home without considering the ramifications of sex or ethnic discrimination. Those who sought to integrate the analyses of the various forms of social inequality were at first in the minority.

By the 1970s the diverse groups had successfully documented the importance of their subjects' contributions to historical development and demonstrated the existence of social structures of domination over each group. An effort began then to integrate this analysis and to arrive at a more complex, fundamental explanation of the interconnections among these distinct social-historical experiences.

The process of including women's history, black history, Indian, Chicano, Asian, immigrant, and labor histories in the chronicles of United States history has been a first step toward an integrated history. Now we are confronted with the next step of jointly interpreting our interrelated histories. This requires going beyond the empirical combination of facts, names, and dates to the conceptual problem of seeking an explanation of how the diverse experiences were daily woven by individual human beings into a single and common historical reality.

In outlining the factors involved in these interconnected experiences, we must be careful to search for both the subjective, cultural conditions that motivated the individual woman's experiences and perceptions, and the objective, political-economic conditions that shaped the experiences of each social group.

The use of diaries, personal testimonies, oral histories, and literature has proved to be effective for uncovering the first set of conditions: women's personal or subjective experiences. But there are shortcomings to this approach. Women of the poor, slave, or laboring classes do not tend to leave diaries. Different methods and different questions have to be posed if one is to recapture the personal experiences of Indian, Hispanic, black, Asian, and poor white women of the laboring classes.

To find a conceptual interpretation of these diverse personal experiences, we must address the objective conditions of western life. This involves first challenging the traditional Turnerian interpretation of western history as the "frontier" period. The evolution of the West spans hundreds of years of Indian society before the American frontier. It is important to understand Indian social relations and the role of women before the Europeans imposed a class society.

Four centuries of Spanish conquest and settlement left a legacy of cultural development and social relations which is still in force today as, for example, in the legislation of western states.[1] Then, overlapping the three decades of Mexican rule over large parts of the West, comes the relatively brief period of United States conquest, the "frontier" period which has so absorbed myopic western historians. Finally, it is important to keep in mind that western history also comprises the twentieth-century development of women in the West.[2]

THE QUESTION OF CLASS

In studying western history since European penetration, one of the most obvious but often ignored conditions is the existence of social classes.[3] A class system was first introduced in the sixteenth century by the conquering Spaniards into the area that is now the southwestern United States.

Acknowledging the class character of Spanish and Mexican society in the Southwest penetrates the mist of generalizations which inaccurately assume classless homogeneity. Albert Camarillo's study of the Chicano communities in Santa Barbara and Los Angeles, California, delineates the four classes that comprised Mexican society: the elite rich "Californios," wealthy land-owning ranchers whose holdings averaged 25,000 acres; the middle class of small property owners and ranchers; the majority class of artisans and laborers living in humble dwellings; and the Indian population which was converted into laborers for the missions and menial servants for the wealthy Californios.[4]

In this society, what would it mean to talk about the life cycles of women? Certainly women's lives would appear different within the same household, where the wealthy Californios lived with their slave-like Indian female servants. Historian Elinor Burkett encountered this problem when she set out to study the relations of class, race, and sex in Spanish colonial South America. In feminist studies, Burkett notes, we often assume that:

> sex is as important a force in the historical process as class. Thus, we deal with the domestic squabbles of the aristocracy and the survival trials of the black female in the same conference without feeling uncomfortable; frequently forget that the position of the one is maintained only through the exploitation of the other and that such a relationship leaves little concrete room for sisterhood.[5]

If western historians raised these questions they might uncover in verbal records the gulf between the experiences of women of different classes. For example, the following black lullaby from the southern United States laments a black mother's inability to be with her newborn child through early motherhood and nursing because she had to tend to the baby of her mistress.[6]

All the Pretty Little Horses
Hushaby, don't you cry.
Go to sleepy, little baby.
When you wake, you shall have cake,
And all the pretty little horses.
Blacks and bays, dapples and grays,
Coach and six-a little horses.
Way down yonder in the meadow,
There's a poor little lambie;
The bees and the butterflies pickin' out his eyes,
The poor little thing cries, "Mammy."
Hushaby, don't you cry,
Go to sleepy, little baby.

The evidence of working-class women's experience is there, but the prevailing orientations of studying history, even women's history, steer us toward elite or educated women and their written records; then from this limited and class-biased evidence generalizations are drawn and applied to all women.[7]

In fact, if one looks at history through the eyes of the majority of women, the poor and the laboring classes, a very different picture of society emerges; the picture is far more complete, for elite eyes take *their* world as the standard and assume that all society exists, or should exist, in their image.

But to see through the eyes of the women on the bottom is to see not only the lives of the vast majority, but also to look upward through all levels of society; the flaws and contradictions of the upper classes and of the social structure they maintain become exposed from this perspective. The elite class perspective tends to be biased, myopic, and class-centered; the majority laboring class perspective tends to be more critical and encompassing.

WESTWARD EXPANSION

A second major historical consideration in studying the objective conditions that shaped women's experiences is the process of United States "westward expansion," which ultimately resulted in the appropriation of Indian, French, Spanish, and Mexican territories by the United States and the subordination of local ethnic groups as dispossessed cultural or national "minorities."

The process of westward expansion brings into play a host of major economic, political, and social developments. In a historical and economic sense the conquest of the West can be interpreted as corresponding to the similar process undergone by the western European countries in the sixteenth, seventeenth, and eighteenth centuries; known as the original or "primitive" accumulation of land and resources, this process constituted the preliminary stage for the development of industrial capitalist society.[8] In what sense is the conquest of the West a primitive accumulation?[9] And what is the significance of this process for women's experiences in the West?

Frederick Jackson Turner wrote that "the existence of an area of free land, its continuous recession, and the advance of American settlement westward, explain American development." Yet in the process of westward expansion the leading political actors clearly recognized the true character of that expansion: not an acquisition of an unclaimed territory free for the taking, not the expansion of "free land," but a military and political conquest of an already inhabited territory.[10]

Without the United States Army, in fact, the West could never have been "taken" by the settlers and pioneers. What effect did the army, both in the conquest and in its subsequent preservation, have on women in the West? What effect did it have on creating, altering, or maintaining class, ethnic, or racial divisions? Indian reservations in California were inevitably placed next to army posts and outposts.[11] What impact did the army have on Indian women who survived the devastating wars of extermination against their people?

The railroads were also instrumental in the penetration of the West. The building of the railroads was a key to expansion, not just as a means of military transportation but more fundamentally because of what lay behind the conquest: the penetration of the West by eastern capital. Linking the West Coast to the East Coast not only opened up the ports and raw materials of the West for exploitation by eastern bankers, industrialists, and land speculators but, far beyond that, opened up the Asian subcontinent for exploitation in such a way that it placed the United States at the crossroads of international commerce between the Far East and western Europe. Thus, the military

conquest of the Indian and Mexican West and the construction of the transcontinental railroads opened up both a national market and an international empire for giant eastern capitalists.[12]

The building of the transcontinental railroads affected women of diverse ethnic and class backgrounds in a variety of ways; the full effects remain to be studied. We know, for example, that the railroads, after the military, provided one of the most effective ways of destroying American Indian people's subsistence on the Plains, by establishing the policy of paying sharpshooters to kill the buffalo.

The railroads stimulated mass immigration from Europe into the United States and mass migration into the West and Southwest. The construction of the railroads was accomplished by exploiting immigrant laborers: the Chinese, Japanese, and Mexicans on the West Coast, the Irish and European immigrants on the East Coast.[13]

Yet the treatment of European immigrant laborers was qualitatively different, in a political sense, from that of the Asian and Mexican immigrants.[14] Chinese laborers, for example, were brought in as bound labor, as "coolies," a politically unfree form of contract labor. They were forbidden to bring their wives or families. This restriction had a negative and long-lasting impact on the development of Chinese communities in the West, and it led to the importation of Chinese women in the most brutal form of "white slave traffic," an experience quite distinct from that of European immigrant women in the East.[15]

The importation of Mexican labor by the railroads has also left a deep legacy. As with the placement of Indian reservations next to army forts, maps show that the *colonias* or Mexican settlements in the first half of the twentieth century were invariably located along the railroad routes, since whole Mexican families were imported by the companies to clear, lay, and maintain the tracks. The railroad companies would segregate their work force along ethnic lines and establish Mexican colonies of boxcar residences in certain places along the track; thus, the phrase "the wrong side of the tracks" came to be applied to Mexican barrios.[16] In the growing search for roots among Chicanas and Chicanos, the oral histories and family records that are surfacing reveal, in instance after instance, the ties to the railroads among our parents, grandparents, and great-grandparents.[17]

Today many Chicano barrios are still alongside the "wrong side of the tracks." They developed on the original sites of the old railroad-track Mexican colonies; in cities throughout the Southwest from California to Texas, these barrios are still distinguished by adobe houses, unpaved dirt streets, lack of sidewalks, often in direct proximity to walled, modern, Anglo middle-class housing tracts with multitiered, air-conditioned, carpeted homes.

PROPERTY, PATRIARCHY, AND THE NUCLEAR FAMILY

What did the settlement of the land itself mean for women of different classes and ethnicity? Much of the preliminary analysis on women in the West focuses on pioneer women, and their lives are studied through the diaries or literature they left behind. But the majority of women in the nineteenth-century West neither read nor wrote English. Barbara Mayer Wertheimer points out that the ordinary American could not pack up and head West. "It took capital, about $1,500, to outfit a wagon, buy supplies, and tide the family over until the land began to produce. This was an impossible sum for most working-class families to come by."[18]

Without detracting from the courage and endurance of these pioneer women, we have to ask what the takeover and settlement of western lands really represent for the majority of Indian, Mexican, and immigrant women in the West. A more comprehensive answer has to be found by studying first what western conquest and settlement represented in American economic and historical development. The West was not really developed by individual pioneering men and women seeking land. Rather, the West was made economically exploitable by federal intervention in the form of massive land grants to railroads, mining companies, timber companies, and land speculators, and by virtue of federal legislation and funding that subsidized these private profit-making ventures and speculators at public expense.[19]

Industrial and financial magnates did not operate simply out of greed for lucrative profits; they were driven by the economic necessity for expansion, which is at the heart of this system of competition and property. When the United States broke away from England in 1783, capitalist expansion was faced with three obstacles: the plantation slave economy of the South, which held onto a bound labor force, raw materials, and productive lands; the Indian tribes and

nations, which had been pushed together into the West; and the Mexican Southwest.

These barriers could be overcome only by the usurpation and appropriation that have characterized the birth of capitalism wherever it has appeared. This process essentially involves breaking up the existing economic system (e.g., feudalism, tribal societies, peasant communities), concentrating land and wealth in the hands of a few entrepreneurs, and uprooting the native peoples from their land and mode of living to provide a source of wage labor.

A bloody Civil War was launched to remove the first obstacle. Wars against the Indians removed the second, and an unprovoked war against Mexico eliminated the third obstacle. After the defeat of the slave plantation economy, Indian tribal societies, and Mexican feudalism in the Southwest, the United States engaged in accelerated expansion and conquest of western territories. This process involved plunder, massacres, swindling, and bribery. It succeeded in imposing capitalist private property and, equally important, individualism and the patriarchal nuclear family, which is so necessary to sustain this form of property.

Various methods were used to impose this system of property and family in the West. In the accumulation of Indian lands, force was not the only technique applied. Andrew Jackson and subsequent presidents attempted to deprive the Indians of their lands by refusing to deal with them as tribes or to negotiate treaties with them as nations. Instead the government forced the Indians, through bribery, treachery, and legislation, to deal with the government as individuals; this policy set them up against each other with the incentive of immediate cash payment to individuals selling plots of land. By forcing the foreign system of private property onto them, the government was attempting to destroy the fundamental communal basis of Indian tribes.

The General Allotment Act, or Dawes Act, of 1883 sought to push the Indians out of the way of western penetration and open up their lands to exploitation, by alloting parcels of tribal land to individuals. The bill was condemned by Senator Henry Teller of Colorado as "a bill to despoil the Indians of their lands and to make them vagabonds on the face of the earth," yet Congress passed it with the justification that "Indians needed to become competitive." Senator Henry Dawes, principal proponent of the measure, argued that Indians "needed to become selfish."[20]

Two centuries earlier the French colonizers in Canada had been amazed at the egalitarianism and freedom among the women and men of the Montagnais tribe, at their disdain for formal authority and domination, and at the respect and independence between husbands and wives. Yet the Jesuit policy of colonization sought to "give authority to one of them to rule the others," and to teach them "to elect and obey 'Captains,' inducing them to give up their children for schooling, and above all, attempting to introduce the principle of binding monogamy and wifely fidelity and obedience to male authority."[21]

In a similar manner the United States recognized that to break down Indian resistance it was necessary to undermine the tribal and clan social organization of the Indians and to enforce upon them the individual nuclear family, with the husband the authority figure over the women and children. This attempt had the multiple purposes of forcing the Indians to alienate their communal tribal lands, breaking their economic and social clan organization, transforming them into individualist and competitive capitalist farmers, and providing the nuclear family institution through which the ideology of private property, individualism, and dominant–subordinate relations could be passed on.

Other American people—the small farmers, European immigrants, and settlers—also were subject to official policies promoting individualism in the process of westward expansion. The Homestead Act of 1862, which preceded the Dawes Act by almost three decades, forced individuals and individual families to settle independently; no land was made available for whole communities. On the other hand, huge tracts of land were made available only to the big companies penetrating the West: the railroads, banks, land speculators, and mining companies. While the individual homesteaders were told, "The government bets 160 acres against the entry fee of $14 that the settler can't live on the land for five years without starving to death,"[22] the financial and industrial giants were granted all the land they wanted; the government even provided capital for the infrastructural construction they needed to operate and extract their private profits.

The fostering of private property, individualism, and the nuclear family in the West thus resulted on the one hand in the breakup of the population into individual, isolated, competitive minuscule units: nuclear families; and the concentration of wealth and power in the hands of an increasingly smaller elite on the other—monopolies. For monopolization to take place, it was necessary to fragment the population through the imposition of private property.

The United States government promoted this process in the West. Neither the government's nor the monopolies' intention, however, was to perpetuate small-scale production and independence. Rather, they brought people in to clear the land, develop the resources, and make the area productive and, when this was done, usurped this settled population from their small plots and transformed them into the wage-labor force needed in the West. Both stages were accomplished by fostering private property, individual ownership of land, and the privatization of the nuclear family.

EXPLOITATION OF WOMEN'S DOMESTIC LABOR

The patriarchal nuclear family was important, not just as a means of preserving and transferring private property and the values associated with it, but also, for the families of the laboring classes, as a means of privately producing through the domestic labor of women the goods and services necessary to sustain the agricultural or industrial labor force needed by capitalist enterprises.[23]

Among Mexican immigrant families in the early twentieth-century Southwest, women's domestic labor was exploited indirectly by large employers as a means of subsidizing the payment of discriminatory and substandard wages to their Mexican workers.[24] This policy was refined by the monopolies engaged in developing the Southwest; these companies in the extractive, infrastructural, and agricultural industries first imported Mexican immigrants in large numbers at the turn of the century.[25]

The monopolistic pattern of southwestern land ownership and industry in many places retained vestiges of the feudal system, such as tenant or sharecropping systems in agriculture or debt peonage in company mining towns. These practices retarded the assimilation of Mexican immigrants into the working class, and had the effect of perpetuating the bondage of the wife and children under the patriarchal family. Patriarchal family relations were particularly strong in rural areas. Women who were hired as agricultural laborers to pick cotton were never paid their own wages; rather, these were paid to the father, husband, or brother. Because of this system of "family wages," feudal relations in the countryside were not easily broken down, and wage labor did not offer women the economic independence that weakened patriarchal relations as did urban or industrial employment.[26]

Even in urban areas, Mexican families found themselves segregated and living in boxcars or makeshift housing. Mario Garcia, in a study of Mexican families in El Paso, Texas, at the turn of the century, documented how their reduced standard of living provided a justification for the payment of wages far below the "American standard." Mexican families were forced to live "75 percent cheaper than Americans" by a series of economic and political mechanisms. Racial discrimination and starvation wages confined Mexicans to the worst slums, with overcrowded, inferior housing in adobes or shacks. These settlements were denied public services (water, paved streets, electricity, sewers) because the Anglo property owners refused to pay taxes to provide them and because the city, in turn, argued that Mexican residents were not property owners and taxpayers, and therefore not entitled to services.[27]

Given this living situation, the domestic labor of women and children was particularly arduous. They hauled water long distances from the river in buckets, hand-ground corn for hours, gathered and chopped wood for fuel, to make up for the lack of adequate wages and public services.

This extreme exploitation of family labor and the intense immiseration of the laboring communities caused high infant mortality rates, infectious diseases, and malnourishment, while providing the justification for lower wages. It also provided a pool of severely underpaid Mexican female servants whose dusk-to-dawn exploitation in the homes of Anglo-American families freed the women of these families to seek outside employment and enter the industrial world. The economic advancement of many Anglo-American women in the Southwest was carried out on the backs of Mexican-American women, as it was in the South on the backs of black women, and the immediate beneficiaries were the banks and monopolies dominating the South and West.

THE QUESTION OF RESEARCH AND SOCIAL CHANGE

My discussion has not centered on individual heroines of different ethnic or class backgrounds nor on the important subject of women's struggles to change the conditions of ethnic, class, racial, or sex discrimination. I have sought to demonstrate the necessity of taking into consideration the larger, more fundamental political-economic forces in the development of the West, which must be studied if one is to understand the experiences of *all* women.

The forces that had come to dominate the West at the end of the nineteenth century have continued to shape the experiences of women in the twentieth century, the more so as economic concentration and its influence through the growth of government power have expanded. In 1962, the wealthiest 10 percent of the United States population controlled close to 70 percent of all personal wealth, while the other 90 percent of the population shared a little over 30 percent.[28] Even this small share of the pie was unevenly divided. Poverty in the United States was concentrated in the South and West, and among blacks and Mexican-Americans. In 1960, for example, official figures showed that in the Southwest 35 percent of the Spanish-surnamed families and 42 percent of non-white families were living in poverty. Among Anglo families, only 16 percent were listed in poverty, and yet this represented a very large number, since Anglos comprised 66 percent of all poor in the Southwest.[29]

Today we know that poverty and unemployment have worsened, that two out of every three persons in poverty are women, and that black women and Chicanas are among those most affected. This situation continues as the "minority" peoples of the Southwest are rapidly becoming the majority.

The trend toward greater inequality is growing. Richard M. Cyert, president of Pittsburgh's Carnegie-Mellon University, which houses the most advanced research and experimentation center in the robotics fields, recently stated. "I don't think there's any question that we're moving toward a society where income distribution will be even more unequal than it is at present and where unemployment is going to be even greater than it is now."[30]

The issue of inequality confronts anyone seeking to develop a historically accurate, comprehensive analysis that integrates the experiences of the majority of poor and working-class women, the experiences of black, Chicana, Indian, Asian, and immigrant women. We have been dealing with the divisions among us: while these divisions of race and class have existed, we also have to deal with the fundamental unity among us.

Our task is to discover both the causes of the artificial, socially created divisions that have kept us apart and ways to make our fundamental unity a reality. If we are concerned with social change, if our research is to involve a commitment to shedding light on the historical roots of contemporary problems and inequalities so that these inequalities can be abolished, then our research will have to address the issues of inequality, exploitation, and the related political question of democracy. For the history of the West, as the history of the United States, is a history of exploitation of the labor, land, and resources of diverse groups of peoples: Indians, indentured servants, black slaves, farmers, the working class,

immigrants, and, not least, the exploitation of women in the home.

For this reason it is also a history of the unfolding struggle over democratic rights and against the powerful minority of antidemocratic forces who have sought to monopolize political power to ensure their economic concentration. This struggle for democracy has involved the Indians' struggle for their land and sovereignty; the struggle of immigrants, of blacks, of Chicanos; working-class and socialist struggles; and, integral to all of these, women's struggle for equality and political emancipation.

ACKNOWLEDGMENTS

Special thanks to Nancy Paige Fernandez, of the Program in Comparative Culture at the University of California at Irvine, for her thoughtful critique of my first draft, and to Lisa Rubens, Lyn Reese, Deanne Thompson, and all the other women at the Women's West Conference whose warm encouragement and extensive discussions and comments enlightened my analysis and understanding.

NOTES

1. E.g., community-property laws for married couples in many southern and western states (especially in former Spanish and French territories); and the Texas "cuckoo law," which allowed a husband to kill his wife's lover if he caught them "in the act." On community property consult Barbara Allen Babcock et al., *Sex Discrimination and the Law* (Boston: Little, Brown, 1975), pp. 604–13. On the Texas "cuckoo law" see "The 'Equal Shooting Rights,'"*Texas Observer*, Mar. 16, 1965; and "Origins of the Cuckoo Law," Apr. 2, 1965. The latter article observes, "Like so many of our especially Texan legal institutions (our homestead law, our venue statute, the independent executor, our adoption law, and our community property system), our legal attitude toward the cuckold's right to take vengeance for an affront to his conjugal honor is Spanish in origin." More accurately, they are feudal in origin.

2. If we include the twentieth century, certain "academic" problems are resolved, such as that there were few black women in "the West" narrowly defined as the frontier period. If we define the West more fully, the presence of black women emerges as a real issue. How, for example, did the development of Jim Crow in the South in the early twentieth century under the sponsorship of the large propertied and monied interests affect women when Jim Crow was imposed on black, Mexican, and Asian communities in the West?

3. Louis M. Hacker, in "Sections—or Classes?" *The Nation* 137, no. 355 (26 July 1933): 108–10, leveled a sharp critique at the Turnerian thesis of a unique and democratic frontier environment in the West. See also Barry D. Karl, "Frederick Jackson Turner: The Moral Dilemma of Professionalization," *Reviews in American History* 3 (March 1975): 1–7.

4. Albert Camarillo, *Chicanos in a Changing Society: From Mexican Pueblos to American Barrios in Santa Barbara and Southern California, 1848–1930* (Cambridge, Mass.: Harvard University Press, 1979). Other studies of sixteenth- to nineteenth-century Mexican families or women include Leonard Pitt, *The Decline of the Californios: A Social History of the Spanish-Speaking Californians, 1846–1890* (Berkeley: University of California Press, 1971); Richard Griswold del Castillo, *The Los Angeles Barrio, 1850–1890: A Social History* (Berkeley: University of California Press, 1979); Richard Griswold del Castillo, *La Familia: Chicano Families in the Urban Southwest, 1848 to the Present* (Notre Dame, Ind.: University of Notre Dame Press, 1984); Frances Leon Swadesh, *Los Primeros Pobladores, Hispanic Americans of the Ute Frontier* (Notre Dame, Ind.: University of Notre Dame Press, 1974); Ramon A. Gutierrez, *Marriage, Sex, and the Family: Social Change in Colonial New Mexico, 1690–1846* (Ph.D. diss., University of Wisconsin, Madison, 1980); Ramon A. Gutierrez, "From Honor to Love: Transformation of the Meaning of Sexuality in Colonial New Mexico," in Raymond T. Smith, ed., *Love,*

Honor, and Economic Fate: Interpreting Kinship Ideology and Practice in Latin America (Chapel Hill: University of North Carolina Press, 1983); Ramon A. Gutierrez, "Marriage and Seduction in Colonial New Mexico," in Adelaida del Castillo, ed., *Between Borders: Essays on Mexicana/Chicana Women's History,* Chicana Studies Research Center (Encino, CA: Floricanto Press, 1990); Gloria E. Miranda, "*Gente De Razon* Marriage Patterns in Spanish and Mexican California: A Case Study of Santa Barbara and Los Angeles," *Southern California Quarterly* 39, no. 1 (March 1957): 149–66; Jane Dysart, "Mexican Women in San Antonio, 1830-1860: The Assimilation Process," *Western Historical Quarterly* 7, no. 4 (October 1976): 365–75; Fray Angelico Chavez, "Dona Tules, Her Fame and Her Funeral," *Palacio* 57 (August 1950): 227–34; Marcela Lucero Trujillo, "The Spanish Surnamed Woman of Yester Year," in José Otero and Evelio Echevarria, eds., *Hispanic Colorado* (Fort Collins, Colo.: Centennial Publications, 1977); Daniel J. Garr, "A Rare and Desolate Lane: Population and Race in Hispanic California," *Western Historical Quarterly* 6, no. 2 (April 1975): 133–48. A masterful bibliography on the "Borderlands," containing hundreds of references for further research, is Charles C. Cumberland, *The United States-Mexican Border: A Selective Guide to the Literature of the Region,* published by *Rural Sociology* as vol. 25, no. 2 (June 1970): 230 pp. The work includes references to Spanish-Indian relations in the region.

5. Elinor C. Burkett, "In Dubious Sisterhood: Race and Class in Spanish Colonial South America," *Latin American Perspectives* 4, nos. 1–2 (Winter–Spring, 1977): 18–26.

6. "All the Pretty Little Horses," in Middleton Harris et al., *The Black Book* (New York: Random House, 1974), p. 65. The book is a photographic documentary history of the Black experience in the United States, including documents and graphics of blacks in the West.

7. For example, Barbara Welter's "The Cult of True Womanhood: 1820-1860," *American Quarterly* 18, no. 2 (1966): 151–74, reprinted in Michael Gordon, ed., *The American Family in Socio-Historical Perspective* (New York: St. Martin's Press, 1973). Welter assumes an upper-class, native WASP homogeneity of all women in America: "It was a fearful obligation, a solemn responsibility, which the nineteenth century *American woman* had—to uphold the pillars of the temple with her frail *white hand*" (p. 225, emphasis added). Her article provides no discussion of property or of women and the family's relation to property. In her only (indirect) reference to the economic character of American society and its class divisions, she blithely passes by without acknowledging these contradictions: "America was a land of precarious fortunes. . . . the woman who had servants today, might tomorrow, because of a depression or panic, be forced to do her own work. . . . she was to be the same cheerful consoler of her husband in their cottage as in their mansion" (p. 238).

In fact, this section contains the only references to the existence of other classes of women: " . . . the value of a wife in case of business reverses . . . of course she had a little help from 'faithful Dinah' who absolutely refused to leave her beloved mistress" (pp. 238–239). Welter cites quotations linking the Cult of True Womanhood to a certain order of society ("that a stable order of society depended upon her maintaining her traditional place in it" [p. 242]), yet she never questions that order, never examines that society and why its maintenance depended on women's domestic subordination.

8. Cf. Leo Huberman, *Man's Worldly Goods: The Story of the Wealth of Nations* (New York: Monthly Review Press, 1936); Maurice Dobb, *Studies in the Development of Capitalism* (New York: International Publishers, 1947). An incisive presentation of primitive accumulation and its devastating impact on peasant families in Europe is found in Karl Marx, *Capital,* vol. 1, part 8, "The So-Called Primitive Accumulation."

9. Raul A. Fernandez, in *The United States–New Mexico Border: A Politico-Economic Profile* (Notre Dame, Ind.: University of Notre Dame Press, 1977), presents an analysis of the complex character of this process in the Southwest. Ray Allen Billington's classic *Westward Expansion* traces the historical facts of the process of westward expansion, though from the perspective of Frederick Jackson Turner's "frontier thesis."

10. Both Jefferson Davis and Captain Randolph B. Marcy compared the conquest of the West with the French imperialist conquest of Algeria, and both argued that the United States Army should apply the French tactics in that conquest to the conquest of the Indians in the West. Walter Prescott Webb, *The Great Plains* (Lincoln: University of Nebraska Press, ca. 1931), pp. 194, 195, 196.

11. Lynwood Carranco, *Genocide and Vendetta: The Round Valley Wars in Northern California* (Norman: University of Oklahoma Press, 1981). An excellent survey of government-Indian relations is found in D'Arcy McNichols, *Native American Tribalism: Indian Survivals and Renewals* (published for the Institute of Race Relations, London, by Oxford University Press, 1973). Indian women's resistance in the face of both the Spanish and United States conquests is presented in Victoria Brady, Sarah Crome, and Lyn Reese's "Resist and Survive, Aspects of Native Women of California," (MS Sarah Crome, Institute for the Study of Social Change, University of California, Berkeley, Calif.)

12. For a very explicit account of the connections between this internal conquest and the creation of a foreign empire by the United States, see Scott Nearing, *The American Empire* (New York: Rand School of Social Science, 1921). See also Leo Huberman, *We, the People* (New York, London: Harper Brothers, 1947).

13. A good overview of immigration in the United States is found in Barbara Kaye Greenleaf, *America Fever: The Story of American Immigration* (New York: New American Library, 1974).

14. Rosalinda M. González, "Capital Accumulation and Mexican Immigration to the United States" (Ph.D. diss., University of California at Irvine, 1981), offers a political–economic analysis of the discriminatory treatment of Asian and Mexican immigrants that differs from the traditional explanations in terms of racism.

15. Dorothy Gray, "Minority Women in the West, Juanita, Biddy Mason, Donaldina Cameron," in *Women of the West* (Millbrae, Calif.: Les Femmes Publishing, 1976), pp. 62–75; *Asian Women* (Berkeley: University of California, Dwinelle Hall, 1971); Ruthanne Lum McCunn, *An Illustrated History of the Chinese in America* (San Francisco: Design Enterprises, 1979).

16. Case studies of these barrios and their twentieth-century development appear in Arthur J. Rubel, *Across the Tracks: Mexican-Americans in a Texas City* (Austin: University of Texas Press, 1966); and Ricardo Romo, *East Los Angeles, History of a Barrio* (Austin: University of Texas Press, 1983). The historical development of the Chicano people is examined in Carey McWilliams's classic *North from Mexico: The Spanish Speaking People of the United States* (New York: Greenwood Press, 1968); Rodolfo Acuna, *Occupied America: A History of Chicanos* (New York: Harper & Row, 1981); and the excellent bilingual pictorial history by Chicano Communications Center, *450 Years of Chicano History in Pictures* (South Pasadena, Calif.: Bilingual Educations Services, n.d.). A case study of how monopoly-motivated reforms of the Progressive Era were applied to Mexican immigrant communities at the turn of the century is found in Gilbert G. Gonzalez, *Progressive Education: A Marxist Interpretation* (Minneapolis: Marxist Educational Press, 1982). A historical analysis of Chicanas is presented in Martha P. Cotera, *Diosa y Hembra: The History and Heritage of Chicanas in the U.S.* (Austin, Tex.: Information Systems Development, 1976).

17. See, e.g., the beautiful and poignant description in Jose Lona's "Biographical Sketch of the Life of an Immigrant Woman," in Maria Linda Apodaca, "The Chicana Woman: An Historical Materialist Analysis," *Latin American Perspectives* 4, nos. 1–2: 70–89. The Institute of Oral History at the University of Texas at El Paso has a growing collection of over 500 taped interviews, many of which relate to the railroads.

18. Barbara Mayer Wertheimer, *We Were There: The Story of Working Women in America* (New York: Pantheon Books, 1977), p. 249. Lillian Schlissel, in *Women's Diaries of the Westward Journey* (New York: Schocken Books, 1982), pointed out that most of the western pioneers were landowners and that their parents had also been landowners, "a class of 'peasant proprietors' " (pp. 10–11).

19. See, e.g., Gabriel Kolko, *Railroads and Regulation* (Westport, Conn.: Greenwood Press, 1976); Robert Wiebe, *The Search for Order, 1877–1920* (New York: Hill and Wang, 1968); James Weinstein, *The Corporate Idea in the Liberal State, 1900–1918* (Boston: Beacon Press, 1968); Matthew Josephson, *The Robber Barons* (New York: Harcourt Brace, 1934); and Matthew Josephson, *The Money Lords* (New York: Weybright and Talley, 1972).

20. McNichols, *Native American Tribalism*. For a brief description on the negative effects on tribal solidarity from the imposition of individualism and the nuclear family on Indian society, see the first two chapters of Keith Basso's *The Cibecue Apache* (New York: Holt, Rinehart and Winston, 1970).

21. Eleanor Leacock, "Women in Development: Anthropological Facts and Fictions, " *Latin American Perspectives* 4, nos. 1–2.

22. Sheryll and Gene Pattersen-Black, *Western Women in History and Literature* (Crawford, Neb.: Cottonwood Press, 1978), p. 5.

23. An important article by Joan Jensen, "Cloth, Bread, and Boarders: Women's Household Production for the Market," *The Review of Radical Political Economics* 12, no. 2 (Summer 1980): 14–24, examines women's household production from the late-eighteenth to early-twentieth centuries. Jensen concludes that it increased the economic productivity of the family through women's provision of services and the home production of produce for domestic consumption and for local and regional markets. In rural areas the domestic labor of women allowed men to increase production of cash crops for urban markets without increasing food costs. "Low food costs combined with taking in boarders allowed the males of American urban families to work for lower wages than they might have required had women not contributed to the family income."

24. Rosalinda M. González, "Mexican Immigrants in the United States: Cultural Conflict and Class Transformation," *Labor History*, forthcoming; and Rosalinda M. González, "Chicanas and Mexican Immigrant Families, 1920–1940" in Joan Jensen and Lois Scharf, eds., *Decades of Discontent: The Women's Movement, 1920–1940* (Westport, Conn.: Greenwood Press, 1983).

25. Many of the leading entrepreneurs in western expansion also had their stakes in foreign conquest. In the Southwest, for example, Adolph Spreckles, who built his fortune in California and Hawaii sugar plantations, merged with Henry C. Havemeyer, the eastern sugar king, to form the sugar trust, which was obtaining concessions in Mexico to grant it complete monopolization. Spreckles was a close friend of the Southern Pacific Railroad, which under the leadership of Henry Huntington and subsequently under William Harriman was gobbling up railroads in the United States and Mexico and absorbing steamship lines and ports. John Kenneth Turner, *Barbarous Mexico* (Austin: University of Texas Press, 1969); Carey McWilliams, *Factories in the Field* (Santa Barbara, Calif.: Peregrine Publishers, 1971).

26. Ruth Allen, *The Labor of Women in the Production of Cotton* (Austin, Tex.: University of Texas Press, 1931).

27. Mario T. Garcia, *Desert Immigrants: The Mexicans of El Paso, 1880–1920* (New Haven, Conn.: Yale University Press, 1981).

28. Institute for Labor Education and Research, *What's Wrong with the U.S. Economy?* (Boston: South End Press, 1982), pp. xi, 32.

29. Leo Grebler et al., in "A Preview of Socioeconomic Conditions," *The Mexican American People* (New York: The Free Press, 1970), pp. 13–34.

30. Donald Dewey, "Robots Reach Out," *United* (August 1983): 92–99.

Where I Come From Is Like This

Paula Gunn Allen

I

Modern American Indian women, like their non-Indian sisters, are deeply engaged in the struggle to redefine themselves. In their struggle they must reconcile traditional tribal definitions of women with industrial and postindustrial non-Indian definitions. Yet while these definitions seem to be more or less mutually exclusive, Indian women must somehow harmonize and integrate both in their own lives.

An American Indian woman is primarily defined by her tribal identity. In her eyes, her destiny is necessarily that of her people, and her sense of herself as a woman is first and foremost prescribed by her tribe. The definitions of woman's roles are as diverse as tribal cultures in the Americas. In some she is devalued, in others she wields considerable power. In some she is a familial/clan adjunct, in some she is as close to autonomous as her economic circumstances and psychological traits permit. But in no tribal definitions is she perceived in the same way as are women in western industrial and postindustrial cultures.

In the West, few images of women form part of the cultural mythos, and these are largely sexually charged. Among Christians, the madonna is the female prototype, and she is portrayed as essentially passive: her contribution is simply that of birthing. Little else is attributed to her and she certainly possesses few of the characteristics that are attributed to mythic figures among Indian tribes. This image is countered (rather than balanced) by the witch/goddess/whore characteristics designed to reinforce cultural beliefs about women, as well as western adversarial and dualistic perceptions of reality.

The tribes see women variously, but they do not question the power of femininity. Sometimes they see women as fearful, sometimes peaceful, sometimes omnipotent and omniscient, but they never portray women as mindless, helpless, simple, or oppressed. And while the women in a given tribe, clan, or band may be all these things, the individual woman is provided with a variety of images of women from the interconnected supernatural, natural, and social worlds she lives in.

As a half-breed American Indian woman, I cast about in my mind for negative images of Indian women, and I find none that are directed to Indian women alone. The negative images I do have are of Indians in general and in fact are more often of males than of females. All these images come to me from non-Indian sources, and they are always balanced by a positive image. My ideas of womanhood, passed on largely by my mother and grandmothers, Laguna Pueblo women, are about practicality, strength, reasonableness, intelligence, wit, and competence. I also remember vividly the women who came to my father's store, the women who held me and sang to me, the women at Feast Day, at Grab Days, the women in the kitchen of my Cubero home, the women I grew up with; none of them appeared weak or helpless, none of them presented herself tentatively. I remember a certain reserve on those lovely brown faces; I remember the direct gaze of eyes framed by bright-colored shawls draped over their heads and cascading down their backs. I remember the clean cotton dresses and carefully pressed hand-embroidered aprons they always wore; I remember laughter and good food, especially the sweet bread and the oven bread they gave us. Nowhere in my mind is there a foolish woman, a dumb woman, a vain woman, or a plastic woman, though the Indian women I have known have shown a wide range of personal style and demeanor.

My memory includes the Navajo woman who was badly beaten by her Sioux husband; but I also remember that my grandmother abandoned her Sioux husband long ago. I recall the stories about the Laguna woman beaten regularly by her husband in the presence of her children so that the children would not believe in the strength and power of femininity. And I remember the women who drank, who got into fights with other women and with the men, and who often won those battles. I have memories of tired women, partying women, stubborn women, sullen women, amicable women, selfish women, shy women, and aggressive women. Most of all I remember the women who laugh and scold and sit uncomplaining in the long sun on feast days and who cook wonderful food on wood stoves, in beehive mud ovens, and over open fires outdoors.

Among the images of women that come to me from various tribes as well as my own are White Buffalo Woman, who came to the Lakota long ago and brought them the religion of the Sacred Pipe, which they still practice; Tinotzin the goddess, who came to Juan Diego to remind him that she still walked the hills of her people and sent him with her message, her demand, and her proof to the Catholic bishop in the city nearby. And from Laguna I take the images of Yellow Woman, Coyote Woman, Grandmother Spider (Spider Old Woman), who brought the light, who gave us weaving and medicine, who gave us life. Among the Keres she is known as Thought Woman, who created us all and who keeps us in creation even now. I remember Iyatiku, Earth Woman, Corn Woman, who guides and counsels the people to peace and who welcomes us home when we cast off this coil of flesh as huskers cast off the leaves that wrap the corn. I remember Iyatiku's sister, Sun Woman, who held metals and cattle, pigs and sheep, highways and engines and so many things in her bundle, who went away to the east saying that one day she would return.

II

Since the coming of the Anglo-Europeans beginning in the fifteenth century, the fragile web of identity that long held tribal people secure has gradually been weakened and torn. But the oral tradition has prevented the complete destruction of the web, the ultimate disruption of tribal ways. The oral tradition is vital; it heals itself and the tribal web by adapting to the flow of the present while never relinquishing its connection to the past. Its adaptability has always been required, as many generations have experienced. Certainly the modern American Indian woman bears slight resemblance to her forebears—at least on superficial examination—but she is still a tribal woman in her deepest being. Her tribal sense of relationship to all that is continues to flourish. And though she is at times beset by her knowledge of the enormous gap between the life she lives and the life she was raised

to live, and while she adapts her mind and being to the circumstances of her present life, she does so in tribal ways, mending the tears in the web of being from which she takes her existence as she goes.

My mother told me stories all the time, though I often did not recognize them as that. My mother told me stories about cooking and childbearing; she told me stories about menstruation and pregnancy; she told me stories about gods and heroes, about fairies and elves, about goddesses and spirits; she told me stories about the land and the sky, about cats and dogs, about snakes and spiders; she told me stories about climbing trees and exploring the mesas; she told me stories about going to dances and getting married; she told me stories about dressing and undressing, about sleeping and waking; she told me stories about herself, about her mother, about her grandmother. She told me stories about grieving and laughing, about thinking and doing; she told me stories about school and about people; about darning and mending; she told me stories about turquoise and about gold; she told me European stories and Laguna stories; she told me Catholic stories and Presbyterian stories; she told me city stories and country stories; she told me political stories and religious stories. She told me stories about living and stories about dying. And in all of those stories she told me who I was, who I was supposed to be, whom I came from, and who would follow me. In this way she taught me the meaning of the words she said, that all life is a circle and everything has a place within it. That's what she said and what she showed me in the things she did and the way she lived.

Of course, through my formal, white, Christian education, I discovered that other people had stories of their own—about women, about Indians, about fact, about reality—and I was amazed by a number of startling suppositions that others made about tribal customs and beliefs. According to the un-Indian, non-Indian view, for instance, Indians barred menstruating women from ceremonies and indeed segregated them from the rest of the people, consigning them to some space specially designed for them. This showed that Indians considered menstruating women unclean and not fit to enjoy the company of decent (nonmenstruating) people, that is, men. I was surprised and confused to hear this because my mother had taught me that white people had strange attitudes toward menstruation: they thought something was bad about it, that it meant you were sick, cursed, sinful, and weak

AIN'T I A WOMAN?

Sojourner Truth

Well, children, where there is so much racket there must be something out of kilter. I think that `twixt the negroes of the South and the women of the North, all talking about rights, the white men will be in a fix pretty soon. But what's all this here talking about?

That man over there says that women need to be helped into carriages, and lifted over ditches, and to have the best place everywhere. Nobody ever helps me into carriages, or over mud-puddles, or gives me any best place! An ain't I a woman? Look at me! Look at my arm! I have ploughed and planted, and gathered into barns, and no man could head me! And ain't I a woman? I could work as much and eat as much as a man—when I could get it—and bear the lash as well! And ain't I a woman? I have borne thirteen children, and seen them most all sold off to slavery, and when I cried out with my mother's grief, none but Jesus heard me! and ain't I a woman?

Then they talk about this thing in the head; what's this they call it? [Intellect, someone whispers.] That's it, honey. What's that got to do with women's rights or negro's rights? If my cup won't hold but a pint, and yours holds a quart, wouldn't you be mean not to let me have my little half-measure full?

Then that little man in black there, he says women can't have as much rights as men, 'cause Christ wasn't a woman! Where did your Christ come from? Where did your Christ come from? From God and a woman! Man had nothing to do with Him.

If the first woman God ever made was strong enough to turn the world upside down all alone, these women together ought to be able to turn it back, and get it right side up again! And now they is asking to do it, the men better let them.

Obliged to you for hearing me, and now old Sojourner ain't got nothing more to say.

and that you had to be very careful during that time. She taught me that menstruation was a normal occurrence, that I could go swimming or hiking or whatever else I wanted to do during my period. She actively scorned women who took to their beds, who were incapacitated by cramps, who "got the blues."

As I struggled to reconcile these very contradictory interpretations of American Indians' traditional beliefs concerning menstruation, I realized that the menstrual taboos were about power, not about sin or filth. My conclusion was later borne out by some tribes' own explanations, which, as you may well imagine, came as quite a relief to me.

The truth of the matter as many Indians see it is that women who are at the peak of their fecundity are believed to possess power that throws male power totally out of kilter. They emit such force that, in their presence, any male-owned or -dominated ritual or sacred object cannot do its usual task. For instance, the Lakota say that a menstruating woman anywhere near a yuwipi man, who is a special sort of psychic,

spirit-empowered healer, for a day or so before he is to do his ceremony will effectively disempower him. Conversely, among many if not most tribes, important ceremonies cannot be held without the presence of women. Sometimes the ritual woman who empowers the ceremony must be unmarried and virginal so that the power she channels is unalloyed, unweakened by sexual arousal and penetration by a male. Other ceremonies require tumescent women, others the presence of mature women who have borne children, and still others depend for empowerment on postmenopausal women. Women may be segregated from the company of the whole band or village on certain occasions, but on certain occasions men are also segregated. In short, each ritual depends on a certain balance of power, and the positions of women within the phases of womanhood are used by tribal people to empower certain rites. This does not derive from a male-dominant view; it is not a ritual observance imposed on women by men. It derives from a tribal view of reality that distinguishes tribal people from feudal and industrial people.

Among the tribes, the occult power of women, inextricably bound to our hormonal life, is thought to be very great; many hold that we possess innately the blood-given power to kill—with a glance, with a step, or with a judicious mixing of menstrual blood into somebody's soup. Medicine women among the Pomo of California cannot practice until they are sufficiently mature; when they are immature, their power is diffuse and is likely to interfere with their practice until time and experience have it under control. So women of the tribes are not especially inclined to see themselves as poor helpless victims of male domination. Even in those tribes where something akin to male domination was present, women are perceived as powerful, socially, physically, and metaphysically. In times past, as in times present, women carried enormous burdens with aplomb. We were far indeed from the "weaker sex," the designation that white aristocratic sisters unhappily earned for us all.

I remember my mother moving furniture all over the house when she wanted it changed. She didn't wait for my father to come home and help—she just went ahead and moved the piano, a huge upright from the old days, the couch, the refrigerator. Nobody had told her she was too weak to do such things. In imitation of her, I would delight in loading trucks at my father's store with cases of pop or fifty-pound sacks of flour. Even when I was quite small I could do it, and it gave me a belief in my own physical strength that advancing middle age can't quite erase. My mother used to tell me about the Acoma Pueblo women she had seen as a child carrying huge ollas (water pots) on their heads as they wound their way up the tortuous stairwell carved into the face of the "Sky City" mesa, a feat I tried to imitate with books and tin buckets. ("Sky City" is the term used by the Chamber of Commerce for the mother village of Acoma, which is situated atop a high sandstone table mountain.) I was never very successful, but even the attempt reminded me that I was supposed to be strong and balanced to be a proper girl.

Of course, my mother's Laguna people are Keres Indian, reputed to be the last extreme mother-right people on earth. So it is no wonder that I got notably nonwhite notions about the natural strength and prowess of women. Indeed, it is only when I am trying to get non-Indian approval, recognition, or acknowledgment that my "weak sister" emotional and intellectual ploys get the better of my tribal woman's good sense. At such times I forget that I just moved the piano or just wrote a competent paper or just completed a financial transaction satisfactorily or have supported myself and my children for most of my adult life.

Nor is my contradictory behavior atypical. Most Indian women I know are in the same bicultural bind: we vacillate between being dependent and strong, self-reliant and powerless, strongly motivated and hopelessly insecure. We resolve the dilemma in various ways: some of us party all the time; some of us drink to excess; some of us travel and move around a lot; some of us land good jobs and then quit them; some of us engage in violent exchanges; some of us blow our brains out. We act in these destructive ways because we suffer from the societal conflicts caused by having to identify with two hopelessly opposed cultural definitions of women. Through this destructive dissonance we are unhappy prey to the self-disparagement common to, indeed demanded of, Indians living in the United States today. Our situation is caused by the exigencies of a history of invasion, conquest, and colonization whose searing marks are probably ineradicable. A popular bumper sticker on many Indian cars proclaims: "If You're Indian You're In," to which I always find myself adding under my breath, "Trouble."

III

No Indian can grow to any age without being informed that her people were "savages" who interfered with the march of progress pursued by respectable, loving, civilized white people. We are the villains of the scenario when we are mentioned at all. We are absent from much of white history except when we are calmly, rationally, succinctly, and systematically dehumanized. On the few occasions we are noticed in any way other than as howling, blood-thirsty beings, we are acclaimed for our noble quaintness. In this definition, we are exotic curios. Our ancient arts and customs are used to draw tourist money to state coffers, into the pocketbooks and bank accounts of scholars, and into support of the American-in-Disneyland promoters' dream.

As a Roman Catholic child I was treated to bloody tales of how the savage Indians martyred the hapless priests and missionaries who went among them in an attempt to lead them to the one true path. By the time I was through high school I had the idea that Indians were people who had benefited mightily from the advanced knowledge and superior morality of the Anglo-Europeans. At least I had, perforce, that idea to lay beside the other one that derived from my daily experience of Indian life, an idea less dehumanizing and more accurate because it came from my mother and the other Indian people who raised me. That idea was that Indians are a people who don't tell lies, who care for their children and their old people. You never see an Indian orphan, they said. You always know when you're old that someone will take care of you— one of your children will. Then they'd list the old folks who were being taken care of by this child or that. No child is ever considered illegitimate among the Indians, they said. If a girl gets pregnant, the baby is still part of the family, and the mother is too. That's what they said, and they showed me real people who lived according to those principles.

Of course the ravages of colonization have taken their toll; there are orphans in Indian country now, and abandoned, brutalized old folks; there are even illegitimate children, though the very concept still strikes me as absurd. There are battered children and neglected children, and there are battered wives and women who have been raped by Indian men. Proximity to the "civilizing" effects of white Christians has not improved the moral quality of life in Indian country, though each group, Indian and white, explains the situation differently. Nor is there

much yet in the oral tradition that can enable us to adapt to these inhuman changes. But a force is growing in that direction, and it is helping Indian women reclaim their lives. Their power, their sense of direction and of self will soon be visible. It is the force of the women who speak and work and write, and it is formidable.

Through all the centuries of war and death and cultural and psychic destruction have endured the women who raise the children and tend the fires, who pass along the tales and the traditions, who weep and bury the dead, who are the dead, and who never forget. There are always the women, who make pots and weave baskets, who fashion clothes and cheer their children on at powwow, who make fry bread and piki bread, and corn soup and chili stew, who dance and sing and remember and hold within their hearts the dream of their ancient peoples—that one day the woman who thinks will speak to us again, and everywhere there will be peace. Meanwhile we tell the stories and write the books and trade tales of anger and woe and stories of fun and scandal and laugh over all manner of things that happen every day. We watch and we wait.

My great-grandmother told my mother: Never forget you are Indian. And my mother told me the same thing. This, then, is how I have gone about remembering, so that my children will remember too.

READING 4

The Master's Tools Will Never Dismantle the Master's House

Audre Lorde

I agreed to take part in a New York University Institute for the Humanities conference a year ago, with the understanding that I would be commenting upon papers dealing with the role of difference within the lives of american [sic] women: difference of race, sexuality, class, and age. The absence of these considerations weakens any feminist discussion of the personal and the political.

It is a particular academic arrogance to assume any discussion of feminist theory without examining our many differences, and without a significant input from poor women, Black and Third World women, and lesbians. And yet, I stand here as a Black lesbian feminist, having been invited to comment within the only panel at this conference where the input of Black feminists and lesbians is represented. What this says about the vision of this conference is sad, in a country where racism, sexism, and homophobia are inseparable. To read this program is to assume that lesbian and Black women have nothing to say about existentialism, the erotic, women's culture and silence, developing feminist theory, or heterosexuality and power. And what does it mean in personal and political terms when even the two Black women who did present here were literally found at the last hour? What does it mean when the tools of a racist patriarchy are used to examine the fruits of that same patriarchy? It means that only the most narrow perimeters of change are possible and allowable.

The absence of any consideration of lesbian consciousness or the consciousness of Third World women leaves a serious gap within this conference and within the papers presented here. For example, in a paper on material relationships between women, I was conscious of an either/or model of nurturing which totally dismissed my knowledge as a Black lesbian. In this paper there was no examination of mutuality between women, no systems of shared support, no interdependence as exists between lesbians and women-identified women. Yet it is only in the patriarchal model of nurturance that women "who attempt to emancipate themselves pay perhaps too high a price for the results," as this paper states.

For women, the need and desire to nurture each other is not pathological but redemptive, and it is within that knowledge that our real power is rediscovered. It is this real connection which is so feared by a patriarchal world. Only within a patriarchal structure is maternity the only social power open to women.

Interdependency between women is the way to a freedom which allows the *I* to *be*, not in order to be used, but in order to be creative. This is a difference between the passive *be* and the active *being*.

Advocating the mere tolerance of difference between women is the grossest reformism. It is a total denial of the creative function of difference in our lives. Difference must be not merely tolerated, but seen as a fund of necessary polarities between which our creativity can spark like a dialectic. Only then does the necessity for interdependency become unthreatening. Only within that interdependency of different strengths, acknowledged and equal, can the power to seek new ways of being in the world generate, as well as the courage and sustenance to act where there are no charters.

Within the interdependence of mutual (nondominant) differences lies that security which enables us to descend into the chaos of knowledge and return with true visions of our future, along with the concomitant power to effect those changes which can bring that future into being. Difference is that raw and powerful connection from which our personal power is forged.

As women, we have been taught either to ignore our differences or to view them as causes for separation and suspicion rather than as forces for change. Without community there is no liberation, only the most vulnerable and temporary armistice between an individual and her oppression. But community must not mean a shedding of our differences, nor the pathetic pretense that these differences do not exist.

Those of us who stand outside the circle of this society's definition of acceptable women; those of us who have been forged in the crucibles of difference—those of us who are poor, who are lesbians, who are Black, who are older—know that *survival is not an academic skill*. It is learning how to stand alone, unpopular and sometimes reviled, and how to make common cause with those others identified as outside the structures in order to define and seek a world in which we can all flourish. It is learning how to take our differences and make them strengths. *For the master's tools will never dismantle the master's house.* They may allow us temporarily to beat him at his own game, but they will never enable us to bring about genuine change. And this fact is threatening only to those women who still define the master's house as their only source of support.

Poor women and women of Color know there is a difference between the daily manifestations of marital slavery and prostitution because it is our daughters who line 42nd Street. If white american [sic] feminist theory need not deal with the differences between us, and the resulting difference in our oppressions, then how do you deal with the fact that the women who clean your houses and tend your children while you attend conferences on feminist theory are, for the most part, poor women and women of Color? What is the theory behind racist feminism?

In a world of possibility for us all, our personal visions help lay the groundwork for political action. The failure of academic feminists to recognize difference as a crucial strength is a failure to reach beyond the first patriarchal lesson. In our world, divide and conquer must become define and empower.

Why weren't other women of Color found to participate in this conference? Why were two phone calls to me considered a consultation? Am I the only possible source of names of Black feminists? And although the Black panelist's paper ends on an important and powerful connection of love between women, what about interracial cooperation between feminists who don't love each other?

In academic feminist circles, the answer to these questions is often, "We did not know who to ask." But that is the same evasion of responsibility, the same copout, that keeps Black women's art out of women's exhibitions, Black women's work out of most feminist publications except for the occasional "Special Third World Women's Issue," and Black women's texts off your reading lists. But as Adrienne Rich pointed out in a recent talk, white feminists have educated themselves about such an enormous amount over the past ten years, how come you haven't also educated yourselves about Black women and the differences between us—white and Black—when it is key to our survival as a movement?

Women of today are still being called upon to stretch across the gap of male ignorance and to educate men as to our existence and our needs. This is an old and primary tool of all oppressors to keep the oppressed occupied with the master's concerns. Now we hear that it is the task of women of Color to educate white women—in the face of tremendous resistance—as to our existence, our differences, our relative roles in our joint survival. This is a diversion of energies and a tragic repetition of racist patriarchal thought.

Simone de Beauvoir once said: "It is in the knowledge of the genuine conditions of our lives that we must draw our strength to live and our reasons for acting."

Racism and homophobia are real conditions of all our lives in this place and time. *I urge each one of us here to reach down into that deep place of knowledge inside herself and touch that terror and loathing of any difference that lives there. See whose face it wears.* Then the personal as the political can begin to illuminate all our choices.

READING 5

Teaching About Being an Oppressor: Some Personal and Political Considerations

Steven P. Schacht

I believe the truth about any subject only comes when all sides of the story are put together, and all their different meanings make a new one. Each writer writes the missing parts of the other writer's story. And the whole truth is what I am after

—Walker 1983, p. 49

Women's studies programs have been established on the vast majority of college and university campuses in the United States over the past twenty-five years. While the founding and continued existence of these programs has frequently been met with resistance, they have also realized untold successes. Women's studies programs have seriously challenged every academic discipline's conceptualizations of gender, ethnicity, class, and sexuality. These programs have also reinvigorated several fields of studies' ongoing dialogues—many of which had long since grown tired and stale. Correspondingly, it has been one of the fastest growing academic fields. In many ways women's studies has forever changed the face of academia.

A perhaps somewhat latent but nevertheless important outcome of this transformation has been the impact that women's studies (and feminism in general) have had on people like myself. That is being a white heterosexual[1] male from an upper-middle class background meant I was born into a social status that afforded me limitless opportunities to obtain immeasurable amounts of male prestige, privilege, power, and concordant wealth. Yet, as I enter my middle-age years (often another privileged male social status in our society) I find myself covertly and overtly rejecting the oppressive roles a male dominated society has cast for me, and replacing them with a feminist center and personal way of being (Schacht and Ewing 1998; Schacht 2000a).

This essay explores my attempts as a white male to meaningfully contribute to the Women's Studies programs on the various campuses where I have taught and to the larger feminist movement. Recognizing that I must travel a disparate path than women to realize a feminist worldview (Schacht and Ewing 1997), I similarly acknowledge that as a male (pro)feminist[2] instructor, the potential contribution I can make to women's studies is also quite different than that of female instructors (Schacht 2000b). The experiential knowledge I bring into my classes is very much situated in that of an incredibly privileged societal member: I am male, white, heterosexual, and from an upper-middle-class background (Haraway 1988). While being privileged has significantly decreased the likelihood of me being oppressed—as defined by Young (1988), I honestly can claim no experience of me being oppressed—it has correspondingly increased the likelihood of me being an oppressor. That is, both in action and mere presence, much of my life has been spent being oppressive to others. Accordingly, much of my privilege and status has been purchased at the expense of societal subordinates, as they were the real estate and obvious requisites for me being superior and doing masculinity: it was through the humiliation and degradation of others (sometimes in the form of their bruised and bloodied bodies), [3] the resultant terror and pain in their eyes, and the typical powerlessness and helplessness of their response that I came to experience and fallaciously believe myself to be superior to so many others.

A great deal of what feminists have written about and is taught in women's studies courses, however, is about experiences of being oppressed and the unjust basis of all too common societal realities. Since I lack any experiences of being oppressed, it would initially appear that I would have little to contribute to women's and other subordinated people's emancipation. Yet I believe that it is exactly through my experiences of

being an oppressor that I can contribute to the creation of a more just world. By telling my different story of the how's and why's of being an oppressor, I hope to become a meaningful collaborator in the "whole story being written," ultimately done in hopes that new, non-oppressive stories might be envisioned and acted upon.

ON BEING MALE AND OVER-PRIVILEGED

As I have written elsewhere (Schact 2000a, 2000b). I increasingly try to teach my classes using a feminist pedagogy. This has meant that both the materials I use in my all my courses and the way I approach the classroom have changed significantly over the past fifteen years that I have been teaching. While I have previously explored in detail how I have personally benefitted from a feminist instructional approach and students' positive responses to my attempts, I have yet to clearly consider what exactly it is that I am personally trying to accomplish as a white heterosexual male professing feminism in my classes?

There are obviously numerous ways I could answer this question. Moreover, I would guess that many of my answers would be quite consistent with what women feminist instructors hope to accomplish in their classes. Ultimately, however, I hope to teach the participants of my courses that the reason that women, people of color, the poor, and so forth are truly disadvantaged is that certain individuals, such as myself, are truly over-privileged in our society. More specifically, combining the feminist materials I use in my classes that explore the various ways certain people are categorically oppressed and exploited with my experiences as a white male from an upper-middle-class background, I attempt to share with the participants of my courses the ways in which much of the privilege that has been conferred upon me has been unearned, how I have benefitted from others' oppression, the often unjust nature of the rewards I have received, and what I am personally trying to do to change this.

Peggy McIntosh (2000), in her classic and frequently reprinted article "White Privilege and Male Privilege," explores the numerous ways that white people enjoy unearned skin privilege. Since I frequently use this article in my classes, I believe it provides an excellent model of how I attempt to explain the oppressive basis of my being (male, in particular, as this is the primary focus of my essay) to the participants of my classes. Her essay lists numerous (although far from exhaustive) ways that her being white confers unearned privilege to her on a daily basis. As she also notes, the conditions she chooses "attach somewhat more to skin-color privilege than to class, religion, ethnic status, or geographical location" and are ones that as far as she can tell her "African American coworkers, friends, and acquaintances . . . cannot count on most of these conditions" (p. 477)

In her analysis McIntosh makes the important distinction between "positive advantages" and "negative advantages." Positive advantages are things such as adequate housing, nutrition, and health care that all people should be entitled to. As she argues, we should work to extend these types of advantages to all people and to make them the norms of a just society. Since many of these positive advantages, however, are only available to certain people, they remain an unearned and unfair privilege. On the other hand, negative types of advantage are ones that, because of certain peoples' blind acceptance and/or unwillingness to reject them, further reinforce the hierarchical realities of our society. These are privileges that not only subordinate and oppress people but that also often further reinforce and enhance the status of the dominant party who is exercising them.

Although I explore both types of advantages in my classes, I most strongly emphasize the negative privileges that men have bestowed upon themselves in our society. The following list is a sampling of status conferring conditions I discuss in my classes that through my own past experience—as either a witness to or an active participant of—I have learned I can count on during any given day. As such, although academic research can be found in support of all these conditions, since they are based on my experiences, I accordingly prefer to list them as just that, my observations and realizations. In keeping with McIntosh's framework, these are all unearned privileges granted to me that women are largely and, in some cases, entirely denied. Because of the limits of my own partial and situated perspective, this list should obviously be considered far from exhaustive.

1. I can be reasonably sure that, for most jobs I might apply for, I will not only have a better chance of getting them than a comparably qualified woman, but I will be paid more than a woman doing the same job. In addition to having more and better-paying employment opportunities available to me than women, should I decide to venture into a traditional female vocation (e.g., nursing or schoolteacher) I can still count on being paid better and promoted more often that my female counterparts.

2. When I go to lease/buy a car or home (or to have work done on them), I can expect to not only be treated in a far more professional manner than a woman (who is often patronized in these business transactions), but in most cases to ultimately pay less for the product or service.

3. When I read the newspaper or watch the nightly news, I can largely assume that the vast majority of the stories will be about the accomplishments of men. Moreover, throughout the media I can rest assured that most positive portrayals are about men and their importance. Conversely, when women are made visible, it typically will be in a trivializing manner: as models (sex objects) to sell some good or service, or in the form of some self-help/defective-being product all "real" women need (e.g., cosmetics and weight loss products).

4. Should I enjoy watching sports, I am virtually guaranteed that all the important, most-skilled participants will also be men who are paid unbelievable sums of money to reinforce my masculine and seemingly superior sense of being. Alternatively, I am almost equally guaranteed that when women are presented at these events it most often will be in the form of them being sidelined cheerleaders for the far more important men on the field. And in the few events that women are exclusively found, they will most typically be presented in a manner that largely denigrates their skills in comparison to men's. Moreover, I am virtually guaranteed that all the sporting teams I might cheer for will have virile names to further reinforce my masculine sense of importance. Sometimes when these same names are applied to their female counterparts, one's left with quite strange results: the women's basketball team at my alma mater is called the Lady Rams.

5. If I am sexually active, even promiscuous, I can largely count on not being seen as a slut, a whore, or a prostitute. To the contrary, most typically I will be held in high regard, perhaps seen as a "stud," with such behavior attesting to my superior sense of being.

6. I can largely count on clothes fashions that ensure my mobility and reinforce my status as an impor-

tant person whereas women often are expected to wear restrictive clothing designed to objectify their status as a subordinate in our society. Moreover, since women's fashions are largely designed by men, I am virtually assured that the fashions available to me will both stay in style longer and cost less money.

7. I am not expected to spend my discretionary income on makeup skin lotion, and age defying potions to cover my flaws, nor am I expected to spend money on dieting products (unless severely obese), all so I can be seen as attractive and socially acceptable.

8. If I am married or even cohabiting, I can count on my "wife" doing most of the housework and being responsible for most of the childcare should we have children, regardless of whether she works or not.

9. Should my "wife" unexpectedly become pregnant—or for that matter, any women I might have sex with—I can rest assured that it will be almost entirely seen as her fault and responsibility to take care of especially if the pregnancy is not desired on my part.

10. Should I decide to rape a woman in my quest to feel superior, I can rest assured that it is highly unlikely that she will report my misogynist criminal activity to the police. If, however, I should incur the unfortunate charge of rape, unlike any other crime, I can count on my accuser's life and status to simultaneously be on trial to determine if she is worthy of being named my "victim."

11. To demonstrate my superiority, should I feel the need to physically assault my "wife" (or other women that I might purport to love), even to the point I might kill her, I can be reasonably assured that I will largely not be held accountable for my actions. Conversely, should a woman partake in these same actions against me, especially murder, I can count on her being held far more accountable for her actions.

12. Moreover, should abusing my "wife" not be sufficient, I can additionally turn my perversely exercised authority on my children. Should I get caught, unless it is someone else's child, I know that the most typical punishment will be for my children to be removed from my home, and that my "wife" will also largely be held accountable and blamed for my actions, thus diffusing some, if not most, of my responsibility for what I have done.

13. Should I decide to divorce my spouse, or have this decision forced upon me, if children are involved, I can count on her being the primary caretaker of them (unless I should desire otherwise), and to correspondingly experience an increase in my standard of living often with the full knowledge that hers will significantly drop.

14. Should I not have a woman immediately at my disposal to denigrate and further support my false notions of superiority, I can easily and cheaply go out and purchase or rent pornographic depictions to serve as a surrogate for this purpose. If this does not sufficiently reinforce my feelings of superiority, I can go to a strip club, a peep show, or a mud wrestling/wet t-shirt contest to have live depictions of female subordination (in the flesh), or even better yet, go out and purchase a prostitute for these same purposes.

15. When venturing out in public I can reasonably rest assured that I will not be sexually harassed or sexually assaulted. Conversely, should I come across a woman in these same contexts, I can largely count on a simple terrorist/manly man stare on my part to make her feel uncomfortable in my presence. The same also holds true for most public drinking places. If I am especially brave, I can expose myself to a woman or masturbate in front of her to even further reinforce my masculinity, and forever implant this image into her head, yet largely count on not getting caught or punished.

16. Should I have specialized medical problems, I can rest assured that the majority of research dollars being spent are to find cures for male health problems using largely male research subjects (an extreme example of this would be Viagra, which was developed for male impotence that has promising yet unproven usage possibilities for female sexual dysfunction).

17. Should I feel the desire to search for positive role models in positions of authority, nearly everywhere I look I can easily find a male to fill this need. If my identification with these specific male role models is not sufficient to bolster my perceived self-importance, I can easily further reinforce this perception by largely seeing most women in subordinate positions throughout our society.

18. When I listen to my radio or watch music videos, I can be assured that most of the performers

I will listen to will be males who often explicitly denigrate women in the verses of their songs. Moreover, most of the few female artists who make it on the airways will be conversely singing songs that reinforce male dominance and female subordination.

19. When attending school I can often count on the teacher (he or she) to perceive my inquires and presence as more important than the females that are in attendance.

20. At the schools I attend I can often count on more monies being spent on the activities men traditionally partake in, especially sports (even with the passage of Title IX over 25 years ago), and in general have wider array of activities available for me to participate in.

21. I can also be pretty confident that my parents will be supportive of a wider array of activities for me to partake in, spend more money on them, and give me more freedom to explore my surroundings.

22. When undertaking conversations with women, I can largely count on my voice being heard more often by both of us, my comments to be more validated, and should I feel the need to interrupt a woman while she is talking (further reinforcing the importance of my voice) I will in all likelihood be generously forgiven for my transgression.

23. Should I ever feel the need to verbally denigrate someone to boost my masculinity and false sense of being, I will have available an endless cache of derogatory terms that refer explicitly to women to accomplish this task. Conversely, the few derogatory terms that refer explicitly to my male gender I can often use in a positive, affirming manner. "Scott, you're such a 'dick head' or 'prick,' buddy."

24. If I so choose, I can count on numerous all male contexts to be available to me for my pleasure and affirmation. And although there are a few exclusive female settings (some auxiliaries to men's groups), I can still count on the ones I might attend to almost always be perceived as more important, replete with activities to support this assertion.

25. Finally, should I choose not to partake in any of the above conditions, the mere fact that I can make this choice is in itself indicative and quite telling of the privilege upon which it is predicated. Moreover, I can still count on other

men partaking in them, which ultimately still maintains my superior status in society. All that is expected of me is to remain silent and I, too, will cash in on my patriarchal dividend.

I am guessing that it is quite easy for the reader to see the unjust nature of each of the above conditions. Although a handful of participants in my classes will sometimes challenge their prevalence and/or applicability to their own experiences, most easily ascertain the unjust nature of these and numerous other privileges. Once each of these unfair negative advantages is presented and discussed, I always reserve a significant amount of class time to discuss what each of us might do to resist their occurrence. For the female participants of my classes this is usually accomplished by exploring the various attitudes women hold—internalized oppression—and corresponding behaviors that women often undertake to support such outcomes. For the male participants this usually involves me exploring ways men might release the firm grip they have on maintaining their existence—quite literally in some cases—and coming up with more just approaches to life

RELEASE THE PENIS AND LET THE BLOOD FLOW TO THE BRAIN. ISN'T IT AMAZING THE THINGS ONE MIGHT ASCERTAIN?

We live in a society where ignorance truly is bliss, especially for those with unearned male privilege and status, which in turn often provide men with an excuse to deny the existence of the very real and harmful sexist hierarchical realities that surround us and the active role men must play in their maintenance. While some men are willing to admit that women are disadvantaged in our society, very few men are willing to acknowledge that they are over-privileged (McIntosh 2000). After all, to actually do so would mean that men would not only have to admit the unearned and unjust basis of their advantage but perhaps even personally change and give up some of their privilege. In the highly competitive world we live in giving up any advantages—earned or unearned—one might have in the game of life would seem foolish at best to the vast majority of men.

And yet, as a partner, a mother, a sister, a daughter or just a friend, most men have significant women in their lives that they deeply care about, love, and sometimes even view as equals. I believe herein lies the true promise of the feminist pedagogy that I bring to my classes. Instead of abstractly talking about male dominance and women's subordination, I attempt to put a face, on oppression, I offer my own experiences of doing unearned male privilege, and recognize the harm it inflicted on others—both female and male. Often courageous male students will also offer their experiences of male dominance. In all classroom discussions female students freely and frequently offer their experiences of being oppressed by men. These revelations are combined with constant reminders by me that the "who's" and "what's" we are talking about are our partners, parents, siblings, children, friends, and each of us. What emerges are the lived images of the oppressor and oppressed. These "faces" demonstrate how all too common oppression is, how harmful it is for so many, and why each of us—women and men—should join together to bring about its end.

By making men aware of the unearned advantages that society confers upon them, coupled with the knowledge of how this is oppressive to the significant women in their lives, many men are left in an ideological bind: how can they personally express concern and respect for the welfare of these women all the while supporting realities that cause women's oppression in large societal settings? While I realistically have no meaningful way to measure the answer to this question, I have witnessed many men (although admittedly not all) in my classes very much loosen the otherwise firm grip they have on justifying and living the male privilege that society so unjustly confers upon them. A world without unearned male privilege would be a significant step in the pursuit of a non-oppressive, egalitarian future.

REFERENCES

Haraway, Donna. 1998. "Situated Knowledges. The Science Question in Feminism and the Privilege of a Partial Perspective." *Feminist Studies* 14. 575–591.

McIntosh, Peggy, 2000. "White Privilege and Male Privilege. A Personal Account of Coming to See Correspondences through Work in Women's Studies." pp. 475–485 in *The Social Construction of Difference and Inequality*, edited by Tracy E. Ore. Mountain View, CA: Mayfield.

Schacht, Steven P., and Doris Ewing. 1997. "The Many Paths of Feminism: Can Men Travel Any of Them?" *Journal of Gender Studies* 6(2): 159–176.

———. 1998. *Feminism and Men Reconstructing Gender Relations*. New York: New York University Press.

Schacht, Steven P. 2000a, "Paris is Burning: How Society's Stratification Systems Make Drag Queens of Us All." *Race, Gender & Class* 7(1): 147–166.

———. 2000b. "The Promise of Men Using a Female Pedagogy: The Possibilities and Limits of a Partial and Situated Perspective.' Unpublished manuscript.

Walker, Alice. 1983. *In Search of Our Mothers' Garden*. New York: Harcourt-Brace-Jovanovich.

Young, Iris. 1998. "The Five Faces Of Oppression." *Philosophical Forum*. 19: 270–90.

ENDNOTES

1. While in my classes and personal interactions I increasingly refer to and identify myself as queer and/or simply sexual, since my partner is a woman and acknowledging that most people still view and treat me as "heterosexual," I am using the term accordingly here and throughout this essay.

2. I use "(pro)feminist" as an inclusive way to recognize both men who identify as profeminist and a perhaps equal number of other men who think of themselves as male feminists.

3. The ethos of the various male groups I belonged to prescribed that one should never be violent towards a woman. Accordingly, although I have severely injured innumerable men, I never have been physically violent towards a woman. Nevertheless, when I was younger I often did use economic resources to be controlling and abusive to many women.

Theoretical Perspectives

Theory is simply an effort to understand and explain the social world. Theories of gender are attempts to outline the major processes and social structures that give rise to the differences and inequalities between women and men and to analyze how these gender inequalities are connected to other major inequalities of race, class, sexuality, and nationality. You may notice as you read some of these selections that the language of theory is a bit different from some other forms of writing. Some of these readings may seem "harder" to you, and in fact, the language in some of them is more complex as the authors attempt to make sense of abstract and complicated social processes and as they summarize others' attempts to do so. We hope that you will not be intimidated by this. Every student is smart enough to understand "theory," and the effort you put into reading these works will be rewarded in two ways: you will grasp the fascinating and provocative ideas the authors put forward, and you will gain a sense of your own competence. We are all theorists of gender, after all, whether we construct our theories in formal academic language or in everyday discussions with our friends.

Feminist scholars generally distinguish between sex, or the biological or innate characteristics of males and females, and *gender,* or the social statuses and meanings assigned to women and men. Gender is one of the most important social distinctions. Societies define men and women as separate and distinct categories, and gender or sex-based stratification is ubiquitous. An individual's gender is one of the first things we notice about her or him, and our own gender is central to our sense of who we are. Not only individuals but also behaviors (aggression, nurturing), traits (strong, delicate), and even objects (pink or blue clothes) are viewed in gendered terms. As we saw in the previous section, gender distinctions overlap with race, class, sexuality, nationality, and other inequalities. Feminist scholars seek to understand how societies construct the meaning of being a woman or a man and how gender affects individual identities, the ways people interact with each other, and inequality.

Explanations of gender inequality fall into two basic schools of thought: the essentialist and the social constructionist. The essentialist position holds that the behaviors of men and women are rooted in biological and genetic factors, including differences in hormonal patterns, physical size, aggressiveness, the propensity to "bond" with members of the same sex, and the capacity to bear children. For the essentialist, the sexual division of labor in human societies is rooted in the sexual determination to be found in all species, from ants to deer to felines to primates. Viewing such differences as a natural outgrowth of human evolution, essentialists contend that sex-based inequality and the natural superiority of the male are inevitable, functional, and necessary for the survival of the species.

The second school of thought, the social constructionist approach, bases its position on a growing body of historical and anthropological research that points to wide variations in gender behavior and in the sexual division of labor among human societies throughout time. Social constructionists contend that the diversity of cultural understandings of gender is too great to be explained by biological factors. Instead, they argue, male dominance appears to be inevitable because cultural ideas and beliefs have arisen to justify and perpetuate sex-based stratification systems that entitle men to greater power, prestige, and wealth than women. While such ideologies do not cause gender inequality, they certainly justify it as natural.

The readings in this section present various approaches to understanding gender. In " 'Night to His Day': The Social Construction of Gender," Judith Lorber outlines a social constructionist approach. She defines gender as a social institution that rests on the "socially constructed statuses" of "man" and "woman." Even the apparently dimorphic physical characteristics of the two sexes, Lorber argues, are socially interpreted and emphasized. How does the social institution of gender create *sameness* among members of each gender and *difference* between women and men? How are the genders ranked in a hierarchy that privileges men over women?

In "The Medical Construction of Gender," Suzanne Kessler illustrates the powerful role medicine plays in the social construction of the categories of male and female. Kessler challenges the notion that the biological distinctions between women and men are natural rather than subject to social construction. Drawing from interviews with medical experts who have had extensive clinical experience managing babies born with genitals that are neither clearly male nor clearly female, Kessler discusses the standard practices used by the medical establishment to define the gender of intersexed infants. The primary consideration in physi-

cians' gender assignments and corrective surgery is the ability to construct correctly formed genitals, not the other potential gender markers such as chromosomes, hormones, or psychological factors. Kessler argues that the equation of gender with a two-genital culture helps create and maintain the view that gender consists of two mutually exclusive types—female and male—despite biological evidence of greater natural variation in actual gender markers. Do you agree with the medical view that gender must be assigned immediately, decisively, and irreversibly when an intersexed child is born? What role, if any, do you think social factors should play in making decisions about gender identity? What does Kessler's article suggest about the relationship (if any) between biological differences and societal gender systems?

In addition to the labor market, other social institutions are central to the construction of gender. Central among these is what Adrienne Rich, in a classic article, called "compulsory heterosexuality."[1] Rich argued that heterosexuality is enforced through the organization of marriage, threats of violence against women who are unprotected by men, the legal system, and cultural norms. Under this system, women's romantic relationships with other women pose a threat to male dominance. Other close emotional connections between women—friendships, family relationships—also are a form of resistance to the societal demand that women cast their lot emotionally with men. Adrienne Rich and others encourage us to consider heterosexuality as a cultural ideology and social institution that proscribes and devalues all forms of female friendship and community as it perpetuates women's subordination to men. The concept of compulsory heterosexuality reminds us to consider the role of sexuality in systems of gender inequality. As you read the other selections in this section, can you find examples of how sexuality is connected to the patterns of gender inequality they describe?

Patricia Hill Collins, the foremost proponent of a Black Feminist theoretical perspective, discusses how gender looks different depending on one's social position, in "Some Group Matters:

Intersectionality, Situated Standpoints, and Black Feminist Thought." Standpoint theory, one of her topics in this article, suggests that a group's social position shapes its outlook on the world. Collins asks how we can reconcile this position with a social constructionist approach. That is, if we believe that race and gender are real only because they have been created by society, how is it that African-American women and white women, for example, see their lives differently? And how do we bring together a theory that stresses commonalities between members of a given racial or gender group with the reality that individuals experiences differ widely? Collins outlines an intersectional theory that recognizes that no single category—be it race, gender, sexuality, or class—can fully define any individual's experience, because we are all members of multiple, intersecting categories. Yet the different forms of oppression affect people's lives in different ways. Race and class have both historically included segregated living and working locations, whereas gender operates more through family and intimate relationships. As a result, standpoint theories may be more accurate for race and class perspectives because women cannot readily develop a group consciousness or culture. While some recent feminist theories seek to do away with the idea of standpoint theory in favor of seeing all social groups as fragmented and unable to share a meaningful point of view, Collins argues that this ignores the experiences of race and class groups that share a history—and a present reality—of segregation. The challenge, then, is to recognize shared group locations and differences in experience simultaneously. How does Collins suggest this can be done? Can you develop an intersectional analysis of some practices or organizations from your social environment? For example, how do race, class, and gender intersect to create the student body or student organizations at your school? What about the composition of the faculty, or the work experiences you have had? To what extent do you think people with shared racial, class, or gender identity have a common perspective on the world?

As you consider the various ways of thinking about gender presented in these articles, with which do you agree? As you read the selections in the rest of the book, consider the questions raised here about what gender is, the extent to which women share commonalities of oppression or experience, how gender intersects with other forms of inequality such as race, class, or nationality, and how gender is part of our cultural systems of meaning and our institutions and social structures.

NOTE

1. Adrienne Rich, "Compulsory Heterosexuality and Lesbian Experience," *Blood, Bread, and Poetry: Selected Prose 1979–1985* (New York: Norton, 1986).

"Night to His Day": The Social Construction of Gender

Judith Lorber

Talking about gender for most people is the equivalent of fish talking about water. Gender is so much the routine ground of everyday activities that questioning its taken-for-granted assumptions and presuppositions is like thinking about whether the sun will come up.[1] Gender is so pervasive that in our society we assume it is bred into our genes. Most people find it hard to believe that gender is constantly created and recreated out of human interaction, out of social life, and is the texture and order of that social life. Yet gender, like culture, is a human production that depends on everyone constantly "doing gender" (West and Zimmerman 1987).

And everyone "does gender" without thinking about it. Today, on the subway, I saw a well-dressed man with a year-old child in a stroller. Yesterday, on a bus, I saw a man with a tiny baby in a carrier on his chest. Seeing men taking care of small children in public is increasingly common—at least in New York City. But both men were quite obviously stared at—and smiled at, approvingly. Everyone was doing gender—the men who were changing the role of fathers and the other passengers, who were applauding them silently. But there was more gendering going on that probably fewer people noticed. The baby was wearing a white crocheted cap and white clothes. You couldn't tell if it was a boy or a girl. The child in the stroller was wearing a dark blue T-shirt and dark print pants. As they started to leave the train, the father put a Yankee baseball cap on the child's head. Ah, a boy, I thought. Then I noticed the gleam of tiny earrings in the child's ears, and as they got off, I saw the little flowered sneakers and lace-trimmed socks. Not a boy after all. Gender done.

Gender is such a familiar part of daily life that it usually takes a deliberate disruption of our expectations of how women and men are supposed to act to pay attention to how it is produced. Gender signs and signals are so ubiquitous that we usually fail to note

(everywhere)

them—unless they are missing or ambiguous. Then we are uncomfortable until we have successfully placed the other person in a gender status; otherwise, we feel socially dislocated. In our society, in addition to man and woman, the status can be *transvestite* (a person who dresses in opposite-gender clothes) and *transsexual* (a person who has had sex-change surgery). Transvestites and transsexuals carefully construct their gender status by dressing, speaking, walking, gesturing in the ways prescribed for women or men—whichever they want to be taken for—and so does any "normal" person.

For the individual, gender construction starts with assignment to a sex category on the basis of what the genitalia look like at birth.[2] Then babies are dressed or adorned in a way that displays the category because parents don't want to be constantly asked whether their baby is a girl or a boy. A sex category becomes a gender status through naming, dress, and the use of other gender markers. Once a child's gender is evident, others treat those in one gender differently from those in the other, and the children respond to the different treatment by feeling different and behaving differently. As soon as they can talk, they start to refer to themselves as members of their gender. Sex doesn't come into play again until puberty, but by that time, sexual feelings and desires and practices have been shaped by gendered norms and expectations. Adolescent boys and girls approach and avoid each other in an elaborately scripted and gendered mating dance. Parenting is gendered, with different expectations for mothers and for fathers, and people of different genders work at different kinds of jobs. The work adults do, as mothers and fathers and as low-level workers and high-level bosses, shapes women's and men's life experiences, and these experiences produce different feelings, consciousness, relationships, skills—ways of being that we call feminine or masculine.[3] All of these processes constitute the social construction of gender.

Gendered roles change—today fathers are taking care of little children, girls and boys are wearing unisex clothing and getting the same education, women and men are working at the same jobs. Although many traditional social groups are quite strict about maintaining gender differences, in other social groups they seem to be blurring. Then why the one-year-old's earrings? Why is it still so important to mark a child as a girl or a boy, to make sure she is not taken for a boy or he for a girl? What would happen if they were? They would, quite literally, have changed places in their social world.

To explain why gendering is done from birth, constantly and by everyone, we have to look not only at the way individuals experience gender but at gender as a social institution. As a social institution, gender is one of the major ways that human beings organize their lives. Human society depends on a predictable division of labor, a designated allocation of scarce goods, assigned responsibility for children and others who cannot care for themselves, common values and their systematic transmission to new members, legitimate leadership, music, art, stories, games, and other symbolic productions. One way of choosing people for the different tasks of society is on the basis of their talents, motivations, and competence—their demonstrated achievements. The other way is on the basis of gender, race, ethnicity—ascribed membership in a category of people. Although societies vary in the extent to which they use one or the other of these ways of allocating people to work and to carry out other responsibilities, every society uses gender and age grades. Every society classifies people as "girl and boy children," "girls and boys ready to be married," and "fully adult women and men," constructs similarities among them and differences between them, and assigns them to different roles and responsibilities. Personality characteristics, feelings, motivations, and ambitions flow from these different life experiences so that the members of these different groups become different kinds of people. The process of gendering and its outcome are legitimated by religion, law, science, and the society's entire set of values.

In order to understand gender as a social institution, it is important to distinguish human action from animal behavior. Animals feed themselves and their young until their young can feed themselves. Humans have to produce not only food but shelter and clothing. They also, if the group is going to continue as a social group, have to teach the children how their particular group does these tasks. In the process, humans reproduce gender, family, kinship, and a division of labor—social institutions that do not exist among animals. Primate social groups have been referred to as families, and their mating patterns as monogamy, adultery, and harems. Primate behavior has been used to prove the universality of sex differences—as built into our evolutionary inheritance (Haraway 1978). But animals' sex differences are not at all the same as humans' gender differences; animals' bonding is not kinship; animals' mating is not ordered by marriage; and animals' dominance hierarchies are not the equivalent of human stratification systems. Animals group on sex and age, relational categories that are physiologically, not socially, different. Humans create gender and age-group categories that are socially, and not necessarily physiologically, different.[4]

For animals, physiological maturity means being able to impregnate or conceive; its markers are coming into heat (estrus) and sexual attraction. For humans, puberty means being available for marriage; it is marked by rites that demonstrate this marital eligibility. Although the onset of physiological puberty is signaled by secondary sex characteristics (menstruation, breast development, sperm ejaculation, pubic and underarm hair), the onset of social adulthood is ritualized by the coming-out party or desert walkabout or bar mitzvah or graduation from college or first successful hunt or dreaming or inheritance of property. Humans have rituals that mark the passage from childhood into puberty and puberty into full adult status, as well as for marriage, childbirth, and death; animals do not (van Gennep 1960). To the extent that infants and the dead are differentiated by whether they are male or female, there are different birth rituals for girls and boys and different funeral rituals for men and women (Biersack 1984, 132–33). Rituals of puberty, marriage, and becoming a parent are gendered, creating a "woman," a "man," a "bride," a "groom," a "mother," a "father." Animals have no equivalents for these statuses.

Among animals, siblings mate and so do parents and children; humans have incest taboos and rules that encourage or forbid mating between members of different kin groups (Lévi-Strauss 1956, [1949] 1969). Any animal of the same species may feed another's young (or may not, depending on the species). Humans designate responsibility for particular children by kinship; humans frequently limit responsibility for children to the members of their kinship group or make them into members of their kinship group with adoption rituals.

Animals have dominance hierarchies based on size or on successful threat gestures and signals. These hierarchies are usually sexed, and in some species, moving to the top of the hierarchy physically changes the sex (Austad 1986). Humans have stratification patterns based on control of surplus food, ownership of property, legitimate demands on others' work and sexual services, enforced determinations of who marries whom, and approved use of violence. If a woman replaces a man at the top of a stratification hierarchy, her social status may be that of a man, but her sex does not change.

Mating, feeding, and nurturant behavior in animals is determined by instinct and imitative learning and ordered by physiological sex and age (Lancaster 1974). In humans, these behaviors are taught and symbolically reinforced and ordered by socially constructed gender and age grades. Social gender and age statuses sometimes ignore or override physiological sex and age completely. Male and female animals (unless they physiologically change) are not interchangeable; infant animals cannot take the place of adult animals. Human females can become husbands and fathers, and human males can become wives and mothers, without sex-change surgery (Blackwood 1984). Human infants can reign as kings or queens.

Western society's values legitimate gendering by claiming that it all comes from physiology—female and male procreative differences. But gender and sex are not equivalent, and gender as a social construction does not flow automatically from genitalia and reproductive organs, the main physiological differences of females and males. In the construction of ascribed social statuses, physiological differences such as sex, stage of development, color of skin, and size are crude markers. They are not the source of the social statuses of gender, age grade, and race. *Social statuses* are carefully constructed through prescribed processes of teaching, learning, emulation, and enforcement. Whatever genes, hormones, and biological evolution contribute to human social institutions is materially as well as qualitatively transformed by social practices. Every social institution has a material base, but culture and social practices transform that base into something with qualitatively different patterns and constraints. The economy is much more than producing food and goods and distributing them to eaters and users; family

and kinship are not the equivalent of having sex and procreating; morals and religions cannot be equated with the fears and ecstasies of the brain; language goes far beyond the sounds produced by tongue and larynx. No one eats "money" or "credit"; the concepts of "god" and "angels" are the subjects of theological disquisitions; not only words but objects, such as their flag, "speak" to the citizens of a country.

Similarly, gender cannot be equated with biological and physiological differences between human females and males. The building blocks of gender are *socially constructed statuses.* Western societies have only two genders, "man" and "woman." Some societies have three genders—men, women, and *berdaches* or *hijras* or *xaniths.* Berdaches, hijras, and xaniths are biological males who behave, dress, work, and are treated in most respects as social women; they are therefore not men, nor are they female women; they are, in our language, "male women."[5]There are African and American Indian societies that have a gender status called *manly hearted women*—biological females who work, marry, and parent as men; their social status is "female men" (Amadiume 1987; Blackwood 1984). They do not have to behave or dress as men to have the social responsibilities and prerogatives of husbands and fathers; what makes them men is enough wealth to buy a wife.

Modern Western societies' *transsexuals* and *transvestites* are the nearest equivalent of these crossover genders, but they are not institutionalized as third genders (Bolin 1987). Transsexuals are biological males and females who have sex-change operations to alter their genitalia. They do so in order to bring their physical anatomy into congruence with the way they want to live and with their own sense of gender identity. They do not become a third gender; they change genders. Transvestites are males who live as women and females who live as men but do not intend to have sex-change surgery. Their dress, appearance, and mannerisms fall within the range of what is expected from members of the opposite gender, so that they "pass." They also change genders, sometimes temporarily, some for most of their lives. Transvestite women have fought in wars as men soldiers as recently as the nineteenth century; some married women, and others went back to being women and married men once the war was over.[6] Some were discovered when their wounds were treated; others not until they died. In order to work as a jazz musician, a man's occupation, Billy Tipton, a woman, lived most of her life as a man. She died recently at seventy-four, leaving a wife and three adopted sons for whom she was husband and father, and musicians with whom she had played and traveled, for whom she was "one of the boys" (*New York Times* 1989).[7] There have been many other such occurrences of women passing as men to do more prestigious or lucrative men's work (Matthaei 1982, 192–93).[8]

Genders, therefore, are not attached to a biological substratum. Gender boundaries are breachable, and individual and socially organized shifts from one gender to another call attention to "cultural, social, or aesthetic dissonances" (Garber 1992, 16). These odd or deviant or third genders show us what we ordinarily take for granted—that people have to learn to be women and men. Men who cross-dress for performances or for pleasure often learn from women's magazines how to "do femininity" convincingly (Garber 1992, 41–51). Because transvestism is direct evidence of how gender is constructed, Marjorie Garber claims it has "extraordinary power . . . to disrupt, expose, and challenge, putting in question the very notion of the 'original' and of stable identity" (1992, 16).

GENDER BENDING

It is difficult to see how gender is constructed because we take it for granted that it's all biology, or hormones, or human nature. The differences between women and men seem to be self-evident, and we think they would occur no matter what society did. But in actuality, human females and males are physiologically more similar in appearance than are the two sexes of many species of animals and are more alike than different in traits and behavior (Epstein 1988). Without the deliberate use of gendered clothing, hairstyles, jewelry, and cosmetics, women and men would look far more alike.[9] Even societies that do not cover women's breasts have gender-identifying clothing, scarification, jewelry, and hairstyles.

The ease with which many transvestite women pass as men and transvestite men as women is corroborated by the common gender misidentification in Westernized societies of people in jeans, T-shirts, and sneakers. Men with long hair may be addressed as "miss," and women with short hair are often taken for men unless they offset the potential ambiguity with deliberate gender markers (Devor 1987, 1989). Jan

Morris, in *Conundrum*, an autobiographical account of events just before and just after a sex-change operation, described how easy it was to shift back and forth from being a man to being a woman when testing how it would feel to change gender status. During this time, Morris still had a penis and wore more or less unisex clothing; the context alone made the man and the woman:

> Sometimes the arena of my ambivalence was uncomfortably small. At the Travellers' Club, for example, I was obviously known as a man of sorts—women were only allowed on the premises at all during a few hours of the day, and even then were hidden away as far as possible in lesser rooms or alcoves. But I had another club, only a few hundred yards away, where I was known only as a woman, and often I went directly from one to the other, imperceptibly changing roles on the way—"Cheerio, sir," the porter would say at one club, and "Hello, madam," the porter would greet me at the other. (1975, 132)

Gender shifts are actually a common phenomenon in public roles as well. Queen Elizabeth II of England bore children, but when she went to Saudi Arabia on a state visit, she was considered an honorary man so that she could confer and dine with the men who were heads of a state that forbids unrelated men and women to have face-to-unveiled-face contact. In contemporary Egypt, lower-class women who run restaurants or shops dress in men's clothing and engage in unfeminine aggressive behavior, and middle-class educated women of professional or managerial status can take positions of authority (Rugh 1986, 131). In these situations, there is an important status change: These women are treated by the others in the situation as if they are men. From their own point of view, they are still women. From the social perspective, however, they are men.[10]

In many cultures, gender bending is prevalent in theater or dance—the Japanese kabuki are men actors who play both women and men; in Shakespeare's theater company, there were no actresses—Juliet and Lady Macbeth were played by boys. Shakespeare's comedies are full of witty comments on gender shifts. Women characters frequently masquerade as young men, and other women characters fall in love with them; the boys playing these masquerading women, meanwhile, are acting out pining for the love of men characters.[11] In *As You Like It*, when Rosalind justifies her protective cross-dressing, Shakespeare also comments on manliness:

> Were it not better,
> Because that I am more than common tall,
> That I did suit me all points like a man:
> A gallant curtle-axe upon my thigh,
> A boar-spear in my hand, and in my heart
> Lie there what hidden women's fear there will,
> We'll have a swashing and martial outside,
> As many other mannish cowards have
> That do outface it with their semblances.
>
> (I, i, 115–22)

Shakespeare's audience could appreciate the double subtext: Rosalind, a woman character, was a boy dressed in girl's clothing who then dressed as a boy; like bravery, masculinity and femininity can be put on and taken off with changes of costume and role (Howard 1988, 435).[12]

M Butterfly is a modern play of gender ambiguities, which David Hwang (1989) based on a real person. Shi Peipu, a male Chinese opera singer who sang women's roles, was a spy as a man and the lover as a woman of a Frenchman, Gallimard, a diplomat (Bernstein 1986). The relationship lasted twenty years, and Shi Peipu even pretended to be the mother of a child by Gallimard. "She" also pretended to be too shy to undress completely. As "Butterfly," Shi Peipu portrayed a fantasy Oriental woman who made the lover a "real man" (Kondo 1990b). In Gallimard's words, the fantasy was "of slender women in chong sams and kimonos who die for the love of unworthy foreign devils. Who are born and raised to be perfect women. Who take whatever punishment we give them, and bounce back, strengthened by love, unconditionally" (Hwang 1989, 91). When the fantasy woman betrayed him by turning out to be the more powerful "real man," Gallimard assumed the role of Butterfly and, dressed in a geisha's robes, killed himself: "because 'man' and 'woman' are oppositionally defined terms, reversals . . . are possible" (Kondo 1990b, 18).[13]

PORTRAIT OF A MAN

Loren Cameron

I suppose I have told the same old story countless times now. I mean, every transsexual man I've ever met tells the same story: "I never felt like a girl; I played with boys' toys and liked boys' games, etc." Then a rehash about pubescent anxiety, how your body betrays you and you begin to develop very clever coping mechanisms to manage the stress. Like bad posture to hide your budding breasts and big boots and baggy shirts—and lesbianism, if you're lucky.

That was my story, anyway. I figured out early on that I had somehow gotten a square peg, and I wasn't too happy about it. Right from the start this skin of mine just didn't fit. Maybe it was because Mom was going through a divorce when she carried me in her womb. Maybe she was having some survival issues, causing her to put me awash in testosterone.

Or maybe it was those G.I. Joes I played with. Did you ever have one? They had the best uniforms. Lots of outfits to choose from—and boots, don't forget the boots. Big guns and grenades and cool scars. (Scars. I see a real early influence here.) Or it could be that I noticed I always got KP duty and was never promoted above the rank of private when I played Army with the boys on my block. Girls were never allowed to go into combat.

I don't really know what felt so out of whack, and I don't think I really care. I guess there are as many reasons why a transsexual is transsexual as there are people in the world. All that matters is that it's my body and I can do what I want with it.

(continued)

It's too bad that my days in Lesbiana had to come to an end. After about ten years of Butch Camp. I graduated to Boy World, big time. All of a sudden, one year I woke up and realized that the boobs had to go. What's more, I wanted a beard too. And a nice, hard, lean body to go with it. A penis? I would settle for an oversize clitoris; it was cheaper, and it works better.

I guess that mean I wanted to be a man. But that felt so alien in the beginning of my change. I was still very socialized as Butch Lesbian. (That isn't the same as Female. Do ya get it?) I felt like a boy in the first few years, and I looked like one too: lots of pimples and a breaking voice, a bad temper and a randy disposition. I remember one occasion when I was shopping for clothes with my girl-friend Isabella. She was High Femme (I was still into femmes in those days), a few inches taller, and a little older than I was. We were in the boys' clothing department at Macy's, which was the only place I could find shirts to fit me. (Besides, I was in my second adolescence.) The salesperson looked at Isabella and then at me and said, "Oh, is that your son?" I was mortified. I was twenty-nine years old; Isabella was thirty-six. People used to think she was some kind of pervert or something. She was a real trouper, stayed with me through teenage zits, disapproving lesbians, and hetero assumptions. Life was pretty weird in those first years of transi-tion, but it was exciting as well.

It was then that I picked up a camera for the first time. Around '93, I guess. I was taking really bad snapshots of myself to send to friends and family. You know, the kind that are sort of out of focus and lop off the top of your head because you're holding the camera at arm's length. I really got it that visuals were essential to help the folks back home keep up with me as I went through this strange body transformation, this chemical and surgical reinvention of self. That's when I realized that visuals were useful in helping everybody else understand it too.

I knew I had to photograph us. Transsexuals, I mean. Us—that's what was new and different about the idea. I was going to be a photographer who was like them. I believed that we needed that, to see images of ourselves by one of us whose eye through the lens looked for a reflection. Self-portraiture. An eye that didn't see anything odd or freakish. An eye that looked for beauty.

I began meeting more transsexual people, listen-ing to their stories of change, and I started taking their pictures. I took more photos of myself and watched eagerly as the hormones, body building, and chest surgery sculpted my female form more and more into a male one. I was proud of what I saw, in me and in them. We all had one thing in common, if nothing else: We were hell-bent on becoming the people we believed ourselves to be. We had to; we didn't feel it was a matter of choice.

By 1996 my book *Body Alchemy* was published. It's a collection of photographs that will show you just about everything you ever wanted to know about female-to-male bodies and is chock-full of proud, handsome trans men. I have tried to repre-sent some measure of my community in an effort to provide bolstering and informative images with text for both trans and nontrans readers. I feel it has been a needed contribution in a new wave of transsexual activism, very much a part of a bur-geoning movement that began about the time I was figuring out what an f-stop was.

Finally, nearly twelve years later, I am feeling just fine. I look in the mirror, and I see the man I've worked so hard to grow up to be. My body has that muscular and hard build like those comic-book heroes that I always wanted to look like. (Well, maybe not quite as big, especially in the crotch. Did you ever notice how big they look in those tights?) My beard, at long last, has filled in, while my head begins to bald, and my photogra-phy career goes skipping down its path. I've got a delicious pup of a girlfriend (partner) who, ironi-cally (or maybe not so ironically), is a very hand-some butch, indeed. Everybody thinks that Stephanie is my son—or my boy—and that I am some kind of old pervert queer. I tell you, being a man can be a very confusing thing sometimes.

But despite the ease with which gender boundaries can be traversed in work, in social relationships, and in cultural productions, gender statuses remain. Transvestites and transsexuals do not challenge the social construction of gender. Their goal is to be feminine women and masculine men (Kando 1973). Those who do not want to change their anatomy but do want to change their gender behavior fare less well in establishing their social identity. The women Holly Devor called "gender blenders" wore their hair short, dressed in unisex pants, shirts, and comfortable shoes, and did not wear jewelry or makeup. They described their everyday dress as women's clothing: One said, "I wore jeans all the time, but I didn't wear men's clothes" (Devor 1989, 100). Their gender identity was women, but because they refused to "do femininity," they were constantly taken for men (1987, 1989, 107–42). Devor said of them: "The most common area of complaint was with public washrooms. They repeatedly spoke of the humiliation of being challenged or ejected from women's washrooms. Similarly, they found public change rooms to be dangerous territory and the buying of undergarments to be a difficult feat to accomplish" (1987, 29). In an ultimate ironic twist, some of these women said "they would feel like transvestites if they were to wear dresses, and two women said that they had been called transvestites when they had done so" (1987, 31). They resolved the ambiguity of their gender status by identifying as women in private and passing as men in public to avoid harassment on the street, to get men's jobs, and, if they were lesbians, to make it easier to display affection publicly with their lovers (Devor 1989, 107–42). Sometimes they even used men's bathrooms. When they had gender-neutral names, like Leslie, they could avoid the bureaucratic hassles that arose when they had to present their passports or other proof of identity, but because most had names associated with women, their appearance and their cards of identity were not conventionally congruent, and their gender status was in constant jeopardy.[14] When they could, they found it easier to pass as men than to try to change the stereotyped notions of what women should look like.

Paradoxically, then, bending gender rules and passing between genders do not erode but rather preserve gender boundaries. In societies with only two genders, the gender dichotomy is not disturbed by transvestites, because others feel that a transvestite is only transitorily ambiguous—is "really a man or woman underneath." After sex-change surgery, transsexuals end up in a conventional gender status—a "man" or a "woman" with the appropriate genitals (Eichler 1989). When women dress as men for business reasons, they are indicating that in that situation, they want to be treated the way men are treated; when they dress as women, they want to be treated as women:

By their male dress, female entrepreneurs signal their desire to suspend the expectations of accepted feminine conduct without losing respect and reputation. By wearing what is "unattractive" they signify that they are not intending to display their physical charms while engaging in public activity. Their loud, aggressive banter contrasts with the modest demeanor that attracts men. . . . Overt signalling of a suspension of the rules preserves normal conduct from eroding expectations. (Rugh 1986, 131)

FOR INDIVIDUALS, GENDER MEANS SAMENESS

Although the possible combinations of genitalia, body shapes, clothing, mannerisms, sexuality, and roles could produce infinite varieties in human beings, the social institution of gender depends on the production and maintenance of a limited number of gender statuses and of making the members of these statuses similar to each other. Individuals are born sexed but not gendered, and they have to be taught to be masculine or feminine.[15] As Simone de Beauvoir said: "One is not born, but rather becomes, a woman . . . ; it is civilization as a whole that produces this creature . . . which is described as feminine." (1952, 267).

Children learn to walk, talk, and gesture the way their social group says girls and boys should. Ray Birdwhistell, in his analysis of body motion as human communication, calls these learned gender displays *tertiary sex characteristics* and argues that they are needed to distinguish genders because humans are a weakly dimorphic species—their only sex markers are genitalia (1970, 39–46). Clothing, paradoxically, often hides the sex but displays the gender.

In early childhood, humans develop gendered personality structures and sexual orientations through their interactions with parents of the same and opposite gender. As adolescents, they conduct their sexual behavior according to gendered scripts. Schools, parents, peers, and the mass media guide young people into gendered work and family roles. As adults, they take on a gendered social status in their society's stratification system. Gender is thus both ascribed and achieved (West and Zimmerman 1987).

The achievement of gender was most dramatically revealed in a case of an accidental transsexual—a baby boy whose penis was destroyed in the course of a botched circumcision when he was seven months old (Money and Ehrhardt 1972, 118–23). The child's sex category was changed to "female," and a vagina was surgically constructed when the child was seventeen months old. The parents were advised that they could successfully raise the child, one of identical twins, as a girl. Physicians assured them that the child was too young to have formed a gender identity. Children's sense of which gender they belong to usually develops around the age of three, at the time that they start to group objects and recognize that the people around them also fit into categories—big, little; pink-skinned, brown-skinned; boys, girls. Three has also been the age when children's appearance is ritually gendered, usually by cutting a boy's hair or dressing him in distinctively masculine clothing. In Victorian times, English boys wore dresses up to the age of three, when they were put into short pants (Garber 1992, 1–2).

The parents of the accidental transsexual bent over backward to feminize the child—and succeeded. Frilly dresses, hair ribbons, and jewelry created a pride in looks, neatness, and "daintiness." More significant, the child's dominance was also feminized:

> The girl had many tomboyish traits, such as abundant physical energy, a high level of activity, stubbornness, and being often the dominant one in a girls' group. Her mother tried to modify her tomboyishness: ". . . I teach her to be more polite and quiet. I always wanted those virtues. I never did manage, but I'm going to try to manage them to—my daughter—to be more quiet and ladylike." From the beginning the girl had been the dominant twin. By the age of three, her dominance over her brother was, as her mother described it, that of a mother hen. The boy in turn took up for his sister, if anyone threatened her. (Money and Ehrhardt 1972, 122)

This child was not a tomboy because of male genes or hormones; according to her mother, she herself had also been a tomboy. What the mother had learned poorly while growing up as a "natural" female she insisted that her physically reconstructed son–daughter learn well. For both mother and child, the social construction of gender overrode any possibly inborn traits.

[Editors' note: For a variety of social, psychological, and medical reasons, this often-cited case of gender reassignment was not, in fact, a success. As a teenager, the child discovered that he had been born male and chose to return to living in the male sex category. Studies of other cases of gender reassignment show that as adults some individuals remain in their assigned gender, while others return to their original sex category. See John Colapinto, *As Nature Made Him: The Boy Who Was Made a Girl* (New York: Harper Collins, 2000) for a discussion of the twins case. Suzanne Kessler (Reading 7) discusses the complex factors that influence the gender reassignment of infants.]

People go along with the imposition of gender norms because the weight of morality as well as immediate social pressure enforces them. Consider how many instructions for properly gendered behavior are packed into this mother's admonition to her daughter: "This is how to hem a dress when you see the hem coming down and so to prevent yourself from looking like the slut I know you are so bent on becoming" (Kincaid 1978).

Gender norms are inscribed in the way people move, gesture, and even eat. In one African society, men were supposed to eat with their "whole mouth, wholeheartedly, and not, like women, just with the lips, that is halfheartedly, with reservation and restraint" (Bourdieu [1980] 1990, 70). Men and women in this society learned to walk in ways that proclaimed their different positions in the society:

> The manly man . . . stands up straight into the face of the person he approaches, or wishes to welcome. Ever on the alert, because ever threatened, he misses nothing of what happens around him. . . . Conversely, a well brought-up woman . . . is expected to walk with a slight stoop, avoiding every misplaced movement of her body, her head or her arms, looking down, keeping her eyes on the spot where she will next put her foot, especially if she happens to have to walk past the men's assembly. (70)

Many cultures go beyond clothing, gestures, and demeanor in gendering children. They inscribe gender directly into bodies. In traditional Chinese society, mothers bound their daughters' feet into three-inch stumps to enhance their sexual attractiveness. Jewish fathers circumcise their infant sons to show their covenant with God. Women in African societies remove the clitoris of prepubescent girls, scrape their labia, and make the lips grow together to preserve their chastity and ensure their marriageability. In Western societies, women augment their breast size with silicone and reconstruct their faces with cosmetic surgery to conform to cultural ideals of feminine beauty. Hanna Papanek (1979) notes that these practices reinforce the sense of superiority or inferiority in the adults who carry them out as well as in the children on whom they are done: The genitals of Jewish fathers and sons are physical and psychological evidence of their common dominant religious and familial status; the genitals of African mothers and daughters are physical and psychological evidence of their joint subordination.[16]

Sandra Bem (1981, 1983)argues that because gender is a powerful "schema" that orders the cognitive world, one must wage a constant, active battle for a child not to fall into typical gendered attitudes and behavior. In 1972, *Ms.* magazine published Lois Gould's fantasy of how to raise a child free of gender-typing. The experiment calls for hiding the child's anatomy from all eyes except the parents' and treating the child as neither a girl nor a boy. The child, called X, gets to do all the things boys *and* girls do. The experiment is so successful that all the children in X's class at school want to look and behave like X. At the end of the story, the creators of the experiment are asked what will happen when X grows up. The scientists' answer is that by then it will be quite clear what X is, implying that its hormones will kick in and it will be revealed as a female or male. That ambiguous, and somewhat contradictory, ending lets Gould off the hook; neither she nor we have any idea what someone brought up totally androgynously would be like sexually or socially as an adult. The hormonal input will not create gender or sexuality but will only establish secondary sex characteristics; breasts, beards, and menstruation alone do not produce social manhood or womanhood. Indeed, it is at puberty, when sex characteristics become evident, that most societies put pubescent children through their most important rites of passage, the rituals that officially mark them as fully gendered—that is, ready to marry and become adults.

Most parents create a gendered world for their newborn by naming, birth announcements, and dress. Children's relationships with same-gendered and different-gendered caretakers structure their self-identifications and personalities. Through cognitive development, children extract and apply to their own actions the appropriate behavior for those who belong in their own gender, as well as race, religion, ethnic group, and social class, rejecting what is not appropriate. If their social categories are highly valued, they value themselves highly; if their social categories are low status, they lose self-esteem (Chodorow 1974). Many feminist parents who want to raise androgynous children soon lose their children to the pull of gendered norms (Gordon 1990, 87–90). My son attended a carefully nonsexist elementary school, which didn't even have girls' and boys' bathrooms. When he was seven or eight years old, I attended a class play about "squares" and "circles" and their need for each other and noticed that all the girl squares and circles wore makeup, but none of the boy squares and circles did. I asked the teacher about it after the play, and she said, "Bobby said he was not going to wear makeup, and he is a powerful child, so none of the boys would either." In a long discussion about conformity, my son confronted me with the question of who the conformists were, the boys who followed their leader or the girls who listened to the woman teacher. In actuality, they both were, because they both followed same-gender leaders and acted in gender-appropriate ways. (Actors may wear makeup, but real boys don't.)

For human beings there is no essential femaleness or maleness, femininity or masculinity, womanhood or manhood, but once gender is ascribed, the social order constructs and holds individuals to strongly gendered norms and expectations. Individuals may vary on many of the components of gender and may shift genders temporarily or permanently, but they must fit into the limited number of gender statuses their society recognizes. In the process, they recreate their society's version of women and men: "If we do gender appropriately, we simultaneously sustain, reproduce, and render legitimate the institutional arrangements. . . . If we fail to do gender appropriately, we as individuals—not the institutional arrangements—may be called to account (for our character, motives, and predispositions)" (West and Zimmerman 1987, 146).

The gendered practices of everyday life reproduce a society's view of how women and men should act (Bourdieu [1980] 1990). Gendered social arrangements are justified by religion and cultural productions and backed by law, but the most powerful means of sustaining the moral hegemony of the dominant gender ideology is that the process is made invisible; any possible alternatives are virtually unthinkable (Foucault 1972; Gramsci 1971).[17]

FOR SOCIETY, GENDER MEANS DIFFERENCE

The pervasiveness of gender as a way of structuring social life demands that gender statuses be clearly differentiated. Varied talents, sexual preferences, identities, personalities, interests, and ways of interacting fragment the individual's bodily and social experiences. Nonetheless, these are organized in Western cultures into two and only two socially and legally recognized gender statuses, "man" and "woman."[18] In the social construction of gender, it does not matter what men and women actually do; it does not even matter if they do exactly the same thing. The social institution of gender insists only that what they do is *perceived* as different.

If men and women are doing the same tasks, they are usually spatially segregated to maintain gender separation, and often the tasks are given different job titles as well, such as executive secretary and administrative assistant (Reskin 1988). If the differences between women and men begin to blur, society's "sameness taboo" goes into action (G. Rubin 1975, 178). At a rock-and-roll dance at West Point in 1976, the year women were admitted to the prestigious military academy for the first time, the school's administrators "were reportedly perturbed by the sight of mirror-image couples dancing in short hair and dress gray trousers," and a rule was established that women cadets could dance at these events only if they wore skirts (Barkalow and Raab 1990, 53).[19] Women recruits in the U.S. Marine Corps are required to wear makeup—at a minimum, lipstick and eye shadow—and they have to take classes in makeup, hair care, poise, and etiquette. This feminization is part of a deliberate policy of making them clearly distinguishable from men Marines. Christine Williams quotes a twenty-five-year-old woman drill instructor as saying: "A lot of the recruits who come here don't wear makeup; they're tomboyish or athletic. A lot of

them have the preconceived idea that going into the military means they can still be a tomboy. They don't realize that you are a *Woman* Marine" (1989, 76–77).[20]

If gender differences were genetic, physiological, or hormonal, gender bending and gender ambiguity would occur only in hermaphrodites, who are born with chromosomes and genitalia that are not clearly female or male. Since gender differences are socially constructed, all men and all women can enact the behavior of the other, because they know the other's social script: "'Man' and 'woman' are at once empty and overflowing categories. Empty because they have no ultimate, transcendental meaning. Overflowing because even when they appear to be fixed, they still contain within them alternative, denied, or suppressed definitions" (Scott 1988, 49). Nonetheless, though individuals may be able to shift gender statuses, the gender boundaries have to hold, or the whole gendered social order will come crashing down.

Paradoxically, it is the social importance of gender statuses and their external markers—clothing, mannerisms, and spatial segregation—that makes gender bending or gender crossing possible—or even necessary. The social viability of differentiated gender statuses produces the need or desire to shift statuses. Without gender differentiation, transvestism and transsexuality would be meaningless. You couldn't dress in the opposite gender's clothing if all clothing were unisex. There would be no need to reconstruct genitalia to match identity if interests and lifestyles were not gendered. There would be no need for women to pass as men to do certain kinds of work if jobs were not typed as "women's work" and "men's work." Women would not have to dress as men in public life in order to give orders or aggressively bargain with customers.

Gender boundaries are preserved when transsexuals create congruous autobiographies of always having felt like what they are now. The transvestite's story also "recuperates social and sexual norms" (Garber 1992, 69). In the transvestite's normalized narrative, he or she "is 'compelled' by social and economic forces to disguise himself or herself in order to get a job, escape repression, or gain artistic or political 'freedom'" (Garber 1992, 70). The "true identity," when revealed, causes amazement over how easily and successfully the person passed as a member of the opposite gender, not a suspicion that gender itself is something of a put-on.

GENDER RANKING

Most societies rank genders according to prestige and power and construct them to be unequal, so that moving from one to another also means moving up or down the social scale. Among some North American Indian cultures, the hierarchy was male men, male women, female men, female women. Women produced significant durable goods (basketry, textiles, pottery, decorated leather goods), which could be traded. Women also controlled what they produced and any profit or wealth they earned. Since women's occupational realm could lead to prosperity and prestige, it was fair game for young men—but only if they became women in gender status. Similarly, women in other societies who amassed a great deal of wealth were allowed to become men—"manly hearts." According to Harriet Whitehead (1982):

> Both reactions reveal an unwillingness or inability to distinguish the sources of prestige—wealth, skill, personal efficacy (among other things)—from masculinity. Rather there is the innuendo that if a person performing female tasks can attain excellence, prosperity, or social power, it must be because that person is, at some level, a man. . . . A woman who could succeed at doing the things men did was honored as a man would be. . . . What seems to have been more disturbing to the culture—which means, for all intents and purposes, to the men—was the possibility that women, within their own department, might be onto a good thing. It was into this unsettling breach that the berdache institution was hurled. In their social aspect, women were complimented by the berdache's imitation. In their anatomic aspect, they were subtly insulted by his vaunted superiority. (108)

In American society, men-to-women transsexuals tend to earn less after surgery if they change occupations; women-to-men transsexuals tend to increase their income (Bolin 1988, 153–60; Brody 1979). Men who go into women's fields, like nursing, have less prestige than women who go into men's fields, like physics. Janice Raymond, a radical feminist, feels that transsexual men-to-women have advantages over female women because they were not socialized to be subordinate or oppressed throughout life. She says:

> We know that we are women who are born with female chromosomes and anatomy, and that whether or not we were socialized to be so-called normal women, patriarchy has treated and will treat us like women. Transsexuals have not had this same history. No man can have the history of being born and located in this culture as a woman. He can have the history of *wishing* to be a woman and of *acting* like a woman, but this gender experience is that of a transsexual, not of a woman. Surgery may confer the artifacts of outward and inward female organs but it cannot confer the history of being born a woman in this society. (1979, 114)

Because women who become men rise in the world and men who become women fall, Elaine Showalter (1987) was very critical of the movie *Tootsie*, in which Dustin Hoffman plays an actor who passes as a woman in order to be able to get work. "Dorothy" becomes a feminist "woman of the year" for standing up for women's rights not to be demeaned or sexually harassed. Showalter feels that the message of the movie is double-edged: "Dorothy's 'feminist' speeches . . . are less a response to the oppression of women than an instinctive situational male reaction to being treated like a woman. The implication is that women must be taught by men how to win their rights. . . . It says that feminist ideas are much less threatening when they come from a man" (123). Like Raymond, Showalter feels that being or having been a man gives a transsexual man-to-woman or a man cross-dressed as a woman a social advantage over those whose gender status was always "woman."[21] The implication here is that there is an experiential superiority that doesn't disappear with the gender shift.

For one transsexual man-to-woman, however, the experience of living as a woman changed his/her whole personality. As James, Morris had been a soldier, foreign correspondent, and mountain climber; as Jan, Morris is a successful travel writer. But socially, James was far superior to Jan, and so Jan developed the "learned helplessness" that is supposed to characterize women in Western society:

> We are told that the social gap between the sexes is narrowing, but I can only report that having, in the second half of the twentieth century, experienced life in both roles, there seems to me no aspect of

existence, no moment of the day, no contact, no arrangement, no response, which is not different for men and for women. The very tone of voice in which I was now addressed, the very posture of the person next in the queue, the very feel in the air when I entered a room or sat at a restaurant table, constantly emphasized my change of status.

And if other's responses shifted, so did my own. The more I was treated as woman, the more woman I became. I adapted willy-nilly. If I was assumed to be incompetent at reversing cars, or opening bottles, oddly incompetent I found myself becoming. If a case was thought too heavy for me, inexplicably I found it so myself. . . . Women treated me with a frankness which, while it was one of the happiest discoveries of my metamorphosis, did imply membership of a camp, a faction, or at least a school of thought; so I found myself gravitating always towards the female, whether in sharing a railway compartment or supporting a political cause. Men treated me more and more as junior, . . . and so, addressed every day of my life as an inferior, involuntarily, month by month I accepted the condition. I discovered that even now men prefer women to be less informed, less able, less talkative, and certainly less self-centered than they are themselves; so I generally obliged them. (1975, 165–66)[22]

COMPONENTS OF GENDER

By now, it should be clear that gender is not a unitary essence but has many components as a social institution and as an individual status.[23]

As a social institution, gender is composed of:

Gender statuses, the socially recognized genders in a society and the norms and expectations for their enactment behaviorally, gesturally, linguistically, emotionally, and physically. How gender statuses are evaluated depends on historical development in any particular society.

Gendered division of labor, the assignment of productive and domestic work to members of different gender statuses. The work assigned to those of different gender statuses strengthens the society's evaluation of those statuses—the higher the status, the more prestigious and valued the work and the greater its rewards.

Gendered kinship, the family rights and responsibilities for each gender status. Kinship statuses reflect and reinforce the prestige and power differences of the different genders.

Gendered sexual scripts, the normative patterns of sexual desire and sexual behavior, as prescribed for the different gender statuses. Members of the dominant gender have more sexual prerogatives; members of a subordinate gender may be sexually exploited.

Gendered personalities, the combinations of traits patterned by gender norms of how members of different gender statuses are supposed to feel and behave. Social expectations of others in face-to-face interaction constantly bolster these norms.

Gendered social control, the formal and informal approval and reward of conforming behavior and the stigmatization, social isolation, punishment, and medical treatment of nonconforming behavior.

Gender ideology, the justification of gender statuses, particularly, their differential evaluation. The dominant ideology tends to suppress criticism by making these evaluations seem natural.

Gender imagery, the cultural representations of gender and embodiment of gender in symbolic language and artistic productions that reproduce and legitimate gender statuses. Culture is one of the main supports of the dominant gender ideology.

For an individual, gender is composed of:

Sex category, to which the infant is assigned at birth based on appearance of genitalia. With prenatal testing and sex-typing, categorization is prenatal. Sex category may be changed later through surgery or reinspection of ambiguous genitalia.

Gender identity, the individual's sense of gendered self as a worker and family member.

Gendered marital and procreative status, fulfillment or nonfulfillment of allowed or disallowed mating, impregnation, childbearing, kinship roles.

Gendered sexual orientation, socially and individually patterned sexual desires, feelings, practices, and identification.

Gendered personality, internalized patterns of socially normative emotions as organized by family structure and parenting.

Gendered processes, the social practices of learning, being taught, picking up cues, enacting behavior already learned to be gender appropriate (or inappropriate, if rebelling, testing), developing a gender identity, "doing gender" as a member of a gender status in relationships with gendered others, acting deferent or dominant.

Gender beliefs, incorporation of or resistance to gender ideology.

Gender display, presentation of self as a certain kind of gendered person through dress, cosmetics, adornments, and permanent and reversible body markers.

For an individual, all the social components are supposed to be consistent and congruent with perceived physiology. The actual combination of genes and genitalia, prenatal, adolescent, and adult hormonal input, and procreative capacity may or may not be congruous with each other and with sex-category assignment, gender identity, gendered sexual orientation and procreative status, gender display, personality, and work and family roles. At any one time, an individual's identity is a combination of the major ascribed statuses of gender, race, ethnicity, religion, and social class, and the individual's achieved statuses, such as education level, occupation or profession, marital status, parenthood, prestige, authority, and wealth. The ascribed statuses substantially limit or create opportunities for individual achievements and also diminish or enhance the luster of those achievements.

GENDER AS PROCESS, STRATIFICATION, AND STRUCTURE

As a social institution, gender is a process of creating distinguishable social statuses for the assignment of rights and responsibilities. As part of a stratification system that ranks these statuses unequally, gender is a major building block in the social structures built on these unequal statuses.

As a *process*, gender creates the social differences that define "woman" and "man." In social interaction throughout their lives, individuals learn what is expected, see what is expected, act and react in expected ways, and thus simultaneously construct and maintain the gender order: "The very injunction to be a given gender takes place through discursive routes: to be a good mother, to be a heterosexually

desirable object, to be a fit worker, in sum, to signify a multiplicity of guarantees in response to a variety of different demands all at once" (Butler 1990, 145). Members of a social group neither make up gender as they go along nor exactly replicate in rote fashion what was done before. In almost every encounter, human beings produce gender, behaving in the ways they learned were appropriate for their gender status, or resisting or rebelling against these norms. Resistance and rebellion have altered gender norms, but so far they have rarely eroded the statuses.

Gendered patterns of interaction acquire additional layers of gendered sexuality, parenting, and work behaviors in childhood, adolescence, and adulthood. Gendered norms and expectations are enforced through informal sanctions of gender-inappropriate behavior by peers and by formal punishment or threat of punishment by those in authority should behavior deviate too far from socially imposed standards for women and men.

Everyday gendered interactions build gender into the family, the work process, and other organizations and institutions, which in turn reinforce gender expectations for individuals.[24] Because gender is a process, there is room not only for modification and variation by individuals and small groups but also for institutionalized change (Scott 1988, 7).

As part of a *stratification* system, gender ranks men above women of the same race and class. Women and men could be different but equal. In practice, the process of creating difference depends to a great extent on differential evaluation. As Nancy Jay (1981) says: "That which is defined, separated out, isolated from all else is A and pure. Not-A is necessarily impure, a random catchall, to which nothing is external except A and the principle of order that separates it from Not-A" (45). From the individual's point of view, whichever gender is A, the other is Not-A; gender boundaries tell the individual who is like him or her, and all the rest are unlike. From society's point of view, however, one gender is usually the touchstone, the normal, the dominant, and the other is different, deviant, and subordinate. In Western society, "man" is A, "wo-man" is Not-A. (Consider what a society would be like where woman was A and man Not-A.)

The further dichotomization by race and class constructs the gradations of a heterogeneous society's stratification scheme. Thus, in the United States, white is A, African American is Not-A; middle class is A, working class is Not-A, and "African-American women occupy a position whereby the inferior half of a series of these dichotomies converge" (Collins 1990, 70). The dominant categories are the hegemonic ideals, taken so for granted as the way things should be that white is not ordinarily thought of as a race, middle class as a class, or men as a gender. The characteristics of these categories define the Other as that which lacks the valuable qualities the dominants exhibit.

In a gender-stratified society, what men do is usually valued more highly than what women do because men do it, even when their activities are very similar or the same. In different regions of southern India, for example, harvesting rice is men's work, shared work, or women's work: "Wherever a task is done by women it is considered easy, and where it is done by [men] it is considered difficult" (Mencher 1988, 104). A gathering and hunting society's survival usually depends on the nuts, grubs, and small animals brought in by the women's foraging trips, but when the men's hunt is successful, it is the occasion for a celebration. Conversely, because they are the superior group, white men do not have to do the "dirty work," such as housework; the most inferior group does it, usually poor women of color (Palmer 1989).

Freudian psychoanalytic theory claims that boys must reject their mothers and deny the feminine in themselves in order to become men: "For boys the major goal is the achievement of personal masculine identification with their father and sense of secure masculine self, achieved through superego formation and disparagement of women" (Chodorow 1978, 165). Masculinity may be the outcome of boys' intrapsychic struggles to separate their identity from that of their mothers, but the proofs of masculinity are culturally shaped and usually ritualistic and symbolic (Gilmore 1990).

The Marxist feminist explanation for gender inequality is that by demeaning women's abilities and keeping them from learning valuable technological skills, bosses preserve them as a cheap and exploitable reserve army of labor. Unionized men who could be easily replaced by women collude in this process because it allows them to monopolize the better paid, more interesting, and more autonomous jobs: "Two factors emerge as helping men maintain their separation from women and their control of technological occupations. One is the active gendering of jobs and people. The second is the continual

creation of sub-divisions in the work processes, and levels in work hierarchies, into which men can move in order to keep their distance from women" (Cockburn 1985, 13).

Societies vary in the extent of the inequality in social status of their women and men members, but where there is inequality, the status "woman" (and its attendant behavior and role allocations) is usually held in lesser esteem than the status "man." Since gender is also intertwined with a society's other constructed statuses of differential evaluation—race, religion, occupation, class, country of origin, and so on—men and women members of the favored groups command more power, more prestige, and more property than the members of the disfavored groups. Within many social groups, however, men are advantaged over women. The more economic resources, such as education and job opportunities, are available to a group, the more they tend to be monopolized by men. In poorer groups that have few resources (such as working-class African Americans in the United States), women and men are more nearly equal, and the women may even outstrip the men in education and occupational status (Almquist 1987).

As a *structure*, gender divides work in the home and in economic production, legitimates those in authority, and organizes sexuality and emotional life (Connell 1987, 91–142). As primary parents, women significantly influence children's psychological development and emotional attachments, in the process reproducing gender. Emergent sexuality is shaped by heterosexual, homosexual, bisexual, and sadomasochistic patterns that are gendered—different for girls and boys, and for women and men—so that sexual statuses reflect gender statuses.

When gender is a major component of structured inequality, the devalued genders have less power, prestige, and economic rewards than the valued genders. In countries that discourage gender discrimination, many major roles are still gendered; women still do most of the domestic labor and child-rearing, even while doing full-time paid work; women and men are segregated on the job and each does work considered "appropriate"; women's work is usually paid less than men's work. Men dominate the positions of authority and leadership in government, the military, and the law; cultural productions, religions, and sports reflect men's interests.

In societies that create the greatest gender difference, such as Saudi Arabia, women are kept out of sight behind walls or veils, have no civil rights, and often create a cultural and emotional world of their own (Bernard 1981). But even in societies with less rigid gender boundaries, women and men spend much of their time with people of their own gender because of the way work and family are organized. This spatial separation of women and men reinforces gendered differentness, identity, and ways of thinking and behaving (Coser 1986).

Gender inequality—the devaluation of "women" and the social domination of "men"—has social functions and a social history. It is not the result of sex, procreation, physiology, anatomy, hormones, or genetic predispositions. It is produced and maintained by identifiable social processes and built into the general social structure and individual identities deliberately and purposefully. The social order as we know it in Western societies is organized around racial, ethnic, class, and gender inequality. I contend, therefore, that the continuing purpose of gender as a modern social institution is to construct women as a group to be the subordinates of men as a group. The life of everyone placed in the status "woman" is "night to his day—that has forever been the fantasy. Black to his white. Shut out of his system's space, she is the repressed that ensures the system's functioning" (Cixous and Clément [1975] 1986, 67).

THE PARADOX OF HUMAN NATURE

To say that sex, sexuality, and gender are all socially constructed is not to minimize their social power. These categorical imperatives govern our lives in the most profound and pervasive ways, through the social experiences and social practices of what Dorothy Smith calls the "everyday/everynight world" (1990, 31–57). The paradox of human nature is that it is *always* a manifestation of cultural meanings, social relationships, and power politics; "not biology, but culture, becomes destiny" (Butler 1990, 8). Gendered people emerge not from physiology or sexual orientation but from the exigencies of the social order, mostly from the need for a reliable division of the work of food production and the social (not physical) reproduction of new members. The moral imperatives of religion and cultural representations guard the boundary lines among genders and ensure that what is demanded, what is permitted, and what is tabooed for the people in each gender are well known and followed by most (Davies 1982). Political power, control of scarce resources, and, if necessary, violence uphold the gendered social order in the face of resistance and rebellion. Most people, however, voluntarily go along with their society's prescriptions for those of their gender status, because the norms and expectations get built into their sense of worth and identity as a certain kind of human being, and because they believe their society's way is the natural way. These beliefs emerge from the imagery that pervades the way we think, the way we see and hear and speak, the way we fantasize, and the way we feel.

There is no core or bedrock human nature below these endlessly looping processes of the social production of sex and gender, self and other, identity and psyche, each of which is a "complex cultural construction" (Butler 1990, 36). *For humans, the social is the natural.* Therefore, "in its feminist senses, gender cannot mean simply the cultural appropriation of biological sexual difference. Sexual difference is itself a fundamental—and scientifically contested—construction. Both 'sex' and 'gender' are woven of multiple, asymmetrical strands of difference, charged with multifaceted dramatic narratives of domination and struggle" (Haraway 1990, 140).

NOTES

1. Gender is, in Erving Goffman's words, an aspect of *Felicity's Condition:* "any arrangement which leads us to judge an individual's . . . acts not to be a manifestation of strangeness. Behind Felicity's Condition is our sense of what it is to be sane" (1983, 27). Also see Bem 1993; Frye 1983, 17–40; Goffman 1977.

2. In cases of ambiguity in countries with modern medicine, surgery is usually performed to make the genitalia more clearly male or female.

3. See J. Butler 1990 for an analysis of how doing gender *is* gender identity.

4. Douglas 1973; MacCormack 1980; Ortner 1974; Ortner and Whitehead 1981; Yanagisako and Collier 1987. On the social construction of childhood, see Ariès 1962; Zelizer 1985.

5. On the hijras of India, see Nanda 1990; on the xaniths of Oman, Wikan 1982, 168–86; on the American Indian berdaches, W. L. Williams 1986. Other societies that have

similar institutionalized third-gender men are the Koniag of Alaska, the Tanala of Madagascar, the Mesakin of Nuba, and the Chukchee of Siberia (Wikan 1982, 170).

6. Durova 1989; Freeman and Bond 1992; Wheelwright 1989.

7. Gender segregation of work in popular music still has not changed very much, according to Groce and Cooper 1990, despite considerable androgyny in some very popular figures. See Garber 1992 on the androgyny. She discusses Tipton on pp. 67–70.

8. In the nineteenth century, not only did these women get men's wages, but they also "had male privileges and could do all manner of things other women could not: open a bank account, write checks, own property, go anywhere unaccompanied, vote in elections" (Faderman 1981, 44).

9. When unisex clothing and men wearing long hair came into vogue in the United States in the mid-1960s, beards and mustaches for men also came into style again as gender identifications.

10. For other accounts of women being treated as men in Islamic countries, as well as accounts of women and men cross-dressing in these countries, see Garber 1992, 304–52.

11. Dollimore 1986; Garber 1992, 32–40; Greenblatt 1987, 66–93; Howard 1988. For Renaissance accounts of sexual relations with women and men of ambiguous sex, see Laqueur 1990, 134–39. For modern accounts of women passing as men that other women find sexually attractive, see Devor 1989, 136–37; Wheelwright 1989, 53–59.

12. Females who passed as men soldiers had to "do masculinity," not just dress in a uniform (Wheelwright 1989, 50–78). On the triple entendres and gender resonances of Rosalind-type characters, see Garber 1992, 71–77.

13. Also see Garber 1992, 234–66.

14. Bolin describes how many documents have to be changed by transsexuals to provide a legitimizing "paper trail" (1988, 145–47). Note that only members of the same social group know which names are women's and which men's in their culture, but many documents list "sex."

15. For an account of how a potential man-to-woman transsexual learned to be feminine, see Garfinkel 1967, 116–85, 285–88. For a gloss on this account that points out how, throughout his encounters with Agnes, Garfinkel failed to see how he himself was constructing his own masculinity, see Rogers 1992.

16. Paige and Paige (1981, 147–49) argue that circumcision ceremonies indicate a father's loyalty to his lineage elders—"visible public evidence that the head of a family unit of their lineage is willing to trust others with his and his family's most valuable political asset, his son's penis" (147). On female circumcision, see El Dareer 1982; Lightfoot-Klein 1989; van der Kwaak 1992; Walker 1992. There is a form of female circumcision that removes only the prepuce of the clitoris and is similar to male circumcision, but most forms of female circumcision are far more extensive, mutilating, and spiritually and psychologically shocking than the usual form of male circumcision. However, among the Australian aborigines, boys' penises are slit and kept open, so that they urinate and bleed the way women do (Bettelheim 1962, 165–206).

17. The concepts of moral hegemony, the effects of everyday activities (praxis) on thought and personality, and the necessity of consciousness of these processes before political change can occur are all based on Marx's analysis of class relations.

18. Other societies recognize more than two categories, but usually no more than three or four (Jacobs and Roberts 1989).

19. Carol Barkalow's book has a photograph of eleven first-year West Pointers in a math class, who are dressed in regulation pants, shirts, and sweaters, with short haircuts. The caption challenges the reader to locate the only woman in the room.

20. The taboo on males and females looking alike reflects the U.S. military's homophobia (Berube and D'Emilio 1984). If you can't tell those with a penis from those with a vagina, how are you going to determine whether their sexual interest is heterosexual or homosexual unless you watch them having sexual relations?

21. Garber feels that *Tootsie* is not about feminism but about transvestism and its possibilities for disturbing the gender order (1992, 5–9).

22. See Bolin 1988, 149–50, for transsexual men-to-women's discovery of the dangers of rape and sexual harassment. Devor's "gender blenders" went in the opposite direction. Because they found that it was an advantage to be taken for men, they did not deliberately cross-dress, but they did not feminize themselves either (1989, 126–40).

23. See West and Zimmerman 1987 for a similar set of gender components.

24. On the "logic of practice," or how the experience of gender is embedded in the norms of everyday interaction and the structure of formal organizations, see Acker 1990; Bourdieu [1980] 1990; Connell 1987; Smith 1987.

REFERENCES

Acker, Joan. 1990. Hierarchies, jobs, and bodies: A theory of gendered organizations. *Gender & Society* 4: 139–58.

Almquist, Elizabeth M. 1987. Labor market gendered inequality in minority groups. *Gender & Society* 1: 400–14.

Amadiume, Ifi. 1987. *Male daughters, female husbands: Gender and sex in an African society.* London: Zed Books.

Ariés, Philippe. 1962. *Centuries of childhood: A social history of family life,* translated by Robert Baldick. New York: Vintage.

Austad, Steven N. 1986. Changing sex nature's way. *International Wildlife,* May–June, 29.

Barkalow, Carol, with Andrea Raab. 1990. *In the men's house.* New York: Poseidon Press.

Bem, Sandra Lipsitz. 1981. Gender schema theory: A cognitive account of sex typing. *Psychological Review* 88: 354–64.

———. 1983. Gender schema theory and its implications for child development: Raising gender-aschematic children in a gender-schematic society. *Signs* 8: 598–616.

———. 1993. *The lense of gender: Transforming the debate on sexual inequality.* New Haven: Yale University Press.

Bernard, Jessie. 1981. *The female world.* New York: Free Press.

Bernstein, Richard. 1986. France jails 2 in odd case of espionage. *New York Times,* 11 May.

Berube, Allan, and John D'Emilio. 1984. The military and lesbians during the McCarthy years. *Signs* 9: 759–75.

Bettelheim, Bruno. 1962. *Symbolic wounds: Puberty rites and the envious male.* London: Thames and Hudson.

Biersack, Aletta. 1984. Paiela "women-men": The reflexive foundations of gender ideology. *American Ethnologist* 11: 118–38.

Birdwhistell, Ray L. 1970. *Kinesics and context: Essays on body motion communications.* Philadelphia: University of Pennsylvania Press.

Blackwood, Evelyn. 1984. Sexuality and gender in certain Native American tribes: The case of cross-gender females. *Signs* 10: 27–42.

Bolin, Anne. 1987. Transsexualism and the limits of traditional analysis. *American Behavioral Scientist* 31: 41–65.

———. 1988. *In search of Eve: Transsexual rites of passage.* South Hadley, Mass.: Bergin & Garvey.

Bourdieu, Pierre. [1980] 1990. *The logic of practice.* Stanford, Calif.: Stanford University Press.

Brody, Jane E. 1979. Benefits of transsexual surgery disputed as leading hospital halts the procedure. *New York Times,* 2 October.

Butler, Judith. 1990. *Gender trouble: Feminism and the subversion of identity.* New York and London: Routledge.

Chodorow, Nancy. 1974. Family structure and feminine personality. In Rosaldo and Lamphere.

———. 1978. *The reproduction of mothering.* Berkeley: University of California Press.

Cixous, Hélène, and Catherine Clement. [1975] 1986. *The newly born woman,* translated by Betsy Wing. Minneapolis: University of Minnesota Press.

Cockburn, Cynthia. 1985. *Machinery of dominance: Women, men and technical know-how.* London: Pluto Press.

Collins, Patricia Hill. 1990. *Black feminist thought: Knowledge, consciousness, and the politics of empowerment.* Boston: Unwin Hyman.

Connell, R. [Robert] W. 1987. *Gender and power: Society, the person, and sexual politics.* Stanford, Calif.: Stanford University Press.

Coser, Rose Laub. 1986. Cognitive structure and the use of social space. *Sociological Forum* 1: 1–26.

Davies, Christie. 1982. Sexual taboos and social boundaries. *American Journal of Sociology* 87: 1032–63.

de Beauvoir, Simone. 1953. *The second sex,* translated by H. M. Parshley. New York: Knopf.

Devor, Holly. 1987. Gender blending females: Women and sometimes men. *American Behavioral Scientist* 31: 12–40.

———. 1989. *Gender blending: Confronting the limits of duality.* Bloomington: Indiana University Press.

Dollimore, Jonathan. 1986. Subjectivity, sexuality, and transgression: The Jacobean connection. *Renaissance Drama,* n.s. 17: 53–81.

Douglas, Mary. 1973. *Natural symbols.* New York: Vintage.

Durova, Nadezhda. 1989. *The calvary maiden: Journals of a Russian officer in the Napoleonic wars,* translated by Mary Fleming Zirin. Bloomington: Indiana University Press.

Eichler, Margrit. 1989. Sex change operations: The last bulwark of the double standard. In *Feminist Frontiers,* edited by Laurel Richardson and Verta Taylor. New York: Random House.

El Dareer, Asma. 1982. *Woman, why do you weep? Circumcision and its consequences.* London: Zed Books.

Epstein, Cynthia Fuchs. 1988. *Deceptive distinctions: Sex, gender and the social order.* New Haven: Yale University Press.

Faderman, Lillian. 1981. *Surpassing the love of men: Romantic friendship and love between women from the Renaissance to the present.* New York: William Morrow.

Foucault, Michel. 1972. *The archeology of knowledge and the discourse on language,* translated by A. M. Sheridan Smith. New York: Pantheon.

Freeman, Lucy, and Alma Halbert Bond. 1992. *America's first woman warrior: The courage of Deborah Sampson.* New York: Paragon.

Frye, Marilyn. 1983. *The politics of reality: Essays in feminist theory.* Trumansburg, N.Y.: Crossing Press.

Garber, Marjorie. 1992. *Vested interests: Cross-dressing and cultural anxiety.* New York and London: Routledge.

Garfinkel, Harold. 1967. *Studies in ethnomethodology.* Engelwood Cliffs, N.J.: Prentice-Hall.

Gilmore, David D. 1977. *The arrangement between the sexes.* Theory and Society 4: 301–33.

———. 1990. *Manhood in the making: Cultural concepts of masculinity.* New Haven: Yale University Press.

Goffman, Erving. The arrangement between the sexes. *Theory and Society* 4: 301–33.

Goffman, Erving. Felicity's condition. *American Journal of Sociology* 89: 1–53.

Gordon, Tuula. 1990. *Feminist mothers.* New York: New York University Press.

Gramsci, Antonio. 1971. *Selections from the prison notebooks,* translated and edited by Quintin Hoare and Geoffrey Nowell Smith. New York: International Publishers.

Greenblatt, Stephen. 1987. *Shakespearean negotiations: The circulation of social energy in Renaissance England.* Berkeley: University of California Press.

Groce, Stephen B., and Margaret Cooper. 1990. Just me and the boys? Women in local-level rock and roll. *Gender & Society* 4: 220–29.

Haraway, Donna. 1978. Animal sociology and a natural economy of the body politic. Part I: A political physiology of dominance. *Signs* 4: 21–36.

———. 1990. Investment strategies for the evolving portfolio of primate females. In Jacobus, Keller, and Shuttleworth.

Howard, Jean E. 1988. Crossdressing, the theater, and gender struggle in early modern England. *Shakespeare Quarterly* 39: 418–41.

Hwang, David Henry. 1989. *M Butterfly.* New York: New American Library.

Jacobs, Sue-Ellen, and Christine Roberts. 1989. Sex, sexuality, gender, and gender variance. In *Gender and anthropology,* edited by Sandra Morgen. Washington, D.C.: American Anthropological Association.

Jay, Nancy. 1981. Gender and dichotomy. *Feminist Studies* 7: 38–56.

Kando, Thomas. 1973. *Sex change: The achievement of gender identity among feminized transsexuals.* Springfield, Ill.: Charles C. Thomas.

Kincaid, Jamaica. 1978. Girl. *The New Yorker,* 26 June.

Kondo, Dorinne K. 1990a. *Crafting selves: Power, gender, and discourses of identity in a Japanese workplace.* Chicago: University of Chicago Press.

———. 1990b. *M. Butterfly:* Orientalism, gender, and a critique of essentialist identity. Cultural Critique, no. 16 (Fall): 5–29.

Lancaster, Jane Beckman. 1974. *Primate Behavior and the Emergence of Human Culture.* New York: Holt, Rinehart and Winston.

Laqueur, Thomas. 1990. *Making sex: Body and gender from the Greeks to Freud.* Cambridge, Mass.: Harvard University Press.

Lévi-Strauss, Claude. 1956. The family. In *Man, Culture, and Society,* edited by Harry L. Shapiro, New York: Oxford.

———. [1949] 1969. *The Elementary Structures of Kinship,* translated by J. H. Bell and J. R. von Sturmer. Boston: Beacon Press.

Lightfoot-Klein, Hanny. 1989. *Prisoners of ritual: An odyssey into female circumcision in Africa.* New York: Harrington Park Press.

MacCormack, Carol P. 1980. Nature, culture and gender: A critique. In *Nature, culture and gender,* edited by Carol P. MacCormack and Marilyn Strathern. Cambridge, England: Cambridge University Press.

Matthaei, Julie A. 1982. *An Economic History of Women's Work in America.* New York: Schocken.

Mencher, Joan. 1988. Women's work and poverty: Women's contribution to household maintenance in South India. In Dwyer and Bruce.

Money, John, and Anke A. Ehrhardt. 1972. *Man & Woman, Boy & Girl.* Baltimore, Md.: Johns Hopkins University Press.

Morris, Jan. 1975. *Conundrum.* New York: Signet.

Nanda, Serena. 1990. *Neither man nor woman: The hijiras of India.* Belmont, Calif.: Wadsworth.

New York Times. 1989. Musician's death at 74 reveals he was a woman. 2 February.

Ortner, Sherry B. 1974. Is female to male as nature is to culture? In Rosaldo and Lamphere.

Ortner, Sherry B., and Harriet Whitehead. 1981. Introduction: Accounting for sexual meanings. In Ortner and Whitehead (eds.).

Paige, Karen Ericksen, and Jeffrey M. Paige 1981. *The politics of reproductive ritual.* Berkeley: University of California Press.

Palmer, Phyllis. 1989. *Domesticity and Dirt: Housewives and Domestic Servants in the United States, 1920–1945.* Philadelphia: Temple University Press.

Papanek, Hanna. 1979. Family status production: The "work" and "non-work" of women. *Signs* 4: 775–81.

Raymond, Janice G. 1979. *The Transsexual Empire: The Making of the She-male.* Boston: Beacon Press.

Reskin, Barbara F. 1988. Bringing the men back in: Sex differentiation and the devaluation of women's work. *Gender & Society* 2: 58–81.

Rogers, Mary F. 1992. They were all passing: Agnes, Garfinkel, and company. *Gender & Society* 6: 169–91.

Rosaldo, Michelle Zimbalist, and Louise Lamphere (eds.). 1974. *Woman, culture, and society.* Stanford, CA: Stanford University Press.

Rubin, Gayle. 1975. The traffic in women: Notes on the political economy of sex. In *Toward an Anthropology of Women,* ed. Rayna R[app] Reiter. New York: Monthly Review Press.

Rugh, Andrea B. 1986. *Reveal and Conceal: Dress in Contemporary Egypt.* Syracuse, N.Y.: Syracuse University Press.

Scott, Joan Wallach. 1988. *Gender and the Politics of History.* New York: Columbia University Press.

Showalter, Elaine. 1987. Critical cross-dressing: Male feminists and the woman of the year. In *Men in Feminism,* edited by Alice Jardine and Paul Smith. New York: Methuen.
Smith, Dorothy E. 1987. *The everyday world as problematic: A feminist sociology.* Toronto: University of Toronto Press.
———. 1990. *The Conceptual Practices of Power: A Feminist Sociology of Knowledge.* Toronto: University of Toronto Press.
van der Kwaak, Anke. 1992. Female circumcision and gender identity: A questionable alliance? *Social Science and Medicine* 35: 777–87.
van Gennep, Arnold. 1960. *The Rites of Passage,* trans. Monika B. Vizedom and Gabrielle L. Caffee. Chicago: University of Chicago Press.
Walker, Molly K. 1992. Maternal reactions to fetal sex. *Health Care for Women International* 13: 293–302.
West, Candace, and Don Zimmerman. 1987. Doing gender. *Gender & Society* 1: 125–51.
Wheelright, Julie. 1989. *Amazons and Military Maids: Women Who Cross-dressed in Pursuit of Life, Liberty and Happiness.* London: Pandora Press.
Whitehead, Harriet. 1982. The Bow and the Burden Strap: A New Look at Institutionalized Homosexuality in Native North America. In *Sexual meanings: The cultural construction of gender and sexuality,* edited by Sherry B. Ornter and Harriet Whitehead. New York: Cambridge University Press.
Wikan, Unni. 1982. *Behind the veil in Arabia: Women in Oman.* Baltimore, Md.: Johns Hopkins University Press.
Williams, Christine L. 1989. *Gender differences at work: Women and men in nontraditional occupations.* Berkeley: University of California Press.
Williams, Walter L. 1986. *The spirit and the flesh: Sexual diversity in American Indian culture.* Boston: Beacon Press.
Yanagisako, Sylvia Junko, and Jane Fishburne Collier. 1987. Toward a unified analysis of gender and kinship. In *Gender and kinship: Essays toward a unified analysis,* edited by Jane Fishburne Collier and Sylvia Junko Yanagisako. Berkeley: University of California Press.
Zelizer, Viviana A. 1985. *Pricing the priceless child: The changing social value of children.* New York: Basic Books.

READING 7

The Medical Construction of Gender

Suzanne Kessler

The birth of intersexed infants, babies born with genitals that are neither clearly male nor clearly female, has been documented throughout recorded time.[1] In the late twentieth century, medical technology has become sufficiently advanced to allow scientists to determine chromosomal and hormonal gender, which is typically taken to be the real, natural, biological gender, usually referred to as "sex."[2] Nevertheless, physicians who handle cases of intersexed infants consider several factors beside biological ones in determining, assigning, and announcing the gender of a particular infant. Indeed, biological factors are often preempted in physicians' deliberations by such cultural factors as the "correct" length of the penis and capacity of the vagina.

In the literature on intersexuality, issues such as announcing a baby's gender at the time of delivery, postdelivery discussions with the parents, and consultations with patients in adolescence are considered only peripherally to the central medical issues—etiology, diagnosis, and surgical procedures.[3] Yet members of medical teams have standard practices for managing intersexuality, which rely ultimately on cultural understandings of gender. The process and guidelines by which decisions about gender (re)construction are made reveal the model for the social construction of gender generally. Moreover, in the face of apparently incontrovertible evidence—infants born with some combination of "female" and "male" reproductive and sexual features—physicians hold an incorrigible belief that female and male are the only "natural" options. This paradox highlights and calls into question the idea that female and male are biological givens compelling a culture of two genders.

Ideally, to undertake an extensive study of intersexed infant case management, I would like to have had direct access to particular events, for example the deliveries of intersexed infants and the initial discussions among physicians, between physicians and parents, between parents, and among parents and family and friends of intersexed infants. The rarity with which intersexuality occurs, however, made this unfeasible.[4] Alternatively, physicians who have had considerable experience dealing with this condition were interviewed. I do not assume that their "talk" about how they manage such cases mirrors their "talk" in the situation, but their words do reveal that they have certain assumptions about gender and that they impose those assumptions via their medical decisions on the patients they treat.

Interviews were conducted with six medical experts (three women and three men) in the field of pediatric intersexuality: one clinical geneticist, three endocrinologists (two of them pediatric specialists), one psychoendocrinologist, and one urologist. All of them have had extensive clinical experience with various intersexed syndromes, and some are internationally known researchers in the field of intersexuality. They were selected on the basis of their prominence in the field and their representing four different medical centers in New York City. Although they know one another, they do not collaborate on research and are not part of the same management team. All were interviewed in the spring of 1985 in their offices. The interviews lasted between forty-five minutes and one hour. Unless further referenced, all quotations in this chapter are from these interviews.[5]

THE THEORY OF INTERSEXUALITY MANAGEMENT

The sophistication of today's medical technology has led to an extensive compilation of various intersex categories based on the various causes of malformed genitals. The "true hermaphrodite" condition, where both ovarian and testicular tissue are present either in the same gonad or in opposite gonads, accounts for fewer than 5 percent of all cases of ambiguous genitals:[6] More commonly, the infant has either ovaries or testes, but the genitals are ambiguous. If the infant has two ovaries, the condition is referred to as female pseudohermaphroditism. If the infant has two testes, the condition is referred to as male pseudohermaphroditism. There are numerous causes of both forms of pseudohermaphroditism, and although there are life-threatening aspects to some of these conditions, having ambiguous genitals per se is not harmful to

the infant's health.[7]Although most cases of ambiguous genitals do not represent true hermaphroditism, in keeping with the contemporary literature I will refer to all such cases as intersexed.

Current attitudes toward the intersex condition have been primarily influenced by three factors. First are the developments in surgery and endocrinology. Diagnoses of specific intersex conditions can be made with greater precision. Female genitals can be constructed that look much like "natural" ones, and some small penises can be enlarged with the exogenous application of hormones, although surgical skills are not sufficiently advanced to construct a "normal"-looking and -functioning penis out of other tissue.[8] Second, in the contemporary United States, the influence of the feminist movement has called into question the valuation of women according to strictly reproductive functions, and the presence or absence of functional gonads is no longer the only or the definitive criterion for gender assignment. Third, psychological theorists focus on "gender identity" (one's sense of oneself as belonging to the female or male category) as distinct from "gender role" (cultural expectations of one's behavior as "appropriate" for a female or male).[9] The relevance of this new gender identity theory for rethinking cases of ambiguous genitals is that gender must be assigned as early as possible if gender identity is to develop successfully. As a result of these three factors, intersexuality is considered a treatable condition of the genitals, one that needs to be resolved expeditiously.

According to all of the specialists interviewed, management of intersexed cases is based upon the theory of gender proposed first by John Money, J. G. Hampson, and J. L. Hempson in 1955 and developed in 1972 by Money and Anke A. Ehrhardt. The theory argues that gender identity is changeable until approximately eighteen months of age.[10] "To use the Pygmalion allegory, one may begin with the same clay and fashion a god or a goddess."[11] The theory rests on satisfying several conditions: The experts must ensure that the parents have no doubt about whether their child is male or female; the genitals must be made to match the assigned gender as soon as possible; gender-appropriate hormones must be administered at puberty; and intersexed children must be kept informed about their situation with age-appropriate explanations. If these conditions are met, the theory proposes, the intersexed child will develop a gender identity in accordance with the gender assignment (regardless of the chromosomal gender) and will not question her or his assignment and request reassignment at a later age.

Supportive evidence for Money and Ehrhardt's theory is based on only a handful of repeatedly cited cases, but it has been accepted because of the prestige of the theoreticians and its resonance with contemporary ideas about gender, children, psychology, and medicine. Gender and children are malleable; psychology and medicine are the tools used to transform them. This theory is so strongly endorsed that it has taken on the character of gospel. "I think we [physicians] have been raised in the Money theory," one endocrinologist said. Another claimed, "We always approach the problem in a similar way and it's been dictated, to a large extent, by the work of John Money and Anke Ehrhardt because they are the only people who have published, at least in medical literature, any data, any guidelines." It is provocative that this physician immediately followed this assertion with: "And I don't know how effective it really is." Contradictory data are rarely cited in reviews of the literature, were not mentioned by any of the physicians interviewed, and have not reduced these physicians' belief in the theory's validity.[12]

The doctors interviewed concur with the argument that gender must be assigned immediately, decisively, and irreversibly, and that professional opinions be presented in a clear and unambiguous way. The psychoendocrinologist said that when doctors make a statement about the infant, they should "stick to it." The urologist said, "If you make a statement that later has to be disclaimed or discredited, you've weakened your credibility." A gender assignment made decisively, unambiguously, and irrevocably contributes, I believe, to the general impression that the infant's true, natural "sex" has been discovered, and that something that was there all along has been found. It also serves to maintain the credibility of the medical profession, reassure the parents, and reflexively substantiate Money and Ehrhardt's theory.

Also according to this theory, if corrective surgery is necessary, it should take place as soon as possible. If the infant is assigned the male gender, the initial stage of penis repair is usually undertaken in the first year, and further surgery is completed before the child enters school. If the infant is assigned the female gender, vulva repair (including clitoral reduction) is usually begun by three months of age. Money suggests that if reduction of phallic tissue were delayed beyond the neonatal period, the infant would have traumatic memories of having been castrated.[13] Vaginoplasty, in those females having an adequate internal structure (e.g., the vaginal canal is near its expected location), is done between the ages of one and four years. Girls who require more complicated surgical procedures might not be surgically corrected until preadolescence.[14] The complete vaginal canal is typically constructed only when the body is fully grown, following pubertal feminization with estrogen, although some specialists have claimed surgical success with vaginal construction in the early childhood years.[15] Although physicians speculate about the possible trauma of an early-childhood "castration" memory, there is no corresponding concern that vaginal reconstructive surgery delayed beyond the neonatal period is traumatic.

Even though gender identity theory places the critical age limit for gender reassignment between eighteen months and two years, the physicians acknowledge that diagnosis, gender assignment, and genital reconstruction cannot be delayed for as long as two years, since a clear gender assignment and correctly formed genitals will determine the kind of interactions parents will have with their child.[16] The geneticist argued that when parents "change a diaper and see genitalia that don't mean much in terms of gender assignment, I think it prolongs the negative response to the baby. . . . If you have clitoral enlargement that is so extraordinary that the parents can't distinguish between male and female, it is sometimes helpful to reduce that somewhat so that the parent views the child as female." Another physician concurred: Parents "need to go home and do their job as child rearers with it very clear whether it's a boy or a girl."

DIAGNOSIS

A premature gender announcement by an obstetrician, prior to a close examination of an infant's genitals, can be problematic. Money and his colleagues claim that the primary complications in case management of intersexed infants can be traced to mishandling by medical personnel untrained in sexology.[17] According to one of the pediatric endocrinologists interterviewed, obstetricians improperly educated about intersexed conditions "don't examine the babies closely enough at birth and say things just by looking, before separating legs and looking at everything, and jump to conclusions, because 99 percent of the time it's correct. . . . People get upset, physicians I mean. And they say things that are inappropriate." For example, he said that an inexperienced obstetrician might blurt out, "I think you have a boy, or no, maybe you have a girl." Other inappropriate remarks a doctor might make in postdelivery consultation with the parents include, "You have a little boy, but he'll never function as a little boy, so you better raise him as a little girl." As a result, said the pediatric endocrinologist, "the family comes away with the idea that they have a little boy, and that's what they wanted, and that's what they're going to get." In such cases, parents sometimes insist that the child be raised male despite the physicians' instructions to the contrary. "People have in mind certain things they've heard, that this is a boy, and they're not likely to forget that, or they're not likely to let it go easily." The urologist agreed that the first gender attribution is critical: "Once it's been announced, you've got a big problem on your hands." "One of the worst things is to allow them [the parents] to go ahead and give a name and tell everyone, and it turns out the child has to be raised in the opposite sex."[18]

Physicians feel that the mismanagement of such cases requires careful remedying. The psychoendocrinologist asserted, "When I'm involved, I spend hours with the parents to explain to them what has happened and how a mistake like that could be made, *or not really a mistake but a different decision*" [my emphasis]. One pediatric endocrinologist said, "I try to dissuade them from previous misconceptions and say, `Well, I know what they meant, but the way they said it confused you. This is, I think, a better way to think about it.'" These statements reveal physicians' efforts not only to protect parents from concluding that their child is neither male nor female or both, but also to protect other physicians' decision-making processes. Case management involves perpetuating the notion that good medical decisions are based on interpretations of the infant's real "sex" rather than on cultural understandings of gender.

"Mismanagements" are less likely to occur in communities with major medical centers where specialists are prepared to deal with intersexuality and a medical team (perhaps drawing physicians from more than one teaching hospital) can be quickly assembled. The team typically consists of the original referring doctor (obstetrician or pediatrician), a pediatric endocrinologist, a pediatric surgeon (urologist or gynecologist), and a geneticist. In addition, a psychol-

ogist, psychiatrist, or psychoendocrinologist might play a role. If an infant is born with ambiguous genitals in a small community hospital without the relevant specialists on staff, the baby is likely to be transferred to a hospital where diagnosis and treatment are available. Intersexed infants born in poor rural areas where there is less medical intervention might never be referred for genital reconstruction. Many of these children, like those born in earlier historical periods, will grow up and live through adulthood with the genital ambiguity—somehow managing.

The diagnosis of intersexed conditions includes assessing the chromosomal sex and the syndrome that produced the genital ambiguity and may include medical procedures such as cytologic screening, chromosomal analysis; assessing serum electrolytes; hormone, gonadotropin, and steroids evaluation; digital examination; and radiographic genitography.[19] In any intersexed condition, if the infant isdetermined to be a genetic female (having an XX chromosome makeup), then the treatment—genital surgery to reduce the phallus size—can proceed relatively quickly, satisfying what the doctors believe are psychological and cultural demands. For example, 21-hydroxylase deficiency, a form of female pseudohermaphroditism and one of the most common conditions, can be determined by a blood test within the first few days.

If, on the other hand, the infant is determined to have at least one Y chromosome, then surgery may be considerably delayed. A decision must be made whether to test the ability of the phallic tissue to respond to human chorionic gonadotropin (HCG), a treatment intended to enlarge the microphallus enough to be a penis. The endocrinologist explained, "You do HCG testing and you find out if the male can make testosterone. . . . You can get those results back probably within three weeks. . . . You're sure the male is making testosterone—but can he respond to it? It can take three months of waiting to see whether the phallus responds."

If the Y-chromosome infant cannot make testosterone or cannot respond to the testosterone it makes, the phallus will not develop, and the Y-chromosome infant will not be considered to be a male after all. Should the infant's phallus respond to the local application of testosterone or a brief course of intramuscular injections of low-potency androgen, the gender assignment problem is resolved, but possibly at some later cost, since the penis will not grow again at puberty when the rest of the body develops.[20] Money's case-management philosophy assumes that while it may be difficult for an adult male to have a much smaller than average penis, it is very detrimental to the morale of the young boy to have a micropenis.[21] In the former case, the male's manliness might be at stake, but in the latter case, his essential maleness might be. Although the psychological consequences of these experiences have not been empirically documented, Money and his colleagues suggest that it is wise to avoid the problems of both the micropenis in childhood and the still-undersized penis postpuberty by reassigning many of these infants to the female gender.[22] This approach suggests that for Money and his colleagues, chromosomes are less relevant in determining gender than penis size, and, by implication, that "male" is defined not by the genetic condition of having one Y and one X chromosome or by the production of sperm but by the aesthetic condition of having an "appropriately" sized penis.

The tests and procedures required for diagnosis (and consequently for gender assignment) can take several months.[23] Although physicians are anxious not to make premature gender assignments, their language suggests that it is difficult for them to take a completely neutral position and to think and speak only of *phallic tissue* that belongs to an infant whose gender has not yet been determined or decided. Comments such as "seeing whether the male can respond to testosterone" imply at least a tentative male gender assignment of an XY infant. The psychoendocrinologist's explanations to parents of their infant's treatment program also illustrate this implicit male gender assignment. "Clearly this baby has an underdeveloped phallus. But if the phallus responds to this treatment, we are fairly confident that surgical techniques and hormonal techniques will help this child to look like a boy. But we want to make absolutely sure and use some hormone treatments and see whether the tissue reacts." The mere fact that this doctor refers to the genitals as an "underdeveloped" phallus rather than an overdeveloped clitoris suggests that the infant has been judged to be, at least provisionally, a male. In the case of the undersized phallus, what is ambiguous is not whether this is a penis but whether it is "good enough" to remain one. If, at the end of the treatment period, the phallic tissue has not responded, what had been a potential penis (referred to in the medical literature as a "clitoropenis") is

now considered an enlarged clitoris (or "penoclitoris"), and reconstructive surgery is planned as for the genetic female.

The time-consuming nature of intersex diagnosis and the assumption, based on the gender identity theory, that gender be assigned as soon as possible thus present physicians with difficult dilemmas. Medical personnel are committed to discovering the etiology of the condition in order to determine the best course of treatment, which takes time. Yet they feel an urgent need to provide an immediate assignment and genitals that look and function appropriately. An immediate assignment that will need to be retracted is more problematic than a delayed assignment, since reassignment carries with it an additional set of social complications. The endocrinologist interviewed commented: "We've come very far in that we can diagnose, eventually, many of the conditions. But we haven't come far enough. . . . We can't do it early enough. . . . Very frequently a decision is made before all this information is available, simply because it takes so long to make the correct diagnosis. And you cannot let a child go indefinitely, not in this society you can't. . . . There's pressure on parents [for a decision], and the parents transmit that pressure onto physicians."

A pediatric endocrinologist agreed: "At times you may need to operate before a diagnosis can be made. . . . In one case parents were told to wait on the announcement while the infant was treated to see if the phallus would grow when treated with androgens. After the first month passed and there was some growth, the parents said they had given the child a boy's name. They could only wait a month."

Deliberating out loud on the judiciousness of making parents wait for assignment decisions, the endocrinologist asked rhetorically, "Why do we do all these tests if in the end we're going to make the decision simply on the basis of the appearance of the genitalia?" This question suggests that the principles underlying physicians' decisions are cultural rather than biological, based on parental reaction and the medical team's perception of the infant's societal adjustment prospects given the way the child's genitals look or could be made to look. Moreover, as long as the decision rests largely on the criterion of genital appearance, and male is defined as having a "good-sized" penis, more infants will be assigned to the female gender than the male.

THE WAITING PERIOD: DEALING WITH AMBIGUITY

During the period of ambiguity between birth and assignment, physicians not only must evaluate the infant's prospects of becoming a good male but also must manage the parents' uncertainty about a genderless child. Physicians advise that parents postpone announcing the gender of the infant until a gender has been explicitly assigned. They believe that parents should not feel compelled to disclose the baby's "sex" to other people. The clinical geneticist interviewed said that physicians "basically encourage them [parents] to treat it [the infant] as neuter." One of the pediatric endocrinologists reported that in France parents confronted with this dilemma sometimes give the infant a neuter name such as Claude. The psychoendocrinologist concurred: "If you have a truly borderline situation, and you want to make it dependent on the hormone treatment . . . then the parents are . . . told, 'Try not to make a decision. Refer to the baby as "baby." Don't think in terms of boy or girl.'" Yet, when asked whether this is a reasonable request to make of parents in our society, the physician answered: "I don't think so. I think parents can't do it."[24]

New York State requires that a birth certificate be filled out within forty-eight hours of delivery, but the certificate need not be filed with the state for thirty days. The geneticist tells parents to insert "child of" instead of a name. In one case, parents filled out two birth registration forms, one for each gender, and they refused to sign either until a final gender assignment had been made.[25] One of the pediatric endocrinologists claimed, "I heard a story, I don't know if it's true or not. There were parents of a hermaphroditic infant who told everyone they had twins, one of each gender. When the gender was determined, they said the other had died."

The geneticist explained that when directly asked by parents what to tell others about the gender of the infant, she says, "Why don't you just tell them that the baby is having problems and as soon as the problems are resolved we'll get back to you." A pediatric endocrinologist echoes this suggestion in advising parents to say, "Until the problem is solved, [we] would really prefer not to discuss any of the details." According to the urologist, "If [the gender] isn't announced, people may mutter about it and may grumble about it, but they haven't got anything to get

their teeth into and make trouble over for the child, or the parents, or whatever." In short, parents are asked to sidestep the infant's gender rather than admit that the gender is unknown, thereby collaborating in a web of white lies, ellipses, and mystifications.[26]

Even as physicians teach parents how to deal with those who may not find the infant's condition comprehensible or acceptable, they also must make the condition comprehensible and acceptable to the parents, normalizing the intersexed condition for them. In doing so, they help the parents consider the infant's condition in the most positive way. There are four key aspects to this "normalizing" process.

First, physicians teach parents usual fetal development and explain that all fetuses have the potential to be male or female. One of the endocrinologists explains, "In the absence of maleness, you have femaleness. . . . It's really the basic design. The other [intersex] is really a variation on a theme." This explanation presents the intersex condition as a natural phase of fetal development. Another endocrinologist "like[s] to show picture[s] to them and explain that at a certain point in development males and females look alike and then diverge for such and such reason." The professional literature suggests that doctors use diagrams that illustrate "nature's principle of using the same anlagen to produce the external genital parts of the male and female."[27]

Second, physicians stress the normalcy of other aspects of the infant. For example, the geneticist tells parents, "The baby is healthy, but there was a problem in the way the baby was developing." The endocrinologist says the infant has "a mild defect, [which] just like anything could be considered a birth defect, a mole, or a hemangioma." This language not only eases the blow to the parents but also redirects their attention. Terms like "hermaphrodite" or "abnormal" are not used. The urologist said that he advised parents "about the generalization of sticking to the good things and not confusing people with something that is unnecessary."

Third, physicians (at least initially) imply that it is not the gender of the child that is ambiguous but the genitals. They talk about "undeveloped," "maldeveloped," or "unfinished" organs. From a number of the physicians interviewed came the following explanations:

At a point in time the development proceeded in a different way, and sometimes the development isn't complete and we may have some trouble . . . in determining what the *actual* sex is. And so we have to do a blood test to help us. [my emphasis]

The baby may be a female, which you would know after the buccal smear, but you can't prove it yet. If so, then it's a normal female with a different appearance. This can be surgically corrected.

The gender of your child isn't apparent to us at the moment.

While this looks like a small penis, it's actually a large clitoris. And what we're going to do is put it back in its proper position and reduce the size of the tip of it enough so it doesn't look funny, so it looks right.

Money and his colleagues report a case in which parents were advised to tell their friends that the reason their infant's gender was reannounced from male to female is that "the baby was . . . 'closed up down there.' [. . .] When the closed skin was divided, the female organs were revealed, and the baby discovered to be, *in fact*, a girl." [my emphasis] It was mistakenly assumed to be a male at first because "there was an excess of skin on the clitoris."[28]

The message in these examples is that the trouble lies in the doctor's ability to determine the gender, not in the baby's gender per se. The real gender will presumably be determined/proven by testing, and the "bad" genitals (which are confusing the situation for everyone) will be "repaired." The emphasis is not on the doctors' creating gender but in their completing the genitals. Physicians say that they "reconstruct" the genitals rather than "construct" them. The surgeons reconstitute from remaining parts what should have been there all along. The fact that gender in an infant is "reannounced" rather than "reassigned" suggests that the first announcement was a mistake because the announcer was confused by the genitals. The gender always was what it is now seen to be.[29]

Finally, physicians tell parents that social factors are more important in gender development than biological ones, even though they are searching for biological causes. In essence, the physicians teach the parents Money and Ehrhardt's theory of gender development.[30] In doing so, they shift the emphasis from the discovery of biological factors that are a sign of the "real" gender to providing the appropriate social conditions to produce the "real" gender. What remains unsaid is the apparent contradiction in the assumption that a "real" or "natural" gender can be or needs to be produced artificially. The physician/parent discussions make it clear to family members that gender is not a biological given [even though, of course, the physicians' own procedures for diagnosis assume that it is] and that gender is fluid: The psychoendocrinologist paraphrased an explanation to parents thus: "It will depend, ultimately, on how everybody treats your child and how your child is looking as a person. . . . I can with confidence tell them that generally gender [identity] clearly agrees with the assignment." A pediatric endocrinologist explained: "I try to impress upon them that there's an enormous amount of clinical data to support the fact that if you sex-reverse an infant . . . the majority of the time the alternative gender identity is commensurate with the socialization, the way that they're raised, and how people view them, and that seems to be the most critical."

The implication of these comments is that gender identity (of all children, not just those born with ambiguous genitals) is determined primarily by social factors, that the parents and community always co struct the child's gender. In the case of intersexed infants, the physicians merely provide the right genitals to go along with the socialization. Of course at so-called normal births, when the infant's genitals are unambiguous, the parents are not told that the child's gender is ultimately up to socialization. In those cases, doctors do treat gender as a biological given.

SOCIAL FACTORS IN DECISION MAKING

Most of the physicians interviewed claimed that personal convictions of doctors ought to play no role in the decision-making process. The psychoendocrinologist explained:

I think the most critical factors [are] what is the possibility that this child will grow up with genitals which look like that of the assigned gender and which will ultimately function according to gender. . . . That's why it's so important that it's a well-established team, because [personal convictions] can't really enter into it. It has to be what is surgically and endocrinologically possible for that baby to be able to make it. . . . It's really much more within medical criteria. I don't think many social factors enter into it.

While this doctor eschews the importance of social factors in gender assignment, she argues forcefully that social factors are extremely important in the development of gender identity. Indeed, she implies that social factors primarily enter the picture once the infant leaves the hospital.

In fact, doctors make decisions about gender on the basis of shared cultural values that are unstated, perhaps even unconscious, and therefore considered objective rather than subjective. Money states the fundamental rule for gender assignment: "Never assign a baby to be reared, and to surgical and hormonal therapy, as a boy, unless the phallic structure, hypospadiac or otherwise, is neonatally of at least the same caliber as that of same-aged males with small–average penises."[31] Elsewhere, he and his colleagues provide specific measurements for what qualities as a micropenis: "A penis is, by convention, designated as a micropenis when at birth its dimensions are three or more standard deviations below the mean. . . . When it is correspondingly reduced in diameter with corpora that are vestigial, . . . it unquestionably qualifies as a micropenis."[32] A pediatric endocrinologist claimed that although "the [size of the] phallus is not the deciding factor, . . . if the phallus is less than two centimeters long at birth and won't respond to androgen treatments, then it's made into a female." There is no clearer statement of the formula for gender assignment than the one given by one well-published pediatric surgeon: "The decision to raise the child with male pseudohermaphroditism as a male or female is dictated entirely by the size of the phallus."[33]

These guidelines are clear, but they focus on only one physical feature, one that is distinctly imbued with cultural meaning. This becomes especially apparent in the case of an XX infant with normal female reproductive gonads and a "perfect" penis. Would the size and shape of the penis, in this case, be the deciding factor in assigning the infant as a "male," or would the "perfect" penis be surgically destroyed and female genitals created? Money notes that this dilemma would be complicated by the anticipated reaction of the parents to seeing "their apparent son lose his penis."[34] Other researchers concur that parents are likely to want to raise a child with a normal-shaped penis (regardless of size) as "male," particularly if the scrotal area looks normal and if the parents have had no experience with intersexuality.[35] Elsewhere, Money argues in favor of not neonatally amputating the penis of XX infants since fetal masculinization of brain structures would predispose them "almost invariably [to] develop behaviorally as tomboys, even when reared as girls."[36] This reasoning implies first that tomboyish behavior in girls is bad and should be avoided and second that it is preferable to remove the internal female organs, implant prosthetic testes, and regulate the "boy's hormones for his entire life than to overlook or disregard the perfection of the penis."[37]

The ultimate proof to the physicians that they intervened appropriately and gave the intersexed infant the correct gender assignment is that the reconstructed genitals look normal and function normally in adulthood. The vulva, labia, and clitoris should appear ordinary to the woman and her partner(s), and the vagina should be able to receive a normal-sized penis. Similarly, the man and his partner(s) should feel that his penis (even if somewhat smaller than the norm) looks and functions in an unremarkable way. Although there are no published data on how much emphasis the intersexed person, him- or herself, places upon genital appearance and functioning, physicians are absolutely clear about what they believe is important. The clinical geneticist said, "If you have . . . a seventeen-year-old young lady who has gotten hormone therapy and has breast development and pubic hair and no vaginal opening, I can'teven entertain the notion that this young lady wouldn't want to have corrective surgery." The urologist summarized his criteria: "Happiness is the biggest factor. Anatomy is part of happiness." Money states, "The primary deficit [of not having sufficient penis]—and destroyer of morale—lies in being unable to satisfy the partner."[38] Another team of clinicians reveals its phallocentrism and argues that the most serious mistake in gender assignment is to create "an individual unable to engage in genital [heterosexual] sex."[39]

The equation of gender with genitals could have emerged only in an age when medical science can create genitals that appear to be normal and to function adequately, and an emphasis on the good phallus above all else could have emerged only in a culture that has rigid aesthetic and performance criteria for what constitutes maleness. The formulation "Good penis equals male; absence of good penis equals female" is treated in the literature and by the physicians interviewed as an objective criterion, operative in all cases. There is a striking lack of attention to the size and shape requirements of the female genitals, other than that the clitoris not be too big and that the vagina be able to receive a penis.[40]

In the late nineteenth century, when women's reproductive function was culturally designated as their essential characteristic, the presence or absence of ovaries (whether or not they were fertile) was held to be the ultimate criterion of gender assignment for hermaphrodites. As recently as 1955, there was some concern that if people with the same chromosomes or gonads paired off, even if they had different genitals, that "might bring the physician in conflict with the law for abetting the pursuit of (technically) illegal sex practices."[41] The urologist interviewed recalled a case from that period of a male child reassigned to "female" at the age of four or five because ovaries had been discovered. Nevertheless, doctors today, schooled in the etiology and treatment of the various intersex syndromes, view decisions based primarily on chromosomes or gonads as wrong, although, they complain, the conviction that the presence of chromosomes or gonads is the ultimate criterion "still dictates the decisions of the uneducated and uninformed."[42] Presumably the educated and informed now know that decisions based primarily on phallic size, shape, and sexual capacity are right.

While the prospect of constructing good genitals is the primary consideration in physicians' gender assignments, another extramedical factor was repeatedly cited by the six physicians interviewed—the specialty of the attending physician. Although intersexed infants are generally treated by teams of specialists, only the person who coordinates the team is actually responsible for the case. This person, acknowledged by the other physicians as having chief responsibility, acts as spokesperson to the parents. Although all of the physicians claimed that these medical teams work smoothly, with few differences of opinion, several of them mentioned decision-making orientations that are grounded in particular medical specializations. One endocrinologist stated, "The easiest route to take, where there is ever any question, . . . is to raise the child as female. . . . In this country, that is usual if the infant falls into the hands of a pediatric endocrinologist. . . . If the decision is made by the urologists, who are mostly males, . . . they're always opting, because they do the surgery, they're always feeling they can correct anything." Another endocrinologist concurred: "[Most urologists] don't think in terms of dynamic processes. They're interested in fixing pipes and lengthening pipes, and not dealing with

hormonal, and certainly not psychological issues. . . . `What can I do with what I've got?'" Urologists were defended by the clinical geneticist: "Surgeons here, now I can't speak for elsewhere, they don't get into a situation where the child is a year old and they can't make anything."

Whether or not urologists "like to make boys," as one endocrinologist claimed, the following example from a urologist who was interviewed explicitly links a cultural interpretation of masculinity to the medical treatment plan. The case involved an adolescent who had been assigned the female gender at birth but was developing some male pubertal signs and wanted to be a boy. "He was ill-equipped," said the urologist, "yet we made a very respectable male out of him. He now owns a huge construction business—those big cranes that put stuff up on the building."

POSTINFANCY CASE MANAGEMENT

After the infant's gender has been assigned, parents generally latch onto the assignment as the solution to the problem—and it is. The physician as detective has collected the evidence, as lawyer has presented the case, and as judge has rendered a verdict. Although most of the interviewees claimed that parents are equal participants in the whole process, they gave no instances of parental participation prior to the gender assignment.[43] After the physicians assign the infant's gender, the parents are encouraged to establish the credibility of that gender publicly by, for example, giving a detailed medical explanation to a leader in their community, such as a physician or pastor, who will explain the situation to curious casual acquaintances. Money argues that "medical terminology has a special layman's magic in such a context, it is final and authoritative and closes the issue."[44] He also recommends that eventually the mother "settle [the] argument once and for all among her women friends by allowing some of them to see the baby's reconstructed genitalia." Apparently, the powerful influence of normal-looking genitals helps overcome a history of ambiguous gender.

Some of the same issues that arise in assigning gender recur some years later when, at adolescence, the child may be referred to a physician for counseling.[45] The physician then tells the adolescent many of the same things his or her parents had been told years before, with the same language. Terms like "abnormal," "disorder," "disease," and "hermaphroditism" are avoided; the condition is normalized and the child's gender is treated as unproblematic. One clinician explains to his patients that sex organs are different in appearance for each person, not just those who are intersexed. Furthermore, he tells the girls "that while most women menstruate, not all do . . . that conception is only one of a number of ways to become a parent; [and] that today some individuals are choosing not to become parents."[46] The clinical geneticist tells a typical female patient: "You are female. Female is not determined by your genes. Lots of other things determine being a woman. And you are a woman but you won't be able to have babies."

A case reported by one of the pediatric endocrinologists involving an adolescent female with androgen insensitivity provides an intriguing insight into the postinfancy gender-management process. She was told at the age of fourteen "that her ovaries weren't normal and had been removed. That's why she needed pills to look normal. . . . I wanted to convince her of her femininity. Then I told her she could marry and have normal sexual relations. . . . [Her] uterus won't develop but [she] could adopt children." The urologist interviewed was asked to comment on this handling of the counseling. "It sounds like a very good solution to it. He's stating the truth, and if you don't state the truth . . . then you're in trouble later." This is a strange version of "the truth," however, since the adolescent was chromosomally XY and was born with normal testes that produced normal quantities of androgen. There *were* no ovaries or uterus. Another pediatric endocrinologist, in commenting on the management of this case, hedged the issue by saying that he would have used a generic term like "the gonads." A third endocrinologist said she would say that the uterus had never formed.

Technically, these physicians are lying when, for example, they explain to an adolescent XY female with an intersexed history that her "ovaries . . . had to be removed because they were unhealthy or were producing 'the wrong balance of hormones.'"[47] We can presume that these lies are told in the service of what physicians consider a greater good— keeping individual/concrete genders as clear and uncontaminated as the notions of female and male are in the abstract. One clinician suggests that with some female patients it eventually may be possible to talk to them "about their gonads having some structures and features that are testicular-like."[48] This call for honesty may be based, at least partly, on the possibil-

ity of the child's discovering his or her chromosomal sex inadvertently from a buccal smear taken in a high school biology class. Today's litigious climate may be another encouragement.

In sum, the adolescent is typically told that certain internal organs did not form because of an endocrinological defect, not because those organs could never have developed in someone with her or his sex chromosomes. The topic of chromosomes is skirted.

There are no published studies on how these adolescents experience their condition and their treatment by doctors. An endocrinologist interviewed mentioned that her adolescent patients rarely ask specifically what is wrong with them, suggesting that they are accomplices in this evasion. In spite of the "truth" having been evaded, the clinician's impression is that "their gender identities and general senses of well-being and self-esteem appear not to have suffered."[49]

LESSONS FROM INTERSEX MANAGEMENT

Physicians conduct careful examinations of the intersexed infant's genitals and perform intricate laboratory procedures. They are interpreters of the body, trained and committed to uncovering the "actual" gender obscured by ambiguous genitals. Yet they also have considerable leeway in assigning gender, and their decisions are influenced by cultural as well as medical factors. What is the relationship between the physician as discoverer and the physician as determiner of gender? Where is the relative emphasis placed in discussions with parents and adolescents and in the consciousness of the physicians? It is misleading to characterize the doctors whose words are provided here as presenting themselves publicly to the parents as discoverers of the infant's real gender but privately acknowledging that the infant has no real gender other than the one being determined or constructed by the medical professionals. They are not hypocritical. It is also misleading to claim that the physicians' focus shifts from discovery to determination over the course of treatment: first the doctors regard the infant's gender as an unknown but discoverable reality; then the doctors relinquish their attempts to find the real gender and treat the infant's gender as something they must construct. They are not medically incompetent or deficient. Instead, I am arguing that the peculiar balance of discovery and determination throughout treatment permits physicians to handle very problematic cases of gender in the most unproblematic of ways.

This balance relies fundamentally on a particular conception of "natural."[50] Although the "deformity" of intersexed genitals would be immutable were it not for medical interference, physicians do not consider it natural. Instead, they think of, and speak of, the surgical/hormonal alteration of such "deformities" as natural because such intervention returns the body to what it ought to have been if events had taken their typical course. The nonnormative is converted into the normative, and the normative state is considered natural.[51] The genital ambiguity is remedied to conform to a "natural," that is, culturally indisputable gender dichotomy. Sherry Ortner's claim that the culture/nature distinction is itself a construction—a product of culture—is relevant here. Language and imagery help create and maintain a specific view of what is natural about the two genders and, I would argue, about the very idea of gender—that it consists of two exclusive types: female and male.[52] The belief that gender consists of two exclusive types is maintained and perpetuated by the medical community in the face of incontrovertible physical evidence that this is not mandated by biology.

The lay conception of human anatomy and physiology assumes a concordance among clearly dimorphic gender markers—chromosomes, genitals, gonads, hormones—but physicians understand that concordance and dimorphism do not always exist. Their understanding of biology's complexity, however, does not inform their understanding of gender's complexity. In order for intersexuality to be managed differently than it currently is, physicians would have to take seriously Money's assertion that it is a misrepresentation of epistemology to consider any cell in the body authentically male or female.[53] If authenticity for gender resides not in a discoverable nature but in someone's proclamation, then the power to proclaim

something else is available. If physicians recognized that implicit in their management of gender is the notion that finally, and always, people construct gender, as well as the social systems that are grounded in gender-based concepts, the possibilities for real societal transformations would be unlimited. Unfortunately, neither in their representations to the families of the intersexed nor among themselves do the physicians interviewed for this study draw such far-reaching implications from their work. Their "understanding" that particular genders are medically (re)constructed in these cases does not lead them to see that gender *is always* constructed. Accepting genital ambiguity as a natural option would require that physicians also acknowledge that genital ambiguity is "corrected" not because it is threatening to the infant's life but because it is threatening to the infant's culture.

Rather than admit to their role in perpetuating gender, physicians "psychologize" the issue by talking about the parents' anxiety and humiliation in being confronted with an anomalous infant. They talk as though they have no choice but to respond to the parents' pressure for a resolution of psychological discomfort and as though they have no choice but to use medical technology in the service of a two-gender culture. Neither the psychology nor the technology is doubted, since both shield physicians from responsibility. Indeed, for the most part, neither physicians nor parents emerge from the experience of intersex case management with a greater understanding of the social construction of gender. Society's accountability, like their own, is masked by the assumption that gender is a given. Thus, the medical management of intersexuality, instead of illustrating nature's failure to ordain gender in these isolated, "unfortunate" instances, illustrates physicians' and Western society's failure of imagination—the failure to imagine that each of their management decisions is a moment when a specific instance of biological "sex" is transformed into a culturally constructed gender.

NOTES

1. For historical reviews of the intersexed person in ancient Greece and Rome, see Leslie Fiedler, *Freaks: Myths and Images of the Second Self* and Vern Bullough, *Sexual Variance in Society and History*. For the Middle Ages and Renaissance, see Michel Foucault, *History of Sexuality*. For the eighteenth and nineteenth centuries, see Michel Foucault, *Herculine Barbin* and Alice Domurat Dreger, *Hermaphrodites*

and the Medical Invention of Sex. For the early twentieth century, see Havelock Ellis, *Studies in the Psychology of Sex*.

2. Traditionally, the term "gender" has designated psychological, social, and cultural aspects of maleness and femaleness, and the term "sex" has specified the biological and presumably more objective components. Twenty years ago, Wendy McKenna and I introduced the argument that

"gender" should be used exclusively to refer to anything related to the categories "female" and "male," replacing the term "sex," which would be restricted to reproductive and "lovemaking" activities (Kessler and McKenna). Our reasoning was (and still is) that this would emphasize the socially constructed, overlapping nature of all category distinctions, even the biological ones. We wrote about gender chromosomes and gender hormones even though, at the time, doing so seemed awkward. I continue this practice here, but I follow the convention of referring to people with mixed biological gender cues as "intersexed" or "intersexuals" rather than as "intergendered" or "intergenderals." The latter is more consistent with my position, but I want to reflect both medical and vernacular usage without using quotation marks each time.

3. See, for example: M. Bolkenius, R. Daum, and E. Heinrich, "Paediatric Surgical Principles in the Management of Children with Intersex"; Kenneth I. Glassberg, "Gender Assignment in Newborn Male Pseudohermaphrodites"; and Peter A. Lee et al., "Micropenis. I. Criteria, Etiologies and Classification."

4. It is difficult to get accurate statistics on the frequency of intersexuality. Chromosomal abnormalities (like XOXX or XXXY) are registered, but those conditions do not always imply ambiguous genitals, and most cases of ambiguous genitals do not involve chromosomal abnormalities. None of the physicians interviewed would venture a guess on frequency rates, but all claimed that intersexuality is rare. One physician suggested that the average obstetrician may see only two cases in twenty years. Another estimated that a specialist may see only one a year or possibly as many as five a year. A reporter who interviewed physicians at Johns Hopkins Medical Center wrote that they treat, at most, ten new patients a year (Melissa Hendricks, "Is It a Boy or a Girl?"). The numbers are considerably greater if one adopts a broader definition of intersexuality to include all "sex chromosome" deviations and any genitals that do not look, according to the culturally informed view of the moment, "normal" enough. A urologist at a Mt. Sinai School of Medicine symposium on Pediatric Plastic and Reconstructive Surgery (New York City, 16 May 1996) claimed that one of every three hundred male births involves some kind of genital abnormality. A meticulous analysis of the medical literature from 1955 to 1997 led Anne Fausto-Sterling and her students to conclude that the frequency of intersexuality may be as high as 2 percent of live births, and that between 0.1 and 0.2 percent of newborns undergo some sort of genital surgery (Melanie Blackless et al., "How Sexually Dimorphic Are We?"). The Intersex Society of North America (ISNA) estimates that about five intersex surgeries are performed in the United States each day.

5. Although the interviews in this chapter were conducted more than ten years ago, interviews with physicians conducted in the mid- to late 1990s and interviews conducted with parents of intersexed children during that same time period (both reported on in later chapters) indicate that little has changed in the medical management of intersexuality. This lack of change is also evident in current medical management literature. See, for example, F. M. E. Slijper et al., "Neonates with Abnormal Genital Development Assigned the Female Sex: Parent Counseling," and M. Rohatgi, "Intersex Disorders: An Approach to Surgical Management."

6. Mariano Castro-Magana, Moris Angulo, and Platon J. Collipp, "Management of the Child with Ambiguous Genitalia."

7. For example, infants whose intersexuality is caused by congenital adrenal hyperplasia can develop severe electrolyte disturbances unless the condition is controlled by cortisone treatments. Intersexed infants whose condition is caused by androgen insensitivity are in danger of eventual malignant degeneration of the testes unless these are removed. For a complete catalog of clinical syndromes related to the intersexed condition, see Arye Lev-Ran, "Sex Reversal as Related to Clinical Syndromes in Human Beings."

8. Much of the surgical experimentation in this area has been accomplished by urologists who are trying to create penises for female-to-male transsexuals. Although there have been some advancements in recent years in the ability to create a "reasonable-looking" penis from tissue taken elsewhere on the body, the complicated requirements of the organ (requiring both urinary and sexual functioning) have posed surgical problems. It may be, however, that the concerns of the urologists are not identical to the concerns of the patients. While data are not yet available from the intersexed, we know that female-to-male transsexuals place greater emphasis on the "public" requirements of the penis (for example, being able to look normal while standing at the urinal or wearing a bathing suit) than on its functional requirements (for example, being able to achieve an erection) (Kessler and McKenna, 128–132). As surgical techniques improve, female-to-male transsexuals (and intersexed males) might increase their demands for organs that look and function better.

9. Historically, psychology has tended to blur the distinction between the two by equating a person's acceptance of her or his genitals with gender role and ignoring gender identity. For example, Freudian theory posited that if one had a penis and accepted its reality, then masculine gender role behavior would naturally follow (Sigmund Freud, "Some Psychical Consequences of the Anatomical Distinctions between the Sexes").

10. Almost all of the published literature on intersexed infant case management has been written or co-written by one researcher, John Money, professor of medical psychology and professor of pediatrics, emeritus, at Johns Hopkins University and Hospital, where he is director of the Psychohormonal Research Unit. Even the publications that

are produced independently of Money reference him and reiterate his management philosophy. Although only one of the physicians interviewed has published with Money, they all essentially concur with his views and give the impression of a consensus that is rarely encountered in science. The one physician who raised some questions about Money's philosophy and the gender theory on which it is based has extensive experience with intersexuality in a nonindustrialized culture where the infant is matured differently with no apparent harm to gender development. Even though psychologists fiercely argue issues of gender identity and gender role development, doctors who treat intersexed infants seem untouched by these debates. There are still, in the late 1990s, few renegade voices from within the medical establishment. Why Money has been so single-handedly influential in promoting his ideas about gender is a question worthy of a separate substantial analysis. His management philosophy is conveyed in the following sources: John Money, J. G. Hampson, and J. L. Hampson, "Hermaphroditism: Recommendations Concerning Assignment of Sex, Change of Sex, and Psychologic Management"; John Money, *Sex Errors of the Body: Dilemmas, Education, Counseling*; John Money, Reynolds Potter, and Clarice S. Stoll, "Sex Reannouncement in Hereditary Sex Deformity: Psychology and Sociology of Habilitation"; Money and Ehrhardt; John Money, "Psychologic Consideration of Sex Assignment in Intersexuality"; John Money, "Psychological Counseling: Hermaphroditism"; John Money, Tom Mazur, Charles Abrams, and Bernard F. Norman, "Micropenis, Family Mental Health, and Neonatal Management: A Report on Fourteen Patients Reared as Girls"; and John Money, "Birth Defect of the Sex Organs: Telling the Parents and the Patient."

11. Money and Ehrhardt, 152.

12. One exception is the case followed by Milton Diamond in "Sexual Identity, Monozygotic Twins Reared in Discordant Sex Roles and a BBC Follow-up" and, with Keith Sigmundson, in "Sex Reassignment at Birth: Long-term Review and Clinical Applications."

13. Money, "Psychologic Consideration of Sex Assignment in Intersexuality."

14. Castro-Magana, Angulo, and Collipp.

15. Victor Braren et al., "True Hermaphroditism: A Rational Approach to Diagnosis and Treatment."

16. Studies of nonintersexed newborns have shown that, from the moment of birth, parents respond to their infant based on her or his gender. Jeffrey Rubin, F. J. Provenzano, and Z. Luria, "The Eye of the Beholder: Parents' Views on Sex of Newborns."

17. Money, Mazur, Abrams, and Norman.

18. There is evidence from other kinds of sources that once a gender attribution is made, all further information buttresses that attribution, and only the most contradictory new information will cause the original gender attribution to be questioned. Kessler and McKenna.

19. Castro-Magana, Angulo, and Collipp.

20. Money, "Psychologic Consideration of Sex Assignment in Intersexuality."

21. Technically, the term "micropenis" should be reserved for an exceptionally small but well-formed structure, a small, malformed "penis" should be referred to as a "microphallus" (Peter A. Lee et al.).

22. Money, Mazur, Abrams, and Norman, 26. A different view is argued by another leading gender-identity theorist: "When a little boy (with an imperfect penis) knows he is a male, he creates a penis that functions symbolically the same as those of boys with normal penises" (Robert J. Stoller, *Sex and Gender*).

23. W. Ch. Hecker, "Operative Correction of Intersexual Genitals in Children."

24. This way of presenting advice fails to understand that parents are part of a larger system. A pediatric endocrinologist told biologist Anne Fausto-Sterling that parents, especially young ones, are not independent actors. They rely on the advice of grandparents and older siblings, who, according to the physician, are more hysterical and push for an early gender assignment before all the medical data are analyzed (private communication, summer 1996).

25. Elizabeth Bing and Esselyn Rudikoff, "Divergent Ways of Parental Coping with Hermaphrodite Children."

26. These evasions must have many ramifications in everyday social interactions between parents, family, and friends. How people "fill in" the uncertainty such that interactions remain relatively normal is an interesting question that warrants further study. One of the pediatric endocrinologists interviewed acknowledged that the published literature discusses intersex management only from the physicians' point of view. He asks, "How [do parents] experience what they're told, and what [do] they remember . . . and carry with them?" One published exception to this neglect of the parents' perspective is a case study comparing two different coping strategies. The first couple, although initially distressed, handled the traumatic event by regarding the abnormality as an act of God. The second couple, more educated and less religious, put their faith in medical science and expressed a need to fully understand the biochemistry of the defect. Bing and Rudikoff.

27. Tom Mazur, "Ambiguous Genitalia: Detection and Counseling," and Money "Psychologic Consideration of Sex Assignment in Intersexuality," 218.

28. Money, Potter, and Stoll, 211.

29. The term "reassignment" is more commonly used to describe the gender changes of those who are cognizant of their earlier gender, e.g., transsexuals—people whose gender itself was a mistake.

30. Although Money and Ehrhardt's socialization theory is uncontested by the physicians who treat intersexuality and is presented to parents as a matter of fact, there is actually much debate among psychologists about the effect of

prenatal hormones on brain structure and ultimately on gender-role behavior and even on gender identity. The physicians interviewed agreed that the animal evidence for prenatal brain organization is compelling but that there is no evidence in humans that prenatal hormones have an inviolate or unilateral effect. If there is any effect of prenatal exposure to androgen, they believe it can easily be overcome and modified by psychosocial factors. It is this latter position, not the controversy in the field, that is communicated to the parents. For an argument favoring prenatally organized gender differences in the brain, see Milton Diamond, "Human Sexual Development: Biological Foundations for Social Development"; for a critique of that position, see Ruth Bleier, *Science and Gender. A Critique of Biology and Its Theories on Women.*

31. Money, "Psychological Counseling: Hermaphroditism," 610.

32. Money, Mazur, Abrams, and Norman, 18.

33. P. Donahoe, "Clinical Management of Intersex Abnormalities."

34. John Money, "Hermaphroditism and Pseudohermaphroditism."

35. Mojtaba Beheshti, Brian E. Hardy, Bernard M. Churchill, and Denis Daneman, "Gender Assignment in Male Pseudohermaphrodite Children." Of course, if the penis looked normal and the empty scrotum was overlooked, it might not be discovered until puberty that the male child was XX with a female internal structure.

36. Money, "Psychologic Consideration of Sex Assignment in Intersexuality," 216.

37. Weighing the probability of achieving a "perfect" penis against the probable trauma such procedures may entail is another social factor in decision making. According to an endocrinologist interviewed, if it seems that an XY infant with an inadequate penis would require as many as ten genital operations over a six-year period in order to have an adequate penis, the infant would be assigned the female gender. In this case, the endocrinologist's practical and compassionate concerns would override purely genital criteria.

38. Money, "Psychologic Consideration of Sex Assignment in Intersexuality," 217.

39. Castro-Magana, Angulo, and Collipp, 180.

40. It is unclear how much of this bias is the result of a general cultural devaluation of the female and how much is the result of physicians' belief in their ability to construct anatomically correct and functional female genitals.

41. John F. Oliven, *Sexual Hygiene and Pathology: A Manual for the Physician.*

42. Money, "Psychologic Consideration of Sex Assignment in Intersexuality," 215. Remnants of this anachronistic view can still be found, however, when doctors justify the removal of contradictory gonads on the grounds that they are typically sterile or at risk for malignancy (J. Dewhurst and D. B. Grant, "Intersex Problems.") Presumably, if the gonads were functional and healthy, their removal would provide an ethical dilemma for at least some medical professionals.

43. Although one set of authors argued that the views of the parents on the most appropriate gender for their child must be taken into account (Dewhurst and Grant, 1192), the physicians interviewed here denied direct knowledge of this kind of participation. They claimed that they personally had encountered few, if any, cases of parents who insisted on their child being assigned a particular gender. Yet each had heard about cases where a family's ethnicity or religious background biased them toward males. None of the physicians recalled whether this preference for male offspring meant the parents wanted a male regardless of the "inadequacy" of the penis, or whether it meant that the parents would have greater difficulty with a less-than-perfect-male than with a "normal" female.

44. Money, "Psychological Counseling: Hermaphroditism," 613.

45. As with the literature on infancy, most of the published material on adolescents is on surgical and hormonal management rather than on social management. See, for example, Joel J. Roslyn, Eric W. Fonkalsrud, and Barbara Lippe, "Intersex Disorders in Adolescents and Adults."

46. Mazur, 421.

47. Dewhurst and Grant, 1193.

48. Mazur, 422.

49. Ibid.

50. For an extended discussion of different ways of conceptualizing what is natural, see Richard W. Smith, "What Kind of Sex Is Natural?"

51. This supports sociologist Harold Garfinkel's argument that we treat routine events as our *due* as social members and that we treat gender, like all normal forms, as a moral imperative. It is no wonder, then, that physicians conceptualize what they are doing as natural and unquestionably "right." Harold Garfinkel, *Studies in Ethnomethodology.*

52. Sherry B. Ortner, "Is Female to Male as Nature Is to Culture?"

53. Money, "Psychological Counseling: Hermaphroditism," 618.

REFERENCES

Beheshti, Mojtaba, Brian E. Hardy, Bernard M. Churchill, and Denis Daneman. "Gender Assignment in Male Pseudohermaphrodite Children." *Urology* 22, no. 6 (December 1983): 604–607.

Bing, Elizabeth and Esselyn Rudikoff. "Divergent Ways of Parental Coping with Hermaphrodite Children." *Medical Aspects of Human Sexuality* (December 1970): 73–88.

Blackless, Melanie, Anthony Charuvastra, Amanda Derryck, Anne Fausto-Sterling, Karl Lauzanne, and Ellen Lee. "How Sexually Dimorphic Are We?" Unpublished manuscript, 1997.

Bleier, Ruth. *Science and Gender: A Critique of Biology and Its Theories on Women.* New York: Pergamon Press, 1984.

Bolkenius, M., R. Daum, and E. Heinrich. "Paediatric Surgical Principles in the Management of Children with Intersex." *Progress in Pediatric Surgery* 17 (1984): 33–38.

Braren, Victor, John J. Warner, Ian M. Burr, Alfred Slonim, James A. O'Neill Jr., and Robert K. Rhamy. "True Hermaphroditism: A Rational Approach to Diagnosis and Treatment." *Urology* 15 (June 1980): 569–574.

Bullough, Vern. *Sexual Variance in Society and History.* New York: John Wiley and Sons, 1976.

Castro-Magana, Mariano, Moris Angulo, and Platon J. Collipp. "Management of the Child with Ambiguous Genitalia." *Medical Aspects of Human Sexuality* 18, no. 4 (April 1984): 172–188.

Dewhurst, J., and D. B. Grant. "Intersex Problems." *Archives of Disease in Childhood* 59 (July–December 1984): 1191–1194.

Diamond, Milton. "Human Sexual Development: Biological Foundations for Social Development." In *Human Sexuality in Four Perspectives,* ed. Frank A. Beach, 22–61. Baltimore: The Johns Hopkins University Press, 1976.

———. "Sexual Identity, Monozygotic Twins Reared in Discordant Sex Roles and a BBC Follow-Up." *Archives of Sexual Behavior* 11, no. 2 (1982): 181–186.

———, and Keith Sigmundson. "Sex Reassignment of Birth: Long-term Review and Clinical Applications." *Archives of Pediatric and Adolescent Medicine* 151 (May 1997): 298–304.

Donahoe, P. "Clinical Management of Intersex Abnormalities." *Current Problems in Surgery* 28 (1991): 519–579.

Dreger, Alice Domurat. *Hermaphrodites and the Medical Invention of Sex.* Cambridge: Harvard University Press, 1998.

Ellis, Havelock. *Studies in the Psychology of Sex.* New York: Random House, 1942.

Fiedler, Leslie. *Freaks: Myths and Images of the Second Self.* New York: Simon and Schuster, 1978.

Foucault, Michael. *Herculine Barbin.* New York: Pantheon Books, 1978.

———. *History of Sexuality.* New York: Pantheon Books, 1980.

Freud, Sigmund. "Some Psychical Consequences of the Anatomical Distinctions between the Sexes" (1925). In *The Complete Psychological Works,* trans. and ed. J. Strachy, vol. 18. New York: Norton, 1976.

Garfinkel, Harold. *Studies in Ethnomethodology.* Englewood Cliffs, N.J.: Prentice Hall, 1967.

Glassberg, Kenneth I. "Gender Assignment in Newborn Male Pseudohermaphodites." *Urologic Clinics of North America* 7 (June 1980): 409–421.

Hecker, W. Ch. "Operative Correction of Intersexual Genitals in Children." *Progress in Pediatric Surgery* 17 (1984): 21–31.

Hendricks, Melissa. "Is It a Boy or a Girl?" *Johns Hopkins Magazine* 45, no. 5 (November 1993): 10–16.

Kessler, Suzanne J., and Wendy McKenna. *Gender: An Ethnomethodological Approach.* New York: Wiley-Interscience, 1978; Chicago: University of Chicago Press, 1985.

Lee, Peter A., Thomas Mazur, Robert Danish, James Amrhein, Robert M. Blizzard, John Money, and Claude J. Migeon. "Micropenis: I. Criteria, Etiologies and Classification." *The Johns Hopkins Medical Journal* 146 (1980): 156–163.

Lev-Ran, Arye. "Sex Reversal as Related to Clinical Syndromes in Human Beings." In *Handbook of Sexology II: Genetics, Hormones and Behavior,* ed. John Money and H. Musaph, 157–173. New York: Elsevier, 1978.

Mazur, Tom. "Ambiguous Genitalia: Detection and Counseling." *Pediatric Nursing* 9 (November/December 1983): 417–431.

Money, John. "Birth Defect of the Sex Organs: Telling the Parents and the Patient." *British Journal of Sexual Medicine* 10 (March 1983): 14.

———. "Hermaphroditism and Pseudohermaphroditism." In *Gynecologic Endocrinology,* ed. Jay J. Gold, 449–464. New York: Hoeber, 1968.

———. "Psychologic Consideration of Sex Assignment in Intersexuality." *Clinics in Plastic Surgery* 1 (April 1974): 215–222.

———. "Psychological Counseling: Hermaphroditism." In *Endocrine and Genetic Diseases of Childhood and Adolescence,* ed. L. I. Gardner, 609–618. Philadelphia: W. B. Saunders, 1975.

———. *Sex Errors of the Body: Dilemmas, Education, Counseling.* Baltimore: The Johns Hopkins University Press, 1968. Reprint, 1994.

———, and Anke A. Ehrhardt. *Man & Woman, Boy & Girl.* Baltimore: The Johns Hopkins University Press, 1972.

———, J. G. Hampson, and J. L. Hampson. "Hermaphroditism: Recommendations Concerning Assignment of Sex, Change of Sex, and Psychologic Management." *Bulletin of The Johns Hopkins Hospital* 97 (1955): 284–300.

———, Tom Mazur, Charles Abrams, and Bernard F. Norman. "Micropenis, Family Mental Health, and Neonatal Management: A Report on Fourteen Patients Reared as Girls." *Journal of Preventive Psychiatry* 1, no. 1 (1981): 17–27.

———, Reynolds Potter, and Clarice S. Stoll. "Sex Reannouncement in Hereditary Sex Deformity: Psychology and
Sociology of Habilitation." *Social Science and Medicine* 3
(1969): 207–216.

Oliven, John F. *Sexual Hygiene and Pathology: A Manual for the
Physician.* Philadelphia: J. B. Lippincott Co., 1955.

Ortner, Sherry B. "Is Female to Male as Nature Is to
Culture?" In *Woman, Culture, and Society,* ed. Michelle
Zimbalist Rosaldo and Louise Lamphere, 67–87.
Stanford, Calif.: Stanford University Press, 1974.

Rohatgi, M. "Intersex Disorders: An Approach to Surgical
Management." *Indian Journal of Pediatrics* 59 (1992):
523–530.

Roslyn, Joel J., Eric W. Fonkalsrud, and Barbara Lippe.
"Intersex Disorders in Adolescents and Adults." *The
American Journal of Surgery* 146 (July 1983): 138–144.

Rubin, Jeffrey, F. J. Provenzano, and Z. Luria. "The Eye of
the Beholder: Parents' Views on Sex of Newborns."
American Journal of Orthopsychiatry 44, no. 4 (1974):
512–519.

Slijper, F. M. E., S. L. S. Drop, J. C. Molenaar, and R. J.
Scholtmeijer. "Neonates with Abnormal Genital
Development Assigned the Female Sex: Parent
Counseling." *Journal of Sex Education and Therapy* 20, no. 1
(1994): 9–17.

Smith, Richard W. "What Kind of Sex is Natural?" In
The Frontiers of Sex Research, ed. Vern Bullough, 103–111.
Buffalo: Prometheus, 1979.

Stoller, Robert J. *Sex and Gender,* vol. 1. New York:
J. Aronson, 1968.

READING 8

Some Group Matters: Intersectionality, Situated Standpoints, and Black Feminist Thought

Patricia Hill Collins

In developing a Black feminist praxis, standpoint theory has provided one important source of analytical guidance and intellectual legitimation for African-American women.[1] Standpoint theory argues that group location in hierarchical power relations produces shared challenges for individuals in those groups. These common challenges can foster similar angles of vision leading to a group knowledge or standpoint that in turn can influence the group's political action. Stated differently, group standpoints are situated in unjust power relations, reflect those power relations, and help shape them.

I suspect that one reason that the ideas of standpoint theory (in contrast to the vocabulary deployed by standpoint theorists, including the term *standpoint theory* itself) resonate with African-American women's experiences lies in the resemblance of standpoint theory to the norm of racial solidarity. Created in response to institutionalized racism and associated with Black nationalist responses to such oppression (see, e.g., Franklin 1992; Van Deburg 1992), racial solidarity within Black civil society requires that African-Americans stick together at all costs. The civil rights

and Black Power movements certainly demonstrated the effectiveness of Black politics grounded in racial solidarity. In the former, racial solidarity among African-Americans lay at the center of a multiracial civil rights effort. In the latter, racial solidarity was expressed primarily through all-Black organizations. Collectively these movements delivered tangible political and economic gains for African-Americans as a group (but not for all members within the group). Differences could be expressed *within* the boundaries of Blackness but not *across* those same boundaries. In this sense, the notion of a Black women's standpoint gains meaning in the context of a shared Black consciousness dedicated to sustaining racial solidarity. Notions of racial solidarity and a shared Black women's standpoint both invoke explicitly political objectives. Just as adhering to racial solidarity was important for Black emancipation in the United States, so might a collective Black women's standpoint be seen as essential for Black feminist praxis. Since Black women, like African-Americans overall, are oppressed as a group, collective as compared to individualized strategies remain important.

Much has happened since the 1970s. Depending on their placement in hierarchies of age, gender, economic class, region of the country, and sexuality, African-American women encounter new challenges associated with the new politics of containment in the United States. These changes require fresh ideas that analyze the complexities of contemporary lived Black experience and suggest adequate political responses to them. The intellectual climate currently housing Black feminist thought has also changed. In academic contexts influenced by postmodern rubrics of decentering, deconstruction, and difference, the norm of racial solidarity itself has come under increasing attack. Within Black cultural studies in particular, critiques now stress how racial solidarity has far too often been constructed on the bedrock of racial authenticity and essentialism (see, e.g., Dyson 1993; West 1993), leading some to emphasize the pitfalls of unquestioned racial solidarity for African-American women (Terrelonge 1984; Richie 1996). Academic feminism in North America takes aim at similar targets. Whereas Black academics question the utility of racial solidarity in addressing social issues of lived Black experience, feminist theorists increasingly criticize standpoint theory on theoretical grounds (Hekman 1997). Collectively, many Black and/or feminist academics question the assumptions that underlie solidarities of all sorts. This has great implication for Black feminist praxis generally, and a Black women's standpoint situated in unjust power relations in particular.

Given these shifting patterns, the situated standpoints that Black women collectively construct, and even the question of whether African-American women self-define as a group, become vitally important. In historical contexts in which racial segregation more visibly organized geographic, symbolic, and political space assigned to African-Americans, the links between a group's common positionality in power relations, the shared experiences that accompanied this commonality, the mechanisms for constructing group standpoints, and the significance of group standpoints for political activism were fairly straightforward. Under the changed conditions that accompany the new politics of containment, however, these links are neither clear nor assumed. Despite the historical significance of the ideas of standpoint theory to African-American women, questions remain concerning the efficacy of group-based identities of this sort for contemporary political struggles. In situations in which increasingly sophisticated practices, such as

controlling populations through constant surveillance (Foucault 1979), as well as strategies of everyday racism (Essed 1991) and symbolic racism (Jhally and Lewis 1992), obscure the continued effects of institutionalized injustices of all sorts, political theories that seem to advocate pulling together and storming the factory gates can seem simplistic. Moreover, the decreasing effectiveness of an identity politics currently associated with standpoint theory raises questions of its continued relevance. Are group-based identities that emerge from standpoint theory and the politics they generate still empowering for African-American women? Do group-based identities such as those advocated by standpoint theory ultimately disempower African-American women because they unduly suppress differences and heterogeneity among Black women? Quite simply, in what ways, if any, does standpoint theory remain relevant for Black feminist thought?

INTERSECTIONALITY AND SOCIAL GROUPS

Since standpoint theory remains predicated on the notion of a group with shared experiences and interests, addressing these questions requires revisiting the connections between African-American women's identities as individuals and Black women's historically constituted group identity. Individuals can assemble associations by coming together as already formed persons. African-American women who join sororities come as individuals and participate as voluntary members. In contrast, a historically constituted group identity is neither fleeting nor chosen. As Iris Marion Young points out, "One *finds oneself* as a member of a group, which one experiences as always already having been" (1990, 46; emphasis in original). For example, for the vast majority of the population in the United States, race creates immutable group identities. Individuals cannot simply opt in or out of racial groups, because race is constructed by assigning bodies meaningful racial classifications. Gender marks the body in a similar fashion.[2] Within the framework provided by their historically constituted group identity, individuals take up and perform their classification in diverse ways. African-American women, for example, all encounter some variation of what is expected of them as "Black women." How individual Black women construct their identities within these externally defined boundaries varies tremendously.

However, it also occurs in response to the shared challenges that all Black women encounter.

Within unjust power relations, groups remain unequal in the powers of self-definition and self-determination. Race, class, gender, and other markers of power intersect to produce social institutions that, in turn, construct groups that become defined by these characteristics. Since some groups define and rule others, groups are hierarchically related to one another. Within this overarching hierarchical structure, the ways in which individuals find themselves to be members of groups in group-based power relations matters. In some cases, individuals may be aware that their classification in a particular group matters, but they have little contact with other group members or believe that group membership is not important in everyday lived experience. Other groups have clearly defined histories, traditions, and patterned forms of behavior dedicated to ensuring that individual members "find themselves" as members of groups quite early in life.[3]

I stress this difference between the individual and the group as units of analysis because using these two constructs as if they were interchangeable clouds understanding of a host of topics, in this case, assessing the contributions of group-based experiences in constructing standpoints.[4] The type of reductionist thinking that uses individual experience to theorize group processes falters, because the treatment of the group in standpoint theory is not synonymous with a "family resemblance" of individual choice expanded to the level of voluntary group association. The notion of standpoint refers to groups having shared histories based on their shared location in unjust power relations—standpoints arise neither from crowds of individuals nor from groups analytically created by scholars or bureaucrats. Common location within power relations, not the result of collective decision making of individuals, creates African-American women as a group. What collective decision making does produce is a determination of the *kind* of group African-American women will be in a given social context.

Under race-only or gender-only conceptual frameworks, it is fairly easy to see how unjust power relations create social groups. Within binary thinking, men rule women and Whites dominate Blacks in schools, the labor market, government organization, and other social institutions. However, the emerging paradigm of intersectionality problematizes this entire process of group construction. As a heuristic device, intersectionality references the ability of social phenomena such as race, class, and gender to mutually construct one another. One can use the framework of intersectionality to think through social institutions, organizational structures, patterns of social interactions, and other social practices on all levels of social organization. Groups are constructed within these social practices, with each group encountering a distinctive constellation of experiences based on its placement in hierarchical power relations. African-American women, for example, can be seen both as a group that occupies a distinctive social location within power relations of intersectionality and as one wherein intersectional processes characterize Black women's collective self-definitions and actions. Whereas race-only or gender-only perspectives classify African-American women as a subgroup of either African-Americans or women, intersections of race, class, and gender, among others, create more fluid and malleable boundaries around the category "African-American women." Within this logic, Black women as a historically constituted group in the United States are no less real—how the group is theoretically defined, however, changes markedly.

Intersectionality thus highlights how African-American women and other social groups are positioned within unjust power relations, but it does so in a way that introduces added complexity to formerly race-, class-, and gender-only approaches to social phenomena. The fluidity that accompanies intersectionality does not mean that groups themselves disappear, to be replaced by an accumulation of decontextualized, unique individuals whose personal complexity makes group-based identities and politics that emerge from group constructions impossible. Instead, the fluidity of boundaries operates as a new lens that potentially deepens understanding of how the actual mechanisms of institutional power can change dramatically even while they reproduce longstanding group inequalities of race, class, and gender. As Kimberle Crenshaw points out, "Intersectionality captures the way in which the particular location of black women in dominant American social relations is unique and in some senses unassimilable into the discursive paradigms of gender and race domination" (1992, 404). In this sense, African-American women's group history and location can be seen as points of convergence within structural, hierarchical, and changing power relations.

Given the tendency of state power to manipulate groups that rely too heavily on narrowly defined identity politics, it is especially important to keep intersectional analyses of group construction in mind. In their assessment of how the government policy of positive action (affirmative action) in Great Britain effectively weakened racial and ethnic identity politics, Floya Anthias and Nira Yuval-Davis (1992) identify an important pitfall confronting groups that allow themselves to be constructed around essentialist definitions. When state distribution of social rewards in relation to group membership fosters a situation of group competition for scarce resources, policing the boundaries of group membership becomes much more important. Anthias and Yuval-Davis illustrate how initial efforts to express self-defined group standpoints can easily be co-opted by state powers that recognize and use identity politics for their own interests.

Retaining this focus on groups constructed within and through intersectionalities remains important for another reason. Intersectionality works better as a substantive theory (one aimed at developing principles that can be proved true or false) when applied to individual-level behavior than when documenting group experiences. The construct of intersectionality works well with issues of individual agency and human subjectivity and thus has surface validity in explaining everyday life. Individuals can more readily see intersections of race, gender, class, and sexuality in how they construct their identities as individuals than in how social institutions rely on these same ideas in reproducing group identities. On the level of the individual, using race, class, gender, sexuality, and national belonging as mutually constructing categories of experience that take on shifting meanings in different contexts makes sense. It is perfectly reasonable to compare, for example, an individual African-American woman to an individual white American woman and to ask how each constructs an identity informed by intersections of race, class, and gender across varying social contexts. On the level of the individual, these kinds of comparisons work, because the unit of comparison—the individual—is deemed equivalent, constant, and not in need of analysis.

Unfortunately, the compatibility of intersectionality with individual-level analyses can foster the consequence of elevating individualism above group analyses. This valorization of individualism to the point where group and structural analyses remain relegated to the background has close ties to American liberalism. Despite the significance of racial, ethnic, economic, and other types of groups in U.S. society, individualism continues as a deep taproot in American law and social theory. David Goldberg describes the roots of liberalism:

> Liberalism is committed to *individualism* for it takes as basic the moral, political, and legal claims of the individual over and against those of the collective. It seeks *foundations* in *universal* principles applicable to all human beings or rational agents. . . . In this, liberalism seeks to transcend particular historical, social, and cultural differences: It is concerned with broad identities which it insists unite persons on moral grounds, rather than with those identities which divide. . . . Liberalism takes itself to be committed to equality. (1993, 5; emphasis in original)

Whether we are talking about the explicit individualism of bourgeois liberalism or the explicit individualism permeating postmodern renditions of difference, individualistic models define freedom as the absence of constraints, including those of mandatory group membership. Freedom occurs when individuals have rights of mobility into and out of groups—the right to join clubs and other voluntary associations or to construct their subjectivity as multiple and changing. Little mention is made of the collective struggles that preceded any group's gaining individual rights of this sort. Within this logic, race, class, gender, and the like become defined as personal attributes of individuals that they should be able to choose or reject. Thus, because it fails to challenge the assumptions of individualism, intersectionality when applied to the individual level can coexist quite nicely with both traditional liberalism and a seemingly apolitical postmodernism.

When discussing intersectionality and group organization, however, assumptions of individualism obscure hierarchical power relations of all sorts, from race- and gender-only perspectives through more complex frameworks such as intersectionality. Can one argue that African-American women and White American women as *groups* are so equivalent that one can take the reality of the social group itself as an assumption that does not need to be examined? Moreover, not only does intersectionality, when applied to the level of groups, become more difficult to conceptualize, but because groups do not operate as individuals do, intersectionality on the group level becomes difficult to study. When examining structural power relations, intersectionality functions better as a conceptual framework or heuristic device describing what kinds of things to consider than as one describing any actual patterns of social organization. The goal is not to prove intersectionality right or wrong, nor to gather empirical data to test the existence of intersectionality. Rather, intersectionality provides an interpretive framework for thinking through how intersections of race and class, or race and gender, or sexuality and class, for example, shape any group's experience across specific social contexts. The existence of multiple axes within intersectionality (race, class, gender, sexuality, nation, ethnicity, age) means neither that these factors are equally salient in all groups' experiences nor that they form uniform principles of social organization in defining groups. For example, institutionalized racism constitutes such a fundamental feature of lived Black experience that, in the minds of many African-American women, racism overshadows sexism and other forms of group-based oppression. In contrast, if the literature on the social construction of Whiteness is any indication (see, e.g., Frankenberg 1993), despite their comfort with identifying themselves as women, many White women in the United States have difficulty seeing themselves as already part of Whites as a group. Although African-American women and White American women participate in the same system of institutionalized racism and sexism, each group assigns a different salience to race and gender. Race and class and gender may *all* be present in *all* social settings in the United States, yet groups will experience and "see" them differently. Within this logic, examining historically constructed groups that exist not in theory but in everyday practice requires having an open mind about what types of groups will actually be uncovered.

Given the significance of both group membership and intersectionality, African-American women's group classification and its connection to intersectional analyses of Black women's common history become important. African-American women participate in two distinctive yet overlapping ways of organizing groups in the United States, one organized around a race-class axis and the other around the axis of gender. Because both operate as defining principles of American national identity—recall the race-gender categories of "free White men," "free White women," and "Slaves"—both constitute groups in which Black women find themselves members quite early in life. However, despite the significance of, on the one hand, race-class groupings and, on the other, gender groupings as core forms of social organization, race, class, and gender mutually construct one another in historically distinctive ways.

Although race, class, and gender may share equal billing under the paradigm of intersectionality as a heuristic device, most African-American women would identify race as a fundamental, if not the most important, feature shaping the experiences of Black women as a group. Race operates as such an overriding feature of African-American experience in the United States that it not only overshadows economic class relations for Blacks but obscures the significance of economic class within the United States in general. Even though race and economic class are intertwined, mutually constructing, and intersecting categories, race is often manipulated to divert attention from economic class concerns (Katz 1989; Quadagno 1994). At the same time, race and economic class are such tightly bundled constructs in shaping actual economic outcomes in the United States that one construct loses meaning without referencing the other. Recall that in interpreting the intent of the framers of the Constitution, Chief Justice Roger Taney referred to African slaves as "a subordinate and inferior class of beings" (qtd. in Estell 1994, 130). In this remark, Taney uses a language of class to describe a racialized population and thus illustrates how race and class often stand as proxy for one another. For the sake of argument, I'll refer to this relationship as one of articulation between race and class or, for the context of the United States, race-class intersectionality.[5]

As women and men, African-Americans also encounter gender as a fundamental organizing principle of social structure. Race and economic class not only articulate with one another but also intersect with gender. Although race and gender both mark the body in similar (but not identical) ways, in the United States they are organized in social relations quite differently. Race-class intersections operate primarily through distancing strategies associated with racial and economic segregation. Groups remain separated from one another and do not see themselves as sharing common interests. Blacks and Whites, labor and management are defined in oppositional terms. Although race-class groups may be in close proximity—slavery certainly represented full employment for Blacks coupled with close proximity to Whites—they do not see themselves as sharing common interests. For African-Americans in particular, segregated spaces of all sorts—in particular, housing segregation with its concomitant effects on educational opportunities, employment prospects, and public facilities—accentuate these oppositional relationships. In contrast, gender is organized via inclusionary strategies where, via family, neighborhood, and religious groups, women live in close proximity to or belong to common social units with men. Women are encouraged to develop a commonality of interest with men, despite the gender hierarchy operating within this category of belonging.

Examining how race and class, on the one hand, and gender, on the other, have been historically organized in the United States suggests that they represent two divergent ways of constructing groups, each with different implications for the meaning of standpoint theory. African-American women's positionality within both race-class collectivities and gender collectivities as two overlapping yet distinct forms of group organization, provides a potentially important lens for evaluating standpoint theory overall. Specifically, standpoint theory seems useful in analyzing issues associated with a new politics of containment that places Black women in segregated housing, schools, and jobs designed to keep them on the economic "bottom." But standpoint theory seems less applicable to gender relations in the United States. Because women are separated from one another by race and class, they face different challenges both in conceptualizing themselves as a group at all and in seeing themselves as a group similar to race-class groups. This suggests that standpoint theory might be better suited for particular types of groups or, alternately, that groups formed via different mechanisms have varying relationships with standpoint theory.

I realize that in an intellectual climate in which viewing race, class, gender, sexuality, and nation as intersecting categories of analysis has now become more accepted, highlighting differences between race-class and gender as forms of organization may seem counterintuitive to some and intellectually conservative to others. However, despite my commitment to intersectionality as an important conceptual framework, continuing to leave intersectionality as an undertheorized construct contributes to old hierarchies (and some new ones) being reformed under what I see as a new myth of equivalent oppressions.

In the United States, to be a Black woman is not the same as to be a White gay man or a working-class Latino. Similarly, Black women's collective experiences differ from those of White gay men and working-class Latinos. Although these experiences are all connected, they are not equivalent. Moreover, in a situation in which far too many privileged academics feel free to claim a bit of oppression for themselves—if all oppressions mutually construct one another, then we're all oppressed in some way by something— oppression talk obscures actual unjust power relations. Within these politics, some groups benefit more from an assumed equivalency of oppressions than others. Although this approach is valid as a heuristic device, treating race, class, and gender as if their intersection produces equivalent results for all oppressed groups obscures differences in how race, class, and gender are hierarchically organized, as well as the differential effects of intersecting systems of power on diverse groups of people.

Black women's social location in the United States provides one specific site for examining these cross-cutting relationships among race, class, and gender as categories of analysis. Its particularity may also shed light on how rethinking the connections between social group formation and intersectionality points to the potential relevance of standpoint theory for Black feminist praxis. In the next two sections of this chapter, I examine two groups in which African-American women "find themselves"—race-class groups in the United States, and gender-organized groups shaping women's experiences. My analysis is not meant to be exhaustive but instead sketches out some patterns for beginning to examine how intersectionality might relate to situated standpoints.

RACE-CLASS GROUP FORMATION: STANDPOINT THEORY REVISITED

Reviewing the origins of standpoint theory in a more general theory of economic class relations associated with the critical social theory of Karl Marx sheds light on race-class intersectionality in the United States generally and standpoint theory in particular. Although current scholarly attention restricts its attention to standpoint theory, the idea of experiential bases of knowledge is much broader than Marxist social theory. Social theorists as diverse as American functionalist Robert Merton, German critical theorist Karl Mannheim, and French postmodernist Michel

Foucault all explore the experiential base of knowledge to some degree. Marxist social thought, however, most clearly situates knowledge within unjust power relations.[6]

Although Marx may be better known for his analyses of capitalism and socialism, I find that revisiting Marx's historical work provides new directions for conceptualizing how race and economic class mutually construct one another in the United States.[7] Marx's 1852 essay *The Eighteenth Brumaire of Louis Bonaparte* provides a historical examination of how economic class relations both constrained and shaped human agency during a period of social uprising in France. The following passage from this work contains several interrelated ideas that collectively provide an interpretive context for understanding how economic class represents a specific type of group formation.

> In so far as millions of families live under economic conditions of existence that separate their mode of life, their interests and their culture from those of the other classes, and put them in hostile opposition to the latter, they form a class. In so far as there is merely a local interconnection among these small-holding peasants, and the identity of their interests begets no community, no national bond and no political organization among them, they do not form a class. They are consequently incapable of enforcing their class interest in their own name. (Marx 1963, 124)

Four features of economic class analysis are germane to conceptualizing how race-class intersectionality in the United States constitutes a particular type of group formation. First, although economic class remains rooted in economic analysis, dual meanings of economic class exist. On a specific level, economic class refers to the economic status of historically identifiable groups in capitalist political economies such as the United States. Concentrations of economic power (owning income-producing property), political power (running workplaces and the government), and ideological power (controlling the schools, media, and other forms of representation) distinguish economic classes from one another (Higginbotham and Weber 1992). Analyses that define the middle class as comprising managerial and professional workers, the working class as encompassing factory workers and clerical workers, and the underclass as populated by workers who move between secondary labor-market jobs, government transfer payments, and the informal economy represent one important dimension of economic class relationships. Relying on analyses of segmented labor markets, industrial sectors, or other indices of placement in political economy, these approaches attribute economic class outcomes to economic causes (Baran and Sweezy 1966; Edwards 1979; Wilson 1978, 1987).

Ways of conceptualizing class relations exist other than those accompanying the familiar labor market, industrial sector, and human capital variables. Understanding classes whose "economic conditions of existence" distinguish them from other groups requires situating those groups in the specific history of their society. This history might resemble the familiar bourgeoisie and proletariat of Marxist conflict theory constructed from studies of industrializing, racially homogeneous nineteenth-century European societies. However, in the post-colonial, desegregated contexts of advanced capitalism, Marxist class categories seemingly lose validity. The approach taken to constructing class, however, remains valuable. Rather than starting with a theory of how capitalist economies predetermine economic classes, analysis *begins* with how social groupings are actually organized within historically specific capitalist political economies. Class categories are constructed from the actual cultural material of historically specific societies. This is exactly the method that Marx used in constructing his class categories—the bourgeoisie and proletariat were not theoretically derived categories but emerged from historical analysis.[8]

Analyzing class relations via historically concrete, lived experience sheds light on race-class intersectionality in the United States. One might ask whether African-Americans "live under economic conditions of existence that separate their mode of life, their interests and their culture from those of other classes" or, alternately, whether African-Americans continue to bear the intergenerational costs associated with the denial of citizenship stemming from their being branded "a subordinate and inferior class of beings." For African-Americans, group positionality is determined less by theoretical categories constructed within assumptions of distinct discourses of class or race, and more by actual lived Black experience. Although economic outcomes remain fundamental to conceptualizing Black economic class relations, such relations may not be defined *solely* by labor markets, industrial sectors, and other economic criteria. A more complex analysis of class formation might encompass an intersectional analysis attentive to institutionalized racism, slavery as a mode of production, and other factors shaping the social location of African-Americans as a group. The forces constructing African-Americans as a group living under economic conditions that distinguish them from other groups in the United States are far more complex than simple economic determinism.

This leads to a second feature essential for exploring how race-class intersectionality in the United States might foster a specific type of group formation—the necessity of historic specificity in examining both economic class relations and any standpoints that might ensue. Nowhere is it written that only two or three classes exist. Yet this parsimonious number persists. It seems just as reasonable to argue that actual class relations are much more complex. Since Marxist class analysis is heavily influenced by its origins in racially homogeneous European societies as well as its construction of class categories from the individual's relationship to capital and labor, it underemphasizes the importance of race in conceptualizing class. However, given how institutionalized racism and capitalism have constructed one another in the United States (Marable 1983), restricting analysis to a few economic classes shorn of racial meaning oversimplifies a series of complex relationships. Rather than taking a class analysis developed for one specific historical context—for example, Marx's discussion of the bourgeoisie and proletariat developed for nineteenth-century France or industrializing England—and applying it uncritically to other social settings, one might assume that differently organized class differences will *always* characterize unjust power relations.

This shift in perspective that both views class relations in more than purely economic terms and generates class categories from actual lived experience creates space to examine how social hierarchies construct group or class relationships with visible economic dimensions. It also creates space to think about class in relation to race, nationality, and ethnicity (see, e.g., Anthias and Yuval-Davis 1992). Within the United States, race, ethnicity, and nationality have long been intertwined in historically complex ways in producing pronounced economic inequalities among groups (Takaki 1993). Moreover, the institutional mechanisms by which unjust power relations of class, race, nation, and ethnicity are organized are similar—

namely, separation and exclusion. Issues of purity and separation, whether of geographical space or occupational and employment space, or in school curricula, the media, or other forms of symbolic space, appear central to maintaining unjust power relations of race, class, nation, and ethnicity in the United States. Despite a rhetoric of individualism associated with liberalism, Americans seem to be profoundly group-oriented. As sociologist Joseph Scott succinctly puts it, "Group rights are the American practice; individual rights are the American promise" (1984, 178).

If groups with historically identifiable histories and traditions have become the focus of class analysis (class cannot operate in the abstract—it always works through actual lived experience), African-Americans participate in class relations in particular ways. The complexity of class analysis is limited only by the degree of specificity used to delineate groups with shared "economic conditions of existence." Class relations can thus be drawn with broad brush strokes, as in the case of nineteenth-century industrializing England, or more finely crafted into intersectional categories such as race-class intersectionality in the late-twentieth-century United States. Within this logic, race-class groups are constructed less from theoretical models advanced by governmental officials and academics, and more from actual group histories.

A third feature of class analysis that is especially germane to both group formation and race-class intersectionality in the United States concerns the nature of class as a construct. Class does not describe a "thing" but rather a *relationship* among social groups unequal in power. Classes represent bounded categories of the population, groups set in a relation of opposition to one another. Within Marxist social theory, group relationships describe power relations such that one group's privilege is predicated upon another group's disadvantage. One group or class exploits the other, excludes the other from equitable social rewards, or somehow benefits from the other's disadvantage. The main insight here concerns the relationship between group structure, group membership, and unjust power relations. Groups become defined largely by their placement within historically specific power relations, not from choices exercised by individual group members concerning issues of identity and belonging.

From this perspective, it makes little sense to talk about the middle class as an entity or a thing unto itself, because such a class could not exist without other economic classes to which it is linked in relationships of, at best, mutuality and, at worst, exploitation. In a similar fashion, historically in the United States, the notion of Whiteness as a meaningful group category was formed in relation to Blackness as a separate and allegedly inferior way of constructing groups. Moreover, these group relationships within race-class intersectionality persist over time. Although patterns of race-class intersectionality may be distinctive for any given era, the basic oppositional relationships among groups constructed within and linked by these intersections remain constant. As long as the basic relationship of intergenerational disadvantage and privilege in which White and Black individuals "find themselves" persists, the relationship is one of class.

I stress the intergenerational nature of this process of mutually constructing privilege and disadvantage because, in the United States, such relationships remain organized through family units. With the important exception of feminist analyses of the family, the concept of family remains simultaneously underanalyzed and fundamental to how people conceptualize groups of all sorts. In his discussion of class, Marx identifies families as the unit of class analysis. Recall the passage quoted earlier: "In so far as millions of *families* live under economic conditions of existence that separate their mode of life, their interests and their culture from those of the other classes, and put them in hostile opposition to the latter, they form a class" (1963, 124; emphasis added). Consider how differently that passage would read if the term *individuals* were substituted for the term *families*. In this passage, classes are constructed not from the building blocks of *individuals* but from those of *families*, the same building blocks of nations, races, and ethnic groups. Thus, class, race, and nation all become linked in a common cognitive framework that relies on separation and exclusion to define family groups. This shift from the individual to the family as the basic unit of class analysis leads to very different notions of how hierarchical power relations become reproduced over time. As the long-standing debate on Black family deviance indicates, most Americans seem comfortable with the idea of the intergenerational transfer of property from one generation to the next, as long as the property under consideration is *cultural* capital. Any resulting inequalities can then be attributed to the workings of good or bad parenting.

However, analyzing how the intergenerational transfer of *wealth*, or actual capital, participates in shaping these same outcomes leads to different conclusions (Collins 1997). Here one encounters inherited patterns of opportunity or disadvantage, based on the class position of one's family. Moreover, if family is used to conceptualize other types of groups—race as family, nation as a large extended family, ethnicity as a large kinship group—then relations within the family and the treatment of family members and outsiders become significant to social relations of all sorts (Collins forthcoming 1998b).

Rather than trying to determine the essential features that distinguish African-Americans from other social groups, a more fruitful approach might explore how African-Americans participate in race-class intersectionality in the United States at any given time, especially in oppositional relationships with other groups. This approach accommodates a dual emphasis on fixity and change. On the one hand, intergenerational patterns of family inequality in which Whites and Blacks largely replicate the economic status of their parents signal the fixed nature of race-class intersectionality in the United States. On the other hand, because history is seen as changing, race-class formations also change, as the new politics of containment suggests, often in quite dramatic ways. Within such changes, opportunities for struggle continually are being remade. Historicizing race-class relations as specific power relations in this way not only highlights how race-class relations change over time but also reintroduces the question of human agency in bringing about such changes.

Exercising agency in response to and/or in behalf of a group requires *recognizing* groups by seeing how past circumstances have profound effects on the present. Thus, a final dimension of class approaches to group formation specifically related to race-class intersectionality in the United States concerns the centrality of group culture and consciousness in developing self-defined group standpoints. Shared disadvantage and shared interests are not sufficient—*separate* modes of life that distinguish groups from one another remain important. Although structural features such as shared location in the economy can bring people into proximity who have common economic interests, they do not become classes without some sort of self-defined group knowledge. Individuals within the group must develop and proclaim a consciousness of their connections with one another, and the group itself must come to see its relationships with other groups within this same system of power relations:[9] "In so far as there is merely a local interconnection among these small-holding peasants, and the identity of their interests begets no *community*, no national bond and no political organization among them, they do not form a class" (Marx 1963, 124; emphasis added). In other words, a group consolidates its class interests through community infrastructures that actively reproduce its particular group interests for its own membership.

Historically, African-Americans have recognized themselves as a group in this way, with shared interests constructed in opposition to those of more powerful Whites as a dominant group. The longevity of Black nationalism in Black civil society stems in part from its repeated denouncements of institutionalized racism, coupled with an insistence that Blacks center political action on lived Black experience. Recall that Black cultural nationalism encourages African-Americans to claim an independent Black culture. Aiming to develop a radical Black consciousness that recognizes how existing race-class relations are unjust, such a culture is designed to give voice to Black political struggle. In exploring these relations, African-American legal scholar Derrick Bell has the Curia, fictional Black women judges, point to the importance of situated standpoints for theories of Black liberation:

> Some of you . . . will leave here seeking theories of liberation from white legal philosophers, who are not oppressed, who do nor perceive themselves as oppressors, and who thus must use their impressive intellectual talent to imagine what you experience daily. Black people, on the other hand, come to their task of liberation from the battleground of experience, not from the rarefied atmosphere of the imagination. (1987, 253)

Bell's fictional account in which the Curia chides Black people who fail to trust their own experiences with racism, who deny the perspectives that often emerge from these experiences, and who look to Whites for answers resonates with the type of independent thinking advocated by Black nationalist leader Malcolm X, who once advised a group of Black youth to think for themselves (Collins 1992). Within this framework, culture, consciousness, and political struggle become inextricably intertwined.

Overall, the ideas of standpoint theory seem more suited to groups structured via segregated spaces such as residential racial segregation, employment discrimination, and other exclusionary practices characterizing race-class intersectionality in the United States. Despite its insights into the workings of power through segregated spaces, this race-class approach to group construction routinely fails to address hierarchy *within* groups that are differentially positioned within unjust power relations. This failure to address internal hierarchy has great implications for constructing group standpoints. Even though a social group may occupy a distinctive structural location within hierarchical power relations, it can simultaneously remain quite uninformed about unjust power relations operating within its own boundaries. Thus, one fundamental challenge lies in ensuring that neither group practices nor any ensuing standpoints replicate other hierarchies, particularly those of gender and sexuality.

GENDER AND GROUP FORMATION

Because women in the United States are distributed *across* groups formed within race-class intersectionality, gender raises different issues. Long-standing exclusionary practices that separate women by race, economic condition, citizenship status, and ethnicity result in social groups that *include* women, organized via these categories. For example, Black women and White women do not live in class-stratified women's neighborhoods, separated from men and children by processes such as gender steering, bank redlining that results in refusal to lend money to women's neighborhoods, inferior schools in women's inner-city neighborhoods due to men moving to all-male suburban areas, and the like. Instead, for the most part, Black and White women live in racially segregated, economically stratified neighborhoods (Massey and Denton 1993). The experiences they garner in such communities, especially via the powerful social institution of family, reflect the politics of race-class intersectionality in the United States. Stated differently, although women in the United States may share much as women, residential patterns, schools, and employment opportunities that routinely sort women into clearly defined categories of race, economic class, ethnicity, and citizenship status mean that few opportunities exist for having the type of intimate, face-to-face contact that would reveal women's "shared economic conditions," if they exist at all, let alone for organizing around those conditions.

At the same time, as a collectivity, women experience distinctive gendered mechanisms of control that remain specific to women's patterns of inclusion within race-class groups. Specifically, regardless of actual family composition, all women encounter the significance of American society's preoccupation with family. As a familiar and seemingly natural form of group organization, the idea of family serves as a particular foundation on which many types of groups are built (Collins 1998a). Members of all sorts of collectivities are often encouraged to treat one another as "family," a perspective illustrated by family references to, for example, the "brothers" in gangs, the "sisterhood" of feminist struggle, the Black "mothers" of the church, and the founding "fathers" of America. Recall that Marx himself falls back on the image of the family as the smallest social unit having a shared interest. By definition, families stick together against outsiders. Within idealized notions of family, family units protect and balance the interests of all of their members—the strong care for the weak, and members contribute to and benefit from family membership in proportion to their capacities. Though there may be differentiation within the family, family members share a common origin through blood and a commonality of interests.

By providing compelling arguments that family functions as a primary site for conceptualizing and organizing women's oppression, feminist scholarship challenges these assumptions. Analyses of bourgeois family structure or the traditional family ideal, in particular, unpack the relationship between particular ideas of family and gender oppression. Defined as a natural or biological arrangement based on heterosexual attraction, a normative and ideal family consists of a heterosexual couple who produce their own biological children. Formed through a combination of marital and blood ties, the traditional family ideal views this nuclear unit as having a specific authority structure, arranged in this order: a father-head earning an adequate family wage, a stay-at-home wife and mother, and children. Assuming a relatively fixed sexual division of labor, wherein women's roles are defined as primarily in the home and men's in the public world of work, the traditional family ideal assumes the separation of work and family. Viewing the family as a private haven from a public world, family is seen as held together through primary emotional bonds of love and caring (Andersen 1991; Thorne 1992).

Feminist scholarship reveals that despite a rhetoric of equality in this ideal, a good part of women's subordination is organized via family ties. In contrast to idealized versions of family, actual families remain organized around varying patterns of hierarchy. As Anne McClintock observes, "The family image came to figure *hierarchy within unity* as an organic element of historical progress, and thus became indispensable for legitimating exclusion and hierarchy within nonfamilial social forms such as nationalism, liberal individualism and imperialism" (1995, 45). Thus, because the family is perceived as a private sphere that is naturally and not socially constructed, relying on the traditional family ideal as a model for group organization replicates a naturalized hierarchy. For women, domination and love remain intimately linked. Through their contribution of socializing family members into an appropriate set of "family values," women participate in naturalizing the hierarchy within the assumed unity of interests symbolized by the family while laying the foundation for systems of hierarchy outside family boundaries. As people often learn their place within hierarchies of race, gender, ethnicity, sexuality, nationality, and class from their experiences within family units, they simultaneously learn to view such hierarchies as natural social arrangements, as compared to socially constructed ones. As feminist analyses of family suggest, women's families remain central to their subordination. Moreover, because women's shared economic conditions as women remain organized within families across race-class groups, women remain disadvantaged in seeing their connections with other similarly situated women.

Developing group culture and consciousness for all women as a collectivity involves extracting them from historically constituted groups within which family serves as part of the conceptual glue giving meaning to race, class, ethnicity, and nation. It also involves creating a new group identity based on gender affiliation. For women as a collectivity, building this type of group constitutes an intellectual and political project distinctly different from that confronting groups organized via the segregated spaces of race, class, ethnicity, and nation. Moreover, differences in group construction and the challenges that face different types of groups have implications for any ensuing standpoints. Using standpoint theory both as a tool for analyzing gender relations in the United States and as a strategy for organizing women raises a different and complex set of issues. Because women are distributed across a range of race-class groups, all women confront the initial task of developing a shared understanding of their common interests as women. However, they must do so in close proximity to, and often in sexualized love relationships with, members of the group that allegedly oppresses them. Since women must first construct a self-definition as a member of a group, ideas may precede the building of actual group relations. Women certainly know other women within their own race, economic, ethnic, and/or citizenship groups, but most have difficulty seeing their shared interests across the vast differences that characterize women as a collectivity. The process of constructing a group standpoint for women differs dramatically from that confronting groups with histories of group-based segregated spaces. Women come to know themselves as members of a political collectivity through ideas that construct them as such.

By invoking the rhetoric of family in constructing women's groups and any hoped-for standpoints that might follow, a feminist politics may inadvertently undermine the logic of its own organization. The longed-for group solidarity promised under the rubric of "sisterhood" posited by contemporary feminists seems designed to build a community among women that is grounded in shared conditions of existence. However, imagining multicultural, multiethnic, multiracial, multiclass women's groups predicated on family-based notions of sisterhood is much easier than building such communities across lived, institutionalized segregation. The path from women conceptualized as a numerically superior "minority group," through feminist organizing designed to generate a shared consciousness of women's oppression or standpoint under the banner of sisterhood, to building actual women's groups organized around sisterhood encountered considerable resistance, much of it from African-American women and other similarly situated women (Dill 1983).

White American feminist critiques of standpoint theory may emerge in part from discouragement with the seeming failure of feminist struggles for sisterhood. In part, the increasing attraction of postmodernism for many White American feminists may lie in its deconstructive move. By arguing that multiracial, multicultural women's collectivities are neither desirable nor possible, postmodernism seems to offer a way out. Turning attention away from challenging women's oppression to deconstructing the modern subject provides conceptual space to sidestep the theoretical failures of Western feminism. If women cannot be organized as a group, then groups themselves must go, and everything associated with them, including standpoints. Although this theoretical move seems highly plausible when directed toward the fragile solidarity of women, applying similar deconstructive moves to groups organized through segregated spaces of race and economic class remains far less convincing. Despite well-intentioned gestures (e.g., placing "race" in quotation marks to signal the socially constructed notion of race as a category of analysis), declaring a moratorium on using the word *race* does not make housing segregation, underfunded inner-city schools, and employment discrimination any less real.

Because groups respond to the actual social conditions that they confront, it stands to reason that groups constructed by different social realities will develop equally different analyses and political strategies. For example, White American feminist thinkers who theorize that feminist standpoints are untenable may be inadvertently expressing the standpoint of a group that has no need of such thinking. Moreover, despite the support and leadership of many women's studies professionals for intersectional analyses, such support may evaporate quickly if any real sharing of power appears on the horizon. Ironically, within unexamined assumptions of individualism, intersectionality can be reconfigured so that it makes things worse. Just as academic talk of centers and margins flattened and in some cases erased hierarchical power relations, the construct of intersectionality used to analyze differences among women can be similarly depoliticized. When extracted from hierarchical power relations, recognizing differences among women can become so watered down that power simply vanishes.

In a fundamental way, African-American women are caught in the cross fire of two different ways of organizing groups. Race, class, nation, and ethnicity all rely heavily on segregation and other exclusionary practices to maintain hierarchy. In contrast, because women often find themselves in close proximity to men, gender relies more heavily on surveillance and other inclusionary strategies of control targeted toward the proximate other. Because it reproduces the naturalized hierarchy that also informs the self-definitions of race-class groups, the idea of family permeates both types of group organization. On the one hand, due to its overreliance on a gender-blind racial solidarity constructed via family metaphors, Black civil society fosters a problematic paradigm of sacrifice for African-American women. On the other hand, because structural power attached to race-class intersectionality in the United States can be recast within apolitical frameworks of differences among women, White American feminist theories in particular maintain the illusion of gender solidarity while allowing hierarchy to be reformulated via actual practices. For African-American women, hierarchy flourishes in *both* approaches to constructing groups.

SITUATED STANDPOINTS AND BLACK FEMINIST THOUGHT

How might these complexities introduced by intersectionalities and group organization shed light on the relationship between standpoint theory and Black feminist thought? A more intricate view both of African-American women as a group and of any accompanying Black women's standpoint might emerge by first agreeing that African-American women have a shared (though not uniform) location in hierarchical power relations in the United States. The existence of group interests means neither that all individuals within the group have the same experiences nor that they interpret them in the same way. Acknowledging a shared location means neither that African-American women's experiences become collapsed into stereotypes of welfare queens or Black Lady Overachievers, nor that images of "natural," "African," or "real" Black women that are conjured up in Black nationalist discourse constitute what is shared. A paradigm of intersectionality stressing how race, class, and gender mutually construct one another suggests that unitary standpoints of the type associated with traditional racial solidarity are neither possible nor desirable. However, if groups themselves need not be organized via essentialist principles, neither do group-derived standpoints. Group-based experiences, especially those shared by African-American women as collectivity, create the conditions for a shared standpoint that in turn can stimulate collective political action. But they guarantee neither that such standpoints will follow nor that efforts to develop

standpoints constitute the most effective way of empowering a group in a given context.

Shared group location is better characterized by viewing Black women's social location as one of a heterogeneous commonality embedded in social relations of intersectionality. Despite heterogeneity among African-American women that accompanies such intersections, differences in Black women's experiences generated by differences of age, sexual orientation, region of the country, urban or rural residence, color, hair texture, and the like theoretically can all be accommodated within the concept of a shared standpoint. When it comes to oppression, there are essentials. A passage in *The Eighteenth Brumaire* speaks to this critical element of what might actually be shared: "Men make their own history, but they do not make it just as they please; they do not make it under circumstances chosen by themselves, but under circumstances directly encountered, given and transmitted from the past" (Marx 1963, 15). "Shared" refers to the "circumstances directly encountered, given and transmitted from the past," not to uniform, essentialist responses to those conditions. Stated differently, a shared standpoint need not rest on a list of essential rules or Black feminist articles of faith to which Black women must subscribe in order to be considered a true sister. Rather, it rests on the recognition that when it comes to being African-American women in the United States, as Fannie Lou Hamer points out, "we're in this bag together" (qtd. in Lerner 1972, 613).

By primarily emphasizing only one historically specific dimension of hierarchical power relations, namely, economic classes in industrializing political economies, Marx posited that, however unarticulated and inchoate, oppressed groups possessed a particular standpoint concerning the "bag" they were in, that is, their own oppression. Contemporary analyses of social structure that stress the complexity created by intersections of race, economic class, gender, ethnicity, sexuality, and nationality ask how to invoke a comparable complexity in defining and studying groups. What we now have is increasing sophistication about how to discuss group location not in singular "fighting words" paradigms of economic class, race, or gender, but with a growing recognition of the significance of intersectionality. This suggests that the complexity characterizing African-American women's group identity under a new politics of containment will generate a comparably sophisticated Black women's standpoint.

As the preceding discussion of race-class and gender groups suggests, actually thinking through this complexity represents a daunting task. However, at a minimum, it points to the need to develop a more sophisticated language for discussing social groups that takes power relations into account. Traditional discussions of standpoint theory leave this notion of group unexamined, if they make mention of it at all, allowing unexamined family metaphors to fill the void.

Because actual family relations are rarely fair and just, using family as metaphor for constructing an understanding of group processes can duplicate inequalities that are embedded in the very definition of what constitutes a well-functioning group. This has profound implications for any group that understands its internal dynamics through the lens of "family." Since the 1970s, increasing numbers of African-American women have recognized how this notion of naturalized hierarchy within a family constitutes a problematic organizing principle for the organization of actual Black families. However, challenging conceptions of Black civil society that naturalize hierarchy among African-American men and women has proved more difficult. This recognition requires questioning long-standing norms that simultaneously have used family language to define African-Americans as a race and have often conceptualized Black political struggle via the rhetoric of family.

Protesting gender hierarchies internal to Black civil society certainly framed the feminism of African-American women participating in the civil rights and Black Power movements of the 1960s and 1970s. As Frances Beale succinctly observed in "Double Jeopardy: To Be Black and Female," her groundbreaking 1970 essay,

> Unfortunately, there seems to be some confusion in the movement today as to who has been oppressing whom. Since the advent of black power, the black male has exerted a more prominent leadership role in our struggle for justice in this country. He sees the system for what it really is for the most part, but where he rejects its values and mores on many issues, when it comes to women, he seems to take his guidelines from the pages of the *Ladies' Home Journal.* (Beale 1995, 147–48)

Beale's comments reveal how African-American women's placement in political struggles organized by both race and gender reveal two overlapping and important uses of family in constructing groups. On the one hand, a Black civil society in which race-as-family metaphors are used to construct group identity misses potentially problematic internal hierarchies such as those of gender and sexuality. On the other hand, African-American women who see themselves as part of a women's collectivity organized around women's subordination within families confront the ongoing difficulties of organizing across deeply entrenched patterns of segregated space.

In thinking through these relationships, it may prove useful to revisit standard sociological categories of macro-, meso-, and micro-levels of social organization yet to view them as organized within and through power relations. Hierarchical power relations operate on all three levels—no one level "rules" the others. Collectively, these levels of social structure frame what Black women as a group are, what they do, and what they might think. On the macro level, schools, labor markets, the media, government, and other social institutions reproduce a social position or category of "Black woman" that is assigned to all individuals who fit criteria for membership. One does nor choose to be a "Black woman." Rather, one "finds oneself" classified in this category, regardless of differences in how one got there. On the meso level, Black women as a group encounter accumulated wisdom learned from past interactions between what was expected of them as Black women and what they actually did. On this level, Black women develop strategies for how African-American women grapple with these socially assigned positions. On the micro level, specific contexts of everyday life provide each Black woman multiple opportunities to play the social role of "Black woman" as it has been scripted or to negotiate new patterns. In this sense, each Black woman constructs the type of Black woman she chooses to be in different situations. All of these levels work together recursively, shaping one another to create specific social outcomes.

In analyzing the question of situated group standpoints, the meso level provides considerable insight on how Black women's group organization mediates between categories that are socially assigned to Black women and options that individual African-American women perceive in constructing their unique ways of being Black women. Although all Black women remain defined by the social role of Black women, how individual African-American women act in specific situations depends on at least two factors. The distinctive patterns of their individual biographies constitute one important factor. In addition, their access to historically created and shared Black feminist wisdom, for want of a better term, matters. This is of immense importance for Black feminist thought, because it suggests that Black women's collective, lived experiences in negotiating the category "Black woman" can serve a purpose in grappling with the new politics of containment. Despite its importance, scholarship on this meso level that examines Black women's agency in accessing cultural knowledge to construct individual expressions of self within socially defined categories of "Black woman" remains modest. What does exist, however, is provocative. Signithia Fordham's study of "loud Black girls" in education (1993) reveals strategies deployed by Black women who routinely encounter institutional silencing. Jacqueline Bobo's study of Black women as cultural readers (1995) informs us that Black women do not sit passively by, watching movies and believing everything they see. Rather, they actively negotiate cultural meanings.

Developing Black feminist thought as critical social theory requires articulating a situated standpoint that emerges from rather than suppresses the complexity of African-American women's experiences as a group on this meso level. British sociologist Stuart Hall's notion of articulation works well here— the idea of "unity and difference," of "difference in complex unity, without becoming a hostage to the privileging of difference as such" (qtd. in Slack 1996, I22). Such a standpoint would identify the ways in which being situated in intersections of race,

economic class, and gender, as well as those of age, sexuality, ethnicity, and region of the country, constructs relationships *among* African-American women as a group. At the same time, a situated standpoint would reflect how these intersections frame African-American women's distinctive history as a collectivity in the United States. This involves examining how intersectionality constructs relationships *between* African-American women and other groups. Thus, the challenge confronting African-American women lies in constructing notions of a Black female collectivity that remain sensitive to Black women's placement in distinctively American hierarchical power relations, while simultaneously resisting replication of these same relations within the group's own ranks.

The ability of Black feminist thought to make useful contributions to contemporary freedom struggles hinges on its ability to develop new forms of visionary pragmatism. Within the new politics of containment that confronts African-American women, visionary pragmatism in turn hinges on developing greater complexity within Black women's knowledge. In this regard, remaining situated is essential. Vision can be conjured up in the theoretical imagination, yet pragmatic actions require being responsive to the injustices of everyday life. Rather than abandoning situated standpoints, becoming situated in new understandings of social complexity is vital. Despite the importance of this project, changes in Black civil society, coupled with the growing importance of academia as a site where Black feminist thought is produced and circulated, raise real questions concerning the future of this type of functional knowledge. Whether Black feminist standpoints survive remains to be seen.

NOTES

1. Standpoint theory alone cannot explain Black women's experiences. Instead, it constitutes one of many conceptual frameworks that I use in analyzing Black feminist thought. Despite the overtly claimed and clearly stated eclecticism of my own work, I remain amazed at repeated efforts to categorize my ideas in one theoretical framework or another, generally without full knowledge of the scope of my work. I interpret this pressure to classify works in this fashion as a shortcut way of analyzing social phenomena. Grounded in circular reasoning, one identifies what one

perceives as the essence of one approach, classifies thinkers and/or their works in those categories, and then accepts or rejects their ideas based on one's initial classification. Intellectual work typically reflects much more complexity than this, and Black women's intellectual traditions in the United States certainly cannot be adequately addressed by any one approach (standpoint theory or any other).

2. Although bodies receive race and gender classifications, people routinely try to escape from, blur, or challenge the legitimacy of the boundaries between their

assigned category and others. The history of racial and gender "passing" (when Blacks "pass" as White and women "pass" as men) speaks to one way of transgressing boundaries. The strength of these performances reveals how classifications are rooted not in nature but in power relations. Similarly, the current attention to racially mixed individuals (as evidenced by the ongoing debate to change the racial categories of the U.S. census) and to intersexed individuals (those whose sex cannot easily be assigned at birth) also speaks to the permeability of racial and sexual borders. Although these cases are transgressive, installing these specific acts as a new transgressive politics writ large seems shortsighted. It's like chipping away at the edges of a giant mountain, claiming that each chip weakens the structure while failing to realize that the mountain of race and gender classification is far from crumbling.

3. Iris Marion Young contends that the New Left social movements of the 1960s and 1970s introduced new meanings of oppression by stressing group location in social institutions: "In its new usage, oppression designated the disadvantage and injustice some people suffer not because a tyrannical power coerces them, but because of the everyday practices of a well-intentioned liberal society" (1990, 41). Oppression became less associated with individual intentionality and more with the everyday workings of social structures that manufactured groups in hierarchies. In my brief analysis of intergenerational transfer of group privilege later in this chapter, I build on Young's notion of group-based oppression carried out by social institutions. As Young continues, "We cannot eliminate this structural oppression by getting rid of the rulers or making some new laws, because oppressions are systematically reproduced" (41).

4. This slippage between the individual and the group as units of analysis also fosters a reductive and problematic reading of "voice" as symbolic of group consciousness. Individual "voice" is not the same as group "voice" or standpoint. Typically, this reduction operates by imagining how *individuals* negotiate self-definitions and then claiming that through a "family resemblance," *collectivities* undergo a similar process. Because collectivities certainly do construct stories in framing their identity, this approach appears plausible. However, can the individual stand as proxy for the group and the group for the individual? Moreover, can this particular version of the individual serve as the exemplar for collective group identity? If an individual reasons from his or her own personal experiences that "since *we* are all the same under the skin, therefore, what *I* experience must be the same as what *everybody else* experiences," a certain perception of group narrative structure emerges. If an individual believes that his or her personal experiences in coming to voice—especially the inner voices within his or her individual consciousness, which are hidden from hierarchal power relations—not only reflect a common human experience but,

more to the point, serve as an exemplar for how *group* consciousness and decision making operate, then individual experience becomes the model for comprehending group processes. This approach minimizes the significance of conflict between groups in generating group narratives. In the model wherein individuals conduct inner dialogues among various parts of their "selves," the process of mediating conflicting identities occurs within each individual. The individual always holds complete power or agency over the consciousness that he or she constructs in his or her own mind and over the voice that she or he uses to express that consciousness.

5. For the moment, I am deliberately choosing to use the term *intersectionality* instead of its related term *articulation*, even though articulation approximates my understanding of intersectionality. In her essay "The Theory and Method of Articulation in Cultural Studies," Jennifer Daryl Slack examines the meaning of articulation in the work of British sociologist Stuart Hall. Recognizing the difficulty of developing a precise definition of articulation, Slack notes that articulation "isn't *exactly* anything" (1996, 117; emphasis in original). Although articulation is obviously a very powerful concept that closely parallels what I am calling intersectionality, there may be a difference between them. Slack describes the relationship between ideas and social structure that she sees emerging in cultural studies and that is captured by articulation: "The context is not something *out there, within which practices occur or which influence the development of practices*. Rather, *identities, practices, and effects generally, constitute the very context in which they are practices, identities or effects*" (125; emphasis in original). Although I value the effort to infuse a more dynamic dimension into analyses of social phenomena, this definition seems too much of a closed loop for me. I prefer, at least analytically, to retain the distinction between context and ideas that Slack collapses into one. Thus, the notion of intersectionality seems more closely wedded to notions of articulation that assume an independent existence for social structure. For additional insight into Hall's use of the term *articulation*, see Grossberg (1996).

6. Many thinkers have worked within a sociology-of-knowledge framework. At first glance, the links between a sociology of knowledge associated with Robert Merton and a standpoint theory associated with Karl Marx may seem surprising. Merton is typically associated with a structural-functionalism that omits questions of power. Although Merton is known for his contributions to the sociology of science, he treats science as one knowledge among many. Merton has been central in bringing ideas of the sociology of knowledge, historically associated more with theoretical and historicist traditions of Europe than with empiricist traditions in American sociology, to American sociology. As Merton suggests in his important essay "Paradigm for the Sociology of Knowledge," originally published in 1945, "The perennial problem of the implications of existential

influences upon knowledge for the epistemological status of knowledge has been hotly debated from the very outset" (Merton 1973, 13).

In contrast, Marx's entire focus seems to be hierarchy. The fundamental questions that link diverse thinkers in this field are flexible enough to accommodate a considerable variability on the connections between knowledge and social structure. Merton places far less emphasis than Marx on the hierarchical or power dimensions of social structure. In contrast, Marx focuses on the power dimensions of social structure; his ideas that are now known as standpoint theory are designed to explore the connections between hierarchical power relations and ensuing knowledges or standpoints. Moreover, thinking through the connections between knowledge and power is an especially sociological concern, because sociology examines social structures. French philosopher Michel Foucault (1977) points out that it is not a question of emancipating truth from systems of power. Rather, the issue lies in detaching the power of truth from its hegemonic institutional contexts. Foucault suggests that rather than being outside power or deprived of power, truth remains grounded in real-world politics. Each society has its own "regime of truth" or "general politics" of truth. These regimes consist of the types of discourses harbored by a particular society that it causes to function as true; epistemological criteria that distinguish truth from falsehoods; and legitimating mechanisms that determine the status of those charged with constructing truth (Foucault 1977). Using a more general definition of class as group leads one in a different direction. Like Robert Merton (1973), I see Karl Mannheim's work (1954) as extending the idea of class as a group with a connection to knowledge, to broader types of social groups. Thus, although the language of standpoint remains affiliated with Marxist social theory, the idea of knowledge emerging from groups differentially placed in social conditions transcends its origins in Marxism.

7. The literature on economic class is vast, and I make no attempt to review it here. Both Grimes (1991) and Vanneman and Cannon (1987) provide useful resources for summarizing and critiquing American scholarship on economic class. In brief, within American social science, economic class is routinely associated with either Karl Marx (social class) or Max Weber (status). The status-attainment perspective has garnered the most attention in American social science. Sacks (1989) takes the position that economic class should be conceptualized as group relationships and that efforts to assign a class category to individuals in order to examine economic class consciousness overlook the more significant features of economic class analysis. Thus, the approach that I use in developing a context for standpoint theory is already a minority position. For a discussion of the origins of feminist standpoint epistemology in a Marxist standpoint theory of labor, see Smith (1987), especially pp. 78–81.

8. Bourdieu makes a similar point about the differences between the ideas in Marxist social theory and the use to which those ideas are put: "Marxism, in the reality of its social use, ends up by being a mode of thought completely immune to historical criticism, which is a paradox, given the potentialities and indeed, the demands inherent in Marx's thought" (1990, 17).

9. Current debates that juxtapose class and culture as if these were two oppositional and distinct processes may create artificial boundaries where none exist. Economic class is typically theorized on the level of macrosociological structures—labor markets, industrial sectors, and the like. In contrast, historically, studies of group culture have emphasized ethnic and tribal cultures emerging from small-group interactions. This, seeming division of the themes of economics, political science, and sociology as being best suited for one type of issue, namely, economic class, and the humanities of history, literary studies, English, and literature as dealing with another, reflects the problems inherent in relying too heavily on disciplinary approaches to each concept. Sociology claimed the concept of social class and, from its inception, has studied economic class as a structural phenomenon largely divorced from culture. In contrast, until the advent of British cultural studies and its subsequent impetus on communications studies generally to take on the theme of mass culture, culture remained largely the province of anthropologists who carried out studies of culture in other societies.

REFERENCES

Andersen, Margaret. 1991. "Feminism and the American Family Ideal." *Journal of Comparative Family Studies* 22(2), summer: 235–46.

Anthias, Floya, and Nira Yuval-Davis. 1992. *Racialized Boundaries: Race, Nation, Gender, Colour, and Class in the Anti-racist Struggle.* New York: Routledge.

Baran, Paul, and Paul Sweezy. 1966. *Monopoly Capital.* New York: Monthly Review Press.

Beale, Frances. 1995 [1970]. "Double Jeopardy: To Be Black and Female." In *Words of Fire: An Anthology of African American Feminist Thought,* edited by Beverly Guy-Sheftall, 146–55. New York: New Press.

Bell, Derrick. 1987. *And We Are Not Saved: The Elusive Quest for Racial Justice.* New York: Basic Books.

Bobo, Jacqueline. 1995. *Black Women as Cultural Readers.* New York: Columbia University Press.

Bourdieu, Pierre. 1990. *In other words: Essays towards a Reflexive Sociology.* Stanford: Stanford University Press.

Collins, Patricia Hill. 1992. "Learning to Think for Ourselves: Malcolm X's Black Nationalism Reconsidered." In *Malcolm X: In Our Own Image,* edited by Joe Wood, 59–85. New York: St. Martin's.

———. 1997. "African-American Women and Economic Justice: A Preliminary Analysis of Wealth, Family, and Black Social Class." *University of Cincinnati Law Review* 65(3): 825–52.

———. 1998a. "Intersections of Race, Class, Gender, and Nation: Some Implications for Black Family Studies." *Journal of Comparative Family Studies* 29(1): 27–36.

———. Forthcoming, 1998b."It's All in the Family: Intersections of Gender, Race, Class, and Nation." *Hypatia.*

Crenshaw, Kimberle Williams. 1992. "Whose Story Is It Anyway? Feminist and Antiracist Appropriations of Anita Hill." In *Race-ing Justice, En-gendering Power,* edited by Toni Morrison, 402–40. New York: Pantheon.

Dill, Bonnie Thornton. 1983. "Race, Class, and Gender: Prospects for an All-Inclusive Sisterhood." *Feminist Studies* 9(1): 131–50.

Dyson, Michael Eric. 1993. *Reflecting Black: African-American Cultural Criticism.* Minneapolis: University of Minnesota Press.

Edwards, Richard. 1979. *Contested Terrain: The Transformation of the Workplace in the Twentieth Century.* New York: Basic Books.

Essed, Philomena. 1991. *Understanding Everyday Racism: An Interdisciplinary Theory.* Newbury Park, Calif.: Sage.

Estell, Kenneth. 1994. *The African-American Almanac.* 6th ed. Detroit: Gale Research. "Excerpts from Tapes in Discrimination Lawsuit." 1996. *New York Times,* November 4, D4.

Fordham, Signithia. 1993. "'Those Loud Black Girls': (Black) Women, Silence, and Gender 'Passing' in the Academy." *Anthropology and Education Quarterly* 24 (1): 3–32.

Foucault, Michel. 1977. "The Political Function of the Intellectual." *Radical Philosophy.* 17 (summer):12–14.

———. 1979. *Discipline and Punish: The Birth of the Prison.* Translated by Alan Sheridan. New York: Schocken.

Frankenberg, Ruth. 1993. *White Women, Race Matters: The Social Construction of Whiteness.* Minneapolis: University of Minnesota Press.

Franklin, V. P. 1992. *Black Self-Determination: A Cultural History of African-American Resistance.* Chicago: Lawrence Hill.

Goldberg, David Theo. 1993. *Racist Culture: Philosophy and the Politics of Meaning.* Cambridge, Mass.: Blackwell.

Grimes, Michael D. 1991. *Class in Twentieth-Century American Sociology.* New York: Praéger.

Grossberg, Lawrence. 1996. "On Postmodernism and Articulation: An Interview with Stuart Hall." In *Stuart Hall: Critical Dialogues in Cultural Studies,* edited by David

Morley and Kuan-Hsing Chen, 131–50. New York: Routledge.

Hekman, Susan. 1997. "Truth and Method: Feminist Standpoint Theory Revisited." *Signs* 22(2): 341–65.

Higginbotham, Elizabeth, and Lynn Weber. 1992. "Moving Up with Kin and Community: Upward Social Mobility for Black and White Women." *Gender and Society* 6(3): 416–40.

Jhally, Sut, and Justin Lewis. 1992. *Enlightened Racism.* Boulder: Westview.

Katz, Michael B. 1989. *The Undeserving Poor: From the War on Poverty to the War on Welfare.* New York: Pantheon.

Lerner, Gerda, ed. 1972. *Black Women in White America: A Documentary History.* New York: Vintage.

Mannheim, Karl. 1954 [1936]. *Ideology and Utopia: An Introduction to the Sociology of Knowledge.* New York: Harcourt, Brace & World.

Marable, Manning. 1983. *How Capitalism Underdeveloped Black America.* Boston: South End.

Marx, Karl. 1963 [1852]. *The Eighteenth Brumaire of Louis Bonaparte.* New York: International.

Massey, Douglas S., and Nancy A. Denton. 1993. *American Apartheid: Segregation and the Making of the Underclass.* Cambridge: Harvard University Press.

McClintock, Anne. 1995. *Imperial Leather: Race, Gender, and Sexuality in the Colonial Conquest.* New York: Routledge.

Merton, Robert K. 1973. *The Sociology of Science: Theoretical and Empirical Investigations.* Chicago: University of Chicago Press.

Quadagno, Jill. 1994. *The Color of Welfare: How Racism Undermined the War on Poverty.* New York: Oxford University Press.

Richie, Beth E. 1996. *Compelled to Crime: The Gender Entrapment of Battered Black Women.* New York: Routledge.

Sacks, Karen Brodkin. 1989. "Toward a Unified Theory of Class, Race, and Gender." *American Ethnologist* 16 (3): 534–50.

Scott, Joseph W. 1984. "1984: The Public and Private Governance of Race Relations." *Sociological Focus* 17 (3): 175–87.

Slack, Jennifer Daryl. 1996. "The Theory and Method of Articulation in Cultural Studies." In *Stuart Hall: Critical Dialogues in Cultural Studies,* edited by David Morley and Kuan-Hsing Chen, 112–27. New York: Routledge.

Smith, Dorothy E. 1987. *The Everyday World as Problematic: A Feminist Sociology.* Boston: Northeastern University Press.

Takaki, Ronald. 1993. *A Different Mirror: A History of Multicultural America.* Boston: Little, Brown.

Terrelonge, Pauline. 1984. "Feminist Consciousness and Black Women." In *Women: A Feminist Perspective.* 3rd ed. Edited by Jo Freeman, 557–67. Palo Alto, Calif.: Mayfield.

Thorne, Barrie. 1992. "Feminism and the Family: Two Decades of Thought." In *Rethinking the Family: Some*

Feminist Questions, edited by Barrie Thorne and Marilyn Yalom, 3–30. Boston: Northeastern University Press.

Van Deburg, William L. 1992. *New Day in Babylon: The Black Power Movement and American Culture, 1965–1975.* Chicago: University of Chicago Press.

Vanneman, Reeve, and Lynn Weber Cannon. 1987. *The American Perception of Class.* Philadelphia: Temple University Press.

West, Cornel. 1993. *Race Matters.* Boston: Beacon.

Wilson, William Julius. 1978. *The Declining Significance of Race.* Chicago: University of Chicago Press.

———. 1987. *The Truly Disadvantaged.* Chicago: University of Chicago Press.

Young, Iris Marion. 1990. *Justice and the Politics of Difference.* Princeton: Princeton University Press.

WOMANIST

Alice Walker

Womanist

1. From *Womanish.* (Opp. of "girlish," i.e., frivolous, irresponsible, not serious.) A black feminist or feminist or feminist of color. From the black folk expression of mothers to female children, "You acting womanish," i.e., like a woman. Usually referring to outrageous, audacious, courageous or *willful* behavior. Wanting to know more and in greater depth than is considered "good" for one. Interested in grown-up doings. Acting grown up. Being grown up. Interchangeable with another black folk expression: "You trying to be grown." Responsible. In charge. *Serious.*

   . . .

2. *Also:* A woman who loves other women, sexually and/or nonsexually. Appreciates and prefers women's culture, women's emotional flexibility (values tears as natural counterbalance of laughter), and women's strength.

Sometimes loves individual men, sexually and/or nonsexually. Committed to survival and wholeness of entire people, male *and* female. Not a separatist, except periodically, for health. Traditionally universalist, as in: "Mama, why are we brown, pink, and yellow, and our cousins are white, beige, and black?" Ans.: "Well, you know the colored race is just like a flower garden, with every color flower represented." Traditionally capable, as in: "Mama, I'm walking to Canada and I'm taking you and a bunch of other slaves with me." Reply: "It wouldn't be the first time."

   . . .

3. Loves music. Loves dance. Loves the moon. *Loves* the Spirit. Loves love and food and roundness. Loves struggle. *Loves* the Folk. Loves herself. *Regardless.*

   . . .

4. Womanist is to feminist as purple to lavender.

PART TWO

Gender, Culture, and Socialization

Everyone is born into a *culture*—a set of shared ideas about the nature of reality, standards of right and wrong, and concepts for making sense of social interactions. These ideas are put into practice in behaviors and material objects. As totally dependent infants we are *socialized*—taught the rules, roles, and relationships of the social world we will inherit. In the process of growing up, we learn to think, act, and feel as we are "supposed to." As adults, we are embedded in our culture's assumptions and images of gender.

One of the earliest and most deeply seated ideas to which we are socialized is that of gender identity: the idea that "I am a boy" or "I am a girl." Because the culture promotes strong ideas about what boys and girls are like, we learn to think of ourselves in terms of our gender identity (our "boyness" or "girlness") and adopt behaviors that are sex-assigned in our culture. Thus, for example, a girl who plays quietly with dolls is viewed as behaving in a feminine or "ladylike" manner and a boy who plays with trucks is seen as appropriately masculine, "all boy." Consciously or unconsciously, adults and peers categorize children as boys or girls, respond to and regard them differently, and encourage them to adopt behaviors and attitudes on the basis of their sex. We raise, in effect, two different kinds of children: girls and boys.

Parents are strong socializing influences, and they provide the first and most deeply experienced socialization. Despite claims to the contrary, American parents treat girls and boys differently. Boys and girls have different toys, names, and room decor, and they are played with in different ways. Even the stores in which parents shop for children's toys or clothing have separate aisles for boys' and girls' items. Even if parents monitor their actions in the hope of preventing sexism from affecting their child, other socializing influences—peers, schools, mass media—bear down on girls and boys.

One of the primary socializing influences is *language*. When we learn to talk we also learn the thought patterns and communication styles of our culture. Those patterns and styles reinforce differentiation by sex and perpetuate sex stereotyping, although the kind of stereotyping may vary from language to language. All languages teach their culture's ideas about men and women. They do it "naturally": as one learns a language, one learns the viewpoint of one's culture.

In the English language, for example, the generic *man* is supposed to include males and females, as well as people of all races and ethnicities, but in linguistic practice it does not. People other than white and male are linguistically tagged in writing and in speech. For example, occupational categories are sex- or race-tagged if the person's sex or race does not fit cultural stereotypes about who will be in those occupations. Consider: doctor/woman doctor/black woman doctor; nurse/male nurse/Asian male nurse. Linguistic tags teach normative expectations about who should occupy particular positions in society and about the normality or legitimacy of white men's claim to powerful positions.

As societies become more complex, increasingly the mass media have become centralized agents that transmit dominant cultural beliefs. Movements toward cultural heterogeneity are thwarted through the homogenizing effects of television in particular. TV presents sex stereotypes in their purest and simplest forms. Whether the program is about African-American families, lawyers at work, white teenagers, or talking animals, the stereotyping messages about sex and race are endlessly repetitive. Children in the United States spend more time watching television than they spend in school or interacting with parents or peers. Moreover, they believe that what they see on television is an accurate representation of how the world is and should be organized. White middle-class male dominance and sexualized, passive femininity are the repetitive themes.

The socialization effected by the family, language, and the mass media is continued in the educational system. Schools are formally charged with teaching the young. While teaching them reading, writing, and arithmetic, however, the schools also teach the conventional views of gender. They do so through the pattern of staffing (male principals and custodians, female teachers and food servers), curriculum, the sex segregation of sports and activities, and different expectations for boys and girls. Children themselves reinforce these messages through sex-segregated play and teasing of children who do not conform.

Socialization—whether through the home, the school, language, or the mass media—creates and sustains gender differences. Boys are taught that they will inherit the privileges and prestige of manhood, and that they must be tough, aggressive, and interested in trucks, airplanes, and sports. Girls, in contrast, learn that they are less socially valuable than boys, and that they should be quiet, pretty, and interested in dolls, fashion, and boys. Subcultures that promote values and beliefs different from the mainstream do exist, and individuals do not necessarily internalize every message from the dominant culture. Nevertheless, traditional cultural views of gender are ubiquitous and powerful.

Through powerful social institutions, then, children learn and consume a culture. Our culture is one that views men and masculinity as superior to women and femininity. It is a system that assigns different behaviors and attitudes to males and females and that further distinguishes between people of different racial and ethnic groups. As adults we continue to be shaped by the books and magazines we read, the movies we see, the music we enjoy and the people with whom we spend time. The ways that gender is portrayed or represented in the culture—in mass media, schools, public discussions—provide us with our only conceptual tools for thinking about men and women. It becomes nearly impossible to think about gender without being shaped by the images that surround us.

The readings in this part of *Feminist Frontiers 6* illustrate and explain different aspects of cultural constructions of gender and the socialization process. These systems of meaning shape how we understand ourselves and the social institutions that form our society. The readings document both the prevalence of conventional understanding in the culture and the presence of alternative messages. As you read, consider what kinds of influences conventional representations of gender have and what sources exist for challenging these images.

Representation, Language, and Culture

Images of gender are pervasive in our lives. In our language, mass media, and daily lives, we encounter particular images of what it means to be a woman or a man. Often we take these images for granted, and the ways that women and men are represented seem natural or inevitable. Language and media representations of gender shape the way we view ourselves and our relationships to each other and to the world around us. This section explores the images of women and men expressed in language and mass media.

Laurel Richardson's "Gender Stereotyping in the English Language" demonstrates the major ways in which sexism pervades the structure and standard usage of modern American English. Her analysis reveals different expectations of women and men embedded in the language and shows how we internalize and reinforce gender differences, as we read, write, and speak English or hear it spoken. The reading raises questions about the relationships between language and social life, including connections between linguistic change and other forms of social change. What are some examples of sexist or nonsexist language? Do you think using nonsexist language affects people's attitudes about women? How?

Language is one among many aspects of cultural conceptions of women. In many societies, standards of beauty and eroticism require women's bodies to conform to unrealistic and distorted ideals.

Debra Gimlin describes one of the consequences of cultural messages of beauty on women: the high rates of cosmetic surgery. In "Cosmetic Surgery: Paying for Your Beauty," she discusses the phenomenal rise in the United States of elective cosmetic surgeries such as liposuction, breast augmentation (and reduction), blepharoplasty (eyelid surgery), facelift, and chemical peel. Ninety percent of patients undergoing such procedures are women. Criticism of such surgeries focus not only on the risks and costs, but also on the increasing pressure for women to take advantage of medical advances to fight aging, imperfection, and ethnic deviations from an Anglo-Saxon ideal of beauty.

Yet Gimlin, in interviewing women who had undergone plastic surgery at a Long Island clinic, challenges the notion that women are simply dupes of the culture. She finds that women set realistic and limited goals—not the attainment of perfect beauty—when they seek plastic surgery, and that the surgery is often successful in making them feel better about their bodies and themselves. At the same time, they feel the need to construct elaborate defenses for having made this choice. Gimlin offers a complex view of cosmetic surgery. Do you think cosmetic surgery is a reasonable choice for women? How important are cultural ideals in making women dislike parts of their bodies? Can you imagine seeking cosmetic surgery for yourself?

Some of the women Gimlin interviewed disliked their Jewish or Italian noses or Asian eyes. Race, ethnicity, and class have a great deal to do with American ideas of beauty. Ingrid Banks, author of a book called *Hair Matters*, argues in "Hair Still Matters", that hair continues to carry complex meanings for African-American women. From Venus Williams's controversial beaded braids to the butch haircut of Rebecca (on the television show *The Practice*), African-American women's hair makes statements about race, gender, sexuality, and culture. Banks listens to the voices of African-American women talking about how hair is perceived by others and how they feel about their own hair. And she connects the issue of hair to global issues of beauty and women's bodies. Given cultural images of white women with long flowing hair, is it surprising that long hair signals femininity for many African-American women? What do different hairstyles signal about the people who choose to wear them? Do you judge people's femininity and sexuality based on hairstyle?

Bell hooks, in "Selling Hot Pussy: Representations of Black Female Sexuality in the Cultural Marketplace," continues this consideration. Hooks argues that contemporary images of black female bodies perpetuate racist assumptions about black women that can be traced to slavery, when white Europeans developed a fascination with the bodies of black people. When black women are included in films, television, and advertising, they usually play sluts or mammies. Almost always, the black women playing these roles are biracial or light-skinned. Drawing from the songs and performances of entertainers such as Tina Turner, Anita Baker, and Diana Ross, hooks shows that black women are represented in magazines, popular music, and advertising in ways that tend to reinforce prevailing stereotypes of them as highly sexualized. What images of black women are embedded in your favorite movies, TV shows, music videos, and popular songs? Are there any that present new and different representations of the black female body and black female sexuality?

Cultural representations of gender and sexuality are central to racial, patriarchal, and class domination. Focusing on the lives of Asian Americans in the United States, Yen Le Espiritu examines the way cultural symbols pertaining to masculinity and femininity are used to objectify and exploit Asian-American women and men. In "Ideological Racism and Cultural Resistance," Espiritu describes the way both Asian-American women and men have been femininized, contributing to the group's marginalization and role as the compliant "model minority" in contemporary U.S. cultural ideology.

She views the rise of Asian-American nationalist culture, which presents images of Asian-American men as strong, independent, and self-defined, as a form of resistance to the ideological assaults on their gender identities. At the same time, the masculinist underpinnings of Asian nationalist culture and politics marginalize Asian-American women and their needs. Can you think of some examples of movies, TV shows, videos, and popular music that portray Asian-American men and women in feminine terms? Can you think of examples of other social movements that accentuate men's identities and interests and marginalize women and their interests?

We cannot emphasize too strongly the importance of language and media images in the construction of our understanding of women's and men's positions in society. We are exposed to these images continually. Because the language we have acquired and the images we use are so deeply rooted and inseparable, it is very difficult for us to break free of them, to see and describe the world and our experiences in nonsexist ways. Yet women and other subordinate groups do attempt to construct alternative systems of meaning and draw strength from cultures of resistance. The power to define has a major influence on our conceptions of others and ourselves.

Gender Stereotyping in the English Language

❧ Laurel Richardson

Everyone in our society, regardless of class, ethnicity, sex, age, or race, is exposed to the same language, the language of the dominant culture. Analysis of verbal language can tell us a great deal about a people's fears, prejudices, anxieties, and interests. A rich vocabulary on a particular subject indicates societal interests or obsessions (e.g., the extensive vocabulary about cars in America). And different words for the same subject (such as *freedom fighter* and *terrorist, passed away* and *croaked, make love* and *ball*) show that there is a range of attitudes and feelings in the society toward that subject.

It should not be surprising, then, to find differential attitudes and feelings about men and women rooted in the English language. Although English has not been completely analyzed, six general propositions concerning these attitudes and feelings about males and females can be made.

First, in terms of grammatical and semantic structure, women do not have a fully autonomous, independent existence; they are part of man. The language is not divided into male and female with distinct conjugations and declensions, as many other languages are. Rather, *women* are included under the generic *man*. Grammar books specify that the pronoun *he* can be used generically to mean *he or she*. Further, *man,* when used as an indefinite pronoun, grammatically refers to both men and women. So, for example, when we read *man* in the following phrases we are to interpret it as applying to both men and women: "man the oars," "one small step for man, one giant step for mankind," "man, that's tough," "man overboard," "man the toolmaker," "alienated man," "garbageman." Our rules of etiquette complete the grammatical presumption of inclusivity. When two persons are pronounced "man and wife," Miss Susan Jones changes her entire name to Mrs. Robert Gordon (Vanderbilt, 1972). In each of these correct usages, women are a part of man; they do not exist autonomously. The exclusion of women is well expressed in Mary Daly's ear-jarring slogan "the sisterhood of man" (1973:7–21).

However, there is some question as to whether the theory that *man* means everybody is carried out in practice (see Bendix, 1979; Martyna, 1980). For example, an eight-year-old interrupts her reading of "The Story of the Cavemen" to ask how we got here without cavewomen. A ten-year-old thinks it is dumb to have a woman post*man.* A beginning anthropology student believes (incorrectly) that all shamans ("witch doctors") are males because her textbook and professor use the referential pronoun *he.*

But beginning language learners are not the only ones who visualize males when they see the word *man.* Research has consistently demonstrated that when the generic *man* is used, people visualize men, not women (Schneider & Hacker, 1973; DeStefano, 1976; Martyna, 1978; Hamilton & Henley, 1982). DeStefano, for example, reports that college students choose silhouettes of males for sentences with the word *man* or *men* in them. Similarly, the presumably generic *he* elicits images of men rather than women. The finding is so persistent that linguists doubt whether there actually is a semantic generic in English (MacKay, 1983).

Man, then, suggests not humanity but rather male images. Moreover, over one's lifetime, an educated American will be exposed to the prescriptive *he* more than a million times (MacKay, 1983). One consequence is the exclusion of women in the visualization, imagination, and thought of males and females. Most likely this linguistic practice perpetuates in men their feelings of dominance over and responsibility for women, feelings that interfere with the development of equality in relationships.

Second, in actual practice, our pronoun usage perpetuates different personality attributes and career aspirations for men and women. Nurses, secretaries, and elementary school teachers are almost invariably referred to as *she;* doctors, engineers, electricians, and presidents as *he*. In one classroom, students referred to an unidentified child as *he* but shifted to *she* when discussing the child's parent. In a faculty discussion of the problems of acquiring new staff, all architects, engineers, security officers, faculty, and computer programmers were referred to as *he*; secretaries and file clerks were referred to as *she*. Martyna (1978) has noted that speakers consistently use *he* when the referent has a high-status occupation (e.g., doctor, lawyer, judge) but shift to *she* when the occupations have lower status (e.g., nurse, secretary).

Even our choice of sex ascription to nonhuman objects subtly reinforces different personalities for males and females. It seems as though the small (e.g., kittens), the graceful (e.g., poetry), the unpredictable (e.g., the fates), the nurturant (e.g., the church, the school), and that which is owned and/or controlled by men (e.g., boats, cars, governments, nations) represent the feminine, whereas that which is a controlling forceful power in and of itself (e.g., God, Satan, tiger) primarily represents the masculine. Even athletic teams are not immune. In one college, the men's teams are called the Bearcats and the women's teams the Bearkittens.

Some of you may wonder whether it matters that the female is linguistically included in the male. The inclusion of women under the pseudogeneric *man* and the prescriptive *he*, however, is not a trivial issue. Language has tremendous power to shape attitudes and influence behavior. Indeed, MacKay (1983) argues that the prescriptive *he* "has all the characteristics of a highly effective propaganda technique": frequent repetition, early age of acquisition (before age six), covertness (*he* is not thought of as propaganda), use by high-prestige sources (including university texts and professors), and indirectness (presented as though it were a matter of common knowledge). As a result, the prescriptive affects females' sense of life options and feelings of well-being. For example, Adamsky (1981) found that women's sense of power and importance was enhanced when the prescriptive *he* was replaced by *she*.

Awareness of the impact of the generic *man* and prescriptive *he* has generated considerable activity to change the language. One change, approved by the Modern Language Association, is to replace the prescriptive *he* with the plural *they*—as was accepted practice before the eighteenth century. Another is the use of *he or she*. Although it sounds awkward at first, the *he or she* designation is increasingly being used in the media and among people who have recognized the power of the pronoun to perpetuate sex stereotyping. When a professor, for example, talks about "the lawyer" as "he or she," a speech pattern that counteracts sex stereotyping is modeled. This drive to neutralize the impact of pronouns is evidenced further in the renaming of occupations: a policeman is now a police officer, a postman is a mail carrier, a stewardess is a flight attendant.

Third, linguistic practice defines females as immature, incompetent, and incapable and males as mature, complete, and competent. Because the words *man* and *woman* tend to connote sexual and human maturity, common speech, organizational titles, public addresses, and bathroom doors frequently designate the women in question as *ladies*. Simply contrast the different connotations of *lady* and *woman* in the following common phrases:

> Luck, be a lady (woman) tonight.
> Barbara's a little lady (woman).
> Ladies' (Women's) Air Corps.

In the first two examples, the use of *lady* desexualizes the contextual meaning of *woman*. So trivializing is the use of *lady* in the last phrase that the second is wholly anomalous. The male equivalent, *lord*, is never used, and its synonym, *gentleman*, is used infrequently. When *gentleman* is used, the assumption seems to be that certain culturally condoned aspects of masculinity (e.g., aggressivity, activity, and strength) should be set aside in the interests of maturity and order, as in the following phrases:

> A gentlemen's (men's) agreement.
> A duel between gentlemen (men).
> He's a real gentleman (man).

Rather than feeling constrained to set aside the stereotypes associated with *man*, males frequently find the opposite process occurring. The contextual connotation of *man* places a strain on males to be continuously sexually and socially potent, as the following examples reveal:

> I was not a man (gentleman) with her tonight.
> This is a man's (gentleman's) job.
> Be a man (gentleman).

Whether males, therefore, feel competent or anxious, valuable or worthless in particular contexts is influenced by the demands placed on them by the expectations of the language.

Not only are men infrequently labeled *gentlemen,* but they are infrequently labeled *boys.* The term *boy* is reserved for young males, bellhops, and car attendants, and as a putdown to those males judged inferior. *Boy* connotes immaturity and powerlessness. Only occasionally do males "have a night out with the boys." They do not talk "boy talk" at the office. Rarely does our language legitimize carefreeness in males. Rather, they are expected, linguistically, to adopt the responsibilities of manhood.

On the other hand, women of all ages may be called *girls.* Grown females "play bridge with the girls" and indulge in "girl talk." They are encouraged to remain childlike, and the implication is that they are basically immature and without power. Men can become men, linguistically, putting aside the immaturity of childhood; indeed, for them to retain the openness and playfulness of boyhood is linguistically difficult.

Further, the presumed incompetence and immaturity of women are evidenced by the linguistic company they keep. Women are categorized with children ("women and children first"), the infirm ("the blind, the lame, the women"), and the incompetent ("women, convicts, and idiots"). The use of these categorical designations is not accidental happenstance; "rather these selectional groupings are powerful forces behind the actual expressions of language and are based on distinctions which are not regarded as trivial by the speakers of the language" (Key, 1975:82). A total language analysis of categorical groupings is not available, yet it seems likely that women tend to be included in groupings that designate incompleteness, ineptitude, and immaturity. On the other hand, it is difficult for us to conceive of the word *man* in any categorical grouping other than one that extends beyond humanity, such as "Man, apes, and angels" or "Man and Superman." That is, men do exist as an independent category capable of autonomy; women are grouped with the stigmatized, the immature, and the foolish. Moreover, when men are in human groupings, they are invariably first on the list ("men and women," "he and she," "man and wife"). This order is not accidental but was prescribed in the sixteenth century to honor the worthier party.

Fourth, in practice women are defined in terms of their sexual desirability (to men); men are defined in terms of their sexual prowess (over women). Most slang words in reference to women refer to their sexual desirability to men (e.g., *dog, fox, broad, ass, chick*).

Slang about men refers to their sexual prowess over women (e.g., *dude, stud, hunk*). The fewer examples given for men is not an oversight. An analysis of sexual slang, for example, listed more than a thousand words and phrases that derogate women sexually but found "nowhere near this multitude for describing men" (Kramarae, 1975:72). Farmer and Henley (cited in Schulz, 1975) list five hundred synonyms for *prostitute,* for example, and only sixty-five for *whoremonger.* Stanley (1977) reports two hundred twenty terms for a sexually promiscuous woman and only twenty-two for a sexually promiscuous man. Shuster (1973) reports that the passive verb form is used in reference to women's sexual experiences (e.g., *to be laid, to be had, to be taken*), whereas the active tense is used in reference to the male's sexual experience (e.g., *lay, take, have*). Being sexually attractive to males is culturally condoned for women and being sexually powerful is approved for males. In this regard, the slang of the street is certainly not countercultural; rather, it perpetuates and reinforces different expectations in females and males as sexual objects and performers.

Further, we find sexual connotations associated with neutral words applied to women. A few examples should suffice. A male academician questioned the title of a new course, asserting it was "too suggestive." The title? "The Position of Women in the Social Order." A male tramp is simply a hobo, but a female tramp is a slut. And consider the difference in connotation of the following expressions:

> *It's easy.*
> *He's easy.*
> *She's easy.*

In the first, we assume something is "easy to do"; in the second, we might assume a professor is an "easy grader" or a man is "easygoing." But when we read "she's easy," the connotation is "she's an easy lay."

In the world of slang, men are defined by their sexual prowess. In the world of slang and proper speech, women are defined as sexual objects. The rule in practice seems to be: If in doubt, assume that *any* reference to a women has a sexual connotation. For both genders, the constant bombardment of prescribed sexuality is bound to have real consequences.

Fifth, women are defined in terms of their relations to men; men are defined in terms of their relations to the world at large. A good example is seen in the words *master* and *mistress*. Originally these words had the same meaning—"a person who holds power over servants." With the demise of the feudal system, however, these words took on different meanings. The masculine variant metaphorically refers to power over something; as in "He is the master of his trade"; the feminine variant metaphorically (although probably not in actuality) refers to power over a man sexually, as in "She is Tom's mistress." Men are defined in terms of their power in the occupational world, women in terms of their sexual power over men.

The existence of two contractions for Mistress (*Miss* and *Mrs.*) and but one for Mister (*Mr.*) underscores the cultural concern and linguistic practice: women are defined in relation to men. Even a divorced woman is defined in terms of her no-longer-existing relation to a man (she is still *Mrs. Man's Name*). But apparently the divorced state is not relevant enough to the man or to the society to require a label. A divorced woman is a *divorcée,* but what do you call a divorced man? The recent preference of many women to be called *Ms.* is an attempt to provide for women an equivalency title that is not dependent on marital status.

Sixth, a historical pattern can be seen in the meanings that come to be attached to words that originally were neutral: those that apply to women acquire obscene and/or debased connotations, but no such pattern of derogation holds for neutral words referring to men. The processes of *pejoration* (the acquiring of an obscene or debased connotation) and *amelioration* (the reacquiring of a neutral or positive connotation) in the English language in regard to terms for males and females have been studied extensively by Muriel Schulz (1975).

Leveling is the least derogative form of pejoration. Through leveling, titles that originally referred to an elite class of persons come to include a wider class of persons. Such democratic leveling is more common for female designates than for males. For example, contrast the following: *lord—lady; baronet—dame; governor—governess.*

Most frequently what happens to words designating women as they become pejorated, however, is that they come to denote or connote sexual wantonness. *Sir* and *mister*, for example, remain titles of courtesy, but at some time *madam, miss,* and *mistress* have come to designate, respectively, a brothelkeeper, a prostitute, and an unmarried sexual partner of a male (Schulz, 1975:66).

Names for domestic helpers, if they are females, are frequently derogated. *Hussy,* for example, originally meant "housewife." *Laundress, needlewoman, spinster* ("tender of the spinning wheel"), and *nurse* all referred to domestic occupations within the home, and all at some point became slang expressions for prostitute or mistress.

Even kinship terms referring to women become denigrated. During the seventeenth century, *mother* was used to mean "a bawd"; more recently *mother* (*mothuh f—*) has become a common derogatory epithet (Cameron, 1974). Probably at some point in history every kinship term for females has been derogated (Schulz, 1975:66).

Terms of endearment for women also seem to follow a downward path. Such pet names as Tart, Dolly, Kitty, Polly, Mopsy, Biddy, and Jill all eventually became sexually derogatory (Schulz, 1975:67). *Whore* comes from the same Latin root as *care* and once meant "a lover of either sex."

Indeed, even the most neutral categorical designations—*girl, female, woman, lady*—at some point in their history have been used to connote sexual immorality. *Girl* originally meant "a child of either sex"; through the process of semantic degeneration it eventually meant "a prostitute." Although *girl* has lost this meaning, *girlie* still retains sexual connotations. *Woman* connoted "a mistress" in the early nineteenth century; *female* was a degrading epithet in the latter part of the nineteenth century; and when *lady* was introduced as a euphemism, it too became deprecatory. "Even so neutral a term as *person,* when it was used as substitute for *woman,* suffered [vulgarization]" (Mencken, 1963: 350, quoted in Schulz, 1975:71).

Whether one looks at elite titles, occupational roles, kinship relationships, endearments, or age–sex categorical designations, the pattern is clear. Terms referring to females are pejorated—"become negative in the middle instances and abusive in the extremes" (Schulz, 1975:69). Such semantic derogation, however, is not evidenced for male referents. *Lord, baronet, father, brother, nephew, footman, bowman, boy, lad, fellow, gentleman, man, male,* and so on "have failed to undergo the derogation found in the history of their corresponding feminine designations" (Schulz, 1975:67). Interestingly, the male word, rather than undergoing derogation, frequently is replaced by a female referent when the speaker wants to debase a male. A weak man, for example, is referred to as a *sissy* (diminutive of *sister*), and an army recruit during basic training is called a *pussy*.

And when one is swearing at a male, he is referred to as a *bastard* or a *son of a bitch*—both appellations that impugn the dignity of a man's mother.

In summary, these verbal practices are consistent with the gender stereotypes that we encounter in everyday life. Women are thought to be a part of man, nonautonomous, dependent, relegated to roles that require few skills, characteristically incompetent and immature, sexual objects, best defined in terms of their relations to men. Males are visible, autonomous and independent, responsible for the protection and containment of women, expected to occupy positions on the basis of their high achievement or physical power, assumed to be sexually potent, and defined primarily by their relations to the world of work. The use of the language perpetuates the stereotypes for both genders and limits the options available for self-definition.

REFERENCES

Adamsky, C. 1981. "Changes in pronominal usage in a classroom situation." *Psychology of Women Quarterly* 5:773–79.

Bendix, J. 1979. "Linguistic models as political symbols: Gender and the generic 'he' in English." In J. Orasanu, M. Slater, and L. L. Adler, eds., *Language, Sex and Gender: Does la différence Make a Difference?* pp. 23–42. New York: New Academy of Science Annuals.

Cameron, P. 1974. "Frequency and kinds of words in various social settings, or What the hell's going on?" In M. Truzzi, ed., *Sociology for Pleasure*, pp. 31–37. Englewood Cliffs, N.J.: Prentice Hall.

Daly, M. 1973. *Beyond God the Father*. Boston: Beacon Press.

DeStefano, J. S. 1976. Personal communication. Columbus: Ohio State University.

Hamilton, N., & Henley, N. 1982. "Detrimental consequences of the generic masculine usage." Paper presented to the Western Psychological Association meetings, Sacramento.

Key, M. R. 1975. *Male/Female Language*. Metuchen, N.J.: Scarecrow Press.

Kramarae, Cheris. 1975. "Woman's speech: Separate but unequal?" In Barrie Thorne and Nancy Henley, eds., *Language and Sex: Difference and Dominance*, pp. 43–56. Rowley, Mass.: Newbury House.

MacKay, D. G. 1983. "Prescriptive grammar and the pronoun problem." In B. Thorne, C. Kramarae, and N. Henley, eds., *Language, Gender, and Society*, pp. 38–53. Rowley, Mass.: Newbury House.

Martyna, W. 1978. "What does 'he' mean? Use of the generic masculine." *Journal of Communication* 28:131–38.

Martyna, W. 1980. "Beyond the 'he/man' approach: The case for nonsexist language." *Signs* 5:482–93.

Mencken, H. L. 1963. *The American Language*. 4th ed. with supplements. Abr. and ed. R. I. McDavis. New York: Knopf.

Schneider, J., & Hacker, S. 1973. "Sex role imagery in the use of the generic 'man' in introductory texts: A case in the sociology of sociology." *American Sociologist* 8:12–18.

Schulz, M. R. 1975. "The semantic derogation of women." In B. Thorne and N. Henley, eds., *Language and Sex: Difference and Dominance*, pp. 64–75. Rowley, Mass.: Newbury House.

Shuster, Janet. 1973. "Grammatical forms marked for male and female in English." Unpublished paper. Chicago: University of Chicago.

Stanley, J. P. 1977. "Paradigmatic woman: The prostitute." In D. L. Shores, ed., *Papers in Language Variation*. Birmingham: University of Alabama Press.

Vanderbilt, A. 1972. *Amy Vanderbilt's Etiquette*. Garden City, N.Y.: Doubleday.

WHY I'M NOT A LADY (AND NO WOMAN IS)

Sherryl Kleinman

Ladies have pale skin,
wear white gloves
they sweep across the top
of the armoire
to make sure the
darker-skinned woman
who cleaned it
didn't forget or cheat.

A lady doesn't sit
with one leg dangling
over the arm of the chair
like she just doesn't give a damn.

Ladies don't fix cars, build bridges, wire houses.
Ladies become First Lady, not President.

Sit up straight, young lady!
Cross your legs (shave them first).
Remove (surgically if necessary)
that frown from your forehead.
Lower your voice.
Smile.

(If anyone asks why you
snuck down to the Ladies Room,
say you had to powder your nose.)

Call yourself a lady
and he'll protect you,
he'll respect you,
he won't leave.
But who protects the cleaning lady?

Wonder why we don't have

"Ladies Studies"
at the university?

I'll remain a woman,
keep the basic word
that got so dirty
she wants to clean herself off
and be called lady.

Until a real woman
can earn one dollar on the man's dollar;
Until a real woman can call her body her own;
Until a real woman can love a woman in peace,
love a man without fear;
Until a real woman can walk the dark streets
with her mind on the stars and not on her back,

I will know that lady is a lie.

READING 10

Cosmetic Surgery: Paying for Your Beauty

Debra L. Gimlin

After several unsuccessful attempts to schedule an appointment, I finally managed to meet with Jennifer, a twenty-nine-year-old grade school teacher who volunteered to talk with me about her cosmetic surgery. On a typically cold November afternoon, I spoke with Jennifer in her apartment on the south shore of Long Island. Jennifer is 5 feet 6 inches tall and has long, straight blonde hair and expressive light blue eyes. That day she was dressed in an oversized gray pullover and black sweatpants. While we talked, she peeled and sliced the crudites that would be her contri-

bution to the potluck engagement party that she was attending later that evening.

During our conversation, I noticed that by far the most prominent feature in her small studio apartment was the enormous black and chrome stair-climbing machine set slightly off from the center of the living room/bedroom. I learned that Jennifer spends forty minutes each day on this machine and works out with weights at a nearby gym three to four times a week. She eats no meat, very little oil or fat, and no sweets, and she drinks very little alcohol. Despite her rigorous body work routine, Jennifer's legs have remained a disappointment to her. Rather than lean and muscular, they look, by her account, thick and shapeless—particularly around her lower thighs and knees. Jennifer says that her decision to have liposuction was motivated primarily by her inability to reshape her legs through diet and exercise. During the procedure, the fatty deposits were removed from the insides of Jennifer's knees, making her legs appear slimmer and more toned.

Jennifer acknowledged her own significant ambivalence about taking surgical steps to alter her body. If possible, she would have preferred to shape her legs through aerobics, weight training, and dieting, rather than through liposuction, which Jennifer described as a final and desperate option. By her account, plastic surgery was the only way to alter physical attributes that she referred to as "genetic flaws," features that she could change through no other available means. Expressing some shame, as she says, "for taking the easy way out," Jennifer's guilt is not so great that she regrets having surgery. Indeed, she plans to have a second liposuction in the near future, this time to remove the fatty tissue from her upper and inner thighs.

Cosmetic surgery stands, for many theorists and social critics, as the ultimate invasion of the human body for the sake of physical beauty. It epitomizes the astounding lengths to which contemporary women will go to obtain bodies that meet current ideals of attractiveness. As such, plastic surgery is perceived by many to be qualitatively different from aerobics, hair styling, or even dieting. In this view, cosmetic surgery is not about controlling one's own body but is instead an activity so extreme, so invasive that it can only be interpreted as subjugation. Even more than women who may participate in other types of body-shaping activities, those who undergo cosmetic surgery appear to many observers—both casual and academic—to be so obsessed with physical appearance that they are willing to risk their very existence to become more attractive.

Not surprisingly, cosmetic surgery has been attacked by the scores of feminist writers who criticize body work generally.[1] While these attacks may be well deserved, the cosmetic surgery industry is expanding rapidly nevertheless. Board-certified plastic surgeons performed more than 2.2 millions procedures in 1999, a 44 percent increase since 1996 and striking 153 percent increase since 1992. Liposuction, the most common cosmetic procedure in the United States, was performed 230, 865 times (up 57 percent since 1996 and

264 percent since 1992), at a cost of approximately $2,000 per patient. Breast augmentation, with its price tag of nearly $3,000, was the second most common procedure, at 167,318 (a 51 percent increase since 1996). Blepharoplasty (eyelid surgery), the third most common, was performed on 142,033 patients at a cost of just under $3,000, followed by facelift (72,793) at over $5,000, and chemical peel (51,519), at nearly $1,300.[2] Ninety percent of these operations are performed on women, as are virtually all breast augmentations and reductions, 87 percent of liposuctions, 91 percent of face-lifts, and 85 percent of blepharoplastics. In 1999, American women had 167,318 breast augmentations, 120,160 blepharoplasties, 201,083 liposuction procedures, and 66,096 face-lifts.[3]

Although strategies for surgically altering the body's appearance have been available for centuries, the practice has only recently become a mass phenomenon. Until recently, patients were most often men disabled by war or industrial accidents. Now the recipients are overwhelmingly women who are dissatisfied with their looks.[4] Today, aesthetic operations make up 45 percent of all plastic surgery.[5]

Cosmetic surgery is one of the fastest-growing specialities in American medicine.[6] Although the total number of physicians in the United States has little more than doubled in the last quarter of a century, the number of plastic surgeons has increased fourfold. At the end of World War II, there were only about 100 plastic surgeons in the country; in 1965, there were 1,133. By 1990, that number had tripled to 3,850. Moreover, these figures may underrepresent the total number of individuals performing aesthetic procedures today. Because it is not necessary to be a licensed plastic surgeon to perform cosmetic surgery, procedures such as face-lifts, eyelid corrections, and chemical peels may be performed by other specialists, such as dermatologists.[7]

Criticisms of surgical alternation of the female body multiply nearly as rapidly as the procedures themselves. One of the main critiques of cosmetic surgery derives from the dangers involved. Cosmetic surgery is undeniably painful and risky, and each operation involves specific potential complications. For instance, pain, numbness, bruising, discoloration, and depigmentation frequently follow a liposuction, often lingering up to six months after the operation. Face-lifts can damage nerves, leaving the patient's face permanently numb. More serious complications include fat embolisms, blood clots, fluid depletion, and even death. Health experts estimate that the chance of serious side effects from breast augmentation are between 30 percent and 50 percent. The least dramatic and most common of these include decreased sensitivity in the nipples, painful swelling or congestion of the breasts, and hardening of the breasts that makes it difficult to lie down comfortably or to raise the arms without shifting the implants.[8] More serious is the problem of encapsulation, in which the body reacts to foreign materials by forming a capsule of fibrous tissue around the implants. This covering can sometimes be broken down manually by the surgeon, but, even when successful, the procedure is extremely painful. When it is unsuccessful, the implants must be removed; in some cases, the surgeon must chisel the hardened substance from the patient's chest wall.

Clearly, the recipient of cosmetic surgery may emerge from the operation in worse shape than when she went in. Unsuccessful breast augmentations are often disfiguring, leaving the patient with unsightly scars and deformation. An overly tight facelift produces a "zombie" look, in which the countenance seems devoid of expression. Following liposuction, the skin can develop a corrugated, uneven texture.

Finally, some criticisms of plastic surgery focus on the implications of such procedures for contemporary conceptualizations of the body and identity. Cosmetic surgery has expanded alongside specific technological developments, including advances in medical equipment like magnifying lenses, air drills for severing bone and leveling skin, and improved suturing materials, all of which enable surgical interventions to be performed with better results and less trauma for the patient.[9] According to some critics, these developments, and the increasing flexibility in body altering that they permit, are linked to cultural discourses likening the body to what Susan Bordo has called "cultural plastic." The body is now understood as having a potential for limitless change, "undetermined by history, social location or even individual biography."[10] Not only has the body come to stand as a primary symbol of identity, but it is a symbol with an unlimited capacity for alteration and modification. The body is not a dysfunctional object requiring medical intervention but a commodity, not unlike "a car, a refrigerator, a house, which can be continuously upgraded and modified in accordance with new interests and greater resources."[11] The body is a symbol of selfhood, but its relation to its inhabitant is shaped primarily by the individual's capacity for material consumption.

Of the various forms of body work, plastic surgery is surely the hardest to justify. The physical dangers

are real. The symbolic damage done to all women by the apparent surrender of some to unattainable ideals of beauty is significant. Yet the criticisms also leave out a good deal. Most important, the criticisms operate either at the grand level of cultural discourse or the highly grounded level of physiological effect. As a result, they overlook the experience of the women who have plastic surgery. In this chapter, after first discussing the role of the doctor as a gatekeeper to plastic surgery, I focus on that experience.

First—and most important to those who undergo it—plastic surgery often works. This fact stands in contrast to a rhetoric that concentrates on the unattainable character of contemporary beauty ideals, portraying plastic surgery as a Sisyphean task. Critics of plastic surgery imply that those who undergo it will complete one operation only to discover some new flaw. Yet this is not the case. Somewhat to my surprise, many of the women I interviewed expressed enormous satisfaction with their procedures. While some did, indeed, intend to return for additional operations, others seemed content to have fixed a particular "flaw." I do not mean to argue that all contemporary ideals of beauty are, in fact, attainable. They are not. Neither do I mean to argue that women in contemporary America can escape the nagging self-doubts caused by those unattainable ideals. They cannot. But the ambitions of those women who undergo plastic surgery often stop far short of attaining ideal beauty. And given these limited ambitions—and within the cultural space marked out for the expression of female beauty—plastic surgery frequently achieves the exact goals intended by those who undergo it.

Second, criticisms of plastic surgery directed at gender issues often understate the extent to which this activity involves gender at an intersection with age, race, ethnicity, and even class. Many women surely undertake plastic surgery, most notably in the case of breast enlargement, to enhance distinctively female attributes. Others, however—Jewish and Italian women who have rhinoplasty, Chinese and Japanese women who have their eyes reshaped—do so in a distinctively ethnic context. And many others have plastic surgery in an attempt to reproduce the bodies of their youth. If plastic surgery speaks to the depredations of gender domination, we should recognize that it also speaks to the depredations of Anglo-Saxon ideals of beauty and the idealization of youth.

Third, the criticisms of plastic surgery ignore the complicated process by which the women who undergo surgical procedures integrate them into their identities. If not in feminist theory, then in popular culture, there lies an implicit notion that the benefits of plastic surgery are somehow inauthentic and, therefore, undeserved. Although the critics of plastic surgery insist that appearance should not be the measure of a woman's worth, the women who have plastic surgery are nonetheless participants in a culture in which appearance is taken as an expression of an inner state. To be able to purchase a new nose or wider eyes or thinner thighs seems, then, to sever the relationship between inner states and their outer expression. Where the women in aerobics classes are working hard to detach their identities from their bodies, the women who undergo plastic surgery must work even harder to reattach their identities to their new appearances. On the one hand, they are using plastic surgery to tell a story about themselves: I am the woman with svelte thighs or a button nose. On the other hand, they must also tell a story about plastic surgery in order to counter the charges of its inauthenticity. They must somehow show, to themselves even more than to others, that the new appearance is both deserved and a better indicator of the self than the old appearance—an appearance necessarily repositioned as "accidental." The result, then, is that the woman who has plastic surgery finds herself in a double bind. She is unhappy with her appearance, and so she takes the only steps she can to improve it. No matter how successful her efforts are—or how pleased she is with their outcome—the woman must ultimately defend her decision to purchase appearance and identity.

RESEARCH AND METHODS

The research for this chapter involved fieldwork in a Long Island plastic surgery clinic and interviews with the surgeon and twenty of his female patients. Finding a location to study cosmetic surgery proved difficult because many women hesitate to admit that they have undergone such procedures and physicians are bound by doctor-patient confidentiality. Having organized my research around interviews and fieldwork in identifiable physical locations, I knew that I wanted to talk with a single surgeon's female patients, rather than a "snowball" sample of surgery clients, whom I could have located easily through advertisements in local newspapers, gyms, universities, or hairstyling salons. As a result, I needed to find a cosmetic surgeon who would permit me access to patients. My search for this doctor took nearly six months, during which time I contacted over twenty clinics and interviewed seven physicians.

I eventually chose to focus on the clinic of Dr. John Norris, a local surgeon specializing in aesthetic procedures. My discussions with the six other physicians proved to be a rich source of data about the cosmetic surgery industry and cosmetic surgeons themselves. I learned, for example, that cosmetic surgeons are frequently critical of their female clientele, seeing them as obsessed and impossible to please. Moreover, often believing that the physical imperfections that their clients observe are insignificant, surgeons sometimes suspect their patients of trying to solve emotional problems by altering their bodies.

I met John Norris at the gym where I studied aerobics. As a member of the gym, I spent a considerable amount of time there each week, both in research and on my own body work. John and his wife, Monica, were gym regulars who, like me, tended to exercise in the mornings, and I saw them several times each week. Even though I had met him previously, I contacted John formally, as I did the other cosmetic surgeons in the area. I explained my project to his receptionist and made an appointment to speak with him. After our second meeting, I asked John to allow me to interview twenty of his female clients. He agreed and asked his receptionist to contact women who might be willing to talk with me. After obtaining his patients' approval, John provided me with their names and telephone numbers. This procedure surely biased my sample in favor of successful cases. In addition to interviewing patients (one of whom I was able to interview both before and after she had surgery), I conducted several interviews with John. I also attended informational sessions at another local clinic to learn more about many of these procedures.

John conducts his enormously successful practice in two offices, one on Long Island and the other in Manhattan. I spoke with him at some length about his interest in aesthetic plastic surgery. He explained that although he had originally aspired to be a sculptor, he soon decided that a career in art would not provide an adequate income. As his interest in science developed, John opted instead for a medical career and for what he now refers to as the "excitement of sculpting human appearance." Believing that his work helps his patients to feel more satisfied with the way they look, more desirable, and more confident in their professional and private lives, John says that he derives enormous satisfaction from his career.

John is interested not only in "sculpting" the appearances of others; he is himself heavily involved in the culture of body work. In particular, John has participated in bodybuilding since he was fifteen years old and, at age fifty-one, still participates regularly in bodybuilding competitions. Moreover, John has personally undergone plastic surgery to remove the "love handles" that he says will develop at his waistline unless he maintains a body composition of no more than 3 percent body fat. As his medical career has progressed, John's training and competition have both fueled and been fueled by his interest in using surgery to rework the aesthetics of the body. While he began his career doing reconstructive and burn-correcting surgery in addition to cosmetic procedures, he now focuses almost exclusively on aesthetic plastic surgery, which he finds equally rewarding and more enjoyable.

Similar to the staff of Pamela's Hair Salon [discussed in another part of *Body Work: Beauty and Self-image in American Culture* (Berkeley: University of California Press, 2002), from which this reading is taken], John is a "true believer" in beauty ideology. Like the stylists, John not only dispenses the means of altering appearance but also is deeply involved in reworking his own appearance. Nevertheless, he is differentiated from them by his higher social status. Like Pamela's staff, John is able both to assess his clients' appearance "flaws" and to suggest particular techniques for correcting them. But, unlike Pamela's staff—and primarily because of his status as a medical professional—John's patients nearly always accept his advice. Simply put, John is different from Pamela's stylists because he not only dispenses "beauty" to his patients but also shapes the choices they make about their appearances.

Moreover, John regularly denies surgical candidates access to the body work he provides. He is selective in choosing his clientele, screening patients to ensure that they are suitable for the operations they request. Listening to the client's description of her physical imperfections, John determines whether or not her complaint is reasonable—whether or not her nose is really inappropriate for her face, her breasts are really too small, her ankles are really too thick, and so on. In making such judgments, John (like the beauticians at Pamela's) blurs the line between technique and aesthetics, effectively broadening his area of expertise. While understanding his activity as a process of determining the "appropriateness" of surgical candidates, he actually selects patients based in large part on his personal taste and sense of aesthetics. As a purveyor of body work, John positions himself not only as a surgeon but also as an expert in contemporary standards for female beauty.

In deciding whether patients are suitable candidates for the procedures they request, John judges not only the aesthetics of their appearance but also their psychological health. By his own account, John attempts to determine whether patients are trying to deal with personal crises (such as divorce) through plastic surgery. John says that when he talks with potential patients about their motivations for having cosmetic surgery, many express sadness or fear regarding a significant personal relationship, even to the point of breaking down in tears in his office. This reaction, he claims, suggests that patients should seek the services of "some other type" of professional presumably, a psychologist or marital counselor—rather than those of a cosmetic surgeon.

John has come to categorize patients in four conceptual types, distinguished primarily by their motivations for having surgery. The first of the groups includes individuals who are "self-motivated and realistic." These patients pursue surgery as a means of bringing their appearances in line with their inner self. Claiming that their bodies fail to represent them as the people they truly are, individuals in this group explain their desire for cosmetic surgery with statements such as "I don't feel like an old person. I don't want to look like one," or "I exercise and diet. I want to look like I do." These candidates, according to John, are adequately prepared for cosmetic surgery, with expectations that will likely be met by the procedures they undergo.

The second type of patient seeks out plastic surgery to please someone else. In John's description, this patient—usually a woman—is going through a painful breakup and, hoping that changing her appearance will reignite her partner's interest, turns to plastic surgery as a "last-ditch effort" to save her relationship. Breast augmentation—which, John notes with some amusement, is the surgical procedure most likely to precede divorce—is a common request among members of this category. John typically refuses to perform such procedures on patients who hope to use plastic surgery to solve some personal problem.

The third group in John's typology involves children, usually brought to the office by their parents. According to John, these patients' parents frequently say things such as "She has her father's nose," which the parents, rather than the children themselves, judge as unattractive and requiring change. John makes it a practice to ask the adolescents what they think about the particular body part. According to him, they tend to be relatively satisfied with the "nose" or other problematic feature, finding it far less objectionable than the parents do. John advises parents not to "fix what isn't broken," to give the child a few years to "grow into" the feature and then broach the topic of surgery again if they feel it necessary.

The last group includes individuals John refers to as "flighty," who want surgery for any number of "bizarre" reasons. As an example, John described one woman who wanted to have rhinoplasty because a favorite movie star had undergone the procedure. In another case, a potential patient requested breast augmentation in order to look more like a celebrity her boyfriend admired. In such cases, John refuses to operate because he considers these individuals to be psychologically unstable and impossible to satisfy.

All told, John claims that he rejects two or three requests per week. His ability and willingness to deny service suggest another comparison between the plastic surgeon and the hairstylist: John is less dependent on his clientele than are the beauticians at Pamela's, who have little choice concerning whose hair they style or how they style it. At the same time, John's decisions to reject patients are linked to his medical and legal responsibility for the surgeries that he performs. Indeed, his motivations for denying surgical procedures suggest a wariness about trying to satisfy the desires of individuals whose expectations are unreasonable and who might hold him legally responsible for their inevitable dissatisfaction. In this sense, John is even more vulnerable to his clients than are the stylists at Pamela's. While a beautician might lose a client who dislikes her haircut, John could potentially lose much more to a patient who claims that he is responsible for some physical deformity, particularly if that patient decides to sue.

The patients I interviewed ranged in age from twenty-four to fifty. The procedures they underwent included breast augmentations, nose jobs, face-lifts, eye-reshaping procedures, tummy tucks, and liposuctions. All of the women were Asian American or European American; three were of Semitic ancestry; and all but one (a full-time mother) held salaried jobs or were students at the time of the interviews. They were employed as opticians, medical technicians, receptionists, insurance agents, teachers, office administrators, hairstylists, and secretaries.

THE STORY OF A FACE-LIFT: ANN MARIE

Ann Marie, a slender, soft-spoken fifty-year-old medical technician with upswept blonde hair, was one of the first patients I interviewed. Married to her current and only husband for nearly thirty years, Ann Marie carries herself with a careful gentility. Dressed in snug-fitting woolen pants, low-heeled brown pumps and a fuzzy light mauve sweater, Ann Marie invites me into her small, tidy home and asks if I would like coffee. Anxious to begin my first interview, I refuse. Ann Marie brings her own drink back from the kitchen in a tiny, flower-painted china cup and saucer and begins telling me about her experiences with plastic surgery.

Ann Marie is not at all shy about discussing her face-lift. She actually seems eager to tell me the reasons for her decision. Her appearance began to change in her late thirties and forties when she developed "puffiness underneath the eyes" and "drooping upper eyelids." Most unattractive, by Ann Marie's account, "the skin of my throat started getting creepy." In her words, "You get to an age" when "you look in the mirror and see lines that were not there before." Because her physical appearance had begun to reflect the aging process, she explains, "All of a sudden, the need [for cosmetic surgery] was there."

While Ann Marie describes her need for a face-lift as "sudden," she had planned to have the procedure long before. She recalls that "about ten years ago," she spoke with several close friends about having a face-lift at some point in the future. She explains, "We talked about it a long time ago. I guess I have never accepted the axiom of growing old gracefully. I have always sworn I would never picture myself as a chubby old lady." Ann Marie and her friends "talked and decided that when the time was just right, we would definitely do it." Ann Marie is the only member of the group who actually went through with surgery.

Despite her resolve, Ann Marie did not enter into cosmetic surgery lightly. Instead, for several years she "thought about it from time to time. There was a lot to be considered." Among the issues she contemplated were the physical dangers involved in the operation, the risk of looking worse after the surgery than before, and the importance of choosing a well-qualified doctor with an excellent reputation. She explains, "You are putting your face in the hands of a surgeon; there is the possibility of absolute disaster, very possibly permanently. You have to choose the surgeon very carefully."

Ann Marie chose John Norris to perform the face-lift. Largely because he had performed an emergency procedure for her just over one year earlier, Ann Marie claims that she felt completely comfortable with him. "John was recommended to me by my dermatologist. I had an infection on my face; it was quite serious. The dermatologist told me I had to go to a plastic surgeon, and John was the only one he would recommend." Because of the dermatologist's recommendation and her satisfaction with John's earlier work, Ann Marie returned to him for the face-lift. She visited his office in Long Island for a consultation and, not long after her appointment, decided to go ahead with the procedure.

During their first meeting, Ann Marie had what she refers to as two "surprises": one was the price of the operation and the other the news that she would have to stop smoking. According to Ann Marie, John explained that "you will not heal as well if you continue to smoke. Because it impedes circulation, smoking decreases your ability to heal properly." She says, "The most difficult part was to stop smoking. I was puffing away a pack and a half a day for over twenty years." John told Ann Marie that she would not be able to smoke for three months before the surgery. She says, "I thought, What? I will never be able to do this. But I did, I stopped cold. That was the real sacrifice for me."

While giving up cigarettes may have been the greatest sacrifice for Ann Marie, there were clearly many others. For a full year, Ann Marie had to work "one day job, one night job, occasionally a third job" to afford the surgery. She had to "bank" four weeks of overtime at her primary job so she could take time off to recover from the procedure. She also postponed repairs on her home. She explains, "There were things my house needed, but my feeling was, I needed a face-lift more than my house did."

By providing me with a long and detailed account of her need for a face-lift and the sacrifices she was willing to make to have the procedure, Ann Marie hints at an awareness that her behavior is somehow subject to criticism, that it might be construed by others as superficial or shallow. With a hint of defensiveness, Ann Marie explains that she "needed" the face-lift—despite its financial costs and physical risks—not merely because she is concerned with her appearance, but because of pressures in "the work-field." She says, "Despite the fact that we have laws against age discrimination, employers do find ways of getting around it. I know women my age who do not get jobs or are relieved of jobs because of age. . . . [The face-lift] will ensure my work ability." Ann Marie, by her account, decided to have cosmetic surgery not due to narcissism but to concern for her professional well-being. Justifying her behavior as a career decision, she implies that she is sensitive to the social disapproval of plastic surgery, that she knows that the behavior requires some justification.

Even though Ann Marie believes that looking younger will help her professionally, she also admits that she has "not seen anything that has really changed in that area." Instead, the procedure has affected her primarily "on a personal basis, a social basis." Explaining these effects in more detail, she says, "I meet people I haven't seen for two or three years who will say, 'There is something different about you, but I don't know what it is.' I met a sister of a very good friend of mine in June, which is five months after my surgery. She looked at me and said, 'I don't know you.' I said, 'Of course you do. I've known you nearly all of my life.' She realized who I was and was astounded at my appearance."

This incident, along with several similar ones, has, by Ann Marie's account, improved her self-image. By attributing these experiences—and the resulting improvement in her self-perception—to her face-lift, Ann Marie justifies her decision to have cosmetic surgery. In contemporary Western culture, "feeling good" about oneself is understood to be worth considerable effort because it makes us better workers, spouses, and citizens. Among children, self-esteem is credited with the ability to improve grades and to discourage sex and illegal drug use. Ann Marie explains her choice to have plastic surgery as "a matter of personal esteem. If you feel you look better, you feel better about yourself." By granting cosmetic surgery the power to provide self-esteem, Ann Marie—like many of the other women I spoke with—effectively legitimizes an otherwise illegitimate activity.

At the same time, Ann Marie's defensiveness suggests that she is somewhat self-conscious about her choice. She describes her decision to have a face-lift as "not purely vanity," and then adds, "If it is vanity, so what? That does not make me a bad person. I don't want to look bad. I don't want to look my age. I want to look younger. I want smoother skin." By her account, Ann Marie is not "bad" or vain; in fact, she is actually a good person, as evidenced by the other forms of body work in which she participates. She explains, "My weight is only a variance of six pounds heavier from what it was thirty years ago. I keep in shape in addition to the surgery. I jog, I exercise, I diet." Ann Marie has maintained her physical appearance of youth in every way possible—failing only to control the appearance of her facial skin, which she could not keep from "getting creepy." In her account, Ann Marie deserved the surgery—an act tinged with deception—because she has proved her moral character through other (physically demanding and highly symbolic) forms of work on her body. Ann Marie is entitled to an appearance that reflects those efforts, even if that appearance is obtainable only through cosmetic surgery.

"A DEEP, DARK SECRET": HAVING LIPOSUCTION

John arranged for me to speak with a twenty-seven-year-old woman named Bonnie who was planning to have cosmetic surgery. In sharp contrast to the other women I interviewed, Bonnie was hesitant to speak with me about the procedure, because, as she later said, she considered it to be "a deep, dark secret" that she had discussed with no one but her husband of five months. Bonnie worked out at the same gym that both John and I attended. Because she and I were previously acquainted, John suggested that Bonnie speak with me about the procedure she was considering, and she agreed. Over the next six months, Bonnie and I met several times to discuss cosmetic surgery; during that period, she decided to have liposuction, underwent the procedure, and recovered from it.

Having recently completed a master's degree at a New England university, Bonnie moved to the east end of Long Island to take a position as a chemist in a pharmaceutical firm. She explained to me that over the years she had spoken casually to various women about cosmetic surgery and had "fantasized about" having liposuction herself, though she had never considered it seriously. Prior to having the operation, Bonnie told me why she was reluctant to have cosmetic surgery:

It's always seemed to me to be one step too far. I have dieted and exercised my whole life, and sometimes I've gone over the edge and done some things that probably weren't very healthy, but I could always stop myself before I became totally obsessed. I guess I have always thought that I would never get so obsessed that I would allow my body to be cut into just so I could look better. At least that's what I had always hoped. I couldn't imagine myself as one of "them," as one of those weak women who would go that far.

Despite her stated objections to cosmetic surgery and her characterization of its patients as "weak," Bonnie underwent liposuction on the outside of her upper thighs. Bonnie described this area of her body as "flabby, no matter what I do. I exercise five or six times a week; I cycle with my husband. I do all the weight lifting that is supposed to tone up the muscles in those areas. Nothing works!" Nevertheless, Bonnie never seriously investigated the procedure until she finished graduate school and began full-time employment. She explained, "This is the first time I've ever made enough money to think about doing something like this. The liposuction will cost $2,000, which is less than it usually costs because I won't have to have general anesthesia, but it's still a lot of money."

Referring to her new job and home, Bonnie noted that she would never have considered having cosmetic surgery while she was living near her family and friends. "I wouldn't want any of my friends or my family to know about it, only my husband. My family would all be like, 'You don't need to have that done. You're crazy. You are thin enough already.' That doesn't keep me from thinking these lumps on my thighs are really ugly. They are the only thing I see when I look in the mirror."

Bonnie's hesitance to discuss liposuction with her friends stems from her perception of cosmetic surgery as part of a process of "giving in to pressure, giving in to these ideals about how women should look, when none of us real women are ever going to look like that." Bonnie believes that her friends would react to her interest in plastic surgery by making her "feel so ashamed, like I am not strong enough to accept myself like I am."

Unlike most of John's patients, Bonnie articulates her ambivalence about plastic surgery primarily in political rather than personal terms. Her description of her friends' imagined objections is one of many examples of her concern with the political meaning of her actions. In another, Bonnie explains that her own political view of cosmetic surgery is the main source of her conflict over having the procedure. She says, "I am not worried about problems with the operation itself. I know that Dr. Norris has a great reputation. I've talked to other people at the gym who have used him, and they were all really happy. He does so much of this stuff, I'm sure he's really good at it." Bonnie's concerns focus instead on the social and cultural significance of her action. "If I am proud to be a woman, then I should be proud to look like a woman, with a woman's butt and a woman's thighs." Reacting to her own accusations, she notes, "I am proud to be a woman, but I really hate it when I get a glimpse of my backside and I just look big. I feel terrible knowing that it is those areas of my body which are understood to be most 'female' that I dislike the most." Expressing her interest in cosmetic surgery as her only viable option for reducing her dissatisfaction with her appearance, she adds,

> I don't really know how to get around it, though, because I really do not like those parts of my figure. Plastic surgery seems like a pretty good way, and really, a pretty easy way, to deal with that dissatisfaction, to put those negative feelings behind me . . . to move on with the rest of my life. . . . I'd love to get dressed for work in the morning and have only the work in front of me, rather than, you know, what's literally behind me, be the thing that concerns me the most.

Bonnie is explicitly aware that the body and the self are linked. When she says that she dislikes the "female" parts of her figure, one can easily imagine replacing the term "figure" with the term "self." Indeed, it is Bonnie's ambivalence about her female identity that is most troubling to her; eradicating the physical signs of femininity—and the flaws inherent in those attributes—may enable her to construct a self that she believes to be less imperfect, more culturally acceptable, and that will allow her to focus more attention on other activities and concerns, including her career, the sports she enjoys, and her new marriage. At the same time, her decision to undergo liposuction comes at a considerable cost; Bonnie says explicitly that, if possible, she would prefer to change her perceptions rather than her body. The "pressure" she feels, however, limits her ability to rework her self-image, leaving her to choose between plastic surgery and a negative self-concept, two options that are unsatisfying. Bonnie's decision to undergo liposuction suggests that, in the end, the costs associated with plastic surgery are somehow less significant than those attached to her appearance flaws.

Obviously, Ann Marie and Bonnie present two quite disparate facets of the concerns women face as they consider having cosmetic surgery. While Ann Marie struggled to meet the financial and physical requirements of her face-lift, Bonnie agonized over the political dimension of her decision to have liposuction. So distinct are these preoccupations, in fact, that they can be conceptualized as opposite ends of a continuum, along which the perspectives of the other eighteen women I interviewed can be placed. For most of these women, the political implications of cosmetic surgery, though not entirely insignificant, were far less important than they were for Bonnie. The other women I interviewed were more often concerned with the health risks and financial costs of cosmetic surgery and with how they would look after their procedures.

While Ann Marie's and Bonnie's preoperative anxieties took different forms, both constructed elaborate justifications for plastic surgery. Like the other women I interviewed, Bonnie responds to the negative identity implications of plastic surgery by explaining that she has done all that is humanly possible to alter an imperfect body but that no act short of plastic surgery will allow her to live peacefully with herself. Invariably, the women's accounts involve bodies that were flawed in some way for which the individual claimed not to be responsible. Each woman's body was imperfect not because she had erred in her body work but because of aging, genetics, or some other physical condition that she could not control. Their flawed bodies are inaccurate indicators of character, and so they effectively lie about who the women really are. Accounts like these permit women to engage in cosmetic procedures with less guilt. Plastic surgery becomes for them not an act of deception but an attempt to align body with self.

"THE BODY I WAS MEANT TO HAVE": WHY WOMEN HAVE COSMETIC SURGERY

Whereas some writers have dealt with cosmetic surgery as if it were an attempt to attain idealized female beauty in order to gain the approval of men,[12] the women I interviewed claim that their goal in undergoing plastic surgery is neither to become beautiful nor to be beautiful specifically for husbands, boyfriends, or other significant individuals. Rather, they alter their bodies for their own satisfaction, in effect utilizing such procedures to create what they consider a normal appearance, one that reflects a normal self. While I do not accept their accounts without some skepticism, I believe that women who have plastic surgery are not necessarily doing so in order to become beautiful or to please particular individuals. Instead they are responding to highly restrictive notions of normality and the "normal" self, notions that neither apply to the population at large (in fact, quite the reverse) nor leave space for ethnic variation. Plastic surgery "works" for women who have these procedures, but it works only within the context of a culture of appearance that is less about beauty than it is about control based on the physical representations of gender, age, and ethnicity.

My respondents claim that prior to having surgery, some particular physical feature stood in the way of their looking "normal." This feature distinguished them from others and prohibited them from experiencing "a happy, regular life," as Marcy, a twenty-five-year-old student, put it. Marcy decided at twenty-one to have the bony arch in the middle of her nose removed and its tip shortened. Before the procedure, Marcy had never been involved in a romantic relationship, a fact that she attributed to her "hook" nose and unattractive appearance. Marcy says, "I have always felt terrible about how pronounced it was. No matter how I wore my hair, it was in the middle of my face, and everybody noticed it. It's not like I could just wear my bangs long."

Marcy decided to have rhinoplasty near a date that was particularly symbolic for her. "I was having my nose done just before Valentine's Day. I thought to myself, maybe if I have my nose done for Valentine's Day, by next Valentine's Day, I'll have a Valentine!" Although she did not find a Valentine for the following year—she explained that dating "didn't happen until a few years later"—Marcy claimed that over

time, the surgery allowed her to experience pleasure that she would otherwise have missed.

Because Marcy uses cosmetic surgery to make herself more appealing to others, her experience seemingly supports the criticisms of authors like Naomi Wolf. However, Marcy stresses that she does not expect plastic surgery to make her beautiful. Neither does she believe that winning male affection requires her to be beautiful. Quite the contrary, Marcy clearly imagines that a merely normal appearance is sufficient to garner the male attention she desires.

The women describe several ways in which their physical features have kept them from living ordinary lives. For example, Barbara, a twenty-nine-year-old bookkeeper, says that her breasts— which were, by her account, too small to fill out attractive clothing—made her appear "dumpy" and ill-proportioned. Her "flaw" contributed to a negative self-image, which in turn served to limit the education and career goals Barbara set for herself, the friendships she fostered, and the romantic and sexual relationships she pursued. Barbara decided to have her breasts augmented (from a 36A to a 36D) to become, in her words, "more attractive to myself and others." While her larger breasts have in fact made Barbara feel more attractive, she, like other patients I interviewed, nevertheless laments women's inability to be self-confident despite their physical shortcomings. She says, "For women, the appearance is the important thing. That's too bad that we can't worry about not being judged. [Small breasts] made a big difference in how I felt myself being perceived and how I felt about myself as a person."

Because physical attractiveness shapes the way women are "judged," appearance must be protected as women age. Like Ann Marie, several of the patients I interviewed underwent cosmetic procedures aimed at reducing the natural signs of aging. These women claim that aging had changed an acceptable appearance into an unacceptable one that reflected negatively on their identity. For instance, Sue, a forty-four-year-old optician, decided to have the loose skin around her eyes tightened. She discusses her motivations for having the operation: "My eyes had always been all right, nice eyes. I guess I had always liked my face pretty well, but with age, the skin around them started getting puffy. They just didn't look nice anymore. I looked tired, tired and old. That's why I had them fixed." While Sue had, according to her own account, once been satisfied with her appearance, she grew to dislike her face as the signs of aging became apparent. She used cosmetic surgery to regain the face she liked "pretty well."

Several women told me that they chose to have cosmetic surgery not to make themselves beautiful or outstanding in any particular way but simply to regain normal physical characteristics they had lost through aging.[13] Like Sue and Ann Marie, Tina, a forty-eight-year-old receptionist, used cosmetic surgery to combat the physical changes associated with growing older. Tina underwent liposuction to reduce what she referred to as "secretarial spread," the widening of her hips and buttocks that she believed had come with her twenty-five-year career in office management. She explains, "When I was younger, I had nice hips, curvy but narrow enough, and my rear was well-shaped. After a lifetime of sitting, growing older and flabbier, it had gotten really huge." Tina hoped to restore her appearance to its more youthful form. Believing that her only means of doing so was cosmetic surgery, Tina opted to have liposuction rather than surrender to the aging process that had so drastically altered her body.

Youth—or at least a youthful appearance—is not the only characteristic women attempt to construct or regain through aesthetic procedures. Indeed, three of the patients I interviewed—all under the age of thirty—had cosmetic surgery to reduce the physical markers of ethnicity. These women underwent procedures intended to make their physical features more Anglo-Saxon. Marcy, a Jewish woman, notes that her rhinoplasty removed physical features "more frequently associated with Jewish people." Jodie, a twenty-eight-year-old student who also had her nose reshaped, says, "I had this Italian bump on my nose. It required a little shaving. Now, it looks better." By a "better" nose, Jodie implies a more Anglo-Saxon, less Italian, and therefore less ethnic nose. And Kim, a twenty-two-year-old Taiwanese American student, underwent a procedure to make her eyes appear more oval in shape. She said, "[Taiwanese people] regard girls with wide, bright eyes as beautiful. My eyes used to look a little bit as if I was staring at somebody. The look is not soft; it is a very stiff look." While none of these women consciously attempted to detach themselves from ethnicity, they nevertheless chose to ignore the fact that their efforts to appear "normal" explicitly diminished the physical markers of that ethnicity. Seemingly indifferent to this loss, they accept the notion that normalized (i.e., Anglo-Saxon) features are more attractive than ethnic ones.

All the women claimed that plastic surgery was, for them, a logical, carefully thought-out response to distressing circumstances that could not be otherwise remedied. They now perceive themselves to be more socially acceptable, more normal, and, in several cases, more outgoing. As Bonnie explains, "I got exactly what I wanted from this. My body isn't extraordinarily different, but now, I feel like, well, I have a cute bottom. I have a cuter figure. I don't feel like the one with the big butt anymore. And for me, that lets me put my body issues away pretty much."

At the same time, displaying some remnants of her original ambivalence about cosmetic surgery, Bonnie notes, "I wish that I could have said, 'To hell with it, I am going to love my body the way it is' . . . but I had tried to do that for fifteen years, and it didn't work." She adds, "Now, I know I'll never look like Cindy Crawford, but I can walk around and feel like everything is good enough."

Women who undergo plastic surgery report various other benefits. For instance, some say that they can now wear clothes that they could not have worn prior to their operations; others attest to having greater self-confidence or to being more extroverted. Jennifer explains, "When I walk out that door in the morning, my head might be a little bit higher when I'm wearing a certain outfit. Like, before I had [liposuction] done, it used to be, I feel good, but I hope no one will notice that my legs aren't too nice."

These women now wear bathing suits, dresses with low-cut necklines, and feminine and revealing lingerie. Wearing these clothes, and believing themselves to be attractive in them, shapes the women's perceptions of themselves and increases their self-confidence. Tara, a twenty-seven-year-old student, told me that before she had breast augmentation surgery, she avoided wearing bathing suits in public and rarely shopped for bras. She says, "[Breast augmentation] has given me more self-confidence than I ever had. I fit in when I'm with my girlfriends now. Before, I never went to the beach with anybody around. After I had [plastic surgery], I couldn't wait to buy a bra. I could never buy one before because I was so pathetically small." Having plastic surgery made Tara appear more "normal." She is now able to participate in activities from which she previously felt excluded.

Barbara, who also had breast augmentation surgery, recounted a similar experience. She says, "I used to wear super-padded bras when I dressed up, but they just never did it for me. I didn't look like the other women. But now, like tonight, I am going to a party, and I know I'll be able to fill out the dress." She added, "[Breast augmentation] has made me feel very confident. I think that's the difference."

Sandra, a forty-three-year-old office manager who had liposuction to reduce her "thick thighs" and "saddlebag" hips, explains that she underwent the procedure not only to appear youthful and wear feminine clothing, but also to approximate a cultural ideal involving social class. "I used to put on nice clothes and still look like a bag lady, you know, unsophisticated. Now I feel like I can wear good clothes and look like they are appropriate for me. Now, my body fits the clothes." Sandra likens appearance to a tableau of social class, both in the context of the clothing one chooses and the extent to which one's body appears to be "appropriate" for that clothing (and the social standing that it implies). Simply put, before Sandra's surgery, her "flabby" body had less class than her clothing. Her body undermined her efforts to use appearance to stake out a particular social location. In effect, it not only made her clothing an ineffective class identifier but also invalidated her claims to a particular status. Plastic surgery, however, has allowed Sandra to display social class through clothing. Cosmetic surgery legitimizes Sandra's claims to social status.

Other women I interviewed also claimed that cosmetic surgery helped them feel more self-confident. For example, Kim says, "I guess I feel better when I am out with friends, like maybe people will think I am attractive. I feel attractive and I guess, I act more attractive." Thus, the women imagine that they are now perceived more favorably and so behave in a manner that they believe is appropriate for "attractive" women. At the same time, the women recognize that they may simply be imagining others' perceptions of them and that their behaviors may have changed independently of any alteration in the way they are viewed. Kim says, "Maybe nobody even notices, but I feel like I look better. I guess just thinking I look better changes the way I act a little."

Nearly all of the women told me that their romantic partners believed the cosmetic procedures were unnecessary. Before her breast augmentation procedure, Tara's boyfriend voiced significant apprehension. "He was very, very frightened about it. He kept on telling me, 'I love you just the way you are,' that type of thing." And Barbara's fiance blamed himself for her dissatisfaction with her breasts. She recalls, "My fiance thought he was doing something wrong that would make me feel like this about myself." In many cases, the women's partners attempted to convince them not to undergo the surgery. Jennifer says her boyfriend "tried to talk me out of it, but finally he decided, 'If it's going to make you happy, go ahead and do it.'" Some of John's patients report that their partners have had mixed reactions to the results of the procedures. Barbara says that even though she has always considered her husband a "breast man, because his eyes would pop out if he saw a big-breasted woman," he nevertheless told her that she was "perfect" with small breasts. She adds, laughing, "He still says he liked me better before, but I'll tell you, I can't keep him off of me. I keep saying I'm taking them back for a refund."

The frequency with which I heard such assertions points to the considerable importance women attach to having "freely" chosen to have cosmetic surgery, independent of coercion by their lovers or the desire to please someone other than themselves. These assertions make sense in light of the women's accounts of their surgery. Plastic surgery cannot be both something women "deserve" and something that they are forced or manipulated into doing. In their accounts, plastic surgery is positioned as a final option for correcting a tormenting problem. This conception of plastic surgery is clearly inconsistent with an image of acts forced on them by others—particularly others who might actually benefit more from the procedures than do the women themselves.

PLASTIC SURGERY AND INAUTHENTICITY: THE HIGH PRICE OF BODY WORK

In turning "abnormal" bodies into "normal" ones, plastic surgery succeeds: the woman who participates in plastic surgery comes to possess the foundation (i.e., a normal body) of a normative self. However, plastic surgery fails as a method for constructing a positive self-concept because of the negative social and political meanings attached to it. Women participate in cosmetic surgery in a world that limits their choices and in which the flawed body is taken as a sign of a flawed character. Despite the negative connotations of plastic surgery, women opt to engage in such procedures because the alternative is more detrimental to self-image. However, most of the women I interviewed carry with them the burden of their decisions; the process of dealing with that burden exacts from them a considerable price.

Some of the costs of cosmetic surgery—including the danger of physical damage and the high financial price—are obvious to those who have undergone these procedures and perhaps even to those who have not. Most of these women had plastic surgery only after serious consideration (often accompanied by research into the medical technology involved in the operations). Likewise, few could easily afford the surgery they underwent; nearly all of them had to sacrifice some other large purchase or to weather financial hardship. Some have accrued considerable debt, while others had to request financial help from relatives. Only a very few of the women had health insurance that covered part of the cost.

Other costs associated with cosmetic surgery, while less concrete, are no less substantial. Specifically, after surgery, women must attempt to deal with the taint of inauthenticity these procedures imply. Although the body appears more normal, the character becomes suspect, with the self, by implication, becoming deviant. The unacceptable act of cosmetic surgery displaces the normative body as an indicator of character. Although the women I interviewed do not formulate the complexities and contradictions involved in their activities in the way I have here, their accounts show that they struggle with a self-concept that continues to be deviant despite their now-normal appearance. Indeed, the accounts themselves—which attempt to deny inauthenticity by positioning cosmetic surgery as somehow owed to the women who partake of it—show that plastic surgery fails to align body and self.

These accounts suggest a singular conclusion with regard to the success of plastic surgery for establishing the normative identity. Women like Ann Marie and Bonnie—like participants in the aerobics classes [discussed in another part of *Body Work*]—invoke their rigorous body work regimens as evidence of moral rectitude and as the basis for their entitlement to cosmetic surgery. But although cosmetic surgery patients and aerobics participants seem to rely on the same symbols of identity, for women who undergo cosmetic surgery, those symbols fail to mitigate the body's negative implications for self. Had these

women accepted their body work as an adequate indicator of identity, they would not have needed to turn to plastic surgery to correct their bodies' failings. Moreover, still needing to establish the "deceptive" act of plastic surgery as irrelevant to self (and to position the surgically altered, normative body as the true indicator of selfhood), these women revert to accounts that have already proved unsuccessful. Indeed, the negative implications for self inherent in cosmetic surgery require women to resort to accounts that they know—consciously or not—fail to support the normative identity. In so doing, these women attest to the failure of cosmetic surgery to position the transformed body as symbolic of self. Simply put, if plastic surgery were a successful method for constructing identity, these women would argue that the surgically altered body—rather than body work that has proved unsuccessful at shaping the body or establishing the self—serves to symbolize identity.

CONCLUSION

My research points to three general conclusions. The first bears on the reasons women have plastic surgery and suggests a modification of the criticisms of such procedures. The second bears on the ways in which women create accounts of plastic surgery, which are ignored by the criticisms of plastic surgery to date. The third returns more sympathetically to those criticisms.

None of the women I spoke to embarked casually on plastic surgery. The costs associated with these procedures—measured in dollars and the risk of physical damage—are well known. Although physicians may serve as gatekeepers by preventing some women from undergoing surgery, they rarely recruit patients directly. When surgeons actively market their practices—as did John Norris—they tend to do so indirectly, through advertisements in local magazines and shopping malls. And the women I interviewed did not report that they underwent surgery at the urging of a husband, parent, lover, or friend. Rather, the decision to seek surgery seems to have been theirs alone, at least in the immediate circumstances. To be sure, these decisions were shaped by broader cultural considerations—by notions of what constitutes beauty, by distinctively ethnic notions of beauty, and, most important, by the assumption that a woman's worth is measured by her appearance. Yet to portray the women I talked to as cultural dupes, as passively submitting to the demands of beauty, is to misrepresent them badly. A more appropriate image, I would suggest, is to present them as savvy cultural negotiators, attempting to make out as best they can within a culture that limits their options. Those who undergo plastic surgery may (ultimately) be misguided, but they are not foolish. They know what they are doing. Their goals are realistic, and they in fact achieve most of what they set out to accomplish with plastic surgery. Although their actions surely do, in the long run, contribute to the reproduction of a beauty culture that carries heavy costs for them and for all women, in the short run they have succeeded in their own limited purposes.

Second, plastic surgery requires a defense. Much like the women I studied in the aerobics classes, those who underwent plastic surgery are working hard to justify themselves. But the accounts of the women who have plastic surgery are very different from those of the women who attend the aerobics classes. The aerobics women use hard physical work as an indicator of character that allows them to sever their conception of the self from the body. In contrast, the women who have had plastic surgery work hard to reattach the self to the body. First, they must convince themselves that they deserve the surgery, whether by the hard work they put in at the gym or the effort they invest in saving the money for the procedure. In so doing, they make the surgery psychologically and ideologically their own. Second, they must convince themselves that their revised appearance is authentically connected to the self.[14] To do this, they invoke essentialist notions of the self and corresponding notions of the body as accidental, somehow inessential or a degeneration from a younger body that better represented who they truly are.

I do not mean these observations as a defense of plastic surgery so much as an effort to understand that surgery and its implications. Indeed, if we are to distinguish plastic surgery from other forms of body work, we can do so on precisely the grounds I have just suggested. I am not convinced that reducing facial wrinkles is somehow less "real" than dyeing hair from gray to brown or even that eye surgery or rhinoplasty is somehow less authentic than a decision to have straight rather than curly hair. However, what characterizes the efforts of women in aerobics, hair salons, and, as we shall see, in NAAFA, is that they attempt, in somewhat different ways and with varying degrees of success, to neutralize appearance as a measure of character. Far more than the other women I studied, the women who undergo plastic surgery help to reproduce some of the worst aspects of the beauty culture, not so much through the act of the surgery itself as through their ideological efforts to restore appearance as an indicator of character.

My own criticisms of plastic surgery are tempered by observations of the women described in the other chapters of this book. Although I have characterized plastic surgery as a research "site," parallel to an aerobics class or a group of women in a hair salon or the members of NAAFA [National Association to Advance Fat Acceptance; discussed in another part of *Body Work*], this parallel is in certain respects misleading. In the hair salon, in the aerobics class, and especially in NAAFA, I found women working together to find common solutions to a shared problem. But women who underwent plastic surgery were not a group in the same sense. For the most part, they did not know each other. They did not speak to each other. And although they may have had common problems with a common solution, they did not develop this solution cooperatively. In the other settings I studied, the local production of an alternative culture was very much in evidence. In the plastic surgery group, however, there were the aesthetic judgments of the plastic surgeon, the ignored opposition of friends and family, but no culture of its own. The women in the aerobics class, in the hair salon, and especially in NAAFA, all challenged a beauty culture, however haltingly, however partially. In contrast, the women who undergo plastic surgery are simply making do within a culture that they believe judges and rewards them for their looks.

NOTES

1. Ann Dally. *Women under the Knife: A History of Surgery* (London: Hutchinson Radius, 1991); Eugenia Kaw, "Opening Faces: The Politics of Cosmetic Surgery and Asian-American Women," in *Many Mirrors: Body Image and Social Relations*, ed. N. Sank (New Brunswick, N.J.: Rutgers University Press, 1994), 241–65.

2. American Society of Plastic and Reconstructive Surgeons, *1999 Plastic Surgery Procedural Statistics* (Arlington

Heights, Ill.: American Society of Plastic and Reconstructive Surgeons, www.plasticsurgery.org, March 2000); American Society of Plastic and Reconstructive Surgeons, *1999 Average Surgeon's Fees* (Arlington Heights, Ill.: American Society of Plastic and Reconstructive Surgeons, www.plasticsurgery.org., March 2000). Generally, surgeons' fees do not include anesthesia, operating-room facilities, or other related expenses.

3. American Society of Plastic and Reconstructive Surgeons, *1999 Gender Distribution. Cosmetic Procedures* (Arlington Heights, Ill.: American Society of Plastic and Reconstructive Surgeons, www.plasticsurgery.org., March 2000).

4. American Society of Plastic and Reconstructive Surgeons, *1999 Plastic Surgery Procedural Statistics* (Arlington Heights, Ill.: www.plasticsurgery.org, March 2000).

5. Joachim Gabka and Ekkehard Vaubel, *Plastic Surgery Past and Present: Origin and History of Modern Lines of Incision* (Basle: Karger, 1983), 29.

6. Susan Faludi, *Backlash: The Undeclared War on Women* (New York: Crown, 1991), 217.

7. Kathy Davis, *Reshaping the Female Body: The Dilemma of Cosmetic Surgery* (New York: Routledge, 1995), 21.

8. Robert M. Goldwyn, ed., *Long-Term Results in Plastic and Reconstructive Surgery*, 2d ed. (Boston: Little, Brown, 1980).

9. Barbara Meredith, *A Change for the Better* (London: Grafton Books, 1988).

10. Susan Bordo, "'Material Girl': The Effacements of Postmodern Culture," *Michigan Quarterly Review* 29 (1990): 657.

11. Joan Finkelstein, *The Fashioned Self* (Philadelphia: Temple University Press, 1991), 87.

12. Naomi Wolf; *The Beauty Myth: How Images of Beauty Are Used against Women* (New York: William Morrow, 1991).

13. See Davis, *Reshaping the Female Body*, for similar findings.

14. Concern about authenticity may well be class-specific; however, because my sample is based on references from a plastic surgeon, it is likely to include those patients who are least troubled by what they have done.

THE MYTH OF THE PERFECT BODY

ROBERTA GALLER

A woman was experiencing severe abdominal pain. She was rushed to the emergency room and examined, then taken to the operating room, where an appendectomy was performed. After surgery, doctors concluded that her appendix was fine but that she had VD. It never occurred to them that this woman had a sexual life at all, because she was in a wheelchair.

I saw a woman who had cerebral palsy at a neuro-muscular clinic. She was covered with bruises. After talking with her, it became clear that she was a battered wife. I brought her case to the attention of the medical director and social worker, both progressive practitioners who are knowledgeable about resources for battered women. They said, "But he supports her. Who else will take care of her? And besides, if she complains, the court might take custody of her children."

As a feminist and psychotherapist I am politically and professionally interested in the impact of body image on a woman's self-esteem and sense of sexuality. However, it is as a woman with a disability that I am personally involved with these issues. I had polio when I was ten years old, and now with arthritis and some new aches and pains I feel in a rather exaggerated fashion other effects of aging, a progressive disability we all share to some degree.

Although I've been disabled since childhood, until the past few years I didn't know anyone else with a disability and in fact *avoided* knowing anyone with a disability. I had many of the same fears and anxieties which many of you who are currently able-bodied might feel about close association with anyone with a disability. I had not opted for, but in fact rebelled against, the prescribed role of dependence expected of women growing up

(continued)

when I did and which is still expected of disabled women. I became the "exceptional" woman, the "super-crip," noted for her independence. I refused to let my identity be shaped by my disability. I wanted to be known for *who* I am and not just by what I physically cannot do.

Although I was not particularly conscious of it at the time, I was additionally burdened with extensive conflicts about dependency and feelings of shame over my own imperfections and realistic limitations. So much of my image and definition of myself had been rooted in a denial of the impact of my disability. Unfortunately, my values and emphasis on independence involved an assumption that any form of help implied dependence and was therefore humiliating.

As the aging process accelerated the impact of my disability, it became more difficult to be stoic or heroic or ignore my increased need for help at times. This personal crisis coincided in time with the growing national political organization of disabled persons who were asserting their rights, demanding changes in public consciousness and social policy, and working to remove environmental and attitudinal barriers to the potential viability of their lives.

Disabled women also began a dialogue within the feminist community. On a personal level it has been through a slow process of disability consciousness-raising aided by newly found "sisters in disability," as well as through profoundly moving discussions with close, nondisabled friends that we, through mutual support and self-disclosure, began to explore our feelings and to shed the shame and humiliation associated with needing help. We began to understand that to need help did not imply helplessness nor was it the opposite of independence. This increased appreciation of mutual interdependence as part of the human condition caused us to reexamine the feminist idea of autonomy versus dependence.

Feminists have long attacked the media image of "the Body Beautiful" as oppressive, exploitative, and objectifying. Even in our attempts to create alternatives, however, we develop standards which oppress some of us. The feminist ideal of autonomy does not take into account the realistic needs for help that disabled, aging—and,

in fact, most—women have. The image of the physically strong "superwoman" is also out of reach for most of us.

As we began to develop disability consciousness, we recognized significant parallels to feminist consciousness. For example, it is clear that just as society creates an ideal of beauty which is oppressive for us all, it creates an ideal model of the physically perfect person, who is not beset with weakness, loss, or pain. It is toward these distorted ideals of perfection in form and function that we all strive and with which we identify.

The disabled (and aging) woman poses a symbolic threat by reminding us how tenuous that model, "the myth of the perfect body," really is, and we might want to run from this thought. The disabled woman's body may not meet the standard of "perfection" in either image, form, or function. On the one hand, disabled women share the social stereotype of women in general as being weak and passive, and in fact are depicted as the epitome of the incompetent female. On the other hand, disabled women are not viewed as women at all, but portrayed as helpless, dependent children in need of protection. She is not seen as the sexy, but the sexless, object, asexual, neutered, unbeautiful and unable to find a lover. This stigmatized view of the disabled woman reflects a perception of assumed inadequacy on the part of the nondisabled.

For instance, disabled women are often advised by professionals not to bear children, and are (within race and class groupings) more likely to be threatened by or be victims of involuntary sterilization. Concerns for reproductive freedom and child custody, as well as rape and domestic violence, often exclude the disabled woman by assuming her to be an asexual creature. The perception that a disabled woman couldn't possibly get a man to care for or take care of her underlies the instances where professionals have urged disabled women who have been victims of brutal battery to stay with abusive males. Members of the helping professions often assume that no other men would want them.

Disability is often associated with sin, stigma, and a kind of "untouchability." Anxiety, as well as a sense of vulnerability and dread, may cause

(continued)

others to respond to the "imperfections" of a disabled woman's body with terror, avoidance, pity and or guilt. In a special *Off Our Backs* issue on disabled women, Jill Lessing postulated that it is "through fear and denial that attitudes of repulsion and oppression are acted out on disabled people in ways ranging from our solicitous good intentions to total invisibility and isolation."*

Even when the disabled woman is idealized for surmounting all obstacles, she is the recipient of a distancing admiration, which assumes her achievement to be necessary compensation for a lack of sexuality, intimacy, and love. The

*Jill Lessing. "Denial and Disability," *Off Our Backs*, vol. xi, no. 5. May 1981, p. 21.

stereotype of the independent "super-crip," although embodying images of strength and courage, involves avoidance and denial of the realities of disability for both the observer and the disabled woman herself.

These discomforts may evoke a wish that disabled women remain invisible and that their sexuality be a hidden secret. However, disabled (and aging) women are coming out; we are beginning to examine our issues publicly, forcing other women to not only address the issues of disability but reexamine their attitudes toward their own limitations and lack of perfection, toward oppressive myths, standards, and social conditions which affect us all. . . .

READING 11

Hair Still Matters

Ingrid Banks

Williams' beaded braids, though popular with her fans and part of her identity the past few years, have long been a matter of annoyance to some opponents even when they don't come undone. . . . To bead or not to bead, that is the question now facing Williams. For the moment, she plans only to braid them a little tighter. "I shouldn't have to change," she said. "I like my hair."

—*Associated Press, 1999*

INTRODUCTION

I've always liked tennis, as both a player and fan. But who knew back in 1999 when Venus Williams was beginning to light a fire to the women's professional circuit that my interest in tennis and my scholarly research on black women and hair would collide? Though troubled by the racial, gendered, and cultural meanings of Williams being penalized for wearing

beads in her hair during the Australian Open, I knew that once again I had some phat fodder for continuing to argue that hair STILL matters for black women.[1] The expectation to conform to white standards is nothing new in a society that privileges whiteness, and the expectation is becoming magnified for blacks in predominantly white spaces like professional tennis. In fact, in the late 1990s, descriptions of Venus Williams and basketball sensation Allen Iverson often included allusions to their hairstyles, braided and in rows, respectively. The coded racial language of sportscasters' coverage of Williams's tennis matches or Iverson's basketball games is indicative of the fascination and discomfort that white mainstream U.S. society continues to feel regarding African Americans in general, and particular black hairstyles and what they signify, whether real or imagined. Like the Afro, Williams's beaded braids and Iverson's cornrows are exotic to some and threatening to others because they display a black aesthetic that is linked to an authentic or radical blackness in the imagination of many whites. Still, the gendered component of Williams's sanctioning during her 1999 match is equally as important as the racial one. For example, Williams choice of hairstyle was rooted outside of mainstream constructions of femininity. By wearing beaded braids, Williams's expression of racialized gender sent the message to a predominantly white professional women's tennis circuit that mainstream constructions of womanhood are insufficient in understanding black women's relationship to beauty culture. In fact, Williams's hairstyle sent a bold statement that the very notion of what constitutes femininity must not only be contested, but our understanding of womanhood must be expanded. Feminist scholars have done well in unmasking the gender politics of femininity and sexuality that are embedded in how the female body has been, for example, treated in popular media and science (Jaggar and Bord 1989; Bordo 1993). The female body in general, as a site where both empowerment and repression are played out, must be central to feminist projects in the 21st century. From a woman's right to choose what happens to her body with regard to abortion to female circumcision to the covering of women's bodies among Muslims, feminists, locally and globally, must continue to illuminate the contexts under which women's bodies are politicized, as well as depoliticized.

SITUATING HAIR IN ACADEMIA AND POPULAR CULTURE

To be sure, this is not fetish or trendy scholarship. Hair has been of interest to social theorists spanning the 20th century from Freud to Robin D. G. Kelley. Psychoanalysts were waxing theoretical poetic about the sexual symbolism of hair during the earlier period (Freud 1922). In reaction to psychoanalytic readings of hair symbolism, social meanings of hair emerged. More specifically in the latter part of the century, scholars focusing on blacks and hair emphasize the importance of hair among blacks in relationship to Africa (Morrow 1973), enslavement (Patterson 1982), constructions of race (Mercer 1990), skin color, self-esteem, ritual, aesthetics, and adornment, (Mercer 1990), appropriate grooming practices (Tyle 1990), images of beauty, politics, and identity (Grier and Cobbs 1968; Mercer 1990), and the intersection of race and gender (Craig 1997; Kelley 1997).

The scholarship on blacks and hair highlighting the difference that gender makes in understanding hairstyling practices among African Americans provides a similar gender intervention to that within general hair theorizing scholarship (Eilberg-Schwartz and Doniger 1995).

Several works have been written that engage beauty culture and black women (Giddings 1984; Hill Collins 1990; Caraway 1991; Rooks 1996; Craig 2002). In particular, discussions by black women moved the debate about hair among people of African descent to one that also focuses on experience (Okazawa-Rey et al. 1986; Benton Rushing 1988; hooks 1988; Walker 1988; Hill Collins 1990; Caldwell 1991; Norsworthy 1991; Cleage 1993; Wade Gayles 1993; Davis 1994; Jones 1994; Gibson 1995; DuCille 1996; Rooks 1996). In these works the authors discuss personal experiences involving hair that intersect with race, gender, motherhood, freedom, law, appropriation, and identity. In one of the most important texts focusing on black women and hair, *Hair Raising: Beauty, Culture, and African American Women*, Noliwe Rooks (1996) examines black hair care advertisements at the turn of the century in her investigation of how dominant or mainstream ideologies of race and beauty forced African American women to produce and sell beauty products for an African American female market. Rooks makes a strong case for understanding why gendered investigations of hair meanings in black communities are central for understanding how black women negotiate mainstream beauty culture. More recently, provocative texts that examine the history of black hair in the U.S. (Byrd and Tharps, 2001) and personal reflections on hair (Harris and Johnson, 2001) have contributed greatly to scholarship on black women and hair.

Similar to early anthropological writings that do not take into consideration the difference culture and gender make in understandings about hair, early feminist discussions about the relationship between femininity and hair focus on hair as an indelible marker of femininity. For example, Susan Brownmiller (1984) conflates the meanings of hair by reducing the interpretation of "good" hair and "bad" hair to mean the same thing for black women as it does for white women. Brownmiller collapses these terms despite racial and cultural difference. Her analysis demonstrates why these types of comparisons are problematic and how they disclaim the cultural significance of hair for black women by treating the issue as if it were *merely* a women's issue, and not an issue that traverses lines of race and culture.

Black hair is certainly not simply an academic matter. In fact, the debates that scholars engage are clearly indicative of real-world tensions, as the literature on blacks and hair demonstrates. Within the context of black popular culture, hair has always been "pop." Spike Lee films such as *School Daze* and *Jungle Fever*, as well as the prime-time TV shows *Any Day Now, Girlfriends, Moesha, The Parkers, and The Practice*, have engaged the politically charged issue of black women's hair. For example, in Spike Lee's *School Daze*, a scene unfolds in the film that illustrates the intraracial tensions embedded in constructions of "good" hair and "bad" hair. In one episode of Lifetime Television Network's drama *Any Day Now*, a story line involving the different cultural meanings that black and white women ascribe to hair grooming practices illustrates difference race makes in understanding how women relate to beauty culture.

Rap artists such as Lauryn Hill and her former Fugees crew, The Lost Boyz, and The Roots have laced particular songs with explicit references to nappy hair.[2] Preceding the attention given to black hair on prime time and in popular music in the late 20th century and early 21st century was the emergence of the Afro almost three decades ago. Though today the Afro has less political meaning, in the late 1960s it was associated with a movement and a black woman. The movement was black power and the black woman was (and still is, even without her late 1960s, early 1970s Afro) Angela Davis. During an interview for *Hair Matters*, Taylor, a forty-eight year old accountant, reminisced about her desire to wear an "Angela Davis Afro" during the early 1970s. Similar yet different from Davis's recognition that law enforcement officers used her image (i.e., Afro) as a reason to detain and harass black women, Taylor explained that it was her Afro and *assumed* gender that led to her being detained during the early 1970s:

> When Afros came out, I wanted to wear an Afro. So I did everything and I finally got me a great big huge Angela Davis Afro. Whenever I would wear my Afro I'd get pulled over the police because I drove a very sleek car and they always thought from the back of the head that I had to be male a lot of times because we [Black women and Black men] all wore the same hairstyle.

Taylor's understanding of why she was detained by police officers was based on both her Afro and mistaken gender-identity. Whereas Taylor presented an image of the Afro-wearing militant as male, which was supported by the general perception of the black militant at the time, Davis describes how race and gender merged to stigmatize and repress black women, a point that would surface almost twenty years later when black women's hair was at the center of legal battles.

In the late 1980s black female employees went to court to challenge a policy by Hyatt Hotels and American Airlines against the wearing of braids.[3] These companies couched their policy in terms that related to "appropriate" grooming practices, which they argued braids violated. In November 1996, another hair controversy hit a sururban middle school in Chicago. *The Atlanta Journal/Atlanta Constitution* ran a story that highlighted a ban on hairstyles, along with certain clothes and jewelry that school officials defined as "gang related paraphernalia." Hairstyles such as cornrows, dreadlocks, braids, and ponytails for boys would lead to suspension; hairstyles with zigzag parts for girls were disallowed. With a similar argument as the one used against Hyatt Hotels and American Airlines, critics argued that the school's policy appeared to restrict African Americans. To add, the weekly ABC news show *20/20* aired a segment that examined the tensions that many black professional women face when hair is at issue. Oprah Winfrey dedicated an entire show to the "black hair question." As the *Los Angeles Times* reported in an article that examined the rise in natural hairstyles among black women (and men), the *20/20* episode illustrated how "one woman was terminated because management saw her hairstyle as 'extreme,' and another woman was written up because her braids were deemed 'too ethnic'" (George 1998, E4).

MY RESEARCH ON BLACK WOMEN AND HAIR

My research is a departure from previous research and discussions as it serves as the first empirical study that examines why hair matters to black women and girls. Prior to my research, an empirically based book that centers black women's views was absent in the literature and to this end, the study fills a void in the literature. Given that I identified a gap in research on this topic, how did I go about collecting data? By the fall of 1998, I completed forty-three individual interviews and five focus group interviews with African-American women and girls. The interviewees consisted of girls and women ranging from ages 12 to 76, from various walks of life. Individuals were recruited and interviewed in the San Francisco Bay area, Los Angeles, Santa Barbara, and Atlanta. During a focus group interviewee, Wixie, a 45-year-old physician explained to me, "There's always a question of race, money, and sex. But I think for black women, it's race, money, sex, and hair. It transcends a cosmetic [or esthetic] issue because it is at the base historically, culturally, and socially." Indeed, the argument here presents hair as a cultural tool that shapes black women's ideas about race, gender, class, sexuality and images of beauty and power. In addition, my research illustrates that hair matters for black women are never merely arrested within esthetics. Indeed, it serves cultural theorists well in paying close to attention to why hair matters to black women. In stating that hair matters, I argue that identity matters.

HAIR AND FEMININITY

On January 3, 1999, hair, in relationship to Black women, made prime time again on the ABC weekly one-hour drama *The Practice*. The show focuses on a group of attorneys in a Boston law firm. In this particular episode, Lucy, the white female receptionist in her early twenties, asks the black female attorney, Rebecca, if she's a lesbian. Rebecca, somewhat puzzled, replies no, but wonders why anyone would assume she is a lesbian. Lucy replies, "With that rump and no guy in your life, and that crop-cut butchy-do hair [I just assumed you were a lesbian]." Rebecca commences to wonder if the reason she doesn't get asked out is because she "looks butch." Though Rebecca's femininity is marked through her shapely posterior, which is loaded with racialized images of Black women's bodies, her hair becomes the ultimate marker of both her womanhood and sexuality. Ideas about the relationship between hair, femininity, and sexuality, as well as images of beauty and male perceptions of femininity, surfaced as the women and girls addressed the question of whether hair is associated with femininity in any way.

Several of the women explained how long hair is associated with femininity and how their beliefs have been nurtured through the mainstream media or other external forces. For example Pearl, a 45-year-old college counselor, explained that she felt most sexy with long hair:

PEARL: Oh I have [associated hair with femininity]. I think the sexiest hairstyle was for me, and this could come from advertisements, television, anywhere, was when my hair was longer and it was piled on top of my head and I would always have little ringlets on the side. And that could also be from my southern background and that's how southern women wore their hair a long time ago. It could stem from my mom. I'm not exactly sure where those images come from but I would look in the mirror and I would see how I look and say, "God, that is sexy, that looks gorgeous."

Pearl also associated her perception of long hair with her southern roots and mother, but still questioned how she learned what is feminine or sexy. Aria, a 30-year-old undergraduate student, also explained the relationship between long hair, femininity, and constructions of beauty but unlike Pearl, Aria perceived this relationship through gender and racial readings of hair:

ARIA: Oh please, yes. If I said no I'd be lying because for years we have been inundated with magazine pictures of white women and their beautiful bodies and their long flowing locks. We have seen commercials, they're [white women] in the magazine ads. You see them in school flippin' their hair all through the classroom. I mean I sit in class and I see these women changing their hairstyles in a fifty-minute class at least four different times, you know. It's like come on. We have romance novels that accentuate the long, silken tresses so there's so many different mediums that portray [long] hair as beautiful, as feminine, as silky. And then if you have a lack of hair, then your femininity sometimes is questioned.

Aria pointed to the white women on TV, in magazines, and in romance novels with long, flowing hair as representative of femininity in U.S. society. Therefore, femininity is not merely associated with long hair as described by Pearl but with white women. Aria made a connection to the historical construction of womanhood, also known as the "cult of the lady" or the "cult of true womanhood" that represented 19th century U.S. Victorian society (Giddings 1984). Similar to Aria's construction of femininity that does not include black women, this was also the case with the cult of true womanhood. Given that the cult was based on a socioeconomic class hierarchy,[4] as well as racist and sexist ideologies, there was no place for black women regardless of class status in the definition of "true" womanhood.

Aria ends by stating that if a woman lacks hair, her femininity is questioned. This idea was common among the women. They associated their understanding of what short hair means in relationship to sexuality and masculinity. Dianne, a 50-year-old retired material handler, explained that an understanding of what it means to be male and female is embedded in readings of hair length. She also presented a different way of approaching the image of long flowing hair among black women:

DIANNE: Oh yeah. Right or wrong, you'll say stuff like that's a feminine cut, that's not a feminine cut, or whatever. I think to the extent that you have this long flowing hair that's perceived as very feminine. And the shorter you go, the less feminine it seems to be. So I definitely think that there's some association with that. And the whole interesting thing with the long hair [is] that [it] has some tie back to mainstream culture because not a lot of people in our community have this flowing long hair, but that's defined as being feminine. So when [women] go really short, [people say] that looks too mannish or something. My sister got her hair cut really short one time and she was like, "oh now people are going to think that I look like a boy or something."

In Dianne's explanation of the relationship between femininity and hair, she presented a scale in which long hair (feminine) and short hair (masculine) exists at the extremes. "Mannish" is associated with "looking like a boy" and long, flowing hair becomes a powerful feminine trait. However, Dianne questioned placing the image of long flowing hair among black people outside of black communities when she stated that based on her observations, there is not a critical mass of black folk who have long flowing hair. The more telling issue is how black people in general, and black women in particular, understand these meanings and how ideas that link long hair to femininity are actually acted out. In fact Indigo, a 28-year-old independent filmmaker and teacher, explained how

her decision to grow dreadlocks has allowed her to fulfill the dream of having long hair.

INDIGO: I think certainly. I've just begun to take a look at the issue of dreadlocks because I look at myself and all my life I wanted to have long hair and now I get to have it with dreadlocks. The longer I let it grow I can have this long, flowing hair. Of course it won't look like Cheryl Tiegs's hair or, you know, Farah Fawcett's, but it will be my own hair.

Although similar to Aria's observation that white women's hair is the standard of long, flowing hair, Indigo sees length as outweighing texture. She demonstrated her perception of femininity through hair, and although she recognizes the problem in reinforcing the belief that long hair characterizes femininity, she challenged mainstream standards of beauty through the length of her dreadlocks. Although she doesn't have the stuff, in terms of texture and color, as do Tiegs and Fawcett, she does possess the feminine trait, long hair. Thus, Indigo's reading of hair permits black women to sit at the table of femininity, despite historical constructions of what constitutes womanhood and, therefore, beauty. But the desire to have long hair relates to perceptions of what is considered feminine and it is associated with white women. That is, even with long dreadlocks, the model of long hair, and therefore femininity, is white women like Cheryl Tiegs and Farah Fawcett.

Indigo also explained how shaving her head and having short hair shaped her understanding about hair and femininity. Like other women, she discussed the relationship between sexuality or perceived sexuality with hair, particularly in relationship to lesbianism.

INDIGO: For women, you know, it is a very important part of your appearance. Your face, your hair. I mean you can still be feminine and have no hair on your head. But you know, we have these judgments that only certain women can pull that off. I mean actually be bald, and still be considered feminine. I know when I shaved off [my hair or the] many times I've had my hair short, I was trying to compensate with earrings and all this kind of stuff. Trying not to wear as many pants because I felt like I was going to be, you know, categorized as a dyke, or you know, just deemed unattractive.

Cheryl, Jean, Kaliph, and Barbara[5] made similar comments in linking hair to sexuality, as well as being masculine:

CHERYL: Yeah, I think it is, unfortunately. I cut my hair [short] [and] the day I did it I went out to a club with my girl [in the nonromantic sense]. It wasn't that crowded, so we were kinda hangin' out together and I think we went on the dance floor. We weren't even really dancing together but we were, you know, dancing without partners and somebody came up to me and asked me if like we were together as like a lesbian couple. And she [my friend] wears dreads. And I was like, it's the hair, isn't it?

JEAN: Oh yeah, definitely. So you know, especially in this town [San Francisco Bay Area, California] people see a haircut and they say, oh, dyke.

KALIPH: Yes, definitely yes because, and now I'm thinking in terms of length and lack of length. I hear one of the concerns among my friends who wear their hair short and natural, that there is sometimes a misperception around sexuality like, oh you must be a lesbian if you wear your hair like that. And by definition if you're a lesbian that somehow there's a lack of femininity, you know, you're trying to be a man. You're trying to be male, masculine. So I think there is something about hair, particularly length of hair, that speaks to being feminine and being a woman.

BARBARA: In my view, no. But some men will see a woman with short hair, real short hair, and will think negatively. [Like] a butch cut. I've heard that.

Words such as "butch" and "dyke" describe how ideas about sexuality can be read through hair. Sexual identities are often placed on individuals based on hair, which is why Cheryl concluded that it was her short haircut and her friend's dreadlocks that made others think they were a lesbian couple on the dance floor. Kaliph even shared that she has black female friends with close-cropped and natural hair that are concerned with being perceived as lesbian. Kaliph explained that hair length is related not only to sexuality but also to female attractiveness. For example, when Indigo compensated for the lack of hair on her head, she did so by accentuating what she understood as feminine. It was Indigo's concern with being

labeled a lesbian and therefore unfeminine that guided her practice of wearing big earrings and more skirts and dresses. In fact, as if in a dialogue with Indigo, Mrs. Franklin, a 70-year-old retired instructor's assistant, supported this reading of hair and femininity:

MRS. FRANKLIN: Yes, I do [think hair is associated with femininity]. Because I like to see women with hair. Most women when they have their hair short, [they] got to get up in the morning [and start] puttin' on make-up, puttin' on earrings and all this kind of stuff so people won't take a second look and say, "Is that a man or a lady?"

Even though Mrs. Franklin appeared to be making a presumption that women with short hair have to highlight their femininity, her thoughts resonate in Indigo's personal account of her insecurities about how her womanhood, in relationship to sexuality, would be read. What Mrs. Franklin and Indigo demonstrate is that black women understand that femininity cannot be reduced to one thing. Although hair is important in black women's understanding of what constitutes femininity, it is not the only marker. However, their comments also contradict their understanding of a more complicated reading of femininity because if a black woman has long hair, it is not necessary for her to "play up" her femininity by adorning her body in ways that are defined as "feminine." Even if hair is only one of many markers of femininity, or lack thereof, it is definitely one of the most powerful.

Habiba is a 50-year-old writer and teacher. In her reading of the relationship between hair and femininity, she also discussed long hair but used the example of (black) men wearing dreads as indicative of femininity. Femininity is still read through long hair, but Habiba challenged the belief that only women possess feminine characteristics when they have long hair. She also *explicitly* stated that hair is associated with femininity *and* sexuality:

HABIBA: [Hair is associated with femininity] and sexuality. People often times have their hands in each others hair, pubic [for example]. So [hair] is very, very sensual. Very, very feminine. And I think men growing the long hair, men with dreads, are also activating that. What is it? They're activating the feminine side. Yes, yes, yes. For men to have the long hair and the dreads. Oh, that's incredible.

Habiba also provided a different view of the sexual nature of hair. Her reading of the relationship between hair and sexuality involves sensuality. Although her discussion supports how long hair is associated with femininity, Habiba's perception of what it means to be masculine is not questioned when she sees black men with long hair. Unlike the explanations of what it means for a woman to wear particular short hairdos[6] that are perceived as male "do's'" Habiba questioned static notions of gender identities for women and men even as she supported the idea that long hair is associated with femininity. However it is Semple's critique of gender readings of hair (she is a 22-year-old undergraduate student), like that posed by Habiba's, that view long hair as feminine, that present a challenge to how gender is socially constructed. Unlike other women, Semple discussed this matter within the context of black males and how their hairstyling practices relate to how they are perceived:

SEMPLE: Is hair associated with femininity? I mean, I can see where we've maybe been socialized to think certain hairstyles [are feminine]. [The artist formally known as] Prince is always thought of as being out the box because he wants to wear a perm and a short cut. Michael Jackson got a little bob cut and people wanted to feminize that whole image. But at the same time, a brother can grow locks down his back and still be seen as extremely masculine. I mean brothers are wearing braids now and people are still [associating certain hairstyles with femininity]. I mean there's an element of "gang society" who walks around with permed hair and curls in their hair.

Unlike Habiba, Semple sees long dreadlocks worn by black men as indicative of masculinity, not femininity. Styles or lengths that are perceived as feminine do not necessarily question the masculinity or sexuality of black men. Semple's discussion of femininity as being read through the hairstyling practices of black men provided a different lens from which to view how black women understand gender through their ideas about hair. Although Semple discussed the hairstyling practices of Michael Jackson and The Artist as influencing their feminization, it is in her discussion of gang culture and the hairstyling practices among younger black males, particularly those in urban

areas, that undoubtedly influence and have been influenced by hip-hop culture and rap music, that she contested feminine constructions of hair. Although I am in no way suggesting that rap artist Snoop Dog is a gangster, his hairstyling practices sheds light on Semple's critique. When Snoop appeared on the MTV Music Awards show in New York City a few years ago his hair was freshly straightened with lots of "Shirley Temple" curls. A year or two later, he was on the same awards show with straightened hair that touched his shoulders. Despite Snoop's hairstyling practices that imitate popular hairstyling practices by (Black) women, his "manhood" is not called into question. Like other younger black males who are straightening their hair, wearing braids and cornrows, as well as barrettes and rubber bands, their hair, Snoop is still seen as masculine. In a recent DJ Quik music video "Youz a Gangsta," Snoop appears with individual braids with beads dangling elegantly at the end of each braid. DJ Quik's hairstyle changes from cornrows to a straightened style by the end of the video. In another recent video, "Thug Mentality," rap artist Krayzie Bone appears with beautiful cornrows, and one of his possee members stands by his side with the same type of braided and beaded style as Snoop in Dj Quik's video. The video represents the life of a thug, with car chases and gambling rounding out the message of the video. Despite their hairdos, in both of these videos, the masculinity and sexuality of the main characters are never questioned because they are gangstas and thugs. This was true in the 1970s as well within the urban pimp culture scene. No one challenged Ron O'Neal's masculinity in the blaxploitation film *Super Fly*. If anything, he was hypermasculinized and seen as the perfect example of a "brother's brother." That is, a man's man. He had women, money, sharp clothes, a nice apartment, and a fancy car. And he had straightened ("fly") hair.

What Semple's observation suggests is that gender identity is not static, but given the comments by other women who addressed the relationship between hair and femininity, a nonstatic or even a cross-reading of gender does not occur when women's hairstyling practices resemble those that are considered masculine. Whereas all black men are not labeled as feminine or gay when they sport hairdos that are perceived as feminine, when black women wear their hair close-cropped, for example, they are constructed as being unfeminine, unattractive, masculine, and lesbian. As Indigo and Mrs. Franklin's comments demonstrate above, women have to play up their femininity in other ways.

CONCLUSION: FEMININITY, HAIR, AND GLOBALIZATION

Hair still matters, and though differences arise in different cultural and political contexts, for women, hair is never *simply* arrested within the aesthetic. Though global-studies scholars are raising important questions concerning globalization and its relationship to not merely Western societies, but the entire planet, hair went global a while back. "Through the seventies, stock imported from Europe was the only hair product sold to what the industry calls the 'Caucasian Trade.' Now that the European market is drying up, Asian hair goes to all races, in most cases, unless specially ordered. When you buy human hair in lengths for weaving and braiding, in wigs, and as male-replacement product, what you buy nine times out often is Asian hair (Jones, 1994, p. 282) The average woman from Asia growing her hair for profit lives in poverty. It is an eerie feeling to realize that though these women will most likely remain living in a cycle of poverty, their hair exists within a global context.

Hair has gone global culturally as well. During the post-September 11 era, hair matters continue to make news, though within a different global and cultural context than what went down with Venus Williams in Australia in 1999. Consider the eyes of the Western/Christian world not merely on the Taliban restrictions placed on Afghani women, but also on the wider Islamic faith's teachings concerning the presentation of the female body. The hijab (veil) that covers the hair continues to be a source of great debate within and outside feminist circles. With the downfall of the Taliban government, some Afghani women proudly shed the all-encompassing burka (full body veil). However, many women continue to follow Afghan culture by continuing to wear the burka. As feminists, we would be remiss if we discounted the views of Islamic women outside and inside of Afghanistan who continue to don the hijab. Certainly, the issue of covering women's bodies among Muslims cannot be disengaged from patriarchy and the state, but as my research on U.S. black women conveys, women must be given a platform to speak, to theorize, about *their* existence from *their* various standpoints. As 22-year-old Mahbobo Sidiqi stated as she and the other women shed their burkas after entering a classroom at the University of Kabul to sit for college entrance exams along with men in February 2000 "My head is free. . . . No more headaches" (*Miami Herald*, February 7: 2002). Indeed, hair still matters, and it matters for women of color in profound ways as exemplified by what we can learn by recent events in the global culture.

ACKNOWLEDGMENTS

I am indebted to Hung Cam Thai for his insightful comments and unwavering support. He is one of the finest *feminists* that I know.

NOTES

1. Ingrid Banks, *Hair Matters: Beauty, Power, and Black Women's Consciousness* (New York: New York University Press, 2000).

2. See Lauryn Hill's "Doo Wop (That Thing)," the Fugees' "Nappy Hair," and The Lost Boyz album "Love, Peace, and Nappiness".

3. See Paulette Caldwell's (1991) discussion of these cases.

4. For example, poor and working-class women, regardless of race, were not viewed as "true women." Those women who had to work outside of the home for economic necessity were excluded from the definition of a lady.

5. Cheryl is a 22-year-old graduate student, Jean is a 37-year-old architect, Kaliph is a 28 year-old graduate student, and Barbara is a 49-year-old Administrative Assistant II.

6. Not all short hairdos worn by women are viewed as unfeminine; what is meant here is particularly those hairdos that resemble traditional men's hairdos (e.g., short, cropped, buzz cuts).

REFERENCES

Banks, Ingrid, 2000. *Hair Matters: Beauty, Power and Black Women's Consciousness*. New York: University Press.

Benton Rushing, Andrea 1988. "Hair-Raising." *Feminist Studies* 14(2) (Summer): 325–335.

Bordo, Susan. 1993. *Unbearable Weight: Feminism, Western Culture, and the Body*. Berkeley: University of California Press.

Brownmiller, Susan 1984. *Femininity*. New York: London Press/Simon & Schuster.

Byrd, Ayana D., and Lori L. Tharps. 2001. *Hair Story: Untangling the Roots of Black Hair in America*. New York: St. Martin's Press.

Caldwell, Paulette M. 1991. "A Hair Piece: Perspectives on the Intersection of Race and Gender." *Duke Law Review*: 365–397.

Caraway, Nancie. 1991. *Segregated Sisterhood: Racism and the Politics of American Feminism*. Knoxville: University of Tennessee Press.

Cleage, Pearl 1993. "Hairpeace: Requirement for Afro-American Women Writers to Discuss Hair." *African-American Review* 27 (1) (Spring): 37.

Craig, Maxine. 2002. *Ain't I A Beauty Queen? Black Women, Beauty, and the Politics of Race*. New York: Oxford University Press.

———. 1997. "The Decline and the Fall of the Conk; or, How to Read a Process." *Fashion Theory: The Journal of Dress, Body and Culture* 1 (4) (December): 399–419.

Davis, Angela Y. 1994. "Afro Images: Politics, Fashion, and Nostalgia." *Critical Inquiry* 21(1) (Autumn): 37.

DuCille, Ann. 1996 *Skin Trade*. Cambridge: Harvard University Press.

Eilberg-Schwartz, Howard, and Wendy Doniger, eds. 1995. *Off With Her Head! The Denial of Woman's Identity in Myth, Religion, and Culture*. Berkeley: University of California Press.

Freud, Sigmund. 1922. "Medusa's Hair." In *Collected Papers*, 105–106. London: Hogarth Press and the Institute of Psychoanalysis.

George, Lynell. 1998. "The Natural Look." *The Los Angeles Times*, August 6, E1.

Gibson, Aliona. 1995. *Nappy: Growing Up Black and Female in America*. New York: Harlem River Press.

Giddings, Paula. 1984. *When and Where I Enter: The Impact of Black Women on Race and Sex in America*. New York: Bantam Books.

Grier, William H. & Price M. Cobbs. 1968. *Black Rage*. New York: Basic Books.

Harris, Juliette, and Pamela Johnson. 2001. *Tenderheaded: A Comb-Bending Collection of Hair Stories*. New York: Pocket Books.

Hill Collins, Patricia. 1990. *Black Feminist Thought: Knowledge, Consciousness, and the Politics of Empowerment*. London: Harper Collins.

hooks, bell. 1988. Straightening Our Hair." *Z Magazine* (Summer): 14–18.

Jagger, Alison, and Bordo, Susan. 1989. *Gender/Body/Knowledge: Feminist Reconstructions of Knowing*. Newark, NJ: Rutgers University Press.

Jones, Lisa 1994. *Bulletproof Diva: Tales of Race, Sex, and Hair*. New York: Doubleday.

Kelley, Robin D.G. 1997. "Nap Time: Historicizing the Afro." *Fashion Theory: The Journal of Dress, Body and Culture* 1 (4) (December): 339–351.

Mercer, Kobena. 1990. "Black Hair/Style Politics." In *Out There: Marginalization and Contemporary Cultures*, Russell Ferguson et al., eds., 247–264. New York & The New Museum of Contemporary Art & MIT Press.

Morrow, Willie. 1973. *400 Years Without a Comb*. San Diego: Black Publishers of San Diego.

Norsworthy, Kym. 1991. "Hair Discovery." *Real News*, 2(1): 3, 8.

Okazawa-Rey, Margo, et al. 1986. "Black Women and the Politics of Skin Color and Hair." *Women's Studies Quarterly* 14 (1 and 2) (Spring/Summer): 13–14

Patterson, Orlando. 1982. *Slavery and Social Death: A Comparative Study*. Cambridge: Harvard University Press.

Rooks, Noliwe. 1996. *Hair Raising: Beauty, Culture, and African American Women*. New Brunswick, NJ: Rutgers University Press.

Shipp, E. R. 1988. "Are Cornrows Right for Work?" *Essence*, February, 109–110.

Tyler, Bruce M. 1990. "Black Hairstyles: Cultural and Socio-political Implications." *The Western Journal of Black Studies* 14 (4) 235–250.

Wade-Gayles, Gloria. 1993. "The Making of a Permanent Afro." In *Pushed Back to Strength: A Black Woman's Journey Home*, 133–158. Boston: Beacon Press.

Walker, Alice. 1988. "Oppressed Hair Puts a Ceiling on the Brain." In *Living By the Word*, 69–74. Orlando: Harcourt Brace Jovanovich.

Selling Hot Pussy: Representations of Black Female Sexuality in the Cultural Marketplace

✍ bell hooks

Friday night in a small midwestern town—I go with a group of artists and professors to a late-night dessert place. As we walk past a group of white men standing in the entryway to the place, we overhear them talking about us, saying that my companions, who are all white, must be liberals from the college, not regular "townies," to be hanging out with a "nigger." Everyone in my group acts as though they did not hear a word of this conversation. Even when I call attention to the comments, no one responds. It's like I am not only not talking, but suddenly, to them, I am not there. I am invisible. For my colleagues, racism expressed in everyday encounters—this is our second such experience together—is only an unpleasantness to be avoided, not something to be confronted or challenged. It is just something negative disrupting the good time, better to not notice and pretend it's not there.

As we enter the dessert place they all burst into laughter and point to a row of gigantic chocolate breasts complete with nipples—huge edible tits. They think this is a delicious idea—seeing no connection between this racialized image and the racism expressed in the entryway. Living in a world where white folks are no longer nursed and nurtured primarily by black female caretakers, they do not look at these symbolic breasts and consciously think about "mammies." They do not see this representation of chocolate breasts as a sign of displaced longing for a racist past when the bodies of black women were commodity, available to anyone white who could pay the price. I look at these dark breasts and think about the representation of black female bodies in popular culture. Seeing them, I think about the connection between contemporary representations and the types of images popularized from slavery on. I remember Harriet Jacobs' powerful expos of the psycho-sexual dynamics of slavery in *Incidents in the Life of a Slave Girl*. I remember the way she described that

"peculiar" institution of domination and the white people who constructed it as "a cage of obscene birds."

Representations of black female bodies in contemporary popular culture rarely subvert or critique images of black female sexuality which were part of the cultural apparatus of nineteenth-century racism and which still shape perceptions today. Sander Gilman's essay, "Black Bodies, White Bodies: Toward an Iconography of Female Sexuality in Late Nineteenth-Century Art, Medicine, and Literature," calls attention to the way black presence in early North American society allowed whites to sexualize their world by projecting onto black bodies a narrative of sexualization disassociated from whiteness. Gilman documents the development of this image, commenting that "by the eighteenth century, the sexuality of the black, male and female, becomes an icon for deviant sexuality." He emphasizes that it is the black female body that is forced to serve as "an icon for black sexuality in general."

Most often attention was not focused on the complete black female on display at a fancy ball in the "civilized" heart of European culture, Paris. She is there to entertain guests with the naked image of Otherness. They are not to look at her as a whole human being. They are to notice only certain parts. Objectified in a manner similar to that of black female slaves who stood on auction blocks while owners and overseers described their important, salable parts, the black women whose naked bodies were displayed for whites at social functions had no presence. They were reduced to mere spectacle. Little is known of their lives, their motivations. Their body parts were offered as evidence to support racist notions that black people were more akin to animals than other humans. When Sarah Bartmann's body was exhibited in 1810, she was ironically and perversely dubbed "the Hottentot

Venus." Her naked body was displayed on numerous occasions for five years. When she died, the mutilated parts were still subject to scrutiny. Gilman stressed that: "The audience which had paid to see her buttocks and had fantasized about the uniqueness of her genitalia when she was alive could, after her death and dissection, examine both." Much of the racialized fascination with Bartmann's body concentrated attention on her buttocks.

A similar white European fascination with the bodies of black people, particularly black female bodies, was manifest during the career of Josephine Baker. Content to "exploit" white eroticization of black bodies, Baker called attention to the "butt" in her dance routines. Phyllis Rose, though often condescending in her recent biography, *Jazz Cleopatra: Josephine Baker in Her Time,* perceptively explores Baker's concentration on her ass:

> She handled it as though it were an instrument, a rattle, something apart from herself that she could shake. One can hardly overemphasize the importance of the rear end. Baker herself declared that people had been hiding their asses too long. "The rear end exists. I see no reason to be ashamed of it. It's true there are rear ends so stupid, so pretentious, so insignificant that they're good only for sitting on." With Baker's triumph, the erotic gaze of a nation moved downward: she had uncovered a new region for desire.

Many of Baker's dance moves highlighting the "butt" prefigure movements popular in contemporary black dance.

Although contemporary thinking about black female bodies does not attempt to read the body as a sign of "natural" racial inferiority, the fascination with black "butts" continues. In the sexual iconography of the traditional black pornographic imagination, the protruding butt is seen as an indication of a heightened sexuality. Contemporary popular music is one of the primary cultural locations for discussions of black sexuality. In song lyrics, "the butt" is talked about in ways that attempt to challenge racist assumptions that suggest it is an ugly sign of inferiority, even as it remains a sexualized sign. The popular song, "Doin' the Butt," fostered the promotion of a hot new dance favoring those who could most protrude their buttocks with pride and glee. A scene in Spike Lee's film *School Daze* depicts an all-black party

where everyone is attired in swimsuits dancing— doing the butt. It is one of the most compelling moments in the film. The black "butts" on display are unruly and outrageous. They are not the still bodies of the female slave made to appear as mannequin. They are not a silenced body. Displayed as playful cultural nationalist resistance, they challenge assumptions that the black body, its skin color and shape, is a mark of shame. Undoubtedly the most transgressive and provocative moment in *School Daze,* this celebration of buttocks either initiated or coincided with an emphasis on butts, especially the buttocks of women, in fashion magazines. Its potential to disrupt and challenge notions of black bodies, specifically female bodies, was undercut by the overall sexual humiliation and abuse of black females in the film. Many people did not see the film, so it was really the song "Doin' the Butt" that challenged dominant ways of thinking about the body, which encourage us to ignore asses because they are associated with undesirable and unclean acts. Unmasked, the "butt" could be once again worshiped as an erotic seat of pleasure and excitement.

When calling attention to the body in a manner inviting the gaze to mutilate black female bodies yet again, to focus solely on the "butt," contemporary celebrations of this part of the anatomy do not successfully subvert sexist/racist representations. Just as nineteenth-century representations of black female bodies were constructed to emphasize that these bodies were expendable, contemporary images (even those created in black cultural production) give a similar message. When Richard Wright's protest novel *Native Son* was made into a film in the 1980s, the film did not show the murder of Bigger's black girlfriend Bessie. This was doubly ironic. She is murdered in the novel and then systematically eliminated in the film. Painters exploring race as artistic subject matter in the nineteenth century often created images contrasting white female bodies with black ones in ways that reinforced the greater value of the white female icon. Gilman's essay colludes in this critical project: he is really most concerned with exploring white female sexuality.

A similar strategy is employed in the Wright novel and in the film version. In the novel, Bessie is expendable because Bigger has already committed the more heinous crime of killing a white woman. The first and more important murder subsumes the second. Everyone cares about the fate of Mary Dalton, the ruling-class white female daughter; no one cares about the fate of Bessie. Ironically, just at the moment when Bigger decides that Bessie's body is expendable, that he will kill her, he continues to demand that she help him, that she "do the right thing." Bigger intends to use her, then throw her away, a gesture reinforcing that hers is an expendable body. While he must transgress dangerous boundaries to destroy the body of a white female, he can invade and violate a black female body with no fear of retribution and retaliation.

Black and female, sexual outside the context of marriage, Bessie represents "fallen womanhood." She has no protectors, no legal system will defend her rights. Pleading her cause to Bigger, she asks for recognition and compassion for her specific condition.

> Bigger, please! Don't do this to me! Please! All I do is work, work like a dog! From morning till night. I ain't got no happiness. I ain't never had none. I ain't got nothing and you do this to me. . . .

Poignantly describing the lot of working-class poor black women in the 1940s, her words echo those of poet Nikki Giovanni describing the status of black women in the late 1960s. The opening lines to "Woman Poem" read: "You see my whole life is tied up to unhappiness." There is a radical difference, however. In the 1960s, the black female is naming her unhappiness to demand a hearing, an acknowledgment of her reality, and change her status. This poem speaks to the desire of black women to construct a sexuality apart from that imposed upon us by a racist/sexist culture, calling attention to the ways we are trapped by conventional notions of sexuality and desirability:

> It's a sex object if you're pretty and no love or love and no sex if you're fat get back fat black woman be a mother grandmother strong thing but not woman gameswoman romantic woman love needer man seeker dick eater sweat getter fuck needing love seeking woman

"Woman Poem" is a cry of resistance urging those who exploit and oppress black women, who objectify and dehumanize, to confront the consequences of their actions. Facing herself, the black female realizes all that she must struggle against to achieve self-actualization. She must counter the representation of herself, her body, her being as expendable.

Bombarded with images representing black female bodies as expendable, black women have either passively absorbed this thinking or vehemently resisted it. Popular culture provides countless examples of black female appropriation and exploitation of "negative stereotypes" to either assert control over the representation or at least reap the benefits of it. Since black female sexuality has been represented in racist/sexist iconography as more free and liberated, many black women singers, irrespective of the quality of their voices, have cultivated an image which suggests they are sexually available and licentious. Undesirable in the conventional sense, which defines beauty and sexuality as desirable only to the extent that it is idealized and unattainable, the black female body gains attention only when it is synonymous with accessibility, availability, when it is sexually deviant.

Tina Turner's construction of a public sexual persona most conforms to this idea of black female sexuality. In her recent autobiography *I, Tina* she presents a sexualized portrait of herself—providing a narrative that is centrally "sexual confession." Even though she begins by calling attention to the fact that she was raised with puritanical notions of innocence and virtuous womanhood which made her reticent and fearful of sexual experience, all that follows contradicts this portrait. Since the image that has been cultivated and commodified in popular culture is of her as "hot" and highly sexed—the sexually ready and free black woman—a tension exists in the autobiography between the reality she presents and the image she must uphold. Describing her first sexual experience, Turner recalls:

> Naturally, I lost my virginity in the backseat of a car. This was the fifties, right? I think he had planned it, the little devil—he knew by then that he could get into my pants, because there's already been a lot of kissing and touching inside the blouse, and then under the skirt and so forth. The next step was obvious. And me, as brazen as I was, when it came down to finally doing the real thing, it was like: "Uh-oh, it's time." I mean, I was scared. And then it happened.
>
> Well, it hurt so bad—I think my earlobes were hurting. I was just dying, God. And he wanted to do it two or three times! It was like poking an open wound. I could hardly walk afterwards.
>
> But I did it for love. The pain was excruciating; but I loved him and he loved me, and that

made the pain less—Everything was right. So it was beautiful.

Only there is nothing beautiful about the scenario Turner describes. A tension exists between the "cool" way she describes this experience, playing it off to suggest she *was* in control of the situation, and the reality she recounts where she succumbs to male lust and suffers sex. After describing a painful rite of sexual initiation, Turner undermines the confession by telling the reader that she felt good. Through retrospective memory, Turner is able to retell this experience in a manner that suggests she was comfortable with sexual experience at an early age, yet cavalier language does not completely mask the suffering evoked by the details she gives. However, this cavalier attitude accords best with how her fans "see" her. Throughout the biography she will describe situations of extreme sexual victimization and then undermine the impact of her words by evoking the image of herself and other black women as sexually free, suggesting that we assert sexual agency in ways that are never confirmed by the evidence she provides.

Tina Turner's singing career has been based on the construction of an image of black female sexuality that is made synonymous with wild animalistic lust. Raped and exploited by Ike Turner, the man who made this image and imposed it on her, Turner describes the way her public persona as singer was shaped by his pornographic misogynist imagination:

> Ike explained: As a kid back in Clarksdale, he'd become fixated on the white jungle goddess who romped through Saturday matinee movie serials— revealing rag-clad women with long flowing hair and names like Sheena, Queen of the Jungle, and Nyoka—particularly Nyoka. He still remembered *The Perils of Nyoka*, a fifteen-part Republic Picture serial from 1941, starring Kay Alridge in the title role and featuring a villainess named Vultura, an ape named Satan, and Clayton Moore (later to be TV's Lone Ranger) as love interest. Nyoka, Sheena—Tina! Tina Turner—Ike's own personal Wild Woman. He loved it.

Turner makes no comment about her thoughts about this image. How can she? It is part of the representation which makes and maintains her stardom.

Ike's pornographic fantasy of the black female as wild sexual savage emerged from the impact of a white patriarchal controlled media shaping his perceptions of reality. His decision to create the wild black woman was perfectly compatible with prevailing representations of black female sexuality in a white supremacist society. Of course the Tina Turner story reveals that she was anything but a wild woman; she was fearful of sexuality, abused, humiliated, fucked, and fucked over. Turner's friends and colleagues document the myriad ways she suffered about the experience of being brutally physically beaten prior to appearing on stage to perform, yet there is no account of how she coped with the contradiction (this story is told by witnesses in *I, Tina*). She was on one hand in excruciating pain inflicted by a misogynist man who dominated her life and her sexuality, and on the other hand projecting in every performance the image of a wild tough sexuality liberated woman. Not unlike the lead character in the novel *Story of O* by Pauline Reage, Turner must act as though she glories in her submission, that she delights in being a slave of love. Leaving Ike, after many years of forced marital rape and physical abuse, because his violence is utterly uncontrollable, Turner takes with her the "image" he created.

Despite her experience of abuse rooted in sexist and racist objectification, Turner appropriated the "wild woman" image, using it for career advancement. Always fascinated with wigs and long hair, she created the blonde lioness mane to appear all the more savage and animalistic. Blondeness links her to jungle imagery even as it serves as an endorsement of a racist aesthetics which sees blonde hair as the epitome of beauty. Without Ike, Turner's career has soared to new heights, particularly as she works harder to exploit the visual representation of woman (and particularly black woman) as sexual savage. No longer caught in the sadomasochistic sexual iconography of black female in erotic war with her mate that was the subtext of the Ike and Tina Turner show, she is now portrayed as the autonomous black woman whose sexuality is solely a way to exert power. Inverting old imagery, she places herself in the role of dominator.

Playing the role of Aunty Entity in the film *Mad Max: Beyond the Thunderdome*, released in 1985, Turner's character evokes two racist/sexist stereotypes, that of the black "mammy" turned power hungry and the sexual savage who uses her body to seduce and conquer men. Portrayed as lusting after the white male hero who will both conquer and reject her, Aunty Entity is the contemporary reenactment of that mythic black female in slavery who supposedly "vamped" and seduced virtuous white male slave owners. Of course the contemporary white male hero of *Mad Max* is stronger than his colonial forefathers. He does not succumb to the dangerous lure of the deadly black seductress who rules over a mini-nation whose power is based on the use of shit. Turner is the bad black woman in this film, an image she will continue to exploit.

Turner's video "What's Love Got to Do with It" also highlights the convergence of sexuality and power. Here, the black woman's body is represented as potential weapon. In the video, she walks down rough city streets, strutting her stuff, in a way that declares desirability, allure, while denying access. It is not that she is no longer represented as available; she is "open" only to those whom she chooses. Assuming the role of hunter, she is the sexualized woman who makes men and women her prey (in the alluring gaze of the video, the body moves in the direction of both sexes). This tough black woman has no time for woman bonding, she is out to "catch." Turner's fictive model of black female sexual agency remains rooted in misogynist notions. Rather than being a pleasure-based eroticism, it is ruthless, violent; it is about women using sexual power to do violence to the male Other.

Appropriating the wild woman pornographic myth of black female sexuality created by men in a white supremacist patriarchy, Turner exploits it for her own ends to achieve economic self-sufficiency. When she left Ike, she was broke and in serious debt. The new Turner image conveys the message that happiness and power come to women who learn to beat men at their own game, to throw off any investment in romance and get down to the real dog-eat-dog thing. "What's Love Got to Do with It" sung by Turner evokes images of the strong bitchified black woman who is on the make. Subordinating the idea of romantic love and praising the use of sex for pleasure as commodity to exchange, the song had great appeal for contemporary postmodern culture. It equates pleasure with materiality, making it an object to be sought after, taken, acquired by any means necessary. When sung by black women singers, "What's Love Got to Do with It" called to mind old stereotypes which make the assertion of black female sexuality

and prostitution synonymous. Just as black female prostitutes in the 1940s and 1950s actively sought clients in the streets to make money to survive, thereby publicly linking prostitution with black female sexuality, contemporary black female sexuality is fictively constructed in popular rap and R&B songs solely as commodity—sexual service for money and power, pleasure is secondary.

Contrasted with the representation of wild animalistic sexuality, black female singers like Aretha Franklin and younger contemporaries like Anita Baker fundamentally link romance and sexual pleasure. Aretha, though seen as a victim of no-good men, the classic "woman who loves too much" and leaves the lyrics to prove it, also sang songs of resistance. "Respect" was heard by many black folks, especially black women, as a song challenging black male sexism and female victimization while evoking notions of mutual care and support. In a recent PBS special highlighting individual musicians, Aretha Franklin was featured. Much space was given in the documentary to white male producers who shaped her public image. In the documentary, she describes the fun of adding the words "sock it to me" to "Respect" as a powerful refrain. One of the white male producers, Jerry Wexler, offers his interpretation of its meaning, claiming that it was a call for "sexual attention of the highest order." His sexualized interpretations of the song seemed far removed from the way it was heard and celebrated in black communities. Looking at this documentary, which was supposedly a tribute to Aretha Franklin's power, it was impossible not to have one's attention deflected away from the music by the subtext of the film, which can be seen as a visual narrative documenting her obsessive concern with the body and achieving a look suggesting desirability. To achieve this end, Franklin constantly struggles with her weight, and the images in the film chronicle her various shifts in body size and shape. As though mocking this concern with her body, throughout most of the documentary Aretha appears in what seems to be a household setting, a living room maybe, wearing a strapless evening dress, much too small for her breast size, so her breasts appear like two balloons filled with water about to burst. With no idea who shaped and controlled this image, I can only reiterate that it undermined the insistence in the film that she has overcome sexual victimization and remained a powerful singer; the latter seemed more likely than the former.

Black female singers who project a sexualized persona are as obsessed with hair as they are with body size and body parts. As with nineteenth-century sexual iconography, specific parts of the anatomy are designated more sexual and worthy of attention than others. Today much of the sexualized imagery for black female stars seems to be fixated on hair; it and not buttocks signifies animalistic sexuality. This is quintessentially so for Tina Turner and Diana Ross. It is ironically appropriate that much of this hair is synthetic and man-made, artificially constructed as is the sexualized image it is meant to evoke. Within a patriarchal culture where women over forty are not represented as sexually desirable, it is understandable that singers exploiting sexualized representations who are near the age of fifty place less emphasis on body parts that may reflect aging while focusing on hair.

In a course I teach on "The Politics of Sexuality," where we often examine connections between race and sex, we once critically analyzed a *Vanity Fair* cover depicting Diana Ross. Posed on a white background, apparently naked with the exception of white cloth draped loosely around her body, the most striking element in the portrait was the long mane of jet black hair cascading down. There was so much hair that it seemed to be consuming her body (which looked frail and anorexic), negating the possibility that this naked flesh could represent active female sexual agency. The white diaperlike cloth reinforced the idea that this was a portrait of an adult female who wanted to be seen as childlike and innocent. Symbolically, the hair that is almost a covering hearkens back to early pictorial images of Eve in the garden. It evokes wildness, a sense of the "natural" world, even as it shrouds the body, repressing it, keeping it from the gaze of a culture that does not invite women to be sexual subjects. Concurrently, this cover contrasts whiteness and blackness. Whiteness dominates the page, obscuring and erasing the possibility of any assertion of black power. The longing that is most visible in this cover is that of the black woman to embody and be encircled by whiteness, personified by the possession of long straight hair. Since the hair is produced as commodity and purchased, it affirms contemporary notions of female beauty and desirability as that which can be acquired.

According to postmodern analyses of fashion, this is a time when commodities produce bodies, as this image of Ross suggests. In her essay "Fashion and the Cultural Logic of Postmodernity," Gail Faurshou

explains that beauty is no longer seen as a sustained "category of precapitalist culture." Instead, "the colonization and the appropriation of the body as its own production/consumption machine in late capitalism is a fundamental theme of contemporary socialization." This cultural shift enables the bodies of black women to be represented in certain domains of the "beautiful" where they were once denied entry, i.e., high-fashion magazines. Reinscribed as spectacle, once again on display, the bodies of black women appearing in these magazines are not there to document the beauty of black skin, of black bodies, but rather to call attention to other concerns. They are represented so readers will notice that the magazine is racially inclusive even though their features are often distorted, their bodies contorted into strange and bizarre postures that make the images appear monstrous or grotesque. They seem to represent an anti-aesthetic, one that mocks the very notion of beauty.

Often black female models appear in portraits that make them look less like humans and more like mannequins or robots. Currently, black models whose hair is not straightened are often photographed wearing straight wigs; this seems to be especially the case if the model's features are unconventional, i.e., if she has large lips or particularly dark skin, which is not often featured in the magazine. The October 1989 issue of *Elle* presented a short profile of designer Azzedine Alaia. He stands at a distance from a black female body holding the sleeves of her dress. Wearing a ridiculous straight hairdo, she appears naked, holding the dress in front of her body. The caption reads, "THEY ARE BEAUTIFUL AREN'T THEY!" His critical gaze is on the model and not the dress. As commentary it suggests that even black women can look beautiful in the right outfit. Of course when you read the piece, this statement is not referring to the model but is a statement Alaia makes about his clothes. In contemporary postmodern fashion sense, the black female is the best medium for the showing of clothes because her image does not detract from the outfit; it is subordinated.

Years ago, when much fuss was made about the reluctance of fashion magazines to include images of black women, it was assumed that the presence of such representations would in and of themselves challenge racist stereotypes that imply black women are not beautiful. Nowadays, black women are included in magazines in a manner that tends to reinscribe prevailing stereotypes. Darker-skinned models are most likely to appear in photographs where their features are distorted. Biracial women tend to appear in sexualized images. Trendy catalogues like Tweeds and J.Crew make use of a racialized subtext in their layout and advertisements. Usually they are emphasizing the connection between a white European and American style. When they began to include darker-skinned models, they chose biracial or fair-skinned black women, particularly with blonde or light-brown long hair. The nonwhite models appearing in these catalogues must resemble as closely as possible their white counterparts so as not to detract from the racialized subtext. A recent cover of Tweeds carried this statement:

> Color is, perhaps, one of the most important barometers of character and self-assurance. It is as much a part of the international language of clothes as silhouette. The message colors convey, however, should never overwhelm. They should speak as eloquently and intelligently as the wearer. Whenever colors have that intelligence, subtlety, and nuance we tend to call them European.

Given the racialized terminology evoked in this copy, it follows that when flesh is exposed in attire that is meant to evoke sexual desirability it is worn by a nonwhite model. As sexist/racist sexual mythology would have it, she is the embodiment of the best of the black female savage tempered by those elements of whiteness that soften this image, giving it an aura of virtue and innocence. In the racialized pornographic imagination, she is the perfect combination of virgin and whore, the ultimate vamp. The impact of this image is so intense that Iman, a highly paid black fashion model who once received worldwide acclaim because she was the perfect black clone of a white ice-goddess beauty, has had to change. Postmodern notions that black female beauty is constructed, not innate or inherent, are personified by the career of Iman. Noted in the past for features this culture sees as "Caucasian"—thin nose, lips, and limbs-Iman appears in the October 1989 issue of *Vogue* "made over." Her lips and breasts are suddenly full. Having once had her "look" destroyed by a car accident and then remade, Iman now goes a step further. Displayed as the embodiment of a heightened sexuality, she now looks like the racial/sexual stereotype. In one full-page shot, she is naked, wearing only a pair of brocade boots, looking as though she is ready to

stand on any street corner and turn a trick, or worse yet, as though she just walked off one of the pages of *Players* (a porn magazine for blacks). Iman's new image appeals to a culture that is eager to reinscribe the image of black woman as sexual primitive. This new representation is a response to contemporary fascination with an ethnic look, with the exotic Other who promises to fulfill racial and sexual stereotypes, to satisfy longings. This image is but an extension of the edible black tit.

Currently, in the fashion world the new black female icon who is also gaining greater notoriety, as she assumes both the persona of sexually hot "savage" and white-identified black girl, is the Caribbean-born model Naomi Campbell. Imported beauty, she, like Iman, is almost constantly visually portrayed nearly nude against a sexualized background. Abandoning her "natural" hair for blonde wigs or ever-lengthening weaves, she has great crossover appeal. Labeled by fashion critics as the black Brigitte Bardot, she embodies an aesthetic that suggests black women, while appealingly "different," must resemble white women to be considered really beautiful.

Within literature and early film, this sanitized ethnic image was defined as that of the "tragic mulatto." Appearing in film, she was the vamp that white men feared. As Julie Burchill puts it outrageously in *Girls on Film:*

> In the mature Forties, Hollywood decided to get to grips with the meaty and messy topic of multiracial romance, but it was a morbid business. Even when the girls were gorgeous white girls—multiracial romance brought tears, traumas, and suicide. The message was clear: you intelligent white men suffer enough guilt because of what your grandaddy did—you want to suffer some more! Keep away from those girls . . .

Contemporary films portraying biracial stars convey this same message. The warning for women is different from that given men—we are given messages about the danger of asserting sexual desire. Clearly the message from *Imitation of Life* was that attempting to define oneself as sexual subject would lead to rejection and abandonment. In the film *Choose Me,* Rae Dawn Chong plays the role of the highly sexual black woman chasing and seducing the white man who does not desire her (as was first implied in *Imitation of Life*) but instead uses her sexually, beats her, then discards her. The biracial black woman is constantly "gaslighted" in contemporary film. The message her sexualized image conveys does not change even as she continues to chase the white man as if only he had the power to affirm that she is truly desirable.

European films like *Mephisto* and the more recent *Mona Lisa* also portray the almost white, black woman as tragically sexual. The women in the films can only respond to constructions of their reality created by the more powerful. They are trapped. Mona Lisa's struggle to be sexually self-defining leads her to choose lesbianism, even though she is desired by the white male hero. Yet her choice of a female partner does not mean sexual fulfillment, as the object of her lust is a drug-addicted young white woman who is always too messed up to be sexual. Mona Lisa nurses and protects her. Rather than asserting sexual agency, she is once again in the role of mammy.

In a more recent film, *The Virgin Machine,* a white German woman obsessed by the longing to understand desire goes to California where she hopes to find a "paradise of black Amazons." However, when she arrives and checks out the lesbian scene, the black women she encounters are portrayed as mean fat grotesques, lewd and licentious. Contemporary films continue to place black women in two categories, mammy or slut, and occasionally a combination of the two. In *Mona Lisa,* one scene serves as powerful commentary on the way black sexuality is perceived in a racist and imperialist social context. The white male who desires the black prostitute Mona Lisa is depicted as a victim of romantic love who wishes to rescue her from a life of ruin. Yet he is also the conqueror, the colonizer, and this is most evident in the scene where he watches a video wherein she engages in fellatio with the black male pimp who torments her. Both the black man and the black woman are presented as available for the white male's sexual consumption. In the context of postmodern sexual practice, the masturbatoryvoyeuristictechnologically based fulfillment of desire is more exciting than actually possessing any real Other.

There are few films or television shows that attempt to challenge assumptions that sexual relationships between black women and white men are not based solely on power relationships which mirror master/slave paradigms. Years ago, when soap operas first tried to portray romantic/sexual involvement between a black woman and a white man, the station received so many letters of protest from outraged viewers that they dropped this plot. Today many viewers are glued to the television screen watching the soap opera *All My Children* primarily to see if the black woman played by Debbie Morgan will win the white man she so desperately loves. These two lovers are never portrayed in bedroom scenes so common now in daytime soaps. Morgan's character is not just competing with an old white woman flame to get her white man, she is competing with a notion of family. And the story poses the question of whether white male desire for black flesh will prevail over commitments to blood and family loyalty.

Despite this plot of interracial sexual romance on the soaps, there is little public discussion of the connections between race and sexuality. In real life, it was the Miss America pageant where a black woman was chosen to represent beauty and therefore desirability which forced a public discussion of race and sex. When it was revealed that Vanessa Williams, the fair-skinned straightened-hair "beauty," had violated the representation of the Miss America girl as pure and virtuous by having posed nude in a series of photographs showing her engaged in sexual play with a white woman, she lost her crown but gained a different status. After her public "disgrace," she was able to remain in the limelight by appropriating the image of sexualized vamp and playing sexy roles in films. Unmasked by a virtuous white public, she assumed (according to their standards) the rightful erotic place set aside for black women in the popular imagination. The American public that had so brutally critiqued Williams and rejected her had no difficulty accepting and applauding her when she accepted the image of fallen woman. Again, as in the case of Tina Turner, Williams's bid for continued success necessitated her acceptance of conventional racist/sexist representations of black female sexuality.

The contemporary film that has most attempted to address the issue of black female sexual agency is Spike Lee's *She's Gotta Have It.* Sad to say, the black woman does not get "it." By the end of the film, she is still unable to answer the critical question, posed by one of her lovers as he rapes her, "whose pussy is this?" Reworded the question might be: How and when will black females assert sexual agency in ways that liberate us from the confines of colonized desire, of racist/sexist imagery and practice? Had Nola Darling been able to claim her sexuality and name its power, the film would have had a very different impact.

There are few films that explore issues of black female sexuality in ways that intervene and disrupt conventional representations. The short film *Dreaming Rivers,* by the British black film collective Sankofa, juxtaposes the idealized representation of black woman as mother with that of sexual subject, showing adult children facing their narrow notions of black female identity. The film highlights the autonomous sexual identity of a mature black woman which exists apart from her role as mother and caregiver. *Passion of Remembrance,* another film by Sankofa, offers exciting new representations of the black female body and black female sexuality. In one playfully erotic scene, two young black women, a lesbian couple, get dressed to go out. As part of their celebratory preparations they dance together, painting their lips, looking at their images in the mirror, exulting in their black female bodies. They shake to a song that repeats the refrain "let's get loose" without conjuring images of a rotgut colonized sexuality on display for the racist/sexist imagination. Their pleasure, the film suggests, emerges in a decolonized erotic context rooted in commitments to feminist and antiracist politics. When they look in the mirror and focus on specific body parts (their full thick lips and buttocks), the gaze is one of recognition. We see their pleasure and delight in themselves.

Films by African-American women filmmakers also offer the most oppositional images of black female sexuality. Seeing for a second time Kathleen Collin's film *Losing Ground,* I was impressed by her daring, the way she portrays black female sexuality in a way that is fresh and exciting. Like *Passion of Remembrance* it is in a domestic setting, where black women face one another (in Collin's film—as mother and daughter), that erotic images of black female sexuality surface outside a context of domination and exploitation. When daughter and mother share a meal, the audience watches as a radical sexual aesthetics emerges as the camera moves from woman to woman, focusing on the shades and textures of their skin, the shapes of their bodies, and the way their delight and pleasure in themselves is evident in

their environment. Both black women discreetly flaunt a rich sensual erotic energy that is not directed outward, it is not there to allure or entrap; it is a powerful declaration of black female sexual subjectivity.

When black women relate to our bodies, our sexuality, in ways that place erotic recognition, desire, pleasure, and fulfillment at the center of our efforts to create radical black female subjectivity, we can make new and different representations of ourselves as sexual subjects. To do so we must be willing to transgress traditional boundaries. We must no longer shy away from the critical project of openly interrogating and exploring representations of black female sexuality as they appear everywhere, especially in popular culture. In *The Power of the Image: Essays on Representation and Sexuality,* Annette Kuhn offers a critical manifesto for feminist thinkers who long to explore gender and representation:

> In order to challenge dominant representations, it is necessary first of all to understand how they work, and thus where to seek points of possible productive transformation. From such understanding flow various politics and practices of oppositional cultural production, among which may be counted feminist interventions. . . . There is another justification for a feminist analysis of mainstream images of women: may it not teach us to recognize inconsistencies and contradictions within dominant traditions of representation, to identify points of leverage for our own intervention: cracks and fissures through which may be captured glimpses of what in other circumstance might be possible, visions of "a world outside the order not normally seen or thought about?"

This is certainly the challenge facing black women, who must confront the old painful representations of our sexuality as a burden we must suffer, representations still haunting the present. We must make the oppositional space where our sexuality can be named and represented, where we are sexual subjects—no longer bound and trapped.

Ideological Racism and Cultural Resistance: Constructing Our Own Images

✌ Yen Le Espiritu

The slit-eyed, bucktooth Jap thrusting his bayo-net, thirsty for blood. The inscrutable, wily Chinese detective with his taped eyelids and wispy moustache. The childlike, indolent Filipino houseboy. Always giggling. Bowing and scraping. Eager to please, but untrustworthy. The sexless, hairless Asian male. The servile, oversexed Asian female. The Geisha. The sultry, sarong-clad, South Seas maiden. The serpentine, cunning Dragon Lady. Mysterious and evil, eager to please. Effeminate. Untrustworthy. Yellow Peril. Fortune Cookie Psychic. Savage. Dogeater. Invisible. Mute. Faceless peasants breeding too many children. Gooks. Passive Japanese Americans obediently marching off to "relocation camps" during the Second World War.

—Jessica Hagedorn (1993, p.xxii)

Focusing on the material lives of Asian Americans, racist and gendered immigration policies and labor conditions have worked in tandem to keep Asian Americans in an assigned, subordinate place. But as is evident from the stereotypes listed above, besides structural discrimination, Asian American men and women have been subject to ideological assaults. Focusing on the ideological dimension of Asian American oppression, this chapter examines the cultural symbols—or what Patricia Hill Collins (1991) called "controlling images" (pp. 67–68)—generated by the dominant group to help justify the economic exploitation and social oppression of Asian-American men and women over time. Writing on the objectification of black women, Collins (1991) observed that the exercise of political-economic domination by racial elites "always involves attempts to objectify the subordinate group" (p. 69). Transmitted through cultural institutions owned, controlled, or supported by various elites, these "controlling images" naturalize racism, sexism, and poverty by branding subordinate groups as alternatively inferior, threatening, or praiseworthy. These controlling images form part of a larger system of what Donald G. Baker (1983) referred to as "psychosocial dominance" (p. 37). Along with the threat and occasional use of violence, the psychosocial form of control conditions the subject minority to become the stereotype, to "live it, talk it, embrace it, measure group and individual worth in its terms, and believe it" (Chin & Chan, 1972, pp. 66–67). In so doing, minority members reject their own individual and group identity and accept in its stead "a white supremacist complex that establishes the primacy of Euro-American cultural practices and social institutions" (Hamamoto, 1994, p. 2). But the objectification of Asian Americans as the exotic and inferior "other" has never been absolute. Asian Americans have always, but particularly since the 1960s, resisted race, class, and gender exploitation not only through political and economic struggles but also through cultural activism. This chapter surveys the range of oppositional projects in which Asian-American cultural workers have engaged to deconstruct the conceptual apparatus of the dominant group and to defend Asian-American manhood and womanhood. My goal is to understand how the internalization and renunciation of these stereotypes have shaped sexual and gender politics within Asian America. In particular, I explore the conflicting politics of gender between Asian-American men and women as they negotiate the difficult terrain of cultural nationalism—the construction of an antiassimilationist, native Asian-American subject—and gender identities.

YELLOW PERIL, CHARLIE CHAN, AND SUZIE WONG

A central aspect of racial exploitation centers on defining people of color as "the other" (Said, 1979). The social construction of Asian American "otherness"—through such controlling images as the Yellow Peril, the model minority, the Dragon Lady, and the China Doll—is "the precondition for their cultural marginalization, political impotence, and psychic alienation from mainstream American society" (Hamamoto, 1994, p. 5). As indicated by these stereotypes, representations of gender and sexuality figure strongly in the articulation of racism. These racist stereotypes collapse gender and sexuality: Asian men have been constructed as hypermasculine, in the image of the "Yellow Peril," but also as effeminate, in the image of the "model minority," and Asian women have been depicted as superfeminine, in the image of the "China Doll," but also as castrating, in the image of the "Dragon Lady" (Mullings, 1994, pp. 279–280; Okihiro, 1995). As Mary Ann Doane (1991) suggested, sexuality is "indissociable from the effects of polarization and differentiation, often linking them to structures of power and domination" (p. 217). In the Asian-American case, the gendering of ethnicity—the process whereby white ideology assigns selected gender characteristics to various ethnic "others"—casts Asian-American men and women as simultaneously masculine and feminine but also as neither masculine nor feminine. On the one hand, as part of the Yellow Peril, Asian-American men and women have been depicted as a *masculine* threat that needs to be contained. On the other hand, both sexes have been skewed toward the female side: an indication of the group's marginalization in U.S. society and its role as the compliant "model minority" in contemporary U.S. cultural ideology. Although an apparent disjunction, both the feminization and masculinization of Asian men and women exist to define and confirm the white man's superiority (Kim, 1990).

The Yellow Peril

In the United States, Asia and America—East and West—are viewed as mutually exclusive binaries (Kim, 1993, p. viii). Within this exclusive binary system, Asian Americans, even as citizens, are designated Asians, not Americans. Characterizing Asian Americans as "permanent houseguests in the house of America," Sau-Ling Cynthia Wong (1993) stated

that "Asian Americans are put in the niche of the 'unassimilable alien': . . . they are alleged to be self-disqualified from full American membership by materialistic motives, questionable political allegiance, and, above all, outlandish, overripe, 'Oriental' cultures" (p. 6). Sonia Shah (1994) defined this form of "cultural discrimination" as a "peculiar blend of cultural and sexist oppression based on our accents, our clothes, our foods, our values, and our commitments" (p. 182). This cultural discrimination brands Asians as perpetual foreigners and thus perpetuates the notion of their alleged racial unassimilability. For example, although Japanese Americans have lived in the United States since the turn of the century, many television programs, such as "Happy Days" (1974–1984) and "Gung Ho" (1986–1987), have continued to portray them as newly arrived foreigners (Hamamoto, 1994, p. 13).

As the unassimilable alien, Asian Americans embody for many other Americans the "Yellow Peril"—the threat that Asians will one day unite and conquer the world. This threat includes military invasion and foreign trade from Asia, competition to white labor from Asian labor, the alleged moral degeneracy of Asian people, and potential miscegenation between whites and Asians (Wu, 1982, p. 1). Between 1850 and 1940, U.S. popular media consistently portrayed Asian men as a military threat to the security and welfare of the United States *and* as a sexual danger to innocent white women (Wu, 1982). In numerous dime novels, movies, and comic strips, Asians appeared as feral, rat-faced men lusting after virginal white women. Arguing for racial purity, these popular media depicted Asian—white sexual union as "at best, a form of beastly sodomy, and, at worst, a Satanic marriage" (Hoppenstand, 1983, p. 174). In these popular depictions, the white man was the desirable sexual partner and the hero who rescued the white woman from "a fate worse than death" (Hoppenstand, 1983, pp. 174–175). By the mid-1880s, hundreds of garishly illustrated and garishly written dime novels were being disseminated among a wide audience, sporting such sensational titles as *The Bradys and the Yellow Crooks, The Chase for the Chinese Diamonds, The Opium Den Detective* and *The Stranglers of New York.* As portrayed in these dime novels, the Yellow Peril was the Chinatown district of a big city "in which decent, honest white folk never ventured" (Hoppenstand, 1983, p. 177).

In twentieth-century U.S. popular media, the Japanese joined the Chinese as a perceived threat to Europe and the United States (Wu, 1982, p. 2). In

1916, William Randolph Hearst produced and distributed *Petria,* a movie about a group of fanatical Japanese who invade the United States and attempt to rape a white woman (Quinsaat, 1976, p. 265). After the Japanese bombing of Pearl Harbor on December 7, 1941, the entire Yellow Peril stereotype became incorporated in the nation's war propaganda, quickly whipping white Americans into a war fever. Along with the print media, Hollywood cranked up its anti-Japanese propaganda and produced dozens of war films that centered on the Japanese menace. The fiction of the Yellow Peril stereotype became intertwined with the fact of the United States' war with Japan and the two became one in the mindset of the American public (Hoppenstand, 1983, pp. 182–183). It was fear of the Yellow Peril—fear of the rise of nonwhite people and their contestation of white supremacy—that led to the declaration of martial law in Hawaii on December 7, 1941, and to the internment of over 110,000 Japanese on the mainland in concentration camps (Okihiro, 1994, p. 137). In subsequent decades, reflecting changing geopolitical concerns, U.S. popular media featured a host of new Yellow Peril stereotypes. During the 1950s Cold War years, in television programs as well as in movies, the Communist Chinese evildoers replaced the Japanese monster; during the Vietnam war of the 1970s, the Vietnamese Communists emerged as the new Oriental villains.

Today, Yellow Perilism takes the forms of the greedy, calculating, and clever Japanese businessman aggressively buying up U.S. real estate and cultural institutions *and* the superachieving but nonassimilating Asian Americans (Hagedorn, 1993, p. xxii). In a time of rising economic powers in Asia, declining economic opportunities in the United States, and growing diversity among America's people, this new Yellow Perilism—the depiction of Asia and Asian Americans as economic and cultural threats to mainstream United States—supplies white Americans with a united identity and provides ideological justification for U.S. isolationist policy toward Asia, increasing restrictions against Asian (and Latino) immigration,[1] and the invisible institutional racism and visible violence against Asians in the United States (Okihiro, 1994, pp. 138-139).

The Racial Construction of Asian-American Manhood

Like other men of color, Asian-American men have been excluded from white-based cultural notions of the masculine. Whereas white men are depicted both

as virile and as protectors of women, Asian men have been characterized both as asexual *and* as threats to white women. It is important to note the historical contexts of these seemingly divergent representations of Asian-American manhood. The racist depictions of Asian men as "lascivious and predatory" were especially pronounced during the nativist movement against Asians at the turn of the century (Frankenberg, 1993, pp. 75–76). The exclusion of Asian women from the United States and the subsequent establishment of bachelor societies eventually reversed the construction of Asian masculinity from "hypersexual" to "asexual" and even "homosexual." The contemporary model-minority stereotype further emasculates Asian-American men as passive and malleable. Disseminated and perpetuated through the popular media, these stereotypes of the emasculated Asian male construct a reality in which social and economic discrimination against these men appears defensible. As an example, the desexualization of Asian men naturalized their inability to establish conjugal families in pre-World War II United States. Gliding over race-based exclusion laws that banned the immigration of most Asian women and antimiscegenation laws that prohibited men of color from marrying white women, these dual images of the eunuch and the rapist attributed the "womanless households" characteristic of prewar Asian America to Asian men's lack of sexual prowess and desirability.

A popular controlling image applied to Asian-American men is that of the sinister Oriental—a brilliant, powerful villain who plots the destruction of western civilization. Personified by the movie character of Dr. Fu Manchu, this Oriental mastermind combines western science with eastern magic and commands an army of devoted assassins (Hoppenstand, 1983, p. 178). Though ruthless, Fu Manchu lacks masculine heterosexual prowess (Wang, 1988, p. 19), thus privileging heterosexuality. Frank Chin and Jeffrey Chan (1972), in a critique of the desexualization of Asian men in western culture, described how the Fu Manchu character undermines Chinese-American virility:

> Dr. Fu, a man wearing a long dress, batting his eyelashes, surrounded by muscular black servants in loin cloths, and with his habit of caressingly touching white men on the leg, wrist, and face with his long fingernails, is not so much a threat as he is a frivolous offense to white manhood. (p. 60)

In another critique that glorifies male aggression, Frank Chin (1972) contrasted the neuterlike characteristics assigned to Asian men to the sexually aggressive images associated with other men of color. "Unlike the white stereotype of the evil black stud, Indian rapist, Mexican macho, the evil of the evil Dr. Fu Manchu was not sexual, but homosexual" (p. 66). However, Chin failed to note that as a homosexual, Dr. Fu (and by extension, Asian men) threatens and offends white masculinity—and therefore needs to be contained ideologically and destroyed physically.[2]

Whereas the evil Oriental stereotype marks Asian-American men as the white man's enemy, the stereotype of the sexless Asian sidekick—Charlie Chan, the Chinese laundryman, the Filipino houseboy—depicts Asian men as devoted and impotent, eager to please. William Wu (1982) reported that the Chinese servant "is the most important single image of the Chinese immigrants" in American fiction about Chinese Americans between 1850 and 1940 (p. 60). More recently, such diverse television programs as "Bachelor Father" (1957–1962), "Bonanza" (1959–1973), "Star Trek" (1966–1969), and "Falcon Crest" (1981–1990) all featured the stock Chinese bachelor domestic who dispenses sage advice to his superiors in addition to performing traditional female functions within the household (Hamamoto, 1994, p. 7). By trapping Chinese men (and by extension, Asian men) in the stereotypical "feminine" tasks of serving white men, American society erases the figure of the Asian "masculine" plantation worker in Hawaii or railroad construction worker in the western United States, thus perpetuating the myth of the androgynous and effeminate Asian man (Goellnicht, 1992, p. 198). This feminization, in turn, confines Asian immigrant men to the segment of the labor force that performs women's work.

The motion-picture industry has been key in the construction of Asian men as sexual deviants. In a study of Asians in the U.S. motion pictures, Eugene Franklin Wong (1978) maintained that the movie industry filmically castrates Asian males to magnify the superior sexual status of white males (p. 27). As on-screen sexual rivals of whites, Asian males are neutralized, unable to sexually engage Asian women and prohibited from sexually engaging white women. By saving the white woman from sexual contact with the racial "other," the motion-picture industry protects the Anglo-American, bourgeois male establishment from any challenges to its hegemony (Marchetti,

1993, p. 218). At the other extreme, the industry has exploited one of the most potent aspects of the Yellow Peril discourses—the sexual danger of contact between the races—by concocting a sexually threatening portrayal of the licentious and aggressive Yellow Man lusting after the White Woman (Marchetti, 1993, p. 3). Heedful of the larger society's taboos against Asian male-white female sexual union, white male actors donning "yellowface"—instead of Asian male actors—are used in these "love scenes." Nevertheless, the message of the perverse and animalistic Asian male attacking helpless white women is clear (Wong, 1978). Though depicting sexual aggression, this image of the rapist, like that of the eunuch, casts Asian men as sexually undesirable. As Wong (1978) succinctly stated, in Asian male–white female relations, "There can be rape, but there cannot be romance" (p. 25). Thus, Asian males yield to the sexual superiority of the white males who are permitted filmically to maintain their sexual dominance over both white women and women of color. A young Vietnamese-American man describes the damaging effect of these stereotypes on his self-image:

> Every day I was forced to look into a mirror created by white society and its media. As a young Asian man, I shrank before white eyes. I wasn't tall, I wasn't fair, I wasn't muscular, and so on. Combine that with the enormous insecurities any pubescent teenager feels, and I have no difficulty in knowing now why I felt naked before a mass of white people. (Nguyen, 1990, p. 23)

White cultural and institutional racism against Asian males is also reflected in the motion-picture industry's preoccupation with the death of Asians—a filmic solution to the threats of the Yellow Peril. In a perceptive analysis of Hollywood's view of Asians in films made from the 1930s to the 1960s, Tom Engelhardt (1976) described how Asians, like Native Americans, are seen by the movie industry as inhuman invaders, ripe for extermination. He argued that the theme of the nonhumanness of Asians prepares the audience to accept, without flinching, "the leveling and near-obliteration of three Asian areas in the course of three decades" (Engelhardt, 1976, p. 273). The industry's death theme, though applying to all Asians, is mainly focused on Asian males, with Asian females reserved for sexual purposes (Wong, 1978, p. 35). Especially in war films, Asian males, however advantageous their initial position, inevitably perish at the hands of the superior white males (Wong, 1978, p. 34).

The Racial Construction of Asian-American Womanhood

Like Asian men, Asian women have been reduced to one-dimensional caricatures in western presentation. The condensation of Asian women's multiple differences into gross character types—mysterious, feminine, and nonwhite—obscures the social injustice of racial, class, and gender oppression (Marchetti, 1993, p. 71). Both Western film and literature promote dichotomous stereotypes of the Asian woman: Either she is the cunning Dragon Lady or the servile Lotus Blossom Baby (Tong, 1994, p. 197). Though connoting two extremes, these stereotypes are interrelated: Both eroticize Asian women as exotic "others"—sensuous, promiscuous, but untrustworthy. Whereas American popular culture denies "manhood" to Asian men, it endows Asian women with an excess of "womanhood," sexualizing them but also impugning their sexuality. In this process, sexism and racism have been blended together to produce the sexualization of white racism (Wong, 1978, p. 260). Linking the controlling images of Asian men and women, Elaine Kim (1990) suggested that Asian women are portrayed as sexual for the same reason that men are asexual: "Both exist to define the white man's virility and the white man's superiority" (p. 70).

As the racialized exotic "others," Asian-American women do not fit the white-constructed notions of the feminine. Whereas white women have been depicted as chaste and dependable, Asian women have been represented as promiscuous and untrustworthy. In a mirror image of the evil Fu Manchu, the Asian woman was portrayed as the castrating Dragon Lady who, while puffing on her foot-long cigarette holder, could poison a man as easily as she could seduce him. "With her talonlike six-inch fingernails, her skintight satin dress slit to the thigh," the Dragon Lady is desirable, deceitful, and dangerous (Ling, 1990, p. 11). In the 1924 film *The Thief of Baghdad*, Anna May Wong, a pioneer Chinese-American actress, played a handmaid who employed treachery to help an evil Mongol prince attempt to win the hand of the Princess of Baghdad (Tajima, 1989, p. 309). In so doing, Wong unwittingly popularized a common Dragon Lady social type: treacherous women who are partners in crime with men of their own kind. The publication of

Daughter of Fu Manchu (1931) firmly entrenched the Dragon Lady image in white consciousness. Carrying on her father's work as the champion of Asian hegemony over the white race, Fah Lo Sue exhibited, in the words of American studies scholar William F. Wu, "exotic sensuality, sexual availability to a white man, and a treacherous nature" (cited in Tong, 1994, p. 197). A few years later, in 1934, Milton Caniff inserted into his adventure comic strip "Terry and the Pirates" another version of the Dragon Lady who "combines all the best features of past moustache twirlers with the lure of the handsome wench" (Hoppenstand, 1983, p. 178). As such, Caniff's Dragon Lady fuses the image of the evil male Oriental mastermind with that of the Oriental prostitute first introduced some fifty years earlier in the dime novels.

At the opposite end of the spectrum is the Lotus Blossom stereotype, reincarnated throughout the years as the China Doll, the Geisha Girl, the War Bride, or the Vietnamese prostitute—many of whom are the spoils of the last three wars fought in Asia (Tajima, 1989, p. 309). Demure, diminutive, and deferential, the Lotus Blossom Baby is "modest, tittering behind her delicate ivory hand, eyes downcast, always walking ten steps behind her man, and, best of all, devot[ing] body and soul to serving him" (Ling, 1990, p. 11). Interchangeable in appearance and name, these women have no voice; their "nonlanguage" includes uninterpretable chattering, pidgin English, giggling, and silence (Tajima, 1989). These stereotypes of Asian women as submissive and dainty sex objects not only have impeded women's economic mobility but also have fostered an enormous demand for X-rated films and pornographic materials featuring Asian women in bondage, for "Oriental" bathhouse workers in U.S. cities, and for Asian mail-order brides (Kim, 1984, p. 64)

Sexism, Racism, and Love

The racialization of Asian manhood and womanhood upholds white masculine hegemony. Cast as sexually available, Asian women become yet another possession of the white man. In motion pictures and network television programs, interracial sexuality, though rare, occurs principally between a white male and an Asian female. A combination of sexism and racism makes this form of miscegenation more acceptable: Race mixing between an Asian male and a white female would upset not only racial taboos but those that attend patriarchal authority as well (Hamamoto, 1994, p. 39). Whereas Asian men are depicted as either the threatening rapist or the impotent eunuch, white men are endowed with the masculine attributes with which to sexually attract the Asian woman. Such popular television shows as "Gunsmoke" (1955–1975)and "How the West Was Won" (1978–1979) clearly articulate the theme of Asian female sexual possession by the white male. In these shows, only white males have the prerogative to cross racial boundaries and to choose freely from among women of color as sex partners. Within a system of racial and gender oppression, the sexual possession of women and men of color by white men becomes yet another means of enforcing unequal power relations (Hamamoto, 1994, p. 46).

The preference for white male-Asian female is also prevalent in contemporary television news broadcasting, most recently in the 1993–1995 pairing of Dan Rather and Connie Chung as coanchors of the "CBS Evening News." Today, virtually every major metropolitan market across the United States has at least one Asian-American female newscaster (Hamamoto, 1994, p. 245). While female Asian-American anchorpersons—Connie Chung, Tritia Toyota, Wendy Tokuda, and Emerald Yeh—are popular television news figures, there is a nearly total absence of Asian-American men. Critics argue that this is so because the white male hiring establishment, and presumably the larger American public, feels more comfortable (i.e., less threatened) seeing a white male sitting next to a minority female at the anchor desk than the reverse. Stephen Tschida of WDBJ-TV (Roanoke, Virginia), one of only a handful of male Asian-American television news anchors, was informed early in his career that he did not have the proper "look" to qualify for the anchorperson position. Other male broadcast news veterans have reported being passed over for younger, more beauteous, female Asian Americans (Hamamoto, 1994, p. 245). This gender imbalance sustains the construction of Asian-American women as more successful, assimilated, attractive, and desirable than their male counterparts.

To win the love of white men, Asian women must reject not only Asian men but their entire culture. Many Hollywood narratives featuring romances between Anglo-American men and Asian women follow the popular Pocahontas mythos: The Asian woman, out of devotion for her white American lover, betrays her own people and commits herself to the dominant white culture by dying, longing for, or going to live with her white husband in his country. For example, in the various versions of *Miss Saigon,* the contemporary version of *Madame Butterfly,* the tragic Vietnamese prostitute eternally longs for the white boy soldier who has long abandoned her and their son (Hagedorn, 1993, p. xxii). These tales of interracial romance inevitably have a tragic ending. The Asian partner usually dies, thus providing a cinematic resolution to the moral lapse of the Westerner. The Pocahontas paradigm can be read as a narrative of salvation; the Asian woman is saved either spiritually or morally from the excesses of her own culture, just as she physically saves her western lover from the moral degeneracy of her own people (Marchetti, 1993, p. 218). For Asian women, who are marginalized not only by gender but also by class, race, or ethnicity, the interracial romance narratives promise "the American Dream of abundance, protection, individual choice, and freedom from the strictures of a traditional society in the paternalistic name of heterosexual romance" (Marchetti, 1993, p. 91). These narratives also carry a covert political message, legitimizing a masculinized Anglo-American rule over a submissive, feminized Asia. The motion picture *China Gate* (1957) by Samuel Fuller and the network television program "The Lady from Yesterday" (1985), for example, promote an image of Vietnam that legitimizes American rule. Seduced by images of U.S. abundance, a feminized Vietnam sacrifices herself for the possibility of future incorporation into America, the land of individual freedom and economic opportunities. Thus, the interracial tales function not only as a romantic defense of traditional female roles within the patriarchy but also as a political justification of American hegemony in Asia (Marchetti, 1993, p. 108).

Fetishized as the embodiment of perfect womanhood and genuine exotic femininity, Asian women are pitted against their more modern, emancipated western sisters (Tajima, 1989). In two popular motion pictures, *Love Is a Many-Splendored Thing* (1955) and *The World of Suzie Wong* (1960), the white women remain independent and potentially threatening, whereas both Suyin and Suzie give up their independence in the name of love. Thus, the white female characters are cast as calculating, suffocating, and thoroughly undesirable, whereas the Asian female characters are depicted as truly "feminine"—passive, subservient, dependent, and domestic. Implicitly, these films warn white women to embrace the socially constructed passive Asian beauty as the feminine ideal if they want to attract and keep a man. In pitting white women against Asian women, Hollywood affirms white male identity against the threat of emerging feminism and the concomitant changes in gender relations (Marchetti, 1993, pp. 115–116). As Robyn Wiegman (1991) observed, the absorption of women of color into gender categories traditionally reserved for white women is "part of a broader program of hegemonic recuperation, a program that has at its main focus the reconstruction of white masculine power" (p. 320). It is also important to note that as the racialized exotic "other," Asian women do not replace but merely substitute for white women, and thus will be readily dismissed once the "real" mistress returns.

The controlling images of Asian men and Asian women, exaggerated out of all proportion in western representation, have created resentment and tension between Asian-American men and women. Given this cultural milieu, many American-born Asians do not think of other Asians in sexual terms (Fung, 1994, p. 163). In particular, due to the persistent desexualization of the Asian male, many Asian females do not perceive their ethnic counterparts as desirable marriage partners (Hamamoto, 1992, p. 42). In so doing, these women unwittingly enforce the Eurocentric gender ideology that objectifies both sexes and racializes all Asians (see Collins, 1990, pp. 185–186). In a column to *Asian Week,* a weekly Asian-American newspaper, Daniel Yoon (1993) reported that at a recent dinner discussion hosted by the Asian-American Students Association at his college, the Asian-American women in the room proceeded, one after another, to describe how "Asian-American men were too passive, too weak, too boring, too traditional, too abusive, too domineering, too ugly, too greasy, too short, too . . . Asian. Several described how they preferred white men, and how they never had and never would date an Asian man" (p. 16). Partly as a result of the racist constructions of Asian-American womanhood and manhood and their acceptance by Asian Americans, intermarriage patterns are high, with Asian-American women intermarrying at a much higher rate than Asian-American men.[3] Moreover, Asian women involved in intermarriage have usually married white partners (Agbayani-Siewert & Revilla, 1995, p. 156; Min, 1995, p. 22; Nishi, 1995, p. 128). In part, these intermarriage patterns reflect the sexualization of white racism that constructs

white men as the most desirable sexual partners, frowns on Asian male–white women relations, and fetishizes Asian women as the embodiment of perfect womanhood. Viewed in this light, the high rate of outmarriage for Asian-American women is the "material outcome of an interlocking system of sexism and racism" (Hamamoto, 1994, p. 42).[4]

CULTURAL RESISTANCE: RECONSTRUCTING OUR OWN IMAGES

"One day/I going to write/about you," wrote Lois-Ann Yamanaka (1993) in "Empty Heart" (p. 548). And Asian Americans did write—"to inscribe our faces on the blank pages and screens of America's hegemonic culture" (Kim,1993, p. xii). As a result, Asian Americans' objectification as the exotic aliens who are different from, and other than, Euro-Americans has never been absolute. Within the confines of race, class, and gender oppression, Asian Americans have maintained independent self-definitions, challenging controlling images and replacing them with Asian-American standpoints. The civil rights and ethnic studies movements of the late 1960s were training grounds for Asian-American cultural workers and the development of oppositional projects. Grounded in the U.S. black power movement and in anticolonial struggles of Third World countries, Asian-American antihegemonic projects have been unified by a common goal of articulating cultural resistance. Given the historical distortions and misrepresentations of Asian Americans in mainstream media, most cultural projects produced by Asian-American men and women perform the important tasks of correcting histories, shaping legacies, creating new cultures, constructing a politics of resistance, and opening spaces for the forcibly excluded (Kim, 1993, p. xiii; Fung, 1994, p. 165).

Fighting the exoticization of Asian Americans has been central in the ongoing work of cultural resistance. As discussed above, Asian Americans, however rooted in this country, are represented as recent transplants from Asia or as bearers of an exotic culture. The Chinese American playwright Frank Chin noted that New York critics of his play *Chickencoop Chinaman* complained in the early 1970s that his characters did not speak, dress, or act "like Orientals" (Kim, 1982, p. xv). Similarly, a reviewer described Maxine Hong Kingston's *The Woman Warrior* as a tale of "East meets West" and praised the book for its "myths rich and varied as Chinese brocade"—even though *The Woman Warrior* is deliberately antiexotic and antinostalgic (quoted in Kim, 1982, p. xv). In both of these examples, the qualifier *American* has been blithely excised from the term *Asian American*.

Asian-American cultural workers simply do not accept the exotic, one-dimensional caricatures of themselves in U.S. mass media. In the preface of *Aiiieeeee!*, a landmark collection of Asian-American writers (in this case, Chinese, Japanese, and Filipinos), published in the mid-1970s, the editors announced that the anthology, and the title *Aiiieeeee!* itself, challenged the exoticization of Asian Americans:

> The pushers of white American culture. . . . pictured the yellow man as something that when wounded, sad, angry, or swearing, or wondering whined, shouted, or screamed "aiiieeeee!" Asian America, so long ignored and forcibly excluded from creative participation in American culture, is wounded, sad, angry, swearing, and wondering, and this is his AIIIEEEEE!!! It is more than a whine, shout, or scream. It is fifty years of our whole voice. (Chan et al., 1974, p. xii)

The publication of *Aiiieeeee!* gave Asian-American writers visibility and credibility and sparked other oppositional projects. Jessica Hagedorn, a Filipina-American writer, described the legacy of *Aiiieeeee!*: "We could not be ignored; suddenly, we were no longer silent. Like other writers of color in America, we were beginning to challenge the long-cherished concepts of a xenophobic literary canon dominated by white heterosexual males" (Hagedorn, 1993, p. xviii). Inspired by *Aiiieeeee!* and by other "irreverent and blasphemous" American writers, Hagedorn created an anthology of contemporary Asian-American fiction in 1993—"a book I wanted to read but had never been available to me" (Hagedorn, 1993, p. xxx). In the tradition of *Aiiieeeee!*, the title of Hagedorn's anthology, *Charlie Chan Is Dead*, is vigorously political, defying and stamping out the vestiges of a "fake 'Asian' pop icon" (Hagedorn, 1993, p. xxi). In the anthology's preface, Elaine Kim (1993) contested the homogenization of Asian American by juxtaposing the one-dimensional Charlie Chan to the many ways of being Asian American in the contemporary United States:

> Charlie Chan is dead, never to be revived. Gone for good his yellowface asexual bulk, his fortune-cookie English, his stereotypical Orientalist version

of "the [Confucian] Chinese family," challenged by an array of characters, some hip and articulate, some brooding and sexy, some insolent and others innocent, but all as unexpected as a Korean American who writes in French, a Chinese-Panamanian-German who longs too late to know her father, a mean Japanese-American grandmother, a Chinese-American flam-dive, or a teenage Filipino-American male prostitute. Instead of "model minorities," we find human beings with rich and complex pasts and brave, often flamboyant dreams of the future. (p. xiii)

Taking up this theme, Wayne Chang's commercial film *Chan Is Missing* (1981) offers a range of Chinatown characters who indirectly convey the message that Chinese Americans, like other Americans, are heterogeneous (Chan, 1994, p. 530). Portraying Asian Americans in all our contradictions and complexities-as exiled, assimilated, rebellious, noble-Asian-American cultural projects reveal heterogeneity rather than "producing regulating ideas of cultural unity or integration" (Lowe, 1994, p. 53). In so doing, these projects destabilize the dominant racist discourse that constructs Asians as a homogeneous group who are "all alike" and readily conform to "types" such as the Yellow Peril, the Oriental mastermind, and the sexy Suzie Wong (Lowe, 1991).

Asian-American cultural projects also deconstruct the myth of the benevolent United States promised to women and men from Asia. Carlos Bulosan's *America Is in the Heart* (1943/1973), one of the core works of Asian-American literature, challenges the narrative of the United States as the land of opportunity. Seduced by the promise of individual freedom through education, the protagonist Carlos discovers that as a Filipino immigrant in the United States, he is denied access to formal schooling. This disjunction between the promise of education and the unequal access of different racial and economic groups to that education—reinforced by Carlos's observations of the exploitation, marginality, and violence suffered by his compatriots in the United States—challenges his faith in the promise of U.S. democracy and abundance (Lowe, 1994, p. 56). John Okada's *No-No Boy* (1957) is another searing indictment of U.S. racist hysteria. In this portrayal of the aftermath of the internment of Japanese Americans during World War II, the protagonist, Ichiro, angrily refuses to adjust to his postinternment and postimprisonment circumstances, thus dramatizing the Asian-American subject's refusal to accept the subordinating terms of assimilation (Lowe, 1994, p. 59). In the following excerpt from the poem by Cao Tan, "Tomorrow I Will Be Home," a Vietnamese refugee describes the emasculating effect of U.S. society:

> Tomorrow I will be home and someone will ask
> What have you learned in the States?
> If you want to give me a broom
> I'll tell you, I am a first class janitor.
> I wash dishes much faster than the best housewife
> And do a vacuum job better than any child
> Every day I run like a madman in my brand new car
> Every night I bury my head in my pillow and cry. . . .
> > Bich (1989)

To reject the myth of a benevolent United States is also to refute ideological racism: the justification of inequalities through a set of controlling images that attribute physical and intellectual traits to racially defined groups (Hamamoto, 1994, p. 3). In the 1980 autobiographical fiction *China Men,* Maxine Hong Kingston smashed the controlling image of the emasculated Asian man by foregrounding the legalized racism that turned immigrant Chinese "men" into "women" at the turn of the century. In his search for the Gold Mountain, the novel's male protagonist Tang Ao finds instead the Land of Women, where he is caught and transformed into an Oriental courtesan. Because Kingston reveals at the end of the legend that the Land of Women was in North America, readers familiar with Chinese-American history will readily see that "the ignominy suffered by Tang Ao in a foreign land symbolizes the emasculation of Chinamen by the dominant culture" (Cheung, 1990, p. 240). Later in the novel, the father's failure as a provider—his emasculation—inverts the sexual roles in the family. His silence and impotent rage deepen as his wife takes on active power in the family and assumes the "masculine" traits of aggressiveness and authority. As a means of releasing his sense of frustration and powerlessness in racist America, the father lapses into silence, screams "wordless male screams in his sleep," and spouts furious misogynistic curses that frighten his daughter (Sledge, 1980, p. 10). The author/narrator Maxine traces her father's abusive behavior back to his feeling of emasculation in America: "We knew that it was to feed us you had to endure demons and physical labor" (cited in Goellnicht, 1992, p. 201).

Similarly, in Louis Chu's 1961 novel *Eat a Bowl of Tea,* the protagonist's sexual impotence represents the social powerlessness of generations of Chinatown bachelors prevented by discriminatory laws and policies from establishing a traditional family life (Kim, 1982, p. xviii).

More recently, Steven Okazaki's film *American Sons* (1995)[5] tells the stories of four Asian-American men who reveal how incidents of prejudice and bigotry shaped their identity and affected the way they perceived themselves and society. About his film, Okazaki (1995) explained, "Prejudice, bigotry, and violence twist and demean individual lives. *American Sons* looks at difficult issues, such as hate violence, in order to show this intimate and disturbing examination of the deep psychological damage that racism causes over generations." Asian-American men's increasing involvement in hip-hop—a highly masculinized cultural form and a distinctly American phenomenon—is yet another contemporary denouncement of the stereotype of themselves as "effeminate, nerdy, asocial foreigners" (Choe, 1996). By exposing the role of the larger society in the emasculation and oppression of Asian men, Kingston, Chu, and Okazaki invalidated the naturalization and normalization of Asian men's asexuality in U.S. popular culture.

Finally, Asian-American cultural workers reject the narrative of salvation: the myth that Asian women (and a feminized Asia) are saved, through sexual relations with white men (and a masculinized United States), from the excesses of their own culture. Instead, they underscore the considerable potential for abuse in these inherently unequal relationships. Writing in Vietnamese, transplanted Vietnamese writer Tran Dieu Hang described the gloomy existence of Vietnamese women in sexist and racist U.S. society—an accursed land that singles out women, especially immigrant women, for oppression and violence. Her short story "Roi Ngay Van Moi" ("There Will Come New Days," 1986) depicts the brutal rape of a young refugee woman by her American sponsor despite her tearful pleas in limited English (Tran, 1993, pp. 721-73). Marianne Villanueva's short story "Opportunity" (1991) also calls attention to the sexualization and racialization of Asian women. As the protagonist Nina, a "mail-order bride" from the Philippines, enters the hotel lobby to meet her American fiance, the bellboys snicker and whisper *puta,* whore: a reminder that U.S. economic and cultural colonization of the Philippines always forms the backdrop to any relations between Filipinos and Americans (Wong, 1993, p. 53). Characterizing Filipino-American literature as a "literature of exile," Oscar Campomanes (1992) underscored the legacy of U.S. colonization of the Philippines: "The signifiers 'Filipinos' and 'Philippines' evoke colonialist meanings and cultural redactions which possess inordinate power to shape the fates of the writers and of Filipino peoples everywhere" (p. 52). Theresa Hak Kyung Cha's *Dictee* (1982), a Korean-American text, likewise challenges the myth of U.S. benevolence in Asia by tracing the impact of colonial and imperial damage and dislocation on the Korean subject (Lowe, 1994, p. 61). As Sau-Ling Cynthia Wong (1993) suggested, "To the extent that most typical cases of Asian immigration to the United States stem from an imbalance of resources writ large in the world economy, it holds in itself the seed of exploitation" (p. 53).

CONTROLLING IMAGES, GENDER, AND CULTURAL NATIONALISM

Cultural nationalism has been crucial in Asian Americans' struggles for self-determination. Emerging in the early 1970s, this unitary Asian-American identity was primarily racial, male, and heterosexual. Asian-American literature produced in those years highlighted Chinese- and Japanese-American male perspectives, obscuring gender and other intercommunity differences (Kim, 1993). Asian-American male writers, concerned with recuperating their identities as men and as Americans, objectified both white and Asian women in their writings (Kim, 1990, p. 70). In a controversial essay entitled "Racist Love," Frank Chin and Jeffrey Paul Chan (1972) pointed to the stereotype of the emasculated Asian-American man:

> The white stereotype of Asian is unique in that it is the only racial stereotype completely devoid of manhood. Our nobility is that of an efficient housewife. At our worst we are contemptible because we are womanly, effeminate, devoid of all the traditionally masculine qualities of originality, daring, physical courage, creativity. (p. 68)

In taking whites to task for their racist debasement of Asian-American men, however, Chin and Chan succumbed to the influence of Eurocentric gender ideology, particularly its emphasis on oppositional dichotomous sex roles (Collins, 1991, p. 184). In a critique of "Racist Love," King-Kok Cheung (1990) contended that Chin and Chan buttressed patriarchy "by invoking gender stereotypes, by disparaging domestic efficiency as 'feminine,' and by slotting desirable traits such as originality, daring, physical courage, and creativity under the rubric of masculinity" (p. 237). Similarly, Wong (1993) argued that in their influential "Introduction" to *Aiiieeeee! An Anthology of Asian American Writers* (1974), Chan, Chin, Inada, and Wong operated on the premise that a true Asian-American sensibility is "non-Christian, nonfeminine, and nonimmigrant" (p. 8).

Though limited and limiting, a masculinist cultural nationalist agenda appealed to Asian-American activists because of its potential to oppose and disrupt the logic of racial domination. In the following excerpt, Elaine Kim (1993), a pioneer in the field of Asian-American literature, explained the appeal of cultural nationalism:

> Certainly it was possible for me as a Korean-American female to accept the fixed masculinist Asian-American identity posited in Asian-American cultural nationalism, even when it rendered invisible or at least muted women's oppression, anger, and ways of loving and interpreted Korean Americans as imperfect imitations of Chinese Americans; because I could see in everyday life that not all material and psychic violence to women of color comes from men, and because, as my friends used to say, "No Chinese [American] ever called me a 'Gook.'" (p. x)

Kim's statement suggests that for Asian-American women, and for other women of color, gender is only a part of a larger pattern of unequal social relations. Despite the constraints of patriarchy, racism inscribes these women's lives and binds them to Asian-American men in what Collins (1991) called a "love and trouble" tradition (p. 184).

Because the racial oppression of Asian Americans involves the "feminization" of Asian men (Said, 1979), Asian-American women are caught between the need to expose the problems of male privilege and the desire to unite with men to contest the overarching racial ideology that confines them both. As Cheung (1990) suggested, Asian-American women may be simultaneously sympathetic and angry toward the men in their ethnic community: sensitive to the men's marginality but resentful of their sexism (p. 239). Maxine Hong Kingston's writings seem to reflect these conflicting emotions. As discussed above, in the opening legend of *China Men,* the male protagonist Tang Ao is captured in the Land of Women (North America), where he is forced to become a woman—to have his feet bound, his ears pierced, his eyebrows plucked, his cheeks and lips painted. Cheung (1990) argued that this legend is double-edged, pointing not only to the racist debasement of Chinese Americans in their adopted country but also to the subjugation of Chinese women both in China and in the United States (p. 240). Although the effemination suffered by Tang Ao is brutal, it is the same mutilation that many Chinese women were for centuries forced to bear. According to Goellnicht's (1992) reading of Kingston's work, this opening myth suggests that the author both deplores the emasculation of her forefathers by mainstream America and critiques the Confucian patriarchal practices of her ancestral homeland (p. 194). In *China Men,* Kingston also showed no acceptance of sexist practices by immigrant men. The father in this novel/autobiography is depicted as a broken man who attempts to reassert male authority by denigrating those who are even more powerless—the women and children in his family (Cheung, 1990, p. 241; Goellnicht, 1992, p. 200).

Along the same lines, Maxine Hong Kingston's *The Woman Warrior* (1977) reveals the narrator's contradictory attitudes toward her childhood "home," which is simultaneously a site of "woman hatred" and an area of resistance against the racism of the dominant culture. The community that nourishes her imagination and suffuses her with warmth is the same community that relegates women to an inferior position, limiting them to the role of serving men (Rabine, 1987, pp. 477–478). In the following passage, the narrator voices her mixed feelings toward the Chinese-American community:

> I looked at their ink drawings of poor people snagging their neighbors' flotage with long flood hooks and pushing the girl babies on down the river. And I had to get out of hating range. . . . I refuse to shy my way anymore through our China town, which tasks me with the old sayings and the stories. The swordswoman and I are not so dissimilar. May my people understand the resemblance so that I can return to them. (Kingston, 1977, p. 62)

Similarly, in a critique of Asian-American sexual politics, Kayo Hatta's short video *Otemba* (1988) depicts a girl's-eye view of the final days of her mother's pregnancy as her father hopes and prays for the birth of a boy (see Tajima, 1991, p. 26).

Stripped of the privileges of masculinity, some Asian-American men have attempted to reassert male authority by subordinating feminism to nationalist concerns. Lisa Lowe (1991) argued that this identity politics displaces gender differences into a false opposition of "nationalism" and "assimilation." From this limited perspective, Asian-American feminists who expose Asian-American sexism are cast as "assimilationist," as betraying Asian-American "nationalism." Maxine Hong Kingston's *The Woman Warrior* (1977) and Amy Tan's *The Joy Luck Club* (1989) are the targets of such nationalist criticisms. Frank Chin, Ben Tong, and others have accused these and other women novelists of feminizing Asian-American literature by exaggerating the community's patriarchal structure, thus undermining the power of Asian-American men to combat the racist stereotypes of the dominant white culture. For example, when Kingston's *The Woman Warrior* received favorable reviews, Chin accused her of attempting to "cash in on the feminist fad" (Chan, 1994, p. 528). Another Asian-American male had this to say about the movie *The Joy Luck Club:*

> The movie was powerful. But it could have been powerful *and inclusive,* if at least one of the Asian male characters was portrayed as something other than monstrously evil or simply wimpy. We are used to this message coming out of Hollywood, but it disturbed me deeply to hear the same message coming from Amy Tan and Wayne Wang-people of my own color. (Yoon, 1993)

Whereas Chin and others cast this tension in terms of nationalism and assimilationism, Lisa Lowe (1991) argued that it is more a debate between nationalist and feminist concerns in Asian-American discourse. This insistence on a fixed masculinist identity, according to Lowe (1991), "can be itself a colonial figure used to displace the challenges of heterogeneity, or subalternity, by casting them as assimilationist or anti-ethnic" (pp. 33–34).

But cultural nationalism need not be patriarchial. Rejecting the ideology of oppositional dichotomous sex roles, Asian-American cultural workers have also engaged in cross-gender projects. In a recent review of Asian-American independent filmmaking, Renee Tajima (1991) reported that some of the best feminist films have been made by Asian-American men. For example, Arthur Dong's *Lotus* (1987) exposes women's exploitation through the practice of foot-binding (Tajima, 1991, p. 24). Asian-American men have also made use of personal documentary, in both diary and autobiographical form—an approach known to be the realm of women filmmakers. Finally, there is no particular gender affiliation in subject matters: Just as Arthur Dong profiles his mother in *Sewing Woman*; Lori Tsang portrays her father's life in *Chinaman's Choice* (Tajima, 1991, p. 24).

CONCLUSION

Ideological representations of gender and sexuality are central in the exercise and maintenance of racial, patriarchal, and class domination. In the Asian-American case, this ideological racism has taken seemingly contrasting forms: Asian men have been cast as both hypersexual and asexual, and Asian women have been rendered both superfeminine and masculine. Although in apparent disjunction, both forms exist to define, maintain, and justify white male supremacy. The racialization of Asian-American hood and womanhood underscores the interconnections of race, gender, and class. As categories of difference, race and gender relations do not parallel but intersect and confirm each other, and it is the complicity among these categories of difference that enables U.S. elites to justify and maintain their cultural, social, and economic power. Responding to the ideological assaults on their gender identities, Asian-American cultural workers have engaged in a wide range of oppositional projects to defend Asian-American manhood and womanhood. In the process, some have embraced a masculinist cultural nationalism, a stance that marginalizes Asian-American women and their needs. Though sensitive to the emasculation of Asian-American men, Asian-American feminists have pointed out that Asian-American nationalism insists on a fixed masculinist identity, thus obscuring gender differences. Though divergent, both the nationalist and feminist positions advance the dichotomous stance of man or woman, gender or race or class, without recognizing the complex relationality of these categories of oppression. It is only when Asian Americans recognize the intersections of race, gender, and class that we can transform the existing hierarchical structure.

ACKNOWLEDGMENT

The excerpt from Cao Tan's poem "Tomorrow I Will Be Home" appeared in *War and Exile: A Vietnamese Anthology*, edited by N. N. Bich, 1989, Springfield, VA: Vietnam PEN Abroad.

NOTES

1. In 1996, the U.S. Congress deliberated on but did not pass two bills (S. 1394/269 and H.R. 2202) that would have sharply cut legal immigration by removing the family preferences from the existing immigration laws.

2. I thank Mary Romero for pointing this out to me.

3. Filipino Americans provide an exception in that Filipino-American men tend to intermarry as frequently as Filipina-American women. This is so partly because they are more Americanized and have a relatively more egalitarian gender-role orientation than other Asian-American men (Agbayani-Siewert & Revilla, 1995, p. 156).

4. In recent years, Asian Americans' rising consciousness, coupled with their phenomenal growth in certain regions of the United States, has led to a significant increase in inter-Asian marriages (e.g., Chinese Americans to Korean Americans). In California (where 39% of all Asian Pacific Americans reside), inter-Asian marriages increased from 21.1% in 1980 to 64% in 1990 of all intermarriages for Asian-American husbands and from 10.8% to 45% for Asian-American wives during the same time period.

5. I thank Takeo Wong for calling my attention to this film.

REFERENCES

Agbayani-Siewert, P., & Revilla, L. (1995). Filipino Americans. In P. G. Min (Ed.), *Asian Americans: Contemporary Trends and Issues* (pp. 134–168). Thousand Oaks, CA: Sage.

Baker, D. G. (1983). *Race, Ethnicity, and Power: A Comparative Study.* New York: Routledge.

Bich, N. N. (Ed.). (1989). *War and Exile: A Vietnamese Anthology.* Springfield, VA: Vietnam PEN Abroad.

Camponanes, O. (1992) "Filipinos in the United States and their literature of exile." In S. G. Lim and A. Ling (Eds.), *Reading the Literatures of Asian America* (pp. 49–78). Philadelphia: Temple Univ. Press.

Chan, J. P., Chin, F., Inada, L. F., & Wong, S. (1974). *Aiiieeeee! An Anthology of Asian American Writers.* Washington, DC: Howard University Press.

Chan, S. (1994). The Asian-American Movement, 1960s-1980s. In A. S. Chan, D. H. Daniels, M.T. Garcia, and T.P.-Wilson (Eds.), *Peoples of Color in the American West* (pp. 525-533). Lexington, MA: D. C. Heath.

Cheung, K.-K. (1990). The woman warrior versus the Chinaman pacific: Must a Chinese American critic choose between feminism and heroism? In M. Hirsch & E. F. Keller (Eds.), *Conflicts in Feminism* (pp. 234–251). New York: Routledge.

Chin, F. (1972). Confessions of the Chinatown cowboy. *Bulletin of Concerned Asian Scholars, 4*(3), 66.

Chin, F., & Chan, J. P. (1972). Racist love. In R. Kostelanetz (Ed.), *Seeing through Shuck* (pp. 65-79). New York: Ballantine.

Choe, Laura. 1996, February 10. "Versions": Asian Americans in Hip Hop. Paper presented at the California Studies Conference, Long Beach, CA.

Collins, P. H. (1991). *Black Feminist Thought: Knowledge, Consciousness, and the Politics of Empowerment.* New York: Routledge.

Doane, M. A. (1991). *Femme Fatales: Feminism, Film Theory, Psychoanalysis.* New York: Routledge.

Engelhardt, T. (1976). Ambush at Kamikaze Pass. In E. Gee (Ed.), *Counterpoint: Perspectives on Asian America* (pp. 270–279). Los Angeles: University of California at Los Angeles, Asian American Studies Center.

Frankenberg, R. (1993). *White Women, Race Matters: The Social Construction of Whiteness.* Minneapolis: University of Minnesota Press.

Fung, R. (1994). Seeing yellow: Asian identities in film and video. In K. Aguilar-San Juan (Ed.), *The State of Asian America* (pp. 161–171). Boston: South End.

Goellnicht, D. C. (1992). Tang Ao in America: Male subject positions in *China Men.* In S. G. Lim & A. Ling (Eds.), *Reading the Literatures of Asian America* (pp. 191–212). Philadelphia: Temple University Press.

Hagedorn, J. (1993). Introduction: "Role of dead man requires very little acting." In J. Hagedorn (Ed.), *Charlie Chan Is Dead: An Anthology of Contemporary Asian American Fiction* (pp. xxi-xxx). New York: Penguin.

Hamamoto, D. Y. (1994). *Monitored Peril: Asian Americans and the Politics of Representation.* Minneapolis: University of Minnesota Press.

Hoppenstand, G. (1983). Yellow devil doctors and opium dens: A survey of the yellow peril stereotypes in mass media entertainment. In C. D. Geist & J Nachbar (Eds.), *The Popular Culture Reader* (3rd ed., pp. 171–185). Bowling Green, OH: Bowling Green University Press.

Kim, E. (1982). *Asian American Literature: An Introduction to the Writings and Their Social Context.* Philadelphia: Temple University Press.

Kim, E. (1984). Asian American writers: A bibliographical review. *American Studies International, 22,* 2.

Kim, E. (1990). "Such opposite creatures": Men and women in Asian American literature. *Michigan Quarterly Review, 29,* 68–93.

Kim, E. (1993). Preface. In J. Hagedorn (Ed.), *Charlie Chan Is Dead: An Anthology of Contemporary Asian American Fiction* (pp. vii-xiv). New York: Penguin.

Kingston, M. H. (1977). *The Woman Warrior.* New York: Vintage.

Ling, A. (1990). *Between Worlds: Women Writers of Chinese Ancestry.* New York: Pergamon.

Lowe, L. (1991). Heterogeneity, hybridity, multiplicity: Marking Asian American difference. *Diaspora, 1,* 24–44.

Lowe, L. (1994). Canon, institutionalization, identity: Contradictions for Asian American studies. In D. Palumbo-Liu (Ed.), *The Ethnic Canon: Histories, Institutions, and Interventions* (pp. 48-68). Minneapolis: University of Minnesota Press.

Lowe, L. (1996). *Immigrant Acts: On Asian American Cultural Politics.* Durham, NC: Duke University Press.

Marchetti, G. (1993). *Romance and the "Yellow Peril": Race, Sex, and Discursive Strategies in Hollywood Fiction.* Berkeley: University of California Press.

Min, P. G. (1995). Korean Americans. In P. G. Min (Ed.), *Asian Americans: Contemporary Trends and Issues* (pp. 199-231). Thousand Oaks, CA: Sage.

Mullings, L. (1994). Images, ideology, and women of color. In M. Baca Zinn & B. T. Dill (Eds.), *Women of Color in U.S. Society* (pp. 265–289). Philadelphia: Temple University Press.

Nguyen, V. (1990, December 7). Growing up in white America. *Asian Week,* p. 23.

Nishi, S. M. (1995). Japanese Americans. In P. G. Min (Ed.), *Asian Americans: Contemporary Trends and Issues* (pp. 95–133). Thousand Oaks, CA: Sage.

Okazaki, S. (1995). *American Sons.* Promotional brochure for the film of that name.

Okihiro, G. Y. (1994). *Margins and Mainstreams: Asians in American History and Culture.* Seattle: University of Washington Press.

Okihiro, G. Y. (1995, November). *Reading Asian Bodies, Reading Anxieties.* Paper presented at the University of California, San Diego Ethnic Studies Colloquium, La Jolla.

Quinsaat, J. (1976). Asians in the media: The shadows in the spotlight. In E. Gee (Ed.), *Counterpoint: Perspectives on Asian America* (pp. 264–269). Los Angeles: University of California at Los Angeles, Asian American Studies Center.

Rabine, L. W. (1987). No lost paradise: Social gender and symbolic gender in the writings of Maxine Hong Kingston. *Signs: Journal of Women in Culture and Society,* 12, 471–511.

Said, E. (1979). *Orientalism.* New York: Random House.

Shah, S. (1994). Presenting the Blue Goddess: Toward a national, Pan-Asian feminist agenda. In K. Aguilar-San Juan (Ed.), *The State of Asian America: Activism and Resistance in the 1990s (pp. 147-158).* Boston: South End.

Sledge, L. C. (1980). Maxine Kingston's *China Men:* The family historian as epic poet. *MELUS, 7,* 3–22.

Tajima, R. (1989). Lotus blossoms don't bleed: Images of Asian Women. In Asian Women United of California (Ed.), *Making Waves: An Anthology of Writings by and about Asian American Women* (pp. 308–317). Boston: Beacon.

Tajima, R. (1991). Moving the image: Asian American independent filmmaking 1970-1990. In R. Leong (Ed.), *Moving the Image: Independent Asian Pacific American Media Arts* (pp. 10–33). Los Angeles: University of California at Los Angeles, Asian American Studies Center, and Visual Communications, Southern California Asian American Studies Central.

Tong, B. (1994). *Unsubmissive Women: Chinese Prostitutes in Nineteenth-Century San Francisco.* Norman: University of Oklahoma Press.

Tran, Q. P. (1993). Exile and home in contemporary Vietnamese American feminine writing. *Amerasia Journal, 19,* 71–83.

Wang, A. (1988). Maxine Hong Kingston's reclaiming of America: The birthright of the Chinese American male. *South Dakota Review, 26,* 18-29.

Wiegman, R. (1991). Black bodies/American commodities: Gender, race, and the bourgeois ideal in contemporary film. In L. D. Friedman (Ed.), *Unspeakable Images: Ethnicity and the American Cinema* (pp. 308-328). Urbana: University of Illinois Press.

Wong. E. F. (1978). *On Visual Media Racism: Asians in the American Motion Pictures.* New York: Arno.

Wong, S.-L. C. (1993). *Reading Asian American Literature: From Necessity to Extravagance.* Princeton, NJ: Princeton University Press.

Wu, W. F. (1982). *The Yellow Peril: Chinese Americans in American Fiction 1850-1940.* Hamden, CT: Archon.

Yamanaka, L.A. (1993). Empty heart. In J. Hagedorn (Ed.), *Charlie Chan is dead: An anthology of contemporary Asian American Fiction* (pp. 544–550). New York: Penguin.

Yoon, D. D. (1993, November 26). Asian American male: Wimp or what? *Asian Week,* p. 16.

SECTION FOUR

Socialization

We are born into cultures that have definite ideas about men and women and their appropriate attitudes, values, and behaviors. Dominant American culture defines certain traits as masculine or feminine and values behaviors, occupations, and attitudes deemed masculine more highly than those associated with women. It assumes that what men do is right and normal. Women are judged in accordance with how well they conform to the male standard. This way of thinking is known as *androcentrism*. As children, we learn to see ourselves and others as girls or boys and to judge our own and others behaviors according to standards of gender-appropriate behavior. The articles in this section analyze the complex process of gender socialization from various perspectives. Learning about our culture begins in the family. We learn about gender not only from what our parents say, but from what they do. When mothers have primary responsibility for raising children, both girls and boys learn that nurturing is more a responsibility of women than of men. Gender socialization continues in schools, peer groups, and religious institutions, and can be ongoing throughout life, as we learn the expectations of our college contexts, our workplaces, and the families we form as adults.

Because the culture differentiates not only along gender lines but according to race, ethnicity, and class as well, our socialization experiences also differ along these lines. What an African-American mother, for example, needs to teach her sons and daughters to enable them to survive in a white-male-dominated society is different from what a white mother needs to teach her children. These kinds of racial differences, in turn, are compounded by differences in class status. In "'The Means to Put My Children Through': Child-Rearing Goals and Strategies among Black Female Domestic Servants," Bonnie Thornton Dill writes about the complexity of race and gender issues. Contrasting the race and class advantages available to white employers' children with the goals domestic workers held for their own children, Dill outlines the reactions and responses of black female domestic workers who cared for white children to provide income but who reared their own children to enter the middle class.

Gender socialization is carried out in schools as well as in homes. By the time children are in school, they not only have been socialized into their gender but also are able to negotiate how and in which situations gender will be socially salient. Barrie Thorne, in "Girls and Boys Together . . . But Mostly Apart: Gender Arrangements in Elementary Schools," argues for a more complex idea of gender as socially constructed and context specific. In her observations of social relations among children in elementary school, she finds that boys and girls are segregated and seen as different in the classroom and on the playground both because of teachers' actions and because children socialize each other. Did your own experiences in elementary school conform to the patterns Thorne describes?

A new concern with boys has emerged in the past few years. In "What Are Little Boys Made Of?" Michael Kimmel discusses the different ways that popular discourse defines the problems that face boys, from violence to attention deficit disorder to the pressure to appear emotionally invulnerable. Kimmel argues that there are clear problems facing boys, but that these problems stem from cultural expectations and peer pressure to conform to a narrow definition of masculinity. He critiques authors who argue that testosterone or other biological features make boys more violent, or more active, or less adapted to educational settings than girls. Instead, he suggests, boys' lives can be improved by not only addressing the emotional straightjacket forced upon them by gender norms, but by taking a feminist approach to eliminating gender inequality. Do you agree with Kimmel's argument? How are his observations about boys' experiences similar to those that Thorne describes? Can you think of examples from your own experience of the pressures placed on boys to conform to masculinity?

Some parents try to raise children without these gender stereotypes. In "Ideology, Experience, Identity: The Complex Worlds of Children in Fair Families," Barbara Risman describes how children with egalitarian parents understand gender. She suggests that children acquire gender identities and ideologies from both their parents and their peers. When mothers and fathers both work outside the home, share child-raising, and are committed to gender equality, their children also believe that men and women should be equal. Yet, Risman finds, these same children believe that girls and boys are very different from each other, and their own identities are at least partially gender-traditional. What do the children she interviews think boys and girls are like? How do they view their own nonconformity with gender roles? In your observation, are traditional views of what girls and boys are like still prevalent?

"The Means to Put My Children Through": Child-Rearing Goals and Strategies among Black Female Domestic Servants

Bonnie Thornton Dill

This essay explores the family and child-rearing strategies presented by a small group of Afro-American women who held jobs as household workers while raising their children. The data are drawn from a study of the relationship of work and family among American-born women of African descent who were private household workers (domestic servants) for most of their working lives.

The primary method of data collection was life histories, collected through open-ended, in-depth interviews with twenty-six women living in the northeastern United States. All participants were between sixty and eighty years old. A word of caution in reading this essay: The conclusions are not meant to apply to all Black female domestic servants, but represent only my interpretation of the experiences of these twenty-six women.

The life history method is particularly useful in studying Black female domestic workers whose stories and experiences have largely been distorted or ignored in the social science literature.[1] According to Denzin (1970: 220), the method "presents the experiences and definitions held by one person, group, or organization as that person, group, or organization interprets those experiences." As such, it provides a means of exploring the processes whereby people construct, endure, and create meaning in both the interactional and structural aspects of their lives. It aids in the identification and definition of concepts appropriate to a sociological understanding of the subject's experience, and moves toward building theory that is grounded in imagery and meanings

relevant to the subject. Collected through in-depth interviews, life histories are active processes of rendering meaning to one's life—its conflicts, ambiguities, crises, successes, and significant interpersonal relationships. Subjects are not merely asked to "report" but rather to reconstruct and interpret their choices, situations, and experiences.[2] The study of Black Americans cries out for such a sensitized approach to their lives.

The child-rearing goals and strategies adopted by the women who participated in this study are particularly revealing of the relationship of work and family. As working mothers, they were concerned with providing safe and secure care for their children while they were away from home. As working-class people, seeking to advance their children beyond their own occupational achievements, they confronted the problem of guiding them toward goals that were outside of their own personal experience. These issues, as well as others, take on a particular form for women who were household workers primarily because of the nature of their work.

Unlike many other occupations, domestic work brings together, in a closed and intimate sphere of human interaction, people whose paths would never cross were they to conduct their lives within the socioeconomic boundaries to which they were ascribed. These intimate interactions across the barriers of income, ethnicity, religion, and race occur within a sphere of life that is private and has little public exposure—the family.

As household workers, these women often become vital participants in the daily lives of two separate families: their employer's and their own. In fact, they have often been described as being "like one of the family" (Childress, 1956), and yet the barriers between them and their employers are real and immutable ones. In addition, working-class Black women employed by middle- and upper-class white families observe and experience vast differences in the material quality of life in the two homes. With regard to child-rearing, employers could provide luxuries and experiences for their children that were well beyond the financial means of the employee.

This essay, therefore, presents some of the ways in which the women talked about their reactions and responses to the discrepancies in life chances between those of their children and those of their employers. To some extent, these discrepancies became the lens through which we viewed their goals for their children and their child-rearing practices. At the same time, the contrast in objective conditions provides a background against which the women's perceptions of similarities between themselves and their employers are made more interesting.

The data from this study indicate that the relationship between the employee's family life and her work was shaped by four basic factors. First, there was the structure of the work. Whether she worked full-time or part-time and lived in, lived out, or did day work determined the extent to which she became involved in the employer's day-to-day life. It also determined the amount of time she had to share with her own family. Second were the tasks and duties she was assigned. With regard to her own child-rearing goals and strategies, the intermingling of employer and employee lifestyles occurred most frequently among those women who took care of the employer's children. It is through their discussion of these activities that the similarities and differences between the two families are most sharply revealed. A third factor is the degree of employer–employee intimacy. An employee who cared for the employer's children was more likely to have an intimate relationship with her employing family, but not always. Though the employer–employee relationship in domestic service is characterized as a personalized one when compared with other work relationships, this does not presume intimacy between the two parties, that is, a reciprocal exchange of interests and concerns. Among the women who participated in this study, those who did not share much of their own life with their employers appeared to minimize the interaction of work and family. Finally were the employee's goals for her children. Those women who felt that their employers could aid them in achieving the educational or other goals they had set for their children were more likely to encourage an intermingling of these two parts of their lives.

On domestic work and upward mobility:

Strangely enough, I never intended for my children to have to work for anybody in the capacity that I worked. Never. And I never allowed my children to do any baby-sitting or anything of the sort. I figured it's enough for the mother to do it and in this day and time you don't have to do that. . . . So they never knew anything about going out to work or anything. They went to school.

Given the low social status of the occupation, the ambivalent and defensive feelings many of the women expressed about their work and the eagerness with which women left the occupation when other opportunities were opened to them, it is not at all surprising that most of the women in this study said they did not want their children to work in domestic service. Their hopes were centered upon "better" jobs for their children: jobs with more status, income, security, and comfort. Pearl Runner[3] recalled her goals for her children:

My main goal was I didn't want them to follow in my footsteps as far as working. I always wanted them to please go to school and get a good job because it's important. That was really my main object.

Lena Hudson explained her own similar feelings this way:

They had a better chance than I had, and they shouldn't look back at what I was doing. They had a better chance and a better education than I had, so look out for something better than I was doing. And they did. I haven't had a one that had to do any housework or anything like that. So I think that's good.

The notion of a better chance is a dominant one in the women's discussions of their goals for their children. They portray themselves as struggling to give their children the skills and training they did not have; and as praying that opportunities which had not been open to them would be open to their children. In their life histories, the women describe many of the obstacles they encountered in this quest. Nevertheless, there are dilemmas which, though not discussed explicitly, are implicit in their narratives and a natural outgrowth of their aspirations.

First of these is the task of guiding children toward a future over which they had little control and toward occupational objectives with which they had no direct experience. Closely tied to this problem was their need to communicate the undesirability of household work and at the same time maintain their personal dignity despite the occupation. While these two problems are not exceptional for working-class parents in an upwardly mobile society, they were mediated for Black domestic workers through the attitudes toward household work held by members of the Black communities in which the women lived and raised their children.

Had domestic work not been the primary occupation of Black women and had racial and sexual barriers not been so clearly identifiable as the reason for their concentration in this field of employment, these problems might have been viewed more personally and the women's histories might have been more self-deprecating than in fact they were. This particular set of circumstances would suggest that the women at least had the option of directing their anger and frustration about their situation outward upon the society rather than turning it inward upon themselves. Drake and Cayton (1945) confirm this argument in their analysis of domestic work, saying that "colored girls are often bitter in their comments about a society which condemns them to the *white folks'* kitchen" (p. 246). In addition, attitudes in the Black community toward domestic service work mediated some of the more negative attitudes which were prevalent in the wider society. Thus, the community could potentially become an important support in the child-rearing process, reinforcing the idea that while domestic service was low-status work, the people who did it were not necessarily low-status people.

The data in this study do not include the attitudes of the children of domestic servants toward their mothers' occupation. To my knowledge, there has been no systematic study of this issue. However, some biographies and community studies

have provided insight into the range of feelings children express. Drake and Cayton (1945), for example, cite one woman who described her daughter as being "bitter against what she calls the American social system." DuBois talks about feeling an instinctive hatred toward the occupation (1920: 110). I have had employers tell me that their domestics' children hated their children because the employer's kids got the best of their mother's time. I have also heard Black professionals speak with a mixture of pride, anger, and embarrassment about the fact that their mother worked "in the *white folks'* kitchen" so that they could get an education. Clearly, these issues deserve further study.

Throughout these histories, the women identified education as the primary means through which mobility could be achieved. As with many working-class people, education was seen as a primary strategy for upward mobility, a means to a better-paying and more prestigious job. Most of the women who participated in this study had not completed high school (the mean years of schooling completed for the group were 9.2 years). They reasoned that their limited education in combination with racial discrimination had hindered their own chances for upward mobility. Zenobia King explained her attitudes toward education in this way:

In my home in Virginia, education, I don't think, was stressed. The best you could do was be a schoolteacher. It wasn't something people impressed upon you you could get. I had an aunt and cousin who were trained nurses and the best they could do was nursing somebody at home or something. They couldn't get a job in a hospital . . . I didn't pay education any mind really until I came to New York. I'd gotten to a certain stage in domestic work in the country and I didn't see the need for it. When I came, I could see opportunities that I could have had if I had a degree. People said it's too bad I didn't have a diploma.

From Mrs. King's perspective and from those of some of the other women, education for a Black woman in the South before World War II did not seem to offer any tangible rewards. She communicates the idea that an education was not only unnecessary but could perhaps have been a source of even greater frustration and dissatisfaction. This idea was reemphasized by other women who talked about college-educated women they knew who could find no work other than domestic work. In fact, both Queenie Watkins and Corrinne Raines discussed their experiences as trained teachers who could not find suitable jobs and thus took work in domestic service. Nevertheless, Corrinne Raines maintained her belief in education as a means of upward mobility, a belief that was rooted in her family of orientation. She said:

I am the twelfth child [and was] born on a farm. My father was—at that day, you would call him a successful farmer. He was a man who was eager for his children to get an education. Some of the older ones had gotten out of school and were working and they were able to help the younger ones. That's how he was able to give his children as much education as he gave them, because the older ones helped him out.

Given this mixed experience with education and social mobility, it might be expected that many of the women would have expressed reservations about the value of an education for their children's mobility. However, this was not the case. Most of them, reflecting on their goals for their children, expressed sentiments similar to Pearl Runner's:

This is the reason why I told them to get an education. . . . If they want to go to college it was fine because the higher you go the better jobs you get. They understood that because I always taught that into them. Please try to get an education so you can get a good job 'cause it was hard for colored girls to get jobs, period. They had to have an education.

Mrs. Runner's statement is important because it contains the rudiments of an explanation for why she and other women stressed education in the face of discriminatory practices that frequently discounted even their best efforts. Opallou Tucker elaborates on this theme and provides a somewhat more detailed explanation:

It's [domestic work] all right if you want to do it and if you can't do anything else, but it's not necessary now. If you prepare yourself for something that's better, the doors are open now. I know years ago there was no such thing as a Black typist. I remember girls who were taking typing when I was going to school. They were never able to get a job at it. So it really [was] for their own personal use. My third child, and a niece, after they got up some size, started taking typing. And things began to open up after she got grown up. But in my day and time you could have been the greatest typist in the world, but you would never have gotten a job. It's fine to prepare yourself so that when opportunity knocks, you'll be able to catch up.

In these statements, Mrs. Runner and Mrs. Tucker convey a complex and subtle understanding of the interaction of racism and opportunity. They recognize the former as a real and tangible barrier, but they do not give in to it. They describe themselves as having taught their children to be prepared. Education was seen as a means of equipping oneself for whatever breaks might occur in the nation's patterns of racial exclusion. Thus, key to their aspirations for their children was the hope and belief that opportunities would eventually open and permit their children to make full use of the skills and knowledge they encouraged them to attain.

Nevertheless, maintaining these hopes could not have been as easy and unproblematic as hindsight makes it seem. The fact that many of the women who expressed this strong commitment to education at the time of the interview had seen their children complete a number of years of schooling and enter jobs which would never have been open to them when they were young was clearly a source of pride and satisfaction which could only have strengthened their beliefs. Thus, as they recalled their goals and aspirations for their children, they tended to speak with a sense of self-affirmation about their choices, confidence that may not have been present years earlier. As Mrs. Runner expressed,

I tell you I feel really proud and I really feel that with all the struggling that I went through, I feel happy and proud that I was able to keep helping my children, that they listened and that they all went to high school. So when I look back, I really feel proud, even though at times the work was very hard and I came home very tired. But now, I feel proud about it. They all got their education.

Perhaps reflective of their understanding of the complex interaction of racism and opportunity, most of the women described limited and general educational objectives for their children. Although a few women said they had wanted their children to go to college and one sent her son to a private high school with the help of scholarships, most women saw high school graduation as the concrete, realizable objective which they could help their children attain. Willie Lee Murray's story brings out a theme that was recurrent in several other histories:

> My children did not go to college. I could not afford to send them to college. And they told me, my younger one especially, he said: Mommy, I don't want to go to college at your expense. When I go to college, I'll go on my own. I would not think of you workin' all your days—sometimes you go sick and I don't know how you gonna get back. You put us through school and you gave us a beautiful life. We'll get to college on our own.

Mrs. Murray seems to indicate that while she would have liked her children to go to college, she limited her goals and concentrated her energies upon their completing high school.

In addition to limited educational objectives, most of the women did not describe themselves as having had a specific career objective in mind for their children. They encouraged the children to get an education in order to get a better job. Precisely what those jobs would be was left open, to be resolved through the interaction of their son or daughter's own luck, skill, perseverance, and the overall position of the job market vis-à-vis Black entrants.

Closely related to the goals the women expressed about their children's future position in society were their goals relative to their child's development as a person. Concern that their children grow up to be good, decent, law-abiding citizens was a dominant theme in these discussions. Most of the women in the study described their employers as having very specific career goals for their children, usually goals that would have the children following their parents' professional footsteps. In characterizing the differences between their goals and those of their employers, the women stressed the differences in economic resources. Johnnie Boatwright was quite explicit on this point:

> There was a lot of things they [employers] did that I wanted to do for mine, but I just couldn't afford it. . . . Like sending them to school. Then they

could hire somebody; child slow, they could hire a tutor for the child. I wish I could have been able to do what they done. And then too, they sent them to camps, nice camps, not any camp but one they'd pick out. . . . So that's what I wished I could had did for him [her son]. . . . See, whether it was right or wrong, mines I couldn't do it because I didn't have the money to do it. I wasn't able to do it. So that's the way it was. I did what I could and that was better than nothing.

In light of these discrepancies in resources, personal development was an important and realizable goal which may have been an adaptive response to the barriers which constricted the women's range of choices. This was an area over which the women had greater influence and potential control. It was also an area in which they probably received considerable community support, since values in the Black community, as pointed out above, attribute status to success along personal and family dimensions in addition to the basic ones of occupation, education, and income.

While Mrs. Boatwright conveys a sense of resignation and defeat in discussing her inability to do for her son what the employers did for theirs, Pearl Runner is more optimistic and positive about what she was able to do for her children.

> Their money may be a little more, but I felt my goal was just as important as long as they [the children] got their education. They [employers] had the money to do lots more than I did, but I felt that if I kept working, my goals was just as important. I felt my children were just as important.

Feelings like those expressed by both Mrs. Runner and Mrs. Boatwright are reflected throughout the data in the women's comparisons of their aspirations and expectations for their children's future with those of their employers. However, it also seems apparent that their intimate participation in families in which the husbands were doctors, lawyers, stockbrokers, college professors, writers, and housewives provided considerable support for their more limited educational objectives. While not everyone had the specific experience of Lena Hudson, whose employer provided an allowance for her daughter which permitted the girl to stay in high school, the model of the employer's life with regard to the kinds of things they were able to give their children was a forceful one and is repeatedly reflected in the women's discussions of their child-rearing goals.

When asked: "What do you think were the goals that the Wallises [her employers] had for their children? What did they want for their children? What did they want them to become in life?" Lena Hudson replied:

> Well, for *their* children, I imagine they wanted them to become like they were, educators or something that like. What they had in mind for *my* children, they saw in me that I wasn't able to make all of that mark. But raised my children in the best method I could. Because I wouldn't have the means to put *my* children through like they could for *their* children. And they see I wasn't the worst person in the world, and they saw I meant *some* good to my family, you see, so I think that was the standard with them and my family.

Her answers provide insight into the personal and social relationship between the two families and into her recognition of the points of connectedness and distance between them. The way in which she chose to answer the question reflects her feelings about working for the Wallis family and how that helped her accomplish the goals she had set for her own family.

MRS. HUDSON: And in the meantime, they owned a big place up in Connecticut. And they would take my children, and she, the madam, would do for my children just what she did for theirs.

INTERVIEWER: What kinds of things do you think your children learned from that, from the time that they spent with them?

MRS. HUDSON: Well, I think what they learnt from them, to try to live a decent life themselves, and try to make the best out of their life and the best out of the education they had. So I think that's what they got from them.

INTERVIEWER: What would you say you liked most about the work that you did?

MRS. HUDSON: Well, what I liked most about it, the things that I weren't able to go to school to do for my children. I could kinda pattern from the families that I worked for, that I could give my children the best of my abilities. And I think that's the thing I got from them, though they [her children] couldn't become professors, but they could be good in whatever they did.

The warm personal relationship between the two families was based not only on the direct assistance which the Wallises gave Mrs. Hudson, but also on the ways in which she was able to utilize her position in their family to support and sustain her personal goals. Thus, we can understand why she saw work as an ability rather than a burden. Work was a means for attaining her goals; it provided her with the money she needed to be an independent person, and it exposed her and her children to "good" things— values and a style of life which she considered important. To some extent, Lena Hudson found the same things in her work that she found in her church; reinforcement for the standards which she held for her children and for herself.

The women who stressed education for their children and saw their children attain it were most frequently women like Mrs. Hudson who were closely tied to one or two employing families for a long period of time. For the most part, they were the women who had careers in domestic service. However, ties with employers were not crucial even within this small group, because some women said they had received very little support from their employers along these lines. Several women, as indicated above, pointed to a strong emphasis upon education in their families of orientation. Additionally, education as a means of upward mobility is a fundamental element in American social ideology. It appears, therefore, that the importance of the employer–employee relationship was in the support and reinforcement these middle-class families' goals, aspirations, and style of life provided the women. The amount of support varied, of course, with the particular relationship the employee had with her employer's family and the degree of the employer's interest in and commitment to the employee's personal life. On the spectrum presented by the women in this study, Mrs. Hudson's relationship with the Wallis family would be at one end; the relationship between Georgia Sims and the family for whom she worked longest at the other. The following segment of the interview with Mrs. Sims is a good example of a minimally interactive employer–employee relationship:

INTERVIEWER: What were your goals for your children?

MRS. SIMS: Well, to be decent, law-abiding men. That's all.

INTERVIEWER: Do you think there were any similarities between your goals for your children and the goals your employers, the Peterses, had for their children?

MRS. SIMS: Oh, sure! Oh, yes, because I mean you must remember, they had the money; now I didn't have it. Oh, definitely there was different goals between us. [*Note:* Mrs. Sims obviously understood the question to be about *differences* rather than similarities, so the question was asked again.]

INTERVIEWER: Do you think there were any things that were alike in terms of your goals for your children and their goals for their children?

MRS. SIMS: No. Nothing.

INTERVIEWER: Nothing at all?

MRS. SIMS: No.

INTERVIEWER: What kinds of goals did they have for their children?

MRS. SIMS: Oh, I mean education, going on to be, you know, upstanding citizens, and they had the jobs—My children couldn't get up, I mean when they become twenty, twenty-one, they couldn't get up and go out and say, well, I'm gonna get an office job, I'm gonna get this kind of job. No. The best thing they could do is go and be a porter in the subway.

Mrs. Sims was very detached from her occupation. She was not a career household worker. In fact, she described herself as having had very limited contact with her employers, arriving when they were all on their way to work and school and often departing before they returned home. She said that she had no specific child care duties. Thus, her description of the employers' goals for their children is probably more of a projection on her part than it is based on discussion or direct participation in the employers' life.

Two types of child-rearing goals have been identified thus far: goals regarding the child's future position in the society and goals regarding his or her personal development. In addition to these two types of goals, the women aspired to provide their children with some accoutrements of a middle-class lifestyle. Their discussion of these desires often reflects the discrepancies between their lives and those of their employers. Jewell Prieleau describes her employer's children as follows:

Her children always dress nice. Whenever her daughter was going to music school or anyplace, I had to take her in a taxi. Whenever she finish, she had to be picked up. I had to go get her.

In describing her own grandchildren, she said:

I went to three nice department stores and I opened up credit for them so I could send them to school looking nice. I got up early in the morning and sent them off to school. After school I would pick them up in a taxi and bring them here [the job].

Mrs. Prieleau is not the only woman in this study who talked about going into debt to give her children some of the material things that she never had and that were part of her image of a "better life" for her children. Willa Murray told the following story:

I remember when my sons wanted that record player. I said I'm gonna get a record player; I'm gonna do days work. But I had to get AC current for this record player. I called up this lady [her employer] and I said, I'm goin' to Household Finance this morning. If they call you for a reference would you give me some reference. She said, sure. I sat down and the man said come in. He said, Miz Murray, do you have a co-signer. I said, no. He said, well what's your collateral? I said something about the furniture. He said, do you work? I said, yeah, I do days work. He said, days work? You don't have a steady job? I said yes sir, days work. He said, who do you work for? I told him. He said, we'll see what we can do. He gave the hundred and fifty dollars. I came home, phone the electric company, told them they could send the man to put the current in.

In these statements and some of the ones quoted earlier, we begin to see how the employer's style of life influenced these women. However, it cannot be assumed that the women's desires were merely an outgrowth of the employer–employee relationship. The material products which they sought are so widely available in the culture that they are considered general symbols of upward mobility. Upward mobility for their children was the basic goal of most of the women who participated in this study. It was a goal which seems to have existed prior to and apart from their work situation and the values of their employers. Nevertheless, in some cases the women found reinforcement for and regeneration of these goals within the work situation, just as they found supports within their community and family lives.

RAISING THE "WHITE FOLKS' " CHILDREN

The women's discussion of child-rearing strategies, particularly such issues as discipline, exemplify both the class and cultural differences between employer and employee. For private household workers, these differences are expressed within a relationship of inequality. The data collected in this study permitted an examination of employer parent–child interactions as it was perceived and constructed by the household workers. This has benefits as well as liabilities. As outsiders whose child-rearing practices and lifestyle differed from those of the employers, the women in this study provide a particularly revealing picture of parent–child relationships in the employing family. However, they were not mere observers of the process; they participated in it and thereby restructured it. The women's insights, therefore, offer a unique critical perspective that is found only in subordinates' characterizations of their superiors. However, as participants in the process, their observations are limited to the time frame in which they were present and make it virtually impossible to assess the women's impact on the process. Nevertheless, their stories about their own role in rearing the employer's children provide considerable understanding of how they saw their work and, more importantly, how their work affected their own style of parenting. Willa Murray's comments illuminate this:

> Throughout, the people that I worked for taught their children that they can talk back. They would let them [the children] say anything they wanted to say to them. I noticed a lot of times they [the children] would talk back or something and they [the parents] would be hurt. They would say to me, I wish they [the children] wouldn't. I wish they were more like your children. They allowed them to do so much. But they taught them a lot of things. I know one thing, I think I got a lot of things from them. . . . I think I've learnt a lot about [how to do] with my children by letting them do and telling them—like the whites would tell them—that I trust you. I think a lot of Black mothers when we come along, they didn't trust us. They were telling us what we were gonna do. . . . But I think they [whites] talk to their children about what's in life, what's for them, what not to do. And they let them talk, they tell them all the

things that we didn't tell our children. We're beginning to tell our children. . . . The alternative is that I told my children straight, that if a boy and a girl have sexual intercourse—I learned that from the white people—and you don't have anything to protect it, that girl will get a baby. So my children were looking out for that. I learned that from my people. I listened to what they tell [their children].

Talk between parents and children is a dominant theme of Mrs. Murray's comments. She is critical of her employers for permitting their children to "talk back" to them; to question their instructions, to respond impertinently or otherwise mock or demean the parents' authority. Yet, talking *with* the children, reasoning with them, explaining things and hearing their thoughts and opinions on various matters, is behavior which she admired enough to try to emulate. Telling the children that you "trust them" places greater emphasis upon self-direction than upon following orders. Clearly, the line between letting the children talk and permitting them to "talk back" is a difficult one to draw, yet Mrs. Murray draws it in transferring her work-learned behavior to her own child-rearing circumstances.

It should not be surprising that there would be behavioral characteristics which employers would admire in employee children, just as there were traits which Mrs. Murray and others admired in their employers' interactions with their children. In fact, it is striking that each would admire aspects of the other and seek to incorporate them within their own lives while the circumstances that generated those particular patterns were quite different. Nevertheless, reorienting the parent–child relationship in the employer's family was frequently described as a regular part of the worker's child care activity. In fact, the women's discussions of their experiences in caring for their employers' children are variations upon the stories of resistance which characterized their establishing themselves in the employer–employee relationship. Queenie Watkins's description of the following child care incident provides a good example:

> One morning I was feeding Stevie oatmeal and I was eating oatmeal. His uncle, the little girl and I were all sitting at the table together eating. He said, I don't want this and I'm gonna spit it out. I said, you better not, Stevie. With that he just let it all come into my face. I took myself a big mouthful

and let it go right back in his face. He screamed, and his uncle said, what did you do that for? I said, you fight fire with fire. My psychology is to let a child know he can't do to you what you can't do to him. The mother came running. I said, this ends my work here, but she said, just wash Stevie's face. I said, I'm not gonna wash it; let him wash it himself—he wasn't two years old. Finally, I said, I'll take him and wash his face but who's gonna wash my face? His mother started to laugh and said, you're some character. And you know what, he never did that again. He ate his food and I never had to chastise Stevie about anything after that.

Zenobia King told a slightly different story about the way in which she inserted her values into the parent–child relationship of an employing family:

One time the daughter went out and she stayed all day. She didn't tell her mother where she was. And when she came back, her mother jumped on her in a really bad way. She told her she wished she had died out there, etc., etc., and her daughter said if her mother had loved her she would have asked where she was going. So, I separated them. I sent the daughter to one room and the mother to the other and talked to both of them and I brought them back together.

In both of these stories, as in others in this genre, the women see themselves as the instructor of both the children and the parents. They characterize themselves as helping the parent learn how to parent while simultaneously setting rules and regulations as to the kind of treatment they should expect from the children. Queenie Watkins's philosophy of fighting fire with fire was reiterated by Oneida Harris in describing her relations with one of the children whom she cared for:

He was nine years old and he rate me the worst maid they'd ever had because I wouldn't take any of his foolishness. If he kicked me in the shins, I'd kick him back. . . . I said he hasn't any bringing up, and if I stay here he's gonna listen. I said to his mother, if you don't want me, tell me tomorrow and I'll go. So anyway, the next day he would bring me up a little bit; she's the next-to-the-worst maid we ever had. Each week I came up till I was the best one.

As in the stories of resistance, both Queenie Watkins and Oneida Harris depict themselves as setting guidelines for respect from the children in the same way respect was established in the employer–employee relationship. The additional dimension of instructing parents in the ways of handling their children was another recurrent theme in the life histories.

Through these and other similar anecdotes which the women used to describe their participation in caring for their employers' children, they communicate a perception of their employers as uncomfortable in exercising the power associated with the parenting role. To a large degree, they depict their employers as either inconsistent and afraid of their children or ignorant of child-rearing strategies that would develop obedience and respect. The women see this as their forte; in many instances they describe themselves as exercising power on behalf of the parents and teaching the children to obey them and respect their parents. In so doing, they also present themselves as teaching the parents. Willa Murray is keenly aware of the paradoxical nature of this situation when she says: "Now I'm the maid, not the mistress." In the maid–mistress relationship, the latter gives instructions, which the former carries out. In a sense, Willa Murray's story presents a role reversal, one which she finds both surprising and amusing but also appropriate. It is akin to the anecdote in which she described herself telling her employers that they had more education than she did but their behavior was not intelligent. These presentations suggest that despite stereotypic conceptions of the maid–mistress relationship, women in these roles could gain considerable power and influence within a family, particularly where they had worked for a number of years and had considerable responsibility.

The household workers' impact on the parent–child relationship is only one aspect of their child care role. The other, equally important, aspect of this role is their relationship with the children they cared for and the fact, implicit in our earlier discussion, that they describe themselves as surrogate mothers for these children:

There's a long time she [the child] use to thought I was her mamma. She would ask me why is my skin white and yours brown, you my mamma? I tell her I'm not your mamma and I see the hurt coming in her eye. You know, like, she didn't want me to say that. I said there's your mamma in there,

I'm just your nurse. She said no, you my mamma. [Mattie Washington]

I took care of the children. In fact, the children would call me when they had a problem or something, before they would call her [their mother]. [Zenobia King]

He [the boy] looked at me as a mother. When he went away to school he just would not come home if I wasn't there. And even when he was at home, if he was out playing with the boys he'd come in, his mother, grandmother and father would be sitting around, he'd say, where is everybody? His mother would look around and say well if you mean Oneida, I think she's upstairs. Upstairs he'd come. And they couldn't get that. It was sad, you see. They give him everything in the world but love. [Oneida Harris]

I was more like a mother to them, and you see she didn't have to take too much time as a mother should to know her children. They were more used to me because I put them to bed. The only time she would actually be with them was like when I'm off Thursday and on Sundays. They would go out sometimes, but actually I was really the mother because I raised them from little. [Pearl Runner]

Without exception, the women in this study who had child-care responsibilities talked about themselves as being "like a mother" to the employers' children. Their explanations of the development of this kind of relationship tended to follow those of Oneida Harris and Pearl Runner: their employers were frequently unavailable and spent less time with the children than they did. Because they interacted with the children on a daily basis and often had responsibility for their care, discipline, play, and meals, their role was a vital and important one in the eyes of both child and parent. This explains, in part, some of their power in affecting the parent–child relationship, as discussed above. The fact that the women had such an important and pivotal role in the development of the employer's children and at the same time held a job in which they could be replaced gave the entire relationship of parent, child, and housekeeper a particularly intense quality. For the most part, workers developed

their strongest emotional ties to the children in the employing family.

Because the women saw themselves as surrogate mothers, the children whom they cared for could easily become their surrogate children. This is particularly apparent when we compare their comments and discussions about their own and their employers' children. One of the most prevalent patterns was to talk with pride and satisfaction about the accomplishments of their surrogate children. In general, the women would talk about how frequently they heard from these children and whether they got cards, letters, or money at Mother's Day or Christmas. In addition, they would describe the (now grown) children's occupations and family and, if they had pictures available, they would show them to me. This type of commentary provided an interesting parallel to their discussions of their own children. But even more important, it was designed to communicate the closeness that they felt existed between them and the children they had raised; closeness which was maintained over a number of years even after the children were grown.

Surrogate mothering, as pointed out in Opallou Tucker's case study, had the prospect of tying the worker into the emotional life of the employing family. For the women who lived outside the employer's household and were actively engaged in rearing their own children and caring for their own families, as were most of the women in this study, the prospect was minimized. However, for a woman like Mattie Washington, who lived in for most of the thirty years that she worked for one family, the potential for becoming enveloped in their life, at the expense of her own, was much greater.

In most instances, the women described themselves as caretakers, playmates, disciplinarians, confidantes, and friends of the employer's children. Nevertheless, it is clear from their discussions that in most cases the real ties of affection between themselves and their employer came through the children.

The children, therefore, provided the ties that bound the women to their employers as well as the mark of their difference. The role of surrogate mother allowed the women to cross these barriers and, for a fleeting moment, express their love and concern for a child without regard to the obstacles that lay ahead. Also, because most young children readily return love that is freely given and are open and accepting of people without regard to status factors that have meaning for their parents, the workers probably felt that they were treated with greater equality and more genuine acceptance by the children of the household.

NOTES

1. There is a very limited body of literature directly focused upon Black women in domestic service in the United States. Many of these studies are confined to the southern experience. Among the most important containing data on Black women in northern cities are Haynes (1923), Eaton (1967), and Chaplin (1964). Some discussion of the subject was also found in community studies, particularly those conducted before World War II (Drake & Cayton, 1945; Ovington, 1969). Labor studies provided a third source of data (among these were Greene & Woodson, 1930, and Haynes, 1912).

2. This discussion is largely drawn from a paper by Dill and Joselin (1977).

3. The names used for the participants in the study are fictitious.

REFERENCES

Chaplin, D. 1964."Domestic service and the Negro." In A. Shostak and W. Gamberg, eds., *Blue Collar World*. Englewood Cliffs, N.J.: Prentice-Hall.

Childress, A. 1956. *Like One of the Family*. Brooklyn: Independence Publishers.

Denzin, N. K. 1970. *The Research Act*. Chicago: AVC.

Dill, B. T., & Joselin, D. 1977. "The limit of quantitative methods: The need of life histories." Paper presented at the Society for the Study of Social Problems Annual Meetings, Chicago.

Drake, S.C., & Cayton, H. 1945. *Black Metropolis*. New York: Harper & Row.

DuBois, W. E. B. 1920. *Darkwater*. New York: Harcourt Brace.

Eaton, I. 1967. "Negro domestic service in Seventh Ward Philadelphia." In W. E. B. DuBois, *The Philadelphia Negro*. New York: Schocken.

Greene, L. J., & Wooden, C. G. 1930. *The Negro Wage Earner*. Washington, D.C.: Association for the Study of Negro Life and History.

Haynes, G. 1912. *The Negro at Work in New York City: A Study in Economic Progress*. New York: Longmans.

Haynes, G. 1923. "Negroes in domestic service in the United States." *Journal of Negro History* 8:384–442.

Ovington, M. W. 1969. *Half a Man*. New York: Schocken.

READING 15

Girls and Boys Together . . . But Mostly Apart: Gender Arrangements in Elementary Schools

Barrie Thorne

Throughout the years of elementary school, children's friendships and casual encounters are strongly separated by sex. Sex segregation among children, which starts in preschool and is well established by middle childhood, has been amply documented in studies of children's groups and friendships (e.g., Eder & Hallinan, 1978; Schofield, 1981) and is immediately visible in elementary school settings. When children choose seats in classrooms or the cafeteria, or get into line, they frequently arrange themselves in same-sex clusters. At lunchtime, they talk matter-of-factly about "girls' tables" and "boys' tables." Playgrounds have gendered turfs, with some areas and activities, such as large playing fields and basketball courts, controlled mainly by boys, and others—smaller enclaves like jungle-gym areas and concrete spaces for hopscotch or jump rope—more often controlled by girls. Sex segregation is so common in elementary schools that it is meaningful to speak of separate girls' and boys' worlds.

Studies of gender and children's social relations have mostly followed this "two worlds" model, separately describing and comparing the subcultures of girls and boys (e.g., Lever, 1976; Maltz & Borker, 1983). In brief summary: Boys tend to interact in larger, more age-heterogeneous groups (Lever, 1976; Waldrop & Halverson, 1975; Eder & Hallinan, 1978). They engage in more rough and tumble play and physical fighting (Maccoby & Jacklin, 1974). Organized sports are both a central activity and a major metaphor in boys' subcultures; they use the language of "teams" even when not engaged in sports, and they often construct interaction in the form of contests. The shifting hierarchies of boys' groups (Savin-Williams, 1976) are evident in their more frequent use of direct commands, insults, and challenges (Goodwin, 1980).

Fewer studies have been done of girls' groups (Foot, Chapman, & Smith, 1980; McRobbie & Garber, 1975), and—perhaps because categories for description and analysis have come more from male than female experience—researchers have had difficulty seeing and analyzing girls' social relations. Recent work has begun to correct this skew. In middle childhood, girls' worlds are less public than those of boys; girls more often interact in private places and in smaller groups or friendship pairs (Eder & Hallinan, 1978; Waldrop & Halverson, 1975). Their play is more cooperative and turn-taking (Lever, 1976). Girls have more intense and exclusive friendships, which take shape around keeping and telling secrets, shifting alliances, and indirect ways of expressing disagreement (Goodwin, 1980; Lever, 1976; Maltz & Borker, 1983). Instead of direct commands, girls more often use directives which merge speaker and hearer, e.g., "let's" or "we gotta" (Goodwin, 1980).

Although much can be learned by comparing the social organization and subcultures of boys' and of girls' groups, the separate-worlds approach has eclipsed full, contextual understanding of gender and social relations among children. The separate-worlds model essentially involves a search for group sex differences and shares the limitations of individual sex difference research. Differences tend to be exaggerated and similarities ignored, with little theoretical attention to the integration of similarity and difference (Unger, 1979). Statistical findings of difference are often portrayed as dichotomous, neglecting the considerable individual variation that exists; for example, not all boys fight, and some have intense and exclusive friendships. The sex difference approach tends to abstract gender from its social context, to assume that males and females are qualitatively and permanently different (with differences perhaps unfolding through separate developmental lines). These assumptions mask the possibility that gender arrangements and patterns of similarity and difference may vary by situation, race, social class, region, or subculture.

Sex segregation is far from total, and is a more complex and dynamic process than the portrayal of separate worlds reveals. Erving Goffman (1977) has observed that sex segregation has a "with-then apart" structure; the sexes segregate periodically, with separate spaces, rituals, groups, but they also come together and are, in crucial ways, part of the same world. This is certainly true in the social environment of elementary schools. Although girls and boys do interact as boundaried collectivities—an image suggested by the separate-worlds approach—there are other occasions when they work or play in relaxed and integrated ways. Gender is less central to the organization and meaning of some situations than others. In short, sex segregation is not static, but is a variable and complicated process.

To gain an understanding of gender which can encompass both the "with" and the "apart" of sex segregation, analysis should start not with the individual, nor with a search for sex differences, but with social relationships. Gender should be conceptualized as a system of relationships rather than as an immutable and dichotomous given. Taking this approach, I have organized my research on gender and children's social relations around questions like the following: How and when does gender enter into group formation? In a given situation, how is gender made more or less salient or infused with particular meanings? By what rituals, processes, and forms of social organization and conflict do "with–then apart" rhythms get enacted? How are these processes affected by the organization of institutions (e.g., different types of schools, neighborhoods, or summer camps), varied settings (e.g., the constraints and possibilities governing interaction on playgrounds vs. classrooms), and particular encounters?

METHODS AND SOURCES OF DATA

This study is based on two periods of participant observation. In 1976–1977 I observed for eight months in a largely working-class elementary school in California, a school with 8 percent Black and 12 percent Chicana/o students. In 1980 I did fieldwork for three months in a Michigan elementary school of similar size (around 400 students), social class, and racial composition. I observed in several classrooms—a kindergarten, a second grade, and a combined fourth–fifth grade—and in school hallways, cafeterias, and playgrounds. I set out to follow the round of the school day as children experience it, recording their interactions with one another, and with adults, in varied settings.

Participant observation involves gaining access to everyday, "naturalistic" settings and taking systematic notes over an extended period of time. Rather than starting with preset categories for recording, or with fixed hypotheses for testing, participant observers record detail in ways which maximize opportunities for discovery. Through continuous interaction between observation and analysis, "grounded theory" is developed (Glaser & Strauss, 1967).

The distinctive logic and discipline of this mode of inquiry emerges from: (1) theoretical sampling—being relatively systematic in the choice of where and whom to observe in order to maximize knowledge relevant to categories and analysis which are being developed; and (2) comparing all relevant data on a given point in order to modify emerging propositions to take account of discrepant cases (Katz, 1983). Participant observation is a flexible, open-ended and inductive method, designed to understand behavior within, rather than stripped from, social context. It provides richly detailed information anchored in everyday meanings and experience.

DAILY PROCESSES OF SEX SEGREGATION

Sex segregation should be understood not as a given, but as the result of deliberate activity. The outcome is dramatically visible when there are separate girls' and boys' tables in school lunchrooms or sex-separated groups on playgrounds. But in the same lunchroom one can also find tables where girls and boys eat and talk together, and in some playground activities the sexes mix. By what processes do girls and boys separate into gender-defined and relatively boundaried collectivities? And in what contexts, and through what processes, do boys and girls interact in less gender-divided ways?

In the school settings I observed, much segregation happened with no mention of gender. Gender was implicit in the contours of friendship, shared interest, and perceived risk which came into play when children chose companions—in their prior planning, invitations, seeking of access, saving of places, denials of entry, and allowing or protesting of "cuts" by those who violated the rules for lining up. Sometimes children formed mixed-sex groups for play, eating, talking, working on a classroom project, or moving through space. When adults or children explicitly invoked gender—and this was nearly always in ways which separated girls and boys—boundaries were heightened and mixed-sex interaction became an explicit arena of risk.

In the schools I studied, the physical space and curricula were not formally divided by sex, as they have been in the history of elementary schooling (a history evident in separate entrances to old school buildings, where the words "Boys" and "Girls" are permanently etched in concrete). Nevertheless, gender was a visible marker in the adult-organized school day. In both schools, when the public address system sounded, the principal inevitably opened with: "Boys and girls. . . .," and in addressing clusters of children, teachers and aides regularly used gender terms ("Heads down, girls"; "The girls are ready and the boys aren't"). These forms of address made gender visible and salient, conveying an assumption that the sexes are separate social groups.

Teachers and aides sometimes drew upon gender as a basis for sorting children and organizing activities. Gender is an embodied and visual social category which roughly divides the population in half, and the separation of girls and boys permeates the history and lore of schools and playgrounds. In both schools—although through awareness of Title IX, many teachers had changed this practice—one could see separate girls' and boys' lines moving, like caterpillars, through the school halls. In the fourth–fifth-grade classroom the teacher frequently pitted girls against boys for spelling and math contests. On the playground in the Michigan school, aides regarded the space close to the building as girls' territory, and the playing fields "out there" as boys' territory. They sometimes shooed children of the other sex away from those spaces, especially boys who ventured near the girls' area and seemed to have teasing in mind.

In organizing their activities, both within and apart from the surveillance of adults, children also explicitly invoked gender. During my fieldwork in the Michigan school, I kept daily records of who sat where in the lunchroom. The amount of sex segregation varied: it was least at the first-grade tables and almost total among sixth-graders. There was also variation from classroom to classroom within a given age and from day to day. Actions like the following heightened the gender divide: In the lunchroom, when the two second-grade tables were filling, a high-status boy walked by the inside table, which had a scattering of both boys and girls, and said loudly, "Oooo, too many girls," as he headed for a seat at the far table. The boys at the inside table picked up their trays and moved, and no other boys sat at the inside table, which the pronouncement had effectively made taboo. In the end, that day (which was not the case every day), girls and boys ate at separate tables.

Eating and walking are not sex-typed activities, yet in forming groups in lunchrooms and hallways children often separated by sex. Sex segregation assumed added dimensions on the playground, where spaces, equipment, and activities were infused with gender meanings. My inventories of activities and groupings on the playground showed similar patterns in both schools: boys controlled the large fixed spaces designated for team sports (baseball diamonds, grassy fields used for football or soccer); girls more often played closer to the building, doing tricks on the monkey bars (which, for sixth-graders, became an area for sitting and talking) and using cement areas for jump rope, hopscotch, and group games like four-square. (Lever, 1976, provides a good analysis of sex-divided play.) Girls and boys most often played together in kickball, and in group (rather than team) games like four-square, dodgeball, and handball. When children used gender to exclude others from play, they often drew upon beliefs connecting boys to some activities and girls to others: A first-grade boy avidly watched an all-female game of jump rope. When the girls began to shift positions, he recognized a means of access to the play and he offered, "I'll swing it." A girl

responded, "No way, you don't know how to do it, to swing it. You gotta be a girl." He left without protest. Although children sometimes ignored pronouncements about what each sex could or could not do, I never heard them directly challenge such claims.

When children had explicitly defined an activity or a group as gendered, those who crossed the boundary—especially boys who moved into female-marked space—risked being teased. ("Look! Mike's in the girls' line!"; "That's a girl over there," a girl said loudly, pointing to a boy sitting at an otherwise all-female table in the lunchroom.) Children, and occasionally adults, used teasing—especially the tease of "liking" someone of the other sex, or of "being" that sex by virtue of being in their midst—to police gender boundaries. Much of the teasing drew upon heterosexual romantic definitions, making cross-sex interaction risky and increasing social distance between boys and girls.

RELATIONSHIPS BETWEEN THE SEXES

Because I have emphasized the "apart" and ignored the occasions of "with," this analysis of sex segregation falsely implies that there is little contact between girls and boys in daily school life. In fact, relationships between girls and boys—which should be studied as fully as, and in connection with, same-sex relationships—are of several kinds:

1. "Borderwork," or forms of cross-sex interaction which are based upon and reaffirm boundaries and asymmetries between girls' and boys' groups.
2. Interactions which are infused with heterosexual meanings.
3. Occasions where individuals cross gender boundaries to participate in the world of the other sex.
4. Situations where gender is muted in salience, with girls and boys interacting in more relaxed ways.

Borderwork

In elementary school settings, boys' and girls' groups are sometimes spatially set apart. Same-sex groups sometimes claim fixed territories such as the basketball court, the bars, or specific lunchroom tables. However, in the crowded, multifocused, and adult-controlled environment of the school, groups form and disperse at a rapid rate and can never stay totally apart. Contact between girls and boys sometimes lessens sex segregation, but gender-defined groups also come together in ways which emphasize their boundaries.

"Borderwork" refers to interaction across, yet based upon and even strengthening, gender boundaries. I have drawn this notion from Fredrik Barth's (1969) analysis of social relations which are maintained across ethnic boundaries without diminishing dichotomized ethnic status.[1] His focus is on more macro, ecological arrangements; mine is on face-to-face behavior. But the insight is similar: groups may interact in ways which strengthen their borders, and the maintenance of ethnic (or gender) groups can best be understood by examining the boundary that defines the groups, "not the cultural stuff that it encloses" (Barth, 1969:15). In elementary schools there are several types of borderwork: contests or games where gender-defined teams compete; cross-sex rituals of chasing and pollution; and group invasions. These interactions are asymmetrical, challenging the separate-but-parallel model of "two worlds."

Contests   Boys and girls are sometimes pitted against each other in classroom competitions and playground games. The fourth–fifth-grade classroom had a boys' side and a girls' side, an arrangement that reemerged each time the teacher asked children to choose their own desks. Although there was some within-sex shuffling, the result was always a spatial moiety system— boys on the left, girls on the right—with the exception of one girl (the "tomboy" whom I'll describe later), who twice chose a desk with the boys and once with the girls. Drawing upon and reinforcing the children's self-segregation, the teacher often pitted the boys against the girls in spelling and math competitions, events marked by cross-sex antagonism and within-sex solidarity. The teacher introduced a math game; she would write addition and subtraction problems on the board, and a member of each team would race to be the first to write the correct answer. She wrote two scorekeeping columns on the board: "Beastly Boys". . . . "Gossipy Girls." The boys yelled out, as several girls laughed, "Noisy girls! Gruesome girls!" The girls sat in a row on top of their desks; sometimes they moved collectively, pushing their hips or whispering "Pass it on." The boys stood along the wall, some reclining against desks. When members of either group came back victorious from the front of

the room, they would do the "giving five" hand-slapping ritual with their team members.

On the playground a team of girls occasionally played a team of boys, usually in kickball or team two-square. Sometimes these games proceeded matter-of-factly, but if gender became the explicit basis of team solidarity, the interaction changed, becoming more antagonistic and unstable. Two fifth-grade girls played against two fifth-grade boys in a team game of two-square. The game proceeded at an even pace until an argument ensued about whether the ball was out or on the line. Karen, who had hit the ball, became annoyed, flashed her middle finger at the other team, and called to a passing girl to join their side. The boys then called out to other boys, and cheered as several arrived to play. "We got five and you got three!" Jack yelled. The game continued, with the girls yelling, "Bratty boys! Sissy boys!" and the boys making noises—"Weee haw," "Ha-ha-ha"—as they played.

Chasing   Cross-sex chasing dramatically affirms boundaries between girls and boys. The basic elements of chase and elude, capture and rescue (Sutton-Smith, 1971) are found in various kinds of tag with formal rules and in informal episodes of chasing which punctuate life on playgrounds. These episodes begin with a provocation (taunts like "You can't get me!" or "Slobber monster!"; bodily pokes or the grabbing of possessions). A provocation may be ignored or responded to by chasing. Chaser and chased may then alternate roles. In an ethnographic study of chase sequences on a school playground, Christine Finnan (1982) observes that chases vary in number of chasers to chased (e.g., one chasing one or five chasing two); form of provocation (a taunt or a poke); outcome (an episode may end when the chased outdistances the chaser, or with a brief touch, being wrestled to the ground, or the recapturing of a hat or a ball); and use of space (there may or may not be safety zones).

Like Finnan (1982) and Sluckin (1981), who studied a playground in England, I found that chasing has a gendered structure. Boys frequently chase one another, an activity which often ends in wrestling and mock fights. When girls chase girls, they are usually less physically aggressive; they less often, for example, wrestle one another to the ground.

Cross-sex chasing is set apart by special names— "girls chase the boys"; "boys chase the girls"; "the chase"; "chasers"; "chase and kiss"; "kiss chase"; "kissers and chasers"; "kiss or kill"—and by children's animated talk about the activity. The names vary by region and school, but contain both gender and sexual meanings (this form of play is mentioned, but only briefly analyzed, in Finnan, 1982; Sluckin, 1981; Parrott, 1972; and Borman, 1979).

In "boys chase the girls" and "girls chase the boys" (the names most frequently used in both the California and Michigan schools) boys and girls become, by definition, separate teams. Gender terms override individual identities, especially for the other team ("Help, a girl's chasin' me!"; "C'mon, Sarah, let's get that boy"; "Tony, help save me from the girls"). Individuals may also grab someone of their sex and turn them over to the opposing team: Ryan grabbed Billy from behind, wrestling him to the ground. "Hey, girls, get 'im," Ryan called.

Boys more often mix episodes of cross-sex with same-sex chasing. Girls more often have safety zones, places like the girls' restroom or an area by the school wall, where they retreat to rest and talk (sometimes in animated postmortems) before new episodes of cross-sex chasing begin.

Early in the fall in the Michigan school, where chasing was especially prevalent, I watched a second-grade boy teach a kindergarten girl how to chase. He slowly ran backwards, beckoning her to pursue him, as he called, "Help, a girl's after me." In the early grades chasing mixes with fantasy play, e.g., a first-grade boy who played "sea monster," his arms out-flung and his voice growling, as he chased a group of girls. By third grade, stylized gestures—exaggerated stalking motions, screams (which only girls do), and karate kicks—accompany scenes of chasing.

Names like "chase and kiss" mark the sexual meanings of cross-sex chasing, a theme I return to later. The threat of kissing—most often girls threatening to kiss boys—is a ritualized form of provocation. Cross-sex chasing among sixth-graders involves elaborate patterns of touch and touch avoidance, which adults see as sexual. The principal told the sixth-graders in the Michigan school that they were not to play "pom-pom," a complicated chasing game, because it entailed "inappropriate touch."

Rituals of Pollution   Cross-sex chasing is sometimes entwined with rituals of pollution, as in "cooties," where specific individuals or groups are treated as contaminating or carrying "germs." Children have rituals for transferring cooties (usually touching someone else and shouting, "You've got cooties!"), for

immunization (e.g., writing "CV" for "cootie vaccination" on their arms), and for eliminating cooties (e.g., saying "no gives" or using "cootie catchers" made of folded paper) (described in Knapp & Knapp, 1976). While girls may give cooties to girls, boys do not generally give cooties to one another (Samuelson, 1980).

In cross-sex play, either girls or boys may be defined as having cooties, which they transfer through chasing and touching. Girls give cooties to boys more often than vice versa. In Michigan, one version of cooties is called "girl stain"; the fourth-graders whom Karkau (1973) describes used the phrase "girl touch." "Cootie queens" or "cootie girls" (there are no "kings" or "boys") are female pariahs, the ultimate school untouchables, seen as contaminating not only by virtue of gender, but also through some added stigma such as being overweight or poor.[2] That girls are seen as more polluting than boys is a significant asymmetry, which echoes cross-cultural patterns, although in other cultures female pollution is generally connected to menstruation and not applied to prepubertal girls.

Invasions   Playground invasions are another asymmetric form of borderwork. On a few occasions I saw girls invade and disrupt an all-male game, most memorably a group of tall sixth-grade girls who ran onto the playing field and grabbed a football which was in play. The boys were surprised and frustrated, and, unusual for boys this old, finally tattled to the aide. But in the majority of cases, boys disrupt girls' activities rather than vice versa. Boys grab the ball from girls playing four-square, stick feet into a jump-rope and stop an ongoing game, and dash through the area of the bars where girls are taking turns performing, sending the rings flying. Sometimes boys ask to join a girls' game and then, after a short period of seemingly earnest play, disrupt the game. Two second-grade boys begged to "twirl" the jump rope for a group of second-grade girls who had been jumping for some time. The girls agreed, and the boys began to twirl. Soon, without announcement, the boys changed from "seashells, cockle bells" to "hot peppers" (spinning the rope very fast), and tangled the jumper in the rope. The boys ran away laughing.

Boys disrupt girls' play so often that girls have developed almost ritualized responses: they guard their ongoing play, chase boys away, and tattle to the aides. In a playground cycle which enhances sex segregation, aides who try to spot potential trouble before it occurs sometimes shoo boys away from areas where girls are playing. Aides do not anticipate trouble from girls who seek to join groups of boys, with the exception of girls intent on provoking a chase sequence. And indeed, if they seek access to a boys' game, girls usually play with boys in earnest rather than breaking up the game.

A close look at the organization of borderwork—or boundaried interactions between the sexes—shows that the worlds of boys and girls may be separate, but they are not parallel, nor are they equal. The worlds of girls and boys articulate in several asymmetric ways:

1. On the playground, boys control as much as ten times more space than girls, when one adds up the area of large playing fields and compares it with the much smaller areas where girls predominate. Girls, who play closer to the building, are more often watched over and protected by the adult aides.

2. Boys invade all-female games and scenes of play much more than girls invade boys'. This, and boys' greater control of space, correspond with other findings about the organization of gender, and inequality, in our society: compared with men and boys, women and girls take up less space, and their space and talk are more often violated and interrupted (Greif, 1982; Henley, 1977; West & Zimmerman, 1983).

3. Although individual boys are occasionally treated as contaminating (e.g., a third-grade boy who both boys and girls said was "stinky" and "smelled like pee"), girls are more often defined as polluting. This pattern ties to themes that I discuss later: it is more taboo for a boy to play with (as opposed to invade) girls, and girls are more sexually defined than boys.

A look at the boundaries between the separated worlds of girls and boys illuminates within-sex hierarchies of status and control. For example, in the sex-divided seating in the fourth–fifth-grade classroom, several boys recurringly sat near "female space": their desks were at the gender divide in the classroom, and they were more likely than other boys to sit at a predominantly female table in the lunchroom. These boys—two nonbilingual Chicanos and an overweight "loner" boy who was afraid of sports—were at the bottom of the male hierarchy. Gender is sometimes used as a metaphor for male hierarchies; the inferior status of boys at the bottom is conveyed by calling them "girls." Seven boys and one girl were playing basketball. Two younger boys came over and asked to play. While the girl silently stood, fully accepted in the company of players, one of the older boys disparagingly said to the younger boys, "You girls can't play."[3]

In contrast, the girls who more often travel in the boys' world, sitting with groups of boys in the lunchroom or playing basketball, soccer, and baseball with them, are not stigmatized. Some have fairly high status with other girls. The worlds of girls and boys are asymmetrically arranged, and spatial patterns map out interacting forms of inequality.

Heterosexual Meanings

The organization and meanings of gender (the social categories "woman/man," "girl/boy") and of sexuality vary cross-culturally (Ortner & Whitehead, 1981)—and, in our society, across the life course. Harriet Whitehead (1981) observed that in our (Western) gender system, and that of many traditional North American Indian cultures, one's choice of a sexual object, occupation, and dress and demeanor are closely associated with gender. However, the "center of gravity" differs in the two gender systems. For Indians, occupational pursuits provide the primary imagery of gender; dress and demeanor are secondary, and sexuality is least important. In our system, at least for adults, the order is reversed: heterosexuality is central to our definitions of "man" and "woman" ("masculinity/femininity") and the relationships that obtain between them, whereas occupation and dress/demeanor are secondary.

Whereas erotic orientation and gender are closely linked in our definitions of adults, we define children as relatively asexual. Activities and dress/demeanor are more important than sexuality in the cultural meanings of "girl" and "boy." Children are less heterosexually defined than adults, and we have nonsexual imagery for relations between girls and boys. However, both children and adults sometimes use heterosexual language—"crushes," "like," "goin' with," "girlfriends," and "boyfriends"—to define cross-sex relationships. This language increases through the years of elementary school; the shift to adolescence consolidates a gender system organized around the institution of heterosexuality.

In everyday life in the schools, heterosexual and romantic meanings infuse some ritualized forms of interaction between groups of boys and girls (e.g., "chase and kiss") and help maintain sex segregation. "Jimmy likes Beth" or "Beth likes Jimmy" is a major form of teasing, which a child risks in choosing to sit by or walk with someone of the other sex. The structure of teasing and children's sparse vocabulary for relationships between girls and boys are evident in the following conversation, which I had with a group of third-grade girls in the lunchroom. Susan asked me what I was doing, and I said I was observing the things children do and play. Nicole volunteered, "I like running, boys chase all the girls. See Tim over there? Judy chases him all around the school. She likes him." Judy, sitting across the table, quickly responded, "I hate him. I like him for a friend." "Tim loves Judy," Nicole said in a loud, singsong voice.

In the younger grades, the culture and lore of girls contain more heterosexual romantic themes than those of boys. In Michigan, the first-grade girls often jumped rope to a rhyme which began: "Down in the valley where the green grass grows, there sat Cindy [name of jumper], as sweet as a rose. She sat, she sat, she sat so sweet. Along came Jason and kissed her on the cheek. First comes love, then comes marriage, then along comes Cindy with a baby carriage." Before a girl took her turn at jumping, the chanters asked her, "Who do you want to be your boyfriend?" The jumper always proffered a name, which was accepted matter-of-factly. In chasing, a girl's kiss carried greater threat than a boy's kiss; "girl touch," when defined as contaminating, had sexual connotations. In short, starting at an early age, girls are more sexually defined than boys.

Through the years of elementary school, and increasing with age, the idiom of heterosexuality helps maintain the gender divide. Cross-sex interactions, especially when children initiate them, are fraught with the risk of being teased about "liking" someone of the other sex. I learned of several close cross-sex friendships, formed and maintained in neighborhoods and church, which went underground during the school day.

By the fifth grade a few children began to affirm, rather than avoid, the charge of having a girlfriend or a boyfriend; they introduced the heterosexual courtship rituals of adolescence. In the lunchroom in the Michigan school, as the tables were forming, a high-status fifth-grade boy called out from his seat at the table: "I want Trish to sit by me." Trish came over, and almost like a king and queen, they sat at the gen-der divide—a row of girls down the table on her side, a row of boys on his. In this situation, which inverted earlier forms, it was not a loss but a gain in status to publicly choose a companion of the other sex. By affirming his choice, the boy became unteasable (note the familiar asymmetry of heterosexual courtship rituals: the male initiates). This incident signals a temporal shift in arrangements of sex and gender.

Traveling in the World of the Other Sex

Contests, invasions, chasing, and heterosexually defined encounters are based upon and reaffirm boundaries between girls and boys. In another type of cross-sex interaction, individuals (or sometimes pairs) cross gender boundaries, seeking acceptance in a group of the other sex. Nearly all the cases I saw of this were tomboys—girls who played organized sports and frequently sat with boys in the cafeteria or classroom. If these girls were skilled at activities central in the boys' world, especially games like soccer, baseball, and basketball, they were pretty much accepted as participants.

Being a tomboy is a matter of degree. Some girls seek access to boys' groups but are excluded; other girls limit their "crossing" to specific sports. Only a few—such as the tomboy I mentioned earlier, who chose a seat with the boys in the sex-divided fourth–fifth grade—participate fully in the boys' world. That particular girl was skilled at the various organized sports which boys played in different seasons of the year. She was also adept at physical fighting and at using the forms of arguing, insult, teasing, naming, and sports-talk of the boys' subculture. She was the only Black child in her classroom, in a school with only 8 percent Black students; overall that token status, along with unusual athletic and verbal skills, may have contributed to her ability to move back and forth across the gender divide. Her unique position in the children's world was widely recognized in the school. Several times, the teacher said to me, "She thinks she's a boy."

I observed only one boy in the upper grades (a fourth-grader) who regularly played with all-female groups, as opposed to "playing at" girls' games and seeking to disrupt them. He frequently played jump rope and took turns with girls doing tricks on the bars, using the small gestures—for example, a helpful push on the heel of a girl who needed momentum to turn her body around the bar—which mark skillful and earnest participation. Although I never saw him play in other than an earnest spirit, the girls often chased him away from their games, and both girls and boys teased him. The fact that girls seek and have more access to boys' worlds than vice versa, and the fact that girls who travel with the other sex are less stigmatized for it, are obvious asymmetries, tied to the asymmetries previously discussed.

Relaxed Cross-Sex Interactions

Relationships between boys and girls are not always marked by strong boundaries, heterosexual definitions, or interacting on the terms and turfs of the other sex. On some occasions girls and boys interact in relatively comfortable ways. Gender is not strongly salient nor explicitly invoked, and girls and boys are not organized into boundaried collectivities. These "with" occasions have been neglected by those studying gender and children's relationships, who have emphasized either the model of separate worlds (with little attention to their articulation) or heterosexual forms of contact.

Occasions when boys and girls interact without strain, when gender wanes rather than waxes in importance, frequently have one or more of the following characteristics:

1. The situations are organized around an absorbing task, such as a group art project or creating a radio show, which encourages cooperation and lessens attention to gender. This pattern accords with other studies finding that cooperative activities reduce group antagonism (e.g., Sherif & Sherif, 1953, who studied divisions between boys in a summer camp; and Aronson et al., 1978, who used cooperative activities to lessen racial divisions in a classroom).

2. Gender is less prominent when children are not responsible for the formation of the group. Mixed-sex play is less frequent in games like football, which require the choosing of teams, and more frequent in games like handball or dodgeball, which individuals can join simply by getting into a line or a circle. When adults organize mixed-sex encounters—which they frequently do in the classroom and in physical education periods on the playground—they legitimize cross-sex contact.

This removes the risk of being teased for choosing to be with the other sex.

3. There is more extensive and relaxed cross-sex interaction when principles of grouping other than gender are explicitly invoked—for example, counting off to form teams for spelling or kickball, dividing lines by hot lunch or cold lunch, or organizing a work group on the basis of interests or reading ability.

4. Girls and boys may interact more readily in less public and crowded settings. Neighborhood play, depending on demography, is more often sex- and age-integrated than play at school, partly because with fewer numbers, one may have to resort to an array of social categories to find play partners or to constitute a game. And in less crowded environments there are fewer potential witnesses to "make something of it" if girls and boys play together.

Relaxed interactions between girls and boys often depend on adults to set up and legitimize the contact.[4] Perhaps because of this contingency—and the other, distancing patterns which permeate relations between girls and boys—the easeful moments of interaction rarely build to close friendship. Schofield (1981) makes a similar observation about gender and racial barriers to friendship in a junior high school.

IMPLICATIONS FOR DEVELOPMENT

I have located social relations within an essentially spatial framework, emphasizing the organization of children's play, work, and other activities within specific settings and in one type of institution, the school. In contrast, frameworks of child development rely upon temporal metaphors, using images of growth and transformation over time. Taken alone, both spatial and temporal frameworks have shortcomings; fitted together, they may be mutually correcting.

Those interested in gender and development have relied upon conceptualizations of "sex-role socialization" and "sex differences." Sexuality and gender, I have argued, are more situated and fluid than these individualist and intrinsic models imply. Sex and gender are differently organized and defined across situations, even within the same institution. This situational variation (e.g., in the extent to which an encounter heightens or lessens gender boundaries, or is infused with sexual meanings) shapes and constrains individual behavior. Features which a developmental perspective might attribute to individuals and understand as relatively internal attributes unfolding over time may, in fact, be highly dependent on context. For example, children's avoidance of cross-sex friendship may be attributed to individual gender development in middle childhood. But attention to varied situations may show that this avoidance is contingent on group size, activity, adult behavior, collective meanings, and the risk of being teased.

A focus on social organization and situation draws attention to children's experiences in the present. This helps correct a model like "sex-role socialization," which casts the present under the shadow of the future, or presumed "endpoints" (Speier, 1976). A situated analysis of arrangements of sex and gender among those of different ages may point to crucial disjunctions in the life course. In the fourth and fifth grades, culturally defined heterosexual rituals ("goin' with") begin to suppress the presence and visibility of other types of interaction between girls and boys, such as nonsexualized and comfortable interaction and traveling in the world of the other sex. As "boyfriend/girlfriend" definitions spread, the fifth-grade tomboy I described had to work to sustain "buddy" relationships with boys. Adult women who were tomboys often speak of early adolescence as a painful time when they were pushed away from participation in boys' activities. Other adult women speak of the loss of intense, even erotic ties with other girls when they entered puberty and the rituals of dating, that is, when they became absorbed into the situation of heterosexuality (Rich, 1980). When Lever (1976) describes best-friend relationships among fifth-grade girls as preparation for dating, she imposes heterosexual ideologies onto a present which should be understood on its own terms.

As heterosexual encounters assume more importance, they may alter relations in same-sex groups. For example, Schofield (1981) reports that for sixth- and seventh-grade children in a middle school, the popularity of girls with other girls was affected by their popularity with boys, while boys' status with other boys did not depend on their relations with girls. This is an asymmetry familiar from the adult world; men's relationships with one another are defined through varied activities (occupations, sports), while relationships among women—and their public status—are more influenced by their connections to individual men.

A full understanding of gender and social relations should encompass cross-sex as well as within-sex

interactions. "Borderwork" helps maintain separate, gender-linked subcultures, which, as those interested in development have begun to suggest, may result in different milieux for learning. Daniel Maltz and Ruth Borker (1983), for example, argue that because of different interactions within girls' and boys' groups, the sexes learn different rules for creating and interpreting friendly conversation, rules which carry into adulthood and help account for miscommunication between men and women. Carol Gilligan (1982) fits research on the different worlds of girls and boys into a theory of sex differences in moral development. Girls develop a style of reasoning, she argues, which is more personal and relational; boys develop a style which is more positional, based on separateness. Eleanor Maccoby (1982), also following the insight that because of sex segregation, girls and boys grow up in different environments, suggests implications for gender-differentiated prosocial and antisocial behavior.

This separate-worlds approach, as I have illustrated, also has limitations. The occasions when the sexes are together should also be studied, and understood as contexts for experience and learning. For example, asymmetries in cross-sex relationships convey a series of messages: that boys are more entitled to space and to the nonreciprocal right of interrupting or invading the activities of the other sex; that girls are more in need of adult protection, lower in status, more defined by sexuality, and may even be polluting. Different types of cross-sex interaction—relaxed, boundaried, sexualized, or taking place on the terms of the other sex—provide different contexts for development.

By mapping the array of relationships between and within the sexes, one adds complexity to the overly static and dichotomous imagery of separate worlds. Individual experiences vary, with implications for development. Some children prefer same-sex groupings; some are more likely to cross the gender boundary and participate in the world of the other sex; some children (e.g., girls and boys who frequently play "chase and kiss") invoke heterosexual meanings, while others avoid them.

Finally, after charting the terrain of relationships, one can trace their development over time. For example, age variation in the content and form of borderwork, or of cross- and same-sex touch, may be related to differing cognitive, social, emotional, or physical capacities, as well as to age-associated cultural forms. I earlier mentioned temporal shifts in the organization of cross-sex chasing, from mixing with fantasy play in the early grades to more elaborately ritualized and sexualized forms by the sixth grade. There also appear to be temporal changes in same- and cross-sex touch. In kindergarten, girls and boys touch one another more freely than in fourth grade, when children avoid relaxed cross-sex touch and instead use pokes, pushes, and other forms of mock violence, even when the touch clearly expresses affection. This touch taboo is obviously related to the risk of seeming to *like* someone of the other sex. In fourth grade, same-sex touch begins to signal sexual meanings among boys as well as between boys and girls. Younger boys touch one another freely in cuddling (arm around shoulder) as well as mock-violence ways. By fourth grade, when homophobic taunts like "fag" become more common among boys, cuddling touch begins to disappear for boys, but less for girls.

Overall, I am calling for more complexity in our conceptualizations of gender and of children's social relationships. Our challenge is to retain the temporal sweep, looking at individual and group lives as they unfold over time, while also attending to social structure and context and to the full variety of experiences in the present.

ACKNOWLEDGMENTS

I would like to thank Jane Atkinson, Nancy Chodorow, Arlene Daniels, Peter Lyman, Zick Rubin, Malcolm Spector, Avril Thorne, and Margery Wolf for comments on an earlier version of this paper. Conversations with Zella Luria enriched this work.

NOTES

1. I am grateful to Frederick Erickson for suggesting the relevance of Barth's analysis.

2. Sue Samuelson (1980) reports that in a racially mixed playground in Fresno, California, Mexican-American but not Anglo children gave cooties. Racial as well as sexual inequality may be expressed through these forms.

3. This incident was recorded by Margaret Blume, who, for an undergraduate research project in 1982, observed in the California school where I earlier did fieldwork. Her observations and insights enhanced my own, and I would like to thank her for letting me cite this excerpt.

4. Note that in daily school life depending on the individual and the situation, teachers and aides sometimes lessened and at other times heightened sex segregation.

REFERENCES

Aronson, E., et al. 1978. *The Jigsaw Classroom.* Beverly Hills, Calif.: Sage.

Barth, F., ed. 1969. *Ethnic Groups and Boundaries.* Boston: Little, Brown.

Borman, K. M. 1979. "Children's interactions in playgrounds," *Theory into Practice* 18: 251–57.

Eder, D., & Hallinan, M. T. 1978. "Sex differences in children's friendships." *American Sociological Review* 43: 237–50.

Finnan, C. R. 1982. "The ethnography of children's spontaneous play." In G. Spindler, ed., *Doing the Ethnography of Schooling,* pp. 358–80. New York: Holt, Rinehart & Winston.

Foot, H. C., Chapman, A. J., & Smith, J. R. 1980. "Introduction." *Friendship and Social Relations in Children,* pp. 1–14. New York: Wiley.

Gilligan, C. 1982. *In a Different Voice: Psychological Theory and Women's Development.* Cambridge: Harvard University Press.

Glaser, B. G., & Strauss, A. L. 1967. *The Discovery of Grounded Theory.* Chicago: Aldine.

Goffman, E. 1977. "The arrangement between the sexes." *Theory and Society* 4: 301–36.

Goodwin, M. H. 1980. "Directive-response speech sequences in girls' and boys' task activities." In S. McConnell-Ginet, R. Borker, & N. Furman, eds., *Women and Language in Literature and Society,* pp. 157–73. New York: Praeger.

Greif, E. B. 1982. "Sex differences in parent–child conversations." *Women's Studies International Quarterly* 3: 253–8.

Henley, N. 1977. *Body Politics: Power, Sex, and Nonverbal Communication.* Englewood Cliffs, N.J.: Prentice-Hall.

Karkau, K. 1973. *Sexism in the Fourth Grade.* Pittsburgh: KNOW, Inc. (pamphlet).

Katz, J. 1983. "A theory of qualitative methodology: The social system of analytic fieldwork." In R. M. Emerson, ed., *Contemporary Field Research,* pp. 127–48. Boston: Little, Brown.

Knapp, M., & Knapp, H. 1976. *One Potato, Two Potato: The Secret Education of American Children.* New York: W. W. Norton.

Lever, J. 1976. "Sex differences in the games children play." *Social Problems* 23: 478–87.

Maccoby, E. 1982. "Social groupings in childhood: Their relationship to prosocial and antisocial behavior in boys and girls." Paper presented at conference on The Development of Prosocial and Antisocial Behavior, Voss, Norway.

Maccoby, E., & Jacklin, C. 1974. *The Psychology of Sex Differences.* Stanford, Calif.: Stanford University Press.

Maltz, D. N., & Borker, R. A. 1983. "A cultural approach to male–female miscommunication." In J. J. Gumperz, ed., *Language and Social Identity,* pp. 195–216. New York: Cambridge University Press.

McRobbie, A., & Garber, J. 1975. "Girls and subcultures." In S. Hall & T. Jefferson, eds., *Resistance through Rituals,* pp. 209–22. London: Hutchinson.

Ortner, S. B., & Whitehead, H. 1981. *Sexual Meanings.* New York: Cambridge University Press.

Parrott, S. 1972. "Games children play: Ethnography of a second-grade recess." In J. P. Spradley & D. W. McCurdy, eds., *The Cultural Experience,* pp. 206–19. Chicago: Science Research Associates.

Rich, A. 1980. "Compulsory heterosexuality and lesbian existence." *Signs* 5: 631–60.

Samuelson, S. 1980. "The cooties complex." *Western Folklore* 39: 198–210.

Savin-Williams, R. C. 1976. "An ethological study of dominance formation and maintenance in a group of human adolescents." *Child Development* 47: 972–79.

Schofield, J. W. 1981. "Complementary and conflicting identities: Images and interaction in an interracial school." In S. R. Asher & J. M. Gottman, eds., *The Development of Children's Friendships,* pp. 53–90. New York: Cambridge University Press.

Sherif, M., & Sherif, C. 1953. *Groups in Harmony and Tension.* New York: Harper.

Sluckin, A. 1981. *Growing Up in the Playground.* London: Routledge & Kegan Paul.

Speier, M. 1976. "The adult ideological viewpoint in studies of childhood." In A. Skolnick, ed., *Rethinking Childhood,* pp. 168–86. Boston: Little, Brown.

Sutton-Smith, B. 1971. "A syntax for play and games." In R. E. Herron and B. Sutton-Smith, eds., *Child's Play,* pp. 298–307. New York: Wiley.

Unger, R. K. 1979. "Toward a redefinition of sex and gender." *American Psychologist* 34:1085–94.

Waldrop, M. F., & Halverson, C. F. 1975. "Intensive and extensive peer behavior: Longitudinal and cross-sectional analysis." *Child Development* 46: 19–26.

West, C., & Zimmerman, D. H. 1983. "Small insults: A study of interruptions in cross-sex conversations between unacquainted persons." In B. Thorne, C. Kramarae, & N. Henley, eds., *Language, gender, and society.* Rowley, Mass.: Newbury House.

Whitehead, H. 1981. "The bow and the burden strap: A new look at institutionalized homosexuality in Native America." In S. B. Ortner & H. Whitehead, eds., *Sexual Meanings,* pp. 80–115. New York: Cambridge University Press.

What Are Little Boys Made Of?

✍ Michael Kimmel

To hear some tell it, there's a virtual war against boys in America. Best-sellers' subtitles counsel us to "protect" boys, to "rescue" them. Inside, we hear how boys are failing at school, where their behavior is increasingly seen as a problem. Therapists advise anguished parents about boys' fragility, their hidden despair and despondence. Boys, we read, are depressed, suicidal, emotionally shut down.

And why? It depends on whom you ask. The backlash chorus—the cultural rights as well as the authors of some of these books—chant "feminism." Because of feminism, they say, America has been so focused on girls that we've forgotten about the boys. Other writers blame patterns of male development, while still others find in feminism not the problem but its solution.

There's no question that there's a boy crisis. Virtually all the books cite the same statistics: boys are four to five times more likely to kill themselves than girls, four times more likely to be diagnosed as emotionally disturbed, three times more likely to be diagnosed with attention deficit disorder, and 15 times more likely to be victims of violent crime. The debate concerns the nature of the crisis, its causes, and, of course, its remedies. The startling number of advice manuals that have appeared in the past couple of years—almost all by male therapists—alternate between psychological diagnoses and practical advice about how to raise boys.

One group, epitomized by therapist Michael Gurian (*A Fine Young Man, The Wonder of Boys*), suggests that boys are both doing worse than ever and doing worse than girls thanks to feminists' efforts. Gurian argues that as feminists have changed the rules, they've made boys the problem. By minimizing the importance of basic biological differences, and establishing girls' standards as the ones all children must follow, feminists have wrecked boyhood. Along with Australian men's movement guru Steve Biddulph (*Raising Boys*), Gurian argues that our educational system forces naturally rambunctious boys to conform to a regime of obedience. With testosterone surging through their little limbs, boys are commanded to sit still, raise their hands, and take naps.

To hear these critics tell it, we're no longer allowing boys to be boys. We've misunderstood boy biology, and cultural meddling—especially by misinformed women—won't change a thing. It's nature, not nurture, that propels boys towards obnoxious behavior, violence, and sadistic experiments on insects. What makes boys boys is, in a word, testosterone, that magical, catch-all hormone that drives them toward aggression and risk-taking, and challenging this fact gives them the message, Gurian says, that "boyhood is defective."

This facile biological determinism mars otherwise insightful observations. Gurian adroitly points out the nearly unbearable pressure on young boys to conform, to resort to violence to solve problems, to disrupt classroom decorum. But he thinks it's entirely due to biology—not peer culture, media violence, or parental influence. And Biddulph agrees: "Testosterone equals vitality," he writes. All we have to do is "honor it and steer it into healthy directions." This over-reliance on biology leads both writers to overstate the differences between the sexes and ignore the differences among boys and among girls. To argue that boys have a harder time in school ignores all reliable evidence from sources such as Myra and David Sadker's *Failing at Fairness: How America's Schools Cheat Girls*.

These misdiagnoses lead to some rather bizarre excuses for boys' behavior, and to the celebration of all things masculine as the simple product of that pubertal chemical elixir. In *The Wonder of Boys*, Gurian cities bewilderingly incongruous rites of passage, such as "military boot camp, fraternity hazings, graduation day, and bar mitzvah," as essential parts of every boy's life. Hazing and bar mitzvahs? Have you read any reports of boys dying at the hands of other boys at bar mitzvahs? Biddulph explains boys' refusal to listen to adult authority by reference to the "fact" that their ear canals develop in irregular spurts, "leading to a period of hearing loss." And did you know that baritone singers in Welsh choruses have more testosterone than tenors—and have more sex! Where do they get this stuff?

More chilling, though, are their strategies for intervention. Gurian suggests reviving corporal punishment both at home and at school—but only when administered privately with cool indifference and never in the heat of adult anger. (He calls it "spanking responsibly.") Biddulph, somewhat more moderately, proposes that boys start school a year later than girls, so they'll be on a par intellectually.

The problem is, there's plenty of evidence that boys are not "just boys" everywhere and in the same ways. If it's all biological, why is the slightest deviation from expected manly behavior so cruelly punished? Why aren't Norwegian or French or Swiss boys as violent, homophobic, and misogynist as many are in the U.S.? Boys are not doomed to be victims of what Alan Alda once facetiously called "testosterone poisoning." On the contrary, they can become men who express their emotions and treat their partners respectfully, who listen as well as act, and who love and nurture their children.

But how do we get there? Another group of therapists, including Dan Kindlon and Michael Thompson, and William Pollack, eschew testosterone-tinged testimonials and treat masculinity as an ideology to be challenged. For them, we need to understand the patterns of boys' development to more effectively intervene and set boys on the path to a manhood of integrity.

To do that, Kindlon and Thompson write in *Raising Cain,* we must contend with the "culture of cruelty" that forces a boy to deny emotional neediness, "routinely disguise his feelings," and end up emotionally isolated. In *Real Boys,* Pollack calls it the "Boy Code" and the "mask of masculinity"—a kind of swaggering attitude that boys embrace to hide their fears, suppress dependency and vulnerability, and present a stoic front.

These two books are the biggest sellers and their authors the most visible experts on boyhood. Pollack's book is far better. The most influenced by feminism, his observations provide an important parallel to psychologist Carol Gilligan's work on how assertive, confident, and proud girls "lose their voices" when they hit adolescence. At the

same moment, Pollack says, boys find the inauthentic voice of bravado, of constant posturing, of foolish risk-taking and gratuitous violence. The Boy Code teaches them that they are supposed to be in power and thus to act like it. They "ruffle in a manly pose," as Yeats once put it, "for all their timid heart."

Unfortunately, these therapists' explanations don't always track. For one thing they all use examples drawn from their clinical practices but then generalize casually from their clients to all boys. And, alas, "all" is limited almost entirely to middle-class, suburban white boys. Cute blond boys stare at us from the books' covers, while inside the authors ignore large numbers of boys whose pain and low self-esteem may have to do with insecurities and anxieties that are more economically and politically rooted. Gurian's books disingenuously show one boy of color on each cover, but there's nary a mention of them inside. Kindlon and Thompson generalize from their work at an elite prep school.

If all the boys are white and middle class, at least they're not all straight. Most therapists treat homosexuality casually, dropping in a brief reference, "explaining" it as biological, and urging compassion and understanding before returning to the more "important" stuff. Only Pollack devotes a sensitive and carefully thought-out chapter to homosexuality and he actually uses the term "homophobia."

The cause of all this posturing and posing is not testosterone, of course, but privilege. In adolescence, both boys and girls get their first real dose of gender inequality, and that is what explains their different paths. The interventions recommended by Kindlon and Thompson—allowing boys to have their emotions; accepting a high level of activity; speaking their language; treating them with respect; using discipline to guide and build; modeling manhood as emotionally attached (all of which are good suggestions and applicable to girls, also)—don't address male entitlement. Indeed, of the male therapists, only Pollack and James Gilligan (*Violence*) even seem to notice it. For the others, boys' troubles are all about fears suppressed, pain swallowed. Kindlon and Thompson write that the "culture of cruelty imposes a code of silence on boys, requiring them to suffer without speaking of it and to be silent witnesses to acts of cruelty to others.

The books that are written with an understanding of male privilege—and the need to challenge it—are the ones that offer the most useful tools to improve boys' lives. Books by Myriam Miedzian and by Olga Silverstein and Beth Rashbaum, published several years ago, offer critiques of traditional boyhood and well-conceived plans for support and change. Eschewing biological determinism, these books see in feminism a blueprint for transforming both boyhood and manhood. Feminism encourages men—and their sons—to be more emotionally open and expressive, to develop empathic skills, and to channel emotional outbursts away from violence. And feminism demands the kinds of societal changes that make this growth possible.

That's all the more necessary, because there really is a boy crisis in America—not the crisis of inverted proportions that claims boys are the new victims of a feminist-inspired agenda run amok. The real boy crisis usually goes by another name. We call it "teen violence," "youth violence," "gang violence," "violence in the schools," Let's face facts: men and boys are responsible for 85 percent of all violent crimes in this country, and their victims are overwhelmingly male as well. From an early age, boys learn that violence is not only an acceptable form of conflict resolution, but one that is admired. Four times more teenage boys than teenage girls think fighting is appropriate when someone cuts into the front of a line. Half of all teenage boys get into a physical fight each year.

"Rescuing" or "protecting" isn't the answer, say British high school teachers Jonathan Salisbury and David Jackson. As their title, *Challenging Macho Values*, shouts, they want to take issue with traditional masculinity, to disrupt the facile "boys will be boys" model, and to erode boys' sense of entitlement. And for Paul Kivel (*Boys Will Be Men*), raising boys to manhood means confronting racism, sexism, and homophobia—both in our communities and in ourselves. These books are loaded with hands-on practical advice to help adolescents raise issues, confront fears, and overcome anxieties, and to help teachers dispel myths, encourage cooperation, and discourage violent solutions to perceived problems. Salisbury and Jackson's book will be most valuable to teachers seeking to transform disruptive behavior; Kivel's is geared more to parents, to initiate and continue those sensitive and difficult conversations. The most valuable material helps parents and teachers deconstruct sexuality myths and challenge sexual harassment and violence. "We believe that masculine violence is intentional, deliberate, and purposeful," write Salisbury and Jackson. "It comes from an attempt by men and boys

to create and sustain a system of masculine power and control that benefits them every minute of the day." Forget testosterone; it's sexism! Even if these two books are less gracefully written and more relentlessly critical of traditional boyhood, they are the only ones to recognize that not all boys are the same, and that one key to enabling boys to express a wider range of emotions is to challenge the power and privilege that is part of their cultural heritage.

Gilligan and Miedzian, along with James Garbarino (*Lost Boys*), understand that the real boy crisis is a crisis of violence—specifically the cultural prescriptions that equate masculinity with the capacity for violence. Garbarino's fortuitously timed study of youthful offenders locates the origins of men's violence in the way boys swallow anger and hurt. Among the boys he studied, "deadly petulance usually hides some deep emotional wounds, a way of compensating through an exaggerated sense of grandeur for an inner sense of violation, victimization, and injustice." In other words, as one prison inmate put it, "I'd rather be wanted for murder than not wanted at all."

Gilligan is even more specific. In his insightful study of violence, he places its origins in "the fear of shame and ridicule, and the overbearing need to prevent others from laughing at oneself by making them weep instead." The belief that violence is manly is not carried on any chromosome, not soldered into the wiring of the right or left hemisphere, not juiced by testosterone. (Half of all boys don't fight, most don't carry weapons, and almost all don't kill: are they not boys?) Boys learn it. Violence, Gilligan writes, "has far more to do with the cultural construction of manhood than it does with the hormonal substrates of biology."

That's where feminism comes in. Who, after all, has offered the most trenchant critique of that cultural construction but feminists? That's why the books written by women and men that use a feminist perspective (Gilligan, Kivel, Miedzian, Pollack, Salisbury and Jackson, and Silverstein and Rashbaum) are far more convincing than those that either repudiate it (Gurian, Biddulph) or ignore it (Kindlon and Thompson).

Frankly, I think the antifeminists such as Gurian and Biddulph (and the right wing in general) are the real male bashers. When they say boys will be boys, they mean boys will be uncivilized animals. In their view, males are biologically propelled to be savage, predatory, sexually omnivorous creatures, hard-wired for violence. As a man, I find this view insulting.

Feminists imagine, and demand, that men (and boys) can do better. Feminism offers the possibility of a new boyhood and a new masculinity based on a passion for justice, a love of equality, and the expression of a full range of feelings.

INHERIT THE WAR

Grace Paley

The father has been preparing a war for his son's birthday. He started long ago. You have to, you know. People who decide on a war and expect it to happen the minute or week or month they want it to are often disappointed. You also cannot do it alone. The father has a few friends from his war who are willing to help out. They have sons too. There are quite simple ways to begin—probably in childhood. For instance: help the boy develop an easy dislike for your neighbor. Mild prejudice will then rest contentedly in his little breast. As time goes on, it can appear as nothing worse than sleepy contempt for their daughter.

The father remember his war, how long it took *his* father to get it right. He was almost too old. (The father and his friends are now called the Great Generation. This isn't exactly fair. *Their* fathers had fought in an equally famous war and luckily survived to provide a war for the father and his friends.)

This father does need more preparation, and quickly. His son is growing beautifully, but he's reading too much. Some of his ideas seem to come from leftish media . . . the schools are also bad, even treacherous. But he's sure, the father is sure that he can find the old newspapers that he's kept or the right pages of the history book, which are very clever about enumerating insults to our national soul and natural hegemony. The recollection of historical insult is important in the life of great nations, as well as their stunning victories. Of course anxiety about civilian deaths—women and children—always undercuts the enthusiasm of sentimental citizens and tenderhearted boys. But he loves his boy, and he doesn't want him left out. He's talked to many other fathers. They're nearly ready. They've begun their letters to newspapers, their attacks on the wimps in Congress and the administration. Most important, they've selected the enemy and are very clear about it . . .

He has only one year left before his son's eighteenth birthday. His son is not unaware of what is coming. He has that boyish excitement, that intensifying patriotism—his own war, at last.

READING 17

Ideology, Experience, Identity:
The Complex Worlds of Children in Fair Families

Barbara Risman

In this chapter I follow what happens when marital partners committed to fairness become parents. In these households there are few interactional expectations attached to gender. But children grow up not only in their families but also in their schools and with their friends. In this chapter I explore what happens when gendered expectations are changed within the family but not outside of it. What are the consequences for the children's gendered identities, and for their social lives?[1]

There has been no previous research, to my knowledge, on how and whether children raised in egalitarian households differ from those in more traditional families. We found two patterns: the children faced serious inconsistencies between their egalitarian beliefs and their experiences with peers, and their identities seem to be forged more from lived experiences than from ideology (see Risman and Myers 1997 for an earlier discussion of these findings). The disjunction between ideology, experience, and identity seems to be common to all these children's stories. I cannot conclusively show that the patterns identified here are not true for all upper-middle-class white children in contemporary America, but I do not believe that they are. First, as a parent, I have direct access to my daughter's friends and to their families, and I rarely see any evidence that most of those children deal with the same issues as those salient to children in these fair families. Second, I can compare these children's experiences to some new gender research on children and make some educated guesses about what makes these children different.

PREVIOUS LITERATURE: DEVELOPING GENDERED IDENTITIES

Sociologists have only rarely—and quite recently—studied children's gender. Most of the literature that needs to be reviewed originates in other disciplines. When children are studied in both sociology and psychology, the predominant questions center on how children learn to be boys or girls. That is, most of the past literature falls squarely into the individualist level of analysis—seeking to explain how male and female babies develop into gendered boys and girls. This individualist literature on children can be organized analytically by presumptions about children's role in their own socialization. I divide this scholarship into three categories: that which sees children as the primary *actors* in the gendering process; that which sees children's gender as something *imposed* by the larger culture and reinforced by rewards and punishments; and that which argues that children are constrained by longstanding gender norms but which sees children as *participating in and negotiating* the enactment of gender.

Self-Gendering

Theories of cognitive development have addressed children's role in learning gendered expectations. Piaget (1932) and Kohlberg (1966) argued that children play an active role in gender acquisition. Children do not passively absorb information from their parents and peers but seek relevant information, and they organize it into predictable patterns. They begin to do this at a young age in order to make sense of their worlds. According to Kohlberg, children choose gender as a major organizing principle because it jibes with their desire for order. Children come to view gender as "natural" differences between males and females. Piaget and other cognitive development theorists argue that children see same-sex modeling as morally necessary and invariant (Kohlberg 1966; Maccoby 1992; Martin 1993). This perspective puts undue emphasis on the child as a rational actor who freely selects gender from the available options. There is a chicken-and-egg conundrum here. Children are born into the existing social structure and are affected accordingly; they do not randomly reproduce gender. Writers in this perspective have tended to presume that gender dichotomies are not only salient but necessary for the psychological development of children. Thus, while children are seen as actors, this perspective ignores the power of gender stratification on children's cognitive processes. Still, one could imagine that children raised in a family without gender dichotomies might self-gender less systematically.

Socialization Imposed on Passive Recipients

Scholars at the other end of the spectrum have often focused on how the existing gender order constrains the socialization of children. Beginning with Parsons and Bales (1955) and Inkeles (1968), scholars in this tradition see socialization as a one-way conduit of information from adult to child. In particular, parents and other adults apply to children stereotypes of behavior based on the child's sex. This typing begins at birth (Deaux 1984; Fagot, Leinbach, and C. O'Boyle 1992; Hutson 1983; Stern and Karraker 1989). Bandura (1962, 1971) argues that parents, teachers, and peers all reward children for learning the behavior of the same sex. Because they receive positive feedback for "correct" behavior, children imitate same-sex behavior and "encode" it into their behavioral repertoires. Once encoded, the child's gender is set.

Scholars of sex roles assert that the gendering of children is complete at an early age. The acquisition of appropriate gender characteristics and expectations is not optional for the child. The important impact of scholarship on gender socialization is the realization that, because we treat boys and girls differently, they develop different skills and desires (Renzetti and Curan 1992; Richardson 1981). In this view, different treatment helps to create people who *are* socially different. By imposing different constraints and expectations society helps to create a self-fulfilling prophecy that perpetuates gender inequality. However, the socialization perspective of gender learning offers a static picture of gender, with the child as a relatively acquiescent recipient of appropriate models of behavior that in turn offer little room for improvisation and change (Kreps et al. 1994). Within this perspective one would logically argue that children rewarded for gender-atypical behavior would develop less gender-typed personalities and identities.

Acting, Not Just Reacting

Sociologists have begun to argue that gender socialization of children is more than just adults providing role models and sanctions, with children hitting, missing, and eventually getting it "right" (Corsaro 1985; Alanen 1988). Instead, they are finding that children actually participate in the process. This emerging tradition integrates a concern with the development of gendered selves via cognitive schemas with attention to the power of interactional expectations. Children are influenced not only by the adult world (self-gendering and socialization) but also by each other. For example, Borman and O'Reilly (1987) find that kindergarteners in same-sex play groups initiate play in similar ways but that the topics for play vary by gender. That is, boys and girls play different types of games, creating different conversational and negotiation demands. Thorne (1993) observed groups of children in classrooms and school yards, noting how they create and police gender boundaries and form various strata among themselves. She asserts that gender relations are not invariant but can change according to the context and the actors involved. Thorne has criticized most socialization and development frameworks because they presuppose a certain outcome: that boys will learn appropriate masculinities, girls will learn appropriate femininities, and if they fail to do so they will either be punished or relegated to the ranks of deviants. She argues that such a future-oriented perspective distorts children's everyday realities, which are crucial to their ongoing gendered negotiations. "Children's interactions are

not preparation for life," she writes. "They are life itself" (3).

Bem (1993) similarly improves on both cognitive and socialization theories by linking them. She argues that children try to make sense of the world by forming categories, or schemas, but says that these categories are shaped by existing gender categories in society. Gender is subtly transmitted to children by adults both consciously and unconsciously, so that the dominant way of understanding the social world is usually seen as the best way to understand it. Existing gender divisions are nearly hegemonic and often unquestioned by both children and adults. Therefore, questioning the taken-for-granted gendered organization of society is difficult and unlikely.

It seems reasonable that all three processes occur. Children who live in gendered societies no doubt develop gender schemas and will code themselves, as well as the world around them, in gendered terms. But this seems much more likely to be the result of their lived experiences in patriarchal societies than the consequence of an innate drive for cognitive development. While children are developing cognitive gender schemas, adults and older children are treating boys and girls quite differently. Gender socialization is apparent in any observation of children's lives. And while children are being socialized they react to, negotiate, and even reject some societal pressures. Although children are actors in the gendering process, we must not ignore the impact of differential reinforcement of gender-appropriate behavior. The cognitive effects of living in a gendered (and sexist) society, the reality of gender socialization, and the active efforts of boys and girls to negotiate their own worlds interact to shape their daily lives, and perhaps to affect their future options.

Unequal Outcomes: Reproducing Gender Difference and Inequality

Even when we recognize that children are both actors and reactors in the gendering process, we cannot overlook the strong empirical data which suggest that most boys and girls are differentially prepared for adulthood. Boys are still routinely socialized to learn to work in teams and to compete, and girls are still routinely socialized to value nurturing (note the relative numbers of boys and girls in team sports versus those dedicated to the popular Babysitters Club book series). Thorne (1993) has shown convincingly that there is much more crossover gender play than dichotomous thinking presumes, yet other research continues to indicate the consequences of gender socialization on children (Lever 1978; Luttrell 1993; Hawkins 1985; Wilder, Mackie, and Cooper 1985; Signorelli 1990; Maccoby 1992; Hutson 1983). There is also much evidence that gender socialization differs by social class, ethnicity, and religion (Peterson and Rollins 1987; Collins 1990).

Socialization clearly happens both in children's play and in their families. Lever's (1978) classic study of boys' and girls' play offers insight into how boys and girls are prepared for a future in which men are presumed to belong in the public, competitive sphere and women to the private, nurturing sphere. Boys' games were more likely to be outside, involve teams, and be age-integrated. Girls were more likely to play make-believe games with one or two others and to break up a game rather than work through conflict. These differences are well developed by the middle of elementary school. Parents and immediate family are also obviously an important source of transmission for gendered expectations (Maccoby 1992). Research indicates that parents participate in gender-typing by often rewarding gender-typical play and punishing gender-atypical play (Bem 1993; Hutson 1983).

While several scholars have documented that some families are moving toward shared parenting and more liberal gender socialization for children, we have little information about how effective such changes in parenting style might be in a society in which gendering processes continue to occur (Coltrane 1996; Schwartz 1994; Segal 1990). It is to this question of how children in egalitarian families fare that I now turn our attention.

CHILDREN IN FAIR FAMILIES

The parents of the children discussed here have attempted to break the chain of gender inequality that typically begins at birth. These children are living in a context different from that in more mainstream families: most of these parents make a conscious effort *not* to replicate what Connell (1987) calls hegemonic masculinities and emphasized femininities. They have an ideological and practical commitment to organizing their homes and families in an egalitarian manner. Whereas mainstream parents may react with delight when their daughter wants to be Barbie for Halloween and their son wants toy guns for his birth-

day, these parents are likely to be dismayed. Their children are growing up in a world where gender does not dictate who does what or who has more power, at least not in the family. Rather than receiving reinforcement from their parents when they enact hegemonic behavior, these children are likely to encounter disappointment or concern. So how do these children negotiate gender, given their atypical parents?

To understand these children's perspectives on their own lives we had to create cognitively appropriate research instruments. After six months of planning we decided on three separate formats for the children: an interview schedule with questions resembling stories for the four- through six-year-olds; an interview format that included some questions, some writing of poems, and some free play for seven-through ten-year-olds; and interviews that included open-ended questions and some paper-and-pencil items for the older children. There were twenty-six children in these fifteen families, but five were under four years of age, too young to interview. We interviewed twelve boys and nine girls. Ten of the children were between four and six, seven children were between seven and ten, and four children were at least eleven. Three of the four older children were from the same family, so I refrain from making any generalizations about that group.

These children live in complex worlds. They must navigate complicated social and cognitive landscapes. Three themes emerged from our conversations and observations. First, the parents seem to be very successful at transferring their ideological values to their children. The youngsters believe that men and women are equal, or ought to be. Second, these children's experiences at school and with their peers have taught them unequivocally that boys and girls are not similar, nor do they think they should be. Boys and girls are—in these children's minds—totally different kinds of people. Third, identities seem more forged from experiences with peers than from ideology. The boys in particular seem to struggle to reconcile their identities and their beliefs.

Ideology

Sixteen of the twenty-one children we interviewed had entirely adopted their parents' egalitarian or feminist views on gender, and two of the children without such views were four-year-olds whose answers were better described as inconsistent than traditional. The children know that occupations are currently sex-segregated but believe they should not be. They do not see any tasks in families that ought to be exclusively for either men or women. One nine-year-old boy actually became annoyed at the line of questioning about what men and women should do. He rolled his eyes and retorted, "I told you I think anybody can do these jobs. . . . I think that saying just men or just women could do these jobs isn't being equal." In contrast, most four-year-olds assign sex-stereotypic labels to activities, occupations, and playthings (Bornstein and Lamb 1988).

Most of the children, both boys and girls, not only believe that men and women should be free to work in any occupation and should share the family labor, but also understand that male privilege exists in contemporary society. A nine-year-old girl told us that she believes very much in feminism because "I don't think that it is the least bit fair that in most places males have the main power. I think that women play an important part and should be free to do what they want to do." Similarly, a fifteen-year-old told us, in response to a question about what he likes about being a boy, "It's probably easier being a guy. At least it is now because of stereotypes and prejudices and everything." Overall, most of these children were sophisticated true believers in the capabilities of men and women to perform the same jobs and family roles. The influence of their parents as ideological conduits and role models is evident in their attitudes.

Experiences

These children may have liberal attitudes about gender equality for men and women, but when that ideology contradicts their experiences as boys and girls, life wins hands down. Despite their post-gender answers to what is appropriate for adults, these children give stereotypical answers about the differences between boys and girls. In order to find out their gut beliefs about boys and girls we probed their experiences with a variety of techniques. We asked how their lives would be different if a magician turned them into the opposite sex. We provided short scenarios using stereotypically male and female adjectives (e.g., weak, strong, fearful, adventuresome) and asked them to tell us which adjectives described girls and which described boys and why. We asked what they

liked and disliked about being a girl or boy. We asked them to write poems beginning with the line "If I were a boy/girl" using the opposite sex category. We showed them pictures of a boy and a girl, sitting side by side on a sofa, and asked them to tell us a story about each child. We followed up every comment that would help us assess their attitudes.

Although none of the four- to six-year-olds have begun to believe that boys and girls are different, most children from mainstream families clearly have strong gender schemas by this age (Bem 1993). Their egalitarian parents have managed to insulate the preschoolers from typical American norms, perhaps by their choice of paid care-giving arrangements and friends. Once the children reached seven years of age, however, their nonfamilial experiences broadened considerably, as did their ideas about differences between the sexes. We find the descriptions of school-age children remarkably consistent and stereotypical across sex and age categories. Girls are sweet and neat; boys are athletic and disruptive. And these descriptions are consistent with those given by children, presumably from more mainstream families, in other research (Bornstein and Lamb 1988). Table 1 contains adjectives used in direct quotes about boys. The age and sex of the speakers who use each adjective at least once are indicated. Of the sixteen adjectives used, half describe socially disruptive personality traits, often considered aspects of masculinity. The rest are more neutral descriptors but are still stereotypically male. The world that these school-age children know is one in which boys as a group are athletic and mean.

We elicited more comments about boys than about girls—girls are described almost as a second species. But again the comments were remarkably consistent. All of the adjectives describe traditional feminine stereotypes (Table 2). Six of the adjectives are socially valued personality traits, the others more neutral. The children voiced unequivocal belief in major sex differences between boys and girls just minutes after parroting their parents' feminist views about the equality and similarity of men and women.

Three of these children did qualify their stereotypical answers. One eight-year-old boy made a point of telling us that he knew that girls could be into sports or computers, he just did not know any who were. A seven-year-old girl was sure that girls were better behaved and that boys were mean, but she also sometimes wanted to be a boy because they seemed

TABLE 1   ADJECTIVES USED TO DESCRIBE BOYS

Adjective	Speakers by Gender and Age				
Active	7-year-old girl				
Into sports	7-year-old girl	12-year-old boy	10-year-old boy	10-year-old boy	9-year-old girl
Mean	7-year-old girl	15-year-old boy	4-year-old girl		
Bad	7-year-old girl	9-year-old girl			
More free	11-year-old girl				
Sarcastic	15-year-old boy				
Cool	4-year-old girl				
Aggressive	12-year-old boy	10-year-old boy	9-year-old girl		
Athletic	12-year-old boy	10-year-old boy			
Tough	12-year-old boy				
Stronger	6-year-old boy	10-year-old boy			
Into fighting	10-year-old boy	9-year-old girl			
Troublemaking	10-year-old boy	9-year-old girl			
Competitive	9-year-old girl				
Bully	10-year-old boy				
Into computers	4-year-old boy				

TABLE 2   ADJECTIVES USED TO DESCRIBE GIRLS

Adjective	Speakers by Gender and Age		
Nice	10-year-old boy	4-year-old girl	12-year-old boy
Well-behaved	10-year-old boy	7-year-old girl	
Quiet	10-year-old boy	10-year-old boy	7-year-old girl
Cooperative	9-year-old girl		
Good	9-year-old girl		
Sweet	7-year-old girl		
Not into sports	10-year-old boy		
Not sneaky	12-year-old boy		
Nicer to friends	12-year-old boy		
Less free	11-year-old girl		

to have more playful and active games. A ten-year-old boy knew that some girls were "like boys," and he was even letting such a girl try out for his spy club. And one five-year-old boy made the acute observation that girls played different games than boys did when at school on the playground, but when in the neighborhood they played the same games together.

When family experiences collided with experiences with peers, the family influences were dwarfed. For example, a six-year-old boy told us that if a magician were to turn him into a girl, he'd be different because he would have long hair. This boy's father had a ponytail that reached the middle of his back, and the mother's hair was hardly below her ears. A four-year-old boy told us that if a magician were to turn him into a girl, he'd have to do housework—this from the son of a father whose flexible work schedule has allowed him to spend more time in domestic pursuits than his wife does.

It almost seems as if these children believe that boys and girls are opposites but that men and women are magically transformed into equal and comparable people. The children know that men and women are equal; it is boys and girls who are totally different.

Seven of these children spoke explicitly about male privilege among peers or at school. An eleven-year-old girl told us that sometimes she wished to be a boy because when

> teachers need help like to carry a box to their classroom, they always come in and say, like, "Can I borrow a couple of your boys," and never say, "Can I borrow a couple of your students?" And so the girls never get to do any of the stuff and leave the classroom. . . . It's always the boys that get to leave. And, like, little trips and stuff, when we used to go on field trips, the boys would always have to carry a basket of lunches and go ahead, and when they had stuff to bring from the car, it'd always be boys that would get to go to the car. . . . The girls, like, had to stay on the bus and just sit there and wait while some boys got to go there and the girls never got to do it, do that stuff. . . . You get left out because you're a girl. . . . But I'm not wimpy.

A seven-year-old girl told us that she was "more hyper" than most girls and that many of her friends were boys because they were more active and playful. A ten-year-old boy mentioned "racism against

women" in sports. A nine-year-old-girl was an avowed feminist with implicit essentialist notions about girls' innate cooperativeness versus boys' innate combativeness. She thought girls ought to have more power in the world because they were better people.

This is the response an eight-year-old boy gave to us when he was asked to write a poem about what it would be like to be a girl. His understanding of male privilege was widely shared if not usually so well articulated.

If I were a girl I'd have to attract a guy
wear makeup; sometimes.
Wear the latest style of clothes and try to be likable.
I probably wouldn't play any physical sports like football or
soccer.
I don't think I would enjoy myself around men
in fear of rejection
or under the pressure of attracting them.

While both boys and girls "knew" that boys were troublemakers, sarcastic, and athletic, this boy also saw clearly that girls had major disadvantages.

Only a few of the boys were aware that they belonged to a group for which they had internalized negative characteristics. One such boy answered our question about how he was different from other guys this way: "I think I'm taller. I don't like bullying people around that much. . . . When one of my friends starts fighting somebody or arguing with somebody I don't join in. I steer clear of them. I try to get in as few fights as possible." This boy built his identity on sports (his room was a baseball shrine, and his activities were sports, sports, and more sports) but tried to distance himself from the violent aspects of peer-group masculinity. Another boy told us that if he were transformed into a girl he would be nicer to his friends. These boys had internalized negative attitudes toward their own group and, at some level, themselves. In no case did any girl tell us how bad girls were as a group. When girls talked about how they were similar to and different from other girls, their answers were idiosyncratic (e.g., taller or shorter, longer hair, better reader). These children "know" that boys and girls are different, they "know" that boys have advantages, but they also "know" that girls are nicer people.

Identity

These children are very consistent when they explain how boys and girls are different. The unanimity dissolves when we begin to look at how they are forging their own identities. Only six of the children seem to have fashioned selves that unambiguously fit their own stereotyped notions about childhood gender. The interview and observational data collected in these families identify six children who describe themselves in consistently gendered fashion and were so identified in observational data.

The first obvious finding is that these children's attitudes and identities are not necessarily correlated. Of the six children with stereotypical gendered selves, one boy and three girls are also self-consciously egalitarian, even feminist. The two other children in this category had more traditional beliefs about gender.

As the tables show, the children suggested that boys were active, into sports, mean, bad, freer than girls, sarcastic, cool, aggressive, athletic, tough, stronger than girls, into fights, troublemakers, competitive, bullies, and into computers. I use the label "all-boy" boys and "all-girl" girls to describe children who portray characteristics exclusively in one of the two tables. No child manifested every characteristic on our list, but the two children in the all-boy category and the four girls in the all-girl group could not be described with any of the adjectives on the opposite-sex list. For example, there was no indication that the Pretzman boy was mean or a troublemaker—just the opposite. He followed our directions closely and appeared to be very sweet. Yet all his interests were stereotypically masculine—sports, Legos, "Star Trek," computers. He described himself as "strong" and used that criterion to differentiate boys and girls. He didn't play much with girls, and there was no indication of cross-gender behavior or traits either in the interview or as we watched him at home. The twelve-year-old Potadman boy was similar. His main interest and identity seemed to be attached to sports. He answered us with short, not-too-reflective comments. In traditionally masculine fashion, he described his friendships almost entirely in terms of sharing activities.

I categorize the four girls as all-girl because they can be described using the characteristics the children provided for us about girls: nice, well-behaved, quiet, cooperative, good, sweet, not into sports, not sneaky, nice to friends. None of these girls embodied every one of these traits, but it is unlikely that they would be described by any of the traits on the other list. One shared characteristic was their distaste for competitive sports. The eleven-year-old Germane girl provides an easy comparison with the twelve-year-old Potadman boy. Her favorite games were fantasies, her favorite activity was dance, her favorite possessions were dolls and stuffed animals. The Stokes ten-year-old was similarly gendered. Her favorite activities were reading, writing poems, and art. She is adamant about disliking sports, and she knows why: she doesn't like any activity where you have to be pushy or aggressive. The six-year-old Green daughter had three dollhouses, and there was not a "boy" toy in the house. Her parents were very conscious of encouraging her to make her own choices and to develop her own potential; the mother told us she was trying to get her daughter to be willing to play some sports, at least at school during recess.

These six children, raised by egalitarian parents and often holding feminist attitudes themselves, have nevertheless fashioned selves that are unambiguously gendered. The following poem sums up what these children think about even imagining being the opposite sex. The poem was written by the Sykes girl in response to our request to write a verse that begins "If I were a boy": "If I were a boy, I'd know my parents had made a mistake and that I should have been a girl. I'd always feel that I didn't belong because the girls were who I wanted to play with but they wouldn't let me, and I didn't want to be with the boys."

This nine-year-old provides an interesting example of the disjunction between identity and ideology. She lives in one of the most self-consciously feminist and progressive families in our study. They see themselves as outside the mainstream. They have no television set so that their daughter will avoid excess materialism. Both parents and daughter are avowed feminists. The daughter is one of the most feminine in the sample—her long wavy hair flows below her waist. She collects china teacups, hates competitive sports, and loves nature and hiking. She saved a bug from death during my home observation and carried it tenderly outside. In my honor she put on her favorite nightgown, ankle-length and with a pink bow. This child is very smart, and she intends to succeed professionally, maybe in a scientific career. So despite her feminine self-presentation and dislike for most things male, she actually crosses gender boundaries in other ways.

The other fifteen children have also fashioned gendered selves. The boys are much more likely to like sports, the girls to like dance. Despite their parents' role-modeling, despite their own ideology, all these girls are more feminine than masculine and all these boys are more masculine than feminine. But the rest of the children, to varying degrees, cross gender lines in interests and interpersonal style. All but one of the girls is either involved in at least one competitive sport or expects to be when she is a little older. All the boys stand out in some way as exceptions to hegemonic masculinity. An interesting sex difference exists, however. All the girls told us in quite explicit terms just how they were different from other girls, but the boys often denied any differences from other boys—differences that our interview and observational team noted. For example, the Cody daughter knows that she is different from other girls because she loves team sports, and she would like to be a boy except that she knows "they aren't always very nice." A four-year-old girl likes to climb trees as well as play fantasy games about babies. She knows she is "nice, like other girls," but she wants to be "cool," like boys. She told us her future goal was to "be a mommy so I can work hard and like my job." The Cross girl believes that she is more active than other girls, but she is also "real sweet," likes horses, and is nice to her friends (all characteristics that she says make her different from boys). The Relux six-year-old told us that she is "not like other girls particularly." She has friends who are boys, although her best friend is another girl. But she likes being a girl because she can do whatever she wants.

The boys coded as portraying some crossover behaviors and interpersonal style were much less likely than the girls to notice it themselves. Although some of the data reported here come directly from the interviews, this analysis also relies on subtle inconsistencies in their own words, body language, and to some extent intuition of the part of the interview and observational team, as recorded in field notes. The older Potadman boys (fifteen and seventeen years of age) told us of some hopes and dreams that seemed to cross gender stereotypes. The fifteen-year-old baby-sits and loves to vacuum and cook. He would like to stay home with his children if his wife could earn a high enough income. His very tall older brother, whose ponytail reaches below his waist, hates to work out and finds it unfair that women can be considered sexy without being muscular but that men cannot. He writes poetry and never had been much into sports, though he does like volleyball. He describes himself as an intellectual outsider and seems comfortable—if somewhat vulnerable—with the status.

Four little boys also reported androgynous preferences. The four-year-old Cody boy likes many boys' games, particularly baseball. But he also wants to be like his sister, plays housekeeping at day care, and enjoys playing dress-up in his sister's clothes. The four-year-old Trexler son has favorite movie characters: Aladdin and the Little Mermaid. The four-year-old Relux boy thinks that being "silly" is the best part of being a boy. While he likes guns and has mostly boys as friends, his answers to most questions seem gender-neutral. Similarly, the five-year-old Cary boy likes boys' toys and baseball, but many of his favorite activities seem to be gender-neutral, such as board games and playing outside with both boys and girls. His body language and self-presentation led to the description of him as "gentle" in the field notes. The six-year-old Staton son prefers stereotypically boys' toys, and he takes tai kwon do lessons, but, like the fifteen-year-old Potadman boy, he would like to not work at all so that he could "spend more time with his kids." These boys never seemed rough or tough; even when talking about their stereotypical behaviors they seemed warm and caring.

There were two boys whose words contradicted their behavior (as reported by their parents) and our observations. The ten-year-old Oakley boy seemed to try too hard at his self-presentation. He wanted us to think he was tough, mean, and sneaky, a "real" boy. But the boy we met was warm, kind, and soft-spoken, even as he told us about his war games. This son of two writers wanted a blue-collar job for which he could wear "lots of armor" and be tough. But these words didn't square with what we saw: a ten-year-old who played gently with his four-year-old sister. He interrupted his own and his sister's interview to take her to look out the bathroom window so that she did not miss the full moon. They fought during our home interview, and he hurt her by mistake. He was genuinely sorry, offering his "butt" for her to hit in response. When we noticed some Barbie dolls in his closet and asked what kind of games he played with them, he answered, "Oh, I mostly kill them in war games. They're my sisters." But his mother told us that both children played fantasy games with the dolls. He alluded to this himself later: "I like the Ken doll because he is a basketball star." This boy twitched when he spoke about gender preferences. I found the interview poignant: he knew that boys were supposed to be mean and sneaky, and he wanted very much to fulfill those expectations, or at least to make us believe that he did. But we couldn't believe it. He was too nice a child.

Another interviewer had a similar experience with the ten-year-old Woods boy. His identity was sports based: he was a baseball fanatic, and his room was entirely in Carolina Blue. He talked about liking to compete. And yet he described his baby brother in loving terms, and in three straight losses in a card game he showed no competitive spirit or disappointment. He emanated warmth, as did his father. He also differentiated himself from other boys because he was not a bully and did not like to fight.

CONCLUSION

These data illustrate the usefulness of the theoretical model offered in this book. Although gender structure exists at the institutional, interactional, and individual levels, its consequences are far from predetermined. The children discussed here are being raised in social settings in which gender expectations and interactional demands have been consciously changed to value gender equality. And the children in fair families have adopted their parents' egalitarian views. They say that men and women are equal and that no jobs—inside or outside the family—ought to be sex-typed. But beyond these abstract belief statements these children depend on their own lived experiences for understanding gender. And they "know" that boys and girls are very different.

Boys, as a group, are described—even by boys themselves—as not only athletic but also mean and troublesome. Girls are described as sweet, quiet, and well behaved. And yet it is clear that both boys and girls value, at some level, the masculine over the feminine, or at least the privileges that accompany male status. They notice that boys have more freedom at school and that most boys play harder and with more autonomy. Six of these children met their own criteria for being all boy or all girl; the rest exhibited some cross-gender behavior. The girls knew and reported how they were different from other girls; the boys did not. Gendered selves are changing here, but the change is uneven, with attitudes toward others changing faster than identities. Thorne (1993) shows that children from more mainstream families also

cross gender boundaries. Some boys from traditional families also develop soft and gentle selves, and girls from traditional homes can be seen aggressively entering boys' games on the playground. But Thorne gives no indication that children from more traditional families struggle with the inconsistencies among their beliefs, their extrafamilial experiences, and their developing identities.

The parents in fair families are transmitting new cognitive images or gender rules to their children. And though this process is hardly direct or perfectly effective, the children of these families seem to be adopting their parents' gender rules about adult responsibilities. But when it comes to developing their own identities, these children seem to be at least as influenced by the cognitive images and folk knowledge learned from peers as those messages from home. The children struggle with the contradictions between their parentally influenced ideologies and the cognitive images that dominate peer-group culture. In how they fashion their identities, their gendered selves, we can see why social change moves so slowly at the individual level.

Yet the parents in fair families also were raised in peer cultures with traditional cognitive images about gender and somehow have managed to create new ones for themselves. Their children are the product of a gender structure in flux. Most of them, while clearly developing gendered selves, are also crossing gender boundaries even as they subscribe to the ruling cognitive images in their own culture, which still define boys and girls as opposites. Each time a girl admits that she is not like other girls because she likes sports, each time a little boy differentiates himself from boys as a group because he does not like to fight, the cognitive image begins to blur. Eventually, perhaps, with some adult intervention, those childhood cognitive images might crack and dissolve, to be re-created in a post-gendered society. What is even more clear, however, is that as these children grow into adulthood and move into more egalitarian settings, they are well prepared to reconstruct post-gendered identities. There is no reason to believe that the identities and selves they adopt to negotiate their sexist and gendered childhood worlds will determine the selves they adopt later in life, as their social situations and the expectations they face change.

These data are very clear on another important point, too. These children are growing up to be happy, healthy, and well adjusted in egalitarian, gender-atypical families. They are doing well in families in which both parents are committed to labor-force participation and in which fathers are actively nurturing their children. These families dramatically depart from what many fundamentalist Judeo-Christian traditionalists and contemporary political conservatives have argued is the "natural" family—with patriarchal breadwinning fathers and homemaking mothers. Children raised in families with attentive and loving feminist parents do just fine.

But what is also clear is that changing families alone does not allow children to live post-gendered lives. Parents may have the power to change their marriage and their child-rearing techniques, but effective social change requires collective action and coalitions across families, schools, and friendship networks. Social change cannot be effective at the level of identities only; it must occur simultaneously at the level of identities, interactions, and institutions.

NOTE

1. An earlier report of these data about children in fair families is available in Risman and Myers (1997).

REFERENCES

Alanen, L. 1988. "Rethinking Childhood." *Acta Sociologica* 31: 53–67.

Bandura, A. 1962. "Social Learning Through Imitation." In *Nebraska Symposium on Motivation*, vol. 10, 211–274, edited by M. Jones. Lincoln: University of Nebraska Press.

———. 1971. *Psychological Modeling: Conflicting Themes.* Chicago: Aldine-Atherton.

Bem, Sandra L. 1993. *The Lenses of Gender: Transforming the Debate on Sexual Inequality.* New Haven: Yale University Press.

Borman, K. M., and P. O'Reilly. 1987. "Learning Gender Roles in Three Urban U.S. Kindergarten Classrooms." *Child and Youth Services* 8: 43–66.

Bornstein, Marc H., and Michael E. Lamb. 1988. *Developmental Psychology: An Advanced Textbook.* Hillsdale, N.J.: Erlbaum.

Collins, Patricia Hill. 1990. *Black Feminist Thought: Knowledge, Consciousness, and the Politics of Empowerment.* Boston: Unwin, Hyman.

Coltrane, Scott. 1996. *Family Man: Fatherhood, Housework, and Gender Equity.* Oxford: Oxford University Press.

Connell, Robert W. 1987. *Gender and Power: Society, the Person, and Sexual Politics.* Stanford, Calif: Stanford University Press.

Corsaro, W. A. 1985. *Friendship and Peer Culture in the Early Years.* Norwood, N.J.: Ablex.

Deaux, Kay. 1984. "From Individual Differences to Social Categories: Analysis of a Decade's Research on Gender." *American Psychologist* 39:105–116.

Fagot, B. I., M. D. Leinbach, and C. O'Boyle. 1992. "Gender Labeling, Gender Stereotyping, and Parenting Behaviors." *Development Psychology* 28: 225–230.

Hawkins, J. 1985. "Computers and Girls: Rethinking the Issues." *Sex Roles* 13: 165–180.

Hutson, A. H. 1983. "Sex-Typing." In *Handbook of Child Psychology*, vol 4, edited by E. M. Hetherington. New York: Wiley.

Inkeles, A. 1968. "Society, Social Structure, and Child Socialization." In *Socialization and Society*, ed. J. Clausen. Boston: Little, Brown.

Kohlberg, Lawrence. 1966. "A Cognitive-Developmental Analysis of Children's Sex-Role Concepts and Attitudes." In *The Development of Sex Differences*, 82–172, ed. Eleanor Maccoby. Stanford, Calif.: Stanford University Press.

Kreps, G. A., and S. L. Bosworth with J. A. Mooney, S. T. Russell, and K. A. Myers. 1994. *Organizing, Role Enactment, and Disaster: A Structural Theory.* Newark: University of Delware Press.

Lever, Janet. 1978. "Sex Differences in the Complexity of Children's Play and Games." *American Sociological Review* 43: 471–483.

Luttrell, W. 1993. "The Teachers, They All Had Their Pets: Concepts of Gender, Knowledge, and Power." *Signs* 18: 505–546.

Maccoby, E. E. 1992. "The Role of Parents in the Socialization of Children: An Historical Overview." *Developmental Psychology* 28: 1006–1017.

Martin, C. L. 1993. "New Directions for Investigating Children's Gender Knowledge." *Developmental Review* 13: 184–204.

Parsons, T., and R. Bales. 1955. *Family Socialization and Interaction Process.* Glencoe, Ill.: Free Press.

Peterson, G. W., and B. C. Rollins. 1987. "Parent–Child Socialization." In *Handbook of Marriage and the Family*, ed. M. Sussman and S. Steinmetz. New York: Plenum.

Piaget, J. 1932. *The Moral Judgement of the Child*. London: Kegan Paul.

Renzetti, C. M., and D. J. Curran. 1992. *Women and Men in Society*. Boston: Allyn and Bacon.

Richardson, L. W. 1981. *The Dynamics of Sex and Gender*. 2nd ed. Boston: Houghton-Mifflin.

Risman, Barbara, and Kristen Myers. 1997. "As the Twig Is Bent: Children Reared in Feminist Households." *Qualitative Sociology* 20: 2.

Schwartz, Pepper. 1994. *Peer Marriage: How Love between Equals Really Works*. New York: Free Press.

Segal, L. 1990. *Slow Motion: Changing Masculinities, Changing Men*. New Brunswick, N.J.: Rutgers University Press.

Signorelli, N. 1990. "Children, Television, and Gender Roles." *Journal of Adolescent Health Care* 11: 50–58.

Stern, M., and K. H. Karraker. 1989. "Sex Stereotyping of Infants: A Review of Gender Labeling Studies." *Sex Roles* 20: 501–522.

Thorne, Barrie. 1993. *Gender Play*. New Brunswick, N.J.: Rutgers University Press.

Wilder, G., D. Mackie, and J. Cooper. 1985. "Gender and Computers: Two Surveys of Gender-Related Attitudes." *Sex Roles* 13: 215–228.

P A R T   T H R E E

Social Organization of Gender

The processes of gender socialization that begin in early childhood prepare us for participation in society as adult women and men. Socialization alone, however, cannot account for the differences in power and prestige between men and women in almost all societies. Gender encompasses more than the socialized differences between individual women and men. As Judith Lorber pointed out in Section Two, gender also affects the way that social institutions—from family to medicine to politics—are structured. Key to feminist analyses is an understanding of the role of a society's *institutions* in perpetuating gender inequality.

Like other forms of social inequality, *gender inequality* includes the unequal distribution of three different kinds of valued commodities. First, inequality entails differential access to power, defined as the ability to carry out one's will despite opposition. Second, inequality includes differential access to the sources of prestige, defined as the ability to command respect, honor, and deference. Third, differential access to wealth, or economic and material resources, is important to inequality. Those who have access to any one of these resources—power, prestige, or wealth—occupy a position from which they are likely to achieve access to the others and thereby reinforce their status over those who have less. In the case of gender-stratified social systems, men's greater access to power, prestige, and wealth enhances their opportunities to exploit women and decreases women's ability to resist.

Of course, not all men have equal access to prestige, power, or wealth. Men of subordinate racial or ethnic groups, working-class and poor men, and many gay or elderly men are also excluded from socially sanctioned sources of power, prestige, and wealth. Women, too, vary in their degree of access to power, prestige, and wealth; white or upper-class women receive benefits from their class and race even while they are penalized for their gender. Patricia Hill Collins suggests that we think of gender as one system of domination that interacts with other systems of domination such as racism, class inequality, and heterosexism (Collins 1990). The task of feminist scholars is to trace the intersections of gender and other systems of domination, examining the varied ways that gender inequality is expressed and reinforced in social institutions.

Institutions construct systems of inequality in a variety of ways. Economic and legal systems; political, educational, medical, religious, and familial institutions; mass media; and the institutions of science and technology reinforce the ideology of women's inferiority and preserve men's greater access to power, wealth, and prestige. How? The *structures* of institutions are gendered in that they privilege men and those traits labeled masculine and they penalize women and the traits labeled feminine. Such institutions engage in practices that discriminate against women, exclude or devalue women's perspectives, and perpetuate the idea that differences between women and men and the dominance of men are natural. In addition, the control of these institutions usually rests in the hands of men, and social scientists understand that dominant groups tend to behave in ways that enhance their own power.

Institutions establish various kinds of rewards and punishments that encourage women to behave in submissive ways, and such submissive behavior in turn perpetuates the idea that women are naturally submissive. For example, a complex social system in the United States exerts strong pressures on women to marry heterosexually. Families train daughters to be wives and mothers; high school events require opposite-sex dates; college fraternities and sororities promote heterosexual coupling; widespread violence against women encourages them, ironically, to seek male protection; and men's higher incomes mean that heterosexual marriage tends to improve a woman's standard of living.

A woman's failure to marry constitutes a violation of social prescriptions and often leaves her economically disadvantaged and socially suspect. On the other hand, despite women's increasing participation in the paid labor force, in heterosexual marriage the burden of domestic labor still usually falls disproportionately on women, a dynamic that helps maintain the inequality between men and women in the work world.

It is important to reiterate that gender stratification is not the only form of inequality affecting women's and men's lives and the structure of social institutions. Institutions that disadvantage racial or ethnic groups, older people, the disabled, the poor, or particular religious or class-based groups also discriminate against both women and men who belong to those groups. Understanding women's oppression as a function of the social organization of gender necessitates understanding the overlaps between sexism and other forms of subordination.

The following articles examine how particular institutions express, construct, and maintain gender inequality. They analyze the ways that women's subordination is maintained in work, families, sexuality, treatment of and attitudes about bodies, and violence against women. The articles do not simply document women's submission, however. They also describe the ways that women and men in various groups resist oppression and attempt to exercise control over their choices and their lives. To what extent are women or men able to resist the structures of gender, and to what extent are they controlled by gendered institutions?

REFERENCE

Collins, Patricia Hill. 1990. *Black Feminist Thought.* New York: Routledge.

Work

Work for pay influences many aspects of our lives: our economic prosperity, our social status, where we live, our relationships with family members and friends, our health, and our access to health care. Our work experiences influence how we come to view others, ourselves, and the social world around us. Reciprocally, how we are situated in society often influences the kind of work we do and our compensation for that work.

In traditional societies, division of labor based on sex and age did not necessarily correspond to differences in the importance assigned to different tasks: "women's work" might be considered just as socially valuable as "men's work." In societies like the United States, however, social divisions of labor based on gender, race, and age reflect and perpetuate power differences among groups.

This section begins with Alice Kessler-Harris's examination of the historical justifications of pay inequities between women and men. "The Wage Conceived: Value and Need as Measures of a Woman's Worth" explores the ideological bases of the differential economic rewards available to women and men and the implications of both gender ideologies and the economic practices for women's participation in the workforce. Can you think of ways in which these historical justifications for paying women less than men are still influential today?

Inequities between women and men in earnings often exist because the sexes are concentrated in different occupations. In "Sex Segregation in the

U.S. Labor Force," Christine Bose and Rachel Whaley survey the continued concentration of women in predominately female and men in predominately male occupations. The most common occupations for women include secretary, cashier, and nurse, while men are most likely to be employed as truck drivers and carpenters. Bose and Whaley discuss the different ways of measuring sex segregation, the nature of sex segregation in white-collar, pink-collar, clerical, and blue-collar jobs, and the various explanations for the persistence of sex segregation into the twenty-first century. They also argue that sex segregation matters, not just because it contributes to the wage gap, but also because it leads to tokenism and lack of occupational mobility. Thinking about the people you know, how many are in non-sex-segregated jobs? What factors hinder people from finding work outside the traditional gender-appropriate occupations? How important is outright discrimination? What do you think can be done to end sex segregation in the labor force?

In the next article, "Moving Up and Taking Charge," Barbara Reskin and Irene Padavic examine sex differences in promotion and authority. Although the gap between women and men's access to promotions has narrowed over the past thirty years, there are still some groups of women—especially African American women—and women in some kinds of jobs—particularly low-skill ones—who have very little access to promotion. We hear a great deal about the "glass ceiling" that prevents women in high-level positions from rising to the top, but less about the "sticky floor" that keeps women in low-mobility jobs. But even when women have better chances of promotion, they still experience an authority gap at work.

Reskin and Padevic assess four explanations for sex inequalities in promotion and the exercise of authority: sex segregation, human capital inequalities, sex differences in social networks, and discriminatory personnel practices. They also consider potential remedies. They ask, "Will the outlook be better for the college students of today?" What do you think? How many women department chairs, deans, and vice presidents are there at your college or university? What remedies do you think have the best chance of success in closing the promotion and authority gap?

The last article in this section focuses on the experiences of Latina domestic workers in Los Angeles. Here we see up close the consequences of sex segregation and racial/ethnic patterns of employment as Pierrette Hondagneu-Sotelo talks with immigrant women, mostly from Latin America, who work as live-in and live-out nannies and housekeepers and as housecleaners. We see why they choose particular kinds of jobs at different times. New immigrants without the support of family and friends must often take jobs as live-ins, the least desirable position because of the lack of privacy, social isolation, long hours, incessant demands, and low pay. We hear how these Latina women feel about the houses they must clean, the children they care for, the food (or lack thereof) their employers provide. We understand why, as soon as they can, women choose to work on a live-out basis, in their own homes and communities, and why some choose housecleaning as the most autonomous job.

Hondagneu-Sotelo puts these women's experiences into the context of immigration, transnational motherhood, and racial stereotyping. What do the experiences of Latina domestic workers tell us about gender, ethnicity, and employment? What determines whether they see their jobs as good jobs? Think about the relationship between their lives and the lives of the women who employ them.

As these articles demonstrate, women's ethnicities, ages, and class backgrounds affect both the structural opportunities available to them in the labor force and their interpretations of these experiences. What experiences, if any, do women in the labor force share by virtue of their gender?

The Wage Conceived: Value and Need as Measures of a Woman's Worth

❧ Alice Kessler-Harris

When a person complains that a certain wage rate is unduly low, he may be making that judgment in the light of what he thinks is due the kind of person *performing that work, e.g. a married man. Others may regard the same rate as not unreasonable in view of the kind of work* it is.

—*Henry A. Landsberger*[1]

In 1915 New York State's Factory Investigating Commission asked some seventy-five prominent individuals—economists, social reformers, businessmen, and publicists among them—what factors determined the rate of wages. The answers varied. Some suggested that workers' organizations were most important; others believed the size of a business's profits could enhance or restrain the wages of employees. Another key factor was the standard of living anticipated by workers. But the majority of those interviewed believed the efficiency of the worker and the supply of labor constituted by far the two most powerful determinants of wages.[2] These traditional explanations for wage rates would have found favor with the proponents of the economic theory then popular.

Widely accepted wage theory at the turn of the century was rooted in, though not limited to, the law of supply and demand. If that phrase, as economic historian Arnold Tolles implies, does not do economists justice, it does, at least, convey the economists' belief "that the reward for every kind of human effort is controlled by some kind of impersonal and irresistible force, similar to the force of gravity."[3] Theory held that wages would rise or fall in response to employers' fluctuating willingness to pay. That willingness in turn was predicated on what employers thought they could

earn from labor as well as on how much labor was available at different wage rates. Thus, in theory, the demand for labor (measured by the additional revenue labor could produce) and the supply (which took into account the differences in education and training of the worker) together determined the wage.[4]

Despite the apparent certainty of economists such as Professor Roy Blakely of Cornell, who testified before the commission that "wages tend to approximate the value of what they produce,"[5] the theory left room for a substantial degree of subjective judgment on the part of employers as to the value of particular workers. A critical part of the chemical mix that determined the wages of workers in general involved something intangible called "custom." If a male worker was paid according to some formula that reflected the value of what he produced and the difficulty of replacing him, he was also paid according to what he and other workers thought he was worth. Custom, or tradition, played an acknowledged but uncalculated role in regulating the wage. But custom and tradition were gendered. They influenced male and female wages in different ways. And especially in the female wage, they played a far larger role than we have earlier been willing to concede. The women's wage, at least for the early twentieth century, rested in large measure on conceptions of what women needed.

The distinction alerts us to the rich possibilities contained in the wage conceived as a social rather than as a theoretical construct. If the wage is, as most economists readily acknowledge, simultaneously a set of ideas about how people can and should live and a marker of social status, then it contains within it a set of social messages and a system of meanings that influence the way women and men behave. We are all familiar with the capacity of these social meanings to reduce the wages of recent immigrants, of

African-Americans, and of other groups. But, partly because it is so apparently natural, the capacity of the wage to speak to issues of gender is less clear. Yet the language with which the women's wage is conceived throws into relief the same process that exists for men. The wage frames gendered messages; it encourages or inhibits certain forms of behavior; it can reveal a system of meaning that shapes the expectations of men and women and anticipates their struggles over power; it participates in the negotiations that influence the relationships of the sexes inside and outside the family. In all these capacities, the wage functions as a terrain of contest over visions of fairness and justice. This essay will attempt to illustrate some of these processes in the early twentieth century.

The structure of wages that emerged in the course of industrialization in the late nineteenth century reflected a long tradition that revolved around what has become known as the family wage—the sum necessary to sustain family members. That sum had been earned by several family members for most of the history of capitalism. Family income was typically pooled and then redistributed by one family member. But the dream of a family wage that could be earned by a male breadwinner alone had long been an object of struggle among organized working people who thought of it as a mechanism for regulating family life and allowing women to work in their own homes.[6] Ideally, and sometimes in practice, the family wage was a male wage, a wage that went to a male breadwinner.[7]

What then of a woman's wage? It reflected not what was but what ought to be. That men ought to be able to support wives and daughters implied that women need not engage in such support. They ought to be performing home duties. Thus, if a woman earned wages, the normal expectation was that she did so to supplement those of other family wage earners. Theoretically, at least, the decision as to who would and would not earn was regulated by the family unit. The wage belonged to her family. Until the third quarter of the nineteenth century, U.S. law and practice reflected these assumptions. Typically, a woman's wage was legally the property of her husband or father. The average wage of women workers was little more than half of the male wage. And even the most skilled women rarely earned as much as two-thirds of the average paid to unskilled men. If a woman lived independently, her wage was normally not sufficient to support her. Nor was it intended to do so.

The nineteenth century fight for a family wage was thus simultaneously a fight for a social order in which men could support their families and receive the services of women; and women, dependent on men, could stay out of the labor force. Historians have debated the advantages and disadvantages of this mode of thinking, but for our purposes it is important to note only that the family wage reflected popular thinking—a sense of what was right and just.[8] Widely supported by working-class men and women at the end of the nineteenth century, it rested on what seemed to many to be a desirable view of social order.

Its incarnation in the form of the living wage more clearly isolated the female role. Though the content of a living wage varied, like the family wage, it was imbued with gendered expectations. John Ryan, the Catholic priest who was the United States' most prolific exponent of the living wage, for example, asserted the laborer's right to a "decent and reasonable" life that meant to him "the right to exercise one's primary faculties, supply one's essential needs, and develop one's personality."[9] Others were somewhat more specific. British economist William Smart thought the living wage ought to pay for "a well-drained dwelling, with several rooms, warm clothing with some changes of underclothing, pure water, a plentiful supply of cereal food with a moderate allowance of meat and milk and a little tea, etc., some education, and some recreation, and lastly sufficient freedom for his wife from other work to enable her to perform properly her maternal and her household duties."[10] John Mitchell, head of the United Mine Workers union, was somewhat more ambitious. The wage, he thought, ought to be enough to purchase "the American standard of living." This included, but was not limited to, "a comfortable house of at least six rooms," which contained a bathroom, good sanitary plumbing, parlor, dining room, kitchen, sleeping rooms, carpets, pictures, books, and furniture.[11]

For Ryan, as for other proponents of the living wage, the "love and companionship of a person of the opposite sex"[12] was an essential element of what a living wage should purchase. The bottom line, according to Ryan, was the laborer's capacity "to live in a manner consistent with the dignity of a human being."[13] The *Shoe Workers' Journal* proposed that "everything necessary to the life of *a normal man* be included in the living wage: the right to marriage, the right to have children and to educate them."[14]

As the family wage held the promise of female homemaking, the living wage, which explicitly incorporated wife and children, excluded the possibility that female dignity could inhere either in a woman's ability to earn wages or in her capacity to support a family. Because the living wage idealized a world in which men had the privilege of caring for women and children, it implicitly refused women that privilege. And, because it assumed female dependency, to imagine female independence impugned male roles and male egos. Ground rules for female wage earners required only self-support, and even that was estimated at the most minimal level. Champions of the living wage for women counted among her necessities food, clothing, rent, health, savings, and a small miscellaneous fund.[15] Nothing in the arguments for a female living wage vitiates the harsh dictum of John Stuart Mill. The wages of single women, asserted that famous economist, "must be equal to their support, but need not be more than equal to it; the minimum in their case is the pittance absolutely required for the sustenance of one human being."[16] "Women who are forced to provide their own sustenance have a right," echoed Ryan, "to what is a living wage *for them.*" Their compensation, he argued, with apparent generosity, "should be sufficient to enable them to live decently."[17]

At the time Ryan wrote, women constituted close to 25 percent of the industrial workforce. More than one-third of wage-earning women in urban areas lived independently of their families, and three-quarters of those living at home helped to support other family members. False conceptions of women who needed only to support themselves did a particular disservice to Black women, who were eight times as likely to earn wages as white women. For Black women racial discrimination and its attendant poverty meant that more that one-third of those who were married would continue to earn wages, and virtually all of those who earned wages participated in family support.[18] Yet the real needs of these women were rarely acknowledged. Nor did the brief, dismissive commentary on "a woman's living wage" mention recreation or comfort or human dignity or the capacity to care for others.

Ryan readily conceded that men without families to support and/or with other means of support were entitled to draw a living wage because "they perform as much labor as their less fortunate fellows."[19] His proposals generously allocated a living wage to men who never intended to marry because "rights are to be interpreted according to the average conditions of human life."[20] But the same generosity was not evident in notions of the living wage for women workers. Rather, it seemed fair to reduce women to the lowest levels of bestiality. Advocates of the living wage confidently explained that women's "standard of physical comfort, in other words, their standard of life" was lower than that of men." While her ideals were "naturally higher than those of men, her physical wants are simpler. The living wage for a woman is lower than the living wage for a man because it is possible for her as a result of her traditional drudgery and forced tolerance of pain and suffering to keep alive upon less."[21] Women, with a single set of exceptions, were to be paid only according to their most minimal needs. Only to women who were employed in the same jobs as men did Ryan concede the need for equal pay because, he argued, "when women receive less pay than men, the latter are gradually driven out of the occupation."[22]

Ryan failed to acknowledge that in attributing to women "average conditions" that reflected social myth rather than reality he undermined his own cause. While his vision and that of most living wage advocates came from a desire to protect the home, not from antagonism to the pitiable condition of those women who worked for wages, his proposals left the home vulnerable. "The welfare of the whole family," he noted, "and that of society likewise, renders it imperative that the wife and mother should not engage in any labor except that of the household. When she works for hire, she can neither care properly for her own health, rear her children aright, nor make her home what it should be for her husband, her children, herself."[23] Theoretically, that might have been true; but in practice, by reducing women's potential capacity to earn adequate incomes, he diminished their ability to support themselves and their homes.

Without negating the good intentions of Ryan and others on behalf of the family and without imposing anachronistic judgments about their desire to protect the family and to place family needs ahead of women's individual rights, one can still see that the consequences of their rhetoric for women who earned wages were no mere abstractions. They assumed a hard and concrete reality, for example, in discussions of the minimum wage for women that took place between about 1911 and 1913. To alleviate the plight of women workers, social reformers attempted to pass legislation that would force employers to pay a wage sufficient to meet a woman's minimal needs. Between 1912 and 1923, thirteen states and the District of Columbia passed such legislation in one form or another. Each statute was preceded by a preamble that declared the legislators' intentions to offer protection that ranged from providing a sum "adequate for maintenance" to ensuring enough to "maintain the worker in health" and guaranteeing her "moral well-being." Whatever the language of the preamble, and whatever the mechanism by which the wage was ultimately to be decided, the minimum was invariably rooted in what was determined to be a "living" wage for women workers.[24] But the discussion required some estimate of what a living wage might be. Elizabeth Beardsley Butler, who surveyed working women in Pittsburgh in 1907, suggested that a woman could "not live decently and be self supporting" at a wage of less than $7 a week. Three years later Louise Bosworth estimated the living wage of Boston's women ranged from $9 to $11 a week—the first amount would keep a woman from dying of cold or hunger; the second provided the possibility of efficiency at work and some minimal recreation.[25] The question, said social pundit Thomas Russell, was whether "it is to be an amount that shall provide only the bare necessaries of life or shall it include some provision for comforts, recreation, and the future?"[26]

The budgets drawn up by experts generally opted only for the necessities. Arrived at after extensive surveys to uncover the actual expenditures of "working girls," and heavily reliant on language and imagery that reduced women to perpetual girlhood, they included almost nothing beyond the barest sustenance.[27] A typical survey was undertaken by Sue Ainslee Clark in 1908 and published by Clark and Edith Wyatt in the pages of McClure's magazine in 1910.[28] The authors focused on the effortful struggle to make ends meet, turning survival itself into a praiseworthy feat. They exuded sympathy for the girl who "ate no breakfast," whose "luncheon consisted of coffee and rolls for ten cents," and who, as "she had no convenient place for doing her own laundry, . . . paid 21 cents a week to have it done. Her regular weekly expenditure was as follows: lodging, 42 cents; board, $1.40; washing, 21 cents; clothing and all other expenses, $1.97: total, $4."[29] Such estimates encouraged social investigators to define precisely

how much a female wage earner might spend for everything from undergarments to gifts.

The debate over the minimum wage revealed what this outward order dictated: to live alone required the strictest exercise of thrift, self-discipline, and restraint. The budgets warned fiercely against expectations of joy, spontaneity, pleasure, or recreation. Even the carfare that might provide access to a walk in the country was rigidly restricted. The wage prescribed a spartan lifestyle, sufficient, it was hoped, to preserve morality for those destined to earn but not so generous as to tempt those in families to live outside them. It limited fantasy to the price of survival and held open the door of ambition only to a meager independence. Its effects are grimly reflected in a series of snippets selected by and published in Harper's Bazaar in 1908 under the title "The Girl Who Comes to the City."[30]

Offering to pay $5 for each one it used, the magazine solicited brief essays "written by those girl readers who have gone through the experience of coming to the city, and either succeeding or failing there during the last ten years."[31] Success, in these pieces, is measured in small and treasured doses. Mere survival emerges as a potent source of satisfaction. In a period when most experts estimated a living wage at around $9 a week, a pay envelope that amounted to $10 a week could yield happiness. A $2-a-week raise, accompanied by a kind boss, and perhaps the chance to improve oneself by reading occasionally at work seemed to be the height of ambition.[32] At the top of the wage scale, a bookkeeper could aspire to $65 a month, enough to ensure a small cash balance in the bank if one limited social excursions to one night a week and carefully selected clothes from among sale items.[33] The stories reveal justified pride and accomplishment in the ability to sustain oneself. But they also tell us something of the limits imposed on women's aspirations. "I had," boasted one contributor about the period before she returned home, "made both ends meet financially for five months and I had saved a modest sum for the purchase of a winter suit."[34] Even women who needed help in the form of occasional contributions of clothing felt they had managed very nicely.

And yet, in practice, survival was the best, not the worst, that the wage embodied. The estimates made by well-intentioned reformers and the efforts of the most well-meaning women were compromised by the refusal of most employers to concede a woman's need even to support herself. Evidence for this is part of the folklore of the female labor market before World War II and has frequently been recorded by historians.[35] The *Harper's Bazaar* series is no exception. There, as elsewhere, women recalled how difficult it was to ask for reasonable compensation. A stenographer described how a lawyer had refused to pay more because "he expected young women had friends who helped them out." A budding news reporter was told by a potential employer that his "rule is never to employ a woman who must depend entirely upon my salaries."[36]

The aspirations of young women thus fell victim to the self-confirming myths that enforced their dependence. Nineteenth-century British economist William Smart described the process succinctly. Part of the reason a woman's wage is low, he suggested, was "because she does not require a high wage, whether it be because her father partly supports her, or because her maintenance does not cost so much."[37] Employers routinely acted upon this myth. "We try to employ girls who are members of families," a box manufacturer told social investigator and economist Elizabeth Butler, "for we don't pay the girls a living wage in this trade."[38] Historian Joanne Meyerowitz summed up the prevailing attitude this way: "Employers assumed that all working women lived in families where working males provided them with partial support. It profited employers to use this idealized version of the family economy to determine women's wages."[39]

For all the elaborate theory justifying low wages, the bottom line turned out almost always to be the employer's sense of what was acceptable. Men, as Elizabeth Butler noted, came into occupations at a wage paid for the job. Women came into them at a wage deemed appropriate for female workers—not, that is to say, at the customary wage level of the occupation but "at a level analogous to that paid women generally in other occupations."[40] New York City social worker Mary Alden Hopkins told the Factory Investigating Commission that the sex of the employee was one of the most important influences on women's wages. "In laundry work, factory work, some mercantile establishments and home work, efficiency has little and often no effect upon wages," she declared.[41] The hardest woman's job, in her judgment, was the lowest paid, and an increase in worker productivity and employer profits led less often to rewarding workers than to discharging

high-paid workers in favor of those who could be paid less. The young Scott Nearing summarized the process this way: "No one even pretends that there is a definite relation between the values produced by the worker and the wage which he secures."[42] Samuel Gompers would have agreed: "Everyone knows that there is little connection between the value of services and wages paid; the employer pays no more than he must."[43]

While from the economist's perspective this may be a gross oversimplification, employers, workers, and observers all accepted the critical importance of custom in the wage structure. A vice president of the Pullman Company, speaking before the commission that investigated the great strike of 1894, acknowledged as much. Piece rates, he said, were based on the company's estimates of a "reasonable wage for ten hours . . . for a competent workman." If the company discovered "that at the piece price fixed the known less competent and less industrious workmen are regularly making an unreasonable day's wage, it becomes apparent that the piece price allotted is too large."[44] At issue here was what was "reasonable" and "unreasonable," not the productivity or efficiency of the worker. In this context, that part of the content of custom should rest on the sex of the worker appears to be merely natural. An official of International Harvester, testifying before an Illinois investigating commission in 1912, described his company's efforts to set a minimum wage for female employees. His company's desire, he claimed, "was to establish a minimum that would be fair and reasonable." But the constraints of what was deemed reasonable were established as much by the nature and characteristics of the worker as by the company's financial spreadsheets. "The girls affected by lower wages," he said in mitigation, "are mostly of foreign birth. They are not required to dress up for their employment. Many of those to whom we will pay $8 could not earn a dollar downtown."[45] Presumably, the same kind of reasoning led to paying Black women less than white women. Although occupational segregation accounts for most of the wage differential between Black and white women, Black women who worked on the same kinds of jobs routinely received one dollar a week less.

Nor was the weight of custom in setting wages a hidden dimension. Rather, the comments of employers and others reveal it to have been quite conscious and available. Several respondents to the Factory

Investigating Commission's survey noted its influence in setting wage rates, pointing out that wages could not be set without reference to such factors as the "needs of the individual and family," the influence of "local or trade union conditions," and the differential requirements of *"pin-money workers."* Edward Page, an officer of the Merchants' Association of New York, thought that the "customary or habitual rate of wages which prevails in the group to which the workingman belongs and which is usual in the industry under consideration . . . is by far the most important factor in the determination of wages."[46] On their face these factors were gender neutral. But since each embodied deeply rooted aspects of gendered expectations, the wage both reflected and perpetuated gendered behavior.

If the role of custom in fixing wages is not surprising, and we can take for granted that sex played a part, then we need ask only to what degree the sex of the worker influenced custom. When it came to women, one might argue that custom played not the smallest but the largest part in determining the wage. William Smart placed the factors that determined the wages of women in the category of "wants." The wage scale in a modern industrial economy, he suggested, was typically determined by "what a worker does." But for a woman "what the worker is" was the gauge of wages. The difference made him uneasy. "If a male worker," he asked, "is supposed to get a high wage when he produces much, a low wage when he produces little, why should a woman's wage be determined by another principle? We cannot hunt with the individualist hounds and run with the socialist hare."[47]

Yet women's wages at the turn of the century clung stubbornly to what Smart would have called her "wants" rather than to either the value of the product or the level of the worker's productivity. For if custom was inscribed into the wage and the wage was conceived male, what *women* earned was not in the same sense as *males* a "wage." In the minds of employers and of male workers, the wage was to be paid to those who supported families.[48] If part of its function was to reflect the value of the product made, another and equally important part was to make a statement about the value of the worker who made the product. As long as female workers were not—could not be—male workers, their wages could not hope to touch those of their male peers.

We can guess that employers thought of it that way by their responses to questions about how much

they paid women. Louise Bosworth cited the case of a woman who told her employer, "We cannot live on what we earn," and was asked in response, "Then what wages can you live on?"[49] The same paternalistic assumptions appear among employers who testified before the commission that investigated Illinois's *white slave* traffic in 1912. [Editors' note: "White slavery" was the phrase used in the early 1900s to refer to forced prostitution.] The employers interviewed reported unhesitatingly that they paid their male and female workers on the basis of what they estimated each needed. Julius Rosenwald, head of Sears, Roebuck and Company, then a mail-order house, told an investigative commission that "the concern made it a point not to hire girls not living at home at less than $8 a week."[50] A Montgomery Ward vice president echoed the sentiment: "We claim that all our employees without homes are on a self-supporting basis, and if we discover they are not we will put them there in an hour."[51] One department store executive described how his store asked all job applicants to sign a form "giving their estimate of necessary expenses in addition to family particulars. The girls who are not receiving sufficient to live on come to us. There are many instances of such receiving an increase." No one ever investigated the accuracy of the application forms, and even the commission chair was dubious as to who the procedure protected. A girl might readily lie about home support, he noted, "to assure herself of a job."[52] But at bottom, this was less the issue than the prevailing assumption that "girls" could and should be paid at a minimum that relied on family subsidy rather than on what their labor was worth.

If employers and popular opinion are any guide, and the question of what appeared to be reasonable lay at the heart of the wage structure, then all wages—not only those of women—contained a greater proportion of wants than most of us have recognized. Women's wages, then, are only uniquely vulnerable in the sense that they participate in popular definitions of gender that denigrate the needs of one sex. The wage simultaneously framed job-related expectation in the light of existing gender roles and shaped gender experiences to avoid disappointment in view of the prevailing wage structure. More than exploitation of women, or paternalism toward them, the wage reflected a rather severe set of injunctions about how men and women were to live. These injunctions could be widely negated only at the peril of social order. Thus, part of the function of the female wage was to ensure attachment to family. The male wage, in contrast, provided incentives to individual achievement. It promoted geographical mobility and sometimes hinted at the possibility of social mobility as well. The female wage allowed women to survive; the male wage suggested a contribution to national economic well-being. These messages affirmed existing values and integrated all the parties into a set of understandings that located the relationships of working men and women to each other.

Some of these messages are powerful. Existing wage fund theory posited a limited sum available for all wages. It reduced the incentive to provide a higher wage for women by suggesting that their gain would come at the cost of male raises and therefore threaten the family's well-being. Smart put it this way: "Women's wages are, after all, part and parcel of the one share in the distribution of income which falls to labor."[53] What followed from that, of course, was that raising women's wages would merely reduce those of the men in their class by a similar proportion, leaving families in the same place economically and depriving them of maternal care to boot. Samuel Gompers translated this into a warning to members of the American Federation of Labor: "In industries where the wives and children toil, the man is often idle because he has been supplanted, or because the aggregate wages of the family are no higher than the wages of the adult man—the husband and father of the family."[54]

If women's wage gains could come only at the cost of the family, then their low wages affirmed and supported existing family life. As the renowned economist Alfred Marshall put it, a higher wage for women might be "a great gain in so far as it tends to develop their faculties, but an injury in so far as it tempts them to neglect their duty of building up a true home, and of investing their efforts in the personal capital of their children's character and abilities."[55] To Marshall the clear social choice implicit in the wage payment was between individual achievement and family well-being. His statement affirms the use of wages to preserve what is desirable to him: that all women are or will be married, that marriage is a normal state, that women will be continuously supported by men with sufficient wages, and that under these circumstances a wage that might be translated into an incentive not to marry or remain within families poses a challenge. Moreover, Marshall's view reflected the prevailing belief that a man was entitled to a wife to serve him and their home. It contained the assumption that a female who did not have a husband had erred. The differential female wage thus carried a moral injunction, a warning to women to follow the natural order.

The absence, by choice or necessity, of a family of her own did not excuse a woman from adherence to familial duties or morals, nor did it impel a more generous attitude toward wages. In fact, the level of the wage, which signaled an affirmation of family life, simultaneously threw out a challenge to preserve morality. In a March 1913 letter to the *New York Herald*, the head of Illinois's vice commission commented that "our investigations . . . show conclusively that thousands of good girls are going wrong every year merely because they can not live upon the wages paid them by employers."[56] But this was not necessarily an invitation to raise wages. Since not to live within a family was itself immoral, and the wage was seen as primarily a contribution to family life, a higher wage would only contribute to immorality. An ongoing debate over the fine line between a wage high enough to tempt women into supporting themselves and one so low that it could push the unwary into prostitution placed the wage in thrall to morality. Social worker Jeannette Gilder found herself in the awkward position of testifying against a pay raise for working women because "it seems to me to be paying a pretty poor compliment to the young women of this country to suggest that their virtue hangs upon such a slender thread that its price can be fixed somewhere between $6 and $8 a week."[57] And yet those who insisted that a low wage was an invitation to prostitution dominated the debate.

The wage also transmitted messages about the workforce. Employers feared that a rise in women's wages would trigger a demand for higher wages for men. As the wage captured social restrictions on female aspirations at work, so it conveyed the male potential for advancement, promotion, loyalty, and persistence. Contemporaries understood this well. When Elizabeth Butler remarked that "boys are often preferred to girls . . . because they can be relied on to learn the trade and women cannot,"[58] she captured the notion that implicit in the wage is the assumption that a man's wage is an investment in the future, while a woman's wage assumes only that the work at hand will be done. Economist Francis Walker said this in a different way. If a man marries, he "becomes a better and more notable workman on that account." In contrast, if a woman marries, "it is most probable that she will . . . be a less desirable laborer than she was before."[59] Yet these statements promote the self-fulfilling function they simultaneously reflect. Lacking a man's wage, women were not normally given the opportunity to demonstrate that they too could be an investment in the future. Such experiments would be dangerous. Not only would a higher wage for women convey an inaccurate estimate of the potential occupational mobility of females, but it might inhibit the employer's capacity to use wages to construct the workforce to his liking.

Finally, the wage made a familiar statement about female personality. Holding the stereotypical male as the norm, it claimed recompense for the costs of translating female qualities into the marketplace. Francis Walker exaggerated but caught the point when *he* insisted that the wage reflected women's character traits as well as their domestic orientation. It took account, *he* noted, of personalities that were "intensely sensitive to opinion, [and] shrink from the familiar utterances of blame." Coldness and indifference alone, he thought, were often sufficient to repress women's "impulses to activity."[60] These qualities of character exacted supervisory costs of the employer that were recaptured in the lower pay of women. As Charles Cheney, a South Manchester, Connecticut, manufacturer, put it, part of the reason women were paid less than men was because "they are sensitive and require extraordinarily tactful and kindly treatment and much personal consideration."[61]

Restrictive as the messages thrown out by a woman's wage were clearly intended to be, they were by no means the only messages that reached women. The very existence of a wage, the possibility of earning income evoked a contrary set of images: images that derived some support from the promise of American success. The same wage that evoked a struggle to survive and placed a lid on social mobility, the same wage that obscured women's visions of independence and citizenship had the capacity to conjure contrary images as well. It could even point the way to potential equality for women. These tensions are visible in the huge strikes that wracked the garment industry beginning in 1909–10, in the energy of young female labor leaders, and in the quest of more affluent women for lives that combined career and motherhood. Such events indicate that the notion of wages rooted in wants existed in a contested

sphere—tempered by a broader ideology of individualism. They lead us to wonder about the role played by a woman's wage in a period of changing wants and rising levels of personal ambition.

The wage that in some measure helped to affirm and construct gendered expectations in the period before World War I continued to play that role afterward. But the dramatic social changes that came during and after the war, particularly the rise of a consumer culture, created their own pressures on the structure of gender. Because for most people the wage offered access to consumption, it mediated some of the tensions in gender roles that emerged in the 1920s. While public perception of a woman's wage remained conceptually "needs-based," continuing to limit female expectations, it quickly became clear that changing needs demanded some concessions to women's individual aspirations. These mixed messages contributed to arguments among women about who deserved a wage.[62]

In the statistical tables, the war appears as a small blip in the history of working women. New entrants into the labor force were relatively few, and the teens ended with little apparent increase in the numbers of women who earned wages. But the big surprise lay in the numbers of women who switched jobs. About half a million women, it seemed, chose to move into men's jobs. The *New York Times* commented on these figures with surprise: "The world of men woke up and took a second look at the world of women during the World War. It is still looking." And, it continued, "the Great War has in many cases been responsible for a change of premise as well as job."[63]

The primary explanation for these job shifts seems to have been the attraction of the male wage. Historian Maurine Greenwald estimates, for example, that women who became streetcar conductors immediately increased their wages by about *one-third* over those they had earned in traditional female jobs.[64] Daniel Nelson, who has explored the transformation of the factory, notes that after 1915 "the wages offered by machinery and munitions makers" drew an increasing number of women who had worked in traditional women's fields.[65] Though women's productivity was frequently acknowledged to be as high as that of the men they replaced, women were not, on principle, offered the same wage. A twenty-six-city survey by the New York State Industrial Commission at the end of the war revealed that *less* than 10 percent of the women who replaced men received pay equal to that of the men who had preceded them. The commission reported that "in many cases the production of women was equal to that of men, in others it was greater, and in still others, less. The wages paid had little, if anything, to do with productive efficiency."[66] Since women who were paid less than men still earned far more than they could have at women's jobs, few of those who benefited from wartime opportunities complained. But the pressure of a dual wage structure on male wages posed a problem. Fearing a breakdown of social order, men and women began to call for a wage paid for the job—or equal pay. This slogan, as we will see later, was designed primarily to reduce pressure on men's wages.

Though most of the wartime job shifts proved to be temporary, they signaled an incipient dissatisfaction among some wage-earning women over the issue of wages—a dissatisfaction that could no longer be contained by rationalizations over social role. These struggles frequently pitted women who earned wages against those who did not, revealing something about contested definitions of womanhood among white women. For example, when female streetcar conductors in several large cities waged largely futile battles to hang on to their high-paying jobs, they were fighting not only the men who wanted their jobs back but a conception of womanliness that restricted access to outdoor work. And the female printers in New York State who successfully struggled to exempt themselves from legislation that precluded their working during the lucrative night hours simultaneously attacked rigid conceptions of family life.

Such campaigns were opposed by clear signals from government and corporations to women not to expect too much. The Women's Bureau of the Department of Labor offers a case in point. In 1920, when the bureau was created, it received a meagre $75,000 lump-sum appropriation and distributed it as effectively as it could. In 1922 a House proviso "stipulated that no salary in the Women's Bureau should be more than $1800, except three at $2000, and the director's and assistant director's salaries which have been fixed by statute." If effected, the proviso, as the Women's Bureau pointed out, would have left it with "no staff of technically trained, experienced people to direct and supervise its work." But more important, the bureau noted that other agencies of the government paid their male

employees with the same qualifications "very much higher salaries than any that have even been suggested by the Women's Bureau—twice as much in many instances."[67]

Such policies were routine in industry. In the electrical industry of the 1920s, Ronald Schatz reports that "corporations maintained separate pay scales for men and women. Male wage keysheets began where female keysheets left off; the least skilled male workers earned more than the most capable female employee."[68] Still, the point for women was that even this low pay exceeded that of such traditionally female jobs as laundry work and waiting on tables. "For this reason, many young women preferred jobs in electrical factories." When the Ford Motor Company instituted a five-dollar day for its male employees after the war, it deliberately omitted women workers. According to Vice President James Couzens, women "are not considered such economic factors as men."[69]

Corporations carefully distinguished between the kinds of social welfare programs offered as extensions of cash wages to women and men. General Electric and Westinghouse offered men programs that stressed financial and job security, such as a 5 percent bonus every six months after five years of service, a pension after twenty years, and group life insurance and paid vacations after ten years of service. Women, for whom longevity was not encouraged and for whom it was thought not to matter, got programs that emphasized sociability, such as "dances, cooking classes, secretarial instruction, picnics, clubs, and summer camps."[70]

The not-so-subtle relationship between policy and practice is beautifully illustrated in the self-confirming apparatus in effect at the General Electric Company, where President Gerard Swope defended his policies on the grounds that "our theory was that women did not recognize the responsibilities of life and were hoping to get married soon and would leave us, and therefore, this insurance premium deduction from the pay would not appeal to them."[71] As historian Ronald Schatz notes, because GE compelled women to quit if they married, women rarely acquired enough seniority to obtain pensions or vacations with pay. Women's aspirations could not be entirely stilled by these measures. The Ford Motor Company, according to historian Stephen Meyer III, "considered all women, regardless of their family stakes, as youths: that is as single men under twenty-two without

dependents, and therefore ineligible for Ford profits."
Yet "as the result of criticism from women's rights
advocates, the company eventually allowed some
women, who were the heads of households, to participate in its welfare plan."[72]

One result of such policies and an instrument in
their perpetuation as well was that women carefully
rationalized their increasing workforce participation
and defended themselves by comparing their wages
only to those of other women. The model was familiar. The numerous investigating commissions of the
prewar period had already asserted the injustice of
paying women as much as men. Thus, investigators
exploring the feasibility of a higher wage for women
raised such issues as what, for instance, a firm would
"have to pay a man with a family if it paid $2 a day to
girls with no one but themselves to support?"[73] This
does not seem to have inhibited women's desire for
higher incomes. But it seems to have channeled their
grievances away from men who earned far more than
they and toward women instead. Among Western
Electric workers interviewed in the late 1920s, a typical female who complained about wages tended to be
distressed not at her absolute wage but at how it compared with those of other women. As one female
employee complained, "the girl next to me, her job
pays $39.80 per hundred, and mine pays $28.80 and I
work just as hard as she does. I don't see how they
figure that out. She makes ten cents more on every
one she makes."[74]

These powerful and sometimes explicit barriers
extended across race lines and to the social wages
offered by modern corporations. In their presence
Black women were paid less than white women for
the same or similar jobs. Employers utilized them to
sanction distinctions in the amenities they offered to
Black and white women. An early survey of the
tobacco industry in Virginia reflects the value of such
circumscribed comparisons. "Tuesday and Friday,"
the report noted matter of factly, "the white girls have
15 minutes extra in order to dance, but the 15 minutes
is paid for by the firm."[75]

What kept the "wage" pot bubbling, then, was not
women's desire to achieve male pay but their urge to
satisfy more concrete wants. As mass production jobs
and clerical work opened up to white women, some
factory jobs became available to Black women.
New, relatively well-paying jobs and rising real
wages for both men and women contributed to the
advent of the consumer society and helped to create a

new definition of wants that drew on a prevailing
individualism from which women could hardly be
excluded. Marketing techniques, installment
buying, and the increasing value placed on consumption replaced thrift and postponed gratification as
appropriate spirits of the time. New definitions of
wants attracted new groups of women to the workforce and suggested new rationales for staying there.

The changing population of female workers challenged perceptions of a wage that spoke to simpler
needs. To women for whom the prewar women's
wage had offered little apart from the despair of
poverty, the wage now stretched to encompass the
hope of individual achievement measured by material
goals. Defined in prewar practice as the minimum
required to sustain a single woman partially supported by her family, the postwar wage at least suggested the capacity to earn a living.[76] Ronald
Edsforth, who studied auto workers in the 1920s,
notes that government investigators discovered
among the women working in auto factories in the
1920s a "genuinely modern level of individual materialism . . . guiding . . . life-shaping decisions." They
concluded that "jobs in the auto factories were most
desired simply because auto workers' earnings were
high."[77] But even the rising wage was clearly inadequate to reconcile the competing needs of an increasingly heterogeneous group of female wage
earners. Less immigrant than native born, containing
a small but steadily growing proportion of married
women, and with a still tiny but slowly growing representation of Black women in mainstream jobs that
had long been closed to them, women with competing views of the wage attempted to participate in
what some called the "American standard of living."
In the process they helped to establish a new set of
gendered definitions about self and others.

For middle-class, single, adventurous women,
work and a wage meant escape from boredom, a bit
of rebellion, a purpose in life—the means to a relatively autonomous existence. Fueled by the rhetoric of
the women's movement and energized by a successful campaign for the vote, single women, no
longer subsidized by families and increasingly eager
to live outside them, craved the independence
that wages potentially offered. To some,
participation in wage work offered to contribute economic equality to the political citizenship they had
won with suffrage.[78] To others, as economist Theresa
Wolfson suggested, the wage bought the liberty to

live "comparatively free lives outside of their working hours."[79]

For poorer women, including immigrants and women of color, and for most of the married women who earned, the wage became a measure of the capacity to participate in an increasingly pervasive consumer society. "I would like to work," commented one young assembly line worker, "until I get my furniture paid for. My husband is young and hasn't got much of a start yet and I want to help him."[80] A woman's wage represented, still, a supplement to male earnings— an extension of family life. Less a vehicle to sheer survival in the 1920s, it promised access to the new wants generated by an ethic of consumption. If it still continued to preclude freedom for most women, it offered a way to sustain and even enhance family life and exacted, in return, the price of women's continuing commitment to the workforce.[81] It should not surprise us then that the changing material content of the wage did not diminish either the effort to earn it or its importance in women's lives. And it dramatically expanded the numbers of women willing and able to earn wages. A young woman who had worked at the Western Electric company for a year complained that her feet swelled on the job. She didn't want to sit down, however, because "I can't turn out the rates when I sit down." She had, she said, returned to Western Electric after a year at another job because "I couldn't earn near as much money, and I couldn't save any."[82]

Because a woman's wage had to serve the increasingly fragmented needs of a diverse array of women, the rhetoric surrounding it became more complex. It is best uncovered in the efforts of the newly created Women's Bureau of the Department of Labor to represent women workers of all kinds. The bureau's official position consistently upheld wages for women based on the value of the job. Yet its public posture simultaneously affirmed the need for a minimum wage based on the needs of the worker. Wages, wrote Mary Anderson, head of the bureau, "should be established on the basis of occupation and not on the basis of sex or race." At the same time, she added, the minimum wage rate that was available to women only, if at all, "should cover the cost of living in health and decency, instead of a bare existence, and should allow for dependents and not merely for the individual."[83]

The compromise, then, appeared to lie not in abandoning a needs-based assessment of women's wages so much as in an effort to understand that any definition of "wants" encompassed a broad range of human needs. While fewer than 15 percent of all married women, and about 30 percent of Black married women, with wage-earning husbands were regularly employed before the 1930s, those who earned wages had a complicated series of wants. For example, well-paid male and female hosiery workers in the Piedmont Valley of North Carolina and Tennessee flaunted their capacity to buy consumer goods.[84] In the same region, the poorly paid white textile workers could and frequently did hire Black women to take care of their children while white husbands and wives worked in the mills.[85] Black women used their tiny pay to feed and clothe their children and to support those who cared for them in their absence. Such enormous differences in the uses of wages notwithstanding, the image of women paid at a rate regulated by public perceptions of abstract needs helped to perpetuate the sense that, in the competition for jobs among women, what was at stake was not skill or the nature of work but the capacity to contribute to family support. This image perpetuated a low wage for all women. In exactly the way that employers had earlier chosen to believe that young, single women were supported by their parents, so, in the period after World War I, an idealized image of marriage with its attendant financial subsidy served to define a woman's role and threatened to regulate the level of wages for all women.

Partly in consequence, single women, inside and outside the Women's Bureau, were haunted by visions of married women subsidized by their husbands and therefore able to accept lower wages. Public debate over the wage question in the 1920s turned on the issue of whose needs the wage was intended to meet—the married woman working for "pin money" or the independent self-supporting woman of all classes. Neither category encompassed the reality of women workers, more than three-quarters of whom, according to contemporary studies, supported themselves and their families. While in the prewar period, questions about "workers who are in part supported by parents or other members of the family"[86] had captured a certain unease about independent women who transcended traditional roles, the 1920s attack on pin-money workers focused on the distress of single working women who feared competition from women whose families partially supported them. The competition, muted by the prosperity of the 1920s, did not explode until the 1930s. In the meantime, the question of married women in industry was argued pro and con, with such stalwart champions of working women as Mary Gilson, Melinda Scott, and Sophonisba Breckinridge protesting that married women ought not to be in the labor force. Breckinridge proposed instead "a living wage for men based on their own needs and those of their wives and a standard family of three children; disciplinary measures for husbands who are unwilling to work, and state aid for wives of those who cannot work."[87]

In the face of the commitment to a needs-based wage, proponents of individualism and some champions of the Women's Bureau fought a losing battle for "a rate for the job." The new consumerism required a more complex set of messages than simple individualism. While it offered support for raising the wage enough to accommodate both new social relations and new needs, it would not, and did not, challenge conceptions of the wage that sustained family life. Thus, one group of women struggled to elevate a woman's wage by asking that all workers receive value for the job, while a second declared itself in need of protective legislation and advocated a minimum wage to legitimate women's capacity to work at all. A woman's wage still refused to incorporate the capacity to earn a living. At most, it offered a fling at independence to those who did not need to contribute to family support. For the poor it could enhance a family's standard of living. But in no sense was a woman's wage intended to promote the desire for a self-sufficient existence.

Yet to women who worked, the capacity to improve the standard of living was not mere ideology. The reification of an "American" standard of living offered a rationale for continuing wage work among married women. As consumer expectations rose, the purchase of what some might have called pin-money goods became not a luxury but part of the quality of life. Because a woman's wage

appeared as largely contributory, it neither undermined male egos nor fomented female independence. Men understood the wage as an indication of whether they were "getting ahead." Women understood it as an indication of whether they could keep up with their work, their status among their peers, and their position in the eyes of the boss. And yet women's capacity to enhance the family standard contributed to denuding the notion that the family wage either could or should be earned by men alone. At the same time, women established new sources of comparisons that enabled them to maintain status and self-esteem even as they continued to earn less than two-thirds of the wage of the average male worker.

But women's wages, restricted by an ethos of need and locked into comparisons with other women, still could not rise high enough to compete with the wages of men. If the message of the wage differed for men and women, it failed to prevent women from seeking the same kinds of material gains acquired by men. At some level the "woman's wage" decisively relegated females to a plateau of citizenship that could not be equated with that of men. As much as suffrage had seemed to extend citizenship to women, a women's wage suggested the limits of their aspirations and assigned them to sometimes objectionable social roles. A "rate for the job"—a wage equivalent to that of similarly situated men working in the same firm—would have trumpeted a message of aspiration and ambition that few in the 1920s were ready to hear. But the value that a woman worker created was never the central issue of women's wage work. Rather, the wage sought to identify the boundaries within which economic inequality could be used to constrain the prerogatives of citizenship. The sex of a worker remained safely more important than what that worker did. With some few exceptions, equality was not at issue; the wage did not contest male prerogatives in the workplace. Rather, it symbolized the limits of political citizenship.

NOTES

1. Henry A. Landsberger, *Hawthorne Revisited: Management and the Worker, Its Critics, and the Developments in Human Relations in Industry* (Ithaca, N.Y.: Cornell University, 1958), 19.

2. New York State, *Factory Investigating Commission*, Fourth Report (Albany: S.B. Lyon Co., 1915), vol. 1, app. 3, passim. (Hereinafter referred to as FIC.)

3. N. Arnold Tolles, *Origins of Modern Wage Theories* (Englewood Cliffs, N.J.: Prentice-Hall, 1964), 8.

4. This theory, known as marginal productivity theory, was predicated on the assumption of perfect competition and emphasized the demands of employers in calculating the wage. Its classic exposition is John Bates Clark, *The Distribution of Wealth* (New York: Macmillan, 1899).

5. FIC, Fourth Report, vol. 4, 435.

6. In the United States, organized workers agitated for the idea beginning in the 1830s.

7. Melton McLaurin, *Paternalism and Protest: Southern Cotton Mill Workers and Organized Labor, 1875–1905* (Westport, Conn.: Greenwood Press, 1971), 23, describes how the notion of a family wage that rested on the labor of all family members could contribute to expectations of female and child labor. In southern textile mills, "mill management argued that the total annual income of a mill family was far greater than that of a farm family. Thus the 'family wage' was used as a cover for the low wages paid individuals" (23). But this is not the usual understanding. See Martha May, "The Historical Problem of the Family Wage: The Ford Motor Company and the Five Dollar Day," *Feminist Studies,* 8 (Summer 1982), 394–424.

8. For access to the opposing positions, see Jane Humphries, "The Working Class Family, Women's Liberation, and Class Struggle: The Case of Nineteenth Century British History," *Review of Radical Political Economics,* 9 (Fall 1977), 25–41; Michelle Barrett and Mary McIntosh, "The Family Wage: Some Problems for Socialists and Feminists," *Capital and Class,* 11 (1980), 51–72; and Hilary Land, "The Family Wage," *Feminist Review,* 6 (1980), 55–78.

9. John A. Ryan, *A Living Wage: Its Ethical and Economic Aspects* (New York: Macmillan, 1906), 117.

10. William Smart, *Studies in Economics* (London: Macmillan, 1985), 34. Smart added that "in addition perhaps some consumption of alcohol and tobacco, and some indulgence in fashionable dress are, in many places, so habitual that they may be said to be 'conventionally necessary'" (34).

11. Cited by Ryan, *Living Wage,* 130, from the *American Federationist,* 1898.

12. Ryan, *Living Wage,* 117.

13. Ibid., vii.

14. Italics mine. Quoted in May, "Historical Problem of the Family Wage," 402. Samuel Gompers believed the worker's living wage should "be sufficient to sustain himself and those dependent upon him in a manner to maintain his self-respect, to educate his children, supply his household with literature, with opportunities to spend a portion of his life with his family." In Samuel Gompers, "A Minimum Living Wage," *American Federationist,* 5 (April 1898), 26.

15. See, for example, the list compiled by F. Spencer Baldwin in Louise Bosworth, *The Living Wage of Women Workers* (New York: Longmans Green and Co., 1911), 7; see also Elizabeth Beardsley Butler, *Women and the Trades: Pittsburgh, 1907–1908* (Pittsburgh: University of Pittsburgh Press, 1984 [1909]), 346–47.

16. J. Laurence Laughlin, ed., *Principles of Political Economy by John Stuart Mill* (New York: D. Appleton and Company, 1885), 214.

17. Italics mine. Ryan, *Living Wage,* 107.

18. Lynn Y. Wiener, *From Working Girl to Working Mother: The Female Labor Force in the United States, 1820–1980* (Chapel Hill: University of North Carolina, 1985), 19, 26, 84.

19. Ryan, *Living Wage,* 107.

20. Ibid., 120.

21. Kellogg Durland, "Labor Day Symposium," *American Federationist* 12 (September 1905), 619.

22. Ryan, *Living Wage,* 107.

23. Ibid., 133.

24. Dorothy W. Douglas, *American Minimum Wage Laws at Work* (New York: National Consumers' League, 1920), 14.

25. Butler, *Women and the Trades,* 346; Bosworth, *Living Wage of Women Workers,* 9. The Women's Bureau estimated that the minimums in effect from 1913 to 1915 ranged from $8.50 to $10.74. See Bulletin no. 61, *The Development of Minimum Wage Laws in the United States: 1912–1927* (Washington, D.C.: Government Printing Office, 1928).

26. Thomas Herbert Russell, *The Girl's Fight for a Living: How to Protect Working Women from Dangers Due to Low Wages* (Chicago: M.A. Donahue, 1913), 108.

27. Elizabeth Brandeis, "Labor Legislation," vol. 3 of John Commons, *History of Labor in the United States* (New York: Macmillan, 1935), 524–25, makes the point that these budgets were calculated in one of two ways: on the basis of actual expenditures (a problem because women had to live on what they earned, however small) or on the basis of theoretical budgets (a problem because employer-members of boards resisted the inclusion of such items as recreation, "party dress," etc.). They were then "modified" by estimates of prevailing wages, consideration of the amounts of the proposed increases, and possible consequences for business conditions.

28. Sue Ainslee Clark and Edith Wyatt, "Working-Girls' Budgets: A Series of Articles Based upon Individual Stories of Self-Supporting Girls," *McClure's,* 35 (October 1910). Additional articles appeared in *McClure's* in vol. 36 in November and December 1910 and February 1911. They were published in book form under the title *Making Both Ends Meet: The Income and Outlay of New York Working-Girls* (New York: Macmillan, 1911). The classic study is that of Louise Bosworth, cited in note 25.

29. Clark and Wyatt, "Working-Girls' Budgets," *McClure's,* 35 (October 1910), 604. See the discussion of these budgets in Wiener, *From Working Girl to Working Mother,* 75–77; and Joanne Meyerowitz, *Women Adrift: Independent Wage Earners in Chicago, 1880—1930* (Chicago: University of Chicago Press, 1988), 33—35.

30. The magazine advertised for contributions in January 1908 and published from four to six contributions from February 1908 to January 1909. In September 1908 it announced that it was flooded with contributions and would no longer accept any more. There is no way of knowing how heavily these were edited, so they have been used here only to extract a broad gauge of opinion.

31. "The Girl Who Comes to the City," *Harper's Bazaar,* 42 (January 1908), 54.

32. "The Girl Who Comes to the City," 42 (October 1908), 1005; 42 (July 1908), 694.

33. "The Girl Who Comes to the City," 42 (August 1908), 776. The maximum achieved by any of these women was the $100 a month earned by a Washington D.C., civil servant (42 [November 1908], 1141). That sum was sufficient for a single woman not only to live reasonably well but to save and invest some of her income. It was rarely achieved by women.

34. "The Girl Who Comes to the City," 42 (November 1908), 1141; see also October 1908, 1007.

35. See, for example, Alice Kessler-Harris, *Out to Work: A History of Wage Earning Women in the United States* (New York: Oxford, 1982), 99–101; Meyerowitz, *Women Adrift,* 34–36.

36. "The Girl Who Comes to the City," 42 (March 1908), 277; 42 (May 1908), 500. The widespread nature of this assumption is apparent in "Women's Wages," *Nation,* 108 (February 22, 1919), 270–71: "The employer of women today is in a large proportion of cases heavily subsidized; for there is a considerable gap between the $9 a week that is paid to a girl and her actual cost of maintenance. Who makes up the difference? In the employer's mind it is usually the girl's family—which is often mythical."

37. Smart, *Studies in Economics,* 115.

38. Butler, *Women and the Trades,* 346.

39. Meyerowitz, *Women Adrift,* 33.

40. Butler, *Women and the Trades,* 344.

41. FIC, Fourth Report, vol. 4, app. 3, 450.

42. Scott Nearing, "The Adequacy of American Wages," *Annals of the American Academy of Political and Social Sciences,* 59 (May 1915), 2.

43. "Women's Wages and Morality," *American Federationist,* 20 (June 1913), 467.

44. Smart, *Studies in Economics,* 125.

45. Russell, *Girl's Fight for a Living,* 21. On pay differences by race, see Meyerowitz, *Women Adrift,* 36; and Dolores Janiewski, *Sisterhood Denied: Race, Gender and Class in a New South Community* (Philadelphia: Temple University Press, 1985), 110–13.

46. FIC, Fourth Report, vol. 2, app. 3, 468; Don D. Lescohier, then a Minnesota statistician and later to become an eminent gatherer of labor statistics, commented at the same hearings that "custom . . . plays a far larger part in holding wages stationary than we have been accustomed to think" (ibid., 459).

47. Smart, *Studies in Economics,* 116. The radical Scott Nearing, in a minority opinion, held that the male wage was not determined by another principle at all. He protested industry's lack of attention to social relations: "The man with a family is brought into active competition with the man who has no family obligations. The native-born head of a household must accept labor terms which are satisfactory to the foreign-born single man. Industry does not inquire into a

worker's social obligations" (Nearing, "Adequacy of American Wages," 123).

48. Which is not, of course, to imply that all males who earned wages were paid enough to support families. See Janiewski, *Sisterhood Denied,* for illustrations of wages in the southern tobacco and textile industries that required the labor of three or more people to sustain a family.

49. Bosworth, *Living Wage,* 4.

50. Russell, *Girl's Fight for a Living,* 73.

51. Ibid., 108.

52. Ibid., 83.

53. Smart, *Studies in Economics,* 107.

54. Samuel Gompers, "Woman's Work, Rights and Progress," *American Federationist,* 20 (August 1913), 625.

55. Alfred Marshall, *Principles of Economics,* 8th ed. (New York: Macmillan, 1953), 685.

56. Quoted in Russell, *Girl's Fight for a Living,* 16; and see "Women's Wages and Morality," 465.

57. Russell, *Girl's Fight for a Living,* 38; cf. also the testimony of Ida Tarbell in ibid., 39.

58. Butler, *Women and the Trades,* 342–43.

59. Francis Amasa Walker, *The Wages Question: A Treatise on Wages and the Wages Class* (New York: Henry Holt and Company, 1876), 374.

60. Ibid., 378.

61. Quoted in Marjorie Shuler, "Industrial Women Confer," *Woman Citizen,* 8 (January 27, 1923), 25.

62. Such arguments were prefigured in the late nineteenth century by assertions that the greedy were taking jobs from the needy. See Kessler-Harris, *Out to Work,* 99ff.

63. "Women as Wage Earners," *New York Times,* January 28, 1923, 26.

64. Maurine Greenwald, *Women, War, and Work: The Impact of World War One on Women in the United States* (Westport, Conn.: Greenwood Press, 1980), 155. Greenwald notes that a female janitor who might have made $35 a month earned $75–80 a month as a conductor.

65. Daniel Nelson, *Managers and Workers: Origins of the New Factory System in the United States* (Madison: University of Wisconsin Press, 1975), 145.

66. Quoted in "Women and Wages," *The Woman Citizen,* 4 (June 7, 1919), 8. The article went on to report that one plant had "reckoned women's production as 20 per cent greater than that of the men preceding them. But this did not prevent the same plant from cutting down the women's pay one-third."

67. Typescript, "Memoranda Regarding Women's Bureau," in National Archives, Record Group 86, Box 4, File: WTUL Action on Policies. The bureau lost this battle. As a result, its professional staff tended to work more out of loyalty and commitment than for monetary gain. See Judith Sealander, *As Minority Becomes Majority: Federal Reaction to the Phenomenon of Women in the Work Force, 1920–1963* (Westport, Conn.: Greenwood Press, 1983), chap. 3, for the early days of the Women's Bureau.

68. Ronald W. Schatz, *The Electrical Workers: A History of Labor at General Electric and Westinghouse, 1923–60* (Urbana: University of Illinois Press, 1983), 32.

69. Quoted in Stephen Meyer III, *The Five Dollar Day: Labor Management and Social Control in the Ford Motor Company, 1908–1921* (Albany: State University of New York Press, 1981), 140.

70. Schatz, *Electrical Workers*, 20–21.

71. Quoted in Schatz, *Electrical Workers*, 21; Nelson, *Managers and Workers*, 118, confirms that the wage as welfare differed for men and women: "Manufacturers who employed large numbers of women usually emphasized measures to make the factory more habitable. Lunchrooms, restrooms, landscaping and other decorative features conveyed the idea of a home away from home. At the same time, the classes in domestic economy and child rearing, social clubs, outings and dances (women only) assured the worker that she need not sacrifice her femininity when she entered the male world of the factory. But, because the female operative was (or was thought to be) a secondary wage earner and probably a transient, she was not offered pensions, savings programs and insurance plans."

72. Meyer, *Five Dollar Day*, 140; implicit in the Ford policy was a quite conscious attempt to circumscribe the roles and self-perceptions of men as well as of women. Meyer quotes a Ford policy manual from the 1920s to the effect that "if a man wants to remain a profit sharer, his wife should stay at home and assume the obligations she undertook when married" (141). See the commentary on this issue in "Housework Wages," *The Woman Citizen*, 4 (October 4, 1919), 449.

73. Russell, *Girl's Fight for a Living*, 101; the same investigator asked an employer, "If you raised a little girl from $3 to $8 would a man getting $15 feel aggrieved?" (112)—a question that loads the dice by imagining women as no more than children.

74. Microfilm records, Western Electric Plant, Hawthorne Works, Operating Branch M., interviews, Reel 6, July 8, 1929. Records of individuals are not identified or tagged beyond the branch where the interviews were taken. The growing sense of entitlement to comparable wages was captured by an experienced female worker who declared herself satisfied with her work "because it was more interesting and I could make my rate" but nevertheless complained that "I don't see why they didn't raise me anyway like they did the other girls, every half year or every year." In ibid., July 9, 1929. This phenomenon was not specific to women alone. F. J. Roethlisberger and William Dickson, analyzing the Western Electric research, commented, "The results of the interviewing program show very clearly that the worker was quite as much concerned with these differentials, that is the relation of his wages to that of other workmen as with the absolute amount of his wages." See *Management and the Worker: An Account of a Research Program Conducted by the Western Electric Company, Hawthorne Works, Chicago* (Cambridge, Mass.: Harvard University Press, 1946), 543. But nothing in the interviews indicates that women compared their wages with those of men, nor did men with those of women.

75. Mary Schaill and Ethel Best to Mary Anderson, November 5, 1919, Virginia Survey, Bulletin no. 10, National Archives, Record Group 86: Records of the Women's Bureau, Box 2.

76. Pauline Newman, veteran trade unionist, challenged old notions of a living wage in "The 'Equal Rights' Amendment," *American Federationist*, 45 (August 1938), 815. She wrote, "It is not a wage which affords an opportunity for intellectual development; it is not a wage which allows for spiritual growth; it is not a wage on which wage-earning women can enjoy the finer things of life."

77. Ronald Edsforth, *Class Conflict and Cultural Consensus: The Making of a Mass Consumer Society in Flint, Michigan* (New Brunswick, N.J.: Rutgers University Press, 1987), 95.

78. Daniel T. Rodgers, *The Work Ethic in Industrial America: 1850–1920* (Chicago: University of Chicago Press, 1974), 196.

79. Theresa Wolfson, *The Woman Worker and the Trade Unions* (New York: International Publishers, 1926), 42.

80. Microfilm records, Western Electric Plant, Hawthorne Works, Operating Branch M., interviews, Reel 6, July 8, 1929.

81. Wolfson, *Woman Worker*, 42–43.

82. Microfilm records, Western Electric Plant, Hawthorne Works, Operating Branch M., interviews, Reel 6, Folder 1, Box 14, July 1, 1929.

83. Mary Anderson, "Industrial Standards for Women," *American Federationist*, 32 (July 1925), 565.

84. Jacquelyn Dowd Hall et al., *Like a Family: The Making of a Southern Cotton Mill World* (Chapel Hill: University of North Carolina Press, 1987), 255–56.

85. See interviews with Ada Mae Wilson, Mary Ethel Shockley, Ina Wrenn, and Gertrude Shuping in Southern Oral History Project Collection, Martin Wilson Library, University of North Carolina, Chapel Hill. Used with the kind help of Jacquelyn Dowd Hall.

86. The quotation is from FIC, Fourth Report, vol. 4, 440. The percentage of married Black women working and supporting families was far higher than that for white women.

87. Shuler, "Industrial Women Confer," 12.

Sex Segregation in the U.S. Labor Force

Christine E. Bose and Rachel Bridges Whaley

Sex segregation in the workplace is manifested in many ways—in the extent to which women and men are concentrated in different industries, establishments, occupations, and jobs, and in the extent to which any particular job is dominated by workers of one sex. An occupation is usually considered female or male dominated if it is at least 75 percent female or male. For example, 7 of the 10 most common occupations for women are dominated by female workers including secretary (98 percent), cashier (78 percent), and registered nurse (93 percent) (Women's Bureau 1999) (see Table 1). Similarly, the majority of the most common occupations for men are male dominated, such as truck driver (94 percent) and carpenter (98 percent) (U.S. Census Bureau 1998a) (see Table 2). The only occupation among the top 10 (largest numbers) for both men and women is

miscellaneous salaried manager, which is 70 percent male (Women's Bureau 1999). Such occupational "integration" is rare and its positive effects are frequently diluted because the particular jobs offered by employers or firms are sex segregated.

Occupational segregation may entail the physical separation of workers of different social groups (sex and racial or ethnic groups). For example, between 1920 and 1940 in North Carolina's tobacco industry, workers were physically separated and segregated into sex-typed and race-typed tasks. Black women tobacco workers were located in one building or on one floor, designed for "dirty" prefabrication work such as stripping the leaves, and white women were in another building or on another floor, inspecting and packing the product. Meanwhile black men hauled materials between locales and white men

TABLE 1 TEN MOST COMMON OCCUPATIONS FOR WOMEN, 1998

Women's Common Occupations[1]	Percent Women
Secretaries	98
Cashiers	78
Managers and administrators, n.e.c.[1]	30
Sales supervisors and proprietors	40
Registered nurses	93
Nursing aides, orderlies, and attendants	89
Elementary school teachers	84
Bookkeepers, accounting clerks	93
Waiters and waitresses	78
Sales workers, other commodities[2]	68
Average labor-force occupation	46

[1]Not elsewhere, classified or miscellaneous.
[2]Includes foods, drugs, health, and other commodities.

TABLE 2 TEN MOST COMMON OCCUPATIONS FOR MEN, 1998

Men's Common Occupations	Percent Women
Managers and administrators, n.e.c.	30
Truck drivers	5
Sales supervisors and proprietors	40
Construction laborers	16
Freight, stock, and material handlers	24
Janitors and cleaners	35
Fabricators and assemblers	33
Carpenters	1
Cooks	41
Sales representatives, commodities, wholesale	26

SOURCE: U.S. Census, Statistical Abstract accessed on 4/10/00 at http://www.census.gov/prod/99pubs/99statab/sec13.pdf
Note: Occupational categories drawn from this source are slightly less detailed than those for women's occupations.

acted as supervisors and inspectors (Jones 1984). A more recent example can be found in the baking industry. Female bakers are located in retail establishments (e.g., supermarkets) while men make up the majority of wholesale bakers (Steiger and Reskin 1990).

The sex segregation of any occupation can change over time, even while the segregation of the entire labor force remains fairly stable. Occupations are more likely to shift from male to female domination than the reverse. Public-school teaching made this transition in the late nineteenth century; clerical workers, telephone operators, waiters and waitresses, and bank tellers were resegregated by the middle of the twentieth century from male to female jobs. More recently, residential real estate sales and pharmacy work have become female dominated. Women have made significant inroads into other male-dominated jobs such as bartending and insurance adjustment, which now appear to be sex integrated but may be merely in transit to becoming female dominated. According to Barbara Reskin and Patricia Roos (1990), the fundamental reason that a job is resegregated from male to female domination is a shortage of male workers. That shortage occasionally happens when an occupation is rapidly expanding, using up the supply of suitable men. In most cases, however, men are leaving a job that has become less attractive because the work process has been downgraded in terms of skills or the job rewards are less. Consequently, the decrease in prestige and pay of an occupation occurs before women enter it. As a result, women's integration into apparently prestigious male-dominated jobs can be a hollow victory.

MEASURING SEX SEGREGATION

One way to understand the extent to which men and women do different work is to examine the proportion of workers of the same sex in each occupation, as was done above. To this end, it is seen that most men and women work in occupations where workers of the same sex predominate. Indeed, only a fraction of women work in occupations that are dominated by men (Kraut and Luna 1992).

Another method is to examine the extent to which male and female workers are clustered in a small number of occupations. Reskin and Irene Padavic

(1994) report that 33 percent of women workers are employed in the top 10 occupations sex-typed female compared to about 25 percent of men being clustered in the top 10 occupations sex-typed male.

The most common way to measure sex segregation is to calculate an index of sex segregation, also called an *index of dissimilarity*, which ranges from 0 to 100. Its value is interpreted as the percentage of workers of one sex that would have to change occupations so that men and women have the same distribution in each occupation. An index of 0 implies perfect integration while an index of 100 suggests that the sexes are completely segregated from each other. In 1990 the index was 53, which means 53 percent of women workers (or approximately 28 million individuals) would need to be redistributed into other occupations if all occupations were to have the same percentage of women and men that are in the entire labor force (Reskin and Padavic 1994).

Researchers have calculated the occupational sex segregation index, using the preferred detailed Census job categories, for different historical periods. It is generally agreed that the index stayed fairly high and steady, between 65 and 69, from 1900 through 1960 (Gross 1968) and perhaps as late as 1970 (Jacobs 1989). If one focuses on nonagricultural jobs, there was only a six-point decline in sex segregation in the 60 years between 1910 and 1970, dropping from 74 to 68. Though the 1970s, however, it dropped another 8 points to 60 in 1980 (Jacobs 1989b), In the 1980s, the segregation index continued to drop but at a much slower rate (Reskin and Roos 1990).

In 1940 a comparable index of occupational *race* segregation, calculated separately for blacks and whites of each sex, was rather high at 65 among women and 44 among men. These rates actually increased through 1960 but declined thereafter with the advent of affirmative-action legislation. By 1980, the greater racial segregation among working women had declined to match that of men, reaching 26 to men's 30 by 1990 (King 1992; Reskin 1994). During this same 50-year time span, occupational sex segregation rates among both blacks and whites remained almost twice as high as race segregation among men (Reskin and Padavic 1994). Indeed, Joyce Jacobsen (1994) has concluded that the slowed decline in occupational sex segregation, combined with high rates of firm-level segregation, make it unlikely that sex segregation rates will become as low as race segregation rates by the 2000 census.

SEX SEGREGATION IN SPECIFIC CATEGORIES OF OCCUPATIONS

White-Collar Occupations

As a group, white-collar occupations typically command high salaries, prestige, and autonomy. Yet further inspection reveals considerable variation in their earnings as well as considerable sex segregation. There is a hierarchy of occupations within the classification white-collar. Imagine a pyramid. Executives, physicians, lawyers, and college professors are at the top of the pyramid, while nurses, librarians, and elementary school and secondary-school teachers form part of the middle third. The bottom third includes clerical workers, sales workers, and some service workers. More women are in white-collar occupations today than ever before but where?

In 1900 only 9 percent of women workers were employed in professional occupations and only 1 percent in managerial occupations. Ninety years later 17 percent of working women are in a professional specialty and 11 percent are in executive, administrative, and managerial occupations (U.S. Census Bureau 1990). In fact, women are 49 percent of all workers in executive, administrative, and managerial occupations and 53 percent in professfonal specialties, respectively (U.S. Census Bureau 1998a). Does this mean occupational sex segregation is no longer a problem? Unfortunately the answer is no.

Industry, firm, and job segregation channels women into the lower-paid, less autonomous, and less prestigious positions that often lack opportunities for upward advancement. For example, although women are about 50 percent of financial managers, they tend to be segregated in small bank branches rather than in loan and investment departments at headquarters (Silver 1981, cited in Reskin and Phipps 1988). Women are 63 percent of personnel and labor relations managers, a service-focused occupation with median annual earnings of $50,080, but only 35 percent of managers in marketing, advertising, and public relations who earn an average $57,100 a year (U.S. Census Bureau 1998a; U.S. Bureau of Labor Statistics 1997).

Women are currently about 27 percent of all lawyers, a remarkable increase from the 1900 figure of .8 percent. Yet, in a recent study of 200 male and female lawyers, Patricia MacCorquodale and Gary Jensen found that "Not a single respondent, male or female, would choose an equally qualified female attorney over a male attorney when considering who would command more respect in court" (1993, 590). Stereotypes and prejudices influence which firms hire women lawyers, the cases they are given, and whether they make partner. Research suggests that the path to partnership is considerably more demanding for women, who must present themselves as "super lawyers" to dissuade the sexist doubts of current partners (Kay and Hagan 1998, 741).

The barriers that women face when they attempt to move into higher-status positions, with greater responsibility, decision-making power, and authority, are widespread in male-dominated occupations. The phenomenon is so common that it has been termed the *glass-ceiling effect*, a phrase that helps people visualize the very real barrier to upward mobility on the job for women workers. The glass ceiling is created by a variety of organizational barriers and discrimination. . . .

Although the gender balance in the broad categories of executive, administrative, and managerial occupations and professional specialties appears to be about 50–50 and thousands of women are managers, doctors, and college professors, occupational segregation continues to limit women's options. In fact, 70 percent of women professionals, but only 27 percent of men professionals, are employed as teachers, librarians, and counselors or in health assessment and treating occupations such as nurse or dietitian (U.S. Census Bureau 1990).

Pink-Collar Occupations

There is a cluster of white-collar occupations that are more commonly labeled pink-collar occupations because they are female dominated. For example, women are approximately 93 percent of registered nurses, 98 percent of preschool and kindergarten teachers, 84 percent of elementary-school teachers, and 81 percent of librarians (U.S. Census Bureau 1998a; Women's Bureau 1999). These professional jobs are occasionally labeled semiprofessions because they lack some of the characteristics that identify an occupation as professional. Semiprofessions tend to be less prestigious, have less autonomy, and command lower salaries than full professions. Nursing and teaching at the elementary-school level are among the top 10 occupations for women, but women earn an average of only $38,168 as registered nurses and $35,204 as elementary-school teachers. Semiprofessionals are usually located in a bureaucratic setting where persons other than fellow professional workers set most administrative rules and professional norms.

In contrast to the relatively large proportion of women who have attempted to enter traditionally male-dominated occupations (e.g., manager, doctor, or lawyer), men are much less likely to enter the traditionally female-dominated domain of pink-collar occupations. Currently, 8 percent of registered nurses, 16 percent of elementary-school teachers, and 20 percent of librarians are men (U.S. Census Bureau 1998a; Women's Bureau 1999). Contrary to the lower wages that women command when they enter male-dominated occupations, men who enter female-dominated occupations often receive higher wages than women in similar positions. Yet the wage gap is almost negligible in nursing and elementary-school teaching, where women earn 95 percent and 90 percent of what men earn. It is important that both women and men who work in female-dominated occupations earn relatively less than women and men who work in male-dominated occupations; "women's work" is generally devalued and underpaid (England and Herbert 1993). Men in female-dominated occupations often find themselves on the fast track or on a "glass escalator"; upward mobility is encouraged and supported for them, for example, in occupations such as bank teller or airline flight attendant.

Clerical Occupations

The history of clerical work represents an example of the feminization of an occupation. At the beginning of the twentieth century, women were only 4 percent of clerical workers. Clerical work was a small, male-dominated occupation with relatively high prestige; it incorporated a diversity of tasks ranging from correspondence to bookkeeping. As the economy grew to be dominated by business and as paperwork proliferated, the need for clerical workers increased drastically. Employers drew on the ready supply of educated, working-class women who were eager to leave domestic service and factory work and enter these "cleaner" jobs. Companies intentionally divided up and restructured clerical work, creating female-dominated typists, whose jobs were mechanized by the previously invented typewriter, and filers, both having less autonomy than the accounting, bookkeeping, and cashier work initially reserved for men (Davies 1982).

Today women are 99 percent of secretaries, 94 percent of typists, and 97 percent of receptionists (U.S. Census Bureau 1998a), while being only 31 percent of shipping clerks, 41 percent of purchasing managers, and 57 percent of accountants and auditors. Secretarial work now employs more women than any other occupation. Compared to other prevalent women's occupations, the median weekly salary for secretaries ($430) is ranked fifth, well behind the higher earnings of the top-ranked registered nurses ($734) (Women's Bureau 1999). Secretarial work and other clerical positions tend to have short promotion ladders and typically do not lead to professional or managerial positions (Nakano Glenn and Feldberg 1989). Over the last century, clerical work has become tedious, requires power skills, and is highly supervised. Clerical workers are often overeducated and find the work does not allow them to utilize all their skills (Nakano Glenn and Feldberg 1989).

Blue-Collar Occupations

Approximately 39 percent of men and 11 percent of women work in blue-collar occupations, which are counted by the Census under the headings of precision production, craft, and repair occupations and as machine operators, fabricators, and laborers (U.S. Census Bureau 1990) Like most occupational categories, blue-collar work includes a diverse array of occupations ranging from skilled through semiskilled to unskilled. Four blue-collar jobs—truck driver, carpenter, construction laborer, and automobile mechanic—were among the 10 leading occupations for men in 1990. All four are almost completely male dominated ranging from 99 percent (automobile mechanic) to 89 percent male (truck driver). Except for skilled occupations (e.g., electrician, carpenter, and plumber) and supervisory positions, blue-collar work offers little room for autonomy or creativity, requires hard physical labor, and is often dangerous.

Blue-collar work appeals to women although they find it hard to gain access to such positions. Historically, work in the manufacturing sector, particularly in unionized mills and plants, offered several advantages over the service jobs traditionally open to women. A study of women in the steel industry in the 1970s found that they preferred the higher wages, job security, health-care benefits, opportunity for shift work, and slower pace of blue-collar work over the harsh reality of working in sales or waitressing (Fonow 1993). In fact these tangible benefits outweighed the negative experiences in blue-collar work.

EXPLANATIONS OF SEX SEGREGATION

The history of work in the United States and elsewhere reveals a pattern of sex typing, defining some jobs as appropriate for men and others as women's work. But the origins of sex segregation in work are usually attributed to emerging industrialization. Sex segregation was created, in part, by gendered social expectations for women and men. For example, the ideas surrounding men as breadwinners and the "family wage" functioned to keep married women out of the labor force; and when single, divorced, or widowed women worked, these notions kept their wages lower than men's. The assumption was that all women had fathers and then husbands to care for them. Since men were considered the typical employees, part-time work, which women needed to be compatible with children's school hours, was virtually nonexistent except in the form of factory outwork or taking in laundry. Legal barriers constrained women's opportunities as well. Protective legislation limited women's options by defining how many hours, when (day versus night), and in which occupations they could work. In a reciprocal fashion, such segregation reinforced gendered power relations by limiting women's access to good jobs and by increasing their dependency on men. Through these processes, jobs became gendered. In other words, certain job titles as well as work tasks and skills became defined as male as distinct from female. This process is almost unnoticeable except when a job is newly created (and fought over by men and women) or its stereotype changes. A clear example of the latter case is the redefinition of clerical work as women's work by 1940 when, previously, it had been dominated by men.

Present-day researchers explain sex segregation in a variety of ways ranging from theories about individuals' behaviors to those emphasizing labor-market processes and social structure. The earliest sociological explanation focused on individual socialization, suggesting that the gender-stereotypical lessons people learn in childhood about masculine men and feminine women determine the academic fields they study and the occupations they choose. This view, however, is only partially supported. The

jobs available to members of different social groups, such as women, blacks, or Hispanics, play a much greater role in determining our occupational status than any gender (or race) lessons we were taught as children. Workers are constrained by the opportunities available to them, by structural forces external to individuals.

One of the most important economic perspectives that, like socialization theory, focuses on individuals is human capital theory. Human capital is considered to be those characteristics or skills that make a worker more productive and attractive to an employer. To explain why women are predominantly employed in female-dominated occupations, human-capital theorists make many assumptions. First, they assume that all workers choose educational fields and occupations primarily with an eye toward maximizing lifetime earnings. They further assume that women consider work to be secondary to family and are only employed for short periods of time. Following from these assumptions, human-capital theorists expect women to select educational fields that require little investment in training and occupations that require skills that will not depreciate during occasional absences from the labor force. The assumption is that the resulting female-dominated occupations will be low skilled, have short career ladders, be amenable to intermittent employment, and pay more at entry than male-dominated jobs, where pay increases depend on on-the-job training. These assumptions are based on a 1950s understanding of women's roles.

Thus it is not surprising that researchers have shown that the human-capital perspective does not explain occupational sex segregation. It cannot explain why women enter low-skilled, female-dominated jobs when there are low-skilled, male-dominated jobs available. Worse still, most female-dominated occupations do not make it any easier to combine work and family than male-dominated occupations.

Counter to human-capital or socialization theorists, structural theorists argue that features of work can create behaviors, rather than individual behavior shaping occupational characteristics. For example, working in female-dominated occupations that are monotonous, have poor benefits and low wages, and lack autonomy can lead to high turnover rates. Researchers found that the same negative occupational characteristics lead to turnover among male workers, too (Reskin and Hartmann 1986). In other words, jobs can influence the attitudes, ambitions, and job preferences of workers, who are malleable and responsive to changing job situations.

The notion that institutional forces largely determine people's life chances is central to the various social-structural perspectives on occupational sex segregation. Social-control theory points to the social pressures that women and men encounter before and during employment. Both men and women are often discouraged from seeking employment in sex-atypical positions. Steel mill jobs were offered to women only after a federal court ordered steel companies to end discrimination against them. Even then the mills and male workers did not embrace the idea of women workers with open arms. In fact, women applicants reported feeling strongly discouraged by management, who questioned their interest and ability to deal with the negative aspects of the work (Fonow 1993). Men who attempt to enter traditionally female occupations are similarly discouraged by questions concerning their sexual orientation, manhood, and reasons for wanting to work with children or patients (Williams 1992).

In spite of such stereotyping, working people are not merely at the mercy of social institutions. They are also active participants in shaping sex segregation. Both sex typing and race typing of jobs can develop out of workers' struggles over new or existing occupations (Baron 1991; Milkman 1987). When the occupations of typist (originally called typewriter) or computer programmer were created, workers contended over which sex should fill them. When the existing occupation of typesetter changed from using hot-metal type to electronic composition in the 1970s, women actively entered jobs that men chose to leave (Roos 1990). Such resegregation in jobs from male to female is partially, but not entirely, responsible for the gradual decline in sex segregation during the 1980s (Jacobs 1989b).

Other processes, such as hiring procedures, help explain why women find employment in female-dominated occupations. When employers depend upon referrals from current employees for new employees, they tend to receive applications from workers of the same sex and race as those currently employed. The reason is that workers' informal networks of friends and family tend to include people of their own sex or racial group. Thus if an employer asks white men for referrals, names of other white men are proposed. Informal networks have been found to be very helpful for applicants; the sharing of information about job openings and promotion opportunities is critical to gaining access to higher-status and better-paying positions. This benefit, however, appears to be an advantage only for men. When women rely upon informal networks to learn about job openings, more often than not they end up in female-dominated occupations (Drentea 1998). When employers use open-recruitment methods, which they have to do if they are subject to affirmative-action laws, they are more likely to receive applications from workers who differ in sex, race, and ethnicity.

Open recruitment does not guarantee women access to sex-atypical jobs, however. Other organizational barriers make it difficult for women to break away from female-dominated occupations. For example, apprenticeship programs for various blue-collar jobs may have age limits, so that women who try to enter programs after having children are deemed too old, or they may require unnecessary previous experience including high school shop class. Seniority systems that are not plantwide and thus not transferable across departments may discourage women in clerical positions from taking more traditionally male jobs. The use of secretarial and typing pools in large offices hurts women's opportunities to be noticed and considered for promotion. Recent evidence suggests that sex segregation has a feedback effect. That is, employers tend to promote or hire women into management-level positions only if other women currently hold positions at the same level (Cohen, Broschak, and Haveman 1998). In other words, promotion or advancement in management for women occurs more often in female-dominated ladders. Until employers take the "risk" and hire women for positions not currently held by women, current practices will perpetuate sex segregation.

While many organizational or geographic barriers to sex-atypical occupations are grounded in administrative policies that have little to do with an employer's prejudices, discriminatory actions by employers and other male workers play an important role in the perpetuation of segregation. Recall the situation of women lawyers discussed above. Current law firm partners, who make decisions about granting new partnerships, have prejudices that can make it difficult for women to obtain partner status (Kay and Hagan 1998). Although discrimination against workers on the basis of sex and race is illegal, it persists nonetheless, as evidenced by the number of legitimate complaints of discrimination heard by the Equal Employment Opportunity Commission and other institutions.

CONSEQUENCES OF SEX SEGREGATION

Why does it matter that men and women are physically separated at work? What are the implications of sex-typed occupations? Sex segregation in the workplace matters for the same reason that the U.S. Supreme Court outlawed school segregation in 1964; among socially unequal groups, separate is not equal. The separation of men and women, as well as members of different racial or ethnic groups, into different jobs makes it easier to treat them differently and helps maintain stereotypes about men's and women's work-related characteristics (skills, aspirations, experience). It makes possible the devaluation of women's skills and abilities.

The remainder of this chapter briefly highlights some of the major consequences of occupational sex segregation, including the wage gap, tokenism, and hindered mobility. Other consequences include women's lower Social Security and retirement benefits as a result of earning less during employment and having worked in less profitable industries that may not provide pensions (Hogan, Perrucci, and Wilmoth 2000). Sexual harassment appears to be a major consequence of sex segregation. When women are a numerical minority in an office or section of a plant, they are very likely to experience various forms of sexual harassment ranging from hostile environment to sexual coercion. . . .

The wage gap is a major consequence of occupational sex segregation. Among full-time, year-round workers age 25 years and over, women earn an average of 74 cents for every men's dollar (U.S. Bureau of Labor Statistics, 1999). The current wage gap represents a historical narrowing of earnings inequality; between 1930 and 1980 it fluctuated between 55 and 64 percent (Reskin and Padavic 1994, 103). However, only two-fifths of women's wage improvement in the last 20 years is due to an increase in their real wages; the remaining three-fifths is due to the fall in men's real wages.

Occupational sex segregation helps explain the wage gap in several ways. First, women and men work in different occupations. The occupations in which men predominate pay higher wages. Second, even when one compares women and men in

the same occupational grouping, one finds that sex segregation in industries, establishments, departments, and jobs results in lower wages for women workers. Women engineers earn $800 less per week than men engineers (Andersen 1997, 105). The median weekly income for female machine operators is $228, yet for male machine operators it is $415 (Andersen 1997, 105). Although the occupations of engineer and machine operator are male dominated, sales occupations appear well integrated; 50 percent of sales workers are women (U.S. Census Bureau 1998a); however, retail or wholesale, men and women sell different items. In large department stores, for example, men sell large appliances on commission, while women work in noncommission departments such as sportswear. Consequently, the median weekly earning for men in this "integrated" occupational category is $603 while women earn $352 (U.S. Census Bureau 1998b). The broad categorization of sales occupations only appears integrated. Upon closer examination, the segregation of women into the retail industry and into positions such as cashier reveal the extent to which sales occupations are really not integrated. Third, female-dominated jobs often have a shorter career ladder and fewer possibilities for upward job mobility. As a result, women's jobs not only have a glass ceiling but also a "sticky floor" (Berheide 1992).

Researchers have debated the extent to which sex segregation actually explains the wage gap. Other explanations point to human-capital characteristics, job characteristics, and organizational and regional differences. Donald Tomaskovic-Devey (1995) compared the ability of sex composition to explain the wage gap in both jobs and occupations. He found that the number of women employees in jobs explains 46 percent of the earnings differential for women and men while sex composition in occupations explains 33 percent. Similarly, the segregation of men and women into different occupations and industries when they begin their careers explains 42 percent of the earnings gap while gender differences in human capital and occupational aspirations account for only 14 and 10 percent of the gap, respectively (Marini and Fan 1997). . . .

Women and men who enter nontraditional occupations may encounter varieties of "boundary heightening" by majority-group members; this situation also occurs when people of color enter predominantly white organizations (Kanter 1977). When one class of worker makes up only 15 percent of a work group or organization, majority-group members are likely to act in ways that strengthen or make more visible the differences between their own group and the minority group. Much of this activity involves discriminatory treatment that may have direct impact on a token person's work environment, physical and mental well-being, and opportunity for advancement. In the case of female tokens, employee events may take on a decidedly masculine theme involving football or cars to which female co-workers may not even be invited. Thus women may be effectively excluded from the informal networks that prove so important in obtaining better jobs. Dress codes also set women apart in a very visible manner. In addition to boundary-heightening actions, majority-group workers may attempt to discourage women workers altogether. When women first entered steel work, male workers attempted to sabotage their work. Women fire fighters report concerns as to whether co-workers will back them up in dangerous situations. Finally, when women are members of a token group in the workplace they are often "over-supervised" and scrutinized.

The discriminatory treatment of women in male-dominated occupations does not mirror the experience of men in female-dominated occupations. Although female nurses and librarians often interact with male nurses and librarians in stereotypical ways (e.g., asking a male nurse to help change a tire), male tokens receive more rewards as a result of their numerical minority than disadvantages (Williams 1992). For example, rather than being labeled a "bitch" or an "Iron Maiden" for working hard and overachieving, a man in a sex-atypical position will be encouraged to move ahead and will often be placed on the fast track. The glass escalator experienced by many token male employees reveals the extent to which the token's experience is dependent upon gender. Female and male tokens are not treated similarly by co-workers, potential mentors, and bosses.

In sum, the consequences of occupational segregation are substantial. Occupations can provide income, autonomy, security, social status, and upward mobility. Occupational segregation, however, serves as a major institutional factor shaping and limiting women's (and men's) employment options, ultimately, reinforcing a gendered distribution of power and social status.

CONCLUSION

Throughout much of the twentieth century, rates of occupational sex segregation were consistent and high, only declining since 1970 from 68 to 53. In white-collar, pink-collar, clerical, and blue-collar occupations, the jobs at the top of the hierarchy tend to be male dominated; when women are allowed into those specialties, it is usually because the jobs have changed in some way to be less attractive to men. Although occupational segregation per se is not illegal, discriminatory hiring and promotion practices are prohibited in firms covered by affirmative-action legislation. Unfortunately, many states are overturning affirmative-action laws and policies. This trend is likely to slow any progress made toward the inclusion of more women and minorities in highly skewed male occupations. The best-supported explanations for the persistence of occupational sex segregation are those that focus on institutional and socially constructed antecedents rather than individual characteristics or gender differences. Perhaps surprisingly, the rapid, large increase in women's recorded employment over the last few decades has done proportionately little to reduce occupational sex stereotyping and the overall sex segregation of workers. Attitudes about the desirability of women's work may have changed, but the social organization of the specific jobs women hold has not always done so. Some occupations have become more sex integrated or have switched from male to female dominated. Yet other factors have counterbalanced this trend, including the decline of sex-integrated occupations in agriculture or the growth of new and existing sex-segregated occupations in the service sector. The consequence is continuing high rates of sex segregation that foster gender inequities.

REFERENCES

Andersen, Margaret L. (1997). *Thinking About Women: Sociological Perspectives on Sex and Gender.* Boston: Allyn and Bacon.

Baron, Ava. (1991). *Work Engendered: Toward a New History of American Labor.* Ithaca, NY: Cornell University Press.

Berheide, Catherine White. (1992). *"Women still 'stuck' in low level jobs." Women in Public Services: A Bulletin for the Center for Women in Government* 3 (Fall). Albany: Center for Women in Government, State University of New York.

Cohen, Lisa E., Josepf P. Broschak, and Heather A. Haveman. (1998). "And then there were more? The effect of organizational sex composition on the hiring and promotion of managers." *American Sociological Review,* 63: 711–727.

Davies, Margery W. (1982). *Women's Place Is at the Typewriter: Office Work and Office Workers 1870–1930.* Philadelphia: Temple University Press.

Drentea, Patricia. (1998). "Consequences of women's formal and informal job search methods for employment in female-dominated jobs." *Gender & Society,* 12: 321–338.

England, Paula and Melissa S. Herbert. (1993). "The pay of men in 'female' occupations: Is comparable worth only for women?" Pp. 28–48 in *Doing "Women's Work": Men in Nontraditional Occupations.* Christine L. Williams (ed.). Newbury Park, CA: Sage.

Fonow, Mary Margaret. (1993). "Occupation/ steelworker: Sex/female." Pp. 217–222 in *Feminist Frontiers III.* Laurel Richardson and Verta Taylor (eds.). New York: McGraw-Hill.

Gross, Edward. (1968). *"Plus ça change*: The sexual segregation of occupations over time." *Social Problems,* 16: 198–208.

Hogan, Richard, Carolyn C. Perrucci, and Janet M. Wilmoth. (2000). "Gender inequality in employment and retirement income effects of marriage, industrial sector, and self-employment." Pp. 27–54 in *Advances in Gender Research, Vol. 4, Social Change for Women and children.* Vasilikie Demos and Marcia Texler Segal (eds.). Stamford, CT: JAI.

Jacobs, Jerry. (1989). "Long-term trends in occupational segregation by sex." *American Journal of Sociology,* 95: 160–173.

Jacobsen, Joyce P. (1994). "Trends in work force sex segregation. 1960–1990." *Social Science Quarterly,* 75(1): 204–211.

Jones, Beverly W. (1984). "Race, sex, and class; black female tobacco workers in Durham, North Carolina, 1920–1940, and the Development of Female Consciousness." Pp. 228–233 in *Feminist Frontiers IV.* Laurel Richardson, Verta Taylor, and Nancy Whittier (eds.). New York: McGraw-Hill.

Kanter, Rosabeth Moss. (1977). *Men and Women of the Corporation.* New York: Basic.

Kay, Fiona M. and John Hagan. (1998). "Raising the bar: The gender stratification of law-firm capital." *American Sociological Review,* 63: 728–743.

King, Mary C. (1992). "Occupational segregation by race and sex, 1940–88." *Monthly Labor Review,* 115: 30–36.

Kraut, Karen and Molly Luna. (1992). *Work and Wages: Facts on Women and People of Color in the Workforce.* Washington, DC: National Committee on Pay Equity.

MacCorquodale, Patricia and Gary Jensen. (1993). "Women in the law: Partners or tokens?" *Gender & Society,* 7: 582–593.

Marini, Margaret Mooney and Pi-Ling Fan. (1997). "The gender gap in earnings at career entry." *American Sociological Review,* 62: 588–604.

Milkman, Ruth. (1987). *Gender at Work: The Dynamics of Job Segregation by Sex During World War II.* Urbana: University of Illinois Press.

Nakano Glenn, Evelyn and Roslyn L. Feldberg. (1989). "Clerical work: The female occupation." Pp. 287–311 in *Women: A Feminist Perspective.* Jo Freeman (ed.). Mountain View, CA: Mayfield.

Reskin, Barbara F. (1994). "Segregating workers: Occupational differences by sex, race, and ethnicity." Paper presented at the annual meeting of the Population Association of America in San Francisco.

Reskin, Barbara F. and Heidi I. Hartmann. (1986). *Women's Work, Men's Work: Sex Segregation on the Job.* Washington, DC: National Academy Press.

Reskin, Barbara F. and Irene Padavic. (1994). *Women and Men at Work.* Thousand Oaks, CA: Pine Forge.

Reskin, Barbara F. and Polly A. Phipps. (1988). "Women in male-dominated professional and managerial occupations." Pp. 190–205 in *Women Working: Theories and Facts in Perspective,* Second Edition. Ann Helton Stromberg and Shirley Harkess (eds.). Mountain View, CA: Mayfield.

Reskin, Barbara F. and Patricia A. Roos (eds.). (1990). *Job Queues, Gender Queues: Explaining Women's Inroads into Male Occupations.* Philadelphia: Temple University Press.

Roos, Patricia A. (1990). "Hot-metal to electronic composition: Gender, technology, and social change." Pp. 275–298 in *Job Queues, Gender Queues: Explaining Women's Inroads into Male Occupations.* Barbara F. Reskin and Patricia A. Roos (eds.). Philadelphia: Temple University Press.

Silver, Catherine Bodare. (1981). "Public bureaucracy and private enterprise in the U.S.A. and France: Contexts for the attainment of executive positions by women." In *Access to Power: Cross-National Studies of Women and Elites.* Cynthia Fuchs Epstein and Rose Laub Coser (eds.). London: George Allen and Unwin.

Steiger, Thomas and Barbara F. Reskin. (1990). "Baking and baking off: Deskilling and the changing sex makeup of bakers." Pp. 257–274 in *Job Queues, Gender Queues: Explaining Women's Inroads into Male Occupations.* Barbara F. Reskin and Patricia A. Roos (eds.). Philadelphia: Temple University Press.

Tomaskovic-Devey, Donald. (1995). "Sex composition and gendered earnings inequality: A comparison of job and occupational models." Pp. 23–56 in *Gender Inequality at Work.* Jerry A. Jacobs (ed.). Thousand Oaks, CA: Sage.

U.S. Bureau of Labor Statistics. (1997). "Table 1. Table A-1. National employment and wage data from the occupational employment statistics survey by occupation, 1997."

[Web Page]. Accessed 3 August 1999. Available at http://stats.bls.gov;80/news.release/ocwage.t01.htm.

———. (1999). "D-20 median weekly earnings of full-time wage and salary workers by selected characteristics." [Web Page]. Accessed 13 August 1999. Available at http://www.bls.gov/cpseeq.htm.

U.S. Census Bureau. (1990). "Table 20. Occupation of employed persons: 1990." P. 20 in *Census of the Population. Social and Economic Characteristics. United States.* Washington, DC: Bureau of the Census.

———. (1998a). *The Official Statistics*™. "No. 672. Employed civilians, by occupations, sex, race, and Hispanic origin: 1983 and 1997." in *Statistical Abstract of the United States.* [Web Page]. Accessed 7 August 1999. Available at http://www.census.gov/prod/3/98pubs/98statab/cc98stab.htm.

———. (1998b). *The Official Statistics*™. "No. 696. Full-time wage and salary workers—number and earnings: 1985 to 1997." *Statistical Abstract of the United States.* [Web Page]. Accessed 7 August 1999. Available at http://www.census.gov/prod/3/98pubs/98statab/cc98stab.htm.

Williams, Christine L. (1992). "The glass escalator: Hidden advantages for men in the 'female' professions." Pp. 193 207 in *Men's Lives*, Third Edition. Michael S. Kimmel and Michael A. Messner (eds.). Boston: Allyn and Bacon.

Women's Bureau, Department of Labor. (1999) "20 leading occupations of employed women: 1998 annual averages." [Web Page]. Accessed 7 August 1999. Available at http://www.dol.gov/dol/wb/public/wb_pubs/201ead98.htm.

The co-authors have equally contributed to this chapter and their order is alphabetical. ♦

READING 20

Moving Up and Taking Charge

Irene Padavic and Barbara Reskin

Until 30 years ago, few employers considered women for promotions that would take them outside the female clerical or assembly-line ghettos. Now women receive promotions as often as men, although they occupy only a tiny fraction of the nation's very top jobs. When they are in higher-level jobs, many women do not have the authority that is typical of these positions. This chapter first examines promotion differences between women and men and then focuses on two aspects of women's and men's differential access to authority: women's greater chances of encountering a "glass ceiling" barring them from jobs that grant power and authority and women's lesser chances of being able to exercise authority even when they hold jobs that normally confer it. We conclude by discussing explanations and remedies for the sex differences we find.

WOMEN, MEN, AND PROMOTIONS

Promotions matter to workers and employers. Given the centrality of work in peoples' lives, career advancement is key for how they think about themselves. Many regard getting ahead at work as a way of showing that they are worthwhile and productive. For their part, employers use promotions to retain valued workers, to fill higher-level positions with workers familiar with the company, and to give workers an incentive to work hard.

National surveys that ask about promotions—the General Social Survey (GSS) and the National Longitudinal Survey of Youth (NLSY)—indicate a small to moderate gender gap in promotions. The GSS asked a random sample of workers across all ages whether they had ever been promoted by their current employer. In 1991 (the most recent year available), 48 percent of men had been promoted, compared to only 34 percent of women (Kalleberg and Reskin 1995). In contrast, in 1998 the NLSY asked workers in their mid-30s and early 40s if their current employer had promoted them within the previous two years. These data indicate that men had a very slight edge over women (21.6 percent of men compared to 20.6 percent of women) (U.S. Bureau of Labor Statistics 1999). Because the NLSY data concern only recent promotions of workers in midcareer, they do not pick up sex differences during the early years of a career, when most promotions occur. Men are promoted at a faster rate during those years, after which the sex gap disappears (Cobb-Clark and Dunlop 1999). Thus, compared to the large differences in promotion rates in the early 1980s (men averaged .83 promotions compared to women's .47; Spaeth 1989), the promotion gap has narrowed considerably.

Among federal government workers, women have been promoted at a higher rate than men: Whereas women made up 45 percent of the federal workforce in 1998, they accounted for 52 percent of all promotions. However, most of women's promotions were in the low- and midlevel ranks, not the senior ones, 62 percent of which went to men, who were 55 percent of the federal workforce (U.S. Office of Personnel Management 1999).

The size of sex differences in promotion rates also depends on characteristics of workers. Consider education. Women high school graduates and women with less than a high school education are far more likely to be promoted than similarly educated men. The reverse is true for college graduates and above. About 35 percent of men college graduates were promoted in 1996, compared to only about 29 percent of similar women. The difference is even more pronounced among those with postgraduate schooling: 34 percent of such men had been promoted, compared to 21 percent of such women (Cobb-Clark and Dunlop 1999).

Being married increases the chances of a man being promoted, but has the opposite effect for women. Having a preschooler also has contrary effects for men and women: Fathers of preschoolers have higher rates of promotion than the average man, and mothers of preschoolers have lower rates than the average woman. Thus, the sex gap in promotions is greater among married than single workers and among parents of preschoolers compared to others (Cobb-Clark and Dunlop 1999).

Women's and men's promotion rates depend partly on their race and ethnicity, with black women particularly disadvantaged relative to white men. Among workers in their mid-30s to early 40s in 1998, for example, only 17 percent of black women had been promoted, compared to 22 percent of white men (U.S. Bureau of Labor Statistics 1999).

Promotion opportunities also vary by occupation. When the media depict people who are promoted, they tend to present high-status workers moving up, such as law firm associates becoming partners or midlevel managers rising to executive positions. But most workers are not in management or professional

jobs. Recall . . . that the most common job for men is truck driver and for women it is secretary. Most promotions are from low- to slightly higher-level positions. Moreover, many workers hold jobs with no promotion possibilities (Davis, Smith, and Marsden 2000). Thus, for many workers, the problem is not the glass ceiling blocking them from top jobs (which we discuss later), but the sticky floor that traps them in low-mobility jobs (Berheide 1992). Generally, female and male workers in the less-skilled occupations—operatives, laborers, and service workers—are less likely to be promoted than workers in higher-skill jobs (Cobb-Clark and Dunlop 1999).

Of people aged 32 to 39 in 1996, men had an advantage among professionals, service workers, and operators (Cobb-Clark and Dunlop 1999). In one professional group—lawyers—men were two to three times more likely to have been promoted to partnership than women (Gorman 2001; Rhode 2001). Not surprisingly, women lawyers tend to be less satisfied with their advancement opportunities and more likely to think that promotion decisions in their firms were made unfairly (Catalyst 2001).

Even in traditionally female jobs (nurse, librarian, elementary school teacher, social worker, and the like), men do not confront blocked opportunities because of their sex. According to male workers, their employers singled them out for an express ride to the top on a "glass escalator" (Williams 1995). Findings from a nationally representative sample from the 1980s confirm this finding: the more women in an occupation, the greater men's—particularly white men's—chances of moving into supervisory positions (Maume 1999: 501). In fact, the odds are that after having spent 12 years in a predominantly female occupation, 44 percent of white men will have been promoted into managerial ranks, compared to only 17 percent of black men, 15 percent of white women, and 7 percent of black women.

Although men as a population seldom encounter barriers to promotion, they nevertheless can face promotion-related problems. Employers may regard men who are unwilling to pursue advancement opportunities because of family reasons as lacking career commitment, just as they perceive women who make similar choices. A senior computer programmer unwilling to be promoted out of his 35-hour-a-week job explained:

I have a six-year-old and a two-year-old. School ends for the older one at 2:30 every day, plus they have "early release" at noon every other Wednesday. My wife can only take so much time off work, and after-school programs only go so far. This isn't a point in my life when I can add the work hours that would come with a promotion, but my boss doesn't understand that. (Jim Madsen, personal communication, 2001)

Men who do not seek advancement, regardless of the reason, may suffer professionally because they violate gender stereotypes of men as oriented to advancement. Some of the men in traditionally female jobs that Williams studied faced pressure to accept promotions, such as the children's librarian who received negative evaluations for not "shooting high enough." He recalled: "I wasn't doing the management-oriented work that they thought I should be doing. And as a result . . . [I] had a lot of bad marks . . . against me" (Williams 1995: 88). Thus, both sexes face promotion problems, but the nature of these problems can vary for men and women.

In sum, sex inequality in access to promotions has declined: If we compare all women and men, the differences between them are small. One group of men appears to face greater obstacles to promotion: men with high school diplomas or less. Segregation probably accounts for this difference: These men are concentrated in lines of work that offer fewer advancement opportunities than those in which women are concentrated.

In other groups, men have an advantage over women: Among those educated to the college degree level and beyond, married people, and parents of preschoolers, men enjoy a promotion advantage. Nowadays, women are not systematically disadvantaged: Some are doing about the same as men, some do better, and some do worse, particularly black women, whose chances of promotion are worse than white men's chances.

WOMEN, MEN, AND AUTHORITY

When it comes to exercising authority on the job, women still fare worse than men. Exercising **authority** means having legitimate power to mobilize people, to get their cooperation, and to secure the resources to do the job (Kanter 1983). Typically in a bureaucracy, authority resides in the job, not in its occupant's personal qualities. A person with job authority sets policy or makes decisions about organizational goals, budgets, production, and subor-

dinates (for example, about hiring, pay, and work schedules).

Women's lesser authority in the workplace appears in two guises. First, women are less likely than men to occupy the high-level positions that offer opportunities to exert power. This blocked mobility to influential jobs has been called a **glass ceiling**. Second, even when women hold positions that typically confer authority, they have less power than men, regardless of whether they are managers, professionals, or blue-collar workers.

The Glass Ceiling in Management

Men are greatly overrepresented among the elite group of top jobholders in organizations, a phenomenon that has been described as a glass ceiling. Although managerial occupations, by definition, confer authority, if women are blocked from the top managerial ranks, they are unable to make the major business or policy decisions. The occupational category of manager includes jobs with wide variation in status and authority, ranging from the extremely low level (such as coffee shop manager) to the extremely top level (such as chief executive officer). And despite improvements, women managers are still greatly underrepresented in the top slots.

In general, the higher the level of authority in an organization, the less likely women are to be represented. In 2000, women held fewer than 13 percent of the corporate officer slots across all Fortune 500 companies, up from about 9 percent in 1995 (Catalyst 2000a). Of the 10 highest-earning companies in 1999, women's share of officer positions ranged from none at Exxon to 31 percent at Phillip Morris. Between those extremes were Citigroup (14 percent); AT&T, Ford, General Motors, Wal-Mart, and Boeing (around 10 percent); and General Electric and IBM (about 6 percent). Although in 50 of the Fortune 500 companies women held one-quarter or more of corporate officer positions, in 90 others no women were represented in these positions.

Women's representation is even lower—just 6 percent—in the "clout" positions that offer the greatest power—chief executive officer [CEO], chair, vice chair, president, chief operating officer, senior executive vice president, and executive vice president. At the very top of the job hierarchy, CEOs in the top 500 corporations, there were just five women in 2001.

Positions on corporate boards of directors provide another route to exercising genuine power, and here,

EXHIBIT I MANAGERIAL EMPLOYMENT BY SEX AND RACE, 1970–2000
**SOURCE: U.S. Census Bureau 1972, table 2; U.S. Census Bureau 1982a; authors' calculations
from the March 1988, 1999, and 2000 Current Population Surveys.**
Note: Figures for 2000 are averages of 1998, 1999, and 2000 Current Population Survey data.

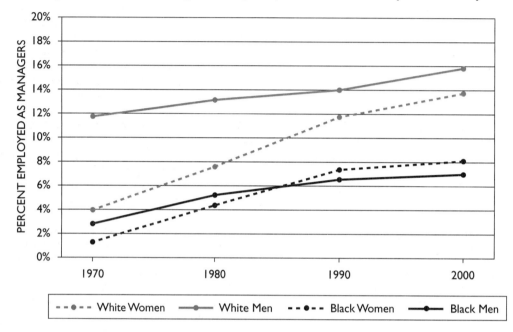

too, women remain sharply under-represented, holding only 12 percent of such seats in the Fortune 500 firms in 2000. Eighty-one of these companies had no women board members (Catalyst 1999).

Industries vary in employing women in positions that confer authority. In industries that employ mostly women, women are more likely to be found in top-level occupations (Catalyst 1999). For example, in 1999 only 3.3 percent of officers in the male-dominated computer peripherals industry were women, but a quarter of officers in the publishing and printing industry were. A study of the United States, Canada, Norway, and Sweden found that women had far greater access to positions of authority in service industries than in industrial ones (Clement and Myles 1994).[1]

Sex Differences by Race and Ethnicity Sex differences in the likelihood of being in managerial occupations vary by race and ethnicity. Exhibit 1 shows improvements over the past 30 years for black women and men and particularly strong gains for white women. At the turn of the twenty-first century, white women

were almost as likely as white men to be managers. Among African Americans, women had a slight edge over men in their likelihood of holding managerial positions. White men were still twice as likely to be managers (15.8 percent of white men found employment as managers) as were black women (8.1 percent) or black men (7 percent).

A different source that uses a category called "officials and managers" provides more detailed race and ethnic information, but because this category differs from "managerial occupations," the data deviate somewhat from those depicted in Exhibit 1. These data from the Equal Employment Opportunity Commission show that men in 1999 were better represented than coethnic women among all race/ethnic groups for which data were available (U.S. Equal Employment Opportunity Commission 2001). The sex gap was largest among whites (16.1 percent of white men held such jobs compared to 8.8 percent of white women). It was smallest among Hispanics (5.2 percent of men and 3.7 percent of women) and blacks (5.5 percent of black men and 3.9 percent of black women). The gap between Asian/Pacific Islander women and men (9.5 percent of men and 5.4 percent of women) and that between American Indian/Alaskan Native men and women (8.5 percent of men and 5.3 percent of women were officials and managers) fell between these extremes.

The Managerial Glass Ceiling in Government Employment Among government workers, too, men have a substantial edge in access to top jobs, although the disparity is smaller than in the private sector. Women accounted for about 52 percent of the workforce in state governments in 1999, but only 30 percent of those serving as top-ranking policy leaders (Center for Women in Government 1999). In the federal government—the nation's largest employer—women made up 45 percent of the workforce at the turn of the twenty-first century and have greatly increased their representation in the top jobs. In 1978, women held only 6 percent of higher-level positions; they held 22 percent of senior executive positions in 1998 (U.S. Merit Systems Protection Board 1996: 16; U.S. Office of Personnel Management 1999). Thus, the authority gap has been shrinking in the federal government, but despite women's gains, men still hold three-quarters of the best jobs.

These sex differences in federal government employment depend on the race of the worker. Minority women remain concentrated in lower grades than white men or men of their same race/ethnicity (U.S. Merit Systems Protection Board 1996, Figure 4; U.S. Office of Personnel Management 2001). Although minority women made up 37 percent of federal government workers, they filled only 19 percent of senior management positions; minority men made up 23 percent of the workers and only 12 percent of such positions (U.S. Office of Personnel Management 2001). And when it comes to the top executive positions, minority women held about 2 percent and minority men held about 8 percent of these jobs (U.S. Merit Systems Protection Board 1996, Table 4). These differences are not the result of different qualifications: Women with levels of education and experience equivalent to those of men of their same race and ethnicity were in lower-ranked jobs.

The Managerial Glass Ceiling Around the World Compared to women in most other countries, American women are doing relatively well: Women's representation in top jobs worldwide is under 5 percent (International Labour Organization 1998). In no country are women represented in top-level jobs on a par with their numbers in all administrative and managerial positions. Out of Germany's 70,000 largest companies, fewer than 3 percent of top executives and board members were women. In Brazil, about 3 percent of top executives were women. In the United Kingdom, women were 4 percent of directors and 2 percent of executive directors in the top 100 companies. In Japan, only 2 percent of top managers of large corporations were women, although including small and medium-sized companies brings the figure up to 13 percent. The United Nations estimates that if current trends continue, women will not achieve parity with men in attaining top jobs for almost another 500 years (Seager 1997: 70).

The Glass Ceiling in Other Occupations

We noted earlier that one reason women have less authority than men is that they are less likely to be in managerial positions. Of course, there are other positions in which people exercise authority, and we now turn to the glass ceiling in other occupations. Women are underrepresented in top jobs in the professions, the military, and unions. In the field of law, at the beginning of the twenty-first century, women were far more likely to be law firm associates than law firm partners, and it is partners who run the show. Nationally, women were 39 percent of law firm associates, but only 15 percent of partners (Rhode 2001). A study of almost 700 Ontario lawyers found that even women lawyers who served the "important" clients and who generated high billings had lower chances of partnership compared to men (Kay and Hagan 1999). At the pinnacle of the legal profession and certainly at the height of decision-making power are federal court judges, fewer than 1 in 6 of whom are women (Rhode 2001).

Other professions show similar patterns. Female medical school graduates who obtained degrees between 1979 and 1993 made up only 10 percent of medical school faculty (DeAngelis 2000). A "stained glass ceiling" in which women clergy were overrepresented in subordinate, low-status positions exists, according to a national study of over 15,000 Episcopal priests and a smaller sample of Presbyterian clergy (Sullins 2000). In the military, women's representation in the officer ranks was about equal to their representation in the enlisted ranks (Manning and Wight 2000: 9), but female and minority officers were concentrated in less-prestigious administrative and supply areas and underrepresented in tactical operations, from which two-thirds of the general and flag officers are drawn *(New York Times 1999)*. The Federal Bureau of Investigation (FBI) refused even to hire women as agents until after its director, J. Edgar Hoover, died in 1972 (Johnston 1993). The lingering effect of this practice is that women FBI agents near the end of the twentieth century were far less likely than men agents to be in the highest ranks: 92 percent of criminal investigators in the Bureau's highest grades were men (U.S. Government Accounting Office 1995, Figure 1.2).

Unions have increased the proportion of women in top jobs, but room for improvement remains. At the turn of the twenty-first century, women comprised over 40 percent of union members but only 13 percent of the AFL-CIO Executive Council (Gerstel and Clawson 2001: 290). The executive vice-president of the AFL-CIO was a Hispanic woman in 2001, but at that time only three women had been elected president at the nation's biggest unions: the American Federation of Teachers, the Association of Flight Attendants, and the American Federation of Television and Radio Artists (Fix 2001).

Sex Differences in Opportunities to Exercise Authority

Women who achieve jobs that typically involve decision-making power cannot always exercise the same level of authority as men. Among workers in Atlanta, Boston, and Los Angeles, women were substantially less likely to hold positions of authority than men, regardless of race or ethnicity (Smith and Elliott 2002). White men had a decided advantage in almost every case: They were four times more likely to hold positions that provided authority than were black and Hispanic women, and three times more likely than Asian women, twice as likely as black or Hispanic men, and slightly more likely than Asian men to hold positions that conferred authority.

What does it mean that women have less decision-making authority than men? A study of decision making among a cross section of workers found that women managers participated in decision making by gathering information and making recommendations, but that men usually made the final decisions (Reskin and Roos 1992). Men more often had the authority to make decisions about bread-and-butter issues such as hiring, firing, promoting, and giving raises, and they were more likely to have had a say in decisions that

affected other units. The three-city study we discussed earlier similarly found that among women and men in authority positions, men were more likely than coethnic women to be in jobs offering high levels of authority (Smith and Elliott 2002). Asian men, for example, were two-and-a-half times as likely as Asian women to hold positions of authority, black and Hispanic men almost twice as likely as black and Hispanic women to hold such positions, and white men were half again as likely as white women.

The existence of relatively powerless female managers has led some researchers to question whether women's increasing representation in managerial occupations represents genuine progress or whether they are "glorified secretaries," women with managerial titles but not the responsibilities and authority that usually accompany the titles (Jacobs 1992). A conversation secretly taped by the FBI between the vice-chair and two division presidents in a Fortune 500 corporation illustrates this concept. One executive raised the idea of promoting two women to vice president levels and making another head of a department. Another senior executive responded: "Yeah, [it's] just a title, just a title. Don't mean anything. At least to the outside it does mean something" (Eichenwald 2000).

Coworkers also may actively deny women and minorities the chance to exercise authority. Women in traditionally male blue-collar jobs, for example, encounter problems in exercising authority even when their job explicitly confers it. One woman promoted to construction foreperson while the supervisors were out for a week said:

> It was like *Mutiny on the Bounty*. I mean, I had been working with these guys for months, everybody getting along fine, doing a wonderful job. . . . [But when I was put in charge], by God, . . . if I told them to do something, they'd do their best to find some way not to do it. (Eisenberg 1998: 167)

When a female electrician was appointed to a supervisory role at Atlantic City's convention center, the site's business manager objected: "[N]ow is not the time, the place or the year [n]or will it ever be the year for a woman foreman" (Schultz 1998: 1723). The men she supervised refused to work under her and stood by laughing while she lifted heavy boxes.

Some workers circumvent a lack of authority by becoming their own boss (Powell 1999: 338). Women commonly cite blocks to advancement as a reason for starting their own businesses (Moore and Buttner

1997). In 1997, women-owned businesses made up about one-quarter of all nonfarm businesses in the country, representing an increase of 16 percent in just 5 years, and showed receipts that grew at a faster rate than those of other businesses (U.S. Census Bureau 2001). Businesses owned by minority women, especially Hispanics, have grown at an even faster rate (Moore 1999: 371, 375).[2] Yet women-owned firms tend to be smaller and return lower profits than men-owned firms. Over two-thirds had receipts of under $25,000 per year (compared to 53 percent of all firms), and only 2 percent had receipts of over $1 million (U.S. Census Bureau 2001).

Women-run businesses generate less revenue than men-run businesses because they are smaller and are in the service sector. Many female business owners act as **independent contractors**—workers hired on a freelance basis to do work that regular employees otherwise would do in-house. Most employ just themselves—only 16 percent had paid employees.[3] The average annual earnings of a full-time self-employed female worker were only about $14,000, compared to about $29,000 for an employed female worker (U.S. Census Bureau 1998, 1999, 2000). Another factor that depresses the profits of women-run businesses is that few are able to attract venture capital. Only 5 percent of the $12 billion pool of available venture capital went to women-owned firms in 1999 (an improvement over the 2 percent in previous years; Thomas 2000).

EXPLANATIONS AND REMEDIES FOR THE PROMOTION AND AUTHORITY GAPS

Although there is no longer a systematic promotion gap across the board, there are sectors where it remains. Particularly problematic are the slots high up in organizations: Men are more likely to occupy top positions, and the higher one looks, the bigger the sex disparity. This section examines four explanations for sex inequalities in promotions and authority and the remedies derived from them.

Segregation

Women's and men's segregation into different jobs contributes to women's blocked mobility to the top jobs. Thus, the more segregated the sexes over time or across work settings, the greater should be men's promotion advantage. The mechanism that converts segregation into a promotion gap is the **internal labor market.** Internal labor markets comprise related jobs (or job families) connected by **job ladders** that are promotion or transfer paths between lower- and higher-level jobs.

Insofar as segregation disproportionately concentrates women in dead-end jobs or jobs with short promotion ladders, it commensurately reduces their promotion chances. Men are more likely than women to be on career ladders (Cassirer and Reskin 2000, table 1). In a mid-1990s court case, the Wall Street firm Salomon Smith Barney paid thousands of dollars to settle a claim that (among other charges) it had systematically channeled men into broker-training programs while directing women into sales assistant jobs that offered little hope of promotion to broker (McGeehan 1998). Academia offers other examples. Women faculty members are overrepresented in non-tenure track positions (i.e., instructor, lecturer) that offer no prospects for rising through the ranks (Grant and Ward 1996). Women faculty in law schools, for example, disproportionately work as instructors who teach legal writing and research and professional skills, and instructors are seldom on the tenure ladder (Reskin, Hargens, and Merritt 2001). Men's greater likelihood of being on career ladders is mirrored in their greater optimism about their chances of a promotion: 61 percent of a national sample of 34- to 41-year-old men in 1998 thought being promoted at their present job within 2 years was possible, compared to 56 percent of women (U.S. Bureau of Labor Statistics 1999; see also Cassirer and Reskin 2000).

Sex-segregated internal labor markets can also help explain women's lesser access to jobs that confer authority. Employers designed many traditionally female jobs, such as teacher, without job ladders in order to encourage turnover, thereby keeping wages low. (By giving workers an incentive to stay, job ladders discourage turnover.)

For workers whose jobs are on promotion ladders, men tend to be found on longer ladders that reach higher in the organization where authority is concentrated. In contrast, women are concentrated on shorter ladders, with just one or two rungs above the entry level. Clerical work, for example, is often part of a two-rung system. A typical word-processing office in a small firm consists of many word-processing workers and one supervisor; a travel agency employs many reservation agents and one supervisor (Gutek 1988: 231).

An illustration of how internal labor markets can affect access to top jobs comes from a grocery chain, whose female employees sued for discrimination because it had promoted almost no women or minorities to store manager. A diagram of this chain's internal labor market (Exhibit 2) shows how women's underrepresentation in the top jobs stemmed largely from the sex segregation of lower-level jobs. Job ladders in the predominantly male produce department led to top management. In contrast, the most heavily female departments—bakery/deli and general merchandise—were on short job ladders that were not directly connected to the ladder to top management.

Establishment segregation explains much of women's underrepresentation in the top jobs. Large organizations are more likely to have the resources that allow them to create internal labor markets (Powell 1999). Moreover, their sheer size lets them create more opportunities for deserving workers (Spaeth 1989). Most workers of both sexes work for small employers, not corporations, but women's greater concentration in small, entrepreneurial firms and nonprofit organizations reduces their odds of promotion relative to men (Cobb-Clark and Dunlop 1999; Kalleberg and Reskin 1995).

Women's share of top leadership jobs also affects other women's opportunities to move up and take charge. Jobs that have low female representation at the top tend to have poor female representation at all levels of management (Cohen, Broschak, and Haveman 1998). For instance, junior women in law firms that had higher proportions of women partners had better employment experiences: Compared to those in firms with few senior women, they perceived fewer differences between women and men workers and regarded women as more capable of achieving success (Ely 1995).

Women's share of nonmanagerial jobs also matters. In companies that fill managerial jobs by promoting from within rather than by recruiting from outside the company, a strong representation of women in nonmanagerial positions increased female employees' share of managerial jobs (Reskin and McBrier 2000: 224). This was particularly true in largely male industries, where the recruitment pool outside the company was also mostly male. (Of course, if the insider pool has few women and the outside pool has many, women's chances of becoming managers are greater if the firm engages in recruiting from outside.)

Segregation further contributes to women's underrepresentation in the upper echelons of management and the professions by obscuring women's accomplishments. Women tend to hold "staff" positions, such as human relations and public relations, that offer fewer opportunities to demonstrate competence. Among corporate officers, for example, men occupy 93 percent of the more important "line" positions, which entail profit and loss responsibility, compared to only 7 percent of women (Catalyst 2000a). Staff positions involve little risk and therefore provide few opportunities for workers to display their talents to senior managers. When top executives are looking for people to promote to senior management, they seldom pick vice presidents of personnel management or public relations. They pick vice presidents in product management or sales, who are usually men. By denying women jobs in which workers make important decisions, segregation produces an authority gap.

Women in heavily female industries tend to have greater access to jobs that confer authority than do women in male-dominated industries, as we noted previously. Perhaps the companies' greater experience with female workers makes them less likely to stereotype women and better able to spot talented individuals. Furthermore, jobs in female-intensive industries pay less and are thus less desirable to men. Because of the small pool of male competitors, women get more opportunities to exercise authority than they would in male-dominated industries. In any event, sex segregation contributes to this outcome by concentrating women in some industries.

In general, lowering segregation within establishments would go a long way toward equalizing the sexes' access to advancement and authority. . . . Until it is eliminated, however, steps can be taken to ensure that the contributions of workers relegated to staff jobs are noticed and rewarded with promotions. For example, workers who bring profitable clients or resources into their firms are commonly called "rainmakers." Evaluations that contain "rainmaking equivalency quotients" calibrate the accomplishments of workers in departments that do not produce profits to those in departments that do, thus allowing staff workers the possibility to advance into the upper ranks (Meyerson and Fletcher 1999; see also Nelson and Bridges 1999: 340).

The problem posed by women's concentration on job ladders with low mobility potential can be addressed through companies' creation of "bridge" programs to help workers switch job ladders—for example, move from a clerical ladder to an administrative one—without penalty: In response to a consent decree, for example, Home Depot partially automated

EXHIBIT 2 INTERNAL LABOR MARKET FOR GROCERY STORE CHAIN
Note: Arrows indicate transfer or promotion paths.

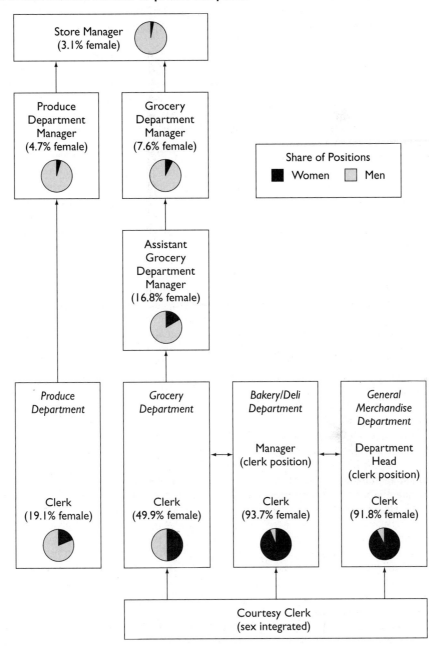

its promotion system. Current employees enter into a computer their job qualifications, which are automatically incorporated into the applicant pool for all jobs that fit their preference and qualifications profile, regardless of the employee's originating department (Sturm 2001: 459).

Sex Differences in Human Capital

The logic behind human-capital theory assumes that sex differences in commitment, education, and experience make women less productive than men (Becker 1985). Lower productivity should lead to poorer promotion rates and fewer opportunities to exercise authority. [However,] women's career commitment does not differ from men's, and women are fast catching up in educational attainment with men. The human-capital claim that women's lesser experience contributes to their underrepresentation at the top of career hierarchies deserves a more careful look, however.

According to this explanation, women as a group lack the experience needed to advance into positions that confer authority. Sociologists conceptualize different levels of experience between two groups in a workplace in terms of the seniority composition of the organization. Many demographic factors affect the sex composition of an organization, and how rapidly these factors change depends on the turnover rate of female and male workers in the higher ranks, the sex composition of the younger pool of workers, the growth (or decline) of jobs in the field, and the sheer number of jobs in the top ranks (Hargens and Long 2002).

Organizations vary on these demographic dimensions. In settings where turnover is high and career spans are short, it should not take as long for the sex composition to become more equal if employers ignore sex in employment decisions; in settings where turnover is low and career spans are long, it takes longer. Thus, the sex composition of the U.S. Supreme Court will change more slowly (because justices have lifetime appointments) than will the sex composition of top jobs in an organization that replaces corporate officers every two or three years. Commenting on the small number of job slots in the top ranks of her firm, an African American woman engineer at General Electric said, "There are only so many management slots. It gets to the point where your moves are lateral, not vertical" (Walsh 2000). Establishments with more top slots or greater turnover in managerial jobs offer more opportunities. Thus, even in the complete absence of discrimination today, it can take decades for women to achieve parity with men in the top ranks when turnover is low.

There is merit to this logic and to the human capital claim that women as a group receive less training and have less experience both within an establishment and within the labor force. These differences need to be equalized for the sex gap in promotions and authority to disappear. On the other hand, it is important to recognize that employers as well as workers contribute to how much and what kinds of experience workers acquire. In many settings, employers prevent women from acquiring experiences needed for advancement. For example, military promotion to the rank of commissioned officer is usually reserved for people with ground combat experience, but Congress and the military ban women from combat (Manning and Wight 2000: 18). In banking, managers who hope for a top spot need extensive experience in commercial lending. Only recently have substantial numbers of women bank managers been given the chance to work in commercial lending, so few women could acquire the expertise needed to rise beyond middle management. In the same way, the sex segregation of blue-collar production jobs denies women the experience they need to rise to management positions in manufacturing firms. Moreover, the biases of people responsible for training can block opportunities. A black female electrician recalled her "training": "I did all the grunt work—digging ditches, moving trash, unloading tractor trailers for days in and days out. You didn't use your tools that much. I had to . . . clean out their toilets and mop their floors. . . . The electricians would tell me, 'This is the way you move up'" (Eisenberg 1998: 149)

In an increasingly global economy, international experience is crucial for advancement in many firms. Eighty percent of the human resources executives in a study of 75 Fortune 500 companies said that developing global talent will be a top priority over the next five years (Catalyst 2000b). Women, however, are far less likely than men to receive international assignments. Women are 49 percent of all managers and professionals but are only 13 percent of American managers who are sent abroad (Catalyst 2000b). Many companies think twice before sending a woman to a foreign assignment, partly because they fear that sexist attitudes abroad will hinder their employee's ability to get the job done. For example, a woman with excellent performance evaluations and rapport with clients said that her career was stalling because of management's refusal to have an African-American woman represent it overseas (Hesse-Biber and Carter 2000: 164).

What remedies based on human capital explanations are likely to work? Women still lag behind men in the years of experience that would put them in line for the top positions. Clearly, if a qualification such as training or experience truly is essential to do a high-level job, women who don't have it won't advance. Thus, adding women at lower levels where they can gain experience and enter the pipeline leading to future high level jobs is necessary for progress. But it is not sufficient. Also necessary is the removal of barriers that block women's access to training and experience. For example, because having *job-specific* experience is important for promotions, employers who concentrate women in different jobs than men will reduce these women's job-relevant experience, thereby lowering their promotion chances. As for experience abroad, the courts have ruled that customer preference does not justify treating women and men employees differently. To the extent that employers take seriously a commitment to abide by antidiscrimination laws and to create an equal-opportunity environment, concerns about customers' or foreign firms' comfort levels will be more or less a barrier. Enforcement matters, too: If regulatory agencies more closely monitored women's opportunities for assignments overseas, for example, women would face fewer such barriers. In sum, the equalization of women's and men's opportunities for moving up and taking charge varies depending on organizations' personnel policies and practices and on enforcement agencies' activities.

Sex Differences in Social Networks

Filling jobs through social networks ("word-of-mouth" recruiting) tends to reproduce the characteristics of the existing workforce because people's networks tend to include others like themselves (Lin 2000). As this chapter has shown, at the highest levels, most organizations are male dominated. Thus, if the pool of people being considered is made up of members of decision makers' social networks, women usually will be disadvantaged. A woman manager alluded to the advantages men have in networks by describing what she called the "armpit track" into the upper reaches of management: "They put [a man] under their armpit and say come fly with me up to the executive suite" (Bell and Nkomo 2001: 153).

Most employers fill managerial jobs through informal networks, according to a nationally representative survey of establishments. . . . Half had frequently recruited managers via referrals or direct invitations to apply; only 7 percent had not used these methods, and the establishments using informal recruitment methods were less likely to have women in managerial positions than organizations that used "open" recruitment methods (Reskin and McBrier 2000: 221–22).

Some organizations have sought to remedy social-network exclusion by actively seeking to expose workers to a broader array of networks. Encouraging the formation of networks of women and minority employees from across the organization is one way to do this (Sessa 1992; Walsh 2000). Caucus groups at the Xerox Corporation, for example, helped promote women's upward mobility (Sessa 1992).

Mentoring programs can help get around social network exclusion by providing connections to influential people in the organization who can advocate for people they mentor, teach them the ropes, and provide them with "reflected power" (the status that comes with being associated with powerful people; Kanter 1977; McGuire 2000: 501). Having a powerful person publicly support a woman helps protect her from blatant and subtle discrimination. Moreover, mentoring allows some outsiders into the networks of powerful people, which provides them with information on job openings and corporate politics. Workers with mentors experience clear advantages over other workers: They are promoted at a higher rate, earn more, have greater work satisfaction and commitment, and have more power at work (Lin 2000: 787; Ragans 1999: 347).

Organizations' Personnel Practices

Organizations improve women's access to promotions and to top jobs when they engage in practices that minimize decision makers' abilities to act on their stereotypes and preferences. . . . All decision makers automatically come up with mental schemas in evaluating others. If decision makers, who typically are male, have the discretion to act on these stereotypes or any preferences for certain types of people— usually people like themselves—then women's prospects for advancement will be diminished. Women's prospects improve in organizations that check this discretion.

Supervisors' stereotypes of women as lacking the qualities needed in higher-level jobs—which abound—can damage women's promotion chances. A large body of research documents how stereotypes of women as less able than men to make hard-nosed decisions and as lacking the qualities needed for leadership roles hinder women's career progress (Heilman 1995: 8–9). Consistent with this evidence are women's reports of stereotypes interfering with promotions. Women coal miners, for example, said that supervisors' negative stereotypes about their work capabilities affected their success in obtaining higher-skilled mining jobs (Tallichet 2000). One told how foremen "have it in their minds that we are the weaker sex." The mine superintendent told her that "men have a more mechanical approach" to their work and that the women were stuck in the menial rather than the more skilled mining jobs because it was "natural." At a major accounting firm, decision makers' stereotypes meant that women were routinely passed over for assignments that would provide the experience they needed to move up. According to a member of the task force studying the problem:

> The pervasive issue was people in leadership positions in our firm [who] were exclusively male making assumptions about women, like "I wouldn't want to put her on that kind of client because it's a dirty manufacturing environment, and that's just not the right place for her" or "That client's in a real nasty part of town." Or making assumptions on behalf of the client, like "Well, the client's not really going to be comfortable with her." If you asked the people who were doing that if they were doing that, I think they'd say no. It was very subliminal and unconscious, but it was happening a lot. (Sturm 2001: 494)

Motherhood can also disqualify women from authority positions in settings where employers hold stereotypes that pregnancy and motherhood "soften" women (Williams 2000: 69). An attorney complained that since she returned from maternity leave, her superiors refused to give her the high-level work she had been doing: "I want to say, look, I had a baby, not a lobotomy" (Williams 2000: 69). A self-study by Deloitte & Touche revealed that some managers admitted they kept top assignments from women out of fear that they might quit for family reasons (Williams 2000: 89). One woman summed up the problem: "Let's face it, how is an employer going to think a woman is manager material if he thinks her maternal instincts have primacy over business priorities?" (Kleiman 1993). If allowed to influence job assignments, stereotypes like these seriously under-

mine women's authority on the job as well as their chances for advancement.

A tendency to act on such stereotypes is more common in some situations than others (Powell 1999: 91; Reskin 2002). When women are already fairly well represented in the higher ranks, for example, decision makers tend to act in a more gender-neutral way in conferring promotions, resulting in less bias in favor of men (Perry, Davis-Blake, and Kulik 1994). Thus, as we noted earlier, female managers' promotion chances are better for jobs that already have some women (Cohen et al. 1998), in part because the women who came before have shown that women can perform the job.

Staffing jobs in which the nature of the work is uncertain or ambiguous present a situation likely to bring out favoritism toward men because decision makers attempt to eliminate uncertainty by promoting people who have social characteristics like their own (Kanter 1977). Kanter called this practice **homosocial reproduction**. Presumably, employers believe that similar people are likely to make the same decisions they would. This belief—along with in-group favoritism . . . leads employers to seek to advance others who are the same sex, race, ethnicity, social class, and religion and who belong to the same clubs, share the same sexual orientation, attended the same colleges, and enjoy the same leisure activities. Homosocial reproduction is especially likely in risky ventures, such as launching a new TV series. Denise Bielby and William Bielby (1992) argued that, because most studio and network executives are male, they view male writers and producers as "safer" than women with equally strong qualifications and are more likely to give men rather than women long-term deals and commitments for multiple series. Executives' acting on stereotypes about someone who seems different—a woman, perhaps, or a Hispanic—results in a cadre of top managers who look alike and think alike.

Organizations can shrink the promotion and authority gaps by replacing informal personnel practices with formal ones that restrict opportunities to act on bias. Firms with written rules and procedures, written hiring and firing procedures, written job descriptions, written performance records, and written evaluations have a better record in placing women in management jobs than firms that do not, because these bureaucratic practices discourage favoritism (Reskin and McBrier 2000: 223–24)[4]

Using formal criteria can also help ensure that decisions are based only on relevant information for each candidate and not on casual impressions or hearsay, which stereotypes tend to distort (Reskin 2002). The case of Ann Hopkins, who had been denied partnership in the former Big Six accounting firm of Price Waterhouse, offers an example. Despite having brought more money into the firm than any other contender for promotion had done, Hopkins was denied promotion to partner. According to the Supreme Court, which ruled in her favor in 1990, the senior partners based their evaluation on her personality and appearance and ignored her accomplishments. Hopkins had been advised that her chances for promotion would improve if she would "walk more femininely, talk more femininely, wear makeup, have [her] hair styled and wear jewelry" (White 1992: 192). Formal evaluation procedures based on established criteria would have allowed her accomplishments to take center stage.

Similarly, a lack of formal personnel practices meant that Lucky Grocery Stores did not formally post announcements of promotion opportunities because male store managers thought they knew which employees were interested in promotion. The result was that few women were promoted, prompting a successful lawsuit by women who had been passed over (*Slender et al. v. Lucky* 1992). A contrasting case shows how formalized procedures can enhance equality: After a lawsuit, Home Depot instituted a program whereby managers must interview at least three applicants for every position, thus minimizing the possibility that jobs are "wired" for certain candidates.

Employers have many incentives for revamping organizational cultures, that impede the career progress of women and minorities (Powell 1999: 332). A stake in complying with laws and government regulations is one reason. Meeting the needs of an increasingly diverse customer base is another. A desire to recruit and retain the best workers is a third powerful motivation to disrupt systems that discourage these workers. For example, when Proctor & Gamble followed up on highly valued employees who had quit, it discovered that two-thirds were women and that many had quit out of frustration with their advancement opportunities. Because it wanted to keep its best employees, the company revamped its promotion system and saw women's quit rates fall to the level of men's and their satisfac-

tion levels rise substantially (Parker-Pope 1998). Similarly, when Deloitte and Touche learned that women who quit cited a lack of mentors, having been barred from plum assignments, work-family balance problems, and having been excluded from informal networks and from social events with clients, it instituted policies to eradicate the glass ceiling and to make jobs more flexible. As a result, women's turnover rates dropped from 26 to 15 percent (Williams 2000: 90).

The social forces within an organizational culture that maintain sex differences in opportunities to move up and take charge are resistant to change, however, and formal policies are not a panacea. In some firms, especially smaller ones, these policies are merely symbolic, and decision makers still choose managers through social networks (Reskin and McBrier 2000).

Raising the price that employers pay to discriminate has prompted some firms to eliminate several of the obstacles described in this chapter. Despite the wastefulness of excluding potentially productive people from influential jobs on the basis of their sex and color, many employers have done just that. Organizations have multiple goals, and they act on the ones that have the highest priority. Because the bottom line is usually the top priority, fines and other financial sanctions raise equal opportunity on employers' agendas.

Litigation increases this price. Although individual lawsuits rarely result in court wins (because the plaintiff loses or because the case results in a settlement, not a verdict), large awards in class action cases spur employers to reconsider their employment practices. For example, a 1991 lawsuit led Marriott Corporation to pay $3 million to women managers who had been denied promotions. At fault was the company's informal promotion policy and a work culture that "froze women out" (Goozner 1991). Lawsuits against grocery store chains in the 1990s also have resulted in large settlements: Publix supermarkets agreed in 1997 to pay over $81 million to settle a lawsuit claiming that it had kept women in dead-end jobs, Albertson's paid $29 million in 1996, and Safeway paid $7.5 million in 1994.

Legislation can reduce the authority gap when it is implemented and enforced. Congress established the Glass Ceiling Division within the U.S. Department of Labor in 1991 with the charge to eliminate barriers to women's and minorities' promotions to top posts. Its "glass ceiling reviews" of some companies with

federal contracts and its awards to exemplary companies are expected to increase voluntary compliance
with the law (U.S. Employment Standards
Administration 1997).

SUMMARY

We have seen considerable variation in
women's progress in closing the promotion and
authority gaps over the past 30 years. The promotion
gap has narrowed considerably. For some populations and in some settings, it seems to have disappeared; for other groups and in other settings, it is
still appreciable. Thus, women who haven't completed high school now have an advantage over similar men, but men who are college educated and married still have an advantage over similar women.

Another group that stands out is black women, who
face a disadvantage in promotions compared to white
men. As for the authority gap, women have made
some gains, but their representation in top jobs in
management and the professions is uneven. Will the
outlook be better for the college students of today?
We don't know. History shows that women's and
minorities' access to jobs that confer authority does
not improve automatically. It improved during the
1970s through the efforts of federal agencies, advo-
cacy groups, and companies voluntarily establishing
Equal Employment Opportunity programs (Reskin
1998). It then stalled in the 1990s. Further progress
depends on similar efforts and on organizations'
recognition of the gains to be made from instituting
programs to ensure equality in access to top jobs for
all their workers.

NOTES

1. Compared to women in the United States and Canada,
Norwegian and Swedish women were less likely to hold jobs
involving authority (Clement and Myles 1994). The high
level of part-time employment among the women in these
countries accounts for this difference (Kalleberg and Reskin
1995).

2. Note that growth rates are high because the numbers
these percentages are based on are so small.

3. These few firms accounted for 88 percent of the gross
receipts for women-owned businesses.

4. A different strategy for getting around the negative
effects of favoritism draws on people's tendency to create
"us" and "them" categories (Reskin 2002). Organizations can
encourage workers to identify with sex- and race-integrated
task groups, so that the "us" category becomes "we who are
working on this project" (Brewer 1997).

REFERENCES

Becker, Gary S. 1985. "Human Capital, Effort, and the Sexual
    Division of Labor." *Journal of Labor Economics* 3
    (Supplement): S33–58.

Bell, Ella and Stella Nkomo. 2001. *Our Separate Ways: Black
    and White Women and the Struggle for Professional Identity*,
    Boston, MA: Harvard Business School Press.

Berheide, Catherine W. 1992. "Women Still 'Stuck' in Low-
    Level Jobs." *Women in Public Services: A Bulletin for the
    Center for Women in Government* 3 (Fall).

Bielby, Denise D. and William T. Bielby. 1992. "Cumulative
    Versus Continuous Disadvantage in an Unstructured
    Labor Market." *Work and Occupations* 19: 366–87.

Brewer, Marilynn B. 1997. "The Social Psychology of
    Intergroup Relations: Can Research Inform Practice?"
    Journal of Social Issues 53: 197–211.

Cassirer, Naomi and Barbara F. Reskin. 2000. "High Hopes:
    Organizational Location, Employment Experiences, and
    Women's and Men's Promotion Aspirations." *Work and
    Occupations* 27: 438–63.

Catalyst. 1999. *Catalyst Census of Women Board Directors of the
    Fortune 1000.* New York: Catalyst.

———. 2000a. *2000 Catalyst Census of Women Corporate
    Officers and Top Earners.* New York: Catalyst. www.
    catalystwomen.org/press/releases/release111300.html.

Catalyst. 2000b. *Passport to Opportunity: U.S. Women
    in Global Business.* New York: Catalyst. http://www.cata-
    lystwomen.org/press/passportmediakit/ factsglobal.html.

———. 2001. *Women in Law: Making the Case.* New York:
    Catalyst. www.catalystwomen.org/press/factsheets/
    factslaw.html.

Center for Women in Government. 1999. *Appointed Policy
    Makers in State Government.* www.cwig.albany.edu.

Clement, Wallace and John Myles. 1994. *Relations of Ruling:
    Class and Gender in Postindustrial Societies.* Montreal:
    McGill-Queens University Press.

Cobb-Clark, Deborah and Yuonne Dunlop, 1999. "The Role
    of Gender in Job Promotions." *Monthly Labor Review* 122:
    32–38.

Cohen, Lisa E., Joseph P. Broschak, and Heather A.
    Haveman. 1998. "And Then There Were More? The
    Effects of Organizational Sex Composition on Hiring and
    Promotion." *American Sociological Review* 64: 711–27.

Davis, James A., Tom W. Smith, and Peter V. Marsden. 2000. *General Social Survey, 1972-2000* [machine-readable data file]. NORC ed. Chicago: National Opinion Research Center, producer. Storrs, CT: The Roper Center for Public Opinion Research. http://csa.berkeley.edu:7502/archive.htm.

DeAngelis, Catherine D. 2000. "Women in Academic Medicine: New Insights, Same Sad News." *New England Journal of Medicine* 342 (6): Feb. 10.

Eichenwald, Kurt. 2000. *The Informant.* New York: Random House Inc. Excerpt found at www.thislife.org/pages/trax/text/adm2.html.

Eisenberg, Susan. 1998. *We'll Call You if We Need You.* Ithaca, NY: ILR.

Ely, Robin J. 1995. "The Power in Demography: Women's Social Construction of Gender Identity at Work." *Academy of Management Journal* 38: 589–634.

Fix, Janet L. 2001. "Labor's Changing Face; Women and the Union Issues They Care About Are on the Move." *The San Diego Union-Tribune,* May 7, p. D1.

Gerstel, Naomi and Dan Clawson. 2001. "Unions' Responses to Family Concerns." *Social problems* 48: 277–97.

Goozner, Merrill. 1991. "$3 Million Sex-Bias Accord at Marriott." *Chicago Tribune,* March 6, sec. 3, p. 3.

Gorman, Elizabeth H. 2001. *Gender and Organizational Selection Decisions: Evidence from Law Firms.* Cambridge, MA: Unpublished doctoral dissertation, Harvard University.

Grant, Linda and Kathryn B. Ward. 1996. "Women in Academia." Pp. 165–67 in *Women and Work: A Reader,* edited by P.J. Dubeck and K. Borman. New Brunswick, NJ: Rutgers University Press.

Gutek, Barbara. 1988. "Women in Clerical Work." Pp. 225–40 in *Women Working: Theory and Facts in Perspective,* edited by A. H. Stromberg and S. Harkess. Mountain View, CA: Mayfield.

Hargens, Lowell and J. Scott Long. 2002. "Demographic Inertia and Women's Representation Among Faculty in Higher Education." *Journal of Higher Education* 73 (July / August): 494–517.

Heilman, Madeline E. 1995. "Sex Stereotypes and Effects in the Workplace: What We Know and What We Don't Know." *Journal of Social and Behavioral Sciences* 10 (6): 3–26.

Hesse-Biber, Sharlene and Gregg L. Carter. 2000. *Working Women in America: Split Dreams.* New York: Oxford University Press.

International Labour Organization. 1988. *Breaking through the Glass Ceiling: Women in Management.* Report for discussion at the Tripartite Meeting. Geneva: ILO.

Jacobs, Jerry A. 1992. "Women's Entry Into Management: Trends in Earnings, Authority, Values, and Attitudes Among Salaried Managers." *Administrative Science Quarterly* 37: 282–301.

Johnston, David. 1993. "FBI Agent to Quit Over Her Treatment in Sexual Harassment Case." *New York Times,* October 11, p. A7.

Kalleberg, Arne and Barbara F. Reskin. 1995. "Gender Differences in Promotion in the United States and Norway." *Research in Social Stratification and Mobility* 14: 237–264.

Kanter, Rosabeth Moss. 1977. *Men and Women of the Corporation.* New York: Basic Books.

———. 1983. "Women Managers: Moving Up in a High Tech Society." Pp. 21–36 in *The Woman in Management: Career and Family Issues,* edited by J. Farley. Ithaca: New York State School of Industrial and Labor Relations, Cornell University.

Kay, Fiona M. and John Hagan. 1999. "Cultivating Clients in the Competition for Partnership: Gender and the Organizational Restructuring of Law Firms in the 1990s" *Law & Society Review* 33: 517–55.

Kleiman, Carol. 1993. "Women End Up Sacrificing Salary for Children." *Tallahassee Democrat,* March 3, p, D8.

Lin, Nan. 2000. "Inequality in Social Capital." *Contemporary Sociology* 29: 785–95.

Manning, Lori and Vanessa R. Wight. 2000. *Women in the Military: Where They Stand,* 3rd ed. Washington, DC: Women's Research and Education Institute.

Maume, David J., Jr. 1999. "Glass ceilings and Glass Escalators: Occupational Segregation and Race and Sex Differences in Managerial Promotions." *Work and Occupations* 26: 483-509.

McGeehan, Patrick. 1998. "Travelers Seeks to Fix Damage After Smith Barney Sex Case." *Wall Street Journal,* April 10, p. C1.

McGuire, Gail M. 2000. "Gender, Race, Ethnicity, and Networks: The Factors Affecting the Status of Employees' Network Members." *Work and Occupations* 27: 500–23.

Meyerson, Deborah and Joyce Fletcher. 1999. "A Modest Manifesto for Shattering the Glass Ceiling." *Harvard Business Review,* Jan-Feb: 127-36 (reprint R00107).

Moore, Dorothy P. 1999. "Women Entrepreneurs: Approaching a New Millennium." Pp. 371–90 in *Handbook of Gender and Work,* edited by G. N. Powell. Thousand Oaks, CA: Sage.

Moore, Dorothy P. and E. H. Buttner. 1997. *Women Entrepreneurs: Moving Beyond the Glass Ceiling.* Thousand Oaks, CA: Sage.

Nelson, Robert L. and William P. Bridges. 1999. *Legalizing Gender Inequality: Courts, Markets, and Unequal Pay for Women in America.* New York: Cambridge University Press.

New York Times. 1999. "Race and Gender in the Military." November 25, P. A 36.

Parker-Pope, Tara. 1998. "Inside P&G, a Pitch to Keep Women Employees." *Wall Street Journal,* September 9, pp. B1, B6.

Perry, Elissa L., Allison Davis-Blake, and Carol T. Kulik. 1994. "Explaining Gender-Based Selection Decisions: A Synthesis of Contextual and Cognitive Approaches." *Academy of Management Review* 19: 786–820.

Powell, Gary N. 1999. "Reflections on the Glass Ceiling: Recent Trends and Future Prospects." Pp. 325–46 in *Handbook of Gender and Work*, edited by G. N. Powell. Thousand Oaks, CA: Sage.

Ragans, Belle R. 1999. "Gender and Mentoring Relationships: Review and Research Agenda for the Next Decade." Pp. 347–70 in *Handbook of Gender and Work*, edited by G. N. Powell, Thousand Oaks, CA: Sage.

Reskin, Barbara F. 1998. *The Realities of Affirmative Action in Employment.* Washington, DC: American Sociological Association.

———. 2002. "Retheorizing Employment Discrimination and Its Remedies." In *New Directions in Economic Sociology*, edited by M. F. Guillen, R. Collins, P. England, and M. Meyer. New York: Russell Sage.

Reskin, Barbara F., Lowell L. Hargens, and Deborah J. Merritt. 2001. "Explaining Sex Differences in the Labor Market for Legal Academe." Presented at the Annual Meeting of the American Sociological Association, Anaheim, CA.

Reskin, Barbara F. and Debra McBrier. 2000. "Why Not Ascription? Organizations' Employment of Male and Female Managers." *American Sociological Review* 25: 335–61.

Reskin, Barbara F. and Patricia A. Roos. 1990. *Job Queues, Gender Queues: Explaining Women's Inroads Into Male Occupations.* Philadelphia: Temple University Press.

Rhode, Deborah. L. 2001. *Unfinished Agenda: Women and the Legal Profession.* Chicago, IL: American Bar Association, Commission on Women in the Profession.

Schultz, Vicki. 1998. "Reconceptualizing Sexual Harassment." *The Yale Law Journal* 107(6): 1682–1805.

Seager, Joni. 1997. *The State of Women in the World Atlas.* New York: Penguin.

Sessa, Valerie I. 1992. "Managing Diversity at the Xerox Corporation: Balanced Workforce Goals and Caucus Groups." Pp. 37–64 in *Diversity in the Workplace*, edited by S. E. Jackson and Associates. New York: Guilford.

Smith, Ryan and James R. Elliott. 2002. "Does Ethnic Concentration Influence Employers' Access to Authority? An Examination of Contemporary Urban Labor Markets." *Social Forces* 81: forthcoming.

Spaeth, Joe L. 1989. *Determinants of Promotion in Different Types of Organizations.* Unpublished manuscript. Urbana: University of Illinois.

Stender et al. v. Lucky. 1992. "Findings of Fact and Conclusion of Law," *Federal Reporter, vol. 803, Feb. Supplement, p. 259.*

Sturm, Susan. 2001. "Second Generation Employment Discrimination: A Structural Approach." *Columbia Law Review* 101: 458–568.

Sullins, Paul. 2000. "The Stained Glass Ceiling: Career Attainment for Women Clergy." *Sociology of Religion* 61: 243–266.

Tallichet, Suzanne E. 2000. "*Barriers to Women's Advancement in Underground Coal Mining.*" Rural Sociology 65: 234–52.

Thomas, Paulette. 2000. "At 'Camp,' Women Learn to Pitch Deals to Investors." *Wall Street Journal*, July 18.

U.S. Bureau of Labor Statistics. 1999. "National Longitudinal Survey of Youth 1979 Cohort, 1979–1998 (rounds 1–18)" [computer file]. Columbus, OH: Center for Human Resource Research, the Ohio State University.

U.S. Census Bureau. 1972. "U.S. Census of Population, 1970," Subject Reports, 7C, Occupational Characteristics. Washington, D.C: Census Bureau.

U.S. Census Bureau. 1982a. "Census of Population and Housing, 1980: Public Use Microdata Samples U.S." (Machine-readable data files, prepared by the Bureau of the Census.) Washington, DC: Census Bureau.

U.S. Census Bureau. 1998. Microdata from the Annual Demographic Survey of the March 1998 Current Population Surveys.

———. 1999. Microdata from the Annual Demographic Survey of the March 1998 Current Population Surveys.

———. 2000. Microdata from the Annual Demographic Survey of the March 1998 Current Population Surveys.

———. 2001. "1997 Revenues for Women-Owned Businesses Show Continued Growth, Census Bureau Reports." www.census.gov/press-release/www/2001/cb01-61.html.

U.S. Employment Standards Administration. 1997. "OFCCP Glass Ceiling Initiative: Are There Cracks in the Ceiling?" June. Office of Federal Contract Compliance Programs. www.dol.gov/dol/esa/public/media/reports/ofccp/gccover.htm.

U.S. Equal Employment Opportunity Commission. 2001. "Job Patterns for Minorities and Women in Private Industry (EEO1)." www.eeoc.gov/stats.

U.S. Government Accounting Office. 1995. "Progress of Women and Minority Criminal Investigators at Selected Agencies." April. Washington, DC: U.S. GAO.

U.S. Merit Systems Protection Board. 1996. "Fair and Equitable Treatment: A Progress Report on Minority Employment in the Federal Government." Washington, DC: U.S. Merit Systems Protection Board.

U.S. Office of Personnel Management. 1999. "Women in the Federal Government: A Statistical Profile." apps.opm.gov/publications/pages/default_search.htm.

U.S. Office of Personnel Management. 2001. "Demographic Profile of the Federal Workforce, 2000 edition." Sept.7. www.opm.gov/feddata/demograph/demograph.htm.

Walsh, Mary Williams. 2000. "Where G.E. Falls Short: Diversity at the Top." *New York Times*, Sept. 3, p. C1.

White, Jane. 1992. *A Few Good Women: Breaking the Barriers to Top Management.* Englewood Cliffs, NJ: Prentice Hall.

Williams, Christine L. 1995. *Still a Man's World: Men Who Do "Women's Work."* Berkely, CA: University of California Press.

Williams, Joan 2000. *Unbending Gender: Why Family and Work Conflict and What to Do About It.* New York: Oxford University Press.

THE REALITIES OF AFFIRMATIVE ACTION IN EMPLOYMENT

Barbara Reskin

Affirmative action policies and practices reduce job discrimination against minorities and white women, although their effects have not been large. Some critics charge that affirmative action's positive effects have been offset by its negative effects on white men, on productivity, and on the merit system.

For many people, the most troubling aspect of affirmative action is that it may discriminate against majority-group members (Lynch 1997). According to 1994 surveys, 70 to 80 percent of whites believed that affirmative action sometimes discriminates against whites (Steeh and Krysan 1996, p. 139). Men are more likely to believe that a woman will get a job or promotion over an equally or more qualified man than they are to believe that a man will get a promotion over an equally or more qualified women (Davis and Smith 1996).

Several kinds of evidence indicate that whites' fears of reverse discrimination are exaggerated. Reverse discrimination is rare both in absolute terms and relative to conventional discrimination.[1] On every measured outcome, African-American men were much more likely than white men to experience discrimination, and Latinos were more likely than non-Hispanic men to experience discrimination (Heckman and Siegelman 1993, p. 218). Statistics on the numbers and outcomes of complaints of employment discrimination also suggest that reverse discrimination is rare.

According to national surveys, relatively few whites have experienced reverse discrimination. Only 5 to 12 percent of whites believe that their race has cost them a job or a promotion, compared to 36 percent of African Americans (Steeh and Krysan 1996, pp. 139–40). Of 4,025 Los Angeles workers, 45 percent of African Americans and 16 percent of Latinos said that they had been refused a job because of their race, and 16 percent of African Americans and 8 percent of Latinos reported that they had been discriminated against in terms of pay or a promotion (Bobo and Suh 1996, Table 1). In contrast, of the 863 whites surveyed, less than 3 percent had ever experienced discrimination in pay or promotion, and only one mentioned reverse discrimination. Nonetheless, two-thirds to four-fifths of whites (but just one-quarter of African Americans) surveyed in the 1990s thought it likely that less qualified African Americans won jobs or promotions over more qualified whites (Taylor 1994a; Davis and Smith 1994: Steeh and Krysan 1996, p. 139)[2]

Alfred Blumrosen's (1996, pp. 5–6) exhaustive review of discrimination complaints filed with the Equal Employment Opportunity Commission offers additional evidence that reverse discrimination is rare. Of the 451,442 discrimination complaints filed with the EEOC between 1987 and 1994, only 4 percent charged reverse discrimination (see also Norton 1996, pp. 44–5).[3] Of the 2,189 discrimination cases that federal appellate courts decided between 1965 and 1985, *less* than 5 percent charged employers with reverse discrimination (Burstein 1991, p. 518).

Allegations of reverse discrimination are less likely than conventional discrimination cases to be supported by evidence. Of the approximately 7,000 reverse-discrimination complaints filed with the EEOC in 1994, the EEOC found only 28 credible (Crosby and Herzberger 1996, p. 55). Indeed, U.S.

(continued)

district and appellate courts dismissed almost all the reverse-discrimination cases they heard between 1990 and 1994 as lacking merit.

How can we reconcile the enormous gulf between whites' perceptions that they are likely to lose jobs or promotions because of affirmative action and the small risk of this happening? The white men who brought reverse-discrimination suits presumably concluded that their employers' choices of women or minorities could not have been based on merit, because men are accustomed to being selected for customarily male jobs (*New York Times*, March 31, 1995).[4] Most majority-group members who have not had a firsthand experience of competing unsuccessfully with a minority man or woman or a white woman cite media reports as the source of their impression that affirmative action prompts employers to favor minorities and women (Hochschild 1995, pp. 144, 308).[5] It seems likely that politicians' and the media's emphasis on "quotas" has distorted the public's understanding of what is required and permitted in the name of affirmative action (Entman 1997).

There is no evidence that affirmative action reduces productivity or that workers hired under affirmative action are less qualified than other workers. In the first place, affirmative action plans that compromise valid educational and job requirements are illegal. Hiring unqualified workers or choosing a less qualified person over a more qualified one because of their race or sex is illegal and is not condoned in the name of affirmative action (U.S. Department of Labor, Employment Standards Administration n.d. (b), p. 2). Second, to the extent that affirmative action gives women and minority men access to jobs that more fully exploit their productive capacity, their productivity and that of their employers should increase.

Although many Americans believe that affirmative action means that less qualified persons are hired and promoted (Verhovek 1997, p. 32), the evidence does not bear this out. According to a study of more than 3,000 workers hired in entry-level jobs in a cross-section of firms in Atlanta, Boston, Detroit, and Los Angeles, the performance evaluations of women and minorities hired under affirmative action did not differ from those of white men or female or minority workers for whom affirmative action played no role in hiring (Holzer and Neumark 1998). In addition, Columbus, Ohio, female and minority police officers hired under an affirmative action consent decree performed as well as white men (Kern 1996). Of nearly 300 corporate executives surveyed in 1979, 72 percent believed that minority hiring did not impair productivity (*Wall Street Journal* 1979); 41 percent of CEOs surveyed in 1995 said affirmative action improved corporate productivity (Crosby and Herzberger 1996, p. 86).[6]

The consequences of affirmative action reach beyond workers and employers by increasing the pools of skilled minority and female workers. When affirmative action prompts employers to hire minorities or women for positions that serve the public, it can bring services to communities that would otherwise be underserved. For example, African-American and Hispanic physicians are more likely than whites and Anglos to practice in minority communities (Komaromy et al. 1996). Graduates of the Medical School at the University of California at San Diego who were admitted under a special admissions program were more likely to serve inner-city and rural communities and saw more poor patients than those admitted under the regular procedures (Perm, Russell, and Simon 1986).

Women's and minorities' employment in non-traditional jobs also raises the aspirations of other members of excluded groups by providing role models and by signaling that jobs are open to them. Some minorities and women do not pursue jobs or promotions because they expect to encounter discrimination (Mayhew 1968, p. 313). By reducing the perception that discriminatory barriers block access to certain lines of work, affirmative action curtails this self-selection (Reskin and Roos 1990, p. 305). In addition, the economic gains provided by better jobs permit beneficiaries to invest in the education of the next generation.

The tension between affirmative action and merit is the inevitable result of the conflict between our national values and what actually occurs in the nation's workplaces. As long as discrimination is

(*continued*)

more pervasive than affirmative action, it is the real threat to meritocracy. But because no one will join the debate on behalf of discrimination, we end up with the illusion of a struggle between affirmative action and merit.

NOTES

1. Lynch's (1989, p. 53) search for white male Southern Californians who saw themselves as victims of reverse discrimination turned up only 32 men.

2. Younger whites, those from more privileged backgrounds, and those from areas with larger black populations—especially black populations who were relatively well off—were the most likely to believe that blacks benefited from preferential treatment (Taylor 1994b).

3. Two percent were by white men charging sex, race, or national-origin discrimination (three-quarters of these charged sex discrimination), and 1.8 percent were by white women charging race discrimination (Blumrosen 1996, p. 5).

4. Occupational segregation by sex, race, and ethnicity no doubt contributes to this perception by reinforcing the notion that one's sex, color, or ethnicity is naturally related to the ability to perform a particular job.

5. The disproportionate number of court-ordered interventions to curtail race and sex discrimination in cities' police and fire departments (Martin 1991) and the large number of court challenges by white men (Bureau of National Affairs 1995, pp. 5–12) probably contributed to the public's impression that hiring quotas are common.

6. No data were provided on the proportion who believed that affirmative action hampered productivity.

REFERENCES

Blumrosen, Alfred W. 1996. *Declaration*. Statement Submitted to the Supreme Court of California in Response to Proposition 209, September 26.

Bobo, Larry, and Susan A. Suh. 1996. "Surveying Racial Discrimination: Analyses from a Multi-Ethnic Labor Market." Working Paper No. 75, Russell Sage Foundation, New York.

Bureau of National Affairs. 1995. *Affirmative Action after Adarand: A Legal, Regulatory, Legislative Outlook.* Washington, DC: The Bureau of National Affairs.

Burstein, Paul. 1991. " 'Reverse Discrimination' Cases in the Federal Courts: Mobilization by a Counter-movement." *Sociological Quarterly* 32: 511–28.

Crosby, Faye J., and Sharon D. Herzberger. 1996. "For Affirmative Action." Pp. 3–109 in *Affirmative Action: Pros and Cons of Policy and Practice*, ed. R. J. Simon. Washington, DC: American University Press.

Davis, James A., and Tom W. Smith. 1994. *General Social Survey* [MRDF]. Chicago, IL: National Opinion Research Center [producer, distributor].

———.1996. *General Social Survey* [MRDF]. Chicago, IL: National Opinion Research Center [producer, distributor].

Entman, Robert M. 1997. "Manufacturing Discord: Media in the Affirmative Action Debate." *Press/Politics* 2: 32–51.

Heckman, James J., and Peter Siegelman. 1993. "The Urban Institute Audit Studies: Their Methods and Findings." Pp. 187–229 in *Clear and Convincing Evidence. Measurement of Discrimination in America*, ed. M. Fix and R. J. Struyk. Washington, DC: The Urban Institute.

Hochschild, Jennifer. 1995. *Facing Up to the American Dream*. Princeton, NJ: Princeton University Press.

Holzer, Harry J. and David Neumark. Forthcoming 1998. "Are Affirmative Action Hires Less Qualified? Evidence from Employer–Employee Data on New Hires." *Journal of Labor Economics*.

Kern, Leesa. 1996. "Hiring and Seniority: Issues in Policing in the Post-Judicial Intervention Period." Department of Sociology, Ohio State University, Columbus, OH: Unpublished manuscript.

Komaromy, Miriam, Kevin Grumbach, Michael Drake, Karen Vranizan, Nicole Lurie, Dennis Keane, and Andrew Bindman. 1996. "The Role of Black and Hispanic Physicians in Providing Health Care for Underserved Populations." *New England Journal of Medicine* 334: 1305–10.

Lynch, Frederick R. 1989. *Invisible victims: White Males and the Crisis of Affirmative Action*. New York: Greenwood.

———. 1997. *The Diversity Machine: The Drive to Change the White Male Workplace*. New York: Free Press.

Martin, Susan E. 1991. "The Effectiveness of Affirmative Action: The Case of Women in Policing." *Justice Quarterly* 8: 489–504.

Mayhew, Leon. 1968. *Law and Equal Opportunity: A Study of Massachusetts Commission against Discrimination*. Cambridge, MA: Harvard University Press.

(continued)

New York Times. 1995. "Reverse Discrimination Complaints Rare. Labor Study Reports." *New York Times*, March 31, p. A23.

Norton, Eleanor Holmes. 1996. "Affirmative Action in the Workplace." Pp. 39–48 in *The Affirmative Action Debate*, ed. G. Curry. Reading, MA: Addison-Wesley.

Penn, Nolan E., Percy J. Russell, and Harold J. Simon. 1986."Affirmative Action at Work: A Survey of Graduates of the University of California at San Diego Medical School." *American Journal of Public Health* 76: 1144–46.

Reskin, Barbara F., and Patricia Roos. 1990. *Job Queues, Gender Queues*. Philadelphia, PA: Temple University Press.

Steeh, Charlotte, and Maria Krysan. 1996. "The Polls—Trends. Affirmative Action and the Public, 1970–1995." *Public Opinion Quarterly* 60: 128–58.

Taylor, Marylee C. 1994a. "Beliefs about the Preferential Hiring of Black Applicants: Sure It Happens, But I've Never Seen It." Pennsylvania State University, University Park, PA. Unpublished manuscript.

———. 1994b. "Impact of Affirmative Action on Beneficiary Groups: Evidence from the 1990 General Social Survey." *Basic and Applied Social Psychology* 15: 143–78.

U.S. Department of Labor, Employment Standards Administration, Office of Federal Contract Compliance Programs [cited as OFCCP]. The Rhetoric and the Reality about Federal Affirmative Action at the OFCCP." Washington, DC: U.S. Department of Labor.

Verhovek, Sam Howe. 1997. "In Poll, Americans Reject Means but Not Ends of Racial Diversity." *New York Times*, December 14, 1, 32.

Wall Street Journal. 1979. "'Labor Letter: A Special News Report on People and Their Jobs in Offices, Fields and Factories: Affirmative Action Is Accepted by Most Corporate Chiefs." *Wall Street Journal*. April 3, p. 1.

READING 21

Maid in L.A.

ɕ Pierrette Hondagneu-Sotelo

The title of this chapter was inspired by Mary Romero's 1992 book, *Maid in the U.S.A.*, but I am also taking the pun to heart: most Latina immigrant women who do paid domestic work in Los Angeles had no prior experience working as domestics in their countries of origin. Of the 153 Latina domestic workers that I surveyed at bus stops, in ESL classes, and in parks, fewer than 10 percent reported having worked in other people's homes, or taking in laundry for pay, in their countries of origin. This finding is perhaps not surprising, as we know from immigration research that the poorest of the poor rarely migrate to the United States; they simply cannot afford to do so.

Some of the Latina immigrant women who come to Los Angeles grew up in impoverished squatter settlements, others in comfortable homes with servants. In their countries of origin, these women were housewives raising their own children, or college students, factory workers, store clerks, and secretaries; still others came from rural families of very modest means. Regardless of their diverse backgrounds, their transformation into housecleaners and nanny/housekeepers occurs in Los Angeles. I emphasize this point because images in popular culture and the media more or less identify Latinas with domestic workers—or, more precisely, as "cleaning gals" and "baby-sitters," euphemisms that mask American discomfort with these arrangements. Yet they take on these roles only in the United States, at various points in their own migration and settlement trajectories, in the context of private households, informal social networks, and the larger culture's racialized nativism.

Who are these women who come to the United States in search of jobs, and what are those jobs like? Domestic work is organized in different ways, and in this chapter I describe live-in, live-out, and housecleaning jobs and profile some of the Latina immigrants who do them and how they feel about their work. The chapter concludes with a discussion of why it is that Latina immigrants are the primary recruits to domestic work, and I examine what they and their employers have to say about race relations and domestic work.

LIVE-IN NANNY/HOUSEKEEPER JOBS

For Maribel Centeno, newly arrived from Guatemala City in 1989 at age twenty-two and without support-ive family and friends with whom to stay, taking a live-in job made a lot of sense. She knew that she wouldn't have to spend money on room and board, and that she could soon begin saving to pay off her debts. Getting a live-in job through an agency was easy. The *señora*, in her rudimentary Spanish, only asked where she was from, and if she had a husband and children. Chuckling, Maribel recalled her initial misunderstanding when the *señora*, using her index finger, had drawn an imaginary "2" and "3" in the palm of her hand. "I thought to myself, well, she must have two or three bedrooms, so I said, fine. 'No,' she said. 'Really, really big.' She started counting, 'One, two, three, four . . . two-three rooms.' It was twenty-three rooms! I thought, huy! On a piece of paper, she wrote '$80 a week,' and she said, 'You, child, and entire house.' So I thought, well, I have to do what I have to do, and I happily said, 'Yes.'"

"I arrived on Monday at dawn," she recalled, "and I went to the job on Wednesday evening." When the *señora* and the child spoke to her, Maribel remem-bered "just laughing and feeling useless. I couldn't understand anything." On that first evening, the *señora* put on classical music, which Maribel quickly identified. "I said, 'Beethoven.' She said, 'Yeah,' and began asking me in English, 'You like it?' I said 'Yes,' or perhaps I said, 'Si,' and she began playing other cassettes, CDs. They had Richard Clayderman and I recognized it, and when I said that, she stopped in her tracks, her jaw fell open, and she just stared at me. She must have been thinking, 'No schooling, no preparation, no English, how does she know this music?'" But the *señora*, perhaps because of the lan-guage difficulty, or perhaps because she felt upstaged by her live-in's knowledge of classical music, never did ask. Maribel desperately wanted the *señora* to respect her, to recognize that she was smart, edu-cated, and cultivated in the arts. In spite of her best status-signaling efforts, "They treated me," she said, "the same as any other girl from the countryside." She

never got the verbal recognition that she desired from the *señora*.

Maribel summed up her experiences with her first live-in job this way: "The pay was bad. The treatment was, how shall I say? It was cordial, a little, uh, not racist, but with very little consideration, very little respect." She liked caring for the little seven-year-old boy, but keeping after the cleaning of the twenty-three-room house, filled with marble floors and glass tables, proved physically impossible. She eventually quit not because of the polishing and scrubbing, but because being ignored devastated her socially.

Compared to many other Latina immigrants' first live-in jobs, Maribel Centeno's was relatively good. She was not on call during all her waking hours and throughout the night, the parents were engaged with the child, and she was not required to sleep in a child's bedroom or on a cot tucked away in the laun-dry room. But having a private room filled with amenities did not mean she had privacy or the ability to do simple things one might take for granted. "I had my own room, with my own television, VCR, my pri-vate bath, and closet, and a kind of sitting room—but everything in miniature, Thumbelina style," she said. "I had privacy in that respect. But I couldn't do many things. If I wanted to walk around in a T-shirt, or just feel like I was home, I couldn't do that. If I was hungry in the evening, I wouldn't come out to grab a banana because I'd have to walk through the family room, and then everybody's watching and having to smell the banana. I could never feel at home, never. Never, never, never! There's always something invisible that tells you this is not your house, you just work here."

It is the rare California home that offers separate maid's quarters, but that doesn't stop families from hiring live-ins; nor does it stop newly arrived Latina migrant workers from taking jobs they urgently need. When live-ins cannot even retreat to their own rooms, work seeps into their sleep and their dreams. There is no time off from the job, and they say they feel confined, trapped, imprisoned.

"I lose a lot of sleep," said Margarita Gutiérrez, a twenty-four-year-old Mexicana who worked as a live-in nanny/housekeeper. At her job in a modest-sized condominium in Pasadena, she slept in a corner of a three-year-old child's bedroom. Consequently, she found herself on call day and night with the child, who sometimes went several days without seeing her mother because of the latter's schedule at an insurance company. Margarita was obliged to be on her job twenty-four hours a day; and like other live-in nanny/housekeepers I interviewed, she claimed that she could scarcely find time to shower or brush her teeth. "I go to bed fine," she reported, "and then I wake up at two or three in the morning with the girl asking for water, or food." After the child went back to sleep, Margarita would lie awake, thinking about how to leave her job but finding it hard to even walk out into the kitchen. Live-in employees like Margarita literally have no space and no time they can claim as their own.

Working in a larger home or staying in plush, private quarters is no guarantee of privacy or refuge from the job. Forty-four-year-old Elvia Lucero worked as a live-in at a sprawling, canyon-side residence, where she was in charge of looking after twins, two five-year-old girls. On numerous occasions when I visited her there, I saw that she occupied her own bedroom, a beautifully decorated one outfitted with delicate antiques, plush white carpet, and a stenciled border of pink roses painstakingly painted on the wall by the employer. It looked serene and inviting, but it was only three steps away from the twins' room. Every night one of the twins crawled into bed with Elvia. Elvia disliked this, but said she couldn't break the girl of the habit. And the parents' room lay tucked away at the opposite end of the large (more than 3,000 square feet), L-shaped house.

Regardless of the size of the home and the splendor of the accommodations, the boundaries that we might normally take for granted disappear in live-in jobs. They have, as Evelyn Nakano Glenn has noted, "no clear line between work and non-work time," and the line between job space and private space is similarly blurred[1] Live-in nanny/housekeepers are at once socially isolated and surrounded by other people's territory; during the hours they remain on the employers' premises, their space, like their time, belongs to another. The sensation of being among others while remaining invisible, unknown and apart, of never being able to leave the margins, makes many live-in employees sad, lonely, and depressed. Melancholy sets in and doesn't necessarily lift on the weekends.

Rules and regulations may extend around the clock. Some employers restrict the ability of their live-in employees to receive telephone calls, entertain friends, attend evening ESL classes, or see boyfriends during the workweek. Other employers do not impose these sorts of restrictions, but because their homes are located on remote hillsides, in suburban enclaves, or in gated communities, their live-in nanny/housekeepers are effectively kept away from anything resembling social life or public culture. A Spanish-language radio station, or maybe *a telenovela*, may serve as their only link to the outside world.

Food—the way some employers hoard it, waste it, deny it, or just simply do not even have any of it in their kitchens—is a frequent topic of discussion among Latina live-in nanny/housekeepers. These women are talking not about counting calories but about the social meaning of food on the job. Almost no one works with a written contract, but anyone taking a live-in job that includes "room and board" would assume that adequate meals will be included. But what constitutes an adequate meal? Everyone has a different idea, and using the subject like a secret handshake, Latina domestic workers often greet one another by talking about the problems of managing food and meals on the job. Inevitably, food enters their conversations.

No one feels the indignities of food more deeply than do live-in employees, who may not leave the job for up to six days at a time. For them, the workplace necessarily becomes the place of daily sustenance. In some of the homes where they work, the employers are out all day. When these adults return home, they may only snack, keeping on hand little besides hot dogs, packets of macaroni and cheese, cereal, and peanut butter for the children. Such foods are considered neither nutritious nor appetizing by Latina immigrants, many of whom are accustomed to sitting down to meals prepared with fresh vegetables, rice, beans, and meat. In some employers' homes, the cupboards are literally bare. Gladys Villedas recalled that at one of her live-in jobs, the *señora* had graciously said, " 'Go ahead, help yourself to anything in the kitchen.' But at times," she recalled, "there was nothing, nothing in the refrigerator! There was nothing to eat!" Even in lavish kitchens outfitted with Subzero refrigerators and imported cabinetry, food may be scarce. A celebrity photographer of luxury homes that appear in posh magazines described to a reporter what he sees when he opens the doors of some of Beverly Hills' refrigerators: "Rows of cans of Diet Coke, and maybe a few remains of pizza."[2]

Further down the class ladder, some employers go to great lengths to economize on food bills. Margarita Gutiérrez claimed that at her live-in job, the husband did the weekly grocery shopping, but he bought things in small quantities—say, two potatoes that would be served in half portions, or a quarter of a watermelon to last a household of five all week. He rationed out the bottled water and warned her that milk would make her fat. Lately, she said, he was taking both her and the children to an upscale grocery market where they gave free samples of gourmet cheeses, breads, and dips, urging them all to fill up on the freebies. "I never thought," exclaimed Margarita, formerly a secretary in Mexico City, "that I would come to this country to experience hunger!"

Many women who work as live-ins are keenly aware of how food and meals underline the boundaries between them and the families for whom they work. "I never ate with them," recalled Maribel Centeno of her first live-in job. "First of all, she never said, 'Come and join us,' and secondly, I just avoided being around when they were about to eat." Why did she avoid mealtime? "I didn't feel I was part of that family. I knew they liked me, but only because of the good work I did, and because of the affection I showered on the boy; but apart from that, I was just like the gardener, like the pool man, just one more of their staff." Sitting down to share a meal symbolizes membership in a family, and Latina employees, for the most part, know they are not just like one of the family.

Food scarcity is not endemic to all of the households where these women work. In some homes, ample quantities of fresh fruits, cheeses, and chicken stock the kitchens. Some employer families readily share all of their food, but in other households, certain higher-quality, expensive food items may remain off-limits to the live-in employees, who are instructed to eat hot dogs with the children. One Latina live-in nanny/housekeeper told me that in her employers' substantial pantry, little "DO NOT TOUCH" signs signaled which food items were not available to her; and another said that her employer was always defrosting freezer-burned leftovers for her to eat, some of it dating back nearly a decade.

Other women felt subtle pressure to remain unobtrusive, humble, and self-effacing, so they held back from eating even when they were hungry. They talked a lot about how these unspoken rules apply to fruit. "Look, if they [the employers] buy fruit, they buy three bananas, two apples, two pears. So if I eat one, who took it? It's me," one woman said, "they'll know it's me." Another nanny/housekeeper recalled:

"They would bring home fruit, but without them having to say it, you just knew these were not intended for you. You understand this right away, you get it." Or as another put it, "*Las Americanos* have their apples counted out, one for each day of the week." Even fruits growing in the garden are sometimes contested. In Southern California's agriculture-friendly climate, many a residential home boasts fruit trees that hang heavy with oranges, plums, and peaches, and when the Latina women who work in these homes pick the fruit, they sometimes get in trouble.[3] Eventually, many of the women solve the food problem by buying and bringing in their own food; early on Monday mornings, you see them walking with their plastic grocery bags, carting, say, a sack of apples, some chicken, and maybe some prepared food in plastic containers.

The issue of food captures the essence of how Latina live-in domestic workers feel about their jobs. It symbolizes the extent to which the families they work for draw the boundaries of exclusion or inclusion, and it marks the degree to which those families recognize the live-in nanny/housekeepers as human beings who have basic human needs. When they first take their jobs, most live-in nanny/housekeepers do not anticipate spending any of their meager wages on food to eat while on the job, but in the end, most do—and sometimes the food they buy is eaten by members of the family for whom they work.

Although there is a wide range of pay, many Latina domestic workers in live-in jobs earn less than minimum wage for marathon hours: 93 percent of the live-in workers I surveyed in the mid-1990s were earning less than $5 an hour (79 percent of them below minimum wage, which was then $4.25), and they reported working an average of sixty-four hours a week.[4] Some of the most astoundingly low rates were paid for live-in jobs in the households of other working-class Latino immigrants, which provide some women their first job when they arrive in Los Angeles. Carmen Vasquez, for example, had spent several years working as a live-in for two Mexican families, earning only $50 a week. By comparison, her current salary of $170 a week, which she was earning as a live-in nanny/housekeeper in the hillside home of an attorney and a teacher, seemed a princely sum.

Many people assume that the rich pay more than do families of modest means, but working as a live-in in an exclusive, wealthy neighborhood, or in a twenty-three-room house, provides no guarantee of a high salary. Early one Monday morning in the fall of 1995, I was standing with a group of live-in nanny/housekeepers on a corner across the street from the Beverly Hills Hotel. As they were waiting to be picked up by their employers, a large Mercedes sedan with two women (a daughter and mother or mother-in-law?) approached, rolled down the windows, and asked if anyone was interested in a $150-a-week live-in job. A few women jotted down the phone number, and no one was shocked by the offer. Gore Vidal once commented that no one is allowed to fail within a two-mile radius of the Beverly Hills Hotel, but it turns out that plenty of women in that vicinity are failing in the salary department. In some of the most affluent Westside areas of Los Angeles—in Malibu, Pacific Palisades, and Bel Air—there are live-in nanny/housekeepers earning $150 a week. And in 1999, the *Los Angeles Times* Sunday classified ads still listed live-in nanny/housekeeper jobs with pay as low as $100 and $125.[5] Salaries for live-in jobs, however, do go considerably higher. The best-paid live-in employee whom I interviewed was Patricia Paredes, a Mexicana who spoke impeccable English and who had legal status, substantial experience, and references. She told me that she currently earned $450 a week at her live-in job. She had been promised a raise to $550, after a room remodel was finished, when she would assume weekend housecleaning in that same home. With such a relatively high weekly salary she felt compelled to stay in a live-in job during the week, away from her husband and three young daughters who remained on the east side of Los Angeles. The salary level required that sacrifice.

But once they experience it, most women are repelled by live-in jobs. The lack of privacy, the mandated separation from family and friends, the round-the-clock hours, the food issues, the low pay, and especially the constant loneliness prompt most Latina immigrants to seek other job arrangements. Some young, single women who learn to speak English fluently try to move up the ranks into higher-paying live-in jobs. As soon as they can, however, the majority attempt to leave live-in work altogether. Most live-in nanny/housekeepers have been in the United States for five years or less; among the live-in nanny/housekeepers I interviewed, only two (Carmen Vasquez and the relatively high-earning Patricia Paredes) had been in the United States for longer than that. Like African American women ear-

lier in the century, who tired of what the historian Elizabeth Clark-Lewis has called "the soul-destroying hollowness of live-in domestic work,"[6] most Latina immigrants try to find other options.

Until the early 1900s, live-in jobs were the most common form of paid domestic work in the United States, but through the first half of the twentieth century they were gradually supplanted by domestic "day work."[7] Live-in work never completely disappeared, however, and in the last decades of the twentieth century, it revived with vigor, given new life by the needs of American families with working parents and young children—and, as we have seen, by the needs of newly arrived Latina immigrants, many of them unmarried and unattached to families. When these women try to move up from live-in domestic work, they see few job alternatives. Often, the best they can do is switch to another form of paid domestic work, either as a live-out nanny/housekeeper or as a weekly housecleaner. When they do such day work, they are better able to circumscribe their work hours, and they earn more money in less time.[8]

LIVE-OUT NANNY/HOUSEKEEPERS

When I first met twenty-four-year-old Ronalda Saavedra, she was peeling a hard-boiled egg for a dog in the kitchen of a very large home where I was interviewing the employer. At this particular domestic job, the fifth she had held since migrating from El Salvador in 1991, she arrived daily around one in the afternoon and left after the children went to bed. On a typical day, she assisted the housekeeper, a middle-aged woman, with cleaning, laundry, and errands, and at three o'clock she drove off in her own car to pick up the children—a nine-year-old boy, whom she claimed was always angry, and his hyperactive six-year-old brother.

Once the children were put to bed, Ronalda Saavedra drove home to a cozy apartment that she shared with her brother in the San Fernando Valley. When I visited her, I saw that it was a tiny place, about half the size of the kitchen where we had first met; but it was pleasantly outfitted with new bleached oak furniture, and the morning sunshine that streamed in through a large window gave it a cheerful, almost spacious feel. Ronalda kept a well-stocked refrigerator, and during our interview she served me *pan dulce*, coffee, and honeydew melon.

Like many other women, Ronalda had begun her work stint in the United States with a live-in job, but she vastly preferred living out. She slept through the night in peace, attended ESL classes in the morning, ate what she wanted when she wanted it, and talked daily on the phone with her fiancé. All this was possible because live-out jobs are firmly circumscribed. Even when women find it difficult to say no to their employers when they are asked, at the last minute, to stay and work another hour or two, they know they will eventually retreat to their own places. So while the workday tasks and rhythms are similar to those of live-ins, the job demands on live-outs stop when they exit the houses where they work and return to their own homes, usually small and sometimes crowded apartments located in one of Los Angeles' many Latino neighborhoods. For such women with husbands or with children of their own, live-out jobs allow them to actually live with their family members and see them daily.

Live-out nanny/housekeepers also earn more money than live-ins. Most of them work eight or nine hours a day, and of those I surveyed, 60 percent worked five days a week or fewer. Their mean hourly wages were $5.90—not an exorbitant wage by any means, but above the legal minimum, unlike the wages of their peers in live-in jobs. Ronalda earned $350 for her forty-hour workweek, making her hourly wage $8.75. On top of this, her employer gave her an additional $50 to cover gasoline expenses, as Ronalda spent a portion of each afternoon driving on errands, such as going to the dry cleaners, and ferrying the children home from school and then to and from soccer practices, music lessons, and so on. In the suburban landscape of Los Angeles, employers pay an extra premium for nanny/housekeepers who can provide this shuttling service. Only Latina nanny/housekeepers with experience, strong references, English skills, and an impressive array of certificates and licenses enjoy earnings that reach Ronalda's level.

Today, most Americans who hire a domestic worker to come into their homes on a daily basis do so in order to meet their needs for *both* housecleaning and child care. Most Latina nanny/housekeepers work in households where they are solely responsible for these tasks, and they work hard to fit in the cleaning and laundry (most of them don't cook) while the children are napping or at school. Some of them feel, as one woman said, that they need to be "octopuses," with busy arms extended simultaneously in all directions. A big part of their job requires taking care of the children; and various issues with the children present nanny/housekeepers with their greatest frustrations. Paradoxically, they also experience some of their deepest job satisfaction with these children with whom they spend so much time.

After what may be years of watching, feeding, playing with, and reprimanding the same child from birth to elementary school, day in and day out, some nanny/housekeepers grow very fond of their charges and look back nostalgically, remembering, say, when a child took her first steps or first learned nursery rhymes in Spanish. Ronalda, an articulate, highly animated woman who told stories using a lot of gestures and facial expressions, talked a great deal about the children she had cared for in her various jobs. She imitated the voices of children she had taken care of, describing longingly little girls who were, she said, "*muy* nice" or "*tan* sweet," and recalled the imaginary games they would play. Like many other nanny/housekeepers, she wept freely when she remembered some of the intimate and amusing moments she had spent with children she no longer saw. She also described other children who, she said, were dour, disrespectful, and disobedient.

Many live-out nanny/housekeepers made care work—the work of keeping the children clean, happy, well nourished, and above all safe—a priority over housecleaning duties. This sometimes created conflicts with their employers, who despite saying that their children should come first still expected a spotless house. "The truth is," explained Teresa Portillo, who looked after a child only on the weekends, "when you are taking care of children, you can't neglect anything, absolutely nothing! Because the moment you do, they do whatever little *travesura*, and they scrape their knees, cut themselves or whatever." Nanny/housekeepers fear they will be sent to jail if anything happens to the children.

Feeding the children is a big part of the job. Unlike their live-in peers, when live-out nanny/housekeepers talk about food, they're usually concerned with what the children eat or don't eat. Some of them derive tremendous pleasure and satisfaction from bringing the children special treats prepared at their own homes—maybe homemade flan or *pan con crema*, or simply a mango. Some nanny/housekeepers are also in charge, to their dismay, of feeding and cleaning the children's menagerie of pets. Many feel disgusted when they have to bathe and give eyedrops to old, sick dogs, or clean the cages of iguanas, snakes, lizards, and various rodents. But these tasks are trivial in comparison to the difficulties they encounter with hard-to-manage children. Mostly, though, they complain about permissive, neglectful parents.

Not all nanny/housekeepers bond tightly with their employers' children, but most are critical of what they perceive as their employers' careless parenting—or, more accurately, mothering, for their female employers typically receive the blame. They see mothers who may spend, they say, only a few minutes a day with their babies and toddlers, or who return home from work after the children are asleep. Soraya Sanchez said she could understand mothers who work "out of necessity," but all other mothers, she believed, hired nanny/housekeepers because they just didn't like being with their own kids. "*La Americana* is very selfish, she only thinks about herself," she said. "They prefer not to be with their children, as they find it's much easier to pay someone to do that." Her critique was shared by many nanny/housekeepers; and those with children of their own, even if they didn't live with them, saw their own mothering as far superior. "I love my kids, they don't. It's just like, excuse the word, 'shitting kids'" said Patricia Paredes. "What they prefer is to go to the salon, get their nails done, you know, go shopping, things like that. Even if they're home all day, they don't want to spend time with the kids because they're paying somebody to do that for them." For many Latina nanny/housekeepers, seething class resentments find expression in the rhetoric of comparative mothering.

When Latina immigrant women enter the homes of middle-class and upper-middle-class Americans, they encounter ways of raising children very different from those with which they are familiar. As Julia Wrigley's research has shown, the child-rearing values of many Latina and Caribbean nannies differ from those of their employers, but most are eager to do what middle-class parents want—to adopt "time out" discipline measures instead of swatting, or to impose limits on television viewing and Nintendo.[9] Some of them not only adapt but come to genuinely admire and appreciate such methods of child rearing. Yet they, too, criticize the parenting styles they witness close up in the homes where they work.

Some nanny/housekeepers encounter belligerent young children, who yell at them, call them names,

and throw violent temper tantrums; and when they do, they blame the parents. They are aghast when parents, after witnessing a child scratch or bite or spit at them, simply shrug their shoulders and ignore such behavior. Parents' reactions to these incidents were a litmus test of sorts. Gladys Villedas, for example, told me that at her job, a five-year-old "grabbed my hair and pulled it really hard. Ay! It hurt so much I started crying! It really hurt my feelings because never in my own country, when I was raising my children, had this happened to me. Why should this happen to me here?" When she complained to her employer, she said the employer had simply consulted a child-rearing manual and explained that it was "a stage." Not all nanny/housekeepers encounter physically abusive children, but when they do, they prefer parents who allow them the authority to impose discipline, or who back them up by firmly instructing their children that it is not okay to kick or slap the nanny. Nanny/housekeepers spoke glowingly about these sorts of employers.

When nanny/housekeepers see parent-child interactions in the homes where they work, they are often put off and puzzled by what they observe. In these moments, the huge cultural gulf between Latina nanny/housekeepers and their employers seems even wider than they had initially imagined. In the home where Maribel Centeno was working as a live-out nanny/housekeeper, she spent the first few hours of her shift doing laundry and housecleaning, but when a thirteen-year-old boy, of whom she was actually very fond, arrived home from school, her real work began. It was his pranks, which were neither malicious nor directed at her, and parental tolerance of these, that drove her crazy. These adolescent pranks usually involved items like water balloons, firecrackers, and baking soda made to look like cocaine. Recently the boy had tacked up on his parents' bedroom door a condom filled with a small amount of milk and a little sign that read, "Mom and Dad, this could have been my life." Maribel thought this was inappropriate behavior; but more bewildering and disturbing than the boy's prank was his mother's reaction—laughter. Another nanny/housekeeper had reacted with similar astonishment when, after a toddler tore apart a loaf of French bread and threw the pieces, balled like cotton, onto the floor, the father came forward not to reprimand but to record the incident with a camcorder. The regularity with which their employers waste food astounds them, and drug use also raises their eyebrows. Some nanny/housekeepers are instructed to give Ritalin and Prozac to children as young as five or six, and others tell of parents and teens locked in their separate bedrooms, each smoking marijuana.

Nanny/housekeepers blame permissive and neglectful parents, who they feel don't spend enough time with their own children, for the children's unruly behavior and for teen drug use. "The parents, they say 'yes' to everything the child asks," complained one woman. "Naturally," she added, "the children are going to act spoiled." Another nanny/housekeeper analyzed the situation this way: "They [the parents] feel guilty because they don't spend that much time with the kids, and they want to replace that missed time, that love, with toys."

Other nanny/housekeepers prided themselves on taming and teaching the children to act properly. "I really had to battle with these children just to get them to pay attention to me! When I started with them, they had no limits, they didn't pick up their toys, and they couldn't control their tempers. The eldest—oof! He used to kick and hit me, and in public! I was mortified," recalled Ronalda Saavedra. Another woman remarked of children she had looked after, "These kids listened to me. After all, they spent most of the time with me, and not with them [the parents]. They would arrive at night, maybe spend a few moments with the kids, or maybe the kids were already asleep." Elvia Areola highlighted the injustice of rearing children whom one will never see again. Discussing her previous job, she said, "I was the one who taught that boy to talk, to walk, to read, to sit! Everything! She [the child's mother] almost never picked him up! She only picked him up when he was happy." Another nanny/housekeeper concluded, "These parents don't really know their own children. Just playing with them, or taking them to the park, well, that's not raising children. I'm the one who is with them every day."

Nanny/housekeepers must also maneuver around jealous parents, who may come to feel that their children's affections have been displaced. "The kids fall in love with you and they [the parents] wonder why. Some parents are jealous of what the kids feel toward you," said Ronalda Saavedra, "I'm not going to be lying, 'I'm your mommy,' but in a way, children go to the person who takes care of them, you know? That's just the way it is." For many nanny/housekeepers, it is these ties of affection that make it possible for them to do their job by making it rewarding. Some of them

say they can't properly care for the children without feeling a special fondness for them; others say it just happens naturally. "I fall in love with all of these children. How can I not? That's just the way I am," one nanny/ housekeeper told me. "I'm with them all day, and when I go home, my husband complains that that's all I talk about, what they did, the funny things they said." The nanny/housekeepers, as much as they felt burdened by disobedient children, sometimes felt that these children were also a gift of sorts, one that parents—again, the mothers—did not fully appreciate. "The babies are so beautiful!" gushed Soraya Sanchez. "How is it that a mother can lose those best years, when their kids are babies. I mean, I remember going down for a nap with these little babies, how we'd cuddle. How is it that a person who has the option of enjoying that would prefer to give that experience to a stranger?" Precisely because of such feelings, many Latina immigrants who have children try to find a job that is compatible with their own family lives. Housecleaning is one of those jobs.

HOUSECLEANERS

Like many working mothers, every weekday morning Marisela Ramírez awoke to dress and feed her preschooler, Tomás, and drive him to school (actually, a Head Start program) before she herself ventured out to work, navigating the dizzying array of Los Angeles freeways. Each day she set off in a different direction headed for a different workplace. On Mondays she maneuvered her way to Pasadena, where she cleaned the stately home of an elderly couple; on Tuesdays she alternated between cleaning a home in the Hollywood Hills and a more modest-sized duplex in Glendale; and Wednesdays took her to a split-level condominium in Burbank. You had to keep alert, she said, to remember where to go on which days and how to get there!

By nine o'clock she was usually on the job, and because she zoomed through her work she was able to finish, unless the house was extremely dirty, by one or two in the afternoon. After work, there were still plenty of daylight hours left for Marisela to take Tomás to the park, or at least to take him outside and let him ride down the sidewalk on his kid-sized motorized vehicle before she started dinner. Working as a housecleaner allowed Marisela to be the kind of wife and mother she wanted to be. Her job was something she did, she said, "because I have to"; but unlike her peers who work in live-in jobs, she enjoyed a fairly regular family life of her own, one that included cooking and eating family meals, playing with her son, bathing him, putting him to bed, and then watching *telenovelas* in the evenings with her husband and her sister. On the weekends, family socializing took center stage, with *carne asadas* in the park; informal gatherings with her large Mexican family, which extended throughout Los Angeles; and music from her husband, who worked as a gardener but played guitar in a weekend *ranchera* band.

Some might see Marisela Ramírez as just another low-wage worker doing dirty work, but by her own account—and gauging by her progress from her starting point—she had made remarkable occupational strides. Marisela had begun working as a live-in nanny/housekeeper in Los Angeles when she was only fifteen years old. Ten years later, the move from live-in work to housecleaning had brought her higher hourly wages, a shorter workweek, control over the pace of work, and flexibility in arranging when she worked. Cleaning different houses was also, she said, less boring than working as a nanny/housekeeper, which entailed passing every single day "in just one house, all week long with the same routine, over and over."

For a while she had tried factory work, packaging costume jewelry in a factory warehouse located in the San Fernando Valley, but Marisela saw housecleaning as preferable on just about every count. "In the factory, one has to work very, very fast!" she exclaimed. "And you can't talk to anybody, you can't stop, and you can't rest until it's break time. When you're working in a house, you can take a break at the moment you wish, finish the house when you want, and leave at the hour you decide. And it's better pay. It's harder work, yes," she conceded, "but it's better pay."

"How much were you earning at the factory?" I asked.

"Five dollars an hour; and working in houses now, I make about $11, or even more. Look, in a typical house, I enter at about 9 A.M., and I leave at 1 P.M., and they pay me $60. It's much better [than factory work]." Her income varied, but she could usually count on weekly earnings of about $300. By pooling these together with her husband's and sister's earnings, she was able to rent a one-bedroom bungalow roofed in red tile, with a lawn and a backyard for Tomás's sandbox and plastic swimming pool. In Mexico, Marisela had only studied as far as fifth

grade, but she wanted the best for Tomás. Everyone doted on him, and by age four he was already reading simple words.

Of the housecleaners I surveyed, the majority earned, like Marisela, between $50 and $60 per housecleaning, which usually took about six hours. This suggests an average hourly wage of about $9.50, but I suspect the actual figure is higher.[10] Women like Marisela, who drive their own cars and speak some English, are likely to earn more than the women I surveyed, many of whom ride the buses to work. Marisela was typical of the housecleaners whom I surveyed in having been in the United States for a number of years. Unlike nanny/housekeepers, most of the housecleaners who were mothers themselves had all their children with them in the United States. Housecleaning, as Mary Romero has noted, is a job that is quite compatible with having a family life of one's own.

Breaking into housecleaning is tough, often requiring informal tutelage from friends and relatives. Contrary to the image that all women "naturally" know how to do domestic work, many Latina domestic workers discover that their own housekeeping experiences do not automatically transfer to the homes where they work. As she looked back on her early days in the job, Marisela said, "I didn't know how to clean or anything. My sister taught me." Erlinda Castro, a middle-aged women who had already run her own household and raised five children in Guatemala, had also initially worked in live-in jobs when she first came to Los Angeles. Yet despite this substantial domestic experience, she recalled how mystified she was when she began housecleaning. "Learning how to use the chemicals and the liquids" in the different households was confusing, and, as friends and employers instructed her on what to do, she began writing down in a little notebook the names of the products and what they cleaned. Some women learn the job by informally apprenticing with one another, accompanying a friend or perhaps an aunt on her housecleaning jobs.

Establishing a thriving route of *casas* requires more than learning which cleaning products to use or how to clean quickly and efficiently. It also involves acquiring multiple jobs, which housecleaners typically gain by asking their employers if they have friends, neighbors, or acquaintances who need someone to clean their houses; and because some attrition is inevitable, they must constantly be on the lookout for more *casas*. Not everyone who wants to can fill up her entire week.

To make ends meet when they don't have enough houses to clean, Latina housecleaners in Los Angeles find other ways to earn income. They might prepare food-say, tamales and *crema*—which they sell door-to-door or on the street; or they might sell small amounts of clothing that they buy wholesale in the garment district, or products from Avon, Mary Kay cosmetics, and Princess House kitchenware. They take odd jobs, such as handing out flyers advertising dental clinics or working at a swap meet; or perhaps they find something more stable, such as evening janitorial work in office buildings. Some housecleaners work swing shift in garment factories, while others work three days a week as a nanny/housekeeper and try to fill the remaining days with housecleaning jobs. Some women supplement their husband's income by cleaning only one or two houses a week, but more often they patch together a number of jobs in addition to housecleaning.

Housecleaning represents, as Romero has written, the "modernization" of paid domestic work. Women who clean different houses on different days sell their labor services, she argues, in much the same way that a vendor sells a product to various customers.[11] The housecleaners themselves see their job as far preferable to that of a live-in or live-out nanny/housekeeper. They typically work alone, during times when their employers are out of the home; and because they are paid "by the job" instead of by the hour, they don't have to remain on the job until 6 or 7 P.M., an advantage much appreciated by women who have families of their own. Moreover, because they work for different employers on different days, they are not solely dependent for their livelihood on one boss whom they see every single day. Consequently, their relationships with their employers are less likely to become highly charged and conflictual; and if problems do arise, they can leave one job without jeopardizing their entire weekly earnings. Since child care is not one of their tasks, their responsibilities are more straightforward and there are fewer points of contention with employers. Housecleaning is altogether less risky.

Housecleaners also see working independently and informally as more desirable than working for a commercial cleaning company. "The companies pay $5 an hour," said Erlinda Castro, whose neighbor worked for one, "and the women have to work their

eight hours, doing up to ten, twenty houses a day! One does the vacuuming, the other does the bathroom and the kitchen, and like that. It's tremendously hard work, and at $5 an hour? Thank God, I don't have to do that." Two of the women I interviewed, one now a live-out nanny/housekeeper and the other a private housecleaner, had previously worked for cleaning services, and both of them complained bitterly about their speeded-up work pace, low pay, and tyrannical bosses.

Private housecleaners take enormous pride in their work. When they finish their job, they can see the shiny results, and they are proud of their job autonomy, their hours, their pay, and, most important, what they are able to do with their pay for themselves and for their families. Yet housecleaning brings its own special problems. Intensive cleaning eventually brings physical pain, and sometimes injury. "Even my bones are tired," said fifty-three-year-old Lupe Vélez; and even a relatively young woman like Celestina Vigil at age thirty-three was already reporting back problems that she attributed to her work. While most of them have only fleeting contact with their employers, and many said they work for "good people," just about everyone has suffered, they said, "inconsiderate persons" who exhort them to work faster, humiliate them, fail to give raises, add extra cleaning tasks without paying extra, or unjustly accuse them of stealing or of ruining a rug or upholstery. And the plain old hard work and stigma of cleaning always remain, as suggested by the answer I got when I asked a housecleaner what she liked least about her job. "The least?" she said, with a wry smile. "Well, that you have to clean."

DOMESTIC JOB TRAJECTORIES AND TRANSNATIONAL MOTHERHOOD

As we have seen, private paid domestic work is organized into sub occupations, each with different pay scales, tasks, and hours.[12] Although they share many similarities, each job arrangement has its own different problems and rewards. In this section I discuss the movement between the three suboccupations and some of the family characteristics of the women who fill these jobs.

Some researchers have called live-in domestic work "the bridging occupation," because in various periods and places, it allowed rural migrant women to acculturate to the city and learn new ways of living.[13] Unlike Irish immigrant women or the black women who went from the South to the North to work as domestics in the early twentieth century, and unlike many private domestics in Europe and Latin America in the past, most Latina immigrants doing paid domestic work in the United States are *not* new to the city. Yet for many of them in Los Angeles today, especially those who are single and have very limited options for places to work and live, live-in jobs do serve as an initial occupational step. As Table 1 shows, new arrivals and women who have lived in the United States five years or less concentrate in live-in jobs (60 percent). In contrast, the majority of housecleaners (83 percent) and live-out nanny/housekeepers (69 percent) have lived in the United States for more than five years. Some begin their live-in jobs literally within forty-eight hours after arriving in Los Angeles, while some housecleaners have lived in the United States for twenty years or more. For newly arrived immigrant women without papers, a live-in job in a private home may feel safer, as private homes in middle- and upper-middle-class neighborhoods are rarely, if ever, threatened by Immigration and Naturalization Service raids.[14]

As the years pass, the women who took live-in jobs learn some English, gain knowledge of other job possibilities, and learn to use their social networks to their occupational advantage. Most of them eventually move out of live-in work. Some return to their countries of origin, and others look to sales, factory work, or janitorial work. But given the low pay of those jobs—in 1999, garment workers in Los Angeles were earning $5.00 an hour, and nonunion janitors with six years of experience were earning $6.30 an hour—many of them transition into some form of domestic day work.[15]As they abandon their live-in positions for live-out nanny/housekeeper and housecleaner jobs, their wages increase. For these women, the initial misery suffered in their live—in jobs makes other domestic work look if not good then at least tolerable—and certainly better than where they started.

For Latina immigrants in Los Angeles today, live-in domestic work does serve as an occupational bridge of sorts, but it often leads only to other types of domestic jobs. These individual trajectories match historical transformations in the occupation. Much as live-in jobs were once the dominant form of paid domestic work, and then gave way to arrangements in which domestics continued to work daily for one employer but lived with their own families, and finally to modernized "job work" or periodic housecleaning, so many Latina immigrants today traverse these three different types of jobs. Some roughly follow the historical order, moving from live-in to live out nanny/housekeeper jobs, and then to housecleaning, but their modest occupational mobility does not always follow such a linear course.

As Mexican and Central American immigrant women move into live-out and housecleaning jobs, their family lives change. With better pay and fewer hours of work, they become able to live with their own family members. Among those I surveyed, about 45 percent of the women doing day work were married, but only 13 percent of the live-ins were married. Most women who have husbands and children with them in Los Angeles do not wish to take live-in jobs; moreover, their application for a live-in job is likely to

TABLE I   TYPE OF DOMESTIC WORK, LENGTH OF RESIDENCE IN THE UNITED STATES, AND MEAN HOURLY WAGES

	Live-ins (percent) ($n = 30$)	Live-outs (percent) ($n = 64$)	Housecleaners (percent) ($n = 59$)
Five years or less in United States	60	31	17
More than five years in United States	40	69	83
Mean hourly wage	$3.80	$5.90	$9.50

be rejected if they reveal that they have a husband, a boyfriend, or children living in Los Angeles. As one job seeker in an employment agency waiting room put it, "You can't have a family, you can't have anyone [if you want a live-in job]." Live-out nanny/housekeepers often face this family restriction too, as employers are wary of hiring someone who may not report for work when her own children come down with the flu.

Their subminimum wages and long hours make it impossible for many live-in workers to bring their children to Los Angeles; other live-ins are young women who do not have children of their own. Once they do have children who are either born in or have immigrated to Los Angeles, most women try to leave live-in work to be with them. Not all the women can do so, and sometimes their finances or jobs force them to send the children "back home" to be reared by grandmothers. Clearly, performing domestic work for pay, especially in a live-in job, is often incompatible with caring for one's own family and home.[16]

The substantial proportion of Latina domestic workers in Los Angeles whose children stay in their countries of origin are in the same position as many Caribbean women working in domestic jobs on the East Coast, and as the Filipinas who predominate in domestic jobs in many cities around the globe. This is what I label "transnational motherhood" . . . ; in a 1997 article Ernestine Avila and I coined this term as we examined how Latina immigrant domestic workers are transforming their own meanings of motherhood to accommodate these spatial and tem-poral separations.[17] As Table 2 suggests, these arrangements are most common among women with live-in jobs, but live-in domestic workers and single mothers are not the only ones who rely on them.[18]

These transnational arrangements are not alto-gether new. The United States has a long history of incorporating people of color through coercive systems of labor that do not recognize family rights, including the right to care for one's own family members. As others have pointed out, slavery and contract labor systems were organized to maximize economic productivity, and offered few supports to sustain family life.[19] Today, international labor migration and the job characteristics of paid domestic work, especially live-in work, virtually impose transnational motherhood on many Mexican and Central American women who have children of their own.

At the other end of the spectrum are the housecleaners, who earn higher wages than live-ins (averaging $9.50 an hour vs. $3.80) and who work fewer hours per week than live-ins (twenty-three vs. sixty-four). The majority of them (76 percent) have all their children in the United States, and they are the least likely to experience transnational spatial and temporal separations from their children. Greater financial resources and more favorable job terms enhance house-cleaners' abilities to bring their children to the United States. As we have seen, weekly housecleaning is dominated by relatively well-established women with more years of experience in the United States, who speak some English, who have a car, and who have job references. Because their own

TABLE 2 TYPE OF DOMESTIC WORK, MARITAL STATUS, AND LOCATION OF CHILDREN

	Live-ins (percent) (n = 30)	Live-outs (percent) (n = 64)	Housecleaners (percent) (n = 59)
Single (included the widowed, divorced, or separated)	87	55	54
Married	13	45	46
	Domestic Workers with Children		
	(n = 16)	(n = 53)	(n = 45)
All children in United States	18	58	76
At least one child "back home"	82	42	24

position is more secure, they are also more likely to have their children here. And because they tend to work fewer hours per week, have greater flexibility in scheduling, and earn higher wages than the live-ins, they can live with and care for their children.

With respect to their ability to care for their own children, live-out nanny/housekeepers fall between live-ins and weekly cleaners—predictably, since they are also in an intermediate position in their earnings, rigidity of schedule, and working hours. Live-out domestic workers, according to the survey, earn $5.90 an hour and work an average workweek of thirty-five hours, and 42 percent of those who are mothers reported having at least one of their children in their country of origin.

THE DOMINANCE OF CENTRAL AMERICAN AND MEXICAN IMMIGRANT WOMEN

Paid domestic work has long been a racialized and gendered occupation, but why today are Central American women hugely over-represented in these jobs in Los Angeles in comparison with Mexicans (whose immigrant population is of course many times larger)? In the survey I conducted of 153 Westside Latina domestic workers, 75 percent of the respondents were from Central America; of those, most were from El Salvador and Guatemala. And in census counts, Salvadoran and Guatemalan women are, respectively, twelve times and thirteen times more likely than the general population to be engaged in private domestic work in Los Angeles.[20] Numerous studies paint a similar picture in other major U.S. cities, such as Washington, D.C., Houston, and San Francisco; one naturally wonders why this should be so.[21]

In Los Angeles, the heavy concentration of Central American women in paid domestic work is partially explained by the location of L.A.'s primary Central American immigrant neighborhood, the Pico-Union/Westlake area, just west of the small, high-rise downtown. As UCLA sociologist David Lopez and his colleagues explain, "A large proportion of Central Americans tend to reside closer to the middle-class neighborhoods of the Westside and the San Fernando Valley . . . while Mexicans are concentrated in the more isolated areas east and south of Downtown Los Angeles.[22] It is certainly quicker to drive or take a bus to the Westside from the Pico Union area than it is

from East L.A. But there is more to this story than spatial location and L.A. transportation systems: distinct migration patterns have also influenced these occupational concentrations.

Mexican migration to the United States goes back over a hundred years, initially driven by labor recruitment programs designed to bring in men to work in agriculture. Since the late 1960s, it has shifted from a primarily male population of temporary or sojourner workers to one that includes women and entire families; these newcomers have settled in rural areas, cities, and suburbs throughout the United States, but disproportionately in California. Many Mexican women who migrated in the 1970s and 1980s were accompanied by their families and were aided by rich social networks; the latter helped prevent the urgency that leads new immigrants to take live-in jobs. Even those unmarried Mexican women who did migrate on their own, despite being opposed and sometimes stigmatized by their family and community, were often assisted by friends and more sympathetic family members. By the 1990s, more unmarried Mexican women were going north, encouraged in part by help from female friends and kin. When Mexican women arrive in the United States, many of them enjoy access to well-developed, established communities whose members have long been employed in various industries, particularly agriculture, construction, hotels, food-processing plants, and garment factories. Compared to their Central American peers, Mexican women are more likely to have financial support from a husband; because fewer Mexican immigrant women must work outside their home, they have lower rates of overall participation in the labor force than do Central American women.[23] Their social networks also give Mexican women greater variety in their employment options; paid domestic work is only one of their alternatives.

Salvadoran and Guatemalan women migrating to the United States have done so under different circumstances than Mexican women. For Central Americans coming to *el norte*, there was no long-standing labor program recruiting men who could then bring, or encourage the migration of, their wives and daughters. In fact, as Terry Repak's study shows, some of the early pioneers of Salvadoran migration to Washington, D.C., were women, themselves informally recruited by individual members of the diplomatic corps precisely because they were desired as private domestics.[24] More significantly, Salvadoran and Guatemalan women and men left their countries in haste, often leaving their children behind, as they fled the civil wars, political violence, and economic upheaval of the 1980s. Theirs are immigrant communities that subsisted without legal status for nearly two decades, grew rapidly, and remain very poor. Even Guatemalan and Salvadoran women who arrived in the United States in the late 1980s and early 1990s could not count on finding communities of well-established compatriots who could quickly and efficiently situate them in jobs in restaurants, hotels, factories, or other industries. In fact, as some of the most compelling ethnographies of Salvadorans in San Francisco and on Long Island have shown, Central Americans' relatively shallow U.S. roots have left their social networks extremely impoverished and sometimes fractured.[25] For Central American women arriving on their own, without husbands and children in tow, desperate and lacking information about jobs—and at a crucial historical moment when American families were seeking to resolve their own child care and housekeeping problems—live-in jobs were both attractive and available.

Family structures and marriage patterns may have also contributed to the preponderance of Central American women in paid domestic work. El Salvador has traditionally had one of the lowest marriage rates in the hemisphere, especially among the urban poor, where common-law marriages and legacies of internal and intra–Central America labor migration—mostly for work on coffee plantations—have encouraged the formation of female-headed households.[26] Thus Salvadoran women have been more likely to migrate on their own and accept live-in jobs.[27] Their large numbers in this lowest rung of domestic work would then explain their eventual disproportionate concentration in all types of private paid domestic work, following the pattern discussed above.

The experience of Central American women might also be compared to that of Asian immigrant women, who have been entering the United States at increasing rates. The latter are an extremely heterogeneous group, but on average—and this is particularly true of Chinese, Indian, and Filipina women—they arrive with much higher levels of education, better English language skills, and more professional credentials than do their Latina peers. They are also more likely to have legal status; and members of some groups, especially Korean immigrant women, enjoy access to

jobs in family businesses and ethnic enclaves.[28] At the same time, the generally poorer and less-educated women from Vietnam, Laos, and Cambodia have been able to withstand periods of underemployment and unemployment because they are officially sanctioned political refugees and therefore enjoy access to welfare and resettlement assistance from the federal government. While some individual Asian immigrant women are working in paid domestic work, they have not developed social networks that channel them into this niche.

It is particularly striking that Filipina immigrants predominate in this occupation elsewhere around the globe, but not in the United States. Worldwide, about two-thirds of Filipina migrants in countries as different as Italy, Canada, Hong Kong, Taiwan, Singapore, Saudi Arabia, and Jordan, do paid domestic work; but in the United States, their high levels of education and fluent English enable most of them to enter higher status occupations that require more skills than does domestic work. In 1990, 71 percent of the Filipinas in the United States were working in managerial, professional, technical/sales, and administrative support jobs, and only 17 percent were employed in service jobs.[29] They are disproportionately concentrated in the health professions, the result of formal recruitment programs designed to fill U.S. nursing shortages.[30] Experience in the health professions leads many Filipinas to take jobs in elder care; and though some work as nanny/housekeepers in Los Angeles, many of them as live-ins, in my numerous discussions with employers, Latina employees, attorneys, and owners and employees of domestic employment agencies, no one ever mentioned Filipina housecleaners.

Nevertheless, Filipina immigrants are doing paid domestic work in the United States. Interviews conducted by Rhacel Parreñas with twenty-six Filipina domestic workers in Los Angeles reveal that many of these women have college diplomas and are working in homes because they are older and face age discrimination; they tend to earn more as care providers for the elderly ($425 per week) and more as nanny/housekeepers ($350 per week) than do Latina immigrants in these same jobs.[31] When it comes to caring for their children, some employers prefer Filipina nanny/housekeepers because they speak English well (English is the official language of schools and universities in the Philippines), and because they tend to be highly educated. Paradoxically, these qualities may predispose some employers to *not* choose Filipinas as domestic employees. At three domestic employment agencies, the owners told me that they rarely placed Filipina job applicants, because they were deemed "uppity," demanding, and likely to lie about their references. Racial preferences, as the next section suggests, shape the formation of Latina domestic workers and their employment in Los Angeles.

NARRATIVES OF RACIAL PREFERENCES

In a race-conscious society, everyone has racial preferences and prejudices, and Latina domestic workers and the women who employ them are no exception. When choosing someone to work in their homes, many employers prefer Latinas, because as "others" in language, race-ethnicity, and social class, they are outside white, English-speaking, middle-class social circles and are thus seen as unlikely to reveal family secrets and intimacies. If they do tell someone about the family fight they witnessed, that someone is likely to be another Latina nanny or a member of their own family—in either case, no one who matters to the employers. This fear of exposure sometimes prevents employers from choosing white, English-speaking job candidates. "She was non-Hispanic, and I wasn't sure if I could trust her," said one woman of a prospective employee. Another employer had been advised not to hire a white woman as a nanny/housekeeper because an immigrant would be less likely to recognize her philanthropic family's name and to engage in bribery or kidnapping. Other women told me that they did not want a European au pair or midwestern (white) teenager taking care of their children because they would probably be young, irresponsible teens, more interested in cavorting with boyfriends, cruising the beach, and stargazing in Hollywood than in doing their job. Employers may also prefer to hire Latina nannies, as research conducted by Julia Wrigley suggests, because they view them as more submissive than whites.[32]

While some of the older employers I interviewed had hired African American housecleaners and domestics in the past, none were now doing so. Of the relatively few black women working in paid domestic work in contemporary Los Angeles, most are immigrants from Belize and Brazil, and some employers remain adamantly opposed to hiring black women to work in their homes. One domestic employment agency owner told me that some clients had requested that he never send black women to inter-

view for a job. And at an informal luncheon, arranged by one of the employer interviewees, one of them cleared her throat and then offered, with some awkward hesitation, "Uhm, ah, I would never hire a black woman. I'd be too scared to, and I'd be especially scared if her boyfriend came around." The women, all of them relatively upper-class white matrons, had nodded in silent agreement. The old stereotype of the bossy black maid is apparently alive and well, now joined by newer terrifying images associated with young black men; but since African-American women are not pursuing domestic work jobs in Los Angeles, most employers need never confront their own racial fears directly. It is, after all, Latina immigrant women who are queuing up for domestic jobs in private homes.

When I talked with them, most employers expressed genuine appreciation for the effort, dedication, and work that these women put into their homes and children. They viewed Latina domestic workers as responsible, trustworthy, and reliable employees who have "a really strong work ethic." And while plenty of employers spoke at length about Latina women as ideally suited to caring for children, relying on images of Latinas as exceptionally warm, patient, and loving mothers, there was no similar racialized image of cleanliness. No one said, for instance, "She cleans like a Mexican." Such a phrase may sound offensive, but the absence of any such generalization is striking when nearly everyone hired to do cleaning in Los Angeles is Mexican or Central American.

Indeed, some of the employers I interviewed did make this kind of statement—to associate their own northern European heritage with superior cleaning and hygiene. A few of them offered remarks such as "People associate very clean homes with Dutch people," or "My mother's German and she cleans, you know, like Germans clean." These women did not necessarily claim that they were excellent cleaners, only that they belonged to racial-ethnic groups associated with cleanliness. None of them described their domestic employees as "dirty," but the adjective has been commonly featured in racial epithets directed at Mexicans in the Southwest and at domestic workers just about everywhere. The historian Phyllis Palmer, who has written compellingly about dirt, domesticity, and racialized divisions among women, notes that while dirt and housework connote inferior morality, white middle-class women transcend these connotations by employing women different from themselves to do the work. "Dirtiness," Palmer notes, "appears always in a constellation of the suspect qualities that, along with sexuality, immorality, laziness, and ignorance, justify social rankings of race, class and gender. The 'slut,' initially a shorthand for 'slattern' or kitchen maid, captures all of these personifications in a way unimaginable in a male persona.[33]

Employers are not the only ones who hold strong racial-ethnic preferences and prejudices. Latina domestic workers at the bus stops, at the agencies, and in the public parks readily agreed on who were their worst employers: Armenians, Iranians, Asians, Latinos, blacks, and Jews, especially Israeli Jews. "I'll never work again for *un chino!*" or "*Los armenios* [Armenians] are the worst," they tell each other. These statements were echoed in the individual interviews, as well as by the preferences job candidates register at employment agencies, and they seem to mirror what Latino men who work as day laborers think about their similarly racialized employers in Los Angeles.[34] Anyone marked as "nonwhite," it seems, is at risk of being denounced as a cheap, abusive, and oppressive employer, one to be avoided at all costs.

There are a number of factors at work here. Many of the employers in these racial-ethnic groups are immigrants themselves, albeit entrepreneurial and professional immigrants with substantially more resources than the Latinas they hire to care for their homes and children. Many had belonged to elites in their countries of origin, accustomed to having servants in their homes who would be expected to perform all sorts of jobs on demand. Some of them bring these expectations with them when they come to the United States. When Latina domestic workers are expected to massage the señora's feet with oil, or scrub the kitchen floor on their hands and knees, they take offence. Others are wholly unprepared to iron Hindu saris, or to follow kosher food preparation and serving practices in the homes of Orthodox Jews. At the same time, the immigrant and ethnic employers may have been accustomed in their countries of origin to paying slave wages, and the tenuous financial situations of some makes them unable to pay minimum wage. Some newly arrived women who find their first job working as a live-in for other working-class Latino immigrant families may receive as little as $25 or $50 a week in exchange for their round-the-clock services.

Latina immigrants also operate under racist assumptions, many of which they learn in the United States. They quickly pick up the country's racial hierarchies and racist stereotypes. "Jews are cheap," "Mexican Americans and blacks are lazy," or "*Los chinos* are too bossy," they say. The regional racial hierarchy also fixes Jews, Armenians, and Iranians in low positions. "*Los Americanos*," the term they typically use to refer to employers marked only "white," are almost never singled out by ethnicity and are rarely criticized or negatively labeled as a group.

Conversely, Latina domestic workers single out the race of particular employers who happen to be both "bad employers" and "racialized" as nonwhite. One Mexican housecleaner who maintained that Latino employers were among the most exploitative was Lupe Vélez. When I probed why she felt this way, she cited as evidence her experiences with one employer, a man from Monterrey, Mexico. A large, verbally abusive man, he had called her a pig, he went out of his way to deny her food when he sat down to eat with his family, and he had unfairly accused her of scratching and ruining a stove top. These deeply felt, painful experiences were recounted tearfully.

Yet as we talked longer, I discovered that in Los Angeles, Lupe had worked in three different Latino homes; she spoke of a Mexican American teacher who had treated her well and paid her fairly. Mutual fondness, respect, and closeness had grown between the two, who had unsuccessfully conspired at matchmaking between their young adult children. How could she maintain that Latinos were the "worst" employers when in fact a Mexican American had been among her best employers? In recalling her bad experience with the Mexican man, Lupe Vélez singled out his racial-ethnic identity. As she recalled that painful experience, his being Mexican and consistently acting abusively toward her became the most salient features about him. She applied "Latino," a racial marker, to this man, labeled an abusive, bad employer, but not to the teacher whom she had favored.

I suspect that when Latina domestic workers denounce Jewish employers, a similar process is at work. In those cases, they may only identify as Jewish those employers who are abusive and who are, as Orthodox Jews or recently emigrated Israeli Jews, unambiguously marked as Jewish. They might not recognize the other Jews for whom they work. Or perhaps Latina domestic workers' disdain for Jewish employers is testimony to the force of contemporary anti-Semitism. It is no small irony that a major provider of legal services for Latina domestic workers in Los Angeles is a Jewish nonprofit organization.[35]

Some Latina domestic workers related counternarratives, criticizing their peers for relying on racial stereotypes and hasty racial judgments. One Salvadoran housecleaner cited her Moroccan employer as one of the most gracious because she always served her a hot lunch, sitting down to chat with her; another related her appreciation of an African American bachelor, an ex-basketball player, who kept a messy house but paid her very generously; still another felt warmly toward her Korean employer who did not pay well, but who passed many choice housecleaning jobs on to her. Yet the voices of these women were drowned out by the louder, frequently blanket condemnations that other Latina domestic workers offered about their racially

marked minority and immigrant employers. Amid the public clamor of racialized nativism that propelled California ballot initiatives against health and education services for undocumented immigrants and their children, against affirmative action, and against bilingual education (Propositions 187, 209, and 227 respectively), Latina immigrant domestic workers learn their own version of regional racism.

In this chapter, I conveyed briefly some of the life textures and the daily trials and triumphs experienced by Latina immigrants who work as housecleaners, live-out nanny/housekeepers, and live-in nanny/ housekeepers. The Mexican, Salvadoran, and Guatemalan women who occupy these jobs come from diverse class, regional, and cultural locations, and they bring different expectations to their jobs. Once in the United States, however, they share a set of similar experiences part because of the way that their domestic work is structured.

NOTES

1. Glenn 1986: 141.

2. Lacher 1997: 1.

3. One nanny/housekeeper told me that a señora had admonished her for picking a bag of fruit, and wanted to charge her for it; another claimed that her employer had said she would rather watch the fruit fall off the branches and rot than see her eat it.

4. Many Latina domestic workers do not know the amount of their hourly wages; and because the lines between their work and nonwork tend to blur, live-in nanny/housekeepers have particular difficulty calculating them. In the survey questionnaire I asked live-in nanny/housekeepers how many days a week they worked, what time they began their job, and what time they ended, and I asked them to estimate how many hours off they had during an average workday (39 percent said they had no time off, but 32 percent said they had a break of between one and three hours). Forty-seven percent of the women said they began their workday at 7 A.M. or earlier, with 62 percent ending their workday at 7 P.M. or later. With the majority of them (71 percent) working five days a week, their average workweek was sixty-four hours. This estimate may at first glance appear inflated; but consider a prototypical live-in nanny/house keeper who works, say, five days a week, from 7 A.M. until 9 P.M., with one and a half hours off during the children's nap time (when she might take a break to lie down or watch television). Her on-duty work hours would total sixty-four and a half hours per week. The weekly pay of live-in nanny/housekeepers surveyed ranged from $130 to $400, averaging $242. Dividing this figure by sixty-four yields an hourly wage of $3.80. None of the live-in nanny/housekeepers were charged for room and board—

and, as we will see in chapter 8, this practice is regulated by law—but 86 percent said they brought food with them to their jobs. The majority reported being paid in cash.

5. See, e.g., Employment Classified Section 2, *Los Angeles Times*, June 6, 1999, G9.

6. Clark-Lewis 1994: 123. "After an average of seven years," she notes in her analysis of African American women who had migrated from the South to Washington, D.C., in the early twentieth century, "all of the migrant women grew to dread their live-in situation. They saw their occupation as harming all aspects of their life" (124). Nearly all of these women transitioned into day work in private homes. This pattern is being repeated by Latina immigrants in Los Angeles today, and it reflects local labor market opportunities and constraints. In Houston, Texas, where many Mayan Guatemalan immigrant women today work as live-ins, research by Jacqueline Maria Hagan (1998) points to the tremendous obstacles they face in leaving live-in work. In Houston, housecleaning is dominated by better-established immigrant women, by Chicanas and, more recently, by the commercial cleaning companies—so it is hard for the Maya to secure those jobs. Moreover, Hagan finds that over time, the Mayan women who take live-in jobs see their own social networks contract, further reducing their internal job mobility.

7. Several factors explain the shift to day work, including urbanization, interurban transportation systems, and smaller private residences. Historians have also credited the job preferences of African American domestic workers, who rejected the constraints of live-in work and chose to live with their own families and communities, with helping to promote this shift in the urban North after 1900 (Katzman 1981;

Clark-Lewis 1994: 129–35). In many urban regions of the United States, the shift to day work accelerated during World War I, so that live-out arrangements eventually became more prevalent (Katzman 1981; Palmer 1989). Elsewhere, and for different groups of domestic workers, these transitions happened later in the twentieth century. Evelyn Nakano Glenn (1986: 143) notes that Japanese immigrant and Japanese American women employed in domestic work in the San Francisco Bay Area moved out of live-in jobs and into modernized day work in the years after World War II.

8. Katzman 1981; Glenn 1986.

9. Wrigley 1995.

10. Keep in mind that the survey questionnaire was administered at three different types of sites: bus stops, ESL evening classes, and parks where nannies congregate with the children in their charge. Housecleaners who drive and have their own cars, and who speak some English, typically earn more money and are able to clean more houses per week. Because my survey is biased toward Latina domestic workers who ride the buses and attend ESL classes, those housecleaners earning higher wages are not taken into account.

11. Romero 1992.

12. In addition to the jobs of live-in nanny/housekeepers, live-out nanny/housekeepers, and weekly or biweekly housecleaners, an increasingly important and growing segment of the domestic workforce is engaged in elder care. That, too, is organized in different ways; and though the occupation lies beyond the parameters of this study (much of it is formally organized and contracted for by the state or medical organizations), some Latina immigrants are privately contracted for jobs as elders' companions and caretakers, as *damas de compañífa.*

13. Smith 1973; McBride 1976.

14. The only news report of INS raids involving nannies working in private homes in Los Angeles that came to my attention as I did this research involved a nanny working for a top-ranking Latino INS agent, Jorge Guzman. In 1996 armed plainclothes INS agents illegally raided Guzman's home, and allegedly fondled and made sexual advances toward the domestic worker. Guzman claimed that the raid was part of a ten-year program of internal anti-Latino harassment directed at him. After he filed suit, the U.S. Justice Department agreed to pay him $400,000 to settle (McDonnell 1999).

15. Personal communication, Cynthia Cranford, March 1999; Cleeland 1999.

16. Rollins 1985; Glenn 1986; Romero 1992. See Romero 1997 for a study focusing on the perspective of domestic workers' children. Although the majority of respondents in that study were children of day workers, and none appear to have been children of transnational mothers, they still recall that their mothers' occupation had significant costs for them.

17. Hondagneu-Sotelo and Avila 1997.

18. Central American women seem more likely than Mexican women to leave their children in their country of origin, even if their husbands are living with them in the United States, perhaps because of the multiple dangers and costs associated with undocumented travel from Central America to the United States. The civil wars of the 1980s, continuing violence and economic uncertainty, greater difficulties and costs associated with crossing multiple national borders, and stronger cultural legacies of socially sanctioned consensual unions may also contribute to this pattern for Central Americans.

19. Glenn 1986; Dill 1988.

20. The figures on Salvadoran and Guatemalan women are taken from an analysis of the 1990 census data by the sociologists David E. Lopez, Eric Popkin, and Edward Telles (1996); they also found that Mexican immigrants were only 2.3 times as likely as those in the general population to be engaged in paid domestic work.

21. See Salzinger 1991; Hagan 1994, 1998; Repak 1995.

22. Lopez, Popkin, and Telles 1996: 298.

23. According to 1990 PUMS Census data, about 70 percent of Central American women between the ages of 24 and 60 in Los Angeles County are in the labor force, while only 56 percent of their Mexican peers are. Among this same group, 71 percent of Mexican immigrant women but only 56 percent of their Central American peers are married and living with a spouse. To put it oven more starkly, 28 percent of Mexican immigrant women and 43 percent of Central American women report living with family members or adults other than their spouses.

24. Repak 1995.

25. Mahler 1995; Menjívar 2000.

26. Some studies estimate that as many as 50 percent of poor households in San Salvador were formed by "free unions" rather than marriage by law. This pattern is related not just to internal and intra-Central American labor migration but also to urban poverty, as there is no need to secure inheritance rights when there is no property to share (Nieves 1979; Repak 1995).

27. Countries with traditions of consensual marriages afford women more migration opportunities (Donato 1992).

28. A survey conducted in Los Angeles and Orange County in 1986 revealed that 45 percent of Korean immigrants were self-employed; many were business owners in the Korean ethnic economy (Min 1996: 48).

29. Mar and Kim 1994.

30. Between 1966 and 1985 nearly 25,000 Filipina nurses came to work in the United States, and another 10,000 came between 1989 and 1991. Filipinas who were formally recruited through government programs then informally recruited their friends and former nursing school classmates (Ong and Azores 1994).

31. Parreñas 2001

32. Wrigley 1995.

33. Palmer 1989: 140.

34. Personal communication with UCLA professor Abel Valenzuela, fall 1998.

35. Bet Tzedek Legal Services.

REFERENCES

Clark-Lewis, Elizabeth. 1994. *Living In, Living Out: African American Domestics in Washington, D.C. 1910–1940.* Washington, D.C.: Smithsonian Institution Press.

Cleeland, Nancy. 1999. "Garment Jobs: Hard, Bleak, and Vanishing." *Los Angeles Times*, March 11, A1, A14–16.

Dill, Bonnie Thornton. 1988. "'Making Your Job Good Yourself': Domestic Service and the Construction of Personal Dignity." In *Women and the Politics of Empowerment*, edited by Ann Bookman and Sandra Morgen, 33–52. Philadelphia: Temple University Press.

Donato, Katharine. 1992. "Understanding U.S. Immigration: Why Some Countries Send Women and Others Send Men." In *Seeking Common Ground: Multidisciplinary Studies of Immigrant Women in the United States*, edited by Donna Gabaccia, 159–84. Westport, Conn.: Praeger.

Glenn, Evelyn Nakano. 1986. *Issei, Nisei, Warbride.* Philadelphia: Temple University Press.

Hagan, Jacqueline Maria. 1994. *Deciding to Be Legal: A Maya Community in Houston.* Philadelphia: Temple University Press.

———. 1998. "Social Networks, Gender, and Immigrant Incorporation." *American Sociological Review* 63: 55–67.

Hondagneu-Sotelo, Pierrette, and Ernestine Avila. 1997. "'I'm Here, But I'm There': The Meanings of Latina Transnational Motherhood." *Gender and Society* 11: 548–71.

Katzman, David M. 1981. *Seven Days a Week: Women and Domestic Service in Industrializing America.* Urbana: University of Illinois Press.

Lacher, Irene. 1997. "An Interior Mind." *Los Angeles Times*, March 16, E1, E3.

Lopez, David E., Eric Popkin, and Edward Telles. 1996. "Central Americans: At the Bottom, Struggling to Get Ahead." In *Ethnic Los Angeles*, edited by Roger Waldinger and Mehdi Bozorgmehr, 279–304. New York: Russell Sage Foundation.

Mahler, Sarah J. 1995. *American Dreaming: Immigrant Life on the Margins.* Princeton: Princeton University Press.

Mar, D., and M. Kim. 1994. "Historical Trends." In *The State of Asian Pacific America: Economic Diversity, Issues, and Policies*, edited by Paul Ong. 13–30. Los Angeles: LEAP Asian Pacific American Public Policy Institute and UCLA Asian American Studies Center.

McBride, Theresa. 1976. *The Domestic Revolution: The Modernization of Household Service in England and France, 1820–1920.* New York: Holmes and Meier.

McDonnell, Patrick J. 1999. "U.S. to Pay $400,000 to INS Agent in Bias Suit." *Los Angeles Times*, January 21, B1, B5.

Menjívar, Cecilia. 2000. *Fragmented Ties: Salvadoran Immigrant Networks in America.* Berkeley: University of California Press.

Min, Pyong Gap. 1996. *Caught in the Middle: Korean Communities in New York and Los Angeles.* Berkeley: University of California Press.

Nieves, Isabel, 1979. "Household Arrangements and Multiple Jobs in San Salvador." *Signs* 5: 139–50.

Ong, Paul, and Tania Azores. 1994. "Health Professionals on the Front Line." In *The State of Asian Pacific America: Economic Diversity, Issues, and Policies*, edited by Paul Ong, 139–63. Los Angeles: LEAP Asian Pacific American Public Policy Institute and UCLA Asian American Studies Center.

Palmer, Phyllis. 1989. *Domesticity and Dirt: Housewives and Domestic Servants in the United States, 1920–1945.* Philadelphia: Temple University Press.

Parrenas, Rhacel Salazar. 2001. *Servants of Globalization: Women, Migration, and Domestic Work.* Stanford University Press.

Repak, Terry A. 1995. *Waiting on Washington: Central American Workers in the Nation's Capital.* Philadelphia: Temple University Press.

Rollins, Judith. 1985. *Between Women: Domestics and Their Employers.* Philadelphia: Temple University Press.

Romero, Mary. 1992. *Maid in the U.S.A.* New York: Routledge.

Romero, Mary. 1997. "Who Takes Care of the Maid's Children? Exploring the Costs of Domestic Service." In *Feminism and Families*, edited by Hilde L. Nelson, 63–91. New York: Routledge.

Salzinger, Leslie. 1991. "A Maid by Any Other Name: The Transformation of 'Dirty Work' by Central American Immigrants." In *Ethnography Unbound: Power and Resistance in the Modern Metropolis*, by Michael Burawoy et al., 139–60. Berkeley: University of California Press.

Smith, Margo L. 1973. "Domestic Service as a Channel of Upward Mobility for the Lower-Class Woman: The Lima Case." In *Female and Male in Latin America: Essays*, edited by Ann Pescatello, 192–207. Pittsburgh: University of Pittsburgh Press.

Wrigley, Julia. 1995. *Other People's Children.* New York: Basic Books.

Families

Families are a fundamental social unit. In families we develop a sense of ourselves as individuals and as members of a primary group. We internalize messages about our position in our communities, our nations, and the world. We are taught systems of belief, usually consistent with the society in which we live, about appropriate roles for particular kinds of people. For example, we learn to think differently about men and women, elders and children, and people of various races, classes, and social statuses. We also learn how we are expected to treat the people we encounter in the world around us.

It is within families that members of a society first develop ideas and feelings about themselves as gendered individuals. When we are children, the socialization we receive contains strong messages about the appropriate attitudes and behaviors for males and females. When we are adults, families are where we spend much of our time, divide up the work of meeting our physical and emotional needs, and care for others, such as children or aging family members. Families usually divide up these interpersonal roles according to what is considered appropriate for men or for women. Yet families come in many forms, even within one society. The normative family structure of a married mother and father with children no longer represents the majority of families. Instead, a family may be a single parent with children, a couple with no children, lesbian or gay parents and their children, or a group of people who decide to share a household. As a result, individuals' experiences in families vary widely.

Feminist scholars examine the family as a major source of the reproduction of sexism in society. Researchers ask questions about how the organization of family life supports women's oppression in society through its ideologies, economics, distribution of domestic tasks, and intimate relations. Reciprocally, researchers examine the impact of demographic, technological, economic, and political structures on women's and men's power and positions in their families.

At the same time, feminist researchers examine families as a source of women's strength and resistance. Alternative family forms are one way to restructure family lives; in addition, families may provide a source of resistance to other forms of oppression, such as racism or poverty. Feminist family studies emphasize the ways that race, ethnicity, sexuality, and class influence our family experiences.

In the first selection in Section Six, Rosanna Hertz examines how couples and single parents balance work and family. She focuses on couples who emphasize both parents' participation in family life over their paid employment, in contrast to most heterosexual couples who rely either on mothers' care-giving or on hired help. Middle-class couples with professional jobs who share parenting often do so because of their belief that fathers should be involved. They are likely to have flexible work schedules or to be able to work at home, allowing both women and men more time with children. Working-class couples, in contrast, may come to shared parenting through the husband's underemployment, which brings men more into the home, and may work different shifts so that one parent is home most of the time. Although the second group would not have chosen shared parenting, men nevertheless became nurturing parents and began to transform societal ideas of child-raising as the exclusive province of women. Single mothers, on the other hand, have fewer options because they have to support themselves and their children. Some middle-class single mothers save money so that they can afford to take time off from work after their children were born, while others turn to credit cards or renting space in their homes as a source of extra funds. Many working-class single mothers work several jobs in order to make enough money, but rely on extended families for child care and often have no health insurance. Support networks of relatives and friends are indispensable to single mothers as they try to balance both work and family. All of these strategies not only affect the nature of family life, but shape the workplace and how employees do their jobs. Thus, we see that family and work are interconnected.

What kind of work and family strategies do you engage in yourself? What kinds did your family employ when you were growing up? How would you like to balance family and work, ideally, and what kinds of jobs and support systems would you need in order to do so?

The ways that heterosexual women balance work and family vary according to class, ethnicity, culture, and nationality. Denise Segura analyzes how Chicana and Mexicana immigrant mothers view their lives as employed mothers in "Working at Motherhood: Chicana and Mexicana Immigrant Mothers and Employment." She finds that many Mexicana immigrants in the study viewed working for pay as an important part of motherhood because the income helped support their families. Many Chicana mothers, in contrast, who had grown up in the United States, had been socialized with the American notion of a separation between spheres of work and family and therefore expressed more ambivalence about combining employment and mothering. The article illustrates how the meaning and practice of motherhood

are culturally constructed and thus vary among different groups of women. How is the relationship between working outside the home and raising children defined in the culture in which you grew up?

In "For Better or Worse: Gender Allures in the Vietnamese Global Marriage Market," Hung Cam Thai shows how ideas of gender shape marriage strategies in quite different ways for Vietnamese male migrants to the United States and for women living in Vietnam. Women in Vietnam, he argues, are expected to "marry up" to men who are more highly educated, better employed, and older. But women who pursue higher education may lose their opportunity to marry up—in effect, "pricing themselves out" of the marriage market because by the time they finish their education, they are not only too highly educated but also too old to marry up. Reluctant to marry down in Vietnam and sacrifice their status and independence, they look for spouses who have immigrated to the United States, hoping to find a more egalitarian gender system there. Men in the United States, in contrast, often find themselves in low-status and low-paying jobs, despite education or higher class status in Vietnam. For them, a wife from Vietnam provides the hope of a traditional marriage in which they can gain the respect that they have lost in the workplace. As Thai shows, these women and men bring very different hopes to their marriages, both shaped by complicated intersections of gender, nationality, class, and culture. What do you think will happen to couples like these? How do their expectations compare to those of other cultures and communities with which you are familiar?

Suzanna Danuta Walters also shows how different groups reinterpret motherhood and family, in "Wedding Bells and Baby Carriages: Heterosexuals Imagine Gay Families, Gay Families Imagine Themselves." Unlike the other readings in this section, Walters focuses on how the mass media portray lesbian and gay families, and how these portrayals shape the way people think about family and sexuality. Walters contrasts the visibility and acceptance of gay weddings on TV with the virulent opposition gay marriage faces in political reality. Yet, as she describes, the lesbian and gay community itself is divided over the political implications of gay marriage. Some argue that legalizing gay marriage would serve to stabilize and integrate lesbians and gay men into the larger society, while others argue that the institution of marriage has served to reinforce sexism and to penalize and stigmatize people who remain single. Gay parenting, like marriage, has become more visible in the mass media, and it has also increased in reality as more lesbians and gay men choose to have children. Here, too, while media portrayals emphasize gay parents' "normalcy"— that is, their similarity to heterosexual parents— political discourse criticizes them as perverted and bad role models, and legal systems in many states place gay parents at risk of losing custody of their children. For both marriage and parenting, the ten-

sion for gay men and lesbians is between assimilating to heterosexual models and attempting to form new models of family. Why do you think the media portrayals and the politics of gay marriage and parenting are so different from each other? Do you think that gay marriage and parenting will change the institutions of family more generally? In what ways?

For most women, these articles suggest, family relationships are a complicated mixture of accommodation and resistance to gender oppression. How do women accept traditional definitions of their family roles? How do they make choices about the relationship of paid employment to mothering? How do they gain power and fulfillment through family relationships, and how do these relationships constrict them?

Working to Place Family at the Center of Life: Dual-Earner and Single-Parent Strategies

ঌ Rosanna Hertz

Most scholars have focused on the ways in which employment structures family life. Economic resources and employment status are frequently noted as major correlates (if not predictors) of parents' beliefs about parenting and child care (for example, who should do it and how it ought to be arranged). This holds true even in studies of child care arrangements where parents' beliefs about motherhood are positioned as independent variables. While my own empirical studies look at how workplaces cause families to organize in particular ways, in each of these studies I have also encountered numerous couples and individuals who are pushing workplaces to accommodate them or who are creating their own careers and businesses in order to place children and child rearing before employment. For the sake of clarity, I will use the term "work" to refer to paid employment; work in the home is referred to as "housework." In this article, I move these couples out of the margins and into the spotlight to examine how and why they navigate the work world despite indifferent and, in some cases, hostile employment policies. I use the cases from two recent studies as examples: a study of 95 dual-earner couples and a study of 52 single, unwed mothers.[1]

THE BROADER WORK-FAMILY CONTEXT

Family benefits (for example, flex-time, on-site day care, and parental leaves) are more common now than when I wrote *More Equal Than Others: Women and*

NOTE: The author thanks Robert J. Thomas for his generous comments and editorial assistance and Faith I. Ferguson for sharing data collection and initial analysis on the single-mother study. She thanks Bradley Googins and Marcie Pitt-Catsouphes for detailed suggestions that improved the flow of her arguments. Wellesley College provided transcription costs for the interviews in both studies.

Men in Dual-Career Marriages over a decade ago.[2] However, while organizations may acknowledge that most employees have families, families have yet to exert a dramatic influence on organizational policies. In part, the lack of a strong push to make work family-friendly can be attributed to the ability of employers to make special (that is, unique or onetime) concessions to individual employees. For example, flexible work hours may be granted to valued professional or technical women (Catalyst 1997), but such concessions generally do not translate into flextime for everyone.[3] More broadly, a concept of social contract like that found in many Western European economies is notably absent in policy circles (much less in corporate personnel departments) in the United States. However, less obvious (but no less important) is the fact that not all employees utilize benefits even when they are offered; for example, men rarely make use of paternity leave benefits. As long as a core group of employees continues to advance without the use of the new family benefits, the structure and the culture of the workplace are likely to remain unchallenged. In short, employers remain the silent (and relatively intransigent) partners in the life of all families (Hertz 1986).

Without a doubt, family structure has changed dramatically, and economic and workplace factors have an important role to play in explaining the change in family structures.[4] However, there remains a great deal to be learned about the effect of family on work, on one hand, and of family ideology on work choices, on the other. For instance, it is not at all clear that women are trading home for employment as a less stressful environment (cf. Hochschild 1997). More likely, women work outside the home because they and their families cannot get by on one paycheck. Indeed, as Coontz (1992, 18–19) notes, polls show that the pressures for balancing work and family, particularly for women, are enormous and that a large percentage of women would trade a day's pay for an extra day off. Additionally, studies of shift-work families demonstrate that wives remain in the workforce after children are born but change to working shifts (Presser and Cain 1983; Presser 1988). Working opposite shifts from those of their husbands allows them to care for their children (Hertz and Charlton 1989) and does not compete with views of being a "visible" mom in ways that working days did (Garey 1995; Hertz 1997).

Our relative ignorance about the effect of family on work stems at least in part from the fact that most scholars continue to focus their research on a narrow slice of employed families: the most successful (and elite) dual-career and dual-earner couples. Left aside are couples who—for reasons of ideology or economic circumstance—may actually be placing family ahead of workplace demands. For example, insufficient attention has been paid to dual-earner couples who have faced the effects of job loss by one or both spouses. For these couples, job loss for husbands may, in fact, be causing couples to rethink the primacy of work outside the home over family. Moreover, the most under-represented category of family are those single (never married) women and men who have families that they support. While the fastest-growing category of U.S. families may be single moms, the focus continues to be on teen mothers and not those who are active in the labor market, economically self-sufficient, and over the age of 20.

The two groups whose experiences I analyze in this article offer up an interesting comparison. The first group consists of married dual-earner couples who have put into practice an egalitarian approach to parenting. The second group consists of women who are financially self-sufficient and who intentionally became single mothers. Both groups would appear to have made conscious choices to put family ahead of employment. Therefore, they offer a valuable opportunity to examine the conditions under which family affects employment.

DUAL-EARNER COUPLES AND THE NEW PARENTING

In my most recent study of dual-earner couples and their decision-making practices (Hertz 1997), I found three general approaches to child care: the mothering approach, the market approach, and the new parenting

approach. The mothering approach assumes that the person best suited to raise the couple's children is the wife, who should be with them at home. The market approach involves hiring other people to care for one's own children. The new parenting approach is exemplified by the belief that the family ought to be organized around caring for the children—with the critical distinction that both parents are full participants. While this approach was the least common of the three, it posed the strongest challenge to a traditional family division of labor and to conventional definitions of job and career.

The two groups of couples found to most often practice the new parenting approach came from very different economic and social situations. One group was made up of couples in which both spouses held middle-range managerial and professional jobs that allowed them to request more flexible work time or fewer workdays. As valued employees whose jobs did not involve extensive direct supervision, their requests for flexibility were met with individual concessions but not policy changes. Other employees were asking to be evaluated on a per project or task-completion basis. This contract with bosses allowed individuals to structure their own work schedules and pace, shifting the work culture to performance evaluation as separate from employee visibility. The arrangement did not require income reduction. A shift to a project-based evaluation afforded parents (particularly mothers but also a small but growing number of fathers) afternoons with children in order to coach sport teams and chauffeur children to enrichment activities.

The other group was the working-class, dual-earner families where husbands were underemployed. These fathers had held blue-collar jobs before those jobs were eliminated by downsizing.[5] For these couples in particular, underemployment and/or major shifts in occupation and employer became a catalyst for reshaping—if not rethinking—traditional gender-based divisions of labor. These couples were crafting strategic responses to a turbulent and shifting labor market. Tag-team parenting typified by shift workers involved parents who worked opposite shifts in order to care for children themselves. Overlapping shift workers used a neighbor or family member for transition periods.

Couples in the upper middle class (who occupied positions often at the top of organizations and tended to have the most authority and responsibility for lower-level employees) were among the least likely to restructure their employment in order to adopt the new parenting approach. Though they might have chosen to seek alternative employment, few did, reasoning that they would have had to give up salient parts of their careers in the process of redefining their work and family goals. The other groups of couples less likely to adopt the new parenting approach to child care comprised those who worked in settings that were highly structured (inflexible) or highly demanding of their time.

In the following, I discuss two different situations where coparenting strategies are used to keep family at the center. In the first group, coparenting reflects beliefs about the importance of shared parenting itself. In the second situation, coparenting evolves as an option for keeping family at the center of daily life when both parents need to work outside the home (although some of these families might choose not to coparent if their economic circumstances were different).

Reorganizing Employment to Maximize Parenting

This group of parents shared a belief that equal parental contributions to child care represented a superior solution to the market (for example, day care) or the mothers' complete withdrawal from the labor force. They believed that men and women should work outside and inside the home and share responsibility for child rearing. Individuals attempted to modify their jobs and employment commitments in order to regulate the demands that paid work makes and, thus, to restore some semblance of control—even if it meant loss of income.

Couples emphasized that men have historically been shortchanged as nurturers. Husbands talked about achieving parity with wives in their desire to experience fatherhood. Men modified their work schedules in order to be actively involved in child care. Usually they did this by working longer hours four days a week in order to have the fifth day to care for their child. Occasionally, this fifth day included taking the child to the office for a meeting or holding the meeting at home. But this reorganization of time did not lead to a cut in pay. For her part, the wife found a new, less demanding job working part-time three days a week. Not only

did the individual spouses alter their work schedules, but the total number of hours the couple worked each week was reduced because of a belief by the couple that both parents should be child oriented as a priority.

Underemployment as a Route to Shared Parenting

The couples previously described arranged work scheduling to fit coparenting as a core belief. In this second dual-earner couple situation, the couples emphasized their belief in keeping family at the center. It was possible to observe couples implementing the new parenting approach in practice while not forsaking the ideology that only mothers are really capable of "maternal thinking" (Ruddick 1980). Indeed, oftentimes women with underemployed husbands struggled with the idea of sharing mothering. Still, many women whose husbands settled for jobs with less than full-time hours conceded that their husbands had mastered maternal practice. Husbands, in turn, frequently remarked that this approach to parenting was one they never imagined themselves doing.

Economic downturns and corporate downsizing in the 1980s (Hodson and Sullivan 1990) and major sectoral shifts in the mid-1990s led these couples to piece together new employment and child care arrangements from which active fathering was a by-product. These couples did not consciously choose to work less (and earn less) in order to do more for their children directly. They worried about a further erosion in their economic standing. Wives commonly worked in jobs in the service sector, particularly as caregivers such as nurses. Since many wives had secure jobs with benefits and some over-time, they often brought home a larger paycheck. Unable to find a comparable job to the one they had lost, many husbands were forced to take temporary, unskilled, or part-time work; others found entry-level jobs with a new employer and industry. Retraining programs, these men reported, had not led to well-paying full-time jobs comparable to the ones they had lost, even with the booming economy of the late 1990s. Both jobs may be important to the household economy, but the larger paycheck is symbolic of an inability to fulfill beliefs about one's identity.

One father, who was 39 years old with two children and who worked part-time as a home health aide, explained how his employment history had devolved:

> I think [for] *many* of the long-term unemployed, [for] people like me who don't show up in the statistics, life goes on. So you do other things, you work part-time, either delivering pizza, which I did for three years, or bagging mail for the post office, whatever. But life goes on, so you have to adjust yourself because first of all, no one's gonna hire you. Once you're over 30, no one's gonna hire you for any real job. So what's the sense? . . . Your buddy who mows lawns for a living is offering you $10 an hour. So you do what you have to do. And you just fall into a whole other world that you forget exists when you worked for a large company, working 9–5 for six years.

The wife, aged 35, was a nurse who typically worked the night shift, from 7 P.M. to 7 A.M. She worried that, if she lost her overtime, she would have to find a second nursing job. (Not only did she not want to work a second job, but she would have preferred to stay home part-time, an unlikely reality in the near future.) She explained how underemployment had affected her husband's sense of masculinity: "And of course his ego was all shot to hell. He's not the family provider he wants to be and he's not doing exactly what he wanted, what he set in his mind. All his goals are rearranged."

Couples in which the wife was employed full-time while the husband was employed part-time often wished that the wife could opt to work fewer hours outside the home. Since she was the source of medical benefits, however, these couples were unable to reduce her employment to part-time without sacrificing these benefits. While middle-class white women continued to think of themselves as having the option of staying at home or entering the labor force, ideological and structural barriers prevented men from having similar choices (Gerson 1993).

Dual-Earner Couples: Summary

Regardless of which path they traveled to shared child care, the practice of new parenting transformed these men into more nurturing and sensitive caregivers who were teaching their young children how to navigate the world (Coltrane 1996). Indeed, it is ironic that many of the couples who are on the cutting edge of transforming maternal thinking are doing so not because of an ideological belief but as the result of constraints associated with corporate downsizing and economic restructuring. In both instances, however, couples rethink family life, particularly caring for children, as they cobble together identities that are no longer unidimensional. Underemployed couples continue to wish their home and work time could be more evenly divided but not because they wish wives would become full-time mothers.

SINGLE MOTHERS

The single mothers I discuss in this section were all economically self-sufficient and chose to parent without a partner. The majority described themselves as strongly committed to employment prior to motherhood. They had occupations as diverse as lawyers, corporate consultants, waitresses, and aerobics instructors. Most worked within the service sector in feminized occupations (such as nurses, secretaries, social workers, elementary school teachers). The remainder were self-employed and pieced together a living wage.

While single parents in general have been glossed over by researchers interested in work and family dilemmas, these women represent a potentially valuable source of insight into the effects of family on work. There are two reasons for this. First, family was highly valued by these women. This is powerfully portrayed in the stories the women told about the lengths to which they went to build a family (for example, enduring the uncertainties of donor insemination or the bureaucratic travails of trying to adopt as a single parent). Therefore, we should expect them to be quite dedicated to shaping employment to fit family. Second, single mothers have no one immediately available to share the tasks within the home or to shoulder the burden of earning a living. They have few easy ways to expand their financial resources, and the increase in financial costs that women experience when they double the size of their households is dramatic. For instance, child care for an infant at a day care center in metropolitan Boston is $12,000 per year (family day care is $8000 per year) and medical coverage for a family plan is usually triple the cost of an individual plan. (This leaves aside diapers, formula, car seats, strollers, and clothing, just to mention major items.) Therefore, single mothers are likely to have the least slack (the least flexible alternatives) in order to adjust family to the demands of work outside the home.

Regardless of income, these women believe themselves to be part of the middle class. This belief—even when it masks structural inequalities in the labor force—is important because it symbolizes a sense of having a future, not simply getting by from one paycheck to the next. As women said repeatedly, they worked hard to ensure that they were visible middle-class consumers. Reducing their income when children arrive—for all but the wealthiest women—would mean slipping down the economic ladder and potentially losing footing within the middle class. Cutting back, therefore, was not a viable solution (Hertz and Ferguson 1998).[6]

Like the dual-earner couples described in the preceding section who practiced the new parenting approach, these single mothers come from two very different points in the economic spectrum. First, there are the women who worked in top jobs in their chosen fields and who had spent years competing with their peers in dual-earner families (or childless peers). Once they wanted to start a family, they turned away from the attractions of job success that had motivated and rewarded them. Second, there are women who worked at the bottom of the labor force hierarchy and were employed in several part-time (sometimes full-time) jobs with no medical or child care benefits when their children were born. They had to keep (or find) one job with benefits or slip down the economic ladder and collect welfare and other subsidies. Slipping to welfare dependency went against the grain of their own values: these women had worked to keep themselves independent, and many were among the last of their high school girlfriends to have children.

Unlike the dual-earner couples, however, these single mothers have fewer resources internal to the family to call on in trying to balance work and family. They are more likely to cultivate external resources—in broader kin and friendship networks—to help them put family first. The implications of this form of community building will be taken up later, in the conclusion.

In the following, I discuss the three strategies adopted by these single mothers in order to place family life at the center: financing their own "mother time"; multiple jobs; and community supports.

Women Professionals: Financing Their Own Mother Time

Armed with college and advanced degrees, these women professionals typically described themselves as workaholics prior to having children—always available to work extra hours. Once children arrived, however, they had to decide whether to set a more flexible work schedule or to reduce the inflated number of hours of "face time" that their work culture expected of them (see Landers, Rebitzer, and Taylor 1996). The work culture of competition and fear of job loss made it seem essential to be in the office from 7 A.M. till late at night. Often the last to leave the office, they used employment to fill the void of a family life.

When children arrived, many of the women cut back significantly on their work hours and, at least symbolically, demonstrated greater commitment to family over work. Quite a few took extended leaves. However, unlike Swedish families who take long parental leaves, the women in my study were financing their own parental leaves and extended periods of part-time work through savings they consciously set aside years before, knowing that someday they would have children. This gave them the time to be with their children without altering their lifestyles. When the savings ran low, they turned to credit card debt or reluctantly increased their work hours. To make up for lost mother time, they might spend their lunch hour with their child at the day care provider's.

Technical or professional skills sometimes allowed women who worked in larger organizations to argue for flexible arrangements, including working a shorter workweek (with longer days), or working part of the week in the office and part from home, or cutting back to limited travel. A manager who recently decided to change firms explained how this move enabled her to be an agent in shaping her work life, but she admitted that she could do this because of her advanced technical skills:

I'm going to have one-third of the number of people reporting to me than I used to and I'm going to walk out of work at 5:15 P.M. . . . And that was a very conscious choice. I didn't want a job that was going to consume me right now because I know that my priority needs to be taking care of Ben. . . . So it's constantly this balance of how much time at work and with my child. How deep does the foot go in? Is it the toe; up to the ankle; up to the knee?

How deep am I in the work world with still my arms and my head free to be with Ben and it's a balance that I anticipate continually needing to adjust as the years play out.

However, in their attempts to strike a balance between work and family responsibilities, many traded off job advancement or opportunities for more interesting work projects in order to be out of the office by dinner time. The new goal is "streamlining": trying to "become more efficient" in order to "structure their work time better." But, since many of their managers measure time in the office—not work accomplished—the women who left early reported losing out, a trade-off they were willing to make. Sometimes they started their own businesses or freelanced on a project basis as a way to set their own work hours and avoid the stress of a work culture that may be family friendly but not woman friendly.[7] Even the women who take on piece-rate projects, which they believe gives them independence from the dictates of corporate structures, know there are only so many hours they can shave off a day and still maintain their lifestyle. Some try to increase the rates they charge; others take a part-time job that carries medical benefits (a huge expense for the self-employed) and do contract work with the remaining allocated work hours each week.

Even more create income by turning assets like space in their homes to barter for services or rent. For instance, one woman lived in a large Victorian house with her child and retired father. When he died, however, they lost his contribution to the mortgage. Assessing her life, she decided she could either find a more lucrative job and be away from her daughter all day or turn the house into a seasonal inn. Turning space into economic value gave her continued autonomy from a more structured job situation and allowed her to blur the boundaries between work and family. Other women bought triple-decker buildings and rented out two of the apartments in order to reduce housing costs. Lacking the savings to purchase a building, others took in roommates in order to cut costs.

Women Working Multiple Jobs

Good mothering for women who hold several jobs more closely resembles the experiences of minority and immigrant women in the United States (as well as other mothers around the world). For these women, being a good provider and having a close family member care for a child is being a good mother (cf. Glenn, Nakano, and Forcey 1994, especially the chapters by Collins and Segura). For instance, one woman who was a day care provider at a for-profit day care center worked just under the number of hours necessary for her boss to pay her benefits. She had begun working at this center as an intern in high school, and by the time she had her child (at age 26) she had worked 10 years at the same workplace. With no benefits and an unpaid maternity leave, she took off a few weeks and then returned to work. Her child spent four days a week being cared for at her mother's home and three days a week at her own home. Without her mother's help, the cost would have made it impossible to remain employed. The day care center director gave this valued employee one free day a week of child care. The child did have medical coverage through the state, while the mother remained uninsured. To earn additional money, when her child was at her mother's, she baby-sat in the evenings, and during the summer on weekends she cleaned cottages at a vacation resort. Between her mother's ability to watch her child, the free day of child care, and the extra jobs, she managed to save money.

Those at the bottom of the labor force hierarchy, typically high-school-educated women, worked long hours and often held several part-time jobs from which they derived no benefits. Prior to having a child, they cared about piecing together enough hours of work to live decently.[8] Others worked day jobs and then night jobs (for instance, during the day they worked as an administrative assistant, and then they waitressed at night or worked as phone operators for a catalogue company). Working two or three jobs in this fashion in the Boston area gave women incomes of $25,000–$30,000 a year with no benefits, making them vulnerable labor force participants.

With the arrival of a child, however, benefits become essential. Making good money without benefits might be doable without a child, but having a child can dramatically change one's financial situation from independence to welfare dependence in a matter of months. The majority of women who parent without a partner do not have the choice of leaving the labor force. Besides a brief maternity leave (and even these may be forfeited if unpaid), these women have no option but to work for income. Some women go the route of expanding their work hours by working multiple jobs, but extra hours spent at work is a disheartening trade-off for time spent with children. Moreover, they are likely to earn entry-level wages, and the extra jobs are usually seasonal or erratic.

When workplaces do not give all their employees benefits (such as health care), these women turn to government subsidies (such as Medicaid), which are a necessary but poor substitute. In my study, those women without families to help out were likely to resort to collecting welfare until they could reorganize their lives to hold a job and parent a child at the same time. Every woman in this study who received welfare also went to two-year college programs with the hopes of acquiring skills that would get them out of the cycle of multiple jobs and hired into a job with advancement and benefits.

In short, every mother in this study wanted to reduce work hours. They cut back at work if it did not lead to downward mobility. Some who found that they could not make ends meet once children grew older took the children to their extra jobs (such as housecleaning and baby-sitting). These women took these extra jobs despite their personal cost because the chosen lifestyle—for the poorest women, remaining off of state aid—required a minimum level of cash available only through paid work.

Creating a Support Network

Single mothers cannot expand their time available for parenting or their income to support their families by crafting an arrangement with a family partner—because there is no partner. Therefore, as I found in my study, single employed mothers are apt to create networks of external resources (that is, external to their household) to substitute for the flexibility afforded to dual-earner couples. For example, nearby relatives are frequently tapped for child care; when kin are not available (as happens far more frequently these days), fictive kin like godparents are woven into the family as sources of spiritual and material support. Even more creatively, single mothers often build a "repertory family" (Hertz and Ferguson 1997) by pulling together an ensemble of people who provide some combination of emotional and psychological support, economic contributions, and performance of routine household chores and maintenance. This way, they spread the risk of losing a key person by having a network of people in their lives.

The women I found to be most likely to create an external support network were those employed in female-dominated occupations earning wages at the border of the working and middle classes. They were highly social, resourceful, and adept at relationship building. Many of these women had or sought out middle-class sponsorship—help from other women they had met through previous jobs—particularly in sustaining a modicum of middle-class social and cultural opportunities for their children, such as invitations to birthday parties, inclusion in car pools and sports leagues, and participation in community events. Finally, they were skilled at finding "pennies from heaven," that is, at establishing rapport by revealing their circumstances to people they trusted who sometimes became significant gift-givers (Hertz and Ferguson 1998).

CONCLUSION

The objective of this article was to study the effect of family on work by comparing the experiences of two distinctly different family forms: dual-earner couples who had adopted an egalitarian approach to parenting and women who had chosen to become parents without marital partners. These families, I suggested, were most likely to offer insight into the way family is made to have priority over employment. Two conclusions, deserving of additional study, should be emphasized.

First, most parents either have or evolve a belief system about how children should be raised—whether, for example, mothers should work outside the home while children are toddlers—but not all families have the means or the opportunity to enact those beliefs. Indeed, the very concept of balancing work and family may be better viewed as a euphemism for competing ideologies about child rearing. Positioning in the external labor market and, more specifically, within a particular organization's internal labor market strongly influences whether individual women and men implement (or even contemplate implementing) their ideologies about parenting. People employed in a workplace with flexible hours and benefits are freer to live out their beliefs about parenting. When flexible work schedules or work-related benefits are not available, it is far more difficult for mothers and fathers to actively parent even when they want to.

Second, ideology is important, but benefits matter. While women with professional training or job skills, regardless of marital status, may be able to negotiate individual deals for themselves on the basis of their own value or nonsubstitutability to the organization, couples with two high-status jobs have a major source of leverage not available to single mothers: that is, the cushion (or indirect advantage) that derives from the other spouse's benefits package (and paycheck). The couple can decide how to distribute their combined time between paid work and parenting, or one spouse can decide to go solo and open up a business. As long as one partner has benefits, the other can create flexibility, including staying home with children or starting up a business. Thus, while marriage may constrain the unbridled pursuit of one career to the possible disadvantage of the other, it also buffers the negative impacts of reversals in one or the other career. The practice of combining two careers—not the articulation of a nonsexist ideology—shapes decisions and informs change (Hertz 1986).

The couple can make decisions that might not be deemed optimal from the perspective of individual employers. Put differently, the couple is utilizing two work organizations even though it may appear to the employer that only the individual is making the decision. Gender is not the determining factor as to which partner might decide to try something different. Passion or vocation is more likely to be the concern between spouses when one decides to become an entrepreneur, a consistent finding in my studies of dual-earner couples since 1986. But if both spouses remain in traditional organizations, the wives will more likely (though not always, as the new parenting approach demonstrates) be the ones to ask for part-time or flexible work arrangements. Therefore, these couples are able to exercise their family and child care ideologies in ways that single mothers (divorced or unwed) with the same human capital and similar child care ideology cannot.

Unwed single mothers who have professional and managerial careers are more likely to take longer maternity leaves in order to be with their hard-won children, and they are more likely to think up creative solutions to deal with organizations that demand either on-site constant face time or frequent client-related travel; both work cultures limit the ability of parents to parent. These women may become the new entrepreneurs because of their organizing skills. They are more likely than their dual-earner peers to believe that raising children is not solely the responsibility of parents, but that workplaces and communities need to provide an adequate supply of day care slots for children—not just model day care for a few employees. For instance, communities need to rethink lengthening the school year and providing after-school programs as an accepted reality in community life so that children can keep up with the amount of information and skills essential to successfully entering the labor force but also so that parents are not constantly forced to make ad hoc arrangements for half days and school vacations. After-school programs have become the new neighborhoods our children play in; these programs need not simply a paid staff but community volunteers—perhaps retired individuals—who can share special talents and vocations with the young. In this regard, privatized corporate day care has been more willing to operate during hours that are more accommodating to parents. Once children enter school, parents complain about the quality of public school education (shortened school days and year), which continues to ignore the needs of employed parents. Ironically, work sites may have day care on the premises, but the supply of slots may not equal the demand for care for children under school age. Nevertheless, we have begun to find ways to enhance parents' employment when their children are very young. Through public education, communities must take the next step from kindergartens that end by 11 A.M. to schools that end by 2 P.M.

For those dual-earner parents of preschool children and for younger couples who have experienced downsizing and underemployment—similar to single mothers—the lack of benefits is crucial. Benefits are crucial for all families but particularly those who, without spouses, manage to make a living through piecing together a variety of jobs. A world in which benefits existed for everyone would give families more choice in how to position themselves in the workplace. New employment alternatives (in some cases, new employment alternatives mean unconventional jobs and employment contracts; in others "new" just means different jobs in the same organization) are important if people are to feel they have a choice. If they are unsatisfied as a couple with work arrangements, family life becomes stressful, and work, simply clocked hours to pay the bills. Remember the nurse who wanted to stay home part-time but worked extra shifts because her husband could not find a job with adequate benefits.

In this regard, the unit of analysis is the couple, not the individual work site. Cafeteria-style benefits may allow couples to choose from the alternatives provided by two different workplaces to maximize their ability to spend time with children. But, as a society, we must also acknowledge that an important and growing part of the labor force is and will be single parents who need ways to be productive employees and good mothers: this recognition may force communities to become more than empty spaces and, instead, to become places where children can be left in safe environments so mothers can become and remain self-sufficient.

The aim of this article has been to highlight families that have tended to be overlooked in research on work-family issues and to better understand why and how they may shape their work lives to fit their beliefs about family. As I have tried to show, ideologies about family and coparenting motivated employed parents to develop creative strategies to keep family at the center. At the same time, close examination of how these families put family first demonstrates that work-family policies and programs rarely address the broader meaning of balancing work and family life. Indeed, it may rest with employees to collectively alter the future of workplace cultures by placing families first—rather than waiting for policies (public or private) to address their needs.

NOTES

1. The data for the dual-earner study were collected between 1993 and 1995 in Massachusetts. Husbands and wives were interviewed in-depth separately but simultaneously. A total of 36 percent of the couples were working class; the other three-fifths were middle and upper middle class. See Hertz 1997 for a more complete description of sampling and methods. The single mothers are part of an ongoing data collection. The first wave of data, collected between 1995 and 1997, was based upon in-depth interviews with 52 single mothers stratified by route to motherhood. With social class defined by education, occupation, and income, currently the sample is 24 percent working class and 76 percent middle class. See Hertz and Ferguson 1998 for a more complete description of sampling and methods.

2. For the 837 major U.S. employers that provided information about work-family benefits in the 1990–91 Hewitt Associates SpecBook (*Work and Family Benefits* 1991), child care was the most prevalent benefit: 64 percent of the employers offered some kind of child care assistance to their employees; 89 percent of those who offered child care assistance offered dependent care spending accounts; and 41 percent offered resource and referral services. Only 9 percent of the employers provided an employer-sponsored child care center. Elder care programs were more limited: only 32 percent of the employers provided assistance to their employees. Of those providing elder care assistance, 88 percent offered dependent care spending accounts.

3. Flextime is a catchall category including time alterations ranging from arriving or leaving a half hour earlier than the official start or end of the work day, to broad blocks of time away from the workplace (for example, in the middle of the day) or banking time for use as time off in the future. Flexible scheduling arrangements are offered by 54 percent of the employers in the 1990–91 Hewitt Associates SpecBook (*Work and Family Benefits* 1991). The most common arrangements offered by these employers are flextime (provided by 76 percent of the employers) and part-time employment (provided by 67 percent of the employers). But fewer employers had scheduling on an individual basis (4 percent), work at home (15 percent), compressed work schedules (23 percent), or job sharing (31 percent).

4. In the 1950s, the archetypal family had a stay-at-home wife, who was responsible for the children and chores. Today, only 14 percent of U.S. households consist of a married couple where only the husband earns income. The dual-earner and single-parent families of today can no longer count on a family member's running the household and taking care of the needs of each member. The most visible evidence of a changing family structure is reflected in women's workforce participation. In 1993, fully 60 percent of all women with children under age 6 worked for pay. Of those women with children aged 6 to 17 years, 75 percent were employed. This represents a marked increase from 1966, when 44 percent of women with children this age were employed (Hayghe and Bianchi 1994).

5. See Bluestone and Rose 1997 on the divided labor force.

6. The median income for the 52 women in this study was $40,000 per year, which approximated the median income for all families in Massachusetts (U.S. Bureau of the Census 1993, 23–145).

7. Family-friendly policies apply to both men and women. However, since women are more likely than men to actually care for family members, women pay a price in terms of face time, overtime, and other symbolic expressions of organizational commitment. They may do the actual job just as well as men but still be perceived as less dedicated to the job or the company.

8. It is beyond the scope of this article to discuss the economics of the part-time worker, but, clearly, not offering compensation benefits reduces the organization's costs.

REFERENCES

Bluestone, Barry and Stephen Rose. 1997. Overworked and Underemployed: Unraveling an Economic Enigma. *American Prospect* 31(Mar.–Apr.): 58–69.

Catalyst. 1997. *A New Approach to Flexibility: Managing the Work/Time Equation.* New York: Catalyst.

Coltrane, Scott. 1996. *Family Man: Fatherhood, Housework, and Gender Equity.* New York: Oxford University Press.

Coontz, Stephanie. 1992. *The Way We Never Were.* New York: Basic Books.

Garey, Anita Ilta. 1995. Constructing Motherhood on the Night Shift: "Working Mothers" as "Stay at Home Mom." *Qualitative Sociology* 18 (4): 415–37.

Gerson, Kathleen. 1993. *No Man's Land: Men's Changing Commitments to Family and Work.* New York: Basic Books.

Glenn, Evelyn, Grace Chang Nakano, and Linda Rennie Forcey, eds. 1994. *Mothering: Ideology, Experience and Agency.* New York: Routledge.

Hayghe, Howard V. and Suzanne M. Bianchi. 1994. Married Mothers' Work Patterns: The Job-Family Compromise. *Monthly Labor Review* 117(6): 24–30.

Hertz, Rosanna. 1986. *More Equal than Others: Women and Men in Dual-Career Marriages.* Berkeley: University of California Press.

———. 1997. A Typology of Approaches to Child Care: The Centerpiece of Organizing Family Life for Dual-Earner Couples. *Journal of Family Issues* 18(4): 355–85.

Hertz, Rosanna and Joy Charlton. 1989. Making Family under a Shiftwork Schedule: Air Force Security Guards and Their Wives. *Social Problems* 36: 491–507.

Hertz, Rosanna and Faith I. Ferguson. 1997. Kinship Strategies and Self-Sufficiency among Single Mothers by Choice: Post Modern Family Ties. *Qualitative Sociology* 20(2): 187–227.

———. 1998. Only One Pair of Hands: Ways That Single Mothers Stretch Work and Family Resources. *Community, Work and Family* 1(1): 13–37.

Hochschild, Arlie Russell. 1997. *The Time Bind: When Work Becomes Home and Home Becomes Work.* New York: Metropolitan Books.

Hodson, Randy and Teresa Sullivan. 1990. *The Social Organization of Work.* Belmont, CA: Wadsworth.

Landers, Renee M., James B. Rebitzer, and Lowell J. Taylor. 1996. Rat Race Redux: Adverse Selection in the Determination of Work Hours in Law Firms. *American Economic Review* 86(3): 329–48.

Presser, Harriet B. 1988. Shiftwork and Childcare Among Young Dual-Earner American Parents. *Journal of Marriage and the Family* 50: 133–48.

Presser, Harriet B. and V. S. Cain. 1983. Shiftwork Among Dual-Earner Couples with Children. *Science* 219: 876–79.

Ruddick, Sara. 1980. Maternal Thinking. *Feminist Studies* 6(3): 343–67.

U.S. Bureau of the Census. 1993. *Population Profile of the U.S. Current Population Reports,* Special Series.

Work and Family Benefits Provided by Major U.S. Employers in 1990–91. 1991. Hewitt Associates SpecBook.

THE MOMMY TEST

Barbara Ehrenreich

My, my, girls, what's all the fuss over the new "mommy test"? Hundreds of eager young female job seekers have written to me in the last few weeks alone, confident of being able to pass the drug test, the polygraph test, Exxon's new Breathalyzer test— but panicked over the mommy test. Well, the first thing you have to grasp if you hope to enter the ranks of management is that corporations have a perfect *right* to separate the thieves from the decent folk, the straights from the druggies, and, of course, the women from the mommies.

For starters, you should know that thousands of U.S. women, even those afflicted with regular ovulatory cycles and patent fallopian tubes, have been taking—and *passing*—the mommy test for decades. In fact, it used to be almost the first question (just after "Can you type?") in the standard female job interview: "Are you now, or have you ever, cotemplated marriage, motherhood, or the violent overthrow of the U.S. government?"

Today, thanks to women's lib, you won't be out on the street even if you fail. All right, there are

(continued)

disadvantages to the mommy track: mandatory milk and cookies at ten, quiet time at three, and so forth. But many women are happy to get a paycheck of any kind, even if it is a gift certificate to Toys 'R' Us. And if you *still* want to be on the fast track, with the grown-ups and the men, here are a few simple tips for acing the mommy test:

1. Be prepared for tricky psychological questions, such as: Would you rather *(a)* spend six straight hours in a windowless conference room with a group of arrogant, boorish men fighting over their spreadsheets, or *(b)* scrape congealed pabulum off a linoleum floor? (The answer, surprisingly is *a*.) Or try this one: Would you rather *(a)* feed apple juice to a hungry baby, or *(b)* figure out how to boost profits by diluting the company's baby apple juice product with wastewater from the local nuclear power plant? But you get the idea. . . .
2. Bring proof of infertility: your uterus in a mason jar, for example. Alternatively, tell the interviewer that you already had a child, but— and at this point you stare pensively into space—it didn't work out. . . .
3. Your interviewer will no doubt have framed photos of his own wife and children displayed prominently on his desk. Do not be misled, this is *part of the test*. Be sure to display appropriate levels of disgust and commiseration. You might ask, in a pitying tone, "Oh, did you marry a *mommy?*"
4. If, you actually are a mommy, and have small children of your own who, for some reason, are still living with you, the case is almost hopeless. Unless you can prove that, as a result of some bioengineering feat or error on their birth certificates, you are actually their daddy and hence have no day-to-day responsibility for their care.

But the key thing is *attitude*. If you go for your job interview in a hostile, self-pitying rnood, if you're convinced that the mommy test is an example of discrimination or prejudice, believe me, it will show. And there isn't prejudice against mommies today, not really. They're no longer subject to the extreme residential segregation imposed in the fifties, when mommies were required to live in special suburban compounds, far from the great centers of commerce. Today, you'll find them living just about everywhere, even in jaunty little cardboard structures within walking distance of Wall Street.

Today, it is no longer necessary (as it was for poor Nancy Reagan) for a woman who aspires to public recognition to renounce all knowledge of, and contact with, her children. We even have a special day devoted to the distribution of flowers on the graves of dead mothers, as well as to those mothers who, for some reason, still linger on.

However, even if we acknowledge all the tremendous contributions mothers have made— and there were mommies at Plymouth Rock, at Gettysburg, possibly even at the Republican National Convention—we must admit that they have, as a race, shown remarkably little aptitude for the fine points of corporate management. When have you ever seen a get-rich-quick book titled *Leveraged Buyouts: A Mother's Secrets,* or *Swimming with the Sharks: A Mommy's Guide to Eating the Competition (And Finishing Every Last Bite)?*

But the bottom line (not to be confused, gals, with the mark left by overly tight Pampers!) is: Even if you respect mommies, like mommies, and are aware of the enormous diversity among them, would you really want to work with one? This is the question that thousands of top U.S. male managers have had to face: Would you want to be at a $100 power lunch and risk being told to polish your plate? Hence the mommy track. It just makes *sense* to segregate them in special offices equipped with extra umbrellas, sweaters, raincoats, and toothbrushes—for their own safe as much as anything.

Personally, I think the mommy track may be just the first step in a new wave of corporate cost cutting. There's a new approach based on the experience of a brilliant young fast-track executive who got pregnant unbeknownst to herself and handily delivered in the ladies' room during a break in the third-quarter sales conference. The baby was raised on phenobarbital and take-out food until it outgrew the lower right-hand desk drawer, at which point our fast tracker hired a babysitter—to take over her corporate responsibilities!

For the truth is, all you eager young job seekers, that no one knows for sure what the management

(continued)

of top U.S. corporations does all day or well into the night. Sitting at desks has been observed. Sitting at meetings has been observed. Initialing memos has been observed. Could a woman—even a mommy—do all this? Certainly, and with time left over for an actual job of some sort. So the question that our corporate leaders must ultimately face is: What does our vast army of pin-striped managers do anyway, and could it be done by a reliable baby-sitter?

————— READING 23 —————

Working at Motherhood: Chicana and Mexicana Immigrant Mothers and Employment[1]

✌ Denise A. Segura

In North American society, women are expected to bear and assume primary responsibility for raising their children. This socially constructed form of motherhood encourages women to stay at home during their children's early or formative years, and asserts activities that take married mothers out of the home (for instance, paid employment) are less important or "secondary" to their domestic duties.[2] Motherhood as a social construction rests on the ideological position that women's biological abilities to bear and suckle children are "natural," and therefore fundamental to women's "fulfillment." This position, however, fails to appreciate that motherhood is a culturally formed structure whose meanings can vary and are subject to change.

Despite the ideological impetus to mother at home, over half of all women with children work for wages.[3] The growing incongruence between social ideology and individual behaviors has prompted some researchers to suggest that traditional gender role expectations are changing (for example, greater acceptance of women working outside the home).[4] The profuse literature on the "ambivalence" and "guilt" employed mothers often feel when they work outside the home, however, reminds us that changes in expectations are neither absolute nor uncontested.

Some analysts argue that the ambivalence felt by many employed mothers stems from their discomfort in deviating from a socially constructed "idealized mother," who stays home to care for her family.[5] This image of motherhood, popularized in the media, schoolbooks, and public policy, implies that the family and the economy constitute two separate spheres, private and public. Hood argues, however, that the notion of a private–public dichotomy largely rests on the experiences of white, leisured women and lacks immediate relevance to less privileged women (for instance, immigrant women, women of color), who have historically been important economic actors both inside and outside the home.[6] The view that the relationship between motherhood and employment varies by class, race, and/or culture raises several important questions. Do the ideology of motherhood and the "ambivalence" of employed mothers depicted within American sociology and feminist scholarship pertain to women of Mexican descent in the United States? Among these women, what is the relation between the ideological constructions of motherhood and employment? Is motherhood mutually exclusive from employment among Mexican-heritage women from different social locations?

In this chapter I explore these questions using qualitative data gathered from thirty women of

Mexican descent in the United States—both native-born Chicanas (including two Mexico-born women raised since preschool years in the US) and resident immigrant Mexicanas.[7] I illustrate that notions of motherhood for Chicanas and Mexicanas are embedded in different ideological constructs operating within two systems of patriarchy. Contrary to the expectations of acculturation models, I find that Mexicanas frame motherhood in ways that foster a more consistent labor market presence than do Chicanas. I argue that this distinction—typically bypassed in the sociological literature on motherhood, women and work, or Chicano Studies—is rooted in their dissimilar social locations—that is, the "social spaces" they engage within the social structure created by the intersection of class, race, gender, and culture.[8]

I propose that Mexicanas, raised in a world where economic and household work often merged, do not dichotomize social life into public and private spheres, but appear to view employment as one workable domain of motherhood. Hence, the more recent the time of emigration, the less ambivalence Mexicanas express regarding employment. Chicanas, on the other hand, raised in a society that celebrates the expressive functions of the family and obscures its productive economic functions, express higher adherence to the ideology of stay-at-home motherhood and correspondingly more ambivalence toward full-time employment—even when they work.

These differences between Mexicanas and Chicanas challenge current research on Mexican-origin women that treats them as a single analytic category (for instance, "Hispanic") as well as research on contemporary views of motherhood that fails to appreciate diversity among women. My examination of the intersection of motherhood and employment among Mexican immigrant women also reinforces emerging research focusing on women's own economic and social motivations to emigrate to the United States (rather than at the behest of husbands and/or fathers).[9]

My analysis begins with a brief review of relevant research on the relationship between motherhood and employment. Then I explore this relationship in greater detail, using in-depth interview data. I conclude by discussing the need to recast current conceptualizations of the dilemma between motherhood and employment to reflect women's different social locations.

THEORETICAL CONCERNS

The theoretical concerns that inform this research on Chicana/Mexicana employment integrate feminist analyses of the hegemonic power of patriarchy over work and motherhood with a critique of rational choice models and other models that overemphasize modernity and acculturation. In much of the literature on women and work, familial roles tend to be portrayed as important constraints on both women's labor market entry and mobility. Differences among women related to immigrant status, however, challenge this view.

Within rational choice models, motherhood represents a prominent social force behind women's job decisions. Becker and Polachek, for example, argue that women's "preference" to mother is maximized in jobs that exact fewer penalties for interrupted employment, such as part-time, seasonal, or clerical work.[10] According to this view, women's pursuit of their rational self-interest reinforces their occupational segregation within low-paying jobs (for example, clerical work) and underrepresentation in higher-paying, male-dominated jobs that typically require significant employer investments (for example, specialized training). Employers may be reluctant to "invest" in or train women workers who, they perceive, may leave a job at any time for familial reasons.[11] This perspective views motherhood as a major impediment to employment and mobility. But it fails to consider that the organization of production has developed in ways that make motherhood an impediment. Many feminist scholars view this particular development as consistent with the hegemonic power of patriarchy.

Distinct from rational choice models, feminist scholarship directs attention away from individual preferences to consider how patriarchy (male domination/female subordination) shapes the organization of production, resulting in the economic, political, and social subordination of women to men.[12] While many economists fail to consider the power of ideological constructs such as "family" and "motherhood" in shaping behavior among women, employers, and the organization of production itself, many feminist scholars focus on these power dynamics.

Within feminist analyses, motherhood as an ideology obscures and legitimizes women's social subordination because it conceals particular interests within the rubric of a universal prerogative (reproduction).

The social construction of motherhood serves the interest of capital by providing essential childbearing, child care, and housework at a minimal cost to the state, and sustains women as a potential reservoir of labor power, or a "reserve army of labor."[13] The strength of the ideology of motherhood is such that women continue to try to reconcile the "competing urgencies"[14] of motherhood and employment despite the lack of supportive structures at work or within the family.

Because employers view women as mothers (or future mothers), they encounter discrimination in job entry and advancement.[15] Because women are viewed as mothers, they also work a "second shift" at home.[16] The conflict between market work and family work has caused considerable ambivalence within women. Berg, for example, notes that one of the dominant themes in analyzing women and work is the "guilt" of employed mothers based on "espousing something different" from their own mothers.[17]

The notion Berg describes of "conflict" or "guilt" rests on several suppositions. The first assumption is that motherhood is a unilaterally oppressive state; the second, that employed mothers feel guilt; and the third, that today's employed mothers do not have working mothers (which partially explains their "guilt feelings"). Inasmuch as large numbers of working-class, immigrant, and racial ethnic women have long traditions of working in the formal and informal economic sectors, such assumptions are suspect.

Research on women of Mexican descent and employment indicates their labor force participation is lower than that of other women when they have young children.[18] Moreover, Chicanas and Mexicanas are occupationally segregated in the lowest-paying of female-dominated jobs.[19] Explanations for their unique employment situation range from analyses of labor market structures and employer discrimination[20] to deficient individual characteristics (for instance, education, job skills)[21] and cultural differences.[22]

Analyses of Chicana/Mexicana employment that utilize a cultural framework typically explain the women's lower labor force participation, higher fertility, lower levels of education, and higher levels of unemployment as part of an ethnic or cultural tradition.[23] That is, as this line of argument goes, Chicano/Mexican culture emphasizes a strong allegiance to an idealized form of motherhood and a patriarchal ideology that frowns upon working wives and mothers and does not encourage girls to pursue higher education or employment options. These attitudes are supposed to vary by generation, with immigrant women (from Mexico) holding the most conservative attitudes.[24]

There are two major flaws in the research on Chicana/Mexicana employment, however. First, inconsistency in distinguishing between native-born and resident immigrant women characterizes much of this literature. Second, overreliance on linear acculturation persists. Both procedures imply either that Chicanas and Mexicanas are very similar, or that they lie on a sort of "cultural continuum," with Mexican immigrants at one end holding more conservative behaviors and attitudes grounded in traditional (often rural) Mexican culture, and U.S.-born Chicanos holding an amalgamation of cultural traditions from Mexico and the United States.[25] In terms of motherhood and employment, therefore, Mexicanas should have more "traditional" ideas about motherhood than U.S.-born Chicanas. Since the traditional ideology of motherhood typically refers to women staying home to "mother" children rather than going outside the home to work, Mexicanas theoretically should not be as willing to work as Chicanas or North American women in general—unless there is severe economic need. This formulation, while logical, reflects an underlying emphasis on modernity—or the view that "traditional" Mexican culture lags behind North American culture in developing behaviors and attitudes conducive to participating fully in modern society.[26] Inasmuch as conventional North American views of motherhood typically idealize labor market exit to care for children, embracing this prototype may be more conducive to maintaining patriarchal privilege (female economic subordination to men) than facilitating economic progress generally. In this sense, conceptualizations of motherhood that affirm its economic character may be better accommodating to women's market participation in the United States.

The following section discusses the distinct views of motherhood articulated by Chicanas and Mexicanas and their impact on employment attitudes and behaviors. In contrast to the notion that exposure to North American values enhances women's incentives to work, proportionately more Chicanas than Mexicanas express ambivalence toward paid employment when they have children at home. I analyze these differences among a selected sample of clerical, service, and operative workers.

METHOD AND SAMPLE

This paper is based on in-depth interviews with thirty Mexican-origin women—thirteen Chicanas and seventeen Mexicanas—who had participated in the 1978 to 79 or 1980 to 81 cohorts of an adult education and employment training program in the greater San Francisco Bay Area.[27] All thirty respondents had been involved in a conjugal relationship (either legal marriage or informal cohabitation with a male partner) at some point in their lives before I interviewed them in 1985, and had at least one child under eighteen years of age. At the time of their interviews, six Chicanas and fourteen Mexicanas were married; seven Chicanas and three Mexicanas were single parents.

On the average, the married Chicanas have 1.2 children at home; the Mexicanas report 3.5 children. Both Chicana and Mexicana single mothers average 1.6 children. The children of the Chicanas tend to be preschool age or in elementary school. The children of the Mexicanas exhibit a greater age range (from infant to late adolescence), reflecting their earlier marriages and slightly older average age.

With respect to other relevant characteristics, all but two Mexicanas and five Chicanas had either a high school diploma or its equivalent (GED). The average age was 27.4 years for the Chicanas and thirty-three years for the Mexicanas.[28] Upon leaving the employment training program, all the women secured employment. At the time of their interviews, about half of the Chicanas ($n = 7$); and three-fourths of the Mexicanas ($n = 12$) were employed. Only two out of the seven (28 percent) employed Chicanas worked full-time (thirty-five or more hours per week) whereas nine out of the twelve (75 percent) employed Mexicanas worked full-time. Most of the Chicanas found clerical or service jobs (for example, teacher assistants); most of the Mexicanas labored in operative jobs or in the service sector (for example, hotel maids), with a small minority employed as clerical workers.

I gathered in-depth life and work histories from the women to ascertain:

1. What factors motivated them to enter, exit, and stay employed in their specific occupations;
2. whether familial roles or ideology influenced their employment consistency; and
3. whether other barriers limited their job attachment and mobility.

My examination of the relationship between motherhood and employment forms part of a larger study of labor market stratification and occupational mobility among Chicana and Mexican immigrant women.[29]

MOTHERHOOD AND EMPLOYMENT

Nearly all of the respondents, both Chicana and Mexicana, employed and nonemployed, speak of motherhood as their most important social role. They differ sharply in their employment behaviors and views regarding the relationship between motherhood and market work. Women fall into four major groups. The first group consists of five *Involuntary Nonemployed Mothers,* who are not employed but care full-time for their children. All of these women want to be employed at least part-time. They either cannot secure the job they want and/or feel pressured to be at home mothering full-time.

The second group consists of six *Voluntary Nonemployed Mothers* who are not employed but remain out of the labor force by *choice.* They feel committed to staying at home to care for preschool and/or elementary school age children.

The third category, *Ambivalent Employed Mothers,* includes eleven employed women. They have either preschool or elementary school age children. Women in this group believe that employment interferes with motherhood and feel "guilty" when they work outside the home. Despite these feelings, they are employed at least part-time.

The fourth group, *Nonambivalent Employed Mothers,* includes eight employed women. What distinguishes these women from the previous group is their view that employment and motherhood seem compatible social dynamics irrespective of the age of their children. All eight women are Mexicanas. Some of these women believe employment could be problematic, however, *if* a family member could not care for their children or be at home for the children when they arrived from school.

Chicanas tend to fall in the second and third categories, whereas Mexicanas predominate in the first and fourth groups. Three reasons emerged as critical in explaining this difference:

1. the economic situations of their families;
2. labor market structure (four-fifths of the nonemployed Mexicanas were involuntarily unemployed); and
3. women's conceptualizations of motherhood, in particular, their expressed *need* to mother.

Age of the women and number of children did not fall into any discernible pattern; therefore, I did not engage them in depth within my analysis.

First, I consider the situation of the Voluntary Nonemployed Mothers, including three married Chicanas, one single-parent Mexicana, and one single-parent Chicana. All but one woman exited the labor market involuntarily (for reasons such as layoffs or disability). All five women remain out of the labor force by choice. Among them, the expressed need to mother appears strong—overriding all other concerns. They view motherhood as mutually exclusive from employment. Lydia, a married Chicana with a small toddler, articulates this perspective:

> Right now, since we've had the baby, I feel, well he [her husband] feels the same way, that I want to spend this time with her and watch her grow up. See, because when I was small my grandmother raised me so I felt this *loss* [her emphasis] when my grandmother died. And I've never gotten that *real love*, that mother love from my mother. We have a friendship, but we don't have that "motherly love." I want my daughter to know that I'm here, especially at her age, it's very important for them to know that when they cry that mama's there. Even if it's not a painful cry, it's still important for them to know that mommy's there. She's my number one—she's all my attention. . . . so working-wise, it's up to [her husband] right now.

Susana, a Chicana single parent with a five-year-old child, said:

> I'm the type of person that has always wanted to have a family. I think it was more like I didn't have a family-type home when I was growing up. I didn't have a mother and a father and the kids all together in the same household all happy. I didn't have that. And that's what I want more than anything! I want to be different from my mother, who has worked hard and is successful in her job. I don't want to be successful in the same way.

Lydia, Susana, and the other voluntarily unemployed Chicanas adamantly assert that motherhood requires staying home with their children. Susana said: "A good mother is there for her children all the time when they are little and when they come home from school." All the Chicanas in this category believe that motherhood means staying home with

children—even if it means going on welfare (AFDC). This finding is similar to other accounts of working-class women.[30]

The sense shared among this group of women that motherhood and employment are irreconcilable, especially when children are of preschool age, is related to their social locations. A small minority of the Chicanas had been raised by nonemployed mothers ($n = 3$). They feel they should stay at home with their children as long as it's economically feasible. Most of the Chicanas, however, resemble Lydia and Susana, who had been raised by employed mothers. Although these women recognize that their mothers had worked out of economic need, they believe they did not receive sufficient love and care from their mothers. Throughout their interviews, this group of Chicanas expressed hostility and resentment against their employed mothers for leaving them with other caretakers. These feelings contribute to their decisions to stay at home with their children, and/or their sense of "guilt" when they are employed. Their hostility and guilt defy psychoanalytic theories that speculate that the cycle of gender construction locking women into "exclusive mothering" roles can be broken if the primary caretaker (the mother) undertakes more diverse roles.[31] Rather, Chicanas appear to value current conceptionalizations of motherhood that prioritize the expressive work of the mother, as distinct from her economic activities.

This group of Chicanas seems to be pursuing the social construction of motherhood that is idealized within their ethnic community, their churches, and society at large.[32] Among Chicanos and Mexicanos the image of *la madre* as self-sacrificing and holy is a powerful standard against which women often compare themselves.[33] The Chicana informants also seem to accept the notion that women's primary duty is to provide for the emotional welfare of the children, and that economic activities which take them outside the home are secondary. Women's desire to enact the socially constructed motherhood ideal was further strengthened by their conviction that many of their current problems (for instance, low levels of education, feelings of inadequacy, single parenthood) are related to growing up in families that did not conform to the stay-at-home mother/father-as-provider configuration. Their evaluation of the close relationship between motherhood and economic or emotional well-being of offspring parallels popular emphasis on the primacy of individual efforts and the family environment to emotional vigor and achievement.[34]

Informants in this group speak to a complex dimension of mothering and gender construction in the Chicano/Mexicano communities. These women reject their employed mothers' organization of family life. As children, most had been cared for by other family members, and now feel closer to their grandmothers or other female relatives than to their own biological mothers. This causes them considerable pain—pain they want to spare their own children. Many, like Susana, do not want to be "successful" in the tradition of their own employed mothers. Insofar as "success" means leaving their children with other caretakers, it contradicts their conceptualization of motherhood. Rather, they frame "success" in more affective terms: having children who are happy and doing well in school. This does not suggest that Chicanas disagree with the notion that having a good job or a lucrative career denotes "success." They simply feel that successful careers could and should be deferred until their children are older (for instance, in the upper grades of elementary school) and doing well academically and emotionally.

Only one married Mexicana, Belen, articulated views similar to those of the Chicanas. Belen left the labor market in 1979 to give birth and care for her newborn child. It is important to note that she has a gainfully employed husband who does not believe mothers should work outside the home. Belen, who has two children and was expecting a third when I interviewed her, said:

> I wanted to work or go back to school after having my first son, but my husband didn't want me to. He said, "No one can take care of your child the way you can." He did not want me to work. And I did not feel right having someone else care for my son. So I decided to wait until my children were older.

Belen's words underscore an important dynamic that impacted on both Mexicana and Chicana conceptualizations of motherhood: spousal employment and private patriarchy. Specifically, husbands working in full-time, year-round jobs with earnings greater than those of their wives tended to pressure women to mother full-time. Women who succumb to this pressure become economically dependent on their husbands and reaffirm male authority in the organization of the family. These particular women tend to consider motherhood and employment in similar

ways. This suggests that the form the social construction of motherhood takes involves women's economic relationship to men as well as length of time in the United States.

Four Mexicanas and one Chicana were involuntarily nonemployed. They had been laid off from their jobs or were on temporary disability leave. Three women (two Mexicanas/one Chicana) were seeking employment; the other two were in the last stages of pregnancy but intended to look for a job as soon as possible after their child's birth. All five women reported feeling "good" about being home with their children but wanted to rejoin the labor force as soon as possible. Ideologically these women view motherhood and employment as reconcilable social dynamics. As Isabel, an unemployed production worker, married with eight children, said:

> I believe that women always work more. We who are mothers work to maintain the family by working outside, but also inside the house caring for the children.

Isabel voiced a sentiment held by all of the informants—that women work hard at motherhood. Since emigrating to the U.S. about a decade ago, Isabel had been employed nearly continuously, with only short leaves for childbearing. Isabel and nearly all of the Mexicanas described growing up in environments where women, men, and children were important economic actors. In this regard they are similar to the Nonambivalent Employed Mothers—all of whom are also Mexicanas. They tended not to dichotomize social life in the same way as the Voluntary Nonemployed Chicanas and Ambivalent Employed informants.

Although all of the Chicanas believe that staying home best fulfills their mother roles, slightly fewer than half actually stay out of the labor market to care for their young children. The rest of the Chicanas are employed and struggling to reconcile motherhood with employment. I refer to these women as Ambivalent Employed Mothers. They express guilt about working and assert they *would not work* if they did not have to for economic reasons. Seven of these women are Chicanas; four are Mexicanas.

To try and alleviate their guilt and help meet their families' economic goals, most of the Chicanas work in part-time jobs. This option permits them to be home when their children arrive from school. Despite this, they feel guilty and unhappy about working. As Jenny, a married Chicana with two children, ages two and four, who is employed part-time, said:

> Sure, I feel guilty. I *should* [her emphasis] be with them [her children] while they're little. He [her husband] really feels that I should be with my kids all the time. And it's true.

Despite their guilt, most of the women in this group remain employed because their jobs offer them the means to provide for family economic betterment—a goal that transcends staying home with their children. However, women's utilization of economic rationales for working sometimes served as a smokescreen for individualistic desires to "do something outside the home" and to establish a degree of autonomy. Several women, for example, stated that they enjoyed having their "own money." When I asked these women to elaborate, they typically retreated to a familistic stance. That is, much of *her* money is used *for the family* (for example, child care, family presents, clothing). When money is used *for the woman* (makeup, going out with the girls) it is often justified as necessary for her emotional well-being, which in turn helps her to be a good wife and mother.

The Mexicana mothers who are employed express their ambivalence somewhat differently from the Chicanas. One Mexicana works full-time; the other three are employed part-time. Angela, a Mexicana married with one child and employed full-time as a seamstress, told me with glistening eyes:

> Always I have had to work. I had to leave my son with the baby-sitter since he was six months old. It was difficult. Each baby-sitter has their own way of caring for children, which isn't like yours. I know the baby-sitter wouldn't give him the food I left. He always had on dirty diapers and was starving when I would pick him up. But there wasn't any other recourse. I had to work. I would just clean him and feed him when I got home.

Angela's "guilt" stemmed from her inability to find good, affordable child care. Unlike most of the Mexicanas, who had extensive family networks, Angela and her husband had few relatives to rely on in the U.S. Unlike the Chicana informants, Angela did not want to exit the labor market to care for her child. Her desire is reinforced by economic need; her

husband is irregularly employed.[35] For the other three Mexicanas in this group, guilt as an employed mother appears to have developed with stable spousal employment. That is, the idea of feeling guilty about full-time employment emerged *after* husbands became employed in secure, well-paying jobs and "reminded" them of the importance of stay-at-home, full-time motherhood. Lourdes, who was married with eight children and working as a part-time hotel maid said:

> I was offered a job at a—factory, working from eleven at night to seven in the morning. But I had a baby and so I wasn't able to work. I would have liked to take the job because it paid $8.25 an hour. I couldn't though, because of my baby. And my husband didn't want me to work at night. He said, "If we both work at night, who will take care of the children?" So I didn't take the job.

To thwart potential guilt over full-time employment and to ease marital tension (if she had taken this job she would have earned more money than her husband), Lourdes declined this high-paying job. When her child turned two, she opted to work part-time as a hotel maid. Lourdes, and the other Mexicanas employed part-time, told me that they *would* work full-time *if* their husbands supported their preferences. Mexicanas' ambivalence, then, is related to unease about their children's child care situations, as well as to anger at being held accountable to a narrow construction of motherhood enforced by their husbands.

All Ambivalent Employed Mothers report worrying about their children while at work. While this does not necessarily impair their job performance, it adds another psychological or emotional burden on their shoulders. This burden affects their ability to work full-time (overtime is especially problematic) or seek the means (especially schooling) to advance in their jobs.

Women seem particularly troubled when they have to work on weekends. This robs them of precious family time. As Elena, a Chicana single parent with two children, ages nine and three, who works part-time as a hotel maid, said:

> Yes, I work on weekends. And my kids, you know how kids are—they don't like it. And it's hard. But I hope to find a job soon where the schedule is

fixed and I won't have to work on weekends—because that time should be for my kids.

There is a clear sense among the women I interviewed that a boundary between *time for the family* and *market time* should exist. During times when this boundary folds, women experience both internal conflict (within the woman herself) and external conflict (among family members). They regard jobs that overlap on family time with disfavor and unhappiness. When economic reasons compel women to work during what they view as family time, they usually try to find as quickly as possible a different job that allows them to better meet their mother roles.

Interestingly, the Chicanas appear less flexible in reconciling the boundaries of family time and market time than the Mexicanas. That is, Chicanas overwhelmingly "choose" part-time employment to limit the amount of spillover time from employment on motherhood and family activities. Mexicanas, on the other hand, overwhelmingly work full-time ($n = 9$) and attempt to do both familial caretaking and market work as completely as possible.

This leads us to consider the fourth category I call Nonambivalent Employed Mothers. This category consists of Mexicana immigrants, both married and single-parent (six and two women, respectively). Mexicanas in this group do not describe motherhood as a *need* requiring a separate sphere for optimal realization. Rather, they refer to motherhood as one function of womanhood compatible with employment insofar as employment allows them to provide for their family's economic subsistence or betterment. As Pilar, a married Mexicana with four children, employed full-time as a line supervisor in a factory, said: "I work to help my children. That's what a mother should do." This group of Mexicanas does not express *guilt* over leaving their children in the care of others so much as *regret* over the limited amount of time they could spend with them. As Norma, a Mexicana full-time clerical worker who is married with two children ages three and five, said:

I don't feel guilty for leaving my children because if I didn't work they might not have the things they have now. . . . Perhaps if I had to stay at home I would feel guilty and frustrated. I'm not the type that can stay home twenty-four hours a day. I don't think that would help my children any because I would feel pressured at being cooped up

[*encerrada*] at home. And that way I wouldn't have the same desire to play with my daughters. But now, with the time we have together, we do things that we want to, like run in the park, because there's so little time.

All of the Mexicanas in this group articulate views similar to Norma's. Their greater comfort with the demands of market and family work emanates from their social locations. All of the Mexicanas come from poor or working-class families, where motherhood embraced both economic and affective features. Their activities were not viewed as equal to those of men, however, and ideologically women saw themselves as *helping* the family rather than *providing* for it.

Few Mexicanas reported that their mothers were wage-laborers ($n = 3$); rather, they described a range of economic activities they remembered women doing "for the family."[36] Mexicanas from rural villages ($n = 7$) recounted how their mothers had worked on the land and made assorted products or food to sell in local marketplaces. Mexicanas from urban areas ($n = 5$) also discussed how their mothers had been economically active. Whether rural or urban, Mexicanas averred that their mothers had taught them to "help" the family as soon as possible. As Norma said:

My mother said: "It's one thing for a woman to lie around the house but it's a different thing for the work that needs to be done. As the saying goes, Work is never done; the work does you in [*El trabajo acaba con uno; uno nunca acaba con el trabajo*].

Lourdes and two other Mexicanas cleaned houses with their mothers after school. Other mothers sold clothes to neighbors, cooked and sold food, or did assorted services for pay (for example, giving penicillin shots to neighbors). The Mexicanas do not view these activities as "separate" or less important than the emotional nurturing of children and family. Rather, they appreciate both the economic and the expressive as important facets of motherhood.

Although the Mexicanas had been raised in worlds where women were important economic actors, this did not signify gender equality. On the contrary, male privilege, or patriarchy, characterizes the organization of the family, the economy, and the polity in both rural and urban Mexican society.[37] In the present study, Mexicanas indicated that men wielded greater authority in the family, the community, and the state than women. Mexicanas also tended to uphold male privilege in the family by viewing both domestic work and women's employment as "less important" than the work done by men. As Adela, a married Mexicana with four children, said: "Men are much stronger and do much more difficult work than women." Mexicanas also tended to defer to husbands as the "head" of the family—a position they told me was both "natural" and "holy."[38]

WORKING AT MOTHERHOOD

The differences presented here between the Chicanas and Mexicanas regarding motherhood and employment stem from their distinct social locations. Raised in rural or working-class families in Mexico, the Mexicanas described childhoods where they and their mothers actively contributed to the economic subsistence of their families by planting crops, harvesting, selling homemade goods, and cleaning houses. Their situations resonate with what some researchers term a family economy, where all family members work at productive tasks differentiated mainly by age and sex.[39] In this type of structure, there is less distinction between economic life and domestic life. Motherhood in this context is both economic and expressive, embracing employment as well as child-rearing.

The family economy the Mexicanas experienced differs from the family organization that characterizes most of the Chicanas' childhoods. The Chicanas come from a world that idealizes a male wage earner as the main economic "provider," with women primarily as consumers and only secondarily as economic actors.[40] Women in this context are mothers first, wage earners second. Families that challenge this structure are often discredited, or perceived as dysfunctional and the source of many social problems.[41] The ambivalence Chicanas recurrently voice stems from their belief in what Kanter calls "the myth of separate worlds."[42] They seek to realize the popular notion or stereotype that family is a separate structure—a haven in a heartless world. Their attachment to this ideal is underscored by a harsh critique of their own employed mothers and themselves *when* they work full-time. Motherhood framed within this context appears irreconcilable with employment.

There are other facets to the differences between Chicanas and Mexicanas. The Mexicanas, as immigrant women, came to the United States with a vision of improving the life chances of their families and themselves. This finding intersects with research on "selective immigration." That is, Mexican immigrants tend to possess higher levels of education than the national average in Mexico, and a wide range of behavioral characteristics (for instance, high achievement orientation) conducive to success in the United States.[43]

The Mexicanas emigrated hoping to work—hence their high attachment to employment, even in physically demanding, often demeaning jobs. Mexican and Chicano husbands support their wives' desires to work *so long as* this employment does not challenge the patriarchal structure of the family. In other words, so long as the Mexicanas: (1) articulate high attachment to motherhood *and* family caretaker roles, (2) frame their employment in terms of family economic goals, and (3) do not ask men to do equal amounts of housework or child care, they encounter little resistance from husbands or other male family members.

When Mexican and Chicano husbands secure good jobs, however, they begin pressuring wives to quit working or to work only part-time. In this way, Mexican and Chicano men actively pursue continuity of their superordinate position within the family. This suggests that the way motherhood is conceptualized in both the Mexican and Chicano communities, particularly with respect to employment, is wedded to male privilege, or patriarchy. Ironically, then, Mexicanas' sense of employment's continuity with motherhood enhances their job attachment but does not challenge a patriarchal family structure or ethos.

Similarly, Chicanas' preference for an idealized form of motherhood does not challenge male privilege in their community. Their desire to stay at home to mother exercised a particularly strong influence on the employment behavior of single-parent Chicanas and women with husbands employed in relatively good jobs. This preference reflects an adherence to an idealized, middle-class lifestyle that glorifies women's domestic roles, as well as to maintenance of a patriarchal family order. Chicanas feel they should stay at home to try and provide their children with the mothering they believe children should have—mothering that many of them had not experienced. Chicanas also feel compelled by husbands and the larger community to maintain the status of men as "good providers." Men earning wages adequate to provide for their families' needs usually urged their wives to leave the labor market. While the concept of the good provider continues to be highly valued in our society, it also serves as a rationale that upholds male privilege ideologically and materially, and reinforces the myth of separate spheres that emanates from the organization of the family and the economy.

CONCLUSION

By illustrating how Chicanas and Mexicanas differ in their conceptualizations and organization of the motherhood and employment nexus, this study demonstrates how motherhood is a culturally formed structure with various meanings and subtexts. The vitality of these differences among a group whose members share a common historical origin and many cultural attributes underscores the need for frameworks that analyze diversity among all groups of women. Most essential to such an undertaking is a critique of the privileging of the "separate spheres" concept in analyses of women and work.

The present study provides additional coherence to recent contentions that the private–public dichotomy lacks immediate relevance to less privileged women (for instance, Chicana and Mexican immigrant women). In the process of illustrating how Chicanas and Mexicanas organized the interplay between motherhood and employment, it became clear that a more useful way of understanding this intersection might be to problematize motherhood itself. Considering motherhood from the vantage point of women's diverse social locations revealed considerable heterogeneity in how one might speak of it. For example, motherhood has an economic component for both groups of women, but it is most strongly expressed by Mexicana immigrants. The flavor of the expressive, however, flows easily across both groups of women, and for the Mexicanas embraces the economic. What this suggests is that the dichotomy of the separate spheres lacks relevance to Chicanas and Mexicanas and other women whose social origins make economic work necessary for survival.

This leads us to consider the relative place and function of the ideology of motherhood prevalent in our society. Motherhood constructed to privilege the woman who stays at home serves a myriad of functions. It pushes women to dichotomize their lives

rather than develop a sense of fluidity across roles, responsibilities, and preferences. Idealized, stay-at-home motherhood eludes most American women with children. As an ideology, however, it tells them what "should be," rendering them failures *as women* when they enter the labor market. Hence the feelings of ambivalence that characterized employed mothers' lives for the most part—except those who had not yet internalized these standards. The present research provided examples of such women, along with the understanding that other women from different social locations may demonstrate distinct ways of organizing the motherhood–employment nexus as well.

Feminist analyses of women and work emphasize the role of patriarchy to maintain male privilege and domination economically and ideologically. It is important to recognize that male privilege is not experienced equally by all men, and that patriarchy itself can be expressed in different ways. The present study found that notions of motherhood among Mexicanas and Chicanas are embedded in different ideological constructs operating within two systems of patriarchy. For Mexicanas, patriarchy takes the form of a corporate family model, with all members contributing to the common good. For Chicanas, the patriarchal structure centers more closely around a public–private dichotomy that idealizes men as economic providers and women primarily as caretakers-consumers.

The finding that women from more "traditional" backgrounds (such as rural Mexico) are likely to approach full-time employment with less ambivalence than more "American" women (such as the Chicanas) rebuts linear acculturation models that assume a negative relationship between ideologies (such as motherhood) constructed within "traditional" Mexican society and employment. It also complements findings on the negative relationship between greater length of time in the United States and high aspirations among Mexicans.[44] This suggests that employment problems (for example, underemployment, unemployment) are related less to "traditional" cultural configurations than to labor market structure and employment policies. Understanding the intersections between employment policy, social ideology, and private need is a necessary step toward expanding possibilities for women in our society.

NOTES

1. This article is a revised version of "Ambivalence or Continuity? Motherhood and Employment among Chicanas and Mexican Immigrant Women," *AZTLAN, International Journal of Chicano Studies Research* (1992). I would like to thank Maxine Baca Zinn, Evelyn Nakano Glenn, Arlie Hochschild, Beatriz Pesquera, and Vicki Ruiz for their constructive feedback and criticism of earlier drafts of this paper. A special thanks goes to Jon Cruz for his assistance in titling this paper. Any remaining errors or inconsistencies are my own responsibility. This research was supported in part by a 1986–87 University of California President's Postdoctoral Fellowship.

2. Betsy Wearing, *The Ideology of Motherhood, A Study of Sydney Suburban Mothers* (Sydney: George Allen and Unwin, 1984); Barbara J. Berg, *The Crisis of the Working Mother, Resolving the Conflict between Family and Work* (New York: Summit Books, 1986); Nancy Folbre "The Pauperization of Motherhood: Patriarchy and Public Policy in the United States," *Review of Radical Political Economics* 16 (1984). The view that mothers should not work outside the home typically pertains to married women. Current state welfare policies (e.g., Aid to Families with Dependent Children [AFDC], workfare) indicate that single, unmarried mothers belong in the labor force, not at home caring for their children full-time. See Naomi Gerstel and Harriet Engel Gross, "Introduction," in N. Gerstel and H. E. Gross, eds., *Families and Work* (Philadelphia: Temple University Press, 1987), pp. 1–12; Deborah K. Zinn and Rosemary C. Sarri, "Turning Back the Clock on Public Welfare," in *Signs: Journal of Women in Culture and Society* 10 (1984), pp. 355–370; Nancy Folbre "The Pauperization of Motherhood;" Nancy A. Naples, "A Socialist Feminist Analysis of the Family Support Act of 1988," AFFILIA 6 (1991), pp. 23–38.

3. Allyson Sherman Grossman, "More than Half of All Children Have Working Mothers," Special Labor Force Reports—Summaries, *Monthly Labor Review* (February 1982), pp. 41–43; Howard Hayghe, "Working Mothers Reach Record Number in 1984," *Monthly Labor Review* 107 (December 1984), pp. 31–34; U.S. Bureau of The Census "Fertility of American Women: June 1990," *Current Population Report*, Series P-20, No. 454, (Washington D.C.: United States Government Printing Office, 1991). In June 1990, over half (53.1 percent) of women between the ages of 18 and 44 who had had a child in the last year were in the labor force. This proportion varied by race: 54.9 percent of white women, 46.9 percent of Black women, and 44.4 percent of Latinas were in the labor force. See U.S. Bureau of the Census (1991), p. 5.

4. Simon and Landis report that a 1986 Gallup Poll indicates that support for married women to work outside the home is considerably greater than 1938 levels: 76 percent of women and 78 percent of men approve (1989: 270). Comparable 1938 levels are 25 percent and 19 percent,

respectively, of women and men. The 1985 Roper Poll finds the American public adhering to the view that a husband's career supersedes that of his wife: 72 percent of women and 62 percent of men agree that a wife should quit her job and relocate if her husband is offered a good job in another city (1989: 272). In the reverse situation, 20-percent of women and 22 percent of men believe a husband should quit his job and relocate with his wife (1989: 272). Simon and Landis conclude: "The Women's Movement has not radicalized the American woman: she is still prepared to put marriage and children ahead of her career and to allow her husband's status to determine the family's position in society" (1989: 269). Rita J. Simon and Jean M. Landis, "Women's and Men's Attitudes about a Woman's Place and Role," *Public Opinion Quarterly* 53 (1989), pp. 265–276.

5. Arlie Hochschild with Anne Machung, *The Second Shift, Working Parents and the Revolution at Home* (New York: Viking Penguin Books, 1989); Kathleen Gerson, *Hard Choices* (Berkeley: University of California Press, 1985); Barbara J. Berg, *The Crisis of the Working Mother, Resolving the Conflict between Family and Work* (New York: Summit Books, 1986). The concept of "separate spheres" is approached in a variety of ways and often critiqued. See Michele Barrett, *Women's Oppression Today, Problems in Marxist Feminist Analysis* (London: Verso Press, 1980); Nona Glazer "Servants to Capital: Unpaid Domestic Labor and Paid Work," *Review of Radical Economics* 16 (1984), pp. 61–87. Zaretsky contends that distinct family and market spheres arose with the development of industrial capitalism: "Men and women came to see the family as separate from the economy, and personal life as a separate sphere of life divorced from the larger economy." See Eli Zaretsky, *Capitalism, The Family and Personal Life* (New York: Harper Colophon Books, 1976), p. 78. This stance is substantially different from that of early radical feminist approaches, including Firestone, who argued that the separation antedates history. See Shulamith Firestone, *The Dialectic of Sex* (New York: Bantam Books, 1970). Other scholars assert that the relations of production and reproduction are intertwined and virtually inseparable. See Heidi Hartmann, "Capitalism, Patriarchy and Job Segregation by Sex," in Martha Blaxall and Barbara Reagan, eds., *Women and the Work Place* (Chicago: University of Chicago Press, 1976), pp. 137–169.

6. Hood argues that the "ideal" of stay-at-home motherhood and male provider has historically been an unrealistic standard for families outside the middle and upper classes. She points out that early surveys of urban workers indicate between 40 and 50 percent of all families supplemented their income with the earnings of wives and children. See Jane C. Hood, "The Provider Role: Its Meaning and Measurement," *Journal of Marriage and the Family* 48 (May 1986), pp. 349–359.

7. It should be noted that native-born status is not an essential requirement for the ethnic label "Chicana/o."

There are numerous identifiers used by people of Mexican descent, including: Chicana/o, Mexican, Mexican-American, Mexicana/o, Latina/o, and Hispanic. Often people of Mexican descent use two or three of the above labels, depending on the social situation (e.g., "Mexican-American" in the family or "Chicana/o" at school). See John A. Garcia, "Yo Soy Mexicano . . . : Self-identity and Sociodemographic Correlates," *Social Science Quarterly* 62 (March, 1981), pp. 88–98; Susan E. Keefe and Amado M. Padilla, *Chicano Ethnicity* (Albuquerque, NM: University of New Mexico Press, 1987). My designation of study informants as either "Chicana" or "Mexicana" represents an analytic separation that facilitates demonstrating the heterogeneity among this group.

8. Patricia Zavella, "Reflections on Diversity among Chicanos," *Frontiers* 2 (1991), p. 75.

9. See Rosalia Solorzano-Torres, "Female Mexican Immigrants in San Diego County," in V. L. Ruiz and S. Tiano, eds., *Women on the U.S.-Mexico Border: Responses to Change* (Boston: Allen and Unwin, 1987), pp. 41–59; Reynaldo Baca and Bryan Dexter, "Mexican Women, Migration and Sex Roles," *Migration Today* 13 (1985), pp. 14–18; Sylvia Guendelman and Auristela Perez-Itriago, "Double Lives: The Changing Role of Women in Seasonal Migration," *Women's Studies* 13 (1987), pp. 249–271.

10. Gary S. Becker, "Human Capital, Effort, and the Sexual Division of Labor," *Journal of Labor Economics* 3 (1985 Supplement), pp. S33–S58; Gary S. Becker, *A Treatise on the Family* (Cambridge, MA: Harvard University Press, 1981); Solomon W. Polachek, "Occupational Self-Selection: A Human Capital Approach to Sex Differences in Occupational Structure," *Review of Economics and Statistics* 63 (1981), pp. 60–69; S.Polachek, "Occupational Segregation among Women: Theory, Evidence, and a Prognosis" in C. B. Lloyd, E. S. Andrews and C. L. Gilroy, eds., *Women in the Labor Market* (New York: Columbia University Press, 1981), pp. 137–157; S. Polachek, "Discontinuous Labor Force Participation and Its Effect on Women's Market Earnings," in C. Lloyd, ed., *Sex Discrimination and the Division of Labor* (New York: Columbia University Press, 1975), pp. 90–122. Becker's classic treatise, *Human Capital,* uses the following example borrowed from G. Stigler, "The Economics of Information," *Journal of Political Economy* (June 1961): "Women spend less time in the labor force than men and, therefore, have less incentive than residents of the area to invest in knowledge of specific consumption activities." See Gary S. Becker, *Human Capital* (Chicago: University of Chicago Press, 1975), p. 74.

11. Some institutional economists argue that "statistical discrimination" is one critical labor market dynamic that often impedes women and minorities. See Kenneth Arrow, "Economic Dimensions of Occupational Segregation: Comment I," *Signs; Journal of Women in Culture and Society* 1 (1987), pp. 233–237; Edmund Phelps, "The Statistical Theory of Racism and Sexism," in A. H. Amsden, ed., *The Economics*

of Women and Work (New York: St. Martin's Press, 1980), pp. 206–210. This perspective suggests that prospective employers often lack detailed information about individual applicants and therefore utilize statistical averages and normative views of the relevant group(s) to which the applicant belongs in their hiring decisions (e.g., college-educated men tend to be successful and committed employees; all women are potential mothers; or women tend to exit the labor force for childbearing).

Bielby and Baron pose an important critique to the underlying rationale of statistical discrimination. They argue that utilizing perceptions of group differences between the sexes is "neither as rational nor as efficient as the economists believe." That is, utilizing stereotypical notions of "men's work" and "women's work" is often costly to employers and therefore irrational. This suggests that sex segregation is embedded in organizational policies which reflect and reinforce "belief systems that are also rather inert." See William T. Bielby and James N. Baron, "Undoing Discrimination: Job Integration and Comparable Worth," in C. Bose and G. Spitze, eds., *Ingredients for Women's Employment Policy* (New York: State University of New York Press, 1987), p. 216, pp. 221–222.

12. Annette Kuhn, "Structure of Patriarchy and Capital in the Family," in A. Kuhn and Annemarie Wolfe, eds., *Feminism and Materialism: Women and Modes of Production* (London: Routledge and Kegan Paul, 1978); Heidi Hartmann, "Capitalism, Patriarchy, and Job Segregation by Sex," in Martha Blaxall and Barbara Reagan, eds., *Women and the Work Place* (Chicago: University of Chicago Press, 1976), pp. 137–169; H. Hartmann, "The Family as the Locus of Gender, Class, and Political Struggle: The Example of Housework," *Signs: Journal of Women in Culture and Society* 6 (1981), pp. 366–394; Michele Barrett, *Women's Oppression Today, Problems in Marxist Feminist Analysis* (London: Verso Press, 1980).

13. Lourdes Beneria and Martha Roldan, *The Crossroads of Class and Gender, Industrial Homework, Subcontracting, and Household Dynamics in Mexico City* (Chicago: The University of Chicago Press, 1987); L. Beneria and Gita Sen, "Accumulation, Reproduction, and Women's Role in Economic Development: Boserup Revisited," in E. Leacock and H. I. Safa, eds., *Women's Work: Development and Division of Labor by Gender* (Massachusetts: Bergin and Garvey Publishers, 1986), pp. 141–157; Dorothy Smith, "Women's Inequality and the Family," in N. Gerstel and H. E. Gross, eds., *Families and Work* (Philadelphia: Temple University Press, 1987), pp. 23–54.

14. This phrase was coined by Arlie R. Hochschild and quoted in Lillian B. Rubin, *Intimate Strangers, Men and Women Together* (New York: Harper and Row, 1983).

15. Rosabeth Moss Kanter, *Men and Women in the Corporation* (New York: Basic Books, 1977). Bielby and Baron note: "Employers expect certain behaviors from women (e.g., high turnover) and therefore assign them to routine

tasks and dead-end jobs. Women respond by exhibiting the very behavior employers expect, thereby reinforcing the stereotype." Bielby and Baron, "Undoing Discrimination: Job Integration and Comparable Worth," p. 221.

16. Arlie Hochschild with Anne Machung, *The Second Shift, Working Parents and the Revolution of Home* (New York: Viking Penguin Books, 1989).

17. Barbara J. Berg, *The Crisis of the Working Mother, Resolving the Conflict between Family and Work* (New York: Summit Books, 1986), p. 42.

18. Howard Hayghe, "Working Mothers Reach Record Number in 1984," *Monthly Labor Review* 107 (December 1984), pp. 31–34; U.S. Bureau of the Census, "Fertility of American Women: June 1990" in Current Population Report, Series P-20, No. 454 (Washington D.C.: United States Government Printing Office, 1991); U.S. Bureau of Census Report, "Fertility of American Women: June 1986" in Current Population Report, Series P-20. No. 421 (Washington, D.C.: United States Government Printing Press). In June 1986 (the year closest to the year I interviewed the respondents where I found relevant data), 49.8 percent of all women with newborn children were in the labor force. Women demonstrated differences in this behavior: 49.7 percent of white women, 51.1 percent of Black women, and 40.6 percent of Latinas with newborn children were in the labor force. See U.S. Bureau of the Census "Fertility of American Women: June 1986" (1987), p. 5.

19. Bonnie Thornton Dill, Lynn Weber Cannon, and Reeve Vanneman, "Pay Equity: An Issue of Race, Ethnicity, and Sex" (Washington D.C.: National Commission on Pay Equity, February, 1987); Julianne Malveaux and Phyllis Wallace, "Minority Women in the Workplace," in K. S. Koziara, M. Moskow, and L. Dewey Tanner, eds., *Women and Work: Industrial Relations Research Association Research Volume* (Washington D.C.: Bureau of National Affairs, 1987), pp. 265–298; Vicki L. Ruiz, "'And Miles to go. . . .': Mexican Women and Work, 1930–1985" in L. Schlissel, V. L. Ruiz, and J. Monk, eds., *Western Women, Their Land, Their Lives* (Albuquerque: University of New Mexico Press, 1988), pp. 117–136.

20. Mario Barrera, *Race and Class in the Southwest: A Theory of Racial Inequality* (Notre Dame, IN: University of Notre Dame Press, 1979); Tomas Almaguer, "Class, Race, and Chicano Oppression," in *Socialist Revolution* 5 (1975), pp. 71–99; Denise Segura, "Labor Market Stratification: The Chicana Experience," *Berkeley Journal of Sociology* 29 (1984), pp. 57–91.

21. Marta Tienda and P. Guhleman, "The Occupational Position of Employed Hispanic Women," in G. J. Borjas and M. Tienda, eds., *Hispanics in the U.S. Economy* (New York: Academic Press, 1985), pp. 243–273.

22. Edgar J. Kranau, Vicki Green, and Gloria Valencia-Weber, "Acculturation and the Hispanic Woman: Attitudes towards Women, Sex-Role Attribution, Sex-Role Behavior, and Demographics," *Hispanic Journal of Behavioral Sciences* 4 (1982), pp. 21–40; Alfredo Mirande and Evangelina Enriquez, *La Chicana, The Mexican American Woman* (Chicago: The University of Chicago Press, 1979).

23. Kranau, Green, and Valencia-Weber, "Acculturation and the Hispanic Woman," pp. 21–40; Alfredo Mirande, *The Chicano Experience: An Alternative Perspective* (Notre Dame: University of Notre Dame Press, 1985).

24. Vilma Ortiz and Rosemary Santana Cooney, "Sex-Role Attitudes and Labor Force Participation among Young Hispanic Females and Non-Hispanic White Females," *Social Science Quarterly* 65 (June 1984), pp. 392–400.

25. Susan E. Keefe and Amado M. Padilla, *Chicano Ethnicity* (Albuquerque, NM: University of New Mexico Press, 1987); Richard H. Mendoza, "Acculturation and Sociocultural Variability," in J. L. Martinez Jr. and R. H. Mendoza, eds., *Chicano Psychology*, 2nd ed. (New York: Academic Press, 1984), pp. 61–75.

26. Maxine Baca Zinn, "Mexican-American Women in the Social Sciences," *Signs: Journal of Women in Culture and Society* 8 (1982), pp. 259–272. M. Baca Zinn, "Employment and Education of Mexican-American Women: The Interplay of Modernity and Ethnicity in Eight Families," *Harvard Educational Review* 50 (February 1980), pp. 47–62. M. Baca Zinn, "Chicano Family Research: Conceptual Distortions and Alternative Directions," *Journal of Ethnic Studies* 7 (1979) pp. 59–71.

27. For additional information on the methods and sample selection, I refer the reader to Denise A. Segura, "Chicanas and Mexican Immigrant Women in the Labor Market: A Study of Occupational Mobility and Stratification," unpublished Ph.D. dissertation, Department of Sociology, University of California, Berkeley (1986).

28. The ages of the Chicanas range from 23 to 42 years. The Mexicanas reported ages from 24 to 45. The age profile indicates that most of the women were in peak childbearing years.

29. Denise A. Segura, "Chicanas and Mexican Immigrant Women in the Labor Market."

30. For an example, see Betsy Wearing, *The Ideology of Motherhood, A Study of Sydney Suburban Mothers* (Sydney: George Allen and Unwin, 1984).

31. For an example, see Nancy Chodorow, *The Reproduction of Mothering* (Berkeley: University of California Press, 1979).

32. Manuel Ramirez III and Alfredo Castaneda, *Cultural Democracy, Bicognitive Development, and Education* (New York: Academic Press, 1974); Robert F. Peck and Rogelio Diaz-Guerrero, "Two Core-Culture Patterns and the Diffusion of Values Across Their Borders," *International Journal of Psychology* 2 (1967), pp. 272–282; Javier I. Escobat and E. T. Randolph, "The Hispanic and Social Networks," in R. M. Becerra, M. Karno, and J. I. Escobar, eds., *Mental Health and Hispanic Americans: Clinical Perspectives* (New York: Grune and Stratton, 1982).

33. Alfredo Mirande and Evangelina Enriquez, *La Chicana, The Mexican American Woman* (Chicago: The University of Chicago Press, 1979); Margarita Melville, "Introduction" and "Matrascence" in M. B. Melville, ed., *Twice a Minority: Mexican American Women* (St. Louis: The C. V. Mosby Co., 1980), pp. 1–16; Gloria Anzaldúa, *Borderlands, La Frontera: The New Mestiza* (San Francisco: Spinsters/Aunt Lute Book Co., 1987); Linda C. Fox, "Obedience and Rebellion: Re-Vision of Chicana Myths of Motherhood," *Women's Studies Quarterly* (Winter, 1983), pp. 20–22.

34. Talcott Parsons and Robert Bales, *Family, Socialization, and Interaction Processes* (New York: Free Press, 1955); Robert H. Bradley and Bettye M. Caldwell, "The Relation of Infants' Home Environments to Achievement Test Performance in First Grade: A Follow-up Study," *Child Development* 55 (1984), pp. 803–809; Toby L. Parcel and Elizabeth G. Menaghan, "Maternal Working Conditions and Child Verbal Facility: Studying the Intergenerational Transmission of Inequality from Mothers to Young Children," *Social Psychology Quarterly* 53 (1990), pp. 132–147; Avshalom Caspi and Glen H. Elder, "Emergent Family Patterns: The Intergenerational Construction of Problem Behavior and Relationships," in R. Hinde and J. Stevenson Hinde, eds., *Understanding Family Dynamics* (New York: Oxford University Press, 1988).

35. For a full discussion of the interplay between economic goals and economic status of the respondents and their employment decisions, I refer the reader to Denise Segura, "The Interplay of Familism and Patriarchy on Employment among Chicana and Mexican Immigrant Women," in the *Renato Rosaldo Lecture Series Monograph* 5 (Tucson, AZ: The University of Arizona, Center for Mexican American Studies, 1989), pp. 35–53.

36. Two of the Mexicanas reported that their mothers had died while they were toddlers and therefore they were unable to discuss their economic roles.

37. Patricia M. Fernandez-Kelly, "Mexican Border Industrialization, Female Labor-Force Participation and Migration," in J. Nash and M. P. Fernandez-Kelly, eds., *Women, Men, and the International Division of Labor* (Albany: State University of New York Press, 1983), pp. 205–223; Sylvia Guendelman and Auristela Perez-Itriago, "Double Lives: The Changing Role of Women in Seasonal Migration," *Women's Studies* 13 (1987), pp. 249–271; Reynaldo Baca and Dexter Bryan, "Mexican Women, Migration and Sex Roles," *Migration Today* 13 (1985), pp. 14–18.

38. Research indicates religious involvement plays an important role in gender beliefs. See Ross K. Baker, Laurily K. Epstein, and Rodney O. Forth, "Matters of Life and Death: Social, Political, Religious Correlates of Attitudes on Abortion," *American Politics Quarterly* 9 (1981), pp. 89–102; Charles E. Peek and Sharon Brown, "Sex Prejudice among White Protestants: Like or Unlike Ethnic Prejudice?" *Social Forces* 59 (1980), pp. 169–185. Of particular interest for the present study is that involvement in fundamentalist Christian churches is positively related to adherence to traditional gender role ideology. See Clyde Wilcox and Elizabeth Adell Cook, "Evangelical Women and Feminism: Some Additional Evidence," *Women and Politics* 9 (1989), pp. 27–49; Clyde Wilcox, "Religious Attitudes and Anti-Feminism: An Analysis of the Ohio Moral Majority," *Women and Politics* 48 (1987), pp. 1041–1051. Half of the Mexicanas (and all but two Chicanas) adhered to the Roman Catholic religion; half belonged to various fundamentalist Christian churches (e.g., Assembly of God). Two Chicanas belonged to other Protestant denominations. I noticed that the women who belonged to the Assembly of God tended to both work full-time in the labor market and voice the strongest convictions of male authority in the family. During their interviews many of the women brought out the Bible and showed me the biblical passages that authorized husbands to "rule" the family. Catholic women also voiced traditional beliefs regarding family structure but did not invoke God.

39. Frances Rothstein, "Women and Men in the Family Economy: An Analysis of the Relations Between the Sexes in Three Peasant Communities," *Anthropological Quarterly* 56 (1983), pp. 10–23; Ruth Schwartz Cowan, "Women's Work, Housework, and History: The Historical Roots of Inequality in Work-Force Participation," in N. Gerstel and H. E. Gross, eds., *Families and Work* (Philadelphia: Temple University, 1987), pp. 164–177; Louise A. Tilly and Joan W. Scott, *Women, Work, and Family* (New York: Holt, Rinehart, and Winston, 1978).

40. Jessie Bernard, "The Rise and Fall of the Good Provider Role," *American Psychologist* 36 (1981), pp. 1–12; J. Bernard, *The Future of Motherhood* (New York: Penguin Books, 1974); Jane C. Hood, "The Provider Role: Its Meaning and Measurement," *Journal of Marriage and the Family* 48 (May, 1986), pp. 349–359.

41. Lorraine O. Walker and Mary Ann Best, "Well-Being of Mothers with Infant Children: A Preliminary Comparison of Employed Women and Homemakers," *Women and Health* 17 (1991), pp. 71–88; William J. Doherty and Richard H. Needle, "Psychological Adjustment and Substance Use among Adolescents Before and After a Parental Divorce," *Child Development* 62 (1991), pp. 328–337; Eugene E. Clark and William Ramsey, "The Importance of Family and Network of Other Relationships in Children's Success in School," *International Journal of Sociology of the Family* 20 (1990), pp. 237–254.

42. Rosabeth Moss Kanter, *Men and Women of the Corporation* (New York: Basic Books, 1977).

43. John M. Chavez and Raymond Buriel, "Reinforcing Children's Effort: A Comparison of Immigrant, Native-Born Mexican American and Euro-American Mothers," *Hispanic Journal of Behavioral Sciences* 8 (1986), pp. 127–142; Raymond Buriel, "Integration with Traditional Mexican-American Culture and Sociocultural Adjustment" in J. L. Martinez, Jr. and R. H. Mendoza, eds., *Chicano Psychology,* 2nd ed.

(New York: Academic Press, 1984), pp. 95–130; Leo R. Chavez, "Households, Migration and Labor Market Participation: The Adaptation of Mexicans to Life in the United States," *Urban Anthropology* 14 (1985), pp. 301–346.

44. Raymond Buriel, "Integration with Traditional Mexican-American Culture and Sociocultural Adjustment," in J. L. Martinez, Jr. and R. H. Mendoza, eds., *Chicano Psychology*, 2nd ed. (New York: Academic Press, 1984), pp. 95–130. In their analysis of differences in educational goals among Mexican-Americans, Buriel and his associates found that: "third-generation Mexican Americans felt less capable of fulfilling their educational objectives." See Raymond Buriel, Silverio Caldaza, and Richard Vasquez, "The Relationship of Traditional Mexican American Culture to Adjustment and Delinquency among Three Generations of Mexican American Adolescents," *Hispanic Journal of Behavioral Sciences* 4 (1982), p. 50. Similar findings were reported by Nielsen and Fernandez: "We find that students whose families have been in the U.S. longer have *lower* [their

emphasis] aspirations than recent immigrants." See Francois Nielsen and Roberto M. Fernandez, *Hispanic Students in American High Schools: Background Characteristics and Achievement* (Washington D.C.: United States Government Printing Office, 1981), p. 76.

In their analysis of Hispanic employment, Bean and his associates reported an unexpected finding—that English-proficient Mexican women exhibit a greater "constraining influence of fertility" on their employment vis-à-vis Spanish-speaking women. They speculate that more acculturated Mexican women may have "a greater desire for children of higher quality," and therefore "be more likely to devote time to the informal socialization and education of young children." They wonder "why this should hold true for English-speaking but not Spanish-speaking women." See Frank D. Bean, C. Gray Swicegood, and Allan G. King, "Role Incompatibility and the Relationship between Fertility and Labor Supply among Hispanic Women" in G. J. Borjas and M. Tienda, eds., *Hispanics in the U.S. Economy* (New York: Academic Press, 1985), p. 241

READING 24

For Better or Worse: Gender Allures in the Vietnamese Global Marriage Market[1]

❧ Hung Cam Thai

[1] This is a revised version of another paper previously published under the title "Clashing Dreams: Highly–Educated Vietnamese Brides and Their Low-Wage Overseas Husbands," in *Global Woman* (New York: Metropolitan Books, 2003), edited by Arlie Russell Hochschild and Barbara Ehrenreich. Versions of this paper were also presented at the 2002 annual meetings of American Sociological Association in Chicago, and at the 2003 annual meetings of the West and the Pacific Regional Association for Asian American Studies in Pomona, California. I would like to very much thank Arlie Russell Hochschild, Barbara Ehrenreich, Verta Taylor, and Leila Rupp for comments on previous drafts. Thanks to Ingrid Banks for conversations and feedback. And to Barrie Thorne for guidance at every step of the way.

Men and women like Minh and Thanh have dreams, but their dreams clash. He wants the best of tradition and she wants the best of modernity. He believes the respect he has been searching for did not arrive with him when he migrated to the United States

almost 20 years ago, but instead was left back safely in Vietnam. She feels that the marital respect she needs is waiting for her in the United States and that she will get it when she joins him through marriage migration. Minh, 37, represents one of the more than two million *Viet Kieus*, or Vietnamese people living overseas, who make up an aging diaspora that largely began in the mid-1970s, after the postwar years. He is also one of over a million *Viet Kieus* who returned to visit family and friends during the year 2000, a dramatic increase from the 160,000 who did so in 1993 (Nhat 1999). Thanh, 32, will soon join Minh as one of over 200,000 women *and* men worldwide who come to the United States each year through marriage migration, the number one mechanism for contemporary *legal* migration to the United States. In general, females have dominated in U.S-bound migration since the 1930s (Houstoun, Kramer, and Barrett 1984) and, historically, women more often than men have migrated as spouses (Thornton 1992). Women currently make up more than 65 percent of all marriage migrants. While male marriage migrants make up about a quarter of all men who enter the United States each year, female marriage migrants make up over 40 percent of all women who enter (USINS 1999a; USINS 1999b).

During 14 months of fieldwork done in phases in Vietnam and in the United States from 1997 to 2001, I got to know couples like Minh and Thanh. In addition to understanding their distinct national and local cultures, I paid particular attention to some of their most private matrimonial thoughts—thoughts that they have not yet disclosed to each other. For they are in a migration waiting period, a period in which the women are waiting to be united with their husbands through migration. In this distinct and emergent global marriage market, the immigrant Vietnamese men typically go to Vietnam to marry through arrangement and subsequently return to their places of residence in the Vietnamese diaspora (most are from the United States, Canada, France, and Australia) to initiate paperwork to sponsor their wives. During this waiting period, I came to know them by first entering the lives of the brides in Vietnam and later the U.S.-based grooms.

The marriage of Minh and Thanh characterizes a distinct and growing global stream over the past 40 years of immigrant or immigrant-origin men returning to their home countries for marriage partners through processes of family-forming migration (Lievans 1999), thus significantly transforming gender and race relations in the communities of both origin and destination. Same-ethnic individuals constitute an estimated two-thirds of all marriage migration couples, and among international marriage migrants of U.S. non-citizen permanent residents, who are presumably immigrants, almost 90 percent of them are women (Thornton 1992; USINS 1999a; USINS 1999b). Like many international marriages between same-ethnic individuals, especially in Asia, the marriage of Minh and Thanh was arranged. While there are varying flexible meanings of marriage arrangements and class compositions, I focus on marriages of the two "unmarriageables"—highly educated women in Vietnam and overseas Vietnamese men who do low-wage work. These couples make up roughly 55 percent (*n* = 38) of the 69 marriages I studied.

GLOBALIZATION AND MARRIAGE SQUEEZES ACROSS THE VIETNAMESE DIASPORA

Before I began this study, I was fully aware that Vietnamese people worldwide are pressed unusually, if not uniquely, by what demographer Daniel Goodkind (1997) calls the "double marriage squeeze," which has resulted from a high male mortality rate during the Vietnam War and the larger number of men than women who emigrated during the last quarter of the 20th century. A shortage of one sex or the other in the age group in which marriage generally occurs is often termed a marriage squeeze (Guttentag and Secord 1983). The Vietnamese double marriage squeeze specifically refers to the low ratio of males to females in Vietnam and the unusually high ratio of males to females in the Vietnamese diaspora, especially in Australia and in the United States. For example, by 1999, among people between the ages of 30 to 34 years in Vietnam, statistically speaking, there were approximately 92 men for every 100 women. At the other end of the diaspora in 2000, among Vietnamese Americans between 25 to 29 years, there were 129 men for every 100 women; for the age group of 30 to 34, there were about 135 men for every 100 women. While these numbers are important, they tell only part of the story about the recent dramatic rise in Vietnamese transpacific marriages. The link between demographic numbers, intensified transnational and global processes in Vietnam and worldwide, new contours of kinship, and the intersection of gender and class in marriage markets throughout the Vietnamese diaspora provides a much more in-depth look at social processes involved in the emergence of a Vietnamese transpacific marriage market.

The most striking aspect about marriages of the two unmarriageables like Minh and Thanh is that they have globalized and reversed the marriage gradient, an old and almost universal pattern that women "marry up" and men "marry down," which is to say women marry older men who earn more money and have more education and, conversely, men marry younger women who earn less money and have less education (Fitzgerald 1999). But depending on the measure one uses in the marriages I studied, it is difficult to tell who is "from below." In demographic marriage market language (Guttentag and Secord 1983), women worldwide often find that the pool of marriageable men declines as they move up the educational ladder. Thanh is part of this emerging group of highly educated women in Vietnam who have delayed or avoided marriage with local men. These women have found the pool of marriageable men in Vietnam, who are employed and successful relative to them, to be too small. More importantly, Thanh's status as a highly educated woman made her unmarriageable to many men still influenced by the Asian and Confucian ideologies of hierarchical relations in terms of gender, age, and class. Like highly educated African-American women, women like Thanh in Vietnam are a "surplus" relative to their educated male counterparts. Minh, on the other hand, belongs to a group of surplus men, accumulated in part by the scattering of post-war Vietnamese migration, who are unable to find marriage partners partly because of their current low-wage work status. Some of these men, though certainly not all, experienced tremendous downward mobility as they migrated overseas.

Men like Minh who work in the low-wage labor market made up 80 percent of the men in my study. These men generally work for hourly wages, though some work in ethnic enterprises where salaries are negotiated "under the table." For the most part, they work long hours for low pay. In contrast, women like Thanh represent almost 70 percent of the brides. These women come from college-educated backgrounds, with about 40 percent having advanced degrees and working as doctors, lawyers, computer programmers, and the like. The remaining 60 percent are teachers, service sector workers in foreign companies, etc. To be sure, not all college-educated women in my study married low-wage working men, and not all low-wage working men married college-educated women. Men like Minh and women like Thanh are unmarriageable along both gender and class lines. Statistically, because of the double marriage squeeze, there is simply a surplus of women relative to men in Vietnam and a surplus of *Viet Kieu* men relative to *Viet Kieu* women overseas. But their unmarriageability does not end there. If the demography of the double marriage squeeze is a structural condition propelling these transpacific marriages, the cultural belief in the marriage gradient is perhaps a more powerful force driving these marriages. Vietnamese women and men worldwide have not dared to break the marriage-gradient norm in their local marriage market. They believe, as other unmarriageables do, that by globalizing the gradient, they have somehow solved the potential problem of breaking the marriage-gradient norm. That is, if a man is from a first-world country, he has the "up," while a woman from third-world Vietnam has the "down." And though it is no surprise that the economic divide between the "first-world" and "third-world" would inherently penetrate deeply into the private lives of Vietnamese transpacific couples, it is not always clear *who* has the third-world life in marriages of the two unmarriageables.

Globalization seems like a perfect solution to the dual problem facing the Vietnamese diaspora of "too few women here" and "too few men there," yet there is an untold story about the unanticipated collision of gender ideologies and strategies many of these couples will face.

Couples like Minh and Thanh—the unmarriageables—will bump into a clash of dreams as the women join their husbands overseas. Looking far across the Pacific, both were enamored, not necessarily by the economic, but powerfully by the gender allures of the other side: on one end of the Vietnamese diaspora, for educated women like Thanh, a man living overseas in a modern country will respect women more than men still held back by ancient traditions in Vietnam; on the other end of the diaspora, for low-wage working men like Minh, it is precisely these ancient traditions that he desired and perceived are still maintained by women in Vietnam, the sort of traditions that he believes have been eroded by America's modernity.

Both have turned to the old and new, relying foremost on the tradition of marriage arrangements vis-à-vis family members to introduce them to each other. Yet, it is the new globalizing culture of Vietnam that offered them that opportunity. In 1986, after having no contact with the outside world for over a decade, the Vietnamese government adopted a new economic policy known as *doi moi*. It did not end state ownership, but encouraged private enterprise, free markets, and global engagement. Particularly in the 1990s, Saigon was reemerging as a major international city, first within the Asian landscape and soon to the rest of the world. At the time, Vietnam was in the news and was projected to be one of Asia's next "tigers" (Pierre 2000). Recognizing an enticing labor and consumer market of 80 million people, foreign companies were eager to move their factories there and make their products known. Globalization rapidly opened impersonal markets of capital, goods, and labor, and in conjunction with these markets, it also opened a rather personal market of emotions and marriages. Like global corporations and factories that recently moved to Vietnam because of its large supply of labor, one of the reasons *Viet Kieu* men go there for brides is because they have a much larger selection of marriage partners. However, unlike locals who eagerly work at foreign factories mainly for the monetary rewards, Vietnamese transpacific brides don't always share the same reasons for choosing to marry *Viet Kieu* men.

THE HIGHLY EDUCATED BRIDE'S STORY

Twenty years ago, Thanh's father was a math teacher at Le Buon Phong, a prestigious high school in Saigon. After the war, Thanh's uncle, her mother's younger brother, and his family were among the few thousands of Vietnamese who were airlifted out of Vietnam on April 30, 1975, when Saigon surrendered to North Vietnamese military troops. They eventually settled in Houston, one of the larger Vietnamese enclaves in the United States, and started a successful restaurant business specializing in *pho*, the popular Vietnamese beef noodle soup. Remittances—money sent back—from Thanh's uncle helped her parents open a small candy factory in the late 1980s which now has over 40 employees. Like the "new class of everywhere" in the global economy, her parents are now members of a class that represents a small but very visible percentage of families in Vietnam who enjoy access to overseas resources, such as Thanh's uncle and the remittances he sends home. They are part of a *Viet Kieu economy*, of which remittance plays an important role, that has grown from roughly $35 million in 1993 to an estimated $2 billion in 2000 (Pierre 2000). The remittance upward mobility is of course associated with Thanh's educational and social mobility. It has helped Thanh, her parents' only child, earn not only a good high school education, but also continue to study law and take lessons at international English schools in Saigon.

After graduating from Le Buon Phong High School, Thanh and a small group of her female friends did not choose early marriage, a path that most of their peers took soon after high school. Although Thanh and her friends did want to marry one day, they all wanted to further their schooling. Of her seven close female friends from high school, only one did not go to college. That friend opted for early marriage. The rest, including Thanh, quietly took various

professional routes. Most went into fields traditionally reserved for women, including education and nursing. Two went on for higher education. Thanh obtained a law degree, and the other friend went on to become a prestigious physician at Vinh Bien, a private hospital catering to Saigon's middle class. Four of the seven, now in their early 30s, remain single. The pathways of Thanh and her four friends who chose singlehood illustrate a quiet gender revolution among highly educated women in Vietnam. These women have opted for singlehood in a culture where marriage is not only presumed, but often coerced. And if marriage is not achieved by a certain age, women and men are often dismissively referred to as simply "*e*," a derogatory term referring to commodities that are unmarketable. In contrast, women (often young and beautiful) and men (often educated and financially secure) who fare well on the marriage market are considered "*dat*," or scarce goods. As Thanh explained to me:

> I am already "e" in Vietnam. You know, at thirty-two here, it's hard to find a decent husband. I knew that when I decided to get a good education here that many men would be intimidated by me. But it was important to me to get an education, and I know that for women, marriage is more important. In Asian cultures, but maybe in Vietnam especially, the men do not want their wives to be better than them. I think for me it's harder, too, because my parents are successful here so on the outside [to the outsider] we are very successful.

In truth, Thanh is not completely "e" for there have been several men who, sometimes with their families, have come to propose marriage to her. In contemporary Vietnam, arranging marriage remains common practice, though more so in villages than in urban areas. For women in Vietnam, especially those who have passed the social marriageability age, individual and family success often come with being unmarriageable. Thanh had several proposals for marriage arrangements when she was in her mid-20s before she got her law degree, all from men who wanted to marry down socially and economically. Now, at age thirty-two and highly educated, she believes that marrying up is no longer an option as there are few available men in that category. Marrying down is not an appealing choice either, although she has many suitors in that category. Speaking in the marriage gradient mode, Thanh explains:

> When I look up, there are few men "up there" who I could see as suitable husbands. But those men, the few men I know who have more education and who are more successful than I am, usually want to marry young, beautiful women. To them, I am now too old. The backward thing about life is that the men below are very unappealing. And of course there are many of them! There are many, many non-quality men I could choose from, but that's what they are—non-quality.

Thanh's marriage procrastination was partially anchored in her confused class and gender status, for her educational and remittance upward mobility puts her one up locally, but one down globally. On the one hand, if by tradition, a man is to be above her, he must be the one to provide economically, but given that she married a low-wage worker, she may end up being the one to seek economic security through her own means. On the other hand, by traditional Vietnamese culture, Thanh knows her high educational status would not necessarily help her escape the gender subordination in marital life in Vietnam for few men she knows respect women in the everyday contours of marriage. On our third and final interview, Thanh and I walked along the Saigon River early one evening. As the city's buildings rose arrogantly in the background through the din of countless motorcycles, cycles, and taxis, she explained to me, with a sense of disconsolation:

> In Vietnam, it is hard being single, female, and old. People will criticize and laugh at you. People always ask me, "Where are your husband and children? And when I think about that, I realize that I have two choices. I can marry a man in Vietnam who is much less educated and less successful than me who I will have to support and who will likely abuse me emotionally or physically or dominate me in every possible way. Or I can marry a *Viet Kieu* man. *At least Viet Kieu men live in modern countries where they respect women.*

Ultimately, Thanh' s priority, as an educated woman, in the selection of a marriage partner is for someone to respect her and for a marriage in which a man does not control her like most men in Vietnam she observes do. As Thanh explained to me:

> When I find a nice man "below" me who I could marry, he wouldn't want to marry me because he's afraid that I'll take control of the house or that if anything goes wrong in the marriage, I could turn to my family for help. Most men in Vietnam want to control their wives, they want their wives to be subordinate even when she is more successful and educated. That leaves me with very few choices in Vietnam, you see, because I for sure don't want a man to take control of me.

THE LOW-WAGE WORKING GROOM'S STORY

Through complicated logics of transnationality, Thanh found a suitable spouse across the Pacific. But if Thanh's desire for respect was prompted by her educational and remittance upward mobility, her husband's need for respect was prompted by his migratory downward mobility. Minh, whose hands, facial expressions, and graying hair make him seem older than his 37 years, was the only member of his family to leave Vietnam during "wave II" of the boat refugee exodus that took place after the war (Zhou and Bankston 1998). As the eldest son, he holds a position of distinction and responsibility of six siblings in a family of educators. Both of his parents were teachers of philosophy at Le Buon Phong, where they have known Thanh's parents for many years. Today, three of Minh's sisters are teachers and his two brothers are successful merchants in Saigon.

In 1985, at the age of 21, Minh, then a man of intellectual ambition and curiosity, had just completed his third year of engineering school when his parents asked him if he wanted to go to America. They didn't know anyone overseas at the time, but they knew of several people, among the many hundreds of thousands of refugees, who had fled and safely reached a Western country. Of those who successfully made the trip, over 90 percent eventually settled in France, Australia, Canada, or the United States (Merli 1997). Minh's parents also knew that as many as half of the refugees on any particular boat trip did not succeed. They died along the way due to starvation, pirate attacks, and often, in the case of women and children, rape and murder en route to a refugee camp. Many were also caught by the Vietnamese government and severely punished with long prison sentences. Nevertheless, his parents were confident that he would make it and have a better life abroad. After all, they spent their entire life savings to put him on one of the safest and most reputable boats run by private individuals, to leave the Mekong Delta for Western lands of opportunity via refugee camps in Southeast Asia. Like the Underground Railroad established for slave escapes during the American civil war, details about these refugee boats were kept secret. But unlike the railroads, the boats were made accessible only to wealthy or well-connected families. Many who were not wealthy, such as Minh's family, managed to pool their resources so that one person could go, usually a son. They saw this as an investment made with a hope of high returns, as in the case of Minh's family.

Today, Minh considers himself one of the lucky ones. After surviving two years—a lifetime to Minh— in a refugee camp in Malaysia, he was selected in 1987 for entry to the United States. Many people he met at the camp ended up in less desirable places, like Finland, Belgium, or Hungary. As with current migration from Vietnam, the United States was then considered the top destination choice, followed by Canada, France, and Australia. Minh arrived in rural Wyoming under the sponsorship of a local Catholic church. Like many of the churches scattered across the United States who sponsored Indochinese refugees from the late 1970s to the mid-1990s (Zhou and Bankston 1998), his church sponsored only one individual. He spent the first five years of his life in America as the only person of color in a rural town in Wyoming, the name of which he doesn't even want to remember. Like many Vietnamese refugees of the past three decades, Minh decided to migrate a second time. He wanted to go to Little Saigon, the most highly concentrated Vietnamese enclave outside of Vietnam, located in a seemingly quiet Los Angeles suburb, though today plagued by urban problems reported regularly by the media (Leonard and Tran 2000a; 2000b; *Los Angeles Times* 1995; Marosi and Tran 2000; Paddock and Dizon 1991; Terry 1999). But he had little money and no connections in or around Los Angeles. Then one day, in one of the Vietnamese-produced newspapers in the United States that flourished following the influx of refugees, Minh read about a Chinese restaurant called the Panda Garden that needed dishwashers. Unfortunately, it was not in Los Angeles but in a small town called Quincy, ninety

miles from Seattle. Minh heard that Seattle also had many Vietnamese people and he thought a move there would bring him closer to other refugees.

Eleven years later, at age 37, Minh still lives in Quincy and works at the Panda Garden. He is now a deep fryer and an assistant cook, which is several steps up from the dishwashing position he was first given. Although to him, an assistant cook carries less stigma than a dishwasher, it is far from the engineering career he envisaged in his pre-migration years. Though known as one of the best and most authentic ethnic restaurants in town, the Panda mainly serves a "white American" clientele who, according to the owners, probably wouldn't know the differences between authentic Chinese food and Sara Lee frozen dinners. Quincy is similar to many suburban towns in Middle America—not quite rural, but far from urban. People who live here drive to Seattle to shop and eat if they have money, but stay in town if they want to see a movie. Minh knows five other Vietnamese people in the town, all men, and three of them work with him at the restaurant. He shares a modest three-bedroom apartment with the barest of furnishings with these co-workers.

Similar to many *Viet Kieu* people, Minh is a good example of a giver caught in the irony of a remittance-ship. Receivers of remittances enjoy first-world consumption, while their givers often only enjoy it when they go to Vietnam: on returning to a first-world setting, some givers like Minh, regress to a third-world consumption pattern. Like Thanh's family, Minh's family enjoys remittances, albeit much smaller ones than Thanh's family enjoys from her uncle. He earns approximately $1,400 a month in Quincy and sends $500 of that back to his family. That amount is much higher than the average of $160 the grooms in my study send to their wives and/or families on a monthly basis. At $900, his remaining budget would be considered way below the poverty level anywhere in the United States. But his family has more than enough constant capital from his remittances to keep connected in the small, though conspicuous, circles of families who have overseas kin networks.

And while Minh's family enjoy their new consumption patterns, Minh finds himself lacking the luxury they afford—most importantly the luxury of having the kind of respect he was used to before migration, particularly the kind of respect he once had in intimate markets. Minh remembered vividly that in his early 20s, he had been considered a good catch among his peers. He was heading for an engineering career and was from a well-respected family. Recounting stories of masculinity from his early adulthood, Minh told me that young men he knew had not one, but several, girlfriends at a time, and that it was accepted and celebrated. After all, life after the war was particularly difficult for many families he knew. But he was relatively fortunate, for his parents were well-respected teachers with a small, but steady, income and, therefore, could afford to spend small amounts of money on leisure activities and materials that bought them some status in their pre-remittance circles. As he told me in one conversation when we were talking, with beers and cigarettes in our hands, rather loudly in the hot and sizzling kitchen where he worked:

> Life here now is not like life in Vietnam back then. My younger brothers and sisters used to respect me a lot because I was going to college and I was about to get my degree. Many young women I met at the time liked me, too, because I came from a good family and I had status [dia di]. But now, because I don't have a good job here, people don't pay attention to me. That's the way my life has been since I came to the United States And I don't know if I'm lucky or unlucky, but I think it's hard for a [Vietnamese] man to find a wife here if he doesn't make good money. If you have money, everyone will pay attention [to you], but if you don't, you have to live by yourself.

For the most part, that's what Minh has done in the 16 years since he arrived in the United States. In his social world, Minh believes money can, and often does, buy love, and that if you don't have much of it, you live "by yourself." His yearly income puts him just above the poverty level for a single man, but when I did a budget analysis of his expenditures, I discovered that after remittances, his available funds place him well below the poverty level. The long hours that often accompany low-wage work have also made it particularly difficult for him to meet and court marriage partners. If Minh worked long hours for a law firm or a large business corporation, he would not only get financial rewards, but also the status and prestige which men often use as a trade-off in marriage markets. If he were a blue collar white man in Quincy, he could go to church functions, bowling alleys, or bars to meet and court women in the local

marriage market. For Minh—a single immigrant man—who does low-wage work in a low-status job with long hours in Middle America, the prospect of marriage has been, and remains, low. Like highly educated women such as Thanh, men like Minh are on the market for more than just intimacy. They are on it for respect, a sense of respect for marital life which they perceive they can not find in their local marriage market. For men in general, but especially for working-class men, as sociologist Lillian Rubin (1994) argues in a compelling study, a sense of self is deeply connected to the ability to provide economically for the family. For low-wage workers like Minh, the ability to provide, or lack thereof, is sharply linked to earning respect in marital life. As Minh movingly explained to me:

> I don't know if other men told you this, but I think the main reason why a lot of *Viet Kieu* men go back to Vietnam for a wife is because the women here [*Viet Kieu*] do not respect their husbands if the husbands can not make a lot of money. I think that's why there are a lot of *Viet Kieu* women who marry white men, because the white men have better jobs than us. Many *Viet Kieu* women, even though they are not attractive and would not be worth much if there were a lot of them, would not even look at men like me because we can't buy them the fancy house or the nice cars. *I need my wife to respect me as her husband. If your wife doesn't respect you, who will?*

AND SO THEY MEET

Although Minh was headed for upward mobility in 1985 before he migrated to the United States, and would have become an engineer one day if he had remained in Vietnam, he is now an assistant cook and has spent the bulk of his adult working life in the confines of a small Chinese restaurant in Middle America. He hasn't read a book in recent memory. In fact, he didn't have much to share about what he does, except work, or what he owns, except a used Toyota Tercel he recently bought. Meanwhile, Thanh is a relatively successful lawyer in urban Saigon, where Chanel perfume from Paris and American designer Ann Taylor's shirts are essential components of her daily life. Thanh speaks very good English, the language we used when she and I met in Vietnam; Minh and I spoke Vietnamese when I interviewed him in Quincy, Washington. Thanh is currently attending an international adult English school to obtain her English proficiency degree and her current reading list includes Fitzgerald's *The Great Gatsby*. She often prides herself on the fact that she is not as thin as the average woman in Vietnam, nor does she conform to the stereotypical image of Vietnamese women with long, straight black hair. Instead, Thanh has a perm with red highlights and she spends a large part of her leisure time taking aerobics classes at the Saigonese Women's Union, an emerging activity among Saigon's middle class. Pointing to her access to and practice of modernity, she often joked, "Some people in Vietnam think that I'm a *Viet Kieu* woman."

Minh and Thanh, thus, live in noticeably different social worlds. They were united by a network of kin and acquaintanceship that was spatially separated, yet held together by the histories, memories, and connections of the prewar years. This network of kin helped arrange the marriage of the two and started when Minh's siblings expressed concerns that their eldest brother appeared lonely and "needed" a wife, though they never asked him. After all, he was the eldest brother and the only sibling not yet married and still childless. The average age of marriage for his three younger sisters was 21 and for his two brothers, 24. His next brother's eldest child is now attending her first year at Le Buon Phong High School, a sign to Minh that he's getting old. Minh was often embarrassed when asked, "Why didn't you bring your lady friend back to visit us, too?" What his family did not understand on his first few visits back was that long hours of work, as well as the scarcity of Vietnamese women (relative to men) in the United States in general and Quincy in particular, were reasons why the "lady friend generally was too busy to make the trip home *this time*."

If Minh's choice to return to Vietnam to find a wife was propelled by siblings and then followed by his individual discretion, Thanh's entrance into the transpacific marriage market was the complete opposite. Both faced structural and demographic limitations in their local marriage markets, but in different and reversed ways. On the one hand, Minh knew very *few* Vietnamese-American women, and those he knew usually earned the same amount of, or more, money than he did, which made him a *less* attractive marriage candidate in the United States Research has shown that in the low-wage labor market among Asian Americans, especially in California, women tend to get jobs more easily, work longer hours, and earn more money than men (Espiritu 1999).

In contrast, Thanh knew *many* single men in Saigon, but those she knew were far below her in educational status and made much *less* money than she did working as a part-time lawyer and for her father's factory, all of which made her a *less* attractive marriage candidate in Vietnam. By Vietnamese standards—and for some, by any global standard—women like Thanh come from solidly middle-class backgrounds, through acquired or inherited wealth, educational mobility, or remittances. Thanh's education, combined with the income she and her family generate, have been real trade-offs on the transpacific marriage market. As Thanh explained to me:

> Any *Viet Kieu* man can come here to find a wife. And he can surely find a beautiful woman if he wants because there are many beautiful young women willing to marry anyone to go overseas. I think there is something different when you talk about *Viet Kieu* men coming back here to marry. They look for a real marriage. And a marriage that will last forever. And so it's important to them to check everything about the woman they will marry and her background. These men [*Viet Kieu* men] want a woman who is educated and who comes from an educated family, because that means she comes from a good family. And if her family has money, he knows she just doesn't want to marry him to go overseas because she already has a comfortable life in Vietnam.

Fearful that they may be seen as sex-workers, local women in Vietnam who want a transpacific spouse rarely allow themselves to be courted by foreign men in public spaces as is the case for women in Taiwan, Thailand, Singapore, Malaysia, Hong Kong, and other Asian countries I've visited and learned about. According to most women and men I talked to in Vietnam, *Viet Kieu* men often come back and visit local bars and dance clubs in search of "one-night stands" either with prostitutes or non-prostitutes, but they would never marry women they meet in those public spaces. If women are fearful of the possibility of being sexually exploited, *Viet Kieu* men are wary of being used as a "bridge" to cross the Pacific (Ong 1999). These reasons, as well as the availability of transnational networks, have propelled women in Vietnam and Vietnamese men who live overseas to rely on the old practice of marriage arrangements by family and kin members, rather than engaging in individual courtship, what we call "free love" practices of choosing a marriage partner. As in the case of arranged marriages among other ethnic groups, marriage candidates in the Vietnamese diaspora believe that family members make the best judgements in their interests when looking for a spouse. Here, Thanh explained the logics of marriage arrangements that may seem illogical to a foreigner:

> It's very easy to trick people now. Both men and women can trick each other. Women will pretend to love so they can go abroad and men will pretend to love so they can get a one-night relationship. And so that is why people will choose a family member who could investigate both sides for them. Most of the cases I know are similar to mine. Usually a *Viet Kieu* man says he wants a wife, and then he will call a family here who will search for him. His family member will try to contact friends, neighbors, whoever he can in search of a suitable wife who happens to also be waiting for an overseas man to court her. There's always a lot of women willing to marry a *Viet Kieu* man, even though she may never have thought about it until someone asks them. If you have a family member to choose for you, as my uncle helped me get to know my husband, you will end up with a real marriage. Otherwise, it can be risky for both people if they meet each other on their own.

The marriage arrangement between Minh and Thanh was initiated by Minh's parents, who have known Thanh's family for over two decades. Even though Thanh's father taught at Le Buon Phong two decades ago, and was a friend and colleague of Minh's parents, the current consumption gap between the two families has created a social distance over the years. When Minh's siblings convinced him to search for a wife in Vietnam, he was hesitant at first, but later followed their advice when his parents promised that they would invest time and care in finding the most suitable spouse. According to Minh, however, they were surprised to discover that arranging a marriage for a *Viet Kieu* was more complicated than they had anticipated:

> I thought that it would be easy for them to find someone. I thought all they had to do was mention a few things to their friends, and within days, they could describe a few possible people to me. But my parents told me that they were afraid that women just wanted to use our family to go abroad. We had many people get involved, many people wanted to be matchmakers for the family and added so much anxiety and fear about people's intentions. But the first choice for them was to find a woman from a wealthy family so that they were sure she wasn't just interested in money because if she has money, she would already be comfortable in Vietnam. And it would have been best if she had family in the United States already, because we would know that they already have overseas people who help them out so they would not expect to become dependent on us. In Vietnamese, you know, there is this saying, "When you choose a spouse, you are choosing his/her whole family."

Thanh's family was finally contacted by Minh's parents, a traditional way of arranging marriages in which a groom's parents represent him to propose, often with rituals and a ceremonial language that date back for centuries. Like most brides in my study, Thanh relied on an overseas relative—in this case, Thanh's uncle, Tuan—for advice on Minh's economic and social situation in the United States. The family discovered that Minh was a low-wage worker, but a full-time worker nonetheless. Virtually all of the locals I met in Vietnam viewed overseas men as a two-tiered group: the "successful" who succeeded in owning ethnic enterprises or through obtaining an education, and the "indolent" without full-time jobs who were perceived as being welfare-dependent or as participants in underground economies, such as gambling. Some saw the latter group as men who took up valuable "spots" that others from Vietnam could have filled. "If I had gotten a chance to go," I heard many men say, "I would be so rich by now." Most people, however, did not have an explanation for a man like Minh, who is neither lazy nor extremely successful. Thanh's uncle, Tuan, seemed to know more men in Houston who were not only unemployed, but also alcoholics and gamblers. Her parents were worried that their daughter was unmarriageable as there was certainly no shortage of young and younger women in Vietnam for local men *her* age to marry. In addition, Thanh was already convinced that she was "e." All three were concerned that Thanh was facing a life of permanent singlehood for she was getting old by Vietnamese standards. In the back and front of these pre-arrangement thoughts, all three parties—Thanh's uncle, her parents, and herself—saw the option of marrying Minh, a *Viet kieu* man, more desirable than marrying a local man in Vietnam. For Thanh's parents, Minh's status as a full time worker *and* someone who sent remittances back home to his family translated into a potentially suitable husband. For her uncle, most *Viet Kieu* single men he knew were part of an underclass of which Minh was not a part. For Thanh, Minh's geographical advantage translated into something socially priceless: a man living in a modern country will respect women.

CLASH OF DREAMS

Women like Thanh want a respectful marriage based on principles of gender equality. By these principles, women expect to work for a wage, share in making social and economic decisions for their future households, and have their husbands share in the household division of labor. Above all, they did *not* want to live in multi-generational households serving as the dutiful daughter-in-law and housewife, the two often inseparable and presumed roles historically delegated to women in Vietnam. Many express that reluctance, for they know numerous *Viet Kieu* men who live with their parents or plan to do so in the future when their parents are old. The women's concern about having to live in multi-generational households is anchored in the fact that in Vietnamese culture, and more generally in Asia, elderly parents prefer to, and often do, live with their sons, usually the eldest one. Much less is known about the fact that it is their daughters-in-law, the wives of their sons, who do the fundamental daily caring work.

For Thanh, living with one's in-laws is the most symbolic act of feminine submission. For Minh, a wife's insistence on a nuclear household represents a desire for an equal marriage—and is one of the gendered anxieties of modernity:

> Vietnamese women, they care for their husbands and they are more traditional. I think non-VN women and *Viet Kieu* women, are too modern. They just want to be equal with their husbands and I don't think that it is the way husband and wife should be. [What do you mean?] I mean that husband and wife should not be equal. The wife should listen to husband most of the time. That is how they will have a happy life together. If the woman try to be equal they will have problems. . . . I know many Vietnamese men here who abandon their parents because their wives refuse to live with their parents. If my parents were in America,

I would definitely plan for them to live with me when they are old. But because they are in Vietnam, they are living with one of my brothers.

Instead of seeking peasant village women or uneducated ones like white Europeans and Americans who search for wives through commercialized systems of mail-order brides, men like Minh seek marriage arrangement with educated women as part of a careful gender strategy for a perceived future marital stability. Minh outlines his strategy:

> For me, I want to marry an educated woman because she comes from a good, educated family. It's very hard to find a poor woman or an uneducated woman who comes from an uneducated family, because if they are uneducated [the family] they don't know how to teach their daughters about morals and values. I know many men, *Viet Kieu* and foreign men, who go to Vietnam to marry beautiful young women, but they don't ask why do those women marry them? Those women only want to use their beauty to go overseas and they will leave their husbands when they get the chance. They can use their beauty to find other men. I would never marry a beautiful girl from a poor, uneducated family. You see, the educated women, they know it's important marry and stay married forever. As they say in Vietnam, "tram nam han phuc," [a hundred years of happiness]. Educated women must protect their family's reputation in Vietnam by having a happy marriage, not end in divorce.

UNIMAGINABLE FUTURES

At first glance, Minh and Thanh seem as if they are from different social worlds, two worlds accidentally assembled by a complex Vietnamese history. But once closely acquainted with them, we learn that they are very much alike. First is the class of their past—both sets of their parents were educated and middle class. Second, they are both lonely human faces of globalization who lack the emotional and intimate details that adults of their social worlds enjoy. Most importantly, it seems, because of the gendered meanings embedded in their opposite trails of class mobility, they both long for marital respect, the kind of respect they perceive is scarce in their local marriage market. From Minh's side of the gender scene, he experienced downward mobility quickly and immensely as a result of migration and is eager to get back the respect he has lost. Thanh, a woman who has, in part, priced herself out of the local marriage market by acquiring a higher education, paid for by a remittance upward mobility, wants a man who respects her as an equal and as a woman who embraces modernity. He wants to regain what he sees as something men like him have lost, while she has, in part, challenged the local marriage norm and, in effect, the "control-norm" in the gender world of Vietnam.

The global forces and global histories that have mobilized their marriage—and their clashed dreams—will assuredly usher in marital conflicts. These conflicts will lead to several possibilities as women quietly migrate to join their husbands overseas. In a happy global story, Minh will join in the feminist revolution and leave behind the tradition he never had as he moves forward with his new marriage. I believe some, but few, men will join women in this revolution. In a tragic global story, these couples may end in divorce or worse, women like Thanh will be abused by their husbands. Many women like Thanh have thought about this possibility and have told me that their connection to transnational networks will ensure that they avoid abusive marriages. The most likely possibility for married couples like Minh and Thanh is that men will get what they want in the market of respect and women will consent to

subordination in the name of family and kinship. Thanh will enjoy some aspects of modernity she cannot acquire in Vietnam, but she will be burdened by tradition she doesn't expect to see in the United States. For she will be going from a patriarchal frying pan to a patriarchal fire, but with one big difference. In the United States she has more support for her desire for gender equity where more women dare to quit a marriage if they don't get it. But she has the powerful burden of tradition in Vietnam to hold her back from choosing this option.

In Vietnam, marriage is an important matter not only because it unites two people, but also because it has significant implications for extended networks of kin (Tran 1991). In a culture where divorce is stigmatized and where saving face is a sacred activity especially among the educated and middle class, if Thanh daringly divorces her husband, she will cause her family and kin a loss of reputation in Vietnam and overseas, a risk she told me she is unlikely to take. If she stays in the marriage, she will give up her need for the respect and equality she thinks are waiting for her in the United States. And she will likely serve as the traditional wife Minh needs in order for him to gain back the respect he left back in Vietnam almost 20 years ago. Simply put, Vietnamese politics of kinship promise that couples like Minh and Thanh will remain married—for better or worse.

REFERENCES

Espiritu, Yen Le. 1999. "Gender and Labor in Asian Immigrant Families." *American Behavioral Scientist*: 628–647.

Fitzgerald, Tina Katherine. 1999. *Who Marries Whom? Attitudes in Marital Partner Selection*. Ph.D. Dissertation: University of Colorado.

Goodkind, Daniel. 1997. "The Vietnamese Double Marriage Squeeze." *The Center for Migration Studies of New York* 31: 108–128.

Guttentag, Marcia, and Paul F. Secord. 1983. *Too Many Women? The Sex Ratio Question*. Beverly Hills: Sage Publications.

Houstoun, Marion F., Roger G. Kramer, and Joan Mackin Barrett. 1984. "Female Predominance in Immigration to the United States since 1930s: A First Look." *International Migration Review* 18: 908–963.

Leonard, Jack, and Mai Tran. 2000a. "Agents Target Little Saigon Crime Groups." *Los Angeles Times*, October 7, p. A1.

Leonard, Jack, and Mai Tran. 2000b. "Probes Take Aim at Organized Crime in Little Saigon; Crackdown: Numerous Agencies Target Gambling, Drug Sales, Counterfeit Labels and Credit Card Scams." *Los Angeles Times*, October 7, p. B7.

Lievans, John. 1999. "Family Forming Migration from Turkey and Morocco to Belgium." *International Migration Review* 33: 717–744.

Los Angeles Times. 1995. "Cooler Days in Little Saigon." *Los Angeles Times*, August 8, p. B8.

Marosi, Richard, and Mai Tran. 2000. "Little Saigon Raids Dismantle Crime Ring, Authorities Say; Probe: Asian Syndicate Supplied Most Illegal Gambling Machines in Orange County, Police Say. Fifteen Are Arrested." *Los Angeles Times*, September 29, p. B3

Merli, Giovanna M. 1997. "Estimation of International Migration for Vietnam, 1979–1989." Unpublished Paper, Department of Sociology and Center for Studies in Demography and Ecology. Seattle: University of Washington.

Nhat, Hong. 1999. "Hankering for 'Viet Kieu' Money." P. 12 in *Vietnam Economic News* 9, no. 50 (December).

Ong, Aihwa. 1999. *Flexible Citizenship: The Cultural Logics of Transnationality*. Durham, N.C.: Duke University Press.

Paddock, Richard C., and Lily Dizon. 1991. "3 Vietnamese brothers in shoot-out led troubled lives." P. A3 in *Los Angeles Times*.

Pierre, Andrew J. 2000. "Vietnam's Contradictions." *Foreign Affairs* 79.

Rubin, Lillian. 1994. *Families on the Fault Line: America's Working Class Speaks About the Family, the Economy, Race and Ethnicity*, New York: Harper Collins Press.

Terry, Don. 1999. "Passions of Vietnam War are Revived in Little Saigon; Shop's Ho Chi Minh Poster Sets off Violence." *New York Times*, February 11, p. A20.

Thornton, Michael C. 1992. "The Quiet Immigration: Foreign Spouses Of U.S. Citizens, 1945–1985."

Pp. 64–76 in *Racially Mixed People in America*, edited by Maria P. Root. Newbury Park, CA: Sage Publications.

Tran, Dinh Huou. 1991. "Traditional Families in Vietnam and the Influence of Confucianism." Pp. 27–53 in *Sociological Studies on the Vietnamese Family*, edited by Rita Lijestrom and Tuong Lai. Hanoi: Social Sciences Publishing House.

USINS. 1999a. "International Matchmaking Organizations: A Report to Congress by the Immigration & Naturalization Service." *A Report to Congress*.

USINS. 1999b. *Statistical Yearbook of the Immigration and Naturalization Service, 1997*. Washington, D.C.: U.S. Government Printing Office.

Zhou, Min, and Carl L. Bankston. 1998. *Growing Up American: How Vietnamese Children Adapt to Life in the United States*. New York: Russell Sage Foundation.

READING 25

Wedding Bells and Baby Carriages: Heterosexuals Imagine Gay Families, Gay Families Imagine Themselves

Suzanna Danuta Walters

Is it worth being boring for a Blender? Gay Marriage: You might as well be straight.

> DAM! (Dyke Action Machine) postcards and posters, New York

Just a thought. How soon before expectant parents tell their friends: 'It's twins. A boy and a girl. They're going to be gay. We're calling them Michelangelo and Martina. We've painted the nursery lavender'.

> Sir Ian McKellen, The Guardian

The civilizing influence of family values, with or without children, ultimately may be the best argument for same-sex marriage.

> William Eskridge, Jr., The Case for Same-Sex Marriage

FAMILY: THE FINAL FRONTIER?

It is no coincidence that the "family values" debate emerges in the context of growing discussion and examination of the multiplicity of family forms. In an era when both the feminist and the gay movements have challenged the centrality and desirability of the heterosexual nuclear family, the phrase "family values" emerges to set up an impenetrable dividing line between "us" and "them". However, not only are feminists continuing to question the validity of a uniform notion of "family" but gays and lesbians have begun to come out of the closet about both their own, often poignant, experiences in families and their attempts to form families themselves.

The very place of family is often a fraught one for lesbians and gay men. While the larger social world offers few sites of freedom, the family is often the first place where they experienced homophobia and the place where they felt most betrayed, most alone, most violated. Some of the saddest stories gay people tell are the stories of family—remaining in the closet for fear of rejection, being kicked out, being told you are no longer a son/daughter, being kept away from other kids, being beaten, being told you are sick, telling your mother it is not "her fault," being disinherited, being shunned. It should be no surprise, then, that "family" remains a highly charged arena for lesbians and gay men.[1]

But gay life and identity, defined so much by the problems of invisibility, subliminal coding, double entendres and double lives, have now taken on the dubious distinction of public spectacle. I cannot begin to do it justice here,[2] but suffice it to say that gay family life has not been immune from the extraordinary proliferation of books, TV shows, films, ads, magazine stories, merchandising firms, consumer expos, and Internet chat rooms that have made gay identity (or a media version of it) available to all.

Beyond the odes to diversity and "tolerance," few (except those on the extreme political right) have questioned the value of this almost obsessive "love affair" with gay life. At first glance, these stunning changes seem all for the good. But if gays seem like the paragons of trendiness, then they are being simultaneously depicted as the Antichrist, the sign of a culture in decay, a society in ruins, the perverse eclipse of rational modernity. As religious fundamentalism grows, becomes mainstream and legitimate, so too does hard-edged homophobia. Hate crimes are on the rise—not just in numbers but in the severity and brutality of the acts.[3]

The debates about assimilation are as old as the movement itself, and echo in some ways the conversations about racialised exclusion and inclusion. . . . What *is* new is that these debates are now taking place in full public view, around the water coolers of corporate America, the hallways of university campuses, the barbeque grills of genteel suburbia, and the streets and malls of both urban and rural areas. No longer restricted to closed-door meetings and internecine battles, these internal debates have been irrevocably externalised. If the enemy once was perceived as invisibility itself, then how is the enemy defined in an era of increased visibility? Is the penetrating gaze of the popular a sign of public acceptance or of the homosexual as commodity fetish, as side-show freak?

What profound (and new) alienation must be felt when a gay person looks at a gay wedding cheerfully depicted on TV and then has her/his partner studiously ignored at a family gathering? What does it feel like to be depicted as the cutting edge of chic postmodern style as you are getting fired from your job, rejected by your family, and targeted by right-wing activists? For every successful custody suit, there seem to be two defeats. For every parent who is able successfully to "adopt" her or his non-biological child, others are endlessly delayed or deferred. And it takes great financial resources to be able to access even these tenuous legal avenues.

For all the confusion and localism of gay family rulings and legislation, dominant themes do emerge. Whether it is marriage or parenting, both well-meaning heterosexuals *and* mainstream gays seem to stress gay sameness to straights. Our relationships, our desires, our parenting styles are again and again presented as replicas of heterosexual patterns, as if gay families exist in a sort of alternate universe that isn't really alternate at all. While odes to family *diversity* abound, real invocations of family *difference* are muted.

HONEYMOON IN HAWAII: THE GREAT MARRIAGE DEBATE

Into this strange register of the visible enters the soundbite-ish "gay marriage debate," a debate played out in the pages of gay journals but also on our TV sets, in glossy mainstream magazines, in prime-time news specials, in legal argumentation, in everyday talk. The peculiarly public display that is the wedding ritual emphasises the centrality of the visible to marriage, in a way that domestic partnerships or even commitment ceremonies can never quite manifest. Weddings are highly commercialised public signs; it is no accident that this imagery has captivated public imagination, pushing aside the more mundane and everyday images of lesbian and gay life by making visible that which we cannot have.

Nowhere is this new gay visibility more pronounced—and more problematic—than in television. Gay weddings have appeared in numerous series, including *Friends* (with Candace Gingrich, the lesbian half-sister of Republican standard-bearer Newt, playing the lesbian minister), the since-cancelled *Northern Exposure*, and *Roseanne*. For all the obvious newness of these representations, most have forgone the taboo gay kiss and presented gay marriage ceremonies as cuddly, desexualised mirrors of the more familiar heterosexual ritual. Notably absent are the odes to same-sex love and the revisions of traditional vows that most assuredly accompany many gay commitment ceremonies. The *Friends* wedding—while carefully sensitive—went out of its way to portray the gay wedding as an exact replica of its heterosexual counterpart, only with two bridal gowns. The episode focused more on the heterosexual response to the gay environment than on the gay participants themselves. Indeed, the gay wedding was framed by a secondary plot line concerning the impending divorce of a character's traditional mom, implicitly linking heterosexuality and homosexuality in a liberal scenario of sameness.

It is interesting to note that in the three major "gay weddings" handled on TV, it is a heterosexual character who brings the nervous and fighting homosexual couple together when the nuptials are threatened. In *Friends, Northern Exposure,* and even the more innovative *Roseanne,* one of the series regulars has a "heart-to-heart" with one member of the bickering gay couple and helps convince the wavering one to go through with the wedding. Often, it is the character who is initially most resistant to the wedding. The confidential tête-à-tête between gay outsider and heterosexual insider thus renders not only homosexuality but *homophobia* benign and palatable. The appalled Maurice (of *Northern Exposure*), who complains about "tutti fruttis" ruining the very concept of marriage by engaging in a same-sex version of it, becomes not a bigoted homophobe but rather a befuddled and ultimately good-hearted traditionalist. The straight character gets reformed and redeemed through a demonstrated expertise in pre-wedding cold feet, thereby avoiding reckoning with a previously impregnable homophobia. This redemption, alongside the approving and supportive stance of all the other heterosexual characters, also avoids reckoning with the actual homophobia that surrounds such events.

In this scenario, straight people know more about family life and relationships and are needed to pass that knowledge on to their floundering gay brethren. The implication is that gays are simply not knowledgeable about the "real-life" issues of forming families, making commitments, raising kids.[4] This reintroduces the old canard about homosexuals as childlike, immature, unformed versions of heterosexuals. This backlash scenario argues to "accept"

homosexuals, but not as full-fledged people who can handle their own lives.

In addition, there is a certain hubris in the straight homophobe playing Dear Abby to the jittery gay person. Do these gay people on TV never have *any* gay friends to consult in their travails? Isolation and assimilation are often the price of tokenism. But at least the *Cosby* family had each other. Gay people on TV appear to have sprung full-blown from the Zeus' head of heterosexuality. The social, polical, and cultural context that "births" gay people gives way to the fiction of the fully formed fag, parented by bravely reconstructed heterosexuals. Homophobia is reduced to ignorance, bewilderment, and discomfort. In the television land of gay life, the perpetrators of homophobia—aside from the obvious gaybashers—are basically good-hearted souls whose liberal inclinations win out in the end.

Contrast this delusional neo-liberalism with the realities of anti-gay politics. The same year that witnessed ratings-successful gay weddings on TV also saw the US Congress overwhelmingly support an anti-gay marriage bill and a putatively "pro-gay" President sign it. State after state votes to restrict marriage to heterosexuals, and polls suggest most Americans agree with the decisions and not with the television shows they watch so assiduously. Even the extraordinary victory in Vermont—granting gays the closest thing we have to marriage-like status—has not slowed down the juggernaut of reactionary activism. For the religious Right, gay marriage is the proverbial line in the sand. A full-page ad by the Family Research Council quite explicitly locates marriage as the glue that holds society together—and keeps out the undesirables. Above a picture of a crumbling wedding cake, the ad encapsulates "family values" rhetoric and reveals its political heritage: "The institution of marriage was built to last . . . It was made in heaven . . . Recognized by the state . . . Sanctioned by faith and honored by the community. It has gone hand-in-hand with the rise of civilization. Marriage has survived Marxism. Outlasted Free Love. Outlived Woodstock. Toughed-out the Playboy philosophy. Even endured radical feminism." Opponents of gay marriage link the supposed evils of same-sex love to all the other supposed evils of a secular humanist society—the ogre of sixties-style sex, drugs, and rock-n-roll meets up with the shibboleth of radical feminism and encounters the Godzilla of gay marriage. Because the Right has used this as a "wedge" issue in recent elections, gays must fight on this turf, responding to right-wing hysteria with assurances of shared "family values" and reverence for traditional marriage. It is difficult to hear the more radical gay voices. In this truncated battle, the complicated and difficult politics of marriage evaporates in a sea of assimilationist paeans to divine coupledom.

A PLACE AT THE ALTAR: THE EQUALITY ARGUMENT

What are gays themselves saying about the contested institution of marriage? There are really two debates. The first is the familiar one between gays arguing for rights to marriage and heterosexuals attempting to limit legally recognised marriage to heterosexual couples. On this debate, one can take a position without much ado. The dominant and public gay argument is one of equality: how can one justify denying one group of people access to a practice, simply on the basis of sexual preference? That marriage rights would confer benefits—both social and economic—to many lesbians and gays is undeniable. Given the structure of our social and legal system (including our tax system, inheritance laws, health benefits and responsibilities, childcare and custody and parenting issues, to name just a few), it is understandable that many gay couples desire the same rights and responsibilities, benefits, and assumptions, that married heterosexuals receive. Numerous writers have spelled out the financial and legal ramifications and argue that gay access to marriage is not only just and fair, but would confer tangible benefits that far outweigh additional responsibilities or burdens (Chambers 2000).

This argument is persuasive and important. However, there is a more complex issue that often gets ignored in the media, and that is the differences among gays *themselves* over marriage. The rest of this chapter will engage in a much more critical analysis of gay *desire* to join such dubious institutions, and of the ideological positions and cultural assumptions that surround such desire. No one—gay or straight—is born with some inherent desire to throw themselves on the altar, pledging fidelity to one true love and filing joint income taxes. No gene for that. So gay desire to marry must be interrogated, its seeming transparency compromised in order to reveal the complex of cultural and political imaginings that have produced a moment such as this.

TO TAME THE WILD BEAST: GAY MARRIAGE AS ANTIDOTE

Many gays, such as conservative writer and former editor of the *New Republic* Andrew Sullivan, strongly believe that the right to marry is crucial to the "maturity" of the gay movement. Writing in 1989, Sullivan argues against domestic partnerships and for legalising gay marriage. He is wary of the legal ramifications of domestic partnerships (who qualifies?) but is even more concerned that the concept undermines the centrality and hegemony of the marriage institution, arguing that "society has good reason to extend legal advantages to heterosexuals who choose the formal sanction of marriage over simply living together" (1989: 20). His argument, like that of many other conservative gays, is a familiar and vaguely Victorian one: marriage tames and civilises the wild beast that is Man. Without it, we would be awash in a sea of sexual depravity, flitting madly about from partner to partner, never tending to the business of the day. Like his "family values" counterparts on the Christian right, Sullivan sees marriage as the "anchor . . . in the chaos of sex and relationships to which we are all prone" (1989: 20).

Sullivan's arguments for marriage are framed within an understanding of the gay movement that interprets the "Stonewall generation" as washed-out radicals, too blinded by their own perverse desire for "liberation" to grow up and assimilate. But brave young souls like himself have reckoned with this immaturity and now agree that "a need to rebel has quietly ceded to a desire to belong" (1989: 20). More recently, Sullivan has testified before the House Judiciary subcommittee hearings on the Defense of Marriage Act, arguing that to be in favour of same-sex marriage is to be very pro-family, pro-stability, pro-monogamy and pro-responsibility. His is, as he himself admits, a conservative argument for gay marriage, a claim that same-sex marriage will have two beneficent outcomes: forcing homosexuals into more "committed" and monogamous relationships, and reinforcing the centrality and dominance of marriage as the primary social unit.

While heterosexual commentators give credence to the anti-marriage position, they too often end up arguing that gays should be allowed to marry in order to encourage "harmony and stability" and in order to "serve the common good" (Yardley 1996). Even conservative columnists such as Clarence Page support gay marriage, for the same reasons conservative *gays* do: it helps support those gays who are "law-abiding, productive and well-educated" and who "go to church" and believe in "family values" Page 1996). Gays will honor the institution and, after all, there is "a compelling social interest and arguably a state interest in encouraging homosexuals to settle down in stable, monogamous, responsible and spiritually fulfilling relationships" (Page 1996).

Georgetown University law professor William Eskridge published a more sophisticated and nuanced treatise on gay marriage that unfortunately and perhaps unwittingly echoes the Sullivan argument. Eskridge supports Sullivan's argument about the "civilizing" influence of marriage on gay men in particular, men whose wanton promiscuity needs to be tamed (1996: 78). Eskridge also joins Sullivan in framing the argument around a very particular and truncated historical narrative. Eerily like mainstream heterosexual stories of gay life, Eskridge creates a history of radical gay activists and sexual liberationists giving way to commitment-bound, home-owning, AIDS-fearing "guppies" for whom marriage is the bright light at the end of the tunnel. Not only does this falsely paint a picture of the demise of gay radicalism (it is still alive and well), it also completely ignores the reality of non-white, poor, working-class gays—the majority of course. So marriage will civilize nasty promiscuous gay men (and what of lesbians?) and, in so doing, will make them more "acceptable" (his language) to straights. Like Sullivan, Eskridge argues for marriage over domestic partnership, because "most lesbians and gay men want something more than domestic partnership; they want to be in a committed relationship at some point in their lifetime" (1996: 78). For these gay men, marriage is the *real* sign of a "committed relationship." In making his argument for gay marriage as "pro-family," Eskridge unintentionally joins in the chorus of single-mother-bashing that has characterised the "family values" debate since Dan Quayle let fly at Murphy Brown, claiming that "some studies have found that children of lesbian couples are better adjusted than children of single heterosexual mothers, presumably because there are two parents in the household. If this finding can be generalized, it yields the ironic point that state prohibitions against same-sex marriages may be antifamily and antichildren" (1996: 13). So, in arguing that gay marriage promotes a sound environment for raising children, Eskridge falls into the worst sort of conservative assumptions of two-parent "stability" over just about anything else.

In this conservative argument for gay marriage, there is an implicit and often explicit denigration of radical attempts to challenge marriage and the family. During the early days of both the women's movement and the gay movement, a critique of the family and marriage was integral to a critique of patriarchy and heterosexism. The Gay Liberation Front made a statement in 1969, right after Stonewall, that was crystal clear in its denunciation of marriage: "We expose the institution of marriage as one of the most insidious and basic sustainers of the system" (cited in Eskridge 1996: 53). For writers like Eskridge, Sullivan, and Bruce Bawers (and, one might add, most heterosexuals) this kind of statement is one they would like to forget. For them it is a remnant of an "extremist" and liberationist past that must be transcended if gays are to enter fully into mainstream society and take their rightful place alongside Mr and Mrs Cleaver. But for many others, these are glorious statements of which we are proud. They indicate a thoughtful and thoroughgoing critique of social institutions that have played a serious role in the subjugation of women and the enforcement of heterosexuality. To be liberated from these institutions—and then perhaps to create new and sturdier ones—seems a worthy and ethical goal. For if marriage itself reinforces structural inequalities within families, it also "privileges" state-regulated long-term pairing over other forms of intimacy and connectedness. Many in the gay movement—like their counterparts in the women's movement—have been critical of marriage not only for its gender inequity and history of violence, but for the ways it *devalues* other ways of being sexual, loving, and nurturing.

If gays succeed in sanctifying the couple as the primary social unit, the one that gets financial and legal benefits, does that set up a hierarchy of intimacy that replicates the heterosexual one, rather than challenging or altering it? Gay marriage might grant visibility and "acceptance" to gay marrieds, but it will not necessarily challenge homophobia or the nuclear family. Indeed, it might demonise non-married gays as the "bad gays" un-civilized, promiscuous, irresponsible, while embracing the "good gays" who settle down and get married. Participation in this institution not only assimilates us into the dominant heterosexist way of relating, but gives further credence to an institution that has been built on the backs of sexism and heterosexism.

While there is no measurable correlation between desire to marry and desire to assimilate, testimonies and anecdotal evidence suggest that many gays who desire marriage ceremonies are precisely those gays most interested in demonstrating their essential sameness with heterosexuals. A piece in the *Washington Post* entitled "Every girl's dream" describes the ceremony of two women ("On this untraditional wedding day, the traditional jitters and the traditional tears"). Like all narratives of gay mimesis, the article draws you in by describing the couple the morning before the wedding, like any other couple, then hits you with the bombshell: "Angela is a bride. So is her fiancée" (Blumenfeld 1996: 1). Parents comment on how it is just like a "regular wedding" and bride Elise expresses her desire to do it exactly like the "real people." The "brides" observe a vow of celibacy the week prior to the "wedding" and the whole event is recounted in loving and supportive detail. Is the dream of a seamless inclusion really so foolproof?

If, as many have argued, gay rights and women's rights are intertwined, then any gay argument for marriage that ignores or downplays the relationship of the marriage institution to institutionalized male dominance is problematic at best. Indeed, in recent years we have seen a restigmatising of single women and single mothers—portrayed either as pathetically lonely career gals gone sour (*Ally McBeal, Sex in the City*) or as the cancer in the body of domesticity, creating social havoc through reckless child-rearing and neglectful daycare. While feminists pushed legislation to make it easier to leave marriages, the push now is to make it more difficult, through challenges to no-fault divorce and a rise in fundamentalist "covenant marriages." If feminists are right—that marriage is one of the cornerstones of the patriarchal family and a central site for the reproduction of gendered ideologies and behaviors—then gay inclusion must be examined through that feminist lens. In other words, gay access to marriage must be understood in terms of both sexual exclusion *and* gender domination.

If granted inclusion in the marriage club, will gays and lesbians be pressured to marry like their heterosexual counterparts? Marriage is hardly a choice (Polikoff 1996). Like its partner in crime, heterosexuality, marriage is largely *compulsory*: if the economic benefits don't get you, the social ones surely will. The institution of marriage is inextricably tied to the heterosexual nuclear family, and to the merger of parenting and partnering, intimacy and financial interdependency, that is so central to our truncated vision of "family." Marriage is not an isolated institution, nor some innate desire. Lesbians and gays should do all they can to dismantle those conflations and to continue to envision and enact ways of caring and loving that reinvent family, intimacy, parenting. Working to end marriage as a legal institution, and to provide instead meaningful social and financial supports for relations of dependency and need, would do much more to challenge the noxious politics of family values than getting married ourselves.

FAMILIAR FAMILIES: THE "GAYBY" BOOM AND FAMILY VALUES

For many lesbians and gays, certainly those of the pre-Stonewall era, gayness itself seemed to close off the possibility of having children. Gayness seemed so outside of the realm of family that not being able to have children appeared the inevitable price to pay for a life on the margins. In earlier times, then, most gay people had children within heterosexual relationships, relationships in which they often hid their desires and led painful double lives. In story after story of older gays, one of the constant refrains has to do with children and family. The stress of coming out to parents was exacerbated by a recognition that the parent would be experiencing the loss not only of the presumed heterosexual son/daughter, but of the prospect of grandchildren as well. Parents often report this as one of their biggest fears upon hearing that their child is gay: assuming that gayness disenables reproduction.

Earlier, more pathologizing renderings of homosexuality clearly marked gays as bad candidates for parenthood. If gayness was thought of as arrested development (as in much of psychoanalytic theory) then how could gays be parents? If gayness was thought of as inherited disease, then it might be transferred to progeny. If gayness was understood as predatory and inclined towards conversion, then kids would be forced into "the life" by their recruiting parents. There were no cultural role models, no familial portraits of gays and lesbians, no inkling in the vast social landscape that it could be done.

Let's be clear: lesbians and gays have always had children. What we are witnessing now, though, is the growing phenomenon of lesbians and, to a lesser extent, gay men, having children *as gay people*, outside the conventions of heterosexuality and marriage.

There have always been gay people who have been out enough—and brave enough—to live their lives the way they wanted to, including having children. The current gayby boom, however, seems to be the result of a confluence of factors: the availability of sperm banks and other reproductive technology, the growth of the lesbian and gay movement, and the emergence of couples and individuals who never were "in" the closet and never had to extricate themselves from straight relationships, families, marriages. Gay parents are now a visible, present force to be reckoned with, forming organizations and support groups, participating in PTAs and Little Leagues.

In the midst of all the hype about the gayby boom and the happy stories of gay parenting, it is important to remember that children are still routinely taken away from parents simply because the parent is gay. The celebrated Virginia case of Sharon Bottoms is typical. A mother—living with another woman—has to undergo a custody battle with *her* mother, who claims her lesbianism constitutes her an "unfit" mother. The court agrees, awarding custody to the grandmother solely on the basis of the mother's sexuality.

The National Center for Lesbian Rights, Lambda Legal Defense Fund, and other gay legal organizations regularly defend mothers and fathers in custody cases, around visitation rights, and in second-parent adoptions. Gay women are routinely denied access to alternative insemination and both lesbians and gay men are routinely turned down in attempts to foster and adopt. Legal victories are often fleeting and can be reversed at a moment's notice.

AND A WHITE PICKET FENCE: SELLING GAY SAMENESS

Given heterosexual mistreatment of gay parents, what remain surprising are the narratives by both gays and straights that relegate this mistreatment to a sidebar while focusing on the overwhelming "truth" of assimilated sameness. In article after article on gays with children, the reader is presented with strikingly similar formats. Articles typically go something like this: "Sunshine streams into the kitchen as a small, tow-headed boy and his parents bite into breakfast muffins rich with cherries from their backyard orchard in Cockeysville, Md. It's a Kodak moment of the '90's: Dad, Daddy and Duncan" (Smith 1995). In itself, there is nothing so terribly wrong with the story of Duncan: the lives of gay families often do look

much the same as the lives of straight families. Kids have to be fed, diapered, bathed, loved, taught, bundled off to school, disciplined, nurtured. Barney rules, wherever you go. Yet the power of such family narratives is indisputable. Wolkowitz for instance, describes how they operate to assimilate and neutralize even the conflicts and horrors of atomic weapons, in the autobiographies of women married to Manhattan Project scientists. And in the context of structural discrimination, things take on a different hue. Duncan is—of course—like every other kid. But he is a kid who will have to face homophobic comments (and perhaps worse) from other kids, parents, schoolteachers. He will rarely see his life depicted in textbooks and teaching aids, much less on TV. His parents do not have the same rights as other parents; they can lose jobs, be denied housing, not be promoted. He can even be removed from his parents because of their sexual orientation. In addition, it just might be the case that his parents don't *want* their lives to look like that of the Cleavers. Perhaps they want to build *new* kinds of families with *different* kinds of values.

Finally, gay parents are visible and are not made out to be lurking demons and perverts. What could be wrong with this? When the media make gays "safe" for American cultural consumption, are they not confining gays to a new kind of closet and denying the realities of homophobia? In "reducing" homophobia through assimilation there is a danger of making homosexuality itself invisible again—"straight, with a twist." Aside from the obvious and tedious attacks by the right, denouncing gay parents as immoral and dangers to the very concept of family, most reportage is supportive and steers clear of overt bigotry. What the articles do share is an almost identical narrative structure. In dozens if not hundreds of pieces on gay families the writers could be interchangeable such is the continuity of style and substance. Here are some more samples:

> To look at her, Alanna Gabrielle Handler seems an altogether conventional baby. Just 14 weeks old, she scrunches her tiny face and inspires the usual oohs and ahhs. The nursery in her family's Van Nuys apartment is pastel and girlish and graced with a banner proclaiming, "Welcome Alanna— Grandma and Grandpa." But Alanna is not a typical infant. She was not conceived the traditional way and her parents are not a conventional

couple—or should we say trio? No, Alanna is different. She is a tribute to lesbian romance and a product of artificial insemination, a baby whose very existence challenges traditional views of nature and family. And for the gay rights movement, she is a tiny bundle of hope. (Harris 1991)

Four-year-old Trevor wants to touch the ceiling. He leaps, grunts and tries to climb the wall, but soon figures out he's not going to get there on his own. "If you put me on your shoulders, I can touch the ceiling," he tells his dad. Dad is dubious—but a good sport. The shouldering is successful. But the pair are still inches away from their destination. Enter Daddy. He lifts his son easily onto his taller shoulders and raises the little boy's arms. Mission accomplished. Innocent of the social implications of being the adopted son of gay parents, Trevor is quite content to have two fathers . . . In all but one respect, they are the classic American family. The couple say that despite what stereotypes might suggest about a male child raised by gay men, Trevor is "all boy." He loves trucks, guns, sports and playing in the dirt, and wants to be a policeman. (Loebs 1995)

When mainstream narratives aren't extolling the sameness of homosexual family life, they are concerned with how children of gay parents will reckon with their own sexuality. A number of articles raise the issue of whether children raised by gay parents will themselves be gay or otherwise "do worse" than other kids. To counter hetero fears of a bumper crop of gay kids emerging from the gayby boom, gay researchers have argued that children of gay parents are "no worse" off than kids of hetero parents: "children born to or adopted by lesbians are psychologically healthy" (Tuller 1992). But fears of queer parents producing queer kids persist, and reporters feel compelled to comment on "conflicting evidence" such as a 1986 study of thirty-four gay households that indicated that the children became homosexual or bisexual 15 per cent of the time; and a 1990 study that found that 16 per cent of the daughters of lesbian mothers identified themselves as lesbian. One writer sees these findings as "worst-case scenarios," but is relieved to note that "other studies come up with figures below ten per cent for children of gays and lesbians" (Latz Griffin 1992), This kind of discourse implies a "natural" desire to raise children as heterosexual and figures gayness in kids raised by gays as a "worst-case scenario." Like the discourse that argues children of single parents fare "as well" as children of two-parent households, it inadvertently lends itself to a reassertion of the centrality and desirability of heterosexuality and dual parenting.

AND BABY MAKES . . . TWO: ONE MOTHER'S STORY

As I entered the growing ranks of lesbian mothers, I was forced to reckon with the ways in which alternative families elicit the most thoroughgoing heterosexual fear. I want to raise my daughter to believe that families come in many forms, that two parents are not necessary and that couples of the same gender or single parents may provide all the "role models" needed for healthy development. I try to raise her in a community of like-minded people and, in doing so, to break the hold that the "Cleaver Family" model still has on our cultural imagination. Even for less politically minded gay parents, the choice to raise a child must entail a challenge to many accepted notions of family life and family formation. Times certainly have changed in this regard, and my experience of lesbian motherhood is, I believe, illustrative of some transformations and issues both between straights and gays and within the gay community itself.

I will never forget the time I brought my daughter—barely four months old—to a Kol Nidre service at the local lesbian and gay synagogue. She was dressed in her hippest outfit (leopard print pants and top with matching cap) and all eyes were upon her. From the beginning of the service, as we milled about the church (borrowed for the occasion), to the end schmoozing outside on the steps, I felt suffused—almost overwhelmed—by the warmth and beloved attention that came Emma's way. Now, I could attribute this to her exceptional beauty and charm, but—as a wee infant—her delightful manner had yet to emerge. Something was certainly going on. As hands reached out to touch her hair softly and the line formed for the post-service viewing, I was struck by the delight my community seemed to have in this child. Now most people do coo and chuckle over a cute baby. And God knows my daughter is cute. But the response to Emma seemed much more engaged and deliberate—as if to acknowledge our disenfranchisement from this option and to celebrate it at long last. An elderly heterosexual couple came up to talk with me, tears in their eyes. Their son had recently died of AIDS—he had been a member of this congregation. They wanted to thank me for bringing Emma, for having Emma. An older lesbian approached me and talked to me about "the old days" when it was simply assumed that gay people did not parent, at least not as gay people. Her regrets were clear, even as she talked about her recent decision to attempt adoption. A thirty something couple approached me for info, comparing notes on sperm banks and pondering the possibility of play groups in the future. This is only one event among many and Kol Nidre is already an overweighted holiday, filled as it is with memories of those gone and the mournful tones of the cantor's invocation of Kaddish. But I was to find events like this repeated and repeated over the course of Emma's young life, as she was welcomed into the world by a newly awakened gay community. In Provincetown, the lesbian moms banded together on a section of Herring Cove, staking out baby territory amidst the friendly hordes of topless young women. In demonstrations and Pride Days, babies figure prominently, adorned with appropriate bumper stickers affixed to their overburdened strollers. And everywhere, everywhere questions. How did you do it? Did you go to a doctor? What sperm bank did you use? Did you tell them you were a lesbian? Did they turn you down? Did you experience hostility or discrimination? How did you pick the donor? What was the hospital scene like? What are you going to tell her? Many of these discussions were like any others around pregnancy and birth. But others were particular to this time and place, to this situation, to lesbians choosing children. My particular situation is perhaps unique (and perhaps not) but it does raise some important questions for how we think about family. For me, having a child was never an attempt to replicate heterosexual parenting. Because I came from a progressive family and was raised in an era of possibilities, it never occurred to me that being a lesbian would stop me having children. I was simply waiting for the right time. While more and more women are planning when and if to have children, the deliberation that goes into lesbian motherhood by choice is profound. Not dependent on the "right man" to turn up, lesbians choosing children call their own shots, in a context where lesbian mothers still produce terror, anger, discrimination. So they make the choice with the knowledge of the hardship that will likely ensue.

Curiously, my pregnancy—and later my child—often made me invisible as a lesbian.

Heterosexuals—and some gay people—wrongly assumed I was straight because of the belly pushing out in front or the diaper bag over my shoulder. A colleague looked at me quizzically and wondered if I had "intended" to get pregnant. In disbelief I told her I just got drunk and had my way with a bunch of sailors and forgot to use birth control. So unable was she to reckon with my lesbianism and my pregnancy simultaneously, that one had to disappear and since my belly wasn't going anywhere . . . I simply didn't fit into her mainstream narrative of parenting. While this type of homophobia increased, other forms relented. As I became more recognizable to my colleagues as a woman (real women have babies, therefore I must be a woman, even if I was a lesbian—not a woman), their discomfort with my homosexuality decreased, but not for the "right" reasons. Simply, they now *recognised* me—a pregnant woman—and that familiarity made me more accessible.

This new "tolerance" is problematic; does it help demarcate two separate classes of gay people—those acceptable to straights through their assumption of presumably straight practices, and those unacceptable through their insistence on "doing it their way"? Does it avoid reckoning with the real problem—the homophobia of straights? Indeed, I often feel profoundly misunderstood as a lesbian mother. I am no less radical than I was before Emma. I don't want my family "compared" to heterosexual nuclear families and I'm angered by well-meaning studies that set out to prove that children of gay parents are "no worse off" than children of straight parents. And I'm not really sure I see my family simply as a benign alternative in a sea of welling diversity. I see it in more grandiose terms, as forging intimacy and connection in ways that will enhance the life of the child and of those she comes in contact with. By separating parenting from socially enforced rules of partnering, I believe there are possibilities for familial constructions that are less mired in the violence, inequality, longing that characterize so many families.

BEYOND INCLUSION: RETHINKING INTIMACY, SEX, COMMUNITY

Anthropologist Kath Weston (1991) and others have written convincingly of the ways in which lesbians and gay men, so often disenfranchised from their families of origin, have created "families of choice" that serve many of the personal, emotional and social functions of more traditional familial formations. In creating vast and intricate networks of friends and lovers, ex-lovers and their partners and friends, gay people have forged intimacies and connections chat often seem more lasting and durable than the tenuous family of origin. Weston argues that these "families of choice" are not merely replicas of heterosexual families but create new forms of mutual responsibility, outside the typically gendered roles inhabited by women and men in heterosexual families.

This is not a banal argument for diversity of familial forms. It is about advocating models of love, support, and intimacy that actively dethrone the sexual/familial couple and present instead ever-expanding webs of relationships—ex-lovers, their partners or lovers, old friends, blood kin. Indeed, one can see this as a gay gift to the bankrupt models of middle-class white heterosexuality that "tend to isolate couples from their larger families and sometimes from friends—especially if they are ex-lovers" (Browning 1997: 133).

Gay family issues will, I believe, be the last holdout in the battle for gay and lesbian rights. As much as straights and many gays might want to argue that there is "no difference" between the way gays create families and the way heterosexuals do, it is hard to believe that the structures of exclusion and discrimination that surround gay life will not in some way impact gay family life. Embedded institutions are funny things. True, no institution is impenetrable or completely inelastic to change. Nevertheless, powerful and hierarchical ones such as the military or marriage are not easily altered. Is it possible that the creation of gay families through marriage or commitment ceremonies is the nail in the assimilationist coffin, linking gays irrevocably with mainstream heterosexuality? Or do these moves shake up heterosexual dominance like nothing else, permanently altering the very definition of family? If gays marry from within the dominant heterosexual frameworks, invoking dangerous ideologies of familialism, faith, and fidelity, the prospect of internal combustion fizzles out. If gays claim the right to parent based on their similarity to heterosexuals, we just may find our suburbs expanding to include June and June Cleaver. Obviously, not all gay parents are hetero clones, but those are the only gay parents we see in the news. These pervasive narratives of sameness could serve to keep the brass ring of gay liberation out of reach as gays settle for simple acceptance and a ride on the family merry-go-round. I'd much rather see a Utopian future of unmarried love and lust—for our heterosexual brothers and sisters too—than a dystopian future where marriage and familialism continue to trump values of community and care.

NOTES

1. It is ironic that one of the coded ways gays have of acknowledging other gays is to ask if they "are family."

2. For a more thorough account of the explosion of gay visibility, read my forthcoming book *All the Rage: The Story of Gay Visibility in America* (Walters 2001).

3. According to statistics from the Human Rights Campaign (garnered from the FBI), hate crimes against lesbians and gays (or those perceived as lesbian or gay) increased to 14 per cent of the total of all reported hate crimes in 1997, up from 11.6 per cent in 1996. In addition, attacks against lesbians and gays are becoming more violent, indicated most dramatically by the brutal murder of Wyoming gay student Matthew Shepard in October 1998.

4. The construction of gays as congenitally unable to negotiate the vicissitudes of adulthood (read marriage and kids) is a common theme not only in TV neoliberal discourse, but in gay conservative discourse as well. See particularly Sullivan (1997) and Bawer (1996).

Portions of this chapter are published as 'Take my domestic partner, please: gays and marriage in the age of the visible', in R. Reimann and M. Bernstein (eds) *Queer Families, Queer Politics: Challenging Culture and Society*, New York: Columbia University Press, 2001.

REFERENCES

Bawer, B. (ed.) (1996) *Beyond Queer: Challenging Gay Left Orthodoxy*. New York: Free Press.

Blumenfeld, L. (1996) "Every girl's dream." *The Washington Post* 20 November: D1–2.

Browning, F. (1997) "Why marry?" In A. Sullivan (ed.), *Same-sex Marriage: Pro and Con*. New York: Vintage.

Chambers, D. (2000) "What if? The legal consequences of marriage in the United States today and the legal needs of lesbian and gay male couples" In R. Reimann and M. Bernstein (eds). *Queer Families, Queer Politics: Challenging Culture and the State*. New York: Columbia University Press.

Eskridge, W. N. (1996) *The Case for Same-sex Marriage: From Sexual Liberty to Civilized Commitment*. New York: Free Press.

Harris, S. (1991) "2 moms or 2 dads – and a baby." *Los Angeles Times*, 20 October: Al.

Latz Griffin, J. (1992) "The gay baby boom," *Chicago Tribune*, 3 September: Cl.

Loebs, C. (1995) "Gay partners with children: adoption a challenge in climate of intolerance, legal ambiguities." *The Arizona Republic*, 27 July: 1.

Page, C. (1996) "Same-sex marriages strengthen the institution, not demonise it". *The Phoenix Gazette*, 23 May: B5.

Polikoff, N. (1996) "Marriage as choice? Since when?" *Gay Community News* 24, 3–4: 26–7.

Smith, L. (1995) "Gay parents have typical worries." *Baltimore Sun*, 23 July: 11E.

Sullivan, A. (1989) "Here comes the groom." *New Republic* August: 20.

———. (ed.) (1997) *Same-sex Marriage: Pro and Con*. New York: Vintage.

Tuller, D. (1992) "Lesbian families—study shows healthy kids." *San Francisco Chronicle*, 23 November: A13.

Walters, S. (2001) "Take my domestic partner, please: gays and marriage in the age of the visible." In R. Reimann and M. Bernstein (eds), *Queer Families, Queer Politics: Challenging Culture and Society*. New York: Columbia University Press.

Weston, K. (1991) *Families We Choose: Lesbians, Gays, Kinship*. New York: Columbia University Press.

Yardley, J. (1996) "The march of time." *The Washington Post*, 9 December: E2.

A MEMBER OF THE FUNERAL

Nancy Naples

Standing at my father's freshly dug grave holding the American flag the funeral director had just handed to me, I had the feeling I was in a bad made-for-TV movie. Since my mother was too sick with Alzheimer's to attend and I was the oldest of the six siblings, I was given the "honor." As I watched my three sisters, two brothers, their spouses, and my fifteen nieces and nephews slowly make their way back to the cars with other members of my large "hetero-normal" extended family, I at once ached to be accepted as a part of their world and longed for my "real" family.

I flashed back to the last time I stood by this grave side. It was also a somewhat dreary fall day. My brother Donald, who was the nearest in age to me (born less than a year and a half after me) and who was closest to me in other ways as well, had died in a car crash. At this time, my father decided to buy a plot in the local cemetery in their suburban community just north of New York City that would fit eight family members—fewer than

needed if all of us wanted to be buried there, more if everyone else was buried with their own nuclear family. So now two of the plots are inhabited. I wondered who besides my mother would join them. I presumed that all the other siblings would be buried with their nuclear families. Maybe my father thought that since I was "single," namely, had no "family" of my own, it would make sense for me to join them when the time came.

The significance of my singleness in the context of all the two-parent male and female families who made up the funeral procession was not lost on my two aunts. Earlier at the funeral parlor I overheard one of my aunts say to another aunt, "You know, the one I feel the most sorry for is Nancy. She has nobody." Their hushed and worried exchange amused me somewhat, although I also felt a great deal of sadness since, as many gays and lesbians, I am rich with loving and intimate friends who I consider my "real" family. Yet in fact I was indeed alone at my father's funeral. Where was everybody?

(continued)

When my brother Donald died in 1985, two of my most treasured "real" family were there for me. My lover Nina, who died in 1987 of breast cancer, and Peter, my brother-in-spirit who died of AIDS in 1996, were with me and were important witnesses over the years to the difficulties I had negotiating relationships with my family. Nina and Peter most assuredly would have been by my side had they been alive. Yet since neither Nina nor Peter were my legal or biological relations, their presence would have done little to shake the perception of my aloneness in the heteronormative world of my family.

Nina was my first female lover. We met in graduate school and I fell madly in love with her. Nina was incorporated into my family as my "best friend." No questions were asked about why I was no longer seeing my boyfriend Mark, nor did anyone ever ask why I never had another boyfriend after him. This seemed like an obvious question since I had dated boys since eighth grade, been married once, and lived with another man for several years. Nor did I take the initiative to explain. I just believed deep in my bones that coming out to my parents and siblings at the time would only strain my already conflict-ridden relationship with them. I did not feel that I had anything to gain from doing so and had much more to lose.

Not surprisingly, the unspoken but palpable homophobia I felt from my family was deeply woven into my own psyche. I colluded in the silence about it while Nina was alive. However, after she died I desperately wanted them to acknowledge who she was in my life and what her loss meant for me. I remember my mother commenting on what a good friend and social worker (my previous career) I was, given my central role in Nina's care, which included taking her to doctors' appointments and chemo treatments, sleeping over at the hospital during the last months of her life, and acting as executor of her will. Not even the fact that she left me all her worldly possessions, could shake my family's construction of my "friendship" with Nina.

Given the diversity among my siblings, coming out to them was much easier as well as much harder than I anticipated. The reactions ranged from downright hostility and rejection to ambivalent acceptance (the subtle message was that as long as I did not speak too much about my life as a lesbian, they could accept it). My brother John, the most hostile one, was violently angry and said in an attacking tone that having a sister who was a lesbian was a great embarrassment for him and that he would surely lose friends because of it. My brother Paul refused to hear it at all. Lisa and Melissa, the youngest of the clan, were mildly accepting, although over the years it became clear that, as Lisa put it, they would rather "not think about it." Karen, the remaining sister, was the most profoundly disturbed by it. Karen became a born-again Christian in her early twenties and was very invested in the anti-homosexual position her church promulgated. Her comments about how homosexuality was a sin against God and that gays were sexually promiscuous, carriers of diseases, and a basic threat to the moral fabric of society greatly distressed me even though I was well versed in the religious right's view of what they disparagingly call the "homosexual lifestyle."

Regardless of their individual responses to my coming out as a lesbian, each sibling strongly warned me against telling my parents. I think they all firmly believed that, as my brother John said, "it would kill daddy"—a projection of their own fears and a threat that is frequently used to keep gays and lesbians in their closets. Of course I did not really believe that the simple statement about my sexual orientation would kill my father or mother. However, on one level I felt I had nothing to gain by taking the risk and, on another level, I figured my father already knew. After all, he was a firefighter in the West Village for twenty-five years, even helping to put out the fires of Stonewall. I rationalized that if he wanted to deal with my lesbian identity, he would bring it up himself. So we developed an unspoken contract. I would not name my relationships with women as lesbian and he would accept my girlfriends into his home, no questions asked. I thought that was fair for the most part. In retrospect, I realize that I somehow bought into the fear that my lesbian self was a shameful secret that might have the power if not to kill, at least to deeply harm others.

(continued)

Over the more than ten years since I came out as a lesbian to my siblings, I tried to find a way to be a part of the family while also trying to protect myself from their rejection of my lesbian self. I maintained normalized relationships with all but my brother John and related to the other brother, Paul, through my sister-in-law, who seemed to be more open. I stopped celebrating Christmas and Thanksgiving with them. I would limit my visits to one or two days, staying over no more than one or two nights. I showed up unaccompanied for most events such as Christenings, weddings, baby showers, and physical and mental health crises even when I was in a relationship. I continued to keep my worlds relatively separate with a few moments of connection until 1997 when my mother's Alzheimer's escalated and we had to put her in a nursing home. This precipitated more intense and regular contact with my family. This difficult event overlapped with the start of a new relationship with Sharon, a woman who said that she would not mind being integrated into my family.

So now fast forward to the week of my father's death, which was quite unexpected. When I got the call from my youngest sister, Melissa, that I better get "home," I did not even think about what it would be like to stay with my siblings during the emotionally painful days leading up to my father's death. I rented a car at the airport and drove to Melissa's home in New Jersey. The first couple of days were difficult but manageable. All six of us seemed to be getting along pretty well. Each day I spoke to my soon-to-be ex-lover, Sharon (we were in the process of breaking up), who was trying to be supportive. Each day Sharon offered to come. I so wanted to take her up on her offer. After all, my siblings all had their spouses and children with them. I had neither lover nor friend. But I also knew, given the view of homosexuality held by my sister Karen, that it would be difficult to have my ex-lover with me, although I had no idea how messy it would become.

When Karen and her children began discussing the possibility of moving up to my father's house so they could be closer to the other cousins, I finally saw an opportunity to invite Sharon to join me. When I mentioned that she was coming, Karen threw a fit. She ranted, "How could you bring this into the family at such a time? What about the children? This is a time for the family to be together. It's not a time for us to have to deal with this." I tried to explain that Sharon was my family and that I needed the support. And, further, I was a lesbian whether my lover was with me or not. She refused to calm down and, in a huff, went up to pack hers and her children's bags.

Melissa, the youngest sibling, came to me pleading, "Nancy, do something!" So I took a deep breath, went to my sister Karen and said, "Fine, I'll tell Sharon not to come." I thought that this was the only way we could get through the next couple of days. I felt defeated and so alone but I was, after all, the older sister, a role that I performed uncritically for much of my life. After this incident, I could no longer stay with them. I quietly packed my bags and said that I would go stay with my friends in Manhattan. That night, my father died.

The following day I spent a long time describing the events to some of my close friends. I also contacted Sharon and asked her once again if she would come to be with me. She finally agreed but we did not decide whether or not she would attend the wake and funeral. I felt a bit aimless that day and thought that, even though it would have been easier to avoid it, I should drive to my father's house and together with my siblings confront the reality of his death.

Very quickly after I arrived it became clear to me that my lesbianism and the fear that my lover would come to the wake and funeral was the central topic of conversation. I went into the living room and all but my brother Paul were sitting there. My sister Lisa then turned to me and said, "We want to know what it is going to be like when your lover comes. Are you two going to be touching or whatever?" As John and my two youngest sisters tried to explain their concerns, I painfully noted the smug look on my sister Karen's face. Now she was not the sole voice, the religious fanatic with some extreme view but, rather, just another of my siblings, who all felt that it was an awful thing for me to be a lesbian. I wondered what they thought Sharon and I would do at the funeral parlour. Everyone but Karen had met her, but paranoia had overtaken them and they clearly were not thinking rationally.

(continued)

I, of course, felt attacked, horrified and desperately alone in my father's house. I got up and started packing my things to leave. Lisa came in and tried to explain why she thought it was a good thing for us to have this discussion, that my lesbianism was no longer a taboo subject, that she loved me, and that my lover would always be welcome in her house. I was appalled at the thought that there should have to be any question about this. I replied that they should deal with their own irrational fears about my sexuality but to leave me out of their conversations in the future. How unloving and hateful could a group of people be—people who are supposed to love me and want the best for me! I understood then that I was tolerated as part of the family as long as they thought I was alone, had no one to love me, to hold me, to comfort me. I understood even more deeply that the precious intimate friendships I had constructed over the years were truer expressions of "real" family than my biological family ever had been.

Well, after my father's funeral everyone returned to his house for a luncheon. I returned with them, flag in hand, and spent my remaining hours in his house talking to my aunts and several of my favorite cousins. After they left, I wasn't sure what to do. I wandered from room to room, looked in closets, found the hardcover copy of my book that I had recently given my father, and took one of his flannel shirts off a hanger. I decided to call my ex-lover. She and my friend Jen had, in fact, made it to the first night of the wake. Need I add that, not surprisingly, nothing dramatic happened. None of my siblings' fears about how our presence together might disrupt the dignified nature of the wake were realized. I did feel compelled to keep my physical distance from her. Sharon decided to leave the next morning. We both agreed that was best. But I was glad she came, even for the one night. I mourned the fantasy that one day I would be an accepted member of my biological family. Yet letting go of the need to keep my hetero-normal self alive, I have come to more fully embrace and gain sustenance from my "real" family who have been there all along.

Sexualities

The processes of socialization encourage women and men to develop different views of and approaches to sexuality and intimate relationships. Women learn strong interpersonal and emotional skills in preparation for roles as wives and mothers and for employment in professions associated with nurturing, such as teaching and nursing. At the same time, women's and men's different positions in social institutions mean that we enter our intimate and sexual relationships with different amounts and kinds of resources, power, networks, and expectations. In addition, we are surrounded by a culture that portrays women and men as having intrinsically different sexual needs, desires, and obligations. The readings in this section discuss how sexualities are gendered, showing how even such a seemingly personal matter as sexuality is *socially constructed* in various ways in different contexts.

Leila Rupp, in "Finding the Lesbians in Lesbian History," discusses the evidence we have about female same-sex sexuality in the past. She uses the term *same-sex sexuality* to make clear the difficulties of identifying who was a "lesbian" in places and at times that did not have that word. Pointing to three phenomena—romantic love, transgendered behavior, and sexual acts—she shows the ways that cultural attitudes about women and women's lack of access to public worlds shaped the expressions of same-sex desires. What do we mean when we think of someone as a lesbian today? Does it have to do with love, gender, and/or sex? Do lesbians in the twenty-first century United States have something in common with the women Rupp describes, do you think?

Susan Bordo, in "In Hiding and On Display," turns to a very different subject: the penis. Beginning with her personal experience as an adolescent, Bordo ponders the changing visibility of the penis in American society, from a powerful but hidden symbol of masculinity to a central and visible player in all sorts of media events, from Lorena Bobbitt's severing of her abusive husband's penis to the films *The Crying Game* and *Boogie Nights* to discussions on the floor of the U.S. Senate to the hit television series *Ally McBeal*. As a woman scholar, Bordo takes on the subject of the male body from an outsider's perspective, and the issues she raises say a lot about gender, bodies, and culture in contemporary American society. Why, do you think, is the penis more visible in our culture these days? Is that positive or negative? If you are a woman, how do you think men react to the examples Bordo discusses? If you are a man, how do you react?

The next article, "Doing Desire: Adolescent Girls' Struggles for/with Sexuality," by Deborah Tolman, examines how another group of females—adolescent girls—understand their sexuality. Adolescents have been the subject of considerable recent public debate over sexuality, with many politicians suggesting that teenage sexual activity should be discouraged. Yet, Tolman notes, adolescence is the life stage during which we begin to develop our sexual selves and form a sense of our intimate connections to others. Tolman examines how adolescent girls construct desire, tracing the complex mix of pleasure and desire with danger and fear, and highlighting differences of sexual orientation. As a result of the cultural repression of women's sexuality, Tolman argues, adolescent girls are "denied full access to the power of their own desire." How do the girls Tolman discusses come to understand their sexual selves in this context? Can you think of examples of how teenage sexuality is understood in discussions of public policy or sex education?

In "Becoming 100% Straight," Michael Messner turns our gaze to adolescent male sexuality. Using his own experience as a student athlete, he rethinks his conviction that he had always been 100 percent heterosexual by analyzing a crush he developed on another boy and his subsequent hostile reaction to him. Contrasting his own story to that of Tom Waddell, a closeted gay male athlete, he raises questions about the connections among heterosexuality, masculinity, and sport. He argues that men perform masculinity and heterosexuality through sport, and he asks why and what kind of consequences follow from that performance. How do you read Messner's story of his turn against Timmy? How important do you think sport is for young men today? Do you think sport has similar or different consequences for women as they perform femininity and heterosexuality?

Like family life, sexuality and intimate relationships are both a source of support and strength for women and a location of oppression. What do these readings suggest about how women find sexuality to be a means of fulfillment and an expression of self-definition? In contrast, how do the readings show sexuality to be a means of social control? In short, how are women oppressed and how do they resist in their intimate and sexual lives?

Finding the Lesbians in Lesbian History: Reflections on Female Same-Sex Sexuality in the Western World

♨ Leila J. Rupp

The central question facing students of lesbian history is: Where are the lesbians? This is not just a question of sources, despite the fact that one often feels a bit like Gretel, desperately searching for the bread-crumb trail leading out of the woods. So many of the sources for lesbian history have been destroyed, both by women fearful of leaving a trace and by hostile outsiders determined to wipe out any evidence of the existence of women who loved and had sex with other women. Blanche Wiesen Cook reports that Lorena Hickok—who remembered "the feeling of that soft spot just north-east of the corner of your mouth against my lips" in one of her surviving missives—and Esther Lape fed to the fire letters they had exchanged with Eleanor Roosevelt after the First Lady's death.[1] And in sixteenth-century Geneva, a jurist recommended leaving out the customary description of the crime for women sentenced to death for same-sex sexual relations lest other women, equally weak-willed and lascivious, be tempted to follow their example.[2] But the trail has not entirely vanished. The problem is less one of sources than of definition: who, among the women whose stories we can find, can be called a "lesbian"?

The question comes up at all because, until the late nineteenth century, the concept and identity of "lesbian" in the modern sense did not exist. Of course, women had long loved and engaged in sexual relationships with other women, and the existence of such behaviors was no secret, despite attempts to keep it quiet. But loving a woman did not place one in a category based on sexual object choice—that is, the sex of one's partner was not all-determining—until Western culture devised a classification scheme that differentiated people known as "heterosexuals" from those considered "homosexuals." If we confine "lesbians" to those who have claimed the label and identity, if only to themselves, our history is very short.

Historians interested in female same-sex sexuality, along with lesbian activists, have taken different approaches to the question of who counts and who does not. Adrienne Rich's concepts of "lesbian existence" and the "lesbian continuum," which include woman-identified women who resisted compulsory heterosexuality in a variety of ways, have proven influential.[3] However, the "sex radical" position in the "sex wars" of the 1980s has called attention to the denial of sexuality implicit in such a definition.[4] In her classic article, Blanche Wiesen Cook claimed as lesbians all "women who love women, who choose women to nurture and support and to create a living environment in which to work creatively and independently."[5] But do we then forget about sex? Is it not important?

These are questions with which lesbian historians must grapple. The historical evidence that we have, at this point in time, tends to reveal three different phenomena connected to "lesbian history" or, put more precisely, the history of female same-sex love and sexuality: romantic love between women, transgendered behavior, and sexual acts. In almost all cases, we are left still unsure what the evidence really means in light of our modern conception of lesbian life and lesbian identity.[6]

A few examples illustrate the problem. We now know a great deal about "romantic friendships" and "Boston marriages" between eighteenth- and nineteenth-century middle- and upper-class women in the industrialized Western world.[7] Although scholars are beginning to question just how acceptable they were, passionate attachments between women, often lasting through marriages, were at the very least relatively common and openly discussed without disapproval. Thus Molly Hallock Foote wrote to her friend Helena in the early 1870s: "I wanted so to put my arms round my girl of all the girls in the world and tell her . . . I love her as wives do love their husbands, as *friends* who have taken each other for life."

And when Helena decided to marry, Molly wrote to proclaim her love and passion and also addressed her fiancé: "Do you know sir, that until you came along I believe that she loved me almost as girls love their lovers. *I know I loved her so.* Don't you wonder that I can stand the sight of you."[8] Although this last suggests that, for Molly at least, marriage did interfere with her romantic friendship, the fact remains that Molly and Helena's love was not something to be hidden from the men in their lives.

To take another example, African-American poet Angelina Weld Grimké, the grandniece of abolitionists Sarah and Angelina Grimké, formed a romantic friendship with her school friend Mamie Burrill. In 1896, Burrill wrote to Grimke': "Could I just come to meet thee once more, in the old sweet way, just coming at your calling, and like an angel bending o'er you breathe into your ear, 'I love you.'" Angelina, later that year, expressed her own longing: "Oh Mamie[,] if you only knew how my heart beats when I think of you and it yearns and pants to gaze, if only for one second upon your lovely face."[9] But Grimké, perhaps because of the increasing suspicion towards women's relationships that accompanied the creation of the deviant category of the lesbian and her own experience of a broken heart, came to obscure her desires in her published poetry. Yet in unpublished lyrics and published verses addressed to a gender-unspecified lover, Grimké poured out the pain of an unidentified lost love.

Women's expressions of love for one another, during a period in which such declarations did not immediately point to a sexual relationship, leave us uncertain about the actual nature of such ties. Did women, conceptualized by the mainstream society as lacking in sexual desire, love and kiss and caress and sleep with each other but not "have sex?" Does it matter?

We also have evidence of women who crossed the gender line by taking on the clothing, work, and social roles of men and marrying women. Catharine Linck, in eighteenth-century Germany, disguised herself as a man to serve in the army. After her stint in the military, she took on a man's job and married

a woman, making a dildo and testicles from leather and pigs' bladders in order, as the court in a similar case put it, to "counterfeit the office of a husband." She was discovered when her wife, after an argument, confessed to her mother that Catharine was a woman. Like other women in early modern Europe who claimed both the occupational and sexual privileges of men, she was executed for her crimes.[10]

On the other side of the Atlantic and more than 150 years later, a French-born San Francisco woman by the name of Jeanne Bonnet took to wearing men's clothes. Arrested frequently for her penchant for male dress, Bonnet refused to pay a penny of her fines and instead went to jail, proclaiming her intention never to change her ways. In 1875, she organized a gang of ex-prostitutes who swore off men, arousing the ire of their pimps. Waiting for a gang member who was probably her lover, she was shot to death in 1876.[11]

By the turn of the century in the United States and Europe, as Bonnet's story begins to suggest, cross-dressing women, in the past always isolated from one another, began to come together in urban areas. Within the sexual underworld of big cities, women who dressed as men but did not try to pass as one came to be known as "dikes," from the term for a man all dressed up or "diked out" for a night on the town. Both urban working-class women and wealthy women in bohemian circles affected male dress for a variety of reasons, giving rise to the association made by such sexologists as Havelock Ellis between same-sex sexuality and gender "inversion."[12] At the height of the Harlem Renaissance, the African-American cultural flowering of the 1920s, bisexual and lesbian performers such as Ma Rainey and Gladys Bentley sang of "bulldaggers," connecting a preference for male attire and female company, as in Rainey's "Prove It on Me Blues": "Went out last night with a crowd of my friends, /They must've been women, 'cause I don't like no men./It's true I wear a collar and a tie. . . ."[13]

If transgressions of the gender line outraged mainstream Euroamerican society and found tolerance in the heady days of the Harlem Renaissance, some Native American cultures, primarily in western North America, included a cross-gender role, at least before the late nineteenth century. Women known as *hwame* (Mohave), *kwiraxame* (Maricopa), *tw!nnaek* (Klamath), *koskalaka* (Lakota), or *warrhameh* (Cocopa) took on the mannerisms, clothing, and work typical of men, and they also married women. Although the cross-gender role had complex spiritual meanings, it is significant that the sex and gender systems of these cultures, prior to the impact of Euroamerican imperialism, made a place for such individuals. Although the cross-gender female became a social male, her sexual behavior with her wife was not considered heterosexual but rather rated its own terminology.[14]

Although in many of the cases of women who crossed the gender line we also have evidence of sexual activity, we are left with many puzzling questions. Did the early modern European and U.S. women who defied their societies and risked death or imprisonment to take on the roles of men do so in order to pursue relationships with women? Or were their motives primarily social and economic, but passing as a man required sexual interaction with women? Does it matter? What about their wives? Should the *hwame* and *koskalaka,* who took on a cross-gendered lifestyle in a spiritual context, be considered lesbians?

Finally, we come to examples of sexual acts between women. As already suggested by the case of Catharine Linck, our evidence generally comes from court records, notoriously difficult documents to analyze. For one thing, women accused of sexual acts had every reason to deny having committed them, and women caught with other women had cause to portray themselves as innocent victims. In the case of Benedetta Carlini, a seventeenth-century Italian abbess, and Bartolomea Crivelli, a younger and less powerful sister in the convent, Crivelli testified to the investigating Church authorities that Carlini had forced her into "the most immodest acts." According to their report, "Benedetta would grab her by the arm and throw her by force on the bed. Embracing her, she would put her under herself and kissing her as if she were a man, she would speak words of love to her. And she would stir on top of her so much that both of them corrupted themselves."[15]

As in the case of Catharine Linck, we have evidence of a sexual act, but what does it mean? Another court case, this one from the early nineteenth century, raises some of the same questions but also makes a link between sexual behavior and romantic friendship. In the case made famous by Lillian Hellman's play, *The Children's Hour,* two Scottish schoolteachers confronted an accusation by one of their students that they came to each others' beds, lay one on top of the other, kissed, and shook the beds. The student, Jane Cumming, born of a liaison between an Indian woman and an aristocratic Scottish man serving the

Empire in the East, reported that Jane Pirie said one night, "You are in the wrong place," and her friend, Marianne Woods, replied, "I know" and asserted that she was doing it "for fun." Another night, she said, Pirie whispered, "Oh, do it, darling." And Cumming described, through her tears, the noise that she heard as similar to "putting one's finger into the neck of a wet bottle."[16] Such testimony forced the judges in this case to make an impossible choice between believing that respectable romantic friends might engage in such behavior or that decent schoolgirls could make up such tales. As one judge put it, "Are we to say that every woman who has formed an intimate friendship and has slept in the same bed with another is guilty? Where is the innocent woman in Scotland?"[17] Only Jane Cumming's Indian heritage helped to resolve the dilemma. Surely, many of the judges decided, she had learned of such behavior in India and used her knowledge to get out of a school she found too strict.

If not evidence of actual sexual behavior, this case at least brings to our attention a conception of lesbian sexuality. The question for the court was whether Pirie and Woods kissed, caressed, and fondled "more than could have resulted from ordinary female friendship," suggesting a line into sexuality that could be crossed.[18] That such relations did exist in the guise of romantic friendship is confirmed in the remarkable nineteenth-century diary of Englishwoman Anne Lister, an upper-class, independent, mannish woman who described her numerous sexual affairs with women, some of them married. In 1819, she detailed an encounter with the love of her life, Marianne, who married for economic and social status but continued her affair with Lister, eventually passing on a venereal disease contracted from her husband through his own extramarital exploits: "From the kiss she gave me it seemed as if she loved me as fondly as ever. By & by, we seemed to drop asleep but, by & by, I perceived she would like another kiss & she whispered, 'Come again a bit, Freddy.' . . . But soon, I got up a second time, again took off, went to her a second time &, in spite of all, she really gave me pleasure, & I told her no one had ever given me kisses like hers."[19]

Fed up with waiting for Marianne's all-too-healthy husband to die, Lister went off to Paris in 1824, where she almost immediately began to court a widow, Mrs. Barlow, staying at the same pension. One night, Mrs. Barlow came to her room and climbed into bed with her: "I was contented that my naked left thigh should rest upon her naked left thigh and thus she let me grabble her over her petticoats. All the while I was pressing her between my thighs. . . . Now and then I held my hand still and felt her pulsation, let her rise towards my hand two or three times and gradually open her thighs, and felt . . . that she was excited."[20]

Such explicit descriptions of sexuality, recounted in a woman's own words outside the walls of a courtroom, are a historical treasure. Most of the evidence we have of women's sexuality, like the cases of Benedetta Carlini and Woods and Pirie, is far more ambiguous. Lister was a woman who, before the invention of the term "homosexuality" in 1869 and before the emergence of the first lesbian cultures around the turn of the century, not only loved and desired women but saw this as her defining characteristic. She knew the term "Saffic," considered her attraction to women natural, and proclaimed proudly that "I love, & only love, the fairer sex & thus beloved by them in turn, my heart revolts from any other love than theirs."[21]

Her experiences bring together the previously disparate worlds of romantic friends, transgendered women, and same-sex lovers. The standard story of lesbian history in the Western world tells of class-divided experiences, with peasant and working-class women such as Catharine Linck and Jeanne Bonnet serving as forerunners of the butches and femmes of

the 1950s, and middle- and upper-class women such as Molly Foote and Angelina Weld Grimké foreshadowing the lesbian feminists of the 1970s. Anne Lister's story makes clear that this is far too simple a depiction. We have assumed that, because women did not have access to public space in the same ways that men who cruised the parks and public latrines and taverns of eighteenth-century European cities did, same-sex communities could not form until the turn of the nineteenth century. But perhaps the first "lesbian communities" can be found in the drawing rooms of respectable society as well as in the ranks of prostitutes and other women within the sexual underworld of big cities.

There is no simple way to find the lesbians in lesbian history, just as there is no agreed-upon definition of a lesbian in late twentieth-century U.S. society. That the test of romantic love, or rejection of traditional femininity, or genital sexual relations with another woman, or even identity is not sufficient to "find the lesbians" has become clear through an understanding of cultural differences within the contemporary lesbian world.[22] We must continue to search for the bread crumbs that have not been gobbled up and, valuing each one for what it can tell us, find our way out of the dangerous forest of ignorance about women's same-sex love and sexuality in the past.

NOTES

1. Blanche Wiesen Cook, *Eleanor Roosevelt: Volume One, 1884–1933* (New York: Viking, 1992), 479, 15.

2. Judith Brown, "Lesbian Sexuality in Medieval and Early Modern Europe," in *Hidden from History: Reclaiming the Gay and Lesbian Past,* edited by Martin B. Duberman, Martha Vicinus, and George Chauncey, Jr. (New York: New American Library, 1989), 75.

3. Adrienne Rich, "Compulsory Heterosexuality and Lesbian Existence," *Signs* 5 (1980): 631–60.

4. The struggle over sexual expressiveness and regulation between, on one side, feminists who emphasized the dangers of sexuality and the need to fight pornography as a form of violence against women and, on the other side, those who stressed its pleasures, became a national issue after the 1982 "Scholar and the Feminist IX" conference at Barnard College. See Carol S. Vance, *Pleasure and Danger: Exploring Female Sexuality* (Boston: Routledge & Kegan Paul, 1984), 441–53, and Lynne Segal and Mary McIntosh, *Sex Exposed: Sexuality and the Pornography Debate* (New Brunswick, NJ: Rutgers University Press, 1993).

5. Blanche Wiesen Cook, "Female Support Networks and Political Activism: Lillian Wald, Crystal Eastman and Emma Goldman," *Crysalis* 3 (1977): 43–61.

6. Martha Vicinus, "'They Wonder to Which Sex I Belong': The Historical Roots of Modern Lesbian Identity," *Feminist Studies* 18 (1992): 467–98, also considers these questions.

7. See Carroll Smith-Rosenberg, "The Female World of Love and Ritual: Relations between Women in Nineteenth-Century America," *Signs* 1 (1975): 1–29; Lillian Faderman, *Surpassing the Love of Men: Romantic Friendship and Love between Women from the Renaissance to the Present* (New York: William Morrow, 1981) and *Scotch Verdict* (New York: Quill, 1983); Lisa Moore, "'Something More Tender Still than Friendship': Romantic Friendship in Early Nineteenth-Century England," *Feminist Studies* 18 (1992): 499–520.

8. Quoted in Smith-Rosenberg, 7–8.

9. Quoted in Gloria T. Hull, *Color, Sex, and Poetry: Three Women Writers of the Harlem Renaissance* (Bloomington: Indiana University Press, 1987), 139.

10. See Faderman, *Surpassing the Love of Men,* 51–52.

11. The San Francisco Lesbian and Gay History Project, "'She Even Chewed Tobacco': A Pictorial Narrative of Passing Women in America," in *Hidden From History.*

12. George Chauncey, Jr., "From Sexual Inversion to Homosexuality: Medicine and the Changing Conceptualization of Female Deviance," *Salmagundi* 58–59 (Fall 1982–Winter 1983): 114–46.

13. Quoted in Sandra R. Lieb, *Mother of the Blues: A Study of Ma Rainey* (Amherst: University of Massachusetts Press, 1981), 124. See also Eric Garber, "A Spectacle in Color: The Lesbian and Gay Subculture of Jazz Age Harlem," in *Hidden from History,* 318–31.

14. See Evelyn Blackwood, "Sexuality and Gender in Certain Native American Tribes: The Case of Cross-Gender Females," *Signs* 10 (1984): 27–42, and Paula Gunn Allen, *The Sacred Hoop* (Boston: Beacon Press, 1986).

15. Quoted in Judith Brown, *Immodest Acts: The Life of a Lesbian Nun in Renaissance Italy* (New York: Oxford University Press, 1986), 117–18.

16 Faderman, *Scotch Verdict,* 147.

17. Ibid., 281.

18. Ibid., 82.

19. Anne Lister, *I Know My Own Heart: The Diaries of Anne Lister* (1791–1840), edited by Helena Whitbread (London: Virago, 1988), 104.

20. Anne Lister, *No Priest But Love: The Journals of Anne Lister from 1824–1826,* edited by Helena Whitbread (New York: New York University Press, 1992), 65.

21. Lister, *I Know My Own Heart,* 145.

22. See, for example, Makeda Silvera, "Man Royals and Sodomites: Some Thoughts on the Invisibility of Afro-Caribbean Lesbians," *Feminist Studies* 18 (1992): 521–32, and Carla Trujillo, *Chicana Lesbians: The Girls Our Mothers Warned Us About* (Berkeley, CA: Third Woman Press, 1991).

READING 27

In Hiding and on Display

❧ Susan Bordo

IN THE DARK WITH MEN'S BODIES

Becky Stone was the first of my friends to actually *see* one. We were fifteen, and Becky was going steady with a nice boy who "stopped" when asked, so she was allowed certain explorations too dangerous for the rest of us. I was incredibly jealous of the liberties she enjoyed. But I was also terrified of "having" to look at it myself.

My direct acquaintance, up to that point, had been entirely tactile, furtive, and fragmentary, like the blind man's picture of the elephant. I only knew what came in contact with me in the dark; the rest was left to my imagination, which often got things wrong. From Jeffrey Schwartz, pressing himself against me as we danced in my basement, I had learned that the thing could become hard, and was capable of asserting itself at a surprising angle from the body. I was twelve; from that moment on I imagined that my science teacher, whose pants had an odd crease in front—probably caused by a wallet—was perpetually erect.

Then I was fourteen, and Bobby Cohen was lying heavily on top of me in someone else's basement, his nose running. He did not seem to be having a good time as he humped away. He had a bad cold, and I'm sure would rather have been home (as I wished I was); but something was at stake here more important than pleasure, clearly, for both of us. We were both fully clothed; I stuck my hand in between his body and mine (but over his clothes) and pressed it against him, if only to take an intermission from the incessant humping. A sharp thrill went through me, which I decided to ignore, put on hold for another time. I knew that I could only absorb so much knowledge from this new realm, or I might be scared off forever.

Becky was more relaxed about these things than I. When she finally gave in—her boyfriend had been pleading with her for weeks to "take it out" of his pants—she came back shrieking, giggling, with details that inspired horror, awe, revulsion. "It shoots straight up from a bunch of hair!" That seemed wrong, unnatural, like a particularly ugly mixed metaphor or a mythological beast whose parts were mismatched. I shuddered at the thought that someday I would have to look at one too. But actually, the opportunities for that were minimal growing up in the late fifties and early sixties, at least at my high school, where most heterosexual exploration was organized around forays, skirmishes, invasions into the territory of *our* bodies—women's bodies.

"Did you take it off?" "Did you see it?" "Did you touch it?" Boys compared notes after dates. To become a man, a boy went through a certain education (however flawed or distorted) in women's bodies. Our panties were skins to be peeled, the fasteners on our bras latches to be unlocked; getting underneath or inside might have been for purposes of conquest or "scoring" but it also gave information. My girlfriends and I were so preoccupied with the proper management of this male education (for it seemed to be in our hands) that we often forgot about our own.

Was I odd to have reached puberty without having seen a penis? It is true that my father was especially modest, and I suspect that my friends with brothers at home were more knowledgeable than I. But the vaguely repellent mystery of my father's body—what horrible thing was lurking down there, under his baggy boxer shorts?—was not solved for me by looking around the world outside my family. The fact is that although my father's prissiness about his body may have been extreme among actual men, it seemed to be perfectly mirrored in the attitudes, symbols, stories, and images of the culture around me.

It caused a furor in 1961 at Mattel, Inc., when female executives argued that Barbie's new partner Ken ought to have a bulge in his groin. Barbie's own breasts, if translated into human proportions, would have made her Jayne Mansfield. She had been modeled almost exactly on the German *"Bild Lilli"* doll, originally marketed as a mini sex toy for adult men: big breasts, cinched waist, long legs, and slightly lascivious face. Her biographer, M. G. Lord, describes her body as *"la différence* incarnate." But try to endow Ken with *his* "difference incarnate" and all hell broke loose. The designers had to try out three versions of Ken's crotch in an effort to appease nervous male executives. Charlotte Johnson, Barbie's clothing designer, recalls:

"One was—you couldn't even see it. The next one was a little bit rounded, and the next one really *was*. So the men—especially one of the vice presidents—were terribly embarrassed. So Mrs. Handler and I picked the middle one as being the one that was

nice-looking. And he said he would never have it in the toy line unless we painted Jockey shorts over it."

Some might argue that the squeamish executives only wanted to protect innocent children from a too sexually explicit plaything. After all, these dolls weren't designed as a course in sex instruction. But we're not talking here about testicles, shaft, head—just a little plastic mound. And if keeping sexual messages muted was the issue, then how did Barbie get away with being a bosomy vamp while even an anatomically vague allusion to Ken's sexuality was so problematic?

If one didn't get to see one at home or in the backseat of a car, where *did* a girl get to see one? Museum statues often had fig leaves. On the ones that didn't, the penis itself was so diminutive and innocuous that I doubted *it* could possibly be the same thing my father was hiding. Medical books were short on photographs of penises; even a realistic drawing was hard to come by. No classroom lectures on safe sex, with life-size models to fit with condoms. The boys saw films of oozing sores (but not one healthy member) in their health classes; we girls only got the female reproductive tract and pep talks on how wonderful it was to have a period.

When I was growing up, male movie stars and models provided no instruction either. Beautiful male bodies, of course, were not absent from popular cultural representation—particularly if you include athletes and movie stars as well as classical figures. Sexy male physiques—Paul Newman, William Holden, Yul Brynner—were available for fantasy even when I was growing up. But until very recently—outside of homoerotic photography and porn—a naked (usually hairless) male chest was the most one could expect to see, and that rarely. It wasn't until 1972, remember, that *Cosmopolitan* published that daring centerfold of Burt Reynolds, his penis hidden demurely behind his hands. "Equality at last!" Helen Gurley Brown declared.

By today's standards that centerfold certainly doesn't look like much; the fact that it was regarded as such a breakthrough is a good indication of how revolutionary the mere suggestion of unclothed penile regions was in those days. Now that I've become a student of such matters I realize that the Reynolds centerfold, as tame as it now seems, *did* represent something of a cultural turning point. It wasn't only (or even primarily) feminism that was responsible, though. As the politically oriented rebellions of the sixties gave way to the sex-and-lifestyle conceptions of liberation of the seventies, men's bodies began to be drawn into the ever-widening vortex of late-twentieth-century consumerism. Men could be encouraged to spend their money on fashion, hairstyles, jewelry, too! And what's more, there were plenty of previously ignored consumers out there—both male and female—who liked to look at male bodies.

Five years after the Reynolds centerfold made its appearance, Hollywood put its first hunk in (discreetly black) briefs on the screen (John Travolta, playing Tony Manero in *Saturday Night Fever*), and Calvin Klein, inspired by muscular yet sinewy gay male aesthetics, brought the beauty of men in tight jeans—and a bit later, clinging underwear—to a mass market. No naked penises, true. But a new willingness to visually foreground the sexuality of male hips and buttocks, and, ultimately, male genitals. The representational frontiers of the male body had been expanded; geographically, it now included a southern hemisphere. Consumer culture had discovered and begun to develop the untapped resources of the male body. . . .

At the beginning of the nineties, things began to bubble and brew in unprecedented ways, bringing many of these elements up to the surface of American cultural life. 1991: Long Dong Silver—not only a porno character but a racially stereotyped one at that— referred to in extended (so to speak) discussion on the floor of the United States Senate. 1992: *The Crying Game*. First, one guy asks another to take his penis out of his pants to help him urinate, then we get a close-up of an actual penis—and on the body of what we thought was a woman! 1993: John Bobbitt's member is cut off by his wife (and chucked out the car window like a cigar butt), making real for thousands of men what had previously existed only in Philip Roth novels, therapy sessions, and bad nightmares.

It was as though the repressed had decided to erupt with a vengeance, straight from the collective unconscious, in all its most disturbing, marginal, anxiety-laden forms. "I've had enough of this closet. I'm going to throw open the door, and *really* make them squirm." And squirm we did. After Lorena made her point, the men of this nation (notwithstanding the fact that penis-severing is very, very rare—I personally haven't read of another besides Lorena's) became a country of Alexander Portnoys, nervously awaiting the moment when some woman would come at them with "the knife." Freud had told us all about it, hadn't

he: the little boy whose organ is "so dear to him" will have it "taken away from him if he shows his interest in it too plainly." But that was supposed to be a fantasy! Although Freud did speculate, didn't he, that in "the human family's primeval period," castration actually was used as a punishment against naughty boys? He was right! And it's happening again!

Lorena was for some men what Mark Fuhrman would later become for some blacks—a symbol of the most heinous violence human beings can do to each other. One man wrote to *People* magazine that "being a male in America today is like being a Jew in Nazi Germany." Another wrote, in the *Los Angeles Times*, that "her abuse of him was so barbaric that the fact she was allegedly abused is hardly an issue." Rush Limbaugh and other conservative commentators hallucinated armies of hatchet-faced feminazis for whom castration was an exquisitely just revolutionary act, and Lorena a heroine for all battered women. (In fact, the few feminist intellectuals who cheered for Lorena and saw her action as a "wake-up call" to men included Katie Roiphe and Camille Paglia—not exactly the male-hating "victim-feminists" whom Rush had in mind.)

Our culture was disproportionately obsessional too about "the scene" in Neil Jordan's *The Crying Game*, in which archetypally femme-y singer Dil takes off a satin robe and reveals a penis beneath. In an earlier scene, Dil's ex-lover Jody, chiding his embarrassed captor Fergus into unzipping his pants to help him pee (his own hands are cuffed, since he's being held prisoner), had reminded Fergus that "it's just a piece of meat." Public responses to the movie, however, revealed that the penis is much more than that for us. "Don't give away the secret!" "Don't tell the surprise!" The degree of cultural collusion maintained about "*the* scene," in a society where leakage of information is a national disease, was truly remarkable. Not even the shower scene in *Psycho*—shocking at the time not only because of its violence but because it killed off the star so early in the film—was so carefully guarded. At times, the hysteria to conceal "the secret" of *The Crying Game* bordered on crazy absurdity, as when Roger Ebert furiously scolded Gene Siskel for revealing it on their "If We Picked the Oscars" show, even though film clips had just been shown in which Jaye Davidson, nominated for best supporting *actor*, appears as a woman.

Critics were dazzled. "In the middle of the London sequence, Jordan surprises us so thoroughly that we have to reconsider everything we have felt up to this point," wrote *New York* magazine critic David Denby. Wow. Not all of us, it's true, were quite so surprised, or felt we had to reconsider *everything*. Savvier viewers suspected Dil's biological sex from the start, on the basis of Jaye Davidson's thick neck and wrists, deep voice, and numerous other small but telling cues. Some continued to see Dil as an attractive woman even after her penis had been exposed. They agreed with Dil that the fact that she has a penis is just "details, baby, details" (as she notes drolly in another scene); penis or no penis, she's still a girl according to the cultural grammar of gender. But for most viewers, including Dil's hopeful lover Fergus (who promptly throws up at the sight of Dil's organ), the presence of that penis was definitive—the "absolute insignia of maleness," as psychoanalyst Robert Stoller has described it—and (unlike Fergus, whose stomach eventually settles down) we just couldn't get the sight of it on the "wrong body" out of our minds.

It may seem only natural to those who equate gender with biology that the presence of a penis would confirm that the body who has it is male. But not all sexual body parts scream out their gender as definitively as the penis does. Psychologists Suzanne Kessler and Wendy McKenna showed subjects two sketches: one with all the expected female sexual attributes—breasts, hips, long hair—but *with* a penis, and one without breasts, hips, or body hair but *with* a vagina. They found that the presence of the penis was the single most powerful, *the* definitive cue for deciding which gender the figure was: 96 percent of their subjects judged the figure with the penis as male *despite* breasts and other female cues, while 33 percent of their subjects were able to ignore the vagina as a female cue in the other figure. *The Crying Game* unnerved people by confronting them with a body that unsettled their assumptions about gender—and raised the possibility of it all being organized very differently.

If Lorena Bobbitt stirred up castration anxiety, and *The Crying Game* elicited what might be called gender anxiety, the Clarence Thomas hearings thrust in our faces not only the prevalence of sexual harassment but also a historical legacy of sexually tinged racism. Since 1991, we've nationally televised so many grotesque absurdist moments involving sexual body parts—including news conferences on Bill Clinton's "distinctive" penile features—that it may take some straining to remember how bizarre it was to hear the words "Long Dong Silver" actually coming out of Orrin Hatch's prune mouth. He led up to it laboriously, strategically. "And she said 'He described pornography with people engaging in oral sex.' Is *that* a black stereotype?" "No," replied Thomas. Hatch: "People engaging in acts of sex with animals?" Thomas: "No." Hatch: "'Long Dong Silver.' Is *that* a black stereotype? Something like 'Long Dong Silver'?" When Thomas said yes, Hatch performed the outraged innocent with gusto. "Well! I'm concerned! . . . This really bothers me!"

Hatch's shock was feigned for effect of course. Nonetheless, it was an unprecedented moment, the prissy little senator from Utah—Utah!—forced to say "dong" in order to achieve his political goals. The senators didn't even like to say the word "penis" let alone refer to a gigantic black one. While they thought nothing of dragging Anita Hill through hours of humiliating testimony about pubic hairs on Coke cans and various genres of pornography, they could bring themselves to say the p-word—and with obvious discomfort—only when forced to, quoting from Anita Hill's testimony. Hill's own lawyers too, arguing that "the decorum of the Senate favored delicacy," avoided the term "penis." Their preferred term was "private parts." Even today, we sometimes have trouble with the words for male genitals. ("Stop cancer *down there*," coyly states the July 1997 cover of *Men's Fitness*.) We've become far less delicate, however, about public intrusions into private sexual behavior. We may still employ the euphemisms, but not even— no, let me rephrase that, *especially* not—the President of the United States is actually permitted to have "parts" that are even remotely considered private.

The senator's discomfort was nothing compared with Thomas's. "Yes," Thomas had replied through clenched teeth in response to Hatch's deliberately leading question, "the size of sexual organs would be something . . ." It was an awful moment, no matter whose side one was on. Thomas could barely get the words out, groping to make the stereotype clear while at the same time distancing himself from it; his use of the subjunctive mood (as though he were describing a possible universe), the vagueness of "the size": unconscious protection against his own contamination by the image he was exploiting. Thomas was hoping that the charge that he'd been tarred by racial stereotypes might win him his seat on the Supreme Court—and it did. But he also knew that racist imagery, once released from the collective unconscious, is apt to run amok. And so it did. Thomas won, but a sympathetic *People* magazine story which appeared later that week, showing Thomas piously reading the bible on the couch with his wife, Virginia, made Thomas's crotch the visual focus of every photograph. . . .

It sometimes seems as though popular culture has gone directly from near-censorship to blatant sexual fetishization—even idolatry—of the male organ. The wildly popular television comedy series *Ally McBeal* devoted two episodes to Ally's temptation by (and ultimate affair with) an artist's model who is so fabulously endowed that Ally's foxy roommate Renee, doing a clay sculpture of him in class, has to ask for more clay. We don't get to see the original (only the bulging eyes and open mouths of Ally and Renee), but at one point Renee's clay simulacrum falls to the floor (gravity has screwed up her attempts to do the statue "to scale") looking pretty darn lifelike. After class, at a restaurant, Ally and Renee wave rubbery sausages about, as they discuss whether the model's member was an implant or natural ("*super*natural," suggests Renee). When Ally accepts a date with the guy, her female colleagues—who have spent hours standing around discussing the size of this guy's penis—snigger "Don't get hurt!" They don't mean emotionally.

Sexual politics as well as consumerism have clearly played a role here. Between 1991 and Long Dong Silver and 1998 and Long John Silver (as one of the women refers to the model) watercooler talk about big penises has apparently become not only "correct" but obligatory for demonstrating that the heroines of your show are not *those* kind of feminists. You know, the Anita Hill kind. Any tendencies in that direction are always countered on *Ally McBeal*—not with an "argument" (this is postmodern television, not some dreary old *L.A. Law*), but with irony. Ally, for example, feels guilty for being attracted to the model with the shlong. Less repressed Renee (she's a black woman, after all) points out that men have been no less superficially magnetized by big breasts (including her own "golden, lofty globes"), so why not go for it. "But we're women," Ally sputters, "we're different . . . we have double standards to live up to." The show itself is dedicated to blasting those double standards to pieces—when the mood strikes it—and keeping gender very, very traditional when *that* suits it. In another scene in the same show, Ally—having successfully defended a young man who broke another guy's jaw for insulting his girlfriend—admits while strolling

with the artist's model that she too would "want my date to rip off the head" of any guy who insulted her. As I've said, Ally is a postmodern show. It gets to have it any way it likes.

So, although the women on the show are post-Hill feminists, the men on the show are post-Thomas guys too—at least when it comes to boasts about their own penis size. "Does size really matter?" Billy (Ally's ex, now married to another female lawyer at the firm) asks the giggling women, as they stand around discussing the model's "trunk." As is the case for many ordinary guys in the real world, the super-endowed model has bred insecurity—*not* identification—in Billy. The girls (these are not the kind of girls to be offended by being called that) assure Billy that finger size is more than enough for them. But they're lying, as their giggles demonstrate to Billy. Later, in bed, he's unable to maintain an erection with his wife—which touches her, since until then she'd always been the insecure one in the relationship. But in the meantime, across town, Ally is having primally satisfying sex with Long John Silver, interspersed with scenes of her colleagues (male and female alike) watching a boxing match on television, celebrating their earlier legal vindication of man's "warrior nature," smoking big stinky cigars, lustily urging their favorite to take the other guy out.

Depending on your perspective, the contradictions of *Ally McBeal* are either wonderfully true to the complexity of contemporary life or a shameless, cynical media potpourri, with Teflon politics to which nothing sticks. In the case of the big penis show, however, the show's contradictions accurately (if unquestioningly) reflect our current ambivalence about masculinity, itself reflected in the different guises with which the penis has come out of the closet in our culture. On the one hand, there are the underwear models with jaws and balls of steel—the phallic mythology of Superman masculinity, still vital if not entirely intact in this culture. Think, for example, of our definition of "erectile dysfunction," a term which has entered everyday conversation with the marketing of the miracle drug Viagra. With so much controversy about Viagra . . . , it's becoming somewhat politically incorrect to use the old term "impotence." That's all to the good. But instead, we say "dysfunction" and then define it as the inability to achieve an erection that is adequate for "satisfactory sexual performance"! Not pleasure. Not feeling. *Performance.* Eighty-five-year-old men are having Viagra heart attacks trying to keep those power tools running.

On the other hand, there's the less than masterful reality of Everyman, also coming out of the closet. In the second half of the 1990s, we've seen men depicted learning what it's like—in the charming and successful. *The Full Monty*—to be on public display *without* that gleaming phallic armor. We've heard male insecurities about penis size verbalized on national television. (*Seinfeld* was the first to break that ground, with Costanza's frenetic efforts—on one of the show's most hilarious episodes—to make sure that Jerry's date for a beach weekend, who had accidentally seen his unclothed penis as he came out of the water, will know that he's not *really* as small as he looked. "Shrinkage!" he keeps insisting.) We've even seen a penis caught in a zipper, in the over-the-top comedy *There's Something About Mary*. Now what could be less masterful than that?

Superman and Everyman, however, don't live together in real life as cozily as they do on *Ally McBeal*. For Superman haunts Everyman, threatens his undoing, as Paul Thomas Anderson's *Boogie Nights*—my own favorite coming-out film—dramatizes. The film is the story of the rise and fall of a mythically endowed (or so we are led to fantasize throughout the movie, from the amazed eyes of those who gaze on him) young porn star, Dirk Diggler. Diggler (a stage name) is played by Mark Wahlberg, who used to go by a stage name of his own—Marky Mark, who in his former cultural incarnation as rapper and underwear model did his own bit in bringing the penis out for popular consumption. Burt Reynolds, that centerfold innovator, plays director and porn-film producer Jack Horner. (This film is a field day for what poststructuralists call "intertextuality.")

"There's something wonderful waiting to get out of those jeans," Horner tells young Dirk. And as long as Diggler is revered as the biggest, hottest kid on the block, he does just fine. But he loses his grip in the face of competition, and begins to have trouble getting it up. This dilemma is no scriptwriter's contrivance. With the "money shot" (ejaculation) the culminating moment of virtually all porn films, the pressure for erection on command is constant for the male porn star. Susan Faludi reports a conversation in which an aspiring actor asked an experienced actress for pointers in the business. "Just get it hard," she told him. But this, of course, is more easily said than done, and frequently the actor—with the whole crew tapping their feet—must "wait for wood." Often, the actors fail and "break down on the set" (lose their

erections) and lose the gig. Thus the world of pornography, which (as Ira Levine has put it) dramatizes "the triumph of the dick," at the same time tyrannizes the actors who are expected to enact that triumph.

On the surface, a commercial underground where men pray for "wood" and lose their jobs if they cannot achieve erection on command is far removed from the lives of most men. On a deeper level, however (and as *Boogie Nights* illustrates), the world of the porn actor is simply the most literalized embodiment—and a perfect metaphor—for a masculinity that demands constant performance from men. When Wahlberg first heard about the script to *Boogie Nights*, it unnerved him, reminded him of his own life, and "all the stuff I wanted to get away from." Wahlberg was a male model, of course, and one famous for his endowments. But a man doesn't have to have made his fortune through his member in order to identify with Dirk Diggler's predicament. (The man with whom I saw the movie—a college professor—told me his palms were sweating throughout it, anticipating the inevitable failure.)

Even before Diggler takes up a career that depends on it, his sense of self is constellated around his penis; he pumps up his ego by looking in the mirror and—like a coach mesmerizing his team before a game—intoning mantras about his superior gifts. That works well, so long as he believes it. But unlike a real power tool, the motor of male worth can't simply be switched on and off. Unwavering, unbending power may be intoxicating as long as the fortress holds; but as soon as it cracks, the whole structure falls to pieces. And it's bound to crack; it's just too much to expect from a human penis—or a human being. In the final shot of the movie, we see Diggler's fabled organ itself. It's a prosthesis, actually. (Some men thought that was a cheat—until I reminded them of breast implants.) But prosthesis or not and despite its dimensions, Diggler's penis is no masterful tool. It points downward, weighted with expectation, with shame, looking tired and used.

I don't have a penis, and I don't intend to speak in this book as an expert on those who do. My own experience with the male body is as a woman, a perspective that will be kept at the forefront rather than obscured. This has advantages as well as drawbacks. There are things I can never know by virtue of the fact that I don't have my own "ignoble little brother." But by the same token, I have no need to disown, deny, or despise myself for his mischief.

A certain empathy for the special predicaments of the male body, ironically, may come easier to someone who *doesn't* have one.

At the same time, it may be that this most male of bodily sites—the penis—holds the most promise for a deeper identification between men and women. Dirk Diggler's predicament—shame, exhaustion with cultural expectations, the failure of the body to live up to those expectations—these are all experiences a woman can relate to. I have been amazed at how much unexpected kinship I've felt with men while writing this book, and how many old myths I have been led to revisit and revise. In the process, I've come to see that the pop psychologists are dead wrong. For all our differences, so entertaining and lucrative to emphasize nowadays, men and women do *not* come from different planets. One of my goals in writing this book is to demonstrate that.

BIBLIOGRAPHY

Beauvoir, Simone de. (1952). *The Second Sex*. New York: Vintage Books.

Bordo, Susan. (1993). "Reading the Male Body," *Michigan Quarterly Review*, Vol. 32, No. 4, Fall (Ann Arbor: University of Michigan), pp. 696–737.

Faludi, Susan. (1994). "The Naked Citadel," *The New Yorker*, September 5, pp. 62–81.

Hollander, Anne. (1994). *Sex and Suits: The Evolution of Modern Dress*. New York: Kodansha International.

Horrocks, Roger. (1994). *Masculinity in Crisis*. New York: St. Martin's Press.

Kessler, Suzanne J., and Wendy McKenna. (1978). *Gender: An Ethnomethodological Approach*. Chicago: University of Chicago Press.

Lord, M. G. (1994). *Forever Barbie: The Unauthorized Biography of a Real Doll*. New York: Avon Books.

Roth, Philip. (1974). *My Life as a Man*. Bantam Books: New York.

Roth, Philip. (1969). *Portnoy's Complaint*. New York: Bantam Books.

Sheets-Johnstone, Maxine. (1994). *The Roots of Power: Animate Form and Gendered Bodies*. Chicago: Open Court.

Solomon-Godeau, Abigail. (1995). "Male Trouble." In Maurice Berger, Brian Wallis, and Simon Watson (eds.). *Constructing Masculinity*. New York: Routledge, pp. 69–76.

Updike, John. (1993). "The Disposable Rocket," *Michigan Quarterly Review*, Vol. 32, No. 4, Fall, pp. 517–520.

READING 28

Doing Desire: Adolescent Girls' Struggles for/with Sexuality

☙ **Deborah L. Tolman**

In order to perpetuate itself, every oppression must corrupt or distort those various sources of power within the culture of the oppressed that can provide energy for change. For women, this has meant suppression of the erotic as a considered source of power and information within our lives.

(Lorde 1984, 53)

Recent research suggests that adolescence is the crucial moment in the development of psychological disempowerment for many women (e.g., Brown and Gilligan 1992; Gilligan 1990). As they enter adolescence, many girls may lose an ability to speak about what they know, see, feel, and experience evident in childhood as they come under cultural pressure to be "nice girls" and ultimately "good women" in adolescence. When their bodies take on women's contours, girls begin to be seen as sexual, and sexuality becomes an aspect of adolescent girls' lives; yet "nice" girls and "good" women are not supposed to be sexual outside of heterosexual, monogamous marriage (Tolman 1991). Many girls experience a "crisis of connection," a relational dilemma of how to be oneself and stay in relationships with others who may not want to know the truth of girls' experiences (Gilligan 1989). In studies of adolescent girls' development, many girls have demonstrated the ironic tendency to silence their own thoughts and feelings for the sake of relationships, when what they think and feel threatens to be disruptive (Brown and Gilligan 1992). At adolescence, the energy needed for resistance to crushing conventions of femininity often begins to get siphoned off for the purpose of maintaining cultural standards that stand between women and their empowerment. Focusing explicitly on embodied desire, Tolman and Debold (1993) observed similar patterns in the process of girls learning to look at, rather than experience, themselves, to know themselves from the perspective of men, thereby losing touch with their own bodily feelings and desires. It is at this moment in their development that many women will start to experience and develop ways of responding to their own sexual feelings. Given these realities, what are adolescent girls' experiences of sexual desire? How do girls enter their sexual lives and learn to negotiate or respond to their sexuality?

Despite the real gains that feminism and the sexual revolution achieved in securing women's reproductive rights and increasing women's sexual liberation (Rubin 1990), the tactics of silencing and denigrating women's sexual desire are deeply entrenched in this patriarchal society (Brown 1991). The Madonna/whore dichotomy is alternately virulent and subtle in the cultures of adolescents (Lees 1986; Tolman 1992). Sex education curricula name male adolescent sexual desire; girls are taught to recognize and to keep a lid on the sexual desire of boys but not taught to acknowledge or even to recognize their own sexual feelings (Fine 1988; Tolman 1991). The few feminist empirical studies of girls' sexuality suggest that sexual desire is a complicated, important experience for adolescent girls about which little is known. In an ethnographic study, Fine noticed that adolescent girls' sexuality was acknowledged by adults in school, but in terms that denied the sexual subjectivity of girls; this "missing discourse of desire" was, however, not always absent from the ways girls themselves spoke about their sexual experiences (Fine 1988). Rather than being "educated," girls' bodies are suppressed under surveillance and silenced in the schools (see also Lesko 1988). Although Fine ably conveys the

existence of girls' discourse of desire, she does not articulate that discourse. Thompson collected 400 girls' narratives about sexuality, romance, contraception, and pregnancy (Thompson 1984, 1990) in which girls' desire seems frequently absent or not relevant to the terms of their sexual relationships. The minority of girls who spoke of sexual pleasure voiced more sexual agency than girls whose experiences were devoid of pleasure. Within the context of girls' psychological development, Fine's and Thompson's work underscores the need to understand what girls' experiences of their sexual desire are like.

A psychological analysis of this experience for girls can contribute an understanding of both the possibilities and limits for sexual freedom for women in the current social climate. By identifying how the culture has become anchored in the interior of women's lives—an interior that is birthed through living in the exterior of material conditions and relationships—this approach can keep distinct women's psychological responses to sexual oppression and also the sources of that oppression. This distinction is necessary for avoiding the trap of blaming women for the ways our minds and bodies have become constrained.

METHODOLOGICAL DISCUSSION

Sample and Data Collection

To examine this subject, I interviewed thirty girls who were juniors in an urban and a suburban public high school ($n = 28$) or members of a gay and lesbian youth group ($n = 2$). They were 16.5 years old on average and randomly selected. The girls in the larger study are a heterogeneous group, representing different races and ethnic backgrounds (Black, including Haitian and African American; Latina, including Puerto Rican and Colombian; Euro-American, including Eastern and Western European), religions (Catholic, Jewish, and Protestant), and sexual experiences. With the exception of one Puerto Rican girl, all of the girls from the suburban school were Euro-American; the racial/ethnic diversity in the sample is represented by the urban school. Interviews with school personnel confirmed that the student population of the urban school was almost exclusively poor or working class and the students in the suburban school were middle and upper-middle class. This information is important in that my focus is on how girls' social environments shape their understanding of their sexuality. The fact that girls who live in the urban area experience the visibility of and discourse about violence, danger and the consequences of unprotected sex, and that the suburban girls live in a community that offers a veneer of safety and stability, informs their experiences of sexuality. Awareness of these features of the social contexts in which these girls are developing is essential for listening to and understanding their narratives about sexual experiences.

The data were collected in one-on-one, semistructured clinical interviews (Brown and Gilligan 1992). This method of interviewing consists of following a structured interview protocol that does not direct specific probes but elicits narratives. The interviewer listens carefully to a girl, taking in her voice, and responding with questions that will enable the girl to clarify her story and know she is being heard. In these interviews, I asked girls direct questions about desire to elicit descriptions and narratives. Most of the young women wove their concerns about danger into the narratives they told.

Analytic Strategy

To analyze these narratives, I used the Listening Guide—an interpretive methodology that joins hermeneutics and feminist standpoint epistemology (Brown et al. 1991). It is a voice-centered, relational method by which a researcher becomes a listener, taking in the voice of a girl, developing an interpretation of her experience. Through multiple readings of the same text, this method makes audible the "polyphonic and complex" nature of voice and experience (Brown and Gilligan 1992, 15). Both speaker and listener are recognized as individuals who bring thoughts and feelings to the text, acknowledging the necessary subjectivity of both participants. Self-consciously embedded in a standpoint acknowledging that patriarchal culture silences and obscures women's experiences, the method is explicitly psychological and feminist in providing the listener with an organized way to respond to the coded or indirect language of girls and women, especially regarding topics such as sexuality that girls and women are not supposed to speak of. This method leaves a trail of evidence for the listener's interpretation, and thus leaves room for other interpretations by other listeners consistent with the epistemological stance that there is multiple meaning in such stories. I present a

way to understand the stories these young women chose to tell me, our story as I have heard and understood it. Therefore, in the interpretations that follow I include my responses, those of an adult woman, to these girls' words, providing information about girls' experiences of sexual desire much like countertransference informs psychotherapy.

Adolescent Girls' Experiences of Sexual Desire

The first layer of the complexity of girls' experiences of their sexual desire was revealed initially in determining whether or not they felt sexual feelings. A majority of these girls (two-thirds) said unequivocally that they experienced sexual desire; in them I heard a clear and powerful way of speaking about the experience of feeling desire that was explicitly relational and also embodied. Only three of the girls said they did not experience sexual feelings, describing silent bodies and an absence of or intense confusion about romantic or sexual relationships. The remaining girls evidenced confusion or spoke in confusing ways about their own sexual feelings. Such confusion can be understood as a psychic solution to sexual feelings that arise in a culture that denigrates, suppresses, and heightens the dangers of girls' sexuality and in which contradictory messages about women's sexuality abound.

For the girls who said they experienced sexual desire, I turned my attention to how they said they responded to their sexual feelings. What characterized their responses was a sense of struggle; the question of "doing desire"—that is, what to do when they felt sexual desire—was not straightforward for any of them. While speaking of the power of their embodied feelings, the girls in this sample described the difficulties that their sexual feelings posed, being aware of both the potential for pleasure and the threat of danger that their desire holds for them. The struggle took different shapes for different girls, with some notable patterns emerging. Among the urban girls, the focus was on how to stay safe from bodily harm, in and out of the context of relational or social consequences, whereas among the suburban girls the most pronounced issue was how to maintain a sense of themselves as "good" and "normal" girls (Tolman 1992). In this article, I will offer portraits of three girls. By focusing on three girls in depth, I can balance an approach to "variance" with the kind of case study presentation that enables me to illustrate both similarities and differences in how girls in the larger sample spoke about their sexual feelings. These three girls represent different sexual preferences—one heterosexual, one bisexual, and one lesbian.[1] I have chosen to forefront the difference of sexual preference because it has been for some women a source of empowerment and a route to community; it has also been a source of divisiveness among feminists. Through this approach, I can illustrate *both* the similarities and differences in their experiences of sexual desire, which are nested in their individual experiences as well as their social contexts. Although there are many other demarcations that differentiate these girls—social class, race, religion, sexual experience—and this is not the most pervasive difference in this sample,[2] sexual preference calls attention to the kinds of relationships in which girls are experiencing or exploring their sexual desire and which take meaning from gender arrangements and from both the presence and absence of institutionalization (Fine 1988; Friend 1993). Because any woman whose sexuality is not directly circumscribed by heterosexual, monogamous marriage is rendered deviant in our society, all adolescent girls bear suspicion regarding their sexuality, which sexual preference highlights. In addition, questions of identity are heightened at adolescence.

Rochelle Doing Desire   Rochelle is a tall, larger, African-American girl who is heterosexual. Her small, sweet voice and shy smile are a startling contrast to her large body, clothed in white spandex the day of our interview. She lives in an urban area where violence is embedded in the fabric of everyday life. She speaks about her sexual experience with a detailed knowledge of how her sexuality is shaped, silenced, denigrated, and possible in relationships with young men. As a sophomore, she thought she "had to get a boyfriend" and became "eager" for a sexual relationship. As she describes her first experience of sexual intercourse, she describes a traditional framing of male–female relationships:

> I felt as though I had to conform to everything he said that, you know, things that a girl and a guy were supposed to do, so like, when the sex came, like, I did it without thinking, like, I wish I would have waited . . . we started kissing and all that stuff and it just happened. And when I got, went

home, I was like, I was shocked, I was like, why did I do that? I wish I wouldn't a did it.

Did you want to do it?

Not really. Not really. I just did it because, maybe because he wanted it, and I was always like tryin' to please him and like, he was real mean, mean to me, now that I think about it. I was like kind of stupid, cause like I did everything for him and he just treated me like I was nothing and I just thought I had just to stay with him because I needed a boyfriend so bad to make my life complete but like now it's different.

Rochelle's own sexual desire is absent in her story of defloration—in fact, she seems to be missing altogether. In a virtual caricature of dominant cultural conventions of femininity, Rochelle connects her disappearance at the moment of sex—"it just happened"—to her attempts to fulfill the cultural guidelines for how to "make [her] life complete." She has sex because "he wanted it," a response that holds no place for whether or not she feels desire. In reflecting on this arrangement, Rochelle now feels she was "stupid . . . to do everything for him" and in her current relationship, things are "different." As she explains: "I don't take as much as I did with the first guy, cause like, if he's doin' stuff that I don't like, I tell him, I'll go, I don't like this and I think you shouldn't do it and we compromise, you know. I don't think I can just let him treat me bad and stuff."

During the interview, I begin to notice that desire is not a main plot line in Rochelle's stories about her sexual experiences, especially in her intimate relationships. When I ask her about her experiences of sexual pleasure and sexual desire, she voices contradictions. On one hand, as the interview unfolds, she is more and more clear that she does not enjoy sex: "I don't like sex" quickly becomes "I hate sex . . . I don't really have pleasure." On the other hand, she explains that

> there are certain times when I really really really enjoy it, but then, that's like, not a majority of the times, it's only sometimes, once in a while . . . if I was to have sex once a month, then I would enjoy it . . . if I like go a long period of time without havin' it then, it's really good to me, cause it's like, I haven't had something for a long time and I miss it. It's like, say I don't eat cake a lot, but say, like every two months, I had some cake, then it would be real good to me, so that's like the same thing.

Rochelle conveys a careful knowledge of her body's hunger, her need for tension as an aspect of her sexual pleasure, but her voiced dislike of sex suggests that she does not feel she has much say over when and how she engages in sexual activity.

In describing her experiences with sexuality, I am overwhelmed at how frequently Rochelle says that she "was scared." She is keenly aware of the many consequences that feeling and responding to her sexual desire could have. She is scared of being talked about and getting an undeserved reputation: "I was always scared that if I did that (had sexual intercourse) I would be portrayed as, you know, something bad." Even having sex within the confines of a relationship, which has been described by some girls as a safe haven for their sexuality (Rubin 1990; Tolman 1992), makes her vulnerable; she "could've had a bad reputation, but luckily he wasn't like that"; he did not choose to tell other boys (who then tell girls) about their sexual activity. Thinking she had a sexually transmitted disease was scary. Because she had been faithful to her boyfriend, having such a disease would mean having to know that her boyfriend cheated on her and would also make her vulnerable to false accusations of promiscuity from him. Her concern about the kind of woman she may be taken for is embedded in her fear of using contraception: "When you get birth control pills, people automatically think you're having sex every night and that's not true." Being thought of as sexually insatiable or out of control is a fear that many girls voice (Tolman 1992); this may be intensified for African-American girls, who are creating a sexual identity in a dominant cultural context that stereotypes Black women as alternately asexual and hypersexual (Spillers 1984).

Rochelle's history provides other sources of fear. After her boyfriend "flattened [her] face," when she realized she no longer wanted to be with him and broke off the relationship, she learned that her own desire may lead to male violence. Rochelle confided to me that she has had an abortion, suffering such intense sadness, guilt, and anxiety in the wake of it that, were she to become pregnant again, she would have the baby. For Rochelle, the risk of getting pregnant puts her education at risk, because she will have to sacrifice going to college. This goal is tied to security for her; she wants to "have something of my own before I get a husband, you know, so if he ever tries leavin' me, I have my own money." Given this wall of fears, I am not surprised when Rochelle describes a

time when simply feeling desire made her "so scared that I started to cry." Feeling her constant and pervasive fear, I began to find it hard to imagine how she can feel any other feelings, including sexual ones.

I was thus caught off guard when I asked Rochelle directly if she has felt desire and she told me that she does experience sexual desire; however, she explained "most of the time, I'm by myself when I do." She launched, in breathless tones, into a story about an experience of her own sexual desire just the previous night:

> Last night, I had this crank call. . . . At first I thought it was my boyfriend, cause he likes to play around, you know. But I was sitting there talking, you know, and thinking of him and then I found out it's not him, it was so crazy weird, so I hang the phone up and he called back, he called back and called back. And then I couldn't sleep, I just had this feeling that, I wanted to have sex so so bad. It was like three o'clock in the morning. And I didn't sleep the rest of the night. And like, I called my boyfriend and I was tellin' him, and he was like, what do you want me to do, Rochelle, I'm sleeping! [Laughs.] I was like, okay, okay, well I'll talk to you later, bye. And then, like, I don't know, I just wanted to, and like, I kept tossin' and turnin'. And I'm trying to think who it was, who was callin' me, cause like, it's always the same guy who always crank calls me, he says he knows me. It's kinda scary. . . . I can't sleep, I'm like, I just think about it, like, oh I wanna have sex so bad, you know, it's like a fever, drugs, something like that. Like last night, I don't know, I think if I woulda had the car and stuff, I probably woulda left the house. And went over to his house, you know. But I couldn't, cause I was baby-sitting.

When I told her that it sounds a little frightening but it sounds like there's something exciting about it, she smiled and leaned forward, exclaiming, "Yeah! It's like sorta arousing." I was struck by the intensity of her sexual feelings and also by the fact that she is alone and essentially assured of remaining alone due to the late hour and her responsibilities. By being alone, not subject to observation or physical, social, emotional, or material vulnerability, Rochelle experienced the turbulent feelings that are awakened by this call in her body. Rochelle's desire has not been obliterated by her fear; desire and fear both reverberate through her psyche. But she is not completely alone in this experience of desire, for her feelings occur in response to another person, whom she at first suspects is her boyfriend speaking from a safe distance, conveying the relational contours of her sexual desire. Her wish to bring her desire into her relationship, voiced in her response of calling her boyfriend, is in conflict with her fear of what might happen if she did pursue her wish—getting pregnant and having a baby, a consequence that Rochelle is desperate to avoid.

I am struck by her awareness of both the pleasure and danger in this experience and how she works the contradiction without dissociating from her own strong feelings. There is a brilliance and also a sadness in the logic her body and psyche have played out in the face of her experiences with sexuality and relationships. The psychological solution to the dilemma that desire means for her, of feeling sexual desire only when she cannot respond as she says she would like to, arises from her focus on these conflicts as personal experiences, which she suffers and solves privately. By identifying and solving the dilemma in this way, Rochelle is diminished, as is the possibility of her developing a critique of these conflicts as not just personal problems but as social inequities that emerge in her personal relationships and on her body. Without this perspective, Rochelle is less likely to become empowered through her own desire to identify that the ways in which she must curtail herself and be curtailed by others are socially constructed, suspect, and in need of change.

Megan Doing Desire   Megan, a small, freckled, perky Euro-American, is dressed in baggy sweats, comfortable, unassuming, and counterpointed by her lively engagement in our interview.[3] She identifies herself as "being bisexual" and belongs to a gay youth group; she lives in a city in which wealth and housing projects coexist. Megan speaks of knowing she is feeling sexual desire for boys because she has "kind of just this feeling, you know? Just this feeling inside my body." She explains: "My vagina starts to kinda like act up and it kinda like quivers and stuff, and like I'll get like tingles and and, you can just feel your hormones (laughing) doing something weird, and you just, you get happy and you just get, you know, restimulated kind of and it's just, and Oh! Oh!" and "Your nerves feel good." Megan speaks about her sexual desire in two distinct ways, one for boys and one for girls. In our interview, she speaks most

frequently about her sexual feelings in relation to boys. The power of her own desire and her doubt about her ability to control herself frighten her: "It scares me when I'm involved in a sexual situation and I just wanna go further and further and cause it just, and it scares me that, well, I have control, but if I even just let myself not have control, you know? . . . I'd have sex and I can't do that." Megan knows that girls who lose control over their desire like that can be called "sluts" and ostracized.

When asked to speak about an experience of sexual desire, Megan chooses to describe the safety of a heterosexual, monogamous relationship. She tells me how she feels when a boyfriend was "feeling me up"; not only is she aware of and articulate about his bodily reactions and her own, she narrates the relational synergy between her own desire and his:

> I just wanted to go on, you know? Like I could feel his penis, you know, 'cause we'd kinda lied down you know, and, you just really get so into it and intense and, you just wanna, well you just kinda keep wanting to go on or something, but it just feels good. . . . His penis being on my leg made, you know, it hit a nerve or something, it did something because it just made me start to get more horny or whatever, you know, it just made me want to do more things and stuff. I don't know how, I can't, it's hard for me to describe exactly how I felt, you know like, (intake of breath) . . . when he gets more excited then he starts to do more things and you can kind of feel his pleasure and then you start to get more excited.

With this young man, Megan knows her feelings of sexual desire to be "intense," to have a momentum of their own, and to be pleasurable. Using the concrete information of his erection, she describes the relational contours of her own embodied sexual desire, a desire that she is clear is her own and located in her body but that also arises in response to his excitement.

Although able to speak clearly in describing a specific experience she has had with her desire, I hear confusion seep into her voice when she notices that her feelings contradict or challenge societal messages about girls and sexuality:

> It's so confusing, 'cause you have to like say no, you have to be the one to say no, but why should you be the one to, cause I mean maybe you're

enjoying it and you shouldn't have to say no or anything. But if you don't, maybe the guy'll just keep going and going, and you can't do that, because then you would be a slut. There's so [much] like, you know, stuff that you have to deal with and I don't know, just I keep losing my thought.

Although she knows the logic offered by society—that she must "say no" to keep him from "going and going," which will make her "a slut"—Megan identifies what is missing from that logic, that "maybe you're"—she, the girl—"the one who is enjoying it." The fact that she may be experiencing sexual desire makes the scripted response—to silence his body—dizzying. Because she does feel her own desire and can identify the potential of her own pleasure, Megan asks the next logical question, the question that can lead to outrage, critique, and empowerment: "Why should you have to be the one to [say no]?" But Megan also gives voice to why sustaining the question is difficult; she knows that if she does not conform, if she does not "say no"—both to him and to herself—then she may be called a slut, which could lead to denigration and isolation. Megan is caught in the contradiction between the reality of her sexual feelings in her body and the absence of her sexual feelings in the cultural script for adolescent girls' sexuality. Her confusion is an understandable response to this untenable and unfair choice: a connection with herself, her body, and sexual pleasure or a connection with the social world.

Megan is an avid reader of the dominant culture. Not only has she observed the ways that messages about girls' sexuality leave out or condemn her embodied feelings for boys, she is also keenly aware of the pervasiveness of cultural norms and images that demand heterosexuality:

Every teen magazine you look at is like, guy this, how to get a date, guys, guys, guys, guys, guys. So you're constantly faced with I have to have a boyfriend, I have to have a boyfriend, you know, even if you don't have a boyfriend, just [have] a fling, you know, you just want to kiss a guy or something. I've had that mentality for so long.

In this description of compulsory heterosexuality (Rich 1983), Megan captures the pressure she feels to have a boyfriend and how she experiences the insistence of this demand, which is ironically in conflict with the mandate to say no when with a boy. She is aware of how her psyche has been shaped into a "mentality" requiring any sexual or relational interests to be heterosexual, which does not corroborate how she feels. Compulsory heterosexuality comes between Megan and her feelings, making her vulnerable to a dissociation of her "feelings" under this pressure.

Although she calls herself bisexual, Megan does not describe her sexual feelings for girls very much in this interview. In fact, she becomes so confused that at one point she says she is not sure if her feelings for girls are sexual:

I mean, I'll see a girl I really really like, you know, because I think she's so beautiful, and I might, I don't know. I'm so confused. . . . But there's, you know, that same mentality as me liking a guy if he's really cute, I'm like, oh my God, you know, he's so cute. If I see a woman that I like, a girl, it's just like wow, she's so pretty, you know. See I can picture like hugging a girl; I just can't picture the sex, or anything, so, there's something being blocked.

Megan links her confusion with her awareness of the absence of images of lesbian sexuality in the spoken or imagistic lexicon of the culture, counterpointing the pervasiveness of heterosexual imagery all around her. Megan suggests that another reason that she might feel "confused" about her feelings for girls is a lack of sexual experience. Megan knows she is feeling sexual desire when she can identify feelings in her own body—when her "vagina acts up"—and these feelings occur for her in the context of a sexual relationship, when she can feel the other person's desire. Because she has never been in a situation with a girl that would allow this embodied sexual response, she posits a connection between her lack of sexual experience with girls and her confusion.

Yet she has been in a situation where she was "close to" a girl and narrates how she does not let her body speak:

There was this one girl that I had kinda liked from school, and it was like really weird 'cause she's really popular and everything. And we were sitting next to each other during the movie and, kind of her leg was on my leg and I was like, wow, you know, and that was, I think that's like the first time that I've ever felt like sexual pleasure for a girl. But it's so impossible, I think I just like block it out, I mean, it could never happen. . . . I just can't know what I'm feeling. . . . I probably first mentally just say no, don't feel it, you know, maybe. But I never start to feel, I don't know. It's so confusing. 'Cause finally it's all right for me to like a girl, you know? Before it was like, you know, the two times that I really, that it was just really obvious that I liked them a lot, I had to keep saying no no no no no, you know, I just would not let myself. I just hated myself for it, and this year now that I'm talking about it, now I can start to think about it.

Megan both narrates and interprets her dissociation from her embodied sexual feelings and describes the disciplinary stance of her mind over her body in how she "mentally" silences her body by saying "no," preempting her embodied response. Without her body's feelings, her embodied knowledge, Megan feels confused. If she runs interference with her own sexual feelings by silencing her body, making it impossible for her to feel her desire for girls, then she can avoid the problems she knows will inevitably arise if she feels sexual feelings she "can't know"—compulsory heterosexuality and homophobia combine to render this knowledge problematic for her. Fearing rejection, Megan keeps herself from feelings that could lead to disappointment, embarrassment, or frustration, leaving her safe in some ways, yet also psychologically vulnerable.

Echoing dominant cultural constructions of sexual desire, Megan links her desire for girls with feelings of fear: "I've had crushes on some girls . . . you can picture yourself kissing a guy but then if you like a girl a lot and then you picture yourself kissing her, it's just like, I can't, you know, oh my God, no (laughs), you know it's like scary . . . it's society . . . you never would think of, you know, it's natural to kiss a girl." Megan's fear about her desire for girls is different from the fears associated with her desire for boys; whereas being too sexual with boys brings the stigma of being called a "slut," Megan fears "society" and being thought of as "unnatural" when it comes to her feelings for girls. Given what she knows about the heterosexual culture in which she is immersed—the pressure she feels to be interested in "guys" and also given what she knows about homophobia—there is an inherent logic in Megan's confused response to her feelings for girls.

Melissa Doing Desire   Melissa, dressed in a flowing gypsy skirt, white skin pale against the lively colors she wears, is clear about her sexual desire for girls, referring to herself as "lesbian"; she is also a member of a gay/lesbian youth group. In speaking of her desire, Melissa names not only powerful feelings of "being excited" and "wanting," but also more contained feelings; she has "like little crushes on like millions of people and I mean, it's enough for me." Living in a world defined as heterosexual, Melissa finds that "little crushes" have to suffice, given a lack of opportunity for sexual exploration or relationship: "I don't know very many people my age that are even bisexual or lesbians . . . so I pretty much stick to that, like, being hugely infatuated with straight people. Which can get a little touchy at times . . . realistically, I can't like get too ambitious, because that would just not be realistic."

At the forefront of how Melissa describes her desire is her awareness that her sexual feelings make her vulnerable to harm. Whereas the heterosexual girls in this study link their vulnerability to the outcomes of responding to their desire—pregnancy, disease, or getting a bad reputation—Melissa is aware that even the existence of her sexual desire for girls can lead to anger or violence if others know of it: "Well I'm really lucky that like nothing bad has happened or no one's gotten mad at me so far, that, by telling people about them, hasn't gotten me into more trouble than it has, I mean, little things but not like, anything really awful. I think about that and I think it, sometimes, I mean, it could be more dangerous." In response to this threat of violence, Melissa attempts to restrain her own desire: "Whenever I start, I feel like I can't help looking at someone for more than a few seconds, and I keep, and I feel like I have to make myself not stare at them or something." Another strategy is to express her desire covertly by being physically affectionate with other girls, a behavior that is common and acceptable; by keeping her sexuality secret, she can "hang all over [girls] and stuff and they wouldn't even think that I meant anything by it." I am not surprised that Melissa associates feeling sexual desire with frustration; she explains that she "find(s) it safer to just think about the person than what I wanna do, because if I think about that too much and I can't do it, then that'll just frustrate me," leading her to try to intervene in her feelings by "just think[ing] about the person" rather than about the more sexual things she "want(s) to do." In this way,

Melissa may jeopardize her ability to know her sexual desire and, in focusing on containing what society has named improper feelings, minimize or exorcise her empowerment to expose that construction as problematic and unjust.

My questions about girls' sexual desire connect deeply with Melissa's own questions about herself; she is in her first intimate relationship, and this interview proves an opportunity to explore and clarify painful twinges of doubt that she had begun to have about it. This relationship began on the initiative of the other girl, with whom she had been very close, rather than out of any sexual feelings on Melissa's part. In fact, Melissa was surprised when her friend had expressed a sexual interest, because she had not "been thinking that" about this close friend. After a history of having to hold back her sexual desire, of feeling "frustrated" and being "hugely infatuated with straight people," rather than having the chance to explore her sexuality, Melissa's response to this potential relationship was that she "should take advantage of this situation." As the interview progresses, Melissa begins to question whether she is sexually attracted to this girl or "it's just sort of like I just wanted something like this for so long that I'm just taking advantage of the situation."

When I ask Melissa questions about the role of her body in her experience of sexual desire, her confusion at first intensifies:

Is that [your body] part of what feels like it might be missing?

(eight-second pause) It's not, well, sometimes, I mean I don't know how, what I feel all the time. It's hard like, because I mean I'm so confused about this. And it's hard like when it's actually happening to be like, OK, now how do I feel right now? How do I feel right now? How am I gonna feel about this? . . . I don't know, 'cause I don't know what to expect, and I haven't been with anyone else so I don't know what's supposed to happen. So, I mean I'm pretty confused.

The way she speaks about monitoring her body suggests that she is searching for bodily feelings, making me wonder what, if anything, she felt. I discern what she does not say directly; that her body was silent in these sexual experiences. Her hunger for a relationship is palpable: "I really wanted someone really badly, I think, I was getting really sick of being by

myself. . . . I would be like God, I really need someone." The desperation in her voice, and the sexual frustration she describes, suggest that her "want" and "need" are distinctly sexual as well as relational.

One reason that Melissa seems to be confused is that she felt a strong desire to be "mothered," her own mother having died last year. In trying to distinguish her different desires in this interview, Melissa began to distinguish erotic feelings from another kind of wanting she also experienced: she said that "it's more of like but I kind of feel like it's really more of like a maternal thing, that I really want her to take care of me and I just wanna touch someone and I just really like the feeling of just how I mean I like, when I'm with her and touching her and stuff. A lot, but it's not necessarily a sexual thing at this point." In contrast to her feelings for her girlfriend, Melissa describes feeling sexually attracted to another girl. In so doing, Melissa clarifies what is missing in these first sexual adventures, enabling her to know what had bothered her about her relationship with her girlfriend:

I don't really think I'm getting that much pleasure, from her, it's just, I mean it's almost like I'm getting experience, and I'm sort of having fun, it's not even that exciting, and that's why I think I don't really like her . . . because my friend asked me this the other day, well, I mean does it get, I mean when you're with her does it get really, I don't remember the word she used, but just really, like what was the word she used? But I guess she meant just like, exciting [laughing]. But it doesn't, to me. It's weird, because I can't really say that, I mean I can't think of like a time when I was really excited and it was like really, sexual pleasure, for me, because I don't think it's really like that. I mean not that I think that this isn't good because, I don't know, I mean, I like it, but I mean I think I have to, sort of realize that I'm not that much attracted to her, personally.

Wanting both a relationship and sexual pleasure, a chance to explore closeness and her sexual curiosity, and discovering that this relationship leaves out her sexual desire, Melissa laments her silent body: "I sort of expect or hope or whatever that there would be some kind of more excited feeling just from feeling sexually stimulated or whatever. I would hope that there would be more of a feeling than I've gotten so far." Knowing consciously what she "knows" about the absence of her sexual feelings in this relationship has left her with a relational conflict of large proportions for her: "I'm not that attracted to her and I don't know if I should tell her that. Or if I should just kind of pretend I am and try to . . . anyway." I ask her how she would go about doing that—pretending that she is. She replies, "I don't think I could pretend it for too long." Not being able to "pretend" to have feelings that she knows she wants as part of an intimate relationship, Melissa faces a dilemma of desire that may leave her feeling isolated and lonely or even fraudulent.

ADOLESCENT GIRLS' SEXUAL DESIRE AND THE POSSIBILITIES OF EMPOWERMENT

All of the girls in this study who said they felt sexual desire expressed conflict when describing their responses to their sexual feelings—conflict between their embodied sexual feelings and their perceptions of how those feelings are, in one way or another, anathema or problematic within the social and relational contexts of their lives. Their experiences of sexual desire are strong and pleasurable, yet they speak very often not of the power of desire but of how their desire may get them into trouble. These girls are beginning to voice the internalized oppression of their women's bodies; they knew and spoke about, in explicit or more indirect ways, the pressure they felt to silence their desire, to dissociate from those bodies in which they inescapably live. Larger societal forces of social control in the form of compulsory heterosexuality (Rich 1983), the policing of girls' bodies through school codes (Lesko 1988), and media images play a clear part in forcing this silence and dissociation. Specific relational dynamics, such as concern about a reputation that can easily be besmirched by other girls and by boys, fear of male violence in intimate relationships, and fear of violent repercussion of violating norms of heterosexuality are also audible in these girls' voices.

To be able to know their sexual feelings, to listen when their bodies speak about themselves and about their relationships, might enable these and other girls to identify and know more clearly the sources of oppression that press on their full personhood and their capacity for knowledge, joy, and connection. Living in the margins of a heterosexual society, the

bisexual and lesbian girls voice an awareness of these forces as formative of the experiences of their bodies and relationships; the heterosexual girls are less clear and less critical about the ways that dominant constructions of their sexuality impinge on their embodied and relational worlds. Even when they are aware that societal ambivalence and fears are being played out on their minds and bodies, they do not speak of a need for collective action, or even the possibility of engaging in such activities. More often, they speak of the danger of speaking about desire at all. By dousing desire with fear and confusion, or simple, "uncomplicated" denial, silence, and dissociation, the girls in this study make individual psychological moves whereby they distance or disconnect themselves from discomfort and danger. Although disciplining their bodies and curbing their desire are a very logical and understandable way to stay physically, socially, and emotionally safe, they also heighten the chance that girls and women may lose track of the fact that an inequitable social system, and not a necessary situation, renders women's sexual desire a source of danger rather than one of pleasure and power in their lives. In "not knowing" desire, girls and women are at risk for not knowing that there is nothing wrong with having sexual feelings and responding to them in ways that bring joy and agency.

Virtually every girl in the larger study told me that no woman had ever talked to her about sexual desire and pleasure "like this"—in depth, listening to her speak about her own experiences, responding when she asked questions about how to masturbate, how to have cunnilingus, what sex is like after marriage. In the words of Rubin: "The ethos of privacy and silence about our personal sexual experience makes it easy to rationalize the refusal to speak [to adolescents]" (1990, 83; Segal 1993). Thompson (1990) found that daughters of women who had talked with them about pleasure and desire told narratives about first intercourse that were informed by pleasure and agency. The recurrent strategy the girls in my study describe of keeping their desire under wraps as a way to protect themselves also keeps girls out of authentic relationships with other girls and women. It is within these relationships that the empowerment of women can develop and be nurtured through shared experiences of both oppression and power, in which collectively articulated critiques are carved out and voiced. Such knowledge of how a patriarchal society systematically keeps girls and women from their own desire can instigate demand and agency for social change. By not talking about sexual desire with each other or with women, a source for empowerment is lost. There is a symbiotic interplay between desire and empowerment: to be empowered to desire one needs a critical perspective, and that critical perspective will be extended and sustained through knowing and experiencing the possibilities of desire and healthy embodied living. Each of these girls illustrates the phenomenon observed in the larger study—the difficulty for girls in having or sustaining a critical perspective on the culture's silencing of their sexual desire. They are denied full access to the power of their own desire and to structural supports for that access.

Common threads of fear and joy, pleasure and danger, weave through the narratives about sexual desire in this study, exemplified by the three portraits. Girls have the right to be informed that gaining pleasure and a strong sense of self and power through their bodies does not make them bad or unworthy. The experiences of these and other adolescent girls illustrate why girls deserve to be educated about their sexual desire. Thompson concludes that "to take possession of sexuality in the wake of the anti-erotic sexist socialization that remains the majority experience, most teenage girls need an erotic education" (1990, 406). Girls need to be educated about the duality of their sexuality, to have safe contexts in which they can explore both danger and desire (Fine 1988), and to consider why their desire is so dangerous and how they can become active participants in their own redemption. Girls can be empowered to know and act on their own desire, a different educational direction than the simplistic strategies for avoiding boys' desire that they are offered. The "just say no" curriculum obscures the larger social inequities being played out on girls' bodies in heterosexual relationships and is not relevant for girls who feel sexual feelings for girls. Even adults who are willing or able to acknowledge

that girls experience sexual feelings worry that knowing about their own sexual desire will place girls in danger (Segal 1993). But keeping girls in the dark about their power to choose based on their own feelings fails to keep them any safer from these dangers. Girls who trust their minds and bodies may experience a stronger sense of self, entitlement, and empowerment that could enhance their ability to make safe decisions. One approach to educating girls is for women to speak to them about the vicissitudes of sexual desire—which means that women must let themselves speak and know their own sexual feelings, as well as the pleasures and dangers associated with women's sexuality and the solutions that we have wrought to the dilemma of desire: how to balance the realities of pleasure and danger in women's sexuality.

Asking these girls to speak about sexual desire, and listening and responding to their answers and also to their questions, proved to be an effective way to interrupt the standard "dire consequences" discourse adults usually employ when speaking at all to girls about their sexuality. Knowing and speaking about the ways in which their sexuality continues to be unfairly constrained may interrupt the appearance of social equity that many adolescent girls (especially white, middle-class young women) naively and trustingly believe, thus leading them to reject feminism as unnecessary and mean-spirited and not relevant to their lives. As we know from the consciousness-raising activities that characterized the initial years of second-wave feminism, listening to the words of other girls and women can make it possible for girls to know and voice their experiences, their justified confusion and fears, their curiosities. Through such relationships, we help ourselves and each other to live in our different female bodies with an awareness of danger, but also with a desire to feel the power of the erotic, to fine-tune our bodies and our psyches to what Audre Lorde has called the "yes within ourselves" (Lorde 1984, 54).

NOTES

1. The bisexual girl and the lesbian girl were members of a gay/lesbian youth group and identify themselves using these categories. As is typical for members of privileged groups for whom membership is a given, the girls who feel sexual desire for boys and not for girls (about which they were asked explicitly) do not use the term "heterosexual" to describe themselves. Although I am aware of the debate surrounding

the use of these categories and labels to delimit women's (and men's) experience, because my interpretive practice is informed by the ways society makes meaning of girls' sexuality, the categories that float in the culture as ways of describing the girls are relevant to my analysis. In addition, the bisexual and lesbian girls in this study are deeply aware of compulsory heterosexuality and its impact on their lives.

2. Of the thirty girls in this sample, twenty-seven speak of a desire for boys and not for girls. This pattern was ascertained by who appeared in their desire narratives and also by their response to direct questions about sexual feelings for girls, designed explicitly to interrupt the hegemony of heterosexuality. Two of the thirty girls described sexual desire for both boys and girls and one girl described sexual desire for girls and not for boys.

3. Parts of this analysis appear in Tolman (1994).

REFERENCES

Brown, L. 1991. Telling a girl's life: Self authorization as a form of resistance. In *Women, Girls and Psychotherapy: Reframing Resistance,* ed. C. Gilligan, A. Rogers, and D. Tolman. New York: Haworth.

Brown, L., E. Debold, M. Tappan, and C. Gilligan. 1991. Reading narratives of conflict for self and moral voice: A relational method. In *Handbook of Moral Behavior and Development: Theory, Research, and Application,* ed. W. Kurtines and J. Gewirtz. Hillsdale, NJ: Lawrence Erlbaum.

Brown, L., and C. Gilligan. 1992. *Meeting at the Crossroads: Women's Psychology and Girls' Development.* Cambridge, MA: Harvard University Press.

Fine, Michelle. 1988. Sexuality, schooling and adolescent females: The missing discourse of desire. *Harvard Educational Review* 58:29–53.

Friend, Richard. 1993. Choices, not closets. In *Beyond Silenced Voices,* ed. M. Fine and L. Weis. New York: State University of New York Press.

Gilligan, Carol. 1989. Teaching Shakespeare's sister. In *Making Connections: The Relational World of Adolescent Girls at Emma Willard School,* ed. C. Gilligan, N. Lyons, and T. Hamner. Cambridge, MA: Harvard University Press.

———. 1990. Joining the resistance: Psychology, politics, girls and women. *Michigan Quarterly Review* 29:501–36.

Lees, Susan. 1986. *Losing Out: Sexuality and Adolescent Girls.* London: Hutchinson.

Lesko, Nancy. 1988. The curriculum of the body: Lessons from a Catholic high school. In *Becoming Feminine: The Politics of Popular Culture,* ed. L. Roman. Philadelphia: Falmer.

Lorde, Audre. 1984. The uses of the erotic as power. In *Sister Outsider: Essays and Speeches.* Freedom, CA: Crossing Press.

Rich, Adrienne. 1983. Compulsory heterosexuality and lesbian existence. In *Powers of Desire: The politics of sexuality,* ed. A. Snitow, C. Stansell, and S. Thompson. New York: Monthly Review Press.

Rubin, Lillian. 1990. *Erotic Wars: What Happened to the Sexual Revolution?* New York: HarperCollins.

Segal, Lynne. 1993. Introduction. In *Sex Exposed: Sexuality and the Pornography Debate,* ed. L. Segal and M. McIntosh. New Brunswick, NJ: Rutgers University Press.

Spillers, Hortense. 1984. Interstices: A small drama of words. In *Pleasure and Danger: Exploring Female Sexuality,* ed. C. Vance. Boston: Routledge and Kegan Paul.

Thompson, Sharon. 1984. Search for tomorrow: On feminism and the reconstruction of teen romance. In *Pleasure and Danger: Exploring Female Sexuality,* ed. C. Vance. Boston: Routledge and Kegan Paul.

———. 1990. Putting a big thing in a little hole: Teenage girls' accounts of sexual initiation. *Journal of Sex Research* 27:341–61.

Tolman, Deborah L. 1991. Adolescent girls, women and sexuality: Discerning dilemmas of desire. *Women, Girls, and Psychotherapy: Reframing Resistance,* ed. C. Gilligan, A. Rogers, and D. Tolman. New York: Haworth.

———. 1992. Voicing the body: A psychological study of adolescent girls' sexual desire. Unpublished dissertation, Harvard University.

———. 1994. Daring to desire: Culture and the bodies of adolescent girls. In *Sexual Cultures: Adolescents, Communities and the Construction of Identity,* ed. J. Irvine. Philadelphia: Temple University Press.

Tolman, Deborah, and Elizabeth Debold. 1993. Conflicts of body and image: Female adolescents, desire, and the nobody. In *Feminist Treatment and Therapy of Eating Disorders,* ed. M. Katzman, P. Failon, and S. Wooley. New York: Guilford.

SEX ED: HOW DO WE SCORE?

Carolyn Mackler

The 12:55 bell rings at Ridgewood High School and a flock of freshman filter into Evelyn Rosskamm Shalom's Health 9 class. Greeting the sea of navy blue baseball caps and capri pants, Shalom announces that today's lesson will commence with the "question box" and instructs students to proceed as quietly as possible to the Magic Carpet. In a stampede evocative of July in Pamplona, twenty-five pairs of Nikes and clunky sandals clamor onto a dingy gray rug at the back of the room and, with one brave male exception, self-segregate by gender: girls on one side, boys on the other, a puerile triad huddled in the back. Shalom, joking about her recent fiftieth birthday, treats herself to a metal chair at the mouth of the circle and produces slips of folded white paper.

"Any more to add before I begin?" she asks, casually tucking a wayward strand of auburn hair behind one ear.

Braces-revealing smirks ripple through the crowd, especially among the Peanut Gallery trio, who menacingly ooze "spitball" from every pore of their bodies.

Shalom quickly scans a crumpled selection. "Have I already answered: 'Why do people have oral sex?'"

The Peanut Gallery erupts and a handful of midpubescents dutifully nod their heads. Shalom, a sixteen-year veteran of Ridgewood High School who has been described as someone who rules a class with velvet-gloved discipline, allows the rascals a heartbeat to blow off stream before skillfully channeling their discomfort into a lively debate in response to the next questions: "What is the right age to have sex?" Once Shalom takes the floor to address the query, a hush falls over the Magic Carpet. The only discernable sound is the buzzing of florescent lights above. Fifty eyes are intent on Shalom. Even the Peanut Gallery is hooked.

So goes a typically health class at Ridgewood High School in suburban New Jersey. The Ridgewood school district is renowned for its comprehensive and thorough family-life education curriculum. Following a 1980 statewide mandate that all New Jersey schoolchildren were to have sex education, Ridgewood Public Schools formed an advisory committee to consult with the school regarding its ever-evolving curriculum. Ridgewood students receive health education every year of their public school careers, beginning with instruction from a certified nurse specialist in elementary school and progressing to classes taught by high school teachers, such as Shalom, who has a master's degree in health education.

Fade from the Magic Carpet to a school district in Franklin County, North Carolina, where, in the fall of 1997, a scissors-toting parent-volunteer was summoned to the high school to slice chapters 17, 20, and 21 out of ninth-graders' health textbooks. The culpable text—covering contraception, sexually transmitted diseases (STDs), and relationship—didn't comply with the statewide abstinence-only curriculum, ruled the school board. Apparently, in a state where in 1996 there were 25,240 recorded pregnancies among fifteen-to-nineteen-year-olds, the board hoped that if they obliterated a discourse on condoms, getting down wouldn't dawn on youngsters.

Unfortunately, this sort of scene is business as usual with the politically explosive issue of school-based sex education. While a uniform national curriculum does not exist, barrels of federal money are being siphoned into abstinence-only-until-marriage programs, frequently laden with wrath-of-God scare tactics. Comprehensive sexuality education the likes of Ridgewood's, designed to reinforce sexuality as a positive and healthy part of being human, is available to only about 5 percent of school children in the United States. Sexuality education is an across-the-school-boards contentious subject, bound to generate controversy, even among well-meaning feminists; sexuality is not a one-size-fits-all equation, and the message appropriate for one kid may not work for the girl or boy at the adjacent desk.

(continued)

And then there's the Great Antipleasure Conspiracy. Translation: adults swindling kids (especially girls) by trying to convince them that sex is no fun, in the hope that they won't partake, a practice exemplified by the shocking omission of the clitoris—whose sole function is to deliver female pleasure—from most high school biology textbooks. The notion of women experiencing erotic pleasure—or possessing full sexual agency—clearly scares the boxer shorts off conservative education. Analogous to attempting to eradicate pizza by withholding Italy from a map of Europe, not including the clitoris in a textbook depiction of female genitalia is a frighteningly misleading excuse for education.

Tiptoeing around any of these issues—from pleasure to power to pregnancy prevention—is denying youngsters their basic right to health information. It is catapulting them into life-threatening sexual scenarios without sufficient tools to protect themselves. It is jeopardizing their chance to lay sturdy foundations for a sexually healthy adulthood. It's time to wake up and smell the hormones.

Ridgewood boasts one of the most progressive school districts in a "mixed landscape," explains Susan N. Wilson, the executive coordinator of the Network for Family Life Education, a nonprofit organization based at the Rutgers School for Social Work in Piscataway, New Jersey, that promotes comprehensive sexuality education in schools and communities. Wilson . . . explains that over the past several years there has been progress in the quantity of sex education in the schools. "In most places, it exists; something is being taught," she says, "but there are many school districts where students receive the bare minimum—HIV education—and very, very late in their school lives." Wilson points out that many politicians have embraced AIDS education with open arms. "In a true intertwining of church and state, they've jumped at the chance to reveal that sex does, in fact, equal death."

Debra Haffner, president of the Sexuality Information and Education Council of the United States (SIECUS), a nonprofit group that advocates for sexuality education and sexual rights, describes how most young people in this country get hurried through sex-abuse prevention in early grade school, the Puberty Talk in fifth grade, a lesson on HIV and STDs in middle school, and possibly a health elective in high school. "There's currently a great emphasis on abstinence in this country," she adds, "partially driven by federal programs, but partially driven by the conservative influence in communities."

Abstinence-only lessons, though varying from classroom to classroom, often revolve around a "pet your dog, not your date" theme. One resoundingly sexist message is that the onus of restricting foreplay should fall on the girl, encouraging her to use "self-control" rather than "birth control." A pseudoscientific chart from Sex Respect, a fear-based abstinence curriculum, depicts how male genitalia become aroused during "necking", while female genitalia lag behind until "petting". The girl-cum-gatekeeper's pleasure gets swept to the side, leaving her to ward filthy, boys-will-be-boys paws off her silky drawers.

The overwhelming bulk of scientific research underscores the failure of abstinence-only education in doing anything but eclipsing the erotic with the neurotic. A recent report by the National Campaign to Prevent Teen Pregnancy revealed that "the weight of the current evidence indicates that these abstinence programs do not delay the onset of intercourse." In a country where a mere 6.9 percent of men and 21 percent of women ages eighteen to fifty-nine hold out for their honeymoon, force-feeding "Just Say No" to teenagers sends them scurrying to the playground or onto the Web in search of information—usually to find misinformation—and frolicking under the covers all the same. But the risks of leaving kids without sufficient skills and facts range from the obvious—pregnancy and STDs—to sexual abuse, date rape, and sexual powerlessness.

Reducing adolescent pregnancy and the risk of sexually transmitted diseases is clearly paramount. But Susan Wilson, who's convinced that the right wants to "stamp out" teen sexuality altogether, wonders whether the effort is "on a collision course with healthy sexuality."

Debra Haffner echoes similar sentiments. "My mentor from twenty years ago used to call that

(continued)

'Sex is dirty. Save it for someone you love,'" she scoffs. "We cannot ingrain in young people the message that sexual intercourse violates another person, kills people, and leaves you without a reputation, and then expect that the day they put a wedding band on their finger they're going to forget all that."

She pauses and adds wryly, "It just creates adults who are in sex therapy because they can't have fulfilling relationships with their spouses and partners."

In 1996, SIECUS published the second edition of its *Guidelines for Comprehensive Sexuality Education: K–12*, which it had originally developed earlier in the decade with a task force that included the Centers for Disease Control and Prevention, Planned Parenthood Federation of America, and the National School Boards Association. The guidelines serve as a framework to facilitate the development of a comprehensive sex education program arising from the belief that "young people explore their sexuality as a natural process of achieving sexual maturity." Accordingly, emphasis should be placed on informed decision making about intercourse by acknowledging—not condemning—the broad range of adolescent sexual behaviors.

The SIECUS sexuality education model is designed to spiral through the school years, with age-appropriate lessons at all grade levels. . . . Proponents of comprehensive sexuality education believe that by high school, teenagers should have processed enough information to make responsible choices surrounding sex. And the research is on their side: studies reveal that teenagers who partake in discussions that include all options, from chastity belts to condoms, often delay sexual intercourse or reduce its frequency. By cultivating in adolescents a sense of sexual self-determination—with empowerment and gratification and honest communication being central—things tend to fall into place; unwanted pregnancy and sexually

transmitted diseases remain on the periphery, not at the hub of their ideas about human sexuality.

Back to the Great Antipleasure Conspiracy. There's reluctance even among liberal adults—most likely due to their own discomfort surrounding sexuality—to acknowledge that the majority of sex is for recreation, not procreation. Scarier still is the notion of pleasuring oneself. Wilson points out that masturbation is a subject "avoided assiduously by teachers." It is essential for schools to employ educators who will not blanch at the mention of, say, a clitoris (and who, like Shalom, boycott clitoris-free textbooks). "Nobody invests money in training," says Wilson, who points out that often sex ed teachers hit the chalkboard with only a weekend workshop under their belt. "A basic course in human sexuality for everyone in the helping professions should be commonplace."

It doesn't take a logician to deduce that the future of sex education is in serious jeopardy, but perhaps it's going to take feminists to do something about it. With a paucity of children receiving comprehensive sexuality education and gobs of federal money flying into reactionary, fear-based instruction, there's plenty of action to be taken, in the form of rallying school districts, educators, politicians, and parents to support education designed to empower, enlighten, and, yes, even excite youth about sexuality. And while we'll be sorry to see sex therapists hard-pressed for clients, we can envision a world where girls and boys grow into adults who regard their sexuality as anything but a one-way ticket to disease and unplanned pregnancy.

As I lean across Shalom's metal desk to hit the off button on my tape recorder, she interjects one final comment. "I see how kids respond to this stuff every single day," she reports. "They are just waiting for adults to share the tools with them. And it's not 'share the tools so I can go out and do it,' it's 'please help me learn how to grow up.'"

Becoming 100% Straight

✍ Michael A. Messner

In 1995, as part of my job as the President of the North American Society for the Sociology of Sport, I needed to prepare a one-hour long Presidential Address for the annual meeting of some 200 people. This presented a challenge to me: how might I say something to my colleagues that was challenging, at least somewhat original, and above all, not boring. Students may think that their professors are especially boring in the classroom, but believe me, we are usually much worse at professional meetings. For some reason, many of us who are able to speak to our students in the classroom in a relaxed manner, and using relatively jargon-free language, seem at these meetings to become robots, dryly reading our papers—packed with impressively unclear jargon—to our yawning colleagues.

Since I desperately wanted to avoid putting 200 sport studies scholars to sleep, I decided to deliver a talk which I entitled "studying up on sex." The title, which certainly did get my colleagues' attention, was intended as a play on words—a double entendre. "Studying up" has one, generally recognizable colloquial meaning, but in sociology, it has another. It refers to studying "up" in the power structure. Sociologists have perhaps most often studied "down"—studied the poor, the blue or pink-collar workers, the "nuts, sluts and perverts," the incarcerated. The idea of "studying up" rarely occurs to sociologists unless and until we are living in a time when those who are "down" have organized movements that challenge the institutional privileges of elites. So, for instance, in the wake of labor movements, some sociologists like C. Wright Mills studied up on corporate elites. And recently, in the wake of racial/ethnic civil rights movements, some scholars like Ruth Frankenberg have begun to study the social meanings of "whiteness." Much of my research, inspired by feminism, has involved a studying up on the social construction of masculinity in sport. Studying up, in these cases, has raised some fascinating new and important questions about the workings of power in society.

However, I realized, when it comes to understanding the social and interpersonal dynamics of sexual orientation in sport, we have barely begun to scratch the surface of a very complex issue. Although sport studies has benefited from the work of scholars like Helen Lenskyj, Brian Pronger, and others who have delineated the experiences of lesbians and gay men in sports, there has been very little extension of these scholars' insights into a consideration of the social construction of heterosexuality in sport. In sport, just as in the larger society, we seem obsessed with asking "how do people become gay?" Imbedded in this question is the assumption that people who identify as heterosexual, or "straight," require no explanation, since they are simply acting out the "natural" or "normal" sexual orientation. It's the "sexual deviants" who require explanation, we seem to be saying, while the experience of heterosexuals, because we are considered normal, seems to require no critical examination or explanation. But I knew that a closer look at the development of sexual orientation or sexual identity reveals an extremely complex process. I decided to challenge myself and my colleagues by arguing that although we have begun to "study up" on corporate elites in sport, on whiteness, on masculinity, it is now time to extend that by studying up on heterosexuality.

But in the absence of systematic research on this topic, where could I start? How could I explore, raise questions about, and begin to illuminate the social construction of heterosexuality for my colleagues? Fortunately, I had for the previous two years been working with a group of five men (three of whom identified as heterosexual, two as gay) who were mutually exploring our own biographies in terms of our earlier bodily experiences that helped to shape our gender and sexual identities. We modeled our project after that of a German group of feminist women, led by Frigga Haug, who created a research method which they call "memory work." In short, the women would mutually choose a body part, such as "hair," and each of them would then write a short story, based on a particularly salient childhood memory that related to their hair (for example, being forced by parents to cut your hair, deciding to straighten one's curly hair, in order to look more like other girls, etc.). Then, the group would read all of the stories, discuss them one-by-one, with the hope of gaining some more general understanding of, and raising new questions about, the social construction of "femininity." What resulted from this project was a fascinating book called *Female Sexualization*, which my men's group used as an inspiration for our project.

As a research method, memory work is anything but conventional. Many sociologists would argue that this is not really a "research method" at all, because the information that emerges from the project can't be used very confidently as a generalizable "truth," and especially because in this sort of project, the researcher is simultaneously part of what is being studied. How, my more scientifically oriented colleagues might ask, is the researcher to maintain his or her objectivity in this project? My answer is that in this kind of research, objectivity is not the point. In fact, the strength of this sort of research is the depth of understanding that might be gained through a systematic group analysis of one's experience, one's *subjective* orientation to social processes. A clear understanding of the subjective aspect of social life—one's bodily feelings, emotions, and reactions to others—is an invaluable window that allows us to see and ask new sociological questions about group interaction and social structure. In short, group memory work can provide an important, productive, and fascinating insight into aspects of social reality, though not a complete (or completely reliable) picture.

So, as I pondered the lack of existing research on the social construction of heterosexuality in sport, I decided to draw on one of my own stories from my memory work men's group. Some of my most salient memories of embodiment are sports memories. I grew up the son of a high school coach, and I eventually played point guard on my dad's team. In what follows, I juxtapose one of my stories with that of a gay former Olympic athlete, Tom Waddell, whom I had interviewed several years earlier for a book that I wrote on the lives of male athletes.

TWO SEXUAL STORIES

Many years ago I read some psychological studies that argued that even for self-identified heterosexuals, it is a natural part of their development to have gone through "bisexual" or even "homosexual" stages of life. When I read this, it seemed theoretically reasonable, but it did not ring true in my experience. I have always been, I told myself, 100% heterosexual! The group process of analyzing my own autobiographical stories challenged this conception I had developed of myself, and also shed light on the way that the institutional context of sport provided a context for the development of my definition of myself as "100% straight." Here is one of the stories.

When I was in the 9th grade, I played on a "D" basketball team, set up especially for the smallest of high school boys. Indeed, though I was pudgy with baby fat, I was a short 5′2″, still pre-pubescent with no facial hair and a high voice that I artificially tried to lower. The first day of practice, I was immediately attracted to a boy I'll call Timmy, because he looked like the boy who played in the Lassie TV show. Timmy was short, with a high voice, like me. And like me, he had no facial hair yet. Unlike me, he was very skinny. I liked Timmy right away, and soon we were together a lot. I *noticed* things about him that I didn't notice about other boys: he said some words a certain way, and it gave me pleasure to try to talk like him. I remember liking the way the light hit his boyish, nearly hairless body. I thought about him when we weren't together. He was in the school band, and at the football games, I'd squint to see where he was in the mass of uniforms. In short, though I wasn't conscious of it at the time, I was infatuated with Timmy—I had a crush on him. Later that basketball season, I decided—for no reason that I could really articulate then—that I hated Timmy. I aggressively rejected him, began to make fun of him around other boys. He was, we all agreed, a geek. He was a faggot.

Three years later, Timmy and I were both on the varsity basketball team, but had hardly spoken a word to each other since we were freshmen. Both of us now had lower voices, had grown to around 6 feet tall, and we both shaved, at least a bit. But Timmy was a skinny, somewhat stigmatized reserve on the team, while I was the team captain and starting point guard. But I wasn't so happy or secure about this. I'd always dreamed of dominating games, of being the hero. Halfway through my senior season, however, it became clear that I was not a star, and I figured I knew why. I was not aggressive enough.

I had always liked the beauty of the fast break, the perfectly executed pick and roll play between two players, and especially the long twenty-foot shot that touched nothing but the bottom of the net. But I hated and feared the sometimes brutal contact under the basket. In fact, I stayed away from the rough fights for rebounds and was mostly a perimeter player, relying on my long shots or my passes to more aggressive teammates under the basket. But now it became apparent to me that time was running out in my quest for greatness: I needed to change my game, and fast. I decided one day before practice that I was gonna get aggressive. While practicing one of our standard plays, I passed the ball to a teammate, and then ran to the spot at which I was to set a pick on a defender. I knew that one could sometimes get away with setting a face-up screen on a player, and then as he makes contact with you, roll your back to him and plant your elbow hard in his stomach. The beauty of this move is that your own body "roll" makes the elbow look like an accident. So I decided to try this move. I approached the defensive player, Timmy, rolled, and planted my elbow deeply into his solar plexus. Air exploded audibly from Timmy's mouth, and he crumbled to the floor momentarily.

Play went on as though nothing had happened, but I fell bad about it. Rather than making me feel better, it made me feel guilty and weak. I had to admit to myself why I'd chosen Timmy as the target against whom to test out my new aggression. He was the skinniest and weakest player on the team.

At the time, I hardly thought about these incidents, other than to try to brush them off as incidents that made me feel extremely uncomfortable. Years later, I can now interrogate this as a *sexual* story, and as a *gender* story unfolding within the context of the heterosexualized and masculinized institution of sport. Examining my story in light of research conducted by Alfred Kinsey a half-century ago, I can recognize in myself what Kinsey saw as a very common **fluidity and changeability of sexual desire over the life-course.** Put simply, Kinsey found that large numbers of adult, "heterosexual" men had previously, as adolescents and young adults, experienced sexual desire for males. A surprisingly large number of these men had experienced sexual contact to the point of orgasm with other males during adolescences or early adulthood. Similarly, my story invited me to consider what

is commonly called the **"Freudian theory of bisexuality."** Sigmund Freud shocked the post-Victorian world by suggesting that all people go through a stage, early in life, when they are attracted to people of the same sex. Adult experiences, Freud argued, eventually led most people to shift their sexual desire to what Freud called an appropriate "love object"—a person of the opposite sex. I also considered my experience in light of what lesbian feminist author Adrienne Rich called **institution of compulsory heterosexuality.** Perhaps the extremely high levels of homophobia that are often endemic in boys' and men's organized sports led me to deny and repress my own homoerotic desire through a direct and overt rejection of Timmy, through homophobic banter with male peers, and through the resultant stigmatization of the feminized Timmy. And eventually, I considered my experience in light of what the radical theorist Herbert Marcuse called the **sublimation of homoerotic desire** into an aggressive, violent act as serving to construct a clear line of demarcation between self-and-other. Sublimation, according to Marcuse, involves the driving underground, into the unconscious, of sexual desires that might appear dangerous due to their socially stigmatized status. But sublimation involves more than simple repression into the unconscious—it involves a transformation of sexual desire into something else—often into aggressive and violent acting out toward others, acts that clarify boundaries between one's self and others and therefore lessen any anxieties that might be attached to the repressed homoerotic desire.

Importantly, in our analysis of my story, my memory group went beyond simply discussing the events in psychological terms. My story did suggest some deep psychological processes at work, perhaps, but it also revealed the importance of social context—in this case, the context of the athletic team. In short, my rejection of Timmy and the joining with teammates to stigmatize him in ninth grade stands as an example of what sociologist R. W. Connell calls **moment of engagement with hegemonic masculinity,** where I actively took up the male group's task of constructing heterosexual/masculine identities in the context of sport. The elbow in Timmy's gut three years later can be seen as a punctuation mark that occurred precisely because of my fears that I might be failing at this goal.

It is helpful, I think, to compare my story with gay and lesbian "coming out" stories in sport. Though we have a few lesbian and bisexual coming out stories among women athletes, there are very few gay male coming out stories. Tom Waddell, who as a closeted gay man finished sixth in the decathlon in the 1968 Olympics, later came out and started the Gay Games, an athletic and cultural festival that draws tens of thousands of people every four years. When I interviewed Tom Waddell over a decade ago about his sexual identity and athletic career, he made it quite clear that for many years sports *was* his closet. Tom told me,

> When I was a kid, I was tall for my age, and was very thin and very strong. And I was usually faster than most other people. But I discovered rather early that I liked gymnastics and I liked dance. I was very interested in being a ballet dancer . . . [but] something became obvious to me right away—that male ballet dancers were effeminate, that they were what most people would call faggots. And I thought I just couldn't handle that . . . I was totally closeted and very concerned about being male. This was the fifties, a terrible time to live, and everything was stacked against me. Anyway, I realized that I had to do something to protect my image of myself as a male—because at that time homosexuals were thought of primarily as men who wanted to be women. And so I threw myself into atheletics—I played football, gymnastics, track and field . . . I was a *jock*—that's how I was viewed, and I was comfortable with that.

Tom Waddell was fully conscious of entering sports and constructing a masculine/heterosexual athletic identity precisely because he feared being revealed as gay. It was clear to him, in the context of the 1950s, that being revealed as gay would undercut his claims to the status of manhood. Thus, though he described the athletic closet as "hot and stifling," he remained in the closet until several years after his athletic retirement. He even knowingly played along with locker room discussions about sex and women, knowing that this was part of his "cover":

> I wanted to be viewed as male, otherwise I would be a dancer today. I wanted the male, macho image of an athlete. So I was protected by a very hard shell. I was clearly aware of what I was doing . . . I often felt compelled to go along with

a lot of locker room garbage because I wanted that image—and I know a lot of others who did too.

Like my story, Waddell's story points to the importance of the athletic institution as a context in which peers mutually construct and re-construct narrow definitions of masculinity—and heterosexuality is considered to be a rock-solid foundation of this conception of masculinity. But unlike my story, Waddell's story may invoke what sociologist Erving Goffman called a "dramaturgical analysis": Waddell seemed to be consciously "acting" to control and regulate others' perceptions of him by constructing a public "front stage" persona that differed radically from what he believed to be his "true" inner self. My story, in contrast, suggests a deeper, less consciously strategic repression of my homoerotic attraction. Most likely, I was aware on some level of the dangers of such feelings, and was escaping the dangers, disgrace, and rejection that would likely result from being different. For Waddell, the decision to construct his identity largely within sport was a decision to step into a fiercely heterosexual/masculine closet that would hide what he saw to be his "true" identity. In contrast, I was not so much stepping into a "closet" that would hide my identify—rather, I was stepping out into an entire world of heterosexual privilege. My story also suggests how a *threat* to the promised privileges of hegemonic masculinity—my failure as an athlete—might trigger a momentary sexual panic that could lay bare the constructedness, indeed, the *instability* of the heterosexual/masculine identity.

In either case—Waddell's or mine—we can see how, as young male athletes, heterosexuality and masculinity were not something we "were," but something we were *doing*. It is very significant, I think, that as each of us was "doing heterosexuality," neither of us was actually "having sex" with women (though one of us desperately wanted to!). This underscores a point made by some recent theorists, that heterosexuality should not be thought of simply as sexual acts between women and men; rather, **heterosexuality is a constructed identity, a performance, and an institution** that is not necessarily linked to sexual acts. Though for one of us it was more conscious than for the other, we were both "doing heterosexuality" as an ongoing practice through which we sought (a) to avoid stigma, embarrassment, ostracism, or perhaps worse if we were even suspected of being gay; and (b) to link ourselves into systems of power, status, and privilege that appear to be the birthright of "real men" (i.e., males who are able to successfully compete with other males in sport, work, and sexual relations with women). In other words, each of us actively scripted our own sexual/gender performances, but these scripts were constructed within the constraints of a socially organized (institutionalized) system of power and pleasure.

QUESTIONS FOR FUTURE RESEARCH

As I prepared to tell my above sexual story publicly to my colleagues at the sport studies conference, I felt extremely nervous. Part of the nervousness was due to the fact that I knew some of my colleagues would object to my claim that telling personal stories can be a source of sociological insights. But a larger part of the reason for my nervousness was due to the fact that I was revealing something very personal about my sexuality in such a public way. Most of us aren't used to doing this, especially in the context of a professional conference. But I had learned long ago, especially from feminist women scholars, and from gay and lesbian scholars, that biography is linked to history, and that part of "normal" academic discourse has been to hide "the personal" (including the fact that the researcher is himself or herself a person, with values, feelings, and, yes, biases) behind a carefully constructed facade of "objectivity." Rather than trying to hide—or be ashamed of—one's subjective experience of the world, I was challenging myself to draw on my experience of the world as a resource. Not that I should trust my experience as the final word on "reality"—white, heterosexual males like myself have made the mistake for centuries of calling their

own experience "objectivity," and then punishing anyone who does not share their world view as "deviant." Instead, I hope to use my experience as an example of how those of us who are in dominant sexual/racial/gender/class categories can get a new perspective on the "constructedness" of our identities by juxtaposing our subjective experiences against the recently emerging world views of gay men and lesbians, women, and people of color.

Finally, I want to stress that, juxtaposed, my and Tom Waddell's stories do not shed much light on the question of why some individuals "become gay" while others "become" heterosexual or bisexual. Instead, I'd like to suggest that this is a dead-end question, and that there are far more important and interesting questions to be asked:

- How has heterosexuality, as an institution and as an enforced group practice, constrained and limited all of us—gay, straight, and bi?
- How has the institution of sport been an especially salient institution for the social construction of heterosexual masculinity?
- Why is it that when men play sports they are almost always automatically granted masculine status, and thus assumed to be heterosexual, while when women play sports, questions are raised about their "femininity" and their sexual orientation?

These kinds of questions aim us toward an analysis of the workings of power within institutions—including the ways that these workings of power shape and constrain our identities and relationships—and point us toward imagining alternative social arrangements that are less constraining for everyone.

REFERENCES

Haug, Frigga. 1987. *Female Sexualization: A Collective Work of Memory*. London: Verso.

Katz, Jonathan Ned. 1995. *The Invention of Heterosexuality*. New York: Dutton.

Messner, Michael A. 1992. *Power at Play: Sports and the Problem of Masculinity*. Boston: Beacon Press.

———. 1994. "Gay Athletes and the Gay Games: An interview with Tom Waddell," in M. A. Messner & D. F. Sabo (Eds.),

Sex, Violence and Power in Sports: Rethinking Masculinity (pp. 113–119). Freedom, CA: The Crossing Press.

Pronger, Brian. 1990. *The Arena of Masculinity: Sports, Homosexuality, and the Meaning of Sex*. New York: St. Martin's Press.

S E C T I O N   E I G H T

Bodies

It might seem that women's physical bodies and health are biological matters rather than social. In fact, however, factors like access to health care, working conditions, and nutrition are all socially determined. In addition, cultural ideologies about women's bodies affect how we perceive our own bodies, as well as how social institutions regulate women's bodies and health. Women's bodies are contested terrain, the subject of struggle over political rights, reproductive health care, and medical research. Much feminist scholarship and activism focuses on health issues. The ability to control reproduction, to live and work in conditions not injurious to their health, and to receive safe, effective, and affordable medical care are central to women's welfare. Feminists have devoted considerable energy to changing public health policy on women's behalf and to increasing research funding to women's health issues during the last two decades.

In the 1970s, a women's health movement developed in the United States as an outgrowth of the feminist and consumer health movements. Women's health advocates criticized and challenged the medical establishment's tendency to view women as abnormal and inherently diseased simply because the female reproductive cycle deviates from the male. Women today across the world are asserting the right to control their own bodies by exposing and resisting the medical abuse of women in forms ranging from forced sterilization and sex selection against females to pharmaceutical experimentation. Women are also increasing their control over their own health care by enhancing access to

information and specialized training that allow them to more accurately assess their health care needs and make informed decisions about medical treatment. These movements focused on improving women's health care have recently worked alongside other movements, such as those organizing against AIDS or working for improved nutrition and preventive health care for the poor in the United States and Third World countries.

This section explores the social construction of women's bodies, the role of medicine in the maintenance of gender inequality, and issues related to women's health, including what illness tells us about women's position in society.

Suzanne Kessler's article in Section Two ("The Medical Construction of Gender") showed that the medical system actively constructs sex categories. In "Hormonal Hurricanes: Menstruation, Menopause, and Female Behavior," Anne Fausto-Sterling discusses additional ways that medicine shapes our understandings of gender. She examines traditional research on menstruation and menopause and finds that it reflects a deep bias against women by advancing the view that women are "slaves of their reproductive physiologies." Reviewing feminist studies of premenstrual syndrome and menopause, Fausto-Sterling suggests other approaches to women's health issues. Her work forces us to realize that social contexts deeply affect medical interpretations of the female reproductive cycle. Can you think of additional examples of how beliefs about gender are reflected in medical approaches to women's or men's reproductive health?

Social contexts also shape and create health problems. Becky Wangsgaard Thompson examines the social roots of women's eating problems in "'A Way Outa No Way': Eating Problems among African-American, Latina, and White Women." Thompson argues that compulsive eating, compulsive dieting, anorexia, and bulimia are coping strategies that women employ in response to sexual abuse, poverty, heterosexism, racism, and "class injuries." Eating problems thus are not just about conforming to a norm of physical appearance but are also a "serious response to injustices." Thompson's article illustrates how examining women's multiple oppressions—race, class, and sexuality, as well as gender—can alter feminist analyses. What kinds of social change would be necessary to eliminate eating problems?

Laurie Nsiah-Jefferson, in "Reproductive Laws, Women of Color, and Low-Income Women," examines the impact of race, class, and ethnicity on women's reproductive rights. The reproductive rights movement has not always reached poor women and women of color, and regulations such as time limits on abortion have a disproportionate effect on women who are young, lack financial means, or live in remote areas of the country. Nsiah-Jefferson argues that the real need is for family planning programs that are sensitive to cultural differences so that the number of unintended pregnancies can be reduced.

Other aspects of reproductive rights are also affected by class, race, and ethnicity. Vulnerability to charges of "fetal abuse," exposure to reproductive hazards at work, involuntary sterilization, and denial of new reproductive technologies are all more likely for poor women and women of color. All of these conditions pose challenges for the contemporary reproductive rights movement. How should the movement address these issues? What is the best way to make sure that all women can choose whether to have children or not?

The final article in this section explores the complex subject of Muslim women in sports. "The Muslim Female Heroic: Shorts or Veils," by Jennifer Hargreaves, begins by contrasting the heroine's welcome awaiting Nawal El Moutawakel, when she arrived back in Morocco with an Olympic gold medal in 1984, with the jeers that greeted Hassiba Boulmerka in Algeria in 1992, also returning home after an Olympic victory. Hargreaves points out that responses to Muslim women athletes differ between countries and cultures, over time, and among varieties of Islam, but the central issues remain proper attire, behavior, and mode of participation.

Muslim athletes are struggling in different ways to find an acceptable Islamic position on female participation in sport. Hargreaves makes clear that this is not a story of repressed Muslim women, but of Islamic feminists of different stripes making a difference. What does resistance to women's participation in sport tell us about different Islamic attitudes about the body and sex-integrated activity? How do Islamic feminists respond? Can you think of similar examples in American culture of cultural resistance to women's participation in spheres of activity?

Hormonal Hurricanes: Menstruation, Menopause, and Female Behavior

Anne Fausto-Sterling

Woman is a pair of ovaries with a human being attached, whereas man is a human being furnished with a pair of testes.

—Rudolf Virchow, MD (1821–1902)

Estrogen is responsible for that strange mystical phenomenon, the feminine state of mind.

—David Reuben, MD, 1969

In 1900, the president of the American Gynecological Association eloquently accounted for the female life cycle:

Many a young life is battered and forever crippled in the breakers of puberty; if it crosses these unharmed and is not dashed to pieces on the rock of childbirth, it may still ground on the ever-recurring shadows of menstruation and lastly upon the final bar of the menopause ere protection is found in the unruffled waters of the harbor beyond the reach of the sexual storms.[1]

Since then we have amassed an encyclopedia's worth of information about the existence of hormones, the function of menstruation, the regulation of ovulation, and the physiology of menopause. Yet many people, scientists and nonscientists alike, still believe that women function at the beck and call of their hormonal physiology. In 1970, for example, Dr. Edgar Berman, the personal physician of former Vice President Hubert Humphrey, responded to a female member of Congress:

Even a Congresswoman must defer to scientific truths . . . there just are physical and psychological inhibitants that limit a female's potential. . . . I would still rather have a male John F. Kennedy make the Cuban missile crisis decisions than a female of the

same age who could possibly be subject to the curious mental aberrations of that age group.[2]

In a more grandiose mode, Professor Steven Goldberg, a university sociologist, writes that "men and women differ in their hormonal systems . . . every society demonstrates patriarchy, male dominance, and male attainment. The thesis put forth here is that the hormonal renders the social inevitable."[3]

At the broadest political level, writers such as Berman and Goldberg raise questions about the competency of *any and all* females to work successfully in positions of leadership, while for women working in other types of jobs, the question is, Should they receive less pay or more restricted job opportunities simply because they menstruate or experience menopause? And further, do women in the throes of premenstrual frenzy frequently try to commit suicide? Do they really suffer from a "diminished responsibility" that should exempt them from legal sanctions when they beat their children or murder their boyfriends?[4] Is the health of large numbers of women threatened by inappropriate and even ignorant medical attention—medical diagnoses that miss real health problems, while resulting instead in the prescription of dangerous medication destined to create future disease?

The idea that women's reproductive systems direct their lives is ancient. But whether it was Plato, writing about the disruption caused by barren uteri wandering about the body,[5] Pliny, writing that a look from a menstruating woman will "dim the brightness of mirrors, blunt the edge of steel, and take away the polish from ivory,"[6] or modern scientists writing about the changing levels of estrogen and progesterone, certain messages emerge quite clearly. Women, by nature emotionally erratic, cannot be trusted in positions of responsibility. Their dangerous, unpredictable furies warrant control by the medical profession,[a] while ironically, the same "dangerous" females also need protection because their reproductive systems, so necessary for the procreation of the race, are vulnerable to stress and hard work.

"The breakers of puberty," in fact, played a key role in a debate about higher education for women, a controversy that began in the last quarter of the nineteenth century and still echoes today in the halls of academe. Scientists of the late 1800s argued on physiological grounds that women and men should receive different types of education. Women, they believed, could not survive intact the rigors of higher education. Their reasons were threefold: first, the education of young women might cause serious damage to their reproductive systems. Energy devoted to scholastic work would deprive the reproductive organs of the necessary "flow of power," presenting particular problems for pubescent women, for whom the establishment of regular menstruation was of paramount importance. Physicians cited cases of women unable to bear children because they pursued a course of education designed for the more resilient young man.[7] In an interesting parallel to modern nature—nurture debates, proponents of higher education for women countered biological arguments with environmental ones. One anonymous author argued that, denied the privilege afforded their brothers of romping actively through the woods, women became fragile and nervous.[8]

Opponents of higher education for women also claimed that females were less intelligent than males, an assertion based partly on brain size itself but also on the overall size differences between men and women. They held that women cannot "consume so much food as men . . . [because] their average size remains so much smaller; so that the sum total of food converted into thought by women can never equal the sum total of food converted to thought by men. It follows, therefore, that *men will always think more than women.*"[9] One respondent to this bit of scientific reasoning asked the thinking reader to examine the data: Aristotle and Napoleon were short, Newton, Spinoza, Shakespeare, and Comte delicate and of medium height, Descartes and Bacon sickly, "while unfortunately for a theory based upon superior digestion, Goethe and Carlyle were confirmed dyspeptics."[10] Finally, as if pubertal vulnerability and lower intelligence were not enough, it seemed to nineteenth-century scientists that menstruation rendered women "more or less sick and unfit for hard work" "for one quarter of each month during the best years of life."[11]

Although dated in some of the particulars, the turn-of-the-century scientific belief that women's reproductive functions make them unsuitable for higher education remains with us today. Some industries bar fertile women from certain positions because of workplace hazards that might cause birth defects, while simultaneously deeming equally vulnerable men fit for the job.[b] Some modern psychologists and biologists suggest that women perform more poorly than do men on mathematics tests because hormonal sex differences alter male and female brain structures; many people believe women to be unfit for certain professions because they menstruate. Others argue that premenstrual changes cause schoolgirls to do poorly in their studies, to become slovenly and disobedient, and even to develop a "nymphomaniac urge [that] may be responsible for young girls running away from home . . . only to be found wandering in the park or following boys."[12]

If menstruation really casts such a dark shadow on women's lives, we ought certainly to know more about it—how it works, whether it can be controlled, and whether it indeed warrants the high level of concern expressed by some. Do women undergo emotional changes as they progress through the monthly ovulatory cycle? And if so, do hormonal fluctuations bring on these ups and downs? If not—if a model of biological causation is appropriate—how else might we conceptualize what happens?

THE SHADOWS OF MENSTRUATION: A READER'S LITERATURE GUIDE

The Premenstrual Syndrome

> SCIENCE UPDATE: PREMENSTRUAL STRAIN LINKED TO CRIME
>
> —*Providence Journal*

> ERRATIC FEMALE BEHAVIOR TIED TO PREMENSTRUAL SYNDROME
>
> —*Providence Journal*

> VIOLENCE BY WOMEN IS LINKED TO MENSTRUATION
>
> —*National Enquirer*

Menstruation makes news, and the headlines summarize the message. According to Dr. Katharina

Dalton, premenstrual syndrome (PMS) is a medical problem of enormous dimensions. Under the influence of the tidal hormonal flow, women batter their children and husbands, miss work, commit crimes, attempt suicide, and suffer from up to 150 different symptoms, including headaches, epilepsy, dizziness, asthma, hoarseness, nausea, constipation, bloating, increased appetite, low blood sugar, joint and muscle pains, heart palpitations, skin disorders, breast tenderness, glaucoma, and conjunctivitis.[13] Although the great concern expressed in the newspaper headlines just quoted may come from a single public relations source,[14] members of the medical profession seem eager to accept at face value the idea that "70 to 90 percent of the female population will admit to recurrent premenstrual symptoms and that 20 to 40 percent report some degree of mental or physical incapacitation."[15]

If all this is true, then we have on our hands nothing less than an overwhelming public health problem, one that deserves a considerable investment of national resources in order to develop understanding and treatment. If, on the other hand, the claims about premenstrual tension are cut from whole cloth, then the consequences are equally serious. Are there women in need of proper medical treatment who do not receive it? Do some receive dangerous medication to treat nonexistent physiological problems? How often are women refused work, given lower salaries, taken less seriously because of beliefs about hormonally induced erratic behavior? In the game of PMS the stakes are high.

The key issues surrounding PMS are so complex and interrelated that it is hard to know where to begin. There is, as always, the question of evidence. To begin with we can look, in vain, for credible research that defines and analyzes PMS. Despite the publication of thousands of pages of allegedly scientific analyses, the most recent literature reviews simultaneously lament the lack of properly done studies and call for a consistent and acceptable research definition and methodology.[16] Intimately related to the question of evidence is that of conceptualization. Currently held theoretical views about the reproductive cycle are inadequate to the task of understanding the emotional ups and downs of people functioning in a complex world. Finally, lurking beneath all of the difficulties of research design, poor methods, and muddy thinking is the medical world's view of the naturally abnormal woman. Let's look at this last point first.

If you're a woman you can't win. Historically, females who complained to physicians about menstrual difficulties, pain during the menstrual flow, or physical or emotional changes associated with the premenstruum heard that they were neurotic. They imagined the pain and made up the tension because they recognized menstruation as a failure to become pregnant, to fulfill their true role as a woman.[17] With the advent of the women's health movement, however, women began to speak for themselves.[18] The pain is real, they said; our bodies change each month. The medical profession responded by finding biological/hormonal causes, proposing the need for doctor-supervised cures. A third voice, however, entered in: that of feminists worried about repercussions from the idea that women's natural functions represent a medical problem capable of preventing women from competing in the world outside the home. Although this multisided discussion continues, I currently operate on the premise that some women probably do require medical attention for incapacitating physical changes that occur in synchrony with their menstrual cycle. Yet in the absence of any reliable medical research into the problem it is impossible to diagnose true disease or to develop rational treatment. To start with, we must decide what is normal.

The tip-off to the medical viewpoint lies in its choice of language. What does it mean to say "70 to 90 percent of the female population will admit to recurrent premenstrual symptoms"?[19] The word *symptom* carries two rather different meanings. The first suggests a disease or an abnormality, a condition to be cured or rendered normal. Applying this connotation to a statistic suggesting 70 to 90 percent symptom formation leads one to conclude that the large majority of women are by their very nature diseased. The second meaning of *symptom* is that of a sign or signal. If the figure of 70 to 90 percent means nothing more than that most women recognize signs in their own bodies of an oncoming menstrual flow, the statistics are unremarkable. Consider then the following, written in 1974 by three scientists:

It is estimated that from 25 percent to 100 percent of women experience some form of premenstrual or menstrual emotional disturbance. Eichner makes the discerning point that the few women who do not admit to premenstrual tension are basically unaware of it but one only has to talk to their husbands or co-workers to confirm its existence.[20]

Is it possible that up to 100 percent of all menstruating women regularly experience emotional disturbance? Compared to whom? Are males the unstated standard of emotional stability? If there is but a single definition of what is normal and men fit that definition, then women with "female complaints" must by definition be either crazy or in need of medical attention. A double bind indeed.

Some scientists explicitly articulate the idea of the naturally abnormal female. Professor Frank Beach, a pioneer in the field of animal psychology and its relationship to sexuality, suggests the following evolutionary account of menstruation. In primitive hunter–gatherer societies adult women were either pregnant or lactating, and since life spans were so short they died well before menopause; low-fat diets made it likely that they did not ovulate every month; they thus experienced no more than ten menstrual cycles. Given current life expectancies as well as the widespread use of birth control, modern women may experience a total of 400 menstrual cycles. He concludes from this reasoning that "civilization has given women *a physiologically abnormal status* which may have important implications for the interpretation of psychological responses to periodic fluctuations in the secretion of ovarian hormones"—that is, to menstruation (emphasis added).[21] Thus the first problem we face in evaluating the literature on the premenstrual syndrome is figuring out how to deal with the underlying assumption that women have "a physiologically abnormal status."

Researchers who believe in PMS hold a wide variety of viewpoints (none of them supported by scientific data) about the basis of the problem. For example, Dr. Katharina Dalton, the most militant promoter of PMS, says that it results from a relative end-of-the-cycle deficiency in the hormone progesterone. Others cite deficiencies in vitamin B₆, fluid retention, and low blood sugar as possible causes. Suggested treatments range from hormone injection to the use of lithium, diuretics, megadoses of vitamins, and control of sugar in the diet[22] (see Table 1 for a complete list). Although some of these treatments are harmless, others are not. Progesterone injection causes cancer in animals. What will it do to humans? And a recent issue of the *New England Journal of Medicine* contains a report that large doses of vitamin B₆ damage the nerves, causing a loss of feeling in one's fingers and toes.[23] The wide variety of PMS "causes" and "cures" offered by the experts is confusing, to put it mildly. Just what *is* this syndrome

TABLE 1   ALLEGED CAUSES AND PROPOSED TREATMENTS OF PMS

Hypothesized Causes of Premenstrual Syndrome	Various PMS Treatments (used but not validated)
Estrogen excess	Oral contraceptives (combination estrogen and progesterone pills)
Progesterone deficiency	
Vitamin B deficiency	Estrogen alone
Vitamin A deficiency	Natural progesterone
Hypoglycemia	Synthetic progestins
Endogenous hormone allergy	Valium or other tranquilizers
Psychosomatic	Nutritional supplements
Fluid retention	Minerals
Dysfunction of the neurointermediate lobe of the pituitary	Lithium
	Diuretics
Prolactin metabolism	A prolactin inhibitor/ dopamine agonist
	Exercise
	Psychotherapy, relaxation, education, reassurance

SOURCES: Robert L. Reid and S. S. Yen, "Premenstrual Syndrome," *American Journal of Obstetrics and Gynecology* 139 (1981): 85–104; and Judith Abplanalp, "Premenstrual Syndrome: A Selective Review," *Women and Health* 8 (1983): 107–24.

that causes such controversy? How can a woman know if she has it?

With a case of the measles it's really quite simple. A fever and then spots serve as diagnostic signs. A woman said to have PMS, however, may or may not have any of a very large number of symptoms. Furthermore, PMS indicators such as headaches, depression, dizziness, and loss or gain of appetite show up in everyone from time to time. Their mere presence cannot (as would measle spots) help one to diagnose the syndrome. In addition, whether any of these signals connote disease depends upon their severity. A slight headache may reflect nothing more than a lack of sleep, but repeated, severe headaches could indicate high blood pressure. As one researcher, Dr. Judith Abplanalp, succinctly put it: "There is no one set of symptoms which is considered to be the hallmark of or standard criterion for defining the premenstrual syndrome."[24] Dr. Katharina Dalton agrees but feels one can diagnose PMS quite simply by applying the term to "any symptoms or complaints which regularly come just before or during early menstruation but are absent at other times of the cycle."[25] Dalton contrasts this with men suffering from potential PMS "symptoms," because, she says, they experience them randomly during the month while women with the same physical indications acknowledge them only during the premenstruum.

PMS research usually bases itself on an ideal, regular, twenty-eight-day menstrual cycle. Researchers eliminate as subjects for study women with infrequent, shorter, or longer cycles. As a result, published investigations look at a skewed segment of the overall population. Even for those women with a regular cycle, however, a methodological problem remains because few researchers define the premenstrual period in the same way. Some studies look only at the day or two preceding the menstrual flow, others look at the week preceding, while workers such as Dalton cite cases that begin two weeks before menstruation and continue for one week after. Since so few investigations use exactly the same definition, research publications on PMS are difficult to compare with one another.[26] On this score if no other, the literature offers little useful insight, extensive as it is.

Although rarely stated, the assumption is that there is but *one* PMS. Dalton defines the problem so broadly that she and others may well lump together several phenomena of very different origins, a possibility heightened by the fact that investigators rarely assess the severity of the symptoms. Two women, one suffering from a few low days and the other from suicidal depression, may both be diagnosed as having PMS. Yet their difficulties could easily have different origins and ought certainly to receive different treatments. When investigators try carefully to define PMS, the number of people qualifying for study decreases dramatically. In one case a group used ten criteria (listed in Table 2) to define PMS only to find that no more than 20 percent of those who had volunteered for their research project met them.[27] In the absence of any clearly agreed-upon definition(s) of PMS, examinations of the topic should at least state clearly the methodology used; this would enable comparison between publications and allow us to begin to accumulate some knowledge about the issues at hand (Table 2 lists suggested baseline information). At the moment the literature is filled with individual studies that permit neither replication nor comparison with one another—an appro-

TABLE 2   TOWARD A DEFINITION PREMENSTRUAL SYNDROME

Experimental criteria (rarely met in PMS studies):

Premenstrual symptoms for at least six preceding cycles

Moderate to severe physical and psychological symptoms

Symptoms *only* during the premenstrual period, with marked relief at onset of menses

Age between 18 and 45 years

Not pregnant

Regular menses for six pervious cycles

No psychiatric disorder; normal physical examination and laboratory test profile

No drugs for preceding four weeks

Will not receive anxiolytics, diuretics, hormones, or neuroleptic drugs during the study

Minimal descriptive information to be offered in published studies of PMS (rarely offered in the current literature):

Specification of the ways in which subjects were recruited

Age limitations

Contraception and medication information

Marital status

Parity

Race

Menstrual history data

Assessment instruments

Operational definition of PMS

Pschiatric history dat

Assessment of current psychological state

Criteria for assessment of severity of symptoms

Criteria for defining ovulatory status of cycle

Cutoff criteria for "unacceptable" subjects

SOURCE: Judith Abplanalp, "Premenstrual Syndrome: A Selective Review," *Women and Health* 8 (1983): 107–24.

priate state, perhaps, for an art gallery but not for a field with pretensions to the scientific.

Despite the problems of method and definition, the conviction remains that PMS constitutes a widespread disorder, a conviction that fortifies and is fortified by the idea that women's reproductive function, so different from that of "normal" men, places them in a naturally diseased state. For those who believe that 90 percent of all women suffer from a disease called PMS, it becomes a reasonable research strategy to look at the normally functioning menstrual cycle for clues about the cause and possible treatment. There are, in fact, many theories but no credible evidence about the origins of PMS. In Table 1 I've listed the most frequently cited hypotheses, most of which involve in some manner the hormonal system that regulates menstruation. Some of the theories are ingenious and require a sophisticated knowledge of human physiology to comprehend. Nevertheless, the authors of one recent review quietly offer the following summary: "To date no one hypothesis has adequately explained the constellation of symptoms composing PMS."[28] In short, PMS is a disease in search of a definition and cause.

PMS also remains on the lookout for a treatment. That many have been tried is attested to in Table 1. The problem is that only rarely has the efficacy of these treatments been tested with the commonly accepted standard of a large-scale, double-blind study that includes placebos. In the few properly done studies "there is usually (1) a high placebo response and (2) the active agent is usually no better than a placebo."[29] In other words, women under treatment for PMS respond just as well to sugar pills as to medication containing hormones or other drugs. Since it is probable that some women experience severe distress caused by malfunctions of their menstrual system, the genuinely concerned physician faces a dilemma. Should he or she offer treatment until the patient says she feels better even though the drug used may have dangerous side effects; or should a doctor refuse help for as long as we know of no scientifically validated treatment for the patient's symptoms? I have no satisfactory answer. But the crying need for some scientifically acceptable research on the subject stands out above all. If we continue to assume that menstruation is itself pathological, we cannot establish a baseline of health against which to define disease. If, instead, we accept in theory that a range of menstrual normality exists, we can then set about designing studies that define the healthy female reproductive cycle. Only when we have some feeling for *that* can we begin to help women who suffer from diseases of menstruation.

Many of those who reject the alarmist nature of the publicity surrounding PMS believe nevertheless that women undergo mood changes during their menstrual cycle. Indeed, most western women would agree. But do studies of large segments of our population support this generality? And if so, what causes these ups and downs? In trying to answer these questions we confront another piece of the medical model of human behavior, the belief that biology is primary, that hormonal changes cause behavioral ones, but not vice versa. Most researchers use such a linear, unicausal model without thinking about it. Their framework is so much a part of their belief system that they forget to question it. Nevertheless it is the model from which they work, and failure to recognize and work skeptically with it often results in poorly conceived research combined with implausible interpretations of data. Although the paradigm of biological causation has until very recently dominated menstrual-cycle research, it now faces serious and intellectually stimulating challenge from feminist experts in the field. . . .

MENOPAUSE: THE STORM BEFORE THE CALM

An unlikely specter haunts the world. It is the ghost of former womanhood . . . "unfortunate women abounding in the streets walking stiffly in twos and threes, seeing little and observing less. . . . The world appears [to them] as through a grey veil, and they live as docile, harmless creatures missing most of life's values." According to Dr. Robert Wilson and Thelma Wilson, though, one should not be fooled by their "vapid cow-like negative state" because "there is ample evidence that the course of history has been changed not only by the presence of estrogen, but by its absence. The untold misery of alcoholism, drug addiction, divorce, and broken homes caused by these unstable estrogen-starved women cannot be presented in statistical form."[30]

Rather than releasing women from their monthly emotional slavery to the sex hormones, menopause involves them in new horrors. At the individual level one encounters the specter of sexual degeneration, described so vividly by Dr. David Reuben: "The vagina begins to shrivel, the breasts atrophy, sexual desire disappears. . . . Increased facial hair, deepening voice, obesity . . . coarsened features, enlargement of the clitoris, and gradual baldness complete the tragic picture. Not really a man but no longer a functional woman, these individuals live in the world of intersex."[31] At the demographic level, writers express foreboding about women of the baby-boom generation, whose life span has increased from an average forty-eight years at the turn of the century to a projected eighty years in the year 2000.[32] Modern medicine, it seems, has played a cruel trick on women. One hundred years ago they didn't live long enough to face the hardships of menopause but today their increased longevity means they will live for twenty-five to thirty years beyond the time when they lose all possibility of reproducing. To quote Dr. Wilson again: "The unpalatable truth must be faced that all postmenopausal women are castrates."[33]

But what medicine has wrought, it can also rend asunder. Few publications have had so great an effect on the lives of so many women as have those of Dr. Robert A. Wilson, who pronounced menopause to be a disease of estrogen deficiency. At the same time in an influential popular form, in his book *Feminine Forever*, he offered a treatment: estrogen replacement therapy (ERT).[34] During the first seven months following publication in 1966, Wilson's book sold one hundred thousand copies and was excerpted in *Vogue* and *Look* magazines. It influenced thousands of physicians to prescribe estrogen to millions of women, many of whom had no clinical "symptoms" other than cessation of the menses. As one of his credentials Wilson lists himself as head of the Wilson Research Foundation, an outfit funded by Ayerst Labs, Searle, and Upjohn, all pharmaceutical giants interested in the large potential market for estrogen. (After all, no woman who lives long enough can avoid menopause.) As late as 1976 Ayerst also supported the Information Center on the Mature Woman, a public relations firm that promoted estrogen replacement therapy. By 1975 some six million women had started long-term treatment with Premarin (the Ayerst Labs brand name for estrogen), making it the fourth or fifth most popular drug in the United States. Even today, two million of the forty million postmenopausal women in the United States contribute to the $70 million grossed each year from the sale of Premarin-brand estrogen.[35] The "disease of menopause" is not only a social problem: it's big business.[36]

The high sales of Premarin continue despite the publication in 1975 of an article linking estrogen treatment to uterine cancer.[37] Although in the wake of that publication many women stopped taking estrogen and many physicians became more cautious about prescribing it, the idea of hormone replacement therapy remains with us. At least three recent publications in medical journals seriously consider whether the benefits of estrogen might not outweigh the dangers.[38] The continuing flap over treatment for this so-called deficiency disease of the aging female forces one to ask just what *is* this terrible state called menopause? Are its effects so unbearable that one might prefer to increase, even ever so slightly, the risk of cancer rather than suffer the daily discomforts encountered during "the change of life"?

Ours is a culture that fears the elderly. Rather than venerate their years and listen to their wisdom, we segregate them in housing built for "their special needs," separated from the younger generations from which we draw hope for the future. At the same time we allow millions of old people to live on inadequate incomes, in fear that serious illness will leave them destitute. The happy, productive elderly remain invisible in our midst. (One must look to feminist publications such as *Our Bodies, Ourselves* to find women who express pleasure in their postmenopausal state.) Television ads portray only the arthritic, the toothless, the wrinkled, and the constipated. If estrogen really is the hormone of youth and its decline suggests the coming of old age, then its loss is a part of biology that our culture ill equips us to handle.

There is, of course, a history to our cultural attitudes toward the elderly woman and our views about menopause. In the nineteenth century physicians believed that at menopause a woman entered a period of depression and increased susceptibility to disease. The postmenopausal body might be racked with "dyspepsia, diarrhea . . . rheumatic pains, paralysis, apoplexy . . . hemorrhaging . . . tuberculosis . . . and diabetes," while emotionally the aging female risked becoming irritable, depressed, hysterical, melancholic, or even insane. The more a woman violated social laws (such as using birth control or promoting female suffrage), the more likely she would be to suffer a disease-ridden menopause.[39] In the twentieth century, psychologist Helene Deutsch wrote that at menopause "woman has ended her existence as a bearer of future life and has reached her natural end—her partial death—as a servant of the species."[40] Deutsch believed that during the postmenopausal years a woman's main psychological task was to accept the progressive biological withering she experienced. Other well-known psychologists have also accepted the idea that a woman's life purpose is mainly reproductive and that her postreproductive years are ones of inevitable decline. Even in recent times postmenopausal women have been "treated" with tranquilizers, hormones, electroshock, and lithium.[41]

But should women accept what many see as an inevitable emotional and biological decline? Should they believe, as Wilson does, that "from a practical point of view a man remains a man until the end," but that after menopause "we no longer have the 'whole woman'—only the 'part woman' "?[42] What is the real story of menopause?

The Change: Its Definition and Physiology

In 1976, under the auspices of the American Geriatric Society and the medical faculty of the University of Montpellier, the First International Congress on the Menopause convened in the south of France. In the volume that emerged from that conference, scientists and clinicians from around the world agreed on a standard definition of the words *menopause* and *climacteric*. "Menopause," they wrote, "indicates the final menstrual period and occurs during the climacteric. The climacteric is that phase in the aging process of women marking the transition from the reproductive stage of life to the nonreproductive stage."[43] By consensus, then, the word *menopause* has come to mean a specific event, the last menstruation, while *climacteric* implies a process occurring over a period of years.[c]

During the menstrual cycle, the blood levels of a number of hormones rise and fall on a regular basis. At the end of one monthly cycle, the low levels of estrogen and progesterone trigger the pituitary gland to make follicle-stimulating hormone (FSH) and luteinizing hormone (LH). The FSH influences the cells of the ovary to make large amounts of estrogen, and induces the growth and maturation of an oocyte. The LH, at just the right moment, induces ovulation and stimulates certain ovarian cells to form a progesterone-secreting structure called a corpus luteum. When no pregnancy occurs the life of the corpus luteum is limited and, as it degenerates, the lowered level of steroid hormones calls forth a new round of follicle-stimulating and luteinizing hormone synthesis, beginning the cycle once again. Although the ovary produces the lion's share of these steroid hormones, the cells of the adrenal gland also contribute, and this contribution increases in significance after menopause.

What happens to the intricately balanced hormone cycle during the several years preceding menopause is little understood, although it seems likely that gradual changes occur in the balance between pituitary activity (FSH and LH production) and estrogen synthesis.[44] One thing, however, is clear: menopause does not mean the *absence* of estrogen, but rather a gradual lowering in the availability of *ovarian* estrogen. Table 3 summarizes some salient information about changes in steroid hormone levels during the menstrual cycle and after menopause. In looking at the high point of cycle synthesis and then comparing it to women who no longer menstruate, the most dramatic change is seen in the estrogenic hormone estradiol.[d] The other estrogenic hormones, as well as progesterone and testosterone, drop off to some extent but continue to be synthesized at a level comparable to that observed during the early phases of the menstrual cycle. Instead of concentrating on the notion of estrogen deficiency, however, it is more important to point out that (1) postmenopausally the body makes different kinds of estrogen; (2) the

TABLE 3   HORMONE LEVELS AS A PERCENTAGE OF MID-MENSTRUAL-CYCLE HIGH POINT

Stage of Menstrual Cycle	TYPE OF ESTROGEN			Progesterone	Testosterone	Androstenedione
	Estrone	Estradiol	Estriol			
Premenopausal stage						
Early (menses)	20%	13%	67%	100%	55%	87%
Mid (ovulation)	100	100	—	—	100	100
Late (premenstrual)	49	50	100	—	82	—
Postmenopausal stage	17	3	50	50	23	39

SOURCE: Wulf H. Utian, *Menopause in Modern Perspectives* (New York: Appleton-Century-Crofts, 1980), 32.

ovaries synthesize less and the adrenals more of these hormones; and (3) the monthly ups and downs of these hormones even out following menopause.

While estrogen levels begin to decline, the levels of FSH and LH start to increase. Changes in these hormones appear as early as eight years before menopause.[45] At the time of menopause and for several years afterward, these two hormones are found in very high concentrations compared to menstrual levels (FSH as many as fourteen times more concentrated than premenopausally, and LH more than three times more). Over a period of years such high levels are reduced to about half their peak value, leaving the postmenopausal woman with one-and-one-half times more LH and seven times more FSH circulating in her blood than when she menstruated regularly.

It is to all of these changes in hormone levels that the words *climacteric* and *menopause* refer. From these alterations Wilson and others have chosen to blame estrogen for the emotional deterioration they believe appears in postmenopausal women. Why they have focused on only one hormone from a complex system of hormonal changes is anybody's guess. I suspect, however, that the reasons are (at least) twofold. First, the normative biomedical disease model of female physiology looks for simple cause and effect. Most researchers, then, have simply assumed estrogen to be a "cause" and set out to measure its "effect." The model or framework out of which such investigators work precludes an interrelated analysis of all the different (and closely connected) hormonal changes going on during the climacteric. But why single out estrogen? Possibly because this hormone plays an important role in the menstrual cycle as well as in the development of "feminine" characteristics such as breasts and overall body contours. It is seen as the quintessential female hormone. So where could one better direct one's attention if, to begin with, one views menopause as the loss of true womanhood?

Physical changes do occur following menopause. Which, if any, of these are caused by changing hormone levels is another question. Menopause research comes equipped with its own unique experimental traps.[46] The most obvious is that a postmenopausal population is also an aging population. Do physical and emotional differences found in groups of postmenopausal women have to do with hormonal changes or with other aspects of aging? It is a difficult matter to sort out. Furthermore, many of the studies on menopause have been done on preselected populations, using women who volunteer because they experience classic menopausal "symptoms" such as the hot flash. Such investigations tell us nothing about average changes within the population as a whole. In the language of the social scientist, we have no baseline data, nothing to which we can compare menopausal women, no way to tell whether the complaint of a particular woman is typical, a cause for medical concern, or simply idiosyncratic.

Since the late 1970s feminist researchers have begun to provide us with much-needed information. Although their results confirm some beliefs long held by physicians, these newer investigators present them in a more sophisticated context. Dr. Madeleine Goodman and her colleagues designed a study in which they drew information from a large population of women ranging in age from thirty-five to sixty. All had undergone routine multiphasic screening at a health maintenance clinic, but none had come for problems concerning menopause. From the complete clinic records they selected a population of women who had not menstruated for at least one year and compared their health records with those of women who still menstruated, looking at thirty-five different variables, such as cramps, blood glucose levels, blood calcium, and hot flashes, to see if any of these symptoms correlated with those seen in postmenopausal women. The results are startling. They found that only 28 percent of Caucasian women and 24 percent of Japanese women identified as postmenopausal "reported traditional menopausal symptoms such as hot flashes, sweats, etc., while in nonmenopausal controls, 16 percent in Caucasians and 10 percent in Japanese also reported these same symptoms."[47] In other words, 75 percent of menopausal women in their sample reported no remarkable menopausal symptoms, a result in sharp contrast to earlier studies using women who identified themselves as menopausal.

In a similar exploration, researcher Karen Frey found evidence to support Goodman's results. She wrote that menopausal women "did not report significantly greater frequency of physical symptoms or concern about these symptoms than did pre- or postmenopausal women."[48] The studies of Goodman, Frey, and others[49] draw into serious question the notion that menopause is generally or necessarily associated with a set of disease symptoms. Yet at least three physical changes—hot flashes, vaginal dryness and irritation, and osteoporosis—and one emotional one—depression—remain associated in the minds of many with the decreased estrogen levels of the climacteric. Goodman's work indicates that such changes may be far less widespread than previously believed, but if they are troublesome to 26 percent of all menopausal women they remain an appropriate subject for analysis.

We know only the immediate cause of hot flashes: a sudden expansion of the blood flow to the skin. The technical term to describe them, *vasomotor instability*, means only that nerve cells signal the widening of blood vessels, allowing more blood into the body's periphery. A consensus has emerged on two things: (1) the high concentration of FSH and LH in blood probably causes hot flashes, although exactly how this happens remains unknown; and (2) estrogen treatment is the only currently available way to suppress the hot flashes. One hypothesis is that by means of a feedback mechanism, artificially raised blood levels of estrogen signal the brain to tell the pituitary to call off the FSH and LH. Although estrogen does stop the hot flashes, its effects are only temporary; remove the estrogen and the flashes return. Left alone, the body eventually adjusts to the changing levels of FSH and LH. Thus a premenopausal woman has two choices in dealing with hot flashes: she can either take estrogen as a permanent medication, a course Wilson refers to as embarking "on the great adventure of preserving or regaining your full femininity,"[50] or suffer some discomfort while nature takes its course. Since the longer one takes estrogen, the greater the danger of estrogen-linked cancer, many health care workers recommend the latter.[51]

Some women experience postmenopausal vaginal dryness and irritation that can make sexual intercourse painful. Since the cells of the vaginal wall contain estrogen receptors, it is not surprising that estrogen applied locally or taken in pill form helps with this difficulty. Even locally applied, however, the estrogen enters into the bloodstream, presenting the same dangers as when taken in pill form. There are alternative treatments, though, for vaginal dryness. The Boston Women's Health Collective, for example, recommends the use of nonestrogen vaginal creams or jellies, which seem to be effective and are certainly safer. Continued sexual activity also helps—yet another example of the interaction between behavior and physiology.

Hot flashes and vaginal dryness are the *only* climacteric-associated changes for which estrogen unambiguously offers relief. Since significant

numbers of women do not experience these changes and since for many of those that do the effects are relatively mild, the wisdom of ERT must be examined carefully and on an individual basis. Both men and women undergo certain changes as they age, but Wilson's catastrophic vision of postmenopausal women—those ghosts gliding by "unnoticed and, in turn, notic[ing] little"[52]—is such a far cry from reality that it is a source of amazement that serious medical writers continue to quote his work.

In contrast to hot flashes and vaginal dryness, osteoporosis, a brittleness of the bone which can in severe cases cripple, has a complex origin. Since this potentially life-threatening condition appears more frequently in older women than in older men, the hypothesis of a relationship with estrogen levels seemed plausible to many. But as one medical worker has said, a unified theory of the disease "is still nonexistent, although sedentary lifestyles, genetic predisposition, hormonal imbalance, vitamin deficiencies, high-protein diets, and cigarette smoking all have been implicated."[53] Estrogen treatment seems to arrest the disease for a while, but may lose effectiveness after a few years.[54]

Even more than in connection with any physical changes, women have hit up against a medical double bind whenever they have complained of emotional problems during the years of climacteric. On the one hand physicians dismissed these complaints as the imagined ills of a hormone-deficient brain, while on the other they generalized the problem, arguing that middle-aged women are emotionally unreliable, unfit for positions of leadership and responsibility. Women had two choices: to complain and experience ridicule and/or improper medical treatment, or to suffer in silence. Hormonal changes during menopause were presumed to be the cause of psychiatric symptoms ranging from fatigue, dizziness, irritability, apprehension, and insomnia to severe headaches and psychotic depression. In recent years, however, these earlier accounts have been supplanted by a rather different consensus now emerging among responsible medical researchers.

To begin with, there are no data to support the idea that menopause has any relationship to serious depression in women. Postmenopausal women who experience psychosis have almost always had similar episodes premenopausally.[55] The notion of the hormonally depressed woman is a shibboleth that must be laid permanently to rest. Some studies have related irritability and insomnia to loss of sleep from night-time hot flashes. Thus, for women who experience hot flashes, these emotional difficulties might, indirectly, relate to menopause. But the social, life history, and family contexts in which middle-aged women find themselves are more important links to emotional changes occurring during the years of the climacteric. And these, of course, have nothing whatsoever to do with hormones. Quite a number of studies suggest that the majority of women do not consider menopause a time of crisis. Nor do most women suffer from the so-called "empty nest syndrome" supposedly experienced when children leave home. On the contrary, investigation suggests that women without small children are less depressed and have higher incomes and an increased sense of well-being.[56] Such positive reactions depend upon work histories, individual upbringing, cultural background, and general state of health, among other things.

In a survey conducted for *Our Bodies, Ourselves*, one which in no sense represents a balanced cross section of U.S. women, the Boston Women's Health Collective recorded the reactions of more than two hundred menopausal or postmenopausal women, most of whom were suburban, married, and employed, to a series of questions about menopause. About two-thirds of them felt either positively or neutrally about a variety of changes they had undergone, while a whopping 90 percent felt okay or happy about the loss of childbearing ability![57] This result probably comes as no surprise to most women, but it flies in the face of the long-standing belief that women's lives and emotions are driven in greater part by their reproductive systems.

No good account of adult female development in the middle years exists. Levinson,[58] who studied adult men, presents a linear model of male development designed primarily around work experiences. In his analysis, the male climacteric plays only a secondary role. Feminist scholars Rosalind Barnett and Grace Baruch have described the difficulty of fitting women into Levinson's scheme: "It is hard to know how to think of women within this theory—a woman may not enter the world of work until her late thirties, she seldom has a mentor, and even women with life-long career commitments rarely are in a position to reassess their commitment pattern by age forty," as do the men in Levinson's study.[59]

Baruch and Barnett call for the development of a theory of women in their middle years, pointing out

that an adequate one can emerge only when researchers set aside preconceived ideas about the central role of biology in adult female development and listen to what women themselves say. Paradoxically, in some sense we will remain unable to understand more about the role of biology in women's middle years until we have a more realistic *social* analysis of women's postadolescent psychological development. Such an analysis must, of course, take into account ethnic, racial, regional, and class differences among women, since once biology is jettisoned as a universal cause of female behavior, it no longer makes sense to lump all women into a single category.

Much remains to be understood about menopause. Which biological changes, for instance, result from ovarian degeneration and which from other aspects of aging? How does the aging process compare in men and women? What causes hot flashes and can we find safe ways to alleviate the discomfort they cause? Do other aspects of a woman's life affect the number and severity of menopausally related physical symptoms? What can we learn from studying the experience of menopause in other, especially nonwestern, cultures? A number of researchers have proposed effective ways of finding answers to these questions.[60] We need only time, research dollars, and an open mind to move forward.

CONCLUSION

The premise that women are by nature abnormal and inherently diseased dominates past research on menstruation and menopause. While appointing the male reproductive system as normal, this viewpoint calls abnormal any aspect of the female reproductive life cycle that deviates from the male's. At the same time, such an analytical framework places the essence of a woman's existence in her reproductive system. Caught in her hormonal windstorm, she strives to attain normality but can do so only by rejecting her biological uniqueness, for that too is essentially deformed: a double bind indeed. Within such an intellectual structure no medical research of any worth to women's health can be done, for it is the blueprint itself that leads investigators to ask the wrong questions, look in the wrong places for answers, and then distort the interpretation of their results.

Reading through the morass of poorly done studies on menstruation and menopause, many of which express deep hatred and fear of women, can be a discouraging experience. One begins to wonder how it can be that within so vast a quantity of material so little quality exists. But at this very moment the field of menstrual-cycle research (including menopause) offers a powerful antidote to that disheartenment in the form of feminist researchers (both male and female) with excellent training and skills, working within a new analytical framework. Rejecting a strict medical model of female development, they understand that men and women have different reproductive cycles, *both* of which are normal. Not binary opposites, male and female physiologies have differences *and* similarities. These research pioneers know too that the human body functions in a social milieu and that it changes in response to that context. Biology is not a one-way determinant but a dynamic component of our existence. And, equally important, these new investigators have learned not only to *listen* to what women say about themselves but to *hear* as well. By and large, these researchers are not in the mainstream of medical and psychological research, but we can look forward to a time when the impact of their work will affect the field of menstrual-cycle research for the better and for many years to come.

NOTES

a. In the nineteenth century, control took the form of sexual surgery such as ovarietomies and hysterectomies, while twentieth-century medicine prefers the use of hormone pills. The science of the 1980s has a more sophisticated approach to human physiology, but its political motives of control and management have changed little. For an account of medicine's attitudes toward women, see Barbara Ehrenreich and Deidre English, *For Her Own Good: 150 Years of Experts' Advice to Women* (New York: Doubleday, 1979); and G. J. Barker-Benfield, *The Horrors of the Half-Known Life* (New York: Harper & Row, 1977).

b. The prohibited work usually carries a higher wage.

c. There is also a male climacteric, which entails a gradual reduction in production of the hormone testosterone over the years as part of the male aging process. What part it plays in that process is poorly understood and seems frequently to be ignored by researchers, who prefer to contrast continuing male reproductive potency with the loss of childbearing ability in women.[61]

d. Estrogens are really a family of structurally similar molecules. Their possibly different biological roles are not clearly delineated.

REFERENCES

1. Carroll Smith-Rosenberg and Charles Rosenberg, "The Female Animal: Medical and Biological Views of Woman and Her Role in 19th Century America," *Journal of American History* 60 (1973): 336.

2. Edgar Berman, Letter to the Editor, *New York Times*, 26 July 1970.

3. Steven Goldberg, *The Inevitability of Patriarchy* (New York: William Morrow, 1973), 93.

4. Herbert Wray, "Premenstrual Changes," *Science News* 122 (1982): 380–81.

5. Ilza Veith, *Hysteria: The History of a Disease* (Chicago: University of Chicago Press, 1965).

6. Pliny the Elder, quoted in M. E. Ashley and Montagu, "Physiology and Origins of the Menstrual Prohibitions," *Quarterly Review of Biology* 15 (1940): 211.

7. Smith-Rosenberg and Rosenberg, "The Female Animal"; Henry Maudsley, "Sex in Mind and in Education," *Popular Science Monthly* 5 (1874): 200; and Joan Burstyn, "Education and Sex: The Medical Case against Higher Education for Women in England 1870–1900," *Proceedings of the American Philosophical Society* 177 (1973): 7989.

8. Carroll Smith-Rosenberg, "The Hysterical Woman: Sex Roles and Role Conflict in 19th Century America," *Social Research* 39 (1972): 652–78.

9. M. A. Hardaker, "Science and the Woman Question," *Popular Science Monthly* 20 (1881): 583.

10. Nina Morais, "A Reply to Ms. Hardaker on: The Woman Question," *Popular Science Monthly* 21 (1882): 74–75.

11. Maudsley, "Sex in Mind and in Education," 211.

12. Katharina Dalton, *Once a Month* (Claremont, Calif.: Hunter House, 1983), 78.

13. Ibid.; Katharina Dalton, *The Premenstrual Syndrome* (London: William Heinemann Medical Books, 1972).

14. Andrea Eagan, "The Selling of Premenstrual Syndrome," *Ms.* Oct. 1983, 26–31.

15. Robert L. Reid and S. S. Yen, "Premenstrual Syndrome," *American Journal of Obstetrics and Gynecology* 139 (1981): 86.

16. J. Abplanalp, R. F. Haskett, and R. M. Rose, "The Premenstrual Syndrome," *Advances in Psychoneuro-endocrinology* 3 (1980): 327–47.

17. Dalton, *Once a Month.*

18. Boston Women's Health Collective, *Our Bodies, Ourselves* (New York: Simon and Schuster, 1979).

19. Reid and Yen, "Premenstrual Syndrome," 86.

20. John O'Connor, M. Shelley Edward, and Lenore O. Stern, "Behavioral Rhythms Related to the Menstrual Cycle," in *Biorhythms and Human Reproduction*, ed. M. Fern et al. (New York: Wiley, 1974), 312.

21. Frank A. Beach, Preface to chapter 10, in *Human Sexuality in Four Perspectives* (Baltimore: Johns Hopkins University Press, 1977), 271.

22. M. B. Rosenthal, "Insights into the Premenstrual Syndrome," *Physician and Patient* (April 1983): 46–53.

23. Herbert Schaumberg et al., "Sensory Neuropathy from Pyridoxine Abuse," *New England Journal of Medicine* 309 (1983): 446–48.

24. Judith Abplanalp, "Premenstrual Syndrome: A Selective Review," *Women and Health* 8 (1983): 110.

25. Dalton, *Once a Month*, 12.

26. Abplanalp, Haskett, and Rose, "The Premenstrual Syndrome"; and Abplanalp, "Premenstrual Syndrome: A Selective Review."

27. Abplanalp, "Premenstrual Syndrome: A Selective Review."

28. Reid and Yen, "Premenstrual Syndrome," 97.

29. G. A. Sampson, "An Appraisal of the Role of Progesterone in the Therapy of Premenstrual Syndrome," in *The Premenstrual Syndrome*, ed. P. A. vanKeep and W. H. Utian (Lancaster, England: MTP Press Ltd. International Medical Publishers, 1981), 51–69; and Sampson, "Premenstrual Syndrome: A Double-Bind Controlled Trial of Progesterone and Placebo," *British Journal of Psychiatry* 135 (1979): 209–15.

30. Robert A. Wilson and Thelma A. Wilson, "The Fate of the Nontreated Postmenopausal Woman: A Plea for the Maintenance of Adequate Estrogen from Puberty to the Grave," *Journal of the American Geriatric Society* 11 (1963): 352–56.

31. David Reuben, *Everything You Always Wanted to Know about Sex but Were Afraid to Ask* (New York: McKay, 1969), 292.

32. Wulf H. Utian, *Menopause in Modern Perspectives* (New York: Appleton-Century-Crofts, 1980).

33. Wilson and Wilson, "The Fate of the Nontreated Postmenopausal Woman," 347.

34. Robert A. Wilson, *Feminine Forever* (New York: M. Evans, 1966).

35. Marilyn Grossman and Pauline Bart, "The Politics of Menopause," in *The Menstrual Cycle*, vol. 1, ed. Dan, Graham, and Beecher.

36. Kathleen MacPherson, "Menopause as Disease: The Social Construction of a Metaphor," *Advances in Nursing Science* 3 (1981): 95–113; A. Johnson, "The Risks of Sex Hormones as Drugs," *Women and Health* 2 (1977): 8–11.

37. D. Smith et al., "Association of Exogenous Estrogen and Endometrial Carcinoma," *New England Journal of Medicine* 293 (1975): 1164–67.

38. H. Judd et al., "Estrogen Replacement Therapy," *Obstetrics and Gynecology* 58 (1981): 267–75; M. Quigley, "Postmenopausal Hormone Replacement Therapy: Back to Estrogen Forever?" *Geriatric Medicine Today* 1 (1982): 78–85; and Thomas Skillman, "Estrogen Replacement: Its Risks and Benefits," *Consultant* (1982): 115–27.

39. C. Smith-Rosenberg, "Puberty to Menopause: The Cycle of Femininity in 19th Century America," *Feminist Studies* 1 (1973): 65.

40. Helene Deutsch, *The Psychology of Women* (New York: Grune and Stratton, 1945), 458.

41. J. H. Osofsky and R. Seidenberg, "Is Female Menopausal Depression Inevitable?" *Obstetrics and Gynecology* 36 (1970): 611.

42. Wilson and Wilson, "The Fate of the Nontreated Postmenopausal Woman," 348.

43. P. A. vanKeep, R. B. Greenblatt, and M. Albeaux-Fernet, eds., *Consensus on Menopause Research* (Baltimore: University Park Press, 1976), 134.

44. Utian, *Menopause in Modern Perspectives.*

45. Ibid.

46. Madeleine Goodman, "Toward a Biology of Menopause," *Signs* 5 (1980): 739–53.

47. Madeleine Goodman, C. J. Stewart, and F. Gilbert, "Patterns of Menopause: A Study of Certain Medical and Physiological Variables among Caucasian and Japanese Women Living in Hawaii," *Journal of Gerontology* 32 (1977): 297.

48. Karen Frey, "Middle-Aged Women's Experience and Perceptions of Menopause," *Women and Health* 6 (1981): 31.

49. Eve Kahana, A. Kiyak, and J. Liang, "Menopause in the Context of Other Life Events," in *The Menstrual Cycle*, vol. 1, ed. Dan, Graham, and Beecher, 167–78.

50. Wilson, *Feminine Forever*, 134.

51. A. Voda and M. Eliasson, "Menopause: The Closure of Menstrual Life," *Women and Health* 8 (1983): 137–56.

52. Wilson and Wilson, "The Fate of the Nontreated Postmenopausal Woman," 356.

53. Louis Avioli, "Postmenopausal Osteoporosis: Prevention vs. Cure," *Federation Proceedings* 40 (1981): 2418.

54. Voda and Eliasson, "Menopause: The Closure of Menstrual Life."

55. G. Winokur and R. Cadoret, "The Irrelevance of the Menopause to Depressive Disease," in *Topics in*

Psychoendocrinology, ed. E. J. Sachar (New York: Grune and Stratton, 1975).

56. Rosalind Barnett and Grace Baruch, "Women in the Middle Years: A Critique of Research and Theory," *Psychology of Women Quarterly* 3 (1978): 187–97.

57. Boston Women's Health Collective, *Our Bodies, Ourselves.*

58. D. Levinson et al., "Periods in the Adult Development of Men: Ages 18–45," *The Counseling Psychologist* 6 (1976): 21–25.

59. Barnett and Baruch, "Women in the Middle Years," 189.

60. Ibid.; Goodman, "Toward a Biology of Menopause"; and Voda, Dinnerstein, and O'Donnell, eds., *Changing Perspectives on Menopause.*

61. Marcha Flint, "Male and Female Menopause: A Cultural Put-on," in *Changing Perspectives on Menopause*, ed. A. M. Voda, M. Dinnerstein, and S. O'Donnell (Austin: University of Texas Press, 1982).

IF MEN COULD MENSTRUATE

Gloria Steinem

A white minority of the world has spent centuries conning us into thinking that a white skin makes people superior—even though the only thing it really does is make them more subject to ultraviolet rays and to wrinkles. Male human beings have built whole cultures around the idea that penis envy is "natural" to women—though having such an unprotected organ might be said to make men vulnerable, and the power to give birth makes womb envy at least as logical.

In short, the characteristic of the powerful, whatever they may be, are thought to be better than the characteristics of the powerless—and logic has nothing to do with it.

What would happen, for instance, if suddenly, magically, men could menstruate and women could not?

The answer is clear—menstruation would become an enviable, boast-worthy, masculine event:

Men would brag about how long and how much.

Boys would mark the onset of menses, that longed-for proof of manhood, with religious ritual and stag parties.

Congress would fund a National Institute of Dysmenorrhea to help stamp out monthly discomforts.

Sanitary supplies would be federally funded and free. (Of course, some men would still pay for the prestige of commercial brands such as John Wayne Tampons, Muhammad Ali's Rope-a-dope Pads, Joe Namath Jock Shields—"For Those Light Bachelor Days," and Robert "Barretta" Blake Maxi-Pads.)

Military men, right-wing politicians, and religious fundamentalists would cite menstruation ("*men*struation") as proof that only men could serve in the Army ("you have to give blood to take blood"), occupy political office ("can women be aggressive without that steadfast cycle governed by the planet Mars?"), be priests and ministers ("how could a woman give her blood for our sins?"), or rabbis ("without the monthly loss of impurities, women remain unclean").

Male radicals, left-wing politicians, and mystics, however, would insist that women are equal, just different; and that any woman could enter the ranks if only she were willing to self-inflict a major wound every month ("you *must* give blood for the revolution"), recognize the preeminence of menstrual issues, or subordinate her selfness to all men in their Cycle of Enlightenment.

Street guys would brag ("I'm a three-pad man") or answer praise from a buddy ("Man, you lookin' *good!*") by giving fives and saying, "Yeah, man, I'm on the rag!"

TV shows would treat the subject at length. ("Happy Days": Richie and Potsie try to convince Fonzie that he is still "The Fonz," though he has missed two periods in a row.) So would newspapers.

(continued)

(SHARK SCARE THREATENS MENSTRUATING MEN. JUDGE CITES MONTHLY STRESS IN PARDONING RAPIST.) And movies. (Newman and Redford in *Blood Brothers!*)

Men would convince women that intercourse was *more* pleasurable at "that time of the month." Lesbians would be said to fear blood and therefore life itself—though probably only because they needed a good menstruating man.

Of course, male intellectuals would offer the most moral and logical arguments. How could a woman master any discipline that demanded a sense of time, space, mathematics, or measurement, for instance, without that in-built gift for measuring the cycles of the moon and planets— and thus for measuring anything at all? In the rarefied fields of philosophy and religion, could women compensate for missing the rhythm of the universe? Or for their lack of symbolic death-and-resurrection every month?

Liberal males in every field would try to be kind: the fact that "these people" have no gift for measuring life or connecting to the universe, the liberals would explain, should be punishment enough.

And how would women be trained to react? One can imagine traditional women agreeing to all these arguments with a staunch and smiling masochism. ("The ERA would force housewives to wound themselves every month": Phyllis Schlafly. "Your husband's blood is as sacred as that of Jesus—and so sexy, too!": Marabel Morgan.) Reformers and Queen Bees would try to imitate men, and *pretend* to have a monthly cycle. All feminists would explain endlessly that men, too, needed to be liberated from the false idea of Martian aggressiveness, just as women needed to escape the bonds of menses envy. Radical feminists would add that the oppression of the nonmenstrual was the pattern for all other oppressions. ("Vampires were our first freedom fighters!") Cultural feminists would develop a bloodless imagery in art and literature. Socialist feminists would insist that only under capitalism would men be able to monopolize menstrual blood. . . . In fact, if men could menstruate, the power justifications could probably go on forever.

If we let them.

'I'M TAKING BACK MY PUSSY!': A TRANSGRESSION OF PRIVATIZED GYNECOLOGICAL BOUNDARIES

Claire T. Porter

In this essay, I weave together my personal experiences "in the stirrups" with empirical evidence and theory on the medical maltreatment of women, I do not write this account with claims of authority or objectivity. Just as Lisa M. Tillman-Healy (1996, 78) takes readers into the secret world of bulimic young women by describing her own experiences with bulimia, I mean to take readers through "normal" gynecological procedures by describing my own experiences as a gynecological patient. I identify my embodied self as a locus of abuses done to women in the practice of modern medicine, rather than contriving a distance between my body and my thought process in privatized

medical experiences. In writing this essay, I am informed by data that rest in my body-memory of being poked, prodded, scraped and ogled.

My analysis of the events described herein has evolved over time, from viewing my doctors' behavior as acceptable to viewing it as abusive. Rethinking and reliving these events, I attend to what is often dismissed in social science writing: the way the body remembers. The tension I feel grow up through my thighs, buttocks, and pelvic floor, the tightening of my lower back (which compels me to jump up from my chair every few minutes and do the yogic "cat" stretch), the numbness that creeps into my crotch as I re-live memories of

(continued)

strangers' eyes taking me in, and the eventual clench that freezes my jaw when I try to fathom why my doctors would not explain to me what would be happening to me under anesthetic are all omnipresent memory-sensations as I write. Thus, as I relive these events I rely on a methodological framework based on a process of privileging bodily knowledge in the process of creating an intellectual analysis.

Lying on the maroon vinyl examining table, with my behind hanging off the end and my feet elevated, stirrups apart, I feel a spinning sensation in my head. This scene is surreal. I want to hold onto something tightly. I want to shut my legs and never open them again. I want to giggle hysterically, flush red with embarrassment, and clamp my thighs shut. A strange man is looking at the most private and sensuous part of my body. The doctor is a thirty-something man with a degree from the University of Alabama. I can see his degree on the wall from where I lie. His eyes, which cut from side to side, make me nervous, add to the dizzy feeling in my head. As he attempts to stick the speculum in me, I unintentionally clench against the cold metal shoe horn. He repeats, "Stop tensing. Stop tensing." His command only makes me tense harder. It is as if there is no opening "down there" at all, that he has to carve one out with that thing I am sure he keeps in the refrigerator. But he finally gets it in.

As he opens the speculum and my vagina, he says casually, "I saw you in that play y'all did over there at the college." He puts something else in me that causes a disconcerting scraping sensation. I interject, "You mean The Scarlett Pimpernell'?" "Yes. The one where you had to wear that old fashioned-dress." My teeth are clenched in reaction to dull scraping. It is hard for me to have this conversation. "I mean, you looked gorgeous." I can feel his breath in warm puffs on my thighs as he speaks. I think about how I had to tape up my breasts and then apply makeup to my cleavage so that they appeared to bulge out of the costume. He is going to be sadly disappointed when he does my breast exam.

As he yanks the speculum out of me, leaving me feeling stretched and gooey with lubricant

jelly, he tells me I have a cyst. I will have to have this cyst surgically removed, he says. The doctor explains, the same casual tone in his voice, that the surgeon will slice my abdomen open from pelvic bone to pelvic bone, get the thing out, and then do "exploratory" surgery in my uterus and ovaries. My head is spinning.

The exam is over, but I cannot shake the feeling of being exposed and vulnerable. I have used half a box of tissues to wipe away all the jelly from my genital area. Then I pull on my clothes fast. The doctor returns and invites me to sit on a chair beside a small desk. He launches into a list of appointments he has made for me at labs to get tests, something about a vaginal laproscopic exam, which I had never heard of. I interrupt his monologue to ask him what a vaginal laproscopy entails. He smirks, "A tube with a little camera in it will be inserted in your vagina . . . kind of like a penis." At the word penis he blurts out a laugh. "Oh," I say. I laugh to match his.

He has to be my friend. My face feels oily under the vibrating fluorescent lights of his office, and I am unable to focus on any one object in the room . . . but I know I should be able to handle this. He just wants to make me feel comfortable, to have a sense of humor about this whole ordeal. He did not mean to make me feel embarrassed by the penis remark. I am just overly sensitive. It is not his fault that I am misinterpreting his comments. As I continue to watch his mouth move in a monologue about barium enemas, my face flushes darker until I feel like a vein in my right cheek may explode. I look at him. He has a reddish-brown tufted mustache and blotchy skin that makes me think first of rednecks. Then an image of Hitler comes to mind. Hatred erupts. The last thing I want is for him to know he has made me feel gross and even more exposed. This is my memory of my first gynecological exam.

The lived experiences that I have had in the gynecologic industry are far from rare. If one were to quantify experiences of medical abuse, to attempt to place on a scale from "bad" to "atrocious" my medical treatment, I do not believe that mine

(continued)

would score much beyond bad. The purpose of describing my own experiences "in the stirrups," and subsequently in surgery, is not to present myself as a woman who has been mistreated in an unusual way. I suspect that thousands of women have been treated far worse. Such a scale would be contrary to the purpose of revealing such intimate and humiliating experiences. As with all types of abuse, competitions among individuals or groups to determine who has been abused the most and the worst derail the discussion and diminish more nuanced understandings about the nature of the abuse. Rather than attempting to quantify experiences of medical abuse, my purpose is to explore the methodological use of bodily experience as sociological inquiry.

Waves of humiliation surge up as I go through the process of writing, re-reading, re-writing, and so on, the above account of my first gynecological exam. I realize that I have involuntarily crossed my legs. As I write, read, re-think, and re-write how my doctor had to force the speculum into me, I involuntarily clench my pelvic muscles all over again. Why do I do this to myself? Further, why do I publicize this vulnerability and coerce readers to participate in my memory, to relive it, too? And finally, why deny readers distance by writing in a present, active tense, pulling them into the immediacy of the examination? I detail these experiences using the theoretical framework of emotional sociology (Ellis and Bochner 1992, 99). My goal, by writing and reliving these experiences, is to create an atmosphere where the voice of the body is privileged and central rather than dismissed from the discourse. If the voice of the body becomes central to informing analytical, theoretical stances, then practices that are experienced as violations of the body are recognizable as problematic and unjust, and hence in need of repair.

In publicizing the personal in this essay I also follow the Black feminist theoretical principle discussed by bell hooks and Tanya McKinnon (1996, 36), who state that it is a necessary act of transgression of institutionalized power to talk in the open about private, taboo, and "unspeakable" experiences, even if doing so requires a sacrifice of privacy. hooks and McKinnon assert that activist-oriented theoretical frameworks develop when privatized

abuses are publicized. They state, "The ways in which privacy is constructed and the meaning of public and private legitimize and uphold structures of domination, particularly sexism" (822). Thus, writing about what happened to me in the private space of an OB/GYN office can transgress the institutional protection that this space is afforded in society. The exploitation of women has been commonplace in the gynecological and obstetrics industries for several hundred years (Raymond, 1993, 37). In that sense, the speculum can be viewed as an instrument meant to colonize the female reproductive tract.

It still drives me nuts that I did not kick that gynecologist in the face for objectifying me when his hands were all over my pubic area. It would have been unacceptable in our androcentric, heterosexist culture for a male or female doctor, in the midst of examining a man's penis, to comment on how "gorgeous" he looked during a sporting event. I feel a wave of guilt as I think of my own harsh reaction to my mother when she described to me a gynecologist who, she explained, "tried to turn me on with his hand" during an exam. I had turned on her, asking, "Why didn't you do anything?" She had responded "I told him 'that's enough.'" I had frowned at her, believing her to be weak, even flaky, to let herself be taken advantage of that way. But after my own experience, I can understand perfectly why just that verbal rebuke was difficult for her to muster, and actually showed her bravery. I am suddenly overcome with depression at the way mom and I and most other women are made to feel, like control of our own bodies is impossible in the presence of authoritative doctors, who supposedly know us better than we know ourselves.

It is the morning of my operation. A white gown replaces my clothes. Mom helps me get it on, ties the strings in the back. I am disoriented by having had to take out my contacts and by all the people walking around me while my behind is exposed. I ask several nurses why I have to take off my bra if the surgery is all the way "down there." They all say the same things: "You just have to. It's standard policy." Then, without warning the nurse sticks me in the behind with a needle. I yip and then turn red. She says "sorry" in a flat voice and

(continued)

fades away into the blur of people and voices. I call after her to ask what the shot is for. She says it's the anaesthetic for the surgery. Mom tells me what a piece of cake this will be, that I'll be out in no time. People and voices are getting swirled into a syrupy mess. The shot must be putting me under. Then an African-American man in white smiles close to my face and says jauntily, "She's ready to Go!" He is pulling me along. I hear the click of mom's heels and the man humming and the rush of the wind over my face as the cart rolls along. All in slow motion. Then, I am in another room with two women in white, who lift me onto a table. Oh my God, they're about to operate but the shot did not work! I am not under yet! I hear a buzzing whir sound. It sounds like a circular saw. I struggle but my body has turned into inert pudding. I manage to move my mouth, strange sounds coming out.

I repeat to the two women, "Wait! I'm not under yet! I'm not under yet!" They are both laughing in big snorts and cackles, lifting up my gown. I struggle to get away from the buzzing whir and their laughing. Everything is swirling and twirling together, and I fall away.

Muffled voices are calling my name. I am at the bottom of the lake in Pocono, and my mom's side of the family, decked out in absurdly bright cocktail attire, are calling me from the water's edge. That must be why they sound blurred and sluggish. It is so nice and warm down here, but they must want me to swim in to shore. That bright light up there is getting brighter and brighter. . . . I burst through to the light, and moan. I want to vomit. I feel a slicing, throbbing pain in my stomach. A large picture window streams in morning light, white washing the bed I am lying in. So many people, I cannot focus on any one. Is it morning?

Where's Roger? I want to hold his hand and sob, it hurts so bad. Women in white are talking to me: "Claire, you can push this button whenever it hurts, and pain killers will go though the tube into your arm." Somehow, my hand has traveled to the little red button with the speed of light and my index finger clicks it over and over again. Pain is mixed with confusion and the frustration of not being able to control my body. I fall back into the warm water.

This time, I fight the swim up to the light. Up there is pain. But a current is sucking me upwards. Exhausted, I let it whisk me up. My mom and a nurse are talking to me as I try to make it three feet to the toilet. Every time I lift my leg off the floor, a searing pain strikes my abdomen. The nurse is lecturing me, ". . . and how well you heal now will determine how well you do with your pregnancies." I manage a grin here. She assumes I will be having babies. It is a given. I have a womb, therefore I will have babies. Their serious faces both seem silly, verging on absurd. I let out a too-loud giggle and then snort- laugh at their perturbed faces.

A week has gone by since my operation. My mother takes me to the surgeon's examining table in Atlanta. The nurse comes in to "prep" me, and drapes a white sheet over my bare below-the-waist region. When the doctor comes through the door, a young man in a similar white lab coat is at his side. He whips off the sheet as a magician pulls the tablecloth from beneath the plates, while saying only "hello" to me, with no eye contact. The young resident does not make eye contact with me, but I see his eyes wandering over my whole body. I know that look. I feed off that look. He wants me. I feel a rush of adrenaline. He thinks I am pretty, maybe even beautiful. I could seduce him, make him beg. . . . This is sick. He knows nothing about me. He does not know me, but he wants me? How dare he just peruse my naked body, appraising me like a luxury car he wants to test drive. Do I even matter? Do I even exist except as a body?!

"Closely connected with the absence of self is the dispensing of existence experienced by women. . . . Women undergoing these procedures report a sense of nonbeing" (Raymond 1993, xv). I cannot help feeling that my body, especially the most private areas of it, has been taken away from me. This surgeon and the horny resident both assess my pubic area. Now the vision of my genitals is held in their brains. I feel I possess my sex less and less and feel them both smug in the fact that they own it. What a power trip for them. Bastards.

A hilariously out-of-place image pops into my mind as I lie there being examined: I am in a Wonder Woman costume standing beside me as

(continued)

I lie on the table. I throw my golden lasso over my stolen pelvis, announcing valiantly, "I'm taking back my pussy!" I try to hold onto the power of this fantasy, that I am not only the prone me on the table but also a "Wonder Me" who can save myself, but it seems to escape me almost as soon as I imagine it. I have that achy feeling circling the rims of my eyes that means my body wants me to cry. But I am too disconnected. To cry, I have to feel truly righteous in the knowledge that I am wronged. How can I feel that I am wronged by the renowned surgeon and his assistant who have saved my womb? They are doctors, and doctors do not harm; they heal. That is the whole point. So none of my body's aches or my sense of bodily dispossession is even worth entertaining. These are unjustifiable feelings. So I shut them down and float with the sense of nothingness.

Tracing my scar, which grins along the border of my now-growing-back-in pubic hair, with his ungloved index finger, my surgeon says to the resident at his side, "Would you look at that? It's healing perfectly. Practically imperceptible." He smiles up at me then. "You'll be able to look just as good in bikinis."

"Doctors add to the exposure, often by making comments that promote the sexual objectification of the experience for the woman" (Raymond 1993, 37).

My surgeon then turns to the intern without covering me back up. They speak about the importance of certain procedures. The nurse stands by frowning at them and then at me. After what seems like forever, she covers me with the sheet, snapping it out over me so that it billows. As she does this, she glowers at the two doctors. They remain oblivious, still talking about procedures. The nurse's obvious disgust for the doctors' disregard for my privacy gives me a jolt of indignation. I want to scream, "I don't wear bikinis, asshole. Why don't you try to swim in that shit!" But I feel so exposed and powerless, that if I open my mouth, my voice will be sucked away in that antiseptic white void.

Making women sexually attractive to men and willing and able to bear children are the two pinnacles of a "spermatic economy," according to

G. J. Barker-Benfield (1976, 13). In the logic of the "spermatic economy," women exist for sex: as sex objects and/or breeders (cited in Raymond 1993, 34). Thus, what was relevant to my doctors was that they had "healed" me well so that I could still make babies and would still be attractive to men (e.g., I could still wear bikinis without my scar showing).

Four years after my first exam and subsequent surgery, I have just finished a pelvic exam with a woman gynecologist. By virtue of her gender, I am told she will transform the exam into an empowering experience. It does not seem that different, though. I am still on my back while procedures are performed on my body as though I am an object. Afterwards, she invites me to sit down and talk. Perhaps this is where the empowerment will come. She wants to engage in a dialogue with me.

She starts the dialogue by asserting that she wants very much to put me on "the pill." She is already scribbling out a prescription. I tell her she need not bother, that birth control pills affect every organ of the body, and that they have not been around long enough for anyone to know what the long term side effects are. She frowns and says, "But he must be sick and tired of using condoms". "Well, I'm not," I respond curtly. Why is it always so much easier to be curt to a woman in authority than a man?

She backs off, still frowning, and begins to look through my medical history, lying in a yellow folder. "Oh. You had an ectopic pregnancy when you were eighteen?" She sounds mildly surprised "No, but I had a cyst removed then." "An ectopic pregnancy is a kind of cyst. Didn't they tell you?" she asks, with what sounds like a lilt of pity in her voice. I bristle. "I must have just forgotten it was that kind of cyst." I reply. The light-headed vulnerable feeling has returned, as I am transported back to my first pelvic exam. I cannot really hear anything she says to me after this. I just keep thinking about the two words: "ectopic" and "pregnancy." I hate her all of a sudden, this bitch who wants to show up my ignorance. Who pretends that she is different just because she is a woman. And I hate myself for ever having believed that it would be different, for daring to hope that it could be, for putting myself in such a vulnerable position.

(continued)

It is weeks before I can comprehend that, at the time of my surgery, the doctors must have chosen not to tell me that I had an ectopic pregnancy. Were they trying to protect me from being embarrassed, since to have an ectopic pregnancy was proof that I was sexually active? My embarrassment never seemed to have been a concern of theirs at other humiliating medical moments. Or, did they just figure that I did not need to know the technical details of why I was being sliced open? Maybe they arrogantly assumed it would be way over my head. Even worse, had my parents also known, but complied with the doctors in not explaining to me? Then comes rushing in the strange knowledge that I had been pregnant, that a fetus had lived inside me, if only for a few days, and that it had somehow made a mistake in navigation. I felt sad for that ball of energy that had some fleeting existence in me, and was then cut out and incinerated.

I am not a distanced sociologist discussing the pervasive maltreatment of women in the medical industry. Rather, I am a woman who is sometimes still humiliated by this dehumanizing treatment. I wonder if medical reform is possible. What I do believe is that transgressing the boundaries of the public with the protected privacy of the medical establishment, as advocated by hooks with McKinnon (1996), holds promise as a route to eroding the protected power of the medical establishment.

REFERENCES

Barker-Benfield, G.J. 1976. *The Horrors of the Half-Known Life: Male Attitudes Toward Women and Sexuality in the Nineteenth Century.* New York: Harper & Row.

Ellis, Carolyn and Arthur P. Bochner. 1992. "Telling and performing personal stories: the constraints of choice in abortion." Pp. 79–101 in *Investigating Subjectivity: Research on Lived Experience*, edited by Carolyn Ellis and Michael Flaherty. Newbury Park, CA: Sage Publications.

hooks, bell with Tanya McKinnon. 1996. "Sisterhood: beyond public and private." *Signs* 21 (4): 814–829.

Raymond, Janice G. 1993. *Women As Wombs: Reproductive Technologies and the Battle Over Women's Freedom.* New York: HarperCollins.

Tillman-Healy, Lisa M. 1996 "A Secret life in a Culture of Thinness: Reflections on Body, Food, and Bulimia." Pp. 76–108 in *Composing Ethnography: Alternative Forms of Qualitative Writing*, edited by Carolyn Ellis and Arthur P. Bochner. Walnut Creek, CA: AltaMira Press.

READING 31

"A Way Outa No Way": Eating Problems among African-American, Latina, and White Women

Becky Wangsgaard Thompson

Bulimia, anorexia, binging, and extensive dieting are among the many health issues women have been confronting in the last twenty years. Until recently, however, there has been almost no research about eating problems among African-American, Latina, Asian-American, or Native American women, working-class women, or lesbians.[1] In fact, according to the normative epidemiological portrait, eating problems are largely a white, middle, and upper-class heterosexual phenomenon. Further, while feminist research has documented how eating problems are fueled by sexism, there has been almost no attention to how other systems of oppression may also be implicated in the development of eating problems.

In this article, I reevaluate the portrayal of eating problems as issues of appearance based in the "culture of thinness." I propose that eating problems begin as ways women cope with various traumas, including sexual abuse, racism, classism, sexism, heterosexism, and poverty. Showing the interface between these traumas and the onset of eating problems explains why women may use eating to numb pain and cope with violations to their bodies. This theoretical shift also permits an understanding of the economic, political, social, educational, and cultural resources that women need to change in correcting their relationship to food and their bodies.

EXISTING RESEARCH ON EATING PROBLEMS

There are three theoretical models used to explain the epidemiology, etiology, and treatment of eating problems. The biomedical model offers important scientific research about possible physiological causes of eating problems and the physiological dangers of purging and starvation (Copeland 1985; Spack 1985). However, this model adopts medical treatment strategies that may disempower and traumatize women (Garner 1985; Orbach 1985). In addition, this model ignores many social, historical, and cultural factors that influence women's eating patterns. The psychological model identifies eating problems as "multidimensional disorders" that are influenced by biological, psychological, and cultural factors (Garfinkel and Garner 1982). While useful in its exploration of effective therapeutic treatments, this model, like the biomedical one, tends to neglect women of color, lesbians, and working-class women.

The third model, offered by feminists, asserts that eating problems are gendered. This model explains why the vast majority of people with eating problems are women, how gender socialization and sexism may relate to eating problems, and how masculine models of psychological development have shaped theoretical interpretations. Feminists offer the culture-of-thinness model as a key reason why eating problems predominate among women. According to this model, thinness is a culturally, socially, and economically enforced requirement for female beauty. This

imperative makes women vulnerable to cycles of dieting, weight loss, and subsequent weight gain, which may lead to anorexia and bulimia (Chernin 1981; Orbach 1978, 1985; Smead 1984).

Feminists have rescued eating problems from the realm of individual psychopathology by showing how the difficulties are rooted in systematic and pervasive attempts to control women's body sizes and appetites. However, researchers have yet to give significant attention to how race, class, and sexuality influence women's understanding of their bodies and appetites. The handful of epidemiological studies that include African-American women and Latinas casts doubt on the accuracy of the normative epidemiological portrait. The studies suggest that this portrait reflects which particular populations of women have been studied rather than actual prevalence (Andersen and Hay 1985; Gray, Ford, and Kelly 1987; Hsu 1987; Nevo 1985; Silber 1986).

More important, this research shows that bias in research has consequences for women of color. Tomas Silber (1986) asserts that many well-trained professionals have either misdiagnosed or delayed their diagnoses of eating problems among African-American and Latina women due to stereotypical thinking that these problems are restricted to white women. As a consequence, when African-American women or Latinas are diagnosed, their eating problems tend to be more severe due to extended processes of starvation prior to intervention. In her autobiographical account of her eating problems, Retha Powers (1989), an African-American woman, describes being told not to worry about her eating problems since "fat is more acceptable in the Black community" (p. 78). Stereotypical perceptions held by her peers and teachers of the "maternal Black woman" and the "persistent mammy-brickhouse Black woman image" (p. 134) made it difficult for Powers to find people who took her problems with food seriously.

Recent work by African-American women reveals that eating problems often relate to women's struggles against a "simultaneity of oppression" (Clarke 1982; Naylor 1985; White 1991). Byllye Avery (1990), the founder of the National Black Women's Health Project, links the origins of eating problems among African-American women to the daily stress of being undervalued and overburdened at home and at work. In Evelyn C. White's (1990) anthology, *The Black Woman's Health Book: Speaking for Ourselves*, Georgiana Arnold (1990) links her eating problems partly to racism and racial isolation during childhood.

Recent feminist research also identifies factors that are related to eating problems among lesbians (Brown 1987; Dworkin 1989; Iazzetto 1989; Schoenfielder and Wieser 1983). In her clinical work, Brown (1987) found that lesbians who have internalized a high degree of homophobia are more likely to accept negative attitudes about fat than are lesbians who have examined their internalized homophobia. Autobiographical accounts by lesbians have also indicated that secrecy about eating problems among lesbians partly reflects their fear of being associated with a stigmatized illness ("What's Important" 1988).

Attention to African-American women, Latinas, and lesbians paves the way for further research that explores the possible interface between facing multiple oppressions and the development of eating problems. In this way, this study is part of a larger feminist and sociological research agenda that seeks to understand how race, class, gender, nationality, and sexuality inform women's experiences and influence theory production.

METHODOLOGY

I conducted eighteen life history interviews and administered lengthy questionnaires to explore eating problems among African-American, Latina, and white women. I employed a snowball sample, a method in which potential respondents often first learn about the study from people who have already participated. This method was well suited for the study since it enabled women to get information about me and the interview process from people they already knew. Typically, I had much contact with the respondents prior to the interview. This was particularly important given the secrecy associated with this topic (Russell 1986; Silberstein, Striegel-Moore, and Rodin 1987), the necessity of women of color and lesbians to be discriminating about how their lives are studied, and the fact that I was conducting across-race research.

To create analytical notes and conceptual categories from the data, I adopted Glaser and Strauss's (1967) technique of theoretical sampling, which directs the researcher to collect, analyze, and test hypotheses during the sampling process (rather than imposing theoretical categories onto the data). After completing each interview transcription, I gave a copy to each woman who wanted one. After reading their interviews, some of the women clarified or made additions to the interview text.

Demographics of the Women in the Study

The eighteen women I interviewed included five African-American women, five Latinas, and eight white women. Of these women, twelve are lesbian and six are heterosexual. Five women are Jewish, eight are Catholic, and five are Protestant. Three women grew up outside of the United States. The women represented a range of class backgrounds (both in terms of origin and current class status) and ranged in age from nineteen to forty-six years old (with a median age of 33.5 years).

The majority of the women reported having had a combination of eating problems (at least two of the following: bulimia, compulsive eating, anorexia, and/or extensive dieting). In addition, the particular types of eating problems often changed during a woman's life span. (For example, a woman might have been bulimic during adolescence and anorexic as an adult.) Among the women, 28 percent had been bulimic, 17 percent had been bulimic and anorexic, and 5 percent had been anorexic. All of the women who had been anorexic or bulimic also had a history of compulsive eating and extensive dieting. Of the women, 50 percent were compulsive eaters and dieters (39 percent) or compulsive eaters (11 percent) but had not been bulimic or anorexic.

Two-thirds of the women have had eating problems for more than half of their lives, a finding that contradicts the stereotype of eating problems as transitory. The weight fluctuation among the women varied from 16 to 160 pounds, with an average fluctuation of 74 pounds. This drastic weight change illustrates the degree to which the women adjusted to major changes in body size at least once during their lives as they lost, gained, and lost weight again. The average age of onset was eleven years old, meaning that most of the women developed eating problems prior to puberty. Almost all of the women (88 percent) consider themselves as still having a problem with eating, although the majority believe they are well on the way to recovery.

THE INTERFACE OF TRAUMA AND EATING PROBLEMS

One of the most striking findings in this study was the range of traumas the women associated with the origins of their eating problems, including racism, sexual abuse, poverty, sexism, emotional or physical abuse, heterosexism, class injuries, and acculturation.[2] The particular constellation of eating problems among the women did not vary with race, class, sexuality, or nationality. Women from various race and class backgrounds attributed the origins of their eating problems to sexual abuse, sexism, and emotional and/or physical abuse. Among some of the African-American and Latina women, eating problems were also associated with poverty, racism, and class injuries. Heterosexism was a key factor in the onset of bulimia, compulsive eating, and extensive dieting among some of the lesbians. These oppressions are not the same nor are the injuries caused by them. And certainly, there are a variety of potentially harmful ways that women respond to oppression (such as using drugs, becoming a workaholic, or committing suicide). However, for all these women, eating was a way of coping with trauma.

Sexual Abuse

Sexual abuse was the most common trauma that the women related to the origins of their eating problems. Until recently, there has been virtually no research exploring the possible relationship between these two phenomena. Since the mid-1980s, however, researchers have begun identifying connections between the two, a task that is part of a larger feminist critique of traditional psychoanalytic symptomatology (DeSalvo 1989; Herman 1981; Masson 1984). Results of a number of incidence studies indicate that between one-third and two-thirds of women who have eating problems have been abused (Oppenheimer et al. 1985; Root and Fallon 1988). In addition, a growing number of therapists and researchers have offered interpretations of the meaning and impact of eating problems for survivors of sexual abuse (Bass and Davis 1988; Goldfarb 1987; Iazzetto 1989; Swink and Leveille 1986). Kearney-Cooke (1988) identifies dieting and binging as common ways in which women cope with frequent psychological consequences of sexual abuse (such as body image disturbances, distrust of people and one's own experiences, and confusion about one's feelings). Root and Fallon (1989) specify ways that victimized women cope with assaults by binging and purging: bulimia serves many functions, including anesthetizing the negative feelings associated with victimization. Iazzetto's innovative study (1989), based on in-depth interviews and art therapy

sessions, examines how a woman's relationship to her body changes as a consequence of sexual abuse. Iazzetto discovered that the process of leaving the body (through progressive phases of numbing, dissociating, and denying) that often occurs during sexual abuse parallels the process of leaving the body made possible through binging.

Among the women I interviewed, 61 percent were survivors of sexual abuse (eleven of the eighteen women), most of whom made connections between sexual abuse and the beginning of their eating problems. Binging was the most common method of coping identified by the survivors. Binging helped women "numb out" or anesthetize their feelings. Eating sedated, alleviated anxiety, and combated loneliness. Food was something that they could trust and was accessible whenever they needed it. Antonia (a pseudonym) is an Italian-American woman who was first sexually abused by a male relative when she was four years old. Retrospectively, she knows that binging was a way she coped with the abuse. When the abuse began, and for many years subsequently, Antonia often woke up during the middle of the night with anxiety attacks or nightmares and would go straight to the kitchen cupboards to get food. Binging helped her block painful feelings because it put her back to sleep.

Like other women in the study who began binging when they were very young, Antonia was not always fully conscious as she binged. She described eating during the night as "sleep walking. It was mostly desperate—like I had to have it." Describing why she ate after waking up with nightmares, Antonia said, "What else do you do? If you don't have any coping mechanisms, you eat." She said that binging made her "disappear," which made her feel protected. Like Antonia, most of the women were sexually abused before puberty; four of them before they were five years old. Given their youth, food was the most accessible and socially acceptable drug available to them. Because all of the women endured the psychological consequences alone, it is logical that they coped with tactics they could do alone as well.

One reason Antonia binged (rather than dieted) to cope with sexual abuse is that she saw little reason to try to be the small size girls were supposed to be. Growing up as one of the Italian Americans in what she described as a "very WASP town," Antonia felt that everything from her weight and size to having dark hair on her upper lip were physical characteristics she was supposed to hide. From a young age she knew she "never embodied the essence of the good girl. I don't like her. I have never acted like her. I can't be her. I sort of gave up." For Antonia, her body was the physical entity that signified her outsider status. When the sexual abuse occurred, Antonia felt she had lost her body. In her mind, the body she lived in after the abuse was not really hers. By the time Antonia was eleven, her mother put her on diet pills. Antonia began to eat behind closed doors as she continued to cope with the psychological consequences of sexual abuse and feeling like a cultural outsider.

Extensive dieting and bulimia were also ways in which women responded to sexual abuse. Some women thought that the men had abused them because of their weight. They believed that if they were smaller, they might not have been abused. For example when Elsa, an Argentine woman, was sexually abused at the age of eleven, she thought her chubby size was the reason the man was abusing her. Elsa said, "I had this notion that these old perverts liked these plump girls. You heard adults say this too. Sex and flesh being associated." Looking back on her childhood, Elsa believes she made fat the enemy partly due to the shame and guilt she felt about the incest. Her belief that fat was the source of her problems was also supported by her socialization. Raised by strict German governesses in an upper-class family, Elsa was taught that a woman's weight was a primary criterion for judging her worth. Her mother "was socially conscious of walking into places with a fat daughter and maybe people staring at her." Her father often referred to Elsa's body as "shot to hell." When asked to describe how she felt about her body when growing up, Elsa described being completely alienated from her body. She explained,

Remember in school when they talk about the difference between body and soul? I always felt like my soul was skinny. My soul was free. My soul sort of flew. I was tied down by this big bag of rocks that was my body. I had to drag it around. It did pretty much what it wanted and I had a lot of trouble controlling it. It kept me from doing all the things that I dreamed of.

As is true for many women who have been abused, the split that Elsa described between her body and soul was an attempt to protect herself from the pain she believed her body caused her. In her mind, her fat body was what had "bashed in her dreams." Dieting became her solution, but, as is true for many women in the study, this strategy soon led to cycles of binging and weight fluctuation.

Ruthie, a Puerto Rican woman who was sexually abused from twelve until sixteen years of age, described bulimia as a way she responded to sexual abuse. As a child, Ruthie liked her body. Like many Puerto Rican women of her mother's generation, Ruthie's mother did not want skinny children, interpreting that as a sign that they were sick or being fed improperly. Despite her mother's attempts to make her gain weight, Ruthie remained thin through puberty. When a male relative began sexually abusing her, Ruthie's sense of her body changed dramatically. Although she weighed only 100 pounds, she began to feel fat and thought her size was causing the abuse. She had seen a movie on television about Romans who made themselves throw up and so she began doing it, in hopes that she could look like the "little kid" she was before the abuse began. Her symbolic attempt to protect herself by purging stands in stark contrast to the psychoanalytic explanation of eating problems as an "abnormal" repudiation of sexuality. In fact, her actions and those of many other survivors indicate a girl's logical attempt to protect herself (including her sexuality) by being a size and shape that does not seem as vulnerable to sexual assault.

These women's experiences suggest many reasons why women develop eating problems as a consequence of sexual abuse. Most of the survivors "forgot" the sexual abuse after its onset and were unable to retrieve the abuse memories until many years later. With these gaps in memory, frequently they did not know why they felt ashamed, fearful, or depressed. When sexual abuse memories resurfaced in dreams, they often woke feeling upset but could not remember what they had dreamed. These free-floating, unexplained feelings left the women feeling out of control and confused. Binging or focusing on maintaining a new diet were ways women distracted or appeased themselves, in turn, helping them regain a sense of control. As they grew older, they became more conscious of the consequences of these actions. Becoming angry at themselves for binging or promising themselves they would not purge again was a way to direct feelings of shame and self-hate that often accompanied the trauma.

Integral to this occurrence was a transference process in which the women displaced onto their bodies painful feelings and memories that actually derived from or were directed toward the persons who caused the abuse. Dieting became a method of trying to change the parts of their bodies they hated, a strategy that at least initially brought success as they lost weight. Purging was a way women tried to reject the body size they thought was responsible for the abuse. Throwing up in order to lose the weight they thought was making them vulnerable to the abuse was a way to try to find the body they had lost when the abuse began.

Poverty

Like sexual abuse, poverty is another injury that may make women vulnerable to eating problems. One woman I interviewed attributed her eating problems directly to the stress caused by poverty. Yolanda is a Black Cape Verdean mother who began eating compulsively when she was twenty-seven years old. After leaving an abusive husband in her early twenties, Yolanda was forced to go on welfare. As a single mother with small children and few financial resources, she tried to support herself and her children on $539 a month. Yolanda began binging in the evenings after putting her children to bed. Eating was something she could do alone. It would calm her, help her deal with loneliness, and make her feel safe. Food was an accessible commodity that was cheap. She ate three boxes of macaroni and cheese when nothing else was available. As a single mother with little money, Yolanda felt as if her body was the only thing she had left. As she described it,

> I am here, [in my body] 'cause there is no where else for me to go. Where am I going to go? This is all I got . . . that probably contributes to putting on so much weight cause staying in your body, in your home, in yourself, you don't go out. You aren't around other people . . . You hide and as long as you hide you don't have to face . . . nobody can see you eat. You are safe.

When she was eating, Yolanda felt a momentary reprieve from her worries. Binging not only became a logical solution because it was cheap and easy but also because she had grown up amid positive messages about eating. In her family, eating was a celebrated and joyful act. However, in adulthood, eating became a double-edged sword. While comforting her, binging also led to weight gain. During the

three years Yolanda was on welfare, she gained seventy pounds.

Yolanda's story captures how poverty can be a precipitating factor in eating problems and highlights the value of understanding how class inequalities may shape women's eating problems. As a single mother, her financial constraints mirrored those of most female heads of households. The dual hazards of a race- and sex-stratified labor market further limited her options (Higginbotham 1986). In an article about Black women's health, Byllye Avery (1990) quotes a Black woman's explanation about why she eats compulsively. The woman told Avery,

> I work for General Electric making batteries, and, I know it's killing me. My old man is an alcoholic. My kid's got babies. Things are not well with me. And one thing I know I can do when I come home is cook me a pot of food and sit down in front of the TV and eat it. And you can't take that away from me until you're ready to give me something in its place. (p. 7)

Like Yolanda, this woman identifies eating compulsively as a quick, accessible, and immediately satisfying way of coping with the daily stress caused by conditions she could not control. Connections between poverty and eating problems also show the limits of portraying eating problems as maladies of upper-class adolescent women.

The fact that many women use food to anesthetize themselves, rather than other drugs (even when they gained access to alcohol, marijuana, and other illegal drugs), is partly a function of gender socialization and the competing demands that women face. One of the physiological consequences of binge eating is a numbed state similar to that experienced by drinking. Troubles and tensions are covered over as a consequence of the body's defensive response to massive food intake. When food is eaten in that way, it effectively works like a drug with immediate and predictable effects. Yolanda said she binged late at night rather than getting drunk because she could still get up in the morning, get her children ready for school, and be clearheaded for the college classes she attended. By binging, she avoided the hangover or sickness that results from alcohol or illegal drugs. In this way, food was her drug of choice since it was possible for her to eat while she continued to care for her children, drive, cook, and study. Binging is also less expensive than drinking, a factor that is especially significant for poor women. Another woman I interviewed said that when her compulsive eating was at its height, she ate breakfast after rising in the morning, stopped for a snack on her way to work, ate lunch at three different cafeterias, and snacked at her desk throughout the afternoon. Yet even when her eating had become constant, she was still able to remain employed. While her patterns of eating no doubt slowed her productivity, being drunk may have slowed her to a dead stop.

Heterosexism

The life history interviews also uncovered new connections between heterosexism and eating problems. One of the most important recent feminist contributions has been identifying compulsory heterosexuality as an institution which truncates opportunities for heterosexual and lesbian women (Rich 1986). All of the women interviewed for this study, both lesbian and heterosexual, were taught that heterosexuality was compulsory, although the versions of this enforcement were shaped by race and class. Expectations about heterosexuality were partly taught through messages that girls learned about eating and their bodies. In some homes, boys were given more food than girls, especially as teenagers, based on the rationale that girls need to be thin to attract boys. As the girls approached puberty, many were told to stop being athletic, begin wearing dresses, and watch their weight. For the women who weighed more than was considered acceptable, threats about their need to diet were laced with admonitions that being fat would ensure becoming an "old maid."

While compulsory heterosexuality influenced all of the women's emerging sense of their bodies and eating patterns, the women who linked heterosexism directly to the beginning of their eating problems were those who knew they were lesbians when very young and actively resisted heterosexual norms. One working-class Jewish woman, Martha, began compulsively eating when she was eleven years old, the same year she started getting clues of her lesbian identity. In junior high school, as many of her female peers began dating boys, Martha began fantasizing about girls, which made her feel utterly alone. Confused and ashamed about her fantasies, Martha came home every day from school and binged. Binging was a way she drugged herself so that being alone was

tolerable. Describing binging, she said, "It was the only thing I knew. I was looking for a comfort." Like many women, Martha binged because it softened painful feelings. Binging sedated her, lessened her anxiety, and induced sleep.

Martha's story also reveals ways that trauma can influence women's experience of their bodies. Like many other women, Martha had no sense of herself as connected to her body. When I asked Martha whether she saw herself as fat when she was growing up she said, "I didn't see myself as fat. I didn't see myself. I wasn't there. I get so sad about that because I missed so much." In the literature on eating problems, *body image* is the term that is typically used to describe a woman's experience of her body. This term connotes the act of imagining one's physical appearance. Typically, women with eating problems are assumed to have difficulties with their body image. However, the term *body image* does not adequately capture the complexity and range of bodily responses to trauma experienced by the women. Exposure to trauma did much more than distort the women's visual image of themselves. These traumas often jeopardized their capacity to consider themselves as having bodies at all.

Given the limited connotations of the term *body image*, I use the term *body consciousness* as a more useful way to understand the range of bodily responses to trauma.[3] By body consciousness I mean the ability to reside comfortably in one's body (to see oneself as embodied) and to consider one's body as connected to oneself. The disruptions to their body consciousness that the women described included leaving their bodies, making a split between their body and mind, experiencing being "in" their bodies as painful, feeling unable to control what went in and out of their bodies, hiding in one part of their bodies, or simply not seeing themselves as having bodies. Binging, dieting, or purging were common ways women responded to disruptions to their body consciousness.

Racism and Class Injuries

For some of the Latinas and African-American women, racism coupled with the stress resulting from class mobility related to the onset of their eating problems. Joselyn, an African-American woman, remembered her white grandmother telling her she would never be as pretty as her cousins because they were lighter skinned. Her grandmother often humiliated Joselyn in front of others, as she made fun of Joselyn's body while she was naked and told her she was fat. As a young child, Joselyn began to think that although she could not change her skin color, she could at least try to be thin. When Joselyn was young, her grandmother was the only family member who objected to Joselyn's weight. However, her father also began encouraging his wife and daughter to be thin as the family's class standing began to change. When the family was working class, serving big meals, having chubby children, and keeping plenty of food in the house was a sign the family was doing well. But, as the family became mobile, Joselyn's father began insisting that Joselyn be thin. She remembered, "When my father's business began to bloom and my father was interacting more with white businessmen and seeing how they did business, suddenly thin became important. If you were a truly well-to-do family, then your family was slim and elegant."

As Joselyn's grandmother used Joselyn's body as territory for enforcing her own racism and prejudice about size, Joselyn's father used her body as the territory through which he channeled the demands he faced in the white-dominated business world. However, as Joselyn was pressured to diet, her father still served her large portions and bought treats for her and the neighborhood children. These contradictory messages made her feel confused about her body. As was true for many women in this study, Joselyn was told she was fat beginning when she was very young even though she was not overweight. And, like most of the women, Joselyn was put on diet pills and diets before even reaching puberty, beginning the cycles of dieting, compulsive eating, and bulimia.

The confusion about body size expectations that Joselyn associated with changes in class paralleled one Puerto Rican woman's association between her eating problems and the stress of assimilation as her family's class standing moved from poverty to working class. When Vera was very young, she was so thin that her mother took her to a doctor who prescribed appetite stimulants. However, by the time Vera was eight years old, her mother began trying to shame Vera into dieting. Looking back on it, Vera attributed her mother's change of heart to competition among extended family members that centered on "being white, being successful, being middle class, . . . and it was always, `Ay Bendito. She is so fat. What happened?'"

The fact that some of the African-American and Latina women associated the ambivalent messages about food and eating to their family's class mobility

and/or the demands of assimilation while none of the eight white women expressed this (including those whose class was stable and changing) suggests that the added dimension of racism was connected to the imperative to be thin. In fact, the class expectations that their parents experienced exacerbated standards about weight that they inflicted on their daughters.

EATING PROBLEMS AS SURVIVAL STRATEGIES

Feminist Theoretical Shifts

My research permits a reevaluation of many assumptions about eating problems. First, this work challenges the theoretical reliance on the culture-of-thinness model. Although all of the women I interviewed were manipulated and hurt by this imperative at some point in their lives, it is not the primary source of their problems. Even in the instances in which a culture of thinness was a precipitating factor in anorexia, bulimia, or binging, this influence occurred in concert with other oppressions.

Attributing the etiology of eating problems primarily to a woman's striving to attain a certain beauty ideal is also problematic because it labels a common way that women cope with pain as essentially appearance-based disorders. One blatant example of sexism is the notion that women's foremost worry is about their appearance. By focusing on the emphasis on slenderness, the eating-problems literature falls into the same trap of assuming that the problems reflect women's "obsession" with appearance. Some women were raised in families and communities in which thinness was not considered a criterion for beauty. Yet, they still developed eating problems. Other women were taught that women should be thin, but their eating problems were not primarily in reaction to this imperative. Their eating strategies began as logical solutions to problems rather than problems themselves as they tried to cope with a variety of traumas.

Establishing links between eating problems and a range of oppressions invites a rethinking of both the groups of women who have been excluded from research and those whose lives have been the basis of theory formation. The construction of bulimia and anorexia as appearance-based disorders is rooted in a notion of femininity in which white middle- and upper-class women are portrayed as frivolous, obsessed with their bodies, and overly accepting of narrow gender roles. This portrayal fuels women's tremendous shame and guilt about eating problems—as signs of self-centered vanity. This construction of white middle- and upper-class women is intimately linked to the portrayal of working-class white women and women of color as their opposite: as somehow exempt from accepting the dominant standards of beauty or as one step away from being hungry and therefore not susceptible to eating problems. Identifying that women may binge to cope with poverty contrasts the notion that eating problems are class bound. Attending to the intricacies of race, class, sexuality, and gender pushes us to rethink the demeaning construction of middle-class femininity and establishes bulimia and anorexia as serious responses to injustices.

Understanding the link between eating problems and trauma also suggests much about treatment and prevention. Ultimately, their prevention depends not simply on individual healing but also on changing the social conditions that underlie their etiology. As Bernice Johnson Reagon sings in Sweet Honey in the Rock's song "Oughta Be a Woman," "A way outa no way is too much to ask/too much of a task for any one woman" (Reagon 1980).[4] Making it possible for women to have healthy relationships with their bodies and eating is a comprehensive task. Beginning steps in this direction include insuring that (1) girls can grow up without being sexually abused, (2) parents have adequate resources to raise their children, (3) children of color grow up free of racism, and (4) young lesbians have the chance to see their reflection in their teachers and community leaders. Ultimately, the prevention of eating problems depends on women's access to economic, cultural, racial, political, social, and sexual justice.

NOTES

1. I use the term *eating problems* as an umbrella term for one or more of the following: anorexia, bulimia, extensive dieting, or binging. I avoid using the term *eating disorder* because it categorizes the problems as individual pathologies, which deflects attention away from the social inequalities underlying them (Brown 1985). However, by using the term *problem* I do not wish to imply blame. In fact, throughout, I argue that the eating strategies that women develop begin as logical solutions to problems, not problems themselves.

2. By trauma I mean a violating experience that has long-term emotional, physical, and/or spiritual consequences that may have immediate or delayed effects. One reason the term *trauma* is useful conceptually is its association with the diagnostic label *post-traumatic stress disorder (PTSD)* (American Psychological Association 1987). PTSD is one of the few clinical diagnostic categories that recognize social problems (such as war or the Holocaust) as responsible for the symptoms identified (Trimble 1985). This concept adapts well to the feminist assertion that a woman's symptoms cannot be understood as solely individual, considered outside of her social context, or prevented without significant changes in social conditions.

3. One reason the term *consciousness* is applicable is its intellectual history as an entity that is shaped by social context and social structures (Delphy 1984; Marx 1964). This link aptly applies to how the women described their bodies because their perceptions of themselves as embodied (or not embodied) directly relate to their material conditions (living situations, financial resources, and access to social and political power).

4. Copyright © 1980. Used by permission of Songtalk Publishing.

REFERENCES

American Psychological Association. 1987. *Diagnostic and Statistical Manual of Mental Disorders.* 3rd ed. rev. Washington, DC: American Psychological Association.

Andersen, Arnold, and Andy Hay. 1985. Racial and socioeconomic influences in anorexia nervosa and bulimia. *International Journal of Eating Disorders* 4: 479–87.

Arnold, Georgiana. 1990. Coming home: One Black woman's journey to health and fitness. In *The Black Women's Health Book: Speaking for Ourselves*, Evelyn C. White. Seattle, WA: Seal Press.

Avery, Byllye Y. 1990. Breathing life into ourselves: The evolution of the National Black Women's Health Project. In *The Black Women's Health Book: Speaking for Ourselves*, Evelyn C. White. Seattle, WA: Seal Press.

Bass, Ellen, and Laura Davis. 1988. *The Courage to Heal: A Guide for Women Survivors of Child Sexual Abuse.* New York: Harper & Row.

Brown, Laura S. 1985. Women, weight and power: Feminist theoretical and therapeutic issues. *Women and Therapy* 4: 61–71.

————. 1987. Lesbians, weight and eating: New analyses and perspectives. In *Lesbian Psychologies*, the Boston Lesbian Psychologies Collective. Champaign: University of Illinois Press.

Chernin, Kim. 1981. *The Obsession: Reflections of the Tyranny of Slenderness.* New York: Harper & Row.

Clarke, Cheryl. 1982. *Narratives.* New Brunswick, NJ: Sister Books.

Copeland, Paul M. 1985. Neuroendocrine aspects of eating disorders. In *Theory and Treatment of Anorexia Nervosa and Bulimia: Biomedical, Sociocultural, and Psychological Perspectives*, Steven Wiley Emmett. New York: Brunner/Mazel.

Delphy, Christine. 1984. *Close to Home: A Materialist Analysis of Women's Oppression.* Amherst: University of Massachusetts Press.

DeSalvo, Louise. 1989. *Virginia Woolf: The Impact of Childhood Sexual Abuse on Her Life and Work.* Boston, MA: Beacon.

Dworkin, Sari H. 1989. Not in man's image: Lesbians and the cultural oppression of body image. In *Loving Boldly: Issues Facing Lesbians*, Ester D. Rothblum and Ellen Cole. New York: Harrington Park Press.

Garfinkel, Paul E., and David M. Garner. 1982. *Anorexia Nervosa: A Multidimensional Perspective.* New York: Brunner/Mazel.

Garner, David. 1985. Iatrogenesis in anorexia nervosa and bulimia nervosa. *International Journal of Eating Disorders* 4: 701–26.

Glaser, Barney G., and Anselm L. Strauss. 1967. *The Discovery of Grounded Theory: Strategies for Qualitative Research.* New York: Aldine DeGruyter.

Goldfarb, Lori. 1987. Sexual abuse antecedent to anorexia nervosa, bulimia and compulsive overeating: Three case reports. *International Journal of Eating Disorders* 6: 675–80.

Gray, James, Kathryn Ford, and Lily M. Kelly. 1987. The prevalence of bulimia in a Black college population. *International Journal of Eating Disorders* 6: 733–40.

Herman, Judith. 1981. *Father-Daughter Incest.* Cambridge, MA: Harvard University Press.

Higginbotham, Elizabeth. 1986. We were never on a pedestal: Women of color continue to struggle with poverty, racism and sexism. In *For Crying Out Loud*, Rochelle Lefkowitz and Ann Withorn. Boston, MA: Pilgrim Press.

Hsu, George. 1987. Are eating disorders becoming more common in Blacks? *International Journal of Eating Disorders* 6: 113–24.

Iazzetto, Demetria. 1989. When the body is not an easy place to be: Women's sexual abuse and eating problems. Ph.D. diss., Union for Experimenting Colleges and Universities, Cincinnati, Ohio.

Kearney-Cooke, Ann. 1988. Group treatment of sexual abuse among women with eating disorders. *Women and Therapy* 7: 5–21.

Marx, Karl. 1964. *The Economic and Philosophic Manuscripts of 1844.* New York: International.

Masson, Jeffrey. 1984. *The Assault on the Truth: Freud's Suppression of the Seduction Theory.* New York: Farrar, Strauss & Giroux.

Naylor, Gloria. 1985. *Linden Hills.* New York: Ticknor & Fields.

Nevo, Shoshana. 1985. Bulimic symptoms: Prevalence and the ethnic differences among college women. *International Journal of Eating Disorders* 4: 151–68.

Oppenheimer, R., K. Howells, R. L. Palmer, and D. A. Chaloner. 1985. Adverse sexual experience in childhood and clinical eating disorders: A preliminary description. *Journal of Psychiatric Research* 19: 357–61.

Orbach, Susie. 1978. *Fat Is a Feminist Issue.* New York: Paddington.

————. 1985. Accepting the symptom: A feminist psychoanalytic treatment of anorexia nervosa. In *Handbook of Psychotherapy for Anorexia Nervosa and Bulimia*, David M. Garner and Paul E. Garfinkel. New York: Guilford.

Powers, Retha. 1989. Fat is a Black women's issue. *Essence*, Oct., 75, 78, 134, 136.

Reagon, Bernice Johnson. 1980. "Oughta be a woman." On Sweet Honey in the Rock's album *Good News*. Music by Bernice Johnson Reagon; lyrics by June Jordan. Washington, DC: Songtalk.

Rich, Adrienne. 1986. Compulsory heterosexuality and lesbian existence. In *Blood, Bread and Poetry*. New York: Norton.

Root, Maria P. P., and Patricia Fallon. 1988. The incidence of victimization experiences in a bulimic sample. *Journal of Interpersonal Violence* 3: 161–73.

————. 1989. Treating the victimized bulimic: The functions of binge—purge behavior. *Journal of Interpersonal Violence* 4: 90–100.

Russell, Diana E. 1986. *The Secret Trauma: Incest in the Lives of Girls and Women.* New York: Basic Books.

Schoenfielder, Lisa, and Barbara Wieser, eds. 1983. *Shadow on a Tightrope: Writings by Women about Fat Liberation.* Iowa City, IA: Aunt Lute Book Co.

Silber, Tomas. 1986. Anorexia nervosa in Blacks and Hispanics. *International Journal of Eating Disorders* 5: 121–28.

Silberstein, Lisa, Ruth Striegel-Moore, and Judith Rodin. 1987. Feeling fat: A woman's shame. In *The Role of Shame in Symptom Formation*, Helen Block Lewis. Hillsdale, NJ: Lawrence Erlbaum.

Smead, Valerie. 1984. Eating behaviors which may lead to and perpetuate anorexia nervosa, bulimarexia, and bulimia. *Women and Therapy* 3: 37–49.

Spack, Norman. 1985. Medical complications of anorexia nervosa and bulimia. In *Theory and Treatment of Anorexia Nervosa and Bulimia: Biomedical, Sociocultural, and Psychological Perspectives*, Steven Wiley Emmett. New York: Brunner/Mazel.

Swink, Kathy, and Antoinette E. Leveille. 1986. From victim to survivor: A new look at the issues and recovery process for adult incest survivors. *Women and Therapy* 5: 119–43.

Trimble, Michael. 1985. Post-traumatic stress disorder: History of a concept. In *Trauma and Its Wake: The Study and Treatment of Post-traumatic Stress Disorder*, C. R. Figley. New York: Brunner/Mazel.

What's important is what you look like. 1988. *Gay Community News*, July, 24–30.

White, Evelyn C., ed. 1990. *The Black Women's Health Book: Speaking for Ourselves*. Seattle, WA: Seal Press.

———. 1991. Unhealthy appetites. *Essence*, Sept., 28, 30.

R E A D I N G   3 2

Reproductive Laws, Women of Color, and Low-Income Women

Laurie Nsiah-Jefferson

Reproductive rights, like other rights, are not just a matter of abstract theory. How these rights can be exercised and which segments of the population will be allowed to exercise them must be considered in light of existing social and economic conditions. Therefore, concerns about the effects of race, sex, and poverty, as well as law and technology must be actively integrated into all work and discussions addressing reproductive health policy.

. . . Many, though not all, women of color are poor. Women of color are not all one group, just as women of color and poor women are not one group. They have different needs, behaviors, and cultural and social norms. One thing they do share is having been left out of the decision-making process concerning reproductive rights. Although my experience is as a black woman, I will attempt to identify issues that appear to be nearly universal to both women of color and poor women, and point out instances where their perspectives might differ.

There is little information available about the reproductive needs of women of color. In general, the demographic data about non-Caucasian women are clustered together under the heading "nonwhite" as if there were only two racial groups, white and non-white. For example, published abortion statistics are broken down only into two ethnic categories—white and black. As a result of this dichotomization, under-standing of the experience of specific groups such as Native American, Asian/Pacific Islander, and Latina

women is inadequate. This dichotomization is itself evidence of the pressing need for more precise data gathering on issues concerning women of color. The information that is available generally fails to con-sider the obvious cultural and social differences related to differences in ethnicity and national her-itage. In many cases, this has made it difficult to define and address particular problems and to make recommendations about their solutions.

For many women of color, taking control over their reproduction is a new step, and involves issues never before considered. One reason for this is that women of color have not always had access to the pro-choice movement. In the past, it has been difficult for many middle-class white feminists to understand and include the different perspectives and experi-ences of poor and minority women. Thus, it is partic-ularly important that adequate information on the needs and experiences of all women be made avail-able now.

The broader economic and political structures of society impose objective limitations on reproductive choice, that is, decisions as to when, whether, and under what conditions to have a child. Very simply, women of color and poor women have fewer choices than other women. Basic health needs often go unmet in these communities. Poor women and women of color have a continuing history of negative experi-ences concerning reproduction, including their use of birth control pills, the IUD, and contraceptive injections of Depo-Provera;[1] sterilization abuse;[2] impeded access to abortion;[3] coercive birthing procedures and hysterectomy;[4] and exposure to workplace hazards.[5]

. . . Given the history and circumstances of these groups, there are two overarching concerns. One is the desire to make reproductive services, including new technologies, broadly accessible. The other is the need to safeguard against abuse. . . .

TIME LIMITS ON ABORTION

Poor women and women of color often live under circumstances that make it difficult for them to obtain early abortions. . . . Thus, it is important to understand the laws restricting late abortions will continue to have a particular impact on poor women and women of color.

The Disproportionate Need for Post-First-Trimester Abortions

A significantly higher percentage of nonwhite women who get abortions do so after the first trimester, or first 12 weeks, of pregnancy. Of all abortions obtained by white women in 1983, 8.6 percent took place in the 13th week or later, but 12.0 percent of nonwhite women having abortions obtained them in that period.[6] These figures represent the numbers of women who actually succeed in obtaining post-first-trimester procedures, and they may seriously understate actual demand. Financial, geographical, and other barriers to access are likely to have a greater impact on nonwhite women, whose overall abortion rate is more than twice that of whites.[7]

There is little information directly concerning very late abortions. Available data on women who obtain abortions after the first trimester, however, demonstrate that financial factors are very important. The enactment and implementation of the Hyde Amendment terminating federal Medicaid funding for abortions has caused many poor women to delay having abortions while they raise the necessary funds. A study of a St. Louis clinic, for example, showed that, in 1982, 38 persons of the Medicaid-eligible women interviewed who sought abortions after the 10th week attributed the delay between receiving the results of their pregnancy tests and obtaining their abortions to financial problems[8] . . . Even where state Medicaid funding is in theory still available for

abortions, it is often not available in practice. Welfare workers and other state officials do not always inform Medicaid recipients of their right to obtain Medicaid-funded abortions.[9] Not all abortion providers are aware that reimbursement is available from Medicaid. Some providers are unwilling to accept Medicaid. . . . in part because Medicaid reimbursement rates are so low.

Difficulty in locating abortion services also causes delay. . . . The availability of abortion services . . . varies considerably by state.[10] Because abortion facilities are concentrated in metropolitan areas, access to abortion services is particularly difficult for rural women. . . . Although geographic access may not pose a significant problem for women of color from northern states who are concentrated in inner cities, it is a concern for women of color in southern states.

Not only are Native American women who live on reservations denied federal funding for abortions, but no Indian Health Service clinics or hospitals may perform abortions even when payment for those procedures is made privately.[11] The Indian Health Service may be the only health care provider within hundreds of miles of the reservation, and as a result the impact of the regulations can be quite severe.

Women in prison, who are disproportionately poor and of color, may also have great difficulty in gaining access to abortion facilities. Abortion services are rarely available at the prison, and prison authorities are unwilling to release inmates for treatment.[12] Recently adopted federal regulations specifically deny abortion services to federal prisoners.[13]

Even where abortion services exist, lack of information about them deters early abortion. Language barriers and the absence of culturally sensitive bilingual counselors and educational materials make gaining information about abortion services a special problem for Asian/Pacific and Hispanic women. . . .

[Another factor has] been identified as especially important in accounting for very late abortions: youth. . . .

In 1981 . . . 43 percent of all abortions performed after the 20th week of pregnancy were performed on teenagers.[14] Women under 15 years of age are most likely to obtain the latest abortions (those at 21 weeks or more gestation). . . . Teenagers of color often have particular difficulty in obtaining an abortion. One study found that 4 out of 10 black teenagers were unable to obtain a desired abortion, as compared to 2 out of 10 white teenagers.[15] . . .

Time limits on abortion may be imposed by various laws. Currently, there is concern about statutes that impose prohibitions on post-viability abortions or seek to compel the use of the method most likely to preserve fetal life unless the woman's health would be jeopardized. Poor women and women of color bear the brunt of such laws because women with money and power can find ways to circumvent the law, just as they did prior to the legalization of abortion. Affluent women can either travel to a place where a procedure is legal or find a doctor who will certify that their health is at stake. Poor women who do not have such options are denied autonomy because, as the experience with Medicaid provisions allowing reimbursement only for health-threatening situations suggests, few doctors are willing to risk prosecution under these statutes.

Time limits on abortion may result from a provider's decision not to perform procedures past a certain point in pregnancy. Poor women and women of color today have limited access to facilities that provide abortions after the first trimester.[16] Public hospitals are a major source of health care for poor women, yet only 17 percent of all public hospitals report performing abortions in 1985.[17] . . .

The number of abortions needed can be drastically reduced by teaching men and women how to prevent unintended pregnancy. . . . To be effective, family planning services must present information and services in culturally appropriate ways, involving bilingual materials and personnel. Family planning programs must also take account of cultural attitudes and biases about birth control. . . . [S]uch programs must make women of color aware of how the ability to take control of reproductive decisions will benefit their lives.

PRENATAL SCREENING

Prenatal screening offers women the opportunity to obtain limited information about the status of the fetus they are carrying. . . . Of the many social, economic, and political issues that the use of this technology poses, questions of access, cultural and class differences, informed consent, confidentiality, and eugenics are of particular concern to poor women and women of color. . . .

Financial, cultural, social, and geographic factors all affect access to services. A particularly important factor for women of color and poor women is the cost of many prenatal screening procedures. For example, estimates on the cost of amniocentesis range from $400 to $1000. Amniocentesis for genetic purposes should be performed between the 16th and 20th weeks of pregnancy. The federal government directly supports providers of genetic services on a very limited basis.[18] A woman dependent upon Medicaid or the MCHP [Maternal and Child Health Program] may be able to learn the physical condition of her fetus but be unable to afford an abortion, the only "treatment" alternative in almost every case. . . .

[In addition,] [m]any low-income women are unable to avail themselves of prenatal screening because they begin prenatal care too late or receive none at all. Some poor women and women of color request screening as late as 20 weeks into their pregnancies—too late to schedule counseling, undergo the procedure, obtain the results, and have further counseling on the decision of whether to continue the pregnancy. . . . Increased outreach and education can encourage such women to seek out prenatal care earlier in their pregnancies. . . .

Confidentiality in the prenatal screening process is an extremely important issue for people of color who have experienced adverse consequences when intimate information is revealed to third parties. For example, when employers have been given access to information concerning individuals who have the sickle cell trait, they have used it to justify refusals to hire, promote, or retain the employees.[19] Likewise, some insurance companies have refused sickle cell carriers health and life insurance or inflated the cost of their premiums, although there is no evidence that the carriers have a higher risk of disease or a shorter life span.

AIDS screening presents special problems. The Centers for Disease Control have suggested that all fertile women at high risk for contracting AIDS or AIDS-Related-Complex be tested for HIV antibodies. This would include prostitutes, hemophiliacs, intravenous drug users, Haitians, and sex partners of men in high-risk groups.[20] To date, such testing has not been made mandatory. Although some pregnant women are anxious to find out whether they test positively or negatively for the disease, fear of job loss and ostracism as well as fear of the deadly consequences of the disease itself may prevent other women from seeking needed prenatal care if they know that AIDS screening is part of the treatment. Assurances that test results will be kept confidential should help address the first fear.

A related problem involves the need to assure confidentiality in the identification and testing of prospective parents required for prenatal screening. Where children are conceived outside the bonds of matrimony, it may be harder to get both parties tested. The woman may be unable or unwilling to contact the male partner. Moreover, the possibility that the male partner's identity will be revealed to social workers and other public officials mandated to collect child support from fathers often makes the male unwilling to come forward. In addition, teenage prospective parents may be fearful that their parents will learn of their sexual activity as a result of testing. . . .

FETUS AS PATIENT

The topic of fetus as patient involves attempts by medical and legal authorities to compel women to follow doctors' orders, and accept particular medical procedures while pregnant and when they give birth. For example, doctors and hospitals may seek court orders forcing women to undergo surgery on the fetus or to submit to cesarean sections rather than to give birth vaginally. Women may also be subject to criminal prosecution for "fetal abuse" or to civil suit by their children for their behavior while pregnant.

Medical and legal actions in the name of fetal rights raise many issues for poor women and women of color. A basic question is whether it is right to hold individual women responsible for poor outcomes at birth when many women are not able to live under healthful conditions. This topic thus implicates the general socioeconomic conditions poor women and women of color experience that result in their lack of access to basic prenatal care and advanced prenatal, perinatal, and neonatal technologies. Holding individual women responsible under present circumstances is morally unjust, and it diverts attention from the need to correct the serious inequities that permeate today's society.

There is good reason to believe that poor women and women of color will be especially vulnerable to prosecutors' attempts to hold mothers responsible for bad reproductive outcomes. As a general matter, their children experience greater rates of infant mortality and low birth weight, which can result in physical and neurological illness. Infant mortality and morbidity among mothers who live below the poverty line are greatly increased, sometimes to as much as twice the rate experienced by other women. . . .

Socioeconomic conditions are an important element in these poor reproductive outcomes. Low-income women and women of color lack access to prenatal and neonatal care. In addition, many suffer from general ill health, broken families, and lack of social supports. . . .

Recent evidence suggests that hospital authorities' efforts to force pregnant women to accept high-tech procedures will be aimed disproportionately at low-income women and women of color. In 1987, the *New England Journal of Medicine* published a report on the incidence of court-ordered obstetrical interventions, including forced cesarean sections and intrauterine transfusions. The report revealed that 81 percent of the women subjected to such court orders were black, Hispanic, or Asian; 44 percent were not married; 24 percent were not native English speakers; and none were private patients.[21] Attempts to compel submission to procedures such as cesarean section, fetal monitoring, and other technologies presuppose that they have been adequately explained and that the pregnant woman has no good reason for refusing the procedure. Neither assumption may be warranted. . . .

REPRODUCTIVE HAZARDS IN THE WORK PLACE

The reproductive health of minority and poor women may be impaired directly, through job-related hazards, or indirectly, as a consequence of having low-paying jobs without benefits. Thus their reproductive health, like their general health, is affected by their status as workers, as members of a minority group, and as women. Women of color and poor women often have the most hazardous jobs, risking physical, chemical, and psychological injury.[22] Their low income may restrict their access to health care, and force them to live in neighborhoods contaminated by environmental pollutants and to exist on inadequate diets. Many work in positions with low pay and long hours, without benefits such as health insurance, maternity leave, vacation time, or sick pay.[23] Moreover, poverty and discrimination increase stress. Women who are heads of households are particularly likely to suffer hardships.[24]

Poor women and women of color generally have limited recourse when their rights are violated. They have been excluded from trade unions that could have improved their circumstances in the past, and they are afraid to unionize now for fear of losing their jobs. . . .

[For example], [w]omen working in low-income jobs in the health field are exposed to heavy lifting and to chemical hazards such as sterilizing gases, anesthetic gases, X-rays, and drugs.[25] As a result, black hospital workers suffer an even higher rate of primary and secondary infertility than black people generally. Similarly, although little research has been done specifically on reproductive hazards encountered by minority or other hospital workers, nonprofessional hospital workers may be at elevated risk for certain types of cancers (especially breast cancer) because of exposure to radiation and various chemical agents. Cancer-causing agents usually also cause spontaneous abortion.

The textile industry is another source of danger to poor women of color. . . . Most women who work in such jobs are afraid to complain for fear of being fired or reported to immigration authorities as illegal aliens.

Women of color are also found in laundry and cleaning establishments. In 1980, 40 percent of all clothing ironers and pressers, and 23 percent of all laundry and dry cleaning operatives were black.[26] Jobs in this sector also pose serious health risks.

Many minorities, especially blacks and Chicanos, work in agriculture. Of the estimated five million migrant and seasonal workers, 75 percent are Chicano, and 20 percent are black.[27] These workers are exposed to pesticides that cause liver, renal, and reproductive damage.[28]

For some poor women and women of color, the financial precariousness of their work poses the greatest hazard. Women in low-paying positions, whether in agriculture or as domestics, in private homes, tend to have no health or other benefits, such as sick leave or vacation. As a result, many women are forced to work throughout their pregnancies and to return to work immediately after giving birth irrespective of the risks to their health. For example, some jobs require women to stand on their feet all day, although continuous standing can cause complications during pregnancy. Moreover, many of these jobs pay just enough to prevent women from being eligible for Medicaid and the prenatal care services it covers.

Although there is a definite need to protect women from reproductive and other health hazards in the workplace, there is also a danger that protection will take the form of denying them their jobs. Some companies will exclude women of reproductive age from the workplace rather than make working conditions safe. Others may offer a woman another job, usually at reduced pay. Employer policies of this type have a severe impact on poor women and women of color. . . .

Laws and regulations now on the books at the federal and state level are supposed to protect workers from hazards and discrimination in the workplace. These laws theoretically guarantee workers the right to know about their working environment and protect those who speak out against hazards.[29] Unfortunately, these laws are rarely enforced adequately.[30] In addition, domestic and agricultural workers, who are disproportionately poor and minority, are excluded from their coverage. . . .

INTERFERENCE AND REPRODUCTIVE CHOICE

. . . The problem of sterilization abuse illustrates the range of ways poor women and women of color experience interference with their reproductive choice. At times, poor women and women of color have been subjected to blatant coercion; at other times, their "choice" of sterilization has been based on inadequate or no informed consent, the effects of poverty, differential government funding schemes, and lack of birth control information.

Blatant sterilization abuse was exposed in the 1970s. Public assistance officials tricked illiterate black welfare recipients into consenting to the sterilization of their teenage daughters.[31] Native American women under 21 years of age were subjected to radical hysterectomies, and informed consent procedures were ignored.[32] Doctors agreed to deliver the babies of black Medicaid patients on the condition that the women would be sterilized.[33] Doctors have also conditioned the performance of abortions on "consent" to sterilization.[34]

But one must question how voluntary the choice of sterilization is in other cases as well. Complete information is crucial to voluntary choice, yet many women elect sterilization under the mistaken belief that the procedure is reversible. Medical personnel often encourage that belief by referring to the procedure as "tying the tubes"; many women assume that what can be tied, can be untied later.[35] . . .

Physicians' attitudes are one reason why some poor women and women of color may still be subject to involuntary sterilization. Some doctors, oblivious to their patients' preferences and cultural differences in attitudes towards family size and legitimacy, regard "excessive" childbearing by poor women and women of color as deviant or inappropriate. Doctors convey these attitudes to their patients, who come to believe that they will not be accepted as patients unless they conform to the medical profession's analysis of their behavior and problems.[36] Classism and racism lead physicians and other health care providers to urge sterilization on patients they believe incapable of using other methods effectively. For example, a Boston clinic serving primarily black clients reported that 45 percent of its black clients "chose" tubal ligation as a method of birth control after their first child was born.[37] . . .

Sterilization rates as high as 65 percent of Hispanic women have been reported in the northeast United States.[38] . . . Native American women fare no better. It is estimated that between 30 percent and 42 percent of all Native Americans have been sterilized, resulting in a steadily declining birth rate.[39]

Unnecessary surgery is another form of sterilization abuse. The number of conditions that require removal of female reproductive organs are relatively few, and fibroid tumors are not generally considered in that category. However, many women have gone to a physician for treatment of fibroids—a condition especially common among black women—and been told that a hysterectomy was the only cure.[40] In other cases, doctors have advocated hysterectomy for women they perceive as having too many children,[41] or to provide interns and residents with experience.[42] Unfortunately, such practices appear to persist despite the restrictions on Medicaid reimbursement of hysterectomies for these purposes in effect since 1975.[43] . . .

High unemployment and profound economic insecurity have likewise led to the "choice" of sterilization as a method of contraception. Women who feel they must forgo permanently the possibility of having children they would like to have because they cannot afford a child or even the cost of delivery have been deprived of their reproductive choice. . . .

Access to New Reproductive Technologies

Because the health care in the United States is organized on a for-profit basis, the needs of poor and minority women receive little attention generally. Access to reproductive technologies is particularly problematic. For example, each in vitro fertilization procedure costs from $3500 to $5000 per attempt, and most couples make several attempts at achieving pregnancy. Private insurers rarely cover such procedures, so the new technologies are often beyond the reach of even middle-class women. In regard to poor and minority women, governmental concern appears to be focused primarily on reducing fertility rather than improving it. . . .

Social criteria for services impose additional barriers to access. Most in vitro clinics are highly selective, accepting only married, heterosexual women with adequate resources.[44] This is a problem for many potential clients since, for example, in 1985, 57.3 percent of black women were not married.[45] . . .

Childlessness is a very serious concern in communities of color. As a result of cultural norms and restricted opportunities for women to have a profession or a career, motherhood and family life are generally valued very highly. Therefore, losing the option of procreating and parenting can be devastating to a poor woman or a woman of color.[46]

Sociocultural factors make it difficult for some poor women and women of color to obtain treatment for infertility. Shame and fear may make it hard for them to discuss their reproductive difficulties. Moreover, physicians and other health personnel may want to involve the woman's partner in the treatment process and expect him to be knowledgeable about her menstrual cycle, and other aspects of her physical condition. This may present particular problems for some poor women and women of color, who live in cultures in which certain subjects are essentially taboo and in which distinct roles are assigned to men and women. Some women fear losing their mate if they prove infertile. At the same time, infertility testing may be problematic for men in such cultures, especially when their feelings of masculinity are at least partially based on their ability to father children.

Sociocultural factors also shape alternatives to reproductive technologies as the response to unwanted childlessness. Adoption in poor or minority communities is not always the same as the adoption referred to by the agencies serving the primarily white middle class. In many instances, poor or minority women have not formally adopted children, but have raised the children of other family members who, for a variety of reasons, were unable to care for them. This extended family concept is prevalent in many cultures of color and in some white ethnic communities.

Formal adoption is less common, primarily because, until recently, adoption agencies excluded people of color from the adoption process and imposed other socio-economic barriers. Minorities believe in the concept of adoption, but may be wary of the bureaucracy of adoption administrators.[47] In the past 10 years, more adoption officials have attempted to recruit minority families to adopt children, and formal adoption is becoming a more viable alternative to childlessness.[48] . . .

CONCLUSION

Poor women and women of color have pressing needs for health services, including productive health services. They also have a history of maltreatment by the health care delivery system. For such women, making existing rights a reality and meeting the challenges posed by new modes of reproduction and reported advances in prenatal and perinatal technology are crucially related to these needs and history. Reproductive laws and policies for the 1990s must respond to the concerns of all women. . . .

NOTES

1. Clarke, Subtle Forms of Sterilization Abuse: A Reproductive Rights Analysis, in R. Arditti, R. Klein & S. Minden, eds., Test Tube Women (1984), 188, 199; Birth Control Blamed For Health Problems, Intern Extra (Apr. 7, 1984), 60; Native Americans Given Depo-Provera, 8: 1 (1987) *Listen Real Loud*, A-7.

2. Levin & Taub, Reproductive Rights, in C. Lefcourt ed., *Women and the Law* (1987) 10A-27–28.

3. E. Blaine, The Impact on Women of Color of Restricting Medicaid Funding for Abortion, testimony presented to the National Women's Health Network (1985).

4. See generally Arnold, Public Health Aspects of Contraceptive Sterilization, in S. Newman & Z. Klein, eds., *Behavioral-Social Aspects of Contraceptive Sterilization* (1978).

5. See generally Mullings, Women Of Color and Occupational Health, in W. Chavkin, ed., *Double Exposure* (1984).

6. Telephone interview with spokesperson, Alan Guttmacher Inst. (Sept. 23, 1987).

7. Henshaw, Characteristics of U.S Women Having Abortions 1982–1983, *Fam. Plan. Persps.* 19:1 (1986), 5, 6. Abortion rate data must be understood in the context of non-white women's significantly higher fertility rate, a rate that was, for example, 35 percent higher than that for white women in 1981. Centers for Disease Control, *Abortion Surveillance 1981* (Nov. 1985), Table 14 at 37.

8. In 1982, 50 percent of all Medicaid-eligible women at the clinic had abortions at 10 weeks or later. The abortion rate at 10 weeks or later for women not eligible for (or not needing) Medicaid was only 37 percent. Post 13-week abortions were excluded from this portion of the study. See Henshaw, Characteristics of U.S. Women, 172.

9. An unpublished survey of welfare caseworkers in the northern counties of New Jersey indicated that, out of the 42 caseworkers interviewed, only six demonstrated adequate knowledge of the availability of state-funded Medicaid reimbursement for abortion. S. Cohen, *Welfare Caseworkers and information About Restored State Medicaid Funding For Abortion: Summary of Sample Survey* (A.C.L.U. of N.J. May 1984).

10. "In 17 states, fewer than half of all women of reproductive age live in counties with identified abortion providers. In four States—Kentucky, Mississippi, South Dakota, and West Virginia—less than 30 percent of such women live in counties with any abortion provider." Kentucky and West Virginia, of course, have significant poor populations, and Mississippi has both a large poor and a large black population. Henshaw, Forrest & Blaine, Abortion Services in the United States 1981 and 1982, *Fam. Plan. Persps.* 16:3 (1984), 119, 122.

11. In 1982, the U.S. Department of Health and Human Services (DHHS) promulgated and implemented regulations designed to bring abortion policy in the Indian Health Service in line with that in other DHHS-administered health programs. Under these regulations, abortions may be performed only when the woman's life is endangered. Alan Guttmacher Inst., *Issues in Brief* 5: 6 (1985), 1, 2.

12. See generally *Monmouth County Correctional Inst. Inmates* v. *Lanzaro*, 834 F.2d 326 (3d Cir. 1987).

13. See 28 C.F.R. 551.23 (during fiscal year 1987 the Bureau of Prisons may pay for an abortion only where the life of the mother would be endangered if the fetus were carried to term or if the pregnancy is the result of rape).

14. Centers for Disease Control, *Abortion Surveillance 1981*, Table 14 at 37.

15. Alan Guttmacher Inst., *Teenage Pregnancy: The Problem That Hasn't Gone Away* (1981).

16. Henshaw, Forrest & Van Vort, Abortion Services in the United States, 1984 and 1985, *Fam. Plan. Persps.* 19: 2 (1987) [hereinafter Abortion Services 1984 and 1985].

17. *Id.*

18. Title 11 of the Public Health Service Act (the Genetic Diseases Act) provided for direct federal support until the Reagan administration altered the regulations. The state governments now receive these funds through the categorical block grants (Maternal and Child Health Program). Disbursement of funds is discretionary within a range of services. Telephone interview with spokesperson, Alan Guttmacher Inst. (Jan. 16, 1988).

19. Hubbard & Henifin, Genetic Screening of Prospective Parents and of Workers, in Humber & Almeder, ed., *Biomedical Ethics Reviews* (1984), 92, 100.

20. Recommendations for Assisting in the Prevention of Perinatal Transmission of Human T-Lymphotropic Virus Type III Lymphadenopaty-Associated Virus and Acquired Immune Deficiency Syndrome, *Morbidity & Mortality Weekly Rep.* 34:48 (1985), 721, 724.

21. Kolder, Gallagher & Parsons, Court-Ordered Obstetrical Interventions, *New Eng. J. Med.* 316 (1987), 1192, 1192–1196.

22. One indication of the general health problems people of color face is that black workers are almost one and one-half times more likely than white workers to be severely disabled by job-related injuries and illnesses. *Chicago Rep.* 10:3 (1981), 1, 2.

23. See generally U.S. Comm'n on Civ. Rts., *Health Insurance Coverage & Employment Opportunities for Minorities Women*, Clearinghouse Publication No. 72 (Sept, 1982).

24. See Mullings, Women of Color, 125 (Mullings points out, even in two-parent households, a black woman often bears greater responsibility for providing sustenance to her family than the average white woman).

25. Mass. Coalition for Occupational Health & the Boston Women's Health Book Collective, *Our Jobs, Our Health* 15, 40–42 (1983).

26. Westcott, Blacks in the 1970's: Did They Scale the Job Ladder, *Monthly Lab. Rev.* 105:6 (1982), 29, 32.

27. See *Women's Occupational Health Resource Center News* 3: 5 (1981), 4.

28. Kutz, Yobs & Strassman, Stratification of Organochlorine Insect Residues in Human Adipose Tissue, *J. Occupational Med.* 19:9 (1977), 619, 619–622; Davis, The Impact of Workplace Health and Safety on Black Workers: Assessment and Prognosis, *Lab. L.J.*, 31:12 (1980), 723, 729.

29. See generally Bertin, Reproductive Hazards in the Workplace, in Humber & Almeder eds., *Biomedical Ethics Reviews* (1984).

30. *Id.*

31. See Levin & Taub, Reproductive Rights, at 10A-27–28.

32. Alliance Against Women's Oppression, "Caught in the Crossfire: Minority Women and Reproductive Rights," (Jan. 1983), p. 1, 5.

33. *Walker* v. *Price*, 560 F.2d 609 (4th Cir. 1977).

34. Clarke, *Subtle Forms of Sterilization Abuse*, at 197.

35. One study reported that 45 percent of the sterilized black women interviewed did not know the procedure was irreversible. Forty percent of the sample said they regretted being sterilized. *Id.* at 195.

36. *Id.*

37. Martha Eliot Health Center, *Reproductive Health Report* (1985), 1–2.

38. In 1981, a psychologist found that 65 percent of the Puerto Rican women in Hartford and 55 percent of all Latin women in Springfield, Mass. had been sterilized. Personal communication from Dr. Vickie Barres, Brookside Family Health center, Jamaica Plain, Boston, Apr. 1985.

39. Alliance Against Women's Oppression, "Caught in the Crossfire", at 1.

40. D. Scully, *Men Who Control Women's Health: The Miseducation of Obstetrician-Gynecologists* (1980), 120–140.

41. Clarke, *Subtle Forms of Sterilization Abuse*, at 193–194.

42. Scully, *supra* note 40, at 120–140.

43. Clarke, *Men Who Control Women's Health*, at 205 n. 12.

44. G. Corea, *The Mother Machine: Reproductive Technologies from Artificial Insemination to Antisocial Wombs* (1985), 145.

45. Bureau of the Census, U.S. Dept. of Com., Table No. 49, Marital Status of Black and Spanish Origin Population: 1970–85, *Statistical Abstract of the U.S.* (1987), 40. In 1985, 32 percent of black women were never married, 11 percent were divorced and 14.3 percent were widowed.

46. Corea, *The Mother Machine*, at 169–172.

47. Telephone interview with Devera Foreman, Philadelphia Chapter-Association of Black Psychologists (1986).

48. *Id.*

ASSESSING OLDER LESBIANS' HEALTH NEEDS

Sharon Deevey

During the course of [my] research. I worked as a contingent staff nurse on a geropsychiatric unit in a local private hospital. One shift I was assigned to care for a sixty-year-old retired nurse named Ann who had been diagnosed with depression. The psychiatrist's admitting note reported that Ann had "no family," but had lived for thirty-five years with a female roommate.

After I had met Ann, I returned to the nursing station and speculated quietly that this particular patient might be an older lesbian woman. The other nurses knew about my research and one of them asked, "What makes you think that?"

"Well," I said, not exactly sure myself, "because she has lived for thirty-five years with her roommate, and . . . she has a Gertrude Stein haircut!" How could I explain the "sense" of recognizing someone like myself?

From my research about older gay and lesbian people, I knew to avoid direct discussion of sexual orientation with older clients. Gay men and lesbian women who grew up before the Gay Liberation Movement are frequently unwilling or unable to discuss their personal lives with strangers. In the 1940s and 1950s, exposure of "homosexuality" almost guaranteed loss of family, job, and basic safety.

Ann was on suicide precautions and needed to be escorted when leaving the unit. I went with her to the laundry room, and while she washed her clothes, I chatted with her and learned something of her situation.

She had met her roommate thirty-five years ago when Dorie moved in next door. They'd been friends right away, had moved from the small town where they'd lived to the city of Columbus, and had helped each other through school. Ann had worked in several nursing jobs, and Dorie was a retired dietitian.

Things were hard now, Ann reported, because they could not get around much. Their younger woman friend who had been living with them had become seriously ill with cancer and had returned to her family in California. Dorie needed cataract surgery and could not see to drive. Ann had been having crying spells and angry outbursts. She had read about our special geropsychiatric unit and decided to come for help. She spoke very quietly, rarely made eye contact, and answered little more than specifically asked. Both her answers and her guarded manner seemed to confirm my speculation about her lifestyle.

The following weekend, I was assigned to the adjoining locked adult unit. I asked the nurse in charge on the geropsychiatric unit to tell me if Ann's roommate came to visit.

A couple of hours later, the nurse came looking for me. "I think you're right about them," she said. "There's something about seeing them together. . . . Why don't you come over and talk to them during your break?"

They were sitting in the corner of the dayroom, talking quietly. Ann looked up in recognition. Her partner Dorie stood as I introduced myself. She had very short, pure white hair and startlingly blue eyes that I knew could see very little.

After a few introductory pleasantries (while I wracked my brain trying to figure out how to support these women), I said, "You seem to be very important to each other."

"Oh, yes," Dorie said. "Neither of us has any other family . . . just a nephew of mine in Cleveland."

"You need to be clear with your doctor and the nurses about that," I said. "You have the right to be treated as each other's family."

"I'm afraid someone will sneer," Dorie said, looking away. I was right. If they were just roommates they would have no reason to be afraid.

"I can't promise that everyone will understand," I answered, being intentionally vague. "This hospital generally respects what patients want, but you'll have to ask to be treated as family to each other." When I reported the conversation to Ann's primary nurse, she agreed about the importance of supporting the relationship and managing the issue sensitively.

(continued)

Ann was gone the following weekend. In a team meeting, the primary nurse had mentioned the probability of Ann's lesbian sexual orientation to the other team members.

The psychiatrist was adamant. The primary nurse told me that he said no one was to discuss sex with his patient.

"I tried to convince him," she went on, "it's not about sexuality. It's about social isolation, and why Ann's so distrustful of staff and so guarded with other patients in the dayroom. He wouldn't listen.

He just kept repeating, 'No one is to discuss sex with her.'" As it turned out, Ann signed herself out of the hospital against medical advice.

It was the first time I was tempted to follow a patient home from the hospital, but I knew I could not rescue Ann and Dorie by myself. I returned with renewed determination to my research. When I am aging, or ill, and need health care, I can only hope that nurses and physicians will know more about lesbian women and treat me with the same sensitivity and respect they offer anyone else.

READING 33

The Muslim Female Heroic: Shorts or Veils?

ঌ৹   **Jennifer Hargreaves**

INTRODUCTION: SPORT, POLITICS AND RELIGION

When Nawal El Moutawakel from Morocco took the 400-metre hurdles title at the 1984 Los Angeles Olympics, hers was the first gold medal to be won by a woman from the African continent. Nawal had made history. Her achievement was especially remarkable because she was simultaneously the first Arab woman *and* the first Muslim woman to win a gold medal. For different reasons, and in different contexts, Nawal El Moutawakel was hailed as heroic. Disregarding the reality that the category "Muslim" is heterogeneous and that attitudes to women's involvement in public sport vary from country to country, she was reported in the Western media to have triumphed over a unified, restricted "way of life" that normally excludes women from sport. Her success was celebrated as a fundamental break with tradition, a signal of courage, new possibilities, changing attitudes and newfound freedoms. In Morocco, she was a figure of national triumph and Arabic pride, a sign of radical womanhood made possible by forward-looking government. It was unprecedented for a Muslim woman to be conspicuous in "global" sport and in the global sports media and, broadly, Moutawakel's gold medal signalled a momentous symbolic victory for Muslim women across the world.

But eight years later, in 1992, when Hassiba Boulmerka from Algeria arrived home for a heroine's welcome after her victory in the 1500 metres at the Barcelona Olympic Games, she was booed and jeered by a section of the population commonly referred to as Islamic fundamentalists (Mackay, *Guardian* 8/5/98). Although Hassiba's success was also a significant landmark in the history of Muslim women in sport, it symbolized poignantly the struggles over women's bodies throughout the Muslim world and the powerful links between sport, politics and religion.

Nawal El Moutawakel's story is unusual. In contrast to most other girls young women in Morocco and across the Arab world, her parents were to encourage her athletic ambition. Although she trained in the United States for eight months before the Olympics, the bulk of her training had taken place at home in Morocco, and she also received sponsorship and public acclamation from King Hassan II. In an interview with me in 1994, she pointed out that, "although it is much easier in Morocco than in a country like Algeria, there is still a lot of conservatism. After all these years since I won the gold medal, there is no Moroccan woman to follow in my footsteps."

Moutawakel comes from a comparatively liberal, secular Arab state that gave her psychological and financial backing and nurtured her as a symbol of nationhood and progress. Most importantly, Morocco is keen to present an image of vibrant womanhood suited to the global world of the new century. This is a stance which takes issue with the popular Western perception of the backwardness of Islam and its discrimination against women. But Moutawakel is still exceptional. In all Muslim countries, the issue of female participation in sport is tied to strongly held beliefs about the female body embraced by culture, tradition, religion, and politics. For women's bodies in sport, as in other areas of life and culture, the Qur'an has become the measure of right and wrong.[1] But the words of the Qur'an are understood in different ways by different groups—by the ulema,[2] politicians, "ordinary" men and women, and athletes themselves. Hassiba Boulmerka explains how, as a result, the woman's body—*her* body—is the site of power and struggle: "For Muslim women I symbolise freedom but, believe me, many people think it's not appropriate for women to take part in sport dressed in clothes that show parts of our bodies" (Mackay, *Guardian* 8/5/98). An Algerian sports journalist explains more fully:[3]

> For democrats, women's sport is one way of furthering equality between men and women, as well as manifesting a degree of tolerance. For the conservative and religious leaders, sporting women become the first targets in the fight to halt progress, and that is symbolic of all that is bad in Algerian society. (Butcher, *Guardian* 11/1/92)

The tiny number of successful, pioneering Muslim sportswomen, such as Nawal El Moutawakel and Hassiba Boulmerka, are perceived in Western thinking and by liberal Muslims as heroines who offer promise and possibility for their sex; or, conversely, in more traditional Muslim communities they are branded as sinful and decadent women who are distorting the truth of Islam. The struggles over their bodies have local and global dimensions relating to specific national, religious and political discourses, to global Islamic issues, and to the nexus between Islam and the West. This chapter explores the complexities of these struggles. While much of the discussion has relevance to Muslim women all over the world, its chief focus is the Middle East and North Africa—the "heart" of the "Muslim world."

THE MUSLIM WORLD

It has been estimated that there are around 1.3 billion Muslims in the world (Colvin, *Sunday Times* 30/8/98), and that "Islam today is the official religion of twenty-four world states and the religion of over 90 per cent of the population of Saudi Arabia, Egypt, Iraq, Iran, Pakistan and Bangladesh and the dominant faith in offically secular Indonesia and Turkey" (Nagata 1994: 65). Most Muslim people live either in nation states which emerged when Muslim nationalists fought for independence from Western powers and where the official religion is Islam, or in multiethnic and multireligious countries in which Muslims are numerically dominant. But with population mobility there are sizeable Muslim communities in countries with other major religions—in predominantly Hindu India, for example, there are 112 million Muslims, and in dominantly Christian states throughout the whole of the West there are large Muslim populations. In Western Europe there are between six and eight million Muslims:[4] in France and England, Islam is the second most important religion and it is predicted that a similar situation will soon prevail in several other European countries (Gerholm 1994: 190). Altogether there are Muslim populations in about 50 countries in the world, extending to communities as far-flung as Argentina, the Balkan States, Indonesia, the Philippines and South Africa. Islam is the world's fastest-growing religion, with a genuinely global character (Gerholm 1994: 2; Ahmed and Donnan 1994b: 1). . . .

ISLAMISM

In Western analyses, it is argued that Muslim culture has become a legitimation of Arab racial pride and that it has increasingly taken a fundamentalist form (Gellner 1994: xii), associated with the desire to possess and practise a unique, uncompromising religious truth and tradition (Gellner 1992). The development of Muslim women's sport in countries all over the world is inextricably linked to the discourses surrounding Islamic fundamentalism or "Islamism" in different parts of Africa, Europe and the Middle East (Halliday 1994: 93). Although relatively few Muslim women throughout the world live directly under the umbrella of Islamic fundamentalism, they are all influenced in the ways they think and feel and in the ways they live their lives and use their bodies by its global effects, described here by Nagata (1994: 64):

> Islam as an ideology of renewal has been gathering momentum in the Middle East and North Africa since the mid-nineteeth century, but the Islam that strikes chords in the world today is associated with the so-called "resurgence" which moved to center stage in the 1960s and 1970s. This marks the point at which contemporary Islam seriously became a player in the international political domain, seeking power both as an end in itself and as the means of spreading an Islamic way of life.

Since the advent to power of Ayatollah Khomeini in Iran in February 1979, his condemnation to death of Salman Rushdie in 1989 after the publication of *The Satanic Verses*, and the Gulf War in 1991, the Muslim world has been shaken and transformed.[5] Fundamentalist movements have grown, notably in Afghanistan, Algeria, Egypt, and Jordan, and millions of Muslims living in the West have been more outspoken and organized about their Islamic identity. Modern Islamization arose in opposition to European colonialism, and has condemned "Westernization" and the effects of modernization and secularization. For Muslims across the world there is a conflict in the way in which they live their lives between the Islamic tradition and the pervasive influence of Western culture. Since sport insinuates Westernization, it presents women with particular cultural and bodily uncertainties. . . .

WOMEN AND ISLAM

Women occupy a special place in Islam, and the alignment of politics with religion has had a marked and often negative effect on their lives. It has been alleged that in places where Islamic jurisprudence (Shari'ah) is practised, women's rights have been reduced (Weiss 1994: 129; Whitehorn, *Observer* 19/6/94) and that the influence of Islamic fundamentalists, even when not in political control, has resulted in coercive forms of control and made women fearful of victimization (Mahl 1995; Tohidi 1991). Mahl (1995: 14) argues that the control of women is essential to fundamentalist politics, because of "the focus on identity and subsequently on women who are seen as the guardians of identity, of cultural and religious values, of the purity of the blood." Separate development for

men and women is crucial to the fundamentalist credo tying women to their homes, discriminating against them in law, education, health, and employment, and idealizing their reproductive and moral roles (Mahl 1995: 15). Separatism is an ideology which has had crucial consequences for women's sport.

Akber Ahmed (1992: 33) argues that there is a huge distinction between the "noble Islamic ideal" and the continuing oppression of Muslim women. He goes on: "Where their [women's] lot is miserable and they have no rights, as is certain in tribal areas, it is to be attributed to male tyranny, not Islamic advice and is in need of urgent redress" (1992: 43). In common with Hassiba Boulmerka, some Muslim feminists argue that harsh treatment of women is not supported by the Qur'an and that Mohammed offered far more to women than present-day implacable fundamentalists. Halliday (1994: 96) describes Islam as like all great religions;

> a reserve of values, symbols, and ideas from which it is possible to derive a contemporary and social code: the answer as to why this or that interpretation was put upon Islam resides therefore, not in the religion and its texts itself, but in the contemporary needs of those articulating an Islamic politics.

Put bluntly by Ahmed and Donnan (1994b: 14), "Muslim women in particular seem to be squeezed between Islamic fundamentalism and modernity, and between modernity and postmodernity."

Although Muslim fundamentalism has a global constituency, and Muslim women throughout the world are influenced by it, the types and levels of constraint they experience and the opportunities they have to negotiate for changes and freedoms, vary greatly according to the countries and communities they live in. As we have seen in relation to sport, struggles are greater for women in Algeria than for those in Morocco. At one extreme are women in Afghanistan, who are ruthlessly controlled by the Taliban in every aspect of their lives, where girls' schools have been forcibly closed, and where women's sports have been prohibited (O'Kane 1998: 37); in Iran, women are challenging barriers and negotiating new opportunities in sport within a theocracy; in Egypt, women have choices within the laws of the secular state, although many Egyptian feminists argue that, when it comes to "the women's issue," the ideas of the state vary very little from those of Islamists and, in practice, the governing ideology is

Islamist (Karam 1998: 78, 127); in East Africa, where over 30 per cent of the population is Muslim, the traditionally liberal character of Islam has begun to change, closely influenced by and in part funded by fundamentalist movements from other Muslim countries (Anderson 1998: 33), reducing opportunities for women's sport; in Malaysia, there is growing polarization between Muslim and non-Muslim, the officially secular state is Islamicizing, women's sports are tied more and more to religious prescriptions (Nagata 1994); in Syria, there is a greater separation between Islam and the state, women have more opportunities in sport than in other Muslim countries, real attempts have been made to take account of women's demands, and it is mandatory for women to be represented in all sports organizations.

ISLAM AND THE FEMALE BODY

The social construction of women in Islam is linked to the power of symbol and control over the body. This lies at the heart of attitudes to women's sport in the Muslim world. Hijab (religious modesty) is fundamental and precious to all Muslims but, under the influence of fundamentalism, very narrow and rigid interpretations of modesty are being applied and fostered more and more. Helen Watson (1994: 143) explains that

> the [Qur'anic] concept of modesty, sitr al-'aura (literally "covering one's nakedness"), provides the basis for regulation of behaviour, the segregation of sexes, and proper dress. The Qur'an speaks of being "modest in thy bearing" (verse 31; 19) and mentions Allah's reward for men and women who "guard their modesty." . . . Specific instructions for women are set out in verses 24; 30–l: "Tell the believing women to lower their gaze and be modest, and to display of their ornaments only that which is apparent, and to draw their veils over their bosoms and not to reveal their adornments to their husbands and fathers."

Although the Qur'anic concept of modesty applies equally to men and women, in practice it has been used almost exclusively to regulate the attitudes to, and usages of, women's bodies—as a result, the emphasis on traditional female dress has become a pivotal feature of the recent resurgence of Islam (Watson 1994: 144, 151). All styles of dress relate to hijab, but it is the veil that has become the most potent signifier of Muslim womanhood and, arguably, "a basic requirement of Islam" (Karam 1998: 135). The most extreme fundamentalist interpretation of the Qur'an demands that the entire female body, including the face, be concealed from public gaze. In this case, the purdah or curtain, literally as well as symbolically, separates the spaces, the lived worlds, of men women. More typically strict versions require uniform black cloaks and veils, which cover the body, with the exception of the face; less strict interpretations, but which also require veiling, can in some cases allow women to wear trousers or skirts, blouses with long sleeves, and a headscarf; and liberal interpretations tolerate "decent," non-provocative Western dress with no veil.[6]

The veil is a symbol of cultural difference. For non-Muslims it conveys the idea that Western women are liberated and Muslim women, by comparison, are oppressed. The veil represents the "Otherness" of Islam and is condemned in the West as a constricting mode of dress, a form of social control, and a religious sanctioning of women's invisibility and subordinate sociopolitical status. In the eyes of a Western, liberal critic, allowing women to take part in sport freely and in modern sportswear is, in contrast to veiling, liberating and empowering. But, although many Muslim women who are forced to wear the veil feel angry, repressed and resistant, and are often fearful of showing opposition, they are also troubled that anti-fundamentalist sentiments will be interpreted as anti-Islamic ones and will be used to fuel Islamaphobia (Mahl 1995: 14).

Other Muslim women hold a positive view of hijab—for them, wearing the veil is a deliberate choice, a politicized act, rather than a reaction to male power—what Watson (1994: 152) describes as "a sort of feminism in reverse." For them, exposing the female body in sport is immoral and the veil signals a rejection of arguably provocative and public displays of the body. Veiling has been revived by Muslim women living in Britain, France, and Egypt, for example, "as a way of coping with the challenges of contemporary life in those countries, and of emphasizing Islamic identity" (Ahmed and Donnan 1994b: 14). "Unveiling" and taking part in sport is interpreted as a new form of imperial control (Kanneh 1995).

Although Muslim women's subjectivities are constructed within a context of Islamic traditions and values which places the body in a focal position, the anxieties experienced by Muslim women about their bodies arise from the coupling of Islam and politics. Women's attitudes to sport—to ideas about participation or non-participation or about different modes of participation—are all responses to these anxieties. The pursuit of economic modernization and the inevitable shift towards secularization (which has occurred in different Arab states, for example) has provoked Islamist ideologues to use the control of women's bodies, especially by means of veiling, as a visible and tangible symbol of success. In stark contrast, athletic images of Nawal El Moutawakel and Hassiba Boulmerka running in the Olympics in vests and shorts symbolize a loss of control and a failure of belief. The female body in Islam is at the center of cultural contest, scrutiny, and meaning (Kanneh 1995: 347), and Muslim women in sport encapsulate this contest. They consciously and unconsciously manipulate religious beliefs to negotiate their gender roles and the contradictions between tradition and modernity in sport. The way they do so varies according to the context. . . .

HASSIBA BOULMERKA AND ALGERIA

Hassiba Boulmerka grew up in Algeria during a relatively pluralist and secular period of its history. Algeria had gained independence from France in 1962, and for nearly 30 years afterwards moderate Muslim politics enabled many women to challenge religious laws and cultural traditions that they found restricting and discriminatory (Morgan 1998: 347). In this climate, Boulmerka was able to develop her love and talent for running (Layden 1997: 37), although with increasing difficulty because of the growing power of Islamic ideologues, reflected in an attempt in parliament to abolish schoolgirl sport (Hornblower 1992: 91).[7] In the 1988 All-Africa Games, Boulmerka won both the 800- and 1500-metre races, and she became the first Algerian woman to win a World Athletic Championships title when she took the 1500 metres in Tokyo in 1991. Together with fellow Algerian Noureddine Morceli, the men's 1500 gold medal winner, she was welcomed home as a national heroine—fêted at the airport by a cheering crowd, carried on a motorcade through Algiers, and presented with La Medaille du Mérite, the country's highest honour, never before awarded to civilians. The Algerian sports minister, who at the time was a woman—Madame Leila Aslaoui—declared that both victories were "applauded by every single Algerian"

(Butcher, *Guardian* 11/1/92). She was wrong. Unlike Morceli, Boulmerka quickly became a target of condemnation for militant Muslims (characterized as the "more faithful"), who were encouraged by a strengthening of Islamism (Morgan 1998: 347). In mosques throughout the country, fundamentalist imams who were affiliated to the Front Islamique du Salut (FIS)[8]—pronounced a kofr—a public disavowal of Boulmerka (Butcher, *Guardian* 11/1/92). The object of their condemnation was her body—they argued that because she ran in shorts and vest in public, she had broken the rules of the Qu'ran.

Algeria had been one of the most liberal Muslim countries in the world, but the FIS had become a powerful force in the country taking an aggressive stand against the secular, modernizing, and allegedly corrupt ruling Front de la Libération Nationale (FLN). Opposition to new opportunities and freedoms for women was central to FIS philosophy. By the time that Boulmerka went on to win the 1500-metre gold medal at the 1992 Olympics, she had become thoroughly caught up in the growing opposition between state and society. After winning her World Athletic Championships title, she had described her cry of joy as, "A cry from the heart for every Algerian woman, every Arabic woman" (Butcher, *Guardian* 11/1/92); by the time she had won her Olympic gold, she had taken an explicit stance against fundamentalism,[9] talked openly about her suffering and forced residence in Italy in order to escape the threats on her life, and was appealing to other young Algerians to take a similar stance (Morgan 1998: 347). "I'm a danger to the fundamentalists," she is recorded as saying. "I am a symbol to the young that women don't have to hide behind their chadors" (Hornblower 1992). In 1992, when she was 16, Miriam Hemdane, an aspiring athlete, claimed that "Hassiba is our idol. We are in a hostile environment, but she gives us hope" (Hornblower 1992: 91).[10]

The growing tide of Islamist power, and the inability of the secular state to deal with it, has made it impossible for girls and young women to take part in mixed competitions or train in public in Western-style sportswear, or to participate in sport after marriage or even past the age of puberty—if at all. Women who defy tradition and Islamism are, quite literally, in fear of their lives. Through ideological propaganda and terrorism, the armed dissident wing of the Islamist opposition, the GIA, impels the mainstream Islamist organization, the relatively moderate FIS, to keep up its doctrinaire battle against secular tendencies. It is reported that, since 1992, around 75,000 people have lost their lives during Algeria's seven-year civil war, and that Islamist extremists have carried out unimaginable atrocious massacres (Hirst, *Guardian* 5/1/98). Although terrorist violence may seem unrelated to female sport, it has bred a culture of fear in Algeria, propped up by dogmatic adherence to (and unbending interpretations of) Islam, which influence relations of power between men and women and public attitudes to women's bodies. Those who are working for improved opportunities for women's sport know that it is "a particularly sensitive subject, given the political, social and economic crisis that the country is in," and they are often "fearful about having anything they say misconstrued and seen as anti-Islamic" (personal interview 1996). It is claimed that "the freedom and legitimate right of women to play sports in Algeria has been impeded by various social, cultural, political, and economic obstacles, the result of which is a lack of women in competitive sports—only 3,000 during the course of 1994" (Mechti and Sayad 1994).

There has been a notable drop in the numbers of girls and women taking part in sport in Algeria during the 1990s, especially in competitive and elite events, following a previous steady increase in the number of female athletes during approximately a decade and a half from the second part of the 1970s. For example, in 1978 several female athletes took part in the All-Africa Games in Algiers and the women's handball and basketball teams won gold medals. It was during this period that Sakina Boutamine became the first Algerian woman to take part in an Olympic Games—in Moscow in 1980. From the end of the 1980s onwards, there was a rapid decline in participation as girls and young women were discouraged or forbidden from participating, and punished for disobeying. The increase in numbers of female athletes during the 1970s and 1980s followed legislation to encourage female participation in schools and colleges; the decrease during the 1990s coincided with anti-secular pressures, the rise of fundamentalism, and reversed legislation. Figures for school-level volleyball illustrate the trend—in 1986–7, there were 1607 players; by 1990–1, grants and sponsorship were withdrawn and the figure had dropped to 918 (Mechti and Sayad 1994). The changed political climate has been used by men to justify grossly uneven resourcing in sport between men and women, and sportswomen themselves face hostility, prejudice, and censure—for example, Salma Souakhri, who showed great promise at the Barcelona Olympic Games, was thrown out of school and forbidden to finish her Baccalauréat[11] and Yasmina Azzizi, who came fifth in the 1992 Olympic heptathlon, has had shouts of "Whore" aimed at her during training. Obstacles for female athletes in Algeria have become formidable—some give up, others leave the country because of threats to their safety (Mechti and Sayad 1994).

Boulmerka has become a spokeswoman and an ideologue, most specifically for Algerian women in sport, but also for Muslim women throughout the world. But her position is untypical and controversial. She has resisted the popular idea that there has to be a choice between the East and the West, between Islam and rational capitalism, arguing that it is possible to take the best from Islamic and Western philosophies and still be a good Muslim. Morgan (1998: 347) argues that she uses a curious cultural language, steeped in disparate cultural traditions which blends "Western individual initiative and Eastern community-inspired discipline." Certainly, Boulmerka claims to have acquired, through her personal struggles and achievements in sport, a deeper love of her country and an enduring belief in Islam. She wants people in the East and the West to believe with her that "Islamic culture is not the hotbed of fanaticism it is often made out to be and that it is not necessarily hostile either to individual effort or to the plight of women" (Morgan 1998: 348).

Boulmerka's vision of a radical female Muslim identity is fundamentally political and unquestionably heroic because she has spoken out in the face of oppression and threats to her life. Exceptionally, she is targeting those she calls fascists who, she says, "hide behind the veil of Islam in order to impose their political will" (Moore 1992: 53, cited in Morgan 1998: 348). She is not taking issue with what she believes to be the essence of Islam, but with its extreme and politicized versions. Morgan (1998: 348) describes how Boulmerka has infused "the vocabulary of equal rights and women's sports into the cultural vocabulary of Islam." She knows that by doing so she offends the "more faithful" Muslims, but she is adamant that her position is not un-Islamic and does not go against the grain of what it means to be a Muslim woman (Morgan 1998: 348). Boulmerka believes that her faith alone, and not blind obedience to moral dictates, is necessary for godliness and salvation. She is concerned with the same question that preoccupies other radical Muslim women—whether or not it is possible to build a form of Muslim feminism on affirmative readings of the Qu'ran that will enable women to develop their interests in the modern world without rejecting their Muslim faith. Radical/secular feminists argue that Islam *can* be a tool for women's liberation, that the Qur'an does not direct that society be frozen in the seventh-century Arabian mould, but that it should be adaptable to the needs of changing times and circumstances (Nagata 1994: 80; Van der Gaag 1997: 31).

Boulmerka has been labelled both victim and heroine, a courageous individual who, in reality, can do little to effect real change in a country in the grip of extremists. However, her struggles are especially significant in the international context, where the debate about modesty has gained momentum. In some countries, Muslim women who have confined themselves to female-only participation according to conservative interpretations of Islam have made significant advances, but those who want to take part in mixed international events and who are secular Muslims face far greater hurdles and antagonisms. For these women, Boulmerka is a powerful symbol of resistance and change. Influenced by Boulmerka, and following in her footsteps, remarkably, Nouria Merah-Benida of Algeria won the 1500 metres at the 2000 Sydney Olympics. Referring to her gold medal, she said, "It's for the Arab women so that they can develop like the other women of the world" (Williams, *Guardian* 2/10/2000). In her new position as a full member of the International Olympic Committee (IOC), Boulmerka will be in a unique position to argue in support of Muslim women in sport and to put some pressure on Muslim countries to change their policies about women in sport. In the year 2000 she was one of the first ten athletes to be honoured in this way as part of the IOC's latest radical reforms.

Gaining power is necessary for those who seek change, and power comes from organization. With this in mind, Muslim women in sport have set up organizations, held meetings and congresses, instigated competitions, and lobbied for their cause, at both national and international levels. The internationalization of the discourse around Muslim women in sport assists in the creation and legitimation of a power base. . . .

WOMEN'S SPORT ORGANIZATIONS

Because the momentum for Muslim women's sport has taken place within Islamic codes and conditions, and because there is condemnation of secularism in Islamic countries where women's sport is being authorized, any chance for women to take greater control of the process has to occur under the same conditions. It has been argued that relationships between the state, Islamists and women's organizations form important axes within the complex interplay of power and hegemony (Karam 1998: 3). In 1991 in Egypt, for example, the government banned a secular and openly feminist political organization, sequestered its assets and transfered them to an *Islamic* women's organization (Karam 1998: 2), making it obligatory for women in sport in Egypt to work within an Islamic framework. In all Islamic countries, the "official" voices of women's sport are those of women who work in official capacities in sports organizations, government agencies, or schools and universities. They cannot suggest radical, secular changes, for fear of losing their jobs. Even in liberal Islamic states, such as Syria, where women are not obliged to wear the veil, it is difficult for them to speak out against Islamic codes. The more oppressive the conditions, the more important it has been for Muslim women in sport to create their own (women-only) associations which provide them with opportunities to bond together and show organizational strength, explained here by one of the leaders: "Organisations give us some autonomy. On the one hand we may appear to be subservient, but within our own spaces, we are in control and can make some impact." Muslim women in many countries—for example, Bahrain, Bosnia, Egypt, Iran, Iraq, Kuwait, Jordan, Lagos, Lebanon, Malaysia, Morocco, Pakistan, Palestine, the Philippines, Qatar, Nigeria, Syria, Turkey, Ukraine—are seeking empowerment through organizations at both national, regional and international levels. While cross-cultural unity supports Islam and confirms Muslim identity which transcends nation states, it also provides some potential for women to negotiate new gender relations of power within their individual nation states, to enhance the general position of Muslim women in sport, and to secure better funding for women's sport. Regional and international conferences and organizations "strengthen the ties between women working to promote women's sports in different countries."

Professor Nabila Abdelrahman, from Egypt, has played a pioneering role in establishing organizations for Muslim women in sport. In 1995, she planned an International Scientific Conference for Arab Women and Sport (Abdelrahman 1998) in Alexandria.[12] The conference resulted directly in the endorsement of the Brighton Declaration . . . and the establishment of the Arab Women and Sport Association and the Egyptian Women and Sport Association (IWG 1998: 2). The Arab Women and Sport Association aims "to enhance women's participation in sport, prepare women for roles in sport leadership and ensure Arab women are represented in all sports organisations at all levels" (IWG 1998: 3). Following the conference, national sports associations for women were established in twelve Arab countries, who then affiliated themselves to the international group. The chance to belong to a growing movement, encouraged by a sense of promise, has led to the foundation of women's sports organizations in other countries as well. In 1997 and then 1999, Professor Abdelrahman organized the Second and Third International Conferences for Arab women in sport, with the aim of further improving opportunities for Muslim women in sport.[13] Her position as the only woman on the Egyptian Supreme Council of Youth and Sport helped her to secure sponsorship for all three conferences and to attract delegates from all over the Arab world, and to have international guest speakers. The conferences, organized originally for women from Arab countries, have included Muslim women from other areas as well, who have been inspired to set up meetings and events in their own communities. There is a progressive sense of global Islam in the international Muslim women's sports movement, which grows in strength and effectiveness.

MUSLIM WOMEN AND MAINSTREAM SPORT

For most Muslim women in sport the division between the secular and the sacred is blurred and the issue of sports participation is confined to the insular world of Islam. But Muslim women in sport are drawn into the modern, global world of "mainstream" international sport—which encroaches on Muslim values—through the advances that women in sport are making globally, through connections with women in sport in the Western world, and through the visibility and seductive pull of commodified sport, exemplified by the Olympic Games. As Muslim women create for themselves more opportunities within the confines of Islam, and as standards of training, coaching, and performances improve, they find it more and more difficult to manage their

religion and their identity while still pursuing sport. The issue focuses primarily on whether interpretations of the Qur'an can allow Muslim women to compete in global mainstream sport against athletes from countries all over the world, or whether mainstream events should be organized in single-sex competitions with no men present, so that Muslim women can be included. The issue, as we have seen, is not simply an Islam–Western conflict. There are Muslim women, like Nawal El Moutawakel and Hassiba Boulmerka, who believe that it is possible to be a good Muslim in secular contexts, and there are liberal Muslim states which support such a view. For example, in Marrakech, in 1998 (the International Amateur Athletic Federation [IAAF] Year of Women in Athletics), Hassan II, King of Morocco, spoke about the growing role of women in sport and praised the performance of the Moroccan women's team at the 26th World Cross Country Championships. Referring to the link between sport and women's emancipation, he insisted that the sports movement for Muslim women "is taking place within the framework of the cultural and religious traditions of the Arab world." This very same pronouncement could easily be made in other Islamic states, which (in contrast to relatively liberal Morocco) are strongly influenced by fundamentalism, and where women are denied the option of taking part in public meetings. . . .

MUSLIM WOMEN AND THE OLYMPICS

The nexus of Muslim women's bodies, culture, and politics is incorporated in negotiations surrounding participation at the Olympic Games. In her role as president of the ICWSSC, Faezeh Hashemi has urged the IOC to do more to promote sports for Muslim women, and in doing so to be sensitive to their specific needs. Hashemi points out that there are 500 million Muslim women in the world—one quarter of the world's female population—who cannot take part in Olympic competitions in existing conditions, causing the absence of female athletes from the national teams of several Muslim countries at the 1992 and 1996 Olympics. At the IOC International Conference on Women and Sports, held in Lausanne in 1996, she petitioned the IOC to authorize single-sex venues to enable the participation of Muslim women in Olympic competition. She also negotiated with Juan Antonio Samaranch, president of the IOC, to allow Muslim women, when possible, to take part in the

Olympics in "Islamic dress." As an Islamic feminist, she bases her arguments on close readings of the Qu'ran and its satellite texts.[14]

In contrast, there are lobbyists who link the issue of Muslim women in the Olympics to human rights and who are pressing the IOC to ban countries who enter male-only teams. Speaking about the politics of sport at a conference in 1994 in Australia, Marlene Goldsmith (1995: 14) pointed out that "South Africa and Rhodesia are the only countries that have been expelled from international sport because of human rights violations in their countries," and that "it is difficult to explain why racism should be singled out for special treatment as the only human rights issue of sufficient importance to warrant a boycott." She details some of the horrific human rights violations which are inflicted upon females, including genital mutilation; she points out that, in many countries in the developing world, women have fewer rights and opportunities in many areas of life, including education, health, the law, and work; she cites Pakistan as one of the most oppressive societies in relation to women where cultural practices, including eating, health care, and dress codes, seriously discriminate against women and are detrimental to their health—where women suffer from health problems such as osteomalacia, eczema, and ulcers resulting from lack of exposure to sunlight, and osteoporosis from poor diet and little exercise (1995: 17–18). Goldsmith argues that the most oppressed group in relation to international sports participation is women, yet those who suffer some of the worst deprivations and atrocities "remain without defenders in international sporting conclaves . . . because they are represented at such conclaves by governments that repress them" (1995: 18).

The pro-boycott position has been made official through a women's rights activist body, Atlanta (Atlanta Plus), set up originally by three women—two from France, a human rights lawyer and a scientist (the former, Linda Weil-Curiel, is the co-ordinator), and one from Belgium, who is the past Secretary of State for European Affairs.[15] The idea was a response to commentaries at the opening ceremony of the 1992 Barcelona Olympics, which celebrated the ending of apartheid and the re-entry of South Africa into the Olympics but were silent about the 35 delegations that had no female competitors (because religion is misused to serve political ends; because of a lack of top-calibre women athletes; or because countries were poor and devoted their limited sports budgets mostly to men).[16] The main concern of Atlanta is that by permitting countries that disallow women from taking part in sport to participate in the Games, the IOC is contravening its own Olympic Charter.[17] Atlanta is therefore demanding an Olympic ban on those countries.[18]

The IOC has been antagonistic to Atlanta, and only made its reasons in 1995, leading up to the Atlanta Olympic Games. The IOC argue that the position of Atlanta on "gender apartheid" is "an insult to Nelson Mandela, the South African people, and black people as a whole"; that they cannot agree to waging war against religion; that there is no global consensus for punishing such nations; and that they cannot make policy because the UN had taken no stance on the issue.

Atlanta's response is that the IOC is autonomous in this matter, that the rules of the Olympic Charter are their own and therefore can be enforced against governments that flaunt them. Furthermore, they point out that in the past the IOC has given support to male demands—for example, when the Iranians campaigned for "men only" to present medals and refused to walk behind a Spanish woman holding their country's placard. Atlanta also decry the IOC's support of the Women's Solidarity Games which, they claim, Iran used as part of a political campaign to extol their way of life and beliefs.[19] Atlanta has received cross-party support from the German and French parliaments, from the Parliamentary Council of Europe, and from the UN.[20] The original French publicity material has been translated into Arabic, English, and Spanish, and has been sent to hundreds of organizations around the world and the movement has gathered support from women and men in different parts of the world fighting gender discrimination.[21] The objectives of Atlanta were approved at the annual meeting of the (US) Women's Sports Foundation in 1995 and, in the same year, at the "First World-Wide Forum on Physical Activity and Sport," which was organized under the auspices of the United Nations Educational, Scientific and Cultural Organization (UNESCO), the IOC (ironically), the World Health Organization (WHO) and the World Federation of the Sport Gear Industry (WFSGI).

At the 1996 Atlanta Olympics, 26 countries sent all-male delegations.[22] An Atlanta delegation—from Belgium, France, Germany, Greece, Iran, Kenya, and the USA—held a press conference and met with members of the IOC Executive Commission.[23] In 1996, an open letter was sent to Juan Antonio Samaranch, president of the IOC, repeating the boycott demand and proposing that 1 per cent of Olympic ticket money should go to fund women's sport in poor countries (where women do not participate for financial reasons).[24]

In spite of the IOC's hostility, Atlanta maintain that its action has had some success:

- The IOC has added a provision to its Charter concerning gender.
- Iran sent one woman to the Atlanta Olympics and she held the national flag.
- Their support is growing daily—among political bodies, sports organizations, and individuals.

Ironically, however, support is not forthcoming from some leading figures in international women's sports groups, who argue that segregation in sport does not necessarily imply discrimination and that Atlanta should show greater sensitivity to the cultural conditions of each country and to those women trying to secure advances for themselves while facing huge constraints.[25]

Historically, there has been a tendency for religious beliefs and cultural practices to remain private affairs, but in recent times there has been a marked shift so that these subjects are now public concerns. Atlanta has used the effects of globalization to "expose" and politicize a previously insular, religious, and private matter. Although Islamic sport feminists are opposed to the Atlanta initiative because they argue it is politically inspired and proposes an image of Muslim countries as backward and non-democratic, more radical feminists believe that their assertive stance is forcing the IOC to look seriously at the question of female participation in the Olympics and has opened the door for other groups or organizations to lobby in different ways. Cultural relativism suggests that one has to be sensitive to the cultural conditions of each country and that it is wrong for predominantly White, Western, non-Muslim women to interfere in the traditions and values of cultures other than their own. But Atlanta has never claimed to speak for all Muslim women and does not wish to take issue with Islamic culture in general, or the way in which sport is practised in Islamic countries. Their argument is that the IOC supports discrimination because it allows those countries who refuse to comply with the Olympic Charter to take part in the Games. Importantly, Atlanta does give a voice—albeit

a surrogate one—to those women from Islamic states who would otherwise have no voice because gender relations of power are desperately uneven (personal interview). Although the "official" women's voice of sport in Islamic states is supportive of the Islamist position, those women who want free access to international competitions, and who endorse a boycott, cannot state this so publicly, for fear of reprisals. Women in sport from Islamic countries who desire change but lack power need support of "outsiders." It is also argued that a characteristic of feminist work in other fields is making demands that have relevance to women from disparate backgrounds and places across the world, and therefore it is illogical and dishonourable to refrain from intervening on behalf of women in the Muslim world. Because the right to sport has never been as high on the agenda of feminist action as rights to health and work, for example, and because the vested interests in keeping Muslim women out of sport are highly politicized and emotive, it has been especially difficult and complex to counter opposition to advances for them.

The next target for Atlanta was Sydney 2000. The organization was renamed "Atlanta-Sydney Plus." It maintained pressure in order to attain equal access for men and women in respect of the Olympic Ideal, regardless of religion or tradition. Atlanta-Sydney called on the IOC to ban twenty-five countries from the Sydney Olympics including Afghanistan, Botswana, Iraq, Haiti, Kuwait, Libya, Oman, Palestine, Qatar, Rwanda, Saudi Arabia, Senegal, Somalia, Sudan, United Arab Emirates, and Yemen. Action was focused on two levels:

- *Economic*: the IOC should attribute a specific share of the Olympic Solidarity funds which it contributes to the National Olympic Committees for the formation of women athletes. Thus it will be possible to distinguish the hard-core countries which refuse the participation of women from the Games for exclusively ideological reasons and not for economic ones.
- *Political*: the IOC should condemn and sanction, without any ambiguity, all national sports politics founded on segregation of women (separate games, banning women from certain disciplines, prohibiting women and men from practising sports together). This is the sense of the UN Human Rights Commission, of the Council of Europe, and the European Parliament.

Although Atlanta-Sydney Plus had a growing base of support, it also faced vigorous opposition. The IOC refused to change its policy for the Sydney Olympics but, nevertheless, the Atlanta-Sydney initiative highlighted ways in which external forces—specifically what Weiss (1994) describes as the "global superstructure"—are influencing the participation of Muslim women in sport more than ever before.

CONCLUSION

There are three key questions that arise from this investigation of Muslim women in sport: Is the Muslim women's body in sport subject or object? Can only those women who have lived experience of a culture represent or speak about it? Are the heroines of Muslim women's sport those who are working within the Islamic framework or those who struggle for secularized sport?

The predominant Western representation of Muslim women is that they are objects of oppression, subordinated within starkly uneven gender relations of power, and that, whether or not they take part in sport and what form the participation might take, is determined by tradition, religion, and politics. The contrary view is that the West misunderstands Islamic culture and that Muslim women are active subjects, redefining their roles, setting their own agendas, and working for improved opportunities in different fields of life and culture, including sport. In this view, sport is just one of the increasing numbers of women-oriented and women-run movements, reflecting a rise in women's social power and changes in gender attitudes among men and women (Weiss 1994: 129–30).

However, the Western/Islam solution to the subject/object question sets up false oppositions which fail to take account of the great divergences within Islam (and also among Western interpretations of Islam)—"between Muslims who are profoundly critical of the human rights records of certain Muslim countries and those who maintain that such criticisms are merely symptoms of Islamophobia"; "between different interpretations of specific terminology, doctrines and injunctions in the Qur'an and Islamic traditions"; "between the perceptions and experiences of women and men" (Runnymede Trust 1997: 6). Between women, as well, there are huge differences in ideas and practices. Muslim women in sport are not a homogeneous group and Muslim women's sport is not unitary: some Muslim women quest for

freedom but have none; others have been able to manipulate structures and relations of power to advance their cause. Muslim women's bodies are, therefore, both subject *and* object, unstable and in process, tied as they are to political struggle—not just at the level of the personal, but linked to state and religious ideologies which depend for their credibility on discourses about women and their bodies. Muslim women's sport is thus merged with identity and difference, reflected in the varied ways in which women speak about it, argue about it, and analyse it.

As we have seen, the leaders of women's sport in Muslim countries are Islamic feminists—they reject the stereotype of subjugated woman, embrace Islam, and use sport as a means through which they can express a specifically Islamic gender identity. Fatma Al-Hashimy, president of the Iraqi National Women's Sport Federation, established in 1992, and a member of the Iraqi National Olympic Committee, exemplifies the position. Under her presidency, the Iraqi Women's Sport Federation has worked to establish women's sports clubs and to increase participation of women in sport activities, and she was instrumental in the opening, in 1994, of the first College of Physical Education for Women in Iraq. She makes the link between women's sport and Islamic ethics clear when she says:

> We have in our Islamic religion the best ideal, Islam has respected the Woman and encouraged her to take her responsibilities towards her husband, her children and herself; taking care also of the house and the responsibility of employment requires her participation in sport activities. (Al-Hashimy 1997: 38)

The functional fit between traditional gender roles and support of female sport for health in the discourse of Islamic feminists makes it relatively easy for them to work within an Islamic framework to advance the cause of women's sport. Their movement gets further legitimacy because women's rights in Islamic countries has become one of the most emotive of political issues, and there has been a spread of interest through the Arab world in the specific question of women's sport.

The position for secular feminists is very different. They "firmly believe in grounding their discourse outside the realm of religion . . . and placing it, instead, within the international human rights discourse," viewing religion as a private matter for individual women (Karam 1998: 13). As a result, they are characterized as "clones of the West, implementers of imperialist agendas, and—the ultimate deligitimizer—non-believers," and there is no point of contact whatsoever with Islamic feminists (Karam 1998: 13). Women in sport with secular views—those who are angry at having to wear the veil and who want to take part in open events—have no voice, no legitimacy, and, therefore, no power in official women's sport in Islamic countries, so we face the question about representation, about whether outsiders to Islamic culture can speak on their behalf or, more specifically, whether Western feminists can be representative in any way of their needs and desires (Karam 1998: 7).

There is no straightforward answer. Chow (1993: 93) claims that it is untenable if "Western feminism imposes its own interests and methodologies on who do not inhabit the same sociohistorical spaces, thus reducing the latter to a state of reified silence and otherness." But it can also be argued that Muslim women in sport who are forced to be silent in their own cultures should be able to secure some form of representation and support from outside without reduced to "the Other." Muslim women who are opposed to the melding of sport and politics—however subtly this may occur—believe that Islamic feminists in sport are part of a dominant structure of power and control which is fundamentally oppressive. At the moment, the diverse views of Muslim women in sport are not openly expressed and debated and many Muslim women have no chance to determine their own sporting futures. Atlanta-Sydney (n.d.) argues that "Demanding, through sports, an end to segregation or discrimination of which women are victims is exemplary for several reasons, and it is probably the most effective means of getting around the notion of national sovereignty and cultural differences."

The last question about Muslim heroines of sport is therefore also complex. The extent of diversity and the range of different opinions and practices suggests that the sum total of the struggles of Muslim women who are working, albeit in very different ways, for advances in women's sport has been surprisingly effective and that individual struggle has been heroic. There is more openness about women's sport than ever before and there have been achievements which would have been inconceivable a short time ago, often linked to the energy and determination of individual women. For example, Sahar El-Hawary formed and funded an Egyptian women's national indoor soccer team, kitted the players out in cycling shorts under their football strip to avoid criticism from Islamists, struggled to developed a club infrastructure so that she could go on to form a full 11-a-side team that qualified for the African Nations Cup in Nigeria in 1998, after which the Egyptian Football Federation gave them some funding. Sahar El-Hawary's aim was for the team to take part in the Women's Soccer World Cup in America in 1999. She has spent most of her own fortune on women's soccer in Egypt; has wooed and won over bureaucrats who argued that women's soccer was a waste of government resources; travelled throughout Egypt staging games in the most rural areas to convince everyone that women play soccer well; and obtained official sanction from the Ministry of Sport for the first women's soccer league and national team of Egypt and to promote soccer to girls in school. She is the first African Egyptian Arabic woman on the FIFA committee.

Sahar El-Hawary is just one of the women who are leading the movement for change in sport in Islamic countries. They do so in different ways and in different circumstances but, together, they are making it easier for the next generation to redefine more completely the uses of the female Muslim body. By doing so, they are changing public opinion—with which, Bhatia (*Observer* 21/6/98) contends, lies the greatest chance for change.

NOTES

Special thanks to Haleh Afshar for reading and making such helpful comments on the first draft of this chapter.

1. The Qur'an is the Muslim sacred text reportedly based on Allah's (God's) revelations made to the Prophet Mohammed.

2. Ulema (mullahs, imams)—meaning "wise men" who interpret the Qur'an and the teachings of the Prophet Mohammed.

3. The journalist was speaking at a Sports Writers' Conference in December 1991. Algerian intellectuals and reporters were extremely critical of the Imam's declaration against Hassiba Boulmerka.

4. The Muslim population has risen to around 3 million in Germany (mainly Turkish), over 2 million in France (mostly North African), and around 1.5 million in the UK (mainly from Pakistan and Bangladesh).

5. In his book *The Satanic Verses*, Salman Rushdie is alleged to have blasphemed against Islam. Anyone who does so is subject to the death penalty. The Fatwa was lifted ten years later by a relatively liberal government, in September 1998, after the death of the Ayatollah.

6. For example, in Afghanistan women are forced to wear burquas (head-to-toe black capes which cover the face with a thick "grill" to see through) and beaten for showing their ankles (O'Kane 1998: 37); there is a wide range of "styles of veil," from the uniform black cloaks worn by women in post-revolution Iran, to the exclusive "designer" scarves of women of the "new aristocracy" in Egypt' (Watson 1994: 141); in Malaysia, most Malay women have adopted some version of "a headscarf or attractively styled veil which does not cover the face, and a long, loose two-piece dress also in an appealing co-ordination of colours and textures . . . to the point where it may be said to have become Malay national costume" (Nagata 1994: 78–9).

7. Although the attempt failed, as many as one-third of the National Assembly voted in favour.

8. FIS—widely known as *Intergristes* is the party representing Algeria's Muslim fundamentalist movement. In 1991, the FIS won sweeping victories in municipal elections, and in the first round of the national election (Morgan 1998: 347).

9. Boulmerka dedicated her medal to Mohamed Boudiaf, former president of Algeria, who was assassinated, allegedly by fundamentalists, in June 1992.

10. Because Boulmerka wants to be able to return to her home in Algeria, she has become cautious about talking openly about her situation as a Muslim athlete (Holder 1996).

11. The Baccalauréat is the qualifying examination for university taken by high-school students in order to continue into higher education.

12. Professor Abdelrahman organized the conference following her attendance in 1994 at the Brighton Conference and the creation of the Brighton Declaration. . . . The use of the term "scientific" in the conference title denotes the analytical and theoretical framework of the conference. The conference was sponsored by the Ministry of Education, the Ministry of International Co-operation, the Supreme Council of Youth and Sport, and the Arab League. Approximately 70 per cent of the 200 delegates who attended were women, including Egyptian physical educators, the deans and faculty members from all the major Egyptian universities, and representatives from Egyptian sport organizations. From the conference came a list of 15 key recommendations, recognizing the value of sport to Muslim women in society as well as the essential contribution that sport makes to health.

13. The second conference was under the auspices of Mrs Suzan Mubarak, wife of the president of the Arab Republic of Egypt, who has pioneered work for women and children in Egypt and all over the Arab world. It was supported also by the Supreme Council of Youth and Sport. The third conference in 1999 was under the auspices of Dr Kamal El-Ganzourym, prime minister and president of the Supreme Council for Youth and Sport, and in co-operation and participation with numerous national and international sports and educational organizations.

14. The Prophet's Hadith (the body of tradition about Mohammed that supplements the Qu'ran).

15. Details of the founders of Atlanta are as follows: Anne Marie Lizim (Belgium, ex-Secretary of State for European Affairs); Annie Sugier (a nuclear scientist and French feminist); and Linda Weil-Curiel (French human rights lawyer).

16. The following list of delegations to the 1992 Barcelona Olympics are those that were exclusively male: American Samoa (3); Bahrain (13); Botswana (6); Burkina Faso (4); Caiman Islands (10); Cook Islands (2); Djibouti (5); Eastern Samoa (5); Gambia (6); Haiti (7); Iran (40); Iraq (9); Kuwait (36); Laos (6); Lebanon (13); Libya (6); Mauritania (6); Niger (8); Oman (5); Pakistan (27); Panama (5); Qatar (31); Saudi Arabia (9); Solomon Islands (1); Sudan (6); Swaziland (5); Syria (10); Tanzania (9); Togo (6); Tonga (5); Trinidad and Tobago (7); United Arab Emirates (14); Uruguay (23); Virgin Islands (4); Yemen (13).

17. The Olympic Charter states that "The goal of the Olympic Movement is to contribute to building a peaceful and better world by educating youth through sport practised without discrimination of any kind with regard to a country or a person on grounds of race, religion, politics, sex or otherwise."

18. The Atlanta movement has been active since the 1992 Olympic Games, but had its official launch later, in January 1995.

19. In a brochure distributed by Iranian embassies throughout the world, the following statement is made about the Solidarity Games: "The aim of these games is to spread the Muslim system's culture and values . . . and to prevent the corruption resulting from the simultaneous presence of men and women athletes in the same place." At the seminar on Women and Sport held at the Fourth World Conference on Women in Beijing, China, the spokesperson for the Second Muslim Women's Solidarity Games wished that they would serve as a model for the 500 million Muslim women in the world of whom, she alleged, "Iran is morally in charge."

20. The United Nations High Commissioner on Human Rights, Ayala Lasso, said that sex discrimination was a "civic sin" and agreed that Atlanta was correct in asking the IOC to follow their own charter. The Council of Europe Parliamentary Assembly Resolution 1092 (1996) on discrimination against women in the field of sport—and, more particularly, in the Olympic Games—includes statements and recommendations in general support of the philosophy and actions of Atlanta. It views the absence of women in national teams and the organization of women-only games (barring men from attending) to be infringements of fundamental human rights. The Assembly states that "even if there are cultural differences and traditions,

this should be no argument for accepting any policy of discrimination against women in sport." Its final recommendation is as follows:

The Assembly requests that the IOC:
i) firmly and clearly oppose any discrimination against women in sport
ii) refuses to support any sports event based on discrimination, such as the "Solidarity Games for Women in Islamic Countries."

21. The Feminist Majority Foundation, which has become part of the Atlanta movement, circulated a petition to the IOC during Expo '96 for women's empowerment. Its president, Eleanor Smeal and Director of Policy and Research, Jennifer Jackman, mobilized US women to take action against the countries that block women's Olympic participation. Before the Atlanta Olympics, Dr. Parvin Darabi from Iran said, "We would like to stage a demonstration during the opening ceremonies of the Atlanta Olympics to condemn gender apartheid in Iran and other Islamic nations." She was raising money to bring a championship woman athlete from Iran to the Atlanta Olympics to tell her story.

22. At the 1996 Olympics there were no female athletes from the following countries: Afghanistan; Brunei Darussalam; Botswana; Djibouti; Grenada; Guinea-Bissau; Haiti; Iraq; Kuwait; Libya; Mauritania; Nauru; Oman; Palestine; Papua New Guinea; Qatar; Rwanda; Senegal; Somalia; Saudi Arabia; Sudan; Togo; United Arab Emirates; Yemen.

23. The two members of the IOC Executive Commission that met the Atlanta delegation were François Carrard, Director General of the IOC, and Anita DeFrantz. The two groups agreed on certain points, but remained divided on the critical question as to whether all women should be free to compete in all Olympic disciplines, no matter the reasons given by their governments to deprive women of this universal right.

24. The following letter was presented to the IOC on 17 July 1996 in Atlanta, Georgia:

"An Open Letter to Juan Antonio Samaranch on his Birthday"

Sir,

As you are aware, we created Atlanta [Atlanta Plus] in 1992 to protest gender discrimination at the Olympic Games after the shock Opening Ceremony in Barcelona where 35 countries were composed only of men.

In January '95, the answer given to our demand was that *"the Olympic hierarchy would be reluctant to take the lead in combating sex discrimination when other international organizations*

such as the United Nations have not taken strong diplomatic action" (Associated Press, 13 January 1995).

This answer was surprising since the Olympic Charter clearly states that *"all forms of discrimination with respect to a country or a person, whether for reasons of race, religion, politics, sex or any other are incompatible with the Olympic movement."*

Nevertheless, to comply with the IOC "hierarchy's" demand we have obtained from the United Nations Human Rights Commission, the Council of the European Parliament very clear resolutions supporting our views which you will find enclosed.

All women must be gratified that the Atlanta Games include more women than ever before. This makes it more urgent to ensure that women from all countries are allowed to compete.

This is neither a cultural/religious issue nor a woman's-only issue. To put an end to such an unacceptable situation which is in conflict with the Olympic Charter, we request the IOC:

- *to donate one percent per ticket* to a foundation which will distribute the funds to help countries that cannot afford to train women
- to exclude those countries which either practice institutionalized segregation or forbid female participation of women in the Olympics for *ideological reasons.*

Why should men of those countries be allowed to join one of the few universal gatherings of people of all nations when women of the same countries cannot share this joy and pride? Women all around the world look forward to your response.

Sincerely

Anne Marie Lizim
Annie Sugier
Linda Weil-Curiel

25. In an unpublished paper delivered at the Second Scientific Conference for Arab Women's Sport, in Alexandria, Egypt, in 1997, in a reference to the Atlanta lobby, Margaret Talbot claims that the assumption of Atlanta is that "only Islam is the barrier" and that "they [Atlanta] have trivialized and ridiculed women from Islamic countries." She censured Atlanta for not consulting Muslim women from their banned countries list and concludes: "Atlanta Plus see the situation only through their own narrow and arrogant perspectives." Margaret Talbot is president of IAPESGW.

In response to a paper submitted by Atlanta to the International Working Group (IWG . . .), the decision was made not to alter the Brighton Declaration to take account of gender discrimination as requested by Atlanta.

REFERENCES

Ahmed, A. (1992) *Postmodernism and Islam*, London: Routledge.

Ahmed, A. and H. Donnan (eds) (1994a) *Islam, Globalization and Postmodernity*, London: Routledge.

———. (1994b) "Islam in the Age of Postmodernity," in Ahmed, A. and H. Donnan (eds) *Islam, Globalization and Postmodernity*, London: Routledge, pp. 1–20,

Anderson, B. (1983) *Imagined Communities*, 2nd edition, New York: Verso.

Chow, R. (1993) "Violence in the Other Country," in Mohanty, C., A. Russo and L. Torres (eds) *Third World Women and the Politics of Feminism*, Bloomington, IN: Indiana University Press, pp. 81–100.

Gellner, E. (1992) *Postmodernism, Reason and Religion*, London: Routledge.

———. (1994) "Foreword," in Ahmed, A. and H. Donnan (eds) *Islam, Globalization and Postsmodernity*, London: Routledge, pp. xi–xiv.

Gerholm, T. (1994) "Two Muslim Intellectuals in the Postmodern West," in Ahmed, A. and H. Donnan (eds) *Islam, Globalization and Postmodernity*, London: Routledge, pp. 190–212.

Halliday, F. (1994) "The Politics of Islamic Fundamentalism: Iran, Tunisia and the Challenge to the Secular State," in Ahmed, A. and H. Donnan (eds) *Islam, Globalization and Postmodernity*, London: Routledge, pp. 91–113.

Kanneh, K. (1995) "The Difficult Politics of Wigs and Veils: Feminism and the Colonial Body," in Ashcroft, B., G. Griffiths and H. Tiffin (eds) *The Post-Colonial Studies Reader*, London: Routledge, pp. 346–48.

Karam, A. (1998) *Women, Islamisms and the State*, London: Macmillan.

Layden, J. (1997) *Women in Sports*, Los Angeles: General Publishing.

Morgan, W. (1998) "Hassiba Boulmerka and Islamic Green: International Sports, Cultural Differences, and Their Postmodern Interpretation," in Rail, G. (ed) *Sport and Postmodern Times*, Albany: Suny, pp. 345–65.

Nagata, J. (1994) "How to Be Islamic Without Being an Islamic State: Contested Models of Development in Malaysia," in Ahmed, A. and H. Donnan (eds) *Islam, Globalization and Postmodernity*, London: Routledge, pp. 63–90.

Runnymede Trust (1997) *Islamaphobia*, London: Runnymede Trust.

Tohidi, N. (1991) "Gender and Islamic Fundamentalism: Feminist Politics in Iran," in Mohanty, C., A. Russo and L. Torres (eds) *Third World Women and the Politics of Feminism*, Bloomington: Indiana University Press, pp. 251–70.

Watson, H. (1994) "Women and the Veil: Personal Responses to Global Processes," in Ahmed, A. and H. Donnan (eds) *Islam, Globalization and Postmodernity*, London: Routledge, pp. 141–59.

Weiss, A. (1994) "Challenges for Muslim Women in a Postmodern World," in Ahmed, A. and H. Donnan (eds) *Islam, Globalization and Postmodernity*, London: Routledge, pp. 127–40.

JOURNALS, MAGAZINES, CONFERENCE PAPERS, DISSERTATIONS

Because of the large volume of material referred to, it is impossible to list all newspaper and magazine articles, television programmes and Internet information that has provided a background for the research. Newspaper, magazine, and television references are cited in the text only.

Abdelrahman, N. (1991) "Women and Sport in the Islamic Society: An Analytical Study of the Viewpoints of Some Islamic Ulamas and Physical Education Specialists," unpublished paper presented at the First Islamic Countries Sports Solidarity Congress for Women, University of Alexandria, Egypt.

———. (1998) "Egypt," *Bulletin of International Association of Physical Education and Sport for Girls and Women* 8(1): 13, 16.

Al-Hashimy, F. (1997) "The Development of the Women's Sport Movement in Iraq," in "Woman and Child: Future Vision from a Sport Perspective," in *Proceedings of the Second Scientific International Conference for Women and Sport*, Alexandria University, pp. 37–9.

Goldsmith, M. (1995) "Sporting Boycotts as a Political Tool," in AQ Autumn: 11–20.

Holder, D. (1996) "A Woman's Place is at the Games," *Independent on Sunday* 7 July.

Hornblower, M. (1992) "Running Against the Grain," *Times International*, June: 88–91.

IWG (International Working Group) Women and Sport (1998) *From Brighton to Windhoek—Facing the Challenge: Summary Progress Report of the International Women and Sport Movement—1994–1998*, United Kingdom Sports Council.

Macleod, S. (1998) "Our Veils, Ourselves," *Time* 152(4): 29.

Mahl (1995) "Women on the Edge of Time," *New Internationalist* August: 14–16.

Mechti, Z. and N. Sayad (1994) *Ministry For Youth Sports: Algeria: Female Sports "Reality and Perspective,"* unpublished paper.

O'Kane, M. (1998) "Afghanistan," *New Internationalist* 298: 37.

Pourhaddadi, F. (1998) "A Political and Socio-Economic History of the Asian Games," unpublished B.Sc. dissertation, University of Surrey, Roehampton.

Violence against Women

Violence against women manifests itself in many forms. Verbal harassment, sexual imposition, sexual assault, rape, domestic battering, lesbian bashing, and child abuse all contribute to a social climate that encourages women to comply with men's desires or to restrict their activities in order to avoid assault. The threat of violence against women is pervasive across cultures. Feminist analyses of violence against women focus on the extent to which violence serves as a means for the institutionalized control of women and children by men. The articles in this section analyze various forms of violence against women and contrast beliefs and actualities about various kinds of male violence. Often, sexist ideologies encourage us to accept violence against women as either harmless or deserved. Feminist analyses take the position that this violence constitutes a system through which men frighten and therefore control and dominate women.

Patricia Yancey Martin and Robert A. Hummer also explore the implications of heterosexual male bonding in "Fraternities and Rape on Campus." Fraternity members' negative attitudes toward women, rigid ideas about masculinity, and pressures to demonstrate simultaneously their heterosexuality and their utter loyalty to the "brotherhood" create fraternity cultures in which men use women to demonstrate their masculinity and worth. What are some other social contexts in which similar pressures for men to be hypermasculine exist?

Hate crimes are crimes motivated by prejudice against particular groups. Because violence against women is so widespread, we sometimes fail to recognize it as a crime of hate. Gloria Steinem argues that mass killings in schools such as Columbine, Colorado, and Jonesboro, Arkansas, serial killings by criminals such as Edmund Kemper and Son of Sam, and other multiple sadistic killings of strangers are linked to male domination. In "Supremacy Crimes," Steinem argues that we should regard most such crimes not as individual and apolitical assaults by deranged men. Rather, they are crimes against women as a group, committed for the most part by white heterosexual males and motivated by men's desire for power and superiority. Think about the coverage of the mass killings in schools that occurred at the end of the 1990s. Did the media acknowledge the sex of the killers and most of the victims and the role gender might have played in what happened?

Violence against women is shaped by the intersections between race, class, and gender. In "Mapping the Margins: Intersectionality, Identity Politics, and Violence Against Women of Color," Kimberlé Crenshaw examines the relationship between gender and race in domestic violence.

Domestic violence, she shows, is shaped by race in several ways. First, there are proscriptions within communities of color against publicizing or politicizing domestic violence, out of the fear of reinforcing stereotypes of black men as violent. Controversy over feminism (often seen as a white movement) and reluctance to report violence to an often-racist police force further contribute to the problem. At the same time, efforts to address domestic violence by feminists and policy-makers often either ignore women of color or include them in a tokenistic way. Services to help women who are battered, such as shelters, are often inaccessible to women of color because of language barriers or lack of incorporation of women of color into leadership positions in shelters. What does Crenshaw suggest would be necessary to address domestic violence more effectively in all communities? To what extent do the other readings in this section use an intersectional approach to violence, taking into account how it is shaped by race as well as gender?

Violence against women, as all these articles point out, is not simply the act of individual men against individual women. Instead, it is created and perpetuated by social institutions. The final article in this section, "Accountability or Justice? Rape as a War Crime," by Mary Ann Tétreault, documents the use of rape as "an instrument of policy" in wartime. Focusing on the Iraqi invasion of Kuwait and the war in Bosnia-Herzogovina, Tétreault examines the use of rape and charges of rape as political fodder against the enemy, the treatment of rape victims by their own communities and governments, and the responses of war-crimes tribunals to rape charges. She argues that, as in other forms of rape, shame prevents many women from reporting their assaults or seeking damages from war-crimes tribunals. How is rape in wartime similar to and different from rape in the contexts described in the other articles in this section?

Fraternities and Rape on Campus

Patricia Yancey Martin and Robert A. Hummer

Rapes are perpetrated on dates, at parties, in chance encounters, and in specially planned circumstances. That group structure and processes, rather than individual values or characteristics, are the impetus for many rape episodes was documented by Blanchard (1959) thirty years ago (also see Geis 1971), yet sociologists have failed to pursue this theme (for an exception, see Chancer 1987). A recent review of research (Muehlenhard and Linton 1987) on sexual violence, or rape, devotes only a few pages to the situational contexts of rape events, and these are conceptualized as potential risk factors for individuals rather than qualities of rape-prone social contexts.

Many rapes, far more than come to the public's attention, occur in fraternity houses on college and university campuses, yet little research has analyzed fraternities at American colleges and universities as rape-prone contexts (cf. Ehrhart and Sandler 1985). Most of the research on fraternities reports on samples of individual fraternity men. One group of studies compares the values, attitudes, perceptions, family socioeconomic status, psychological traits (aggressiveness, dependence), and so on, of fraternity and nonfraternity men (Bohrnstedt 1969; Fox, Hodge, and Ward 1987; Kanin 1967; Lemire 1979; Miller 1973). A second group attempts to identify the effects of fraternity membership over time on the values, attitudes, beliefs, or moral precepts of members (Hughes and Winston 1987; Marlowe and Auvenshine 1982; Miller 1973; Wilder, Hoyt, Doren, Hauck, and Zettle 1978; Wilder, Hoyt, Surbeck, Wilder, and Carney 1986). With minor exceptions, little research addresses the group and organizational context of fraternities or the social construction of fraternity life (for exceptions, see Letchworth 1969; Longino and Kart 1973; Smith 1964).

Gary Tash, writing as an alumnus and trial attorney in his fraternity's magazine, claims that over 90 percent of all gang rapes on college campuses involve fraternity men (1988, p. 2). Tash provides no evidence to substantiate this claim, but students of violence against women have been concerned with fraternity men's frequently reported involvement in rape episodes (Adams and Abarbanel 1988). Ehrhart and Sandler (1985) identify over fifty cases of gang rapes on campus perpetrated by fraternity men, and their analysis points to many of the conditions that we discuss here. Their analysis is unique in focusing on conditions in fraternities that make gang rapes of women by fraternity men both feasible and probable. They identify excessive alcohol use, isolation from external monitoring, treatment of women as prey, use of pornography, approval of violence, and excessive concern with competition as precipitating conditions to gang rape (also see Merton 1985; Roark 1987).

The study reported here confirmed and complemented these findings by focusing on both conditions and processes. We examined dynamics associated with the social construction of fraternity life, with a focus on processes that foster the use of coercion, including rape, in fraternity men's relations with women. Our examination of men's social fraternities on college and university campuses as groups and organizations led us to conclude that fraternities are a physical and sociocultural context that encourages the sexual coercion of women. We make no claims that all fraternities are "bad" or that all fraternity men are rapists. Our observations indicated, however, that rape is especially probable in fraternities because of the kinds of organizations they are, the kinds of members they have, the practices their members engage in, and a virtual absence of university or community oversight. Analyses that lay blame for rapes by fraternity men on "peer pressure" are, we feel, overly simplistic (cf. Burkhart 1989; Walsh 1989). We suggest, rather, that fraternities create a sociocultural context in which the use of coercion in sexual relations with women is normative and in which the mechanisms to keep this pattern of behavior in check are minimal at best and absent at worst. We conclude that unless fraternities change in fundamental ways, little improvement can be expected.

METHODOLOGY

Our goal was to analyze the group and organizational practices and conditions that create in fraternities an abusive social context for women. We developed a conceptual framework from an initial case study of an alleged gang rape at Florida State University that involved four fraternity men and an eighteen-year-old coed. The group rape took place on the third floor of a fraternity house and ended with the "dumping" of the woman in the hallway of a neighboring fraternity house. According to newspaper accounts, the victim's blood-alcohol concentration, when she was discovered, was .349 percent, more than three times the legal limit for automobile driving and an almost lethal amount. One law enforcement officer reported that sexual intercourse occurred during the time the victim was unconscious: "She was in a life-threatening situation" (*Tallahassee Democrat* 1988b). When the victim was found, she was comatose and had suffered multiple scratches and abrasions. Crude words and a fraternity symbol had been written on her thighs (*Tampa Tribune* 1988). When law enforcement officials tried to investigate the case, fraternity members refused to cooperate. This led, eventually, to a five-year ban of the fraternity from campus by the university and by the fraternity's national organization.

In trying to understand how such an event could have occurred, and how a group of over 150 members (exact figures are unknown because the fraternity refused to provide a membership roster) could hold rank, deny knowledge of the event, and allegedly lie to a grand jury, we analyzed newspaper articles about the case and conducted open-ended interviews with a variety of respondents about the case and about fraternities, rapes, alcohol use, gender relations, and sexual activities on campus. Our data included over 100 newspaper articles on the initial gang rape case; open-ended interviews with Greek (social fraternity and sorority) and non-Greek (independent) students (*n* = 20); university administrators (*n* = 8, five men, three women); and alumni advisers to Greek organizations

(n = 6). Open-ended interviews were held also with judges, public and private defense attorneys, victim advocates, and state prosecutors regarding the processing of sexual assault cases. Data were analyzed using the grounded theory method (Glaser 1978; Martin and Turner 1986). In the following analysis, concepts generated from the data analysis are integrated with the literature on men's social fraternities, sexual coercion, and related issues.

FRATERNITIES AND THE SOCIAL CONSTRUCTION OF MEN AND MASCULINITY

Our research indicated that fraternities are vitally concerned—more than with anything else—with masculinity (cf. Kanin 1967). They work hard to create a macho image and context and try to avoid any suggestion of "wimpishness," effeminacy, and homosexuality. Valued members display, or are willing to go along with, a narrow conception of masculinity that stresses competition, athleticism, dominance, winning, conflict, wealth, material possessions, willingness to drink alcohol, and sexual prowess vis-à-vis women.

Valued Qualities of Members

When fraternity members talked about the kind of pledges they prefer, a litany of stereotypical and narrowly masculine attributes and behaviors was recited and feminine or woman-associated qualities and behaviors were expressly denounced (cf. Merton 1985). Fraternities seek men who are "athletic," "big guys," good in intramural competition, "who can talk college sports." Males "who are willing to drink alcohol," "who drink socially," or "who can hold their liquor" are sought. Alcohol and activities associated with the recreational use of alcohol are cornerstones of fraternity social life. Nondrinkers are viewed with skepticism and rarely selected for membership.[1]

Fraternities try to avoid "geeks," nerds, and men said to give the fraternity a "wimpy" or "gay" reputation. Art, music, and humanities majors, majors in traditional women's fields (nursing, home economics, social work, education), men with long hair, and those whose appearance or dress violate current norms are rejected. Clean-cut, handsome men who dress well (are clean, neat, conforming, fashionable) are preferred. One sorority woman commented that "the top-ranking fraternities have the best looking guys."

One fraternity man, a senior, said his fraternity recruited "some big guys, very athletic" over a two-year period to help overcome its image of wimpiness. His fraternity had won the interfraternity competition for highest grade-point average several years running but was looked down on as "wimpy, dancy, even gay." With their bigger, more athletic recruits, "our reputation improved; we're a much more recognized fraternity now." Thus a fraternity's reputation and status depend on members' possession of stereotypically masculine qualities. Good grades, campus leadership, and community service are "nice" but masculinity dominance—for example, in athletic events, physical size of members, athleticism of members—counts most.

Certain social skills are valued. Men are sought who "have good personalities," are friendly, and "have the ability to relate to girls" (cf. Longino and Kart 1973). One fraternity man, a junior, said: "We watch a guy [a potential pledge] talk to women . . . we want guys who can relate to girls." Assessing a pledge's ability to talk to women is, in part, a preoccupation with homosexuality and a conscious avoidance of men who seem to have effeminate manners or qualities. If a member is suspected of being gay, he is ostracized and informally drummed out of the fraternity. A fraternity with a reputation as wimpy or tolerant of gays is ridiculed and shunned by other fraternities. Militant heterosexuality is frequently used by men as a strategy to keep each other in line (Kimmel 1987).

Financial affluence or wealth, a male-associated value in American culture, is highly valued by fraternities. In accounting for why the fraternity involved in the gang rape that precipitated our research project had been recognized recently as "the best fraternity chapter in the United States," a university official said: "They were good-looking, a big fraternity, had lots of BMWs [expensive, German-made automobiles]." After the rape, newspaper stories described the fraternity members' affluence, noting the high number of members who owned expensive cars (*St. Petersburg Times* 1988).

The Status and Norms of Pledgeship

A pledge (sometimes called an associate member) is a new recruit who occupies a trial membership status for a specific period of time. The pledge period (typically ranging from ten to fifteen weeks) gives fraternity brothers an opportunity to assess and socialize new recruits. Pledges evaluate the fraternity also and decide if they want to become brothers. The socialization experience is structured partly through assignment of a Big Brother to each pledge. Big Brothers are expected to teach pledges how to become a brother and to support them as they progress through the trial membership period. Some pledges are repelled by the pledging experience, which can entail physical abuse; harsh discipline; and demands to be subordinate, follow orders, and engage in demeaning routines and activities, similar to those used by the military to "make men out of boys" during boot camp.

Characteristics of the pledge experience are rationalized by fraternity members as necessary to help pledges unite into a group, rely on each other, and join together against outsiders. The process is highly masculinist in execution as well as conception. A willingness to submit to authority, follow orders, and do as one is told is viewed as a sign of loyalty, togetherness, and unity. Fraternity pledges who find the pledge process offensive often drop out. Some do this by openly quitting, which can subject them to ridicule by brothers and other pledges, or they may deliberately fail to make the grades necessary for initiation or transfer schools and decline to reaffiliate with the fraternity on the new campus. One fraternity pledge who quit the fraternity he had pledged described an experience during pledgeship as follows:

This one guy was always picking on me. No matter what I did, I was wrong. One night after dinner, he and two other guys called me and two other pledges into the chapter room. He said, "Here, X, hold this 25-pound bag of ice at arms' length 'til I tell you to stop." I did it even though my arms and hands were killing me. When I asked if I could stop, he grabbed me around the throat and lifted me off the floor. I thought he would choke me to death. He cussed me and called me all kinds of names. He took one of my fingers and twisted it until it nearly broke. . . . I stayed in the fraternity for a few more days, but then I decided to quit. I hated it. Those guys are sick. They like seeing you suffer.

Fraternities' emphasis on toughness, withstanding pain and humiliation, obedience to superiors, and using physical force to obtain compliance contributes to an interpersonal style that de-emphasizes caring and sensitivity but fosters intragroup trust and loyalty.

If the least macho or most critical pledges drop out, those who remain may be more receptive to, and influenced by, masculinist values and practices that encourage the use of force in sexual relations with women and the covering up of such behavior (cf. Kanin 1967).

Norms and Dynamics of Brotherhood

Brother is the status occupied by fraternity men to indicate their relations to each other and their membership in a particular fraternity organization or group. Brother is a male-specific status; only males can become brothers, although women can become "Little Sisters," a form of pseudomembership. "Becoming a brother" is a rite of passage that follows the consistent and often lengthy display by pledges of appropriately masculine qualities and behaviors. Brothers have a quasifamilial relationship with each other, are normatively said to share bonds of closeness and support, and are sharply set off from nonmembers. Brotherhood is a loosely defined term used to represent the bonds that develop among fraternity members and the obligations and expectations incumbent upon them (cf. Marlowe and Auvenshine [1982] on fraternities' failure to encourage "moral development" in freshman pledges).

Some of our respondents talked about brotherhood in almost reverential terms, viewing it as the most valuable benefit of fraternity membership. One senior, a business-school major who had been affiliated with a fairly high-status fraternity throughout four years on campus, said:

> Brotherhood spurs friendship for life, which I consider its best aspect, although I didn't see it that way when I joined. Brotherhood bonds and unites. It instills values of caring about one another, caring about community, caring about ourselves. The values and bonds [of brotherhood] continually develop over the four years [in college] while normal friendships come and go.

Despite this idealization, most aspects of fraternity practice and conception are more mundane. Brotherhood often plays itself out as an overriding concern with masculinity and, by extension, femininity. As a consequence, fraternities comprise collectivities of highly masculinized men with attitudinal qualities and behavioral norms that predispose them to sexual

coercion of women (cf. Kanin 1967; Merton 1985; Rapaport and Burkhart 1984). The norms of masculinity are complemented by conceptions of women and femininity that are equally distorted and stereotyped and that may enhance the probability of women's exploitation (cf. Ehrhart and Sandler 1985; Sanday 1981, 1986).

Practices of Brotherhood

Practices associated with fraternity brotherhood that contribute to the sexual coercion of women include a preoccupation with loyalty, group protection and secrecy, use of alcohol as a weapon, involvement in violence and physical force, and an emphasis on competition and superiority.

Loyalty, Group Protection, and Secrecy Loyalty is a fraternity preoccupation. Members are reminded constantly to be loyal to the fraternity and to their brothers. Among other ways, loyalty is played out in the practices of group protection and secrecy. The fraternity must be shielded from criticism. Members are admonished to avoid getting the fraternity in trouble and to bring all problems "to the chapter" (local branch of a national social fraternity) rather than to outsiders. Fraternities try to protect themselves from close scrutiny and criticism by the Interfraternity Council (a quasigoverning body composed of representatives from all social fraternities on campus), their fraternity's national office, university officials, law enforcement, the media, and the public. Protection of the fraternity often takes precedence over what is procedurally, ethically, or legally correct. Numerous examples were related to us of fraternity brothers' lying to outsiders to "protect the fraternity."

Group protection was observed in the alleged gang rape case with which we began our study. Except for one brother, a rapist who turned state's evidence, the entire remaining fraternity membership was accused by university and criminal justice officials of lying to protect the fraternity. Members consistently failed to cooperate even though the alleged crimes were felonies, involved only four men (two of whom were not even members of the local chapter), and the victim of the crime nearly died. According to a grand jury's findings, fraternity officers repeatedly broke appointments with law enforcement officials, refused to provide police with a list of members, and refused to cooperate with police and prosecutors investigating the case (*Florida Flambeau* 1988).

Secrecy is a priority value and practice in fraternities, partly because full-fledged membership is premised on it (for confirmation, see Ehrhart and Sandler 1985; Longino and Kart 1973; Roark 1987). Secrecy is also a boundary-maintaining mechanism, demarcating in-group from out-group, us from them. Secret rituals, handshakes, and mottoes are revealed to pledge brothers as they are initiated into full brotherhood. Since only brothers are supposed to know a fraternity's secrets, such knowledge affirms membership in the fraternity and separates a brother from others. Extending secrecy tactics from protection of private knowledge to protection of the fraternity from criticism is a predictable development. Our interviews indicated that individual members knew the difference between right and wrong, but fraternity norms that emphasize loyalty, group protection, and secrecy often overrode standards of ethical correctness.

Alcohol as Weapon   Alcohol use by fraternity men is normative. They use it on weekdays to relax after class and on weekends to "get drunk," "get crazy," and "get laid." The use of alcohol to obtain sex from women is pervasive—in other words, it is used as a weapon against sexual reluctance. According to several fraternity men whom we interviewed, alcohol is the major tool used to gain sexual mastery over women (cf. Adams and Abarbanel 1988; Ehrhart and Sandler 1985). One fraternity man, a twenty-one-year-old senior, described alcohol use to gain sex as follows: "There are girls that you know will fuck, then some you have to put some effort into it. . . . You have to buy them drinks or find out if she's drunk enough."

A similar strategy is used collectively. A fraternity man said that at parties with Little Sisters: "We provide them with 'hunch punch' and things get wild. We get them drunk and most of the guys end up with one." "'Hunch punch,'" he said, "is a girls' drink made up of overproof alcohol and powdered Kool-Aid, no water or anything, just ice. It's very strong. Two cups will do a number on a female." He had plans in the next academic term to surreptitiously give hunch punch to women in a "prim and proper" sorority because "having sex with prim and proper sorority girls is definitely a goal." These women are a challenge because they "won't openly consume alcohol and won't get openly drunk as hell." Their sororities have "standards committees" that forbid heavy drinking and easy sex.

In the gang rape case, our sources said that many fraternity men on campus believed the victim had a drinking problem and was thus an "easy make." According to newspaper accounts, she had been drinking alcohol on the evening she was raped; the lead assailant is alleged to have given her a bottle of wine after she arrived at his fraternity house. Portions of the rape occurred in a shower, and the victim was reportedly so drunk that her assailants had difficulty holding her in a standing position (*Tallahassee Democrat* 1988a). While raping her, her assailants repeatedly told her they were members of another fraternity under the apparent belief that she was too drunk to know the difference. Of course, if she was too drunk to know who they were, she was too drunk to consent to sex (cf. Allgeier 1986; Tash 1988).

One respondent told us that gang rapes are wrong and can get one expelled, but he seemed to see nothing wrong in sexual coercion one-on-one. He seemed unaware that the use of alcohol to obtain sex from a woman is grounds for a claim that a rape occurred (cf. Tash 1988). Few women on campus (who also may not know these grounds) report date rapes, however; so the odds of detection and punishment are slim for fraternity men who use alcohol for "seduction" purposes (cf. Byington and Keeter 1988; Merton 1985).

Violence and Physical Force   Fraternity men have a history of violence (Ehrhart and Sandler 1985; Roark 1987). Their record of hazing, fighting, property destruction, and rape has caused them problems with insurance companies (Bradford 1986; Pressley 1987). Two university officials told us that fraternities "are the third riskiest property to insure behind toxic waste dumps and amusement parks." Fraternities are increasingly defendants in legal actions brought by pledges subjected to hazing (Meyer 1986; Pressley 1987) and by women who were raped by one or more members. In a recent alleged gang rape incident at another Florida university, prosecutors failed to file charges but the victim filed a civil suit against the fraternity nevertheless (*Tallahassee Democrat* 1989).

Competition and Superiority   Interfraternity rivalry fosters in-group identification and out-group hostility. Fraternities stress pride of membership and superiority over other fraternities as major goals. Interfraternity rivalries take many forms, including competition for desirable pledges, size of pledge class, size of membership, size and appearance of fraternity house, superiority in intramural sports, highest grade-point averages, giving the best parties, gaining the best or most campus leadership roles, and, of great importance, attracting and displaying "good-looking women." Rivalry is particularly intense over members, intramural sports, and women (cf. Messner 1989).

FRATERNITIES' COMMODIFICATION OF WOMEN

In claiming that women are treated by fraternities as commodities, we mean that fraternities knowingly, and intentionally, *use* women for their benefit. Fraternities use women as bait for new members, as servers of brothers' needs, and as sexual prey.

Women as Bait

Fashionably attractive women help a fraternity attract new members. As one fraternity man, a junior, said, "They are good bait." Beautiful, sociable women are believed to impress the right kind of pledges and give the impression that the fraternity can deliver this type of woman to its members. Photographs of shapely, attractive coeds are printed in fraternity brochures and videotapes that are distributed and shown to potential pledges. The women pictured are often dressed in bikinis, at the beach, and are pictured hugging the brothers of the fraternity. One university official says such recruitment materials give the message: "Hey, they're here for you, you can have whatever you want," and, "we have the best-looking women. Join us and you can have them too." Another commented: "Something's wrong when males join an all-male organization as the best place to meet women. It's so illogical."

Fraternities compete in promising access to beautiful women. One fraternity man, a senior, commented that "the attraction of girls [i.e., a fraternity's success in attracting women] is a big status symbol for fraternities." One university official commented that the use of women as a recruiting tool is so well entrenched that fraternities that might be willing to forgo it say they cannot afford to unless other fraternities do so as well. One fraternity man said, "Look, if we don't have Little Sisters, the fraternities that do will get all the good pledges." Another said, "We won't have as good a rush [the period during which new members are assessed and selected] if we don't have these women around."

In displaying good-looking, attractive, skimpily dressed, nubile women to potential members, fraternities implicitly, and sometimes explicitly, promise sexual access to women. One fraternity man commented that "part of what being in a fraternity is all about is the sex" and explained how his fraternity uses Little Sisters to recruit new members:

> We'll tell the sweetheart [the fraternity's term for Little Sister], "You're gorgeous; you can get him." We'll tell her to fake a scam and she'll go hang all over him during a rush party, kiss him, and he thinks he's done wonderful and wants to join. The girls think it's great too. It's flattering for them.

Women as Servers

The use of women as servers is exemplified in the Little Sister program. Little Sisters are undergraduate women who are rushed and selected in a manner parallel to the recruitment of fraternity men. They are affiliated with the fraternity in a formal but unofficial way and are able, indeed required, to wear the fraternity's Greek letters. Little Sisters are not full-fledged fraternity members, however; and fraternity national offices and most universities do not register or regulate them. Each fraternity has an officer called Little Sister Chairman who oversees their organization and activities. The Little Sisters elect officers among themselves, pay monthly dues to the fraternity, and have well-defined roles. Their dues are used to pay for the fraternity's social events, and Little Sisters are expected to attend and hostess fraternity parties and hang around the house to make it a "nice place to be." One fraternity man, a senior, described Little Sisters this way: "They are very social girls, willing to join in, be affiliated with the group, devoted to the fraternity." Another member, a sophomore, said: "Their sole purpose is social—attend parties, attract new members, and 'take care' of the guys."

Our observations and interviews suggested that women selected by fraternities as Little Sisters are physically attractive, possess good social skills, and are willing to devote time and energy to the fraternity and its members. One undergraduate woman gave the following job description for Little Sisters to a campus newspaper:

> It's not just making appearances at all the parties but entails many more responsibilities. You're

going to be expected to go to all the intramural games to cheer the brothers on, support and encourage the pledges, and just be around to bring some extra life to the house. [As a Little Sister] you have to agree to take on a new responsibility other than studying to maintain your grades and managing to keep your checkbook from bouncing. You have to make time to be a part of the fraternity and support the brothers in all they do. (*The Tomahawk* 1988)

The title of Little Sister reflects women's subordinate status; fraternity men in a parallel role are called Big Brothers. Big Brothers assist a sorority primarily with the physical work of sorority rushes, which, compared to fraternity rushes, are more formal, structured, and intensive. Sorority rushes take place in the daytime and fraternity rushes at night so fraternity men are free to help. According to one fraternity member, Little Sister status is a benefit to women because it gives them a social outlet and "the protection of the brothers." The gender-stereotypic conceptions and obligations of these Little Sister and Big Brother statuses indicate that fraternities and sororities promote a gender hierarchy on campus that fosters subordination and dependence in women, thus encouraging sexual exploitation and the belief that it is acceptable.

Women as Sexual Prey

Little Sisters are a sexual utility. Many Little Sisters do not belong to sororities and lack peer support for refraining from unwanted sexual relations. One fraternity man (whose fraternity has sixty-five members and eighty-five Little Sisters) told us they had recruited "wholesale" in the prior year to "get lots of new women." The structural access to women that the Little Sister program provides and the absence of normative supports for refusing fraternity members' sexual advances may make women in this program particularly susceptible to coerced sexual encounters with fraternity men.

Access to women for sexual gratification is a presumed benefit of fraternity membership, promised in recruitment materials and strategies and through brothers' conversations with new recruits. One fraternity man said: "We always tell the guys that you get sex all the time, there's always new girls. . . . After I became a Greek, I found out I could be with females at will." A university official told us that, based on his

observations, "no one [i.e., fraternity men] on this campus wants to have 'relationships.' They just want to have fun [i.e., sex]." Fraternity men plan and execute strategies aimed at obtaining sexual gratification, and this occurs at both individual and collective levels.

Individual strategies include getting a woman drunk and spending a great deal of money on her. As for collective strategies, most of our undergraduate interviewees agreed that fraternity parties often culminate in sex and that this outcome is planned. One fraternity man said fraternity parties often involve sex and nudity and can "turn into orgies." Orgies may be planned in advance, such as the Bowery Ball party held by one fraternity. A former fraternity member said of this party:

> The entire idea behind this is sex. Both men and women come to the party wearing little or nothing. There are pornographic pinups on the walls and usually porno movies playing on the TV. The music carries sexual overtones. . . . They just get schnockered [drunk] and, in most cases, they also get laid.

When asked about the women who come to such a party, he said: "Some Little Sisters just won't go. . . . The girls who do are looking for a good time, girls who don't know what it is, things like that."

Other respondents denied that fraternity parties are orgies but said that sex is always talked about among the brothers and they all know "who each other is doing it with." One member said that most of the time, guys have sex with their girlfriends "but with socials, girlfriends aren't allowed to come and it's their [members'] big chance [to have sex with other women]." The use of alcohol to help them get women into bed is a routine strategy at fraternity parties.

CONCLUSIONS

In general, our research indicated that the organization and membership of fraternities contribute heavily to coercive and often violent sex. Fraternity houses are occupied by same-sex (all men) and same-age (late teens, early twenties) peers whose maturity and judgment is often less than ideal. Yet fraternity houses are private dwellings that are mostly off-limits to, and away from scrutiny of, university and community representatives, with the result that fraternity house events seldom come to the attention of outsiders.

Practices associated with the social construction of fraternity brotherhood emphasize a macho conception of men and masculinity, a narrow, stereotyped conception of women and femininity, and the treatment of women as commodities. Other practices contributing to coercive sexual relations and the cover-up of rapes include excessive alcohol use, competitiveness, and normative support for deviance and secrecy (cf. Bogal-Allbritten and Allbritten 1985; Kanin 1967).

Some fraternity practices exacerbate others. Brotherhood norms require "sticking together" regardless of right or wrong; thus rape episodes are unlikely to be stopped or reported to outsiders, even when witnesses disapprove. The ability to use alcohol without scrutiny by authorities and alcohol's frequent association with violence, including sexual coercion, facilitates rape in fraternity houses. Fraternity norms that emphasize the value of maleness and masculinity over femaleness and femininity and that elevate the status of men and lower the status of women in members' eyes undermine perceptions and treatment of women as persons who deserve consideration and care (cf. Ehrhart and Sandler 1985; Merton 1985).

Androgynous men and men with a broad range of interests and attributes are lost to fraternities through their recruitment practices. Masculinity of a narrow and stereotypical type helps create attitudes, norms, and practices that predispose fraternity men to coerce women sexually, both individually and collectively (Allgeier 1986; Hood 1989; Sanday 1981, 1986). Male athletes on campus may be similarly disposed for the same reasons (Kirshenbaum 1989; Telander and Sullivan 1989).

Research into the social contexts in which rape crimes occur and the social constructions associated with these contexts illumine rape dynamics on campus. Blanchard (1959) found that group rapes almost always have a leader who pushes others into the crime. He also found that the leader's latent homosexuality, desire to show off to his peers, or fear of failing to prove himself a man are frequently an impetus. Fraternity norms and practices contribute to the approval and use of sexual coercion as an accepted tactic in relations with women. Alcohol-induced compliance is normative, whereas, presumably, use of a knife, gun, or threat of bodily harm would not be because the woman who "drinks too much" is viewed as "causing her own rape" (cf. Ehrhart and Sandler 1985).

Our research led us to conclude that fraternity norms and practices influence members to view the sexual coercion of women, which is a felony crime, as sport, a contest, or a game (cf. Sato 1988). This sport is played not between men and women but between men and men. Women are the pawns or prey in the interfraternity rivalry game; they prove that a fraternity is successful or prestigious. The use of women in this way encourages fraternity men to see women as objects and sexual coercion as sport. Today's societal norms support young women's right to engage in sex at their discretion, and coercion is unnecessary in a mutually desired encounter. However, nubile young women say they prefer to be "in a relationship" to have sex while young men say they prefer to "get laid" without a commitment (Muehlenhard and Linton 1987). These differences may reflect, in part, American puritanism and men's fears of sexual intimacy or perhaps intimacy of any kind. In a fraternity context, getting sex without giving emotionally demonstrates "cool" masculinity. More important, it poses no threat to the bonding and loyalty of the fraternity brotherhood (cf. Farr 1988). Drinking large quantities of alcohol before having sex suggests that "scoring" rather than intrinsic sexual pleasure is a primary concern of fraternity men.

Unless fraternities' composition, goals, structures, and practices change in fundamental ways, women on campus will continue to be sexual prey for fraternity men. As all-male enclaves dedicated to opposing faculty and administration and to cementing in-group ties, fraternity members eschew any hint of homosexuality. Their version of masculinity transforms women, and men with womanly characteristics, into the out-group. "Womanly men" are ostracized; feminine women are used to demonstrate members' masculinity. Encouraging renewed emphasis on their founding values (Longino and Kart 1973), service orientation and activities (Lemire 1979), or members' moral development (Marlowe and Auvenshine 1982) will have little effect on fraternities' treatment of women. A case for or against fraternities cannot be made by studying individual members. The fraternity qua group and organization is at issue. Located on campus along with many vulnerable women, embedded in a sexist society, and caught up in masculinist goals, practices, and values, fraternities' violation of women—including forcible rape—should come as no surprise.

ACKNOWLEDGMENTS

We gratefully thank Meena Harris and Diane Mennella for assisting with data collection. The senior author thanks the graduate students in her fall 1988 graduate research methods seminar for help with developing the initial conceptual framework. Judith Lorber and two anonymous *Gender & Society* referees made numerous suggestions for improving our article and we thank them also.

NOTE

1. Recent bans by some universities on open-keg parties at fraternity houses have resulted in heavy drinking before coming to a party and an increase in drunkenness among those who attend. This may aggravate, rather than improve, the treatment of women by fraternity men at parties.

REFERENCES

Adams, Aileen, and Gail Abarbanel. 1988. *Sexual Assault on Campus: What Colleges Can Do.* Santa Monica, CA: Rape Treatment Center.

Allgeier, Elizabeth. 1986. "Coercive Versus Consensual Sexual Interactions." G. Stanley Hall Lecture to American Psychological Association Annual Meeting, Washington, DC, August.

Blanchard, W. H. 1959. "The Group Process in Gang Rape." *Journal of Social Psychology* 49: 259–66.

Bogal-Allbritten, Rosemarie B., and William L. Allbritten. 1985. "The Hidden Victims: Courtship Violence among College Students." *Journal of College Student Personnel* 43: 201–4.

Bohrnstedt, George W. 1969. "Conservatism, Authoritarianism and Religiosity of Fraternity Pledges." *Journal of College Student Personnel* 27: 36–43.

Bradford, Michael. 1986. "Tight Market Dries Up Nightlife at University." *Business Insurance* (March 2): 2, 6.

Burkhart, Barry. 1989. Comments in Seminar on Acquaintance/Date Rape Prevention: A National Video Teleconference, February 2.

Burkhart, Barry R., and Annette L. Stanton. 1985. "Sexual Aggression in Acquaintance Relationships." pp. 43–65 in *Violence in Intimate Relationships*, ed. G. Russell. Englewood Cliffs, NJ: Spectrum.

Byington, Diane B., and Karen W. Keeter. 1988. "Assessing Needs of Sexual Assault Victims on a University Campus." pp. 23–31 in *Student Services: Responding to Issues and Challenges*. Chapel Hill: University of North Carolina Press.

Chancer, Lynn S. 1987. "New Bedford, Massachusetts, March 6, 1983–March 22, 1984: The 'Before and After' of a Group Rape." *Gender & Society* 1: 239–60.

Ehrhart, Julie K., and Bernice R. Sandler. 1985. *Campus Gang Rape: Party Games?* Washington, DC: Association of American Colleges.

Farr, K. A. 1988. "Dominance Bonding through the Good Old Boys Sociability Network." *Sex Roles* 18: 259–77.

Florida Flambeau. 1988. "Pike Members Indicted in Rape." (May 19): 1, 5.

Fox, Elaine, Charles Hodge, and Walter Ward. 1987. "A Comparison of Attitudes Held by Black and White Fraternity Members." *Journal of Negro Education* 56: 521–34.

Geis, Gilbert. 1971. "Group Sexual Assaults." *Medical Aspects of Human Sexuality* 5: 101–13.

Glaser, Barney G. 1978. *Theoretical Sensitivity: Advances in the Methodology of Grounded Theory.* Mill Valley, CA: Sociology Press.

Hood, Jane. 1989. "Why Our Society Is Rape-Prone." *New York Times*, May 16.

Hughes, Michael J., and Roger B. Winston, Jr. 1987. "Effects of Fraternity Membership on Interpersonal Values." *Journal of College Student Personnel* 45: 405–11.

Kanin, Eugene J. 1967. "Reference Groups and Sex Conduct Norm Violations." *The Sociological Quarterly* 8: 495–504.

Kimmel, Michael, ed. 1987. *Changing Men: New Directions in Research on Men and Masculinity.* Newbury Park, CA: Sage.

Kirshenbaum, Jerry. 1989. "Special Report, An American Disgrace: A Violent and Unprecedented Lawlessness Has Arisen among College Athletes in all Parts of the Country." *Sports Illustrated* (February 27): 16–19.

Lemire, David. 1979. "One Investigation of the Stereotypes Associated with Fraternities and Sororities." *Journal of College Student Personnel* 37: 54–57.

Letchworth, G. E. 1969. "Fraternities Now and in the Future." *Journal of College Student Personnel* 10: 118–22.

Longino, Charles F., Jr., and Cary S. Kart. 1973. "The College Fraternity: An Assessment of Theory and Research." *Journal of College Student Personnel* 31: 118–25.

Marlowe, Anne F., and Dwight C. Auvenshine. 1982. "Greek Membership: Its Impact on the Moral Development of

College Freshmen." *Journal of College Student Personnel* 40: 53–57.

Martin, Patricia Yancey, and Barry A. Turner. 1986. "Grounded Theory and Organizational Research." *Journal of Applied Behavioral Science* 22: 141–57.

Merton, Andrew. 1985. "On Competition and Class: Return to Brotherhood." *Ms.* (September): 60–65, 121–22.

Messner, Michael. 1989. "Masculinities and Athletic Careers." *Gender & Society* 3: 71–88.

Meyer, T. J. 1986. "Fight Against Hazing Rituals Rages on Campuses." *Chronicle of Higher Education* (March 12): 34–36.

Miller, Leonard D. 1973. "Distinctive Characteristics of Fraternity Members." *Journal of College Student Personnel* 31: 126–28.

Muehlenhard, Charlene L., and Melaney A. Linton. 1987. "Date Rape and Sexual Aggression in Dating Situations: Incidence and Risk Factors." *Journal of Counseling Psychology* 34: 186–96.

Pressley, Sue Anne. 1987. "Fraternity Hell Night Still Endures." *Washington Post* (August 11): B1.

Rapaport, Karen, and Barry R. Burkhart. 1984. "Personality and Attitudinal Characteristics of Sexually Coercive College Males." *Journal of Abnormal Psychology* 93: 216–21.

Roark, Mary L. 1987. "Preventing Violence on College Campuses." *Journal of Counseling and Development* 65: 367–70.

Sanday, Peggy Reeves. 1981. "The Socio-Cultural Context of Rape: A Cross-Cultural Study." *Journal of Social Issues* 37: 5–27.

———. 1986. "Rape and the Silencing of the Feminine." pp. 84–101 in *Rape*, ed. S. Tomaselli and R. Porter. Oxford: Basil Blackwell.

St. Petersburg Times. 1988. "A Greek Tragedy." (May 29): 1F, 6F.

Sato, Ikuya. 1988. "Play Theory of Delinquency: Toward a General Theory of 'Action.'" *Symbolic Interaction* 11: 191–212.

Smith, T. 1964. "Emergence and Maintenance of Fraternal Solidarity." *Pacific Sociological Review* 7: 29–37.

Tallahassee Democrat. 1988a. "FSU Fraternity Brothers Charged" (April 27): 1A, 12A.

———. 1988b. "FSU Interviewing Students about Alleged Rape" (April 24): 1D.

———. 1989. "Woman Sues Stetson in Alleged Rape" (March 19): 3B.

Tampa Tribune. 1988. "Fraternity Brothers Charged in Sexual Assault of FSU Coed." (April 27): 6B.

Tash, Gary B. 1988. "Date Rape." *The Emerald of Sigma Pi Fraternity* 75(4): 1–2.

Telander, Rick, and Robert Sullivan. 1989. "Special Report, You Reap What You Sow." *Sports Illustrated* (February 27): 20–34.

The Tomahawk. 1988. "A Look Back at Rush, A Mixture of Hard Work and Fun" (April/May): 3D.

Walsh, Claire. 1989. Comments in Seminar on Acquaintance/Date Rape Prevention: A National Video Teleconference, February 2.

Wilder, David H., Arlyne E. Hoyt, Dennis M. Doren, William E. Hauck, and Robert D. Zettle. 1978. "The Impact of Fraternity and Sorority Membership on Values and Attitudes." *Journal of College Student Personnel* 36: 445–49.

Wilder, David H., Arlyne E. Hoyt, Beth Shuster Surbeck, Janet C. Wilder, and Patricia Imperatrice Carney. 1986. "Greek Affiliation and Attitude Change in College Students." *Journal of College Student Personnel* 44: 510–19.

MEN CHANGING MEN

Robert L. Allen and Paul Kivel

Batterers need to be penalized for their actions, but the future safety of women and children depends on stopping the violence before it starts. With prevention in mind, Robert Allen and Paul Kivel discuss the work they do with boys and men in the Oakland Men's Project (OMP). Formed in 1979, this California-based group is a nonprofit, multiracial organization of men and women, devoted to community education and eradicating male violence, racism, and homophobia. The group has worked with thousand of boys and men. Its workshops are designed to encourage participants to examine gender roles, violence and discrimination, and alternatives to violence.

Why do men batter women? We have to discard the essay answers. Portraying batterers as ogres only serves to separate "them" from "us". But men who batter and men who don't are not all that different. Male violence is normal in our society and vast numbers of men participate. Men batter because we have been trained to; because there

(continued)

are few social sanctions against it; because we live in a society where the exploitation of people with less social and personal power is acceptable. In a patriarchal society boys are taught to accept violence as a manly response to real or imagined threats, but they get little training in negotiating intimate relationships. And all too many men believe that they have the right to control or expect certain behavior from "their" women and children; many view difficulties in family relationships as threat to their manhood, and they respond with violence.

Young people's definitions of femininity and masculinity often reflect rigid expectations of what they must live up to in order to be a "real" woman or a "real" man. Time and again we hear boys say that they are supposed to be tough, aggressive, in control, that they are not to express any feelings except anger, not to cry, and never to ask for help. And many boys except girls to acquiesce to men and be dependent on them.

How do boys get these ideas about male identity and manhood? Often from parents, but our whole society contributes to the process. As many as one of every six boys is sexually assaulted, and many, many more are hit, yelled at, teased, and goaded into fighting to prove they're tough. At the project, we believe that many boys become convinced that they will be violated until they learn to use force to protect themselves. Then they move to take their pain and anger out on others the way older males have done to them.

In our work we often use role play as a way of getting at some of these issues. One particularly effective exercise involves a ten-year-old and his father: the father arrives home from work and demands that the boy turn off the TV, then berates him for the messiness of his room. The boy tries to explain; the father tells him to shut up, to stop making excuses. Fueling the father's anger is the fact that he's disappointed by the boy's school report card. The father shoves the report card in his son's face and demands to know why he has gotten a "D" in math. The boy says he did his best. The father tells him that he is stupid. The boy protests and begins to stand up. The father shoves him down, saying, "Don't you dare get up in my face!" The boy is visibly upset, and begins to cry. The father explodes: "Now what? You little mama's boy! You sissy! You make me sick. When are you going to grow up and start acting like a man?"

When we do this exercise in schools, it gets the boys' undivided attention because most have experienced being humiliated by an older male. Indeed, the power of this exercise is that it is so familiar. When asked what they learned from such encounters, the boys often say things like: A man is tough. A man is in control. A man doesn't cry. A man doesn't take crap.

We write the boy's comments on a blackboard, draw a box around them, and label it the "Act Like a Man" box. We talk about how males in this culture are socialized to stay in the box. Eventually we ask: What happens if you step out of it, if you stop acting tough enough or man enough? Invariably we hear that you get called names like "fag," "queer," "mama's boy," "punk," "girl." Asked why, the boys say it's a challenge, that they're expected to fight to prove themselves. Homophobia, and fear of being identified with women are powerful messages boys get from an early age, and they are expected to fight to prove that they're tough and not gay—that they're in the box.

Using exercises, like the father/son interchange, helps us examine how the male sex role often sets men up to dominating, controlling, and abusive. We ask: How safe it is to stay in the "Act Like a Man's box? Usually, most admit that it isn't safe, because boys and men continually challenge each other to prove that they're in the box. When a boy or man is challenged, he can prove he's a man either by fighting the challenger or by finding someone "weaker"—a female or a more vulnerable male—to dominate. Hurting girls relieves any anxiety that we may not be tough enough and establishes our heterosexual credentials. It's both a sign of our interest (we're playing attention to them) and a symbol of our difference (we're in control).

Because we are taught that women are primarily sexual objects, this behaviour seems perfectly natural. And many men come to believe that a woman is just another material possession. We initiate dates, pay for our time together, protect them on the streets, and often marry them. We are trained to think that in

(continued)

return, girls should show their appreciation by taking care of us emotionally, putting their own concerns and interest aside, and putting out sexually.

This unspoken contract is one that many heterosexual men operate by, and it often leads to the assumption that women are our dumping ground. If we've had a hard day at work, were embarrassed or humiliated by a boss—challenged in the box—the contract leads us to believe that we can take those feelings out on "our" women, and thus regain our power. If we end up hitting her, then we have to blame her in order to deny our aggression and keep our self-esteem intact. So we say things like: She asked for it. She pushed my buttons. She deserved it.

Invariably it comes as a surprise to us that women don't meekly accept our violence. So we respond by minimizing and justifying our actions: I didn't mean it, You're too sensitive. That's the way guys are. It was just the heat of the moment.

In order to get men to take responsibility for their own actions, we have to get them to talk about what they did, and what they said, and what they felt. Making the connection between how they have been trained and hurt and how they have learned to pass that pain on by hurting women or young people is essential.

To get men to reflect on their experiences and behaviors, we use exercises we call "stand ups." We ask everyone to be silent, and then slowly pose a series of questions or statements, and ask men to stand every time one applies to them. For example, we may ask, Have you ever:

- worried you were not tough enough?
- been called a wimp, queer, or fag?
- been told to "act like a man"?
- been hit by an older man?
- been forced to fight?
- been physically injured and hid the pain?
- been sexually abused, or touched in a way you didn't like?
- used alcohol or drugs to hide your pain?
- felt like blowing yourself away?

Later in the workshop we ask, Have you ever:

- interrupted a woman by talking louder?
- made a comment in public about a woman's body?
- discussed a woman's body with another man?
- been told by a woman that she wanted more affection and less sex from you?
- used your voice or body to intimidate a woman?
- hit, slapped, shoved, or pushed a woman?
- had sex with a woman when you knew she didn't want to?

Each participant is asked to look around and see other men standing, which helps break down their sense of isolation and feeling of shame. Since we are not a therapy group, no one is questioned or confronted about his own experiences. All of our work involves challenging the notion that males are naturally abusive and that females are natural target of male abuse. We give boys and men a way of analyzing social roles by drawing insights from their own experiences, and help them to recognize that social interactions involve making choices, that we can break free or old roles by supporting each other in choosing alternatives to violence.

An important part of our work is getting men and boys to looks at how power, inequality, and the ability to do violence to others are structured into social relationships in this country. We discuss how these inequalities are maintained and how violence against one targeted group encourages violence against others. This is not to excuse men's behavior, it is done in the belief that in order to make better choices, men must understand the framework of power and violence that constantly pressures us to be in control and on top.

There are growing numbers of men who are critical of sexism. All too often they are isolated and fearful of raising their concerns with other men because they worry about being targeted for violence. We try to help them break through the fear and reach out to other men. But we also work to get men to understand how they are damaged by sexism and how male violence against women keeps us from the collective action needed to confront racial, gender-based, and economic injustice.

For us personally this is powerful, life-changing work. We were each drawn to it because of troubling issues in our own lives: issues around our relation-

(continued)

ships with our fathers (one emotionally abusive, the other emotionally distant); relationships with women partners where we found ourselves repeating controlling, sexist behaviors that make us feel guilty, ashamed, defensive; and the fear that we might do to our children what had been done to us as children. Through the work we have discovered that many men share these concerns, but they are hesitant to talk about this with other men. Sadly, we have all learned that "real" men don't admit vulnerability. But despite their initial hesitation, many men are eager to talk about their lives, and to change the controlling and abusive behavior they've been trained to pass on. Doing this work is healing for us and for those we work with.

Men are responsible for battery and for stopping male violence. If we are to counter the myth that men's abuse of women is natural, men must challenge each other to stop the violence. We must defy notions of manhood that lead us to injure or kill those we say we love. We must confront male friends when we see them heading down the destructive path of domestic violence and urge them to get help. While it is critical that domestic violence cases be taken more seriously by the police and criminal justice system, it is equally important to examine and to change underlying social attitudes and practices that promote and excuse domestic violence. This is truly men's work.

READING 35

Supremacy Crimes

↪ Gloria Steinem

From domestic violence to sexual harassment, naming a crime has been the first step toward solving it. But another crime is hiding in plain sight. You've seen the ocean of television coverage, you've read the headlines: "How to Spot a Troubled Kid," "Twisted Teens," "When Teens Fall Apart."

After the slaughter in Colorado that inspired those phrases, dozens of copycat threats were reported in the same generalized way: "Junior high students charged with conspiracy to kill students and teachers" (in Texas); "Five honor students overheard planning a June graduation bombing" (in New York); "More than 100 minor threats reported statewide" (in Pennsylvania). In response, the White House held an emergency strategy session titled "Children, Violence, and Responsibility." Nonetheless, another attack was soon reported: "Youth With 2 Guns Shoots 6 at Georgia School."

I don't know about you, but I've been talking back to the television set, waiting for someone to tell us the obvious: it's not "youth," "our children," or "our teens." It's our sons—and "our" can usually be read as "white," "middle class," and "heterosexual." We know that hate crimes, violent and otherwise, are overwhelmingly committed by white men who are apparently straight. The same is true for an even higher percentage of impersonal, resentment-driven, mass killings like those in Colorado; the sort committed for no economic or rational gain except the need to say, "I'm superior because I can kill." Think of Charles Starkweather, who reported feeling powerful and serene after murdering ten women and men in the 1950s; or the shooter who climbed the University of Texas Tower in 1966, raining down death to gain celebrity. Think of the engineering student at the University of Montreal who resented females' ability to study that subject, and so shot to death fourteen women students in 1989, while saying, "I'm against feminism." Think of nearly all those who have killed impersonally in the workplace, the post office, McDonald's.

White males—usually intelligent, middle class, and heterosexual, or trying desperately to appear so—also account for virtually all the serial, sexually motivated, sadistic killings, those characterized by stalking, imprisoning, torturing, and "owning" victims in death. Think of Edmund Kemper, who began by killing animals, then murdered his grandparents, yet was released to sexually torture and dismember college students and other young women until he himself decided he "didn't want to kill *all* the coeds in the world." Or David Berkowitz, the Son of Sam, who murdered some women in order to feel in control of all women. Or consider Ted Bundy, the charming, snobbish young would-be lawyer who tortured and murdered as many as forty women, usually beautiful students who were symbols of the economic class he longed to join. As for John Wayne Gacy, he was obsessed with maintaining the public mask of masculinity, and so hid his homosexuality by killing and burying men and boys with whom he had had sex.

These "senseless" killings begin to seem less mysterious when you consider that they were committed disproportionately by white, nonpoor males, the group most likely to become hooked on the drug of superiority. It's a drug pushed by a male-dominant culture that presents dominance as a natural right; a racist hierarchy that falsely elevates whiteness; a materialist society that equates superiority with possessions, and a homophobic one that empowers only one form of sexuality.

As Elliott Leyton reports in *Hunting Humans: The Rise of the Modern Multiple Murderer*, these killers see their behavior as "an appropriate—even 'manly'— response to the frustrations and disappointments that are a normal part of life." In other words, it's not their life experiences that are the problem, it's the impossible expectation of dominance to which they've become addicted.

This is not about blame. This is about causation. If anything, ending the massive cultural cover-up of supremacy crimes should make heroes out of boys and men who reject violence, especially those who reject the notion of superiority altogether. Even if one believes in a biogenetic component of male aggression, the very existence of gentle men proves that socialization can override it.

Nor is this about attributing such crimes to a single cause. Addiction to the drug of supremacy is not their only root, just the deepest and most ignored one. Additional reasons why this country has such a high rate of violence include the plentiful guns that make killing seem as unreal as a video game; male violence in the media that desensitizes viewers in much the same way that combat killers are desensitized in training; affluence that allows maximum access to violence-as-entertainment; a national history of genocide and slavery; the romanticizing of frontier violence and organized crime; not to mention extremes of wealth and poverty and the illusion that both are deserved.

But it is truly remarkable, given the relative reasons for anger at injustice in this country, that white, nonpoor men have a near-monopoly on multiple killings of strangers, whether serial and sadistic or mass and random. How can we ignore this obvious fact? Others may kill to improve their own condition—in self-defense, or for money or drugs; to eliminate enemies; to declare turf in drive-by shootings; even for a jacket or a pair of sneakers—but white males addicted to supremacy kill even when it worsens their condition or ends in suicide.

Men of color and females are capable of serial and mass killing, and commit just enough to prove it. Think of Colin Ferguson, the crazed black man on the Long Island Railroad, or Wayne Williams, the young black man in Atlanta who kidnapped and killed black boys, apparently to conceal his homosexuality. Think of Aileen Carol Wuornos, the white prostitute in Florida who killed abusive johns "in self-defense," or Waneta Hoyt, the upstate New York woman who strangled her five infant children between 1965 and 1971, disguising their cause of death as sudden infant death syndrome. Such crimes are rare enough to leave a haunting refrain of disbelief, as evoked in Pat Parker's poem "jonestown": "Black folks do not/ Black folks do not/Black folks do not commit suicide." And yet they did.

Nonetheless, the proportion of serial killings that are not committed by white males is about the same as the proportion of anorexics who are not female. Yet we discuss the gender, race, and class components of anorexia, but not the role of the same factors in producing epidemics among the powerful.

The reasons are buried deep in the culture, so invisible that only by reversing our assumptions can we reveal them.

Suppose, for instance, that young black males—or any other men of color—had carried out the slaughter in Colorado. Would the media reports be so willing to describe the murderers as "our children"? Would there be so little discussion about the boys' race?

Would experts be calling the motive a mystery, or condemning the high school cliques for making those young men feel like "outsiders"? Would there be the same empathy for parents who gave the murderers luxurious homes, expensive cars, even rescued them from brushes with the law? Would there be as much attention to generalized causes, such as the dangers of violent video games and recipes for bombs on the Internet?

As for the victims, if racial identities had been reversed, would racism remain so little discussed? In fact, the killers themselves said they were targeting blacks and athletes. They used a racial epithet, shot a black male student in the head, and then laughed over the fact that they could see his brain. What if *that* had been reversed?

What if these two young murderers, who were called "fags" by some of the jocks at Columbine High School, actually had been gay? Would they have got the same sympathy for being gay-baited? What if they had been lovers? Would we hear as little about their sexuality as we now do, even though only their own homophobia could have given the word "fag" such power to humiliate them?

Take one more leap of the imagination: suppose these killings had been planned and executed by young women—of any race, sexuality, or class. Would the media still be so uninterested in the role played by gender-conditioning? Would journalists assume that female murderers had suffered from being shut out of access to power in high school, so much so that they were pushed beyond their limits? What if dozens, even hundreds of young women around the country

had made imitative threats—as young men have done—expressing admiration for a well-planned massacre and promising to do the same? Would we be discussing their youth more than their gender, as is the case so far with these male killers?

I think we begin to see that our national self-examination is ignoring something fundamental, precisely because it's like the air we breathe: the white male factor, the middle-class and heterosexual one, and the promise of superiority it carries. Yet this denial is self-defeating—to say the least. We will never reduce the number of violent Americans, from bullies to killers, without challenging the assumptions on which masculinity is based: that males are superior to females, that they must find a place in a male hierarchy, and that the ability to dominate *someone* is so important that even a mere insult can justify lethal revenge. There are plenty of studies to support this view. As Dr. James Gilligan concluded in *Violence: Reflections on a National Epidemic,* "If humanity is to evolve beyond the propensity toward violence . . . then it can only do so by recognizing the extent to which the patriarchal code of honor and shame generates and obligates male violence."

I think the way out can only be found through a deeper reversal: just as we as a society have begun to raise our daughters more like our sons—more like whole people—we must begin to raise our sons more like our daughters—that is, to value empathy as well as hierarchy; to measure success by other people's welfare as well as their own.

But first, we have to admit and name the truth about supremacy crimes.

A LETTER FROM CLAUDIA BRENNER

January 1991

Dear Friend,

On May 13, 1988, my lover, Rebecca, was murdered. I survived, with five bullet wounds.

At the trial of the attacker, it was proven that we were attacked because of who we were—two lesbians, two women living our lives and our love for each other.

There is no way to lessen the horror of that moment. . . .

On May 13, Rebecca and I were hiking on the Appalachian trail in Adams County, Pennsylvania. At our campsite that morning, Rebecca was stopped by a man who asked her for a cigarette. He hadn't been there when we arrived at the site the previous evening, and must have arrived very late at night.

(continued)

Later that day, we broke camp and continued our hike. As we checked a map at a fork in the trail, we were surprised to see the same man walking behind us. He had a rifle.

He asked us if we were lost. We said no, and turned left, onto a side trail. He continued along the main trail. The encounter made both Rebecca and me uneasy. We kept looking behind to see if the man was following us, but we never saw him again.

Late that afternoon, Rebecca and I stopped and made camp near a stream. It was a secluded spot, some distance from the trail. We ate, made love, and rested.

Suddenly, there were gunshots. The shots were *so* sudden, *so* loud, *so* violent, *so* world-changing that at first I didn't even realize that they were gunshots and that we were the targets—except there was so much blood.

Because I was between the attacker and Rebecca, I was hit first. I was shot in the upper arm, twice in the neck, in the head and face. Rebecca told me to run behind a nearby tree. As she followed me, Rebecca was shot in the head and back.

The shooting finally stopped. We were both behind a large tree. In my frantic shock and fear, I didn't understand how badly hurt we were. But Rebecca had the presence of mind to tell me what to do. She told me to stop the bleeding. I believe she saved my life.

My only thought was to get us out of there and get help. I brought Rebecca her sneakers, but she couldn't see them. She was losing her vision. I tried to lift her, but she kept slumping to the ground.

Someplace deep within me, I began to understand how badly hurt Rebecca was. If the situation could get worse, it came with the realization that I had to go for help alone. I covered Rebecca, gave her all the first aid I could think of, and started out for help.

Before I left, Rebecca was unconscious. We never had a chance to say goodbye.

Soaked in blood, I walked on the rugged trail about two miles to a forest road. I was completely terrified that whoever had attacked us might be following and attack again. I walked on the road another two miles before I finally saw a car. I stopped the car, and the driver rushed me to the police in nearby Shippensburg.

All I could think about was Rebecca. The State Police immediately began a search for her.

That evening, I was airlifted to the Hershey Medical Center trauma unit. I had emergency surgery that night. The next day I learned that the police had found Rebecca's body. She died from the bullet wound that hit her back and exploded in her liver.

But my ordeal did not end with the horror of Rebecca's death.

The State Police caught the man who murdered Rebecca—the same man who had followed us on the trail—Stephen Roy Carr. We now know that Stephen Roy Carr stalked us, hid eighty-five feet away in the woods while we made camp, shot to kill, and left us for dead.

During the legal proceedings that followed, it became clear that Carr had attacked us because we were lesbians. Carr's lawyer even implied—during the trial and the appeal—that Rebecca and I had provoked the attack.

The implication that Rebecca and I had "teased" Carr with our sexuality, and that we were responsible for this man stalking us, spying on us, and shooting to kill us was not only outrageous, it was disgusting.

Fortunately, the trial judge refused to allow this line of argument. On October 27, 1988, Stephen Roy Carr was convicted of first-degree murder and later sentenced to life in prison without parole.

I survived the attack, but in the months that followed I was consumed with grief and fear. My world centered on the knowledge that Rebecca was dead and that somehow I was alive.

I had always known that the world was not a safe place for lesbians. But somehow, I believed that nothing this terrible would ever happen to me.

I believed that all I needed to do was not to look like a stereotypical lesbian and be discreet about my expressions of affection to other women. That security was shattered by the bullets. . . .

Sincerely,

Claudia Brenner

Mapping the Margins: Intersectionality, Identity Politics, and Violence Against Women of Color

◈ Kimberlé Crenshaw

. . . My objective [is to explore] the race and gender dimensions of violence against women of color. . . . I consider how the experiences of women of color are frequently the product of intersecting patterns of racism and sexism. . . .

[Based on] a brief field study of battered women's shelters located in minority communities in Los Angeles,[1] [I found that in most cases], the physical assault that leads women to these shelters is merely the most immediate manifestation of the subordination they experience. Many women who seek protection are unemployed or under-employed, and a good number of them are poor. Shelters serving these women cannot afford to address only the violence inflicted by the batterer; they must also confront the other multilayered and routinized forms of domination that often converge in these women's lives, hindering their ability to create alternatives to the abusive relationships that brought them to shelters in the first place. Many women of color, for example, are burdened by poverty, child care responsibilities, and the lack of job skills.[2] These burdens, largely the consequence of gender and class oppression, are then compounded by the racially discriminatory employment and housing practices women of color often face, as well as by the disproportionately high unemployment among people of color that makes battered women of color less able to depend on the support of friends and relatives for temporary shelter.[3]

Where systems of race, gender, and class domination converge, as they do in the experiences of battered women of color, intervention strategies based solely on the experiences of women who do not share the same class or race backgrounds will be of limited help to women who because of race and class face different obstacles.[4] Such was the case in 1990 when Congress amended the marriage fraud provisions of the Immigration and Nationality Act to protect immigrant women who were battered or exposed to extreme cruelty by the United States citizens or permanent residents these women immigrated to the United States to marry. Under the marriage fraud provisions of the Act, a person who immigrated to the United States to marry a United States citizen or permanent resident had to remain "properly" married for two years before even applying for permanent resident status,[5] at which time applications for the immigrant's permanent status were required of both spouses. Predictably, under these circumstances, many immigrant women were reluctant to leave even the most abusive of partners for fear of being deported.[6] When faced with the choice between protection from their batterers and protection against deportation, many immigrant women chose the latter. Reports of the tragic consequences of this double subordination put pressure on Congress to include in the Immigration Act of 1990 a provision amending the marriage fraud rules to allow for an explicit waiver for hardship caused by domestic violence.[7] Yet many immigrant women, particularly immigrant women of color, have remained vulnerable to battering because they are unable to meet the conditions established for a waiver. The evidence required to support a waiver "can include but is not limited to, reports and affidavits from police, medical personnel, psychologists, school officials, and social service agencies.[8] For many immigrant women, limited access to these resources can make it difficult for them to obtain the evidence needed for a waiver. And cultural barriers often further discourage immigrant women from reporting or escaping battering situations. Tina Shum, a family counselor at a social service agency, points out that "[t]his law sounds so easy to apply, but there are cultural complications in the Asian community that make even these requirements difficult. . . . Just to find the opportunity and courage to call us is an accomplishment for many."[9] The typical immigrant spouse, she suggests, may live "[i]n an extended family where several generations live together, there may be no privacy on the telephone, no opportunity to leave the house and no understanding of public phones.[10] As a consequence, many immigrant women are wholly dependent on their husbands as their link to the world outside their homes.

Immigrant women are also vulnerable to spousal violence because so many of them depend on their husbands for information regarding their legal status.[11] Many women who are now permanent residents continue to suffer abuse under threats of deportation by their husbands. Even if the threats are unfounded, women who have no independent access to information will still be intimidated by such threats. And even though the domestic violence waiver focuses on immigrant women whose husbands are United States citizens or permanent residents, there are countless women married to undocumented workers (or who are themselves undocumented) who suffer in silence for fear that the security of their entire families will be jeopardized should they seek help or otherwise call attention to themselves.

Language barriers present another structural problem that often limits opportunities of non-English-speaking women to take advantage of existing support services. Such barriers not only limit access to information about shelters, but also limit access to the security shelters provide. Some shelters turn non-English-speaking women away for lack of bilingual personnel and resources.[12]

These examples illustrate how patterns of subordination intersect in women's experience of domestic violence. . . .

A. THE POLITICIZATION OF DOMESTIC VIOLENCE

[T]he political interests of women of color are obscured and sometimes jeopardized by political strategies that ignore or suppress intersectional issues, [This] is illustrated by my [research]. I attempted to review Los Angeles Police Department statistics reflecting the rate of domestic violence interventions by precinct because such statistics can provide a rough picture of arrests by racial group, given the degree of racial segregation in Los Angeles.[13] L.A.P.D., however, would not release the statistics. A representative explained that one reason the statistics were not released was that domestic violence activists both within and outside the Department

feared that statistics reflecting the extent of domestic violence in minority communities might be selectively interpreted and publicized so as to undermine long-term efforts to force the Department to address domestic violence as a serious problem. I was told that activists were worried that the statistics might permit opponents to dismiss domestic violence as a minority problem and, therefore, not deserving of aggressive action.

The informant also claimed that representatives from various minority communities opposed the release of the statistics. They were concerned, apparently, that the data would unfairly represent Black and Brown communities as unusually violent, potentially reinforcing stereotypes that might be used in attempts to justify oppressive police tactics and other discriminatory practices. These misgivings are based on the familiar and not unfounded premise that certain minority groups—especially Black men—have already been stereotyped as uncontrollably violent. Some worry that attempts to make domestic violence an object of political action may only serve to confirm such stereotypes and undermine efforts to combat negative beliefs about the Black community.

This account sharply illustrates how women of color can be erased by the strategic silences of antiracism and feminism. The political priorities of both were defined in ways that suppressed information that could have facilitated attempts to confront the problem of domestic violence in communities of color.

I. Domestic Violence and Antiracist Politics

Within communities of color, efforts to stem the politicization of domestic violence are often grounded in attempts to maintain the integrity of the community. The articulation of this perspective takes different forms. Some critics allege that feminism has no place within communities of color, that the issues are internally divisive, and that they represent the migration of white women's concerns into a context in which they are not only irrelevant but also harmful. At its most extreme, this rhetoric denies that gender violence is a problem in the community and characterizes any effort to politicize gender subordination as itself a community problem. This is the position taken by Shahrazad Ali in her controversial book, *The Blackman's Guide to Understanding the Blackwoman*.[14] In this stridently antifeminist tract, Ali draws a positive correlation between domestic violence and the liberation of

African Americans. Ali blames the deteriorating conditions within the Black community on the insubordination of Black women and on the failure of Black men to control them.[15] Ali goes so far as to advise Black men to physically chastise Black women when they are "disrespectful".[16] While she cautions that Black men must use moderation in disciplining "their" women, she argues that Black men must sometimes resort to physical force to reestablish the authority over Black women that racism has disrupted.[17]

Ali's premise is that patriarchy is beneficial for the Black community, and that it must be strengthened through coercive means if necessary. Yet the violence that accompanies this will to control is devastating, not only for the Black women who are victimized, but also for the entire Black community. The recourse to violence to resolve conflicts establishes a dangerous pattern for children raised in such environments and contributes to many other pressing problems. It has been estimated that nearly forty percent of all homeless women and children have fled violence in the home,[18] and an estimated sixty-three percent of young men between the ages of eleven and twenty who are imprisoned for homicide have killed their mothers' batterers.[19] And yet, while gang violence, homicide, and other forms of Black-on-Black crime have increasingly been discussed within African-American politics, patriarchal ideas about gender and power preclude the recognition of domestic violence as yet another compelling incidence of Black-on-Black crime.

Efforts such as Ali's to justify violence against women in the name of Black liberation are indeed extreme. The more common problem is that the political or cultural interests of the community are interpreted in a way that precludes full public recognition of the problem of domestic violence. While it would be misleading to suggest that white Americans have come to terms with the degree of violence in their own homes, it is nonetheless the case that race adds yet another dimension to why the problem of domestic violence is suppressed within nonwhite communities. People of color often must weigh their interests in avoiding issues that might reinforce distorted public perceptions against the need to acknowledge and address intracommunity problems. Yet the cost of suppression is seldom recognized in part because the failure to discuss the issue shapes perceptions of how serious the problem is in the first place.

The controversy over Alice Walker's novel *The Color Purple* can be understood as an intracommunity debate about the political costs of exposing gender violence within the Black community.[20] Some critics chastised Walker for portraying Black men as violent brutes.[21] One critic lambasted Walker's portrayal of Celie, the emotionally and physically abused protagonist who finally triumphs in the end. Walker, the critic contended, had created in Celie a Black woman whom she couldn't imagine existing in any Black community she knew or could conceive of.[22]

The claim that Celie was somehow an unauthentic character might be read as a consequence of silencing discussion of intracommunity violence. Celie may be unlike any Black woman we know because the real terror experienced daily by minority women is routinely concealed in a misguided (though perhaps understandable) attempt to forestall racial stereotyping. Of course, it is true that representations of Black violence—whether statistical or fictional—are often written into a larger script that consistently portrays Black and other minority communities as pathologically violent. The problem, however, is not so much the portrayal of violence itself as it is the absence of other narratives and images portraying a fuller range of Black experience. Suppression of some of these issues in the name of antiracism imposes real costs. Where information about violence in minority communities is not available, domestic violence is unlikely to be addressed as a serious issue.

The political imperatives of a narrowly focused antiracist strategy support other practices that isolate women of color. For example, activists who have attempted to provide support services to Asian- and African-American women report intense resistance from those communities.[23] At other times, cultural and social factors contribute to suppression. Nilda Rimonte, director of Everywoman's Shelter in Los Angeles, points out that in the Asian community, saving the honor of the family from shame is a priority.[24] Unfortunately, this priority tends to be interpreted as obliging women not to scream rather than obliging men not to hit.

Race and culture contribute to the suppression of domestic violence in other ways as well. Women of color are often reluctant to call the police, a hesitancy likely due to a general unwillingness among people of color to subject their private lives to the scrutiny and control of a police force that is frequently hostile. There is also a more generalized community ethic against public intervention, the product of a desire to create a private world free from the diverse assaults on the public lives of racially subordinated people. The home is not simply a man's castle in the patriarchal sense, but may also function as a safe haven from the indignities of life in a racist society. However, but for this "safe haven" in many cases, women of color victimized by violence might otherwise seek help.

There is also a general tendency within antiracist discourse to regard the problem of violence against women of color as just another manifestation of racism. In this sense, the relevance of gender domination within the community is reconfigured as a consequence of discrimination against men. Of course, it is probably true that racism contributes to the cycle of violence, given the stress that men of color experience in dominant society. It is therefore more than reasonable to explore the links between racism and domestic violence. But the chain of violence is more complex and extends beyond this single link. Racism is linked to patriarchy to the extent that racism denies men of color the power and privilege that dominant men enjoy. When violence is understood as an acting-out of being denied male power in other spheres, it seems counterproductive to embrace constructs that implicitly link the solution to domestic violence to the acquisition of greater male power. The more promising political imperative is to challenge the legitimacy of such power expectations by exposing their dysfunctional and debilitating effect on families and communities of color. Moreover, while understanding links between racism and domestic violence is an important component of any effective intervention strategy, it is also clear that women of color need not await the ultimate triumph over racism before they can expect to live violence-free lives.

2. Race and the Domestic Violence Lobby

Not only do race-based priorities function to obscure the problem of violence suffered by women of color; feminist concerns often suppress minority experiences as well. Strategies for increasing awareness of domestic violence within the white community tend to begin by citing the commonly shared assumption that battering is a minority problem. The strategy then focuses on demolishing this strawman, stressing that spousal abuse also occurs in the white community. Countless first-person stories begin with a statement like, "I was not supposed to be a battered wife." That battering occurs in families of all races and all classes seems to be an ever-present theme of

anti-abuse campaigns. First-person anecdotes and studies, for example, consistently assert that battering cuts across racial, ethnic, economic, educational, and religious lines.[25] Such disclaimers seem relevant only in the presence of an initial, widely held belief that domestic violence occurs primarily in minority or poor families. Indeed some authorities explicitly renounce the "stereotypical myths" about battered women.[26] A few commentators have even transformed the message that battering is not exclusively a problem of the poor or minority communities into a claim that it equally affects all races and classes.[27] Yet these comments seem less concerned with exploring domestic abuse within "stereotyped" communities than with removing the stereotype as an obstacle to exposing battering within white middle- and upper-class communities.

Efforts to politicize the issue of violence against women challenge beliefs that violence occurs only in homes of "others." While it is unlikely that advocates and others who adopt this rhetorical strategy intend to exclude or ignore the needs of poor and colored women, the underlying premise of this seemingly universalistic appeal is to keep the sensibilities of dominant social groups focused on the experiences of those groups. Indeed, as subtly suggested by the opening comments of Senator David Boren (D-Okla.) in support of the Violence Against Women Act of 1991, the displacement of the "other" as the presumed victim of domestic violence works primarily as a political appeal to rally white elites. Boren said:

> Violent crimes against women are not limited to the streets of the inner cities, but also occur in homes in the urban and rural areas across the country.
>
> Violence against women affects not only those who are actually beaten and brutalized, but indirectly affects all women. Today, our wives, mothers, daughters, sisters, and colleagues are held captive by fear generated from these violent crimes—held captive not for what they do or who they are, but solely because of gender.[28]

Rather than focusing on and illuminating how violence is disregarded when the home is "othered," the strategy implicit in Senator Boren's remarks functions instead to politicize the problem only in the dominant community. This strategy permits white women victims to come into focus, but does little to disrupt the patterns of neglect that permitted the problem to continue as long as it was imagined to be a minority problem. The experience of violence of minority women is ignored, except to the extent it gains white support for domestic violence programs in the white community.

Senator Boren and his colleagues no doubt believe that they have provided legislation and resources that will address the problems of all women victimized by domestic violence. Yet despite their universalizing rhetoric of "all" women, they were able to empathize with female victims of domestic violence only by looking past the plight of "other" women and by recognizing the familiar faces of their own. The strength of the appeal to "protect our women" must be its race and class specificity. After all, it has always been someone's wife, mother, sister, or daughter that has been abused, even when the violence was stereotypically Black or Brown, and poor. The point here is not that the Violence Against Women Act is particularistic on its own terms, but that unless the Senators and other policymakers ask why violence remained insignificant as long as it was understood as a minority problem, it is unlikely that women of color will share equally in the distribution of resources and concern. It is even more unlikely, however, that those in power will be forced to confront this issue. As long as attempts to politicize domestic violence focus on convincing whites that this is not a "minority" problem but their problem, any authentic and sensitive attention to the experiences of Black and other minority women probably will continue to be regarded as jeopardizing the movement.

While Senator Boren's statement reflects a self-consciously political presentation of domestic violence, an episode of the CBS news program *48 Hours*[29] shows how similar patterns of "othering" nonwhite women are apparent in journalistic accounts of domestic violence as well. The program presented seven women who were victims of abuse. Six were interviewed at some length along with their family members, friends, supporters, and even detractors. The viewer got to know something about each of these women. These victims were humanized. Yet the seventh woman, the only nonwhite one, never came into focus. She was literally unrecognizable throughout the segment, first introduced by photographs showing her face badly beaten and later shown with her face electronically altered in the videotape of a hearing at which she was forced to testify. Other images associated with this woman included shots of a bloodstained room and blood-soaked pillows. Her boyfriend was pictured handcuffed while the camera zoomed in for a close-up of his bloodied sneakers. Of all the presentations in the episode, hers was the most graphic and impersonal. The overall point of the segment "featuring" this woman was that battering might not escalate into homicide if battered women would only cooperate with prosecutors. In focusing on its own agenda and failing to explore why this woman refused to cooperate, the program diminished this woman, communicating, however subtly, that she was responsible for her own victimization.

Unlike the other women, all of whom, again, were white, this Black woman had no name, no family, no context. The viewer sees her only as victimized and uncooperative. She cries when shown pictures. She pleads not to be forced to view the bloodstained room and her disfigured face. The program does not help the viewer to understand her predicament. The possible reasons she did not want to testify—fear, love, or possibly both—are never suggested. Most unfortunately, she, unlike the other six, is given no epilogue. While the fates of the other women are revealed at the end of the episode, we discover nothing about the Black woman. She, like the "others" she represents, is simply left to herself and soon forgotten.

I offer this description to suggest that "other" women are silenced as much by being relegated to the margin of experience as by total exclusion. Tokenistic, objectifying, voyeuristic inclusion is at least as disempowering as complete exclusion. The effort to politicize violence against women will do little to address Black and other minority women if their images are retained simply to magnify the problem rather than to humanize their experiences. Similarly, the antiracist agenda will not be advanced significantly by forcibly suppressing the reality of battering in minority communities. As the *48 Hours* episode makes clear, the images and stereotypes we fear are readily available and are frequently deployed in ways that do not generate sensitive understanding of the nature of domestic violence in minority communities.

3. Race and Domestic Violence Support Services

Women working in the field of domestic violence have sometimes reproduced the subordination and marginalization of women of color by adopting policies, priorities, or strategies of empowerment that either elide or wholly disregard the particular intersectional needs of women of color. While gender, race, and class intersect to create the particular context in which women of color experience violence, certain choices made by "allies" can reproduce intersectional subordination within the very resistance strategies designed to respond to the problem.

This problem is starkly illustrated by the inaccessibility of domestic violence support services to many non-English-speaking women. In a letter written to the deputy commissioner of the New York State Department of Social Services, Diana Campos, Director of Human Services for Programas de Ocupaciones y Desarrollo Economico Real, Inc. (PODER), detailed the case of a Latina in crisis who was repeatedly denied accommodation at a shelter because she could not prove that she was English-proficient. The woman had fled her home with her teenaged son, believing her husband's threats to kill them both. She called the domestic violence hotline administered by PODER seeking shelter for herself and her son. Because most shelters would not accommodate the woman with her son, they were forced to live on the streets for two days. The hotline counselor was finally able to find an agency that would take both the mother and the son, but when the counselor told the intake coordinator at the shelter that the woman spoke limited English, the coordinator told her that they could not take anyone who was not English-proficient. When the women in crisis called back and was told of the shelter's "rule," she replied that she could understand English if spoken to her slowly. As Campos explains, Mildred, the hotline counselor, told Wendy, the intake coordinator

> that the woman said that she could communicate a little in English. Wendy told Mildred that they could not provide services to this woman because they have house rules that the woman must agree to follow. Mildred asked her, "What if the woman agrees to follow your rules? Will you still not take her?" Wendy responded that all of the women at the shelter are required to attend [a] support group and they would not be able to have her in the group if she could not communicate. Mildred mentioned the severity of this woman's case. She told Wendy that the woman had been wandering the streets at night while her husband is home, and

she had been mugged twice. She also reiterated the fact that this woman was in danger of being killed by either her husband or a mugger. Mildred expressed that the woman's safety was a priority at this point, and that once in a safe place, receiving counseling in a support group could be dealt with.[30]

The intake coordinator restated the shelter's policy of taking only English-speaking women, and stated further that the woman would have to call the shelter herself for screening. If the woman could communicate with them in English, she might be accepted. When the woman called the PODER hotline later that day, she was in such a state of fear that the hotline counselor who had been working with her had difficulty understanding her in Spanish.[31] Campos directly intervened at this point, calling the executive director of the shelter. A counselor called back from the shelter. As Campos reports,

> Marie [the counselor] told me that they did not want to take the woman in the shelter because they felt that the woman would feel isolated. I explained that the son agreed to translate for his mother during the intake process. Furthermore, that we would assist them in locating a Spanish-speaking battered women's advocate to assist in counseling her. Marie stated that utilizing the son was not an acceptable means in communication for them, since it further victimized the victim. In addition, she stated that they had similar experiences with women who were non-English-speaking, and that the women eventually just left because they were not able to communicate with anyone. I expressed my extreme concern for her safety and reiterated that we would assist them in providing her with the necessary services until we could get her placed someplace where they had bilingual staff.[32]

After several more calls, the shelter finally agreed to take the woman. The woman called once more during the negotiation; however, after a plan was in place, the woman never called back. Said Campos, "After so many calls, we are now left to wonder if she is alive and well, and if she will ever have enough faith in our ability to help her to call us again the next time she is in crisis.[33]

Despite this woman's desperate need, she was unable to receive the protection afforded English-speaking women, due to the shelter's rigid commitment to exclusionary policies. Perhaps even more troubling than the shelter's lack of bilingual resources was its refusal to allow a friend or relative to translate for the woman. This story illustrates the absurdity of a feminist approach that would make the ability to attend a support group without a translator a more significant consideration in the distribution of resources than the risk of physical harm on the street. The point is not that the shelter's image of empowerment is empty, but rather that it was imposed without regard to the disempowering consequences for women who didn't match the kind of client the shelter's administrators imagined. And thus they failed to accomplish the basic priority of the shelter movement—to get the woman out of danger.

Here the woman in crisis was made to bear the burden of the shelter's refusal to anticipate and provide for the needs of non-English-speaking women. Said Campos "It is unfair to impose more stress on victims by placing them in the position of having to demonstrate their proficiency in English in order to receive services that are readily available to other battered women."[34] The problem is not easily dismissed as one of well-intentioned ignorance. The specific issue of monolingualism and the monistic view of women's experience that set the stage for this tragedy were not new issues in New York. Indeed, several women of color reported that they had repeatedly struggled with the New York State Coalition Against Domestic Violence over language exclusion and other practices that marginalized the interests of women of color.[35] Yet despite repeated lobbying, the Coalition did not act to incorporate the specific needs of non-white women into its central organizing vision.

Some critics have linked the Coalition's failure to address these issues to the narrow vision of coalition that animated its interaction with women of color in the first place. The very location of the Coalition's headquarters in Woodstock, New York—an area where few people of color live—seemed to guarantee that women of color would play a limited role in formulating policy. Moreover, efforts to include women of color came, it seems, as something of an afterthought. Many were invited to participate only after the Coalition was awarded a grant by the state to recruit women of color. However, as one "recruit" said, "they were not really prepared to deal with us or our issues. They thought that they could simply incorporate us into their organization without rethinking

any of their beliefs or priorities and that we would be happy."[36] Even the most formal gestures of inclusion were not to be taken for granted. On one occasion when several women of color attended a meeting to discuss a special task force on women of color, the group debated all day over including the issue on the agenda.[37]

The relationship between the white women and the women of color on the Board was a rocky one from beginning to end. Other conflicts developed over differing definitions of feminism. For example, the Board decided to hire a Latina staffperson to manage outreach programs to the Latino community, but the white members of the hiring committee rejected candidates favored by Latina committee members who did not have recognized feminist credentials. As Campos pointed out, by measuring Latinas against their own biographies, the white members of the Board failed to recognize the different circumstances under which feminist consciousness develops and manifests itself within minority communities. Many of the women who interviewed for the position were established activists and leaders within their own community, a fact in itself suggesting that these women were probably familiar with the specific gender dynamics in their communities and were accordingly better qualified to handle outreach than other candidates with more conventional feminist credentials.[38]

The Coalition ended a few months later when the women of color walked out.[39] Many of these women returned to community-based organizations, preferring to struggle over women's issues within their communities rather than struggle over race and class issues with white middle-class women. Yet as illustrated by the case of the Latina who could find no shelter, the dominance of a particular perspective and set of priorities within the shelter community continues to marginalize the needs of women of color.

The struggle over which differences matter and which do not is neither an abstract nor an insignificant debate among women. Indeed, these conflicts are about more than difference as such; they raise critical issues of power. The problem is not simply that women who dominate the antiviolence movement are different from women of color but that they frequently have power to determine, either through material or rhetorical resources, whether the intersectional differences of women of color will be incorporated at all into the basic formulation of policy. Thus, the struggle over incorporating these differences is not a petty or superficial conflict about who gets to sit at the head of the table. In the context of violence, it is sometimes a deadly serious matter of who will survive—and who will not. . . .

NOTES

1. During my research in Los Angeles, California, I visited Jenessee Battered Women's Shelter, the only shelter in the Western states primarily serving Black women, and Everywoman's Shelter, which primarily serves Asian women. I also visited Estelle Chueng at the Asian Pacific Law Foundation, and I spoke with a representative of La Casa, a shelter in the predominantly Latino community of East L.A.

2. One researcher has noted, in reference to a survey taken of battered women's shelters, that "many Caucasian women were probably excluded form the sample, since they are more likely to have available resources that enable them to avoid going to a shelter. Many shelters admit only women with few or no resources or alternatives." Mildred Daley Pagelow, *Woman-Battering: Victims and Their Experiences*, 97 (1981). On the other hand, many middle- and upper-class women are financially dependent upon their husbands and thus experience a diminution in their standard of living when they leave their husbands.

3. More specifically, African Americans suffer from high unemployment rates, low incomes, and high poverty rates. According to Dr. David Swinton, Dean of the School of Business at Jackson State University in Mississippi, African Americans "receive three-fifths as much income per person as whites and are three times as likely to have annual incomes below the federally defined poverty level of $12, 675 for a family of four." Urban League Urges Action, *N.Y. Times*, Jan 9, 1991, at A14. In fact, recent statistics indicate that racial economic inequality is "higher as we begin the 1990s than at any other time in the last 20 years." David Swinton, The Economic Status of African Americans: "Permanent" Poverty and Inequality, in *The State of Black America* 1991, 25 (1991).

The economic situation of minority women is, expectedly, worse than that of their male counterparts. Black women, who earn a median of $7,875 a year, make considerably less than Black men, who earn a median income of $12,609 a year, and white women, who earn a median income of $9,812 a year. *Id.* at 32 (Table 3). Additionally, the percentage of Black female-headed families living in poverty (46.5%) is almost twice that of white female-headed families (25.4%). *Id.* at 43 (Table 8). Latino households also earn considerably less than white households. In 1988, the median income of Latino households was $20,359 and for white households, $28,840—a difference of almost $8,000. *Hispanic Americans: A Statistical Sourcebook* 149 (1991), Analyzing by origin, in 1988, Puerto Rican households were the worst off, with 34.1% earning below $10,000 a year and a median

income for all Puerto Rican households of $15,447 per year. *Id.* at 155. 1989 statistics for Latino men and women show that women earned an average of $7,000 less than men. *Id.* at 169.

4. . . . Racial differences marked an interesting contrast between Jenessee's policies and those of other shelters situated outside the Black community. Unlike some other shelters in Los Angeles, Jenessee welcomed the assistance of men. According to the Director, the shelter's policy was premised on a belief that given African Americans' need to maintain healthy relations to pursue a common struggle against racism, anti-violence programs within the African American community cannot afford to be antagonistic to men. For a discussion of the different needs of Black women who are battered, see Beth Richie, Battered Black Women: A Challenge for the Black Community, *Black Scholar* 40 (Mar./Apr. 1985).

5. §U.S.C. §1186a (1988), . . .

6. Immigration activists have pointed out that "[t]he 1986 Immigration Reform Act and the Immigration Marriage Fraud Amendment have combined to give the spouse applying for permanent residence a powerful tool to control his partner. "Jorge Banales, Abuse Among Immigrants; As Their Numbers Grow So Does the Need for Services, *Washington Post*, Oct. 16, 1990, at E5. . . . In one egregious instance described by Beckie Masaki, executive director of the Asian Women's Shelter in San Francisco, the closer the Chinese bride came to getting her permanent residency in the United States, the more harshly her Asian-American husband beat her. Her husband, kicking her in the neck and face, warned her that she needed him, and if she did not do as he told her, he would call immigration officials. Deanna Hodgin, "Mail-Order" Brides Marry Pain to Get Green Cards, *Washington Times*, Apr. 16, 1991, at El.

7. Immigration Act of 1990, Pub. L. No. 101–649, 104 Stat. 4978. . . .

8. H.R.Rep. No. 723(1). 101st Cong., 2d Sess. 79 (1990), *reprinted in* 1990 U.S.C.C.A.N. 6710, 6759.

9. Hodgin, *supra* note 6.

10. *Id.*

11. A citizen or permanent resident spouse can exercise power over an alien spouse by threatening not to file a petition for permanent residency. If he fails to file a petition for permanent residency, the alien spouse continues to be undocumented and is considered to be in the country illegally. These constraints often restrict an alien spouse from leaving. Dean Ito Taylor tells the story of "one client who has been hospitalized—she's had him arrested for

beating her—but she keeps coming back to him because he promises he will file for her. . . . He holds that green card over her head." Hodgin, *supra* note 6. . . .

12. . . . To combat this lack of appropriate services for women of color at many shelters, special programs have been created specifically for women from particular communities. A few examples of such programs include the Victim Intervention Project in East Harlem for Latina women, Jenessee Shelter for African American women in Los Angeles, Apna Gar in Chicago for South Asian women, and, for Asian women generally, the Asian Women's Shelter in San Francisco, the New York Asian Women's Center, and the Center for the Pacific Asian Family in Los Angeles. Programs with hotlines include Sakhi for South Asian Women in New York, and Manavi in Jersey City, also for South Asian women, as well as programs for Korean women in Philadelphia and Chicago.

13. Most crime statistics are classified by sex or race but none are classified by sex and race. Because we know that most rape victims are women, the racial breakdown reveals, at best, rape rates for Black women. Yet, even given this head start, rates for other non-white women are difficult to collect. While there are some statistics for Latinas, statistics for Asian and Native American women are virtually nonexistent. Cf. G. Chezia Carraway, Violence Against Women of Color, *Stan. L. Rev.* 43 (1993); 1301.

14. Shahrazad Ali, *The Blackman's Guide to Understanding the Blackwoman* (1989). Ali's book sold quite well for an independently published title, an accomplishment no doubt due in part to her appearances on the Phil Donahue, Oprah Winfrey, and Sally Jesse Raphael television talk shows. For public and press reaction, see Dorothy Gilliam, Sick, Distorted Thinking, *Washington Post*, Oct. 11, 1990, at D3; Lena Williams, Black Woman's Book Starts a Predictable Storm, *New York Times*, Oct 2, 1990, at C11; see also Pearl Cleague, *Mad at Miles: A Black Women's Guide to Truth* (1990). The title clearly styled after Ali's, *Mad at Miles* responds not only to issues raised by Ali's book, but also to Miles Davis's admission in his autobiography, *Miles: The Autobiography* (1989), that he had physically abused, among other women, his former wife, actress Cicely Tyson.

15. Shahrazad Ali suggests that the "[Blackwoman] certainly does not believe that her disrespect for the Blackman is destructive, nor that her opposition to him has deteriorated the Black nation." S. Ali, *supra* note 14, at viii. Blaming the problems of the community on the failure of the Black woman to accept her "real definition," Ali explains that "[n]o nation can rise when the natural order of the behavior of the male and the female have been altered against their wishes by force. No species can survive if the female of the genus disturbs the balance of her nature by acting other than herself." *Id.* at 76.

16. Ali advises the Blackman to hit the Blackwoman in the mouth, "[b]ecause it is from that hole, in the lower part of her face, that all her rebellion culminates into words. Her

unbridled tongue is a main reason she cannot get along with the Blackman. She often needs a reminder." *Id.* at 169. Ali warns that "if [the Blackwoman] ignores the authority and superiority of the Blackman, there is a penalty. When she crosses this line and becomes viciously insulting, it is time for the Blackman to soundly slap her in the mouth." *Id.*

17. Ali explains that, "[r]egretfully some Blackwomen want to be physically controlled by the Blackman." *Id.* at 174. "The Blackwoman, deep inside her heart" Ali reveals, "wants to surrender but she wants to be coerced." *Id.* at 72. "[The Blackwoman] wants [the Blackman] to stand up and defend himself even if it means he has to knock her out of the way to do so. This is necessary whenever the Blackwoman steps out of the protection of womanly behavior and enters the dangerous domain of masculine challenge." *Id.* at 174.

18. [Women and Violence: Hearings Before the Senate Comm. on the Judiciary on Legislation to Reduce the Growing Problem of Violent Crime Against Women, 101st Cong., 2d Sess., pt. 2, at 142] (statement of Susan Kelly-Dreiss) (discussing several studies in Pennsylvania linking homelessness to domestic violence).

19. *Id.* at 143 (statement of Susan Kelly-Dreiss).

20. Alice Walker, *The Color Purple* (1982). The most severe criticism of Walker developed after the book was filmed as a movie. Donald Bogle, a film historian, argued that part of the criticism of the movie stemmed from the one-dimensional portrayal of Mister, the abusive man. See Jacqueline Trescott, Passions Over Purple; Anger and Unease Over Film's Depiction of Black Men, *Washington Post*, Feb. 5, 1986, at C1. Bogle argues that in the novel, Walker linked Mister's abusive conduct to his oppression in the white world—since Mister "can't be himself, he has to assert himself with the black woman." The movie failed to make any connection between Mister's abusive treatment of Black women and racism, and thereby presented Mister only as an "insensitive, callous man." *Id.*

21. See, e.g., Gerald Early, Her Picture in the Papers: Remembering Some Black Women, *Antaeus*, Spring 1988, at 9; Daryl Pickney, Black Victims, Black Villains, *New York Review of Books*, Jan. 29, 1987, at 17; Trescott, *supra* note 20.

22. Trudler Harris, On the Color Purple, Stereotypes, and Silence, *Black Am. Lit. F.* 18 (1984), 155.

23. The source of the resistance reveals an interesting difference between the Asian-American and African-American communities. In the African-American community, the resistance is usually grounded in efforts to avoid confirming negative stereotypes of African-Americans as violent; the concern of members in some Asian-American communities as to avoid tarnishing the model minority myth. Interview with Nilda Rimonte, Director of the Everywoman Shelter, in Los Angeles, California (April 19, 1991).

24. Nilda Rimonte, A Question of Culture: Cultural Approval of Violence Against Women in the Pacific-Asian Community and the Cultural Defense, *Stan. L. Rev.* 43 (1991),

1311; see also Nilda Rimonte, Domestic Violence Against Pacific Asians, in Asian Women United of California ed., *Making Waves: An Anthology of Writings By and About Asian American Women*; 327, 328 (1989). . . .

When—or, more importantly, how—to take culture into account when addressing the needs of women of color is a complicated issue. Testimony as to the particularities of Asian "culture" has increasingly been used in trials to determine the culpability of both Asian immigrant women and men who are charged with crimes of interpersonal violence. A position on the use of the "cultural defense" in these instances depends on how "culture" is being defined as well as on whether and to what extent the "cultural defense" has been used differently for Asian men and Asian women. See Leti Volpp, (Mis) Identifying Culture: Asian Women and the "Cultural Defense," (unpublished manuscript).

25. See, e.g., Lenore F. Walker, *Terrifying Love: Why Battered Women Kill and How Society Responds*, 101–102 (1989). ("Battered women come from all types of economic, cultural, religious, and racial backgrounds. . . . They are women like you. Like me. Like those whom you know and love."); Murray A. Straus, Richard J. Gelles & Suzanne K. Steinmetz, *Behind Closed Doors: Violence in the American Family*, 31 (1980) ("Wife-beating is found in every class, at every income level."). . . .

26. For example, Susan Kelly-Dreiss states: "The public holds many myths about battered women—they are poor, they are women of color, they are uneducated, they are on welfare, they deserve to be beaten and they even like it. However, contrary to common misperceptions, domestic violence is not confined to any one socioeconomic, ethnic, religious, racial or age group." Hearings on Violent Crime Against Women, *supra* note 18, pt. 2, at 139 (testimony of Susan Kelly-Dreiss, Executive Director, Pennsylvania Coalition Against Domestic Violence). Kathleen Waits offers a possible explanation for this misperception: "It is true that battered women who are also poor are more likely to come to the attention of governmental officials than are their middle- and upper-class counterparts. However, this phenomenon is caused more by the lack of alternative resources and the intrusiveness of the welfare state than by any significantly higher incidence of violence among lower-class families." Kathleen Waits, The Criminal Justice System's Response to Bartering: Understanding the Problem, Forging the Solutions, *Washington U.L. Rev.* 60 (1985), 267, 276–277.

27. However, no reliable statistics support such a claim. In fact, some statistics suggest that there is a greater frequency of violence among the working classes and the poor. See M. Straus, R. Gelles & S. Steinmetz, *supra* note 25, at 31. Yet these statistics are also unreliable because, to follow Waits's observation, violence in middle- and upper-class homes remains hidden from the view of statisticians and governmental officials alike. I would suggest that assertions that the problem is the same across race and class are driven less by actual knowledge about the prevalence of domestic violence in different communities than by advocates' recognition that the image of domestic violence as an issue involving primarily the poor and minorities complicates efforts to mobilize against it.

28. 137 Cong. Rec. S611 (daily ed. Jan. 14, 1991) (statement of Sen. Boren). Senator William Cohen (D-Me.) followed with a similar statement. . . . *Id.* (statement of Sen. Cohen).

29. *48 Hours: Till Death Do Us Part* (CBS television broadcast, Feb. 6, 1991).

30. Letter of Diana M. Campos, Director of Human Services, PODER, to Joseph Semidei, Deputy Commissioner, New York State Department of Social Services (Mar. 26, 1992).

31. The woman had been slipping back into her home during the day when her husband was at work. She remained in a heightened state of anxiety because he was returning shortly and she would be forced to go back out into the streets for yet another night.

32. PODER Letter, *supra* note 30.

33. *Id.*

34. *Id.*

35. Roundtable Discussion on Racism and the Domestic Violence Movement (April 2, 1992). The participants in the discussion—Diana Campos, Director, Bilingual Outreach Project of the New York State Coalition Against Domestic Violence: Elsa A. Rios, Project Director, Victim Intervention Project (a community-based project in East Harlem, New York, serving battered women); and Haydee Rosario, a social worker with the East Harlem Council for Human Services and a Victim Intervention Project volunteer—recounted conflicts relating to race and culture during their association with the New York State Coalition Against Domestic Violence, a state oversight group that distributed resources to battered women's shelters throughout the state and generally set policy priorities for the shelters that were part of the Coalition.

36. *Id.*

37. *Id.*

38. *Id.*

39. Ironically, the specific dispute that led to the walk-out concerned the housing of the Spanish-language domestic violence hotline. The hotline was initially housed at he Coalition's headquarters, but languished after a succession of coordinators left the organization. Latinas on the Coalition board argued that the hotline should be housed at one of the community service agencies, while the board insisted on maintaining control of it. The hotline is now housed at PODER. *Id.*

Accountability or Justice? Rape as a War Crime

✎ Mary Ann Tétreault

WARTIME RAPE AS A NORMATIVE ISSUE

Whether and how to treat rape as a war crime are complex questions. Rape is a contested issue in domestic criminal law, an assault for which the victim is blamed as much or more than the criminal—she asked for it, people say (Brownmiller 1975: 373). This perversity is rationalized as the outcome of cultural traditions that associate female chastity with family honor (e.g., Peristiany 1965; Tillion 1983), and underlies some of the shame associated with being a rape victim. Shame contributes to the low likelihood that the rapist will be charged with his crime if the victim can conceal what has happened to her. Victim reluctance to suffer the social and legal repercussions of rape also shields rapists who commit their crimes during a war (e.g., Asia Watch & Physicians for Human Rights 1993: 1). Even though concealment also limits the support the victim can claim from her family and friends, shame and the fear of social ostracism work for the rapist whether he is an acquaintance, a stranger, or a soldier.

But the victim is not the only person influencing the kind and amount of publicity given to rape. When rape is an instrument of policy, rapists themselves and their bureaucratic superiors publicize the act as part of the crime. Here, the purpose of rape is precisely to shame the victim, her family, and her nation, and to terrorize her entire community. "Rape [is] an act of conquest and subjugation of whole societies, involving deliberate national humiliation as a means of suppression and social control. . . . " (Makiya 1993: 294). This technique is used domestically, against ethnic minorities and opposition groups, as well as against foreign populations. Kanan Makiya notes that the government of Iraq employs "official rapists," civil servants whose job it is to rape selected Iraqi women and thus "dishonor an entire family name" (289). Other regimes, for example Jordan (Makiya 1993), Pakistan (Makiya 1993; Asia Watch 1992), Haiti (Human Rights Watch National Coalition for Haitian Refugees 1994), and India (Asia

Watch & Physicians for Human Rights 1993) also rape female citizens to control dissident populations.

Rape in war is often read as the criminal—or, even worse, the inevitable—behavior of individuals (Brownmiller 1975: 73). It is far more accurate to view wartime rape as an instrument of policy. Military organizations, with their hierarchical chains of command, are designed so that leaders can direct the behavior of subordinates. To argue that rapes committed by soldiers are individual acts, particularly if military rapists go uncharged and unpunished, is simply untenable (Amnesty International 1993: 4). Rather, as is rape domestically when routinely performed by state employees, wartime rape is undertaken to implement strategies of genocide and terror.

Genocide, the obliteration of an enemy's social formation,[1] has been practiced since ancient times and nearly always involves the sexual violation of women (Smith 1994a). Where slavery was institutionalized—for example, in ancient Greece, Old Testament Israel, or premodern Arabia—the defeat of an enemy on his own territory resulted in killing as many men as possible, destroying the city, and capturing women and children to become concubines and slaves (Garlan 1988; Mernissi 1991; Smith 1994a).[2] This practice destroyed the enemy as an organic community.

Rape has replaced capture as the primary sexual instrument of genocide. Following the battle of Culloden in 1746, English troops used rape to destroy the organization of Scottish tribes (clans) supporting a Stuart claimant to the throne (Brownmiller 1975: 38–40). The army of Pakistan systematically raped more than 200,000 Bengali women before being routed by the Indian army in 1971 (Roy 1975); today, the Indian army uses rape against Muslim women in Kashmir (Asia Watch & Physicians for Human Rights 1993). Rape was an integral element of the genocide committed by the Nazis against the Jews and by the Khmer Rouge against other Khmer (Smith 1994b). It is used today in "ethnic cleansing" campaigns in

Bosnia-Herzegovina (Amnesty International 1993; *New York Times* October 22, 1993: A4).

Wartime rape plus coerced pregnancy combine the ancient mechanism of capture with the perennial mechanism of rape to carry out another version of ethnic warfare. Women are raped repeatedly until pregnancies are confirmed and then detained until their pregnancies are too advanced for safe abortions to be performed. Reports from Bosnia indicate that this pattern was followed in camps maintained by the Bosnian Serbs (e.g., Personal Narratives 1992; Burns 1992; Lewin 1993). However, most reports from Bosnia indicate that rape victims are more likely to be killed than held to bear the children of the rapists (Amnesty International 1993: 2; Burns 1993).

A similar pattern of coerced pregnancy has been reported in Rwanda, but with a twist.

[D]uring the atrocities, women of the opposite ethnic group were raped to humiliate and harm them (and they were often killed afterward). In this later phase . . . the preference was for women of the same ethnic group as the perpetrators, this time to reproduce the group. There are many stories . . . of young Tutsi women being held in Kigali by the RPF forces (mostly Tutsi) as walking wombs, where the yearnings of youth mixed with the strategies of statesmen to capture women of reproductive age—especially women of one's [own] ethnicity. . . . [I]n this case the fighting has ended up by conquering women of the same group as the soldiers (Newbury 1995).

This strategy of replenishing the group depends both on ancient beliefs that women are merely the vessels in which men breed their own descendants, and principles followed by many nation-states whereby nationality passes from father to son independently of the mother (Yuval-Davis and Anthias 1989; Tétreault and al-Mughni 1995).

Rape and the threat of rape are also terror tactics that drive people out of their homes and villages, making it easier for enemy forces to extend their control over territory (Thomas and Ralph 1993). Rape is a crime against women that effectively removes male combatants from enemy ranks. The fear of rape explains why men who might otherwise remain to defend their homes will flee with their families to protect their women—and themselves: Though wartime rape of men is uncommon, it is not unknown (Tétreault 1992; Thomas and Ralph 1993; Riding 1993). Families that stay behind risk more than physical security. The rape of a family member devastates family life; those who watch feel impotent and vulnerable because they cannot protect the victims (Bard and Sangrey 1979). In cultures where shame is connected to the loss of female chastity, a raped woman is both humiliated by her attacker and rejected by family members. Indeed, rape in war, like other forms of torture, is frequently performed in front of family members to maximize its effectiveness in achieving social, emotional, and cognitive disorientation, terrorizing the community, and making it easier to control (e.g., Simons 1994; al-Mughni and al-Turkait 1994).

The unparalleled power of rape to effect or mark subjection has been exploited since ancient times. K. J. Dover (1978) notes that herms, stone markers carved to represent the face and erect penis of the god Hermes, also represented the threat of sexual retaliation against anybody encroaching on the territory of Greek property owners. The equation of penetration with subordination was so strong in ancient Athens that a man who permitted his body to be penetrated during homosexual acts risked his citizenship, while the forcible penetration of an Athenian citizen constituted the crime of hubris and required the execution of the offender to restore the victim to his former political status (103–4).

Despite the fact that both men and women can be raped, rape is overwhelmingly a crime committed by men against women. It is a crime intended to have collective and personal consequences. Rape is triggered by deep emotions and incites equally deep-seated reactions connected to the use of sexual symbolism to convey a whole range of concepts other than those dealing strictly with sexual acts. The symbolic connection between female chastity and group integrity, for example, is an important element motivating wartime rape. *Women* are living beings with personal lives and civil statuses; *woman* is the embodiment of complex constructions of community and nationality (Hunt 1984; Yuval-Davis & Anthias 1989; Mosse 1985; Theweleit 1987).

Wartime rape is a political crime against the symbol. It is a sacrilege. The group is shamed by the rape and injured as a result of the shame; however, the victim suffers both as the victim of a crime and as the scapegoat of their shame. This scapegoating has dire consequences for the sexually violated woman

(Roy 1975; Brownmiller 1975; Tètreault 1992), but they are addressed—if they are addressed—as the problems of a person rather than a people. The appalling prevalence of rape in war and the even more appalling masses of evidence that it is neither inevitable nor unconnected to military strategy evoke questions about why wartime rape is personalized rather than treated as the severe human rights abuse that it is.

> Despite the pervasiveness of rape, it often has been a hidden element of war, a fact that is linked inextricably to its largely gender-specific character. The fact that the abuse is committed by men against women has contributed to its being narrowly portrayed as sexual or personal . . . a portrayal that depoliticizes sexual abuse in conflict and results in its being ignored as a war crime (Thomas & Ralph, 1983: 84)

Rape is often a prelude to murder. But whether victims live or die, rape is an engine of enormous devastation. It wreaks simultaneously physical, emotional, and psychological violence against a human being, a family, a community, and a people. It has grave physical consequences—injury, infection, pregnancy, and death (Quindlen 1993a, 1993b)—and lasting psychological consequences ranging from distaste for sexual intimacy and an impaired capacity for trust to insanity and even suicide (Hartman and Burgess 1988; Kilpatrick and Veronen 1983; Mann 1991; al-Mughni and al-Turkait 1994); and initiates a train of collective consequences that can end in the elimination of a community and its unique pattern of organized social and political life (Smith 1994a).

WARTIME RAPE AS A PRACTICAL ISSUE

In this section, I examine two contemporary cases of war in which rape was utilized strategically as part of a campaign of terror and/or genocide. These are the Iraqi invasion of Kuwait and the war in Bosnia-Herzegovina. I consider three aspects of rape as a human rights abuse: its politicization as a conflict strategy; the treatment of rape victims by families, communities, and governments; and two examples of international tribunals where victims can make claims or bring charges against rapists and those responsible for their actions.

Politicization

The politicization of rape is most likely to occur as part of an ongoing conflict, when it can motivate military and civilian populations and possibly alter the strategic balance of forces. Politicization to motivate one's own armies is clearly an incitement to retaliatory behavior against women on the "other side" (Brownmiller 1975: 64–72). Here I look at cases in which parties in a conflict use charges of enemy rape to mobilize external support for their side. Paradoxically, such a strategy tends to devalue the actual suffering of victims, and is rarely pursued either to seek justice for them once the fighting is over or to hold those responsible accountable for their crimes.

Susan Brownmiller (1975) discusses the politicization of wartime rape in the context of the two world wars. During World War I, the German army was charged with the "rape of Belgium" in atrocity stories aimed at aggravating anti-German feelings among civilian populations and Allied troops. After the war, those stories were reevaluated by scholars, who concluded that they were *merely* propaganda. A numbers game ensued—only so many rapes had occurred, fewer than originally reported (46–48). One writer implied that allegations of rape were made for their alliterative value in French rather than because they had actually occurred (47). The initial exaggeration was used to justify this later trivialization; the reality of the rapes disappeared.

The creation of tribunals to try war criminals on the losing side following World War II led to a somewhat different result in the cases of the "rape of Nanking" and the sexual torture of Jewish women under the Nazi regime. The conquest of Nanking was marked by horrible atrocities committed by Japanese troops against the Chinese civilian population. Reports featured the trope "rape of Nanking" because it was so literally as well figuratively true. Yet a 1938 report by a missionary group detailing the consequences of the Japanese invasion and conquest of the city "excluded rape per se" as a category of damage, despite its inclusion of many less damaging injuries (Brownmiller 1975: 57–58).

The Tokyo war crimes tribunal did not call rape victims to testify. However, witnesses testifying to other crimes also reported on the hundreds of rapes they had seen during the carnage. From this testimony, the tribunal estimated that 20,000 rapes had occurred in Nanking during the first month of occupation alone, and that widespread rape continued to be committed, along with other crimes, "at least six weeks after the city had been taken" (cited in Brownmiller 1975: 61).[3]

Adopting a "rape of Belgium/Nanking" strategy, spokespersons for the Kuwaiti government in exile, desperately aware of its dependence on external forces to liberate Kuwait, made repeated claims about Iraqi atrocities that emphasized the rape of Kuwaiti women by Iraqi soldiers during the invasion and occupation.[4] Publication of these stories in the press and on television helped to build popular sympathy in the United States and Europe for the rollback of the invasion.

After liberation, some Kuwaitis who had remained in Kuwait during the occupation questioned the motivation for this strategy and criticized its terrorizing effects on Kuwaitis living under occupation. None disputed the charge that rapes had occurred and several reported that gang rape, other forms of sexual torture, and murder were routinely inflicted on women in the Resistance unfortunate enough to have been taken captive (e.g., Tétreault 1992; al-Mughni and al-Turkait 1994). An initially classified report by US army investigators released in 1993 supports the tenor of contemporary Kuwaiti allegations, though the estimates of numbers of all types of atrocities were lower than what had been alleged during the war. However, in the postliberation environment, the Kuwaiti regime was pressed by US officials to minimize public comments about human rights abuses committed during the occupation to calm Kuwaitis engaged in retributory rampages against scapegoats, primarily Palestinians, accused of being collaborators (Lancaster 1993).

Unlike the Iraqi rapes of Kuwaitis which appear to have been primarily acts of terror, humiliation, and pollution (al-Mughni and al-Turkait 1994),[5] a significant number of the rapes in Bosnia-Herzegovina were committed as part of a strategy of "ethnic cleansing" intended to remove members of "ethnic" groups other than the one represented by whichever army was victorious in a particular territory. As in the case of Jewish women victimized by the Nazis, some women were taken to concentration camps and repeatedly violated; others were raped in their homes, often in front of family members. Many rape victims were also murdered (Amnesty International 1993; In re Jane Doe et al. 1993; Simons 1994; MacKinnon 1993; Lewis 1994; Coll 1994).

The organized quality of so many rapes is revealed by the sequestration of the women in camps, barracks, and motels (*New York Times* 1992) and the recording of rapes on videotape. Catherine MacKinnon (1993) equates the filming of rapes by Serbs with the expression of a culture of pornography.[6] I see this differently, as part of a propaganda campaign to influence the environment of the conflict. The films are less indicative of pornographic qualities in a particular culture than the results of a sexualization of film and video entertainment visible worldwide. The films, by their nature, get viewers' attention, but they are primarily intended to persuade. Their content depends jointly on technical capability and the government's assessment of just how much it can get away with in the process of creating and marketing its message.

The filming of the rapes is not incidental, however. It is part of the propaganda machine. According to MacKinnon, some rapes by Serb soldiers were staged to look as though they had been committed by Croatians (1993: 27). Rape films are shown on Serbian television to whip up popular support for the war, and to Serb soldiers to encourage them to greater efforts (27–28). As a high school student, I watched similar (though, mercifully, far less graphic) films that had been produced during World War II by the US military for the same purposes.[7] MacKinnon notes that the Nazis also made films like this and used them to produce "sexually explicit antisemitic hate propaganda" (30).

In this context, arguments over the pornographic value of a particular country's propaganda have the same unfortunate consequences as the personalization of wartime rape: They shift attention from the issue of wartime rape as a human rights abuse to allegations about its possible psychological causes. The exploitation of photographs and video footage of someone's rape or mutilated or dying body should qualify as a war crime, a violation of the 1949 Geneva Convention prohibiting "outrages upon personal dignity." However, this is a separate issue.

All sides in the Bosnian war have used allegations of rape to mobilize supporters, neutralize opponents, and manipulate the balance of forces in the conflict. All of them have also engaged in rape (Amnesty International 1993: 3; Riding 1993: 1), though the United Nations has accused only Serb commanders of committing rape and other atrocities as part of a policy of genocide (Cohen 1995: 1). Even though there are vast differences in the degree of criminal culpability among the three sides fighting in Bosnia-Herzegovina, to focus on rapes by one side only makes light of the abuses of women raped by non-Serbian forces. Their attackers are virtually acquitted in the court of public opinion: One side commits war crimes while the other is only responding in kind. This is the same attitude that excused an orgy of Russian rapes of German women at the end of World War II (Brownmiller 1975: 66–72; Rubin 1992). In a similarly perverse way, a focus on "cultures of pornography" attenuates the individual and collective responsibility of rapists, their commanding officers, and the political leaders who oversee and condone their actions.

The Treatment of Victims

Immediately following the liberation, the Kuwaiti government sent female military personnel to interview war victims and record their testimony. Two recorders interviewed in 1992 said that they had talked with a number of rape victims, most of whom reported aggravated circumstances. Neither was willing to report the number of rape victims she had interviewed, nor to divulge any specific information regarding any of the rapes. A clinical psychologist also refused to report the number of wartime rape victims among his patients (Tétreault 1992). A recent estimate drawn from multiple sources, including medical records, concludes that approximately 2,000 Kuwaiti women were sexually assaulted by Iraqi military personnel during the conflict (al-Mughni and al-Turkait 1994).

A mechanism for processing claims for war damages was established under UN auspices (see below), but few Kuwaiti women presented claims for damages from wartime rape. Both the discretion of medical and military officials in possession of actual data and the refusal of the women themselves to press their claims have erased rape from discussions of reparation and restitution due Kuwait from Iraq. The primary public reason given for the quiet submersion of the issue of wartime rape in Kuwait is to respect the shame of rape victims and to avoid causing them any more pain than they have suffered already. The clinical psychologist mentioned above put it this way:

[R]ape is a social and ethical stigma for the one [raped] and for their families. Many families keep their victims locked in the house. Married victims are being divorced. Most rape victims are being treated by traditional methods, reading the Quran, or taking them to special religious people. . . . Many cases with reactive anxiety are developing severe psychotic depression—even schizophrenia. . . . Virginity is a very precious concept to a Kuwaiti (Tétreault 1992).

Here we see again the most frequently cited reasons for the nonreporting of rape: social stigma, self-blame, prevention by family members or religious counselors, fear of rejection and repudiation, and severe mental illness. This psychologist also said that he knew of cases where male family members killed rape victims or encouraged them to commit suicide; others committed suicide despite the efforts of friends and family members to stop them (Tétreault 1992). Occasional press reports told similar stories (e.g., Mann 1991). Death is the most effective silencer.

The treatment of rape victims by investigators and medical personnel was generally humane in Kuwait, including the exemplary discretion practiced by individuals collecting their testimonies. Their treatment by families and neighbors was uneven, despite widespread verbal and occasional actual support for reintegrating victims into Kuwaiti society without stigma (Tétreault 1994, p. 301). The treatment of rape victims by the state was ambiguous. On the one hand, medical and social services were made available to rape victims as to other victims of post-traumatic stress (al-Mughni and al-Turkait 1994), while rape victims' plight was not exploited publicly as a foreign policy tool. For example, rape victims have not been featured in Kuwaiti arguments to retain UN sanctions against Iraq.[8]

On the other hand, the political value of wartime rape was not totally forgone by domestic political actors. A whispering campaign alleged that rape had been far more widespread than was reflected in official reports, and that nearly every family that had remained behind was dishonored because it harbored at least one raped woman. Some who had remained in Kuwait during the occupation were convinced that the whispering campaign was a ploy to discredit the resistance and, by implication if not inclusion, others pressing for greater democratization (Tétreault 1992). At the same time, one well-known resistance rape and murder victim, Asrir al-Qabandy, was publicly honored as a martyr for Kuwait.

Given the climate faced by raped women in similar (though far from identical) cultural circumstances, the willingness of so many women in Bosnia-Herzegovina to testify publicly to their sexual abuse by armed forces is remarkable, and the reluctance of the others is understandable. At this juncture, there is not enough information to judge how well or how poorly rape survivors are being treated by families and communities. However, there is little reason to believe that the post-traumatic treatment of Bosnian women is any less hurtful than what happened to many Kuwaiti women. Well-intentioned individuals and groups gathering evidence for future legal actions carried out their inquiries in ways that brought individual raped women to public attention. Requests that survivors "tell their stories over and over again to reporters, even if the telling was traumatic," inflicted another kind of injury (Quindlen 1993b). Some Bosnian rape victims experienced the added trauma of being interviewed on television in the course of fact-gathering expeditions, many during the extensively covered 1992 trip by a delegation from the European Community to investigate charges about rape camps and pregnancies forced on Bosnian Muslim women (Riding 1993).

The outcomes of coerced pregnancies provide evidence that the treatment of Bosnian women by their government is tainted by instrumental concerns. An unknown number of these pregnancies were terminated by abortion and others ended in the delivery and subsequent abandonment of the infants (e.g., *New York Times* January 27, 1993: A3). The Bosnian government forbade the surrender of the infants for overseas adoption, wanting them to remain Bosnians to replace in however pitifully small numbers the tens of thousands of war dead. The babies were sequestered in orphanages financed by foreign donors, while government officials continued to apply pressure on those mothers whose identities were known to accept them into homes in which husbands were unaware of their existence, much less the circumstances of their conceptions (Williams 1993).

War-Crimes Tribunals

Because Iraq was not defeated by coalition forces but merely driven out of Kuwait, it was not considered possible to establish war-crimes tribunals like the ones set up after World War II. However, the invasion triggered a series of resolutions in the United Nations

Security Council reflecting an intention to punish Iraq for violating Kuwait's sovereignty. Significantly with respect to an innovative approach to war crimes, the resolutions created a novel set of institutions to adjudicate damage claims. The Iraqi government has so far refused to contribute actively to reparations funds to pay these damages (Crook 1993: 146).[9] Even so, the claims and payment process is well under way, thanks to the availability of funds to pay damages in the form of Iraqi assets sequestered under UN-directed economic sanctions imposed on August 6, 1990. As a result, some assessment of its utility as a vehicle for bringing justice to victims can be made.

The legal foundation for Iraq's liability is Security Council Resolution 687, a comprehensive cease-fire resolution passed in April 1991 following the end of hostilities. The resolution reaffirmed Iraq's responsibility for all damages caused by its illegal invasion and occupation of Kuwait. This attribution of responsibility to the state rests on principles established under the law of war, specifically the fourth Hague Convention (1907) and its provisions regarding the conduct of war on land, their interpretation by the International Military Tribunal at Nuremberg in 1946, and their reaffirmation in the 1949 Geneva Conventions (Crook 1993: 147; also Reisman and Antoniou 1994). Of particular interest for those concerned with wartime rape, under these principles, "Iraq is responsible for all acts of its armed forces in Kuwait, including acts contrary to military orders or discipline for which a state might not normally be responsible in peacetime" (Crook 1993: 148). The question of whether any crime committed was "private" rather than a "war crime" thus never becomes an issue. The state is accountable in all cases.

The primary institution for collecting and assessing claims against Iraq for direct losses arising from the invasion and occupation of Kuwait is the United Nations Compensation Commission—the UNCC (Crook 1993). Created over the course of a year, the commission began sitting in July 1991, receiving its first set of claims from governments in June 1992. Governments transmitting these consolidated claims set up their own procedures to collect them. In Kuwait, the Public Authority for Assessment of Compensation for Damages Resulting from Iraqi Aggression—PAAC—was created by Amiri decree on May 27, 1991,

to serve as a national authority for Kuwaiti claims. PAAC has the responsibility to submit to the

UNCC consolidated claims of Kuwaiti and certain [Gulf Cooperation Council][10] nationals, including claims of corporations and government institutions that suffered losses" (Asem and al-Mughni 1994: 12).

PAAC opened five offices to process claims for compensation made under six damage categories established by the UNCC. These are claims for having had to leave Kuwait or remain out of Kuwait as a result of the invasion (category A); claims for serious personal injury or the death of a parent, spouse, or child (category B); individual claims for damages up to $100,000 (category C); individual claims for damages over $100,000 (category D); claims by corporations and other entities (category E); and claims by governments and international organizations (category F). Categories A and B carry fixed rates of compensation (Crook 1993; Asem and al-Mughni 1994).[11]

The UNCC/PAAC procedure is highly routinized, though great care is taken to protect claimants' legal rights. Claimants appear at one of the PAAC offices and fill out a form describing their injuries and losses. They must bring proof of damage such as death certificates, medical reports, receipts, statements by witnesses, and other independent corroboration. The claims are evaluated by PAAC staff members and then by a judicial committee to be sure that each meets the "threshold" standard set for each type of claim. During this process, every claim is reviewed by a lawyer. Consolidated claims are forwarded to the UNCC office in Geneva, where they are evaluated further to determine whether the claims appear to be "unauthorized, inflated or unsubstantiated." After a thorough review, a panel of commissioners recommends to the Governing Council of the UNCC the amount to be paid to each government. The Council decides how much will actually be paid (Crook 1993: 153).

This streamlined procedure was directed by Decision 1 of the UNCC Governing Council and reflected the commission's desire to process small claims to compensate injured individuals, many of whom were likely to have very limited resources, as expeditiously as possible (Crook 1993: 152, 154). The establishment of small fixed payments for A and B claims also makes the procedure easier on victims. The relatively small amount of the payments, given the limits of the fund available to pay them, ensures payment to a relatively large proportion of those injured; fixed payments concentrate attention on the fact of damage rather than on collateral—though

important—issues such as the extent of financial losses from hasty departure and how much an individual suffered as the result of a personal injury. The inclusion of grounds such as "serious personal injury" and "mental pain and anguish" for category B claims led to a specification of the injuries that would qualify. Under Decision 3, the Governing Council listed among qualifying injuries "dismemberment, loss of use of an organ or function . . . [and] mental injury arising from sexual assault" (Crook 1993: 153).

Category B payments can be supplemented by making claims under categories C and D, and here the difficulty in defining the scope of "mental pain and anguish" and therefore the extent of Iraq's liability presented problems bearing on the resolution of claims for compensation for sexual assault. Differences in "national approaches" made reaching conclusions based on anything other than what can be easily monetized—for example, losses of income or medical expenses as opposed to feelings of shame and pollution or the pain of family rejection—impossible to achieve. The potentially infinite mental anguish a victim might suffer moved the Council to establish ceilings for claims in seven categories of mental pain and anguish (Decision 8). These include a ceiling of "$5,000 for each incident of sexual assault, aggravated assault or torture. Various family and overall ceilings also apply" (Crook 1993: 154).[12]

Although one might contest the justice of claims limitations or outright disqualification of some categories of damage, the UNCC/PAAC model offers substantial accountability and justice to wronged individuals through a procedure that grants the maximum dignity and privacy to victims of war crimes. At the most basic level, the fundamental principle of state responsibility obviates what is a near impossibility in most instances—that is, victims having to identify particular individuals who inflicted damage on them. It is independent of the whereabouts of war criminals, a critical advantage in cases in which victims have no reason to believe the national courts of their attackers will assist them. The principles and procedures of UNCC/PAAC provide a tribunal that is especially apt for the adjudication of claims of wartime rape: The crime is defined as having been committed to implement state policy; the victim is treated as injured by state policy and not a personal attack. The relative privacy of the proceedings is an additional protection for the sensibilities of victims and their families.

The small number of Kuwaiti claims for damages due to rape, universally attributed to the shame attached to being a rape victim, could be handled differently but in a way that comports with the principles and procedures of UNCC/PAAC. The rules might accommodate a separate, yet conforming, procedure for confirming sexual assault. PAAC officials had hoped to encourage rape victims to come forward by guaranteeing them anonymity. However, only three came forward (personal communications from two PAAC staff members). Rather than requiring rape victims to present their own claims, however, medical records and records obtained by the military recorders could be used as the basis of claims of publicly unnamed persons—Jane Does and John Does—and forwarded by the responsible agencies to PAAC for review. Any money collected could be held in an escrow account from which injured individuals could apply later for their compensation. The spectacle of aged Korean women mobilizing to demonstrate against the Japanese government, and demanding compensation for sexual assaults committed during World War II,[13] demonstrates both the persistence of suffering experienced by rape victims and their greater willingness to make claims when the prospect of public shame loses its power to make them fear for their life chances.

A second strategy for adjudicating war-crimes charges has been initiated in the Bosnian conflict. In Bosnia-Herzegovina, there is neither access by an international tribunal to territories and populations harboring persons accused of war crimes nor an international consensus regarding which, if any, of the belligerents is responsible for illegal acts. The ongoing nature of the conflict is a third and, perhaps in the end, the chief, obstacle to establishing anything like a satisfactory system of justice. Yet to wait for the conclusion of the conflict to move on the issue of war crimes was widely perceived as little more than an invitation for even more of them to be committed (e.g., Rubin 1992; Anthony Lewis 1994).

The ideology of ethnonationalism that shapes the discourse on the war in the former Yugoslavia is practiced as "ethnic cleansing," the elimination of persons on the basis of religion, ideology, dialect, or political allegiance from territory held by one or another victorious army. The discovery of Serb-ran concentration camps in Bosnia in late summer 1992 (Engleberg 1992a–c; Crane-Engel 1994) provided evidence of genocide that was horrifyingly reminiscent of Nazi and Khmer death camps. Although the international situation remained as stalemated as ever with regard to a consensus on the war, making policy on war crimes proved to be possible though difficult.

The United Nations Security Council voted unanimously on October 6, 1992, to create a war-crimes commission, the first such body to be established since World War II. The commission was charged with collecting evidence about possible atrocities committed anywhere in the former Yugoslavia and making decisions about who should be prosecuted for them (Paul Lewis 1992). Diplomats were quoted as saying that the immediate aim of the new resolution was to deter atrocities by "send[ing] a clear message that those responsible for the atrocities and gross violations . . . must be brought to justice" (A1).

Problems with the commission concept were noted immediately by international jurists. Alfred Rubin (1992: A32) criticized the injustice in the mandate of the commission, confined as it was to investigations in the former Yugoslavia: "If the tribunal is a good idea, shouldn't it be open also to complaints against Iraq . . . the Irish Republican Army and the Royal Ulster Constabulary . . . [and] the Palestine Liberation Organization?" The commission's lack of jurisdiction to investigate charges of atrocities committed by armies of nation-states in addition to insurgent groups was also noted: If the PLO, why not the Israeli army? If the IRA or the RUC, why not the British army? And if Iraq, why not the US military? The Tokyo and Nuremburg tribunals were effective because they were the courts of victors; there were no victors in the former Yugoslavia—indeed, the likely winner was the primary target of the commission. Rubin concluded that the commission's flaws left deterrence through exposure as its only function.

Benjamin Ferencz (1992: A32) hoped that the commission would be just the first step toward the establishment of an international criminal court. Such an outcome would meet the objections to the commission made by Rubin and would be a permanent addition to the range of international organizations available to "enforce the rule of law." The logic of this position was compelling. In May 1993, the Security Council voted unanimously to establish a tribunal to hear charges of war crimes committed in the former Yugoslavia. US delegate Madeleine K. Albright stressed during the debate that rape charges would be among those the court would hear (Paul Lewis 1993).

The commission had begun its work without investigators of its own or even subpoena powers, having to rely on information gathered by others, chiefly governments (Robbins 1993: A8). By July 1993, a war-crimes database compiled by law students at De Paul University in Chicago had counted "some 25,000 victims of rape, torture, murder, and ethnic cleansing" (A1). Despite this mounting evidence, disputes among members of the Security Council regarding the religion of a top candidate delayed the naming of the tribunal's chief prosecutor for a year. Like the eventually nominated chief prosecutor Richard Goldstone, a highly respected jurist from South Africa, none of the judges finally appointed was a Muslim.

The tribunal was not permitted to try anyone in absentia. In late 1992, a high US official had accused ten Yugoslavs of being war criminals, a list including Serbian president Slobodan Milosević and Bosnian Serb leader Radovan Karadzić, persons unlikely ever to be indicted, much less brought to trial (Robbins 1993: A8). The tribunal's lack of access to top war criminals has been criticized since its inception. However, on February 13, 1995, the tribunal handed down the first indictment for genocide ever made by an international court, against Zeljko Meakić, commander of the Omarska camp. The specific crimes committed under his direction include rape (Cohen 1995).

CONCLUSIONS

The repeated recurrence of wholesale rape as a strategy of conflict, together with the acute and long-lasting suffering rape inflicts on victims, support the logic and justice of treating rape as a war crime. Yet unlike other human rights abuses that inflict physical and mental harm, rape includes social opprobrium directed toward the victim as part of its repertoire of damage. This quality makes rape technically and morally difficult to prosecute successfully in domestic criminal courts. It is no less so in the context of civil or international conflict. However, the failure to prosecute offenders for wartime rape and other human rights abuses confers a kind of permission for it to continue. Ignoring rape as a war crime also has contributed to the persistent myth that rape is a crime for which the victim bears significant culpability.

It may be the similarity of rape in war to rape in domestic settings that explains the unwillingness of those responsible for charging and prosecuting offenders to treat rape the same way that other

human rights abuses are treated. It is much easier to prove a case of domestic nonsexual assault in criminal court than a case of rape (Brownmiller 1975: 373–74). This is not only because of men's fears that they will be falsely charged with rape but also because of the subordinate status of women and the widespread assumption that men as persons are entitled to a degree of physical dominance over women that women as persons are denied over men (Johnson 1988). Laws and customs permitting men to rape and beat their wives have no counterparts privileging violent criminal behavior by wives against husbands (Barry 1979).

The symbolic role of women and their sexual violation during war contributes to the complexity of formulating war-crimes charges. At the same time, the desire to avoid shame supports the privatization of rape rather than its treatment as an act of war. Still, evidence about rape contributes to charges of human rights abuses committed against civilians during a conflict. Thus, it strengthens claims for reparations and compensation or, failing that, retribution of some kind. A government's position on wartime rape depends on whether politicization is more likely than privatization to promote national interests.

The politicization of wartime rape guarantees neither consideration for the victims nor that the role of rape as a strategy of conflict will be pondered once the war is over. As the example of Nanking shows, even when evidence is overwhelming, an accounting of rapes may be omitted from assessments of damage. This lessens the likelihood that rape will appear on a list of war-crimes charges or as grounds for demands for compensation to victims. Such omissions contribute to collective amnesia about the myriad specific examples of wartime rape that contradict erroneous assumptions that rape is an opportunistic crime committed by depraved or deprived individuals. This assumption feeds deeply held prejudices about the nature of rape and the relative culpability of victims and rapists.

Myths of culpability also affect the treatment of victims. Shame makes victims reluctant to press charges or demand reparations. The ostensible protectors of victims are also culpable: the family that is helpless in the face of attackers, and the state and its army whose impotence failed to shield a civilian population from atrocities. States can defend their failure to press for justice for rape victims by insisting that they are protecting the victims from further pain and harm when, in reality, leaders of nations and their armies prefer that no one remember how they failed to perform their most fundamental obligation to protect.

Ignoring rape as a war crime reinforces assumptions connected to the symbolic role of women and denies what Hannah Arendt (1965) calls their "plurality," their individual identities. It also denies them standing as injured persons before the law. When women are denied justice, rapists, their commanding officers, and their governments escape accountability. Even if rape is included as a class of war crimes, however, accountability and justice will continue to be difficult to achieve. The ability of the United Nations to develop, under UNCC, an innovative procedure that confers so much autonomy on wronged individuals depended on the decision of the UN Security Council that Iraq's invasion and occupation of Kuwait were illegal. The Security Council was the effective court for war-crimes trials against Iraq. Resolutions passed by the Security Council in response to the Iraqi invasion reflected the United Nations' adjudication of the conflict. Having found Iraq guilty of the war and therefore of every crime committed in the war's prosecution, defining, collecting, and establishing the validity of individual claims for damages quickly became routine.

The drawbacks to such a procedure are also clear. Iraqi leaders from the president to field commanders escaped personal accountability for what were, after all, decisions made by people and not by an automation—the Iraqi "state." For victims to whom "justice" includes the trial and punishment of the individuals personally responsible for breaking their bodies and ruining their lives, recognition that they were wronged and monetary compensation for the damages inflicted on them constitute incomplete rather than full justice. A second drawback is that the achievement of more than partial restitution is far from guaranteed. Iraq has so far rejected the opportunity to sell a limited amount of oil under UN supervision for humanitarian purposes, one of which is to provide money to pay damages to war crimes victims. Instead, it has flouted the Security Council's sanctions by smuggling oil out and selling it on black markets. This recalcitrance denies Iraq's responsibility for its war crimes as well as additional money to pay

damage claims. A further impediment to restitution is the dependence of the replenishment of the fund on implementation by member states, some of whose interests conflict with those of war victims, once economic sanctions against Iraq are lifted. Despite these drawbacks, however, the principle of state responsibility and the procedures protecting victims that mark the operation of UNCC/PAAC are models for achieving limited but significant justice for victims of rape and other human rights abuses.

Neither accountability nor justice is an easy proposition for victims of wartime rape in Bosnia-Herzegovina. There is no international consensus on who is responsible for the conflict—whatever degree of accountability is achieved must be accumulated one defendant at a time. Unlike UNCC/PAAC, the tribunal established to try war crimes committed in the former Yugoslavia has yet to prove itself effective in achieving either accountability or justice. Under its rules, the tribunal is unlikely to indict or try those at the top of the pyramid of responsibility for policies that utilized rape as an instrument of terror and genocide, tainting the justice of trials of lower-level individuals directly involved in rape and other human rights abuses. In effect, the tribunal's necessarily retail approach to accountability reprivatizes rape and other human rights abuses as crimes committed by individuals against individuals or, at best, by a group of individuals against a helpless population.

To consider wartime rape as a human rights abuse encourages us to think about other brutal acts of war and question why so many survivors are so willing to forget them. Victims don't forget, of course, but as one moves away from the direct targets of abuse and the people who love them, shame, distaste, and denial characterize the responses of most of the rest. Much has been written about the German population and its callousness to the plight of Jews during the Nazi era. Yet people of every nationality, including Americans, dismiss human rights abuses as reasons for changing their opinions or their behavior when such actions cost money, strategic advantage, or status. Rape is more convoluted but not fundamentally different from other crimes against humanity. For every human rights abuse, accountability is too seldom demanded and justice far too rarely achieved.

ACKNOWLEDGMENTS

The author thanks Jennifer Louise Davis for her research assistance, and Martha Bailey, David Binder, Obrad Kesic, Haya al-Mughni, David Newbury, Roger Smith, Kristin Stilt, and Robin Teske for their advice and helpful comments on earlier drafts.

NOTES

1. A paradigm of genocide is developed by Helen Fein in "Defining Genocide as a Sociological Concept," *Current Sociology* 38:1 (Spring 1990), 25–30. It includes the notion of a collectivity as constituted by ideology or other forms of group identity *in addition to* ethnicity. Thus, the behavior of the Khmer Rouge in Cambodia is genocide even though the ethnic identities of killers and killed were both Khmer. Other chapters in the Fein volume discuss cases of genocide in addition to the ones noted in this text, and explore theories offering causal explanations.

2. That this practice in Greece was not confined to the Homeric period is evident in the Athenian treatment of Melos during the Peloponnesian War—see Thucycides, *The Peloponnesian War*, trans. Rex Warner (Baltimore: Penguin, 1959), 366.

3. The Nuremburg tribunal did not include rape on the list of war crimes. During the war there was no rerun in the European theater of allegations on the same level as stories of the World War I "rape of Belgium." Indeed, given both the volume of propaganda films produced by the Allies during World War II and the volume of evidence amassed afterward, contemporary charges of war crimes made against Germany during the war seem to have been vastly understated. Afterward, "sexual forms of torture, including rape, were documented at the [Nuremburg] trials" (MacKinnon 1993: 30; see also Brownmiller 1975).

4. Although most of the accusations were made on television, some also appeared in the press. See, for example, *New York Times*, December 2, 1990, 19; December 8, 1990, 8; December 16, 1990, 1. Kuwaitis whom I interviewed in 1992 said that during the war, they had heard reports that the number of Kuwaiti women raped amounted to 8,000.

5. The importance of ritual pollution to Iraqi behavior in Kuwait can be inferred from evidence other than the sexual assaults—for example, the many deposits of urine and feces on furniture, desks, documents, and other places in private homes and public buildings, and the type of vandalization of the works of Kuwaiti artists in the National Museum (Tétreault 1992).

6. "In the war-crimes trials for the genocidal war against Bosnia-Herzegovina and Croatia, will those who incited to genocide through rape, sexual torture, and murder—the Serbian pornographers as well as the high policymakers and the underlings—get what they deserve (Mackinnan 1993: 30)?"

7. I recall one in particular that showed Hitler beaming down on a tableful of naked infants that the voiceover said were babies whose young, unmarried, Aryan mothers had been impregnated in special camps by German soldiers specifically selected to breed new members of the German superrace. Of all the footage that I saw, that segment, along with another from a film shot in Russia during a rout of Russian forces by German troops which featured the death of the person holding the camera, are the only ones that I remember out of the scores of hours of propaganda films that I and my classmates were subjected to in the name of social studies education at the height of the Cold War. As an adult, I would classify both of these clips as pornographic, and as powerful incitements to fear and visceral hatred.

8. The victim group that is the primary subject of Kuwaiti arguments opposing the lifting of sanctions is the several hundred Kuwaitis taken prisoner by the Iraqis and never returned.

9. Money to pay claims was to be provided by assessing Iraq a percentage of its income from oil sales but no such sales have been made to date because of continuing UN economic sanctions against Iraq (Crook 1993: 144). A special procedure was established under UN Security Council Resolution 706 (August 15, 1991) authorizing the sale of $1.6 billion worth of oil over six months, with 30 percent of that to go to the fund and the rest to administrative costs and the purchase, under strict supervision, of food, medicine, and other items to meet civilian needs (146). Iraq has refused to comply with the conditions specified in the resolution.

10. The Gulf Cooperation Council is an international organization modeled after the European Community that was established in 1981. Its members are Kuwait, Saudi Arabia, Bahrain, Qatar, Oman, and the United Arab Emirates.

11. In some cases, claims for damages in excess of the limits set in categories A and B were presented as A and B claims. The additional damages were assessed for things like uncompensated medical bills. This procedure enabled small claims to be processed in the A and B categories, whose settlement was the top priority of UNCC.

12. It should be clear that mental pain and anguish were recognized as resulting from injuries other than sexual assault. Ceilings were set in other areas as well. For example,

the Council approved a ceiling of $15,000 for mental pain and anguish resulting from the death of a spouse, child, or parent (Crook 1993: 154).

13. These are the so-called comfort women, who were kidnapped as girls and sequestered in military brothels for the entertainment of Japanese troops. The very existence of the comfort women was denied until very recently, and their claims for reparations have so far been dismissed by the Japanese government. [Editors' note: Some former "comfort women" have now received reparations.] One reason offered for the government's refusal to admit culpability and make even token payments to the survivors is that this would amount to a very large amount of money. This by itself points up the need to institutionalize procedures for assigning responsibility and assessing damages for wartime rape as a means to limit such behavior in the future.

REFERENCES

Amnesty International. 1993. *Bosnia-Herzegovina: Rape and Sexual Abuse by Armed Forces.* New York: Amnesty International.

Arendt, Hannah. 1965. *On Revolution.* New York: Compass.

Asem, Adel, and Haya al-Mughni. 1994. "Claiming for Compensation through the United Nations Compensation Commission: The Case of Kuwait." Paper presented at the International Conference on the Effects of the Iraqi Aggression on Kuwait. Kuwait. April.

Asia Watch and Physicians for Human Rights. 1993. *Rape in Kashmir: A Crime of War.* New York: Asia Watch.

Asia Watch and the Women's Rights Project. 1992. *Double Jeopardy: Police Abuse of Women in Pakistan.* New York: Human Rights Watch.

Bard, Morton, and Diane Sangrey. 1979. *The Crime Victim's Book.* New York: Basic Books.

Barry, Kathleen. 1979. *Female Sexual Slavery.* Englewood Cliffs, N.J.: Prentice Hall.

Brownmiller, Susan. 1975. *Against Our Will: Men, Women and Rape.* New York: Simon and Schuster.

Burns, John F. 1992. "150 Muslims Say Serbs Raped Them in Bosnia." *New York Times* October 3: L5.

Cohen, Roger. 1993. "2 Serbs to Be Shot for Killings and Rapes." *New York Times* March 31: A6.

———. 1995. "Tribunal Charges Genocide by Serbs." *New York Times* February 4: A1–A2.

Coll, Steve. 1994. "War Crimes and Punishment: Bosnia in the Shadow of the Holocaust." *Washington Post Magazine* September 25.

Crane-Engel, Melinda. 1994. "Germany vs. Genocide." *New York Times Magazine* October 30.

Crook, John R. 1993. "The United Nations Compensation Commission—A New Structure to Enforce State Responsibility." *American Journal of International Law* 87.

In re Jane Doe et al. against Radovan Karadžić. United States District Court, Southern District of New York, Civ. 93-0878 PKL. 1993. "Complaint for Genocide: War Crimes and Crimes against Humanity; Summary Execution; Torture; Cruel, Inhuman or Degrading Treatment; Wrongful Death; Assault and Battery; and Intentional Infliction of Emotional Harm. Class Action: Jury Trial Demand." February. "Memorandum in Support of Motion to Dismiss before Answer." May. "Reply Declaration of Lawrence W. Schilling in Support of Defendant's Motions to Dismiss." May. "Plaintiff's Memorandum of Points and Authorities in Opposition to Defendant's Motion to Dismiss before Answer." August. "Plaintiffs' Sur-Reply Brief in Opposition to Defendant's Motion to Dismiss Before Answer." October.

Dover, K. J. 1978. *Greek Homosexuality.* London: Duckworth.

Engelberg, Stephen. 1992a. "Bosnians Provide Accounts of Abuse in Serbian Camps. "*New York Times* August 4: A1.

———. 1992b. "Refugees from Camps Tell of Agony and Terror." *New York Times* August 7: A5.

———. 1992c. "Clearer Picture of Bosnia Camps: A Brutal Piece of a Larger Plan." *New York Times* August 16: 1, 14.

Fein, Helen. 1990. "Genocide: A Sociological Perspective," *Current Sociology* 38: 1 (Spring).

Ferencz, Benjamin B. 1992. Letter to the editor. *New York Times* October: A32

Garlan, Yvon. 1988. *Slavery in Ancient Greece.* Rev. and expanded ed. Trans. Janet Lloyd. Ithaca: Cornell University Press.

Hartman, Carol R., and Ann Wolbert Burgess. 1988. "Rape Trauma and Treatment of the Victim." In *Post-Traumatic Therapy and Victims of Violence*, ed. F. M. Ochberg. New York: Brunner Mazel.

Human Rights Watch National Coalition for Haitian Refugees. 1994. *Rape in Haiti: A Weapon of Terror.* Washington, D.C.: Human Rights Watch.

Hunt, Lynn. 1984. *Politics, Culture, and Class in the French Revolution.* Berkeley: University of California Press.

Johnson, Miriam. 1988. *Strong Mothers, Weak Wives.* Berkeley: University of California Press.

Kilpatrick, Dean G., and Lois J. Veronen. 1983. "Treatment for Rape-Related Problems: Crisis Intervention Is Not Enough." In *Crisis Intervention*, ed. L. H. Cohen, W. Claiborn, and G. Specter. New York: Human Sciences Press.

Lancaster, John. 1993. "Administration Releases Report on Iraqi War Crimes in Kuwait." *Washington Post* March 20: A18.

Lewin, Tamar. 1993. "The Balkans Rapes: A Legal Test for the Outraged." *New York Times* January 15: B15.

Lewis, Anthony. 1994. " 'The Civilized World.' " *New York Times* July 1: A17.

Lewis, Paul. 1992. "U.N. Sets Up War-Crimes Panel on Charges of Balkan Atrocities." *New York Times* October 7: A1, A6.

———. 1993. "Security Council Establishes War-Crimes Tribunal for the Balkans." *New York Times* May 26: A13.

———. 1994. "If There Ever Were a Nuremburg for the Former Yugoslavia. . . . " *New York Times* June 12: E7.

MacKinnon, Catherine A. 1993. "Turning Rape into Pornography: Postmodern Genocide." *Ms.* July/August.

Makiya, Kanan. 1993. *Cruelty and Silence: War, Tyranny, Uprising, and the Arab World.* New York: Norton.

Mann, Judy. 1991. "Kuwaiti Rape a Doubly Savage Crime." *Washington Post* March 29: C3.

Mernissi, Fatima. 1991. *The Veil and the Male Elite: A Feminist Interpretation of Women's Rights in Islam.* Trans. Mary Jo Lakeland. Reading, Mass.: Addison Wesley.

Mosse, George L. 1985. *Nationalism and Sexuality: Respectability and Abnormal Sexuality in Modern Europe.* New York: Howard Fertig.

Al-Mughni, Haya, and Fawzia al-Turkait. 1994. "Dealing with Trauma: Cultural Barriers to Self-Recovery: The Case of Kuwaiti Women." Paper presented at the seminar on The Effective Methods for Encountering the Psychological and the Social Effects of the Iraqi Aggression, sponsored by the Social Development Office of the Amiri Diwan. Kuwait. March.

New York Times. 1992. "Rape—and Soldiers' Morale." Editorial December 7: A18.

New York Times. 1993. January 27: A3.

New York Times. 1993. October 22: A4.

Newbury, David. 1995. Personal communication.

Peristiany, J. G., ed. 1965. *Honor and Shame: The Values of Mediterranean Society.* London: Weidenfeld and Nicolson.

Personal Narratives. 1992. "Rape after Rape after Rape." *New York Times* December 13: E17.

Peterson, V. Spike. 1994. "Gendered Nationalisms." *Peace Review* 6:1.

Quindlen, Anna. 1993a. "Gynocide." *New York Times* March 10: A19.

———. 1993b. "The Rescuers." *New York Times* May 5: A23.

Reisman, W. Michael, and Chris T. Antoniou, eds. 1994. *The Laws of War: A Comprehensive Collection of Primary Documents on International Laws Governing Armed Conflict.* New York: Vintage.

Riding, Alan. 1993. "European Inquiry Says Serbs' Forces Have Raped 20,000." *New York Times* January 9: 1,4.

Robbins, Carla Anne. 1993. "Balkan Judgments: World again Confronts Moral Issues Involved in War-Crimes Trials." *Wall Street Journal* July 13: A1, A8.

Roy, K. K. 1975. "Feelings and Attitudes of Raped Women of Bangladesh towards Military Personnel of Pakistan." In *Victimology: A New Focus*, vol. 5, *Exploiters and Exploited: The Dynamics of Victimization.* Lexington, Mass.: D. C. Heath.

Rubin, Alfred P. 1992. Letter to the editor, *New York Times* October 23: A32.

Simons, Marlise. 1994. "Bosnian Rapes Go Untried by the U.N." *New York Times* December 7: A8.

Smith, Roger W. 1994a. "Genocide and the Politics of Rape: Historical and Psychological Perspectives." Presented at Remembering for the Future: Internation Conference on the Holocaust and Genocide. March 13–17. Berlin.

———. 1994b. "Women and Genocide: Notes on an Unwritten History." *Holocaust and Genocide Studies* 8: 3 (Winter).

Tétreault, Mary Ann. 1992, Interviews in Kuwait, March, September–October.

———. 1994. "Whose Honor? Whose Liberation? Women and the Reconstruction of Politics in Kuwait." In *Women and Revolution in Africa, Asia, and the New World*, ed. Mary Ann Tétreault. Columbia: University of South Carolina Press.

———, and Haya al-Mughni. 1995. "Women, Citizenship, and Nationalism in Kuwait." Paper presented at the annual meeting of the International Studies Association. February 21–25, Chicago.

Theweleit, Klaus. 1987. *Male Fantasies.* Vol. 1: *Women, Floods, Bodies, History*, trans. Stephen Conway. Minneapolis: University of Minnesota Press.

Thomas, Dorothy Q., and Regan E. Ralph. 1993. "Rape in War: The Tradition of Impunity." *SAIS Review* 14: 1 (Spring)

Tillion, Germaine. 1983. *The Republic of Cousins: Women's Oppression in Mediterranean Society*, trans. Quintin Hoare. London: Al Saqi Books.

Williams, Carol J. 1993. "Bosnia's Orphans of Rape: Innocent Legacy of Hatred." *Los Angeles Times* July 24: A1, A12.

Yuval-Davis, Nita, and Floya Anthias, eds. 1989. *Woman-Nation-State.* London: Macmillan.

P A R T   F O U R

Social Change

Thus far we have emphasized the *stability* of gender inequality. We have examined how socialization, social definitions of gender, and the structure and content of all the major institutional arenas of social life converge to produce a world in which males and females are understood as essentially different and are differentially valued and rewarded. The forces that perpetuate gender inequality are so intricately interwoven into the social fabric and so deeply embedded in the identities of individuals that changing them is beyond the power of any one individual, no matter how well-intentioned that individual may be.

Yet societies can and do *change*. Anyone who has lived through the past three decades in the United States cannot help but notice that there has been substantial change in the position, behaviors, and consciousness of women and men. In earlier readings, we discussed some of the dynamic forces that have *unintentionally* recast gender consciousness and inequality, including new cultural meanings, technological innovations, demographic processes, and economic factors. To understand fully how systems of gender inequality change, we must also examine the ways that women have sought collectively and *intentionally* to reduce their disadvantage. Certainly every society or group contains individuals who are nonconformists, but significant and lasting social change is ultimately the result of collective action rather than individual action.

In Part Four, we turn our attention to struggles to transform culture and social institutions in two arenas. Section Ten focuses on the politicization of gender in the state and global politics. Section Eleven documents the rich history and diversity of the women's movement and examines continuity and change in the history of American feminism. To understand the part that women themselves have played in improving their status, we focus, on the one hand, on women's actions "within the system" by conventional and orderly means and, on the other, on women's collective actions "outside the system" by unconventional and disorderly means.

Politics is generally thought to refer to the institutionalized or authoritative system by which a society makes decisions, allocates power, and distributes resources. According to the traditional view, voting, campaigning, lobbying, conducting organizational activities, holding office, and working in political parties are classified as politics because they take place in the context of formal governmental structure.

However, feminist scholars have pointed out that the standard definition of politics is too narrow for understanding women's political participation. It not only assumes a particular type of state and political system but ignores the fact that in most industrialized societies women have been denied access to the formal political process until fairly recently.

In the United States, women were not allowed to vote, hold office, or sit on juries until the twentieth century. Even after women received the vote with the passage of the Nineteenth Amendment to the U.S. Constitution in 1920, their participation in electoral politics, involvement in major political parties, and election to public offices lagged significantly behind men's. African-American women, moreover, remained effectively disenfranchised in southern states by racist voter-registration rules until the late 1960s.

It was not until a half century after women got the vote that the gap between men's and women's party involvement and office holding began to shrink, and even today women fare better in local and state politics than in the national arena. Voting turnout differences between women and men finally disappeared in 1976. But it took until 1980 for women to use the electoral process to express their collective dissatisfaction by voting in line with their interests in women's equality, creating for the first time what has come to be known as the "gender gap."

Elections, participation in party politics, running for office, and lobbying are not, however, the only ways to express grievances, influence public policy, and achieve social change. Politics also includes social movements, protests, and other group actions intended to change cultural beliefs and influence the distribution of power and resources in a state or community. This definition is broad enough to encompass women's long history of participation in collective action on their own behalf through the feminist movement as well as in pursuit of other human rights causes through female reform societies, women's church groups, alternative religious societies, women's clubs, and other social movements.

Social movements are collective attempts to bring about change. They originate outside the established political system, forge links between individuals and groups who share common concerns, and mobilize the people and resources needed to pursue the goal of social change. In democratic societies, social movements and the tactics they employ—marches, boycotts, strikes, demonstrations, protests—are a regular part of the democratic process. Movements act as pressure groups on behalf of people excluded from routine decision-making processes and the dominant power structure; they are a major source of new social patterns and cultural understandings.

Because participants in social movements typically challenge conventional ideas and behaviors, they are often stereotyped by the larger society as deviant and irrational and are accused of exaggerating their claims. If we take a historical perspective on social movements, however, we will often find that today's social institution is likely to have been yesterday's social movement. In other words, social movement participants are not qualitatively different from other kinds of social actors and their actions are governed by the same norms that underlie other groups.

Although popular opinion often presents the women's movement as a relatively recent phenomenon, its roots are well grounded historically. Indeed, the similarities between the views of contemporary feminists and earlier feminists are remarkable. More than 200 years ago, for example, Abigail Adams gave this warning to her husband, John, when he was fashioning the Constitution of the United States:

> In the new code of laws which I suppose will be necessary for you to make, I desire you would remember the ladies and be more generous and favorable to them than your ancestors. Do not put such unlimited power in the hands of husbands. Remember, all men would be tyrants if they could. If particular care and attention is not paid to the ladies, we are determined to foment a rebellion, and will not hold ourselves bound by any laws in which we have no voice or representation.

Unfortunately, John Adams failed to take his wife's warning seriously. He urged her to be patient and said there were more important issues than the rights of "ladies."

As this example illustrates, in the United States, as in much of the industrialized world, the history of feminist activism is long and rich. Until the past three decades, however, knowledge of the women's movement remained mostly buried. Initially most scholars studying the women's movement held that feminism in the United States has come in waves. The first wave began in the nineteenth century as a broad attack on male domination, continued for almost a century, and then died precipitously in 1920 with the passage of the suffrage amendment granting women the right to vote, which by then had become the movement's major goal. Supposedly, a forty-year lull followed before the second wave, or new feminist movement, erupted in the mid-1960s.

As a result of new research, a different interpretation of the history of the American women's movement has recently emerged that emphasizes the continuity and persistence of women's resistance. The newer work recognizes the great waves of mass feminist activism, but it also points to the survival of feminism in less highly mobilized periods. It focuses not only on the continuity of the movement but on changes in feminist ideology, goals, constituency, tactics, and organizational style. In addition to self-proclaimed feminists, working-class women and women of color also have a long history of struggle on their own behalf, in labor unions, socialist and communist groups, women's clubs, and within churches and communities. Any analysis of contemporary feminism and the backlash against it must consider the multiple forms of the enduring struggle against gender inequality.

The readings thus far suggest the depth, pervasiveness, and persistence of gender inequality and the intersection of gender inequality with inequalities of race, class, and sexuality. It is not surprising, then, that contemporary feminism encompasses a wide range of struggles, from local efforts to improve women's daily lives to broad visions of fundamentally restructuring all institutions that perpetuate and sustain male dominance. The media have repeatedly proclaimed the present period the "post-feminist era" and many women disavow the feminist label—yet, as we shall see, women's movements remain very much alive. Feminist groups can be found within every major institution: in the professions, academia, labor, religion, politics, the arts, music, and literature. Feminist groups have mobilized around practically every issue imaginable, including employment and equal pay issues, abortion rights, health, depression, substance abuse, pornography, prostitution, disability rights, spirituality, child care, nuclear weaponry, lesbianism, incest, battering, racism, and older women's rights. Feminists organize around sexual, racial and ethnic, and class identities.

The flourishing of women's organizing in these multiple forms can be considered a "third wave" of feminism that builds on the successes and lessons of earlier activism. Third-wave feminism is characterized by the view that gender is multiple and variable because it is also shaped by race, class, sexuality, nationality, and other factors. Because feminism addresses every facet of social life, it has had a major and lasting impact not only on economic, political, and cultural institutions but also on the consciousness and lives of individual women and men. Third-wave feminism grows as the women and men born after, and shaped by, the sweeping changes wrought by the 1970s women's movement reshape feminism and the larger world.

In Part Four, we examine the diversity of women's participation in politics and contemporary women's movements (both feminist and nonfeminist), emphasizing the continuity and global nature of feminist challenges, as well as changes and differences in feminist goals, constituencies, and tactics. The readings document the multiple forms that feminist resistance can take. They recognize that protest can be directed at the structural, cultural, or individual level and that resistance varies across cultural and national contexts. We conclude with an overview of the American women's movement and a look to the future. As you think about these readings, consider in what ways gender systems are shaped by national governments and transnational politics. In what ways have the efforts of women to transform gender succeeded?

S E C T I O N T E N

Global Politics and the State

National governments, international relations, and transnational economies exert wide-ranging influence on gender systems. Government-controlled economies shape differences in women's and men's wages and the prices of goods that women and men produce and consume. National and international policies on education, welfare, health, and various forms of violence against women affect women's daily lives in profound ways.

Because governmental policies frequently reflect dominant sexist ideologies, they often serve to reinforce the disadvantaged position of women in most countries. The state, in fact, plays a central part in maintaining a social structure of inequality between women and men. The state plays a crucial role in perpetuating inequalities of class (through regulation of the labor market or of minimum wages, for example) and of race (through legislative policies regarding immigration or affirmative action, for example).

Feminist scholars focus on the ways that state actions and policies create and perpetuate gender categories, ideologies of women's inferiority, and differential access of women and men to valued resources and power. The state's role in upholding gender stratification, of course, is inextricably linked to its role in reinforcing race and class stratification, as the articles in this section point out.

The increasing interdependence of the world's countries means that women's lives are shaped not only by the governmental policies of their own country but also by transnational politics and economics as well. A complex web of interrelationships among transnational corporations, states, groups within states, geography, technology, and ideologies of gender, race, ethnicity, and religion shapes relations among women, states, and global politics. In this section, contributors examine the relationships among constructions of gender, women's lives, and the state, both in the United States and internationally.

One of the major topics of analysis for feminist scholars of the state is the ways that governments regulate women's childbearing and family structures. The first reading looks at how the government regulates the lives of poor women with children. In "Surviving the Welfare System: How AFDC Recipients Make Ends Meet in Chicago," Kathryn Edin shows how AFDC payments provide too little money to support women and their children, forcing women to earn additional money by working under-the-table jobs. In contrast to the stereotypes of the lazy welfare mother, Edin shows that surviving on welfare requires hard work and ingenuity. Yet the low-wage jobs most welfare recipients are qualified for provide no better alternative. What kinds of social changes might alleviate the problems Edin describes?

Harriet Woods, in "The Truth About Women and Power," argues that women need to embrace rather than shun the idea of exercising power, and that they need to begin close to their own daily lives. Full citizenship, contrary to the hopes of some of the early suffragists who thought the vote would end women's political subordination, is not enough. Woods urges American women to run for local public office, to see power as something positive, not negative, to work to change institutions in a way that helps women, and to work collectively. She provides concrete advice for making a difference and succeeding in public office in hopes that many more women leaders will emerge. Why do women fear power? Why have other countries, even ones where women have fewer political rights, had women leaders at the top level of government, while the United States has not? Would having a woman president make a difference? What kind?

Although Woods concentrates on American women in politics, she makes connection to women's political participation around the globe. The last two articles in this section focus on the international politics of gender. Cynthia Enloe discusses the international economics and politics of women's labor in "The Globetrotting Sneaker," suggesting that women workers' interests have been left behind as international trade has increased. Taking sneaker manufacturers as an example, Enloe shows how international corporations profit from the labor of underpaid and exploited women workers in Third World countries. She argues that women's acceptance of traditional submissive, family-oriented models for their lives makes them ideal workers for companies that want low-paid, compliant workers. Documenting the activism of women workers in South Korea, Enloe shows that Nike moved its manufacturing from South Korea to countries like China and Indonesia, where there was less organizing by workers. Yet, she suggests, in-

creasing international organizing by women workers holds the potential for social change, particularly if women in the United States join them. Do you agree with Enloe that companies like Nike and Reebok should not employ women at such low wages? How does your standard of living depend on the work of the women workers that Enloe discusses? Where are your sneakers and clothing produced? Where is the clothing sold by your college or university manufactured? What might you and other Americans do to improve the living situation of women workers abroad?

Finally, Amrita Basu shifts our gaze to India, where nationalist Hindu women have been active in some decidedly nonfeminine behavior, including inciting and participating in community violence against Muslim families. Here, as in Kathleen Blee's article on the U.S. Ku Klux Klan in the next section, we see women exercising power in ways that Harriet Woods would find disturbing. Hindu "communalist" women compare themselves favorably to Muslim women under Islamic fundamentalism, in much the same way that many Western women do. Focusing on the Bharatiya Janata Party, Basu shows the way that Hindu nationalist groups both champion Hindu women's rights and also defend conservative views of women's place, including sati (self-immolation of widows), sexual repression, and the sanctity of motherhood. This context is important for understanding Hindu women's activism, not only in nontraditional violence, but in far more traditional gendered activities. How does the global context affect Hindu women's activism in India? What do Hindu women gain from their participation in nationalist movements? How do the nationalist movements encourage and benefit from women's participation?

Once again, this section returns to the question of the commonalities and differences among women. Given the disparities of wealth and power among women around the world, do women have anything in common by virtue of their gender?

Surviving the Welfare System: How AFDC Recipients Make Ends Meet in Chicago

✒ Kathryn Edin

In the discourse surrounding public welfare, recipients of Aid to Families with Dependent Children (AFDC) have often been portrayed as passive dependents who rely on government handouts as their sole source of support. In this view, welfare creates dependency by discouraging people from seeking work, forcing them and their children into a permanent underclass (Mead 1989, Murray 1984, Novak 1987). During the 1980s, this image of the welfare recipient provided a rationale for state legislators to let benefit levels fall far behind inflation and prompted Congress to restrict benefits (with some exceptions) to those who can prove they are seeking work.

Those who argue that welfare engenders dependence ignore the fact that states set welfare benefits too low to live on. Because of this, recipients must work at regular or informal jobs. But they "work" the system as well: they make sure the money they earn does not come to the attention of the welfare department. They conceal outside income because if they told their caseworker they were working or receiving outside assistance, their welfare checks would soon be reduced by nearly the full amount of their earnings, leaving them as poor as before.

Using data from in-depth interviews with fifty Chicago-area welfare recipients. I show that single mothers did not receive enough money from AFDC to support their families. As a result, all the women I interviewed supplemented their checks and concealed this information from their caseworkers. Although many of these mothers had received welfare for most of their adult lives, none liked being on welfare or having to hide outside income, though they believed their actions were economically necessary. Despite their discomfort, most mothers stayed on welfare because they could not find jobs that made them better off.

In sum, many unskilled single mothers spend much of their adult lives on welfare not because welfare warps their personalities or makes them dependent but because while welfare pays badly, low-wage jobs do not pay any better. Most welfare mothers would leave welfare for work if they could end up with significantly more disposable income as a result.

In the pages below I first describe my methods of research. Then I construct budgets of expenses and income for the mothers in my sample. There is a wide shortfall between what they spent and what they received from welfare and food stamps. Finally, I explain how these women closed this gap by relying on friends, family, absent fathers, boyfriends, and most important, by working.

METHOD

My respondents came from Cook County (Chicago and its surrounding suburbs). Cook County provides AFDC benefits that approximate the national average and has a welfare population that is quite diverse. Between 1988 and 1990, a wide variety of individuals introduced me to fifty-nine mothers on AFDC. All but nine agreed to be interviewed for this study. These women represented thirty-three independent networks and resided in about one-third of Chicago's eighty-eight community areas and five suburbs. The sample included both never-married and divorced mothers, mothers at various educational levels, mothers of black, white, Hispanic, and Asian descent, mothers living in private and public housing, mothers of different age groups, and both long-term and short-term recipients.

My sample is 46 percent African-American (as compared to roughly 40 percent of welfare recipients nationally), 38 percent non-Hispanic white (as compared to 39 percent), 10 percent Hispanic, and 6 percent Asian.[1] Because I wanted to maximize my chances of finding recipients who lived on welfare alone, I oversampled those living in public housing (42 percent as compared to 18 percent nationally) (U.S. House of Representatives 1990: 580, 586).

I conducted most of these one- to three-hour interviews in respondents' homes. In initial interviews, I gathered topical life histories. In subsequent interviews, I collected detailed income and expenditure data. I asked respondents to estimate income and expenditures during the previous month. I then asked how much these monthly amounts had varied over the previous twelve months. Usually, respondents had copies of phone, electric, and gas bills on hand, which they showed me. Because their budgets were tight, respondents typically knew what they spent each month. Most knew the exact cost of each food and household item they purchased and spoke at length about which stores had the lowest prices. If they could not remember how much they spent, I asked them to keep track during the next month and report back. I had respondents estimate their monthly income and expenditures at least twice and asked them to account for any discrepancies. Finally, I asked if they had made large one-time purchases during the previous year (VCRs, furniture, appliances, bicycles, etc.). Respondents generally paid for these items in monthly installments. I spread lump-sum payments evenly over twelve months. I interviewed each respondent at least twice, most between three and five times. I tape-recorded, transcribed, coded, and analyzed each interview using a computer database program.

EXPENSES

The average woman in my sample spent $864 a month. Of this, food and housing accounted for $501. These figures appear in the first column of Table 1. The upper portion of the table is devoted to expenses and the lower portion to income. The amount of money paid for housing varied considerably depending on whether the mother lived in subsidized housing, shared housing with others, or paid the market rate for her own apartment. Because this so heavily influenced the budgets of these women, I have broken down the sample by housing category in columns two, three, and four. Those living in private market-rate housing paid $467 for housing compared to $208 for those who doubled up and $123 for those living in subsidized housing. Those living in private and subsidized housing spent about the same amount for food

($267 and $264 respectively), but those sharing housing spent far less because most of these mothers had only one child, whereas other mothers usually had two or three.

From Table 1 we see that those living in private housing spent far less for items other than housing and food. Car payments, disposable diapers, and burial or life insurance costs (included in miscellaneous expenses) account for most of this difference. Since no privately housed mothers lived in suburbs, they did not need cars. As only a few of these mothers had infants, most did not buy diapers. Finally, these primarily white mothers did not purchase burial insurance. Most black mothers—especially those living in Chicago's dangerous housing projects—said they could not do without burial insurance, for which local morticians charged about $20 per month. If we eliminate these three items, other expenses only varied by about $20 between groups.

At the bottom of Table 1, I have calculated several overall measures of expenses compared to income. The first measure, total expenses minus welfare income, shows the net overall shortfall was $343 for all the women. However, it was $432 for women living in private housing but only $320 for those who shared housing and $276 for women living in subsidized housing.[2]

A second measure, the cost of housing and food minus total income from welfare, shows how much money these women had left over each month for all other expenses once they had paid for food and housing. Overall, there was only $10 left over once rent and food were paid for. But for women living in subsidized housing there was $119. For those sharing housing there was $52 left over. In contrast, mothers living in private housing were already $147 in debt: their total welfare benefit failed by a wide margin even to pay for their rent and food.

From this we could say that women living in private housing were $266 worse off ($147 plus $119) each month than their counterparts living in subsidized housing, even though their welfare benefits were higher ($587 versus $506 because of larger average family sizes). Mothers who share housing are $62 ($119 minus $52) worse off than those with subsidies, but $199 ($147 plus $52) better off than those with their own market-rent apartments.

Although those paying market rents were clearly the worst off, all three categories faced the same fundamental reality—the system did not provide

TABLE I   BUDGETS FOR 50 CHICAGO-AREA AFDC FAMILIES BY HOUSING CATEGORY

N	All, 50	Private Housing, 17	Shared Housing, 11	Subsidized Housing, 22
Expenses				
Housing[1]	$264	$467	$208	$123
Food	$247	$267	$181	$264
Other	$353	$285	$372	$396
Phone	$28	$23	$13	$40
Check cashing	$5	$5	$4	$6
Clothing/shoes	$47	$39	$60	$47
School supplies	$10	$8	$9	$12
Toiletries/cleaning	$30	$35	$31	$26
Laundry/dry cleaning	$32	$44	$16	$30
Transportation	$41	$39	$50	$38
Over-the-counter medical costs	$13	$13	$16	$11
Time payments[2]	$19	$22	$21	$15
Entertainment/travel	$22	$15	$22	$28
Cigarettes/alcohol	$27	$17	$30	$34
Lottery	$3	$5	$2	$1
Car payments	$22	$3	$49	$24
Misc.[3]	$54	$17	$48	$85
Total expenses	$864	$1,019	$761	$782
Income				
Welfare				
AFDC	$324	$349	$287	$320
Foods stamps	$197	$238	$154	$186
Income from other sources				
Unearned				
Friends/family	$59	$43	$111	$45
Boyfriends	$76	$123	$18	$69
Absent fathers	$30	$27	$37	$29
Other	$45	$70	$15	$40
Earned				
Work in the regular economy	$128	$88	$162	$141
Work in the underground economy	$38	$81	$19	$14
Total other sources	$376	$432	$362	$338
Total welfare income[4]	$521	$587	$441	$506
Total income all sources	$897	$1019	$803	$844
Shortfall				
Welfare income minus total expenses	−$343	−$432	−$320	−$276
Welfare income minus housing and food	+$10	−$147	+$52	+$119
Total income minus total expenses	−$33	+$0	−$42	−$62

1. Rent or mortgage, gas, and electricity. Gas is the main source of heat in Chicago.
2. Most of these expenses were for furniture or household appliances.
3. This category includes expenditures for baby care (diapers), hair care, cosmetics, jewelry, expenses for special occasions (gifts and party costs), moving expenses and insurance (life and burial). Burial insurance, for example, is common in black neighborhoods and costs about $20 per month.
4. Table has been somewhat changed from original publication, with permission of the author.

enough money to support a family, as several women indicated:

> I don't ever pay off all my bills, so there isn't ever anything left over. As soon as I get my check, it's gone, and I don't have anything left.

> What you have to live off isn't enough. Me myself, I just got back on, and I had been off for about six years because I was working. But having a baby I had to get back on the program. It's just not enough. You just can't live off it especially with three kids or two kids. . . . It is impossible the things you have to do, to last you `til the next month. Me myself, I get $380 for three kids. The rent I pay is just impossible plus my other little bills.

> Oh yeah. It ain't enough! It ain't enough! Get a big sign saying "That is not enough!" We want more! More! It's just not enough what we're getting.

INCOME

My sample's total income averaged $897 a month, of which 58 percent, $521, came from AFDC and food stamps. Half of the remaining 42 percent came from work of various kinds and just under half from absent fathers, boyfriends, and relatives. Respondents obtained the remainder from student loans, insurance settlements, churches, and community organizations. Although no mother received income from all these sources, most combined several strategies to balance their budget. I divide these strategies in two categories: unearned and earned income.

Unearned Income

First, I discuss assistance received from others and not earned by working. This includes assistance from family, friends, boyfriends, absent fathers, churches, community organizations, student loans and grants, and legal settlements.

Assistance from Family and Friends Nineteen recipients received contributions from family and friends. Thirteen respondents had parents, friends, and relatives who consistently helped. For the other six, friends and family helped in emergencies and on special occasions.

Recipients felt it was unreasonable that the welfare department required them to report such assistance. Since families and friends gave support to "put food on the table" or to "pay the light bill before the electricity gets shut off," respondents maintained it was "crazy" to let welfare "take that away from us."

> A lot of people lie; I know that I have had to lie. Like that they get monies. Like my mom. If she gave me $100 to help me get through, to pay the bills that I've had overdue, or to help me get through, or whatever, I'm not going to claim that to the Public Aid!

Although respondents did not work for this assistance, they spent time and energy establishing and maintaining these relationships. Friends and relatives often pressured mothers to meet relational demands, pushed them to become self-supporting, and expected they take steps (i.e., attend educational or training programs) to achieve financial independence.

Boyfriends and Absent Fathers Boyfriends were also a common source of unearned income. When boyfriends "lived in," mothers felt entitled to regular and substantial assistance. In my small sample, about half of the thirteen live-in boyfriends worked at regular jobs. Boyfriends who worked regular jobs were a more reliable source of financial support than those who only hustled on the street or worked in illegal activities.

> It's difficult around here to find a good man. Most of them don't work. They just work the streets, you know. They just steal and deal and stuff. That kind of thing is a drag. I mean, it's very risky, and though it brings in a lot of money, eventually they're going to lose it all and you're going down with them. My first husband worked the streets, and I know now enough to stay away from that kind.

Mothers claimed they had little difficulty convincing boyfriends to assist in supporting children who were, in most cases, not their own. They had more trouble convincing absent fathers to help (see Liebow 1967: 74–102). Although almost every mother sampled cooperated with government officials to establish paternity for her children, many had no court-ordered support award. Further, support orders did not guarantee payment. Even when absent fathers met their obligation, Public Aid required that support payments be made through the department. Upon receiving payment, Public Aid kept all but $50, which it "passed through" to a recipient as exempt income.

Some mothers circumvented these rules and arranged for absent fathers to pay them directly without the knowledge of the welfare department. In this way they kept the full amount. Even then, support was seldom reliable or substantial, since many of the absent fathers in question worked irregularly or for low wages, had children by other women who also needed support, or were in prison. Mothers could not count on such income, and offered this as one reason why they did not report it.

> Well, the son's father had given me a little bit of money, here and there. But I'm not going to report that: that's not a steady income. I can't rely on him.

Almost all mothers were indignant that the welfare department expected them to report such income and felt welfare officials were "cheating" when they deducted support payments from welfare checks.

Churches and Community Agencies   A few tenacious respondents "got an income" by "hitting" or "begging from" churches and community agencies. Most Chicago churches and agencies give away small amounts of food and clothing. Some also give money for specific needs, like eyeglasses or dental work.

> Two weeks before the checks come out I hit the churches. The churches will let you come the week before you are getting your check, so I hit four different churches in a week. I get about $150 worth of groceries plus they give clothes.

In Chicago, enough churches and community groups offer assistance so a recipient can receive cash and in-kind aid from several sources in a single month.

> You know, getting around and getting the car payment or insurance payment made by churches is an income too. I had to go to one church after another. I would try to remember which one I hadn't gone to and ask them. Oh gosh, I think there were three churches that gave me money to get glasses. But [I only needed one pair], so I paid my car payment and insurance too.

Student Grants and Legal Settlements   Two respondents won large cash settlements for injuries. They did not report this income to Public Aid, as they would have been cut off from all assistance until they had depleted these resources. Full-time student mothers partly relied on student loans and grants to make ends meet. By the time they paid tuition and books, they had only a few hundred dollars left per school term. Still, this extra cash was essential.

> After you pay for your books and everything you may get a refund whatever is left so I get about $200 or $300 a semester and I don't report that.

Earned Income

Just over half of those interviewed did not receive substantial outside assistance, and engaged in part-time or full-time unreported work to make ends meet. I divide earned income from unreported work into two categories: work in the regular economy and work in the underground economy.

Work in the Regular Economy   Seven mothers obtained false social security numbers and worked at regular jobs. They earned an average of $5 an hour. Mothers worked as teacher's aides, nurse's aides, fast-food workers, factory workers, and secretaries. Respondents reported that obtaining false social security cards was easy:

> [You'll find welfare mothers in] any factory. They have a whole network. [False] social security cards are easy to come by—they're a dime a dozen. I could take you to a place right now to get one where I used to work. I was told many times, "Just give me $25, and I'll get you a card." [At this factory] about 25 of them was doing it, and they offered to show me. They was making $5, $6 an hour plus the welfare they was getting.

In my sample, regular jobs taken under false identities proved more reliable and profitable than off-the-books work. Respondents expressed frustration that they "had" to conceal the fact they were working regular jobs because they didn't earn enough to forgo welfare.

> [I work] at [a fast-food place] for $4 an hour. It's still not enough. I wish I could go off aid and let them know that I work.

In addition to low pay, respondents cited frequent lay-offs, uncertainty over the number of hours one could work, and lack of health benefits as reasons why they could not report their work. Their claim that "everybody knows" and "everybody does it" strengthened their belief that concealment was legitimate.

Twenty-two respondents worked part-time at regular jobs or odd jobs but were paid in cash off the books. Jobs included bartending, catering, house cleaning, child care, retail work, and sewing. Because these jobs paid cash, there was little chance AFDC could monitor earnings. Thus, although off-the-books jobs paid only about $3 an hour, most mothers preferred them to better-paid jobs requiring social security numbers.

> I really [have] trouble claiming my work. I know and everyone else knows [about off-the-books] work where you can make cash and not tell them about it. . ..It's the only way to survive.

Some employers reportedly colluded with recipients, offering the option of cash work at a slightly lower wage.

Off-the-books jobs ranged from jobs with regular hours at a single place of employment to highly irregular neighborhood odd jobs. Many said they worked odd jobs when other more reliable strategies failed. Odd jobs offered a type of unemployment insurance to those between what respondents sometimes dubbed "real" or more regular jobs. Nonworking mothers pursued odd jobs when they were between boyfriends or when a friend or relative failed to come through. Irregular jobs were also quite important to underground workers—those who made ends meet by selling sex, drugs, and stolen goods—a point addressed below.

Work in the Underground Economy   Ten mothers worked in the underground economy: they engaged in activities that were against the law, in addition to violating the welfare rules. Those who sold drugs usually sold marijuana and made only a modest profit.[3] One respondent sold cocaine, but was murdered by her supplier during the course of the project because she owed him $600. Another mother said she stopped selling crack after a police officer told her the state would take custody of her children if she was caught. Some mothers fenced stolen goods, including meat, jewelry, and VCRs. The highest-paid work these women performed was selling sex, from which they earned about $40 per hour. Five mothers supplemented their welfare in this way.

To keep the frequency of their underground work to a minimum, respondents combined underground jobs with odd jobs they performed on a more routine basis.

> I might ask somebody if I could do their laundry so I could get some cigarettes, or [beg for money on the street]. I have done some of that in my day. And on a hot summer day, I might get an ounce of marijuana, roll some joints. It cost me $30, [and] I get $120 in profit. I don't do it often.
>
> I [buy joints wholesale] from a friend of mine and I sell them and make a profit. I do this about every other month, and I make about $150. I sell drugs, sell articles which aren't mine, pick up cans, do house chores, shovel snow, [and] cut grass.

These women did not call themselves "dealers," "fences," or "prostitutes." In fact, they distinguished themselves from "professionals," those who worked in the underground economy "for a living." Although those women who sold sex described their activities as "turning tricks," "selling ass," or "selling myself," they did not consider these activities prostitution, but rather, "a social thing," or "social prostitution." In keeping with this self-definition, they claimed they did not solicit openly or often. Most developed regular customers, often servicing only one or two for a period of time. This exclusivity lent some measure of legitimacy to the exchange of sex for money.

> I also think a lot of people have affairs with guys who will pay some of their bills. It's like a more legitimate prostitution. There is not really an exchange of money for services. It is more of a social thing. You are sleeping with this person, and in return he is taking care of a few things for you.

Informants claimed they wanted desperately to be good mothers and keep their families together. Most "professional" dealers, fences, and prostitutes they knew were not good parents to their children. Respondents believed the children of professionals were "trouble," and usually "[got] messed up at an early age." Some claimed they knew professionals who lost custody of their children through neglect or imprisonment.

Those working illegal jobs felt it was unacceptable to perform such activities unless they had exhausted all other resources and the well-being of their children was threatened.

> Like if I don't have food, I have to make some extra money by turning a few tricks. I also do hair, baby-sitting, clean the landlord's house, laundry; . . . [from the combination of these activities] I clear close to $200 a month.
>
> Once my bills were pretty high, and I had to pay them. So what I did was give my nephew my whole check and went in with him to get a pound of reefer. And I got my interest out of that, so I was able to pay what I had to pay.
>
> I've sold things that wasn't mine . . . . I've stolen out of the store to feed my kids. I was sent to the court and spent a day in jail for it. The judge understood and let me out.

PASSIVE DEPENDENCY OR MAINSTREAM VALUES?

Many women on welfare told me "I never thought I'd sink so low," or "I dream of the day that I can leave welfare behind." The overwhelming majority wanted to become self-sufficient through work, and a substantial minority had tried leaving welfare for reported work, only to return to welfare when they found they could not pay their bills. Respondents disliked concealing outside income from the welfare department. In nearly every interview, women used phrases like "I had no choice" or "I was forced to" to account for their actions.

Respondents felt particularly guilty about the lies welfare "forced" them to tell to conceal outside income.

> Public Aid is an agency that I believe can teach a person how to lie. If you tell them the truth, you won't get any help. But if you go down there and tell them a lie, you get help. And I can't understand it, and every woman on Public Aid will tell you the same thing. It teaches you to lie. It won't accept the truth. So when you deal with Public Aid, you have to tell them a tale.

Respondents feared they would suffer real material hardship if they didn't "beat the system."

> One thing about being on AFDC . . . you have to think. You have to set up a strategy on how to beat them and not let them beat you. You know it's bad that you have to think of [a strategy] though. And yet you have to go in there and beat the system. You cannot go in there and be totally honest, because you'll lose every time.

Some feared they would go hungry, end up on the streets, or lose custody of their children. Most could not imagine living solely on welfare; no one knew anyone who did.

These mothers insisted lying was out of character for them, something which they would not do normally. One mother remarked, "Public Aid forces you into deceit and dishonesty, things you normally would not think of doing." Respondents chose between being good mothers and good citizens. In every case, concern for their children's welfare outweighed moral qualms.

> [So how did you feel about having to lie?] I felt guilty. I really did. I felt I was cheating my government, but on the other hand I had to think about my family. I was not about to let my children starve or have no clothes on their backs.

The dissonance between conscience and what mothers perceived as necessary dishonesty diminished self-respect. Most respondents spoke passionately about how receiving welfare made them "feel like dirt" or "feel so ashamed I could die." Their struggle to keep their families together increased their sense of being "on the bottom."

> Sometimes you get so desperate you think the only way you can make ends meet is to be a prostitute. I think that is a gut-level feeling. You feel you are on the bottom anyhow.

Although recipients worried about day-to-day material survival, most viewed survival as not merely a matter of having adequate food, shelter, and clothing. They felt there were "psychological" and "social" aspects as well.

> You know, we live in such a materialistic world. Our welfare babies have needs and wants too. They see other kids going to the circus, having toys and stuff like that. You gotta do what you gotta do

to make your kid feel normal. There is no way you can deprive your child.

The above quote captures a common sentiment among the welfare recipients I interviewed: children need to have an occasional treat, and mothers who refuse may deprive their offspring of normalcy. On a more fundamental level, many mothers worried that if they did not provide a few extras—expensive tennis shoes, for example—their children would be tempted to sell drugs to get them.

My boy, he sees these kids that sell drugs. They can afford to buy these [tennis shoes] and he can't. So I have my little side job and [buy them for him]. You got to do it to keep them away from drugs and . . . from the streets.

The mothers themselves needed an occasional extra, too. Many women reported that by spending small amounts on cosmetics, cigarettes, alcohol, or the lottery, they could avoid feeling "like I'm not completely on the bottom," or "my life is not completely hopeless."

By setting benefits so low, welfare denies these needs and increases recipients' perceived isolation from society's mainstream. The following quote, offered by an unusually articulate respondent, reflects the commonly expressed belief that welfare fails to integrate the poor with the larger society.

I don't understand why [Public Aid is] punishing people who are poor if you want to mainstream them. If indeed, the idea is to segregate, to be biased, to create a widening gap between the haves and the have-nots, then the welfare system is working. If it is to provide basic needs, not just financial but psychological and social needs of every human being, then the system fails miserably.

WORK AND WELFARE: A DUAL DILEMMA

For the fifty Chicago-area recipients I interviewed, finding a job that paid more than welfare was nearly impossible. If welfare recipients could not live on their benefits, they could hardly live on wages resembling those benefits. Furthermore, leaving welfare has serious economic costs, since working mothers typically incur more health, transportation, and clothing expenses than their welfare counterparts.

Few of the jobs that unskilled or semiskilled single mothers can get offer health benefits. Although Medicaid currently covers those who leave welfare for work for one year, few employers provide family coverage after that year is up. Those who qualify for coverage usually must make a copayment they cannot afford.

They say that they want mothers to get back off the Aid and work, okay. There's a lot of mothers who want to work—okay—like me, I want to work. And then you work, [your employer] don't give you [medical insurance]. And sometimes, it depends on how much you make, they cut off your medical card, and when you go out and get those jobs you don't make enough to pay rent, then medical and bills. Then they'll probably get laid off, or they won't like it, and then they have to start all over again and it might be months before they get their benefits going again . . . . It's just another hassle.

The added costs of health care, child care, transportation, and clothing often mean wages do not cover expenses. As a result, mothers who want to work feel they cannot.

Just looking at it doesn't make sense to have to go to a job that pays the minimum wage when you consider that $2, [per hour] goes to pay the babysitter so you bring home $2 and you have to put your food, medical, your rent on $2 an hour—you can't make it. So you go down to welfare because it is cheaper to live for single parents.

I have applied all over, looking for [a job]. But a lot of places that are hiring are only paying me [minimum wage], and that's not enough for me to survive. I had a chance at [a fast food] place, but I figured out how much they were paying. . .and it just wasn't enough to cover my bills.

Since most low-wage entry-level workers experience periodic layoffs, mothers feared taking a reported job: if they lost it they would have had to reapply for welfare. In Chicago, eligibles wait four to six weeks for their benefits to start. In the interim, families are left without any means of support. About one-third of those I sampled had lost low-wage jobs in the past. Some had friends and family to tide them over, but others suffered severe material hardship—an experience they did not want to repeat.

I asked respondents how much they would have to make to leave welfare altogether. Mothers said they would not take a job paying less than $7 to $10 per hour. Jobs at this wage are hard to come by, especially for women with few skills.[4]

Recipients' estimates of an adequate hourly wage agree with data from the Consumer Expenditure Survey of 1984–85, which show that single mothers who work spend about $800 more for health care, $300 more for clothing, $500 more for transportation, and $1,200 more for child care than nonworking single mothers do. By adding these figures to the amounts privately-housed welfare mothers spent, I calculate that working mothers without housing subsidies, but with average child care, clothing, and transportation expenses, need to earn at least $14,800 per year to live as well as their welfare counterparts. Unless they too have substantial outside income, working mothers would need to earn $7.50 to $9.00 per hour to reach this amount, depending on how many hours they work (Jencks and Edin 1991). The average welfare mother cannot expect to earn much. Michalopoulos and Garfinkel (1989) estimate an average welfare mother can expect to earn $5.15 per hour (in 1989 dollars). Assuming they have average work-related expenses, this approximately equals the average welfare benefit package.

Beyond its economic costs, work has substantial noneconomic costs. Few day care centers accept newborns or children over twelve, so their mothers must find alternatives. Working mothers who stay home with sick children may lose their jobs, but they cannot send sick children to day care. Working mothers usually are not home when their school-aged children return from school. In the summer, mothers have difficulty finding responsible adults to watch their children. Unless mothers can afford after-school and summer day care, their children forfeit adult supervision for a substantial part of each day.

In Chicago ghetto neighborhoods, unsupervised children are vulnerable to gang activity, drug use, and teen pregnancy. In my sample, one women's twelve-year-old daughter was "sleeping around with a married man" while she was away at work. She found out from the man's wife, who threatened to kill her child. Another quit her job to make sure her fourteen-year-old son stayed in school. While she worked, her son skipped school repeatedly, ran with a dangerous gang, and was arrested for theft.

The following account reflects the frustration mothers experience when they try to function as full-time workers and mothers, especially when the resulting income is inadequate.

[It's] not worth it to go out working when you think about it, you know. It's not worth it 'cause you have kids and then they gonna be sick, and you gonna have to go to the doctor, and mainly that's why lots of mothers don't go out and get jobs because they don't think it's worth it. Going out there and working and then having a lot of problems and then can't even buy groceries and stuff like that.

DISCUSSION

The so-called "welfare trap" is not primarily one of behavioral dependency but one of economic survival. In a society where single mothers must provide financially for their children, where women are economically marginalized into unreliable jobs that pay little more than the minimum wage, where child support is inadequate or nonexistent, and where day care costs and health insurance (usually not provided by employers) are unaffordable for most, it should surprise no one that half the mothers supporting children on their own choose welfare over reported work.

While some argue welfare creates the very problems it tries to alleviate by setting up a system of perverse incentives that reward dependency rather than work (Mead 1989), I argue that the welfare system actually prohibits dependency by paying too little to make this possible.

The evidence presented here challenges the validity of three widely accepted stereotypes about welfare recipients: they do not work, they do not want to work, and their behaviors reflect values different from mainstream society. These findings have important implications for the debate about the underclass and current and future public policy but must be interpreted with care since the sample is not representative of mothers in other cities and states.

The obvious solution to the problem of inadequate benefits or low earnings is to increase one or the other. The expansion of AFDC benefits is politically unlikely. Since most Americans believe single mothers should work, nonworkers will always be considered outside the mainstream (Garfinkel and McLanahan 1986).

Rather than focus on expanding benefits, I suggest we ensure that those who work full-time can earn a living wage. Several leading policy analysts have proposed that we increase single mothers' income through a child support assurance system and wage supplements of various kinds (Ellwood 1988; Garfinkel 1990; Garfinkel and McLanahan 1986; Jencks and Edin 1991; Orr 1991; Wilson 1987). Any set of solutions, however, must take into account that mothers need to roughly double their current poten-tial earnings to make work a viable alternative to welfare.

Other barriers to employment include lack of af-fordable child care, insufficient health insurance cov-erage, and inadequate or nonexistent child support payments (Danzinger and Nichols-Casebolt 1990, Glass 1990; Marshall and Marx 1991). Providing these benefits to more families would significantly lower the cost of working and facilitate the transition from welfare to self-sufficiency through work.

ACKNOWLEDGMENTS

I wish to gratefully acknowledge the help of the fifty welfare households who participated in this study, who must remain anonymous. Christopher Jencks offered invaluable assistance in every phase of this research. Malcolm Spector gave important editing assistance. Arlene Kaplan Daniels, Susan Mayer, and Timothy J. Nelson also made helpful comments. Shirlee Garcia, Sonja Grant, and Deborah Hayes assisted with interviewing, and Julie Mittler contributed administrative support. Correspondence to Edin, 87B Wentworth Street, Charleston, SC 29401.

NOTES

1. As a white researcher, I was concerned that racial and class differences between me and respondents might limit my interviewing effectiveness. Because of this, I hired one Hispanic and two African-American interviewers. All three were former or current welfare recipients, and after careful training they helped me contact and interview 21 of the 27 black and Hispanic respondents in the sample.

2. Benefits in Chicago are slightly higher than average: no state provides benefits generous enough to cover what the 50 Chicago-area mothers reported spending. Cook County mothers needed at least $961 in cash and food stamps to meet their monthly expenses. It is unlikely that rents in any major city average more than $100 less than in Chicago, so welfare families probably did not get by on less than $750 anywhere. In 1988, a family of three received cash and food stamps worth $750 a month in Los Angeles and San Francisco and $701 in New York City, but these cities were all more expensive than Chicago. Benefits were $699 in Detroit, $589 in Philadelphia, $491 in Atlanta, and $412 in Houston and Dallas (U.S. House of Representatives 1990). Detroit is thus the only major city where a family might have gotten by on AFDC and food stamps. Families living in low-cost rural areas of high-benefit states might also get by. National figures and other small-scale studies are consistent with the story of these 50 Chicago-area recip-ients (Edin 1989; Gardiner and Lyman 1984; Halsey, Nold, and Block 1982; Jencks and Edin 1991; Sharff 1987).

3. I asked respondents to estimate the time they spent selling drugs and stolen goods and how much they made. A simple calculation of earnings over time spent shows these jobs paid approximately the minimum wage (from $3 to $5 an hour).

4. Approximately one-third said they would not take a job without benefits because they or their children had ex-pensive health care needs.

REFERENCES

Danzinger, Sandra K., and Ann Nichols-Casebolt. 1990. "Child support in paternity cases." *Social Service Review* 64: 458–74.

Ellwood, David T. 1988. *Poor Support: Poverty in the American Family.* New York: Basic Books.

Gardiner, John A., and Theodore R. Lyman. 1984. *The Fraud Control Game: State Responses to Fraud and Abuse in AFDC and Medicaid Programs.* Bloomington, Ind.: Indiana University Press.

Garfinkel, Irwin. 1990. "A new child support assurance system." Institute for Research on Poverty, Discussion Paper #916-90. Madison, University of Wisconsin.

Garfinkel, Irwin, and Sara McLanahan. 1986. *Single Mothers and Their Children.* Washington, D.C.: The Urban Institute.

Glass, Becky L. 1990. "Child support enforcement: An implementation analysis." *Social Service Review* 64: 542–56.

Halsey, H., F. Nold, and M. Block. 1982. "AFDC: An analysis of grant overpay." Palo Alto, Calif.: Block and Nold Economic Consultants.

Jencks, Christopher, and Kathryn Edin. 1991. "Reforming welfare." In *Rethinking Social Policy,* ed. Christopher Jencks, 204–35. Cambridge, Mass.: Harvard University Press.

Liebow, Elliot. 1967. *Tally's Corner.* Boston: Little, Brown and Company.

Marshall, Nancy L., and Fern Marx. 1991. "The affordability of child care for the working poor." *Families in Society* 72:202–11.

Mead, Lawrence. 1989. "The logic of workfare: The underclass and work policy." In William Julius Wilson, ed., *The Ghetto Underclass: Social Science Perspectives,* 156–69. Newbury Park, Calif.: Sage.

Michalopoulos, Charles, and Irwin Garfinkel. 1989. "Reducing welfare dependence and poverty of single mothers by means of earnings and child support: Wishful thinking and realistic possibilities." Institute for Research on Poverty, Discussion paper #882-89. Madison: University of Wisconsin.

Murray, Charles. 1984. *Losing Ground.* New York: Basic Books.

Novak, Michael. 1987. *The New Consensus on Family and Welfare.* American Enterprise Institute for Public Policy Research. Milwaukee, Wisc.: Marquette University.

Orr, Lloyd D. 1991. "Wage rate subsidies: Some new dimensions." Unpublished manuscript. Bloomington: Indiana University.

Sharff, Jagna Wojcicka. 1987. "The underground economy of neighborhood." In *Cities of the United States,* ed. Leith Mullings, 19–50. New York: Columbia University Press.

U.S. House of Representatives. 1990. "Background material and data on programs within the jurisdiction of the Committee on Ways and Means." Committee on Ways and Means. Washington, DC: Government Printing Office.

Wilson, William Julius. 1987. *The Truly Disadvantaged.* Chicago: University of Chicago Press.

READING 39

The Truth About Women and Power

Harriet Woods

> *It is time to unleash the full capacity . . . of the women of the world.*
>
> —*U.S. Ambassador to the United Nations Madeleine K. Albright, at Beijing, China, September 6, 1995*

For as long as any of us can remember—certainly back to the days when women began to vote—the big question has been whether there ever will be a woman president. In 1966, when Indira Ghandi became prime minister of India, writer Betty Friedan noted with frustration that the thought of a woman president in the United States was still so inconceivable that it seemed like a joke. Today we're in a new era. We've had a woman secretary of state and a woman attorney general. The question no longer is whether there will be a woman president but who she will be, and the precise date of her inauguration.

The problem is that it's the wrong question to be asking. In 1992, a national magazine asked Gloria Steinem to write an article to be called "Why I'm Not Running for President." In declining, she explained that she thought the presidency was chiefly a bully pulpit and that change had to come from below.[1] The focus on the exceptional heroine allows the majority of women to be bystanders; they can avoid personal responsibility for improving society while being groupies for someone at the top. Our history demonstrates that this approach won't work; leadership must start at the grassroots. Speculation on a woman president is good meat for media, but the most significant measure of women's progress isn't a woman president; it's further down the political food chain.

Unfortunately, few Americans pay attention to how many women are in local government or to what percentage of the state legislature is composed of women. But if we don't reach critical mass in state legislatures, it won't happen in Congress, and that means there will be very slim pickings to find a woman president. The prime candidates for president are governors and senators, and they tend to compete after experience in previous office. Five out of six of the new women elected to Congress in 1998 had previously served in state legislatures. As things are, a 1998 project promoting a woman in the White House had a tough time finding even one credible candidate who might have a realistic chance running for president in the year 2000; there should be dozens, as there are among men.

It's true that a woman president, no matter who she is, will be an important signal that women have achieved equal status, and it will encourage more discussion about women politicians, but as women learned in Great Britain, having Margaret Thatcher as prime minister did virtually nothing to remove barriers impeding other women's political and social progress. It took a Labor Party sweep in 1997 when Labor deliberately flooded local tickets with women candidates, to reverse years of exclusion. The number of Labor women in the House of Commons jumped from 63 to 101, pushing the overall percentage of women to 18.2 percent of total members. Stunned Tory members responded "like schoolboys," cupping their hands in front of their chests during a woman member's speech as if "they were weighing melons."[2] Margaret Thatcher never had threatened them so much.

It's popular to note that at least 20 other nations have had women prime ministers or presidents, but most were selected through the parliamentary system, and some of the most celebrated inherited power through family dynasties, such as Indira Ghandi, Benazir Bhutto, and Khaleda Zia, from India, Pakistan, and Bangladesh, respectively. Our system demands a different process of credentialing. We will have a woman president when a savvy politician with fire in her belly, and the ability to raise lots of money, has the stamina to undertake the exhausting national marathon we require to win party nomination and election.

In the meantime, as we approach the new millennium, the hard truth is that there are nowhere near enough women competing for public office. Some 75 percent of incumbents are men, and incumbents are hard to evict. Even with the possibilities of term limits and redistricting, women continue to run uphill because those in power are in a better position to manipulate events to block newcomers. There were 100 fewer women running for legislative seats in 1998 than the 2,279 who ran in 1992. What if there had been double the number of well-qualified women candidates?

What will the numbers be in the years 2002 and 2004? As few as 4,000 or 5,000 serious women candidates in winnable legislative races across the country could wake up the whole political system—especially if they have behind them tens of thousands of well-informed women who understand the power they have and how to use it, and who are committed to being part of the political process. As we have seen, the prospect of a gender gap initially terrified national leaders in the 1980s; just think of the impact of well-informed, determined women running for winnable seats in every local constituency.

Change occurs when a broad segment of society insists that it happen. That is a power question. Who has it, who uses it, for what purposes? And these are questions with which women continue to have difficulty. Just as men want to be the strong leader who is respected and obeyed, women still want to be the "good girl" who makes no one angry. We continue to view one another through gender lenses, and then respond in our behavior in a way that reinforces those signals. That means that despite new opportunities, women still face old expectations. Army generals are supposed to be manly, even when they're female; nurses are supposed to be motherly, even when they're male. Those expectations can turn into barriers.

The truth about women and power is that our status has changed but not the institutions and policy-making structures that make up our world. We should have noticed when we leveled the playing field that it still belonged to somebody else. That isn't because of some male plot; rather, the difficulty is that our institutions continue to reflect past gender stereotypes. They fail to respond to the rapid changes in our culture, and that means much of government and the corporate world seems unattractive and incompatible with our values. We don't want to get involved in government if it seems like mud wrestling, or stay in the corporate rat race at the cost of family life. We are asked to change ourselves when what should be changing are the institutions and social practices.

It is ironic. We fought so long for equal opportunity, and now that doors are open, we find new challenges behind them. There is a niggling ambivalence about men and women's roles that continues to frustrate all of us and inhibits efforts at reform. We must convince men to join us in changing structures they thought worked for them but really no longer work well for anyone. In the political world, prospective candidates tell us they want no part of a system that's drowning in money, torn asunder by ideology and bitter partisanship, and that is entered by running an obstacle course while ducking rotten eggs. In the private sector, women and men increasingly are disillusioned by a corporate philosophy that eats up personal lives. We need not accept this world when we have the power to change it.

During a business breakfast not long ago, a woman who holds an executive position in the finance field mentioned that she really enjoys her status, but she said, of course, she wasn't talking about exerting "power." She didn't like the word; it suggested bullying. Her remarks took me back twenty years to a time when a speech to women using the word "power" caused a furor. There is a major problem here. If those who control the institutions in our society feel comfortable talking about power, with whatever meaning they give the word, and women don't, because of whatever meaning they give to it, then there is a serious disconnect.

I suggested to my breakfast companion that she might be overreacting to a false idea of power; the term just means an ability to get things done, to influence others to act in a way we want, a measurement of effective energy. It doesn't automatically involve force, confrontation, or any other negative quality. Indeed, many men and women provide a different power model that is more strategic, persuasive, and collaborative and that should be valued as much or more. She listened politely, clearly still disinclined to take any risks with her reputation.

"Women see [power] as a means to an end and men see it as an end,"[3] commented former Congresswoman Leslie Byrne of Virginia. She thought it might have something to do with the mothering role that requires women to put another life ahead of their own. Hillary Rodham Clinton told Congresswoman Margolies-Mezvinsky for her book that it might have something to do with boys' experience in sports and the early goal of playing to win. Generalizations are dangerous, but it would seem that many girls have learned to prefer winning because they are liked rather than because they beat someone else out. Gold medal women's soccer and hockey teams may provide a different model. They beat someone else out and they are liked.

"We willingly submit to this societal brainwashing [about power] until we realize [it] is directly in conflict with our own good,"[4] Congresswoman Margolies-Mezvinsky observed about women. To be liked isn't the same as being given power, former Governor Madeleine Kunin remarked. Women too often are appeased by compliments. She recalled a news commentator telling her that he was with her in his heart. "It wasn't his heart I wanted. It was his vote."[5]

Like my businesswoman friend, many women in the 103rd Congress were conscious of being viewed differently because of gender, but unlike her, they understood that women's attitudes in the power debate had very real consequences. "We have to be aggressive without looking aggressive," Karen Shepherd said. "We have to be fierce without looking bitchy."[6] Some didn't want to discuss power, but Congresswoman Carrie Meek of Florida had no problem in talking about it: "I think as [women] begin to push to get more power—and that's what we're doing . . . because power isn't anything that people want to give to you all the time—sometimes you have to take it."[7]

Here is the heart of our dilemma. If women are going to have a bigger voice in decisionmaking, confrontation is inevitable, but women's comfort level makes confrontation unacceptable. They believe that mixing it up in the political arena, whether as candidate or identified supporter, or facing someone down in the executive suite will exact a price they don't want to pay: the loss of peer approval. These women rarely allow themselves to acknowledge the satisfaction that comes from exercising power. They use power every day at home and at work, but they call it something else, so they can say no when asked to use their influence in more controversial arenas.

It is infuriating when one woman after another declines to lend her name to candidates or causes, let alone write a check, while men respond with alacrity in order to further their interests and their power relationships. The "good girl" complex leaves women vulnerable to manipulation by those who understand power very, very well and have reason not to want to share it. These people delight in labeling activist women with such unattractive adjectives as pushy, bitchy, and feminazi, to make others hesitate to emulate them or even to be involved in their causes. They've worked to make "feminist" a worrisome word. Even when women know these labels are distorted and agree with the goals of the women being attacked, they may join in the chorus blaming the women for being too conspicuously aggressive. Good girls don't stir up trouble.

What I failed to communicate to my breakfast companion is that power, like public service, can be tremendously satisfying. It can produce feelings that are downright euphoric. I can remember the first time it happened to me, during the solo flight as a student pilot. I was just seventeen and a few months earlier had discovered a small airfield on the outskirts of Chicago with a makeshift hangar, a few worn single-engine planes and—it was still wartime—a couple of instructors who looked like Air Force washouts. There was money in my pocket from a job in a record store, and I figured that learning to fly couldn't be much more difficult than learning to drive. After all, there were women aviators in the military ferrying airplanes across the country; it seemed like an adventure.

My parents were taken aback at first, but I always could count on mom. She agreed to take a test flight before saying an absolute no; the flight school used its best plane, the one least likely to leak gasoline on a passenger's feet, and the ride was a persuasive success. It wasn't long before my first solo flight. Going up was easy, but looking down at the plane's small shadow moving over the ground evoked a fresh realization of the fragility of the plane, and of life itself. Everything depended on bringing this machine safely down, and that depended on me. I had never felt such power, and such responsibility.

But it was power that served a very narrow purpose. A few years later, there was a different power experience as managing editor of *The Michigan Daily*, a daily campus newspaper in Ann Arbor. *Look* magazine ran a feature on college life in 1949 that included a telling photograph of me sitting on the copy desk, puffing a cigarette and looking tough. I thought that was the appropriate look for a woman boss. Clearly there still was some learning to do. What was important about this powerful position wasn't intimidating everyone as Big Woman on Campus; it was the ability to shape information for thousands of readers. That could change events.

The final lesson came years later on the day the traffic stopped speeding through our residential street. The door-to-door petition drive had been successful in pressuring authorities to act where an individual complaint had not. There was power in empowering others. The women who changed America in the 1960s and 1970s understood this very well. It would be a

mistake to read our history as a chronicle of famous personalities; these women had power because they inspired others to take action, communicating ideas, convening meetings, confronting authority, and educating women to take leadership. The world changed because those taking the lead spoke to greater dreams than any one individual's personal advancement.

It is unclear whether a younger generation understands that kind of power, which is born of a passion to end injustice. The more fortunate of today's women believe they already have the power to control their lives and need nothing more. They believe all barriers are down and there is no reason why they shouldn't reach any goal: Should I design buildings, be a judge, sell insurance, become a minister, a surgeon, master teacher, professional basketball player, or program a computer? Do I start a family now, or later? Or never? Go back to school, work at home, start a business?

The most fortunate women are not just holding jobs; they're doing interesting things in business, the professions, and community organizations. Most expect to work at least part-time during their lifetime, and that gives them a different view of their own value. They can't believe women ever put up with blatant gender discrimination. Patriarchy? What's that?

We rejoice for them, but it's unclear if they really understand their power, or what they can do with it. Will they use their muscle solely for personal goals, or are they also conscious of a responsibility for those less able to act on their own behalf? How much of their political capital are they willing to risk to improve the world around them? Do they understand that they can change conditions that limit them, instead of adapting to them? Former Texas Governor Ann Richards has commented, "You have got to be willing to step up and use the power—not just acquire it."[8]

Conservative groups argue that women are doing wonderfully and need no further interventions. They scold that women should stop acting like victims when they're not. They accuse feminism of creating present work-family tensions by pushing women into careers that require twelve-hour-day schedules with no time to bear or care for children. The conservatives don't propose changing the working conditions; they blame the women and advise them to stop trying to balance job and family, something that is economically impossible for the majority, who depend upon their work income.

We all should celebrate women's progress. The statistics are impressive; it's been only a generation since women couldn't get credit cards in their own name, didn't have coaches and uniforms for team sports, could be battered by husbands without legal recourse, and were often fired for getting pregnant. We can be proud of what we have accomplished. We've proved we aren't passive victims. It hasn't just been religious fundamentalists who have tried to block us or only the hard line conservatives who now praise our progress in order to stop it. Labor unions once opposed the Equal Rights Amendment as a danger to protective provisions in labor contacts. People have been trying to manipulate or control women's choices throughout history, always claiming to be helping us when the real agenda was something else.

Now we're told that gender problems ended with the passage of antidiscrimination laws. There's a great story demonstrating why that's a myth. It spread like wildfire on the Internet in 1999.[9] It seems that three tenured women professors in the School of Science at the Massachusetts Institute of Technology compared notes in 1995 and decided that they were being treated differently from male colleagues, in a way that discouraged their professional advancement. Indeed, their lives were being made miserable; they received less space, salary, awards, resources, and committee assignments than the men did. No one had spoken out because each woman feared being labeled a radical troublemaker in an institution that valued good behavior. Besides, discrimination was illegal, so how could it exist?

They conducted a survey in which other senior women faculty members confirmed their findings, although junior, untenured faculty women with less seniority did not, saying they sensed no discrimination and felt supported on the job. The junior faculty's big worry was the long-term impact on their careers of trying to combine family and work. The feelings of marginalization apparently began as women moved up, assuming tenured positions that placed them in competition for resources.

The surveyors were fortunate to have a sympathetic dean of science who set up a committee to formally pursue the inquiry. The committee's report not only confirmed that inequities existed for tenured women but it found also that the percentage of women faculty (8 percent) had not changed for at least ten years, despite rapidly increasing numbers of women science students. "The pipeline leaks at every stage of careers."

Throughout the inquiry, despite their discontent, the women encouraged a collaborative process that "could serve as a model for increasing the participation of women and also of underrepresented minorities." Their approach led to a reasonably hopeful ending, when the dean took specific actions to improve the status of senior women as well as to address the family-tenure concerns of the junior women, and to also establish a long-range process to increase the number of women on faculty.

"I was unhappy at MIT for more than a decade," a senior woman said. "I thought it was the price you paid if you wanted to be a scientist at an elite academic institution. After the committee formed and the dean responded, my life began to change. My research blossomed, my funding tripled. Now I love every aspect of my job. It is hard to understand how I survived all those years—or why!"

The MIT story struck a chord with women all over the country who knew something was not working in their corporate or professional settings but hesitated to complain. The MIT women were "gifted scientists [who had] themselves convinced that gender had nothing to do with their careers," but ran into a new discrimination that is "subtle but pervasive, and stems from unconscious ways of thinking that have been socialized into us, men and women alike."[10] We want to believe competence will be rewarded, but for that to be true, women must be prepared to expose and remedy the less obvious discrimination that results when we are measured "through the eyes of prejudice," with expectations based on unconscious stereotypes.

An important finding of the study was that different perceptions of gender bias by junior and senior women repeat themselves over generations. Current senior faculty said they too had begun by believing gender discrimination no longer existed. "Gradually, however, their eyes were opened to the realization that the playing field is not level after all, and that they had paid a high price both personally and professionally as a result."[11] Apparently the greater their stature, the greater the threat and the greater the inequities.

What finally propelled this small group of women to action was "the feeling of an injustice, the anger that accumulates from this recognition, and the strong desire to change things for themselves and for future generations of women."[12] They were able to feel that they were using their power not just for personal advancement, but for everyone.

When critics deride continued concern about discrimination, they miss the impact of conscious and unconscious gender judgments that can produce quite different experiences for men and women. We don't want to admit that we may still have different expectations of one another as men and women and that we can and must deal with this. There's a big difference between telling women that they have an equal chance to win in comparable circumstances to men, as we did in the National Women's Political Caucus, and telling them that comparable circumstances always exist, which is nonsense. There's also a big difference between viewing oneself as a passive victim and as someone with the responsibility to confront inequities and bring about change.

Women in America, just like men, are tremendously diverse in their political and social views, but it is astonishing what women can achieve when we do find common cause. For example, millions of women have joined together to fight breast cancer, rallying across political and ideological lines to raise money, insist on better research and care, and to lobby elected officials. True, it is a socially acceptable cause; no one had to explain the life-and-death urgency or manufacture emotion when word spread that congressmen wouldn't even listen to women's concerns. Indignant women didn't worry that they would be labeled "pushy" for their efforts.

A different example of women's collective strength occurred in Missouri in 1998 when an overwhelming turnout of women defeated a ballot measure to expand the legal right to carry concealed weapons. Women's resolve was remarkable given the adverse factors: Television was swamped with commercials favoring the proposal; it was presumed that the National Rifle Association would triumph in a conservative state. Pollsters reported that men were saying yes, and then noticing that their wives were saying no. Still, analysts were amazed when the measure was defeated, and they attributed the loss to a massive turnout of urban and suburban women voters who believed the proposal would mean more guns and simply didn't want any more. They could have stayed home, accepting "the inevitable," but they didn't. They used their political muscle.

What if we applied that muscle to assuring quality child care, universal health care, family planning funds, flexible working conditions, and wiser military policies? In the workplace, the home, the ballot box, and civic causes, women have power to make a difference.

This is more than a matter of numbers in polling places. Women today have technical skills, financial resources, and key positions in the private and public sector where they can be persuasive opinion-makers—if they are willing. Women are making the workplace a more humane environment, and they are providing models for collaboration in legislative negotiation. They are building effective partnerships across all kinds of old barriers. That is power. Why are we so reluctant to give success that name?

My sons are kind and caring human beings; I'm confident that my grandsons will be the same. Younger women can join with a new generation of men who share their concerns about family, workplace, and world, who welcome a society where duties and responsibilities are shared, and who are free of gender bias. Men need reassurance that change won't cost them their opportunities, and that we appreciate their contributions in all appropriate roles. They need, in turn, to appreciate our leadership. Together, we must reach out more aggressively across traditional barriers of party, race, class, culture, and nationality. Too many remain within arbitrary social boundaries, limiting their effectiveness. The struggle to transform society must benefit everyone, or it won't produce permanent benefits for anyone.

Women are rising up all over the world, particularly in third-world nations, where for so long they have been denied equality and dignity. Hillary Clinton's stirring charge in a speech at the Beijing UN conference that women's rights are human rights has brought new attention to issues such as rape as a tool of war, genital mutilation, sexual slavery, economic inequity, murder of girls in the name of family honor, and other forms of intimidation and violence. There are societies in which girls are denied education and women still are denied the vote. We cannot be complacent; fundamentalism is a danger everywhere, including in this country, where a veil of religion is used to give standing to proposals that would return women to second-class status.

Women throughout Africa, India, and Latin America are taking very real risks to speak up; they are surprising everyone by becoming candidates for major office, challenging deeply ingrained cultural patterns. Women are providing differing styles of leadership in a shattered world. In Ireland, in the former Yugoslavia, and in Somalia, women have organized themselves to overcome ethnic and religious hatreds and create dialogue, while traditional male-led groups continue to kill one another. Here at home, we have set our own examples: Women give direction and energy to crisis centers, to overburdened child care centers and clinics, to struggling public schools, and to training programs that teach alternatives to violence as a way of resolving disputes. There is plenty for us to do in the new century.

For American women, there's been a millennium issue for years. Think of the slogans "50–50 by 2000." "A woman president by 2010." Or just the perennial "Wait 'til Next year!" For the past fifty years, women have concentrated on changing an unsatisfactory present into a more perfect tomorrow. We've had to be futurists. Now we're told that the future is here. There's not much point talking about what we want the future to look like if we aren't ready to talk about using the power we have to achieve it. For those who want to have an impact, here are some ideas on how to start, reflecting the lessons of one lifetime's political voyages:

1. Make the connection between your life and the political process. What vital interests of yours need attention? Legislatures write divorce and child-support laws, tax codes, environmental laws, health and mental health regulations, standards for public schools, regulations for small business, and penalties for crime.
2. Make the connection between your own life and the lives of other women. All issues are women's issues, but common sense tells us that women have different life experiences that they share. Get involved in the campaign of a woman candidate whose views are like your own.
3. Have a long-range plan. There's no magic formula for attaining and using power, but those most likely to succeed have thought about where they want to go and who can help them get there. You also should think how you can use your resources and influence in connection with points 1 and 2.
4. Understand that money is power. Until we find a way to curtail the dominance of money in politics, women must learn to use it to get their voices heard. It's a matter of leveraging resources strategically. Governor Richards used to tell women at fund-raisers to donate the value of the clothes they currently were wearing.
5. Be inclusive. Progress isn't about challenging men; it's about empowering ourselves to achieve more together.

The late Barbara Jordan, congresswoman from Texas, wrote: "Things are changing and they are changing fast. Get active in politics wherever you are at whatever level you choose. Get out there and do what you are able to put more of us where we need to be. We will not rest until more women speak for the needs, worries and interests of women. It's about time."[13]

For those who are moved by Barbara Jordan and want to try public service, here is some additional advice culled from the wisdom of women who have reached public office:

1. Begin with a commitment to something you really care about. If you don't believe in what you are doing, neither will anyone else.
2. Start with something you know about. It doesn't matter whether it's school tax campaigns, trash disposal, or managing money—knowledge is a rallying point for leadership.
3. Start where you are. Even if you really want to be governor, begin in your own neighborhood or your own work place. There's a lot to learn, and it's better to make mistakes in friendly territory.
4. Do your homework. It is amazing how many people expect to be leaders without knowing much about the people or area they want to represent. Listen a lot before you start talking.
5. Reach out beyond your present social circle. Broaden acquaintances to other religious, social, and civic groups; spend time with have-nots as well as haves. If you want to be a party's nominee, make the effort to become active.
6. Be strategic. Several years ago in California, women activists adopted an acronym, DIRE, for Death, Indictment, Retirement, Expectation, to evaluate incumbents likely to create openings for future seats. Do the research to build a base where you have the best chance of winning.
7. Be a risk taker. Opportunities arise; the question is who has the courage to use them. Don't jump off cliffs, but saying no is less risky only if you want to stand still.
8. Maintain a sense of humor. It will make others more comfortable and save your sanity. Women politicians have a reputation for being humorless. The answer isn't telling jokes; it is taking criticism less seriously.

I truly believe that women can make a difference by providing principled leadership with a mission: achieving a more humane and equitable society.

We'll feel more comfortable about power when we can see it through our own gender lens and understand that the reason for insisting on change is not just personal. We are at our best when we feel we're helping others. American women fought to end sex discrimination thirty years ago because we understood that if a hostile system was going to change, we would have to change it. Today, too many women expect unresponsive institutions to change without their commitment. It isn't going to happen.

The reason we recall the past is not to dwell in it but to inspire women to take what is useful in order to move forward. Personal success has given younger women much more power than they seem to realize that they have. We want them to use it. Some time in the next millennium, women finally will reach a critical mass of leadership in public and private sectors, in corporations and legislatures. It would be a tragedy if this younger generation of women should sleepwalk through its good fortune.

We have been largely absent from history; government, money, and politics were considered men's business, so women could deny responsibility for failures. That is no longer true. Women are the majority of the voters. Women are major fundraisers for both parties. Women are holding together neighborhoods. Women are making critical decisions on war and peace and at every level of law and business. It is true that we still are far from fully represented in decision-making bodies and that politics remains a male game; but that's no excuse for failing to use the power we have to make this a more livable world.

We will prevail. "Enter any community in any country, and you will find women insisting—often at great risk—on their right to an equal voice and equal access to the levers of power." Those were the words of Madeleine Albright in Beijing at the UN Conference for Women, a gathering that did much to inspire women elsewhere to believe in their own human rights and to encourage them to put their own strengths to work. Here in this country, we have had a head start; society has been transformed over the past thirty years, and that means opportunity is everywhere.

Somewhere, at this very moment, in some neighborhood in America, a woman very like my younger self is confronting a problem that affects her life and family. Perhaps it's the need for a playground for her children; maybe it's a threat to clean water from rural animal waste. She has spoken up, but no one is willing to take action. She's never been a public person, and famous women senators seem a world away. Still, she cares deeply about finding a solution. After agonizing thought, she makes a crucial decision.

She will step up to power, and another woman leader will be born.

NOTES

1. Carolyn G. Heilbrun, *Education of a Woman* (New York: Dial Press, 1995).

2. Sarah Lyall, "Parliament Defines Itself in Gestures of Chivalry," *The New York Times*, December 22, 1997.

3. Marjorie Margolies-Mezvinsky, with Barbara Feinman, *A Woman's Place* (New York: Crown Publishers, 1994), p. 75.

4. Ibid., p. 78.

5. Madeleine Kunin, *Living a Political Life* (New York: Knopf, 1993), p. 280.

6. Margolies-Mezvinksy, *A Woman's Place*, p. 82.

7. Ibid., p. 80.

8. Mark Clayton, "When the Good Ole Boy is a Girl," *The Christian Science Monitor*, February 10, 1998.

9. *A Study on the Status of Women Faculty in Science at MIT*, 1999.

10. Lotte Bailyn, MIT faculty chair, Comments on the Study, March 1999.

11. Ibid.

12. Ibid.

13. Margolies-Mezvinsky, *A Woman's Place*, p. ii.

IRAQ'S LITTLE SECRET

Nicholas D. Kristof

Baghdad, Iraq—The White House is right that Iraq is by far the most repressive country in the entire Middle East—but that's true only if you're a man.

To see how many Arab countries are in some ways even more repressive to women, consider how an invasion might play out. If American ground troops are allowed to storm across the desert from Saudi Arabia into Iraq, then American servicewomen will theoretically not be able to drive vehicles as long as they are in Saudi Arabia and will be advised to wear an abaya over their heads. As soon as they cross the border into enemy Iraq, they'll feel as if they are entering the free world: they can legally drive, uncover their heads, and even call men idiots.

Iraqi women routinely boss men and serve in non-combat positions in the army. Indeed, if Iraq attacks us with smallpox, we'll have a woman to thank: Dr. Rihab Rashida Taha, the head of Iraq's biological warfare program, who is also known to weapons inspectors as Dr. Germ.

A man can stop a woman on the street in Baghdad and ask for directions without causing a scandal. Men and women can pray at the mosque together, go to restaurants together, swim together, court together or quarrel together. Girls compete in after-school sports almost as often as boys, and Iraqi television broadcasts women's sports as well as men's.

"No one thinks that sports are just for men," said Nadia Yasser, the captain of the Iraqi national women's soccer team. "It's true that my mother was a bit concerned at first when I took up soccer, but I insisted, and so she accepted it and just started praying for me."

The point is not to be soft on Saddam Hussein, whose rash wars and policies have killed hundreds of thousands of women as well as men. Iraqi women would be much better off with Saddam gone, and in any case the relative equality of women in Iraq has little to do with his leadership. Iraq has been civilized more than twice as long as Britain, after all (it was old when Babylon arose),

and Iraq got its first woman doctor back in 1922. Then the Iran–Iraq war boosted equality by sending men to the front lines and forced women to fill in as factory workers, bus drivers and government officials.

Still, we shouldn't demonize all of Iraq—just its demon of a ruler—and it's worth pondering this contrast between an enemy that empowers women and allies that repress them. This gap should shame us as well as these allies, reminding us to use our political capital to nudge Arab countries to respect the human rights not just of Kurds or Shiites, but also of women.

More broadly, in a region where women are treated as doormats, Iraq offers an example of how an Arab country can adhere to Islam and yet provide women with opportunities.

"I look at women in Saudi Arabia, and I feel sorry for them," said Thuha Farook, a young woman doctor in Basra. "They can't learn. They can't improve themselves."

At the Basra Maternity and Pediatric Teaching Hospital, 25 of the 26 students in ob-gyn are women. Across town, 54 percent of Basra University's students are female.

Iraqi women who work typically get six months' maternity leave at full pay and another six months at half pay. Subsidized day care is usually available at the workplace. Female circumcision, still common in American allies like Egypt and Nigeria, is absent in Iraq.

To be sure, aside from brutal political repression that is gender-blind, Iraqi women also endure groping on crowded buses and an occasional honor killing, in which a man kills a daughter or sister for being unchaste. Honor killings typically result in a six-month prison sentence in Iraq; they sometimes go completely unpunished in other countries.

A glance around any Baghdad street also demonstrates that Iraq doesn't have hang-ups about the female body that neighboring countries do. A man can travel widely in the Arab world and

(continued)

know about women's legs only by hearsay, but careful reporting in Iraq confirms that Arab women do have knees: In Baghdad I saw women volleyball players who felt uninhibited enough to roll up their sweats.

So as we invade Iraq for its barbaric and repressive ways, our allies in the Muslim world should feel deeply embarrassed that a rogue state offers women more equality than they do.

READING 40

The Globetrotting Sneaker

✤ Cynthia Enloe

Four years after the fall of the Berlin Wall marked the end of the Cold War, Reebok, one of the fastest-growing companies in United States history, decided that the time had come to make its mark in Russia. Thus it was with considerable fanfare that Reebok's executives opened their first store in downtown Moscow in July 1993. A week after the grand opening, store managers described sales as well above expectations.

Reebok's opening in Moscow was the perfect post–Cold War scenario: commercial rivalry replacing military posturing; consumerist tastes homogenizing heretofore hostile peoples; capital and managerial expertise flowing freely across newly porous state borders. Russians suddenly had the "freedom" to spend money on US cultural icons like athletic footwear, items priced above and beyond daily subsistence: at the end of 1993, the average Russian earned the equivalent of $40 a month. Shoes on display were in the $100 range. Almost 60 percent of single parents, most of whom were women, were living in poverty. Yet in Moscow and Kiev, shoe promoters had begun targeting children, persuading them to pressure their mothers to spend money on stylish, western sneakers. And as far as strategy goes, athletic shoe giants have, you might say, a good track record. In the United States many inner-city boys who see basketball as a "ticket out of the ghetto" have become convinced that certain brand-name shoes will give them an edge.

But no matter where sneakers are bought or sold, the potency of their advertising imagery has made it easy to ignore this mundane fact: Shaquille O'Neal's Reeboks are stitched by someone; Michael Jordan's Nikes are stitched by someone; so are your roommate's, so are your grandmother's. Those someones are women, mostly Asian women who are supposed to believe that their "opportunity" to make sneakers for US companies is a sign of their country's progress—just as a Russian woman's chance to spend two months' salary on a pair of shoes for her child allegedly symbolizes the new Russia.

As the global economy expands, sneaker executives are looking to pay women workers less and less, even though the shoes that they produce are capturing an ever-growing share of the footwear market. By the end of 1993, sales in the United States alone had reached $11.6 billion. Nike, the largest supplier of athletic footwear in the world, posted a record $298 million profit for 1993—earnings that had nearly tripled in five years. And sneaker companies continue to refine their strategies for "global competitiveness"—hiring supposedly docile women to make their shoes, changing designs as quickly as we fickle customers change our tastes, and shifting factories from country to country as trade barriers rise and fall.

The logic of it all is really quite simple; yet trade agreements such as the North American Free Trade Agreement (NAFTA) and the General Agreement of Tariffs and Trade (GATT) are, of course, talked about in a jargon that alienates us, as if they were technical matters fit only for economists and diplomats. The bottom line is that all companies operating overseas depend on trade agreements made between their own governments and the regimes ruling the countries in which they want to make or sell their products. Korean, Indonesian, and other women workers around the world know this better than anyone. They are tackling trade politics because they have learned from hard experience that the trade deals their governments sign do little to improve the lives of workers. Guarantees of fair, healthy labor practices, of the rights to speak freely and to organize independently, will usually be left out of trade pacts—and women will suffer. The recent passage of both NAFTA and GATT ensures that a growing number of private companies will now be competing across borders without restriction. The result? Big business will step up efforts to pit working women in industrialized countries against much lower-paid working women in "developing" countries, perpetuating the misleading notion that they are inevitable rivals in the global job market. (See Table 1.)

All the "New World Order" really means to corporate giants like athletic shoemakers is that they now have the green light to accelerate long-standing industry practices. In the early 1980s, the field marshals commanding Reebok and Nike, which are both US-based, decided to manufacture most of their sneakers in South Korea and Taiwan, hiring local women. L.A. Gear, Adidas, Fila, and Asics quickly followed their lead. In short time, the coastal city of Pusan, South Korea, became the "sneaker capital of the world." Between 1982 and 1989 the United States lost 58,500 footwear jobs to cities like Pusan, which attracted sneaker executives because its location facilitated international transport. More to the point, South Korea's military government had an interest in suppressing labor organizing, and it had a comfortable military alliance with the United States. Korean women also seemed accepting of Confucian philosophy, which measured a woman's morality by her willingness to work hard for her family's well-being and to acquiesce to her father's and husband's dictates. With their sense of patriotic duty, Korean women seemed the ideal labor force for export-oriented factories.

US and European sneaker company executives were also attracted by the ready supply of eager Korean male entrepreneurs with whom they could make profitable arrangements. This fact was central to Nike's strategy in particular. When they moved their

TABLE I   HOURLY WAGES IN ATHLETIC FOOTWEAR FACTORIES

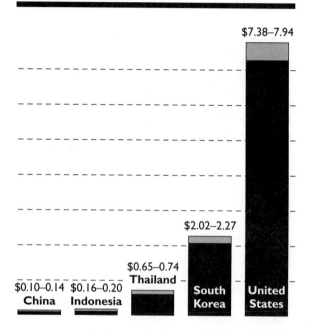

production sites to Asia to lower labor costs, the executives of the Oregon-based company decided to reduce their corporate responsibilities further. Instead of owning factories outright, a more efficient strategy would be to subcontract the manufacturing to wholly foreign-owned—in this case, South Korean—companies. Let them be responsible for workers' health and safety. Let them negotiate with newly emergent unions. Nike would retain control over those parts of sneaker production that gave its officials the greatest professional satisfaction and the ultimate word on the product: design and marketing. Although Nike was following in the footsteps of garment and textile manufacturers, it set the trend for the rest of the athletic footwear industry.

But at the same time, women workers were developing their own strategies. As the South Korean pro-democracy movement grew throughout the 1980s, increasing numbers of women rejected traditional notions of feminine duty. Women began organizing in response to the dangerous working conditions, daily humiliations, and low pay built into their work. Such resistance was profoundly threatening to

TABLE 2   A $70 PAIR OF NIKE PEGASUS: WHERE THE MONEY GOES

Labor $1.66
(Total allocation for the 45 to 50 employees
who work on the one pair of shoes)

┌─ **Subcontractor's profit** $1.19

| | | **Nike markup** $22.95
(After paying subcontractor $14.85,
Nike adds on $22.95 for costs and
profits, selling shoes to retailer
for $37.80) | **Retail markup** $32.20
(Retailer adds on $32.20 for costs
and profits, selling shoes for $70) |

└─ **Administration and overhead** $2.82

Materials $9.18

the government, given the fact that South Korea's emergence as an industrialized "tiger" had depended on women accepting their "role" in growing industries like sneaker manufacture. If women reimagined their lives as daughters, as wives, as workers, as citizens, it wouldn't just rattle their employers; it would shake the very foundations of the whole political system.

At the first sign of trouble, factory managers called in government riot police to break up employees' meetings. Troops sexually assaulted women workers, stripping, fondling, and raping them "as a control mechanism for suppressing women's engagement in the labor movement," reported Jeong-Lim Nam of Hyosung Women's University in Taegu. It didn't work. It didn't work because the feminist activists in groups like the Korean Women Workers Association (KWWA) helped women understand and deal with the assaults. The KWWA held consciousness-raising sessions in which notions of feminine duty and respectability were tackled along with wages and benefits. They organized independently of the male-led labor unions to ensure that their issues would be taken seriously, in labor negotiations and in the prodemocracy movement as a whole.

The result was that women were at meetings with management, making sure that in addition to issues like long hours and low pay, sexual assault at the hands of managers and health care were on the table. Their activism paid off: in addition to winning the right to organize women's unions, their earnings grew. In 1980, South Korean women in manufacturing jobs earned 45 percent of the wages of their male

counterparts; by 1990, they were earning more than 50 percent. Modest though it was, the pay increase was concrete progress, given that the gap between women's and men's manufacturing wages in Japan, Singapore, and Sri Lanka actually *widened* during the 1980s. Last but certainly not least, women's organizing was credited with playing a major role in toppling the country's military regime and forcing open elections in 1987.

Without that special kind of workplace control that only an authoritarian government could offer, sneaker executives knew that it was time to move. In Nike's case, its famous advertising slogan—"Just Do It"—proved truer to its corporate philosophy than its women's "empowerment" ad campaign, designed to rally women's athletic (and consumer) spirit. In response to South Korean women workers' newfound activist self-confidence, the sneaker company and its subcontractors began shutting down a number of their South Korean factories in the late 1980s and early 1990s. After bargaining with government officials in nearby China and Indonesia, many Nike subcontractors set up shop in those countries, while some went to Thailand. China's government remains nominally Communist; Indonesia's ruling generals are staunchly anti-Communist. But both are governed by authoritarian regimes who share the belief that if women can be kept hard at work, low paid, and unorganized, they can serve as a magnet for foreign investors.

Where does all this leave South Korean women—or any woman who is threatened with a factory closure if she demands decent working conditions and a fair wage? They face the dilemma confronted by thousands of women from dozens of countries. The risk of job loss is especially acute in relatively mobile industries; it's easier for a sneaker, garment, or electronics manufacturer to pick up and move than it is for an automaker or a steel producer. In the case of South Korea, poor women had moved from rural villages into the cities searching for jobs to support not only themselves but parents and siblings. The exodus of manufacturing jobs has forced more women into the growing "entertainment" industry. The kinds of bars and massage parlors offering sexual services that had mushroomed around US military bases during the Cold War have been opening up across the country.

But the reality is that women throughout Asia are organizing, knowing full well the risks involved. Theirs is a long-term view; they are taking direct aim at companies' nomadic advantage, by building links among workers in countries targeted for "development" by multinational corporations. Through sustained grassroots efforts, women are developing the skills and confidence that will make it increasingly difficult to keep their labor cheap. Many are looking to the United Nations conference on women in Beijing, China, [1996], as a rare opportunity to expand their cross-border strategizing.

The Beijing conference will also provide an important opportunity to call world attention to the hypocrisy of the governments and corporations doing business in China. Numerous athletic shoe companies followed Nike in setting up manufacturing sites throughout the country. This included Reebok—a company claiming its share of responsibility for ridding the world of "injustice, poverty, and other ills that gnaw away at the social fabric," according to a statement of corporate principles.

Since 1988, Reebok has been giving out annual human rights awards to dissidents from around the world. But it wasn't until 1992 that the company adopted its own "human rights production standards"—after labor advocates made it known that the quality of life in factories run by its subcontractors was just as dismal as that at most other athletic shoe suppliers in Asia. Reebok's code of conduct, for example, includes a pledge to "seek" those subcontractors who respect workers' rights to organize. The only problem is that independent trade unions are banned in China. Reebok has chosen to ignore that fact, even though Chinese dissidents have been the recipients of the company's own human rights award. As for working

conditions, Reebok now says it sends its own inspectors to production sites a couple of times a year. But they have easily "missed" what subcontractors are trying to hide—like 400 young women workers locked at night into an overcrowded dormitory near a Reebok-contracted factory in the town of Zhuhai, as reported last August in the *Asian Wall Street Journal Weekly*.

Nike's cofounder and CEO, Philip Knight, has said that he would like the world to think of Nike as "a company with a soul that recognizes the value of human beings." Nike, like Reebok, says it sends in inspectors from time to time to check up on work conditions at its factories; in Indonesia, those factories are run largely by South Korean subcontractors. But according to Donald Katz in a recent book on the company, Nike spokesman Dave Taylor told an in-house newsletter that the factories are "[the subcontractors'] business to run." For the most part, the company relies on regular reports from subcontractors regarding its "Memorandum of Understanding," which managers must sign, promising to impose "local government standards" for wages, working conditions, treatment of workers, and benefits.

In April, the minimum wage in the Indonesian capital of Jakarta will be $1.89 *a day*—among the highest in a country where the minimum wage varies by region. And managers are required to pay only 75 percent of the wage directly; the remainder can be withheld for "benefits." By now, Nike has a well-honed response to growing criticisms of its low-cost labor strategy. Such wages should not be seen as exploitative, says Nike, but rather as the first rung on the ladder of economic opportunity that Nike has extended to workers with few options. Otherwise, they'd be out "harvesting coconut meat in the tropical sun," wrote Nike spokesman Dusty Kidd, in a letter to the *Utne Reader*. The all-is-relative response craftily shifts attention away from reality: Nike didn't move to Indonesia to help Indonesians; it moved to ensure that its profit margin continues to grow. And that is pretty much guaranteed in a country where "local standards" for wages rarely take a worker over the poverty line. A 1991 survey by the International Labor Organization (ILO) found that 88 percent of women working at the Jakarta minimum wage at the time— slightly less than a dollar a day—were malnourished.

A woman named Riyanti might have been among the workers surveyed by the ILO. Interviewed by the *Boston Globe* in 1991, she told the reporter who had asked about her long hours and low pay: "I'm happy working here. . . . I can make money and I can make friends." But in fact, the reporter discovered that Riyanti had already joined her co-workers in two strikes, the first to force one of Nike's Korean subcontractors to accept a new women's union and the second to compel managers to pay at least the minimum wage. That Riyanti appeared less than forthcoming about her activities isn't surprising. Many Indonesian factories have military men posted in their front offices who find no fault with managers who tape women's mouths shut to keep them from talking among themselves. They and their superiors have a political reach that extends far beyond the barracks. Indonesia has all the makings for a political explosion, especially since the gap between rich and poor is widening into a chasm. It is in this setting that the government has tried to crack down on any independent labor organizing—a policy that Nike has helped to implement. Referring to a recent strike in a Nike-contracted factory, Tony Nava, Nike representative in Indonesia, told the *Chicago Tribune* in November 1994 that the "troublemakers" had been fired. When asked about Nike policy on the issue, spokesman Keith Peters struck a conciliatory note: "If the government were to allow and encourage independent labor organizing, we would be happy to support it."

Indonesian workers' efforts to create unions independent of governmental control were a surprise to shoe companies. Although their moves from South Korea have been immensely profitable [see Table 2], they do not have the sort of immunity from activism that they had expected. In May 1993, the murder of a female labor activist outside Surabaya set off a storm of local and international protest. Even the US State Department was forced to take note in its 1993 worldwide human rights report, describing a system similar to that which generated South Korea's boom twenty years earlier: severely restricted union organizing, security forces used to break up strikes, low wages for men, lower wages for women—complete with government rhetoric celebrating women's contribution to national development.

Yet when President Clinton visited Indonesia last November, he made only a token effort to address the country's human rights problem. Instead, he touted the benefits of free trade, sounding indeed more enlightened, more in tune with the spirit of the post–Cold War era than do those defenders of protectionist trading policies who coat their rhetoric with "America first" chauvinism. But "free trade" as actually being practiced today is hardly *free* for any workers—in the United States or abroad—who have to accept the Indonesian, Chinese, or Korean workplace model as the price of keeping their jobs.

The not-so-new plot of the international trade story has been "divide and rule." If women workers and their government in one country can see that a sneaker company will pick up and leave if their labor demands prove more costly than those in a neighbor country, then women workers will tend to see their neighbors not as regional sisters, but as competitors who can steal their precarious livelihoods. Playing women off against each other is, of course, old hat. Yet it is as essential to international trade politics as is the fine print in GATT.

But women workers allied through networks like the Hong Kong-based Committee for Asian Women are developing their own post–Cold War foreign policy, which means addressing women's needs: how to convince fathers and husbands that a woman going out to organizing meetings at night is not sexually promiscuous; how to develop workplace agendas that respond to family needs; how to work with male unionists who push women's demands to the bottom of their lists; how to build a global movement.

These women refuse to stand in awe of the corporate power of the Nike or Reebok or Adidas executive. Growing numbers of Asian women today have concluded that trade politics have to be understood by women on their own terms. They will be coming to Beijing this September [1996] ready to engage with women from other regions to link the politics of consumerism with the politics of manufacturing. If women in Russia and Eastern Europe can challenge Americanized consumerism, if Asian activists can solidify their alliances, and if US women can join with them by taking on trade politics—the post–Cold War sneaker may be a less comfortable fit in the 1990s.

ACKNOWLEDGMENTS

This article draws from the work of South Korean scholars Hyun Sook Kim, Seung-kyung Kim, Katherine Moon, Seungsook Moon, and Jeong-Lim Nam.

Hindu Women's Activism in India and the Questions It Raises

❧ Amrita Basu

Some of the most powerful images and sounds that live on, since the storm over the Babari Masjid in Ayodhya has abated, are those of Sādhvī Rithambara and Uma Bharati. Their shrill voices filtered through cassette tape recordings goaded Hindu men into violence against Muslims in the course of many riots between 1990 and 1993. On 6 December 1992 these women openly celebrated the destruction of the Babari Masjid. Women's activism has not only found expression among the movement's orators and spokespersons but has also taken hold at the grassroots level. In the early 1990s, thousands of women became skilled in organizing demonstrations, campaigning for elections, and using arms and ammunition.

Perhaps the most startling form of women's activism is their complicity and often direct participation in Hindu violence against Muslim families. In October 1990 in the town of Bijnor in western Uttar Pradesh, Hindu women led a procession through a Muslim neighborhood with *trishūls* (tridents) in hand, shouting bigoted, inflammatory slogans. In the aftermath of the violence in which several hundred people were killed, these women radiated pride at their actions (Basu, 1995b: 35–78; Jeffery, 1994; Jeffery and Jeffery, 1998). In the riots in Bombay in January 1993, Hindu women often justified violence against Muslims. Following police killings of Muslims in the Pratiksha Nagar Housing Colony in Bombay in January 1993, some Hindu women stood on their balconies looking down at the dead bodies of two Muslim women and insisted that these women had died of natural causes, and in any event, "Muslims deserved to die." Hindu women employees of a state-owned corporation threatened to boycott their jobs until the government destroyed a nearby Muslim slum.[1] In a riot in the outskirts of Bhopal during this same period, a woman who was a member of both a municipal corporation and the Bharatiya Janata Party

(BJP) had rushed to the scene of the violence and goaded Hindu men into violence against Muslims.

In the first part of this chapter, I ask whether Hindu women's activism derives its distinctive features from the peculiarities of "communalism," and in particular, traits that distinguish "communalism" from "fundamentalism."[2] Women's activism may be partially explained by the fact that the BJP, which typifies the attributes of "communalism," has supported certain women's rights on the basis of political expediency. However, in the second part of the chapter, I suggest that by overemphasizing the distinctive attributes of "communalism," we risk neglecting its affinities with "fundamentalism." The BJP's "modern" political project resuscitates antimodernist forces, and fundamentalists' claims of authentically representing religious traditions are often shaped by the prevailing political context. . . .

I observed the events of the tumultuous period 1990–1992 while in India studying the growth of Hindu nationalism. I interviewed numerous women who were associated with the Hindu nationalist campaign from the leadership level to rank-and-file members of the three affiliated women's organizations. I visited several towns that had experienced severe riots and interviewed victims and participants in the violence. I joined processions of women as they marched from door to door, campaigning for the BJP in the 1991 parliamentary elections. This chapter draws upon those observations and experiences.

WOMEN'S ACTIVISM AND "COMMUNAL POLITICS"

Certain distinctive features of Hindu "communalism" appear at first glance to promote women's activism. The movement that has emerged since 1989 is led by the BJP, a political party. It is neither controlled nor even deeply influenced by Hindu priests, scriptures, or doctrines. The BJP's major objectives since it was formed in 1980, but with increasing urgency, have been no more complicated than attaining power in New Delhi and in India's regional capitals. The BJP's independence from religious orthodoxy seems to be a key ingredient of women's activism. It frees the party to assume positions that might conflict with Hindu conservatism and to support women's independence when the BJP finds this politically expedient. Other questions, like female seclusion, that are often a staple of "fundamentalist" movements do not figure on the BJP's agenda.

Several scholars have noted that although "fundamentalist" movements are far from monolithic, they tend to converge in their opposition to women's autonomy (Hélie-Lucas, 1994). Most "fundamentalist" movements share a preoccupation with regulating women's sexuality and reproduction (Papanek, 1994). By contrast, Hindu "communalism" is not currently obsessed with controlling Hindu women's sexuality and fertility . . . , (although as I suggest below, it is obsessed with Muslim women's fertility. It does not oppose abortion and birth control or seek to regulate the number and spacing of children. It has not differentiated itself from other political parties with respect to its positions on premarital sexuality, adultery, and widow remarriage.

An excellent example of how the BJP's expediency may serve women's interests is evident from its attempt to steal the thunder of the Congress Party on a scheme it was considering in 1995 to improve the position of women. The Congress government in the State of Haryana announced that it would invest Rs 2,500 (approximately $78) in the name of a newborn girl in a savings scheme that would yield Rs 25,000 when she turned eighteen, the legal age of marriage. (The scheme is restricted to unmarried girls in families with annual incomes below Rs 11,000 and with no more than two children (*Economist*, 11 March 1995: 40)).

Once Congress Party chief Narasimha Rao recognized the electoral potential of this issue and promised to extend the scheme to the whole country, the BJP claimed that it had thought up the idea and implemented it first. The BJP government in Rajasthan had in fact launched a similar scheme in 1993 as a population control measure, not to improve girls' conditions. The Rajasthan government had provided a stipend for girls whose mothers or fathers

had undergone sterilization, a condition that the Haryana government does not impose. However, the BJP is sufficiently concerned with electoral success that it was happy to broaden the scheme so that it would be more beneficial to women if this entailed electoral advantage.

Expediency has also meant that the positions the BJP women's organization assumes are often inconsistent. . . . It is difficult to identify a single one of the vital issues before the women's movement—dowry, *satī*, female feticide—on which it holds a unified position. Thus contrary to what one might expect, neither its positions nor its actions on women's issues are all conservative. Kusum Mehdre, an active member of the Madhya Pradesh women's organization and Minister for Social Welfare, felt that women should attain economic self-sufficiency by assuming nontraditional roles. Accordingly, she had provided them employment in the production of generators, electronics, and leather goods.[3] Purnima Sethi, the convener of the BJP women's organization in Delhi, reported that she had created an agency that provided women with free legal counsel on marriage, divorce, and dowry, so that they could extricate themselves from abusive domestic situations. . . .

"Communalism" also offers a striking contrast with "fundamentalism" in its relationship to secularism. Whereas most "fundamentalist" movements reject the separation of religion and state, Hindu "communalism" accepts this separation in principle and rejects a religious alternative to the secular state. . . .

This point has crucial implications for women because the major alternative to secular law is community-based religious law. In general, safeguards against sexual inequalities are greater in secular than in religious law. By virtue of its supposed commitment to secular principles, the BJP can uphold constitutional protections of sexual equality. The best example of this is the uniform civil code. The BJP has not only emerged as the champion among Indian political parties of a uniform civil code; it has taken over what was historically a major feminist demand. Many feminists now balk at joining hands with the BJP on this issue.

The BJP uses the language of legal and constitutional rights to pit women's rights against minority rights. As Kapur and Cossman (1995: 101) point out, it interprets secularism to mean that Muslims and Hindus should be treated alike, thereby disregarding the vulnerabilities to which Muslims as a minority community are subject. One consequence of juxtaposing the interests of women and minorities is to undermine solidarity among Hindu and Muslim women. "I feel for my Muslim sisters," Uma Bharati commented, "but they do not seem to feel for themselves. Why do they agree to wear the *burqā* (veil)? How can they abide by Muslim law?"[4]

The issue of the uniform civil code provides a lens on some of the most distinctive attributes of Hindu "communalism." Islamic "fundamentalism" in South Asia and the Middle East is inseparable from nationalist opposition to Western domination in its various guises. Women may exemplify what is authentically indigenous and traditional or its antithesis, Westernization and modernity. Deniz Kandiyoti notes that although colonial authorities intervened extensively in the economic and political domains, they provided the colonized greater autonomy in the private sphere. This was the arena that "fundamentalists" claimed as their own (Kandiyoti, 1991: 8; Devji, 1991). "Fundamentalists'" desire to veil or reveil women in Bangladesh and Pakistan has been a reaction to the supposed Western "unveiling" of women (see Feldman, 1998 and Rouse, 1998). Similarly, Valentine Moghadam (1994: 13) notes that "fundamentalists" in Iran consider the veil an antidote to the virus of *gharbzadegi*, which is variously translated as "Westoxication," "Westitis," "Euromania," and "Occidentosis."

Hindu nationalists in India, unlike their counterparts in many predominantly Muslim countries, identify their principal enemies as internal rather than external. Even as India has engaged in the process of economic liberalization, and Western economic and cultural influences have grown, Hindu nationalists have not openly expressed anti-Western sentiment. . . .

The BJP often seeks to define itself in relationship to Muslim "fundamentalism" both by asserting its own superiority and by presenting Hindus as beleaguered victims. Hindu women play a key role in both of these constructions. BJP members often express condescension toward Muslims for practicing *pardā* (female seclusion) and extol the greater freedom of Hindu than of Muslim women. Mridula Sinha, the president of the all-India BJP women's organization, described the downfall of Hindu women in the aftermath of Muslim rule:

In the Vedic era, the status of women used to be much higher than it is today. You can see from the statue of *adhinarishvakar*, which is half Shiva and half Parvati, that the roles of men and women were considered interdependent and complementary. And women made important contributions to four domains: employment, religion, procreation, and the economy. After the Muslim invasion all of this changed: Hindus were forced to marry off their daughters at much younger ages, they adopted seclusion, and women's role in public life declined.[5]

Similarly, Atal Behari Vajpayee states, "Historically women were respected in this culture; indeed women wrote verses of the Vedas and Vedantas. . . . Later on because of foreign invasions various evils cropped up in our society."[6] Hindu nationalists claim that Muslim rule contributed to a decline in Hindu women's position both by force and by example. Hindu men encouraged their wives to retreat into the domestic sphere to protect them from Muslim invaders.

In claiming that the subjugation of Muslim women reveals the backwardness of the Muslim community, the BJP ironically echoes the colonial view that the downtrodden Indian woman signifies the backwardness of Indians. The nineteenth-century social reform movement sought to "uplift" Hindu women in response to this very charge, to demonstrate Indians' fitness to govern themselves. Similarly for the BJP today, the lowly status of Muslim women signifies the inferiority of Muslims.

Joseph Alter (1994) finds in male celibacy an expression of cultural nationalism among Hindus. He argues that Hindus invest in celibacy notions of the fit body, disciplined according to a rigorous regimen that produces a citizen who embodies national integrity and strength. He further argues that the *brahmacharya*, who renounces sexuality, developed in opposition to colonial characterizations of upper-caste Hindu men as emasculated. In response to feelings of powerlessness amidst sociomoral change, Hindu men responded by demonstrating their capacity for self-discipline and self-restraint through celibacy.

In parallel fashion, Hindu "communalists" depict Muslim male sexuality as unrestrained, undisciplined, and antinational. They advocate rigorous measures to control Muslim family size, prohibit polygyny, and punish rapists. Indeed Hindu communalists' most vicious slogans, speeches, and graffiti allude to Muslims' sexual practices. Take, for example, a cassette recorded by Sādhvī Saraswati . . . Saraswati begins by decrying polygyny, which she suggests is sanctioned by Muslim law. It turns Muslim women into sexual objects and breeders and results in large Muslim families. For every five children that Hindus have, Muslims have fifty. She continues:

> And who feeds these fifty children? Hindus do! After Muslims divorce, then the *waqf* (religious charity) boards support the children with taxes that we pay. . . . Within twenty-five years you will be living like a poor minority in this country. . . . Muslims have forty-six countries but Hindus have only one, Nepal! If you become a minority in this country then who will provide refugee status for you? None of the neighboring countries provide the kind of orphanage that India does.

By conjoining the backwardness of Muslims with the weakness of the Indian state, the BJP can extol the superiority of Hindus and the Hindu nation. Women, who figure in "fundamentalist" movements as symbols of tradition and continuity with the past, figure in "communal" movements as symbols of progress and modernity.

DISMANTLING "COMMUNALISM" AND "FUNDAMENTALISM"

As I have argued elsewhere, one of the BJP's major strengths is its ability to speak in many voices (Basu, 1995a). Thus while in some contexts it may present itself as a champion of women's rights, elsewhere it defends conservative Hindu conceptions of women's place. An excellent example both of the BJP's double-speak and of its selective conservatism concerns the issue of *satī* (widow immolation). In the aftermath of the Roop Kanwar satī in Rajasthan in 1987, the BJP was closely associated with the pro-satī lobby. In this context, it played the role that I have argued is often associated with "fundamentalist" positions: it sought justification for satī in Hindu scriptures, idealized women's roles as dutiful wives, and accused feminists of being *azād* (promiscuous) Westernized women. . . .

Perhaps the issue that most reveals the BJP's affinity with "fundamentalist" movements is its anxiety about the moral corruption that modernity entails. For Hindu communalists, political and sexual morality are deeply intertwined. A central theme running through [Hindu nationalist] Rithambara's cassettes is the notion that India has lost its moral bearings. "Things have deteriorated to the point that everything is now

bought and sold, minds, bodies, religion, and even the honor of our elders, sisters, mothers, and sons," she cries out. "We cannot auction our nation's honor in the market of party politics." In a sweeping gesture, Rithambara ingeniously links the corruption of the political process, capitalist development, and sexual objectification.

Another expression of the women's organization concern for sexual morality is around the issue of pornography. Purnima Sethi reported that the BJP women's organization for Delhi state, over which she presided, had organized a major campaign to ban "obscene" publication.[7] It had organized raids of three hundred establishments that were displaying "obscene" material and had pressured the press commissioner into confiscating this material. In Delhi, Lucknow, Bhopal, and other cities, BJP women organized direct-action campaigns that entailed blackening billboards that displayed women's bodies. The BJP has also demanded that the board of film certification censor vulgarity in Indian cinema. According to Shashi Ranjan, president of the BJP film cell, "Mainstream cinema is being shamelessly imbued with innuendo and vulgarity which is threatening to strike at the very core of our culture so steeped in decency and decorum" (*Indian Express*, 8 February 1994).

The Rām Janambhūmi movement and the events that surround it have given expression to some very conservative ideas that cloak themselves in religious garb. The Gita Press in Gorakhpur published a series of cheap, readable books on the proper roles of Hindu women. They are written in the form of treatises that draw upon the authority of religious scriptures. Portions are in Sanskrit, which are then translated into Hindi. Some chapters are written in question-and-answer format: a disciple poses questions to which he or she receives responses, presumably from religious authorities. The books lay out codes of conduct for women around minutiae of social life: how a woman should behave around her relatives, what she should eat while pregnant, what ornaments she should wear after marriage, and whether she should use birth control.

The series' central message for women is the importance of devotion to their families and the dangers that await those who refuse to conform. One book, *How to Lead a Householder's Life* (Ramsukhdas, 1992a), states that misery awaits the bride who chooses her own husband, and sisters who demand a share in their father's property. It counsels the daughter-in-law to accept the harsh treatment of her mother-in-law and "to pay attention to the comfort of her husband, even at the cost of her own comfort." "What should the wife do if her husband beats her and troubles her?" the disciple asks. The response: "The wife should think that she is paying her debt of her previous life and thus her sins are being destroyed and she is becoming pure" (Ramsukhdas, 1992a: 44–50). Another question raised is whether a widow should remarry. The response: it is "beastliness" for the family to remarry her when she is no longer a virgin and thus cannot be offered "as charity" to anyone else. The main point is that a woman's purity must be safeguarded after marriage, when there is the risk of her acting independently. *Nari Siksha* (Women's Education) (Poddar, 1992) voices the same theme in its open support for satī. In these texts the fear of the widow's attainment of economic independence echoes Muslim "fundamentalists'" worries about Shah Bano gaining maintenance payments from her husband.

Another book, *Disgrace of Mother's Prowess* (Ramsukhdas, 1992b), opposes abortion on grounds that it denies the unborn child the possibility of *mokshā* (liberation through rebirth) and thus constitutes a sin. Ramsukhdas argues that the sin of abortion is twice as great as the sin of killing a Brahman. Thus a man whose wife has an abortion must disown her. The only acceptable form of birth control, he continues, is celibacy.

These books echo many of the ideas that are associated with "fundamentalism." First, they juxtapose Indian values with Western values and emphasize the links between women's biological and social roles. *Nari Siksha* in particular engages in a diatribe against Western feminism for supposedly destroying the family and with it the moral backbone of society (Poddar, 1992). It insists upon the sanctity of motherhood for Hindu women and enjoins them to reject Western notions of liberation. *Nari Siksha* states that for a woman to become *satī* (revered as a devoted wife), she must possess *dharma* (faith) and treat her husband like a god. Among other things this entails cooking well for guests and in-laws, rising early to clean the house, and demonstrating deference to in-laws.

It is difficult to know whether the BJP combine has any direct connection to the authors or publishers of these books. But even if these new voices of Hindu conservatism have no direct link to the [nationalist] organizations, the BJP and its affiliates have created a climate that promotes such views.

Although I have used the concepts of "communalism" and "fundamentalism" in hopes of achieving precision, the terms are imprecise and heavily laden with unintended meanings. First, both "fundamentalism" and "communalism" are pejorative terms. It is difficult to understand views that one assumes are irrational. It is also difficult to decouple the concepts of "communalism" and "fundamentalism" from religion, even though the growth of "fundamentalism" and "communalism" have more to do with conflicts over the distribution of power and wealth than with religion per se. Furthermore, the beliefs and practices to which "fundamentalists" and "communalists" refer are selectively filtered from religious doctrines that afford many interpretations.[8]

The connotations of the term "fundamentalism" are especially troublesome. . . . Through habitual usage, "fundamentalism" has come to be identified almost exclusively with Islam, to the disregard of other religious fundamentalisms, among other places in the United States. A tendency to brand the entire Islamic world "fundamentalist" ignores the experiences of the Muslim countries that are not "fundamentalist." It is also erroneous to assume that "fundamentalists," unlike "communalists," are disinterested in political power. Indeed, they have often compromised their principled commitments to women's seclusion on grounds of political expediency. In Pakistan, for example, although the Jama'at-i-Islami had previously opposed the principle of a woman head of state, by 1965 it had supported a woman presidential candidate because of electoral considerations (Mumtaz, 1994: 232). Similarly, despite the decision of the Islamic state in Iran to remove women from public office in the 1980s, it organized four thousand *"basīj"* women into a militia to guard government ministries and banks (Moghadam, 1991: 278). Moreover it would be wrong to assume the absence of women's activism in "fundamentalist" movements. There are several accounts of women's active support for the Iranian revolution, including its veiling of women. Margot Badran (1994) describes a group of conservative women in Egypt who justify women's political participation on grounds of religious commitment. Khawar Mumtaz (1991) shows that in Pakistan in the 1980s and 1990s, "fundamentalist" women associated with the Jama'at-i-Islami opposed feminism for eroding the barriers between male and female worlds because their own activism was premised upon sexual segregation. We simply do not have the evidence to conclude that women's activism is greater in "communal" than in "fundamentalist" movements.

There is also a danger of implying that "communalism" represents a progressive force that encourages women's activism and empowerment, whereas "fundamentalism" does the opposite. This comparison draws on the assumption that Hinduism compares favorably with Islam in its views on women's place. Several scholars have noted that Hinduism rejects notions of women's inherent weakness and considers them powerful and thus potentially dangerous (Wadley, 1977). The varied personalities of female deities in Hinduism may inspire a range of female personas in political life. Ascetic women have the freedom to remain single, travel extensively, and engage in worldly pursuits (Denton, 1991). But even for "ordinary" Hindu women, religious devotion has always provided a culturally sanctioned escape from domestic drudgery and opportunity for self-realization. However, the qualities of Hinduism cannot explain women's activism in communal politics. The BJP has taken a decentered, pluralist religious tradition and rendered it more centralized. Given its willingness to transform Hinduism in such far-reaching ways, the BJP is hardly bound by religious doctrines on questions concerning women. Islam too can be interpreted in diverse ways: some Muslim feminists have emphasized its emancipatory features; fundamentalists have found within it justification for sexually repressive practices.

Both "communalism" and "fundamentalism" are responses to the strains of modernity: the erosion of state legitimacy, the integration of postcolonial economies into the global capitalist system, and the influx of Western cultural influences. But at the same time, both "communalism" and "fundamentalism" seek justification from the past. Both employ gendered images of motherhood to romanticize the past and suggest continuity with it. Hindu "communalism" also finds in motherhood imagery a basis in religion because of the ways in which Hinduism worships mother goddesses. But motherhood imagery is not confined to "communalism" or "fundamentalism"; it is a staple of nationalist movements. Both by virtue of its stated commitments and its actions, the BJP can best be described as a religious nationalist party. The BJP asserts a deep affinity between Hindus and the nation-state. This supposed affinity rests upon the notion that Hindus were the original and thus the most legitimate inhabitants of India. Just as the BJP

employs an organic conception of citizenship, so too it assumes that the Muslim minority, and the Congress Party, which supposedly appeases it, are implicitly antinational. . . .

This chapter opened by remarking on the unusual extent and nature of women's activism around the Rām Janambhūmi issue. I argued that women's activism may be partially explained by the BJP's expedient support for certain (Hindu) women's rights. However, expediency is by definition dual-faceted: it encourages the BJP to take up women's rights, and allows the BJP to ignore, disparage, and undermine them.

The BJP is ultimately less committed to women's rights than to the denial of Muslim rights. While it highlights the inequities of Muslim law, it is remarkably silent about the discriminatory traits of Hindu law.[9] Thus Arun Jaitley defended differences in inheritance rights of sons and daughters on grounds that women's equal rights to inheritance would fragment family landholdings. There are many indications that the BJP's interpretation of a uniform civil code would be modeled on Hindu law. Furthermore, the BJP has championed women's rights in only a narrowly legalistic fashion. Its women's organization has issued statements condemning violence against women but has not campaigned to oppose it. For example, it accepts the dowry system and avoids the issue of dowry deaths.

At this stage it is important to refine the concept of women's activism. Many of the women who took part in processions, campaigns, and riots seemed exhilarated by the opportunity for activism that this provided: leaving their homes, putting aside domestic work, and devoting themselves to a cause. Particularly for lower-middle-class housewives, who form an important part of the BJP's constituency, Hindu nationalist mobilization offered a rare opportunity for self-realization.

But Hindu women's activism has not necessarily challenged patterns of sexual inequality within the home and the world. Nor are women necessarily drawn to the BJP simply because it advocates their rights. Mridula Sinha stated emphatically, "For Indian women, liberation means liberation from atrocities. It doesn't mean that women should be relieved of their duties as wives and mothers. Women should stop demanding their rights all the time and think instead in terms of their responsibilities to the family."[10] Mohini Garg, the all-India secretary of the BJP women's organization, echoed this point: "We want to encourage our members not to think in terms of individual rights but in terms of responsibility to the nation."[11]

Indeed, a striking feature of women's participation in the activities of the BJP's women's organization is women's reenactment of conventional sex-linked roles within the broader public arena. Nirupuma Gour, the organization's secretary in Uttar Pradesh, reported that in preparation for the BJP procession to Ayodhya in October 1990 (the dress rehearsal for 1992), women had developed an elaborate ritual for sending the *"kar sevaks"* (volunteer workers) like warriors to the battlefield.[12] They would congregate at designated spots at the train stations with food, portable stoves, and other paraphernalia. As the men boarded the trains, the women would garland them, place *tilaks* (vermilion marks) on their foreheads, and give them freshly prepared hot food. She said that women were instructed to prepare up to fifty thousand food packets each day. Gour estimates that five to six thousand women arrived in Lucknow from all over the country. Many others could not travel to Ayodhya because transportation was inadequate, but those who reached Lucknow assumed responsibility for protecting men from repression. Thus, for example, when trains approached Ayodhya, the women would sound the alarms to stop them; the men would disembark immediately while the women would confront the train conductors. At Ayodhya, the women would encircle the men to prevent the police from wielding their *lāthīs* (bamboo sticks). When the *kar sevaks* broke through the police cordons and climbed atop the Babari Masjid, however, the women were absent. I asked Mala Rustogi, a member of the Durga Vahini in Lucknow, why the women had not participated in the culmination of their actions. She responded that it would have been undignified for Hindu women to be climbing a mosque in their *sārīs*.[13]

The particular roles that the BJP assigned to women in its very expensive, elaborate electoral campaigns are also significant. Whereas men had primary responsibility for addressing large public gatherings, women engaged in door-to-door campaigning that brought them into contact with housewives who might have been less willing to speak with men.

Women's reenactment of their private roles in the public arena may also play a particularly important place in the context of Hindu nationalism, which has sought to challenge the public/private divide in other ways. The BJP's central platform during the period of its ascendance to power in the late 1980s was its demand that the Congress government demolish the Babari Masjid in Ayodhya and build a Rām temple in its place. Implicit in this demand was the BJP's attempt to accord centrality in political life to questions of religious faith. This proves especially difficult in a democratic context such as India, where the state may intervene to prevent political parties from bringing religious matters into politics. Women are well positioned to further the BJP's project. During the 1991 elections when the election commissioner had prohibited the BJP from shouting religious slogans, I marched with processions of women who appeared to be observing these dictates on the streets. But as soon as they entered the courtyards of people's homes, cries of *"Jāī Shrī Rām!"* (Victory to the Lord Rām!) and *"Mandir vahān banāyenge!"* (We will build a temple there!) filled the air. In this vital phase of Hindu nationalism, women served as emissaries of private-domain religion into the public sphere and of the BJP's supposed religious commitments into the home and family. BJP leaders felt that women's electoral support would affirm the party's religious commitment because, they claimed, women were more devout than men.

What of women themselves? What did they gain from being assigned a role that enabled them to venture out of their homes without challenging norms of sexual subordination? The experiences of Mala Rustogi are instructive. Rustogi said that when she first began working with the Durga Vahini in Lucknow in 1989, she feared the opposition of her husband and in-laws, for her daughter was only three years old at the time. To her surprise, they supported her. She described a newfound sense of pleasure in serving others: "Serving one's husband is expected of women and of course it is important. But serving a third person whom you don't know and aren't expected to serve is much more exciting—for just that reason." Her comment captures some of the traits that were mirrored in women's activism: their experience of self-affirmation through self-sacrifice, and their empowerment through public-sphere activism, which ultimately renewed their commitment to their domestic roles.

Some of the changes under way in Indian society might help explain Hindu women's acceptance of their ambiguous placement between public and private domains. The growth of the BJP coincides with unprecedented economic liberalization, which has truncated the public sphere and redefined the private arena. Women have access to larger markets than ever before, stocked with a range of goods that convey the allure of freedom: ready-made clothes, prepared foods, and gadgets to simplify housework. The Indian women who appear in advertisements for these products have light hair and skin, wear Western or Westernized clothing, and convey a sexy demeanor. Release from domesticity also comes from women's increased employment, particularly among the middle classes in the service sector. Consumerism and employment both lend support to women's growing involvement in the political domain.

The BJP and its women's wing give voice to profound middle-class ambivalence about these social and economic changes. While embracing the modernist project of capitalist expansion, they worry incessantly about the excessive individual freedom that it enables. Indeed, the BJP's changing economic policy is an excellent indicator of this ambivalence. . . . It has sought to promote *svadeshī*, a nationalist response to globalization that encourages self-sufficiency in certain areas of the economy. But it does so without repudiating economic liberalization altogether.

Many of the forms of women's activism that have been identified with Hindu nationalism are mirrored within anticolonial nationalism in India. Within the anticolonial movement we find very similar patterns of women's entering the public sphere without challenging the norms of sexual segregation and seclusion. Although the most exalted images are Gandhian depictions of women's pacifism, there are many instances of women's complicity in violence: in collaborating with the Punjabi revolutionary Bhagat Singh; in the Chatri Sangh in Calcutta in the late 1920s; and in the Chittagong Armoury Raid in the early 1930s. The nationalist revolutionary Subhash Chander Bose formed a women's militia called the Rani of Jhansi Regiment, which trained women in the use of arms and ammunition. Women were also active in revolutionary violence in the Telengana movement in Andhra Pradesh.

Situating Hindu women's activism within a broader context of nationalist mobilization reveals parallels with a range of political movements that make ascribed identity the basis for political mobilization (Moghadam, 1994). There are striking resemblances between Hindu nationalism and some rightwing and fascist movements that harness women's activism around racist and anti-Semitic campaigns.[14]

The extent of women's participation in Islamic movements in the Middle East and North Africa is also striking. Sondra Hale (1994) finds that women have been extremely active in the Islamist party in the Sudan; these women find in the Sharī'a justification for their activism and for asserting their rights as women. Similarly the Muslim Sisters in Egypt justify their activism by reference to Islamic principles. Aisha Abdal-Rahman, a well-known Qur'anic scholar, argues that the "truly Islamic" and the "truly feminist" option is neither immodest dress nor identical roles for the sexes in the name of Islam. "The right path is the one that combines modesty, responsibility and integration into public life with the Qur'anic and naturally enjoined distinctions between the sexes" (Hoffman-Ladd, 1987: 37). Muslim women were active in the "turban movement" in Turkey, which opposed the legal prohibition of the Islamic head scarf for women students; this movement played a vital role in radicalizing the Islamic cause (Toprak, 1994). In all these cases religious idioms provided women with the means of opposing the denigrating forces of Western modernity.

The global dimensions of religious nationalism are striking. The BJP's anti-Muslim propaganda is legitimated by the role of the United States in the Gulf War and the anti-Muslim sentiment that predated and succeeds it, just as Islamic "fundamentalism" finds justification in the U.S. exertion of cultural superiority, political control, and economic dominance in the Middle East. In countries like Iran, leaders can mobilize Muslim sentiment in opposition to Western economic and cultural domination.

In its emphasis on the transnational character of Islamic "fundamentalism," Hindu nationalism finds justification for its own transnational ambitions. The Rām Janambhūmi movement provided the occasion for the development of far-reaching networks among Indians in North America, Africa, Europe, and other regions. These networks can build upon the growth of two groups within the expatriate Indian community: business people who seek ways of demonstrating their nationalist commitments, and self-employed business people for whom Hindu nationalism is a response to racism and discrimination abroad.

CONCLUSION

Certain features of "communalism," such as its support for a uniform civil code, encourage women's activism, but women do not achieve lasting gains from these spurts of activism. Their intense identification with "communal movements" is likely to be short-lived.

The contrasts between "communalism" and "fundamentalism" diminish when we explore the ways in which both are influenced by the economic and political context. Of particular importance are electoral influences. The more committed groups are to exercising power, the more expedient they are likely to be in interpreting religion. This in turn has extremely significant implications for women. The more a group believes itself to be the authentic voice of religion, the more likely it is to treat women as symbols of tradition. Conversely, the more committed a group is to exercising power democratically, the more women count numerically as a means of demonstrating popular support and winning elections. This in turn might entail appealing to women's gender interests.

Furthermore, "communalism" and "fundamentalism" are both essentialist concepts: they infer from religious identities a stable set of values and beliefs. In India, "fundamentalism" is an even more pejorative concept than "communalism." This in turn is partly a reflection of the very influence of Hindu nationalism. The term "fundamentalism" denotes the beliefs and practices of Muslims; "communalism," those of Hindus. The BJP has strengthened the assumption that

Muslims compare particularly unfavorably with Hindus in the treatment of women. Thus the use of the concepts of "fundamentalism" and "communalism" effectively pits Islam against Hinduism. Both terms are so premised on assumptions of primordialism that no amount of creative reinterpretation can sufficiently launder them of it.

In highlighting the modern political ambitions of Hindu "communalism," it is impossible to ignore the complicated ways in which this modernizing project restores, utilizes, and reinterprets traditional forces. Even though the BJP's ambitions are wholly modern—a powerful, expansionist state, integration with the global capitalist system—it also strengthens antimodernist impulses. Thus Vijayraje Scindia at one moment supports a uniform civil code that will accord women legal rights and at another moment suggests that *satī* provides the normative ideal to which Hindu women should aspire.

Hindu nationalists have turned to women as exemplifications of the contradictory qualities they seek to project: a rootedness in the past and a commitment to a modern India in the future. But Hindu women can exemplify these two very different qualities only by taking on another quality: a willingness to render Muslims into dehumanized Others.

NOTES

I received valuable comments on an earlier draft of this chapter from participants at the conference Appropriating Gender: Women and Religious Nationalism in South Asia, held at Rockefeller Conference and Study Center in Bellagio, August 1994; the conference Gender, Nation and the Politics of Culture in India, at Cornell University, 1 April 1995; and at the Peace and World Security Studies workshop at Hampshire College on 3 April 1995. I am particularly grateful to Mary Katzenstein for her encouragement and advice, and to Barbara Metcalf for her forceful denunciation of the concept of fundamentalism. I received research and writing support from the Amherst College Research Award and the John D. and Catherine T. MacArthur Foundation.

1. See Bhaktal (1993: 12–13). Kishwar (1993) describes similar forms of women's violence in the Bombay riots in December 1992 and February 1993, and Shah et al. (1993) describe the complicity of Hindu women in the Surat riots in December 1992.

2. As I indicate later in my paper, I find the terms "communalism" and "fundamentalism" of limited analytic utility

because of their pejorative connotations. I much prefer the terms religious nationalism, or Keddie's "new religious politics" or "religiopolitics" (see Keddie, 1997). However while I use the concept "religious nationalism" whenever possible, I must use the terms communalism and fundamentalism when I seek to compare the two phenomena.

3. Interview with Kusum Mehdre, Bhopal, 14 June 1991.

4. Interview with Uma Bharati, New Delhi, 17 December 1991.

5. Interview with Mridula Sinha, New Delhi, 7 February 1991.

6. Speech delivered at the BJP plenary meeting, Jaipur, December 1991.

7. Interview with Purnima Sethi, New Delhi, 27 March 1991.

8. On this question, see Ahmed (1992). On the Pakistani context, see Gardezi (1990); Mumtaz and Shaheed (1987); Rouse (1986); and Shaheed and Mumtaz (1990).

9. Agnes (1995) similarly points to the failures of the Indian women's movement to redress some of the sexist aspects of Hindu law. If two Hindus marry under the Special

Marriages Act, according to a 1954 amendment, the secular code that grants equal rights to men and women—the Indian Succession Act of 1925—does not apply. Instead, the couple is governed by the Hindu Succession Act, which grants men coparcenary rights (the rights to the family's ancestral property). Under the Hindu Adoption and Maintenance Act, a Hindu wife can neither adopt nor give a child in adoption. In reformed Hindu law, although marriages are in principle monogamous, in practice they may be polygynous, and co-wives are denied the protection that they are afforded in Hindu customary law.

10. Interview with Mridula Sinha, New Delhi, 7 February 1991.

11. Interview with Mohini Garg, New Delhi, 11 April 1991.

12. Interview with Nirupuma Gour, Lucknow, 5 January 1992.

13. Interview with Mala Rustogi (pseudonym), Lucknow, 28 December 1992. Other references to Rustogi's views are drawn from the same interview.

14. There are many parallels between women's activism in Hindu nationalism and in German fascism; see Koonz (1987); Bridenthal, Grossman, and Kaplan (1984). See Blee (1991) and Klatch (1987) for parallels with women's activism in racist and right-wing organizations in the United States.

REFERENCES

Agnes, Flavia. (1995) "Women's Movement Within a Secular Framework: Re-Defining the Agenda." In Tanika Sarkar and Urvashi Butalia (eds.), *Women and the Hindu Right*, 136–57. London: Zed Books; New Delhi: Kali for Women.

Ahmed, Leila. (1992) *Women and Gender in Islam: Historical Roots of a Modern Debate*. New Haven and London: Yale University Press.

Alter Joseph. (1994) "Celibacy, Sexuality and the Transformation of Gender into Nationalism in North India." *Journal of Asian Studies* 53, 1: 46–66.

Badran, Margot. (1994) "Gender Activism: Feminists and Islamists in Egypt." In Valentine M. Moghadam (ed.), *Identity Politics and Women: Cultural Reassertions and Feminisms in International Perspective*, 202–28. Boulder: Westview Press.

Basu, Amrita. (1995a) "Feminism Inverted: The Real Women and Gendered Imagery of Hindu Nationalism." In Tanika Sarkar and Urvashi Butalia (eds.), *Women and the Hindu Right*, 158–80. London: Zed Books; New Delhi: Kali for Women.

———. (1995b) "When Local Riots Are Not Simply Local: Collective Violence and the State in Bijnor, India, 1988-93." *Theory and Society* 24: 35–78.

Bhaktal, Svati Shakravati. (1993) "Sisterhood and Strife." *Women's Review of Books*, 10–11 (July): 12–13.

Blee, Kathleen M. (1991) *Women of the Klan: Racism and Gender in the 1920s*. Berkeley: University of California Press.

Bridenthal, Renate, Atina Grossman, and Marion Kaplan. (1984) *When Biology Becomes Destiny*. New York: Monthly Review Press.

Denton, Lynn Teskey. (1991) "Varieties of Hindu Female Asceticism." In Julia Leslie (ed.), *Roles and Rituals for Hindu Women*, 211–31. Rutherford, N.J.: Fairleigh Dickinson University Press.

Devji, Faisal Fatehali. (1991) "Gender and the Politics of Space: The Movement for Women's Reform in Muslim India, 1857–1900." *South Asia* 14, 1: 141–53.

Feldman, Shelley. (1998) "Representing Islam: Manipulating Gender, Shifting State Practices and Class Frustrations in Bangladesh." In Patricia Jeffery and Amrita Basu (eds.), *Appropriating Gender: Women's Activism and Politicized Religion in South Asia*, 33–59. New York: Routledge.

Gardesi, Fauzia. (1990) "Islam, Feminism, and the Women's Movement in Pakistan: 1981–1991." South Asia Bulletin 10, 2: 18–24

Hale, Sondra. (1994) "Gender, Religious Identity and Political Mobilization in Sudan." In Valentine M. Moghadam (ed.), *Identity Politics and Women: Cultural Reassertions and Feminisms in International Perspective*, 145–66. Boulder: Westview Press.

Hélie-Lucas, Marie-Aimée. (1994) "The Preferential Symbol for Islamic Identity: Women in Muslim Personal Laws." In Valentine M. Moghadam (ed.), *Identity Politics and Women: Cultural Reassertions and Feminisms in International Perspective*, 391-407. Boulder: Westview Press.

Hoffman-Ladd, Valerie. (1987) "Polemics on the Modesty and Segregation of Women in Contemporary Egypt." *International Journal of Middle East Studies* 19: 23–50.

Jeffery, Roger. (1994) "The Bijnor Riots, October 1990: Collapse of a Mythical Special Relationship?" *Economic and Political Weekly* 29, 10: 551–58.

Jeffery, Patricia and Roger Jeffery. (1998) "Gender, Community, and the Local State in Bijnor, India." In Patricia Jeffery and Amrita Basu (eds.), *Appropriating Gender: Women's Activism and Politicized Religion in South Asia*, 123–41. New York: Routledge.

Kandiyoti, Deniz (1991) "Introduction" in Deniz Kandiyoti (ed.), *Women, Islam and the State*. London: Macmillan.

Kapur, Ratna and Brenda Cossman. (1995) "Communalising Gender/Engendering Community: Women, Legal Discourse and the Saffron Agenda." In Tanika Sarkar and Urvashi Butalia (eds.), *Women and the Hindu Right*, 82–120. London: Zed Books; New Delhi: Kali for Women.

Keddie, Nikki. (1997) *The New Religious Politics: Where, When and Why Do "Fundamentalisms" Appear?* Unpublished paper.

Kishwar, Madhu. (1993) "Safety Is Indivisible: The Warning from Bombay Riots." *Manushi* 74–75: 2–8, 24–29, 33-49.

Klatch, Rebecca E. (1987) *Women of the New Right.* Philadelphia: Temple University Press.

Koonz, Claudia. (1987) *Mothers in the Fatherland.* New York: St. Martin's Press.

Moghadam, Valentine M. (1991) "Islamist Movements and Women's Responses in the Middle East." *Gender and History.* 3, 3: 268–86.

———. (1994) "Introduction: Women and Identity Politics in Theoretical and Comparative Perspective." In Valentine M. Moghadam (ed.), *Identity Politics and Women: Cultural Reassertions and Feminisms in International Perspective,* 3–26. Boulder: Westview Press.

Mumtaz, Khawar. (1991) "Khawateen Mahaz-e-Amal and the Sindhiani Tehrik: Two Responses to Political Development in Pakistan." *South Asia Bulletin* 11: 1–2: 101–9.

———. (1994) "Identity Politics and Women: 'Fundamentalism' and Women in Pakistan." In Valentine M. Moghadam (ed.), *Identity Politics and Women: Cultural Reassertions and Feminisms in International Perspective,* 228–42. Boulder: Westview Press.

———, and Farida Shaheed. (1987) *Women of Pakistan: Two Steps Forward, One Step Back?* London: Zed Books.

Papanek, Hanna. (1994) "The Ideal Woman and the Ideal Society: Control and Autonomy in the Construction of Identity." In Valentine M. Moghadam (ed.), *Identity Politics and Women: Cultural Reassertions and Feminisms in International Perspective,* 42–75. Boulder: Westview Press.

Poddar, Hanuman Prasad. (1992) *Nari Siksha.* Gorakhpur: Gita Press.

Ramsukhdas, Swami. (1992a) *How to lead a Householder's Life.* Gorakhpur: Gita Press.

———. (1992b) *Disgrace of Mother's Prowess,* Gorakhpur: Gita Press.

Rouse, Shahnaz. (1986) "Women's Movement in Pakistan: State Class and Gender." *South Asia Bulletin* 5,1: 30–37.

———. (1998). "The Outsider(s) Within: Sovereignty and Citizenship in Pakistan." In Patricia Jeffery and Amrita Basu (eds.), *Appropriating Gender: Women's Activism and Politicized Religion in South Asia,* 53–70. New York: Routledge.

Shah, Kalpana, Smita Shah, and Neha Shah. (1993) "The Nightmare of Surat." *Manushi* 74-75: 50-58.

Shaheed, Farida and Khawar Mumtaz. (1990) "The Rise of the Religious Right and its Impact on Women." *South Asia Bulletin* 10, 2: 9-17.

Toprak, Binnaz. (1994) "Women and Fundamentalism: The Case of Turkey." In Valentine M. Moghadam (ed.), *Identity Politics and Women: Cultural Reassertions and Feminisms in International Perspective,* 293–306. Boulder: Westview Press.

Wadley, Susan. (1977) "Women and the Hindu Tradition." *Signs* 3, 1: 113-25.

———. (1994) *Struggling with Destiny in Karimpur, 1925–1984.* Berkeley: University of California Press.

GLOBALIZATION OF BEAUTY MAKES SLIMNESS TRENDY

Norimitsu Onishi

Lagos, Nigeria—With no success, Nigeria had been sending contestants to the Miss World pageant for years. Winners of the Most Beautiful Girl in Nigeria went year after year to the Miss World competition, and year after year the beauty queens performed remarkably poorly.

Guy Murray-Bruce, the executive director of Silverbird Productions, which runs the Most Beautiful Girl contest, said he had almost resigned himself to the fact that black African women had little chance of winning an international competition in a world dominated by Western beauty ideals.

Then in 2000 he carried out a drastic change of strategy in picking the Most Beautiful Girl and Nigeria's next international representative.

"The judges had always looked for a local queen, someone they considered a beautiful African woman," Mr. Murray-Bruce, 38, said. "So I told the judges not to look for a local queen, but someone to represent us internationally."

The new strategy's success was immediate. The Most Beautiful Girl of 2001, Agbani Darego, went on to clinch the Miss World title in Sun City, South Africa, last October. She became the first African winner in the contest's 51-year history.

(continued)

Her victory stunned Nigerians, whose country had earned a worldwide reputation for corruption and fraud. Now, all of a sudden, Nigeria was No. 1 in beautiful women. Ms. Darego, who was 18 at the time, instantly became a national heroine.

But soon pride gave way to puzzlement. In a culture where Coca-Cola-bottle voluptuousness is celebrated and ample backsides and bosoms are considered ideals of female beauty, the new Miss World shared none of those attributes. She was 6 feet tall, stately and so, so skinny. She was, some said uncharitably, a white girl in black skin.

The perverse reality was that most Nigerians, especially those over 40, did not find the new Miss World particularly beautiful.

The story does not end there, though. In the year since her victory, a social transformation has begun to take hold across this nation, Africa's most populous.

The change is an example of the power of Western culture on a continent caught between tradition and modernity. Older Nigerians' views of beauty have not changed. But among young, fashionable Nigerians, voluptuousness is out and thin is in.

"After Agbani won, girls look up to me and ask me how to get slim," said Linda Ikeji, 22, an English major at the University of Lagos.

"Before, fat girls were the rave of the moment," said Ms. Ikeji, who is 5 feet 8, weighs 130 pounds and now finds work as a part-time model. "Some fat girls thought they had an advantage over me. But Agbani changed everything."

Here in Lagos, the commercial capital, the thin "It" girls are now called lepa, using a Yoruba word that means thin but that was not applied to people before. The lepa girl has had a popular song written about her, called simply "Lepa." Nigeria's booming film industry has capitalized on the trend by producing a movie, "Lepa Shandi"; the title means a girl as slim as a 20-naira bill.

To anyone who has traveled across the continent, especially in West and Central Africa, the cultural shift is striking. In the United States slimness may be an ideal, but many ethnic groups in this region hold festivals celebrating big women. In Niger many women take livestock feed or vitamins to bulk up.

Among the Calabari people in southeastern Nigeria, fat has traditionally held a cherished place. Before their weddings, brides are sent to fattening farms, where their caretakers feed them huge amounts of food and massage them into rounder shapes. After weeks inside the fattening farms, the big brides are finally let out and paraded in the village square.

Ms. Darego, the same Miss World who has helped change young Nigerians' perception of beauty, belongs to the Calabari ethnic group—and thus may seem particularly unattractive to her own people.

"If she was in a crowd of other African women, I wouldn't regard her as a beautiful woman," said Ken Calebs-Olumese, who does not belong to that ethnic group but, as the owner of the exclusive Coliseum nightclub here, knows beautiful women.

"The average African woman is robust, has big hips, a lot of bust," he said. "That's what she offers in terms of beauty. It's in our culture." Mr. Calebs-Olumese, who is 56, drew a blank at the mention of lepa. Still, he acknowledged that he was "speaking from my generation's perspective."

While the transformation in youthful tastes was linked to the Miss World victory, it started, some said, with an earlier event.

"In 1998, M-Net, the South African network seen across Africa on satellite television, opened a search for the "Face of Africa." The winner was promised a three-year, $150,000 modeling contract with the Elite agency in New York.

Not surprisingly, M-Net, which shows mostly American movies and TV shows, chose a skinny, 6-foot-2 teenager from Lagos, Oluchi Onweagba, who was not considered particularly pretty here but became a hit on the runways.

"That was the start," said Frank Osodi, 36, a fashion designer whose studio in the Surulere district in Lagos was a hive for models and beauty queens one recent morning. "Before, if you were thin, people thought you were sick, like an AIDS patient. Now if you have a skinny member in your family, you don't have to be ashamed."

Indeed, parents are now urging their daughters to take part in beauty pageants. In the past, the

(continued)

Most Beautiful Girl competition drew just enough contestants to hold a pageant, Mr. Murray-Bruce said. For the 2001 contest there were only 40; this year there were 400.

No one is predicting whether the youthful preference for thinness represents a fad or a lasting cultural change. But Maureen and Mary-Jane Mekowulu, slim 18-year-old twins who are students at the University of Nsukka in southeastern Nigeria and were visiting their parents here, said they would continue to exercise every morning and abstain from eating after 6 P.M.

"Because of Agbani, people have realized that slim is beautiful," Maureen said of the Miss World.

And the Most Beautiful Girl of 2002 would reinforce that impression, said the contest's producer, Mr. Murray-Bruce. "She's even skinnier than Agbani," he said.

Social Protest and the Feminist Movement

Throughout *Feminist Frontiers* we have begun to understand the breadth and magnitude of the social forces working to differentiate women and men and to disadvantage women. Socialization, the organization of social institutions, and social and economic policies all come together to hinder women's full political participation, self-determination, economic security, and even health and safety.

Despite the ubiquitous nature of sexism, racism, classism, nationalism, homophobia, and the other forms of inequality embedded in our social institutions, women resist. As we have seen, women often fight to undermine the forces of oppression in individual ways. Women also come together to take collective action to pursue social change. This section explores contemporary feminist movements, noting how feminist issues are different in particular cultures and historical contexts.

Not all people who seek to change gender arrangements do so in feminist ways, however, and not all women activists support greater equality. In "The Gendered Organization of Hate: Women in the Ku Klux Klan, " Kathleen Blee discusses white women's involvement in the racist hate movement. Both in the 1920s and in the present, women have made up a significant portion of members in the KKK. Women members are important to the organizational strength of the Klan, helping to recruit and retain members and to socialize children. They join because the KKK appeals to their interests as wives and mothers. In the 1920s, the Klan played on women's concern about moral reform and vice, while in the present, it recruits women by blaming minorities for problems with public schools and safety. In both time periods, the KKK claimed to support gender equality—for white, native-born, non-Jewish women only—in order to recruit women. At the same time, the KKK supported traditional gender ideologies that saw white women as potential victims of sexual violence and emphasized their responsibility for bearing many children to populate the racist movement. What does Blee suggest is necessary in order to work against the racist movement's appeal to women? Do you agree with her that feminist messages could address many of these women's concerns? In general, why do you think women participate in social movements that work against gender equality?

Melanie Heath addresses another movement against feminism, the organization of men known as the Promise Keepers, in "What Promises Can Men Keep? How Men Renegotiate Gender and Racial Ideologies in the Promise Keepers Movement." The Promise Keepers, she argues, incorporate contradictory ideas about gender into their individual identities as men and their official ideology. Participating in the Promise Keepers leads men to adopt a "more expressive and caring masculinity" and to participate more fully in family life, while at the same time retaining their authority as men in the family and the larger society. Similarly, the Promise Keepers encourage men to bond with each other, forming emotional ties rarely found among heterosexual men, but simultaneously reinforce traditional masculinity at events through the absence of women and the creation of a sports-event atmosphere. The Promise Keepers' emphasis on racial reconciliation, Heath argues, is similarly contradictory, encouraging personal bonds across racial boundaries but not challenging structural racial inequality. In what ways do you think the Promise Keepers are a force for gender and racial equality? In what ways do they reinforce inequality? Can you think of examples of other social movements that are contradictory in their approach to gender or racial equality?

As these two articles show, attempts to change gender and race often intersect. From the other side of the political spectrum, African-American lesbian, bisexual, and heterosexual feminist authors have repeatedly emphasized the need to understand the multiple and interlocking nature of racial, sexual, heterosexual, and class domination.

In "Punks, Bulldaggers, and Welfare Queens," Cathy J. Cohen discusses the origins of queer politics, a form of activism that emerged in the 1990s to promote an understanding of sexuality that rejects the idea of static, stable sexual identities and behaviors, such as gay and straight, that have been used to normalize and privilege some groups and to marginalize and subordinate others. Cohen embraces queer activists' in-your-face strategies intended to challenge the invisibility of gay, lesbian, bisexual, and transgendered people and to embrace sexual difference. But she criticizes the narrowness of queer politics for its overemphasis on deconstructing the historically and culturally recognized categories of homosexual and heterosexual. Such a strategy, she argues, exaggerates the similarities between individuals categorized under the label of "heterosexual" and ignores the way other systems of oppression regulate the lives of women and men of all races, classes, and sexualities.

In "The Next Feminist Generation: Imagine My Surprise," Ellen Neuborne describes her experiences as a young woman raised by feminist parents in a world that she believed had been changed by the women's movement. When she encounters sexism at work, she is taken aback to discover that she does not initially resist it. Her "programming" to accept gender inequality is both subtle and pervasive. Neuborne argues that sexism takes different forms now; rather than being expected to make coffee for their male co-workers, women are assigned to less challenging jobs (ostensibly as a favor), or seen as uncommitted employees if they have children. While the second-wave women's movement transformed corporations' official policies to support gender equality, Neuborne suggests that the *practice* of gender equality in the workplace lags far behind. She concludes by telling young women: "[D]on't be fooled into thinking that feminism is old-fashioned. The movement is ours and we need it." Can you think of examples of "programming" in your own experience? How have your workplaces and schools been influenced by feminism? What forms of sexism or gender inequality have you observed? What do you think a feminist movement for the new century might look like?

In the anthology's final reading, Verta Taylor, Nancy Whittier, and Cynthia Fabrizio Pelak present an overview of the multiple ideologies and forms of the feminist movement in the United States from its emergence in the 1960s to the present. "The Women's Movement: Persistence through Transformation" considers the larger social and economic conditions responsible for the rise of women's movements in the Western world and describes the international context of feminism. The analysis focuses on the way feminist movements have changed over time as a result of activists' own ideas and goals and the larger social and political context, including antifeminist countermovements that have arisen to oppose the aims of the women's movement.

Feminism, as this article demonstrates, has a long and vibrant history and strong prospects for the future. Women's movements in the twenty-first century are becoming more diverse than ever and hold great promise for transforming the lives of both women and men for the better. As you finish reading *Feminist Frontiers,* what changes would you like to see in the gender system? How do you propose to accomplish these changes?

The Gendered Organization of Hate: Women in the U.S. Ku Klux Klan

ﾟ Kathleen M. Blee

Among all right-wing extremist groups in U.S. history—that is, groups far outside the political mainstream that favor violent means to achieve antiegalitarian goals—the most successful in recruiting women members have been those that call themselves Ku Klux Klans (KKK). In the 1920s, KKK-affiliated women's Klans brought an estimated five hundred thousand women into the politics of virulent racism, anti-Catholicism, xenophobia, and anti-Semitism, forming what arguably was the largest extremist right-wing women's movement in U.S. history. Today's racist, anti-Semitic, and homophobic Klan is greatly reduced in size, numbering no more than twenty thousand (less than 1 percent of its 1920s membership), but probably at least one-quarter of these members are women.

Given women's significant involvement in the Klan, it is ironic that few political movements have been so active in promoting masculinity as a political virtue. From the all-male gangs in the mid-nineteenth century to the gender-integrated groups today, the KKK has presented itself as a vehicle for challenging threats to the social, economic, and political power of white U.S.-born Protestant (later, Christian) men. Indeed, the Klan explicitly identifies itself as a fellowship, or clan, of besieged and enraged white men. Despite this intense emphasis on masculine political power, however, many women have enlisted in the Klan's white supremacist crusade.

The participation of women in the Ku Klux Klan not only illustrates an interesting paradox in the history of U.S. racist politics, but also permits an examination of more general propositions about gender and the far right In this chapter, I focus on three related issues. First, I examine the gendered nature of women's *participation* in the Klan in the 1920s and today and its implications for women's involvement in other extremist right-wing movements. Second, I explore the *motivation* of women who joined the Ku Klux Klan,

how women are mobilized into right-wing movements that do not reflect, and are even antithetical to, their gendered interests. Third, I consider the *gender ideologies* of the Klan, focusing on how rhetorics of women's rights can support agendas of racial, religious, national, and sexual hatred and bigotry.

As a secret organization, the Klan does not make available its documents or membership lists. Thus, data about the participation, motivations, and gender ideologies of women in the Klan come from a variety of more indirect sources. For the 1920s Klan, I used public and private collections of documents published by the Klan and secondary documents about the Klan. These were supplemented by oral history interviews that I conducted during the mid-1980s with a number of elderly former Klanswomen in Indiana. Information on today's Klan is from my life history interviews in the mid-1990s with women Klan activists, part of a larger project about women in the contemporary U.S. racist movement This is supplemented by my observations at Klan events and analysis of propaganda issued by every existing Klan group over a one-year period.[1]

WOMEN AND THE FAR RIGHT

Scant scholarly attention has been paid to the role of women in racist or extremist right-wing movements in the United States. This dearth of scholarship can be attributed to three conceptual shortcomings. The first problem is the assumption that right-wing extremism is best understood by focusing on its leaders and spokesmen. Due to both the difficulty (and danger) of obtaining reliable information from rank-and-file members of far-right groups and to an assumption that authority in the extreme right is always male dominated and top-down, scholarship on right-wing extremist movements is based almost entirely on written propaganda or interviews with (often self-proclaimed) leaders. This has skewed information on the far-right toward the pronouncements of those who are most visible to the public and away from members who are less open about their participation, resulting in biased data on participants in right-wing extremism.

Relying on the statements of those with organizational tides ensures the invisibility of women in mixed-gender groups of the extreme right. Very few women are official leaders or public spokespersons in the Klan or other such mixed-gender groups in the United States. This is not surprising, given the far-right's emphasis on the importance of men in racist politics and the vitriolic misogyny expressed in the propaganda and political agendas of virtually all right-wing groups in the United States. Yet the absence of women from leadership and public spokesperson roles in the far-right in the United States does not mean that women are not numerous, and even important, rank-and-file members of these movements. Indeed, women are often particularly sought as members by right-wing extremist movements precisely because they are less visible to outsiders, thus helping to shield groups from outside scrutiny and allowing better access to potential recruits. Moreover, the lines of authority in the Klan can be complicated, with leadership (in the sense of providing strategic direction, attracting and socializing new recruits, and organizing internal cohesion) exercised by middle-level leaders, including women, while formal, titled-leaders, generally men, may command the allegiance of fairly few followers.

Second is the conceptual blinder of regarding even those women who hold official public or leadership roles in extremist right-wing groups as simply proxies for more powerful men. Thus, major figures in the history of the far-right in the United States such as Alma White, a Quaker preacher who became a defender of the KKK in the 1920s, or the influential American Nazi devotee of the 1930's, Elizabeth Dilling, have received far less scholarly attention than comparably situated, less influential male figures.[2]

Moreover, U.S. scholars commonly overlook the significance of women as members of right-wing movements, even when the extent of that participation is known. As an example, the existence of numerous women's chapters of the KKK in the 1920s was known to many historians, but without a gender-sensitive lens of analysis, Klanswomen were assumed to be the political or personal pawns of Klansmen,

and scholarly attention was directed exclusively at the Klan's male members.

Third, the absence of women as subjects in scholarship on the extreme right is due to a belief that right-wing movements are intensely and uniformly patriarchal in both their ideologies and their practices. Certainly, support for the social, economic, and political privileges enjoyed by white, or Aryan, men is an outcome of virtually all extremist right-wing politics and an explicit goal of most far-right groups in the United States. However, the gender politics of groups in the far-right also can be complicated. Far-right groups at times have supported gender rights, although always narrowly conceived as the rights of white, or Aryan, women. Such support generally has been a tactic to recruit women members or to broaden the group's appeal to the political mainstream.

Further, the members of right-wing extremist groups can vary in their views about women's rights. Many women in right-wing extremist groups in the United States, including the Klan, espouse views about gender issues that are markedly different from those found in the propaganda of their groups or expressed by male leaders. In the 1920s, for example, a number of prominent women members of the Ku Klux Klan demanded gender equity within the larger Klan movement, over the objection of male Klan leaders. Today, some women in the Klan privately support women's access to abortion or governmental efforts to promote women's advancement at work, even as their groups strenuously denounce women's reproductive rights and state policies like affirmative action. Such complexities of gender ideology within the far-right in the United States are invisible to researchers who do not simultaneously scrutinize the rhetoric of organizational propaganda and the views of rank-and-file members.

THE KU KLUX KLAN

The Ku Klux Klan is a historically discontinuous series of four waves of organized racist activity in the United States. At each period of Klan activism, a number of discrete and often antagonistic Klan groups have claimed to be descendants of the original Klan. Although each Klan is distinct in its leadership and membership, the groups are unified in an agenda of hatred toward African Americans and members of other racial, religious, ethnic, and now, sexual minority groups. They also use similar organizational names, clothing, and rituals. The four most significant waves of Klan activity occurred in the 1860s, 1920s, 1970s, and from 1980 to the present (Bennett 1988; Chalmers 1981).

The initial Klan arose in the mid-1860s, at the end of the Civil War. Born as a violent response by southern whites against efforts at racial and political realignment within the U.S. South during Reconstruction, the first wave of the Klan loosely linked gangs of impoverished rural white male southerners, wealthy plantation owners, and industrialists who feared the loss of their political and economic supremacy. Women did not participate as members in this initial Klan, although white southern women were evoked as symbols of the tradition of racial and sexual supremacy that Klan men were expected to protect. This wave of the Klan was intensely violent, fomenting a bloody sweep of lynchings, assaults, arsons, and destruction and expropriation of property across the former states of the Confederacy, directed at freed African-American slaves, northern representatives of the Reconstruction government, and whites thought to be sympathetic to the new racial order. The first Klan collapsed in the mid-1870s in the face of federal pressure and as a new structure of white supremacist laws, agricultural sharecropping, and a racially exclusive political system shored up the racial structures formerly enforced by the system of slavery (McLean 1994; Blee 1991).

A second wave of the Klan emerged in the mid-1910s and gained strength through the mid-1920s in the period of high immigration from southern and eastern Europe and large-scale migration of African Americans from southern to northern states of the United States. Most scholars estimate the membership of the 1920s Klans at between 2 million and 3 million members, of whom about a half-million were women, making it the largest Klan and perhaps the largest extremist right-wing movement in U.S. history.

Unlike earlier and later waves of the Klan, the second Klan was stronger in many parts of the Midwest, East, and West, including such states as Indiana, Ohio, Oregon, and New York, than in the South. It took root both in large urban areas that were absorbing new immigrants and in racially and religiously homogenous small towns and rural areas that were experiencing few population changes, and it enlisted a substantial proportion, even a majority, of the white, native-born, Protestant population. This Klan drew members from a range of social classes, enlisting small-business owners and professionals together with those from the working and lower classes and, in many areas, was reputedly financed by local wealthy benefactors. In addition to racism against African Americans, the 1920s Klan mobilized sentiment against Catholics, Jews, non-U.S. born immigrants, labor unions, Mormons, and other minority groups (Blee 1991, 57–65).

Women participated in a number of women's Klan groups in the 1920s, the largest being the Women of the Ku Klux Klan. Like male members, Klanswomen came from a range of social positions. They were married and single, employed for wages and housewives, long politically engaged and new to public politics. Although the women's and men's Klans had similar political and racial agendas and rituals, there were outbreaks of conflict and hostility between them, generally over the disbursement of Klan dues. In a few cases, tensions between men's and women's Klan groups became public, spilling over into lawsuits and even physical confrontations between male and female leaders and members. In the states of Arkansas, Michigan, and Pennsylvania, women's and men's Klans battled in court, charging each other with financial mismanagement and illegal practices. Women from an Oregon Klan attacked a male Klan leader when he tried to interfere with their group. This wave of the Klan collapsed precipitously in the late 1920s, as the result of a series of internal financial and sexual scandals and the passage of severe immigration quotas, which undercut one of the Klan's most visible political issues (Chalmers 1981).

The third wave of the Klan appeared in the late 1960s and early 1970s during the turbulent period of social and school racial desegregation in the South. This Klan recruited largely from populations of poorly educated and economically marginal white men in the rural South and unleashed a wave of violence and terror against African Americans. Women played only minor roles in this Klan wave, which had become insignificant by the late 1970s.

Today's Klans emerged in the late 1980s, as part of a broader upsurge in racist activity. This wave of organized racism was fueled by economic restructuring and decline in certain sectors of the economy, notably small-scale agriculture and industrial work, as well as by the increased use of xenophobic, racist, and homophobic rhetoric by politicians from the conservative political mainstream. The Klan and other racist groups also grew in the 1980s because of internal factors within the racist movement. Most important were alliances between previously antagonistic racist and neo-Nazi leaders, made possible in part by decisions by several Klan leaders to deemphasize anti-Catholicism and even to welcome Catholic members along with their traditional base among Protestant fundamentalists. Also influential were efforts by right-wing extremists in central and eastern Europe to forge a transnational "pan-Aryan" movement that would champion the interests of all non-Jewish whites (Aryans) and oppose Jews and all nonwhites, incorporating anti-Semitism into an international racist agenda. A final factor was the growing influence of ideologies of "Christian Identity" in the racist movement that served to cement ideological alliances across racist groups. A pseudoreligion imported to the United States from England, Christian Identity is viciously anti-Semitic and racist, teaching that Jews and African Americans are the offspring of Satan and that white Christians are the true lost tribe of Israel (Barkun 1994; Dobratz and Shanks-Meile 1997).

Most of the several dozen or so groups that now bill themselves as Ku Klux Klans remained small during the 1980s and 1990s, many declining even further in the face of federal investigations of the extreme right after the bombing of the Oklahoma City federal building in 1995. Despite their dwindling size, some contemporary Klan groups, especially those allied with neo-Nazi groups, have become significant players in an amalgamated racist movement. All groups in this movement predict an apocalyptic racial war between African Americans and Aryans. Some groups also advocate race war as a way of undermining racial minorities, while others, who view both Africans American and Aryans as under the grip of powerful but invisible Jewish conspirators, fear that race war will ultimately benefit only Jews.[3]

The composition of the modern Klan is more gender diverse than any Klan since the 1920s. Women are full-fledged members in most Klan groups. In some, they have even become public, although low-level, leaders. Women constitute an estimated 25 percent of the membership of some Klan groups and may make up 50 percent of the new recruits. Like women in the 1920s Klan, today's Klanswomen come from a variety of social class and family statuses. Although it is impossible to determine the exact characteristics of Klan members as a whole, it is clear that both married and nonmarried women, mothers as well as those without children, the employed and those without waged jobs, have joined the Klan in recent decades.

Despite, or perhaps because of, the increasing number of women members, Klan groups, perhaps more than any other segment of the modern extreme right, have experienced conflict between male and female members. Privately, a number of Klanswomen point to disparity between the messages of gender equity espoused in the recruiting materials of some Klans and their treatment as the handmaidens of male members in the Klan. Although all Klan groups maintain the Klan's traditional adherence to moral conservatism, including opposition to divorce and a belief that men's authority should be respected in politics and the home, many of them insist that women are treated as equal to men within the racist movement, including having opportunities to advance to leadership within the Klan. One male Klan leader told me that, "without women, we wouldn't have the Klan,"[4] and at least one Klan features women on its Internet page to demonstrate its gender inclusivity. A major Klan chapter insisted, evidence to the contrary, that "women hold a very high and exalted position in the eyes of the Ku Klux Klan."[5] Further, it claimed to "still believe that our women find their greatest fulfillment as mothers of our children," even though "international finance" [i.e., Jews] has "retarded the advance of white women in this country," who purportedly are pushed into poorly paid jobs when Jewish bosses or bankers make it impossible for white non-Jewish husbands to sustain their families.

In their life histories and private communications, however, Klanswomen say that they regard the gender messages expressed in Klan recruitment materials as a cynical means of bringing women into an organization that does not support women in its internal practices or public politics. They object to what they perceive, but do not label, as a "glass ceiling" in the leadership structure of the Klan in which women are prevented from assuming positions of actual decision making in most Klan groups. As one Klanswoman told me, "The Klan is male oriented, totally sexist. The men still run it, as far as the offices go." Although one woman has received some prominence in one of the major Klans and may even advance to leadership in the near future, she is the daughter of the current Klan head, and many women dismiss her, correctly or not, as her father's political puppet. For their part, Klansmen complain about the increasing presence of women in the Klan, claiming that women are usurping the authority that is rightfully theirs (Coppola 1996, esp. 127–128; Blee 2000, 93–110; Blee 2001).

GENDER AND THE KU KLUX KLAN

To understand the involvement of women in the Ku Klux Klan, I focus on the two periods in which women were most active: the 1920s and today. These time periods also had active Klan chapters in both northern and southern states. It was in these time periods, too, that the Klan had the most elaborate ideologies, specifying not only ideas about race, but also about nationhood, gender, religion, historical change, sexuality, and political leadership. By examining women's participation and motivations and the gender ideologies of these Klans, it is possible to discern more general patterns of women's involvement in extremist right-wing organizing.

Participation

Women's participation in the 1920s Klan was confined to all-women Klan groups that proclaimed their separateness from the male Klan, very different from women's participation in today's mixed-sex Klan groups. Yet the nature of women's involvement in these two waves of the Klan reveals similar, gendered patterns.

One similarity is that both Klans recruited women for strategic purposes. The 1920s Klan was organized at the peak of activism on behalf of women's suffrage. When women were given the right to vote in U.S. federal elections in 1920, they constituted an attractive recruiting pool for Klan leaders. Such practical considerations outweighed the general reluctance of male Klan leaders to enlist women in a male racist fraternity, although they did not quell the antagonism of many men to the intrusion of women into this formerly all-male sphere of politics and violence. Responding to the Klan's appeal, women joined the 1920s Klan to preserve and extend their rights as white Protestants, rights they feared would be eroded by immigrant, African-American, or non-Protestant voters. Indeed, many Klanswomen earlier supported women's enfranchisement in order to counteract the votes that had previously been won by African-American and immigrant men. For them, the transition to Klan politics of racial and religious bigotry and xenophobia was an easy one.

In today's Klan, women are recruited for different, but no less gender-specific, reasons. Faced with declining memberships, Klan leaders have turned to women to bolster the size of their groups relative to those of competing Klans or to stave off organiza-

tional collapse. Too, some Klan leaders regard women members as effective in recruiting their sons and husbands to the Klan's cause. Others see women as more stable and less legally vulnerable than men, pointing to women's lesser propensity to engage in nonracist criminal activity that could attract the attention of law enforcement to the Klan.

Women's involvement in both of these waves of the Klan provoked negative reactions from male Klan members and gender conflict within Klan groups. In the 1920s, the incorporation of women into the Klan, even in gender-segregated Klan groups, was met with derision and hostility by many Klansmen who saw the Klan as a bulwark against all forms of "immoral modernism," including the expansion of women's rights. Male Klan members chided women members, and KKK leaders battled their counterparts in the women's Klans over money and authority. This disdain for women in the Klan was shared by some anti-Klan activists, who ridiculed the KKK for bringing women into politics, out of the home where they rightfully belonged. A prominent anti-Klan newspaper editor from Muncie, Indiana, for example, attacked what he termed the "bob-haired Amazons" of the Klan, chastizing women who "abandoned" husband and children for Klan politics and ridiculing the husbands of Klanswomen who had relinquished their role as family "boss" to their wives (Giel 1967; *Muncie [Indiana] Post-Democrat*, May 23,1924; Blee 1991, 65–69; Blee 2001).

The modern Klan, too, has experienced internal conflicts over issues of gender in its ranks, although these have seldom spilled over into public view. In my interviews, a number of Klanswomen expressed discontent about the condescending and hostile behavior of many male Klan officials and members. These women see Klansmen, in the words of one woman, as "Joe Six-Packs," unable to deal with women as equals. They are particularly critical of men who assume that women are the sexual possessions of men or who expect women to be in the background of racial politics. A Klanswoman complained to me about her husband, saying, "He's been at more rallies than I have. But, you know, I have to work, and I can't really be there and work at the same time. And the bills have got to be paid " Another woman decried what she regarded as the limited vision for women in the Klan, commenting, "Klansmen see women as breeders, and most women in the Klan feel they should produce babies for the white race."

Despite their own commitment to the Klan, these women conclude that they will never encourage their daughters to join such a group. As a Klanswoman told me, if her adult daughter joined the Klan, "there wouldn't be anything for her to do. She could go to a few rallies or picnics, but wouldn't be allowed to go to the real meetings." Once having learned the racist ideas of the Klan, these women see themselves as having a responsibility to the white race to continue in the racist movement, but, surprisingly, they feel no comparable need to instruct their daughters to join racist groups that do not treat women well. Clearly, this is a source of future fragility in a Klan movement increasingly reliant on women recruits. Moreover, as some women continue to rise, although slowly, through the ranks of lower- and middle-level Klan leadership and make claims for positions as Klan spokespersons and leaders, these gender tensions are likely to become a greater source of conflict within the Klan (Blee 1991).

In both of these waves of the Klan, women were involved in activities that served to extend the virulent racism of the Klan, although the nature of these differed. In the 1920s, Klanswomen rarely participated in overt terrorism like night-riding and physical assaults on Klan enemies as Klansmen did, but they were vicious and effective perpetrators of economic, political, and social terrorism. Through organized networks of gossip and boycotts, Klanswomen in Indiana worked to destroy the livelihoods and community acceptance of those they deemed unacceptable in the Klan's vision of America. The jobs and stores of Jews, Catholics, new immigrants, and African Americans were especially vulnerable to such pressures. Across the state, Catholic schoolteachers, Jewish store owners, and African-American workers, facing Klan terror, fled their communities, abandoning careers and businesses in search of safety. In the Klan's campaign to rid Indiana of racial, religious, and national minority groups, the organized effort of Klanswomen was crucial. Women in the Klan spread negative rumors about members of these groups, encouraging others to boycott their stores and shun them personally.

Similarly, Klanswomen today rarely are visible in public violence or terroristic activities in the Klan, but they are active advocates of these actions by Klansmen and work hard to create the organizational strength, effective propaganda, and attention to the recruitment of children and retention of members necessary to continue the Klan over generations.

In one significant way, however, the participation of women in the 1920s differed from that of the modern Klan. In the 1920s Klan, women were brought into all-women's groups that mixed support for the overall Klan agenda of racism, anti-Semitism, anti-Catholicism, and nationalism with ideas of rights for white, Protestant, U.S.-born women. Since this Klan gained strength at the peak of women's suffrage and social reform activism, it recruited many women who combined racist ambitions with substantial histories of involvement in religious, civic, women's rights, and political organizations. These organizational skills and resources, garnered in other social movements, not only made these women effective advocates for the Klan and able to mobilize large numbers of women into its political crusade, but also allowed them to successfully press the Klan to express some support for the political and economic rights of (white, Protestant, U.S.-born) women.

Contemporary women join a very different Klan, one that is small, politically marginal, gender mixed, and in which men hold a firm monopoly on positions of power, titles, and influence. In the decades after the collapse of the 1920s Klan, subsequent waves of Klan organization were virtually all male. Women were incorporated only in background, supportive roles as the wives and girlfriends of Klansmen and the helpmates of the Klan movement. By the 1980s, however, Klan groups started recruiting women directly into the Klan. This strategy has been successful, bringing many women into the Klan, but few have substantial prior involvement in other political movements, and almost none have been given leadership or public roles. As a result, they have relatively little influence over Klan politics and propaganda.

Motivation

The participation or women in the male-supremacist Klan suggests that women can be mobilized into racist movements that seem antithetical to their collective interests. Indeed, far-right agendas—based on appeals to individualism, antiegalitarianism, nationalism, and moralism/traditionalism—appear to offer little to women as a group. Few women would benefit from the patriarchal nature of right-wing agendas, at least to the extent that white class-privileged Protestant men might. Yet, women do join Klan groups and a variety of other extremist right-wing movements. Why?

Evidence from the 1920s and the life history narratives of today's Klanswomen indicate that, like their male counterparts, women are drawn into the Klan in a search for answers to problems they consider pressing in their lives or in society as a whole. But this is a gendered process. In the 1920s, the traditional expectation that home and family life were the province of women provided the Klan a way to attract women members, by presenting itself as a bulwark against the destructive forces of unchecked vice and alcohol on family life. In the propaganda of the 1920s Klan, vice (such as frequenting dance or pool halls, prostitution, gambling, and sexual promiscuity) was associated with Jews and African Americans, and alcohol with Catholics and immigrants. The Klan's focus on vice and alcohol was similar to appeals used by other reform movements of the early twentieth century, including progressive reform movements, but the Klan tied issues of morality to those of race and religion. This is a common and powerful tactic of racist groups, who assert their credibility by focusing on issues of general public concern, then move these in a racist direction.

Today's Klan uses a similar tactic, recruiting women members by emphasizing issues like the declining quality of public schools, then attributing blame for school failure to racial minority and immigrant students, Jewish teachers, and a Jewish-controlled government. One woman explained to me her decision to join the Klan by saying that she got "fed up" that she could not get her children educated properly, adding only as an afterthought that their poor education must have resulted from the presence of Hispanic children in their classroom. Another Klanswoman cited the problem of latchkey children, arguing that "the children of the world now are lost. Mother is having to work now and support them, and they have to sit on the doorstep a couple of hours before their mother ever gets home."

Race, religion, and nationality become simple, concrete solutions to social and political problems that people feel otherwise powerless to correct. Swelling the ranks of the Klan, therefore, are not only women who are motivated by racism, elitism, or bigotry, but also those worried about the effects of crime on themselves and their families, the escalating rate of family dissolution, or the decline of city services—concerns that cannot be easily described as inherently reactionary or progressive (West and Blumberg 1990, 1–40).

Women structure their political opportunities differently than men suggesting why, as West and Blumberg note, women's protest activities—on the left and right alike—are more likely than men's to be linked to issues of economic survival, national/racial/ethnic conflict, humanism/nurturance, or women's rights.

Although the 1920s and 1990s Klans emphasized very different sets of issues, both presented their agendas as consistent with women's interests as mothers, wives, or female citizens, Temma Kaplan's concept of *female consciousness* as the process whereby "recognition of what a particular class, culture, and historical period expect from women, creates a sense of rights and obligations that provides motive force for actions" (1982, 545) is a useful way to think about how women's daily life experiences can be manipulated to bring them into right-wing politics, a process exemplified by the Klan's efforts to position itself as the bulwark against social decay.

GENDER IDEOLOGIES

The ideas about gender found in the propaganda of Klan groups are surprisingly complicated. This is true both today and in the early-twentieth-century Klan. Throughout its history the Klan has been regarded, correctly, as an organization that fosters male supremacism as an integral part of its racist agenda, guarding the privileges of white men against perceived encroachment by white women and minority group members. What Martin Durham in his study of the British fascist National Front terms its "overwhelming masculinity" has been true of the Klan even during periods with significant female membership (1992, 277, citing Mosse 1985).

Despite this historical constancy, however, the propaganda about gender issues issued by the Klan has changed over time in response to changes in the larger political environment. The Klan's ability to combine support for white supremacism with varying positions on gender is attributable to its embrace of what historian George Mosse terms a "scavenger ideology," a system of beliefs formed by annexing pieces of other ideologies (Blee 1991; Koonz 1987; de Grazia 1992).

Thus, in different periods, the racist and anti-Semitic core of the Klan has been surrounded by ideas as disparate as those of alien invasions, animal rights, and temperance. In such an ideological milieu, a variety of contradictory ideas about gender equity also have been able to coexist with dedication to hard-core racism.

Women from groups that the Klan sees as its enemies—racial minorities, Jews, progressive and communist movements, labor unions, immigrants and, in the 1920s, Catholics and Mormons—always have been portrayed by the Klan in demeaning and brutalizing ways, as animalistic, sexually aggressive (or, conversely, asexual), predatory (or, conversely, passive victims of domination and cruelty by non-white, non-Aryan, non-Protestant men), and duplicitous, irresponsible baby breeders (Ware 1996, 79).[6]

The Klan's ideas about white women are more variable. One way that white or Aryan women are depicted by the Klan is as *racial victims*. This idea is captured aptly in scholar Vron Ware's description of the "enduring image of a seemingly passive, but wronged white femininity." The notion of white women as victims is central to every Klan, presented to justify assaults on minority-race men in retaliation for the threat they are declared to pose to innocent white women.

A main claim of the original Reconstruction-era Klan was that it would protect the wives and daughters of Confederate soldiers from retaliatory attack by newly freed African-American men. In the 1920s, the category of those seen as posing danger to white women was broadened to include Jewish businessmen, labor union bosses, and Catholic clergy, together with African-American men. How women were victimized was broadened as well, to include economic and political exploitation. This took many forms, including lurid tales of Catholic priests or Jewish factory owners preying sexually on innocent white Protestant girls, stories of violence inflicted on white women in cities with growing populations of African-American men recently dislocated from the U.S. South, and propaganda that stressed the exploitation of young working women by corrupt labor union officials.

The Klan's message about racial danger to white womanhood has continued unabated over time.[7] Like its predecessors, the newspapers, fliers, websites, and other propaganda of the contemporary Klan proclaims messages about white women's vulnerability to predatory racial minority and conspiratorial Jewish men. Typical and common are cartoons such as those that portray white women as defenseless in the face of vast numbers of nonwhite men streaming across the southern border of the United States from Latin America, anxious to experience the sexual paradise they anticipate in the United States by foisting themselves on young white women, or that depict African-

American men as sex-obsessed beasts waiting to spring on vulnerable white women.[8]

The contemporary Klan, much like Klans of earlier years, combines sexual prudery and sexual titillation to nest admonitions to white women against interracial sex in sexual graphic images, decrying, for example, "young [white] women who fondle these black greasy ballplayers."[9] Klanswomen concur with this message. One Klanswoman told me that "the Klan could do a lot of good, especially with young white girls who keep falling for black guys." The Klan and other racist groups also warn that white women who become involved with racial minority men will be responsible for the "death of the white race."

As one flier, widely distributed across the racist movement, instructs:

"Whiteman, look at the beautiful woman you love. Whitewoman, think about the future for your children. WHITEMAN, THINK. The decision is for this generation. Your children will be outnumbered fifty to one, by colored people who have been inflamed to hatred of our people by the JEWMEDIA . . . YOUR FIRST LOYALTY MUST BE TO YOUR RACE, WHICH IS YOUR NATION!"[10]

Second, the Klan emphasizes white women's responsibilities as racial *wives* and *mothers*.[11] The focus on white motherhood is central to all racist movements because of concerns with racial destiny, racial reproduction, and socialization into racial identities. In her study of France, Claudie Lesselier finds that "at the heart of every racist and/or nationalist system the same function is assigned to women: they are called upon to transmit the blood, tradition, language, and be prepared to fight if necessary" (Lesselier and Venner 1988, 175).

In the 1920s Klan, motherhood was heralded as a status that positioned white women to assume the task of repairing the nation. Drawing on ideas of mothers as the natural housekeepers of the community and the nation, the Klan argued that white native-born Protestant mothers had both the insight and the responsibility to undertake the political work required to restore America to a former glory of white Protestant domination.[12]

As one grand dragon of the Klan declared in 1923, "No longer will man say that in the hand of woman rests the necessity of rocking the cradle only. She has within her hand the power to rule the world "[13] To this end, women were urged to join the Klan to rid their communities of any obstacles to white supremacism. Many women responded enthusiastically to this call, claiming that as mothers of children, they needed to expel Catholic schoolteachers, Jewish-owned businesses, African Americans, and immigrant populations.

In today's Klan, the emphasis on white motherhood largely takes the form of calls for white Aryan women to bear many children. Such pro-natalist rhetoric, reserved exclusively for white non-Jewish women, reflects the Klan's fear that the white race is on the brink of demographic destruction because of high birth rates among minorities and the involvement of white women in interracial affairs. Since the procreative abilities of white Aryan women are seen as the means of securing numerical advantage for the next Aryan generation and safeguarding the purity of Aryan bloodlines, virtually all Klans churn out propaganda stressing Aryan childbearing and endless images of Aryan women as mothers of dependent and innocent family members, especially infants, young children, and older girls. Older boys are rarely depicted in this way as they are not seen as equivalently helpless. The racial procreation entrusted to white women is portrayed as essential to the racial struggle, although still decidedly secondary to the activism of white racist men. As mothers, white women do not have to take conscious racist action. Rather, they safeguard the racial future through their passivity and adherence to conventional gender norms of family life.

Third, at some points in its history, the Klan has found it politically expedient to add issues of *women's rights*—the rights of white Aryan women only, of course—into its ideological stew. The 1920s Klan was organized at a time of heightened political involvement by women. Ever opportunistic, the Ku Klux Klan seized on the rhetoric of the suffrage and reform movements to promote itself as the guarantor of good government and expanded rights for white, U.S.-born, Protestant women. Its chapters championed higher wages for white Protestant working women (although not wages equal to those of white men), billed themselves as opposed to the effects that bootleggers and government corruption had on women and family life, identifying these as the result of Catholic influence in municipal government and police departments, and even urged women to maintain an identity separate from their husbands by keeping their maiden name after marriage. Chapters of the women's Klan even campaigned for an eight-hour

day for mothers, suggesting that motherhood should be regarded as work and thereby deserving of social recognition and social regulation (Comer 1923).

The modern Klan has a more ambivalent rhetoric about women's rights, as it is caught between the social conservatism or its recruits and its desire to bring more women into the Klan. It consistently denounces the feminist movement, declaring it the product of Jewish and lesbian leaders who seek to ruin white Aryan family life. Yet various Klan groups also declare themselves in support of increased rights for white women, both in the racist movement and in society as a whole. To an extent, this is meant to target Klan enemies, by posing white women as beleaguered by affirmative action programs and lenient immigration policies that help racial minorities, supposedly at the expense of white women. But there is also some consideration of white women's rights more directly, seeking to include women in the political campaign for white supremacy as active, if not equal, partners with white men. At present, however, the Klan's emphasis on the importance of women to its mission is more rhetorical than real, and Klanswomen express considerable frustration about their subordinated position in Klan groups. One Klanswoman confided to me her disillusionment with the gender politics of her group, saying that "they acted as if women were equal [to men], but once you are inside the Klan, women are not equal at all."

CONCLUSIONS

What does the case of the U.S. Ku Klux Klan tell us about the mobilization of women into extremist right-wing politics more generally? How might we use this knowledge to counteract the appeal of far-right groups to women? There are three implications from the study of the U.S. Klan. First, research on the far right cannot ignore the participation of women. Scholarship has been distorted by the exclusive focus on men, especially those who proclaim themselves the leaders of the right. Looking more closely at the women who populate rightist groups reveals a wider range of experiences in racist groups. Men and women are recruited in racist groups through different sets of appeals. They have a different relationship to racist group leadership. And they may have strikingly different political views, at least on issues of gender. It is important to understand these gender differences in order to design strategies to prevent the recruitment of women by the far right or to lure them out of extremist right-wing groups. Too, the experiences of discord in racist groups may provide useful insights into how the cohesion of far-right groups could be shattered.

Second, there is a difference between the propagandistic messages of right-wing groups and the motivations that bring women into their ranks. While bombastic and vile attacks on African Americans, Jews, and others are the obvious messages of racist groups, many of their members are attracted by much more mundane concerns, like education, physical safety, and family life. Yet it is also clear that such issues do not need to be the province of the far right. Protecting schools, family, and personal safety are issues that can, and should, be addressed by feminist and progressive movements. This is the best means of ensuring that they do not becoming a mobilizing force for the far-right.

Finally, rightist ideology can be dangerously multifaceted. The far-right is able to broaden its appeal to new audiences by incorporating the rhetoric of political agendas, like those of women's rights, that generally are antithetical to the right. Although this is not common in the extreme right wing, it shows the striking ability of the right to manipulate issues in order to attract recruits. Feminists and political progressives need to recognize the complex ideologies found in right-wing groups to develop an effective counterstrategy and to make more explicit the links between feminism, antiracism, and transnational efforts to safeguard human rights and dignity.

NOTES

1. Greater detail about the methodology of this study can be found in Blee 1991, 596–606; and in Blee 2001.

2. Some biographical information on Alma White can be found in Blee 1991. The one full biography of White (Stanley 1996) does not fully explore White's Klan activity. Jeansonne 1996 includes a discussion of Elizabeth Dilling, but the lack of feminist analysis in this book limits its discussion of gender issues in right-wing politics.

3. From interviews and observations. Also see Cochran 1993, and Ross 1995, 166–181.

4. This quotation, and subsequent quotations from Klansmen and women, are from oral histories and other interviews I conducted in 1994 and 1995. Since the interviews were confidential, no names or identifying details, including dates and places of the interviews, are provided in this chapter.

5. "Women and the Ku Klux Klan," *White Patriot* (1987), 1.

6. An excellent discussion of the role of sexual and gender imagery in another right-wing extremist movement can be found in Bacchetta 1994.

7. There are a large number of Klan publications in which these messages appear. Collections of Klan materials are available at Tulane University, New Orleans Special Collections; the University of Kansas, Wilcox Collection, and the Anti-Defamation League of B'nai B'rith–New York.

8. From untitled fliers distributed by Ku Klux Klan groups.

9. From an untitled flier distributed by a Ku Klan Klan group.

10. Capitalization in the original. From an untitled flier distributed by a Ku Klux Klan.

11. Blee 1997.

12. See, for example, publications by the Women of the Ku Klux Klan, including *Ideals of the Women of the Ku Klux Klan* (n.p. 1923); *Constitution and Laws* (1927); *Women of America!* (n.p., c 1924); Comer 1923, 89; Graff 1924, 7.

13. See *Christian Century*, May 21, 1925, 177–178; *Fiery Cross*, July 6, 1923, 23; and *Imperial Night-Hawk*, September 3, 1924, 6.

REFERENCES

Bacchetta, Paola, 1994a. "'All Our Goddesses Are Armed': Religion, Resistance, and Revenge in the Life of Militant Hindu Nationalist Women" In *Against All Odds: Essays on Women, Religion, and Development from India and Pakistan*, eds. Kamala Bhasin, Ritu Menon, and Nighat Said Khan, 132–156. New Delhi: Kali for Women.

———. 1994b. "Communal Property/Sexual Property: On Representations of Muslim Women in a Hindu Nationalist Discourse" In *Forging Identities: Gender, Communities, and the State*, ed. Zoya Hasan. Boulder, Colo.: Westview.

Barkun, Michael 1994. *Religion and the Racist Right: The Origins of the Christian Identity Movement*. Chapel Hill: University of North Carolina Press.

Bennett, David. 1988. The Party of Fear: From Nativist Movements to New Right in American History. Chapel Hill: University of North Carolina Press.

Birenbaum, Guy. 1992. Le Front national en politique. Paris: Balland

Blee, Kathleen. 1991. Women of the Klan. University of California Press.

———. 1993. "Evidence, Empathy, and Ethics: Lessons from Oral Histories of the Klan." Journal of American History 80, 2 (September).

———. 1997. "Motherhood in the Radical Right." In The Politics of Motherhood: Activist Voices from Left to Right, ed. Alexis Jetter, Annelise Orleck, and Diana Taylor. Hanover, N.H.: University Press of New England.

———. 2000. "White on White: Interviewing Women in U.S. White Supremacist Groups." In Race-ing Research: Methodological and Ethical Dilemmas in Field Research, ed. France Winddance Twine and Jonathan Warren. New York: New York University Press.

———. 2001. Inside Organized Racism: Women and Men in the Racist Movement. University of California Press.

Chalmers, David M. 1981. Hooded Americanism: The History of the Ku Klux Klan. Durham, N.C.: Duke University Press.

Cochran, Floyd. 1993. "Sisterhood of Hate." Privately published and circulated through the Web.

Comer, James. 1923. "A Tribute and a Challenge to American Women" In Papers Read at First Annual Meeting [of the Ku Klux Klan]. n.p.

Coppola, Vincent. Dragons of God: A Journey through Far-Right America. 1996. Atlanta: Longstreet Press

de Grazia,1992. How Facism Rules Women. Italy 1992–1945. Berkeley: University of California Press.

Dobratz, Betty A. and Stephanie L. Shanks-Meile. "White Power, White Pride!" The White Separatist Movement in the United States. New York. Twayne Publishers.

Durham, Martin. 1992. "Gender and the British Union of Fascists." Journal of Contemporary History. 27.

Giel, Lawerence A. 1967. "George R. Dale—Crusader for Free Speech and a Free Press." Ph.D. Diss., Muncie, Ind.: Ball State University.

Graff, F. N. 1924. "A Tribute to the Women of the Ku Klux Klan." Dawn, 26 January 1924.

Jeansonne, Glen, 1996. Women of the Far Right: The Mothers' Movement and Word War II. Chicago: University of Chicago Press.

Kaplan, Temma. 1982. "Female Consciousness and Collective Action: The Case of Barcelona, 1910–1918." Signs: Journal of Women in Culture and Society 7, 3.

Koonz, Claudia. 1987. Mothers in the Fatherland: Women, the Family, and Nazi Politics. New York: St. Martin's Press.

Lesselier, Claudie, and Fiametta Venner, eds. 1988. "The Women's Movement and the Extreme Right in France." In The Nature of the Right: A Feminist Analysis of Order Patterns, ed. Gill Seidel, 173–185. Amsterdam: John Benjamin Publishers.

McLean, Nancy. 1994. Behind the Mask of Chivalry: The Making of the Second Ku Klux Klan. New York: Oxford University Press.

Mosse, George, 1985. Nationalism and Sexuality: Middle class Morality and Sexual Norms in Modern Europe. Madison: University of Wisconsin Press.

Ross, Loretta, 1995. "White Supremacy in the 1990s." In Eyes Right! Challenging the Right Wing Backlash, ed. Chip Berlet. Boston: South End Press.

Stanley, Susie C. 1996. Feminist Pillar of Fire: The Life of Alma White. Cleveland: Pilgrim Press.

Ware, Vron.1996. "Island Racism: Gender, Place, and White Power." Feminist Review 54 (Autumn).

West, Guida, and Rhoda Lois Blumberg. 1990. "Reconstructing Social Protest from a Feminist Perspective." In Women and Social Protest, ed. Guida West and Rhoda Lois Blumberg. New York: Oxford University Press.

What Promises Can Men Keep? How Men Renegotiate Gender and Racial Boundaries in the Promise Keepers Movement

✎ Melanie Heath

A movement built on promises?[1] Since the early 1990s, Promise Keepers has brought Christian men together in football stadiums and in small men's groups to embrace promises: to honor Christ, pursue vital relationships with other men, practice moral and sexual purity, love their families, support their local churches, seek racial harmony, and influence their world (Phillips 1994). From a single meeting in 1991, the Promise Keepers movement grew to twenty-two stadium events nationwide that attracted roughly 1.1 million men in 1996 and, in 1997, staged a million-man assembly called Stand in the Gap (SITG) in Washington D.C. By 1999, the total number of participants at Promise Keepers events was estimated at 3.5 million, an astounding number that might establish Promise Keepers as the largest men's movement ever (Newton forthcoming). Promise Keepers founder Bill McCartney (1994) suggests committing to seven promises promotes the possibility of changing men by helping them to improve relations within their families. A number of scholarly studies and media accounts agree with McCartney's assessment that the movement is producing more sensitive husbands and fathers, but others have characterized it as an anti-feminist backlash that encourages men to regain authority in their families (Messner 1997; Newton forthcoming). These contradictory depictions struggle to assess what kinds of promises men are, in fact, willing to keep. From a feminist perspective, does the Promise Keepers help men to reform or to shore up power in their families and society? To answer this question, I examine how men incorporate both progressive and reactionary ideas into their collective identity as Promise Keepers and consider what the ensuing transformations in their lives imply for social change.

CONTRADICTORY GENDER AND RACIAL IDEOLOGIES

To explore how the identities of men who identify as Promise Keepers promote and/or impede social transformation, I draw on scholarship that links social movements and gender. Social movement scholars have combined gender and social movement literature to theorize how race, class, gender, and sexuality shape identities in the organization of social protest (Brush 1999; Einwohner 1999; Ferree and Roth 1998; Fonow 1998; Hercus 1999; Taylor 1999; Thomas 1999; White 1999). Such theorists have sought to understand how people create collective identities based on shared experiences (Pelak 2002). Taylor and Whittier (1992) conceptualize collective identity based on: (1) forming group boundaries that establish differences between the challenging and dominant group; (2) building an oppositional consciousness through interpretative frameworks to define the challenging group's interests; and (3) negotiating and politicizing everyday actions to resist domination. These three factors interact to form identities based on grievances that mobilize social protest. Yet, there is a lack of research that investigates the formation of identity among groups that mobilize around more reactionary ideas. Morris (1992, 363) asserts that in studying political and social action "social scientists have tended to underemphasize the political consciousness of dominant groups while focusing on the oppositional consciousness of subordinate groups such as workers, blacks, and women." He argues that political consciousness is found not only in struggles to end domination; instead, some groups mobilize to secure privilege and power.

Theorists who examine collective identity among dominant and oppositional movements often assume a distinct boundary between the reactionary or hegemonic and the progressive or oppositional. Yet, contradictory gender and racial ideologies can fuel collective identities and social movements. Connell's (1995) conceptualization of masculinities captures how gender, race, class, and sexuality interact in ideology and practice. He defines hegemonic masculinity as denoting the masculinity that occupies the dominant position in the gender order at any historical moment and articulates with emphasized femininity, a form of femininity that is "defined around compliance with . . . subordination and is oriented to accommodating the interests and desires of men" (1987, 183). Yet, Connell maintains that there is no singular masculinity; rather there are multiple and marginalized masculinities based on race, class, and sexuality that differ from the hegemonic form. For example, white gay men might mobilize around an identity that challenges their marginalized sexuality while both adhering to and contesting certain hegemonic gender and racial ideologies. Collective identities do not singularly affirm or challenge ideologies based on gender, race, class, and sexuality but usually involve a combination of reactionary progressive ideas.

Much media and scholarly attention of Promise Keepers has focused on the reactionary ideas promoted by the movement. Scholars and journalists stress the right-wing leanings of Bill McCartney, former football coach at the University of Colorado, who has vocalized pro-life and antigay sentiments in diverse arenas and has blamed irresponsible male heads of the family for what he characterizes as the moral and social deterioration of U.S. society, a common argument of the religious right (Johnson 2000; Stodghill and Ostling 1997). The right-wing ties of the Promise Keepers movement point to its potential to promote antifeminist and conservative family values. In his analysis of the "terrain of politics" for men's movements, Messner (1997) places the Promise Keepers in the center of the "sphere of antifeminist backlash." He describes how the movement emerges out of a historical ebb and flow of masculinity politics within fundamentalist Christianity in the United States. At the turn of the twentieth century, a religious movement called "Muscular Christianity" swept across the United States with the goal of remasculinizing the church (Kimmel 1996). Led by sports hero Billy Sunday, Muscular Christianity responded to Christian men's fear of being feminized by the church and their shifting place in society that stemmed from feminism and

modernization. Messner characterizes Promise Keepers as the turn of the twenty-first century parallel in its attempt to reestablish men's leadership roles in reaction to the perceived national crisis of the feminization of the American man. With roots in the "moral majority" and other antifeminist, antigay, and antiabortion organizations, Messner argues that the political agenda of this men's movement expresses "a backlash that is antithetical to movements for equality and social justice" (99). From this perspective, Promise Keepers promotes changes in men that are mostly reactionary.

Alternatively, the Promise Keepers movement does tackle the problem of racial segregation within the church, which has potential to bring about progressive social change. Attendance at Promise Keeper rallies has consisted mostly of white, relatively class privileged men, with men of color ranging from 5 to 14 percent (Newton forthcoming). According to a Washington Poll conducted in 1997 at SITG, 49 percent of Promise Keepers earned over $50,000. Twenty-seven percent earned between $30,000 and $50,000, and 14 percent between $15,000 and $30,000. Although disproportionately a movement of white, middle-class men, Promise Keepers introduced the idea of "racial reconciliation" at its inception, building on the theme of the new evangelical reconciliation literature of the early 1990s. Glynn (1998) describes reconciliation as a call to evangelicals to pursue better relations with believers of different races mainly through the medium of public apology. Speakers at Promise Keepers rallies advocate breaking through racial barriers by recognizing the sin of segregation and creating friendships with men of different races. Promise Keepers has also made racial diversity a goal for its leadership; by 1999 one-third of its staff and one-fourth of its Board of Directors were men of color. Despite this focus on diversity, the demographics of participants remained relatively static, calling into question the impact of reconciliation on Promise Keepers and their ideologies (Messner 1997).

More recent studies of Promise Keepers based on field research and interviews, have shown the movement to promote disparate perspectives on gender and race (Williams 2000). In his study of Promise Keepers who met in small groups, Bartkowski (2000) found gender relations to be neither exclusively traditionalist nor solely progressive, but a mixture of the two. Allen (2000) analyzed the perspectives of leaders and participants concerning the Promise Keepers goal to overcome racial divisions among Christian men. He concludes that participants are supportive of the idea of racial healing, but most do not support governmental programs to implement racial equality. Newton (forthcoming) claims that, in some evangelical homes, the idea of men as servants/leaders allows Promise Keepers to become more loving and hardworking mates. Likewise, she argues that the movement's emphasis on building cross-race relations might lead to progressive social change, although its lack of focus on structural inequality would be an Achilles' heel. The tensions between reactionary and more progressive ideas in the movement summon a consideration of how men involved in Promise Keepers negotiate paradoxical gender and racial ideologies in their personal identities.

Contradictory gender and racial ideologies were apparent in the actions of the men who participated at the 1995 Million Man March, which brought an estimated 800,000 mostly African American men to Washington D.C. These men based their collective identity on an oppositional racial consciousness while reinstating a conservative view of gender relations (Messner 1997). Contradictions in ideologies are especially likely to characterize movements that mobilize around a desire to secure privileges based on gender, race, class, and/or sexuality. Blee (1996) finds that, for women in racist movements, activism becomes a defense to fend off social forces that they believe threaten their families. These women hold conflicting gender ideologies as they rely on male racists to provide ideas about white supremacy but also seek to challenge their minority status in a male-dominated movement. Racist women selectively adopt aspects of the racist movement that fit within their belief system and lives, while many criticize the movement for its sexism. They simultaneously reaffirm white privilege and challenge their minority status as women. Other movements borrow elements from progressive movements for reactionary ends. Ferber (2000) uncovers the commonalities between the mythopoetic men's and white supremacist movements as each borrows language from the women's movement to show that it is actually white men who suffer. White men in these movements seek to get in touch with their "true masculine" selves for a sense of empowerment. Ferber asserts that both men's movements represent a backlash against the women's movement and other movements that have destabilized taken-for-granted ideas about identity. Men in these movements struggle with

issues of masculinity as they try to reaffirm their positions of authority in society. Studies such as these underscore the importance of addressing the conflicts that can exist in collective identities.

In this chapter, I address the tensions in Promise Keepers' identities by uncovering the social conditions that lead them to rethink gender and racial ideologies. I apply Taylor and Whittier's (1992) three elements of identity formation—boundaries, consciousness, and negotiation—to reveal the contradictory gender and racial ideologies that shape their identities. I argue that the impact of the Promise Keepers on gender and race relations is likewise contradictory. Promise Keepers fosters men's growth on an interactional level, allowing men to embrace a more expressive and caring masculinity that includes cross-racial bonding. Simultaneously, however, it ignores, and indirectly reinforces, the structural conditions that underpin gender and racial privilege among white men.

STUDYING PROMISE KEEPERS AND THEIR WIVES

From 1997 to 1998, I conducted ethnographic research on Promise Keepers in the Sacramento area. On October 4, 1997, I attended a gathering of about a thousand Promise Keepers at the Capital in Sacramento, California, held in conjunction with SITG in Washington D.C., which was broadcast on several wide-screen televisions. As the men performed activities in concert with the men in Washington, D.C., I stood on the outskirts and talked with several wives who had come to support their husbands. At the end of the day, I informally interviewed seven white men about their reasons for attending. In October, 1998, I attended the "Live a Legacy" rally in Sacramento with over fifty thousand men. During this two-day event, I spoke with eight white men and two men of color about the personal changes they claimed to have made as a result of their involvement in the Promise Keepers.

In 1998, I conducted in-depth interviews lasting approximately two hours with a snowball sample of ten Promise Keepers and their wives in Sacramento, California. I conducted the interviews with both the husband and wife present, which allowed me to get a sense of how the couple interacted (Reinhartz 1992). A disadvantage to interviewing couples jointly might be a reticence on the part of the women and men to discuss their lives and marriages candidly when the other partner is present. On the other hand, interviewing couples together allowed me to observe how they negotiated their interpersonal interactions and gender ideologies. Often, the women were more willing to discuss difficult topics, such as how being more emotional and expressive might be seen as a threat to masculinity. Because the couples did not always agree, I was able to observe how they challenged each other's interpretations. In the end, these interviews document how the couples wished to represent themselves and their relationships to the outside world.

All ten couples lived in the Sacramento area. Four couples attended a Presbyterian church, three a Baptist church, two a Community Baptist church, and one the Church of God. The couples were predominantly middle to upper-middle class: two reported before-tax household incomes of $100,000 or more annually, six reported incomes of $60,000 to $100,000, one reported an income in the $15,000 to $25,000 range, and one reported $15,000 or less. The wife in this last couple was the primary wage earner for the family. Six men who self-identified as white were married to white women, two of the couples self-identified as Black, and the two interracial couples consisted of a white man married to a Latina women and a Latino man married to a white woman. Ages ranged from 26 to 63. Most of the men had professional jobs, including an economist, program analyst, telecommunication analyst, and personnel director. One was not working at the time, and one was a pastor. Of the ten women, six had professional careers, including a teacher, accountant, and nurse. Only two worked full-time, four worked part-time, and four were full-time homemakers. Three men had graduate degrees, three were college graduates, two had some college, and two were high school graduates. For the women, one had a graduate degree, four were college graduates, three had some college, and one was a high school graduate.

Both the husbands and wives in this study subscribed to the conservative Protestant tradition. The beliefs of the respondents match those characterized by contemporary conservative Protestantism, namely a strong commitment to the inerrancy of the Bible (Bartkowski 1997). All of the men interviewed identified themselves as Promise Keepers. All had attended at least one stadium event, and six were involved in what Promise Keepers calls "accountability groups" that consist of three to five men who

meet regularly in the men's home town. In these groups, men utilize study guides to focus on prayer and confession. One man described the purpose of these meetings as an opportunity to hold each other accountable for living a "Godly" life. At one church, men met together at a monthly breakfast, where speakers would discuss concepts that were addressed at the large stadium events. I found that the men and women I interviewed were eager to discuss how the Promise Keepers had brought about changes in the men's lives.

BOUNDARIES

In identifying themselves as Promise Keepers, the men in this study described the changes they made in their lives based on being "born again" or accepting Jesus as their Savior. All ten men I interviewed felt that belonging to the Promise Keepers was about making and keeping promises to God and to others. The men described how the movement helped bind both Christian and non-Christian men together through promise-making practices. Gary, a new father, thought that the Promise Keepers allowed Christian men to support one another. He explained, "I think it is about bringing men together to be accountable to each other, to reach out to non-Christians, and to understand what a Christian community is between men. It's about making promises to one another." Several men asserted that the Promise Keepers provided an arena where Christian men could talk about issues they struggle with, such as how to guard against sexual temptation. These men felt it important to create bonds with other Christian men as a support network.

Many Promise Keepers also identified race as an important issue in pursuing relationships with other Christian and non-Christian men. About a third of the white men and all of the men of color I interviewed informally at rallies mentioned race as a barrier to bringing men together. In my formal interviews, six of the ten men talked about segregation and the need for reconciliation. George, a white man in his sixties, asserted:

> The way our society has gone, it is torn apart with segregation and hate in so many areas involving different people. One goal of Promise Keepers is to heal these differences and make you more accountable in how you act with your fellow men. (George)

The three men of color I interviewed identified the concept of racial reconciliation as central to their participation. James, a 38-year-old Black professional, stated:

> They stress racial reconciliation and it was really good to hear. A couple speakers at the event approached it from a Biblical point of view, challenging men to put barriers aside and see we are all brothers in Christ and not this race or that race. (James)

Ed, a 32-year-old Black man, felt that being involved in the Promise Keepers was "a new experience where a bunch of men from all different races were together, hugging and loving." Being unemployed, he described how interacting with other men gave him hope and support, Whereas the men of color embraced the idea of racial reconciliation as central to their participation, not all the white men adopted the concept as significant to their involvement. Only three of the seven white men I interviewed talked about the need they felt to pursue relationships with men of different races and backgrounds.

Although one focus of Promise Keepers rallies is recognizing differences between men based on race, masculinity and Christianity act as master identities that bring the men together. This is not unexpected, as Promise Keepers is a religious movement. The men felt Promise Keepers rectified the lack of Christian ministries targeting men and helped solve the problem of male independence and isolation that impedes community and sharing. Research shows that heterosexual men do not generally form intimate emotional ties with other men, whereas gay men subvert the norm of masculinity by becoming emotionally involved with one another (Nardi 1992; Weeks, Heaphy, and Donovan 2001). The men I interviewed expressed a need to challenge this norm of masculinity. Jeff, a 39-year-old white father of three, describes how Promise Keepers rallies allow men to express the fragility they feel as men:

> There are 50,000 guys praising the Lord, realizing that we are all fallible, we all make mistakes, and we all need Jesus as our Savior. It's singing, worshiping, hugging, and emotions—things that guys struggle with. (Jeff)

In the dominant culture, sentimentality and openness about emotions might be viewed as non-masculine, effeminate, or "gay." Connell (1995, 78) asserts,

"From the point of view of hegemonic masculinity, gayness is easily assimilated to femininity." Masculinities that are labeled homosexual or feminine are relegated to the bottom of the gender hierarchy among men. By performing activities not conceived of as traditionally male, men and boys can be expelled from the circle of legitimate masculinity. Yet, the men in this study were not afraid to discuss how they were able to feel more emotionally available to other men during the stadium events. The wives agreed that their husbands had become more expressive as a result of the Promise Keepers. In an enthusiastic description, Alice, a 55-year-old "housewife," exclaimed:

> When you see that many men together and there is no game, no sports event—they're all praising the Lord, they're singing, holding hands and no one is looking at them funny—what a wonderful thing. (Alice)

The implication of others looking at the men "funny" is that activities like singing and holding hands might put their masculinity in question or be perceived as gay. Non-Christian men often use disparaging remarks, calling each other "fags" or "pussies," in all-male environments like the locker room, to ensure heterosexual status (Curry 1991; Messner 1992). Offensive language is barred from Christian masculinity, but in its place, Promise Keepers members use the rhetoric of family ties and brotherly love to ensure that male bonding practices are desexualized (Bartkowski 2000).

Another way for Promise Keepers to ensure that male bonding practices do not result in an "effeminate" masculinity is excluding women from rallies and accountability groups, Both husbands and wives asserted that men could be emotionally available to one another because women were not present. Part of the appeal for the men was the fact that the events were held in football stadiums where they could bring their coolers, wear "team hats," and chant team slogans. Gary noted that the rallies were like "getting together for a baseball game but it's to worship the Lord." These activities allow the men to perform sports-type rituals to reaffirm their masculinity (Faludi 1999). If they are hugging, crying, and holding hands, they are doing these things surrounded by the trappings of hegemonic masculinity. The absence of women helps to establish the sport-like atmosphere.

Sally asserted that men would be more self-conscious if women were present:

> I felt that going to Promise Keeper rallies would be a place where men could be themselves and do what men do without worrying about what women will think of them or making an impression. They could be emotional or cry without worrying about women seeing them or feeling like they have to take care of them. (Sally)

Several of the women discussed how being more emotional did not impinge on men's masculinity. Alice stated that women wanted men to be more emotional but "they also wanted men to be *men*." By this statement, she implied that women might perceive men who display too many emotions in settings other than a stadium event as non-masculine. A bounded masculine space enabled these men to express themselves in a manner that did not challenge their masculinity, making limited emotive displays possible in mixed gender settings.

CONSCIOUSNESS

A crucial aspect of consciousness that unites Promise Keepers is resistance to the secular values of non-Christians. Promise Keepers see themselves resisting mainstream masculine values that are incongruent with being a "family man" and taking steps to become more involved with their families. A recurrent theme centered on efforts these men were making to become better husbands and fathers. The ten men I interviewed claimed that Promise Keepers helped challenge them to better themselves to be more responsible and thoughtful in their relationships with their wives and other men. George felt that Promise Keepers had encouraged him to think more about his wife's desires:

> I just have a better feeling about myself and about our relationship. I want to be a better husband. I don't always think about the niceties that a woman would appreciate, but I think I probably would now, more than some guys. (George)

The wives agreed that Promise Keepers helped men be more supportive at home and sensitive in general. Edith, a 36-year-old white professional married to Daniel who is Latino, stated, "What I see is that he al-

ways puts me first, that he is very concerned about my needs." Linda described a change in James: "Before he'd say that he would try to do something, and then it would be totally forgotten. Now, he really tries."

Five men described changes not only in their family lives but also in how they dealt with other men. For three of the white men I interviewed, the question of racial barriers was not something they had grappled with before attending Promise Keepers events. Ted, a white man in his thirties, discussed his own discovery of the painful consequences of racism:

> Many churches have turned their head and said no we're not really racist, but in reality there is a lot of hurt out there I didn't know about. At one event, a Korean minister said Americans tend to be a little bigoted, and even if you don't think you are, that's how we tend to feel about a white person. This was quite enlightening. (Ted)

George credited the Promise Keepers with bringing "to the forefront a conscious awareness of what you should be doing to build relationships" with men of diverse backgrounds. Not all the men, however, had a positive response to this focus on racial barriers. Jim, a white man in his late fifties, expressed frustration with the recurring theme of reconciliation:

> I think it is one of the things they kind of overdo myself. In Oakland, [McCartney] spoke, and I felt that he was preaching to the choir. We got harangued all day a group of speakers, and I felt they were talking to the wrong people. (Jim)

Other studies have found a range of responses to the issue of racial reconciliation from white attendees (Allen 2000; Newton forthcoming). Although the leadership promotes the idea of breaking down racial barriers, the variety of responses by participants reveals that it is not essential to the identity of white men in the Promise Keepers.

Whereas the movement has helped some white men begin to consider racism, its real influence has been to help men rethink their position in their family and society. Although the men willingly submit to God's will for their lives and recognize their frailty, movement literature and sermons remind them of their ability as "born" leaders to be assertive, independent, self-confident, and in control (Beal 1997). While the men I interviewed described personal changes such as a willingness to help their wives with household chores, they also explained that Promise Keepers guided them to take responsibility as the head of their family. While describing men as "born" leaders, both husbands and wives paradoxically believed it difficult for men in contemporary society to perform a leadership role. Alice felt that Promise Keepers events provided a context for establishing a sense of manhood:

> Men . . . for all these years have not had a base. They've been on their own trying to make it, trying to support their family, and they are constantly being sucked in by what the world says they ought to do. Finally, men are going to be men. (Alice)

Alice suggests that "the world" tempts Christian men to act in a manner that is not supportive of their families. Her statement—"Finally, men are going to be men"—points to the idea of an underlying essential nature that all men possess. At the same time, she implies that masculinity is socially constructed in the idea that men need a base to perform gender. Sally explained,

> I think that men don't know exactly where they stand anymore. It used to be that men's roles were solidly defined as the person in charge. Now, women are doing more, and it makes men feel uncertain about what their place is. (Sally)

The wives' assertions that men need to reestablish a masculine identity took on a rehabilitative and patronizing tone, underscoring a fragile masculinity in which men help to "feel like men." Although the men discussed a need to embrace an expressive masculinity, the wives appeared to be the emotional caregivers, enabling the men to be more sensitive. This finding confirms other studies of the evangelical Christian community in which wives promote the concept of male leadership to sustain a harmonious family environment (Gallagher and Smith 1999; Stacey 1998; Stacey and Gerard 1990). Since many men feel uncertain about masculinity, involvement in the Promise Keepers helps reaffirm what it means to be a man.

This gentler notion of masculinity speaks to the cultural image of the "New Man." According to Hondagneu-Sotelo and Messner (2000, 63), there is "a shared cultural image of what the New Man looks like: He is a White, college-educated professional who is a highly involved and nurturant father, 'in touch with' and expressive of his feelings." This notion of hegemonic masculinity is juxtaposed against the "traditional, sexist, and macho" masculinities attributed to some men of color and working class men. The concept of the New Man refers to how white, class-privileged men perform a masculinity that incorporates traditionally feminine characteristics, such as emotionality and sensitivity. Yet, this type of masculinity maintains its hegemonic status as superior to other masculinities, because expressiveness and sensitivity do not necessarily challenge the structural conditions that maintain its dominant status in society.

The focus of the Promise Keepers on men's place in the nuclear family provides a context to organize around an image of a Christian version of the New Man, as opposed to the more authoritarian form of masculinity attributed to some fundamentalist families (Bartkowski 1997). This follows from an understanding of gender in which God has designed differently from women. Cindy, a 44-year-old white teacher, asserted:

> Men were designed to be leaders. This doesn't mean women were meant to be slaves. It just means that when you take that away from a man, you change the way he feels, and that sets the whole domino factor thing going. (Cindy)

Cindy's statement suggests that women must bolster men's masculinity for it to be effective (Stacey 1998). By helping "men to be men," the wives promote a hegemonic masculinity that allows men to be involved husbands and fathers while maintaining their privilege as men.

NEGOTIATION

Both the husbands and wives employed the language of equality while discussing the need for men to retain authority within the family. The references to equality reflect a central organizing principle of the women's movements in the 1960s and 1970s that critiqued unequal gender relations in the family. By incorporating the language of the feminist movements into their conceptualizations of familial roles, these men and women seemed to participate in a postfeminist sensibility. Stacey (1998) suggests that postfeminism is best defined as a gender consciousness and strategy that allows many contemporary women and men to distance themselves from a feminist identity while being profoundly influenced by feminist doctrines. For example, the men described what it means to be head of the household by asserting that leadership does not mean domination, demonstrating an awareness of the critique of the relations of domination and subordination between men and women that have characterized many "traditional" marriages. The wives and husbands managed the language of equality in describing their relationships by focusing on the need to recognize difference.

For these women and men, negotiating masculinity depends on understanding relations as "different but equal." George asserted:

> We are a team. We make our decisions together. I can't state any specific thing I've made the sole decision on. As far as knowledge about what's going on out there I have a heavier lead on that. She's the nurse and I don't know what's going on in nursing. This is not a domineering relationship and it never has been. (George)

For George, the relationship is not one of domination; yet, he declares his superior understanding of how the world operates, relegating his wife's knowledge to the field of nursing. The idea of "different but equal" portrays equality as equal commitment to and responsibility for gendered tasks while skirting the issue of the structural advantages involved in such a division of labor. The men I interviewed focused on responsibilities of being the financial provider or protector. Jim paternalistically declared:

> We are both equal but we have different responsibilities. God didn't make Eve from Adam's head to rule over her or from his foot that he might trample over her, but he took her from his rib, which is close to his heart that he might protect her. (Jim)

Ted explained that the Biblical passage regarding headship is not about male superiority:

> I read that passage and accept it as my responsibility. . . . If God has built it that way and that's how he desires it then I accept that responsibility. But, I don't see that verse saying that a man is better than his wife. (Ted)

Defining equality in negative terms, i.e., the husband is not better, circumvents a positive accounting of what equality might mean. From this perspective, men

maintain their authority while modifying what might be perceived as archaic views on gender relations.

The hegemonic masculinity rearticulated by these men involves gender displays that speak of a softer and gentler man but are still grounded in dominant masculine norms concerning authority, leadership, and heterosexuality. The wives and husbands described a hierarchical ordering that places husbands as an intermediary between God and their wives and children. Linda asserted, "I only have to answer to him (my husband); he has to answer to God, and that is a big responsibility." In this ordering, women are not only subject to God as sinners; they are subject in terms of their gender. The men and women portrayed a clear differentiation for accountability and decision-making based on men's financial responsibilities. Most of the women worked at least part-time, but even in the cases where the women worked full-time and made more money than their husbands did, these couples still described the husband to be ultimately responsible for the finances. Alice, a homemaker in her fifties, claimed, "I think [a decision he would make] would be more of a major financial decision. I think he would be more in the lead in that." Yet, the decision-making processes described by the husbands and wives were much more akin to Stacey and Gerard's (1990) "patriarchy in the last instance," where the man makes the final decision only when an accord cannot be reached. The conversations I had with the couples revealed a complex negotiation process where the men sought to make changes and share decision-making with their wives based on an unquestioned position of authority, Thus, the couples seemed to adhere to a more nominal equality.

Promise Keepers also incorporates the language of equality used by the early civil rights movement to show that all men are equal and to ultimately end "race-thinking." Rick, a white professor, described the reaction of a Black colleague who attended a rally with him:

> My friend is a consummate teacher; his classes are always full. Right before my eyes I saw God directly calling him to supplication. The speaker from an all Black church in Washington, D.C., told the men, "I want each one of you to go out onto the highways and bring in every redneck you can find. I want them to be bright red, nigger haters; those are the ones that I want you to bring." The message is that reconciliation cuts

both ways—Black, white, or whatever color you are, it doesn't matter in the eyes of God. That's the message of the Bible. I looked at my friend, and he was crying. He said, "I've been wrong—it's not about focusing on difference but on similarity." He now teaches his classes differently, and his enrollments are even larger. (Rick)

Rick's interpretation of racial reconciliation is about bringing people together, because "God doesn't see color." The focus on breaking down racial barriers reflects the early civil rights rhetoric of a "race-free" society and the current neo-conservative stance of a "color-blind" society (Omi and Winant 1994). The goal is to move towards a society where racial considerations are never entertained. Instead of seeking institutional, political, or structural solutions to the problem of racism, Promise Keepers focuses on spiritual solutions to purge individuals of the "sin" of racism (Allen 2000). The focus is on building relationships with men of different racial backgrounds.

Although the idea of racial reconciliation has pushed some white men who attend rallies to seriously consider the effects of racial segregation within the church, the lack of focus on institutional racism means that these men do not support political means for change. When I asked Rick about barriers to racial equality such as institutional racism or economic disparities, he responded that "racial reconciliation was about dealing with the wounds caused by racism, and this could only be accomplished through God's love." Not all Promise Keepers thought about race, but the three white men who did consider it were willing to make changes based on a personal and interactional level, ignoring the political system that produces racist ideology and structural inequalities. A focus on equality allows these men to negotiate an identity based on key concepts of the women's and civil rights movements without challenging the structural conditions that these movements sought to transform.

CONCLUSION

Examining identity formation in the Promise Keepers provides several insights into the possibility for social change in movements with members who predominantly occupy threatened positions of privilege in society. First, social changes among groups who hold a privileged, vulnerable position are often attempts to rehabilitate that position. As a movement, Promise Keepers provides a forum for Christian men to grapple with contradictory gender meanings so that these men can make positive changes in their lives around issues of masculinity without challenging their position of authority. On the one hand, the men I interviewed made promises that transformed their ideas about masculinity and facilitated better communication and understanding in their family relationships. They undertook these changes on their own initiative, not because their wives pressured them. Resisting the credo of masculine norms that prescribe inexpressive and unemotional behavior in men, Promise Keepers let loose in stadium events and expressed emotions in ways often marked as homosexual or gay by a heterosexist society. These men based their consciousness on notions of masculinity that encourage them to act in a loving and supportive manner towards their wives, and some sought to grapple with racial prejudice and share with men of diverse backgrounds. A focus on equality in relationships between men and between husbands and wives provided a framework for these men to "do" gender differently on an interactional level from mainstream models of masculinity (West and Zimmerman 1987). The men willingly admitted their mistakes and their need for guidance, and they based their identity as Promise Keepers on what they see as necessary changes in how they do masculinity.

On the other hand, it appears that these men were willing to make changes in their lives on an interactional and personal level because the movement does not challenge them to grapple with the structural conditions which undergird their privilege. In fact, the discussions between the husbands and wives showed that the changes the men made were predicated on maintaining a hierarchical and authoritarian understanding of gender relations. On a structural level, the focus on equality among Promise Keepers appeared nominal. The men's collective identity is bound by practices that reaffirm hegemonic masculinity and heterosexuality through references to essential gender differences, a focus on heterosexual family relationships, and the absence of women and gay men from rallies. As sensitive husbands, Promise Keepers can reap the benefits of building emotional relationships with other men and characterize their marriages as egalitarian without ceasing to be "on top" or to maintain an image of themselves as leaders. This allows the men to make changes in their lives to build a more harmonious family environment without considering the privileges they have as men, such as taking the liberty to portray men's knowledge of what's going on in the world as superior to that of women.

Second, groups that adhere to hegemonic ideas can form a collective identity based on contradictory gender and racial ideologies that renegotiate the terms of resistance used by social protest movements. Promise Keepers employs a discourse of equality that incorporates the language of the women's and civil rights movements, while defusing criticism of hierarchy and structural inequities to focus on personal relationships, emotions, and health. The white men I interviewed felt there should be equality in their relationships with their wives and with men of different racial backgrounds, but their descriptions of equality were couched in ideas concerning leadership and colorblindness. Unlike the men in the mythopoetic and white supremacist movements that Ferber studied, Promise Keepers does not seek to show that it is really white men who suffer. The white men in this study willingly admitted that they needed to make changes in their lives to improve relations with their wives and to build relationships with men of color. However, the manner in which the men portrayed these changes both challenged and reaffirmed hegemonic gender and racial meanings. The men pushed the boundaries of hegemonic masculinity through practices that made them more emotionally supportive of their wives and other men, while they endorsed hegemonic masculinity by embracing ideas about their natural leadership qualities and their essential differences from women. Likewise, several of the white men sought to break down racial barriers by building relationships with men of color but endorsed a therapeutic form of colorblindness that emphasized the need to heal the wounds of racism and ignored institutional racism.

By analyzing the three components of collective identity for Promise Keepers—boundaries, consciousness, and negotiation—I have sought to explain how resistance to hegemonic masculinity can interact with a desire to reinstate men's position of authority in the family and society. In their day-to-day interactions, Promise Keepers seem willing to embrace a softer masculinity that empowers them to be more sensitive and caring husbands and fathers. Yet, they seem willing to make promises and carry out a reformed masculinity because they are able to ignore the structural conditions that empower men and provide pay-offs based on claims to manhood. Ultimately, the prognosis for progressive social change among Promise Keepers is at once promising and disturbing. The best case scenario might be that, as Promise Keepers become more emotionally available, they could continue to resist the trappings of hegemonic masculinity to let go of the idea of leadership and colorblindness and to focus on egalitarian relations. In terms of daily life, these men might become willing to take on many of the activities of the second shift that so many men resist, such as driving the kids to soccer practice or changing the baby's diapers. However, given the lack of attention to addressing men's institutional privileges, few Promise Keepers seem likely to embrace a progressive forum for social change. The rightwing and conservative commitments of the Promise Keepers leadership pointed to by Messner ensure that antifeminist and antigay sentiments will continue to percolate under the surface of invocations for men to transform themselves. Although Promise Keepers seem willing to embrace some meaningful personal changes, the promises they make may ultimately do more to reinforce rather than challenge hegemonic masculinity.

NOTE

1. This is a condensed, revised version of Melanie A. Heath. "Soft-Boiled Masculinity: Renegotiating Gender and Racial Ideologies in the Promise Keepers Movement," *Gender & Society* 17 (2003): 423–44.

REFERENCES

Allen, L. Dean. 2000, "Promise Keepers and Racism: Frame Resonance as an Indicator of Organizational Vitality." *Sociology of Religion* 61: 54–72.

Bartkowski, John P. 1997. "Debating Patriarchy: Discursive Disputes over Spousal Authority among Evangelical Family Commentators." *Journal for the Scientific Study of Religion* 36: 393–410.

———. 2000. "Breaking Walls, Raising Fences: Masculinity, Intimacy and Accountability among the Promise Keepers." *Sociology of Religion* 61: 33–54.

Beal, Becky. 1997. "The Promise Keepers' Use of Sport in Defining 'Christlike' Masculinity." *Journal of Sport and Social Issues* 21: 274–284,

Blee, Kathleen M. 1996. "Becoming a Racist: Women in Contemporary Ku Klux Klan and Neo-Nazi Groups," *Gender & Society* 10: 680–702.

Brush, Paula Stewart. 1999. "The Influence of Social Movements on Articulations of Race and Gender in Women's Autobiographies." *Gender & Society* 13: 120–37.

Cornell, R.W. 1987. *Gender and Power: Society, the Person and Sexual Politics.* Cambridge: Polity.

———. 1995. *Masculinities.* Cambridge: Polity.

Curry, Tim J. 1991. "Fraternal Bonding in the Locker Room: A Profeminist Analysis of Talk about Competition and Women." *Sociology of Sport Journal* 8: 5–21.

Einwohner, Rachel L. 1999. "Gender, Class, and Social Movement Outcomes: Identity and Effectiveness in Two Animal Rights Campaigns." *Gender & Society* 13: 56–76.

Faludi, Susan, 1999. *Stiffed: The Betrayal of the American Man.* New York; Perennial.

Ferber, Abby L. 2000. "Racial Warriors and Weekend Warriors: The Construction of Masculinity in Mythopoetic and White Supremacist Discourse." *Men and Masculinities* 3: 30–56.

Ferree, Myra Marx and Silke Roth. 1998, "Gender, Class, and the Interaction Between Social Movements: A Strike of West Berlin Day Care Workers," *Gender & Society* 12: 626–648.

Fonow, Mary Margaret. 1998, "Protest Engendered: The Participation of Women Steelworkers in the Wheeling-Pittsburgh Steel Strike of 1985." *Gender & Society* 12: 710–28.

Gallagher, Sally K. and Christian Smith. 1999. "Symbolic Traditionalism and Pragmatic Egalitarianism: Contemporary Evangelicals, Families, and Gender." *Gender & Society* 13: 211–33.

Glynn, Patrick. 1998. "Racial Reconciliation: Can Religion Work Where Politics Has Failed?" *American Behavioral Scientist* 41: 834–842.

Hercus, Cheryl 1999. "Identity, Emotion, and Feminist Collective Action." *Gender & Society* 13: 34–55.

Hondagneu-Sotelo, Pierrette and Michael A, Messner. 2000. "Gender Displays and Men's Power: The 'New Man' and the Mexican Immigrant Man." Pp. 63–74 in *Gender Through the Prism of Difference*, edited by M, B. Zinn, P. Hondagneu-Sotelo, and M. A. Messner. Needham Heights: Allyn & Bacon.

Johnson, Stephen D. 2000. "Who Supports the Promise Keepers?" *Sociology of Religion* 61: 93–104.

Kimmel, Michael S. 1996. *Manhood in America: A Cultural History.* New York: Free Press.

McCartney, Bill. 1994. "Seeking God's Favor." Pp. 205–08 in *Seven Promises of a Promise Keeper*, edited by A. Janssen. Colorado Springs: Focus on the Family.

Messner, Michael A. 1992. *Power at Play: Sports and the Problem of Masculinity.* Boston: Beacon Press.

———. 1997. *The Politics of Masculinities: Men in Movements.* Thousand Oaks: Sage.

Morris, Aldon D. 1992. "Political Consciousness and Collective Action." Pp. 351–73 in *Frontiers in Social Movement History*, edited by A. D. Morris and C. M. Mueller. New Haven: Yale University Press.

Nardi, Peter. 1992. "Sex, Friendship, and Gender Roles among Gay Men." in *Men's Friendship*, edited by P. Nardi London: Sage Publications.

Newton, Judith. Forthcoming. *National Manhood and Male Romance.* Lanham: Rowman and Littlefield.

Omi, Michael and Howard Winant 1994. *Racial Formation in the United States from the 1960s to the 1980s.* New York: Routledge.

Pelak, Cythnia Fabrizio. 2002. "Women's Collective Identity Formation in Sports: A Case Study from Women's Ice Hockey." *Gender & Society* 16: 93–114.

Phillips, Randy. 1994. "Seize the Moment." Pp. 1–12 in *Seven Promises of a Promise Keeper*, edited by A. Janssen. Colorado Springs: Focus on the Family Publishing.

Reinharz, Shulamit. 1992. *Feminist Methods in Social Research.* New York: Oxford University Press.

Stacey, Judith. 1998. *Brave New Families.* Berkeley: University of California Press.

Stacey, Judith and Susan Elizabeth Gerard. 1990. "We Are Not Doormats': The Influence of Feminism on Contemporary Evangelicals in the United States." Pp. 98–117 in *Uncertain Terms: Negotiating Gender in American Culture*, edited by F. Ginsburg and A. I Tsing. Boston: Beacon Press.

Stodghill II, Ron and Richard N. Ostling. 1997. "God of Our Fathers: The Promise Keepers are Bringing Their Manly Crusade to Washington." *Time* 150: 34–41.

Taylor, Verta. 1999. "Gender and Social Movements: Gender Processes in Women's Self-Help Movements." *Gender & Society* 13: 8–33.

Taylor, Verta and Nancy Whittier. 1992. "Collective Identity in Social Movement Communities: Lesbian Feminist Mobilization," Pp. 104–29 in *Frontiers in Social Movement Theory*, edited by A. D. Morris and C. M. Mueller. New Haven: Yale University Press.

———. 1995. "Analytical Approaches to Social Movement Culture: The Culture of the Women's Movement." Pp. 163–187 in *Social Movements and Culture*, edited by H. Johnston and B. Klandermans, London: UCL Press.

Thomas, Jan E. 1999. "'Everthing About Us is Feminist': The Significance of Ideology in Organizational Change." *Gender & Society* 13: 101–19.

Weeks, Jeffrey, Brian Heaphy, and Catherine Donovan. 2001. *Same sex intimacies: Families of choice and other life experiments.* London: Routledge.

West, Candace, and Don H. Zimmerman. 1987. "Doing Gender." *Gender & Society* 1: 125–51.

White, Aaronette, M. 1999. "Talking Feminist, Talking Black: Micromobilization Processes in a Collective Protest against Rape." *Gender & Society* 13: 77–100.

Williams, Rhys H, 2000. "Promise Keepers: A Comment on Religion and Social Movements." *Sociology of Religion* 61: 1–10.

Punks, Bulldaggers, and Welfare Queens: The Radical Potential of Queer Politics?

Cathy J. Cohen

On the eve of finishing this essay my attention is focused not on how to rework the conclusion (as it should be) but instead on news stories of alleged racism at Gay Men's Health Crisis (GMHC). It seems that three black board members of this largest and oldest AIDS organization in the world have resigned over their perceived subservient position on the GMHC board. Billy E. Jones, former head of the New York City Health and Hospitals Corporation and one of the board members to quit, was quoted in the *New York Times* as saying, "Much work needs to be done at GMHC to make it truly inclusive and welcoming of diversity. . . . It is also clear that such work will be a great struggle. I am resigning because I do not choose to engage in such struggle at GMHC, but rather prefer to fight for the needs of those ravaged by HIV." (Dunlap).

This incident raises mixed emotions for me, for it points to the continuing practice of racism many of us experience on a daily basis in lesbian and gay communities. But just as disturbingly it also highlights the limits of a lesbian and gay political agenda based on a civil rights strategy, where assimilation into, and replication of, dominant institutions are the goals. Many of us continue to search for a new political direction and agenda, one that does not focus on integration into dominant structures but instead seeks to transform the basic fabric and hierarchies that allow systems of oppression to persist and operate efficiently. For some of us, such a challenge to traditional gay and lesbian politics was offered by the idea of queer politics. Here we had a potential movement of young antiassimilationist activists committed to challenging the very way people understand and respond to sexuality. These activists promised to engage in struggles that would disrupt dominant norms of sexuality, radically transforming politics in lesbian, gay, bisexual, and transgendered communities.

Despite the possibility invested in the idea of queerness and the practice of queer politics, I argue that a truly radical or transformative politics has not resulted from queer activism. In many instances, instead of destabilizing the assumed categories and binaries of sexual identity, queer politics has served to reinforce simple dichotomies between heterosexual and everything "queer." An understanding of the ways in which power informs and constitutes privileged and marginalized subjects on both sides of this dichotomy has been left unexamined.

I query in this essay whether there are lessons to be learned from queer activism that can help us construct a new politics. I envision a politics where one's relation to power, and not some homogenized identity, is privileged in determining one's political comrades. I'm talking about a politics where the *nonnormative* and *marginal* position of punks, bulldaggers, and welfare queens, for example, is the basis for progressive transformative coalition work. Thus, if there is any truly radical potential to be found in the idea of queerness and the practice of queer politics, it would seem to be located in its ability to create a space in opposition to dominant norms, a space where transformational political work can begin.

EMERGENCE OF QUEER POLITICS AND A NEW POLITICS OF TRANSFORMATION

Theorists and activists alike generally agree that it was in the early 1990s that we began to see, with any regularity, the use of the term "queer."[1] This term would come to denote not only an emerging politics, but also a new cohort of academics working in programs primarily in the humanities centered around social and cultural criticism (Morton 121). Individuals such as Judith Butler. Eve Sedgwick, Teresa de Lauretis, Diana Fuss, and Michael Warner produced what are now thought of as the first canonical works of "queer theory." Working from a variety of postmodernist and poststructuralist theoretical perspectives, these scholars focused on identifying and contesting the discursive and cultural markers found within both dominant and marginal identities and institutions which prescribe and reify "heterogendered" understandings and behavior.[2] These theorists presented a different conceptualization of sexuality, one which sought to replace socially named and presumably stable categories of sexual expression with a new fluid movement among and between forms of sexual behavior (Stein and Plummer 182).

Through its conception of a wide continuum of sexual possibilities, queer theory stands in direct contrast to the normalizing tendencies of hegemonic sexuality rooted in ideas of static, stable sexual identities and behaviors. In queer theorizing the sexual subject is understood to be constructed and contained by multiple practices of categorization and regulation that systematically marginalize and oppress those subjects thereby defined as deviant and "other." And, at its best, queer theory focuses on and makes central not only the socially constructed nature of sexuality and sexual categories, but also the varying degrees and multiple sites of power distributed within all categories of sexuality, including the normative category of heterosexuality.

It was in the early 1990s, however, that the postmodern theory being produced in the academy (later to be recategorized as queer theory) found its most direct interaction with the real-life politics of lesbian, gay, bisexual, and transgendered activists. Frustrated with what was perceived to be the scientific "degaying" and assimilationist tendencies of AIDS activism, with their invisibility in the more traditional civil rights politics of lesbian and gay organizations, and with increasing legal and physical attacks against lesbian and gay community members, a new generation of activists began the process of building a more confrontational political formation—labeling it queer politics (Bérubé and Escoffier 12). Queer politics, represented most notoriously in the actions of Queer Nation, is understood as an "in your face" politics of a younger generation. Through action and analysis these individuals seek to make "queer" function as more than just an abbreviation for lesbian, gay, bisexual, and transgendered. Similar to queer theory, the queer politics articulated and pursued by these activists first and foremost recognizes and encourages the fluidity and movement of people's sexual lives. In queer politics sexual expression is something that always entails the possibility of change, movement, redefinition, and subversive performance—from year to

year, from partner to partner, from day to day, even from act to act. In addition to highlighting the instability of sexual categories and sexual subjects, queer activists also directly challenge the multiple practices and vehicles of power which render them invisible and at risk. However, what seems to make queer activists unique, at this particular moment, is their willingness to confront normalizing power by emphasizing and exaggerating their own antinormative characteristics and nonstable behavior. Joshua Gamson, in "Must Identity Movements Self-Destruct? A Queer Dilemma," writes that

> queer activism and theory pose the challenge of a form of organizing in which, far from inhibiting accomplishments, the *destabilization* of collective identity is itself a goal and accomplishment of collective action.
>
> The assumption that stable collective identities are necessary for collective action is turned on its head by queerness, and the question becomes: *When and how are stable collective identities necessary for social action and social change?* Secure boundaries and stabilized identities are necessary not in general, but in the specific, a point social movement theory seems currently to miss. (403, original emphasis)

Thus queer politics, much like queer theory, is often perceived as standing in opposition, or in contrast, to the category-based identity politics of traditional lesbian and gay activism. And for those of us who find ourselves on the margins, operating through multiple identities and thus not fully served or recognized through traditional single-identity-based politics, *theoretical conceptualizations* of queerness hold great political promise. For many of us, the label "queer" symbolizes an acknowledgment that through our existence and everyday survival we embody sustained and multisited resistance to systems (based on dominant constructions of race and gender) that seek to normalize our sexuality, exploit our labor, and constrain our visibility. At the intersection of oppression and resistance lies the radical potential of queerness to challenge and bring together all those deemed marginal and all those committed to liberatory politics.

The problem, however, with such a conceptualization and expectation of queer identity and politics is that in its present form queer politics has not emerged as an encompassing challenge to systems of domination and oppression, especially those normalizing processes embedded in heteronormativity. By "heteronormativity" I mean both those localized practices and those centralized institutions which legitimize and privilege heterosexuality and heterosexual relationships as fundamental and "natural" within society. I raise the subject of heteronormativity because it is this normalizing practice/power that has most often been the focus of queer politics (Blasius 19–20; Warner xxi–xxv).

The inability of queer politics to effectively challenge heteronormativity rests, in part, on the fact that despite a surrounding discourse which highlights the destabilization and even deconstruction of sexual categories, queer politics has often been built around a simple dichotomy between those deemed queer and those deemed heterosexual. Whether in the infamous "I Hate Straights" publication or queer kiss-ins at malls and straight dance clubs, very near the surface in queer political action is an uncomplicated understanding of power as it is encoded in sexual categories: all heterosexuals are represented as dominant and controlling and all queers are understood as marginalized and invisible. Thus, even in the name of destabilization, some queer activists have begun to prioritize sexuality as the primary frame through which they pursue their politics.[3] Undoubtedly, within different contexts various characteristics of our total being—for example, race, gender, class, sexuality—are highlighted or called upon to make sense of a particular situation. However, my concern is centered on those individuals who consistently activate only one characteristic of their identity, or a single perspective of consciousness, to organize their politics, rejecting any recognition of the multiple and intersecting systems of power that largely dictate our life chances.

It is the disjuncture, evident in queer politics, between an articulated commitment to promoting an understanding of sexuality that rejects the idea of static, monolithic, bounded categories, on the one hand, and political practices structured around binary conceptions of sexuality and power, on the other hand, that is the focus of this article. Specifically, I am concerned with those manifestations of queer politics in which the capital and advantage invested in a range of sexual categories are disregarded and, as a result, narrow and homogenized political identities are reproduced that inhibit the radical potential of queer politics. It is my contention that queer activists who evoke a single-oppression framework misrepresent the distribution of power within and outside of gay,

lesbian, bisexual, and transgendered communities, and therefore limit the comprehensive and transformational character of queer politics.

Recognizing the limits of current conceptions of queer identities and queer politics, I am interested in examining the concept of "queer" in order to think about how we might construct a new political identity that is truly liberating, transformative, and inclusive of all those who stand on the outside of the dominant constructed norm of state-sanctioned white middle- and upper-class heterosexuality.[4] Such a broadened understanding of queerness must be based on an intersectional analysis that recognizes how numerous systems of oppression interact to regulate and police the lives of most people. Black lesbian, bisexual, and heterosexual feminist authors such as Kimberle Crenshaw, Barbara Ransby, Angela Davis, Cheryl Clarke, and Audre Lorde have repeatedly emphasized in their writing the intersectional workings of oppression. And it is just such an understanding of the interlocking systems of domination that is noted in the opening paragraph of the now famous black feminist statement by the Combahee River Collective:

> The most general statement of our politics at the present time would be that we are actively committed to struggling against racial, sexual, heterosexual, and class oppression and see as our particular task the development of *integrated* analysis and practice based upon the fact that the major systems of oppression are interlocking. The synthesis of these oppressions creates the conditions of our lives. As Black women we see Black feminism as the logical political movement to combat the manifold and simultaneous oppressions that all women of color face. (272)

This analysis of one's place in the world which focuses on the intersection of systems of oppression is informed by a consciousness that undoubtedly grows from the lived experience of existing within and resisting multiple and connected practices of domination and normalization. Just such a lived experience and analysis have determined much of the progressive and expansive nature of the politics emanating from people of color, people who are both inside and outside of lesbian and gay communities.

However, beyond a mere recognition of the intersection of oppressions, there must also be an understanding of the ways our multiple identities work to limit the entitlement and status some receive from obeying a heterosexual imperative. For instance, how would queer activists understand politically the lives of women—in particular women of color—on welfare, who may fit into the category of heterosexual, but whose sexual choices are not perceived as normal, moral, or worthy of state support? Further, how do queer activists understand and relate politically to those whose same-sex sexual identities position them within the category of queer, but who hold other identities based on class, race and/or gender categories which provide them with membership in and the resources of dominant institutions and groups?

Thus, inherent in our new politics must be a commitment to left analysis and left politics. Black feminists as well as other marginalized and progressive scholars and activists have long argued that any political response to the multilayered oppression that most of us experience must be rooted in a left understanding of our political, economic, social, and cultural institutions. Fundamentally, a left framework makes central the interdependency among multiple systems of domination. Such a perspective also ensures that while activists should rightly be concerned with forms of discursive and cultural coercion, we also recognize and confront the more direct and concrete forms of exploitation and violence rooted in state-regulated institutions and economic systems. The Statement of Purpose from the first Dialogue on the Lesbian and Gay Left comments specifically on the role of interlocking systems of oppression in the lives of gays and lesbians. "By leftist we mean people who understand the struggle for lesbian and gay liberation to be integrally tied to struggles against class oppression, racism, and sexism. While we might use different political labels, we share a commitment to a fundamental transformation of the economic, political and social structures of society."

A left framework of politics, unlike civil rights or liberal frameworks, brings into focus the systematic relationship among forms of domination, where the creation and maintenance of exploited, subservient, marginalized classes is a necessary part of, at the very least, the economic configuration. Urvashi Vaid, in *Virtual Equality,* for example, writes of the limits of civil rights strategies in confronting systemic homophobia:

> civil rights do not change the social order in dramatic ways; they change only the privileges of the group asserting those rights. Civil rights strategies

do not challenge the moral and antisexual underpinnings of homophobia, because homophobia does not originate in our lack of full civil equality. Rather, homophobia arises from the nature and construction of the political, legal, economic, sexual, racial and family systems within which we live. (183)

Proceeding from the starting point of a system-based left analysis, strategies built upon the possibility of incorporation and assimilation are exposed as simply expanding and making accessible the status quo for more privileged members of marginal groups, while the most vulnerable in our communities continue to be stigmatized and oppressed.

It is important to note, however, that while left theorists tend to provide a more structural analysis of oppression and exploitation, many of these theorists and activists have also been homophobic and heterosexist in their approach to or avoidance of the topics of sexuality and heteronormativity. For example, Robin Podolsky, in "Sacrificing Queers and other 'Proletarian' Artifacts," writes that quite often on the left lesbian and gay sexuality and desire have been characterized as "more to do with personal happiness and sexual pleasure than with the 'material basis' of procreation—we were considered self-indulgent distractions from struggle . . . [an example of] 'bourgeois decadence'" (54).

This contradiction between a stated left analysis and an adherence to heteronormativity has probably been most dramatically identified in the writing of some feminist authors. I need only refer to Adrienne Rich's well-known article, "Compulsory Heterosexuality and Lesbian Existence," as a poignant critique of the white, middle-class heterosexual standard running through significant parts of feminist analysis and actions. The same adherence to a heterosexual norm can be found in the writing of self-identified black left intellectuals such as Cornel West and Michael Eric Dyson. Thus, while these writers have learned to make reference to lesbian, gay, bisexual, and transgendered segments of black communities—sparingly—they continue to foreground black heterosexuality and masculinity as the central unit of analysis in their writing—and most recently in their politics, witness their participation in the Million Man March.

This history of left organizing and the left's visible absence from any serious and sustained response to the AIDS epidemic have provoked many lesbian, gay, bisexual and transgendered people to question the relevance of this political configuration to the needs of our communities. Recognizing that reservations of this type are real and should be noted, I still hold that a left-rooted analysis which emphasizes economic exploitation and class structure, culture, and the systemic nature of power provides a framework of politics that is especially effective in representing and challenging the numerous sites and systems of oppression. Further, the left-centered approach that I embrace is one that designates sexuality and struggles against sexual normalization as central to the politics of all marginal communities.

THE ROOT OF QUEER POLITICS: CHALLENGING HETERONORMATIVITY?

In the introduction to the edited volume *Fear of a Queer Planet: Queer Politics and Social Theory*, Michael Warner asks the question: "What do queers want?" (vii). He suggests that the goals of queers and their politics extend beyond the sexual arena. Warner contends that what queers want is acknowledgment of their lives, struggles, and complete existence; queers want to be represented and included fully in left political analysis and American culture. Thus what queers want is to be a part of the social, economic, and political restructuring of this society; as Warner writes, queers want to have queer experience and politics "taken as starting points rather than as footnotes" in the social theories and political agendas of the left (vii). He contends that it has been the absence or invisibility of lived queer experience that has marked or constrained much of left social and political theories and "has posited and naturalized a heterosexual society" in such theories (vii).

The concerns and emerging politics of queer activists, as formulated by Warner and others interested in understanding the implications of the idea of queerness, are focused on highlighting queer presence and destroying heteronormativity not only in the larger dominant society but also in extant spaces, theories, and sites of resistance, presumably on the left. He suggests that those embracing the label of "queer" understand the need to challenge the assumption of heteronormativity in every aspect of their existence:

Every person who comes to a queer self-understanding knows in one way or another that her stigmatization is connected with gender, the fam-

ily, notions of individual freedom, the state, public speech, consumption and desire, nature and culture, maturation, reproductive politics, racial and national fantasy, class identity, truth and trust, censorship, intimate life and social display, terror and violence, health care, and deep cultural norms about the bearing of the body. Being queer means fighting about these issues all the time, locally and piecemeal but always with consequences. (xiii)

Now, independent of the fact that few of us could find ourselves in such a grandiose description of queer consciousness, I believe that Warner's description points to the fact that in the roots of a lived "queer" existence are experiences with domination and in particular heteronormativity that form the basis for genuine transformational politics. By transformational, again, I mean a politics that does not search for opportunities to integrate into dominant institutions and normative social relationships, but instead pursues a political agenda that seeks to change values, definitions, and laws which make these institutions and relationships oppressive.

Queer activists experiencing displacement both within and outside of lesbian and gay communities rebuff what they deem the assimilationist practices and policies of more established lesbian and gay organizations. These organizers and activists reject cultural norms of acceptable sexual behavior and identification and instead embrace political strategies which promote self-definition and full expression. Members of the Chicago-based group Queers United Against Straight-acting Homosexuals (QUASH) state just such a position in the article "Assimilation Is Killing Us: Fight for a Queer United Front" published in their newsletter, WHY I HATED THE MARCH ON WASHINGTON:

Assimilation is killing us. We are falling into a trap. Some of us adopt an apologetic stance, stating "that's just the way I am" (read: "I'd be straight if I could."). Others pattern their behavior in such a way as to mimic heterosexual society so as to minimize the glaring differences between us and them. No matter how much [money] you make, fucking your lover is still illegal in nearly half of the states. Getting a corporate job, a fierce car and a condo does not protect you from dying of AIDS or getting your head bashed in by neo-Nazis. The myth of assimilation must be shattered.

. . . Fuck the heterosexual, nuclear family. Let's make families which promote sexual choices and liberation rather than sexual oppression. We must learn from the legacy of resistance that is ours: a legacy which shows that empowerment comes through grassroots activism, not mainstream politics, a legacy which shows that real change occurs when we are inclusive, not exclusive. (4)

At the very heart of queer politics, at least as it is formulated by QUASH, is a fundamental challenge to the heteronormativity—the privilege, power, and normative status invested in heterosexuality—of the dominant society.

It is in their fundamental challenge to a systemic process of domination and exclusion, with a specific focus on heteronormativity, that queer activists and queer theorists are tied to and rooted in a tradition of political struggle most often identified with people of color and other marginal groups. For example, activists of color have, through many historical periods, questioned their formal and informal inclusion and power in prevailing social categories. Through just such a process of challenging their centrality to lesbian and gay politics in particular, and lesbian and gay communities more generally, lesbian, gay, bisexual, and transgendered people of color advanced debates over who and what would be represented as "truly gay." As Steven Seidman reminds us in "Identity and Politics in a 'Postmodern' Gay Culture: Some Historical and Conceptual Notes," beyond the general framing provided by postmodern queer theory, gay and lesbian—and now queer—politics owes much of its impetus to the politics of people of color and other marginalized members of lesbian and gay communities.

> Specifically, I make the case that postmodern strains in gay thinking and politics have their immediate social origin in recent developments in the gay culture. In the reaction by people of color, third-world-identified gays, poor and working-class gays, and sex rebels to the ethnic/essentialist model of identity and community that achieved dominance in the lesbian and gay cultures of the 1970s, I locate the social basis for a rethinking of identity and politics. (106)

Through the demands of lesbian, gay, bisexual, and transgendered people of color as well as others who did not see themselves or their numerous communi-

ties in the more narrowly constructed politics of white gays and lesbians, the contestation took shape over who and what type of issues would be represented in lesbian and gay politics and in larger community discourse.

While similarities and connections between the politics of lesbians, gay men, bisexuals, and transgendered people of color during the 1970s and 1980s and queer activists of today clearly exist, the present-day rendition of this politics has deviated significantly from its legacy. Specifically, while both political efforts include as a focus of their work the radicalization and/or expansion of traditional lesbian and gay politics, the politics of lesbian, gay, bisexual, and transgendered people of color have been and continue to be much broader in its understanding of transformational politics.

The politics of lesbian, gay, bisexual, and transgendered people of color has often been guided by the type of radical intersectional left analysis I detailed earlier. Thus, while the politics of lesbian, gay, bisexual, and transgendered activists of color might recognize heteronormativity as a primary system of power structuring our lives, it understands that heteronormativity interacts with institutional racism, patriarchy, and class exploitation to define us in numerous ways as marginal and oppressed subjects.[5] And it is this constructed subservient position that allows our sisters and brothers to be used either as surplus labor in an advanced capitalist structure and/or seen as expendable, denied resources, and thus locked into correctional institutions across the country. While heterosexual privilege negatively impacts and constrains the lived experience of "queers" of color, so too do racism, classism, and sexism.

In contrast to the left intersectional analysis that has structured much of the politics of "queers" of color, the basis of the politics of some white queer activists and organizations has come dangerously close to a single-oppression model. Experiencing "deviant" sexuality as the prominent characteristic of their marginalization, these activists begin to envision the world in terms of a "hetero/queer" divide. Using the framework of queer theory in which heteronormativity is identified as a system of regulation and normalization, some queer activists map the power and entitlement of normative heterosexuality onto the bodies of all heterosexuals. Further, these activists naively characterize all those who exist under the category of "queer" as powerless. Thus, in the process of conceptualizing a decentered identity of queerness, meant to embrace all those who stand on the outside of heteronormativity, a monolithic understanding of heterosexuality and queerness has come to dominate the political imagination and actions of many queer activists.

This reconstruction of a binary divide between heterosexuals and queers, while discernible in many of the actions of Queer Nation, is probably most evident in the manifesto "I Hate Straights." Distributed at gay pride parades in New York and Chicago in 1990, the declaration written by an anonymous group of queers begins,

I have friends. Some of them are straight.

Year after year, I see my straight friends. I want to see how they are doing, to add newness to our long and complicated histories, to experience some continuity.

Year after year I continue to realize that the facts of my life are irrelevant to them and that I am only half listened to, that I am an appendage to the doings of a greater world, a world of power and privilege, of the laws of installation, a world of exclusion. `That's not true,' argue my straight friends. There is the one certainty in the politics of power; those left out of it beg for inclusion, while the insiders claim that they already are. Men do it to women, whites do it to blacks, *and everyone does it to queers.*

. . . *The main dividing line, both conscious and unconscious, is procreation . . . and that magic word—Family.* (emphasis added)

Screaming out from this manifesto is an analysis which places not heteronormativity, but heterosexuality, as the central "dividing line" between those who would be dominant and those who are oppressed. Nowhere in this essay is there recognition that "nonnormative" procreation patterns and family structures of people who are labeled heterosexual have also been used to regulate and exclude *them.* Instead, the authors declare. "Go tell them [straights] to go away until they have spent a month walking hand in hand in public with someone of the same sex. After they survive that, then you'll hear what they have to say about queer anger. Otherwise, tell them to shut up and listen." For these activists, the power of heterosexuality is the focus, and queer anger the means of queer politics. Missing from this equation is any attention to, or acknowledgment of, the ways in which

identities of race, class, and/or gender either enhance or mute the marginalization of queers, on the one hand, and the power of heterosexuals, on the other.

The fact that this essay is written about and out of queer anger is undoubtedly part of the rationale for its defense (Berlant and Freeman 200). But I question the degree to which we should read this piece as just an aberrational diatribe against straights motivated by intense queer anger. While anger is clearly a motivating factor for such writing, we should also understand this action to represent an analysis and politics structured around the simple dichotomy of straight and queer. We know, for instance, that similar positions have been put forth in other anonymously published, publicly distributed manifestos. For example, in the document *Queers Read This,* the authors write, "Don't be fooled, straight people own the world and the only reason you have been spared is you're smart, lucky or a fighter. Straight people have a privilege that allows them to do whatever they please and fuck without fear." They continue by stating: "Straight people are your enemy."

Even within this document, which seems to exemplify the narrowness of queer conceptions, there is a surprising glimpse at a more enlightened left intersectional understanding of what queerness might mean. For instance, the authors continue, "being queer is not about a right to privacy; it is about the freedom to be public, to just be who we are. It means everyday fighting oppression; homophobia, racism, misogyny, the bigotry of religious hypocrites and our own self-hatred." Evident in this one document are the inherent tensions and dilemmas many queer activists currently encounter: how does one implement in real political struggle a decentered political identity that is not constituted by a process of seemingly reductive "othering"?

The process of ignoring or at least downplaying queers' varying relationships to power is evident not only in the writing of queer activists, but also in the political actions pursued by queer organizations. I question the ability of political actions such as mall invasions (pursued by groups such as the Queer Shopping Network in New York and the Suburban Homosexual Outreach Program [SHOP] in San Francisco), to address the fact that queers exist in different social locations. Lauren Berlant and Elizabeth Freeman describe mall invasion projects as

[an attempt to take] the relatively bounded spectacle of the urban pride parade to the ambient pleasures of the shopping mall. "Mall visibility actions" thus conjoin the spectacular lure of the parade with Hare Krishna-style conversion and proselytizing techniques. Stepping into malls in hair-gelled splendor, holding hands and handing out fliers, the queer auxiliaries produce an "invasion" that conveys a different message. "We're here, we're queer, *you're* going shopping." (210)

The activity of entering or "invading" the shopping mall on the part of queer nationals is clearly one of attempted subversion. Intended by their visible presence in this clearly coded heterosexual family economic mecca is a disruption of the agreed-upon segregation between the allowable spaces for queer "deviant" culture and the rest of the "naturalized" world. Left unchallenged in such an action, however, are the myriad ways, besides the enforcement of normative sexuality, in which some queers feel alienated and excluded from the space of the mall. Where does the mall as an institution of consumer culture and relative economic privilege play into this analysis? How does this action account for the varying economic relationships queers have to consumer culture? If you are a poor or working-class queer the exclusion and alienation you experience when entering the mall may not be limited to the normative sexual codes associated with the mall, but may also be centered on the assumed economic status of those shopping in suburban malls. If you are a queer of color your exclusion from the mall may, in part, be rooted in racial norms and stereotypes which construct you as a threatening subject every time you enter this economic institution. Queer activists must confront a question that haunts most political organizing: How do we put into politics a broad and inclusive left analysis that can actually engage and mobilize individuals with intersecting identities?

Clearly, there will be those critics who will claim that I am asking too much from any political organization. Demands that every aspect of oppression and regulation be addressed in each political act seem, and are indeed, unreasonable. However, I make the critique of queer mall invasions neither to stop such events nor to suggest that every oppression be dealt with by this one political action. Instead, I raise these concerns to emphasize the ways in which varying relation to power exist not only among heterosexuals, but also among those who label themselves queer.

In its current rendition, queer politics is coded with class, gender, and race privilege, and may have lost its potential to be a politically expedient organizing tool for addressing the needs—and mobilizing the bodies—of people of color. As some queer theorists and activists call for the destruction of stable sexual categories, for example, moving instead toward a more fluid understanding of sexual behavior, left unspoken is the class privilege which allows for such fluidity. Class or material privilege is a cornerstone of much of queer politics and theory as they exist today. Queer theorizing which calls for the elimination of fixed categories of sexual identity seems to ignore the ways in which some traditional social identities and communal ties can, in fact, be important to one's survival. Further, a queer politics which demonizes all heterosexuals discounts the relationships—especially those based on shared experiences of marginalization—that exist between gays and straights, particularly in communities of color.

Queers who operate out of a political culture of individualism assume a material independence that allows them to disregard historically or culturally recognized categories and communities or at the very least to move fluidly among them without ever establishing permanent relationships or identities within them. However, I and many other lesbian and gay people of color, as well as poor and working-class lesbians and gay men, do not have such material independence. Because of my multiple identities, which locate me and other "queer" people of color at the margins in this country, my material advancement, my physical protection and my emotional well-being are constantly threatened. In those stable categories and named communities whose histories have been structured by shared resistance to oppression, I find relative degrees of safety and security.

Let me emphasize again that the safety I feel is relative to other threats and is clearly not static or constant. For in those named communities I also find versions of domination and normalization being replicated and employed as more privileged/assimilated marshal group members use their associations with dominant institutions and resources to regulate and police the activities of other marginal group members. Any lesbian, gay, bisexual, or transgendered person of color who has experienced exclusion from indigenous institutions, such as the exclusion many out black gay men have encountered from some black churches responding to AIDS, recognizes that even within marginal groups there are normative rules determining community membership and power (Cohen). However, in spite of the unequal power relationships located in marginal communities, I am still not interested in disassociating politically from those communities, for queerness, as it is currently constructed, offers no viable political alternative, since it invites us to put forth a political agenda that makes invisible the prominence of race, class, and to varying degrees gender in determining the life chances of those on both sides of the hetero/queer divide.

So despite the roots of queer politics in the struggles of "queer" people of color, despite the calls for highlighting categories which have sought to regulate and control black bodies like my own, and despite the attempts at decentralized grassroots activism in some queer political organizations, there still exist—for some, like myself—great misgivings about current constructions of the term "queer." Personally speaking, I do not consider myself a "queer" activist or, for that matter, a "queer" anything. This is not because I do not consider myself an activist; in fact I hold my political work to be one of my most important contributions to all of my communities. But like other lesbian, gay, bisexual, and transgendered activists of color, I find the label "queer" fraught with unspoken assumptions which inhibit the radical political potential of this category.

The alienation, or at least discomfort, many activists and theorists of color have with current conceptions of queerness is evidenced, in part, by the minimal numbers of theorists of color who engage in the process of theorizing about the concept. Further, the sparse numbers of people of color who participate in "queer" political organizations might also be read as a sign of discomfort with the term. Most important, my confidence in making such a claim of distance and uneasiness with the term "queer" on the part of many people of color comes from my interactions with other lesbian, gay, bisexual, and transgendered people of color who repeatedly express their interpretation of "queer" as a term rooted in class, race, and gender privilege. For us, "queer" is a politics based on narrow sexual dichotomies which make no room either for the analysis of oppression of those we might categorize as heterosexual, or for the privilege of those who operate as "queer." As black lesbian activist and writer Barbara Smith argues in "Queer Politics: Where's the Revolution?":

Unlike the early lesbian and gay movement, which had both ideological and practical links to the left,

black activism and feminism, today's "queer" politicos seem to operate in a historical and ideological vacuum. "Queer" activists focus on "queer" issues, and racism, sexual oppression and economic exploitation do not qualify, despite the fact that the majority of "queers" are people of color, female or working class. . . . Building unified, ongoing coalitions that challenge the system and ultimately prepare a way for revolutionary change simply isn't what "queer" activists have in mind. (13–14)

It is this narrow understanding of the idea of queer that negates its use in fundamentally reorienting the politics and privilege of lesbian and gay politics as well as more generally moving or transforming the politics of the left. Despite its liberatory claim to stand in opposition to static categories of oppression, queer politics and much of queer theory seem in fact to be static in the understanding of race, class, and gender and their roles in how heteronormativity regulates sexual behavior and identities. Distinctions between the status and the acceptance of different individuals categorized under the label of "heterosexual" go unexplored.

I emphasize the marginalized position of some who embrace heterosexual identities not because I want to lead any great crusade to understand more fully the plight of "the heterosexual." Rather, I recognize the potential for shared resistance with such individuals. This potential not only for coalitional work but for a shared analysis is especially relevant, from my vantage point, to "queer" people of color. Again, in my call for coalition work across sexual categories, I do not want to suggest that same-sex political struggles have not, independently, played an essential and distinct role in the liberatory politics and social movements of marginal people. My concern, instead, is with any political analysis or theory which collapses our understanding of power into a single continuum of evaluation.

Through a brief review of some of the ways in which nonnormative heterosexuality has been controlled and regulated through the state and systems of marginalization we may be reminded that differentials in power exist within all socially named categories. And through such recognition we may begin to envision a new political formation in which one's relation to dominant power serves as the basis of unity for radical coalition work in the twenty-first century.

HETEROSEXUALS ON THE (OUT)SIDE OF HETERONORMATIVITY

In this section I want to return to the question of a monolithic understanding of heterosexuality. I believe that through this issue we can begin to think critically about the components of a radical politics built not exclusively on identities, but on identities as they are invested with varying degrees of normative power. Thus, fundamental to my concern about the current structure and future agenda of queer politics is the unchallenged assumption of a uniform heteronormativity from which all heterosexuals benefit. I want again to be clear that there are, in fact, some who identify themselves as queer activists who do acknowledge relative degrees of power, and heterosexual access to that power, even evoking the term "straight queers." "Queer means to fuck with gender. There are straight queers, bi queers, tranny queers, lez queers, fag queers, SM queers, fisting queers in every single street in this apathetic country of ours" (anonymous, qtd. McIntosh 31).

Despite such sporadic insight, much of the politics of queer activists has been structured around the dichotomy of straight versus everything else, assuming a monolithic experience of heterosexual privilege for all those identified publicly with heterosexuality. A similar reductive dichotomy between men and women has consistently reemerged in the writing and actions of some feminists. And only through the demands, the actions, and the writing of many "feminists" and/or lesbians of color have those women who stand outside the norm of white, middle-class, legalized heterosexuality begun to see their lives, needs, and bodies represented in feminist theory (Carby; Collins; hooks). In a similar manner lesbian, gay, bisexual, and transgendered people of color have increasingly taken on the responsibility for at the very least complicating and most often challenging reductive notions of heteronormativity articulated by queer activists and scholars (Alexander; Farajaje-Jones; Lorde; Moraga and Anzaldúa; B. Smith).

If we follow such examples, complicating our understanding of both heteronormativity and queerness, we move one step closer to building the progressive coalition politics many of us desire. Specifically, if we pay attention to both historical and current examples of heterosexual relationships which have been prohibited, stigmatized, and generally repressed, we may begin to identify those spaces of shared or similar oppression and resistance that provide a basis for radical coalition work. Further, we may begin to answer certain questions: In narrowly positing a dichotomy of heterosexual privilege and queer oppression under which we all exist, are we negating a basis of political unity that could serve to strengthen many communities and movements seeking justice and societal transformation? How do we use the relative degrees of ostracization all sexual/cultural "deviants" experience to build a basis of unity for broader coalition and movement work?

A little history (as a political scientist a little history is all I can offer) might be helpful in trying to sort out the various ways heterosexuality, especially as it has intersected with race, has been defined and experienced by different groups of people. It should also help to underscore the fact that many of the roots of heteronormativity are in white supremacist ideologies which sought (and continue) to use the state and its regulation of sexuality, in particular through the institution of heterosexual marriage, to designate which individuals were truly "fit" for full rights and privileges of citizenship. For example, the prohibition of marriages between black women and men imprisoned in the slave system was a component of many slave codes enacted during the seventeenth and eighteenth centuries. M.G. Smith, in his article on the structure of slave economic systems, succinctly states, "As property slaves were prohibited from forming legal relationships or marriages which would interfere with and restrict their owner's property rights" (71–72). Herbert G. Gutman, in *The Black Family in Slavery and Freedom, 1750–1925*, elaborates on the ideology of slave societies which denied the legal sanctioning of marriages between slaves and further reasoned that Blacks had no conception of family.

> The *Nation* identified sexual restraint, civil marriage, and family "stability" with "civilization" itself.
> Such mid-nineteenth-century class and sexual beliefs reinforced racial beliefs about Afro-Americans. As slaves, after all, their marriages had not been sanctioned by the civil laws and therefore "the sexual passion" went unrestrained. . . . Many white abolitionists denied the slaves a family life or even, often, a family consciousness because for them [whites] the family had its origins in and had to be upheld by the civil law. (295)

Thus it was not the promotion of marriage or heterosexuality per se that served as the standard or motivation of most slave societies. Instead, marriage and heterosexuality, as viewed through the lenses of profit and domination, and the ideology of white supremacy, were reconfigured to justify the exploitation and regulation of black bodies, even those presumably engaged in heterosexual behavior. It was this system of state-sanctioned, white male, upperclass, heterosexual domination that forced these presumably black *heterosexual* men and women to endure a history of rape, lynching, and other forms of physical and mental terrorism. In this way, marginal group members, lacking power and privilege although engaged in heterosexual behavior, have often found themselves defined as outside the norms and values of dominant society. This position has most often resulted in the suppression or negation of their legal, social, and physical relationships and rights.

In addition to the prohibition of marriage between slaves, A. Leon Higginbotham, Jr., in *The Matter of Color—Race and the American Legal Process: The Colonial Period*, writes of the legal restrictions barring interracial marriages. He reminds us that the essential core of the American legal tradition was the preservation of the white race. The "mixing" of the races was to be strictly prohibited in early colonial laws. The regulation of interracial heterosexual relationships, however, should not be understood as exclusively relegated to the seventeenth, eighteenth and nineteenth centuries. In fact, Higginbotham informs us that the final law prohibiting miscegenation (the "interbreeding" or marrying of individuals from different "races"—actually meant to inhibit the "tainting" of the white race) was not repealed until 1967:

> Colonial anxiety about interracial sexual activity cannot be attributed solely to seventeenth-century values, for it was not until 1967 that the United States Supreme Court finally declared unconstitutional those statutes prohibiting interracial marriages. The Supreme Court waited thirteen years after its *Brown* decision dealing with desegregation of schools before, in *Loving v. Virginia*, it agreed to consider the issue of interracial marriages. (41)

It is this pattern of regulating the behavior and denigrating the identities of those heterosexuals on the outside of heteronormative privilege, in particular those perceived as threatening systems of white supremacy, male domination, and capitalist advancement, that I want to highlight. An understanding of

the ways in which heteronormativity works to support and reinforce institutional racism, patriarchy, and class exploitation must therefore be a part of how we problematize current constructions of heterosexuality. As I stated previously. I am not suggesting that those involved in publicly identifiable heterosexual behavior do not receive political, economic, and social advantage, especially in comparison to the experiences of some lesbian, transgendered, gay, and bisexual individuals. But the equation linking identity and behavior to power is not as linear and clear as some queer theorists and activists would have us believe.

A more recent example of regulated nonnormative heterosexuality is located in current debates and rhetoric regarding the "underclass" and the destruction of the welfare system. The stigmatization and demonization of single mothers, teen mothers, and, primarily, poor women of color dependent on state assistance has had a long and suspicious presence in American "intellectual" and political history. It was in 1965 that Daniel Patrick Moynihan released his "study" entitled *The Negro Family: The Case for National Action*. In this report, which would eventually come to be known as the Moynihan Report, the author points to the "pathologies" increasingly evident in so-called Negro families. In this document were allegations of the destructive nature of Negro family formations. The document's introduction argues that

> the fundamental problem, in which this is most clearly the case, is that of family structure. The evidence—not final, but powerfully persuasive—is that the Negro family in urban ghettos is crumbling. A middle-class group has managed to save itself, but for vast numbers of the unskilled, poorly educated city working class the fabric of conventional social relationships has all but disintegrated.

Moynihan, later in the document, goes on to describe the crisis and pathologies facing Negro family structure as being generated by the increasing number of single-female-headed households, the increasing number of "illegitimate" births and, of course, increasing welfare dependency:

> In essence, the Negro community has been forced into a matriarchal structure which, because it is so out of line with the rest of the American society, seriously retards the progress of the group as a whole, and imposes a crushing burden on the

Negro male and, in consequence, on a great many Negro women as well. . . . In a word, most Negro youth are in danger of being caught up in the tangle of pathology that affects their world, and probably a majority are so entrapped. . . . Obviously, not every instance of social pathology afflicting the Negro community can be traced to the weakness of family structure. . . . Nonetheless, at the center of the tangle of pathology is the weakness of the family structure. (29–30)

It is not the nonheterosexist behavior of these black men and women that is under fire, but rather the perceived nonnormative sexual behavior and family structures of these individuals, whom many queer activists—without regard to the impact of race, class, or gender—would designate as part of the heterosexist establishment or those mighty "straights they hate."

Over the last thirty years the demonization of poor women, engaged in nonnormative heterosexual relationships, has continued under the auspices of scholarship on the "underclass." Adolph L. Reed, in "The 'Underclass' as Myth and Symbol: The Poverty of Discourse about Poverty," discusses the gendered and racist nature of much of this literature, in which poor, often black and Latina women are portrayed as unable to control their sexual impulses and eventual reproductive decisions, unable to raise their children with the right moral fiber, unable to find "gainful" employment to support themselves and their "illegitimate children," and of course unable to manage "effectively" the minimal assistance provided by the state. Reed writes:

The underclass notion may receive the greatest ideological boost from its gendered imagery and relation to gender politics. As I noted in a critique of Wilson's *The Truly Disadvantaged*, "family" is an intrinsically ideological category. The rhetoric of "disorganization," "disintegration," "deterioration" reifies one type of living arrangement—the ideal type of the bourgeois nuclear family—as outside history, nearly as though it were decreed by natural law. But—as I asked earlier—why exactly is out-of-wedlock birth pathological? Why is the female-headed household an indicator of disorganization and pathology? Does that stigma attach to *all* such households—even, say, a divorced executive who is a custodial mother? If not, what are the criteria for assigning it? The short answer is race

and class bias inflected through a distinctively gendered view of the world. (33–34)

In this same discourse of the "underclass," young black men engaged in "reckless" heterosexual behavior are represented as irresponsible baby factories, unable to control or restrain their "sexual passion" (to borrow a term from the seventeenth century). And unfortunately, often it has been the work of professed liberals like William Julius Wilson, in his book *The Truly Disadvantaged*, that, while not using the word "pathologies," has substantiated in its own tentative way the conservative dichotomy between the deserving working poor and the lazy, Cadillac-driving, steak-eating welfare queens of Ronald Reagan's imagination. Again, I raise this point to remind us of the numerous ways that sexuality and sexual deviance from a prescribed norm have been used to demonize and to oppress various segments of the population, even some classified under the label "heterosexual."

The policies of politicians and the actions of law enforcement officials have reinforced, in much more devastating ways, the distinctions between acceptable forms of heterosexual expression and those to be regulated—increasingly through incarceration. This move toward the disallowance of some forms of heterosexual expression and reproductive choice can be seen in the practice of prosecuting pregnant women suspected of using drugs—nearly 80 percent of all women prosecuted are women of color; through the forced sterilization of Puerto Rican and Native American women: and through the state-dictated use of Norplant by women answering to the criminal justice system and by women receiving state assistance.[6] Further, it is the "nonnormative" children of many of these nonnormative women that Newt Gingrich would place in orphanages. This is the same Newt Gingrich who, despite his clear disdain for gay and lesbian "lifestyles," has invited lesbians and gay men into the Republican party. I need not remind you that he made no such offer to the women on welfare discussed above. Who, we might ask, is truly on the outside of heteronormative power—maybe *most* of us?

CONCLUSION: DESTABILIZATION AND RADICAL COALITION WORK

While all this may, in fact, seem interesting or troubling or both, you may be wondering: What does it have to do with the question of the future of queer politics? It is my argument, as I stated earlier, that one of the great failings of queer theory and especially queer politics has been their inability to incorporate into analysis of the world and strategies for political mobilization the roles that race, class, and gender play in defining people's differing relations to dominant and normalizing power. I present this essay as the beginning of a much longer and protracted struggle to acknowledge and delineate the distribution of power within and outside of queer communities. This is a discussion of how to build a politics organized not merely by reductive categories of straight and queer, but organized instead around a more intersectional analysis of who and what the enemy is and where our potential allies can be found. This analysis seeks to make clear the privilege and power embedded in the categorizations of, on the one hand, an upstanding, "morally correct," white, state-authorized, middle-class, male *heterosexual,* and on the other, a culturally deficient, materially bankrupt, state-dependent, *heterosexual* woman of color, the latter found most often in our urban centers (those that haven't been gentrified), on magazine covers, and on the evening news.

I contend, therefore, that the radical potential of queer politics, or any liberatory movement, rests on its ability to advance strategically oriented political identities arising from a more nuanced understanding of power. One of the most difficult tasks in such an endeavor (and there are many) is not to forsake the complexities of both how power is structured and how we might think about the coalitions we create. Far too often movements revert to a position in which membership and joint political work are based upon a necessarily similar history of oppression—but this is too much like identity politics (Phelan). Instead, I am suggesting that the process of movement building be rooted not in our shared history or identity, but in our shared marginal relationship to dominant power which normalizes, legitimizes, and privileges.

We must, therefore, start our political work from the recognition that multiple systems of oppression are in operation and that these systems use institutionalized categories and identities to regulate and socialize. We must also understand that power and access to dominant resources are distributed across the boundaries of "het" and "queer" that we construct. A model of queer politics that simply pits the grand "heterosexuals" against all those oppressed "queers" is ineffectual as the basis for action in a political environment dominated by Newt Gingrich, the Christian Right, and the recurring ideology of white supremacy. As we stand on the verge of watching those in power dismantle the welfare system through a process of demonizing poor and young, primarily poor and young women of color—many of whom have existed for their entire lives outside the white, middle-class, heterosexual norm—we have to ask if these women do not fit into society's categories of marginal, deviant, and "queer." As we watch the explosion of prison construction and the disproportionate incarceration rates of young men and women of color, often as part of the economic development of poor white rural communities, we have to ask if these individuals do not fit society's definition of "queer" and expendable.

I am not proposing a political strategy that homogenizes and glorifies the experience of poor heterosexual people of color. In fact, in calling for a more expansive left political identity and formation I do not seek to erase the specific historical relation between the stigma of "queer" and the sexual activity of gay men, lesbians, bisexual, and transgendered individuals. And in no way do I mean to, or want to, equate the experiences of marginal heterosexual women and men to the lived experiences of queers. There is no doubt that heterosexuality, even for those heterosexuals who stand outside the norms of heteronormativity, results in some form of privilege and feelings of supremacy. I need only recount the times when other women of color, more economically vulnerable than myself, expressed superiority and some feelings of disgust when they realized that the nice young professor (me) was "that way."

However, in recognizing the distinct history of oppression lesbian, gay, bisexual, and transgendered people have confronted and challenged, I am not willing to embrace every queer as my marginalized political ally. In the same way, I do not assume that shared racial, gender, and/or class position or identity guarantees or produces similar political commitments. Thus, identities and communities, while important to this strategy, must be complicated and destabilized through a recognition of the multiple social positions and relations to dominant power found *within* any one category or identity. Kimberle Crenshaw, in "Mapping the Margins: Intersectionality, Identity Politics, and Violence against Women of Color," suggests that such a project use the idea of intersectionality to reconceptualize or problematize the identities and communities that are "home" to us. She demands that we challenge those identities that seem like home by acknowledging the other parts of our identities that are excluded:

> With identity thus reconceptualized [through a recognition of intersectionality], it may be easier to understand the need to summon up the courage to challenge groups that are after all, in one sense, "home" to us, in the name of the parts of us that are not made at home. . . . The most one could expect is that we will dare to speak against internal exclusions and marginalizations, that we might call attention to how the identity of "the group" has been centered on the intersectional identities of a few. . . . Through an awareness of intersectionality, we can better acknowledge and ground the differences among us and negotiate the means by which these differences will find expression in constructing group politics. (1299)

In the same ways that we account for the varying privilege to be gained by a heterosexual identity, we must also pay attention to the privilege some queers receive from being white, male, and upper class. Only through recognizing the many manifestations of power, across and within categories, can we truly begin to build a movement based on one's politics and not exclusively on one's identity.

I want to be clear that what I and others are calling for is the destabilization, and not the destruction or abandonment, of identity categories.[7] We must reject a queer politics which seems to ignore, in its analysis of the usefulness of traditionally named categories, the roles of identity and community as paths to survival, using shared experiences of oppression and resistance to build indigenous resources, shape consciousness, and act collectively. Instead, I would suggest that it is the multiplicity and interconnectedness of our identities which provide the most promising avenue for the *destabilization and radical politicalization* of these same categories.

This is not an easy path to pursue because most often this will mean building a political analysis and political strategies around the most marginal in our society, some of whom look like us, many of whom do not. Most often, this will mean rooting our struggle in, and addressing the needs of, communities of color. Most often this will mean highlighting the intersectionality of one's race, class, gender, and sexuality and the relative power and privilege that one receives from being a man and/or being white and/or being middle class and/or being heterosexual. This, in particular, is a daunting challenge because so much of our political consciousness has been built around simple dichotomies such as powerful/powerless; oppressor/victim: enemy/comrade. It is difficult to feel safe and secure in those spaces where both your relative privilege and your experiences with marginalization are understood to shape your commitment to radical politics. However, as Bernice Johnson Reagon so aptly put it in her essay, "Coalition Politics: Turning the Century," "if you feel the strain, you may be doing some good work" (362).

And while this is a daunting challenge and uncomfortable position, those who have taken it up have not only survived, but succeeded in their efforts. For example, both the needle exchange and prison projects pursued through the auspices of ACT UP New York point to the possibilities and difficulties involved in principled transformative coalition work. In each project individuals from numerous identities—heterosexual, gay, poor, wealthy, white, black, Latino—came together to challenge dominant constructions of who should be allowed and who deserved care. No particular identity exclusively determined the shared political commitments of these activists; instead their similar positions, as marginalized subjects relative to the state—made clear through the government's lack of response to AIDS—formed the basis of this political unity.

In the prison project, it was the contention of activists that the government which denied even wealthy gay men access to drugs to combat this disease must be regarded as the same source of power that denied incarcerated men and women access to basic health care, including those drugs and conditions needed to combat HIV and AIDS. The coalition work this group engaged in involved a range of people, from formerly incarcerated individuals, to heterosexual men and women of color, to those we might deem privileged white lesbians and gay men. And this same group of people who came together to protest the conditions of incarcerated people with AIDS also showed up to public events challenging the homophobia that guided the government's and biomedical industries response to this epidemic. The political work of this group of individuals was undoubtedly informed by the public identities they embraced, but these were identities that they further acknowledged as complicated by intersectionality and placed within a political framework where their shared experience as marginal, nonnormative subjects could be foregrounded. Douglas Crimp, in his article "Right On, Girlfriend!," suggests that through political work our identities become remade and must therefore be understood as *relational*. Describing such a transformation in the identities of queer activists engaged in, and prosecuted for, needle exchange work, Crimp writes:

> But once engaged in the struggle to end the crisis, these queers' identities were no longer the same. It's not that "queer" doesn't any longer encompass their sexual practices; it does, but it also entails a *relation* between those practices and other circumstances that make very different people vulnerable both to HIV infection and to the stigma, discrimination, and neglect that have characterized the societal and governmental response to the constituencies most affected by the AIDS epidemic. (317–18)

The radical potential of those of us on the outside of heteronormativity rests in our understanding that we need not base our politics in the dissolution of all categories and communities, but we need instead to work toward the destabilization and remaking of our identities. Difference, in and of itself—even that difference designated through named categories—is not the problem. Instead it is the power invested in certain identity categories and the idea that bounded categories are not to be transgressed that serve as the basis of domination and control. The reconceptualization not only of the content of identity categories, but the intersectional nature of identities themselves, must become part of our political practice.

We must thus begin to link our intersectional analysis of power with concrete coalitional work. In real terms this means identifying political struggles such as the needle exchange and prison projects of ACT UP that transgress the boundaries of identity to highlight, in this case, both the repressive power of the state and the normalizing power evident within both dominant and marginal communities. This type of principled coalition work is also being pursued in a more modest fashion by the Policy Institute of the National Gay and Lesbian Task Force. Recently, the staff at the Task Force distributed position papers not only on the topics of gay marriages and gays in the military, but also on right-wing attacks against welfare and affirmative action. Here we have political work based in the knowledge that the rhetoric and accusations of nonnormativity that Newt Gingrich and other right-wingers launch against women on welfare closely resemble the attacks of nonnormativity mounted against gays, lesbians, bisexuals, and transgendered individuals. Again it is the marginalized relation to power, experienced by both of these groups—and I do not mean to suggest that the groups are mutually exclusive—that frames the possibility for transformative coalition work. This prospect diminishes when we do not recognize and deal with the reality that the intersecting identities that gay people embody—in terms of race, class, and gender privilege—put some of us on Gingrich's side of the welfare struggle (e.g., Log Cabin Republicans). And in a similar manner a woman's dependence on state financial assistance in no way secures her position as one supportive of gay rights and/or liberation. While a marginal identity undoubtedly increases the prospects of shared consciousness, only an articulation and commitment to mutual support can truly be the test of unity when pursuing transformational politics.

Finally, I realize that I have been short on specifics when trying to describe how we move concretely toward a transformational coalition politics among marginalized subjects. The best I can do is offer this discussion as a starting point for reassessing the shape of queer/lesbian/gay/bisexual/transgendered politics as we approach the twenty-first century. A reconceptualization of the politics of marginal groups allows us not only to privilege the specific lived experience of distinct communities, but also to search for those interconnected sites of resistance from which we can wage broader political struggles. Only by recognizing the link *between* the ideological, social, political, and economic marginalization of punks, bulldaggers, and welfare queens can we begin to develop political analyses and political strategies effective in confronting the linked yet varied sites of power in this country. Such a project is important because it provides a framework from which the difficult work of coalition politics can begin. And it is in these complicated and contradictory spaces that the liberatory and left politics that so many of us work for is located.

ACKNOWLEDGMENTS

The author would like to thank Mark Blasius, Nan Boyd, Ed Cohen, Carolyn Dinshaw, Jeff Edwards, Licia Fiol-Matta, Joshua Gamson, Lynne Huffer, Tamara Jones, Carla Kaplan, Ntanya Lee, Ira Livingston, and Barbara Ransby for their comments on various versions of this paper. All shortcomings are of course the fault of the author.

NOTES

1. The very general chronology of queer theory and queer politics referred to throughout this article is not meant to write the definitive historical development of each phenomenon. Instead, the dates are used to provide the reader with a general frame of reference. See Epstein for a similar genealogy of queer theory and queer politics.

2. See Ingraham for a discussion of the heterogendered imaginary.

3. I want to be clear that in this essay I am including the destruction of sexual categories as part of the agenda of queer politics. While a substantial segment of queer activists and theorists call for the *destabilization* of sexual categories, there are also those self-avowed queers who embrace a politics built around the *deconstruction* and/or elimination of sexual categories. For example, a number of my self-identified queer students engage in sexual behavior that most people would interpret as *transgressive* of sexual identities and categories. However, these students have repeatedly articulated a different interpretation of their sexual behavior. They put forth an understanding that does not highlight their transgression of categories, but one which instead represents them as individuals who operate outside of categories and sexual identities altogether. They are sexual beings, given purely to desire, truly living sexual fluidity, and not constrained by any form of sexual categorization or identification. This interpretation seems at least one step removed from that held by people who embrace the fluidity of sexuality while still recognizing the political usefulness of categories or labels for certain sexual behavior and communities. One example of such people might be those women who identify as lesbians and who also acknowledge that sometimes they choose to sleep with men. These individuals exemplify the process of destabilization that I try to articulate within this essay. Even further removed from the queers who would do away with all sexual categories are those who also transgress what many consider to be categories of sexual behaviors while they publicly embrace one stable sexual identity (for example, those self-identified heterosexual men who sleep with other men sporadically and secretly).

4. I want to thank Mark Blasius for raising the argument that standing on the outside of heteronormativity is a bit of a misnomer, since as a dominant normalizing process it is a practice of regulation in which we are all implicated. However, despite this insight I will on occasion continue to use this phrasing, understanding the limits of its meaning.

5. See Hennessy for a discussion of left analysis and the limits of queer theory.

6. For an insightful discussion of the numerous methods used to regulate and control the sexual and reproductive choices of women, see Shende.

7. See Jones for an articulation of differences between the destabilization and the destruction of identity categories.

REFERENCES

Alexander, Jacqui. "Redrafting Morality: The Postcolonial State and the Sexual Offences Bill of Trinidad and Tobago." *Third World Women and the Politics of Feminism,* ed. C. T. Mohanty, A. Russo, and L. Torres. Bloomington: Indiana UP, 1991. 133–52.

Berlant, Lauren, and Elizabeth Freeman. "Queer Nationality." Warner 193–229.

Bérubé, Allan, and Jeffrey Escoffier. "Queer/Nation." *Out/Look: National Lesbian and Gay Quarterly* II (Winter 1991): 12–14.

Blasius, Mark. *Gay and Lesbian Politics: Sexuality and the Emergence of a New Ethic.* Philadelphia: Temple UP, 1994.

Butler, Judith. *Gender Trouble.* New York: Routledge, 1990.

Carby, Hazel. *Reconstructing Womanhood: The Emergence of the Afro-American Woman Novelist.* New York: Oxford UP, 1987.

Clarke, Cheryl. "The Failure to Transform: Homophobia in the Black Community." Smith, *Home Girls* 197–208.

Cohen, Cathy J. "Contested Membership: Black Gay Identities and the Politics of AIDS." *Queer Theory/Sociology.* Ed. S. Seidman, Oxford: Blackwell, 1996. 362–94.

Collins, Patricia Hill, *Black Feminist Thought: Knowledge, Consciousness, and the Politics of Sociology Empowerment.* New York: Harper, 1990.

Combahee River Collective. "The Combahee River Collective Statement." Smith, *Home Girls* 272–82.

Crenshaw, Kimberle. "Mapping the Margins: Intersectionality, Identity Politics, and Violence against Women of Color." *Stanford Law Review* 43 (1991): 1241–99.

Crimp, Douglas. "Right On, Girlfriend!" Warner 300–20.

Davis, Angela Y. *Women, Race and Class.* New York: Vintage, 1983.

De Lauretis, Teresa. "Queer Theory: Lesbian and Gay Sexualities." *Differences* 3.2 (Summer 1991): iii–xviii.

Dunlap, David W. "Three Black Members Quit AIDS Organization Board." *New York Times* 11 Jan. 1996: B2.

Dyson, Michael Eric. *Between God and Gangsta Rap.* New York: Oxford UP, 1996.

Epstein, Steven. "A Queer Encounter: Sociology and the Study of Sexuality." *Sociological Theory* 12 (1994): 188–202.

Farajaje-Jones, Elias. "Ain't I a Queer." Creating Change Conference, National Gay and Lesbian Task Force, Detroit, Michigan, 8–12 Nov. 1995.

Fuss, Diana, ed. *Inside/Outside.* New York: Routledge, 1991.

Gamson, Joshua. "Must Identity Movements Self-destruct? A Queer Dilemma." *Social Problems* 42 (1995): 390–407.

Gutman, Herbert G. *The Black Family in Slavery and Freedom, 1750–1925.* New York: Vintage, 1976.

Hennessy, Rosemary. "Queer Theory, Left Politics," *Rethinking MARXISM* 7.3 (1994): 85–111.

Higginbotham, A. Leon, Jr. *In the Matter of Color—Race and the American Legal Process: The Colonial Period.* New York: Oxford UP, 1978.

hooks, bell. *Feminist Theory: From Margin to Center.* Boston: South End, 1984.

Ingraham, Chrys. "The Heterosexual Imaginary: Feminist Sociology and Theories of Gender." *Sociological Theory* 12 (1994): 203–19.

Jones, Tamara. "Inside the Kaleidoscope: How the Construction of Black Gay and Lesbian Identities Inform Political Strategies." Unpublished. Yale University, 1995.

Lorde, Audre, *Sister Outsider: Essays and Speeches by Audre Lorde.* New York: The Crossing P. 1984.

McIntosh, Mary. "Queer Theory and the War of the Sexes." *Activating Theory: Lesbian, Gay, Bisexual Politics,* ed. J. Bristow and A. R. Wilson. London: Lawrence and Wishart, 1993. 33–52.

Moraga, Cherríe, and Gloria Anzaldúa, eds. *This Bridge Called My Back: Writings by Radical Women of Color.* New York: Kitchen Table/Women of Color, 1981.

Morton, Donald. "The Politics of Queer Theory in the (Post) Modern Moment," *Genders* 17 (Fall 1993): 121–15.

Moynihan, Daniel Patrick. *The Negro Family: The Case for National Action.* Washington D.C.: Office of Policy Planning and Research. U.S. Department of Labor, 1965.

Phelan, Shane. *Identity Politics: Lesbian Feminism and the Limits of Community.* Philadelphia: Temple UP, 1989.

Podolsky, Robin. "Sacrificing Queer and other `Proletarian' Artifacts." *Radical America* 25.1 (January 1991): 53–60.

Queer Nation. "I Hate Straights" manifesto. New York, 1990.

Queers United Against Straight-acting Homosexuals. "Assimilation Is Killing Us: Fight for a Queer United Front." WHY I HATED THE MARCH ON WASHINGTON (1993):4.

Ransby, Barbara, and Tracye Matthews. "Black Popular Culture and the Transcendence of Patriarchical Illusions." *Race & Class* 35.1 (July–September 1993): 57–70.

Reagon, Bernice Johnson. "Coalition Politics: Turning the Century." Smith, *Home Girls* 356–68.

Reed, Adolph L., Jr. "The `Underclass' as Myth and Symbol: The Poverty of Discourse about Poverty." *Radical America* 24.1 (January 1990): 21–40.

Rich, Adrienne. "Compulsory Heterosexuality and Lesbian Existence." *Powers of Desire: The Politics of Sexuality,* ed. A. Snitow, C. Stansell and S. Thompson. New York: Monthly Review, 1983. 177–206.

Sedgwick, Eve. *The Epistemology of the Closet.* Berkeley: U of California P, 1990.

Seidman, Steven. "Identity and Politics in a `Postmodern' Gay Culture." Warner 105–42.

Shende, Suzanne. "Fighting the Violence against Our Sisters: Prosecution of Pregnant Women and the Coercive Use of Norplant." *Women Transforming Politics: An Alternative Reader,* ed. C. Cohen, K. Jones, and J. Tronto, New York: New York UP, 1997.

Smith, Barbara. "Queer Politics: Where's the Revolution?" *The Nation* 257.1 (July 5, 1993): 12–16.

———, ed. *Home Girls: A Black Feminist Anthology.* New York: Kitchen Table/Women of Color, 1983.

Smith, M. G. "Social Structure in the British Caribbean about 1820." *Social and Economic Studies* 1.4 (August 1953): 55–79.

"Statement of Purpose." Dialogue on the Lesbian and Gay Left. Duncan Conference Center in Del Ray Beach, Florida. 1–4 April 1993.

Stein, Arlene, and Ken Plummer. "`I Can't Even Think Straight': 'Queer' Theory and the Missing Sexual Revolution in Sociology." *Sociological Theory* 12 (1994): 178–87.

Vaid, Urvashi. *Virtual Equality: The Mainstreaming of Gay & Lesbian Liberation.* New York: Anchor, 1995.

Warner, Michael, ed. *Fear of a Queer Planet: Queer Politics and Social Theory.* Minneapolis: U of Minnesota P, 1993.

West, Cornel. *Race Matters.* Boston: Beacon, 1993.

Wilson, William Julius. *The Truly Disadvantaged: The Inner City, the Underclass, and Public Policy.* Chicago: U of Chicago P, 1987.

The Next Feminist Generation: Imagine My Surprise

⅏ Ellen Neuborne

When my editor called me into his office and told me to shut the door, I was braced to argue. I made a mental note to stand my ground.

It was behind the closed door of his office that I realized I'd been programmed by the sexists.

We argued about the handling of one of my stories. He told me not to criticize him. I continued to disagree. That's when it happened.

He stood up, walked to where I was sitting. He completely filled my field of vision. He said, "Lower your voice when you speak to me."

And I did.

I still can't believe it.

This was not supposed to happen to me. I am the child of professional feminists. My father is a civil rights lawyer. My mother heads the NOW Legal Defense and Education Fund. She sues sexists for a living. I was raised on a pure, unadulterated feminist ethic.

That didn't help.

Looking back on the moment, I should have said, "Step back out of my face and we'll continue this discussion like humans."

I didn't.

I said, "Sorry."

Sorry!

I had no idea twenty-some years of feminist upbringing would fail me at that moment. Understand, it is not his actions I am criticizing; it is mine. He was a bully. But the response was my own. A man confronted me. My sexist programming kicked in. I backed off. I said, "Sorry."

I don't understand where the programming began. I had been taught that girls could do anything boys could do. Equality of the sexes was an unimpeachable truth. Before that day in the editor's office, if you'd asked me how I might handle such a confrontation, I never would have said, "I'd apologize."

I'm a good feminist. I would never apologize for having a different opinion.

But I did.

Programming. It is the subtle work of an unequal world that even the best of feminist parenting couldn't overcome. It is the force that sneaks up on us even as we think that we are getting ahead with the best of the guys. I would never have believed in its existence. But having heard it, amazingly, escape from my own mouth, I am starting to recognize its pattern.

When you are told you are causing trouble, and you regret having raised conflict, that's your programming.

When you keep silent, though you know the answer—programming.

When you do not take credit for your success, or you suggest that your part in it was really minimal—programming.

When a man tells you to lower your voice, and you do, and you apologize—programming.

The message of this programming is unrelentingly clear: Keep quiet.

I am a daughter of the movement. How did I fall for this?

I thought the battle had been won. I thought that sexism was a remote experience, like the Depression. Gloria had taken care of all that in the seventies.

Imagine my surprise.

And while I was blissfully unaware, the perpetrators were getting smarter.

What my mother taught me to look for—pats on the butt, honey, sweetie, cupcake, make me some coffee—are not the methods of choice for today's sexists. Those were just the fringes of what they were really up to. Sadly, enough of them have figured out how to mouth the words of equality while still behaving like pigs. They're harder to spot.

At my first newspaper job in Vermont, I covered my city's effort to collect food and money to help a southern town ravaged by a hurricane. I covered the story from the early fund-raising efforts right up to the day before I was to ride with the aid caravan down South. At that point I was taken off the story and it was reassigned to a male reporter. (It wasn't even his beat; he covered education.) It would be too long a drive for me, I was told. I wouldn't get enough sleep to do the story.

He may as well have said "beauty rest." But I didn't get it. At least not right away. He seemed, in voice and manner, to be concerned about me. It worked. A man got the big story. And I got to stay home. It was a classic example of a woman being kept out of a plum project "for her own good," yet while in the newsroom, hearing this explanation about sleep and long drives, I sat there nodding.

Do you think you would do better? Do you think you would recognize sexism at work immediately?

Are you sure?

Programming is a powerful thing. It makes you lazy. It makes you vulnerable. And until you can recognize that it's there, it works for the opposition. It makes you lower your voice.

It is a dangerous thing to assume that just because we were raised in a feminist era, we are safe. We are not. They are still after us.

And it is equally dangerous for our mothers to assume that because we are children of the movement, we are equipped to stand our ground. In many cases, we are unarmed.

The old battle strategies aren't enough, largely because the opposition is using new weaponry. The man in my office who made a nuisance of himself by asking me out repeatedly did so through the computer messaging system. Discreet. Subtle. No one to see him being a pig. Following me around would have been obvious. This way, he looked perfectly normal, and I constantly had to delete his overtures from my e-mail files. Mom couldn't have warned me about e-mail.

Then there is the danger from other women. Those at the top who don't mentor other women because if they made it on their own, so should subsequent generations. Women who say there is just one "woman's slot" at the top power level, and to get there you must kill off your female competition. Women who maintain a conspiracy of silence, refusing to speak up when they witness or even experience sexism, for fear of reprisals. These are dangers from within our ranks. When I went to work, I assumed other women were my allies.

Again, imagine my surprise.

I once warned a newly hired secretary that her boss had a history of discrimination against young women. She seemed intensely interested in the conversation at the time. Apparently as soon as I walked away, she repeated the entire conversation to her boss. My heart was in the right place. But my brain was not. Because, as I learned that day, sisterhood does not pay the bills. For younger women who think they do not need the feminist movement to get ahead, sisterhood is the first sentiment to fall by the wayside. In a world that looks safe, where men say all the right things and office policies have all the right words, who needs sisterhood?

We do. More than we ever have. Because they are smooth, because they are our bosses and control our careers, because they are hoping we will kill each other off so they won't have to bother. Because of all the subtle sexism that you hardly notice until it has already hit you. That is why you need the movement.

On days when you think the battle is over, the cause has been won, look around you to see what women today still face. The examples are out there.

On college campuses, there is a new game called rodeo. A man takes a woman back to his room, initiates sexual intercourse, and then a group of his friends barges in. The object of this game is for the man to keep his date pinned as long as possible.

Men are still afraid of smart women. When Ruth Bader Ginsburg was nominated to the Supreme Court, the *New York Times* described her as "a woman who handled her intelligence gracefully." The message: If you're smarter than the men around you, be sure to keep your voice down. Wouldn't want to be considered ungraceful.

A friend from high school calls to tell me he's getting married. He's found the perfect girl. She's bright, she's funny and she's willing to take his last name. That makes them less likely to get divorced, he maintains. "She's showing me she's not holding out."

In offices, women with babies are easy targets. I've seen the pattern played out over and over. One woman I know put in ten years with the company, but once she returned from maternity leave, she was marked. Every attempt to leave on time to pick up her baby at day care was chalked up as a "productivity problem." Every request to work part-time was deemed troublemaking. I sat just a few desks away. I witnessed her arguments. I heard the editors gossip when she was absent. One Monday we came into work and her desk had been cleaned out.

Another woman closer to my age also wanted to work part-time after the birth of her son. She was told that was unacceptable. She quit. There was no announcement. No good-bye party. No card for everyone in the office to sign. The week she disappeared from the office, we had a party for a man who was leaving to take a new job. We also were asked to contribute to a gift fund for another man who had already quit for a job in the Clinton administration.

But for the women with babies who were disappeared, nothing happened. And when I talked about the fact that women with babies tended to vanish, I was hauled into my boss' office for a reeducation session. He spent twenty minutes telling me what a great feminist he was and that if I ever thought differently, I should leave the company. No question about the message there: Shut up.

I used to believe that my feminist politics would make me strong. I thought strong thoughts. I held strong beliefs. I thought that would protect me. But all it did was make me aware of how badly I slipped when I lowered my voice and apologized for having a divergent opinion. For all my right thinking, I did not fight back. But I have learned something. I've learned it takes practice to be a strong feminist. It's not an instinct you can draw on at will—no matter how equality-minded your upbringing. It needs exercise. You have to think to know your own mind. You have to battle to work in today's workplace. It was nice to grow up thinking this was an equal world. But it's not.

I have learned to listen for the sound of my programming. I listen carefully for the *Sorrys*, the *You're rights*. Are they deserved? Or did I offer them up without thinking, as though I had been programmed? Have you? Are you sure?

I have changed my ways. I am louder and quicker to point out sexism when I see it. And it's amazing what you can see when you are not hiding behind the warm, fuzzy glow of past feminist victories. It does not make me popular in the office. It does not even make me popular with women. Plenty of my female colleagues would prefer I quit rocking the boat. One

read a draft of this essay and suggested I change the phrase "fight back" to "stand my ground" in order to "send a better message."

But after falling for the smooth talk and after hearing programmed acquiescence spew from my mouth, I know what message I am trying to send: Raise your voice. And I am sending it as much to myself as to anyone else.

I've changed what I want from the women's movement. I used to think it was for political theory, for bigger goals that didn't include my daily life. When I was growing up, the rhetoric we heard involved the theory of equality: Were men and women really equal? Were there biological differences that made men superior? Could women overcome their stigma as "the weaker sex"? Was a woman's place really in the home?

These were ideas. Important, ground-breaking, mind-changing debates. But the feminism I was raised on was very cerebral. It forced a world full of people to change the way they think about women. I want more than their minds. I want to see them do it.

The theory of equality has been well fought for by our mothers. Now let's talk about how to talk, how to work, how to fight sexism here on the ground, in our lives. All the offices I have worked in have lovely, right-thinking policy statements. But the theory doesn't necessarily translate into action. I'm ready to take up that part of the battle.

I know that sitting on the sidelines will not get me what I want from my movement. And it is mine. Younger feminists have long felt we needed to be invited to our mothers' party. But don't be fooled into thinking that feminism is old-fashioned. The movement is ours and we need it.

I am one of the oldest of my generation, so lovingly dubbed "X" by a disdainful media. To my peers, and to the women who follow after me, I warn you that your programming is intact. Your politics may be staunchly feminist, but they will not protect you if you are passive.

Listen for the attacks. They are quiet. They are subtle.

And listen for the jerk who will tell you to lower your voice. Tell him to get used to the noise. The next generation is coming.

The Women's Movement:
Persistence through Transformation

Verta Taylor, Nancy Whittier, and Cynthia Fabrizio Pelak

INTRODUCTION

Popular authors and scholars alike described the 1980s and 1990s as a "postfeminist" era of political apathy during which former feminists traded their political ideals for career mobility and cell phones and younger women single-mindedly pursued career goals and viewed feminism as an anachronism. Yet this was not the first time that commentators proclaimed the death of feminism. In the 1920s, after women won the right to vote, images of young women abandoning the struggle for rights in favor of jobs and good times filled the media. Then as now, feminism changed form, but neither the movement nor the injustices that produced it have vanished. Of all the manifestations of social activism in the 1960s, feminism is one of the few that persist. We explore here continuity and change in the American women's movement from the 1960s to the present. First we consider the structural preconditions of women's movements in the Western world and the international context for activism. Then we focus on the changing ideologies, structures, political contexts, and strategies of the women's movement in the United States. We conclude our discussion by considering historically specific antifeminist countermovements that have emerged in response to challenges of the women's movement.

STRUCTURAL PRECONDITIONS OF WESTERN FEMINIST MOVEMENTS

From a social movement perspective, women have always had sufficient grievances to create the context for feminist activity. Indeed, instances of collective action on the part of women abound in history, especially if one includes female reform societies, women's church groups, alternative religious societies, and women's clubs. However, collective activity on the part of women directed specifically toward improving their own status has flourished primarily in periods of generalized social upheaval, when sensitivity to moral injustice, discrimination, and social inequality has been widespread in the society as a whole (Chafe 1977; Staggenborg 1998a). The first wave of feminism in the United States grew out of the abolitionist struggle of the 1830s and peaked during an era of social reform in the 1890s, and the contemporary movement emerged out of the general social discontent of the 1960s. Although the women's movement did not die between these periods of heightened activism, it declined sharply in the 1930s, 1940s, and 1950s after the passage of the Nineteenth Amendment to the Constitution guaranteeing women the right to vote as a response to the changing social, political, and economic context (Rupp and Taylor 1987). During this period, women who had played important roles in obtaining women's suffrage managed to keep the flames of feminism alive by launching a campaign to pass an Equal Rights Amendment (ERA) to the Constitution.

Despite national differences in feminist movements, scholars identify certain basic structural conditions that have contributed to the emergence of feminist protest in most parts of the western world (Oppenheimer 1973; Huber and Spitze 1983; Chafetz and Dworkin 1986). Broad societal changes in the patterns of women's participation in the paid labor force, increases in women's formal educational attainment, and shifts in women's fertility rates and reproductive roles disrupt traditional social arrangements and set the stage for women's movements. As industrialization and urbanization bring greater education for women, expanding public roles create role and status conflicts for middle-class women, who then develop the discontent and gender consciousness necessary for political action (Chafetz and Dworkin 1986). Specifically, when women, especially married middle-class women, enter the paid labor force, their gender

515

consciousness increases because they are more likely to use men as a reference group when assessing their access to societal rewards. Similarly, women often experience strains and discrepancies in their lives as their gender consciousness is raised through formal education (Klein 1984).

Other important structural factors that serve as preconditions for feminist mobilization include changes in family relationships, marriage, fertility, and sexual mores (Ferree and Hess 1994). Declines in women's childbearing and increases in their age at first marriage can improve women's educational attainment and participation in the paid labor force—which, in turn, raise their gender consciousness (Klein 1984). Moreover, changes in the traditional relationships between women and men in marriage and in sexual mores, such as the shift from authoritarian marriages to romantic or companionate marriages at the turn of the last century in the United States and the "sexual revolution" of the 1960s, can politicize gender relations and create the motivations for feminist mobilization.

Certainly, the specific configuration of structural preconditions underlying the genesis of feminist collective mobilizations varies with historical and geographic context. Not only the political context but also the demographic, economic, and cultural processes that have given rise to feminist movements in the United States are different from those in Third World countries. Such political and cultural variations are reflected in national and regional variations in the way women define their collective interests, in the distinct ideologies, organizational forms, and strategies adopted by feminist movements in different times and places, and ultimately in the possibilities for feminist mobilization. Nonetheless, scholars recognize some important commonalties among women's movements around the world.

FEMINIST MOVEMENTS IN AN INTERNATIONAL CONTEXT

We focus here on the women's movement in the United States. It is nonetheless important to acknowledge the multiple forms of feminist resistance around the world and to underscore the importance of the historical and geographic specificity of feminist activism. Throughout modern history, women in all regions of the world have organized collectively against the injustice and oppression in their lives and com-

munities (Basu 1995). Such mobilizations in diverse political, cultural, and historical contexts have varied widely in their organizations, strategies, ideologies, and structures. Gender oppression for some Third World feminists cannot be divorced from issues and histories of colonization, immigration, racism, or imperialism, and thus feminist activism in some Third World contexts may be organized around a constellation of oppressions rather than specifically around gender oppression (Jayawardena 1986; Mohanty, Russo, and Torres 1991).

In some instances, ideological, organizational, and strategic differences in women's movements lie in fundamental differences in the political culture of a region (Ray 1999). In Calcutta, India, for example, which is dominated by the Communist Party and a strong and traditional left culture, the women's movement functions more as a political party and uses the party structure to address issues such as employment, poverty, and literacy that do not directly threaten the gender status quo. The women's movement in Bombay, on the other hand, which exists in a more open, contested political field and culture, is more explicitly feminist and uses more autonomous forms of organizing to spotlight issues that are more threatening to men, such as violence against women, religious fundamentalism, and women's restricted roles in the family. Although national and regional differences exist, there are important commonalties that link women's movements over time and place (Chafetz and Dworkin 1986; Katzenstein and Mueller 1987; Giele 1995; Miles 1996).

Women's movements, particularly those in industrialized countries, generally have emerged in two waves of heightened activism. In their cross-cultural, historical analysis of forty-eight countries, Chafetz and Dworkin (1986) found that the mass-scale, independent women's movements of the first wave, such as those in European societies and the United States, occurred in the closing decades of the nineteenth century and the first decades of the twentieth century, while the second-wave women's movements have emerged since the 1960s. Major goals of the first wave of activism included women's suffrage, educational opportunities for women, basic legal reforms, inheritance and property rights, and employment opportunities for women. Women's demands during this first wave often were framed around middle-class women's roles as wives and mothers and reinforced gender difference by valorizing women's special virtues and moral superiority over men. Smaller-scale movements during the first wave were more likely to challenge basic role differentiation between women and men and to resist doctrines and images of femininity in the culture.

To the extent that the large-scale changes brought on by urbanization and industrialization in Western countries created dramatic changes in the workplace, the family, and the lives of women and men, it is not surprising there was considerable ideological debate and diversity among first-wave feminists. In the United States, for example, some factions of the nineteenth-century women's movement were grounded in essentialist views of sex differences and were more interested in nonfeminist social reforms, for which the vote was only a prerequisite (Buechler 1990; Giele 1995). Other branches of the nineteenth-century women's movement rejected essentialist notions of gender and, by pursuing more radical changes such as sexual freedom and the expansion of women's roles in the workplace and politics, sought to transform the gender order in more fundamental ways (Cott 1987).

Women's movements of the second wave in western countries, blossoming since the 1960s, have mobilized around an even broader range of issues, such as reproductive rights, sexual and economic exploitation, and violence against women (Chafetz and Dworkin 1986; Ferree and Hess 1994). Modern feminist movements often have developed around women's commonalities, but differences of race, class, ethnicity, and nationality are also expressed in the collective identities deployed by feminists (Moraga and Anzaldúa 1981; Mohanty, Russo, and Torres 1991). African-American women have organized around interlocking structures of oppression that affect women differently depending on their ethnicity, class, or sexual identities (Collins 1990). For example, African-American and Latina women from low-income urban neighborhoods have struggled for quality education, affordable and safe housing, and expanded child care services for their families and communities (Naples 1992).

Since the 1970s, there has been a phenomenal growth in regional, interregional, and international networking among feminist groups (Miles 1996), although the origins of international women's organizations date back to the closing decades of the nineteenth century (Rupp 1997). The United Nations' International Women's Year (1975) and Decade for Women (1975–1985) helped foster global feminist dialogues and stimulated independent, locally based feminist activities in all parts of the world. Since the beginning of the UN Decade for Women, there have been four official UN world conferences of government representatives devoted to women's issues, with four unofficial forums of women's groups running alongside each of these conferences. Since the first forum in Mexico City in 1975, participation by women in the unofficial forums has increased sharply, challenging the notion that feminism has died in recent years.

Although these conferences and forums have been sites of considerable debate and conflict over the meaning of "women's issues" and the definition of feminism, the events have sparked multiple forms and foci of feminist resistance and a global awareness of women's oppression that reaches beyond women's groups. Feminists are forging global relations around a diverse set of issues including "health, housing, education, law reform, population, human rights, reproductive and genetic engineering, female sexual slavery and trafficking in women, violence against women, spirituality, peace and militarism, external debt, fundamentalism, environment, development, media, alternative technology, film, art and literature, publishing, and women's studies" (Miles 1996:142). The trajectory of the US women's movement can be fully understood only in this global context.

THE CONTEMPORARY FEMINIST MOVEMENT: CONTINUITY AND CHANGE

Most scholarly analyses of the women's movement of the late 1960s—what scholars call the "second-wave feminist movement"—divide it into two wings, with origins in the grievances and preexisting organizations of two groups of women: older professional women, who formed bureaucratic organizations with a liberal ideology and adopted legal reform strategies, and younger women from the civil rights and New Left movements, who formed small collective organizations with radical ideology and employed "personal as political" strategies such as consciousness-raising groups (Freeman 1975; Cassell 1977; Ferree and Hess 1994; Buechler 1990). During a period of resurgence dating to the founding of the National Organization for Women (NOW) in 1966, the movement established itself, forming organizations and ideologies and moving into the public eye (Buechler 1990; Ryan 1992). By 1971, major segments of feminism had crystallized: liberal feminism, embodied in the formation of groups such as NOW, the Women's Equity Action League (WEAL) in 1967, and the National Women's Political Caucus (NWPC) in 1971; radical feminism and socialist feminism, emerging from consciousness-raising groups, theory groups, and small action groups such as Redstockings and the Feminists in 1969; and lesbian feminism, organized in such groups as Radicalesbians in 1970 and the Furies (initially called "Those Women") in 1971 (Echols 1989).

The year 1972 was pivotal both for the movement's success and for its opposition. The Equal Rights Amendment (ERA) passed the Congress, and Phyllis Schlafly launched her first antifeminist attacks. This can be considered the movement's heyday because the feminist revolution seemed to be on the move. The campaign to ratify the ERA in the states brought mass mobilization, fostering female solidarity and enlisting women into feminism; women's studies programs proliferated on college campuses; the number and variety of feminist organizations increased phenomenally; and the movement entered the political arena and encountered active opposition (Matthews and DeHart 1990; Ryan 1992). Not only did feminism flourish in the ERA ratification campaign but it spread into the political mainstream, while radical and lesbian feminist organizing heightened outside it.

Following the ERA's defeat in 1982, the women's movement entered a period of the doldrums, in which it developed new structural forms to survive a declining membership and an increasingly nonreceptive environment. The 1980s saw a turning away from the values of equality, human rights, and social justice and even a deliberate backlash against the feminist momentum of the 1970s. Rights won by feminists in the 1960s and 1970s—from affirmative action to legal abortion—were under siege throughout the 1980s and 1990s. Yet the so-called postfeminist era of the 1980s and 1990s no more marks the death of the women's movement than did the earlier premature announcements of feminism's demise. In fact, although the women's movement of the turn of the twenty-first century takes a different form than it did twenty years earlier, it remains vital and influential.

Feminist Ideology

While ideas do not necessarily cause social movements, ideology is a central component in the life of any social movement (Morris and Mueller 1992). The modern feminist movement, like most social movements, is not ideologically monolithic. Feminist ideology encompasses numerous ideological strands that differ in the scope of change sought, the extent to which gender inequality is linked to other systems of domination—especially class, race, ethnicity, and sexuality—and the significance attributed to gender differences. We focus here on the evolution of the dominant ideologies that have motivated participants in the two major branches of the feminist movement from its inception, liberal feminism and radical feminism.

The first wave of the women's movement in the nineteenth century was, by and large, a liberal feminist reform movement. It sought equality within the existing social structure and, indeed, in many ways functioned like other reform movements to reaffirm existing values within the society (Ferree and Hess 1994). Nineteenth-century feminists believed that if they obtained the right to an education, the right to own property, the right to vote, employment rights—in other words, equal civil rights under the law—they would attain equality with men. Scholars have labeled this thinking "individualist" or "equity" feminism, linking the goal of equal rights to gender assumptions about women's basic sameness with men (Offen 1988; Black 1989).

The basic ideas identified with contemporary liberal or "mainstream" feminism have changed little since their formulation in the nineteenth century, when they seemed progressive, even radical (Eisenstein 1981). Contemporary liberal feminist ideology holds that women lack power simply because we are not, as women, allowed equal opportunity to compete and succeed in the male-dominated economic and political arenas but, instead, are relegated to the subordinate world of home, domestic labor, motherhood, and family. The major strategy for change is to gain legal and economic equalities and to obtain access to elite positions in the workplace and in politics. Thus, liberal feminists tend to place as much emphasis on changing individual women as they do on changing society. For instance, teaching women managerial skills or instructing rape victims in "survival" strategies strikes a blow at social definitions that channel women into traditionally feminine occupations or passive behaviors that make them easy targets of aggression from men.

Liberal feminists ironically provided ideological support through the 1970s and 1980s for the massive transformation in work and family life that was occurring as the United States underwent the transition to a postindustrial order (Mitchell 1986; Stacey 1987). Some writers even contend that by urging women to enter the workplace and adopt a male orientation, the equal opportunity approach to feminism unwittingly contributed to a host of problems that further disadvantaged women (especially working-class women and women of color), including the rise in divorce rates, the "feminization" of working-class occupations, and the devaluation of motherhood and traditionally female characteristics (Gordon 1991).

Radical feminist ideology dates to Simone de Beauvoir's early 1950s theory of "sex class," which was developed further in the late 1960s among small groups of radical women who fought the subordination of women's liberation within the New Left (Beauvoir 1952; Firestone 1970; Millett 1971; Atkinson 1974; Rubin 1975; Rich 1976, 1980; Griffin 1978; Daly 1978; Eisenstein 1981; Hartmann 1981; Frye 1983; Hartsock 1983; MacKinnon 1983). The radical approach recognizes women's identity and subordination as a "sex class," emphasizes women's fundamental difference from men, views gender as the primary contradiction and foundation for the unequal distribution of a society's rewards and privileges, and recasts relations between women and men in political terms (Echols 1989). Defining women as a "sex class" means no longer treating patriarchy in individual terms but acknowledging the social and structural nature of women's subordination. Radical feminists hold that in all societies, institutions and social patterns are structured to maintain and perpetuate gender inequality and female disadvantage permeates virtually all aspects of sociocultural and personal life. Further, through the gender division of labor, social institutions are linked so that male superiority depends upon female subordination (Hartmann 1981). In the United States, as in most industrialized societies, power, prestige, and wealth accrue to those who control the distribution of resources outside the home, in the economic and political spheres. The sexual division of labor that assigns child care and domestic responsibilities to women not only ensures gender inequality in the family system but perpetuates male advantage in political and economic institutions as well.

To unravel the complex structure on which gender inequality rests requires, from a radical feminist perspective, a fundamental transformation of all institutions in society. To meet this challenge, radical feminists formulated influential critiques of the family,

marriage, love, motherhood, heterosexuality, sexual violence, capitalism, reproductive policies, the media, science, language and culture, the beauty industry, sports, politics, the law, technology, and more. Radical feminism's ultimate vision is revolutionary in scope: a fundamentally new social order that eliminates the sex-class system and replaces it with new ways—based on women's difference—of defining and structuring experience. Central to the development of radical feminist ideology was the strategy of forming small groups for the purpose of "consciousness-raising." Pioneered initially among New Left women, consciousness-raising can be understood as a kind of conversion in which women come to view experiences previously thought of as personal and individual, such as sexual exploitation or employment discrimination, as social problems that are the result of gender inequality.

By the late 1970s, the distinction between liberal and radical feminism was becoming less clear (Carden 1978; Whittier 1995). Ideological shifts took place at both the individual and organizational levels. Participation in liberal feminist reform and service organizations working on such issues as rape, battering, abortion, legal and employment discrimination, and women's health problems raised women's consciousness, increased their feminist activism, and contributed to their radicalization as they came to see connections between these issues and the larger system of gender inequality (Schlesinger and Bart 1983; Whittier 1995). Women were also radicalized by working through their own personal experiences of sexual harassment, divorce, rape, abortion, and incest (Huber 1973; Klein 1984).

Radicalization has occurred at the group level as well. By the end of the 1970s, liberal feminist organizations such as NOW, the Women's Legal Defense Fund, and the National Abortion Rights Action League (NARAL) which had been pursuing equality within the law, began to adopt strategies and goals consistent with a more radical stance. NOW included in its 1979 objectives not only such legal strategies as the ERA and reproductive choice, but broader issues such as the threat of nuclear energy to the survival of the species, lesbian and gay rights, homemakers' rights, the exploitation of women in the home, and sex segregation in the workplace (Eisenstein 1981). Even the ERA, which sought equality for women within the existing legal and economic structure, was based on the fact that women are discriminated against as a "sex class" (Mansbridge 1986).

Beginning in the mid-1980s, with the defeat of the unifying issue of the ERA and the growing diversification of the movement, feminist ideology de-emphasized the question of women's similarity to or difference from men in favor of "deconstructing" the term *woman*. Women of color, Jewish women, lesbians, and working-class women challenged radical feminists' idea of a "sex class" that implied a distinctive and essential female condition. Since women are distributed throughout all social classes, racial and ethnic groupings, sexual communities, cultures, and religions, disadvantage for women varies and is multidimensional (Spelman 1988). The recognition that the circumstances of women's oppression differ has given way to a new feminist paradigm that views race, class, gender, ethnicity, and sexuality as interlocking systems of oppression, forming what Patricia Hill Collins (1990) refers to as a "matrix of domination."

Some scholars have charged that focusing on women's differences from one another has resulted in a retreat to "identity politics" and the demise of the women's movement. Alice Echols (1989) links disputes over difference and a focus on identity to a concentration on building an alternative women's culture rather than confronting and changing social institutions. In a similar vein, Barbara Ryan (1989) argues that internal debates over the correctness of competing feminist theories and the political implications of personal choices—what she terms "ideological purity"—tore the women's movement apart. But other scholars see the sometimes vehement arguments over women's differences from one another as a sign of life (Taylor and Rupp 1993). Feminists organizing around diverse identities sometimes seek out new arenas of challenge that differ from traditional definitions of political activism and thus extend the reach of feminism. Self-help movements focused on the self and the body, for example—drug and alcohol abuse, incest, postpartum depression, battering, breast cancer—offer a complex challenge to traditional notions of femininity, motherhood, and sexuality and carry the potential to mobilize new constituencies (Taylor and Van Willigen 1996; Gagné 1998).

In any case, ideas alone are an incomplete explanation of either the direction or the consequences of a social movement (Marx and Wood, 1975; McCarthy and Zald 1977). Much depends on a movement's structures and strategies, as well as on the larger political context.

Feminist Organizational Structures

Social movements do not generally have a single central organization or unified direction. Rather, the structure of any general, broad-based social movement is more diffuse—composed of a number of relatively independent organizations that differ in ideology, structure, goals, and tactics. A social movement is characterized by decentralized leadership; it is loosely connected by multiple and overlapping memberships and by friendship networks that work toward common goals (Gerlach and Hine 1970). The organizational structure of the modern feminist movement has conformed to this model from its beginnings (Freeman 1975; Cassell 1977; Ferree and Martin 1995). While the movement as a whole is characterized by a decentralized structure, the various organizations that comprise it vary widely in structure. The diversity of feminist organizational forms reflects both ideological differences and the movement's diverse membership base (Freeman 1979).

There have been two main types of organizational structure in the modern feminist movement since its resurgence, reflecting the two sources of feminist organizing in the late 1960s: bureaucratically structured movement organizations with hierarchical leadership and democratic decision-making procedures, such as the National Organization for Women; and smaller collectively structured groups that formed a more diffuse social movement community held together by a feminist political culture. Collectively organized groups, at least in theory, strove to exemplify a better way of structuring society by constructing a distinctive women's culture that valorized egalitarianism, the expression of emotion, and the sharing of personal experience. It is important to recognize, however, that while the two strands of the women's movement emerged separately, they have not remained distinct and opposed to each other. Most women's movement organizations are mixed in form from the outset. The two structures have increasingly converged as bureaucratic organizations adopted some of the innovations of collectivism and feminist collectives became more formally structured (Staggenborg 1988, 1989; Martin 1990; Ryan 1992; Ferree and Martin 1995; Whittier 1995). In addition, many individual activists are involved in a variety of organizations with differing structures.

The bureaucratically structured and professionalized movement organizations initially adopted by liberal groups such as NOW were well suited to work within the similarly structured political arena and to members' previous experience in professional organizations. The structures that radical feminist groups initially adopted, on the other hand, built on their prior involvement in the New Left (Evans 1979). Collectivist organizations grew from radical feminists' attempts to structure relations among members, processes of decision making, and group leadership in a way that reflected or prefigured the values and goals of the movement (Rothschild-Whitt 1979; Breines 1982). Feminist collectivist organizations made decisions by consensus, rotated leadership and other tasks among members, and shared skills to avoid hierarchy and specialization. Such groups often failed to meet their ideals and did, in fact, spawn unacknowledged hierarchies (Freeman 1972/3). Nevertheless, the conscious effort to build a feminist collective structure has had a lasting impact on the women's movement and has led to the growth of a social movement community (Buechler 1990). That is, the movement consists of not only formal organizations but also more informally organized communities, made up of networks of people who share the movement's political goals and outlook and work toward common aims. The collectivist branch of the women's movement initially sparked the growth of a feminist social movement community in which alternative structures guided by a distinctively feminist women's culture flourished—including bookstores, theater groups, music collectives, poetry groups, art collectives, publishing and recording companies, spirituality groups, vacation resorts, self-help groups, and a variety of feminist-run businesses. This "women's culture," though it includes feminists of diverse political persuasions, has been largely maintained by lesbian feminists. It nurtures a feminist collective identity that is important to the survival of the women's movement as a whole (Taylor and Whittier 1992; Taylor and Rupp 1993).

Both bureaucratic organizations working within mainstream politics and the alternative feminist culture have expanded and converged since the movement's emergence in the 1960s. Organizations such as NOW and NARAL incorporated some of the innovations of collectivism, including consciousness-raising groups, modified consensus decision making, and the use of direct-action tactics and civil disobedience. A host of structural variations emerged, including formally structured groups that use consensus decision making, organizations with deliberately democratic structures, and groups that officially operate by majority-rule democracy but in practice make most decisions by consensus (Staggenborg 1988, 1989; Martin 1990; Ryan 1992; Taylor 1996). At the same time, feminist collectives shifted their focus from consciousness-raising and radical feminist critique to the development of feminist self-help and service organizations such as rape crisis centers, shelters for battered women, job training programs for displaced homemakers, and lesbian peer counseling groups. Moreover, many feminist collectives revised their structure to depend less on consensus decision making and to permit specialization of skills. The widespread acceptance of the feminist analysis of rape as an act of violence and power rather than a strictly sexual act further attested to the impact of the feminist antirape movement. Feminist antirape groups received financial support from government agencies and private foundations to provide rape-prevention and treatment services in public schools and universities (Matthews 1994). The distinction between "working outside the system" and "working within the system," so important in the late 1960s, no longer had the same significance.

In conjunction with the ideological shift from a universal to a differentiated category of "woman," the structures of the women's movement diversified as well. Although individual women of color and working-class women had participated in the founding of NOW and in the early protests against sexism in the civil rights movement, the women's movement attracted primarily white middle-class women. Not that women of color and working-class or poor women experienced no oppression as women or opposed feminist goals. A 1989 *New York Times*/CBS News poll revealed that, while only 64 percent of white women saw a need for a women's movement, 85 percent of African-American women and 76 percent of Hispanic women thought the women's movement was needed (Sapiro 1991). Yet the feminist movement remained predominantly white both because it continued to define its goals based on the concerns of white middle-class women and because many Black women and other women of color placed a priority on working in their own racial communities to advance their collective interests, despite the recognition of sexism within such organizations (Barnett 1993; Robnett 1996).

Independent organizing by women of color did grow during the 1970s, and when African-American activists in the women's movement formed the National Black Feminist Organization in 1973 it grew to a membership of 1,000 within its first year (Deckard 1983). In the 1980s and 1990s, independent feminist organizations and networks of women of color such as the National Black Women's Health Project and the National Coalition of 100 Black Women emerged. Women of color also formed active caucuses within predominantly white feminist organizations, such as the National Women's Studies Association, to work against racism within the women's movement (Leidner 1993). Likewise, Jewish women, who had historically played important roles within the women's movement, organized their own groups in the 1980s and spoke out against antisemitism within the movement (Beck 1980; Bulkin, Pratt, and Smith 1984). Some scholars have argued that the Black feminist movement generally does not mobilize through institutionalized formal organizations but operates through informal networks in local communities. Such informal networks include self-help groups, book clubs, "girlfriend" (women-only) parties and gatherings, and explicitly political groups. For example, in the 1990s, after the much publicized appeal of convicted rapist and professional boxer Mike Tyson one such informal network served as a springboard to launch an antirape education program geared to the Black community (White 1999).

Union women played a significant role in the formation of NOW in 1966 by providing office space and clerical services until NOW's endorsement of the ERA in 1967 forced the women of the United Auto Workers, an organization that at the time opposed the ERA, to withdraw such support. Women committed to both feminism and the union movement, like women of color, formed their own organization, the Coalition of Labor Union Women (CLUW) in 1974 (Balser 1987). CLUW claimed 16,000 members by 1982 and had made progress in its fight to win AFL–CIO support for feminist issues. Union women also participated in deeply gendered ways in labor movement activity such as the 1985 Wheeling-Pittsburgh Steel strike, both affirming and challenging gender (Fonow 1998). The basic class and race composition of the movement may have changed little throughout the 1970s and 1980s, but by the beginning of the twenty-first century "a movement that began as unconsciously class-bound and race-bound has now become consciously class-bound and race-bound" (Buechler 1990:158).

Collective action by the women's movement has created new institutions and moved into almost every major institution of our society. However, in direct proportion to the successes of the women's movement, a countermovement successfully reversed some feminist gains, stalled progress on others, and changed the face of the women's movement.

The Antifeminist Political Context

The early 1980s saw a rapid decrease in the number of feminist organizations and a transformation in the form and activities of the women's movement. In part, this was a response to the successes of the New Right: so powerful were antifeminist sentiments and forces that members of the Republican party were elected in 1980 on a platform developed explicitly to "put women back in their place." After forty years of faithful support of the ERA, the Republican party dropped it from its platform, called for a constitutional amendment to ban abortion, and aligned itself with the economic and social policies of the New Right. After the election of the conservative Reagan administration in 1980, federal funds and grants were rarely available to feminist service organizations, and because other social service organizations were also hard hit by budget cuts, competition increased for relatively scarce money from private foundations. As a result, many feminist programs such as rape crisis centers, shelters for battered women, abortion clinics, and job training programs were forced to close or limit their services.

The failure of the ERA in 1982 seemed to reflect the changed political climate and set the stage for other setbacks throughout the 1980s. Abortion rights, won in 1973 with the Supreme Court's decision in *Roe v. Wade*, were curtailed in 1989 by the Supreme Court's decision in *Webster v. Reproductive Services* permitting states to enact restrictions on abortion (Staggenborg 1991: 137–38). Following the Webster decision, state governments set increasingly tight restrictions on abortion, ranging from "informed consent" laws that required a waiting period before women could obtain abortion surgery, to parental consent laws for under-age women, to outright bans on abortion unless the woman's life was in danger. In 1991, the Supreme Court further limited abortion rights by ruling that federally funded family planning clinics could be barred from providing information on abortion. The antiabortion movement also escalated and hardened its tactics in the late 1980s and 1990s: it bombed abortion clinics, picketed doctors who performed abortions, and attempted to dissuade women entering clinics from having abortions (Staggenborg 1991; Simonds 1996).

Further, women's studies programs in colleges and universities, which had been established in the 1970s in response to feminist agitation, came under attack by conservatives in the late 1980s and early 1990s. A backlash against "multiculturalism" and "political correctness" in academia sought to restore the traditional academic focus on the "great thinkers" of Western European history and thus to maintain the primacy of white male perspectives and experiences. Joining the attack, feminists such as Camille Paglia, Katie Roiphe, and Elizabeth Fox-Genovese drew media attention by holding radical and lesbian feminists responsible for alienating mainstream women and men from the women's movement.

The women's movement suffered not only from such attacks but also from its apparent success. Overt opposition to the feminist movement had been muted in the mid- to late 1970s. Elites in politics, education, and industry gave the appearance of supporting feminist aims through affirmative action programs and the appointment of a few token women to high positions in their respective areas. Meanwhile, the popular image of feminism advanced by the mass media suggested that the women's movement had won its goals. Despite the real-life difficulties women encountered trying to balance paid employment and a "second shift" of housework and child care (Hochschild 1989), the image of the working woman became the feminine ideal. The public discourse implied that since women had already achieved equality with men, they no longer needed a protest movement. Women who continued to press for gender equality were described increasingly in negative terms, as lesbians, man-haters, and, in the words of right-wing talk show host Rush Limbaugh, "feminazis."

But the women's movement did not die. Rather, it went into abeyance in order to survive in a hostile political climate. Movements in abeyance are in a holding pattern, during which activists from an earlier period maintain the ideology and structural base of the movement but few new recruits join (Taylor 1989). A movement in abeyance is primarily oriented toward maintaining itself rather than confronting the established order directly. Focusing on building an alternative culture, for example, is a means of surviving when external resources are not available and the political structure is not amenable to challenge. The structure and strategies of the women's movement have changed, then, as mass mobilization has declined and opposition to feminism has swelled. Nevertheless, feminist resistance continues—just in different forms.

Multiple Strategies and the Challenge to Gender

Gender resistance, challenge, and change can occur at three levels: the individual level of consciousness and interactions, the social structural level, and the cultural level (Collins 1990). This conceptualization of feminist activism allows us to recognize that movements adopt many strategies and to acknowledge the important role of women's movements in the reconstruction of gender.

Resisting Gender Practices   At the level of consciousness and social interactions, individual women can and do resist norms and expectations of the dominant gender system (Thorne 1994, 1995). It is, however, social movements or collectives, rather than isolated individuals, who perform the critical role of refashioning the gender code and calling institutions to account for gender inequality (Huber 1976; Chafetz 1990; Connell 1987). One of the primary goals of the modern feminist movement has been to change the unequal power relations between women and men. A general strategy used by feminists to achieve this goal has been to resist and challenge sexist practices within a diverse set of social contexts, ranging from heterosexual marriage to the gender division of labor in rearing and nurturing children to the gendered workplace and male-dominated medical establishment.

The formation of consciousness-raising groups facilitated the process of resisting and challenging gender practices and politicizing everyday life. Because consciousness-raising enables women to view the "personal as political," for most women it is an identity-altering experience. Becoming a feminist can transform a woman's entire self-concept and way of life: her biography, appearance, beliefs, behavior, and relationships (Cassell 1977; Esterberg 1997). As women's consciousness changes through personalized political strategies, women individually and collectively defy traditionally feminine role expectations for women and, in so doing, reconstruct the meanings of women, femininity, and interpersonal relationships between women and men. For example, some breast cancer activists have chosen to resist societal conceptions of femininity that link women's sexuality to breast beauty by refusing to wear prostheses or displaying mastectomy scars following breast surgery.

Women active in the feminist movement of the 1960s and 1970s continued to shape their lives in the 1980s and 1990s around their feminist beliefs, even when they were not involved in organized feminist activity. They continued to choose leisure activities, significant relationships, dress, and presentation of self consistent with feminist ideology (Whittier 1995). Many held jobs in government, social service organizations, or women's studies departments and other academic programs that allowed them to incorporate their political goals into their work. Even the consciousness and lives of women who did not identify as feminist have been altered by the women's movement. In a study of gender and family life in the Silicon Valley of California, Judith Stacey (1987) found that in the 1980s some women incorporated portions of feminism into traditional family and work structures by combining a feminist emphasis on developing satisfying careers, sharing household work with husbands, and increasing men's emotional expressiveness with fundamentalist Christianity and its focus on the importance of the family. Such women critiqued men's absence from families and lack of emotional expression, reflecting both feminism and traditional religion. The effects of the women's movement stretch far beyond policies and practices that are explicitly labeled feminist.

Another example of women resisting gender practices at the interactional level is found among young African-American women involved in little sister fraternity programs on college campuses in the 1990s. Such women embrace a collective identity built on notions of sisterhood and womanly strength to challenge the sexist practices of fraternities (Stombler and Padavic 1997). Further, these women use the fraternity little sister program to satisfy their own agendas of community service and self-enhancement. Even within the most traditional male-dominated organizations, then, gender relations are not immutable and women are employing diverse strategies to resist gender inequality.

Challenging the Structure of Gender Inequality   The challenge to gender inequality and the dominant gender order is also waged at the social structural level. As we have seen, the liberal bureaucratic strand of the modern feminist movement has employed legal re-

form strategies and engaged in street protests to counter sex discrimination in the economic, education, political, and domestic spheres. The legislative campaigns for equal pay for work of comparable worth and for maternity leave policies in the workplace challenge institutions that essentialize differences between women and men and rank "masculine" values and attributes above those identified as "feminine" (Vogel 1993). The women's movement has created a feminist policy network of elected officials, lobbying organizations, social movement organizations, and individuals who have mobilized to address issues ranging from abortion rights, domestic violence, and pregnancy discrimination to day care, sexual harassment, and welfare rights (Ferree and Hess 1994; Staggenborg 1996; Gagné 1998).

As part of its legislative or legal strategies, the modern feminist movement has engaged in street protests such as picketing, mass demonstrations, and civil disobedience. Even within the conservative political climate of the 1980s, the feminist movement sparked some of the largest feminist demonstrations and actions in years. In April 1989, The National Organization for Women and abortion rights groups organized a national demonstration in Washington, DC, that drew between 300,000 and 600,000 women and men to protest restrictions on abortion. Additional national and local demonstrations followed. Prochoice activists organized electoral lobbying, defended abortion clinics, held conferences, and attempted to form coalitions across racial and ethnic lines and among women of different ages (Staggenborg 1991; Ryan 1992). The National Abortion Rights Action League experienced a growth in membership from 200,000 in 1989 to 400,000 in 1990 (Staggenborg 1991:138). NOW also continued to grow in the late 1980s and 1990s. After a decline in the early 1980s, it reached a membership of 250,000 in 1989 and maintained that membership level throughout the 1990s.

A wide variety of feminist organizations continued to pursue social change at state and local levels in the late 1990s (Ferree and Martin 1995). The Lesbian Avengers, a direct-action group founded in the 1990s with affiliates in several large cities, uses dramatic street theater to focus on issues of sexism and homophobia. For example, outside a police station in Delaware, Lesbian Avengers protested the police department's lack of action to catch a serial rapist by drawing chalk outlines of bodies on the sidewalk to represent women who had been raped during the past year. Veteran feminist organizations, such as NOW, continued to hold public protests in the late 1990s. For instance, in 1999, NOW chapters across the country staged pickets outside Wal-Mart retail stores to protest the corporation's refusal to sell the emergency contraception kit PREVEN to those who wish to prevent unintended pregnancies.

Beyond street politics, feminist activism in the 1980s and 1990s moved into diverse institutional settings. As an indication of the success and influence of feminist mobilization in earlier years, women found niches from which to challenge and transform institutional policies and structures, from pay equity to sexual harassment to occupational sex segregation (Blum 1991). Women in the military, for example, have formed pressure groups such as Women Military Aviators, who fought for the opening up of combat aviation positions for women. In the Catholic Church, radical religious orders have become protected spaces for women who challenge hierarchy within the institutional church (Katzenstein 1998). In major corporations, feminists have joined with gay activists to campaign successfully for domestic partnership benefits for lesbian and gay employees. Such unobtrusive mobilization within institutional boundaries refutes the notion of the death of feminism (Katzenstein 1997). Although the form and location of feminist protest have changed, this does not mean the women's movement has been deradicalized. The transformative potential of feminist activism within institutional settings may in some contexts be greater than that of pressure from outside.

Reconstructing the Culture of Gender   At the cultural level, the feminist social movement community has challenged cultural values, beliefs, and norms around gender and the gender order through building alternative social and cultural institutions for women outside mainstream institutions. The strategy of creating autonomous institutions is rooted in radical feminist ideology, which emphasizes that women need to have places and events away from patriarchal society where they can develop strength and pride as women. Since the early years of the women's movement, an extensive network of institutions has emerged within which a feminist culture flourishes (Taylor and Whittier 1992). Feminist communities contribute to the reconstruction of the culture of gender by challenging the devaluation of the feminine and undermining androcentric values and beliefs at the same time that they rearticulate alternative femininities and woman-centered values and beliefs (Taylor and Rupp 1993).

Into the new century, the feminist cultural community has continued to thrive with events such as an "annual multicultural multiracial conference on aging" for lesbians (*Off Our Backs* 1991: 12), feminist cruises, annual women's music festivals, and women's comedy festivals in different parts of the country (Staggenborg 1998b). Gatherings and conferences include groups such as Jewish lesbian daughters of holocaust survivors, women motorcyclists, fat dykes, pagans, Asian lesbians, practitioners of herbal medicine, and survivors of incest. Newsletters and publications exist for a multitude of groups, among them women recovering from addictions, women's music professionals and fans, lesbian separatists, disabled lesbians, lesbian mothers, feminists interested in sadomasochism, and feminists opposed to pornography.

The growth of the feminist community underscores the flowering of lesbian feminism in the late 1980s and 1990s (Esterberg 1997; Stein 1997). A wide variety of lesbian and lesbian feminist books and anthologies have been published on topics ranging from lesbian feminist ethics to separatism to sexuality to lesbian parenthood to commitment ceremonies for lesbian couples (see, for example, Hoagland 1988; Hoagland and Penelope 1988; Loulan 1990; Butler 1991), reflecting diverse perspectives that have been hotly debated in the pages of lesbian publications and at conferences and festivals. For example, a series of letters to the editor in a national lesbian newsletter during 1991 argued about the correct lesbian feminist response to lesbians serving in the armed forces in the Persian Gulf War: some readers held that the war was a manifestation of patriarchy and that lesbians in the military should be criticized; others argued that lesbian soldiers should be supported because they are lesbians in a homophobic institution, regardless of one's support of or opposition to the war; still others argued that the Gulf War was justified and that lesbian servicewomen should be celebrated for their patriotic service (*Lesbian Connection* 1991). Clearly, the task of building a community based on the identity "lesbian" has proven complex, if not impossible. Nevertheless, the institutional structure of the social movement community has continued to expand, and within the community feminists construct and reinforce a collective identity based on opposition to dominant conceptions of women and lesbians (Taylor and Whittier 1992).

Another example of resistance on the cultural level is the emergence of women's self-help groups, which sprang directly out of the early women's health movement and continue to model support groups on feminist consciousness-raising (Rapping 1996; Simonds 1996). Some feminist writers contend that women's self-help diverts the feminist agenda away from social and political change and directs women, instead, to change themselves (Kaminer 1992). Others argue that explicitly feminist self-help movements, such as strands of the postpartum depression and breast cancer movements, are contributing to the reconstruction of gender through the collective redefinition of womanhood and the cultural articulation of alternative femininities (Taylor 1996; Taylor and Van Willigen 1996; Klawiter 1999). These self-help movements are not depoliticized and purely individually focused; they perform a critical role of challenging institutional gender biases and refashioning the dominant gender code (Taylor 1996; Taylor 1999).

All of these diverse strategies, operating at different levels, challenge traditional societal definitions of femininity and masculinity and the dominant gender order. From the individual to the social structural to the cultural plane, we can see the continuous impact of the women's movement.

Movement Continuity and Change into the Twenty-first Century

Social movement scholars understand that social movements affect one another. The abolitionist movement in the mid-nineteenth century influenced the first wave of the women's movement in the United States, and the civil rights and New Left movements of the 1960s shaped the course of the second wave (Buechler 1990). In turn, the women's movement has had a substantial impact on other social movements. Meyer and Whittier (1994) argue that "the ideas, tactics, style, participants, and organizations of one movement often *spill over* its boundaries to affect other social movements" (277, emphasis in the original). The gay and lesbian movement, transgender, AIDS, recovery from addictions, New Age, and animal-rights movements have been profoundly influenced by feminist values and ideology, including the emphasis on collective structure and consensus, the notion of the personal as political, and the critique of patriarchy extended to the mistreatment of animals and ecological resources (Jasper and Poulsen 1995; Einwohner 1999).

The women's movement also trained a large number of feminist activists in the 1970s (particularly lesbians), who have participated in new social movements and integrated feminism into them (Cavin 1990; Whittier 1995). The gay and lesbian movement, for example, has expanded its health concerns to include breast cancer as well as AIDS and has used strategies of the feminist antirape movement to confront violence against gays and lesbians. In addition, feminists have renewed coalitions with the peace, environmental, socialist, anti-US intervention in Latin America, and antiapartheid movements, transforming these movements both by creating separate feminist organizations that address these issues and by moving into mixed-sex organizations (Whittier 1995). In a sense the women's movement has come full circle, rejoining the 1990s versions of the movements that composed the New Left in the 1960s, when many feminists split off to form a separate autonomous women's movement.

Although the women's movement has changed form and location, the level of mass mobilization and confrontation of the social structural system has clearly declined since the 1980s. Because feminism came to focus more on consciousness and culture and established roots in other social movements of the period, feminist protest is less visible than it was during the heyday of the women's movement. According to some studies (Schneider 1988; Dill unpublished), despite support for feminist goals, many young women do not identify themselves as feminists, apparently because the term is stigmatized. A feminist is seen as someone who deviates from gender norms by being unattractive, aggressive, hostile to men, unfeminine, opposed to marriage and motherhood, and lesbian. Despite the gain made by women in some areas, gender norms are still so rigid and deeply internalized that they successfully deter many women who support the feminist agenda from participating in the movement.

Yet some younger women have joined the women's movement despite the risks entailed in identifying with a stigmatized and unpopular cause. A new generation of women has been recruited to feminism primarily through women's studies courses and through the transmission of feminism from mothers to daughters. The institutionalized gains of the heyday of feminist activism in the 1970s are enabling the women's movement to survive and to disseminate its ideas to new recruits. What direction the self-proclaimed "third-wave" feminists (Kamen 1991; Walker 1992, 1995) will take is not at all clear, but the history of the women's movement suggests that a new constituency will revise feminist ideology, renovate existing structures, respond to a changing political climate, and further develop feminist strategies.

ANTIFEMINIST COUNTERMOVEMENTS

The emergence of organized opposition is one indication of the successes of feminist movements. In general, it is when social movements pose a serious threat to the status quo that countermovements appear (Chafetz and Dworkin 1987). Antifeminist resistance movements mobilized in response to first- and second-wave feminist movements in the United States when feminists began to gain political legitimacy and influence. For example, as the first wave of the women's movement was building support for suffrage in the late nineteenth century, an organized antisuffrage movement began to coalesce (Marshall 1997). Likewise, when the feminist movement of the 1970s was gaining political ground on the ratification of the Equal Rights Amendment, an anti-ERA movement blossomed (Marshall 1984).

Antifeminist countermovements, like feminist movements, are not monolithic. They vary over time and place by ideology, strategy, and organization (Marshall 1985; Buechler 1990; Blee 1991). Chafetz and Dworkin (1987) contend that antifeminist countermovements are composed of two constituencies: vested-interest groups, which are typically male-dominated and oppose feminist change movements on the basis of class interests; and voluntary grassroots associations made up of women who are reacting to the threat to their status as privileged traditional women.

Compared to the scholarship on movements, countermovements have been understudied and undertheorized (Meyer and Staggenborg 1996). Research on organized opposition to feminism by women is also limited (Klatch 1990; Marshall 1997). Women's participation in antifeminist countermovements challenges the radical feminist notion that women are a "sex class" with clearly defined gender interests (Luker 1984; Blee 1991). Scholars often characterize antifeminist women as victims of false consciousness or as women who are passively expressing their husbands' interests. Marshall (1997) argues that these are overly simplistic interpretations and that an appreciation for the ways in which antisuffragist leaders used their

wealth, social networks, and political power to build an oppositional identity in the antisuffrage movement suggests "a conceptual shift of the locus of conflict over suffrage from culture to politics" (p. 13). In this light, antifeminist women should be viewed as political actors who take up gendered class interests independently of their husbands (Marshall 1997).

The interaction between opposing movements is a prominent feature of contemporary US society. Any social movement analysis is incomplete without a consideration of the interdependence of movements and countermovements. For example, we cannot fully understand the tactics, strategies, organizational forms, and feminist identities characteristic of the feminist movement during the 1980s and 1990s without considering the effects of the antiabortion mobilization and the rise of the New Right.

The modern women's movement in the United States has been opposed by a variety of conservative antifeminist groups. In the early 1970s, the Stop ERA campaign initiated by Phyllis Schlafly fought to block passage of the ERA by state legislatures. Through the 1970s, the New Right grew larger and more influential, linking conservative issues like opposition to busing, abortion, gay rights, the ERA, and governmental regulation of business through affirmative action and health and safety programs (Klatch 1990). With the election of Ronald Reagan to the presidency in 1980, the New Right gained state support for its agenda.

The antifeminist movement in the late 1980s and 1990s spent considerable energy opposing abortion, and its successes in that area have been impressive in terms of judicial and legislative gains and disruptive demonstrations at abortion clinics (Staggenborg 1991; Simonds 1996). Over the years a number of aggressive splinter groups, such as Operation Rescue, developed out of the mainstream National Right to Life Committee, which originated within the Catholic Church. The murders of Drs. David Gunn in Pensacola, Florida, and Barnett Slepian in Buffalo, New York, are potent examples of the radical tactics advocated by some antiabortion rights groups.

The prevalence of antifeminist resistance throughout history highlights the significance of the family, sexuality, and reproduction for the maintenance of the dominant social order. The growth of antifeminism, however, does not imply that the women's movement has failed or run its course. On the contrary, it attests to feminism's successful challenge to the status quo.

CONCLUSION

The history of the women's movement and its present survival, despite the challenges it has confronted from within its own ranks and from a conservative political climate, suggest that because feminism is a response to the fundamental social cleavage of gender it will continue to exist (Taylor and Rupp 1993). As one generation of feminists fades from the scene with its ultimate goals unrealized, another takes up the challenge (Rossi 1982).

But each new generation of feminists does not simply carry on where the previous generation left off. Rather, it speaks for itself and defines its own objectives and strategies, often to the dismay and disapproval of feminists from earlier generations. A new generation of feminists may organize a "warm line" for women suffering postpartum depression (Taylor 1996), or construct a public clothesline of T-shirts rep-

resenting the victims of domestic violence to raise awareness of violence against women, or march together in a Take Back the Night event to empower survivors of sexual violence and reclaim the streets for women. They may put on "drag king" performances to challenge the restrictions placed on expressions of women's sexuality, or distribute condoms and dental dams to women for AIDS prevention, or organize "kiss-ins" with Queer Nation. While earlier generations of activists may not view such endeavors as feminist, as Myra Ferree and Beth Hess (1985:182) point out, "feminism is not simply a form of received wisdom" but something that evolves with each new cycle of feminist activism. Just as the women's movement of the twentieth century has endured and persisted through transformation, feminism of the twenty-first century will be characterized by continuity and change.

REFERENCES

Atkinson, T. G. (1974). *Amazon Odyssey*. New York: Links.

Balser, Diane. (1987). *Sisterhood and Solidarity: Feminism and Labor in Modern Times*. Boston: South End Press.

Barnett, Bernice McNair. (1993). Invisible southern black women leaders in the civil rights movement: The triple constraints of gender, race, and class. *Gender & Society, 7,* 162–182.

Basu, Amrita, ed. (1995). *The Challenge of Local Feminisms: Women's Movements in Global Perspective*. Boulder, CO: Westview Press.

Beauvoir, S. de. (1952). *The Second Sex*. New York: Bantam.

Beck, E. T. (1980). *Nice Jewish girls: A Lesbian Anthology*. Watertown, MA: Persephone.

Black, Naomi. (1989). *Social Feminism*. Ithaca, NY: Cornell University Press.

Blee, Kathleen M. (1991). *Women of the Klan: Racism and Gender in the 1920s*. Berkeley, CA: University of California Press.

Blum, Linda M. (1991). *Between Feminism and Labor: The Significance of the Comparable Worth Movement*. Berkeley, CA: University of California Press.

Breines, W. (1982). *Community and Organization in the New Left, 1962–68*. New York: Praeger.

Buechler, Steven M. (1990). *Women's Movements in the United States*. New Brunswick, NJ: Rutgers.

Bulkin, Elly, Minnie Bruce Pratt, & Barbara Smith. (1984). *Yours in Struggle: Three Feminist Perspectives on Anti-Semitism and Racism*. New York: Long Haul Press.

Butler, Becky. (1991). *Ceremonies of the Heart: Celebrating Lesbian Unions*. Seattle, WA: The Seal Press.

Carden, Maren. (1978). The proliferation of a social movement. In Louis Kriesberg, ed., *Research in Social Movements, Conflict, and Change,* vol. 1 (pp. 179–196). Greenwich, CT: JAI Press.

Cassell, J. (1977). *A Group Called Women: Sisterhood and Symbolism in the Feminist Movement*. New York: David McKay.

Cavin, Susan. (1990). The invisible army of women: Lesbian social protests, 1969–88. In Guida West & Rhoda Blumberg, eds. *Women and Social Protest* (pp. 321–332). New York: Oxford University Press.

Chafe, W. H. (1977). *Women and Equality: Changing Patterns in American Culture*. New York: Oxford University Press.

Chafetz, Janet. (1990). *Gender Equity: An Integrated Theory of Stability and Change*. Newbury Park, CA: Sage.

Chafetz, Janet, & Gary Dworkin. (1986). *Female Revolt*. Totowa, NJ: Rowman and Allenheld.

———. (1987). In the face of threat: Organized antifeminism in comparative perspective. *Gender & Society, 1,* 33–60.

Collins, Patricia Hill. (1990). *Black Feminist Thought*. New York: Routledge.

Connell, R. W. (1987). *Gender and Power*. Stanford, CA: Stanford University Press.

Cott, Nancy. (1987). *The Grounding of Modern Feminism*. New Haven, CT: Yale University Press.

Daly, Mary. (1978). *Gyn/ecology*, Boston: Beacon.

Deckard, Barbara Sinclair. (1983). *The Women's Movement*. New York: Harper and Row.

Dill, Kim. Unpublished. "Feminism in the nineties: The influence of collective identity and community on young feminist activists." Master's thesis, The Ohio State University, 1991.

Echols, Alice. (1989). *Daring to Be Bad: Radical Feminism in America 1967–1975*. Minneapolis: University of Minnesota Press.

Einwohner, Rachel L. (1999). Gender, class, and social movement outcomes: Identity and effectiveness in two animal rights campaigns. *Gender & Society*, 13, 56–76.

Eisenstein, Z. (1981). *The Radical Future of Liberal Feminism*. New York: Longman.

Esterberg, Kristin G. (1997). *Lesbian and Bisexual Identities: Constructing Communities, Constructing Selves*. Philadelphia: Temple University Press.

Evans, Sarah. (1979). *Personal Politics*. New York: Knopf.

Ferree, Myra Marx, & Beth B. Hess. [1985] (1994). *Controversy and Coalition: The New Feminist Movement*. Boston: Twayne.

Ferree, Myra Marx, & Patricia Yancey Martin. (1995). *Feminist Organizations: Harvest of the New Women's Movement*. Philadelphia: Temple University Press.

Firestone, S. (1970). *The Dialectic of Sex*. New York: William Morrow.

Fonow, Mary Margaret. (1998). Protest engendered: The participation of women steelworkers in the Wheeling-Pittsburgh steel strike of 1985. *Gender & Society*, 12, 710–728.

Freeman, Jo. (1972/3). The tyranny of structurelessness. *Berkeley Journal of Sociology*, 17, 151–164.

———. (1975). *The Politics of Women's Liberation*. New York: David McKay.

———. (1979). Resource mobilization and strategy: A model for analyzing social movement organization actions. In M. N. Zald & J. D. McCarthy, eds. *The Dynamics of Social Movements* (pp. 167–89). Cambridge, MA: Winthrop.

Frye, Marilyn. (1983). *The Politics of Reality: Essays in Feminist Theory*. Trumansburg, NY: Crossing Press.

Gagné, Patricia. (1998). *Battered Women's Justice: The Movement for Democracy and the Politics of Self-defense*. New York: Twayne Publishers.

Gerlach, L. P., & V. H. Hine. (1970). *People, Power, Change: Movements of Social Transformation*. Indianapolis: Bobbs-Merrill.

Giele, Janet Zollinger. (1995). *Two Paths to Women's Equality: Temperance, Suffrage, and the Origins of Modern Feminism*. New York: Twayne Publishers.

Gordon, Suzanne. (1991). *Prisoners of Men's Dreams*. New York: Little, Brown.

Griffin, S. (1978). *Women and Nature*. New York: Harper & Row.

Hartmann, Heidi. (1981). The family as the locus of gender, class, and political struggle: The example of housework. *Signs*, 6, 366–94.

Hartsock, Nancy. (1983). *Money, Sex, and Power: Toward a Feminist Historical Materialism*. New York: Longman.

Hoagland, Sarah Lucia. (1988). *Lesbian Ethics: Toward New Value*. Palo Alto, CA: Institute of Lesbian Studies.

Hoagland, Sarah Lucia, & Julia Penelope, eds. (1988). *For Lesbians Only*. London: Onlywomen Press.

Hochschild, Arlie. (1989). *The Second Shift*. New York: Avon.

Huber, Joan. (1973). From sugar and spice to professor. In A. S. Rossi & A. Calderwood, *Academic Women on the Move*. New York: Russell Sage Foundation.

———. (1976). Toward a sociotechnological theory of the women's movement. *Social Problems*, 23, 371–388.

Huber, Joan, & Glenna Spitze. (1983). *Sex Stratification: Children, Housework, and Jobs*. New York: Academic.

Jasper, James M., & Jane D. Poulsen. (1995). Recruiting strangers and friends: Moral shocks and social networks in animal rights and anti-nuclear protests. *Social Problems*, 42, 493–512.

Jayawardena, Kumari. (1986). *Feminism and Nationalism in the Third World*. London: Zed Books.

Kamen, Paula. (1991). *Feminist Fatale: Voices from the "Twenty-something" Generation Explore the Future of the Women's Movement*. New York: Donald I. Fine.

Kaminer, Wendy. (1992). *I'm Dysfunctional, You're Dysfunctional: The Recovery Movement and other Self-help Fashions*. Reading, MA: Addison-Wesley.

Katzenstein, Mary Fainsod. (1997). Stepsisters: Feminist movement activism in different institutional spaces. In David Meyer & Sidney Tarrow, eds. *A Movement Society? Contentious Politics for a New Century*. Boulder, CO: Rowland and Littlefield.

———. (1998). *Faithful and Fearless: Moving Feminist Protest inside the Church and Military*. Princeton, NJ: Princeton University Press.

Katzenstein, Mary Fainsod, & Carol McClurg Mueller. (1987). *The Women's Movements of the United States and Western Europe*. Philadelphia: Temple University Press.

Klatch, Rebecca. (1990). The two worlds of women of the new right. In Louise A. Tilly & Patricia Gurin, Eds. *Women, Politics and Change*. New York: Russell Sage Foundation.

Klawiter, Maren. (1999). Racing for the Cure, walking women, and toxic touring: Mapping cultures of action within the Bay Area terrain of breast cancer. *Social Problems*, 46, 104–126.

Klein, Ethel. (1984). *Gender Politics*. Cambridge, MA: Harvard University Press.

Leidner, Robin. (1993). Constituency, accountability, and deliberation: Reshaping democracy in the National Women's Studies Association. *NWSA Journal*, 5, 4–27.

Lesbian Connection (1991). Vols. 13 & 14. Lansing, MI: Ambitious Amazons.

Loulan, JoAnn. (1990). *The Lesbian Erotic Dance*. San Francisco: Spinsters Book Company.

Luker, Kristin. (1984). *Abortion and the Politics of Motherhood*. Berkeley: University of California Press.

MacKinnon, C. A. (1983). Feminism, Marxism, method, and the state: Toward feminist jurisprudence. *Signs*, 8, 635–68.

Mansbridge, Jane. (1986). *Why We Lost the ERA*. Chicago: University of Chicago Press.

Marshall, Susan E. (1984). Keep us on the pedestal: Women against feminism in twentieth-century America. In Jo Freeman, Ed., *Women: A Feminist Perspective* (pp. 568–581). Palo Alto: Mayfield.

———. (1985). Ladies against women: Mobilization dilemmas of antifeminist movements. *Social Problems, 32,* 348-362.

———. (1997). *Splintered Sisterhood: Gender and Class in the Campaign against Woman Suffrage.* Madison, WI: The University of Wisconsin Press.

Martin, Patricia Yancey. (1990). Rethinking feminist organizations. *Gender & Society, 4,* 182–206.

Marx, G. T., & J. L. Wood. (1975). Strands of theory and research in collective behavior. *Annual Review of Sociology,* 1, 363–428.

Matthews, Nancy. (1994). *Confronting Rape: The Feminist Anti-rape Movement and the State.* London: Routledge.

Matthews, Donald G., & Jane Sheffon DeHart. (1990). *Sex, Gender and the Politics of ERA: A State and the Nation.* New York: Oxford.

McCarthy, J. D., & M. N. Zald. (1977). Resource mobilization and social movements: A partial theory. *American Journal of Sociology,* 82, 1212–1239.

Meyer, David S., & Nancy Whittier. (1994). Social movement spillover. *Social Problems, 41,* 277–298.

Meyer, David S., & Suzanne Staggenborg. (1996). Movements, countermovements, and the structure of political opportunity. *American Journal of Sociology,* 101, 1628–1660.

Miles, Angela. (1996). *Integrative Feminisms: Building Global Visions, 1960s–1990s.* New York: Routledge.

Millett, K. (1971). *Sexual Politics.* New York: Avon.

Mitchell, Juliet. (1986). Reflections on twenty years of feminism. In Juliet Mitchell & Ann Oakley, eds. *What Is Feminism?* (pp. 34–48). Oxford: Basil Blackwell.

Mohanty, Chandra Talpade, Ann Russo, & Lordes Torres, eds. (1991). *Third World Women and the Politics of Feminism.* Bloomington, IN: Indiana University Press.

Moraga, Cherríe & Gloria Anzaldúa. (1981). *This Bridge Called My Back: Writings by Radical Women of Color.* Watertown, MA: Persephone.

Morris, Aldon D., & Carol McClurg Mueller, eds. (1992). *Frontiers in Social Movement Theory.* New Haven, CT: Yale University Press.

Naples, Nancy A. (1992). Activist mothering: Cross-generational continuity in the community work of women from low-income neighborhoods. *Gender & Society, 6,* 441–463.

Off Our Backs (1991). Passages 7—Beyond the barriers. Vol. 21 (6), 12.

Offen, Karen. (1988). Defining feminism: A comparative historical approach. *Signs,* 14, 119–157.

Oppenheimer, Valerie Kincade. (1973). Demographic influence on female employment and the status of women. In Joan Huber, Ed. *Changing Women in a Changing Society* (pp. 184–199). Chicago: University of Chicago Press.

Rapping, Elayne. (1996). *The Culture of Recovery: Making Sense of the Recovery Movement in Women's Lives.* Boston: Beacon Press.

Ray, Raka. (1999). *Fields of Protest: Women's Movements in India.* Minneapolis: University of Minnesota Press.

Rich, Adrienne. (1976). *Of Woman Born.* New York: Norton.

———. (1980). Compulsory heterosexuality and lesbian existence. *Signs,* 5, 631–660.

Robnett, Belinda. (1996). African-American women in the civil rights movement, 1954–1965: Gender, leadership, and micromobilization. *American Journal of Sociology,* 101, 1661–1693.

Rossi, Alice S. (1982). *Feminist in Politics: A Panel Analysis of the First National Women's Conference.* New York: Academic Press.

Rothschild-Whitt, Joyce. (1979). The collectivist organization: An alternative to rational-bureaucratic models. *American Sociological Review,* 44, 509–527.

Rubin, G. (1975). "Traffic in women: Notes on the 'political economy' of sex." In *Toward an Anthropology of Women,* Rayne Reiter, ed. New York: Monthly Review Press.

Rupp, Leila J. (1997). *Worlds of Women: The Making of an International Women's Movement.* Princeton, NJ: Princeton University Press.

Rupp, Leila J., & Verta Taylor. (1987). *Survival in the Doldrums: The American Women's Rights Movement, 1945 to 1960s.* New York: Oxford University Press.

Ryan, Barbara. (1989). Ideological purity and feminism: The U.S. women's movement from 1966 to 1975. *Gender & Society,* 3, 239–257.

———. (1992). *Feminism and the Women's Movement.* New York: Routledge.

Sapiro, V. (1991). In Janet Boles, ed. *The Annals of the American Academy of Political and Social Science,* May, 515.

Schlesinger, M. B., & P. Bart. (1983). Collective work and self-identity: The effect of working in a feminist illegal abortion collective. In L. Richardson & V. Taylor, eds. *Feminist Frontiers.* Reading, MA: Addison-Wesley.

Schneider, Beth. (1988). Political generations in the contemporary women's movement. *Sociological Inquiry,* 58, 4–21.

Simonds, Wendy. (1996). *Abortion at Work: Ideology and Practice in a Feminist Clinic.* New Brunswick, NJ: Rutgers University Press.

Spelman, Elizabeth. (1988). *Inessential Woman: Problems of Exclusion in Feminist Thought.* Boston: Beacon Press.

Stacey, Judith. (1987). Sexism by a subtler name? Postindustrial conditions and postfeminist consciousness. *Socialist Review,* 17, 7–28.

Staggenborg, Suzanne. (1988). The consequences of professionalization and formalization in the pro-choice movement. *American Sociological Review,* 53, 585–606.

———. (1989). Stability and innovation in the women's movement: A comparison of two movement organizations. *Social Problems,* 36, 75–92.

———. (1991). *The Pro-choice Movement.* New York: Oxford University Press.

———. (1996). The survival of the women's movement: Turnover and continuity in Bloomington, Indiana. *Mobilization,* 1, 143–158.

————. (1998a). *Gender, Family, and Social Movements.* Thousand Oaks, CA: Pine Forge Press.

————. (1998b). Social movement communities and cycles of protest: The emergence and maintenance of a local women's movement. *Social Problems, 45,* 180–204.

Stein, Arlene. (1997). *Sex and Sensibility: Stories of a Lesbian Generation.* Berkeley, CA: University of California Press.

Stombler, Mindy, & Irene Padavic. (1997). Sister acts: Resisting men's domination in black and white fraternity little sister programs. *Social Problems, 44,* 257–275.

Taylor, Verta. (1989). Social movement continuity: The women's movement in abeyance. *American Sociological Review, 54,* 761–775.

————. (1996). *Rock-a-by Baby: Feminism, Self-help, and Postpartum Depression.* New York: Routledge.

————. (1999). Gender and social movements: Gender processes and women's self-help movements. *Gender & Society, 13,* 8–33.

Taylor, Verta, & Leila Rupp. (1993). Women's culture and lesbian feminist activism: A reconsideration of cultural feminism. *Signs, 19,* 32–61.

Taylor, Verta, & Marieke Van Willigen. (1996). Women's self-help and the reconstruction of gender: The postpartum support and breast cancer movements. *Mobilization: An International Journal, 2,* 123–142.

Taylor, Verta, & Nancy Whittier. (1992). Collective identity in social movement communities: Lesbian feminist mobilization. In Aldon Morris & Carol Mueller, eds. *Frontiers of Social Movement Theory.* New Haven, CT: Yale University Press.

Thorne, Barrie. (1994). *Gender Play: Girls and Boys in School.* New Brunswick, NJ: Rutgers University Press.

————. (1995). Symposium on West and Fenstermaker's 'Doing Difference.' *Gender & Society, 9,* 498–499.

Vogel, Lise. (1993). *Mothers on the Job: Maternity Policy in the U.S. Workplace.* New Brunswick, NJ: Rutgers University Press.

Walker, Rebecca. (1992). Becoming the third wave. *Ms., 2* (January/February), 39–41.

————. (1995). *To Be Real: Telling the Truth and Changing the Face of Feminism.* New York: Anchor.

White, Aaronette M. (1999). Talking feminist, talking back: Micromobilization processes in a collective protest against rape. *Gender & Society, 13,* 77–100.

Whittier, Nancy E. (1995). *Feminist Generations: The Persistence of the Radical Women's Movement.* Philadelphia: Temple University Press.

LINKING ARMS AND MOVEMENTS

Urvashi Vaid

More than 800 lesbians, bisexual women, transgendered women, queer women, and supportive straight women (and a handful of men) gathered at the Lesbian Rights Summit of the National Organization for Women April 23–25 [1999] in Washington, DC. The same weekend a contingent of more than 300 progressive queers of all colors marched on Philadelphia as part of the rally demanding freedom for Mumia Abu-Jamal, the black radical writer and activist many of us believe is falsely accused of murdering a police officer.

A tale of two lesbian movements could be written in the parallel trajectories of these two events. It would be easy, for example, to characterize the NOW meeting as the gathering of the white lesbian-feminist movement—but that would negate the participation and leadership of strong women of color.

And it would be equally easy to dismiss the Mumia mobilization as the Left's issue du jour—but such a characterization would continue the false negation of the critical leadership role that lesbians of color and radical gay men have long played in the Left. It is the links between feminism and queerness that interest me in both of these gatherings.

Lesbian-feminist politics are across the board more multi-issue and progressive than mainstream gay, lesbian, bisexual, and transgender organizing. Dykes and queer girls see the connections and try to organize from the intersection of politics rather than from a single identity. Lesbian-feminist political theory owes much to lesbians of color and to radical women of all colors. The women at the NOW gathering are in many ways the offspring of this progressive tradition among lesbians. There

(continued)

were students, labor activists, mainstream political campaign workers, veteran dykes, and cultural lesbian feminists.

Many of the organizers and supporters of the queer contingent at the Mumia rally represent a who's who of a radical lesbian-feminist movement. Veteran activist and writer Barbara Smith gave a keynote speech noting that queer progressives had always been present inside people-of-color movements.

Lesbian feminism and queer progressive organizing share several points of connection. Both movements share the truth that economic and technological changes help shape our lives and influence public policy choices about the regulation of sexuality. Economic-based decisions shape policy about sex and birth control today. The welfare reform bill passed by Congress and endorsed by the administration contains population control measures such as efforts to reduce the "out of wedlock" birthrate and to promote heterosexual relationships and two-parent families. These measures are designed to control the sexual lives of poor or low-income women. For our queer movement's struggle to create families, those measures are especially dangerous.

There are at least four other links that bind a progressive movement for gay, lesbian, bisexual, and transgender liberation with women's libera-tion. First, there is an intimate connection between homophobia and sexism: Homophobia maintains gender inequality. Labels like "fag" or "dyke" are deployed to police the boundaries of sexual and gender expression.

Second, there is an intimate connection between sexism and gender rigidity and between the gay and lesbian liberation movement and gender nonconformity. Feminists have long argued that biology does not limit men or women to performing preassigned, gender-specific roles. Homophobia persecutes all those who are gender nonconformists—the sissy, the butch, the transgendered person.

Third, feminists and queers have long shared a critique of the limitations and pathologies of the traditional, patriarchal, nuclear family and a commitment to opening up other forms of family.

Fourth, both movements have worked hard to achieve and protect full sexual, reproductive, and personal autonomy and choice for women and men—a struggle that is far from over.

These are the links between the much more traditional politics of NOW's lesbian summit and a more radical lesbian-feminist movement. In the final analysis, both are lesbian movements built on a faith in an intersectional politics that focuses on the need for fundamental change in social institutions.

ACKNOWLEDGMENTS

Paula Gunn Allen, "Where I Come From is Like This" from *The Sacred Hoop: Recovering the Feminine Side in American Indian Traditions.* Copyright © 1986 by Paula Gunn Allen. Reprinted with the permission of Beacon Press.

Robert L. Allen and Paul Kivel, "Men Changing Men" from *Ms.* Magazine (September/October 1994). Copyright © 1994. Reprinted with the permission of *Ms.* Magazine.

Ingrid Banks, "Hair Still Matters." Reprinted with the permission of the author.

Amrita Basu, "Hindu Women's Activism in India and the Questions It Raises" from *Appropriating Gender: Women's Activism and Politicized Religion in South Asia,* edited by Patricia Jeffery and Amrita Basu. Copyright © 1998 by Patricia Jeffery and Amrita Basu. Reprinted with the permission of Routledge, Inc., part of The Taylor & Francis Group.

Kathleen A. Blee, "The Gendered Organization of Hate: Women in the U.S. Ku Klux Klan" from *Right-Wing Women: From Conservatives to Extremists Around the World,* edited by Paola Bacchetta and Margaret Powell. Copyright © 2002 by Routledge. Reprinted with the permission of Routledge, Inc., part of The Taylor & Francis Group.

Susan Bordo, "In Hiding and On Display" from *The Male Body: A New Look at Men in Public and In Private.* Copyright © 1999 by Susan Bordo. Reprinted with the permission of Farrar, Straus & Giroux, LLC.

Christine E. Bose and Rachel Bridges Whaley, "Sex Segregation in the U.S. Labor Force" from *Gender Mosaics: Social Perspectives,* edited by Dana Vannoy. Copyright © 2001 by Roxbury Publishing Company. Reprinted with the permission of the publisher.

Claudia Brenner, "A Letter from Claudia Brenner." Reprinted with the permission of Claudia Brenner.

Loren Cameron, "Portrait of a Man" from *The Advocate* (May 25, 1999). Copyright © 1998 by Loren Cameron. Reprinted with the permission of the publishers. All rights reserved.

Cathy Cohen, "Punks, Bulldaggers, and Welfare Queens: The Radical Potential of Queer Politics?" from *GLQ: A Journal of Lesbian and Gay Studies* 3, no. 4 (1997): 437–65. Copyright

© 1997 by Overseas Publishers Association Amsterdam, B.V. All rights reserved. Reprinted by permission.

Patricia Hill Collins, "Some Group Matters: Intersectionality, Situated Standpoints, and Black Feminist Thought" from *Fighting Words: Black Women and the Search for Justice.* Copyright © 1998 by the Regents of the University of Minnesota. Reprinted with the permission of the University of Minnesota Press.

Kimberlé Crenshaw, "Mapping the Margins: Intersectionality, Identity Politics, and Violence Against Women of Color" from *Stanford Law Review* 1241 (1991). Reprinted with the permission of the author and the *Stanford Law Review,* Stanford University School of Law.

Sharon Deevey, "Assessing Patients' Special Needs" from "Older Lesbian Woman: An Invisible Minority" from *Journal of Gerontological Nursing* 16, no. 5 (May 1990): 38–39. Copyright © 1990 by Charles B. Slack, Inc. Reprinted with the permission of the author and publishers.

Bonnie Thornton Dill, "'The Means to Put My Children Through': Child-Rearing Goals and Strategies Among Black Female Domestic Servants" from *The Black Woman,* edited by La Frances Rodgers-Rose (Newbury Park, Calif.: Sage Publications, 1980). Reprinted with the permission of the author.

Kathryn Edin, "Surviving the Welfare System: How AFDC Recipients Make Ends Meet in Chicago" from *Social Problems* 38, no. 4 (November 1991). Copyright © 1991 by the Society for the Study of Social Problems. Reprinted with the permission of the author and University of California Press Journals.

Barbara Ehrenreich, "The Mommy Test" from *Mother Jones* (July/August 1989). Copyright © 1989 by Foundation for National Progress. Reprinted with the permission of the publishers.

Cynthia Enloe, "The Globe Trotting Sneaker" from *Ms.* Magazine (March/April 1995). Copyright © 1995. Reprinted with the permission of *Ms.* Magazine.

Yen Le Espiritu, "Ideological Racism and Cultural Resistance" from *Asian American Women and Men.* Copyright © 1997 by Sage Publications, Inc. Reprinted with the permission of Alta Mira Press/Rowman & Littlefield, Inc.

Anne Fausto-Sterling, "Hormonal Hurricanes: Menstruation, Menopause, and Female Behavior" adapted from *Myths of Gender: Biological Theories About Women and Men.* Copyright © 1986 by Basic Books, Inc. Reprinted with the permission of Basic Books, a division of Perseus Books LLC.

Marilyn Frye, "Oppression" from *The Politics of Reality: Essays in Feminist Theory.* Copyright © 1983 by Marilyn Frye. Reprinted with the permission of The Crossing Press, Freedom, California.

Roberta Galler, "The Myth of the Perfect Body" from *Pleasure and Danger: Exploring Female Sexuality,* edited by Carole S. Vance. Copyright © 1984 by Roberta Galler. Reprinted with the permission of the author.

Debra Gimlin, "Cosmetic Surgery: Paying for Your Beauty" from *Body Work: Beauty and Self-Image in American Culture.* Copyright © 2002 by the Regents of the University of California. Reprinted with the permission of the University of California Press.

Rosalinda Mendez Gonzalez, "Distinctions in Western Women's Experience: Ethnicity, Class, and Social Change" from *The Women's West,* edited by Susan Armitage and Elizabeth Jameson. Copyright © 1987 by the University of Oklahoma Press. Reprinted with the permission of the publishers.

Jennifer Hargreaves, "The Muslim Female Heroic: Shorts or Veils" from *Heroines of Sport: The Politics of Difference and Identity.* Copyright © 2000 by Jennifer Hargreaves. Reprinted with the permission of International Thomson Publishing Services. This selection contains an excerpt from http://salamiran.org/women/general/womenandsports.html. Reprinted with the permission of The Embassy of The Islamic Republic of Iran.

Melanie Heath, "What Promises Can Men Keep?: How Men Renegotiate Gender and Racial Ideologies in the Promise Keepers Movement." Reprinted with the permission of the author.

Rosanna Hertz, "Working to Place Family at the Center of Life: Dual-Earner and Single-Parent Strategies" from *Annals of the American Academy of Political and Social Science* 562 (March 1999). Copyright © 1999. Reprinted with the permission of Sage Publications, Inc.

Pierrette Honagneu-Sotelo, "Maid in L.A." from *Domestica: Immigrant Workers Cleaning and Caring in the Shadows of Affluence.* Copyright © 2001 by the Regents of the University of California. Reprinted with the permission of the University of California Press.

bell hooks, "Selling Hot Pussy" from *Black Looks: Race and Representation.* Copyright © 1992. Reprinted with the permission of South End Press.

Hung Cam Thai, "For Better or Worse: Gender Allures in the Vietnamese Global Marriage Market." Revised by Verta Taylor and Nancy Whittier from Hung Cam Thai, "Clashing Dreams: Highly-Educated Vietnamese Brides and Their Low-Wage Overseas Husbands" in *Global Women,* edited by Arlie Russell Hochschild and Barbara Ehrenreich (New York: Metropolitan Books, 2003). Reprinted with the permission of the author.

Suzanne J. Kessler, "The Medical Construction of Gender" from *Lessons from the Intersexed.* Copyright © 1990 by The University of Chicago. Copyright © 1998 by Suzanne J. Kessler. Reprinted with the permission of the author and The University of Chicago Press.

Alice Kessler-Harris, "The Wage Conceived: Value and Need as Measures of a Woman's Worth" from *A Woman's Wage: Historical Meanings and Social Consequences.* Copyright © 1990 by Alice Kessler-Harris. Reprinted with the permission of The University Press of Kentucky.

Michael Kimmel, "What Are Little Boys Made Of?" from *Ms.* Magazine (October/November 1999). Copyright © 1999. Reprinted with the permission of the author.

Sherryl Kleinman, "Why I'm Not a Lady (and No Woman Is)." Copyright © 2003 by Sheryl Kleinman. Reprinted with the permission of the author.

Nicholas D. Kristoff, "Iraq's Little Secret" from *The New York Times* (October 1, 2002). Copyright © 2002 by The New York Times Company. Reprinted with permission.

Judith Lorber, "'Night to His Day': The Social Construction of Gender" from *Paradoxes of Gender.* Copyright © 1993 by Yale University. Reprinted with the permission of Yale University Press.

Audre Lorde, "The Master's Tools Will Never Dismantle the Master's House" from *Sister Outsider: Essays and Speeches.* Copyright © 1984 by Audre Lorde. Reprinted with the permission of The Crossing Press, Freedom, California.

Carolyn Mackler, excerpt from "Sex Ed: How Do we Score?" from *Ms.* Magazine (August/September 1999). Copyright © 1999. Reprinted with the permission of *Ms.* Magazine.

Patricia Yancey Martin and Robert A. Hummer, "Fraternities and Rape on Campus" from Gender & Society 3, no. 4 (December 1989). Copyright © 1989 by Sociologists for Women in Society. Reprinted with the permission of Sage Publications, Inc.

Michael A. Messner, "Becoming 100% Straight" from *Inside Sports,* edited by Jay Coakley and Peter Donnelly. Copyright © 1999. Reprinted with the permission of Routledge.

Nancy A. Naples, "A Member of the Funeral" from *Queer Families, Queer Politics: Challenging Culture and the State,* edited by Mary Bernstein and Renate Riemann. Copyright © 2001 by Columbia University Press. Reprinted with the permission of the publishers.

Ellen Neuborne, "The Next Feminist Generation: Imagine My Surprise" (originally titled "Imagine My Surprise") from *Listen Up: Voices from the Next Feminist Generation,* edited by Barbara Findlen. Copyright © 1995 by Ellen Neuborne. Reprinted by permission of Seal Press.

Laurie Nsiah-Jefferson, "Reproductive Laws, Women of Color, and Low Income Women" from *Reproductive Law for the 1990s,* edited by Sherrill Cohen and Nadine Taub. Copyright © 1988. Reprinted with the permission of the author and Humana Press.

Norimitsu Onishi, "Globalization of Beauty Makes Slimness Trendy" from *The New York Times* (October 3, 2002). Copyright © 2002 by The New York Times Company. Reprinted with permission.

Grace Paley, "Inherit the War" from *Ms.* Magazine (December 2001/January 2002). Copyright © 2001. Reprinted with the permission of *Ms.* Magazine.

Claire Porter, "I'm Taking Back My Pussy: A Transgression of Privatized Gynecological Boundaries" from *SWS Network News* 17(3). Reprinted with the permission of the Society for Women in Sociology.

Barbara Reskin and Irene Padavic, "Moving Up and Taking Charge (editors' title, originally titled "Sex Differences in Moving Up and Taking Charge") from *Women and Men at Work,* Second Edition (Thousand Oaks, Calif.: Pine Forge, 2002). Copyright © 2002 by Sage Publications, Inc. Reprinted with the permission of the authors.

Barbara Reskin, excerpt from "The Realities of Affirmative Action in Employment" [Editor's title. Originally titled "The Effects of Affirmative Action on Other Stakeholders"] from *The Realities of Affirmative Action in Employment.* Copyright © 1998 by the American Sociological Association. Reprinted with the permission of the author and the American Sociological Association.

Laurel Richardson, "Gender Stereotyping in the English Language" adapted from *The Dynamics of Sex and Gender: A Sociological Perspective, Third Edition* (New York: Harper & Row, 1987). Copyright © 1981 by Houghton Mifflin Company. Copyright © 1987 by Harper & Row, Publishers, Inc. Reprinted with the permission of the author.

Barbara Risman, "Ideology, Experience, Identity: The Complex Worlds of Children in Fair Families" from *Gender Vertigo: American Families in Transition.* Copyright © 1998 by Yale University. Reprinted with the permission of Yale University Press.

Leila Rupp, "Finding the Lesbians in Lesbian History" from *The New Lesbian Studies: Into the Twenty-First Century,* edited by Bonnie Zimmerman and Toni A.H. McNaron. Copyright © 1996 by Bonnie Zimmerman and Toni A.H. McNaron. Reprinted with the permission of The Feminist Press at the City University of New York, www.feministpress.org.

Steven P. Schacht, "Teaching About Being an Oppressor: Some Personal and Political Considerations" from *Men and Masculinities* 4, no 2 (October 2001): 201–208. Copyright © 2001 by Sage Publications. Reprinted by permission of the author and Sage Publications, Inc.

Denise A. Segura, "Working at Motherhood: Chicana and Mexican Immigrant Mothers and Employment" from *Mothering: Ideology, Experience, and Agency,* edited by Evelyn Nakano Glenn, Grace Chang, and Linda Rennie Forcey. Copyright © 1994 by Routledge. Reprinted with the permission of the author and Routledge, Inc., part of The Taylor & Francis Group.

Gloria Steinem, "If Men Could Menstruate" from *Ms.* Magazine (October 1978). Copyright © 1978 by Gloria Steinem. "Supremacy Crimes" from *Ms.* Magazine (August/September 1999). Copyright © 1999 by Gloria Steinem. Both reprinted with the permission of the author.

Verta Taylor, Nancy Whittier, Cynthia Fabrizio Pelak, "The New Feminist Movement: Persistence Through Transformation." Reprinted with the permission of the authors.

Mary Ann Tetreault, "Accountability or Justice?: Rape as a War Crime" (previously unpublished paper). Reprinted with the permission of the author.

Becky Wangsgaard Thompson, "'A Way Outa No Way': Eating Problems among African American, Latina, and White Women," *Gender & Society* 6, no. 4 (December 1992). Copyright © 1994 by Sociologists for Women in Society. Reprinted with the permission of the author.

Barrie Thorne, "Girls and Boys Together . . . But Mostly Apart: Gender Arrangements in Elementary Schools" from *Relationships and Development,* edited by Willard W. Hartup and Zick Rubin (Hillsdale, New Jersey: Lawrence Erlbaum Associates, 1986). Volume sponsored by the Social Science Research Council. Copyright © 1986 by Lawrence Erlbaum Associates. Reprinted with the permission of the author and publisher.

Deborah L. Tolman, "Doing Desire: Adolescent Girls' Struggles for/with Sexuality" from *Gender & Society* 8, no. 3 (September 1994). Copyright © 1994 by Sociologists for Women in Society. Reprinted with the permission of Sage Publications, Inc.

Urvashi Vaid, "Linking Arms and Movements" from *The Advocate* (June 8, 1999). Copyright © 1999 by Urvashi Vaid.

Alice Walker, "Womanist" from *In Search of Our Mothers' Gardens: Womanist Prose.* Copyright © 1983 by Alice Walker. Reprinted with the permission of Harcourt, Inc.

Suzanna Danuta Walters, "Wedding Bells and Baby Carriages: Heterosexuals imagine gay families, gay families imagine themselves" from *Lines of Narrative: Psychosocial Perspectives,* edited by Molly Andrews, Shelley Day Sclater, Corinne Squire, and Amal Treacher. Copyright © 2000. Reprinted with the permission of Routledge.

Harriet Woods, "The Truth About Women and Power" from *Stepping Up to Power: The Political Journey of American Women.* Copyright © 2000 by Westview Press. Reprinted with the permission of Westview Press, a member of Perseus Books, L.L.C.